June 1999

For Greg, on your graduation

~ may this help you on your way to your next one.

Aloha nui
Graham
Blake
Leigh

ALSO BY MORTIMER J. ADLER

THE GREAT IDEAS

A Lexicon of Western Thought by
MORTIMER J. ADLER

SCRIBNER CLASSICS

SCRIBNER
1230 Avenue of the Americas
New York, NY 10020

First Scribner Classics edition 1999

SCRIBNER and design are trademarks of
Simon & Schuster Inc.

Manufactured in the United States of America

1   3   5   7   9   10   8   6   4   2

Library of Congress Cataloging-in-Publication Data
Adler, Mortimer Jerome, 1902–
The great ideas : a lexicon of Western thought /
by Mortimer J. Adler. —1st Scribner Classics ed.
p.   cm.
Previously published : New York : Macmillan, 1992.
1. Great books of the Western world. I. Title.
AC1.A65   1999
081—dc21   98-46395
CIP

ISBN 0-684-85921-1

To William Benton and Robert Gwinn

CONTENTS

Foreword ix

viii

CONTENTS

FOREWORD

(especially for readers who have never seen the *Syntopicon*)

===

PART ONE

A Twentieth-Century Delusion

A cultural delusion is widespread in the twentieth century. The extraordinary progress in science and technology that we have achieved in this century has deluded many of our contemporaries into thinking that similar progress obtains in other fields of mental activity. They unquestioningly think that the twentieth century is superior to its predecessors in all the efforts of the human mind.

Some of our contemporaries make this inference consciously and explicitly. They do not hesitate to declare that the twentieth century has a better, a more advanced and sounder, solution of moral and political problems, that it is more critically penetrating in its philosophical thought, and that it is superior in its understanding of, and even in its wisdom about, the perennial questions that confront human beings in every generation.

This book of essays about the great ideas and issues and about the great conversation concerning these ideas that can be found in the great books is not for them. Their minds are closed to the possibility that they may be wrong in the inference they have made without examining the evidence to the contrary that this book provides.

But there may be some—perhaps many—among our contemporaries of which this is not true. They may be prone to the twentieth-century delusion as a result of the indoctrination they received from an inadequate schooling, or as a result of the currents of journalistic opinion that fill the press, the radio, and the television. But they may still be open to persuasion that they have mistakenly believed in the superiority of the twentieth century in all fields of intellectual endeavor. It may be possible to show them that, though the twentieth century has made some contribution to the understanding of the great ideas, the significance of that contribution cannot be understood without seeing it in the light of the greater contribution made in earlier epochs of the last twenty-five centuries.

This book is for them because that is precisely what it does. It is the apt remedy for what I have called the twentieth-century delusion, which psychiatrists would call a grandiose delusion. The 102 essays on the great ideas that this book contains dramatically exhibit the great conversation that has been going on across the centuries, in which any unprejudiced and undeluded mind will see the merit of what has been thought and said. Such wisdom as has been achieved is in no way affected or conditioned by time and place.

Unprejudiced and undeluded readers of these essays will, I think, discover for themselves that, with respect to the understanding of the great ideas, differences remain over the centuries. It is almost as if the authors amply quoted in these essays were all sitting around a large table talking face-to-face with one another, differing in their opinions, disagreeing, and arguing.

An auditor of the conversation going on would soon come to regard them as if they were all alike as eminent contemporaries, in spite of their differences in time, place, and language. That auditor would not regard what he heard as voices from the remote past talking about problems no longer of vital concern. Instead, he or she would become fascinated by the fact that all the things he or she heard being said concerned matters of current interest and importance.

This book of 102 essays declares to its readers that our Western civilization is the civilization of the dialogue or symposium, which is the great conversation in the great books about the great ideas.

There is one more thing that I dare to promise readers. They will find that the 102 essays succeed remarkably in presenting the major points of view on almost 3,000 questions without endorsing, applauding, or favoring any of the views presented. That is an accomplishment in which, my friends assure me, I may rightly take the greatest pride.

The Adjective "Great"

Readers of this Foreword may be puzzled and even annoyed by my repeated use of the adjective "great." The great authors are the writers of the great books. They engage in a great conversation. What about? The great ideas. Are all these uses of the adjective related in an orderly way so that one can discern the primary use from which the other uses are derived and by which they are controlled?

I think I have an answer to that question, one that helps me to explain why there will always be controversies about which books, in the literature available to us, deserve to be called "great." There are many different standards or criteria by which persons can judge a book to be great, and its writer a great author. Different groups of persons will, if called upon to do so, construct different lists of books that deserve the status of "great." This is not the case when we consider ideas rather than books. Take the list of the 102 ideas with which the essays in this volume deal. There may be some disagreement about them, but it will be very slight, indeed; there are few of these ideas that anyone would recommend dropping and few that anyone would recommend adding, and those recommended for addition, like EQUALITY, will be found in the Inventory of Terms and will be seen as subordinate to the 102.

If we take the adjective "great" as the qualifier of ideas and as the controlling criterion of our other uses of it, then many things are clarified and little controversy is engendered. The great conversation is the discussion of the great ideas during the last twenty-five centuries of Western culture.

There may be other great ideas and other great conversations about them in three or four of the cultures in the Far East—Hindu, Buddhist, Confucian, and Taoist. But these are not only quite separate from one another, they are also extraneous to the great conversation about the 102 great ideas in Western literature and thought. At this stage in the history of the world, a world cultural community does not exist, and a global set of great ideas cannot be compiled. The future may hold the possibility of one global great conversation, but that lies far ahead of where we are today.

Given the reality of the great conversation for us who have inherited the Western tradition, it is that discussion of the great ideas that determines how we draw the line between books and authors that deserve to be called "great" and those that do not. But, it may be asked, what tangible evidence can be given of the *reality* of the great conversation? What shows us that such a conversation really has taken place from antiquity to the present day?

These ideas were derived from an extremely close analysis of 434 works by 73 authors from Homer to the twentieth century. This analysis was performed by a staff of specialized indexers under my direction, and the works analyzed were later published as *Great Books of the Western World*, about which more will be said later in this Foreword. The editorial staff that I headed found a way of demonstrating the existence of the great conversation. They constructed two indices—one called "The Author-to-Author Index;" the other called "The Author-to-Idea Index."

The first of these indices listed, beginning with the Greek tragic poets and with Herodotus, who came chronologically after Homer, the authors they read and referred to or commented on. As we came down the chronological series of authors, the editorial staff listed all the preceding authors that any author in the series had obviously read and *talked back to*.

Obviously, earlier authors could not refer explicitly to their successors, but often points that they made anticipated what would be considered and challenged later. This Author-to-Author Index shows the great conversation going on across the centuries.

The fifty-four volumes of the first edition of *Great Books of the Western World* in 1952 ended with the works of such late nineteenth- and early twentieth-century authors as Herman Melville, William James, Karl Marx, and Sigmund Freud. Each of these authors was found to have read and commented on twenty-five or more of his predecessors. When six volumes of twentieth-century authors were added to the second edition of *Great Books* in 1990, fewer of these authors appear to have been as well read as their predecessors but for some, such as Alfred North Whitehead, Werner Heisenberg, Max Weber, Claude Lévi-Strauss, and James Joyce, their acquaintance with the works of their eminent predecessors is as clearly evident.

The Author-to-Idea Index provided another demonstration of the reality of the great conversation. The editorial staff listed, from Homer up to the twentieth-century authors, the number of great ideas that each author could be found discussing, counting the appearance of citations of their work in the topics under each idea. Thus, for example, Homer appears in 51 of the 102 great ideas, Herodotus in 71, Plato in 100, Aristotle in all 102, Plutarch in 79, Augustine in 97, Aquinas in 102, Dante in 84, Shakespeare in 79, Montaigne in 90, Francis Bacon in 97, Spinoza in 79, Gibbon in 88, Locke in 98, J. S. Mill in 82, Hegel in 97, Tolstoy in 96, Darwin in 71, Marx in 71, Freud in 91. When we come to the twentieth-century authors, their works, for the most part, are cited in fewer than half of the 102 great ideas.

In a sense, it is the *Syntopicon* itself—the topical index to discussions of the great ideas in the *Great Books*—with its almost 3,000 topics that provides the best evidence for the reality of the great conversation. I hope to be able to demonstrate this in PART TWO by presenting Chapter 50 of the *Syntopicon* on LOVE.

Questions to Be Answered

Readers, into whose hands this book happens to fall, may be naturally inclined to ask the following questions.

Those acquainted only with the book's title are likely to ask:

What is an idea?

What are the great ideas and what makes them great?

Why 102 great ideas? Why not more or fewer than that?

How were they chosen?

Those who open the book and look at its front and rear endpages and its Contents pages will discover that the book contains 102 essays on the great ideas and that these essays have been reproduced from two volumes entitled *The Syntopicon, An Index to the Great Ideas*, two volumes in a set entitled *Great Books of the Western World*. They may now seek the answers to further questions:

What is the *Syntopicon* and how does it provide an index to the great ideas?

How do the essays contained in this book relate to the great books contained in the sixty-volume set?

In the following sections of PART ONE of this Foreword, I will attempt to answer these questions and, perhaps, others that they generate. The answers to these questions will lead to some understanding of the great conversation about the great ideas that is to be found in the *Great Books*. Inquiring readers will then see that by reading the essays in this book they will be introduced to this conversation. They will thus be prepared to participate in the great conversation, by the thinking that they are enabled to do on the thousands of topics that locate the differences and disagreements of the most eminent minds that have contributed to the Western tradition of thought in the last twenty-five centuries. In doing so, they will have taken an important step toward becoming generally educated human beings.

What Is an Idea?

In the vocabulary of daily speech, the word "idea" is generally used to name the subjective contents of our own minds—things that each of us has in his or her own mind. This use of the word predominates in a large portion of modern psychology, concerned as it is with something called "the association of ideas" or "the stream of consciousness"—with the images we experience in dreams or in acts of imagination. It is a kind of omnibus term that covers all the contents of our minds when we have any conscious experience—our sensations and perceptions, our images and memories, and the concepts we form.

But that, obviously, is not the way the word "idea" is being used when we engage one another in the discussion of ideas. In order for a discussion between two or more persons to occur, they must be engaged in talking to one another about something that is a common object of their conjoined apprehension. They do not have a common object to discuss if each of them is speaking only of his own ideas in the subjective sense of the term.

Consider, for example, a number of individuals arguing with one another about liberty and justice, about war and peace, or about government and democracy. They probably differ in the way they subjectively think about these matters. Otherwise, they would not find themselves arguing about them. But it must also be true that they could not be arguing with one another if they did not have a common object to which they were all referring. That common object is an idea in the objective sense of the term.

These two uses of the one word "idea"—the subjective use of it to signify the contents of an individual's conscious mind and the objective use of it to signify something that is a common object being considered and discussed by two or more individuals—may be a source of confusion to many. We might try to eliminate the source of confusion by restricting the use of the word "idea" to its subjective sense and substituting another mode of speech for "idea" in its objective sense. We might always use the phrase "object of thought" instead. Thus, liberty and justice, war and peace, government and democracy might be called objects of thought.

When many years ago, with the help of a large staff gathered at the Institute for Philosophical Research, I wrote two large volumes entitled *The Idea of Freedom*, reviewing and relating everything that had been written in the last twenty-five centuries about that subject, I might have given the two volumes another title, as follows: *Freedom as an Object of Thought*. For if the idea of freedom is not understood as an object of thought, how could we have reviewed and related the thinking that has been done about it in the last twenty-five centuries?

One other example may help to reinforce what has just been said. Let us turn from our thinking to our sense-experience of the world in which we live. We are in a room sitting at a table. On the table is a glass of wine. You are facing the light and I am sitting with my back to it. We have, therefore, different subjective impressions or perceptions of the color of the table and of the wine in the glass. But in spite of our divergent subjective perceptual experiences, we know that we are sitting at one and the same table and looking at one and the same glass of wine. We can put our hands on the table and move it. We can each take sips out of the same glass of wine. Thus we know that the table and the glass of wine are one and the same perceptual *object* for both of us. It is that common object that we can talk about as well as move and use.

If this is clear, then I recommend that we use the word "idea" in its objective sense as a common object of thought that two or more individuals can discuss and either agree or disagree about. To eliminate the word "idea" in its objective sense and always use instead the phrase "object of thought" (thus making the title of this book *102 Objects of Thought*) would be too cumbersome and should be avoided.

We live in two worlds: (1) the sensible world of the common perceptual objects that we move around and use in various ways and (2) the intelligible world of ideas, the common objects of thought that we cannot touch with our bodies or perceive with our senses, but that, as thinking individuals, we can discuss with one another.

What Are the Great Ideas and What Makes Them Great?

Clearly, not all the perceptual objects in the sensible world of our everyday experience are
equally important to us, equally valuable or useful for one purpose or another. The same
is true of the intelligible world of ideas that are objects of thought. There are thousands
upon thousands of ideas in that intelligible world, but only a relatively small number in
that multitude occur again and again as discussables—as foci of human interest and dispute.
Only a small number subsume all the rest, as we shall see presently. The small number that
are the focal points of maximum human interest and importance in every era and epoch
and in every generation are the great ideas. All the others that might be mentioned lead
into them or are in one way or another subordinate to them.

In order to explain more concretely what I have just said, I must tell you how I came to
invent the *Syntopicon*, which is an index to the discussion of the 102 great ideas.

In the summer of 1942, the summer before the siege of Stalingrad, I was preparing to
write a book that, when published in *1943*, bore the title *How To Think About War and
Peace*. In preparation for writing that book, I spent some time going back to great books
I had read that I thought might have something to say on the subject, books by Thucydides,
Plato, Machiavelli, Hobbes, Locke, Kant, Hegel, Tolstoy, and so on.

To my surprise, when I turned to the pages of these books in which I had already marked
and underlined certain passages, I found other passages on war and peace of which I had
taken no notice at all. How could this happen? How could I have missed earlier the fine
passages that I had now discovered?

The answer, I realized, was that on my previous readings of these books, I had other
subjects in mind. I was not thinking about war and peace. If I had been questioning the
authors about what they thought about war and peace on my previous reading of their
work, I could not possibly have missed the passages I had just discovered.

Well, I said to myself, what if the great books were read again and again by a large staff
of readers with every important question in mind? Would we then not discover all the
passages that expressed their authors' thoughts on all these subjects?

I need not here go into all the steps by which the *Syntopicon* project was approved,
financed, and staffed. I need only tell you that when the staff of thirty-five readers were
trained and set to work, with the objective of discovering the passages in the great books
that had something of significance to say about 102 great ideas, they did, in five years,
what amounted to over 400,000 man-hours of reading to assemble all the relevant passages
to which they made index references.

For them to begin this lengthy and arduous endeavor, it was necessary to decide what
these ideas were, and then to compile a list of them. With the assistance of my closest
associates on the staff, I made an initial list of over 500 ideas that were clearly important
in the books we were considering. We went over this list again and again and progressively
boiled it down to 102 ideas—ideas that we determined had been the principal objects of
thought and foci of discussion for the last twenty-five centuries of Western thought, ideas
that truly covered the high points in the intelligible world as we know it, and, most importantly, ideas under which other ideas could be subordinated.

When the *Syntopicon* was finished, we constructed a list of several thousand other ideas
that were subordinate to the 102 we had chosen. This appears in the second volume of the

Syntopicon under the title "Inventory of Terms." I will return to it later in PART TWO of this Foreword.

In short, what makes the 102 ideas we had chosen great ideas is their basic or fundamental character. Though fifty years have elapsed since the 102 great ideas were chosen, nothing that has happened in the last half-century, with one exception, necessitates a single change in that list by addition or subtraction. The one exception is the idea of EQUALITY. New topics have been added under some of the ideas by virtue of advances or changes in twentieth-century thought, but not a single new idea.[1]

I should add here a word about the topics. What we started out with as an index to the great ideas was so different from any other index that had ever been constructed that we made up a new name for what we were producing. We invented the name "Syn-topicon" because the Greek roots of that made-up name mean "collection of topics." Each of the great ideas has many aspects, themes, issues, problems.

For each of them, we developed what we called an "Outline of Topics." Some great ideas have a more intricate and complicated structure than others and, therefore, a longer list of topics than others. As the work progressed, we enlarged and modified these outlines of topics to accommodate relevant passages found in this or that author. We ended up with almost 3,000 topics, organized under the 102 great ideas. The number of the topics under each idea, as well as the number of subordinate terms that refer to these topics, measures the richness and complexity of each of the great ideas.

Why 102 Great Ideas? Why not More or Fewer Than That?

The answer to this question is that the number could have been more or fewer than 102, but probably not much fewer than 92 or much more than 112. In other words, the number of 102 plus or minus 10. Why so?

Let me explain. One of the great ideas is GOVERNMENT. In outlining the topics that present the interior structure of that idea, we could have placed topics dealing with all the major forms of GOVERNMENT, such as TYRANNY AND DESPOTISM, MONARCHY, OLIGARCHY, ARISTOCRACY, and DEMOCRACY. But that would have made the chapter on GOVERNMENT extraordinarily long and unwieldy; so we chose instead to develop separate chapters on the different forms of government mentioned above. By doing so we increased the number of great ideas; if we had made the other choice, we would have decreased the number.

Another example is the chapter on VIRTUE AND VICE. Here we could have included among the topics of that chapter the consideration of particular virtues: COURAGE, TEMPERANCE, PRUDENCE, JUSTICE, and WISDOM. That would have reduced the number of great ideas. But we decided that to do this would make the chapter on VIRTUE AND VICE too long and cumbersome; so we made the other choice.

In short, the number 102 is somewhat arbitrary, in terms of choices that we made for practical reasons. But its arbitrariness is limited. We could not have done the job with only 50 great ideas, or with 150. At no time in all the eight years of work on the production

---

1. The one exception, EQUALITY, appears in the Inventory of Terms; it there refers to many topics under other ideas.

of the *Syntopicon* was there an outcry on the part of the editorial staff that some idea other than the 102 we had chosen was needed to accommodate a large and significant body of Western thought that could not be subsumed under the various topics of the 102 ideas that we had selected. Controversies since engaged in on the publication of the second edition of *The Great Books of the Western World* have, while including much criticism of the choice of authors, conspicuously avoided criticizing the choice of ideas.

I have thus answered as best I can what a great idea is, how the 102 were chosen, and why there are only 102 of them; that is, 102 plus or minus 10.

Why Was Something That Started Out as an Index to the Great Ideas Renamed the *Syntopicon*?

I noted above the brief answer to this question, but further explanation is, perhaps, needed. The nub of the explanation lies in the word "topic."

The Greek word *topos* means a place. There is a mathematical science of topology. But in logic a topic is a place where minds meet in agreement or disagreement about the theme, the issue, or the problem stated in the topic.

When we started out to construct an index to the great ideas as these are discussed in the great books, we came up against a snag that we should have foreseen. All ordinary indices are to books written by a single individual or by a set of coauthors. The terms which are the flags to which the page references in the book are attached are terms to be found in the text. They are the author's own terms. Thus constructed, the terms are arranged in strictly alphabetical order to facilitate the reader's use of the index.

When we started out, we proceeded in the traditional manner of constructing an index. We found that impossible to do. The reason was twofold. In the first place, we were dealing with the works of seventy-four authors, scattered over the last twenty-five centuries, writing in different languages and in different cultural contexts. Different authors used different terms to express the same meaning. No common set of terms could be found for such a disparate and heterogeneous group.

In the second place, we were seeking passages in the great books relevant to 102 great ideas. But as we proceeded we found that the thinking done about great ideas is highly variegated: it touches on different aspects of the idea, different themes, issues, definitions, problems. Unless these were explicitly stated, we could not organize the references to the passages in the great books about a given idea in a significant manner.

To solve these two problems, we had recourse to the logical device known as a topic. A topic is never stated in a sentence, but in an elaborate phrase that neither asserts nor denies anything. It functions like a question to which a variety of opposing or different answers can be given. By using the logical device of the topic, we found ourselves able to do the indexing that could not be done otherwise. Since this was the first time that anyone had ever tried to produce one index to the thought of a large number of authors, it was also the first time that a topical index was constructed.

It was not only the number of authors, but also the structural complexity of the great ideas that necessitated outlining, for each idea, the set of topics that represented its intellectual content—its definitions, issues, problems, and other themes. The actual work of indexing could not be begun until we had at least a first tentative list of the great ideas and tentative outlines of topics for each of them, both list and outlines tentative in the sense that they would be subject to change in the course of the indexing done in the next two or three years. In fact, the Outlines of Topics went through as many as eighteen revisions—topics added, topics rephrased, topics eliminated, in order to accommodate the thought to be found in the great books without prejudice or distortion.

As the work matured, we realized that the word "index" in its well-established traditional sense was not the right word for what we were in the process of constructing. That is why we invented the word "Syntopicon," meaning (as I pointed out earlier) a collection of topics.

How Is the *Syntopicon* Organized?

The *Syntopicon* consists of 102 chapters, one on each of the 102 great ideas. Each chapter has exactly the same structure. It consists of five parts, in the following order: (1) an introductory essay, (2) an Outline of Topics, (3) a section entitled "References," in which, topic by topic, passages relevant to the topics are cited by page references to the *Great Books* in which they are found; (4) a section entitled "Cross-References" in which readers are sent to topics in other chapters that are related to the topics in this chapter, and (5) finally, a section called "Additional Readings," in which the titles of other works, not included in the volumes of *Great Books*, are recommended for reading in connection with this great idea and its component topics. The 102 essays represent the content of the book you are now reading.

The recommended works in the section entitled "Additional Readings" are good books but not great books, because their grasp of the great ideas is limited either in range, or in depth, or both. Thus they contribute only in a subordinate or tangential way to the great conversation that the authors of the great books engage in. Such good books lie on the fringe of the great conversation; they do not fully participate in it. I will have more to say on this point later.

One further point about the structure of the *Syntopicon* is the fact that the 102 ideas are arranged in strictly alphabetical order—from ANGEL at one end to WORLD at the other. This arrangement avoids any judgment about the relation of any one of the great ideas to all the others.

The great ideas can, of course, be grouped by reference to the academic subject-matters to which they appear to have maximum relevance. Thus, for example, such ideas as HAPPINESS, GOOD AND EVIL, VIRTUE AND VICE, DUTY, COURAGE, TEMPERANCE, PRUDENCE, and JUSTICE contribute a great deal to the study of ethics or moral philosophy; such ideas as GOVERNMENT, LAW, MONARCHY, OLIGARCHY, ARISTOCRACY, DEMOCRACY, and TYRANNY AND DESPOTISM contribute to political science and philosophy; such ideas as DESIRE, EXPERIENCE, EMOTION, HABIT, JUDGMENT, LOVE, MEMORY AND IMAGINATION, MIND, PLEASURE AND PAIN, SENSE, SOUL, and WILL would appear to be in the sphere of psychology; such ideas as ASTRONOMY AND COSMOLOGY, INFINITY, MATHEMATICS, MATTERS, MECHANICS, PHYSICS, QUANTITY, SPACE, TIME, and WORLD would appear to be in the sphere of the natural sciences; and so on.

But as our work progressed, we discovered that most of the great ideas have, directly or indirectly, relations with most of the others and that none is without relationships that would be transgressed if they were grouped according to a particular sphere of subject-matter, to which, at first glance, they might appear to have maximum relevance. We, therefore, thought it wise to arrange the great ideas in the completely neutral manner of an alphabetical order, and let readers discover for themselves how, beginning with any one of the 102 great ideas, they are led by circuitous pathways to the consideration of almost all the others.

What Function Did the Introductory Essays Perform in the Construction of the *Syntopicon*?

Since this book in the hands of readers contains only the first element—the introductory essays—in each of the 102 chapters of the *Syntopicon*, this question should be of concern to readers.

In the light of the description of the five parts that constitute the structure of each of the *Syntopicon's* 102 chapters, it would seem obvious that the central—the indispensable—parts in each chapter are the Outline of Topics and the immediately following section, entitled "References," where, topic by topic, the citation of relevant passages in the *Great Books* is set forth.

But why the opening section of each chapter entitled "Introduction"—the 102 essays on the great ideas that compose the present book in the hands of readers? Why did we consider it advisable to include this first part in each of the 102 chapters? Why were they written? What function do they perform?

The first brief answer to this question is that they were written to whet the appetite of readers for the study of the great ideas as they are discussed in the great conversation about them to be found in the pages of the great books collected in the set entitled *Great Books of the Western World.*

There is a longer and more elaborate answer about the function of the essay. I have mentioned earlier that, with help of a large research staff at the Institute for Philosophical Research, and after eight years of work, I wrote and published two volumes entitled *The Idea of Freedom* or, as I said before, two volumes on freedom as an object of thought.

The work done on the *Syntopicon* in the 1940s led to the establishment of an Institute for the purpose of surveying and analyzing what had been thought on each of the great ideas in the twenty-five centuries of Western poetry, fiction, drama, theology, philosophy, and the natural and social sciences; and then presenting this thinking in a dialectically neutral or impartial manner without nodding one's head in the direction of or pointing out where the truth lies among this vast assemblage of differing or opposing views and doctrines. In other words, to encompass all points of view in a manner that is point-of-viewless—not tinged or colored by partiality or partisanship for any one of the many points of view encompassed in the survey.

But it took a large research staff and eight strenuous years of conferences and writing to produce *The Idea of Freedom.*[2] If similar effort and time were to be expended on each of the other 101 great ideas, that accomplishment would take more than a half century. It appeared to be beyond realistic hope of accomplishment.

That being the case, was there any feasible alternative that, if not as good, would at least serve the same purpose? The answer that we came up with was the 102 introductory essays for each of the 102 chapters of the *Syntopicon*. Though the introductory essay in the

---

2. In the 102 ideas of the *Syntopicon*, we chose to use the word "liberty" instead of the word "freedom," pointing out that these two words are strictly synonymous.

Syntopicon's 47th chapter on LIBERTY, which covers little more than six pages, cannot be as comprehensive and as analytically elaborate as the 1,500 pages in the two volumes of *The Idea of Freedom*, it nevertheless can give its readers a fair sampling of the great conversation about liberty (or freedom) by covering in an exposition, enriched by quotations, what has been said, thought, and disputed about the most important topics (some, of course, not all) in the great conversation about that idea.

This, by itself, may be insufficient, but the introduction to the sweep and stress of the great conversation about liberty prepares the reader to go further, with the help of the *Syntopicon*, in the study of the great conversation about that idea.

Even if readers of this book do not go further by using the *Syntopicon* after they have perused these essays, they will at least have become acquainted with the main strands of the great conversation about the 102 great ideas and they may even be able to participate in it themselves; for the essays on the 102 ideas do not tell them what to think, but only what is to be thought about in connection with each of these ideas. Readers are invited—and, I hope, induced—by the reading of them to make up their own minds on the main topics considered in each of these essays.

One further thing must be pointed out here, which careful readers of the essays will find out for themselves. In the assembly of passages on the main topics of each great idea, readers will find more mistakes and errors than truth. The relation between truth and error is a One-Many relation: for any one truth, many errors. Among the answers to most important questions, there is always likely to be only some truth accompanied by a multitude of errors or mistakes, because on any subject whatever is judged to be true will generate judgments about all the wrong answers. The truth on any subject is only well understood when it is understood in the light of all the errors made on the same subject.

I have now responded to the questions that I have thought might be raised by readers of this book when it falls into their hands. PART Two of this Foreword will elaborate on certain points that I have not fully treated in what has gone before.

PART TWO

Displaying *Syntopicon* Chapter 50

In the foregoing pages I have tried to describe the structure of the *Syntopicon*'s 102 chapters and the role that the introductory essays play in them. But showing is always much better than telling. I, therefore, thought it would be extremely helpful to give readers a direct experience of the *Syntopicon* by letting them sample a chapter—Chapter 50 on LOVE.

I have chosen this chapter because the themes, issues, and problems it deals with touch on matters with which almost everyone is acquainted in the course of daily life.

While readers turn the pages of the Outline for Topics for LOVE, I will act as tour guide pointing out things they might fail to notice. I ask readers to postpone reading the essay on LOVE (in Chapter 50 of the present book) until we have gone through the *Syntopicon* chapter.

Chapter 50. LOVE

OUTLINE OF TOPICS

1. The nature of love
    1a. Conceptions of love and hate: as passions and as acts of will
    1b. Love and hate in relation to each other and in relation to pleasure and pain
    1c. The distinction between love and desire: the generous and acquisitive aims
    1d. The aims and objects of love
    1e. The intensity and power of love: its increase or decrease; its constructive or destructive force
    1f. The intensity of hate: envy and jealousy
2. The kinds of love
    2a. Erotic love as distinct from lust or sexual desire
        (1) The sexual instinct: its relation to other instincts
        (2) Infantile sexuality: polymorphous perversity
        (3) Object-fixations, identifications, and transferences: sublimation
        (4) The perversion, degradation, or pathology of love: infantile and adult love
    2b. Friendly, tender, or altruistic love: fraternal love
        (1) The relation between love and friendship
        (2) Self-love in relation to the love of others: vanity and self-interest
        (3) The types of friendship: friendships based on utility, pleasure, or virtue
        (4) Patterns of love and friendship in the family
        (5) Friendship as a habitual association
    2c. Romantic, chivalric, and courtly love: the idealization and supremacy of the beloved
    2d. Conjugal love: its sexual, fraternal, and romantic components
3. The morality of love
    3a. Friendship and love in relation to virtue and happiness
    3b. The demands of love and the restraints of virtue: moderation in love; the order of loves
    3c. The conflict of love and duty: the difference between the loyalties of love and the obligations of justice
    3d. The heroism of friendship and the sacrifices of love
4. The social or political force of love, sympathy, or friendship
    4a. Love between equals and unequals, like and unlike: the fraternity of citizenship
    4b. The dependence of the state on friendship and patriotism: comparison of love and justice in relation to the common good
    4c. The brotherhood of man and the world community
5. Divine love
    5a. God as the primary object of love
        (1) Man's love of God in this life: respect for the moral law
        (2) Beatitude as the fruition of love
    5b. Charity, or supernatural love, compared with natural love
        (1) The precepts of charity: the law of love
        (2) The theological virtue of charity: its relation to the other virtues
    5c. God's love of Himself and of creatures

50. LOVE

REFERENCES

References are listed by volume number (in bold type), author's name, and page number. Bible references are to book, chapter, and verse of the Authorized King James version of the Bible. The abbreviation "esp" calls the reader's attention to one or more especially relevant parts of a whole reference; "passim" signifies that the topic is discussed intermittently rather than continuously in the work or passage cited. Where the work as a whole is relevant to the topic, the page numbers refer to the entire work. For general guidance in the use of *The Syntopicon*, consult the Introduction.

1. The nature of love

1a. Conceptions of love and hate: as passions and as acts of will

New Testament: *I John,* 4:7–8,16,18
 6 Plato, 14–25, 115–129, 149–173
 8 Aristotle, 406–407, 409, 420, 421, 532, 626–628
 11 Plotinus, 310–311, 324–325, 405–411, 654, 676–677
 16 Augustine, 437–438
 17 Aquinas, 120–121, 197–199, 310–311, 435–436, 726–727, 731–732, 733–737, 740–741, 744–749
 18 Aquinas, 483–484
 19 Dante, 67–68
 19 Chaucer, 210–211, 231
 20 Calvin, 183–184
 21 Hobbes, 61
 28 Spinoza, 634, 642–645, 651
 33 Locke, 176–177
 35 Rousseau, 343–345
 39 Kant, 259
 43 Hegel, 137
 45 Balzac, 243–244, 348–349
 46 Eliot, George, 373–374
 47 Dickens, 164–165
 49 Darwin, 312
 51 Tolstoy, 525–526
 53 James, William, 4–5
 54 Freud, 418, 673–674, 783
 59 Joyce, 599

1b. Love and hate in relation to each other and in relation to pleasure and pain

 4 Euripides, 277–295
 6 Plato, 18–19, 21, 121–122, 333–334
 8 Aristotle, 168, 407–410 passim, 420, 423–424, 425, 429, 614
 11 Lucretius, 55–56
 12 Virgil, 143–153
 16 Augustine, 15–16
 17 Aquinas, 726–727, 731–733, 734–735, 743–744, 746–747, 788
 18 Aquinas, 527–530
 19 Dante, 6–7, 67–68
 19 Chaucer, 199, 228
 21 Hobbes, 61–62, 77

 25 Shakespeare, 103–141, 469–470
 28 Spinoza, 634, 636–638, 640–645
 31 Racine, 308
 33 Locke, 176–177
 35 Rousseau, 344
 49 Darwin, 312
 52 Dostoevsky, 295–297, 383–385
 53 James, William, 391–392, 717–718
 54 Freud, 418–421, 659, 708–711, 724–725, 752–754, 766, 789–790
 59 Proust, 355–356
 60 Woolf, 92

1c. The distinction between love and desire: the generous and acquisitive aims

 4 Euripides, 613–614
 6 Plato, 20, 23–24, 115–129, 153–155, 164–165
 7 Aristotle, 89–90
 8 Aristotle, 365, 406–411 passim, 414–417 passim, 420 passim, 421–423
 11 Lucretius, 55
 11 Epictetus, 192–198
 11 Plotinus, 405–411
 16 Augustine, 11–16, 437–438, 744–745
 17 Aquinas, 120–122, 615–616, 724–725, 726–727, 731–732, 733–737, 738–741, 742–743, 749–750
 19 Dante, 63–64
 21 Hobbes, 61
 23 Montaigne, 135–136
 31 Molière, 109–110
 35 Rousseau, 345–346
 51 Tolstoy, 525–526
 54 Freud, 420–421, 617–618, 673–674, 679, 783

1d. The aims and objects of love

Old Testament: *Song of Solomon*
Apocrypha: *Wisdom of Solomon,* 8:1–3 / *Ecclesiasticus,* 4:11–19; 9:8
New Testament: *Colossians,* 3:1–2 / *I Timothy,* 6:10–11 / *I John,* 2:15–16; 4:20–21
 5 Herodotus, 196–197
 6 Plato, 18–24, 120, 126–129, 161–167, 368–375
 8 Aristotle, 407–409, 418–419 passim, 421–423 passim, 423–424, 425–426, 636
 11 Epictetus, 158–160
 11 Plotinus, 322–327, 405–411, 545–546, 624, 654, 676–677

50. LOVE

THE GREAT IDEAS

50. LOVE

THE GREAT IDEAS

50. LOVE

THE GREAT IDEAS

50. LOVE

THE GREAT IDEAS

33 Locke, 1–2
43 Nietzsche, 512
51 Tolstoy, 214–218

5c. God's love of Himself and of creatures

Old Testament: *Deuteronomy,* 7:6–15; 10:15, 18 / *Psalms* passim / *Song of Solomon* / *Isaiah,* 43; 63:7–9 / *Jeremiah,* 13:11; 31 / *Ezekiel,* 16 / *Hosea* / *Jonah,* 4
Apocrypha: *Wisdom of Solomon,* 11:22–26; 12:13–16; 16:20–29 / *Ecclesiasticus,* 11:14–17; 16:11–17:32; 33:10–15
New Testament: *Matthew,* 6:25–34; 7:7–11; 10:29–31 / *Luke,* 11:1–13; 12:6–7,22–28 / *John,* 3:16–21; 13:31–17:26 / *Romans,* 8:29–39 / *Ephesians,* 3:14–20; 5:1–2 / *Titus,* 3:3–7 / *I John,* 3:1–2,16; 4:7–5:5 / *Revelation,* 3:19–21

16 Augustine, 140–141, 308–309, 646–647, 661–662, 685–688, 713–714
17 Aquinas, 30, 109–110, 111–112, 119–124, 197–200, 375–377, 494–495
18 Aquinas, 338–378, 482–484, 490–491
19 Dante, 48, 58, 93, 98–99, 106, 114, 123–124, 127–128, 132–133
19 Chaucer, 210–211, 273
20 Calvin, 90–91
28 Spinoza, 691, 694
29 Milton, 136–143, 161–162
39 Kant, 592
43 Kierkegaard, 414
51 Tolstoy, 271–272
52 Dostoevsky, 161, 197–200 passim
55 Barth, 474–475

CROSS-REFERENCES

For other references regarding:

The basic psychological terms in the analysis of love, *see* DESIRE 3c; EMOTION 1, 2–2c; PLEASURE AND PAIN 7a.
The comparison of love and knowledge, *see* KNOWLEDGE 4d.
The objects of love, *see* BEAUTY 3; DESIRE 1, 2b; GOD 3c; GOOD AND EVIL 1a, 3c; TRUTH 8e; WILL 7d.
Sexual instincts, sexual love, and their normal or abnormal development, *see* DESIRE 4b–4d; EMOTION 1c, 3c–3c(3); HABIT 3–3a; PLEASURE AND PAIN 4b, 7b, 8b–8c; TEMPERANCE 2, 6a–6b.
Conjugal love and its components, *see* FAMILY 7a.
Moral problems raised by love, *see* DUTY 8; JUSTICE 3; OPPOSITION 4d; PLEASURE AND PAIN 8b; SIN 2b; TEMPERANCE 6a–6b; VIRTUE AND VICE 6e.
The role of friendship in the life of the individual, the family, and the state, *see* FAMILY 7c; HAPPINESS 2b(5); STATE 3e; VIRTUE AND VICE 6e.
The brotherhood of man and the world community, *see* CITIZEN 8; MAN 11b; STATE 10f; WAR AND PEACE 11d.
Man's love of God, or charity, as a theological virtue, *see* DESIRE 7b; GOD 3c; VIRTUE AND VICE 8d(3), 8f; WILL 7d; the fruition of this love in eternal beatitude, *see* HAPPINESS 7c–7c(2); IMMORTALITY 5f.
God's love of Himself and of His creatures, *see* GOD 5h; GOOD AND EVIL 2a.

ADDITIONAL READINGS

Listed below are works not included in *Great Books of the Western World,* but relevant to the idea and topics in this chapter. These works are divided into two groups:

  I. Works by authors represented in this collection. This list is in approximate chronological order.
  II. Works by authors not represented in this collection. These authors are listed alphabetically within the era in which they lived.

For full bibliographic citations for the works listed, consult the Bibliography of Additional Readings which follows the last chapter in Volume 2.

I.

Plutarch. "On Envy and Hate," "How to Tell a Flatterer from a Friend," "On Brotherly Love," "Dialogue on Love," in *Moralia*
Augustine. *Of Continence*
———. *Of Marriage and Concupiscence*

Thomas Aquinas. *Quaestiones Disputatae, De Caritate*
———. *Summa Theologica,* PART II-II, QQ 106–107, 114–119, 151–154
———. *Two Precepts of Charity*
Dante. *The Convivio (The Banquet)*

50. LOVE

——. *La Vita Nuova (The New Life)*
Bacon, F. "Of Love," "Of Friendship," "Of Followers and Friends," in *Essayes*
Pascal. *Discours sur les passions de l'amour*
Molière. *Le misanthrope (The Man-Hater)*
Racine. *Andromache*
Hume. *A Treatise of Human Nature*, BK II, PART II
Voltaire. "Charity," "Friendship," "Love," "Love of God," "Love (Socratic Love)," in *A Philosophical Dictionary*
Rousseau. *Julie*
Smith, A. *The Theory of Moral Sentiments*
Kierkegaard. *Either/Or*
——. *Stages on Life's Way*
——. *Works of Love*
Goethe. *Elective Affinities*
——. *The Sorrows of Young Werther*
Balzac. *At the Sign of the Cat and Racket*
Dickens. *David Copperfield*
Tolstoy. *Anna Karenina*
——. *The Law of Love and the Law of Violence*
——. *On Life*
Ibsen. *John Gabriel Borkman*
——. *Peer Gynt*
Freud. *"Civilized" Sexual Morality and Modern Nervousness*
——. *Contributions to the Psychology of Love*
——. *Three Contributions to the Theory of Sex*
James, H. *The Golden Bowl*
——. *The Portrait of a Lady*
Shaw. *Caesar and Cleopatra*
——. *Man and Superman*
Chekhov. *The Sea-Gull*
Proust. *Remembrance of Things Past*
Cather. *My Ántonia*
Lawrence, D. H. *Sons and Lovers*
——. *Women in Love*
Fitzgerald. *The Last Tycoon*
——. *Tender Is the Night*
Faulkner. *Light in August*
Hemingway. *A Farewell to Arms*

II.
THE ANCIENT WORLD (TO 500 A.D.)

Catullus. *The Poems*
Cicero. *Laelius de Amicitia (Of Friendship)*
Horace. *Odes and Epodes*
Ovid. *Amores*
——. *The Art of Love*

THE MIDDLE AGES TO THE RENAISSANCE (TO 1500)

Abelard. *Letters*
Albo. *Book of Principles (Sefer ha-Ikkarim)*, BK III, CH 35
André le Chapelain. *The Art of Courtly Love*
Anonymous. *Amis and Amiloun*
——. *Aucassin and Nicolette*
——. *Sir Gawain and the Green Knight*
——. *The Song of Roland*
——. *Tristan and Iseult*
——. *Valentine and Orson*
Apuleius. *The Golden Ass*

Bernard of Clairvaux. *On Loving God*, CH 7
Boccaccio. *The Decameron*
——. *Il Filocolo*
Chrétien de Troyes. *Arthurian Romances*
Francis of Assisi. *The Little Flowers of St. Francis*, CH 21–22
Gower. *Confessio Amantis*
Guillaume de Lorris and Jean de Meun. *The Romance of the Rose*
Petrarch. *Sonnets*
——. *The Triumph of Love*
Pico della Mirandola, G. *A Platonick Discourse upon Love*
Thomas à Kempis. *The Imitation of Christ*, BK II; BK III, CH 5–10
Villon. *The Debate of the Heart and Body of Villon*

THE MODERN WORLD (1500 AND LATER)

Abe Kōbō. *The Woman in the Dunes*
Ariosto. *Orlando Furioso*
Beattie, A. *Chilly Scenes of Winter*
Bowen. *The Death of the Heart*
——. *The Heat of the Day*
Bradley, F. H. *Aphorisms*
——. *Collected Essays*, VOL I (3)
——. *Ethical Studies*, VII
Brontë, C. *Jane Eyre*
Brontë, E. *Wuthering Heights*
Browning, E. B. *Sonnets from the Portuguese*
Burton. *The Anatomy of Melancholy*, PART III, SECT I–III
Byron. *Don Juan*
Carew. *A Rapture*
Cary. *A Fearful Joy*
Castiglione. *The Book of the Courtier*
Congreve. *The Way of the World*
Corneille. *La Place Royale*
Crashaw. *The Flaming Heart*
D'Arcy. *The Mind and Heart of Love*
Dickinson, E. *Collected Poems*
Donne. *Songs and Sonnets*
Dryden. *All for Love*
Edwards, R. *Damon and Pithias*
Ellis. *Studies in the Psychology of Sex*
Emerson. "Love," in *Essays*, I
Fielding. *Tom Jones*
Flaubert. *Madame Bovary*
García Lorca. *Blood Wedding*
García Márquez. *Love in the Time of Cholera*
Gide. *Strait Is the Gate*
Gourmont. *The Natural Philosophy of Love*
Hardy, T. *Far from the Madding Crowd*
Harris, J. R. *Boanerges*
Hartmann, E. *Philosophy of the Unconscious*, (C) XIII (3)
Hawthorne. *The Blithedale Romance*
Hurd. *Letters on Chivalry and Romance*
John of the Cross. *The Living Flame of Love*
Keats. "The Eve of St. Agnes"
Kundera. *The Joke*
——. *The Unbearable Lightness of Being*

THE GREAT IDEAS

La Fayette. *The Princess of Cleves*
Lewis, C. S. *The Allegory of Love*
Malebranche. *The Search After Truth*, BK IV,
    CH 5-13
Manzoni. *The Betrothed*
Marvell. "To His Coy Mistress"
Menninger. *Love Against Hate*
Meredith. *Modern Love*
Michelangelo. *Sonnets*
Nabokov. *Lolita*
Neruda. *Twenty Love Poems and a Song of Despair*
Nygren. *Agape and Eros*
Patmore. *Mystical Poems of Nuptial Love*
Peirce, C. S. *Collected Papers*, VOL VI, par
    287-317
Poe. "The Fall of the House of Usher"
Richardson, S. *Pamela*
Rossetti. *The House of Life*
Rostand. *Cyrano de Bergerac*
Rougemont. *Love in the Western World*
Santayana. *Interpretations of Poetry and Re-
    ligion*, CH 5
——. *Reason in Society*, CH 1, 7
Scheler. *The Nature of Sympathy*
Schlegel, F. *Lucinde*
Schleiermacher. *Soliloquies*

Schopenhauer. *The World as Will and Idea*, VOL III,
    SUP, CH 44
Scruton. *Sexual Desire*
Sidgwick, H. *The Methods of Ethics*, BK I, CH 7;
    BK III, CH 4
Sidney, P. *Astrophel and Stella*
Spenser. *Epithalamion*
——. *The Faerie Queene*, BK IV
——. *An Hymne of Heavenly Love*
Stendhal. *The Charterhouse of Parma*
——. *Love*
——. *The Red and the Black*
Stephen, L. *The Science of Ethics*
Stevenson. *Virginibus Puerisque*
Synge. *Deirdre of the Sorrows*
Taylor, J. *A Discourse of the Nature, Offices and
    Measures of Friendship*
——. "The Marriage-Ring," in *Twenty-Five
    Sermons*
Tillich. *Love, Power, and Justice*
Tirso de Molina. *The Love Rogue*
Turgenev. *Liza*
Tyler. *Dinner at the Homesick Restaurant*
Wedekind. *Pandora's Box*
Wilde. *The Importance of Being Earnest*
Williams, T. *A Streetcar Named Desire*

I would like to ask readers, after glancing over the Outline of Topics in the Chapter 50 on LOVE, to pick out the particular topics that are of exceptional interest to them; then glance at the references under those topics to see which authors contribute to the discussion of those topics and to note the contribution of twentieth-century authors in Volumes 55 through 60. The Cross-References will show the many other ideas to which the idea of LOVE is related; and the Additional Readings will give a fair sampling of the extensive literature that has been written about LOVE.

Let me first call to the attention of the readers the fact that there are fifty topics in the list of references under the idea of LOVE. But readers should observe that not all of these fifty topics function as headings under which references to relevant passages in the great books are assembled. Three of the thirty-eight topics—1., 3., and 5.—function simply as logical hangers—headings that do not require references but serve only as statements that subsume a number of topical details. All the rest have under them references to passages in the great books, ordered serially by the number of the volumes referred to.

At this point, I must call to the attention of readers the fact that under many of these topics the first reference is to passages in the Old and New Testaments. The Holy Bible is not included in the set of *Great Books* because of the diversity of translations used by Jews, Roman Catholics, and the several Protestant sects; nevertheless, references are inclusive of all canonical and apocalyptical books, thus covering all versions of the Bible.

Turning from the Outline of Topics to the Reference section, readers will see that the authors cited and the passages in their works referred to (without mentioning the titles of these works) have been carefully selected so that their relevance to the topic will be clear and plain. We have eliminated all references that are not focal in this way, but are of merely tangential relevance. Readers will not have to scratch their heads wondering how this or that particular passage is relevant to the topic under which it is cited.

Just by glancing at the Reference section, topic by topic, readers will discover how frequently the names of certain authors appear because their writings touch on so many aspects of LOVE. Readers will also be able to discover the contribution of twentieth-century thought by noting the citation of authors in Volumes 55 through 60.

Finally, readers should turn their attention to the last two sections of Chapter 50—the Cross-References and the Additional Readings. The Cross-References will show readers the relation of the idea of LOVE to specific topics under many other of the great ideas. There are more than twenty-five such connections between LOVE and other ideas, and the connections are specified by the indication of the topic or topics in each case.

The Additional Readings are divided into two sections. Section I recommends other works by authors, some of whose works are included in this set of books. Section II, subdivided chronologically into three periods (antiquity, the Middle Ages, and modern times), lists authors not included in this set of books. The listing is alphabetically arranged. The Additional Readings recommended for the idea of LOVE exceed one hundred titles, so that in the 102 chapters of the *Syntopicon*, the total number of titles recommended exceeds a thousand.

Now that readers have examined the *Syntopicon* chapter reproduced here, let them read the essay on LOVE that will be found in Chapter 50 of the present volume.

I think they will find that this essay calls their attention to the main controversies about LOVE that have occurred in the last twenty-five centuries of Western thought. They will find the great diversity of opinion that exists on certain themes or topics. Since the essays are replete with quotations from the authors cited, they may even discern some traces of wisdom that they would like to explore further. In any case, they will have been given by these essays a foretaste of what they would be able to enlarge and fortify by reading the many other passages that are cited in the Reference section but are not quoted in the essays.

As the author of the 102 essays contained in this book, I think it would not be immodest for me to claim that readers of the essays will find that they have become familiar with the idea, that they have gained sufficient understanding to feel comfortable in discussing it with other individuals, and that the understanding achieved will enable them to look at themselves, their own families, their loved ones, their friends, the equality of men and women, the rearing of children, in a new light that is not only intellectually enlightening but also practically useful.

Two More Useful Features of the *Syntopicon*

If I may be forgiven for what amounts to a sales pitch for *The Great Books of the Western World*, the *Syntopicon* contains two additional features, which are very useful devices. These are placed in the *Syntopicon*'s second volume, immediately following Chapter 102 on WORLD. One is a Bibliography of Addtional Readings; the other is an Inventory of Terms. Both required careful editorial work to produce initially and then to revise and bring up to date for the second edition in 1990. Let me tell the readers first the way in which the Inventory of Terms may prove useful to users of the *Syntopicon*.

I said at the beginning of this Foreword that we started with more than 500 terms when we were compiling a list of the great ideas; after many discussions we reduced that number to the 102 terms that we finally decided on as the names for the 102 great ideas. But the terms not chosen could not be totally ignored. They all had some relation or subordination to the 102 great ideas we had selected. So we went further and compiled a list of terms like the ones we were left with, and constructed a much longer list of secondary and subordinate terms that now comprises the Inventory of Terms. As now completed and recently revised, it contains more than 2,000 terms.

Suppose a person using the *Syntopicon* finds at first that he has no pressing interest in any of the 102 great ideas, though I must confess I think that very unlikely. Nevertheless, suppose readers' initial interests lie elsewhere. If readers then go to the Inventory of Terms, which is arranged alphabetically, they will probably find there a term that is the name for the object of thought in which they are immediately interested. Affixed to that term, they will find references to one or more great ideas to which that term is related or subordinated; and for the one or more ideas, they will be sent to the topic or topics in which that particular matter is considered.

Let me give a few illustrations of how this works, using terms in the Inventory that name matters of current interest, matters that are of great significance today. This has not been the case in prior centuries and so that is why the terms in question were not considered great ideas, for only they have had great significance in *all* of the twenty-five preceding centuries.[3]

We are living, for the first time in the twentieth century, in a society that has a welfare system, in which our national budget includes a large sum for welfare entitlements. We may have questions about how this is working and whether the benefits outweigh the disadvantages. In the Inventory of Terms, readers will find the term "Dole," which will send them to the chapter on LABOR and to the topic 7e. and to WEALTH and the topic 8d.; or they will find the term "Welfare," which will send them to the same two great ideas.

Those interested in the biological and physical sciences may be gratified to find an entry for "DNA," which sends them to ANIMAL and there to topic 10.; or to the idea of EVOLUTION, and there to topic 2a. If physical rather than biological science is their main interest, they will find the term "Quantum mechanics" with reference to CHANCE, topic 3., MECHANICS, topics 8.-8e., and PHYSICS, topic 6.

Another example is applicable to those interested in twentieth-century existentialist philosophy, in which the notion of *angst* or dread is central. They will find the term "Dread" with references to BEING, topic 1. and to EMOTION, topic 2d.

Still two more examples. One is "Sex, sexuality." Under that term, readers will find references to ANIMAL, DESIRE, EVOLUTION, LOVE, and MAN. The other is "Power." Here there are references to twenty of the great ideas.

These few examples should suffice to illustrate the usefulness of the Inventory of Terms, but many more will catch the attention of readers who just thumb through the pages of the Inventory. They will see a great many terms connected with matters in which they have a current interest. In every case they will be sent to one or more great ideas and their component topics, in which such matters are discussed.

I said earlier that each of the *Syntopicon*'s 102 chapters had a final section entitled "Additional Readings," giving the title of works not included in *Great Books* that are worth

---

3. This explains the omission of equality; but equality and inequality appear in the Inventory of Terms, and refer to topics under 9 of the 102 great ideas.

reading in connection with the idea that is the subject of the chapter. In most cases, these lists of recommended readings comprise one hundred or more titles. But the only information given in these lists is the name of the author, the title of the book, and the period of time in which it was written or published.

That is not enough information to enable readers to go to libraries or bookstores to acquire a particular book in which they are especially interested. To assist readers in their search, we compiled what is called "Bibliography of Additional Readings." This is organized alphabetically by the names of the authors. Here readers will find precise information about the date of the works mentioned, their editions or translations, and other facts that enable them to track down the particular book being sought.

Accurate bibliographies are hard to come by. There are few as extensive and detailed as this one, as readers can see for themselves by inspecting it; and this one is also particularly useful to readers whose interest in the great ideas has been sufficiently aroused to investigate the vast literature in which the great ideas are thoroughly discussed.

A Summa Dialectica

The first book I wrote was published in 1928, entitled *Dialectic*. One use of that word "dialectic" signifies the process and the method of conducting conversations in which different views are advanced in regard to clearly stated issues or topics. At the end of that book, I proposed that, after twenty-five centuries of Western thought, some account-taking should be done—a systematic account of the diversity of opposing views that had been expressed on all the major problems and issues that had been confronted and disputed.

I coined the phrase "*Summa Dialectica*" for this projected work, modeling it on the phrase "*Summa Theologica*." In the twelfth and thirteenth centuries many of the great theologians wrote summations of Christian sacred theology. The radical difference between a twentieth-century *Summa Dialectica* that I projected and medieval summations of Christian sacred theology consisted in the radical difference with respect to truth of these two kinds of summation.

The principles of a medieval *Summa Theologica* were the articles of Christian faith, dogmatically declared; and the philosophical effort evoked by faith seeking understanding involved trying to present the best approximation to the truth about these matters that could be attained.

A *Summa Dialectica* would proceed in exactly the opposite fashion. It would try to present the clearest possible statement of disputable problems and issues, but on each of these it would call for suspended judgment about truth and falsity. It would present all points of view without taking any point of view. It would be dialectically neutral or impartial.

Now, more than sixty years later, as I look back at my youthful projection of a *Summa Dialectica* to produce for the *pluralistic* twentieth century what the *Summa Theologica* did for Christendom in the thirteenth century, I see that I may have accomplished it without knowing I was doing it, not as extensively as I had originally projected, but nevertheless essentially that.

I said earlier in this Foreword that *The Idea of Freedom*, produced in two volumes and 1,500 pages by the Institute for Philosophical Research, involved eight years of work by a large staff of persons. To produce similarly extensive work on all the other 101 great ideas would obviously require more than half a millennium. But the essays in this volume may serve as a briefer dialectical summation of Western thought in the great conversation about the 102 great ideas.

The same radical difference between a *Summa Dialectica* and a *Summa Theologica* will be found between this book of essays on the 102 great ideas and the books about great ideas that I have written in the last twenty years. That radical difference is with respect to suspended judgment about where the truth lies and a plain effort to get at the truth; or in other words between a dialectical and a doctrinal approach to the study of the great ideas.

I have written doctrinal books about such great ideas as truth, goodness, and beauty, liberty, equality, and justice, labor, happiness, and virtue, mind, and so on.[4] In each of these works, I have argued for the truth or correctness of one understanding of the idea under consideration, and against divergent, opposed, or inadequate understandings of it.

I did not write in a dialectically neutral or nonpartisan manner, the manner in which I have written the 102 essays that this book contains. That is why I feel somewhat justified in thinking that the present volume of essays, however inadequate it may be, is an approximate realization of my youthful dream of producing a *Summa Dialectica* for twentieth-century readers.

ACKNOWLEDGMENTS

Here I would like to tell the story of how and when the 102 essays were written and revised and also to acknowledge the help I was given in writing them.

When is easier to answer than *How*. For the first edition of the *Syntopicon* in 1952, they were written in the middle 1940's—about 1946–1947. The revision of the *Syntopicon* to accompany the second edition of *Great Books* occurred in 1988 and 1989.

There are three facts about the writing of the essays for the first edition that I must record. When I started writing, what I had before me were the list of the 102 great ideas, first tentative drafts of the 102 Outlines of Topics, and a list of the authors and works to be included in the *Great Books of the Western World*.

A great many of these books I had read before (some many times) from years of conducting great books seminars at Columbia University and the University of Chicago. But for those with which I was not well acquainted, I had on my desk the work done by the editorial staff—the readers and indexers—which gave me fine passages to quote where I found them relevant.

In the second place, I made what I think was a prudent decision to write the essays in the alphabetical order in which they would appear—starting with ANGEL and ending with WORLD. If I had allowed myself to choose to write the easier essays first and to postpone the more difficult ones until later, I might never have finished the job. Since the publication date had been set in advance, and was not that far off, I was under a punishing schedule. I had to finish all 102 essays at a certain time in order to get the whole *Syntopicon* completed and set in type on schedule.

The actual writing of the essays took twenty-six months of sitting at the typewriter with no time off—seven days a week and no vacations or recesses. I have in the course of my

---

4. *Six Great Ideas* (1981), *A Vision of the Future* (1984), *Intellect: Mind Over Matter* (1990).

life written many books—almost half the number of the 102 great ideas—but writing the 102 essays was like writing 102 books. When I write a book, I find the first few chapters the most difficult to write, and as the book gets going, successive chapters gain momentum from the earlier chapters. This makes them progressively easier to write, so that the later chapters almost write themselves; not so in the case of the 102 essays. As one idea succeeded another, no momentum was gained. Each essay had to have its own structure, determined by the thematic development appropriate to that idea and to none of the others. Hence, writing the 102 essays was like writing 102 books. I think it was the most arduous and demanding stint of writing that I have ever undertaken.

The third fact that I wish to record about the initial efforts is that it was not until I reached the ideas in the L section of the alphabetical list (that is, about halfway through the whole), that I discovered to my chagrin that it was only at this point that I had finally developed the appropriate style for writing the essays—a style that involved displaying examples of the great conversation in each essay by amply quoting the words of the authors instead of describing the arguments or differences of opinion in my own words.

Once I had perfected this style of writing, it was easy to go on doing it. But here I was in the middle of the alphabetical sequence. Should I go back and rewrite the first half or keep on writing until I had finished the whole list of ideas? There simply was not enough time left for me to cease going on and return to the revision of the ideas from ANGEL to LAW.

Luckily, I turned to Otto Bird, who was on my editorial staff, and pointed out to him the difference between my style when I had reached the L's and my style in the essays up to that point. He readily perceived the difference between the two styles and said he thought he could submit to me second drafts of those early essays that would approximate the style I thought was the correct one.

As I went on with writing the later essays, he did these redrafts of the first half of the essays, submitted them to me, and it was easy for me to take his suggestions for revision and put them into effect, so that, as they now appear in this volume, I think no one will detect any stylistic difference between the essays in the first half of the alphabetical order and the essays in the second half.

The work of Otto Bird, for which I am most grateful, was not the only help I received in revising the essays before they were published in the *Syntopicon* in 1952. I sent drafts of the essays to Robert M. Hutchins, who was Editor in Chief of *Great Books of the Western World*, and to Senator William Benton, who was its publisher, to William Gorman, who was my closest associate in the production of the *Syntopicon*, and to several other readers. They all returned the essays to me, marked up with their recommendations of changes to be made. I had all of these red-penciled copies of the essays before me when I completed the work of their revision.

The second major revision of the 102 essays occurred, as I have already pointed out, in 1988 and 1989. That was part of the revision of the *Syntopicon* for the second edition of *Great Books*, published in 1990. This revision of the essays was necessitated by the fact that the second edition contained fifteen additional authors in the period from Homer to Ibsen at the end of the nineteenth century, and forty-five twentieth-century authors in Volumes 55–60, representing our nomination of authors who might, in the next century, be recognized as major contributors to Western literature and thought in the twentieth century.

The essays, as written almost fifty years ago, did not mention these new authors in the set and did not display the contributions they made to the great conversation. That could only be accomplished by aptly quoting them at relevant places in the essays. That was a task easier to set for one's self than to accomplish effectively, and smoothly enough so that the new material would not stand out as intrusions. This took almost as much time and effort as did the writing of the first drafts.

The most extensive and radical alterations in the Outlines of Topics occurred with respect to the following ideas: ASTRONOMY AND COSMOLOGY, ELEMENT, EVOLUTION, MATHEMATICS, MECHANICS, SPACE, TIME, WEALTH, and WORLD. Anyone aware of the twentieth-century revolutions in the physical and biological sciences will not be surprised by this. But readers may be surprised to learn that advances in economics called for new topics under the idea of WEALTH; and twentieth-century contributions to philosophy and the social sciences required revising the Outlines of Topics for the following ideas: ANIMAL, CHANCE, DEMOCRACY, LANGUAGE, MATTER, PHILOSOPHY, PHYSICS, RELIGION, SCIENCE, and TRUTH.

Fortunately, I had help from colleagues in accomplishing these revisions for the second edition of the 102 essays, which were especially difficult to do with respect to all the ideas mentioned above. My closest editorial associate in the production of the second edition of *Great Books*, Philip Goetz, did what Robert Hutchins did for me in connection with the first edition: he read all 102 essays and made pertinent and penetrating suggestions for their revision. I also received help in connection with essays in particular fields of learning: from Jeremy Bernstein, Daniel Brown, and John Kenneth Galbraith in revising the essays dealing respectively with ideas in the fields of the physcial and biological sciences, and in the fields of economics and the social sciences.

Finally, I wish to acknowledge my gratitude to Senator William Benton and to Robert Gwinn who, as successive CEOs of Encyclopaedia Britannica, Inc., gave me the encouragement and support that was so indispensable to my completing the task of producing the *Syntopicon*, writing the 102 essays in twenty-six months in the mid-forties, and revising all of them in the late eighties. My gratitude to them is expressed in my dedication of this book to them.

THE GREAT IDEAS

1

Angel

INTRODUCTION

Influenced by a long tradition of religious symbolism in painting and poetry, our imagination responds to the word "angel" by picturing a winged figure robed in dazzling white and having the bodily aspect of a human being.

This image, common to believers and unbelievers, contains features which represent some of the elements of meaning in the abstract conception of angels as this is found in the writings of Jewish and Christian theologians and in related discussions by the philosophers. The human appearance suggests that angels, like men, are persons; that they are most essentially characterized by their intelligence. The wings suggest the function of angels—their service as messengers from God to man. The aura of light which surrounds them signifies, according to established conventions of symbolism, the spirituality of angels. It suggests that to imagine angels with bodies is to use a pictorial metaphor.

Another interpretation might be put upon this aura of light if one considers the role which the notion of angel has played in the history of thought. Wherever that notion has entered into discussions of God and man, of matter, mind, and soul, or knowledge and love, and even of time, space, and motion, it has cast light upon these other topics. The illumination which has been and can be derived from the idea of angels as a special kind of being or nature is in no way affected by doubts or denials of their existence.

Whether such beings exist or not, the fact that they are conceivable has significance for theory and analysis. Those who do not believe in the existence—or even the possible existence—of utopias nevertheless regard them as fictions useful analytically in appraising accepted realities. What an ideal society would be like can be considered apart from the question of its existence; and, so considered, it functions as a hypothesis in political and economic thought. What sort of being an angel would be if one existed can likewise serve as a hypothesis in the examination of a wide variety of theoretical problems.

The idea of angels does in fact serve in precisely this way as an analytical tool. It sharpens our understanding of what man is, how his mind operates, what the soul is, what manner of existence and action anything would have apart from matter. Hence it suggests how matter and its motions in time and space determine the characteristics of corporeal existence. Pascal's remark—that "man is neither angel nor brute, and the unfortunate thing is that he who would act the angel acts the brute"—points to the different conceptions of man which result from supposing him to be either angel or brute rather than neither. Such views of human nature, considered in the chapters on ANIMAL and MAN, cannot be fully explored without reference to theories of the human mind or soul in its relation to matter and to body. As the chapters on MIND and SOUL indicate, theories carrying the names of Plato and Descartes, which attribute to the human mind or soul the being and powers of a purely spiritual substance or entity, seem to place man in the company of the angels. In this tradition Locke applies the word "spirits" equally to human minds and to suprahuman intelligence.

It would be misleading to suppose that the idea of angels is primarily a construction of the philosophers—a fiction invented for their analytical purposes; or that it is simply their conception of a supramundane reality, concerning the existence and nature of which they dispute. In the literature of western civilization, angels first appear by name or reference in the Old and the New Testaments. Readers of the Bible will remember many scenes in which an angel of the Lord performs the mission of acquainting man with God's will. Among the most memorable of such occasions are the visits of the angels to Abraham and Lot and the angelic ministry of Gabriel in the Annunciation to Mary.

In one book of the Bible, Tobias (Tobit, as it is called in the King James Apocrypha), one of the leading characters is the angel Raphael. Through most of the story he appears as a man, but at the end, after he has accomplished his mission, he reveals his identity. "I am the angel Raphael," he declares,

one of the seven, who stand before the Lord.
    And when they had heard these things they were troubled; and being seized with fear they fell upon the ground on their face.
    And the angel said to them: Peace be to you, Fear not.
    For when I was with you, I was there by the will of God: bless ye him and sing praises to him.
    I seemed to eat and to drink with you; but I use an invisible meat and drink, which cannot be seen by men.
    It is time therefore that I return to him that sent me . . .
    And when he had said these things, he was taken from their sight; and they could see him no more.

As a result of scriptural exegesis and commentary, the angels become a fundamental topic for Jewish theologians from Philo to Maimonides, and for such Christian theologians as Augustine, Scotus Erigena, Gregory the Great, Aquinas, Luther, Calvin, Pascal, and Schleiermacher. They figure in the great poetry of the Judeo-Christian tradition—in *The Divine Comedy* of Dante, in *Paradise Lost* of Milton, and in Chaucer's *The Canterbury Tales* and Goethe's *Faust*.

The philosophers, especially in the 17th and 18th centuries, are motivated by Scripture or provoked by theology to consider the existence, the nature, and the activity of angels. Hobbes, for example, attacks the supposition

that angels are immaterial on the ground that the notion of incorporeal substance is self-contradictory and undertakes to reinterpret all the scriptural passages in which angels are described as spirits. After examining a great many, he says that "to mention all the places of the Old Testament where the name of Angel is found, would be too long. Therefore to comprehend them all at once, I say, there is no text in that part of the Old Testament, which the Church of England holdeth for Canonical, from which we can conclude, there is, or hath been created, any permanent thing (understood by the name of *Spirit* or *Angel*) that hath not quantity . . . and, in sum, which is not (taking Body for that which is somewhat or somewhere) Corporeal."

All the passages can be interpreted, Hobbes thinks, simply in the sense in which "angel" means "messenger" and "most often, a messenger of God," which signifies "anything that makes known his extra-ordinary presence." If, instead of existing only when they carry God's word to men, the angels are supposed to have permanent being, then they must be corporeal. As "in the resurrection men shall be permanent and not incorporeal," Hobbes writes, "so therefore also are the angels . . . To men that understand the signification of these words, *substance* and *incorporeal*"—and mean by "incorporeal" having no body at all, not just a *subtle* body—the words taken together "imply a contradiction." Hence Hobbes argues that to say "an angel, or spirit, is (in that sense) an incorporeal substance, is to say in effect that there is no angel or spirit at all. Considering therefore the signification of the word *angel* in the Old Testament, and the nature of dreams and visions that happen to men by the ordinary way of nature," Hobbes concludes that the angels are "nothing but supernatural apparitions of the fancy, raised by the special and extraordinary operation of God, thereby to make his presence and commandments known to mankind, and chiefly to his own people."

Locke seems to take the exactly opposite position. Asserting that we have "no clear or distinct idea of substance in general," he does not think spirits any less intelligible than bodies. "The idea of *corporeal substance*," he writes, "is as remote from our conceptions and apprehensions, as that of *spiritual substance* or spirit; and therefore, from our not having any notion of the substance of spirit, we can no more conclude its non-existence, than we can, for the same reason, deny the existence of body." Just as we form the complex idea of bodies by supposing their qualities, such as figure and motion, or color and weight, to co-exist in some substratum; so by supposing the activities we find in ourselves—such as "thinking, understanding, willing, knowing, and the power of beginning motion, etc."—to co-exist in some substance, "we are able to frame the *complex idea of an immaterial spirit.*"

Not only does Locke think that "we have as clear a perception and notion of immaterial substances as we have of material," but he also finds the traditional doctrine of a hierarchy of angels quite acceptable to reason. "It is not impossible to conceive, nor repugnant to reason, that there may be many species of spirits, as much separated and diversified one from another by distinct properties whereof we have no ideas, as the species of sensible things are distinguished one from another by qualities which we know and observe in them."

Locke goes even further—beyond the mere possibility of angels to the likelihood of their real existence. His reasoning resembles the traditional argument of the theologians on this difficult point. "When we consider the infinite power and wisdom of the Maker," he writes, "we have reason to think that it is suitable to the magnificent harmony of the Universe, and the great design and infinite goodness of the Architect, that the species of creatures should also, by gentle degrees, ascend upward from us toward his infinite perfection, as we see they gradually descend from us downwards."

Such speculations concerning the existence and the order of angels are usually thought to be the province of the theologian rather than the philosopher. But Francis Bacon, like Locke, does not think it unfitting for the philosopher to inquire into such matters. In natural theology—for him a part of philosophy—Bacon thinks it is improper "from the contemplation of nature, and the principles of human reason, to dispute or urge anything with vehemence as to the mysteries of faith." But "it is otherwise," he declares, "as to the nature of spirits and angels; this being neither unsearchable nor forbid, but in a great part level to the human mind on account of their affinity."

He does not further instruct us concerning angels in the *Advancement of Learning,* but in the *Novum Organum* he throws light on their nature as well as ours by touching on one characteristic difference between the human and the angelic mind. Discussing there the theory of induction, he holds that "it is only for God (the bestower and creator of forms), and perhaps for angels or intelligences at once to recognize forms affirmatively at the first glance of contemplation."

UNLIKE MOST of the great ideas with which we are concerned, the idea of angel seems to be limited in its historical scope. It is not merely that since the 18th century the discussion has dwindled, but also that the idea makes no appearance in the great books of pagan antiquity—certainly not in the strict sense of the term, whereby "angel" signifies a creature of God, spiritual in substance and nature, and playing a role in the divine government of the universe.

There are, nevertheless, analogous conceptions in the religion and philosophy of the ancients; and in philosophy at least, the points of resemblance between the analogous concepts are sufficiently strong to establish a continuity of discussion. Furthermore, elements in the thought of Plato, Aristotle, and Plotinus exercise a critical influence on Judeo-Christian angelology.

Gibbon relates how the early Christians made the connection between the gods of polytheism and their doctrine about angels. "It was the universal sentiment both of the church and of heretics," he writes, "that the daemons were the authors, the patrons, and the objects of idolatry. Those rebellious spirits who had been degraded from the rank of angels, and cast down into the infernal pit, were still permitted to roam upon the earth, to torment the bodies and to seduce the minds of sinful men. The daemons soon discovered and abused the natural propensity of the human heart towards devotion, and, artfully withdrawing the adoration of mankind from their Creator, they usurped the place and honors of the Supreme Deity."

In the polytheistic religions of antiquity, the demigods or inferior deities are beings superior in nature and power to man. "The polytheist and the philosopher, the Greek and the barbarian," writes Gibbon, "were alike accustomed to conceive a long succession, an infinite chain of angels, or daemons, or deities, or aeons, or emanations, issuing from the throne of light." In Plato's *Symposium,* for example, Diotima tells Socrates that Love "is intermediate between the divine and the mortal . . . and interprets between gods and men, conveying and taking across to the gods the prayers and sacrifices of men, and to men the commands and replies of the gods; he is the mediator who spans the chasm which divides them." Love, Diotima explains, is only one of "these spirits and intermediate powers" which "are many and diverse."

Such demigods are intermediate by their very nature. Although superhuman in knowledge and action, they still are not completely divine. Occupying a place between men and gods, they are, according to Plato, "by nature neither mortal nor immortal." Their existence is necessary to fill out the hierarchy of natures. They are links in what has come to be called "the great chain of being."

The analogy with the angels arises primarily from this fact of hierarchy. Both pagan and Christian religions believe in an order of supernatural or at least superhuman beings graded in perfection and power. In both, these beings serve as messengers from the gods to men; they act sometimes as guardians or protectors, sometimes as traducers, deceivers, and enemies of man. But the analogy cannot be carried much further than this. The angels, according to Christian teaching, are not inferior gods, or even demigods. As compared with the "intermediate spirits" of pagan religion, they are less human in character, as well as less divine. Nevertheless, the reader of the great poems of antiquity will find a striking parallelism between the heavenly insurrection which underlies the

action of *Prometheus Bound* and the angelic warfare in *Paradise Lost.*

IN THE WRITINGS of Plato, Aristotle, and Plotinus, philosophical inquiry turns from the sensible world of material things to consider the existence and nature of an order of purely intelligible beings. As there is an inherent connection between being perceptible to the senses and being material, so that which is purely intelligible must be completely immaterial. If ideas exist independently—in their own right and apart from knowing or thinking minds—then they constitute such an order of purely intelligible entities.

At this point a number of difficult questions arise. Are the intelligibles also intelligences, *i.e.,* are they an order of knowers as well as a realm of knowables? Can they be regarded as substances? And if so, do they have a mode of action appropriate to their mode of being—action which is other than knowing, action which in some way impinges on the course of events or the motions of the physical world?

Plotinus answers affirmatively that the purely intelligible beings are also pure intelligences, but he does not conceive them as having any power or action except that of knowledge. Another answer to these questions given in antiquity and the Middle Ages is that the intelligences are the celestial motors, the movers of the heavenly bodies. "Since we see," Aristotle writes, "that besides the simple spatial movement of the universe, which we say that the first and unmovable substance produces, there are other spatial movements—those of the planets—which are eternal (for a body which moves in a circle moves eternally), each of *these* movements also must be caused by a substance, both unmovable in itself and eternal." These secondary movers, Aristotle thinks, are "of the same number as the movements of the stars," and not only must they be eternal and unmovable, as is the prime mover, but also "without magnitude" or immaterial.

Plato offers an alternative hypothesis—that the celestial bodies are alive and have souls. This hypothesis, like Aristotle's, tends in the Middle Ages to be restated in terms of the theory of angels. Aquinas reports Augustine as thinking that "if the heavenly bodies are really living beings, their souls must be akin to the angelic nature." He himself holds that "spiritual substances are united to them as movers to things moved," the proof of which, he says, "lies in the fact that whereas nature moves to one fixed end, in which having attained it, it rests; this does not appear in the movement of the heavenly bodies. Hence it follows that they are moved by some intellectual substances."

The question whether intelligences govern the planets also occupies the attention of an astronomer like Kepler. Although he denies any need for such intelligences—among other reasons because planetary motion is not circular but elliptical—he argues that the celestial movements are the work either "of the natural power of the bodies, or else a work of the soul acting uniformly in accordance with those bodily powers." But whether or not they are to be regarded as *movers,* as well as *knowers* and *knowables,* the intelligences represent for ancient and medieval thought a mode of being exempt from the vicissitudes of physical change even as it is separate from matter.

WHEN MODERN philosophers consider spirits or spiritual being, they seldom deal with the ancient speculations about pure intelligibles or separate intelligences without being influenced by the theological doctrine of angels which developed in medieval thought.

The extent of this doctrine may be judged from the fact that the *Summa Theologica* of Aquinas contains a whole treatise on the angels, as well as additional questions on the speech of angels, their hierarchies and orders, the division between the good and the bad angels, and their action on men—the guardianship of the good angels and the assaults of the demons. That these additional questions are contained in the treatise on divine government throws some light on their theological significance.

The primary fact about the angelic nature is immateriality. An angel is immaterial both in its substantial being and in its characteristic activity which, says Aquinas, is "an altogether immaterial mode of operation." Being immaterial, they are also incorruptible. "Nothing is

corrupted except by its form being separated from the matter . . . Consequently," Aquinas writes, "a subject composed of matter and form ceases to be actually when the form is separated from the matter. But if the form subsists in its own being, as happens in the angels, it cannot lose its being." To signify that they are intelligences existing apart from matter, the angels are sometimes called "subsisting forms" and sometimes "separate substances."

Although they are imperishable in being and have immortal life, the angels are not, like God, truly eternal. "The Heaven of Heavens, which you created 'in the Beginning,' that is, before the days began, is some kind of intellectual creature," Augustine writes, but it is in "no way co-eternal with you." As created, the angels have a beginning. Yet, while not eternal, neither are they temporal creatures in continual flux, but, according to Augustine, they "partake in your eternity . . . through the rapture and joy of [their] contemplation of God . . . clinging to you unfailingly" and transcending "every vicissitude of the whirl of time." It is for this reason that the angels are spoken of as "aeviternal." Nevertheless, as Calvin points out, "a fancied divinity has been assigned them" by men because "the minds of many are so struck with the excellence of angelic natures."

The familiar question concerning the number of angels able to stand on a needle's point—if it was ever asked by medieval theologians—merely poses the problem of how an incorporeal substance occupies space. In his Preface to *Saint Joan,* Shaw corrects the myth about the medieval inquiry concerning the number of angels on the point of a needle. "The medieval doctors of divinity who did not pretend to settle how many angels could dance on the point of a needle," he writes, "cut a very poor figure as far as romantic credulity is concerned beside the modern physicists who have settled to the billionth of a millimetre every movement and position in the dance of the electrons." Quantum mechanics, with which Shaw was unacquainted, does not alter his comparison.

The way in which Aquinas discusses "angels in relation to place" discloses how the question serves to raise generally significant issues concerning the nature of space and quantity, and their relation to causality. He points out that a body occupies place in a circumscribed fashion, *i.e.*, its dimensive quantity is contained within the space; whereas "an angel is said to be in a corporeal place by application of the angelic power in any manner whatever to the place . . . An incorporeal substance virtually contains the thing with which it comes into contact, and is not contained by it." To an objector who thinks that since, unlike bodies, angels do not fill a place, several can be in the same place at the same time, Aquinas replies that two angels cannot be in the same place because "it is impossible for two complete causes to be immediately the cause of one and the same thing." Since an angel is where he acts, and since by the power of his action he contains the place at which he acts, "there cannot be but one angel at one place."

Angels are also said to go from one place to another without traversing the intervening space and without the lapse of time. Considering their immateriality, such action is less remarkable for angels to perform than is the action of electrons, which, according to modern quantum mechanics, jump from outer to inner orbits of the atom without taking time or passing through interorbital space.

The immateriality of angels has other consequences which throw comparative light on the conditions of corporeal existence. In the world of physical things we ordinarily think of a species as including a number of individuals. While all men have the same specific nature, they differ numerically or individually. But because angels are immaterial substances, it is held that each angel *is* a distinct species. "Things which agree in species but differ in number," Aquinas explains, "agree in form but are distinguished materially. If, therefore, the angels are not composed of matter and form . . . it follows that it is impossible for two angels to be of one species."

Furthermore, as Aquinas states in another place, among "incorporeal substances there cannot be diversity of number without diversity of species and inequality of nature." Each species is necessarily higher or lower than another, so that the society of angels is a perfect hierarchy in which each member occupies a distinct rank. No two angels are equal as, on the supposition that they share in the same specific humanity, all men are. Yet such names as "seraphim" and "cherubim" and the distinction between archangels and angels indicate an organization of spiritual substances into various groups—according to the tradition, into nine orders or subordinate hierarchies.

The nine orders or ranks of angelic being are described by Dante in the *Paradiso* as distinct circles of love and light. Using these metaphors he thus reports his vision of the heavenly hierarchy. "I saw a point which radiated a light so keen that the eye on which it blazes needs must close because of its great keenness . . . Perhaps as near as a halo seems to girdle the light which paints it, when the vapor that bears it is most dense, at such distance around the point a circle of fire was whirling so rapidly that it would have surpassed that motion which most swiftly girds the universe; and this was girt around by another, and that by a third, and the third by a fourth, by a fifth the fourth, then by a sixth the fifth. Thereon the seventh followed, now spread so wide that the messenger of Juno entire would be too narrow to contain it. So the eighth and the ninth."

Beatrice explains to him how the relation of the circles to one another and to the Point which is God depends upon their measure of love and truth, whereby there is "a wondrous correspondence of greater to more and of smaller to less, in each heaven with respect to its Intelligence." She then amplifies her meaning: "The first circles have shown to you the Seraphim and the Cherubim. Thus swiftly they follow their bonds, in order to liken themselves to the point as most they can, and they can in proportion as they are exalted in vision. Those other loves who go round them are called Thrones of the divine aspect, because they terminated the first triad . . . The next triad that thus flowers in this eternal spring which nightly Aries does not despoil perpetually sings Hosannah with three melodies which sound in the three orders of bliss . . . first Dominions, then Virtues; and the third are Powers. Then in the two penultimate dances, the Principalities and Archangels circle; the last is wholly of Angelic sports. These orders all gaze upward and prevail downward, so that toward God all are drawn, and all do draw."

THE THEORY of angels raises many questions regarding the similarity and difference between them and disembodied souls. But for comparison with men, perhaps the most striking consequences of the theory of angels as bodiless intelligences concern the manner of their knowledge and government. The comparison can be made on quite different views of the nature of man and the soul. In fact, diverse conceptions of man or the soul can themselves be compared by reference to the angelic properties which one conception attributes to human nature and another denies.

Lacking bodies, the angels are without sense perception and imagination. Not being immersed in time and motion, they do not reason or think discursively as men do by reasoning from premises to conclusion. Whereas "human intellects," according to Aquinas, "obtain their perfection in the knowledge of truth by a kind of movement and discursive intellectual operation . . . as they advance from one known thing to another," the angels, "from the knowledge of a known principle . . . straightway perceive as known all its consequent conclusions . . . with no discursive process at all." Their knowledge is intuitive and immediate, not by means of concepts abstracted from experience or otherwise formed, but through the archetypal ideas infused in them at their creation by God. That is why, Aquinas goes on to say, angels "are called *intellectual* beings" as contrasted with such *rational* natures as "human souls which acquire knowledge of truth discursively." If men "possessed the fulness of intellectual light, like the angels, then in the first grasping of principles they would at once comprehend their whole range, by perceiving whatever could be reasoned out from them."

It would appear from this that conceptions of the human intellect which minimize its dependence on sense and imagination, and

which emphasize the intuitive rather than the discursive character of human thought, attribute angelic power to man. The same may be said of theories of human knowledge which account for its origin in terms of innate ideas or implanted principles. Still another example of the attribution of angelic properties to man is to be found in the supposition that human beings can communicate with one another by telepathy. The angels are telepathic; one angel, it is said, can make its ideas known to another simply by an act of will and without any exterior means of communication.

Lacking bodies, the angels are without bodily emotions, free from the human conflict between reason and passion, and completely directed in their love—or the motion of their will—by what they know. In *The Divine Comedy* Beatrice speaks of the angelic society as one in which "the Eternal Love opened into new loves." Adverting to the division between the good and the bad angels, she tells Dante, "Those whom you see here were modest to recognize their being as from the Goodness which had made them apt for intelligence so great: wherefore their vision was exalted with illuminating grace and with their merit, so that they have their will full and established." Yet their vision and love of God is not equal. In heaven, "The Primal Light that irradiates them all is received by them in as many ways as are the splendors to which It joins Itself. Wherefore, since the affection follows upon the act of conceiving, the sweetness of love glows variously in them."

Such a society, governed by knowledge and love, has no need for the application of coercive force, for angels are ordered to one another in such a way that no misunderstandings or disagreements can occur among them. The philosophical anarchist who proposes the ideal of a human society without restraint or coercion seems, therefore, to be angelicizing men, or at least to be wishing for heaven on earth. Conceiving government on earth in other terms, the writers of *The Federalist* remark that "if men were angels, no government would be necessary." If they had considered that the angelic society is governed by love alone and without force, they might have said, "if men were angels, no coercion would be necessary in their government."

ONE OF THE GREAT theological dogmas asserts that, from the beginning, the angels are divided into two hosts—the good and evil spirits. The sin of Lucifer, or Satan, and his followers is that of disobedience, or rebellion against God, motivated by a pride which refuses to be satisfied with being less than God. As Satan himself says, in *Paradise Lost*,

. . . pride and worse Ambition threw me down
Warring in Heav'n against Heav'ns matchless King.
. . . All his good prov'd ill in me,
And wrought but malice; lifted up so high
I 'sdeind subjection, and thought one step higher
Would set me highest, and in a moment quit
The debt immense of endless gratitude . . .
. . . . And that word
Disdain forbids me, and my dread of shame
Among the spirits beneath, whom I seduc'd
With other promises and other vaunts
Then to submit, boasting I could subdue
Th' Omnipotent.

The theologians try to define precisely the nature of Satan's pride in wishing to be God. "*To be as God,*" Aquinas explains, "can be understood in two ways: first, by equality; secondly, by likeness. An angel could not seek to be as God in the first way, because by natural knowledge he knew that this was impossible . . . And even supposing it were possible, it would be against natural desire, because there exists in everything the natural desire to preserve its own nature which would not be preserved were it to be changed into another nature. Consequently, no creature of a lower nature can ever covet the grade of a higher nature, just as an ass does not desire to be a horse."

It must be in the other way, then, Aquinas thinks, that Satan sinned by wishing to be like God. But this requires further explanation. "To desire to be as God according to likeness can happen in two ways. In one way, as to that likeness whereby everything is likened unto God. And so, if anyone desire in this way to be Godlike, he commits no sin; provided that he desires such likeness in proper order, that is to say, that he may obtain it from God. But he would sin were he to desire to be like God

even in the right way, but of his own power, and not of God's. In another way, he may desire to be like God in some respect which is not natural to one; *e.g.*, if one were to desire to create heaven and earth, which is proper to God, in which desire there would be sin."

In this last way, Aquinas asserts, "the devil desired to be as God. Not that he desired to resemble God by being subject to no one else absolutely, for thus he would be desiring his own non-being, since no creature can exist except by participating under God." But he "desired as the last end of his beatitude something which he could attain by virtue of his own nature, turning his appetite away from the supernatural beatitude which is attained by God's grace."

In the original sin of Lucifer and the other fallen angels, as well as in all subsequent intervention by Satan or his demons in the affairs of men, lie the theological mysteries of the origin of evil in a world created by God's love and goodness, and of the liberty of those creatures who, while free, can only do God's will. As indicated in the chapter on SIN, the fall of Adam from grace and innocence involves the same mysteries. Man's destiny is connected with the career of Lucifer in traditional Christian teaching, not only on the side of sin, but also with regard to man's redemption—salvation replacing the fallen angels by the souls of the elect in the heavenly choir.

Among the most extraordinary moments in our literature are those in which Lucifer talks with God about mankind, as in *Paradise Lost;* or about a particular man, as in the Book of Job or in the Prologue in Heaven in *Faust*. Their pagan parallel is the speech of Prometheus to a silent Zeus, but Prometheus, unlike Satan, is man's benefactor and he can defy Zeus because the Fates, whose secret he knows, rule over the gods. Lucifer, on the contrary, seems always to be in the service of God. When he appears to Ivan in *The Brothers Karamazov*, he protests, "I love men genuinely . . . and against the grain I serve to produce events and do what is irrational because I am commanded to." If it were otherwise, the warfare between the powers of light and darkness would have to be construed as a battle between equals, which, according to Christian orthodoxy, is the Manichaean heresy that regards the world as the battleground of the forces of good and evil.

The word "angelic" usually has the connotation of perfect moral goodness, but that must not lead us to forget that the demons are angelic in their nature although of a diabolical or evil will. Nor should the fact of Satan's subservience to God cause us to forget that Christian theology tries not to underestimate the power of the devil in his goings and comings on earth. Satan tried to tempt even Christ, and throughout the New Testament the destruction of the diabolic influence over men occupies a prominent place. The intervention of the devil in man's life provides, if not the theme, the background of Goethe's *Faust*.

As the theory of demonic influence and diabolic possession is an integral part of the traditional doctrine of angels, so, in modern times, demonology has been a major focus of attack upon theological teaching concerning spirits. Moralists have thought it possible to explain human depravity without recourse to the seductions of the devil, and psychiatrists have thought it possible for men to go mad or to behave as if bewitched without the help of evil spirits. The idea of the devil, according to Freud, is a religious fiction—"the best way out in acquittal of God" for those who try "to reconcile the undeniable existence . . . of evil with His omnipotence and supreme goodness."

The characteristic skepticism of our age has been directed against the belief in angels generally. It casts doubt by satire or denies by argument the existence of spirits both good and evil. Yet, all arguments considered, it may be wondered whether the existence of angels—or, in philosophical terms, the existence of pure intelligences—is or is not still a genuine issue. Or are there two issues here, one philosophical and the other theological, one to be resolved or left unresolved on the level of argument, the other to be answered dogmatically by the declarations of a religious faith?

2

Animal

INTRODUCTION

ALPHABETICAL ordering places ANIMAL after ANGEL in this list of ideas. There is a third term which belongs with these two and, but for the alphabet, might have come between them. That term is MAN.

These three terms—and a fourth, GOD, which rounds out the comparison—are conjoined in Shakespeare's statement of what is perhaps the most universal reflection of man upon himself. "What a piece of work is man!" says Hamlet, "How noble in reason! how infinite in faculty! in form and moving, how express and admirable! in action, how like an angel! in apprehension, how like a god! the beauty of the world! the paragon of animals!" Animal, angel, god—in each of these man has seen his image. And at different moments in the history of thought, he has tended to identify himself with one to the exclusion of the others.

Yet predominantly man has regarded himself as an animal, even when he has understood himself to be created in God's image, and to share with the angels, through the possession of intellect, the dignity of being a person. As his understanding of himself has varied, so has he altered his conception of what it is to be an animal.

In terms of a conception of personality which involves the attributes of reason and free will, man has legally, as well as morally and metaphysically, drawn a sharp line between persons and things, and placed brute animals in the class of things. According to the principle of this distinction, being alive or even being sensitive does not give animals, any more than plants and stones, the dignity or status of persons.

When man's animality—either in terms of his biological affinities or his evolutionary origins—has seemed an adequate definition of his nature, man has attributed to animals many of his own traits, his intelligence and freedom, even his moral qualities and political propensities. Nevertheless, he has seldom ceased to regard himself as the paragon of animals, possessing in a higher degree than other animals the characteristic properties of all.

There are exceptions to this, however. One such exception is the worship of animals in primitive cultures. In *The Golden Bough,* Frazer gives numerous examples of the belief that the "external soul"—which holds that "the soul may temporarily absent itself from the body without causing death"—sometimes extends itself into a belief that the soul is deposited in an animal. The result is a kind of animal-man blood-brotherhood: "such a sympathetic relation is supposed to exist that the moment the animal dies the man dies also, and similarly the instant the man perishes so does the beast." Thus, primitive tribes, which are usually identified as hunters, often hold animals in higher regard than most modern societies, which experiment on animals in the name of science.

Animals have also been glorified by man for skeptical or satiric purposes. Montaigne, for example, doubts that man can lay claim to any special attributes or excellences, and further suggests that, in some particulars at least, men are less able and less noble than the beasts. Relying on legends found in Pliny and Plutarch which describe the marvelous exploits of animals, he argues that "it is not by a true judgment, but by foolish pride and stubbornness, that we set ourselves before the other animals and sequester ourselves from their condition and society."

"Why," Montaigne asks, "do we attribute to some sort of natural and servile inclination . . . works which surpass all that we can do by nature and by art?" We have no grounds for believing that "beasts do by natural and obligatory instinct the same things that we do by our choice and cleverness." Rather "we must," he continues, "infer from like results like faculties, and consequently confess that this same reason, this same method that we have for working, is also that of the animals."

Nor can we excuse our presumption of superiority by the fact that we are compelled to look at animals from our human point of view. "When I play with my cat," Montaigne writes, "who knows if I am not a pastime to her more than she is to me?" Suppose animals were to tell us what they thought of us. "This defect that hinders communication between them and us, why is it not just as much ours as theirs? It is a matter of guesswork," Montaigne thinks, "whose fault it is that we do not understand one another; for we do not understand them any more than they do us. By this same reasoning they may consider us beasts, as we consider them."

If Montaigne's view were to prevail, no special significance could be given to "brute" as opposed to "rational" animal. For that matter, the same holds true whenever man is conceived as *just an animal,* paragon or not. Animals are brute only when man is not—only when to be human is to be somehow more than an animal, different in kind, not merely in degree.

Satirists like Swift idealize an animal nature to berate the folly and depravity of man. In his last voyage, Gulliver finds in the land of the Houyhnhnms a race of human-looking creatures, the Yahoos, who by contrast with their noble masters, the horses, are a miserable and sorry lot. Here it is the Yahoos who are brutes, bereft as they are of the intelligence and virtue which grace the splendid Houyhnhnms.

THE COMPARISON of men and animals takes still another direction in the allegories of fable and poetry. From Aesop to the medieval *Bestiaries,* there is the tradition of stories in which animals are personified in order to teach a moral lesson. In *The Divine Comedy* Dante uses specific animals to symbolize the epitome of certain passions, vices, and virtues. The intent of his allegory is, however, never derogatory to man as man. But when Machiavelli allegorizes the qualities required for political power, he advises the prince "knowingly to adopt the beast" and "to choose the fox and the lion." This tends to reduce human society to the jungle where strength and guile compete for supremacy. Other discussions in literature of the differences between animals and human beings can be found in the chapter on MAN.

The comparison of men and animals fails to touch the distinction, or lack of distinction, between animals and plants. This is basic to the definition or conception of animal nature. As in the case of men and animals, this problem can be approached in two ways: *either* from the side of plant life, and with respect to those functions which seem to be common to all living things; *or* from the side of animal life, and with respect to those functions which seem to belong only to animals, never to plants. On either approach the issue remains whether plants and animals are different in kind, not merely in degree.

On the one hand, it may be argued that sensitivity, desire, and locomotion (even perhaps sleeping and waking) are, in some form or degree, to be found in all living things. On the other hand, it may be argued that such functions as nutrition, growth, and reproduction, though obviously common to plants and animals, are performed by animals in a distinctive manner. If plants manifest all the vital powers or activities present in animals; or if in functions common to both, animals differ only in degree, then the scale of life would seem to be a continuous gradation rather than a hierarchy.

The opposite position, which affirms a difference in kind and consequently a hierarchy, is taken by Aristotle. In his biological writings, as well as in his treatise *On the Soul,* he draws a sharp line between plant and animal life by reference to faculties or functions absent in the one and found in the other. Aristotle first points out that "living may mean thinking or perception or local movement and rest, or movement in the sense of nutrition, decay, and growth. Hence," he goes on, "we think of plants also as living, for they are observed to possess in themselves an originative power through which they increase or decrease in all spatial directions; they grow up and down, and everything that grows increases its bulk alike in both directions or indeed in all, and continues to live so long as it can absorb nutriment."

This leads him to assign to plants what he calls a nutritive or vegetative soul, whereby they have the three basic faculties common to all living things—nutrition, growth, and reproduction. But Aristotle does not find in plants any evidence of the functions performed by animals, such as sensation, appetite, and local motion. These are the characteristic powers of the animal soul, called by him the "sensitive soul" because sensation is the source both of animal desire and animal movement.

Galen follows Aristotle in this distinction. In his *On the Natural Faculties* he limits his investigations to the functions common to all living things. He uses the word "natural" for those effects, such as "growth and nutrition ... common to plants as well as animals," which, in his view, are opposed to such activities as "feeling and voluntary motion ... peculiar to animals," that he calls "effects of the soul," or "psychic." It may seem surprising at first that Galen's study of nutrition, growth, and reproduction—not only of the functions themselves but of the bodily organs and processes involved in these functions—should be restricted to their manifestation in animals, and not in plants as well. The reason may be that for the naturalists of antiquity, the biological functions of vegetable matter did not yield their secrets readily enough to observation. A treatise on plants, not written by Aristotle but attributed to his school, begins with the remark that "life is found in animals and plants; but whereas in animals it is clearly manifest, in plants it is hidden and less evident."

This view of the world of living things as divided into the two great kingdoms of plant and animal life prevailed through centuries of speculation and research. But from the time that Aristotle began the work of classification, it has been realized that there exist numer-

ous examples of what Francis Bacon called "bordering instances . . . such as exhibit those species of bodies which appear to be composed of two species, or to be the rudiments between the one and the other."

Within the last hundred years the difficulty of classifying such specimens, particularly those which seem to fall between plant and animal, has raised the question whether the traditional distinction can be maintained. "If we look even to the two main divisions, namely, to the animal and vegetable kingdoms," writes Darwin, "certain low forms are so far intermediate in character that naturalists have disputed to which kingdom they should belong." Yet Darwin does not find the evidence available to him sufficient to determine whether all living things have descended "from one primordial form" or whether the evolution of life is to be represented in two distinct lines of development.

Since Darwin's day the researches of scientists like Jacques Loeb and Herbert Spencer Jennings on the behavior of microorganisms, and the phenomena of tropisms (*e.g.,* the sunflower's turning toward the sun), and the study of what appears to be local motion in plants, have contributed additional evidence relevant to the issue. Some research, however, is still considered open and arguable. Viruses, for example, cannot be classified as plants or animals, although some would argue that they are not organisms at all, for they cannot exist and reproduce without a host organism. As Waddington points out, the discovery of viruses has led to tremendous advances in the study of DNA recombination.

The fact that organisms exist which do not readily fall into either classification may signify continuity rather than separation between plants and animals; but it may also be taken to mean that more acute observations are required to classify these so-called "intermediate forms." Plant tropisms may or may not require us to deny that sensitivity belongs to animals alone. The apparent local motion of plants may be a mode of growth or a random movement rather than a directed change from place to place; and the attachment to place of apparently stationary animals, such as barnacles and mussels, may be different from the immobility of rooted plants.

AGAINST THE BACKGROUND of these major issues concerning plants, animals, and men as continuous or radically distinct forms of life, the study of animal organisms—their anatomy and physiology—acquires much of its critical significance.

Anatomy is an ancient science. Several surgical treatises of Hippocrates display an extensive knowledge of the human skeletal structure and the disposition of some of the organs of the human body. The dissection of animals, as well as gross observation, provides Aristotle with a basis for the comparative anatomy of different species of animal. For Galen as well as Aristotle, much of this anatomical study was motivated by an interest in the structure and relation of the organs involved in the local motion of the body as a whole, and in local motions within the body, such as the motions of the alimentary or reproductive systems.

It remains for a later investigator, schooled in the tradition of ancient biology, to make the startling discovery of the circulation of the blood through the motions of the heart. Harvey not only does this, but he also suggests the functional interdependence of respiration and circulation, based on his observation of the intimate structural connections between heart, arteries, veins, and lungs. His contribution is at once a departure from and a product of the scientific tradition in which he worked, for though his conclusions are radically new, he reaches them by a method of research and reasoning which follows the general principles of Aristotle and Galen. His insistence, moreover, on the necessity of finding a functional purpose for an organic structure stands as the classic rejoinder to Bacon's recommendation that formal and final causes be separated from material and efficient causes in the study of nature. Bacon assigns the first two types of cause to metaphysics, and limits physics to the last two.

Harvey's work on the generation of animals is another example of the continuity between ancient and modern biology. In some respects, Aristotle's researches on the reproductive organs and their functions are more general than Harvey's. They represent for him only part of the large field of comparative anatomy and have significance for the study of mating habits in different classes of animals. Yet on the problem of the act of generation itself, its causes and consequences, especially the phenomena of embryonic development, Harvey's treatise reads partly as a conversation with Aristotle and partly as the record of original observations undertaken experimentally.

"Respect for our predecessors and for antiquity at large," he writes, "inclines us to defend their conclusions to the extent that love of truth will allow. Nor do I think it becoming in us to neglect and make little of their labors and conclusions, who bore the torch that has lighted us to the shrine of philosophy." The ancients, in his opinion, "by their unwearied labor and variety of experiments, searching into the nature of things, have left us no doubtful light to guide us in our studies." Yet, Harvey adds, "no one of a surety will allow that all truth was engrossed by the ancients, unless he be utterly ignorant . . . of the many remarkable discoveries that have lately been made in anatomy." Referring to his own method of investigation, he proposes as a "safer way to the attainment of knowledge" that "in studying nature," we "question things themselves rather than by turning over books."

It is particularly with respect to animal generation that the great books exhibit continuity in the statement of basic problems in biology, as well as indicate the logical conditions of their solution. The issue of spontaneous generation as opposed to procreation runs through Aristotle, Lucretius, Aquinas, Harvey, and Darwin. The problem of sexual and asexual reproduction, with all the relevant considerations of sexual differentiation and sexual characteristics, is to be found in Aristotle, Darwin, and Freud. Questions of heredity, though they are raised with new significance by Darwin and William James, have a lineage as ancient as Plato.

Scientific learning has, of course, advanced in recent times with regard to the nature and behavior of animals. On such topics as heredity, the work of Mendel, Bateson, Morgan, Waddington, Schrödinger, and Dobzhansky is crucial; or, to take another example, our knowledge of the functioning of the respiratory and the nervous system has been greatly enlarged by the researches of Haldane, Sherrington, and Pavlov. Yet even in these areas, the background of recent scientific contributions is to be found in the great books—in the writings, for example, of Harvey, Darwin, and William James.

ANOTHER INTEREST which runs through the whole tradition of man's study of animals lies in the problem of their classification—both with respect to the principles of taxonomy itself, and also in the systematic effort to construct schemes whereby the extraordinary variety of animal types can be reduced to order. In this field Aristotle and Darwin are the two great masters. If the names of Buffon and Linnaeus also deserve to be mentioned, it must be with the double qualification that they are followers of Aristotle on the one hand, and precursors of Darwin on the other. According to Dobzhansky, "the classification of organisms that existed before the advent of evolutionary theories has undergone surprisingly little change in the times following it, and whatever changes have been made depended only to a trifling extent on the elucidation of the actual phylogenetic relationships through paleontological evidence . . . The subdivisions of the animal and plant kingdoms established by Linnaeus are, with few exceptions, retained in the modern classification, and this despite the enormous number of new forms discovered since then."

The Aristotelian classification is most fully set forth in the *History of Animals*. There one kind of animal is distinguished from another by many "properties": by locale or habitat; by shape and color and size; by manner of locomotion, nutrition, association, sensation; by organic parts and members; by temperament, instinct, or characteristic habits of action. With respect to some of these properties, Aristotle treats one kind of animal as differing from another by a degree—by more or less—of the same trait. With respect to other

properties, he finds the difference to consist in the possession by one species of a trait totally lacking in another. He speaks of the lion as being more "ferocious" than the wolf, the crow as more "cunning" than the raven; but he also observes that the cow has an "organ of digestion" which the spider lacks, the lizard an "organ of locomotion" which the oyster lacks. The sponge lives in one manner so far as "locale" is concerned, and the viper in another; reptiles have one manner of locomotion, birds another. So ample were Aristotle's data and so expert were his classifications, that the major divisions and subdivisions of his scheme remain intact in the taxonomy constructed by Linnaeus.

The radical character of Darwin's departure from the Linnaean classification stems from a difference in principle rather than a correction of observational errors or inadequacies. Where Aristotle and all taxonomists before Darwin classify animals by reference to their similarities and differences, Darwin makes inferred genealogy or descent the primary criterion in terms of which he groups animals into varieties, species, genera, and larger phyla.

Naturalists, according to Darwin, "try to arrange the species, genera, and families in each class, on what is called the Natural System. But what is meant by this system? Some authors look at it merely as a scheme for arranging together those living objects which are most alike, and for separating those which are most unlike . . . The ingenuity and utility of this system are indisputable," but Darwin thinks that its rules cannot be explained or its difficulties overcome except "on the view that the Natural System is founded on descent with modification—that the characters which naturalists consider as showing true affinity between any two or more species, are those which have been inherited from a common parent, all true classification being genealogical—that community of descent is the hidden bond which naturalists have been unconsciously seeking, and not some unknown plan of creation, or the enunciation of general propositions, and the mere putting together and separating objects more or less alike."

In Darwin's opinion, classification "must be

strictly genealogical in order to be natural." Only by the principle of descent—"the one certainly known cause of similarity in organic beings"—can we arrange "all organic beings throughout all time in groups under groups"; see "the nature of the relationships by which all living and extinct organisms are united by complex, radiating, and circuitous lines of affinities into a few grand classes"; and understand "the wide opposition in value between analogical or adaptive characters, and characters of true affinity." Furthermore, "the importance of embryological characters and of rudimentary organs in classification" becomes "intelligible on the view that a natural arrangement must be genealogical." By reference to "this element of descent," not only shall we be able to "understand what is meant by the Natural System," but also, Darwin adds, "our classifications will come to be, as far as they can be so made, genealogies; and will then truly give what may be called the plan of creation."

Whereas the Aristotelian classification is static in principle, having no reference to temporal connections or the succession of generations, the Darwinian is dynamic—almost a moving picture of the ever-shifting arrangement of animals according to their affinities through common ancestry or their diversities through genetic variation. Connected with this opposition between static and dynamic principles of classification is a deeper conflict between two ways of understanding the nature of scientific classification itself.

The point at issue is whether the classes which the taxonomist constructs represent distinct natural forms. Do they exist independently as objects demanding scientific definition or are the scientist's groupings somewhat arbitrary and artificial? Do they divide and separate what in nature is more like a continuous distribution with accidental gaps and unevennesses? This issue, in turn, tends to raise the metaphysical question concerning the reality and fixity of species, which relates to the problem of the difference between real and nominal definitions, and the difference between natural and arbitrary systems of classification.

On these matters Aquinas and Locke have much to say, as well as Aristotle and Darwin. Fuller discussion of such questions is to be found in the chapters on DEFINITION and EVOLUTION. Insofar as problems of classification and the nature of species have a bearing on evolution, they are treated in that chapter, as are the related issues of *continuity* or *hierarchy* in the world of living things, and of difference in *degree* or *kind* as between plants and animals, animals and men. The last two problems also occur in the chapters on LIFE AND DEATH and MAN.

The most interesting comment on continuity and discontinuity in the classification of animals is to be found in Dobzhansky. He writes as follows: "Let us examine first an imaginary situation, a living world in which all possible gene combinations are represented by equal numbers of individuals. Under such conditions no discrete groups of forms and no hierarchy of groups could occur, since the single gene differences producing striking phenotypical effects, like some of the mutations in Drosophila, would be the sole remaining source of discontinuity. Disregarding these, the variability would become a perfect continuum. The most 'natural,' although not the only possible, classification would be a sort of multi-dimensional periodic system, with a number of dimensions equal to that of the variable genes." Dobzhansky goes on to say, "Clearly the existing organic world is unlike the above imaginary one . . . only an infinitesimal fraction of the possible gene combinations is realized among the living individuals, or has ever been realized. According to a conservative estimate given by Wright . . . the number of possible combinations of genes is of the order of 10^{1000}, while the estimate of the number of electrons in the visible universe is of the order of 10^{100}."

ON THE THEME of comparisons between animals and men, two further points should be noted.

The first concerns the soul of animals. When soul is conceived as the principle or source of life in whatever is alive, plants and animals can be said to have souls. Like Aristotle, Augustine distinguishes "three grades of soul in universal nature": one which has "only the power of life . . . the second grade in which there is sensation . . . the third grade . . . where intelligence has its throne."

Though he also follows Aristotle in defining three kinds of soul, Aquinas distinguishes four grades of life, and in so doing differentiates between *perfect* and *imperfect* animals. "There are some living things," he writes, "in which there exists only vegetative power, as the plants. There are others in which with the vegetative there exists also the sensitive, but not the locomotive power; such are immovable animals, as shellfish. There are others which besides this have locomotive power, as perfect animals, which require many things for their life, and consequently movement to seek the necessaries of life from a distance. And there are some living things which with these have intellectual power—namely, men."

On this theory, man, viewed in terms of his animal nature, is a perfect animal. Viewed in terms of his reason or intellect, he stands above the highest animals. Yet having a soul is not peculiar to man, just as being alive, or sensitive, or mobile, is not. But when, as with Descartes, soul is identified with intellect—as "a thing which thinks, that is to say a mind . . . or an understanding, or a reason"—and, in addition, soul is conceived as a spiritual and immortal substance, then the conclusion seems to follow that animals do not have souls.

For Descartes, the theory of the animal as a machine or automaton follows as a further corollary. "If there had been such machines, possessing the organs and outward form of a monkey or some other animal without reason," Descartes claims that "we should not have had any means of ascertaining that they were not of the same nature as those animals." Hobbes likewise would account for all the actions of animal life on mechanical principles. "For what is the heart, but a spring," he asks, "and the nerves, but so many strings; and the joints, but so many wheels, giving motion to the whole body?" The animal is thus pictured as an elaborate system of moving parts, inflexibly determined to behave in certain ways under the impact of stimulation by external forces.

The doctrine of the animal automaton is sometimes generalized, as by La Mettrie, a follower of Descartes, to include the conception of man as a machine. The same conclusions which are reached from the denial of soul in animals seem to follow also from the theory that the soul, even in the case of man, is material or a function of matter. According to those who, like Lucretius, hold this view, the phenomena of life, sensation, and thought can be explained by the movement of atomic particles and their interaction.

The second point concerns the relation between instinct and intelligence in animals. The nature of animal instincts (or innate habits) is considered in the chapters on EMOTION and HABIT, as is the nature of animal intelligence in the chapters on MAN and REASONING. But here we face the issue whether instinct functions in animals, as reason does in man, to meet the exigencies of life; or whether in both, though varying in degree, intelligence cooperates with instinct to solve the problems of adjustment to environment.

Those who, like Aquinas, regard instinct and reason as the alternative and exclusive means which God provides for the ends of animal and human life, necessarily tend to interpret animal behavior in all its detail as predetermined by elaborate instinctive endowments. Accordingly, animal behavior, even when voluntary rather than purely the action of physiological reflexes, is said not to be free, or an expression of free choice on the part of the animal; for, as is pointed out in the chapter on WILL, Aquinas calls behavior "voluntary" if it involves some knowledge or consciousness of the objects to which it is directed.

Instinctive behavior, such as an animal's flight from danger or its pursuit of food or a mate, involves sense perception of the objects of these actions, as well as feelings or emotions about them. But though it is "voluntary" in the sense in which Aquinas uses that word, instinctive behavior is, according to him, the exact opposite of action based upon free will. It is completely determined by the inborn pattern of the instinct. It may vary in operation with the circumstances of the occasion, but it does not leave the animal the freedom to act or not to act, or to act this way rather than that. Such freedom of choice, Aquinas holds, depends on reason's ability to contemplate alternatives, to none of which is the human will bound by natural necessity.

Aquinas does not limit human reason and will to a role analogous to the one he ascribes to instinct and emotion in animal life. Their power enables man to engage in speculative thought and to seek remote ends. Nevertheless, on the level of his biological needs, man must resort to the use of his reason and will where other animals are guided by instinct. "Man has by nature," Aquinas writes, "his reason and his hands, which are *the organs of organs,* since by their means man can make for himself instruments of an infinite variety, and for any number of purposes." Just as the products of reason take the place of hair, hoofs, claws, teeth, and horns—"fixed means of defense or of clothing, as is the case with other animals"—so reason serves man's needs, in the view of Aquinas, as instinct serves other animals.

Others, like Darwin, James, and Freud, seem to take a different view. They attribute instinct to men as well as to animals. In their opinion instinctively determined behavior is influenced by intelligence and affected by memory and imagination, in animals as well as in men. They recognize, however, that instinct predominates in some of the lower forms of animal life and acknowledge that the contribution of intelligence is great only among the more highly developed organisms.

"Man has a far greater variety of *impulses* than any lower animal," writes James; "and any one of these impulses taken in itself, is as 'blind' as the lowest instinct can be; but, owing to man's memory, power of reflection, and power of inference, they come each one to be felt by him, after he has once yielded to them and experienced their results in connection with a *foresight* of those results." On the same grounds, James argues that "*every instinctive act, in an animal with memory, must cease to be 'blind' after being once repeated,* and must be accompanied with foresight of its 'end' just so far as that end may have fallen under the animal's cognizance."

If instinct, in animals or men, were sufficient for solving the problems of survival, there would be no need for what James calls "sagacity" on the part of animals, or of learning from experience. Like Montaigne, James assembles anecdotes to show that animals exercise their wits and learn from experience. "No matter how well endowed an animal may originally be in the way of instincts," James declares, "his resultant actions will be much modified if the instincts combine with experience, if in addition to impulses he have memories, associations, inferences, and expectations, on any considerable scale."

In his consideration of "the intellectual contrast between brute and man," James places "the most elementary single difference between the human mind and that of brutes" in the "deficiency on the brute's part to associate ideas by similarity," so that "characters, the abstraction of which depends on this sort of association, must in the brute always remain drowned." Darwin similarly makes the difference in degree between human and animal intelligence a matter of greater or less power to associate ideas. In consequence, human instincts are much more modified by learning and experience than the instincts of other animals, as in turn the higher animals show much greater variability in their instinctive behavior than do lower organisms.

It is not necessary to deny that men alone have reason in order to affirm that, in addition to instinct, animals have intelligence in some proportion to the development of their sensitive powers, especially their memory and imagination. The position of Aristotle and Aquinas seems to involve both points. But if we attribute the extraordinary performances of animals to their intelligence *alone,* rather than primarily to instinct, then we are led to conclude with Montaigne that they possess not merely a sensitive intelligence, but a reasoning intellect.

Montaigne asks, "Why does the spider thicken her web in one place and slacken it in another, use now this sort of knot, now that one, unless she has the power of reflection, and thought, and inference?" And in another place he asks, "What sort of faculty of ours do we not recognize in the actions of the animals? Is there a society regulated with more order, diversified into more charges and functions, and more consistently maintained, than that of the honeybees? Can we imagine so orderly an arrangement of actions and occupations as this to be conducted without reason and foresight?"

GREGARIOUSNESS in animals and the nature of animal communities are considered in the chapter on STATE, in connection with the formation of human society. But so far as human society itself is concerned, the domestication of animals signifies an advance from primitive to civilized life and an increase in the wealth and power of the tribe or city.

Aeschylus includes the taming of animals among the gifts of Prometheus, who yoked beasts of burden "that they might be man's substitute in the hardest tasks," and who "harnessed to the carriage, so that they loved the rein, horses, the crowning pride of the rich man's luxury." *The Iliad* pays eloquent testimony to the change in the quality of human life which accompanied the training of animals to respond to human command. Homer's reference to Castor as "breaker of horses" indicates the sense of conquest or mastery which men felt when they subdued wild beasts; and the oft-repeated Homeric epithet "horsetaming," which is intended as a term of praise for both the Argives and the Trojans, implies the rise of a people from barbarous or primitive conditions—their emancipation from the discomforts and limitations of animal life.

Aristotle points out that one mark of wealthy men is "the number of horses which they keep, for they cannot afford to keep them unless they are rich." For the same reason, he explains, "in old times the cities whose strength lay in their cavalry were oligarchies."

Legend and history are full of stories of the loyalty and devotion of animals to their human masters, and of the reciprocal care and affection which men have given them. But, motivated as it is by their utility for economic or military purposes, the breaking of animals to human will also frequently involves a violent or wanton misuse.

The use, or even the exploitation, of animals by man seems to be justified by the inferiority of the brute to the rational nature. As plants exist for the sake of animals, so animals, according to Aristotle, "exist for the sake of man, the tame for use and food, the wild, if not all, at least the greater part of them, for food, and for the provision of clothing and various instruments." Aristotle's conception of the natural slave, discussed in the chapter on SLAVERY, uses the domesticated animal as a kind of model for the treatment of human beings as tools or instruments.

Though he does not share Aristotle's view that some men are by nature slaves, Spinoza takes a comparable position with regard to man's domination and use of animals. "The law against killing animals," he writes, "is based upon an empty superstition and womanish tenderness, rather than upon sound reason. A proper regard, indeed, to one's own profit teaches us to unite in friendship with men, and not with brutes, nor with things whose nature is different from human nature . . . I by no means deny," he continues, "that brutes feel, but I do deny that on this account it is unlawful for us to consult our own profit by using them for our pleasure and treating them as is most convenient to us, inasmuch as they do not agree in nature with us."

But other moralists declare that men can befriend animals and insist that charity, if not justice, should control man's treatment of beasts. Nor is such contrary teaching confined to Christianity, or to the maxims of St. Francis, who would persuade men to love not only their neighbors as themselves, but all of God's creatures. Plutarch, for instance, argues that although "law and justice we cannot, in the nature of things, employ on others than men," nevertheless, "we may extend our goodness and charity even to irrational creatures." In kindness to dumb animals he finds the mark of the "gentle nature"—the sign of a man's humaneness. "Towards human beings as they have reason, behave in a social spirit," says Marcus Aurelius; but he also writes: "As to animals which have no reason, and generally all things and objects, do thou, since thou hast reason and they have none, make use of them with a generous and liberal spirit."

3

Aristocracy

INTRODUCTION

THE FORMS of government have been variously enumerated, differently classified, and given quite contrary evaluations in the great books of political theory. In the actual history of political institutions, as well as in the tradition of political thought, the major practical issues with respect to the forms of government—the choices open, the ideals to be sought, or the evils to be remedied—have shifted with the times.

In an earlier day—not merely in ancient times, but as late as the 18th century—the form of government called "aristocracy" presented a genuine alternative to monarchy and set a standard by which the defects and infirmities of democracy were usually measured. If aristocracy was not always regarded as *the* ideal form of government, the principle of aristocracy always entered into the definition of the political ideal.

Today, both in theory and practice, aristocracy is at the other end of the scale. For a large part of mankind, and for the political philosopher as well as in prevailing popular sentiment, aristocracy (together with monarchy) has become a subject of historical interest. It is a form of government with a past rather than a future. It no longer measures, but is measured by, democracy. If the aristocratic principle still signifies a factor of excellence in government or the state, it does so with a meaning now brought into harmony with democratic standards.

This change accounts for one ambiguity which the word "aristocracy" may have for contemporary readers. Formerly its primary, if not only, significance was to designate a form of government. It is currently used to name a special social class, separated from the masses by distinctions of birth, talent, property, power, or leisure. We speak of "the aristocracy" as we speak of "the elite" and "the four hundred"; or we follow Marx and Engels in thinking of the "feudal aristocracy" as the class "that was ruined by the bourgeoisie." The *Communist Manifesto* wastes little sympathy on the aristocrats who, while seeking an ally in the proletariat, forgot that "they [too] exploited under circumstances and conditions that were quite different." For Marx and Engels, the aristocracy and the bourgeoisie alike represent the propertied classes, but they differ in the manner in which they came by their property and power. The landed gentry and the feudal nobility got theirs largely by inheritance, the bourgeoisie by industry and trade.

Today, for the most part, we call a man an "aristocrat" if, justly or unjustly, he *claims* a right to certain social distinctions or privileges. It is in this sense, according to Weber, that the German universities regarded "scientific training" as "the affair of an intellectual aristocracy." We seldom use the word "aristocrat" today to indicate a man who *deserves* special political status or preeminence, though we do sometimes use it to name the proponent of any form of government which rests upon the political inequality of men.

Since the discussion of aristocracy in the great books is largely political, we shall here be primarily concerned with aristocracy as a form of government. The general consideration of the forms of government will be found in the chapter on GOVERNMENT. Here and in the other chapters which are devoted to particular forms of government, we shall consider each of the several forms, both in itself and in relation to the others.

THERE IS ONE element in the conception of aristocracy which does not change with changing evaluations of aristocratic government. All of the writers of the great political books agree with Plato that aristocracy is a "government of the few," according as the few rather than the one or the many exercise political power and dominate the state. By this criterion of number, aristocracy is always differentiated from monarchy and democracy.

Though he uses the word "oligarchy" to name what others call "aristocracy," Locke defines the three forms of government by reference to numbers. When the majority themselves exercise the whole power of the community, Locke says, "then the form of the government is a perfect democracy." When they put "the power of making laws into the hands of a few select men . . . then it is an oligarchy; or else into the hands of one man, and then it is a monarchy." Kant proceeds similarly, though again in somewhat different language. "The relation of the supreme power to the people," he says, "is conceivable in three different forms: either *one* in the state rules over all; or *some,* united in relation of equality with each other, rule over all the others; or *all* together rule over each individually, including themselves. The form of the state is therefore either *autocratic,* or *aristocratic,* or *democratic.*"

Hegel claims, however, that "purely quantitative distinctions like these are only superficial and do not afford the concept of the thing." The criterion of number does not seem to suffice when other forms of government are considered. It fails to distinguish monarchy from tyranny or despotism, which may consist of rule by one man, as has usually been the case historically. Number alone likewise fails to distinguish aristocracy from oligarchy. In the deliberations of the Medean conspirators, which Herodotus reports or invents, the rule of "a certain number of the worthiest" is set against both democracy and monarchy and identified as "oligarchy." How, then, shall aristocracy be distinguished from oligarchy?

There seem to be two answers to this question. In the *Statesman,* Plato adds to the characteristic of number the "criterion of law and the absence of law." The holders of political power, whatever their number, may govern either according to the established laws, or by arbitrary caprice in violation of them. "To go against the laws, which are based upon long experience, and the wisdom of counsellors who have graciously recommended them and persuaded the multitude to pass them, would be," the Eleatic Stranger declares in the *Statesman,* "a far greater and more ruinous error than any adherence to written law."

Taking the division of governments according to number, "the principle of law and the absence of law will bisect them all." Monarchy divides into "royalty and tyranny" depending on whether "an individual rules according to law . . . or governs neither by law nor by custom, but . . . pretends that he can only act for the best by violating the laws, while in reality appetite and ignorance are the motives." By the same criterion, the rule of the few divides "into aristocracy, which has an auspicious name, and oligarchy." While democracy is subject to the same division, Plato makes the same name apply to both its good and bad forms.

The second way in which aristocracy differs from oligarchy is also brought out in the *Statesman.* Since "the science of government," according to Plato, is "among the greatest of all sciences and most difficult to acquire . . . any true form of government can only be supposed to be the government of one, two, or, at any rate, of a few . . . really found to possess science." Because of this demand for "science," which presupposes virtue and competence in ruling, monarchy and aristocracy came to be defined as government by the single best man or by the few best men in the community.

A high degree of competence or virtue is, however, not the only mark by which the few may be distinguished from the many. The possession of wealth or property in any sizable amount also seems to divide a small class in the community from the rest, and Plato at times refers to aristocracy simply as the government of the rich. Yet if wealth is the criterion by which the few are chosen to govern, then oligarchy results, at least in contrast to that sense of aristocracy in which the criterion is excellence of mind and character. Aristocracy is called aristocracy, writes Aristotle, "either because the rulers are the best men, or because they have at heart the best interests of the state and of the citizens."

By these additional criteria—never by numbers alone—the ancients conceive aristocracy. When it is so defined, it always appears to be a good form of government, but never the only good form, or even the best. The same criteria also place monarchy among the good forms, and—at least in Plato's *Statesman*—democracy is a third good form, when it is lawful government by the many, the many being competent or virtuous to some degree. In this triad of good forms, aristocracy ranks second best, because government by one man is supposed to be more efficient, or because, in the hierarchy of excellence, the few may be superior, but only the one can be supreme. Aristotle, however, seems to rank aristocracy above monarchy. "If we call the rule of many men, who are all of them good, aristocracy, and the rule of one man royalty," he writes, "then aristocracy will be better for states than royalty."

In the Middle Ages, Huizinga observes, "The life of aristocracies . . . tends to become an all-round game. In order to forget the painful imperfection of reality, the nobles turn to the continual illusion of a high and heroic life. They wear the mask of Lancelot and of Tristram. It is an amazing self-deception."

THE INTRODUCTION of democracy into the comparison tends to complicate the discussion. Not only are the many usually the poor, but they are also seldom considered preeminent in virtue or competence. According to the way in which either wealth or human excellence is distributed, both oligarchy and aristocracy organize the political community in terms of inequalities in status, power, and privilege. This fact leads Rousseau, for example, to use the different kinds of inequality among men as a basis for distinguishing "three sorts of aristocracy—natural, elective, and hereditary."

Natural aristocracy, according to Rousseau, is based on that inequality among men which is due primarily to age and is found among simple peoples, where "the young bowed without question to the authority of experience." Elective aristocracy arose "in proportion as artificial inequality produced by institutions became predominant over natural inequality, and riches or power were put before age." This form, in Rousseau's opinion, is "the best, and is aristocracy properly so called." The third, which is characterized as "the worst of all governments," came about when "the transmission of the father's power along with his goods to his children, by creating patrician families, made government hereditary."

This emphasis upon inequality radically separates aristocracy from democracy. From Aristotle down to Montesquieu, Rousseau, and our own day, equality has been recognized as the distinctive element of democracy. Disregarding slaves who, for the ancients, were political pariahs, Aristotle makes liberty the other mark of democracy—all freemen having, apart from wealth or virtue, an equal claim to political status. As "the principle of an aristocracy is virtue," Aristotle writes, so wealth is the principle "of an oligarchy, and freedom of a democracy."

To the defenders of democracy, ancient or modern, aristocracy and oligarchy stand together, at least negatively, in their denial of the principle of equality. To the defenders of aristocracy, oligarchy is as far removed as democracy, since both oligarchy and democracy neglect or underestimate the importance of virtue in organizing the state. Yet oligarchy more than democracy is the characteristic perversion of aristocracy. It also puts government in the hands of the few, but it substitutes wealth for virtue as the criterion. The democratic critic of aristocracy usually calls attention to the way in which oligarchy tries to wear the mask of aristocracy. However far apart aristocracy and oligarchy may be in definition, he insists that in actual practice they tend to become identical, in proportion as wealth, or noble birth, or social class is taken as the sign of intrinsic qualities which are thought to deserve special political recognition.

Comparing aristocracy and democracy, Tocqueville writes: "An aristocracy is infinitely more skillful in the science of legislation than democracy can ever be. Being master of itself, it is not subject to transitory impulses ... It knows how to make the collective force of all its laws converge on one point at one time. A democracy is not like that; its laws are almost always defective or untimely. Therefore the measures of democracy are more imperfect than those of an aristocracy ... but its aim is more beneficial."

The defenders of aristocracy have admitted the tendency of aristocratic government to degenerate into oligarchy. Its critics are not satisfied with this admission. They deny that aristocracy has ever existed in purity of principle—they deny that the governing few have ever been chosen solely for their virtue. Machiavelli assumes it to be a generally accepted fact that "the nobles wish to rule and oppress the people ... and give vent to their ambitions." Montesquieu, although more optimistic about the possibility of a truly virtuous aristocracy, recognizes its tendency to profit at the expense of the people. To overcome this he would have the laws make it "an essential point ... that the nobles themselves should not levy the taxes ... and should likewise forbid the nobles all kinds of commerce ... and abolish the right of primogeniture among the nobles, to the end that by a continual division of the inheritances their fortunes may be always upon a level."

But perhaps the strongest attack upon aristocracy in all of the great political books is made by J. S. Mill in his *Representative Government*. He admits that "the governments which have been remarkable in history for sustained mental ability and vigour in the conduct of affairs have generally been aristocracies." But he claims that, whatever their abilities, such governments were "essentially bureaucracies," and the "dignity and estimation" of their ruling members were "quite different things from the prosperity or happiness of the general body of the citizens, and were often wholly incompatible with it." When their actions are dictated by "sinister interests," as frequently happens, the aristocratic class "assumes to themselves an endless variety of unjust privileges, sometimes benefiting their pockets at the expense of the people, sometimes merely tending to exalt them above others, or, what is the same thing in different words, to degrade others below themselves." George Orwell sums it up at the end of *Animal Farm* in the memorable line: "All animals are equal, but some animals are more equal than others."

Yet except by those political thinkers who deny the distinction between good and bad government, and hence the relevance of virtue to institutions which are solely expressions of power, the aristocratic principle is seldom entirely rejected. Even when the notion of a pure aristocracy is dismissed as an ideal which can never be fully realized, the aristocratic principle reappears as a counsel of perfection in the improvement of other forms of government.

Even so, one difficulty remains, which tends to prevent aristocracy from being realized in practice, quite apart from any question of its soundness in principle. It lies in the reluctance of the best men to assume the burdens of public office. The parable told in the Book of Judges applies to aristocracy as much as to monarchy.

The trees went forth on a time to anoint a king over them; and they said unto the olive tree, Reign thou over us.
But the olive tree said unto them, Should I leave my fatness, wherewith by me they honor God and man, and go to be promoted over the trees?
And the trees said to the fig tree, Come thou, and reign over us.
But the fig tree said unto them, Should I forsake my sweetness, and my good fruit, and go to be promoted over the trees?
Then said the trees unto the vine, Come thou, and reign over us.
And the vine said unto them, Should I leave my wine, which cheereth God and man, and go to be promoted over the trees?
Then said all the trees unto the bramble, Come thou, and reign over us.
And the bramble said unto the trees, If in truth ye anoint me king over you, then come and put your trust in my shadow: and if not, let fire come out of the bramble, and devour the cedars of Lebanon.

Socrates thinks he has a solution for this problem. In *The Republic*, he proposes a new way to induce good men to rule. Since "money and honor have no attraction for them," necessity, Socrates says, "must be laid upon them, and they must be induced to serve from fear of punishment . . . Now the worst part of the punishment is that he who refuses to rule is liable to be ruled by one who is worse than himself. And the fear of this, as I conceive, induces the good to take office . . . not under the idea that they are going to have any benefit or enjoyment themselves, but as a necessity, and because they are not able to commit the task of ruling to anyone who is better than themselves, or indeed as good."

THE POLITICAL ISSUES, in which monarchy, aristocracy, oligarchy, and democracy represent the major alternatives, cannot be clarified without recourse to the distinction between government by laws and government by men.

It has already been noted that in the *Statesman* Plato makes respect for the laws and violation of the laws the marks of good and bad government respectively. But he also proposes that "the best thing of all is not that the law should rule, but that a man should rule, supposing him to have wisdom and royal power." The imperfections of law could then be avoided, because one or a few men of almost superhuman wisdom would govern their inferiors even as the gods could direct the affairs of men without the aid of established laws. But if no man is a god in relation to other men, then, in Plato's opinion, it is better for laws or customs to be supreme, and for men to rule in accordance with them.

The larger issue concerning rule by law and rule by men is discussed in the chapters on CONSTITUTION and MONARCHY. But here we must observe how the difference between these two types of rule affects the understanding of all other forms of government. This can be seen in terms of Aristotle's distinction between royal and political government, which closely resembles the modern conception of the difference between absolute and despotic government on the one hand, and limited, constitutional, or republican government on the other.

There are passages in which Aristotle regards absolute rule by one or a few superior men as the divine or godlike form of government. When one man or a few excel "all the others together in virtue, and both rulers

and subjects are fitted, the one to rule, the others to be ruled," it is right, in Aristotle's opinion, for the government to be royal or absolute rather than political or constitutional—whether one man rules or a few. "Royal rule is of the nature of an aristocracy," he says. "It is based upon merit, whether of the individual or of his family."

But in other passages Aristotle seems to regard absolute government as a despotic regime, appropriate to the family and the primitive tribe, but not to the state, in which it is better for equals to rule and be ruled in turn. In either case, it makes a difference to the meaning of aristocracy, as also to monarchy, whether it be conceived as absolute or constitutional government.

When it is conceived as absolute government, aristocracy differs from monarchy only on the point of numbers—the few as opposed to the one. Otherwise, aristocracy and monarchy are defended in the same way. The defense usually takes one of two directions. One line of argument which stems from Plato and Aristotle claims that inequality in wisdom or virtue between ruler and ruled justifies absolute rule by the superior. The other line is followed by those who, like Hobbes, maintain that since sovereignty is absolute, unlimited, and indivisible, the difference between kinds of government "consisteth not in the difference of Power, but in the difference of Convenience, or Aptitude to produce the Peace, and Security of the people." When they are conceived as forms of absolute government, aristocracy and monarchy are attacked for the same reason; to those who regard absolutism or despotism in government as unjust because it violates the basic equality of men, an absolute monarchy and a despotic aristocracy are both unjust.

Aristocracy, however, can also be conceived as a form or aspect of constitutional government. Montesquieu, for example, divides governments into "republican, monarchical, and despotic," and under "republican" places those "in which the body, or only a part, of the people is possessed of the supreme power," thus including both democracy and aristocracy. In both, laws, not men, are supreme, but the spirit of the laws is different. In democracy, the "spring," or principle, "by which it is made to act," is virtue resting on equality; in aristocracy, "moderation is the very soul . . . a moderation . . . founded on virtue, not that which proceeds from indolence and pusillanimity." Hegel's comment on this theory deserves mention. "The fact that 'moderation' is cited as the principle of aristocracy," he writes, "implies the beginning at this point of a divorce between public authority and private interest."

For Aristotle, in contrast to Montesquieu, the two major types of constitution are the democratic and the oligarchic, according as free birth or wealth is made the chief qualification for citizenship and public office. Aristocracy enters the discussion of constitutional governments mainly in connection with the construction of the polity or mixed constitution. Although in most states "the fusion goes no further than the attempt to unite the freedom of the poor and the wealth of the rich," he points out that "there are three grounds on which men claim an equal share in the government, freedom, wealth, and virtue."

When the fusion goes no further than the attempt to unite the freedom of the poor and the wealth of the rich, "the admixture of the two elements," Aristotle says, is "to be called a polity." But sometimes the mixture of democracy with oligarchy may include an ingredient of aristocracy, as in "the distribution of offices according to merit." The union of these three elements "is to be called aristocracy or the government of the best," and "more than any other form of government, except the true and the ideal," it has, in Aristotle's judgment, "a right to this name." Polity and aristocracy, as mixed constitutions, are fusions of some of the same elements; hence, he says, it is "obvious that they are not very unlike."

BEGINNING IN the 18th century, and with the rise of representative government, the discussion of aristocracy as a distinct form of government is largely superseded by the consideration of the role which the aristocratic principle plays in the development of republican institutions.

The writers of *The Federalist,* for example,

respond in several places to the charge that the constitution which they are defending shows tendencies toward aristocracy or oligarchy. Yet in their consideration and defense of the new instrument of government as essentially *republican,* they frequently appeal to principles that are aristocratic in nature.

In giving their own meanings to the terms "republic" and "pure democracy"—that is, government by elected representatives on the one hand, and by the direct participation of the whole people on the other—the Federalists also give an aristocratic bent to the very notion of representation. They seem to share the opinion of Montesquieu that "as most citizens have sufficient ability to choose, though unqualified to be chosen, so the people, though capable of calling others to account for their administration, are incapable of conducting administrations themselves."

Thus Madison praises "the delegation of the government . . . to a small number of citizens elected by the rest" as tending "to refine and enlarge the public views, by passing them through the medium of a chosen body of citizens, whose wisdom may best discern the true interest of their country." He further points out that "it may well happen that the public voice, pronounced by the representatives of the people, will be more consonant to the public good than if pronounced by the people themselves, convened for the purpose."

On such a view, the people's representatives in the legislature, or other branches of government, are supposed to be not their minions, but their betters. For the American constitutionalists, as for Edmund Burke, the representative serves his constituents by making independent decisions for the common good, not by doing their bidding. This theory of representation, to which Mill and other democratic thinkers agree in part, supposes that the representative knows better than his constituents what is for their good.

The effort to ensure leadership by superior men may involve the aristocratic principle, yet it is also claimed by Hamilton, Madison, and Jay to be a necessary safeguard for popular government. The senate, for instance, is not only to provide elder statesmen but is also to serve as "a salutary check on the government . . . [which] doubles the security to the people, by requiring the concurrence of two distinct bodies in schemes of usurpation or perfidy, where the ambition or corruption of one would otherwise be sufficient." The electoral college aims directly at placing the immediate election of the president in the hands of "men most capable of analyzing the qualities adapted to the station . . . under circumstances favorable to deliberation." In addition it may serve as an "obstacle . . . opposed to cabal, intrigue, and corruption," which are the "most deadly adversaries of republican government."

In all these respects, as well as in the restrictions on suffrage which it permitted the states to impose, the unamended American constitution appears to have adopted an aristocratic principle in government. Whether the motivation of its proponents was in fact simply aristocratic, or whether it was partly or even largely oligarchic—leadership being the right of men of "good" family and substantial property—will always be a question to be decided in the light of the documents and the relevant historic evidence.

MORE DEMOCRATIC than the American constitutionalists of the 18th century, certainly so with regard to the extension of suffrage, Mill appears to be no less concerned than they are to introduce aristocratic elements into the structure of representative government.

According to Mill, two grave dangers confront a democracy: "Danger of a low grade of intelligence in the representative body, and in the popular opinion which controls it; and danger of class legislation on the part of the numerical majority." Claiming that much of the blame for both dangers lies in the rule of the majority, Mill looks for means to overcome the situation in which "the numerical majority . . . alone possess practically any voice in the State."

His major remedy was a system of proportional representation. This would supposedly constitute a democratic improvement by securing representation for "every minority in the whole nation . . . on principles of equal justice." But it may also serve to increase an aristocratic element, since it "affords the best security for the intellectual qualifications desirable in the representatives." This would be brought about by making possible the election of "hundreds of able men of independent thought, who would have no chance whatever of being chosen by the majority," with the result that Parliament would contain the "very *élite* of the country."

To make still more certain that men of superior political intelligence exert an effect upon government, Mill also proposes a plurality of votes for the educated and the establishment of an upper legislative chamber based on a specially qualified membership. Such proposals seem to indicate Mill's leanings toward aristocracy, not only because they aim at procuring a "government of the best," but also because they are designed to prevent a government based on a majority of "manual labourers" with the consequent danger of "too low a standard of political intelligence."

THE ISSUES RAISED by the theory of aristocracy, or by the aristocratic principle in government, seem to be basically the same in all centuries, however different the terms or the context in which they are expressed. Even when, as today, a purely aristocratic form of government does not present a genuine political alternative to peoples who have espoused democracy, there remains the sense that pure or unqualified democracy is an equally undesirable extreme. The qualifications proposed usually add an aristocratic leaven.

One issue concerns the equality and inequality of men. The affirmation that all men are created equal does not exclude a recognition of their individual inequalities—the wide diversity of human talents and the uneven distribution of intelligence and other abilities. Nor does it mean that all men use their native endowments to good purpose or in the same degree to acquire skill or knowledge or virtue.

To grasp the double truth—that no man is essentially more human than another, though one may have more of certain human abilities than another—is to see some necessity for the admixture of democratic and aristocratic principles in constructing a political constitution. But the issue is whether distributive justice requires, as a matter of right, that the best men should rule or hold public office.

Some political philosophers, like Plato and Aristotle, tend to take the aristocratic view that men of superior ability have a right to govern—that for them to be ruled by their inferiors would be unjust. This theory places greater emphasis on the inequality than on the equality of men. Their democratic opponents insist that the equality of men *as men* is the fundamental fact and the only fact having a bearing on the just distribution of suffrage. That certain individuals have superior aptitude for the exercise of political authority does not automatically confer that authority upon them. The inequality of men in merit or talent does not establish a political right, as does their equality in human nature. The selection of the best men for public office is, on this theory, not a matter of justice, but of expediency or prudence.

Another issue concerns the weight to be given the opinion of the majority as against the opinion of the wise or the expert when, as frequently happens, these opinions diverge or conflict. As the chapter on OPINION indicates, the experts themselves disagree about the soundness of the popular judgment.

Where Thucydides believes that "ordinary men usually manage public affairs better than their more gifted fellows," because "the latter are always wanting to appear wiser than the laws," Herodotus observes that "it seems easier to deceive the multitude than one man." Where Hegel holds it to be "a dangerous and a false prejudice, that the People alone have reason and insight, and know what justice is," Jay declares that "the people of any country (if, like the Americans, intelligent and well-informed) seldom adopt and steadily persevere for many years in an erroneous opinion respecting their interests," and Hamilton adds that "the people commonly *intend* the public good."

Sometimes the same author seems to take both sides of the issue, as Aristotle does when, though he says that "a multitude is a better judge of many things than any individual," he yet prefers government by the one or few who are eminent in wisdom or virtue. Each side, perhaps, contributes only part of the truth. Certainly those who acknowledge a political wisdom in the preponderant voice of the many, but who also recognize another wisdom in the skilled judgment of the few, cannot wish to exclude either from exerting its due influence upon the course of government.

Still another issue has to do with education. Shall educational opportunity be as universal as the franchise? Shall those whose native endowments fit them for political leadership be trained differently or more extensively than their fellow citizens? Shall vocational education be given to the many, and liberal education be reserved for the few?

These questions provide some measure of the extent to which anyone's thinking is aristocratic or democratic—or involves some admixture of both strains. In the great discussion of these questions and issues, there is one ever-present ambiguity. We have already noted it in considering the reality of the line between aristocracy and oligarchy. The agreement or disagreement of Mill and Aristotle, of Burke and Plato, of Hamilton and Paine, of Thorstein Veblen and Vilfredo Pareto, or John Dewey and Matthew Arnold cannot be judged without determining whether the distinction between the many and the few derives from nature or convention.

It is this distinction which Jefferson had in mind when, writing to Adams in 1813, he said, "There is a natural aristocracy among men. The grounds of this are virtue and talents . . . There is also an artificial aristocracy founded on wealth and birth, without either virtue or talents; for with these it would belong to the first class. The natural aristocracy I consider as the most precious gift of nature, for the instruction, the trusts, the government of society . . . The artificial aristocracy is a mischievous ingredient in government, and provision should be made to prevent its ascendancy."

How different from this view of aristocracy is the aristocracy praised by Nietzsche. "The essential thing in a good and healthy aristocracy" is that it "accepts with a good conscience the sacrifice of innumerable men who *for its sake* have to be suppressed and reduced to imperfect men, to slaves and instruments. Its fundamental faith must be that society should *not* exist for the sake of society but only as foundation and scaffolding upon which a select species of being is able to raise itself to its higher task and in general to a higher *existence*"—that of supermen!

4

Art

INTRODUCTION

THE WORD "art" has a range of meanings which may be obscured by the current disposition to use the word in an extremely restricted sense. In contemporary thought, art is most readily associated with beauty; yet its historical connections with utility and knowledge are probably more intimate and pervasive.

The prevalent popular association reflects a tendency in the 19th century to annex the theory of art to aesthetics. This naturally led to the identification of art with one kind of art—the so-called "fine arts," "beaux arts" or "Schöne Künst" (arts of the beautiful). The contraction of meaning has gone so far that the word "art" sometimes signifies one group of the fine arts—painting and sculpture—as in the common phrase "literature, music, and the fine arts." This restricted usage has become so customary that we ordinarily refer to a museum of art or to an art exhibit in a manner which seems to assume that the word "art" is exclusively the name for something which can be hung on a wall or placed on a pedestal.

A moment's thought will, of course, correct the assumption. We are not unfamiliar with the conception of healing and teaching as arts. We are acquainted with such phrases as "the industrial arts" and "arts and crafts" in which the reference is to the production of useful things. Our discussions of liberal education should require us to consider the liberal arts which, however defined or enumerated, are supposed to constitute skills of mind. We recognize that "art" is the root of "artisan" as well as "artist." We thus discern the presence of skill in even the lowest forms of productive labor. Seeing it also as the root of "artifice" and "artificial," we realize that art is distinguished from and sometimes even opposed to nature.

The ancient and traditional meanings are all present in our daily vocabulary. In our thought the first connotation of "art" is fine art; in the thought of all previous eras the useful arts came first. As Huizinga points out, "at the close of the Middle Ages, the connections between art and fashion were closer than at present. Art had not yet fled to transcendental heights; it formed an integral part of social life."

As late as the end of the 18th century, Adam Smith follows the traditional usage which begins with Plato when, in referring to the production of a woolen coat, he says: "The shepherd, the sorter of the wool, the woolcomber or carder, the dyer, the scribbler, the spinner, the weaver, the fuller, the dresser, with many others, must all join their different arts in order to complete even this homely production."

In the first great conversation on art—that presented in the Platonic dialogues—we find useful techniques and everyday skills typifying art, by reference to which all other skills are analyzed. Even when Socrates analyzes the art of the rhetorician, as in the *Gorgias,* he constantly turns to the productions of the cobbler and the weaver and to the procedures of the husbandman and the physician. If the liberal arts are praised as highest, because the logician or rhetorician works in the medium of the soul rather than in matter, they are called arts "only in a manner of speaking" and by comparison with the fundamental arts which handle physical material.

The Promethean gift of fire to men, which raised them from a brutish existence, carried with it various techniques for mastering matter—the basic useful arts. Lucretius, writing in

28

a line that goes from Homer through Thucydides and Plato to Francis Bacon, Smith, and Rousseau, attributes the progress of civilization and the difference between civilized and primitive society to the development of the arts and sciences:

Ships, farms, walls, laws, arms, roads, and all
  the rest,
Rewards and pleasures, all life's luxuries,
Painting, and song, and sculpture—these were
  taught
Slowly, a very little at a time,
By practice and by trial, as the mind
Went forward searching.

At the beginning of this progress Lucretius places man's discovery of the arts of metalworking, domesticating animals, and cultivating the soil. "Metallurgy and agriculture," says Rousseau, "were the two arts which produced this great revolution"—the advance from primitive to civilized life. The fine arts and the speculative sciences come last, not first, in the progress of civilization.

The fine arts and the speculative sciences complete human life. They are not necessary—except perhaps for the good life. They are the dedication of human leisure and its best fruit. The leisure without which they neither could come into being nor prosper is found for man and fostered by the work of the useful arts. Aristotle tells us that is "why the mathematical arts were founded in Egypt; for there the priestly caste was allowed to be at leisure."

THERE IS ANOTHER ambiguity in the reference of the word "art." Sometimes we use it to name the effects produced by human workmanship. We elliptically refer to *works of art* as art. Sometimes we use it to signify the cause of the things produced by human work—that skill of mind which directs the hand in its manipulation of matter. Art is both in the artist and in the work of art—in the one as *cause*, in the other as the *effect*. What is effected is a certain ennoblement of matter, a transformation produced not merely by the hand of man, but by his thought or knowledge.

The more generic meaning of art seems to be that of art as cause rather than as effect. There are many spheres of art in which no

tangible product results, as in navigation or military strategy. We might, of course, call a landfall or a victory a work of art, but we tend rather to speak of the art of the navigator or the general. So, too, in medicine and teaching, we look upon the health or knowledge which results from healing or teaching as natural. We do not find art in them, but rather in the skill of the healer or teacher who has helped to produce that result. Hence even in the case of the shoe or the statue, art seems to be primarily in the mind and work of the cobbler or sculptor and only derivatively in the objects produced.

Aristotle, in defining art as a "capacity to make, involving a true course of reasoning," identifies it with making as distinct from doing and knowing. Though art, like science and moral action, belongs to the mind and involves experience and learning, imagination and thought, it is distinct from both in aiming at production, in being knowledge of *how* to make something or to obtain a desired effect. Science, on the other hand, is knowledge *that* something is the case, or that a thing has a certain nature. Knowledge is sometimes identified with science, to the exclusion of art or skill; but we depart from this narrow notion whenever we recognize that skill consists in *knowing how* to make something.

"Even in speculative matters," writes Aquinas, "there is something by way of work; *e.g.*, the making of a syllogism, or a fitting speech, or the work of counting or measuring. Hence whatever habits are ordained to suchlike works of the speculative reason, are, by a kind of comparison, called arts indeed, but *liberal* arts, in order to distinguish them from those arts which are ordained to works done by the body, which arts are, in a fashion, servile, inasmuch as the body is in servile subjection to the soul, and man as regards his soul is free. On the other hand, those sciences which are not ordained to any suchlike work, are called sciences simply, and not arts."

The discussion of medicine in the great books throws light on the relation of art and science, in their origin as well as their development. The tribal medicine man or shaman, as Lévi-Strauss depicts him, is more a performer than a scientist. The shaman's practice is "a curious mixture of pantomime, prestidigitation, and empirical knowledge, including the art of simulating fainting and nervous fits, the learning of sacred songs," and other unscientific exercises. One of Lévi-Strauss's stories is quite startling: "The shaman hides a little tuft of down in a corner of his mouth, and he throws it up, covered with blood, at the proper moment—after having bitten his tongue or made his gums bleed—and solemnly presents it to his patient and the onlookers as the pathological foreign body extracted as a result of his suckings and manipulations."

Hippocrates writes of medicine as both an art and a science. In his treatise *On Ancient Medicine,* he says, "It appears to me necessary to every physician to be skilled in nature, and strive to know—if he would wish to perform his duties—what man is in relation to the articles of food and drink, and to his other occupations, and what are the effects of each of them on every one. And it is not enough to know simply that cheese is a bad article of food, as disagreeing with whoever eats of it to satiety, but what sort of disturbance it creates, and wherefore, and with what principle in man it disagrees . . . Whoever does not know what effect these things produce upon a man, cannot know the consequences which result from them, nor how to apply them." As a science, medicine involves knowledge of the causes of disease, the different kinds of diseases, and their characteristic courses. Without such knowledge, diagnosis, prognosis, and therapy would be a matter of guesswork—of *chance,* as Hippocrates says—or at best the application of rule of thumb in the light of past experience.

But the scientific knowledge does not by itself make a man a healer, a practitioner of medicine. The practice of medicine requires art in addition to science—art based on science, but going beyond science in formulating *general* rules for the guidance of practice in *particular* cases. The habit of proceeding according to rules derived from science distinguishes for Galen the artist in medicine from the mere empiric. The antithesis of artist and empiric—suggesting the contrast between operation by tested rule and operation by trial and error—parallels the antithesis between scientist and man of opinion.

IT HAS SELDOM, if ever, been suggested that an art can be originally discovered or developed apart from some science of the subject matter with which the art deals. This does not mean that an individual cannot acquire the habit of an art without being taught the relevant scientific knowledge. An art can be learned by practice; skill can be formed by repeated acts. But the teacher of an art cannot direct the learning without setting rules for his pupils to follow; and if the truth or intelligibility of the rules is questioned, the answers will come from the science underlying the art.

According to Kant, "every art presupposes rules which are laid down as the foundation which first enables a product if it is to be called one of art, to be represented as possible." In the case of "fine art," which he distinguishes from other kinds of art as being the product of "genius," Kant claims that it arises only from "a talent for producing that for which no definite rule can be given." Yet he maintains that a "rule" is still at its basis and may be "gathered from the performance, *i.e.,* from the product, which others may use to put their own talent to the test."

Granting that there is no art without science, is the reverse true, and is science possible without art? The question has two meanings. First, are there arts peculiarly indispensable to the development of science? Second, does every science generate a correlative art and through it work productively?

Traditionally, the liberal arts have been considered indispensable to science. This has been held to be particularly true of logic. Because they were intended to serve as the instrument or *the art* for all the sciences, Aristotle's logical treatises, which constitute the first systematic treatment of the subject, deserve the title *Organon* which they traditionally carry. Bacon's *Novum Organum* was in one sense an effort to supply a new logic or art for science, and to institute a renovation of the sciences by the experimental method.

As an art, logic consists of rules for the conduct of the mind in the processes of inquiry, inference, definition, and demonstration, by which sciences are constructed. Scientific method is, in short, the art of getting scientific knowledge. In the experimental sciences, there are auxiliary arts—arts controlling the instruments or apparatus employed in experimentation. The experiment itself is a work of art, combining many techniques and using many products of art: the water clock, the inclined plane, and the pendulum of Galileo; the prisms, mirrors, and lenses of Newton.

The second question—whether all sciences have related arts and through them productive power—raises one of the great issues about the nature of scientific knowledge, discussed in the chapters on PHILOSOPHY and SCIENCE.

For Bacon, and to some extent Descartes, art is the necessary consequence of science. At the beginning of the *Novum Organum,* Bacon declares that "knowledge and human power are synonymous since the ignorance of the cause frustrates the effect; for nature is only subdued by submission, and that which in contemplative philosophy corresponds with the cause, in practical science becomes the rule." The distinction Bacon makes here between the speculative and practical parts of knowledge corresponds to the distinction between science and art, or as we sometimes say, "pure and applied science." He opposes their divorce from one another. If science is the indispensable foundation of art and consists in a knowledge of causes, art in Bacon's view is the whole fruit of science, for it applies that knowledge to the production of effects.

His theory of science and his new method for its development are directed to the establishment of man's "empire over creation" which "is founded on the arts and sciences alone." Just as the present state of the arts accounts for "the immense difference between men's lives in the most polished countries of Europe, and in any wild and barbarous region of the new Indies," so further advances in science promise the untold power of new inventions and techniques.

On Bacon's view, not only the value, but even the validity, of scientific knowledge is to be measured by its productivity. A useless natural science—a science of nature which can-

not be used to control nature—is unthinkable. With the exception of mathematics, every science has its appropriate magic or special productive power. G. H. Hardy notes that "real" mathematics—"higher" mathematics, which produces nothing other than intellectual satisfaction—"must be justified as art if it can be justified at all." Even metaphysics, in Bacon's conception of it, has its "true natural magic, which is that great liberty and latitude of operation which dependeth upon the knowledge of forms."

The opposite answer to the question about science and art is given by Plato, Aristotle, and others who distinguish between speculative and productive sciences. They differ from Bacon on the verbal level by using the word "practical" for those sciences which concern moral and political action rather than the production of effects. The sciences Bacon calls "practical" they call "productive," but under either name these are the sciences of making rather than doing—sciences which belong in the sphere of art rather than prudence. But the significant difference lies in the evaluation of the purely speculative sciences which consist in knowledge for its own sake, divorced from art and morals, or from the utilities of production and the necessities of action.

In tracing the history of the sciences, Aristotle notes that those men who first found the useful arts were thought wise and superior. "But as more arts were invented, and some were directed to the necessities of life, others to recreation, the inventors of the latter were naturally always regarded as wiser than the inventors of the former, because their branches did not aim at utility. Hence, when all such inventions were already established, the sciences which do not aim at giving pleasure or at the necessities of life were discovered, and first in the places where men first began to have leisure . . . So that the man of experience is thought to be wiser than the possessors of any sense-perception whatever, the artist wiser than the man of experience, the master-worker than the mechanic, and the theoretical kinds of knowledge to be more of the nature of Wisdom than the productive." That the theoretic sciences are useless, in the sense of not providing men with the necessities or pleasures of life, is a mark of their superiority. They give what is better than such utility—the insight and understanding which constitute wisdom.

The Baconian reply condemns the conception that there can be knowledge which is merely contemplation of the truth. It announces the revolution which, for Dewey, ushered in the modern world. The pragmatic theory of knowledge had its origin in a conception of science at every point fused with art.

THE ANCIENTS, trying to understand the natural phenomena of change and generation, found that the processes of artistic production provided them with an analytic model. Through understanding how he himself worked in making things, man might come to know how nature worked.

When a man makes a house or a statue, he transforms matter. Changes in shape and position occur. The plan or idea in the artist's mind comes, through his manipulation of matter, to be embodied and realized objectively. To the ancients a number of different causes or factors seemed to be involved in every artistic production—material to be worked on; the activity of the artist at work; the form in his mind which he sought to impose on the matter, thus transforming it; and the purpose which motivated his effort.

In the medical tradition from Aristotle through Galen to Harvey, there is constant emphasis upon the artistic activity of nature. Galen continually argues against those who do not conceive nature as an artist. Harvey consciously compares the activity of nature in biological generation to that of an artist. "Like a potter she first divides her material, and then indicates the head and trunk and extremities; like a painter, she first sketches the parts in outline, and then fills them in with colours; or like the ship-builder, who first lays down his keel by way of foundation, and upon this raises the ribs and roof or deck; even as he builds his vessel does nature fashion the trunk of the body and add the extremities."

Of all natural changes, the one most closely resembling artistic production appears to be generation, especially the production of living things by living things. In both cases, a new individual seems to come into being. But upon further examination, artistic production and natural generation reveal significant differences—differences which divide nature from art.

Aquinas considers both and distinguishes them in his analysis of divine causation. In things not generated by chance, he points out that there are two different ways in which the form that is in the agent is passed on to another being. "In some agents the form of the thing to be made pre-exists according to its natural being, as in those that act by their nature; as a man generates a man, or fire generates fire. Whereas in other agents the form of the thing to be made pre-exists according to intelligible being, as in those that act by the intellect; and thus the likeness of a house pre-exists in the mind of the builder. And this may be called the idea of the house, since the builder intends to build his house like to the form conceived in his mind."

Thus in biological procreation the progeny have the form of their parents—a rabbit producing a rabbit, a horse, a horse. But in artistic production, the product has, not the form of the artist, but the form he has conceived in his mind and which he seeks to objectify. Furthermore, in generation, and in other natural changes as well, the matter which undergoes change seems to have in itself a tendency to become what it changes into, as for example the acorn naturally tends to become an oak, whereas the oaken wood does not have in itself any tendency to become a chair or a bed. The material the artist works on is entirely passive with respect to the change he wishes to produce. The artistic result is in this sense entirely of his making.

The realm of art, or of the artificial, is then opposed to the natural and differentiated from it. Kant, for whom art is distinguished from nature "as making is from acting or operating in general," claims that "by right, it is only production through freedom, *i.e.*, through an act of will that places reason at the basis of its action, that should be termed art." Consequently, art is that which would not have come into being without human intervention. The man-made object is produced by man, not in *any* way, but specifically by his intelligence, by the reason which makes him free.

Animals other than man are apparently productive, but the question is whether they can be called "artists." "A spider conducts operations that resemble those of a weaver, and a bee puts to shame many an architect in the construction of her cells. But," according to Marx, "what distinguishes the worst architect from the best of bees is this, that the architect raises his structure in imagination before he erects it in reality. At the end of every labour-process, we get a result that already existed in the imagination of the labourer at its commencement. He not only effects a change of form in the material on which he works, but he also realizes a purpose of his own that gives the law to his *modus operandi,* and to which he must subordinate his will."

As indicated in the chapter on ANIMAL, some writers, like Montaigne, attribute the productivity of animals to reason rather than to instinct. Art then ceases to be one of man's distinctions from the brutes. But if man alone has reason, and if the productions of art are works of reason, then those who refer to animals as artists speak metaphorically, on the basis of what Kant calls "an analogy with art . . . As soon as we call to mind," he continues, "that no rational deliberation forms the basis of their labor, we see at once that it is a product of their nature (of instinct), and it is only to their Creator that we ascribe it as art."

This in turn leads to the question whether nature itself is a work of art. "Let me suppose," the Eleatic Stranger says in the *Sophist,* "that things which are said to be made by nature are the work of divine art, and that things which are made by man out of these are the work of human art. And so there are two kinds of making and production, the one human and the other divine."

If we suppose that the things of nature are originally made by a divine mind, how does their production differ from the work of human artists, or from biological generation? One answer, given in Plato's *Timaeus,* conceives the original production of things as a

fashioning of primordial matter in the patterns set by the eternal archetypes or ideas. In consequence, the divine work would be more like human artistry than either would be like natural reproduction. The emanation of the world from the One, according to Plotinus, and the production of things out of the substance of God in Spinoza's theory, appear, on the other hand, to be more closely analogous to natural generation than to art.

Both analogies—of creation with art and with generation—are dismissed as false by Christian theologians. God's making is *absolutely* creative. It presupposes no matter to be formed; nor do things issue forth from God's own substance, but out of nothing.

Thus Augustine asks: "By what means did you make heaven and earth?" And he answers: "You did not work as a human craftsman does, making one thing out of something else as his mind directs. His mind can impose upon his material whatever form it perceives within itself by its inner eye . . . Clearly it was not in heaven or on earth that you made them. Nor was it in the air or beneath the sea, because these are part of the domain of heaven and earth. Nor was it in the universe that you made the universe, because until the universe was made there was no place where it could be made . . . Does anything exist by any other cause than that you exist? It must therefore be that *you spoke and they were made.* In your Word alone you created them." According to this view, human art cannot be called creative, and God cannot be called an artist, except metaphorically. "The artist," says Stephen in Joyce's *A Portrait of the Artist as a Young Man,* "like the God of the creation, remains within or behind or beyond or above his handiwork, invisible, refined out of existence, indifferent, paring his fingernails."

The issue concerning various theories of creation, or of the origin of the universe, is discussed in the chapter on WORLD. But here we must observe that, according to the view we take of the similitude between human and divine workmanship, the line we are able to draw between the realms of art and nature becomes shadowy or sharp. A passage from Woolf's *To the Lighthouse* is relevant here.

The artist—a painter—"could see it all so clearly, so commandingly, when she looked: it was when she took her brush in hand that the whole thing changed. It was in that moment's flight between the picture and her canvas that the demons set on her who often brought her to the verge of tears and made this passage from conception to work as dreadful as any down a dark passage for a child. Such she often felt herself—struggling against terrific odds to maintain her courage; to say: 'But this is what I see; this is what I see,' and so to clasp some miserable remnant of her vision to her breast, which a thousand forces did their best to pluck from her."

THE DISCUSSIONS OF ART in the great books afford materials from which a systematic classification of the arts might be constructed, but only fragments of such a classification are ever explicitly presented.

For example, the seven liberal arts are enumerated by various authors, but their distinction from other arts, and their ordered relation to one another, do not receive full explication. There is no treatment of grammar, rhetoric, and logic (or dialectic) to parallel Plato's consideration of arithmetic, geometry, music, and astronomy in *The Republic;* nor is there any analysis of the relation of the first three arts to the other four—traditionally organized as the *trivium* and the *quadrivium.*

However, in Augustine's work *On Christian Doctrine* we have a discussion of these arts as they are ordered to the study of theology. That orientation of the liberal arts is also the theme of Bonaventure's *Reduction of the Arts to Theology.* Quite apart from the problem of how they are ordered to one another, particular liberal arts receive so rich and varied a discussion in the tradition of the great books that the consideration of them must be distributed among a number of chapters, such as LOGIC, RHETORIC, LANGUAGE (for the discussion of grammar), and MATHEMATICS.

The principles of classification of the fine arts are laid down by Kant from "the analogy which art bears to the mode of expression of which men avail themselves in speech, with a view to communicating themselves to one another as completely as possible." Since such expression "consists in word, gesture, and tone," he finds three corresponding fine arts: "the art of speech, formative art, and the art of the play of sensations." In these terms he analyzes rhetoric and poetry, sculpture, architecture, painting and landscape gardening, and music.

A different principle of division is indicated in the opening chapters of Aristotle's *On Poetics.* The principle that all art imitates nature suggests the possibility of distinguishing and relating the various arts according to their characteristic differences *as imitations*— by reference to the *object* imitated and to the *medium* and *manner* in which it is imitated by the poet, sculptor or painter, and musician. "Color and form," Aristotle writes, "are used as means by some . . . who imitate and portray many things by their aid, and the voice is used by others . . . Rhythm alone, without harmony, is the means in the dancer's imitations . . . There is, further, an art which imitates by language alone, without harmony, in prose or in verse." Aristotle's treatise deals mainly with this art—poetry; it does not develop for the other fine arts the analysis it suggests.

Aristotle's principle also suggests questions about the useful arts. Are such arts as shoemaking and house-building imitations of nature in the same sense as poetry and music? Does the way in which the farmer, the physician, and the teacher imitate nature distinguish these three arts from the way in which a statue is an imitation, or a poem, or a house?

The Aristotelian dictum about art imitating nature has, of course, been as frequently challenged as approved. Apart from the issue of its truth, the theory of art as imitation poses many questions which Aristotle left unanswered. If there are answers in the great books, they are there by implication rather than by statement.

THE MOST FAMILIAR distinction between arts— that between the useful and the fine—is also the one most frequently made in modern discussion. The criterion of the distinction needs little explanation. Some of man's productions are intended to be used; others to be contemplated or enjoyed. To describe them in terms of imitation, the products of the useful arts must be said to imitate a natural function (the shoe, for example, the protective function of calloused skin). The imitation merely indicates the use, and it is the use which counts. But in the products of the fine arts, the imitation of the form, quality, or other aspect of a natural object is considered to be the source of pleasure.

The least familiar distinction among the arts is implied in any thorough discussion, yet its divisions are seldom, if ever, named. Within the sphere of useful art, some arts work toward a result which can hardly be regarded as an artificial product. Fruits and grains would grow without the intervention of the farmer, yet the farmer helps them to grow more abundantly and regularly. Health and knowledge are natural effects, even though the arts of medicine and teaching may aid in their production.

These arts, more fully discussed in the chapters on MEDICINE and EDUCATION, stand in sharp contrast to those skills whereby man produces the useful things which, but for man's work, would be totally lacking. In the one case, it is the artist's activity itself which imitates or cooperates with nature's manner of working; in the other, the things which the artist makes by operating on passive materials supplied by nature imitate natural forms or functions.

For the most part, the industrial arts are of the second sort. They transform dead matter into commodities or tools. The arts which cooperate with nature usually work with living matter, as in agriculture, medicine, and teaching. The distinction seems warranted and clear. Yet it is cut across by Smith's division of labor into productive and nonproductive. The work of agriculture is associated with industry in the production of wealth, but whatever other use they may have, physicians and teachers, according to Smith, do not directly augment the wealth of nations. As another economist, Veblen, points out, their "instinct of workmanship . . . disposes men to look with favor upon productive efficiency."

If to the foregoing we add the division of the arts into liberal and servile, the major tra-

ditional distinctions are covered. This last division had its origin in the recognition that some arts, like sculpture and carpentry, could not effect their products except by shaping matter, whereas some arts, like poetry or logic, were free from matter, at least in the sense that they worked productively in symbolic mediums. But by other principles of classification, poetry and sculpture are separated from logic and carpentry, as fine from useful art. Logic, along with grammar, rhetoric, and the mathematical arts, is separated from poetry and sculpture, as liberal from fine art. When the word "liberal" is used to state this last distinction, its meaning narrows. It signifies only the speculative arts, or arts concerned with processes of thinking and knowing.

The adequacy of any classification, and the intelligibility of its principles, must stand the test of questions about particular arts. The great books frequently discuss the arts of animal husbandry and navigation, the arts of cooking and hunting, the arts of war and government. Each raises a question about the nature of art in general and challenges any analysis of the arts to classify them and explain their peculiarities.

THERE ARE TWO OTHER major issues which have been debated mainly with respect to the fine arts.

One, already mentioned, concerns the imitative character of art. The opponents of imitation do not deny that there may be some perceptible resemblance between a work of art and a natural object. A drama may remind us of human actions we have experienced; music may simulate the tonal qualities and rhythms of the human voice registering the course of the emotions. Nevertheless, the motivation of artistic creation lies deeper, it is said, than a desire to imitate nature, or to find some pleasure in such resemblances.

According to Tolstoy, the arts serve primarily as a medium of spiritual communication, helping to create the ties of human brotherhood. According to Freud, it is emotion or subconscious expression, rather than imitation or communication, which is the deepest spring of art; the poet or artist "forces us to become aware of our inner selves in which the same impulses are still extant even though they are suppressed." Freud's theory of sublimation of emotion or desire through art seems to connect with Aristotle's theory of emotional catharsis or purgation. But Freud is attempting to account for the origin of art, and Aristotle is trying to describe an effect proper to its enjoyment.

The theories of communication, expression, or imitation, attempt to explain art, or at least its motivation. But there is also a conception of art which, foregoing explanation, leaves it a mystery—the spontaneous product of inspiration, of a divine madness, the work of unfathomable genius. We encounter this notion first, but not last, in Plato's *Ion*.

THE OTHER MAJOR controversy concerns the regulation of the arts by the state for human welfare and the public good.

Here, as before, the fine arts (chiefly poetry and music) have been the focus of the debate. It is worth noting, however, that a parallel problem of political regulation occurs in the sphere of the industrial arts. On the question of state control over the production and distribution of wealth, Smith and Marx represent extreme opposites, as Milton and Plato are poles apart on the question of the state's right to censor the artist's work. In this debate, Aristotle stands on Plato's side in many particulars, and J. S. Mill with Milton.

The problem of censorship or political regulation of the fine arts presupposes some prior questions. Plato argues in *The Republic* that all poetry but "hymns to the gods and praises of famous men" must be banned from the State; "for if you go beyond this and allow the honeyed muse to enter, either in epic or lyric verse, not law and the reason of mankind, which by common consent have ever been deemed the best, but pleasure and pain will be the rulers in our State." Such a view presupposes a certain theory of the fine arts and of their influence on the citizens and the whole character of the community. Yet because both Plato and Aristotle judge that influence to be far from negligible, they do not see any reason in individual liberty for the state to refrain from interfering with the rights of the artist for the greater good of the community.

To Milton and Mill, the measure of the artist's influence does not affect the question of the freedom of the arts from political or ecclesiastical interference. While admitting the need for protecting the interests of peace and public safety, Milton demands: "Give me the liberty to know, to utter, and to argue freely according to conscience, above all liberties." The issue for them is entirely one of liberty. They espouse the cause of freedom—for the artist to express or communicate his work and for the community to receive from him whatever he has to offer.

5

Astronomy and Cosmology

INTRODUCTION

Astronomy could take its place in this catalog of ideas on the ground that several of the great books are monuments of astronomical science, exemplifying the imaginative and analytic powers which have made it one of the most remarkable triumphs of the human mind. Its claim might further be supported by the fact that other great books—of mathematics, physics, theology, and poetry—have a context of astronomical imagery and theory. But the inclusion of astronomy can be justified by what is perhaps an even more significant fact, namely, that astronomical speculation raises problems and suggests conclusions which have critical relevance for the whole range of the great ideas.

Man has used astronomy to measure, not only the passage of time or the course of a voyage, but also his position in the world, his power of knowing, his relation to God. When man first turns from himself and his immediate earthly surroundings to the larger universe of which he is a part, the object which presses on his vision is the overhanging firmament with its luminous bodies, moving with great basic regularity and, upon closer observation, with certain perplexing irregularities. Always abiding and always changing, the firmament, which provides man with the visible boundary of his universe, also becomes for him a basic, in fact an inescapable, object of contemplation.

Careful and precise astronomical observations antedate the birth of astronomy as a science. The early interest in the heavenly bodies and their motions is often attributed to the usefulness of the predictions which can be made from a knowledge of celestial phenomena.

Whether their motive was entirely utilitarian, or partly religious and speculative, the Egyptians and Babylonians, we learn from Herodotus, undertook patient study of the heavens. They observed and recorded with immense persistence. They calculated and predicted. They turned their predictions to use through the priestly office of prophecy to foretell eclipses, tides, and floods, and they employed their calculations in the mundane arts of navigation and surveying to guide travel and fix boundaries. But they did not, like the Greeks, develop elaborate theories which sought to organize all the observed facts systematically.

With the Greeks, the down-to-earth, everyday utility of astronomy seems to count for less than its speculative grandeur. The dignity which they confer upon astronomy among the disciplines reflects the scope and majesty of its subject matter. The Greek astronomer, concerned as he is with figuring motions that range through the whole of space and are as old as time or as interminable, takes for his object the structure of the cosmos.

Aristotle and Plato pay eloquent tribute to the special worth of astronomy. In the opening chapter of his *Metaphysics,* Aristotle associates astronomical inquiry with the birth of philosophy. "Apart from usefulness," he says, "men delight ... in the sense of sight" and, he adds, "it is owing to their wonder that men both now begin and at first began to philosophise." They wondered first about "the obvious difficulties," but little by little they advanced to "greater matters," and "stated difficulties ... about the phenomena of the moon and sun and stars, and about the genesis of the universe." In his own philosophical thought, Aristotle's treatise *On the Heavens* is not only one of the basic natural sciences but certain of its principles have general significance for all the other parts of his physical science.

A wider view of the importance of astronomy is taken by Plato. In the *Timaeus,* he dwells on "the higher use and purpose for which God has given eyes to us . . . Had we never seen the stars, and the sun, and the heaven," Timaeus says, "none of the words which we have spoken about the universe would ever have been uttered . . . God invented and gave us sight," he continues, "to the end that we might behold the courses of intelligence in the heaven, and apply them to the courses of our own intelligence which are akin to them, the unperturbed to the perturbed; and that we, learning them and partaking of the natural truth of reason, might imitate the absolutely unerring courses of God and regulate our own vagaries."

For Plato, then, man's intellectual relation to the heavens does more than initiate philosophy. Man's self-rule, his purity and peace of soul, is at stake in that relation. That is one reason why, in both *The Republic* and the *Laws,* Plato makes astronomy a required part of the curriculum for the education of rulers. "He who has not contemplated the mind of nature which is said to exist in the stars . . . and seen the connection of music with these things, and harmonized them all with laws and institutions, is not able," the Athenian Stranger says in the *Laws,* "to give a reason for such things as have a reason."

Plato considers the opposition to astronomy on religious grounds by those who think that men who approach celestial phenomena by the methods of astronomy "may become godless because they see . . . things happening by necessity, and not by an intelligent will accomplishing good." His answer points out that one of the "two things which lead men to believe in the gods . . . is the argument from the order of the motion of the stars and of all things under the dominion of the mind which ordered the universe." It was a false understanding of these matters which "gave rise to much atheism and perplexity."

THE ISSUES RAISED by Plato concerning the importance of astronomy for purification and piety, for education and politics, run through the tradition of western thought. Though they are somewhat transformed in the context of Jewish and Christian beliefs, and altered by later developments in the science of astronomy itself, they remain as matters on which an author's strong assent or dissent forcefully reflects his whole intellectual position.

On the one hand, astronomers like Ptolemy, Copernicus, and Kepler, for all their differences on points of scientific theory, seem to concur in reaffirming Plato's conception of the bearing of their science on religion and morals. Lucretius and Augustine, on the other hand, while not agreeing with each other, seem to disagree with Plato. In the tradition of western thought, they represent different types of opposition to the Platonic view.

Where Plato and his followers, including religious Christians like Copernicus and Kepler, hold that true piety profits from astronomical study, Lucretius hopes that astronomy may help to free men from religious superstitions. If when "contemplating that great world/Of heavenly space . . . And pondering the ways of sun and moon," they do so "with a peaceful mind" because they see only the workings of natural law and no evidences of a controlling power in the will of the gods, then men achieve the natural piety of the scientist—different in the opinion of Lucretius from the false worship which is based on fear.

From his own experiences in dealing with the astronomy of the Manichaean sect in relation to their religious doctrine, Augustine insists that the teachings of religion in no way depend upon astronomy. He denies that such knowledge is in any way essential to true piety. "It would be foolish to doubt," he writes, that "a man, though he may not know the track of the Great Bear, is altogether better than another who measures the sky and counts the stars and weighs the elements, but neglects you who allot to all things their size, their number, and their weight."

When Manes, a Manichaean scholar, "was shown to be wrong in what he said about the sky and the stars and the movements of the sun and moon ... although these matters are no part of religious doctrine," his religious teachings, according to Augustine, inevitably suffered ridicule because of his pretension that they derived support from a science of the heavenly bodies. Augustine would disengage theology from astronomy. His position anticipates that later taken by Cardinal Barberini who, during the controversy over the Copernican hypothesis, is reported to have told Galileo that astronomy and religion have quite separate tasks, the one teaching how the heavens go, the other how to go to heaven.

Still another point of view on the importance of astronomy is represented in the skeptical and humanist attitude of Montaigne. "I feel grateful to the Milesian wench" who advised the philosopher Thales "to look rather to himself than to the sky." In saying this, or in quoting with approval the question asked of Pythagoras by Anaximenes—"What sense have I if I can amuse myself with the secret of the stars, having death or slavery ever present before my eyes?"—Montaigne intends more than a preference for the moral over the natural sciences. He regards astronomical inquiry as a prime example of man's "natural and original malady"—presumption. It is presumptuous to suppose that our minds can grasp and plot the course of the heavens when we fail to comprehend things much nearer at hand. Hence Montaigne advises everyone to say, in the spirit of Anaximenes: "When I am battered by ambition, avarice, temerity, and superstition, and have other such enemies of life within me, shall I go dreaming about the revolutions of the earth?"

Kant can be as critical as Montaigne of the frailty of human knowledge. "The investigations and calculations of the astronomers," he writes, have shown us "the abyss of our ignorance in relation to the universe." But Kant—an astronomer himself as well as a moralist—does not, therefore, advise us to forsake the study of the heavens. On the contrary, he recommends it not only for its scientific value, but for its moral significance.

"Two things," Kant declares in a passage which has become famous, "fill the mind with ever new and increasing admiration and awe,

the oftener and more steadily we reflect on them: the starry heavens above and the moral law within." The two fit together to produce a single effect. Astronomy with its view "of a countless multitude of worlds annihilates, as it were, my importance as an *animal* creature." Morality "elevates my worth as an *intelligence* by my personality, in which the moral law reveals to me a life independent of animality and even of the whole sensible world."

Kant's association of the starry heavens with the moral life is not so much an echo of, as a variant upon, Plato's precept that we apply "the courses of intelligence in heaven ... to the courses of our own intelligence." But in one passage of Freud we find an almost complete return to the Platonic insight. "Order has been imitated from nature," he writes; "man's observations of the great astronomical periodicities not only furnished him with a model, but formed the ground plan of his first attempts to introduce order into his own life."

ASTRONOMY HAS connections with biology and psychology, as well as with mathematics and physics. The obvious fact that the sun supports terrestrial life—operating here as a unique and indispensable cause—occasions the inference by Aquinas that it may also operate as a cause in the production of new species by spontaneous generation from putrefying matter. This notion bears some resemblance to the theory in contemporary genetics of the effect of cosmic radiations upon gene mutations.

Unlike these notions in biology, speculations concerning celestial influences upon psychological phenomena seem to cross the line between astronomy and astrology. Sometimes the influence upon man and his actions is found in the constellations attending a nativity; sometimes it is a particular influence of the sort still signified by the meaning of the word "lunacy"; and sometimes omens and auguries are read in the aspect of the heavens.

The chapters on PROPHECY and SIGN AND SYMBOL deal with the issues raised by astrology. Problems more closely associated with astronomical science and speculation are treated in other chapters. The cosmological problem of the origin of the material universe is discussed in the chapters on ETERNITY, TIME, and WORLD; the question of its size in the chapter on SPACE; the question of whether the celestial spheres are themselves alive or are moved by intelligences or spirits in the chapters on ANGEL and SOUL; and the question of the nature of the heavenly bodies in the chapter on MATTER.

This last problem is of crucial significance in the history of astronomy itself. Opposed theories of the motions of the heavenly bodies become correlated with opposed theories concerning their matter—whether that is different in kind from terrestrial matter or the same. It is with reference to these related issues that what has come to be called "the Copernican revolution" represents one of the great crises, certainly one of the most dramatic turning points, in the development of astronomy, and of physics and natural science generally.

The Copernican revolution did not take place by the improvement and enlargement of astronomical observations alone, nor even by the effect of these on alternative mathematical formulations. If it had not been accompanied by the radical shift from ancient to modern physics—especially with regard to the diversity or uniformity of the world's matter—the Copernican hypothesis concerning the celestial motions would have been no more than a mathematical alternative to the Ptolemaic hypothesis. Copernicus seems to advance it only as such, but in the hands of Kepler, Galileo, and Newton it becomes much more than that. They, rather than Copernicus, seem to accomplish the revolution connected with his name.

When their contribution is neglected or inadequately grasped, the Copernican revolution appears to be, as is often popularly supposed, merely a shift in astronomical theory. The problem being to organize mathematically the *apparent* motions of the heavens, Copernicus offers an alternative solution to that of Ptolemy. Instead of treating the earth as stationary and central in the cosmic system, Copernicus attributes three motions to the earth by treating it as a planet which revolves around the sun, spins on its axis, and varies the inclination of its axis with reference to the sun.

What is usually supposed to be revolution-ary about this hypothesis is its effect on man's estimate of himself and his place or rank in the universe. On either of the rival hypotheses, the apparent motions of the heavens remain unaltered, but not man's conception of himself, of his earth, or of the universe in which the earth's orbit cuts so small a figure. As Kant suggests, man's stature seems to shrink. He becomes "a mere speck in the universe" which has been enlarged to infinity, or at least to an unimaginable immensity. He is displaced from its center to become a wanderer with his planet. Humanity's self-esteem, according to Freud, was thus for the first time deeply wounded; he refers to the theory that "is associated in our minds with the name of Copernicus" as the "first great outrage" which humanity "had to endure from the hands of science."

It has been questioned whether this interpretation of the Copernican revolution fits all the documents in the case. Freud may be accurately reporting a popular feeling which, since the 18th century, has become a widespread consequence of Copernican and post-Copernican astronomy. But in earlier centuries when the Ptolemaic system prevailed, or even after Copernicus, the appraisal of man's rank seems to depend more upon the position he occupies in the hierarchy of God's creatures—below the angels and above the brutes—than upon the place or motion of the earth, or the size of the world.

Boethius, for example, finds the Ptolemaic universe large enough to remind man of the infinitesimal space he occupies. Dante, too, comments on the smallness of the earth in the scheme of things. When in his visionary travel Dante reaches the Empyrean, he looks down upon the earth and "with my sight," he tells us, "I returned through all and each of the seven spheres, and saw this globe such that I smiled at its paltry semblance; and that counsel I approve as best which holds it for least."

Kepler, a passionate Copernican deeply concerned with the human significance of astronomy, can be found arguing that the new hypothesis involves something more fitting for man than the old. In his last argument in defense of the Copernican view against that of

Tycho Brahe as well as that of Ptolemy, he declares, "it was not fitting that man, who was going to be the dweller in this world and its contemplator, should reside in one place as in a closed cubicle . . . It was his office to move around in this very spacious edifice by means of the transportation of the Earth his home." In order properly to view and measure the parts of his world, the astronomer "needed to have the Earth a ship and its annual voyage around the sun."

Yet the very fact that Kepler argues in this manner may be interpreted as indicating his sense of the drastic implications for man of the altered structure of the universe. Kepler may even be thought to announce the problem of the so-called "Copernican revolution" when, in denying that the earth can any longer "be reckoned among the primary parts of the great world," since it is only a part of a part, *i.e.*, the planetary region, he deliberately adds the qualification: "But I am speaking now of the Earth in so far as it is a part of the edifice of the world, and not of the dignity of the governing creatures which inhabit it."

Whether or not it was the traumatic blow to the human ego which Freud conjectures, there can be little doubt that the shift from Ptolemy to Copernicus involved a real shock to the imagination. The Ptolemaic system conforms to the look of the world, which is indeed the reason why it is still the one used in practical courses in navigation. Here again Kepler defends Copernicus by explaining why "our uncultivated eyesight" cannot be other than deceived and why it "should learn from reason" to understand that things are really different from the way they appear.

A certain disillusionment may result from this affirmation—repeated by every schoolboy who is taught the Copernican system—that, despite what we see, the sun does not move around the earth, and the earth both rotates and revolves. It undermines the trust men placed in their senses and the belief that science would describe the world as they saw it. In order to "save the appearances," that is, to account for the phenomena, science might henceforward be expected to destroy any naive acceptance of them as the reality.

Furthermore, though the Ptolemaic world was very large, the Copernican universe was much larger. Whereas in the former the radius of the earth was deemed negligible in relation to the radius of the sphere of the fixed stars, in the new universe the radius of the earth's orbit around the sun was negligible in relation to the same radius of the sphere of the fixed stars. It can hardly be doubted that this intensified some men's sense of almost being lost in an abyss of infinity. "I see those frightful spaces of the universe which surround me," Pascal writes, "and I find myself tied to one corner of this vast expanse, without knowing why I am put in this place rather than in another." When he regards the world's immensity as "the greatest sensible mark of the almighty power of God," Pascal experiences an awe which for him is qualified by reverence. Other men may experience the same feeling, but less with reverence than with a gnawing loneliness, born of the doubt that so vast a cosmos—if cosmos it is rather than chaos—can have been beneficently designed as man's habitation.

WHATEVER THE TRUTH about the effect of the Copernican theory in the order of opinion, imagination, and feeling, it did produce a direct result on the intellectual plane. It, more than any other single factor, led to the overthrow of certain crucial doctrines which had been linked together in the physics and astronomy of Aristotle; it thus radically changed the fundamental principles in terms of which man had understood the order and unity of nature. That scientific event deserves not only the name but the fame of the "Copernican revolution."

The revolution in the realm of theory goes much deeper than the substitution of one mathematical construction for another to describe the motions of the world's great bodies. As Freud points out, the heliocentric hypothesis associated with the name of Copernicus was known to the Alexandrian astronomers of antiquity. It is, for example, attributed to Aristarchus of Samos by Archimedes in *The Sand-Reckoner*.

As far as the earth's rotation is concerned, Ptolemy admits it is quite "plausible" to suppose "the heavens immobile and the earth turning on the same axis from west to east very nearly one revolution a day ... As far as the appearances of the stars are concerned," he goes on, "nothing would perhaps keep things from being in accordance with this simpler conjecture."

Why, then, does Ptolemy reject a supposition which is not only plausible but also, in accounting for the appearances, *simpler?* In part the answer may be that he does so because the contrary supposition conforms to our ordinary sense-experience of the earth's immobility and the motions of the heavens from east to west. But that is far from being the most important part of the answer. Ptolemy indicates the crucial part when he tells us that the otherwise plausible supposition of a rotating earth becomes "altogether absurd" when we consider the speed and direction of the motions of bodies within the earth's own atmosphere. His strongest count against the supposition is that it does not conform to the Aristotelian physics which distinguishes between natural and violent motions, assigns certain fixed directions to the natural motions of each of the four elements of matter, and denies that these elementary kinds of terrestrial matter enter into the composition of the heavenly bodies.

That Aristotle's physics and cosmology lie at the very heart of the issue is confirmed by the way in which Kepler later argues for the Copernican theory against Ptolemy. He does not defend its truth on the ground that it accounts for observable facts which the Ptolemaic hypothesis cannot handle. Nor does he prefer it merely because it is mathematically the simpler hypothesis. On the contrary, he specifically notes that anything which can be claimed on mathematical grounds for Copernicus over Ptolemy can be equally claimed for Brahe over Ptolemy. (Brahe's theory was that while the other planets revolve around the sun, the sun, with its planets, revolves around a stationary earth.) According to Kepler, the truth of these competing theories must finally be judged *physically,* not *mathematically,* and when the question is put that way, as it is not by Copernicus himself, Copernicans like Kepler, Galileo, and Newton take issue with

what had been associated with the Ptolemaic theory—the physics of Aristotle.

IN ORDER TO EXAMINE this issue, it is necessary to state briefly here certain features of Aristotle's physics which are more fully discussed in the chapters on CHANGE, ELEMENT, MECHANICS, and PHYSICS.

Just as Ptolemy's astronomy conforms to what we see as we look at the heavens, so Aristotle's physics represents a too simple conformity with everyday sense-experience. We observe fire rising and stones falling. Mix earth, air, and water in a closed container, and air bubbles will rise to the top, while the particles of earth will sink to the bottom. To cover a multitude of similar observations, Aristotle develops the theory of the natural motions and places of the four terrestrial elements— earth, air, fire, and water. Since bodies move naturally only to attain their proper places, the great body which is the earth, already at the bottom of all things, need not move at all. Being in its proper place, it is by nature stationary.

Two other observations exercise a decisive influence on Aristotle's theory. The naked eye sees no type of change in the heavenly bodies *other than* local motion or change of place. Unlike terrestrial bodies, they do not appear to come into being or perish; they do not change in size or quality. Furthermore, whereas the natural local motion of sublunary bodies appears to approximate the path of a straight line, the local motion of the celestial bodies appears to be circular rather than rectilinear.

To cover these observations, Aristotle's theory posits a different kind of matter for celestial and terrestrial bodies. An incorruptible matter must constitute the great orbs which are subject to local motion alone and have the most perfect kind of local motion—that of a circle. Since they are subject to generation and corruption, to change of quality and quantity, and are in local motion along straight lines, terrestrial bodies are of a corruptible matter.

The interconnection of all these points is marked by Aquinas when he summarizes Aristotle's doctrine. "Plato and all who preceded Aristotle," he writes, "held that all bodies are of the nature of the four elements" and consequently "that the matter of all bodies is the same. But the fact of the incorruptibility of some bodies was ascribed by Plato, not to the condition of matter, but to the will of the artificer, God . . . This theory," Aquinas continues, "Aristotle disproves by the natural movements of bodies. For since he says that the heavenly bodies have a natural movement, different from that of the elements, it follows that they have a different nature from them. For movement in a circle, which is proper to the heavenly bodies, is not by contraries, whereas the movements of the elements are mutually opposite, one tending upwards, another downwards . . . And as generation and corruption are from contraries, it follows that, whereas the elements are corruptible, the heavenly bodies are incorruptible."

The same points which Aquinas relates in his defense of the Aristotelian theory, Kepler also puts together when he expounds that theory in order to attack it and the Ptolemaic astronomy which tries to conform to it. "By what arguments did the ancients establish their opinion which is the opposite of yours?" he asks. "By four arguments in especial: (1) From the nature of moveable bodies. (2) From the nature of the motor virtue. (3) From the nature of the place in which the movement occurs. (4) From the perfection of the circle." He then states each of these arguments and answers each in turn.

WHAT IS EXTRAORDINARY about Kepler's attack upon the Ptolemaic astronomy cannot be understood without examining Ptolemy's defense of his theory, a defense which Copernicus meets in Ptolemy's own terms rather than, as Kepler does, by going outside them.

Though his expressed intention was to construct a mathematical theory of the celestial motions which would also conform to Aristotle's physics, Ptolemy, when he finished, recognized that the complications he had been compelled to add in order "to save the appearances" left him with a theory that did not conform to Aristotle's doctrine of the perfect circular motion of the heavenly spheres. Instead of abandoning Aristotle's physics, he

defended his theory on the ground that astronomy, being mathematical rather than physical, could admit such "unrealistic" complications if they served the purposes of calculation and of "saving the appearances."

In the thirteenth and last book of *The Almagest*, when he faces the fact that his mathematical devices have become exceedingly difficult—and strained from the point of view of the Aristotelian reality—Ptolemy writes: "Let no one, seeing the difficulty of our devices, find troublesome such hypotheses . . . It is proper to try and fit as far as possible the simpler hypotheses to the movements of the heavens; and if this does not succeed, then any hypotheses possible. Once all the appearances are saved by the consequences of the hypotheses, why should it seem strange that such complications can come about in the movements of heavenly things?" We ought not to judge the simplicity of heavenly things by comparison with what seems to be simple in the explanation of earthly phenomena. "We should instead judge their simplicity from the unchangeableness of the natures in the heavens and their movements. For thus they would all appear simple, more than those things which seem so here with us."

Ignoring the supposition that simplicity must be judged differently in different spheres, Copernicus challenges Ptolemy on his own grounds when he proposes "simpler hypotheses" to fit "the movements of the heavens." But in doing so, he seems to adopt the traditional view of the mathematical character of astronomical hypotheses. Yet, as will appear, he does not adopt this view in the unqualified form in which Andreas Osiander states it in his preface to *On the Revolutions of the Heavenly Spheres*.

"It is the job of the astronomer," Osiander writes, "to use painstaking and skilled observation in gathering together the history of the celestial movements, and then—since he cannot by any line of reasoning reach the true causes of these movements—to think or construct whatever causes or hypotheses he pleases, such that, by the assumption of these causes, these same movements can be calculated from the principles of geometry, for the past and for the future too.

"It is not necessary," he adds, "that these hypotheses should be true, or even probable; it is enough if they provide a calculus which fits the observations. When for one and the same movement varying hypotheses are proposed, as eccentricity or epicycle for the movement of the sun, the astronomer much prefers to take the one which is easiest to grasp."

What distinguishes Kepler from both Ptolemy and Osiander is the way in which he is concerned with the *truth* of alternative hypotheses in astronomy. He looks upon the truth of a hypothesis as something to be judged not merely in mathematical terms according to the adequacy and simplicity of a calculating device, but to be measured by its conformity to *all* the physical realities. At the very beginning of his *Epitome of Copernican Astronomy,* he flatly declares that "astronomy is part of physics." And in the opening pages of the fourth book, he insists that astronomy has not one, but "two ends: to save the appearances and to contemplate the true form of the edifice of the World." He follows this immediately by observing that, if astronomy had only the first end, Brahe's theory would be as satisfactory as that of Copernicus.

Early in his scientific career, before writing the *Epitome,* Kepler asserts that "one cannot leave to the astronomer absolute license to feign no matter what hypotheses." He complains that astronomers "too often . . . constrain their thought from exceeding the limits of geometry."

It is necessary to go beyond geometry into physics to test the consequences of competing hypotheses which are equally good mathematically. "You must seek the foundations of your astronomy," he tells his fellow scientists, "in a more elevated science, I mean in physics or metaphysics."

Because Kepler thus conceives the task and truth of astronomy, Pierre Duhem in his great history of astronomy calls him a "realistic Copernican." Galileo also, Duhem thinks, was a realistic Copernican. "To confirm by physics the Copernican hypotheses," he writes, "is the center towards which converge Galileo's observations as an astronomer and his terrestrial mechanics."

Newton was the third member of this triumvirate. For him there remained the solution of the problem of deducing Kepler's formulation of the planetary orbits in a manner consistent with Galileo's laws of motion in the dynamics of bodies falling on the earth's surface. But the very posing of this problem itself depended on the insight that terrestrial and celestial mechanics can proceed according to the same principles and laws. That insight entailed the complete overthrow of the ancient physics, with its division of the universe into two distinct parts, having different kinds of matter and different laws of motion.

COPERNICUS, WHO, despite Osiander's apologetics, believed his theory to be true, did not himself face the great point at issue in the Copernican revolution—the material uniformity of the physical universe. We shall subsequently consider the question of the truth of astronomical hypotheses, but whether or not Copernicus and the Copernicans had *in their own day* a right to believe their theory true, it was the acceptance of the Copernican hypothesis as true which led Kepler and Galileo to deny the truth of Aristotelian physics.

If the earth is not at the center and stationary, then the basic doctrine of a natural direction in motion and a natural place of rest for the various elements is completely upset. If the earth is one of the planets, then anything true on the earth—or of the earth, such as Gilbert's theory of the magnetic fields generated by the earth's axial rotation—could be equally true of all the other planets.

"Read the philosophy of magnetism of the Englishman William Gilbert," writes Kepler; "for in that book, although the author did not believe that the Earth moved . . . nevertheless he attributes a magnetic nature to it by very many arguments. Therefore, it is by no means absurd or incredible that any one of the primary planets should be, what one of the primary planets, namely, the Earth, is." Such a statement plainly shows that when the earth becomes a planet, as it does in Copernican theory, no obstacle remains to the assertion of a homogeneity between the earth and the other planets both in matter and motion. The old physical dualism of a supralunar and sublunar world is abandoned.

"Not the movement of the earth," Whitehead remarks, "but the glory of the heavens was the point at issue," for to assert the heavens to be of the same stuff and subject to the same laws as the rest of nature brings them down to the plane of earthly physics. That is precisely what Newton finally does when, in the enunciation of his Third Rule of reasoning in natural philosophy, he dryly but explicitly completes the Copernican revolution. Those "qualities of bodies ... which are found to belong to all bodies within the reach of our experiments, are," Newton maintains, "to be esteemed the universal qualities of all bodies whatsoever."

In the bifurcated world of ancient theory, astronomy had a very special place among the natural sciences, proportionate to the "glory of the heavens." But with Newton it could be completely merged into a general mechanics whose laws of motion have universal application.

In the 19th century, the unification perfected by Newton of terrestrial and celestial mechanics was complemented by a celestial and terrestrial chemical unification. By making a spectral analysis of the light coming from stars, including the sun, and comparing these spectra with those produced by terrestrial elements, it was shown that earthly and heavenly matter were in essence the same—a final refutation of Aristotle's idea that celestial and terrestrial matter are essentially different—the one incorruptible, the other not. One of the more remarkable discoveries of 19th-century astronomy was that of the element helium, which, as its name might suggest, was first identified in solar spectra rather than in studies of the earth.

But the unification of nature which Kepler began and Newton completed, when set against Aristotle's physics, may be even more radical. Newton's theory, because of the amazing way in which it covered the widest variety of phenomena by the simplest, most universal formula, is considered by Kant to have "established the truth of that which Copernicus at first assumed only as an hypothesis." But the larger contribution, in Whitehead's opinion, is "the idea of the neutrality of situation and the universality of physical laws ... holding indifferently in every part."

Whatever position we take today concerning the kind of truth which is possessed by hypotheses in mathematical physics, we now demand, in the spirit of the three Copernicans—Kepler, Galileo, and, above all, Newton—that physical hypotheses account at once for *all* the phenomena of the inanimate universe. Whatever the truth of modern as opposed to ancient physics, the Newtonian universe is so thoroughly established in our minds and feelings that, when we are reminded of the other universe in which men lived before the Copernican revolution, we tend to think it quaint, incredible, preposterous, superstitious, none of which it was.

Finally, from the point of view of our understanding of natural science itself, the astronomical controversy we have been considering is almost an archetypical model. It is necessary, of course, to appreciate the real achievement of Ptolemy as well as of Copernicus and Kepler in order to realize how genuine and difficult the issues were. Facts unknown to all of them may now have closed the dispute decisively, but issues in other spheres of modern science, almost identical in pattern with that great astronomical one, are not yet closed; and to the degree that we are able to reenact in our minds the motion of thought on both sides of the Copernican controversy, we can confront comparable scientific issues—still open—with open minds.

Darwin, for example, finds in the astronomical controversy a precedent to which he can appeal in the defense of natural selection against its adversaries. "The belief in the revolution of the earth on its own axis," he writes, "was until lately not supported by any direct evidence." But the absence of direct evidence does not leave a scientific theory without foundation, Darwin argues, if it has the power to explain several large classes of facts, which "it can hardly be supposed that a false theory would explain" in so satisfactory a manner. Darwin defends the theory of natural selection as having such power. To those who object that "this is an unsafe method of arguing," he replies—citing an example from astronomy—that "it has often been used by the greatest natural philosophers."

THE GREAT BOOKS of astronomy most lucidly exhibit the essential pattern of that kind of natural science which has, in modern times, come to be called "mathematical physics." Though that phrase may be modern, the ancients recognized the special character of the sciences which apply mathematics to nature and which consult experience to choose among hypotheses arising from different mathematical formulations.

Outlining a curriculum for liberal education, Plato, in *The Republic,* groups music and astronomy along with arithmetic and geometry as mathematical arts or sciences. In that context he treats them as pure mathematics. Astronomy is no more concerned with the visible heavens than music is with audible tones. Music is rather the arithmetic of harmonies, astronomy the geometry of motions. But in the *Timaeus* Plato turns mathematical formulas and calculations to use in telling what he calls "a likely story" concerning the formation and structure of the sensible world of becoming. Here, rather than in *The Republic,* we have, according to Whitehead, the initial conception of mathematical physics as well as deep insight into its nature and pattern.

Aristotle criticizes the notion of astronomy as a purely mathematical science. Just as "the things of which optics and mathematical harmonies treat" cannot be divorced from the sensible, so the objects of astronomy are also the visible heavens. "Astronomical experience," Aristotle writes, "supplies the principles of astronomical science." Yet, though its subject matter is physical and its method is in part empirical, astronomy, like optics and harmonics, takes the form of mathematical demonstration; and it is for this reason that Aquinas later calls such disciplines "mixed and intermediate sciences."

The development of astronomy from Plato and Aristotle through Ptolemy, Copernicus, and Kepler to Galileo and Newton thus constitutes an extraordinary set of "case histories" for the study of what J. B. Conant calls the "tactics and strategy" of science, and especially mathematical physics. But astronomy has one peculiar feature which distinguishes it from other branches of mathematical physics. It is empirical rather than experimental. The astronomer does not control the phenomena he observes. He does not, like the physicist, chemist, or physiologist, produce an isolated system of events by means of the laboratory arts.

Harvey comments on this aspect of astronomy when he proposes an experiment that will enable the physiologist to do what the astronomer cannot do, namely, deliberately prepare phenomena for examination by the senses. The astronomer must be content with the appearances as they are given. Defending psychoanalysis against attack "on the ground that it admits of no experimental proof," Freud points out that his critics "might have raised the same objection against astronomy; experimentation with the heavenly bodies is, after all, exceedingly difficult. There one has to rely on observation."

Since the invention of the telescope, the astronomer has had instruments of all sorts to increase the range and accuracy of his observations. As Francis Bacon points out, the telescope enabled Galileo to do more than improve upon the accuracy of prior observations. It brought within the range of observation certain celestial phenomena, hitherto imperceptible to the naked eye, such as the phases of Venus, the satellites of Jupiter, and the constitution of the Milky Way.

Concerning the last of these, Pascal later remarks that the ancients can be excused for the idea they had of the cause of its color. "The weakness of their eyes not yet having been artificially helped, they attributed this color to the great solidity of this part of the sky"; but it would be inexcusable for us, he adds, "to retain the same thought now that, aided by the advantages of the telescope, we have discovered in the Milky Way an infinity of small stars whose more abundant splendor has made us recognize the real cause of this whiteness."

BECAUSE IT IS a mixed science, both empirical and mathematical, astronomy advances not only with the improvement and enlargement of observation but also with new insights or developments in mathematics. Kant gives us striking examples of how the work of the pure mathematicians contributes to the advance of physics and astronomy. Their discoveries are often made without any knowledge of their application to natural phenomena. "They investigated the properties of the parabola," he writes, "in ignorance of the law of terrestrial gravitation which would have shown them its application to the trajectory of heavy bodies . . . So again they investigated the properties of the ellipse without a suspicion that a gravitation was also discoverable in the celestial bodies, and without knowing the law that governs it as the distance from the point of attraction varies, and that makes the bodies describe this curve in free motion."

So amazing are such mathematical anticipations that Kant thinks Plato may be pardoned for supposing that pure mathematics "could dispense with all experience" in discovering the constitution of things. Whether or not Plato goes to this extreme, he does, in *The Republic,* seem to suggest the reverse of Kant's conception of the relationship between mathematics and astronomy. "The spangled heavens should be used as a pattern," he writes, "and with a view to that higher knowledge"—mathematics. Astronomy should be used to instigate discoveries in *pure* mathematics by suggesting good problems and by requiring formulations which transcend an interest in the truth about the heavens.

This twofold relation between mathematical discovery and empirical observation is present in the development of astronomy itself, and of all branches of mathematical physics. But there is another aspect of the relationship which must be taken into account if we are to consider the problem of truth in such sciences. The way in which mathematical formulations fit the phenomena measures the truth of rival hypotheses with respect to the same reality.

The logic of such verification has already been suggested in the discussion of the geocentric and heliocentric hypotheses. It is further considered in the chapter on HYPOTHESIS. To be satisfactory, a hypothesis must—in the language used ever since Simplicius—"save the appearances," that is, account for the relevant phenomena. But two hypotheses (as for example the geocentric and heliocentric) may, at a certain time, do an equally good job of saving the appearances. Then the choice between them becomes a matter of the greater mathematical elegance of one than the other.

That, however, does not give the mathematically superior theory a greater claim to truth. So far as reality is concerned, it is only, in Plato's words, "a likely story"; or as Aquinas points out with reference to the geocentric hypothesis, "the theory of eccentrics and epicycles is considered as established because thereby the sensible appearances of the heavenly movements can be explained; not however, as if this reason were sufficient, since some other theory might explain them."

Two hypotheses may be equally satisfactory for the range of phenomena they were both devised to fit. But only one of them may have the quite amazing virtue of fitting other sets of observations not originally thought to be related to the phenomena for which the hypothesis was devised. The word "consilience" has been used to name the property of a hypothesis which, in addition to saving a limited field of appearances, succeeds in fitting many other phenomena which seem to have become related—to have *jumped together* under its covering explanation. The heliocentric hypothesis, as developed by Newton's laws of motion and theory of gravitation, certainly has this property of consilience to a high degree, for it covers both celestial and terrestrial phenomena, and a wide variety of the latter.

Is the heliocentric hypothesis true then? If the truth of a hypothesis depends on the range of the phenomena it fits or saves, it might seem to be so, for by its consilience it accounts for phenomena that the Ptolemaic theory cannot handle. But though this may cause us to reject the unsuccessful hypothesis, does it establish beyond doubt the truth of the successful one? Or, to put the question another way, is not our judgment here a comparative one rather than absolute? Are we saying more than that one hypothesis is more successful than another in doing what a hypothesis should do? Are we logically entitled to regard that success as the sign of its exclusive truth, or must we restrict ourselves to the more modest statement that, as the better hypothesis, it simply tells a more likely story about reality?

A STRIKING FEATURE of contemporary astronomy is the role evolution plays in it. Stars, it is now argued, are "born" and then "die." More precisely, stars are formed by the gravitational clumping of proto-stellar matter and may, for example, end their existence as black holes or white dwarfs. The cosmos itself is now thought to evolve from a singular explosive state into a highly uniform, frigid, dilute gas.

The last attempt to formulate a non-evolving cosmology was the steady state theory of Sir Fred Hoyle, Hermann Bondi, and others. There was a time when Einstein himself favored some sort of non-evolving cosmology. This fell out of favor with him in the late 1920s with the discovery by Edwin Hubble that the universe is expanding.

In the 1940s George Gamow and his collaborators attempted to give an account of the formulation of the elements during the first four minutes following the primeval explosion, the so-called "Big Bang." In the course of this work, they noted that a remnant of that explosion would be an ambient background of radiation at a temperature of a few degrees above absolute zero. In the 1960s, this radiation was discovered. Its discovery put an end to a non-evolutionary cosmology, such as the steady state theory. At the present time, there is a partial merger between astronomy and cosmology, and the combined discipline is one of the most vigorous contemporary sciences.

6

Beauty

INTRODUCTION

TRUTH, goodness, and beauty form a triad of terms which have been discussed together throughout the tradition of western thought.

They have been called "transcendental" on the ground that everything which *is* is in some measure or manner subject to denomination as true or false, good or evil, beautiful or ugly. But they have also been assigned to special spheres of being or subject matter—the true to thought and logic, the good to action and morals, the beautiful to enjoyment and aesthetics.

They have been called "the three fundamental values" with the implication that the worth of anything can be exhaustively judged by reference to these three standards—and no others. But other terms, such as pleasure or utility, have been proposed, either as additional values or as significant variants of the so-called fundamental three; or even sometimes as more fundamental. Pleasure or utility, for example, has been held by men like Spinoza or J. S. Mill to be the ultimate criterion of beauty or goodness; and for the economist Veblen, there is a purely pecuniary standard of taste in judgments about what is or is not beautiful.

Truth, goodness, and beauty, singly and together, have been the focus of the age-old controversy concerning the absolute and the relative, the objective and the subjective, the universal and the individual. At certain times it has been thought that the distinction of true from false, good from evil, beautiful from ugly, has its basis and warranty in the very nature of things, and that a man's judgment of these matters is measured for its soundness or accuracy by its conformity to fact. At other times the opposite position has been dominant. One meaning of the ancient saying that man is the measure of all things applies particularly to the true, good, and beautiful. Man measures truth, goodness, and beauty by the effect things have upon him, according to what they *seem* to him to be. What seems good to one man may seem evil to another. What seems ugly or false may also seem beautiful or true to different men or to the same man at different times.

Yet it is not altogether true that these three terms have always suffered the same fortunes. For Spinoza goodness and beauty are subjective, but not truth. Because he "has persuaded himself that all things which exist are made for him," man, Spinoza says, judges that to be "of the greatest importance which is most useful to him, and he must esteem that to be of surpassing worth by which he is most beneficially affected." The notions of good and evil, beauty and ugliness, do not conform to anything in the nature of things. "The ignorant," says Spinoza, nevertheless, "call the nature of a thing good, evil, sound, putrid, or corrupt just as they are affected by it. For example, if the motion by which the nerves are affected by means of objects represented to the eye conduces to well-being, the objects by which it is caused are called *beautiful;* while those exciting a contrary motion are called *deformed.*"

BEAUTY HAS BEEN most frequently regarded as subjective, or relative to the individual judgment. The familiar maxim, *de gustibus non disputandum,* has its original application in the sphere of beauty rather than truth and goodness. "Truth is disputable," Hume writes, "not taste . . . No man reasons concerning the justice or injustice of his actions." Thus even when it was supposed that judgments of the

true and the good could have a certain absoluteness or universality—or at least be considered as something about which men might
reach agreement through argument—opinions
about beauty were set apart as useless to dispute. Beauty being simply a matter of individual taste, it could afford no basis for argument
or reasoning—no objective ground for settling
differences of opinion.

From the ancient skeptics down to our own
day, men have noted the great variety of traits,
often sharply opposed, which have been considered beautiful at different times and places.
"We imagine its forms to suit our fancy,"
Montaigne says of beauty. "The Indies paint
it black and dusky, with large swollen lips
and a wide flat nose. And they load the carti-
lage between the nostrils with big gold rings,
to make it hang down to the mouth . . . In
Peru, the biggest ears are the fairest, and
they stretch them artificially as much as
they can . . . Elsewhere there are nations that
blacken their teeth with great care, and scorn
to see the white ones; elsewhere they stain
them red . . . The Italians make beauty plump
and massive, the Spaniards hollow and gaunt;
and among us, one man makes it fair, the
other dark; one soft and delicate, the other
strong and vigorous . . . Even as the preference
in beauty, which Plato attributes to the spherical figure, the Epicureans give rather to the
pyramidal or the square, and cannot swallow a
god in the shape of a ball."

Like Montaigne, Darwin gives an extensive
account of the things men have found beautiful, many of them so various and contradictory that it would seem there could be no
objective basis for judgments of beauty. If any
consensus is found among individuals about
what is beautiful or ugly, the skeptics or rel-
ativists usually explain it by reference to the
prevalence of certain prejudices, or customary
standards, which in turn vary with different
tribes and cultures, and at different times and
places.

Beginning in the sphere of beauty, subjectivism or relativism spreads first to judgments
of good and evil, and then to statements
about truth, never in the opposite direction.
It becomes complete when, as so frequently

happens in our own time, what is good or
true is held to be just as much a matter of
private taste or customary opinion as what is
beautiful.

The problem of the objectivity or subjectivity of beauty can, of course, be separated
from similar problems with regard to truth and
goodness, but any attempt to solve it will necessarily both draw on and bear on the discussion of these related problems. The degree to
which the three problems must be considered
interdependently is determined by the extent
to which each of the three terms requires the
context of the other two for its definition
and analysis.

BEAUTY IS, PERHAPS, not definable in any strict
sense of definition. But there have been, nevertheless, many attempts to state, with the
brevity of definition, what beauty is. Usually
notions of goodness, or correlative notions of
desire and love, enter into the statement.

Aquinas, for example, declares that "the
beautiful is the same as the good, and they
differ in aspect only . . . The notion of good
is that which calms the desire, while the notion of the beautiful is that which calms the
desire, by being seen or known." This, according to Aquinas, implies that "beauty adds to
goodness a relation to the cognitive faculty;
so that *good* means that which simply pleases
the appetite, while the *beautiful* is something
pleasant to apprehend."

Because of its relation to the cognitive
power, Aquinas defines the beautiful as "that
which pleases upon being seen" (*id quod visum placet*). Hence, he continues, "beauty
consists in due proportion, for the senses delight in things duly proportioned . . . because
the sense too is a sort of reason, as is every
cognitive power."

The pleasure or delight involved in the perception of beauty belongs to the order of
knowing rather than to desire or action. The
knowing, furthermore, seems to be different
from that which is proper to science, for it
is concerned with the individual thing rather
than with universal natures, and it occurs intuitively or contemplatively, rather than by judgment and reasoning. There is a mode of truth

peculiar to the beautiful, as well as a special kind of goodness.

Fully to understand what Aquinas is saying about beauty we are required to understand his theory of goodness and truth. But enough is immediately clear to give meaning to Eric Gill's advice to those who are concerned with making things beautiful: "Look after goodness and truth," he says, "and beauty will take care of herself."

To define beauty in terms of pleasure would seem to make it relative to the individual, for what gives pleasure—even contemplative pleasure—to one man, may not to another. It should be noted, however, that the pleasure in question is attributed to the object as its cause. It may be asked, therefore, what in the object is the cause of the peculiar satisfaction which constitutes the experience of beauty? Can the same object just as readily arouse displeasure in another individual, and a consequent judgment of ugliness? Are these opposite reactions entirely the result of the way an individual feels?

Aquinas appears to meet this difficulty by specifying certain objective elements of beauty, or "conditions," as he calls them. "Beauty includes three conditions," he writes: "*integrity* or *perfection*, since those things which are impaired are by that very fact ugly; due *proportion* or *harmony*; and lastly, *brightness* or *clarity*, whence things are called beautiful which have a bright color." Quite apart from individual reactions, objects may differ in the degree to which they possess such properties—traits which are capable of pleasing or displeasing their beholder.

This does not mean that the individual reaction is invariably in accordance with the objective characteristics of the thing beheld. Men differ in the degree to which they possess good perception—and sound critical judgment— even as objects differ in the degree to which they possess the elements of beauty. Once again in the controversy concerning the objectivity or subjectivity of beauty, there seems to be a middle ground between the two extreme positions, which insists upon a beauty intrinsic to the object but does not deny the relevance of differences in individual sensibility.

In *A Portrait of the Artist as a Young Man*, Joyce's Stephen tries to defend Aquinas' definition of beauty as that which pleases on being apprehended. Aquinas, says Stephen, "uses the word *visa* . . . to cover esthetic apprehensions of all kinds, whether through sight or hearing or through any other avenue of apprehension. This word, though it is vague, is clear enough to keep away good and evil which excite desire and loathing." Truth is not beauty, Stephen continues, "but the true and the beautiful are akin. Truth is beheld by the intellect which is appeased by the most satisfying relations of the intelligible: beauty is beheld by the imagination which is appeased by the most satisfying relations of the sensible." Stephen then proceeds to explain the three properties that Aquinas uses to define objective beauty— *integritas, proportio,* and *claritas*—in terms of the *unity* of the object apprehended, the *harmony* of its related parts, and the *radiance* through which the essence of the object reveals itself.

William James would seem to be indicating such a position when, in his discussion of aesthetic principles, he declares: "We are once and for all so made that when certain impressions come before our mind, one of them will seem to call for or repel the others as its companions." As an example, he cites the fact that "a note sounds good with its third and fifth." Such an aesthetic judgment certainly depends upon individual sensibility, and, James adds, "to a certain extent the principle of habit will explain [it]." But he also points out that "to explain *all* aesthetic judgements in this way would be absurd; for it is notorious how seldom natural experiences come up to our aesthetic demands." To the extent that aesthetic judgments "express inner harmonies and discords between objects of thought," the beautiful, according to James, has a certain objectivity; and good taste can be conceived as the capacity to be pleased by objects which *should* elicit that action.

KANT'S THEORY OF the beautiful, to take another conception, must also be understood in the general context of his theory of knowledge, and his analysis of such terms as good, pleasure, and desire. His definition, like that of Aquinas, calls an object beautiful if it satisfies the observer in a very special way—not merely pleasing his senses, or satisfying his desires, in the ways in which things good as means or ends fit a man's interests or purposes. The beautiful, according to Kant, "pleases *immediately . . . apart from all interest.*" The pleasure that results from its contemplation "may be said to be the one and only disinterested and *free* delight; for, with it, no interest, whether of sense or reason, extorts approval."

The aesthetic experience is for Kant also unique in that its judgment "is represented as *universal, i.e.* valid for every man," yet at the same time it is "incognizable by means of any universal concept." In other words, "all judgements of taste are singular judgements"; they are without concept in the sense that they do not apply to a class of objects. Nevertheless, they have a certain universality and are not merely the formulation of a private judgment. When "we call the object beautiful," Kant says, "we believe ourselves to be speaking with a universal voice, and lay claim to the concurrence of every one, whereas no private sensation would be decisive except for the observer alone and *his* liking."

In saying that aesthetic judgments have subjective, not objective, universality, and in holding that the beautiful is the object of a necessary satisfaction, Kant also seems to take the middle position which recognizes the subjectivity of the aesthetic judgment without denying that beauty is somehow an intrinsic property of objects. With regard to its subjective character, Kant cites Hume to the effect that "although critics are able to reason more plausibly than cooks, they must still share the same fate." The universal character of the aesthetic judgment, however, keeps it from being completely subjective, and Kant goes to some length to refute the notion that in matters of the beautiful one can seek refuge in the adage that "every one has his own taste."

The fact that the aesthetic judgment requires universal assent, even though the universal rule on which it is based cannot be formulated, does not, of course, preclude the failure of the object to win such assent from many individuals. Not all men have good taste or, having it, have it to the same degree.

THE FOREGOING CONSIDERATIONS—selective rather than exhaustive—show the connection between definitions of beauty and the problem of aesthetic training. In the traditional discussion of the ends of education, there is the problem of how to cultivate good taste— the ability to discriminate critically between the beautiful and the ugly.

If beauty is entirely subjective, entirely a matter of individual feeling, then, except for conformity to standards set by the customs of the time and place, no criteria would seem to be available for measuring the taste of individuals. If beauty is simply objective—something immediately apparent to observation as are the simple sensible qualities—no special training would seem to be needed for sharpening our perception of it.

The genuineness of the educational problem in the sphere of beauty seems, therefore, to depend upon a theory of the beautiful which avoids both extremes, and which permits the educator to aim at a development of individual sensibilities in accordance with objective criteria of taste.

THE FOREGOING CONSIDERATIONS also provide background for the problem of beauty in nature and in art. As indicated in the chapter on ART, the consideration of art in recent times tends to become restricted to the theory of the fine arts. So too the consideration of beauty has become more and more an analysis of excellence in poetry, music, painting, and sculpture. In consequence, the meaning of the word "aesthetic" has progressively narrowed, until now it refers almost exclusively to the appreciation of works of fine art, where before it connoted any experience of the beautiful, in the things of nature as well as in the works of man.

The question is raised, then, whether natural beauty, or the perception of beauty in nature, involves the same elements and causes as beauty in art. Is the beauty of a flower or of a flowering field determined by the same factors as the beauty of a still life or a landscape painting?

The affirmative answer seems to be assumed in a large part of the tradition. In his discussion of the beautiful in the *Poetics,* Aristotle explicitly applies the same standard to both nature and art. "To be beautiful," he writes, "a living creature, and every whole made up of parts, must not only present a certain order in its arrangement of parts, but also be of a certain magnitude." Aristotle's notion that art imitates nature indicates a further relation between the beautiful in art and nature. Unity, proportion, and clarity would then be elements common to beauty in its every occurrence, though these elements may be embodied differently in things which have a difference in their mode of being, as do natural and artificial things.

With regard to the beauty of nature and of art, Kant tends to take the opposite position. He points out that "the mind cannot reflect on the beauty of nature without at the same time finding its interest engaged." Apart from any question of use that might be involved, he concludes that the "interest" aroused by the beautiful in nature is "akin to the moral," particularly from the fact that "nature . . . in her beautiful products displays herself as art, not as a mere matter of chance, but, as it were, designedly, according to a law-directed arrangement."

The fact that natural things and works of art stand in a different relation to purpose or interest is for Kant an immediate indication that their beauty is different. Their susceptibility to disinterested enjoyment is not the same. Yet for Kant, as for his predecessors, nature provides the model or archetype which art follows, and he even speaks of art as an "imitation" of nature.

The Kantian discussion of nature and art moves into another dimension when it considers the distinction between the beautiful and the sublime. We must look for the sublime, Kant says, "not . . . in works of art . . . nor yet in things of nature, that in their very concept import a definite end, *e.g.* animals of a recognized natural order, but in rude nature merely as involving magnitude." In company with Longinus and Edmund Burke, Kant characterizes the sublime by reference to the limita-

tions of human powers. Whereas the beautiful "consists in limitation," the sublime "immediately involves, or else by its presence provokes, a representation of limitlessness," which "may appear, indeed, in point of form to contravene the ends of our power of judgement, to be ill-adapted to our faculty of presentation, and to be, as it were, an outrage on the imagination."

Made aware of his own weakness, man is dwarfed by nature's magnificence, but at that very moment he is also elevated by realizing his ability to appreciate that which is so much greater than himself. This dual mood signalizes man's experience of the sublime. Unlike the enjoyment of beauty, it is neither disinterested nor devoid of moral tone.

TRUTH IS USUALLY connected with perception and thought, the good with desire and action. Both have been related to love and, in different ways, to pleasure and pain. All these terms naturally occur in the traditional discussion of beauty, partly by way of definition, but also partly in the course of considering the faculties engaged in the experience of beauty.

Basic here is the question whether beauty is an object of love or desire. The meaning of any answer will, of course, vary with different conceptions of desire and love.

Desire is sometimes thought of as fundamentally acquisitive, directed toward the appropriation of a good; whereas love, on the contrary, aims at no personal aggrandizement but rather, with complete generosity, wishes only the well-being of the beloved. In this context, beauty seems to be more closely associated with a good that is loved than with a good desired.

Love, moreover, is more akin to knowledge than is desire. The act of contemplation is sometimes understood as a union with the object through both knowledge and love. Here again the context of meaning favors the alignment of beauty with love, at least for theories which make beauty primarily an object of contemplation. In Plato and Plotinus, and on another level in the theologians, the two considerations—of love and beauty—fuse together inseparably.

It is the "privilege of beauty," Plato thinks,

to offer man the readiest access to the world of ideas. According to the myth in the *Phaedrus,* the contemplation of beauty enables the soul to "grow wings." This experience, ultimately intellectual in its aim, is described by Plato as identical with love.

The observer of beauty "is amazed when he sees anyone having a godlike face or form, which is the expression of divine beauty; and at first a shudder runs through him, and again the old awe steals over him; then looking upon the face of his beloved as of a god, he reverences him, and if he were not afraid of being thought a downright madman, he would sacrifice to his beloved as to the image of a god." When the soul bathes herself "in the waters of beauty, her constraint is loosened, and she is refreshed, and has no more pangs and pains." This state of the soul enraptured by beauty, Plato goes on to say, "is by men called love." This view of love, found in Plato's *Phaedrus,* is cited at length by Thomas Mann in *Death in Venice.*

Sharply opposed to Plato's intellectualization of beauty is that conception which connects it with sensual pleasure and sexual attraction. When Darwin, for instance, considers the sense of beauty, he confines his attention almost entirely to the colors and sounds used as "attractions of the opposite sex." Freud, likewise, while admitting that "psycho-analysis has less to say about beauty than about most things," claims that "its derivation from the realms of sexual sensation . . . seems certain."

Such considerations may not remove beauty from the sphere of love, but, as the chapter on LOVE makes clear, love has many meanings and is of many sorts. The beautiful which is sexually attractive is the object of a love which is almost identical with desire—sometimes with lust—and certainly involves animal impulses and bodily pleasures. "The taste for the beautiful," writes Darwin, "at least as far as female beauty is concerned, is not of a special nature in the human mind."

On the other hand, Darwin attributes to man alone an aesthetic faculty for the appreciation of beauty apart from love or sex. No other animal, he thinks, is "capable of admiring such scenes as the heavens at night, a beautiful landscape, or refined music; but such high tastes are acquired through culture and depend on complex associations; they are not enjoyed by barbarians or by uneducated persons." For Freud, however, the appreciation of such beauties remains ultimately sexual in motivation, no matter how sublimated in effect. "The love of beauty," he says, "is the perfect example of a feeling with an inhibited aim. 'Beauty' and 'attraction' are first of all the attributes of a sexual object."

The theme of beauty's relation to desire and love is connected with another basic theme— the relation of beauty to sense and intellect, or to the realms of perception and thought. The two discussions naturally run parallel.

The main question here concerns the existence of beauty in the order of purely intelligible objects, and its relation to the sensible beauty of material things.

Purely intelligible beauty is to be found in mathematics. "The beauty of a mathematical theorem *depends* a great deal on its seriousness," according to G. H. Hardy. "The mathematician's patterns, like the painter's or the poet's, must be *beautiful;* the ideas, like the colours or the words, must fit together in a harmonious way . . . There is no permanent place in the world for ugly mathematics."

Plotinus, holding that beauty of every kind comes from a "form" or "reason," traces the "beauty which is in bodies," as well as that "which is in the soul" to its source in the "eternal intelligence." This "intelligible beauty" lies outside the range of desire even as it is beyond the reach of sense-perception. Only the admiration or the adoration of love is proper to it.

THESE DISTINCTIONS in types of beauty—natural and artificial, sensible and intelligible, even, perhaps, material and spiritual—indicate the scope of the discussion, though not all writers on beauty deal with all its manifestations.

Primarily concerned with other subjects, many of the great books make only an indirect contribution to the theory of beauty: the moral treatises which consider the spiritual beauty of a noble man or of a virtuous character; the cosmologies of the philosophers or scientists which find beauty in the structure of the world—the intelligible, not sensible, order of the universe; the mathematical works which exhibit, and sometimes enunciate, an awareness of formal beauty in the necessary connection of ideas; the great poems which crystallize beauty in a scene, in a face, in a deed; and, above all, the writings of the theologians which do not try to do more than suggest the ineffable splendor of God's infinite beauty, a beauty fused with truth and goodness, all absolute in the one absolute perfection of the divine being. "The Divine Goodness," observes Dante, "which spurns all envy from itself, burning within itself so sparkles that It displays the eternal beauties."

Some of the great books consider the various kinds of beauty, not so much with a view to classifying their variety, as in order to set forth the concordance of the grades of beauty with the grades of being, and with the levels of love and knowledge.

The ladder of love in Plato's *Symposium* describes an ascent from lower to higher forms of beauty. "He who has been instructed thus far in the things of love," Diotima tells Socrates, "and who has learned to see beauty in due order and succession, when he comes toward the end will suddenly perceive a nature of wondrous beauty ... beauty absolute, separate, simple, and everlasting, which without diminution and without increase, or any change, is imparted to the ever-growing and perishing beauties of all other things. He who from these, ascending under the influence of true love, begins to perceive that beauty, is not far from the end."

The order of ascent, according to Diotima, begins "with the beauties of earth and mounts upwards for the sake of that other beauty," going from one fair form to "all fair forms, and from fair forms to fair practises, and from fair practises to fair notions, until from fair notions" we come to "the notion of absolute beauty and at last know what the essence of beauty is. This, my dear Socrates," she concludes, "is the life above all others which man should live, in the contemplation of beauty absolute."

For Plotinus the degrees of beauty correspond to degrees of emancipation from matter. "The more it goes towards matter ... the feebler beauty becomes." A thing is ugly only because, "not dominated by a form and reason, the matter has not been completely informed by the idea." If a thing could be completely "without reason and form," it would be "absolute ugliness." But whatever exists possesses form and reason to some extent and has some share of the effulgent beauty of the One, even as it has some share through emanation in its overflowing being—the grades of beauty, as of being, signifying the remotion of each thing from its ultimate source.

Even separated from a continuous scale of beauty, the extreme terms—the beauty of God and the beauty of the least of finite things—have similitude for a theologian like Aquinas. The word *visum* in his definition of the beautiful (*id quod visum placet*, "that which pleases upon being seen") is the word used to signify the type of supernatural knowledge promised to the souls of the blessed—the beatific *vision* in which God is beheld intuitively, not known discursively, and in which knowledge united with love is the principle of the soul's union with God.

An analogy is obviously implied. In this life and on the natural level, every experience of beauty—in nature or art, in sensible things or in ideas—occasions something *like* an act of vision, a moment of contemplation, of enjoyment detached from desire or action, and clear without the articulations of analysis or the demonstrations of reason.

7

Being

INTRODUCTION

THE words "is" and "(is) not" are probably the words most frequently used by anyone. They are unavoidable, by implication at least, in every statement. They have, in addition, a greater range of meaning than any other words.

Their manifold significance seems to be of a very special kind, for whatever is said *not to be* in one sense of being can always be said *to be* in another of its senses. Children and practiced liars know this. Playing on the meanings of being, or with "is" and "not," they move smoothly from fact to fiction, imagination to reality, or truth to falsehood.

Despite the obviousness and commonplaceness of the questions which arise with any consideration of the meanings of "is," the study of being is a highly technical inquiry which only philosophers have pursued at length. Berkeley gives one reason why they cannot avoid this task. "Nothing seems of more importance," he says, "towards erecting a firm system of sound and real knowledge . . . than to lay the beginning in a distinct explication of what is meant by *thing, reality, existence;* for in vain shall we dispute concerning the real existence of things, or pretend to any knowledge thereof, so long as we have not fixed the meaning of those words."

In the whole field of learning, philosophy is distinguished from other disciplines—from history, the sciences, and mathematics—by its concern with the problem of being. It alone asks about the nature of existence, the modes and properties of being, the difference between being and becoming, appearance and reality, the possible and the actual, being and nonbeing. Not all philosophers ask these questions; nor do all who ask such questions approach or formulate them in the same way. Nevertheless, the attempt to answer them is a task peculiar to philosophy. Though it often leads to subtleties, it also keeps the philosopher in deepest touch with common sense and the speculative wonder of all men.

As A TECHNICAL concept in philosophy, *being* has been called both the richest and the emptiest of all terms in the vocabulary of thought. Both remarks testify to the same fact, namely, that it is the highest abstraction, the most universal of predicates, and the most pervasive subject of discussion.

William James is in that long line of philosophers which began with the early Greeks when he points out that "in the strict and ultimate sense of the word 'existence,' everything which can be thought of at all exists as some *sort* of object, whether mythical object, individual thinker's object, or object in outer space and for intelligence at large." Even things which do not really exist have being insofar as they are objects of thought—things remembered which once existed, things conceivable which have the possibility of being, things imaginary which have being at least in the mind that thinks them. This leads to a paradox which the ancients delighted in pondering, that even nothing is something, even nonbeing has being, for before we can say "nonbeing is not" we must be able to say "nonbeing is." *Nothing* is at least an object of thought.

Central to 20th-century existentialism is the concern with nothing. "Nothing," writes Heidegger, "is neither an object nor anything that 'is' at all. Nothing occurs neither by itself nor 'apart from' what-is, as a sort of adjunct. Nothing is that which makes the revelation of what-is as such possible for our human existence." Existential angst or dread, according to Heidegger, "reveals Nothing . . . but not as something that 'is' "; yet it "is only made manifest originally in dread." Heidegger goes on to quote Hegel's saying that "pure Being and pure Nothing are . . . one and the same," adding that if concern with being is all-embracing in metaphysics, then "the question of Nothing" also spans "the whole metaphysical field." In the century of existentialist thought, it is not surprising to find T. S. Eliot's *The Waste Land* moving in the realm of nothingness.

Any other word than "being" will tend to classify things. The application of any other name will divide the world into things of the sort denominated as distinct from everything else. "Chair," for example, divides the world into things which are chairs and all other objects; but "being" divides something or anything from nothing and, as we have seen, even applies to nothing.

"All other names," Aquinas writes, "are either less universal, or, if convertible with it, add something above it at least in idea; hence in a certain way they inform and determine it." The concepts which such words express have, therefore, a restricted universality. They apply to *all things of a certain kind,* but not to *all things,* things of every kind or type. With the exception of a few terms inseparably associated with 'being' (or, as Aquinas says, convertible with it), only being is common to all kinds of things. When every other trait peculiar to a thing is removed, its being remains—the fact that it *is* in some sense.

If we start with a particular of any sort, classifying it progressively according to the characteristics which it shares with more and more things, we come at last to being. According to this method of abstraction, which Hegel follows in his *Science of Logic,* 'being' is the emptiest of terms precisely because it is the most common. It signifies the very least that can be thought of anything. On this view, if all we are told of something is that it is—that it has being—we learn as little as possible about the thing. We have to be told that a thing is a material or a spiritual being, a real or an imaginary being, a living or a human being, in order to apprehend a determinate nature. Abstracted from everything else, 'being' has only the positive meaning of excluding 'nonbeing.'

There is an opposite procedure by which the term *being* has the maximal rather than the minimal significance. Since whatever else a thing is, it is a being, its being lies at the very heart of its nature and underlies all its other properties. Being is indeterminate only in the sense that it takes on every sort of determination. Wherever being is found by thought, it is understood as a determined mode of being. To conceive being in this way, we do not remove every difference or determination, but on the contrary, embrace all, since all are differences or determinations of being.

Aquinas, for example, conceives "being taken simply as including all perfections of being"; and in the Judeo-Christian tradition, 'being' without qualification is taken as the most proper name for God. When Moses asked God His name, he received as answer: "I AM THAT I AM . . . Thus shalt thou say unto the children of Israel, I AM hath sent me unto you." Used in this sense, 'being' becomes the richest of terms—the one which has the greatest amplitude of meaning.

BOTH WAYS OF thinking about being are relevant to the problem of the relations among the various meanings of 'being.' Both are also related to the problem of whether being is one or many—the problem first raised by the Eleatics, exhaustively explored in Plato's *Parmenides,* and recurrent in the thought of Plotinus, Spinoza, and Hegel.

The two problems are connected. If everything that is exists only as a part of being as a whole, or if the unity of being requires everything to be the same in being, then whatever diversities there are do not multiply the meanings of *being.* Although he speaks of substance rather than of being, Spinoza argues that "there cannot be any substance excepting God, and consequently none other can be conceived." From this it follows that "whatever is, is in God, and nothing can be or be conceived without God."

Since "there cannot be two or more substances of the same nature or attribute," and since God is defined as a "substance consisting of infinite attributes, each one of which expresses eternal and infinite essence," it is absurd, in Spinoza's opinion, to think of any other substance. "If there were any substance besides God, it would have to be explained," he says, "by some attribute of God, and thus two substances would exist possessing the same attribute," which is impossible.

Spinoza's definition of substance, attribute, and mode or affection, combined with his axiom that "everything which is, is either in itself or in another," enables him to embrace whatever multiplicity or diversity he finds in the world as aspects of one being. Everything which is not substance, existing in and of itself, exists in that one substance as an infinite attribute *or* a finite mode. "The thing extended (*rem extensam*) and the thinking thing (*rem cogitantem*)," he writes, "are either attributes of God or affections of the attributes of God."

If, on the contrary, there is no unitary whole of being, but only a plurality of beings which are alike in being and yet are diverse in being from one another, then our conception of being must involve a system of meanings, a stem of many branches. Descartes, for example, distinguishes between an infinite being, whose essence involves its existence, and finite beings, which do not necessarily exist of themselves but must be caused to exist. The infinite being which is God causes, but does not contain within itself, other finite substances; and among finite things, Descartes holds, "two substances are said to be really distinct, when each of them can exist apart from the other."

In addition to God—"that substance which we understand to be supremely perfect"—Descartes defines two kinds of finite substance. "That substance in which thought immediately resides, I call Mind," he writes; and "that substance, which is the immediate subject of extension in space, and of the accidents that presuppose extension, *e.g.,* figure, situation, movement in space, etc., is called Body." All these substances, and even their accidents, have being, but not being of the same kind or to the same degree. "There are," according to Descartes, "diverse degrees of reality, or (the quality of being an) entity. For substance has more reality than accident or mode; and infinite substance has more than finite substance." Its being is independent, theirs dependent.

The issue between Spinoza and Descartes—a single substance or many—is only one of the ways in which the problem of the unity or diversity of being presents itself. Both Plato and Aristotle, for example, affirm a multiplicity of separate existences, but though both are, in this sense, pluralists, being seems to have one meaning for Plato, many for Aristotle.

According to Plato's distinction between being and becoming, only the immutable essences, the eternal ideas, are beings, and though they are many in number, they all belong to one realm and possess the same type of being. But for Aristotle, not only do perishable as well as imperishable substances exist; not only is there sensible and mutable as well as immaterial and eternal being; but the being which substances possess is not the same as that of accidents; essential is not the same as accidental being; potential being is not the same as being actual; and to be is not the same as to be conceived, that is, to exist in reality is not the same as to exist in mind.

Again and again Aristotle insists that "there are many senses in which a thing is said to be ... Some things are said to be because they are substances, others because they are affections of substance, others because they are in process towards substance, or destructions or privations or qualities of substance, or productive or generative of substance, or of things which are relative to substance, or negations of one of these things or of substance itself. It is for this reason," he continues, "that we say even of non-being that it *is* non-being"; and, in another place, he adds that "besides all these there is that which 'is' potentially or actually."

All these senses of being, according to Aristotle, "refer to one starting point," namely, substance, or that which has being in and of itself. "That which is primarily, *i.e.,* not in a qualified sense," he writes, "must be a substance." But when he also says that "that which 'is' primarily is the 'what' which indicates the substance of a thing," he seems to be using the words "substance" and "essence" interchangeably. This, in turn, seems to be related to the fact that, although Aristotle distinguishes between actual and potential being, and between necessary or incorruptible and contingent or corruptible beings, he, like Plato and unlike Aquinas, Descartes, or Spinoza, does not consider whether the essence and existence of a being are identical or separate.

It may be held that this distinction is implied, since a contingent being is one which is able not to exist, whereas a necessary being cannot *not* exist. A contingent being is, therefore, one whose essence can be divorced from existence; a necessary being, one which *must be* precisely because its essence is identical with its existence. But the explicit recognition of a real distinction between essence and existence seems to be reserved for the later theologians and philosophers who conceive of an infinite being, as Aristotle does not.

The infinity of a being lies not only in its possession of all perfections, but even more fundamentally in its requiring no cause outside itself for its own existence. "That thing," says Aquinas, "whose being differs from its essence, must have its being caused by another ... That which has being, but is not being, is a being by participation." Where Aristotle makes substance the primary type of being, and the "starting-point" of all its other meanings, Aquinas makes the infinite being of God, whose very essence it is to be, the source of all finite and participated beings, in which there is a composition of existence and essence, or "of that *whereby they are* and that *which they are.*"

Since "being itself is that whereby a thing is," being belongs to God primarily and to all other things according to modes of derivation or participation. God and his creatures can be called "beings" but, Aquinas points out, not in the *identically same* sense, nor yet with *utter diversity* of meaning. A similarity—a sameness-in-diversity or analogy—obtains between the unqualified being of God and the being of all other things, which have being subject to various qualifications or limitations.

All other questions about being are affected by the solution of these basic problems concerning the unity of being, the kinds of being, and the order of the various kinds. If they are solved in one way—in favor of unity—certain questions are not even raised, for they are genuine only on the basis of the other solution which finds being diverse. The discussion, in the chapters on SAME AND OTHER, and on SIGN AND SYMBOL, of sameness, diversity, and analogy is, therefore, relevant to the problem of how things are at once alike and unlike in being.

THE GREEKS, NOTABLY Plato and Aristotle, began the inquiry about being. They realized that after all other questions are answered, there still remains the question, What does it mean to say of anything that it *is* or *is not?* After we understand what it means for a thing to be a man, or to be alive, or to be a body, we must still consider what it means for that thing simply to be in any way at all; or to be in one sense, and not to be in another.

The discussion of being, in itself and in relation to unity and truth, rest and motion, runs through many dialogues of Plato. It is central in the *Sophist* and *Parmenides*. The same terms and problems appear in Aristotle's scientific treatise which makes *being* its distinctive subject matter, and which he sometimes calls "first philosophy" and sometimes "theology." It belongs to this science, he declares, "to consider being *qua* being—both what it is and the properties which belong to it *qua* being."

As pointed out in the chapter on METAPHYSICS, it is a historical accident that this inquiry concerning being came to be called "metaphysics." That is the name which, according to legend, the ancient editors gave to a collection of writings in which Aristotle pursued this inquiry. Since they came after the books on physics, they were called "metaphysics" on the supposition that Aristotle intended the discussion of being to follow his treatise on change and motion.

If one were to invent a word to describe the science of being, it would be "ontology," not "metaphysics" or even "theology." Yet "metaphysics" has remained the traditionally accepted name for the inquiry or science which goes beyond physics—or all of natural science—in that it asks about the very existence of things, and their modes of being. Planck acknowledges this when he concedes that "there is a metaphysical reality behind everything that human experience shows to be real," going on to explain that "metaphysical reality does not stand spatially *behind* what is given in experience, but lies fully *within* it."

The traditional connection of metaphysics with theology, discussed in the chapters on METAPHYSICS and THEOLOGY, seems to have its origin in the fact that Aristotle's treatise on being passes from a consideration of sensible and mutable substances to the problem of the existence of immaterial beings, and to the conception of a divine being, purely actual, absolutely immutable.

In a science intended to treat "of that which *is* primarily, and to which all the other categories of being are referred, namely, substance," Aristotle says, "we must first sketch the nature of substance." Hence he begins with what he calls "the generally recognized substances. These are the sensible substances." He postpones until later his critical discussion of "the Ideas and the objects of mathematics, for some say these are substances in addition to the sensible substances"; yet he directs his whole inquiry to the ultimate question "whether there are or are not any besides sensible substances." His attempt to answer this question in the twelfth book makes it the theological part of his *Metaphysics*.

THOUGH THEIR ORDER of discussion is different, the metaphysicians of the 17th century, like Descartes, Spinoza, and Leibniz, deal with many, if not all, major points in the analysis of being which the Greek philosophers initiated and the medieval theologians developed. Later philosophers, whose main concern is with the origin and validity of human knowledge, come to the traditional metaphysical questions through an analysis, not of substance or essence, existence or power, but of our *ideas* of substance and power.

This transformation of the ancient problem of being is stated by Berkeley in almost epigrammatic form. Considering "what is meant by the term *exist*," he argues from the experience of sensible things that "their *esse* is *percipi*, nor is it possible they should have any existence, out of the minds or thinking things which perceive them." Locke, too, although he does not identify being with perception, makes the same shift on the ground that "the first step towards satisfying several inquiries the mind of man was apt to run into, was to make a survey of our own understandings, examine our own powers, and see to what things they were adapted."

Once the problems of being are viewed first in terms of the mind, the questions for the philosopher become primarily those of the relation of our definitions to real and nominal essences, the conditions of our knowledge or existence, and the identification of the real and ideal with perceptible matters of fact and intelligible relations between ideas.

For Kant the basic distinction is between the sensible and supra-sensible, or the phenomenal and noumenal, realms of being. From another point of view, Kant considers the being of things in themselves apart from human experience and the being of natural things or, what is the same for him, the things of experience. The former are unconditioned, the latter conditioned, by the knowing mind which is formative or constitutive of experience.

"The sole aim of pure reason," Kant writes, "is the absolute totality of the synthesis on the side of the conditions . . . in order to preposit the whole series of conditions, and thus present them to the understanding *a priori*." Having obtained these "conditions," we can ascend through them "until we reach the unconditioned, that is, the principles." It is with these ideas of pure reason that metaphysics, according to Kant, properly deals. Instead of *being,* its object consists in "three grand ideas: God, Freedom, and Immortality, and it aims at showing that the second conception, conjoined with the first, must lead to the third as a necessary conclusion."

Hegel, on the other hand, does not approach the problem of being or reality through a critique of knowledge. For Hegel, as for Plotinus before him, the heart of metaphysics lies in understanding that "nothing is actual except the Idea" or the Absolute, "and the great thing is to apprehend in the show of the temporal and the transient, the substance which is immanent, and the eternal which is present." Plotinus calls the absolute, not the Idea, but the All-one, yet he tries to show that the One is the principle, the light, and the life of all things, just as Hegel reduces everything to a manifestation of the underlying reality of the Absolute Idea.

Despite all such changes in terminology, despite radical differences in philosophical principle or conclusion, and regardless of the attitude taken toward the possibility of metaphysics as a science, the central question which is faced by anyone who goes beyond physics, or natural philosophy, is a question about being or existence. It may or may not be asked explicitly, but it is always present by implication.

The question about God, for example, or free will or immortality, is first of all a question about whether such things *exist,* and *how* they exist. Do they have reality or are they only fictions of the mind? Similarly, questions about the infinite, the absolute, or the unconditioned are questions about that primary reality apart from whose existence nothing else could be or be conceived, and which therefore has an existence different from the things dependent on it for their being. Here again the first question is whether such a reality exists.

Enough has been said to indicate why this discussion cannot consider all topics which have some connection with the theory of being. To try to make this Introduction adequate even for the topics outlined here, under which the references to the great books are assembled, would be to make it almost coextensive in scope with the sum of many other Introductions—all, in fact, which open chapters dealing with metaphysical concepts or problems.

It is to be expected, of course, that the special problems of the existence of God, of an immortal soul, and of a free will should be treated in the chapters on GOD, IMMORTALITY, and WILL. But it may not be realized that such chapters as CAUSE, ETERNITY, FORM, IDEA, INFINITY, MATTER, ONE AND MANY, RELATION, SAME AND OTHER, UNIVERSAL AND PARTICULAR—all these and still others cited in the Cross-References below—include topics which would have to be discussed here if we were to try to cover all relevant considerations.

Reasons of economy and intelligibility dictate the opposite course. Limiting the scope of this Introduction to a few principal points in the theory of being, we can also exhibit, through the relation of this chapter to others, the interconnection of the great ideas. The various modes of being (such as essence and existence, substance and accident, potentiality and actuality, the real and the ideal) and the basic correlatives of being (such as unity, goodness, truth) are, therefore, left for fuller treatment in other contexts. But two topics deserve further attention here. One is the distinction between being and becoming, the other the relation of being to knowledge.

THE FACT OF CHANGE or motion—of coming to be and passing away—is so evident to the senses that it has never been denied, at least not as an experienced phenomenon. But it has been regarded as irrational and unreal, an illusion perpetrated by the senses. Galen, for instance, charges the Sophists with "allowing that bread in turning into blood becomes changed as regards sight, taste, and touch," but denying that "this change occurs in reality." They explain it away, he says, as "tricks and illusions of our senses . . . which are affected now in one way, now in another, whereas the underlying substance does not admit of any of these changes."

The familiar paradoxes of Zeno are *reductio ad absurdum* arguments to show that motion is unthinkable, full of self-contradiction. The way of truth, according to Parmenides, Zeno's master in the Eleatic school, lies in the insight that whatever is always was and will be, that nothing comes into being out of nonbeing, or passes out of being into nothingness.

The doctrine of Parmenides provoked many criticisms. Yet his opponents tried to preserve the reality of change, without having to accord it the fullness of being. The Greek atomists, for example, think that change cannot be explained except in terms of permanent beings—in fact eternal ones. Lucretius, who expounds their views, remarks that in any change

Something must stand immovable, it must,
Lest all things be reduced to absolute nothing.
If anything is changed, leaving its limits,
That is the death of what it was before.

The immovable "something" is thought to be the atom, the absolutely indivisible, and hence imperishable, unit of matter. Change does not touch the being of the atoms, but "only breaks their combinations,/Joins them again in other ways." Lucretius believes all things change—that is, all things composite, not the simple bodies of solid singleness.

In a conversation with Cratylus, who favors the Heraclitean theory of a universal flux, Socrates asks, "how can that be a real thing which is never in the same state?" How "can we reasonably say, Cratylus," he goes on, "that there is any knowledge at all, if everything is in a state of transition and there is nothing abiding"?

When he gets Glaucon to admit in *The Republic* that "being is the sphere or subject matter of knowledge, and knowing is to know the nature of being," Socrates leads him to see the correlation of being, not-being, and becoming with knowledge, ignorance, and opinion. "If opinion and knowledge are distinct faculties then the sphere of knowledge and opinion cannot be the same . . . If being is the subject matter of knowledge, something else must be the subject matter of opinion." It cannot be not-being, for "of not-being ignorance was assumed to be the necessary correlative."

Since "opinion is not concerned either with being or with not-being" because it is obviously intermediate between knowledge and ignorance, Socrates concludes that "if anything appeared to be of a sort which is and is not at the same time, that sort of thing would appear also to lie in the interval between pure being and absolute not-being," and "the corresponding faculty is neither knowledge nor ignorance, but will be found in the interval between them." This "intermediate flux" or sphere of becoming, this "region of the many and the variable," can yield only opinion. Being, the realm of the "absolute and eternal and immutable [Ideas]," is the only object that one "may be said to know."

Aristotle would seem to agree with Plato

that change "partakes equally of the nature of being and not-being, and cannot rightly be termed either, pure and simple." He points out that his predecessors, particularly the Eleatics, held change to be impossible, because they believed that "what comes to be must do so either from what is or from what is not, both of which are impossible." It is impossible, so they argued, since "what is cannot come to be (because it *is* already), and from what is not nothing could have come to be." Aristotle concedes the cogency of this argument on one condition, namely, that the terms 'being' and 'not-being' are taken "without qualification." But his whole point is that they need not be taken without qualification and should not be, if we wish to explain change rather than make a mystery of it.

The qualification Aristotle introduces rests on the distinction between two modes of being—the potentiality and actuality correlative with matter and form. In the 20th century, Heisenberg resorts to this distinction and employs the concept of *potentia* in quantum mechanics. He tells us that "physicists have gradually become accustomed to considering the electronic orbits, etc., not as reality but rather as a kind of 'potentia.'"

For Aristotle, this distinction makes it possible for him to maintain that "a thing may come to be from what is not . . . in a qualified sense." He illustrates his meaning by the example of the bronze, which from a mere lump of metal comes to be a statue under the hands of the artist. The bronze, he says, was "potentially a statue," and the change whereby it came to be actually a statue is the process between potentiality and actuality. While the change is going on, the bronze is neither completely potential nor fully actual in respect of *being a statue*.

Like Plato, Aristotle recognizes that there is "something indefinite" about change. "The reason," he explains, "is that it cannot be classed simply as a potentiality or as an actuality—a thing that is merely *capable* of having a certain size is not undergoing change, nor yet a thing that is *actually* of a certain size." Change is "a sort of actuality, but incomplete . . . hard to grasp, but not incapable of existing."

If to exist is to be completely actual, then changing things and change itself do not fully exist. They exist only to the extent that they have actuality. Yet potentiality, no less than actuality, is a mode of being. That potentiality—power or capacity—belongs to being seems also to be affirmed by the Eleatic Stranger in Plato's *Sophist.* "Anything which possesses any sort of power to affect another, or to be affected by another," he says, "if only for a single moment, however trifling the cause and however slight the effect, has real existence . . . I hold," he adds, "that the definition of being is simply power."

The basic issue concerning being and becoming, and the issue concerning eternal as opposed to mutable existence, recurs again and again in the tradition of western thought. They are involved in the distinction between corruptible and incorruptible substances (which is in turn connected with the division of substances into corporeal and spiritual), and with the nature of God as the only purely actual, or truly eternal, being. They are implicit in Spinoza's distinction between *natura naturans* and *natura naturata,* and in his distinction between God's knowledge of things under the aspect of eternity and man's temporal view of the world in process. They are relevant to Hegel's Absolute Idea which, while remaining fixed, progressively reveals itself in the ever changing face of nature and history. In our own day these issues engage John Dewey, George Santayana, and Alfred North Whitehead in controversy, as yesterday they engaged F. H. Bradley, William James, and Henri Bergson.

As ALREADY NOTED, Plato's division of reality into the realms of being and becoming has a bearing on his analysis of knowledge and opinion. The division relates to the distinction between the intelligible and the sensible, and between the opposed qualities of certainty and probability, or necessity and contingency, in our judgments about things. The distinctions between essence and existence and between substance and accident separate aspects or modes of being which function differently as objects for the knowing mind.

Aristotle, for example, holds that "there can be no scientific treatment of the *accidental* . . . for the accidental is practically a mere name. And," he adds, "Plato was in a sense not wrong in ranking sophistic as dealing with that which is not. For the arguments of the sophists deal, we may say, above all, with the accidental." That the accidental is "akin to non-being," Aristotle thinks may be seen in the fact that "things which are in another sense come into being and pass out of being by a process, but things which are accidentally do not." But though he rejects the accidental as an object of science, he does not, like Plato or Plotinus, exclude the whole realm of sensible, changing things from the sphere of scientific knowledge. For him, both metaphysics and physics treat of sensible substances, the one with regard to their mutable *being,* the other with regard to their being *mutable*—their becoming or changing.

For Plotinus, on the other hand, "the true sciences have an intelligible object and contain no notion of anything sensible." They are directed, not "to variable things, suffering from all sorts of changes, divided in space, to which the name of becoming and not being belongs," but to the "eternal being which is not divided, existing always in the same way, which is not born and does not perish, and has neither space, place, nor situation . . . but rests immovable in itself."

According to another view, represented by Locke, substance is as such unknowable, whether it be body or spirit. We use the word "substance" to name the "support of such qualities, which are capable of producing simple ideas in us; which qualities are commonly called accidents." The sensible accidents are all that we truly know and "we give the general name substance" to "the supposed, but unknown, support of those qualities we find existing." Some of these sensible accidents are what Locke calls "primary qualities"—the powers or potentialities by which things affect one another and also our senses.

But to the extent that our senses fail to discover "the bulk, texture, and figure of the minute parts of bodies, on which their constitutions and differences depend, we are fain to make use of their secondary qualities, as the characteristical notes and marks whereby to frame ideas of them in our mind." Nevertheless, powers—which are qualities or accidents, not substances—seem to be, for Locke, the ultimate reality we can know. "The secondary sensible qualities," he writes, "are nothing but the powers" which corporeal substances have "to produce several ideas in us by our sense, which ideas"—unlike the primary qualities— "are not in the things themselves, otherwise than as anything is in its cause."

Hobbes exemplifies still another view. "A man can have no thought," he says, "representing anything not subject to sense." Hobbes does not object to calling bodies "substances," but thinks that when we speak of "an incorporeal body, or (which is all one) an incorporeal substance," we talk nonsense; "for none of these things ever have, or can be incident to sense; but are absurd speeches, taken upon credit (without any signification at all) from deceived Philosophers, and deceived, or deceiving, Schoolmen."

He enumerates other absurdities, such as "the giving of names of bodies to accidents, or of accidents to bodies," *e.g.,* by those who say that "extension is body." Criticism of the fallacy of reification—the fallacy first pointed out by William of Ockham and criticized so repeatedly in contemporary semantics—also appears in Hobbes's warning against making substances out of abstractions or universals "by giving the names of bodies to names or speeches."

WHENEVER A THEORY of knowledge is concerned with how we know reality, as opposed to mere appearances, it considers the manner in which existing beings can be known—by perception, intuition, or demonstration; and with respect to demonstration, it attempts to formulate the conditions of valid reasoning about matters of fact or real existence. But it has seldom been supposed that reality exhausts the objects of our thought or knowledge. We can conceive possibilities not realized in this world. We can imagine things which do not exist in nature.

The meaning of reality—of real as opposed to purely conceptual or ideal being—is derived from the notion of thinghood, of having being outside the mind, not merely in it. In traditional controversies about the existence of ideas—or of universals, the objects of mathematics, or relations—it is not the being of such things which is questioned, but their reality, their existence outside the mind. If, for example, ideas exist apart from minds, the minds of men and God, they have real, not ideal, existence. If the objects of mathematics, such as numbers and figures, have existence only as figments of the mind, they are ideal beings.

The judgment of the reality of a thing, James thinks, involves "a state of consciousness *sui generis*" about which not much can be said "in the way of internal analysis." The focus of this problem in modern times is indicated by James's phrasing of the question, "Under what circumstances do we think things real?" And James gives a typically modern answer to the question.

He begins by saying that "any object which remains uncontradicted is ipso facto believed and posited as absolute reality." He admits that "for most men . . . the 'things of sense' . . . are the absolutely real world's nucleus. Other things," James writes, "may be real for this man or that—things of science, abstract moral relations, things of the Christian theology, or what not. But even for the special man, these things are usually real with a less real reality than that of the things of sense." But his basic conviction is that "our own reality, that sense of our own life which we at every moment possess, is the ultimate of ultimates for our belief. 'As sure as I exist!'— this is our uttermost warrant for the being of all other things. As Descartes made the indubitable reality of the *cogito* go bail for the reality of all that the *cogito* involved, so all of us, feeling our own present reality with absolutely coercive force, ascribe an all but equal degree of reality, first to whatever things we lay hold on with a sense of personal need, and second, to whatever farther things continuously belong with these."

The self or ego is the ultimate criterion of being or reality. "The world of living realities as contrasted with unrealities," James writes, "is thus anchored in the Ego . . . That is the hook from which the rest dangles, the absolute support. And as from a painted hook it has been said that one can only hang a painted chain, so conversely from a real hook only a real chain can properly be hung. *Whatever things have intimate and continuous connection with my life are things of whose reality I cannot doubt. Whatever things fail to establish this connection are things which are practically no better for me than if they existed not at all.*" James would be the first to concede to any critic of his position, that its truth and good sense depend upon noting that word "practically," for it is "the world of 'practical realities'" with which he professes to be concerned.

WE CAN IN CONCLUSION observe one obvious measure of the importance of *being* in philosophical thought. The major *isms* by which the historians of philosophy have tried to classify its doctrines represent affirmations or denials with respect to being or the modes of being. They are such antitheses as realism and idealism; materialism and spiritualism; monism, dualism, and pluralism; even atheism and theism. Undoubtedly, no great philosopher can be so simply boxed. Yet the opposing *isms* do indicate the great speculative issues which no mind can avoid if it pursues the truth or seeks the ultimate principles of good and evil.

8

Cause

INTRODUCTION

EXPLANATION is an inveterate human tendency. Even philosophers who think that we cannot attain to knowledge of causes get involved in explaining why that is so. Nor will their disputes about the theory of causes ever remove the word "because" from the vocabulary of common speech. It is as unavoidable as the word "is." "The impulse to seek causes," says Tolstoy, "is innate in the soul of man."

The question "Why?" remains after all other questions are answered. It is sometimes the only unanswerable question—unanswerable either in the very nature of the case or because there are secrets men cannot fathom. Sometimes, as Dante says, man must be "content with the *quia*," the knowledge *that* something is without knowing *why*. "Why?" is the one question which it has been deemed the better part of wisdom not to ask; yet it has also been thought the one question which holds the key to wisdom. As Virgil writes, in one of his most famous lines, *Felix, qui potuit rerum cognoscere causas* (Happy is the man who has been able to know the causes of things).

The question "Why?" takes many forms and can be answered in many ways. Other knowledge may prove useful in providing the answers. A definition, for example, which tells us what a thing is, may explain why it behaves as it does or why it has certain properties. A narrative, which tells us how something happened by describing a succession of events, may also be part of the total explanation of some event in question.

In other circumstances, a demonstration or statement of grounds or reasons may be explanatory. "How do you know?" is often a concealed form of the "Why" question. To answer it we may have to give our reasons for thinking that something or other is the case; or perhaps give the genesis of our opinion. Things as different as a logical demonstration and a piece of autobiography seem to be relevant in accounting for our convictions; as in accounting for our behavior, we may refer to our purposes and to our past.

THE GREEK WORD for cause, from which our English word "aetiology" is derived, came into the vocabulary of science and philosophy from the language of the law courts. In its legal sense it was used to point out where the responsibility lay. A suit at law is based upon a cause of action; he who demands redress for an injury suffered is expected to place the blame. The charge of responsibility for wrongdoing—the blame or fault which is the cause for legal redress or punishment—naturally calls for excuses, which may include a man's motives.

In the context of these legal considerations, two different meanings of cause begin to appear. One man's act is the cause of injury to another, in the sense of being responsible for its occurrence. If the act was intentional, it probably had a cause in the purpose which motivated it.

These two types of cause appear in the explanations of the historians as well as in trials at law. Herodotus and Thucydides, trying to account for the Persian or the Peloponnesian war, enumerate the incidents which led up to the outbreak of hostilities. They cite certain past events as the causes of war—the factors which predisposed the parties toward conflict, and even precipitated it. The historians do not think they can fully explain why the particular events become the occasions for war except by considering the hopes and ambitions, or,

66

as Thucydides suggests, the fears of the contestants. For the ancient historians at least, finding the causes includes a search for the motives which underlie other causes and help to explain how other factors get their causal efficacy.

Thucydides explicitly distinguishes these two kinds of causes in the first chapter of his history. After noting that the "immediate cause" of the war was the breaking of a treaty, he adds that the "real cause" was one "which was formally most kept out of sight," namely, the "growth of the power of Athens, and the alarm which this inspired in Lacedaemon."

It is sometimes supposed that Thucydides owes his conception of causes to the early medical tradition. That might very well be the case, for Hippocrates constantly seeks the "natural causes" of disease; and in his analysis of the various factors involved in any particular disease, he tries to distinguish between the predisposing and the exciting causes.

But the classification of causes was not completed in the Athenian law courts, in the Greek interpretation of history, or in the early practice of medicine. Causes were also the preoccupation of the pre-Socratic physicists. Their study of nature was largely devoted to an analysis of the principles, elements, and causes of change. Concerned with the problem of change in general, not merely with human action, or particular phenomena such as crime, war, or disease, Greek scientists or philosophers, from Thales and Anaxagoras to Empedocles, Democritus, Plato, and Aristotle, tried to discover the causes involved in any change. Aristotle carried the analysis furthest and set a pattern for all later discussions of cause.

THE EXPLANATION OF a thing, according to Aristotle, must answer all of the queries "comprehended under the question 'why.'" This question can be answered, he thinks, in at least four different ways, and these four ways of saying why something is the case constitute his famous theory of the four causes.

"In one sense," he writes, "that out of which a thing comes to be and which persists, is called 'cause'"—the material cause. "In another sense, the form or the archetype" is a cause—the formal cause. "Again the primary source of the change or coming to rest" is a cause—the efficient cause. "Again the end or 'that for the sake of which' a thing is done" is a cause—the final cause. "This," he concludes, "perhaps exhausts the number of ways in which the term 'cause' is used."

The production of works of art, to which Aristotle himself frequently turns for examples, most readily illustrates these four different kinds of causes. In making a shoe, the material cause is that out of which the shoe is made—the leather or hide. The efficient cause is the shoemaker, or more precisely the shoemaker's acts which transform the raw material into the finished product. The formal cause is the pattern which directs the work; it is, in a sense, the definition or type of the thing to be made, which, beginning as a plan in the artist's mind, appears at the end of the work in the transformed material as its own intrinsic form. The protection of the foot is the final cause or end—that for the sake of which the shoe was made.

Two of the four causes seem to be less discernible in nature than in art. The material and efficient causes remain evident enough. The material cause can usually be identified as that which undergoes the change—the thing which grows, alters in color, or moves from place to place. The efficient cause is always that by which the change is produced. It is the moving cause working on that which is susceptible to change, e.g., the fire heating the water, the rolling stone setting another stone in motion.

But the formal cause is not as apparent in nature as in art. Whereas in art it can be identified by reference to the plan in the maker's mind, it must be discovered in nature in the change itself, as that which completes the process. For example, the redness which the apple takes on in ripening is the formal cause of its alteration in color. The trouble with the final cause is that it so often tends to be inseparable from the formal cause; for unless some extrinsic purpose can be found for a natural change—some end beyond itself which the change serves—the final cause, or that for the sake of which the change took place, is no other than the quality or form which the matter assumes as a result of its transformation.

THIS SUMMARY of Aristotle's doctrine of the four causes enables us to note some of the basic issues and shifts in the theory of causation.

The attack on final causes does not, at the beginning at least, reject them completely. Francis Bacon, for example, divides natural philosophy into two parts, of which one part, "physics, inquireth and handleth the material and efficient causes; and the other, which is metaphysics, handleth the formal and final causes." The error of his predecessors, of which he complains, is their failure to separate these two types of inquiry. The study of final causes is inappropriate in physics, he thinks.

"This misplacing," Bacon comments, "hath caused a deficiency, or at least a great improficiency in the sciences themselves. For the handling of final causes, mixed with the rest in physical inquiries, hath intercepted the severe and diligent inquiry of all real and physical causes, and given men the occasion to stay upon these satisfactory and specious causes, to the great arrest and prejudice of further discovery." On this score, he charges Plato, Aristotle, and Galen with impeding the development of science, not because "final causes are not true, and worthy to be inquired, being kept within their own province; but because their excursions into the limits of physical causes hath bred a vastness and solitude in that tract."

Such statements as "the hairs of the eyelids are for a quickset and fence about the sight," or that "the leaves of trees are for protecting of the fruit," or that "the clouds are for watering of the earth," are, in Bacon's opinion, "impertinent" in physics. He therefore praises the mechanical philosophy of Democritus. It seems to him to inquire into the "particularities of physical causes" better "than that of Aristotle and Plato, whereof both intermingled final causes, the one as a part of theology, the other as a part of logic."

As Bacon's criticisms indicate, the attack on final causes in nature raises a whole series of questions. Does every natural change serve some purpose, either for the good of the changing thing or for the order of nature itself? Is there a plan, analogous to that of an artist, which orders the parts of nature, and their activities, to one another as means to ends? A natural teleology, which attributes final causes to everything, seems to imply that every natural thing is governed by an indwelling form working toward a definite end, and that the whole of nature exhibits the working out of a divine plan or desire.

Spinoza answers such questions negatively. "Nature has set no end before herself," he declares, and "all final causes are nothing but human fictions." Furthermore, he insists, "this doctrine concerning an end altogether overturns nature. For that which is in truth the cause it considers as the effect, and *vice versa*." He deplores those who "will not cease from asking the causes of causes, until at last you fly to the will of God, the refuge of ignorance."

Spinoza denies that God acts for an end and that the universe expresses a divine purpose. He also thinks that final causes are illusory even in the sphere of human action. When we say that "having a house to live in was the final cause of this or that house," we do no more than indicate a "particular desire, which is really an efficient cause, and is considered as primary, because men are usually ignorant of the causes of their desires."

Though Descartes replies to Pierre Gassendi's arguments "on behalf of final causality," by saying that they should "be referred to the efficient cause," his position more closely resembles that of Bacon than of Spinoza. When we behold "the uses of the various parts in plants and animals," we may be led to admire "the God who brings these into existence," but "that does not imply," he adds, "that we can divine the purpose for which He made each thing. And although in Ethics, where it is often allowable to employ conjecture, it is at times pious to consider the end which we may conjecture God set before Himself in ruling the universe, certainly in Physics, where everything should rest upon the securest arguments, it is futile to do so."

The elimination of final causes from natural science leads Descartes to formulate Harvey's discoveries concerning the motion of the heart and blood in purely mathematical terms. But Harvey himself, as Robert Boyle points out in his *Disquisition About the Final Causes of Natural Things,* interprets organic structures in terms of their functional utility; and Boyle defends the soundness of Harvey's method—employing final causes—against Descartes.

Guided as it is by the principle of utility or function, Harvey's reasoning about the circulation of the blood—especially its venal and arterial flow in relation to the action of the lungs—appeals to final causes. He remarks upon the need of arguing from the final cause in his work on animal generation. "It appears advisable to me," he writes, "to look back from the perfect animal, and to inquire by what process it has arisen and grown to maturity, to retrace our steps, as it were, from the goal to the starting place."

Kant generalizes this type of argument in his "Critique of Teleological Judgement." "No one has ever questioned," he says, "the correctness of the principle that when judging certain things in nature, namely organisms and their possibility, we must look to the conception of final causes. Such a principle is admittedly necessary even where we require no more than a *guiding-thread* for the purpose of becoming acquainted with the character of these things by means of observation." Kant criticizes a mechanism which totally excludes the principle of finality—whether it is based on the doctrine of "blind chance" of Democritus and Epicurus, or the "system of fatality" he attributes to Spinoza. Physical science, he thinks, can be extended by the principle of final causes "without interfering with the principle of the mechanism of physical causality."

THE TENDENCY TO dispense with final causes seems to prevail, however, in the science of mechanics and especially in the domain of inanimate nature. Huygens, for example, defines light as "the motion of some sort of matter." He explicitly insists that conceiving natural things in this way is the only way proper to what he calls the "true Philosophy, in which one conceives the causes of all natural effects in terms of mechanical motions."

Mechanical explanation is distinguished by the fact that it appeals to no principles except matter and motion. The material and the moving (or efficient) causes suffice. The philosophical thought of the 17th century, influenced by that century's brilliant accomplishments in mechanics, tends to be mechanistic in its theory of causation. Yet, being also influenced by the model and method of mathematics, thinkers like Descartes and Spinoza retain the formal cause as a principle of demonstration, if not of explanation. Spinoza, in fact, claims that the reliance upon final causes "would have been sufficient to keep the human race in darkness to all eternity, if mathematics, which does not deal with ends, but with the essences and properties of forms, had not placed before us another rule of truth."

Nevertheless, the tendency to restrict causality to efficiency—a motion producing a motion—gains headway. By the time Hume questions man's ability to know causes, the term *cause* signifies only *efficiency,* understood as the energy expended in producing an effect. Hume's doubt concerning our ability to know causes presupposes this conception of cause and effect, which asserts that "there is some connection between them, some power in the one by which it infallibly produces the other." The identification of cause with the efficient type of cause becomes a commonly accepted notion, even among those who do not agree with Hume that "we are ignorant . . . of the manner in which bodies operate on each other"; and that "their force and energy is entirely incomprehensible" to us.

The narrowing of causality to efficiency also appears in the doctrine, more prevalent today than ever before, that natural science describes, but does not explain—that it tells us *how* things happen, but not *why.* If it does not require the scientist to avoid all reference to causes, it does limit him to the one type of causality which can be expressed in terms of sequences and correlations. The exclusion of all causes except the efficient tends furthermore to reduce the causal order to nothing but the relation of cause and effect.

The four causes taken together as the sufficient reason for things or events do not as such stand in relation to an effect, in the sense in which an effect is something separable from and externally related to its cause. That way of conceiving causation—as a relation of cause to effect—is appropriate to the efficient cause alone. When the efficient cause is regarded as the only cause, having a power proportionate to the reality of its effect, the very meaning of *cause* involves relation to an *effect*.

In the other conception of causation, the causal order relates the four causes to one another. Of the four causes of any change or act, the first, says Aquinas, "is the final cause; the reason of which is that matter does not receive form, save in so far as it is moved by an agent, for nothing reduces itself from potentiality to act. But an agent does not move except from the intention of an end." Hence in operation the order of the four causes is final, efficient, material, and formal; or, as Aquinas states it, "first comes goodness and the end, moving the agent to act; secondly the action of the agent moving to the form; thirdly, comes the form."

THE THEORY OF causes, as developed by Aristotle and Aquinas, proposes other distinctions beyond that of the four causes, such as the difference between the essential cause or the cause per se and the accidental or coincidental cause. As indicated in the chapter on CHANCE, it is in terms of coincidental causes that Aristotle speaks of chance as a cause.

A given effect may be the result of a number of efficient causes. Sometimes these form a series, as when one body in motion sets another in motion, and that moves a third; or, to take another example, a man is the cause of his grandson only through having begotten a son who later begets a son. In such a succession of causes, the first cause may be indispensable, but it is not by itself sufficient to produce the effect. With respect to the effect which it fails to produce unless other causes intervene, it is an accidental cause. In contrast, an essential cause is one which, by its operation, immediately brings the effect into existence.

Sometimes, however, a number of efficient causes may be involved simultaneously rather than successively in the production of a single effect. They may be related to one another as cause and effect rather than by mere coinci-

dence. One cause may be the essential cause of another which in turn is the essential cause of the effect. When two causes are thus simultaneously related to the same effect, Aquinas calls one the principal, the other the instrumental cause; and he gives as an example the action of a workman sawing wood. The action of the saw causes a shaping of the wood, but it is instrumental to the operation of the principal cause, which is the action of the workman using the saw.

These two distinctions—between essential and accidental causes and between principal and instrumental causes—become of great significance in arguments, metaphysical or theological, concerning the cause of causes—a first or ultimate cause. Aristotle's proof of a prime mover, for example, depends upon the proposition that there cannot be an infinite number of causes for a given effect. But since Aristotle also holds that the world is without beginning or end and that time is infinite, it may be wondered why the chain of causes cannot stretch back to infinity.

If time is infinite, a temporal sequence of causes reaching back to infinity would seem to present no difficulty. As Descartes points out, you cannot "prove that that regress to infinity is absurd, unless you at the same time show that the world has a definite beginning in time." Though it is a matter of their Jewish and Christian faith that the world had a beginning in time, theologians like Maimonides and Aquinas do not think the world's beginning can be proved by reason. They do, however, think that the necessity of a first cause can be demonstrated, and both adopt or perhaps adapt the argument of Aristotle which relies on the impossibility of an infinite regression in causes.

The argument is valid, Aquinas makes clear, only if we distinguish between essential and accidental causes. "It is not impossible," he says, "to proceed to infinity *accidentally* as regards efficient causes . . . It is not impossible for man to be generated by man to infinity." But, he holds, "there cannot be an infinite number of causes that are *per se* required for a certain effect; for instance, that a stone be moved by a stick, the stick by the hand, and so on to infinity." In the latter case, it should be observed, the cooperating causes are simultaneous and so if there were an infinity of them, that would not require an infinite time. The crux of the argument, therefore, lies either in the impossibility of an infinite number of simultaneous causes, or in the impossibility of an infinite number of causes related to one another as instrumental to principal cause.

Among causes so related, Descartes, like Aquinas, argues that there must be one first or principal cause. "In the case of causes which are so connected and subordinated to one another, that no action on the part of the lower is possible without the activity of the higher; *e.g.*, in the case where something is moved by a stone, itself impelled by a stick, which the hand moves . . . we must go on until we come to one thing in motion which first moves." But for Descartes, unlike Aquinas, this method of proving God as the first cause of all observable effects has less elegance than the so-called "ontological argument" in which the conception of God as a necessary being, incapable of not existing, immediately implies his existence.

The argument from effect to cause is traditionally called *a posteriori* reasoning, in contrast to *a priori* reasoning from cause to effect. According to Aristotle and Aquinas, the latter mode of reasoning can only demonstrate the nature of a thing, not its existence. Aquinas, furthermore, does not regard the ontological argument as a form of reasoning at all, but rather as the assertion that God's existence is self-evident to us, which he denies.

The various forms which these arguments take and the issue concerning their validity are more fully discussed in the chapters on BEING, GOD, and NECESSITY AND CONTINGENCY. But here it is worth noting that Kant questions whether the *a posteriori* method of proving God's existence really differs from the ontological argument. It is, according to him, not only "illusory and inadequate," but also "possesses the additional blemish of an *ignoratio elenchi*—professing to conduct us by a new road to the desired goal, but bringing us back, after a short circuit, to the old path which we had deserted at its call." Hence the causal proof does not, in Kant's opinion, succeed

in avoiding the fallacies which he, along with Maimonides and Aquinas, finds in the ontological argument.

THE ANALYSIS OF CAUSATION figures critically in the speculation of the theologians concerning creation, providence, and the government of the world.

The dogma of creation, for example, requires the conception of a unique type of cause. Even if the world always existed—a supposition which, as we have seen, is contrary to Jewish and Christian faith but not to reason—the religious belief in a Creator would remain a belief in that unique cause without whose action to preserve its being at every moment the world would cease to be.

On the assumption that God created the world in the beginning, it is, perhaps, easy enough to see with Augustine how "the creating and originating work which gave being to all natures, differs from all other types of causation which cause motions or changes, or even the generation of things, rather than their very existence." It may, however, be more difficult to understand the creative action of God in relation to a world already in existence.

But a theologian like Aquinas explains that "as long as a thing has being, so long must God be present to it" as the cause of its being—a doctrine which Berkeley later reports by saying that this makes "the divine conservation . . . to be a continual creation." Aquinas agrees that "the conservation of things by God is not by a new action, but by the continuation of that action whereby He gives being." But in the conservation of things Aquinas thinks that God acts through natural or created causes, whereas in their initiation, being is the proper effect of God alone.

The dogma of divine providence also requires a theory of the cooperation of the first cause with natural or secondary causes. Dante, in describing the direction which providence gives to the course of nature, uses the image of a bow. "Whatever this bow shoots falls disposed to a foreseen end, even as a shaft directed to its mark." That God governs and cares for all things may be supposed to reduce nature to a puppet show in which every action takes place in obedience to the divine will alone. Natural causes would thus cease to be causes or to have any genuine efficacy in the production of their own effects.

Some theologians have tended toward this extreme position, but Aquinas argues contrariwise that natural causes retain their efficacy as instrumental causes, subordinate to God's will as the one principal cause. "Since God wills that effects be because of their causes," he writes, "all effects that presuppose some other effect do not depend solely on the will of God"; and, in another place, he says, "whatsoever causes He assigns to certain effects, He gives them the power to produce those effects ... so that the dignity of causality is imparted even to creatures."

In addition to the role of divine causality in the regular processes of nature, still another kind of divine causation is presupposed by the religious belief in supernatural events, such as the elevation of nature by grace and the deviations from the course of nature which are called "miracles." All these considerations, and especially the matter of God's miraculous intervention in the regular course of nature, have been subjects of dispute among theologians and philosophers (and sometimes physicists and historians). Some of those who do not deny the existence of a Creator, or the divine government of the universe through natural law, nevertheless question the need for divine cooperation with the action of every natural cause, or God's intervention in the order of nature.

Throughout these controversies, the theory of causes defines the issues and determines the lines of opposing argument. But since other basic notions are also involved in the debate of these issues, the further consideration of them is reserved for other chapters, especially GOD, NATURE, and WORLD.

THE DISCUSSION OF CAUSE takes a new turn in modern times. The new issues arise, not from different interpretations of the principle of causality, but from the skeptic's doubts concerning our ability to know the causes of things, and from the tendency of the physical sciences to limit or even to abandon the investigation of causes. A 20th-century geneticist, Dobzhansky, calls our attention to the fact that we use the word "spontaneous," as in the phrase "spontaneous generation" or "spontaneous mutation," to cover up a "thinly veiled admission of the ignorance of the real causes of the phenomena in question."

According to the ancient conception of science, knowledge, to be scientific, must state the causes of things. The essence of scientific method, according to the *Posterior Analytics* of Aristotle, consists in using causes both to define and to demonstrate. Sometimes genus and differentia are translated into material and formal cause; sometimes a thing is defined genetically by reference to its efficient cause, and sometimes teleologically by reference to its final cause.

The degree to which this conception of science is realized in particular fields may be questioned. The treatises of the astronomers, for example, do not seem to exemplify it as much as do Aristotle's own physical treatises or Harvey's work on the circulation of the blood. Yet until modern developments in mathematical physics, the ascertainment of causes seems to be the dominant conception of the scientific task; and until the separation widens between the experimental and the philosophical sciences, the possibility of knowing causes is not generally doubted.

Galileo's exposition of the new mechanics explicitly announces a departure from the traditional interest of the natural philosopher in the discovery of causes. The aim, he says, in his *Concerning Two New Sciences,* is not "to investigate the cause of the acceleration of natural motion, concerning which various opinions have been expressed by various philosophers"; but rather "to investigate and to demonstrate some of the properties of accelerated motion." The "various opinions" about causes are referred to as "fantasies" which it is "not really worth while" for the scientist to examine.

This attitude toward causes, especially efficient causes, characterizes the aim of mathematical physics, both in astronomy and mechanics. For Newton it is enough—in fact, he says, it "would be a very great step in philosophy"—"to derive two or three general principles of motion from phenomena . . . though the causes of those principles were not yet discovered. And, therefore, I scruple not to propose the principles of motion . . . and leave their causes to be found out." In other passages, Newton disparages the search for "hidden or occult causes" as no part of the business of science.

When we pass from classical mechanics to quantum mechanics, causal predictions give way to probability calculations. "The discovery of the quantum of action," Bohr tells us, makes "a detailed causal tracing of atomic processes . . . impossible," because "any attempt to acquire knowledge of such processes involves a fundamentally uncontrollable interference with their course." Quantum mechanics involves a renunciation of "the causal space-time co-ordination of atomic processes."

Hume goes further. He insists that *all* causes are hidden, even in the phenomena studied by classical physics or Newtonian mechanics. By the very nature of what causes are supposed to be and because of the manner in which the human mind knows, man can have no knowledge of how causes really produce their effects. "We never can, by our utmost scrutiny," he says, "discover anything but one event following another, without being able to comprehend any force or power by which the cause operates, or any connexion between it and its supposed effect."

All that men can be referring to when they use the words "cause" and "effect," Hume thinks, is the customary sequence of "one object followed by another, and where all objects similar to the first are followed by objects similar to the second." So far as any knowledge based upon reason or experience can go, the relation of cause and effect is simply one of succession, impressed upon the mind "by a customary transition." That one event leads to another becomes more and more probable—but never more than probable—as the sequence recurs more and more frequently in experience.

Hume's skepticism about causes, and his reinterpretation of the meaning of cause, gains wide acceptance in subsequent thought, especially among natural scientists. William James,

for example, considering "the principle that 'nothing can happen without a cause,'" declares that "we have no definite idea of what we mean by cause, or of what causality consists in. But the principle expresses a demand for *some* deeper sort of inward connection between phenomena than their merely habitual time-sequence seems to be. The word 'cause' is, in short, an altar to an unknown god; an empty pedestal still marking the place for a hoped-for statue. Any really inward belonging-together of the sequent terms," he continues, "if discovered, would be accepted as what the word cause was meant to stand for."

Though Hume holds that we cannot penetrate beyond experience to the operation of real causes imbedded in the nature of things, he does not deny the reality of causation as a principle of nature. On the contrary, he denies that anything happens by chance or that any natural occurrence can be uncaused. "It is universally allowed," Hume says with approval, "that nothing exists without a cause of its existence, and that chance, when strictly examined, is a mere negative word, and means not any real power which has anywhere a being in nature." But "though there is no such thing as *chance* in the world, our ignorance of the real cause of any event has the same influence on the understanding, and begets a like species of belief or opinion."

In other words, Hume's position seems to be that man's ignorance of real causes, and the mere probability of his opinions about customary sequences of "cause" and "effect," indicate human limitations, not limits to causal determination in the order of nature itself. Adversaries of Hume, coming before as well as after him in the tradition of the great books, take issue with him on both points. Nietzsche sides with him: causes are fictions we ourselves invent. "It is *we* alone who have fabricated causes . . . We once more behave as we have always behaved, namely *mythologically*."

Against Hume's determinism, which is no less complete than Spinoza's, Aristotle, for example, affirms the existence of chance or real contingency in the happenings of nature. Against Hume's reduction of statements about causes to probable opinion, Kant insists that, in the metaphysics of nature, such judgments can be made with absolute certainty. These related issues are discussed in the chapters on CHANCE, FATE, and NECESSITY AND CONTINGENCY.

In the development of the natural sciences since Hume's day, his translation of cause and effect into observed sequences or correlations reinforces the tendency, which first appears with Galileo and Newton, to *describe* rather than to *explain* natural phenomena. Yet to the extent that the findings of science bear fruit in technology, man's control over nature seems to confirm Bacon's view of science rather than Hume's—at least to the extent that the application of scientific knowledge to the production of effects implies a knowlege of their causes.

According to Planck, "the law of causality is neither true nor false. It is rather a heuristic principle, a signpost . . . to help us find our bearings in a bewildering maze of occurrences, and to show us the direction in which scientific research must advance in order to achieve fertile results." Concern with causality "impresses the awakening soul of the child and plants the untiring question 'Why?' into his mouth." This "remains a lifelong companion of the scientist and confronts him incessantly with new problems."

THE PRINCIPLE OF CAUSALITY—that nothing happens without a cause or sufficient reason, or, as Spinoza puts it, "nothing exists from whose nature an effect does not follow"—has been made the basis for denials of human freedom as well as of chance or contingency in the order of nature. The problem of man's free will is discussed in the chapters on FATE, LIBERTY, and WILL, but we can here observe how the problem is stated in terms of cause, with respect to both divine providence and natural causation.

If God's will is the cause of everything which happens, if nothing can happen contrary to His will or escape the foresight of His providence, then how is man free from God's foreordination when he chooses between good and evil? If, as the theologians say, "the very act of free choice is traced to God as to a cause," in what sense can the act be called "free"? Is it not necessarily determined to conform to God's will and to His plan? But, on the other hand, if "everything happening from the exercise of free choice must be subject to divine providence," must not the evil that men do be attributed to God as cause?

The problem takes another form for the scientist who thinks only in terms of natural causes, especially if he affirms a reign of causality in nature from which nothing is exempt—just as, for the theologian, nothing is exempt from God's will. Since the realm of nature includes human nature, must not human acts be caused as are all other natural events? Are some human acts free in the sense of being totally uncaused, or only in the sense of being caused differently from the motions of matter? Are causality and freedom opposed principles within the order of nature, appropriate to physical and psychological action; or do they constitute distinct realms—as for Kant, the realms of phenomena and noumena, the sensible and the supra-sensible; or as for Hegel, the realms of nature and history?

The different answers which the great books give to these questions have profound consequences for man's view of himself, the universe, and his place in it. As the issue of necessity and chance is central in physics or the philosophy of nature, so the issue of determinism and freedom is central in psychology and ethics, in political theory and the philosophy of history, and above all in theology. It makes opponents of James and Freud, of Hegel and Marx, of Hume and Kant, of Spinoza and Descartes, of Lucretius and Marcus Aurelius. It raises one of the most perplexing of all theological questions for Augustine, Aquinas, Pascal, and for the two great poets of God's will and man's freedom—Dante and Milton.

9

Chance

INTRODUCTION

ONE sense in which we use the word "chance" does not exclude the operation of causes. The chance event, in this sense, is not uncaused. But within this meaning of chance, there is the question of *how* the chance event is caused.

On one view, what happens by chance is distinguished from what happens by nature in terms of a difference in manner of causation—the difference between the contingent and the necessary. On another view, the chance event does not differ causally from that which happens regularly or uniformly. The difference lies not in the pattern of causes, but in our knowledge of them. The chance event is unpredictable or less predictable because of our ignorance of its causes, not because of any real contingency in the order of nature.

There is still a third sense of "chance" in which it means that which happens totally without cause—the absolutely spontaneous or fortuitous.

These three meanings of *chance* at once indicate the basic issues in which the concept is involved. The third meaning is the most radical. It stands in opposition to the other two. Their opposition to one another can be considered after we examine the sense in which chance excludes every type of cause.

THE DOCTRINE OF absolute fortuitousness is indeterminism in its most extreme form. The familiar phrase, "a fortuitous concourse of atoms," indicates the classical statement of this doctrine and identifies it in the great books with the theory of atomism. It would be more precise to say "with Lucretius' version of that theory," because it is with regard to chance that he departs from the teachings of Democritus and Epicurus and adds an hypothesis of his own.

The swerve of the atoms, according to Lucretius, accounts for the origin of the world, the motions of nature, and the free will of man. But nothing accounts for the swerve of the atoms. It is uncaused, spontaneous, fortuitous.

... while these particles come mostly down,
Straight down of their own weight through
    void, at times—
No one knows when or where—they swerve a little,
Not much, but just enough for us to say
They change direction. Were this not the case,
All things would fall straight down, like drops of
    rain,
Through utter void, no birth-shock would emerge
Out of collision, nothing be created.

Since the atoms differ in shape, size, and weight, it might be supposed that the heavier atoms, falling straight yet more rapidly, would overtake and hit the lighter atoms, thus bringing about their grouping or interlocking. But this supposition, says Lucretius, is contrary to reason. It may hold for things falling through water or thin air, but through the empty void "all things, though their weights may differ, drive/Through unresisting void at the same rate." Therefore heavier things will never be able to fall on the lighter from above nor of themselves bring about the blows sufficient to produce the varied motions by which nature carries things on. Wherefore, Lucretius concludes, the atoms "swerve a little."

Once the atoms have collided, the way in which they are locked together in the patterns of composite things, and all the subsequent motions of these things, can be accounted for by reference to the natural properties of the atoms. The atomic sizes, shapes, and weights determine how they behave singly or in combination. But the swerve of the atoms is not so determined. It is completely spontaneous.

"If cause forever follows after cause," asks Lucretius,

In infinite, undeviating sequence
And a new motion always has to come
Out of an old one, by fixed law; if atoms
Do not, by swerving, cause new moves which break
The laws of fate; if cause forever follows,
In infinite sequence, cause—where would we get
This free will that we have, wrested from fate,
By which we go ahead, each one of us,
Wherever our pleasures urge? Don't we also swerve
At no fixed time or place, but as our purpose
Directs us?

The answer he gives is that there must be in the atoms "some other cause for motion beyond extrinsic thrust or native weight, and this third force is resident in us since we know *nothing can be born of nothing.*"

BEING ABSOLUTELY fortuitous, the swerve of the atoms is absolutely unintelligible. There is no answer to the question why they chance to swerve at undetermined times and places. This unintelligibility may not, however, make the fortuitous unreal or impossible. It can be argued that chance may exist even though, for our limited understanding, it remains mysterious.

The same problem of intelligibility arises with respect to that meaning of chance wherein it is identified with coincidence or contingency. Here, as in the case of the absolutely fortuitous, chance belongs to reality or nature. "Some things always come to pass in the same way, and others for the most part," writes Aristotle as an observer of nature, but there is also "a third class of events besides these two—events which all say are 'by chance.'" Things of this last kind, he goes on to say, are those which "come to pass incidentally"—or accidentally.

According to this theory, a real or objective indeterminism exists. Chance or contingency is not just an expression of human uncertainty born of insufficient knowledge. Contingency, however, differs from the fortuitousness or spontaneity of the atom's swerve, in that it is a product of causes, not their total absence.

Of the contingent event, "there is no definite cause," in Aristotle's opinion, but there is "a chance cause, *i.e.,* an indefinite one."

In the chance happening, two lines of action coincide and thereby produce a single result. This is our ordinary understanding of the way accidents happen. The chance meeting of old friends who run across each other in a railroad station after a separation of many years is a coincidence—a coinciding of the two quite separate and independent lines of action which brought each of them to the same station at the same time, coming from different places, going to different places, and proceeding under the influence of different causes or purposes. That each is there can be explained by the operation of causes. That both are there together cannot be explained by the causes determining their independent paths.

So understood, the chance event exemplifies what Aquinas calls a "clashing of two causes." And what makes it a matter of chance is the fact that "the clashing of these two causes, inasmuch as it is accidental, has no cause." Precisely because it is accidental, "this clashing of causes is not to be reduced to a further preexisting cause from which it follows necessity."

The illustration is not affected by considerations of free will. Whether men have free will or not, whether free acts are caused or are, as Kant suggests, uncaused and spontaneous, the event we call a "chance meeting" remains accidental or, more precisely, a coincidence. Whatever the factors are which control the motions of each man, they operate entirely within that single man's line of action. Prior to the meeting, they do not influence the other man's conduct. If we could state the cause for the coincidence of the two lines of motion, it would have to be some factor which influenced both lines. Were there such a cause and were it known to us, we could not say that the meeting happened by chance. It would still be a coincidence in the merely physical sense of coming together, but it would not be a coincidence causally.

That free will is irrelevant to this meaning of chance can be seen from the fact that the collision of particles which produces atomic fission is regarded as resulting from chance or coincidence in a manner no different from the accidental meeting of friends. Causes control the speeds and directions of the colliding particles, but no cause determines their collision; or, in other words, there is no cause for the coincidence of two separate lines of causation. Contemporary physics affirms a real or objective indeterminism insofar as it does not merely say that the cause of the coincidence is unknown to us, but rather holds that no such cause exists to be known.

Chance appears to be an important factor in other sciences. Biologist C. H. Waddington sees chance as one of the most important characteristics of Darwin's theory of evolution. "The basic feature of Darwinist thought ... is its reliance on chance rather than on a simple determinist type of causation," writes Waddington. "All events that lead to the production of new genotypes, such as mutation, recombination and fertilization, are essentially random." Though Waddington admits that Darwin was probably unaware of this contribution, "it was a major service of Darwinism ... to have broken the hold on our minds of notions of simple causation."

THE CONCEPTION OF THE chance event as an uncaused coincidence of causes is an ancient as well as a modern doctrine. In his *Physics,* Aristotle distinguishes between what happens by nature and what happens by chance in terms of different types of causality. "Chance," he writes, is "reckoned among causes; many things are said both to be and to come to be as a result of chance." But the fact that its effects cannot be "identified with any of the things that come to pass by necessity and always, or for the most part" at once distinguishes the causality of chance from that of nature.

"The early physicists," Aristotle observes, "found no place for chance among the causes which they recognized ... Others there are who, indeed, believe that chance is a cause, but that it is inscrutable to human intelligence, as being a divine thing and full of mystery." But to Aristotle himself "it is clear that chance is an incidental cause" and "that the causes of

what comes to pass by chance are infinite." For this reason, he explains, "chance is supposed to belong to the class of the indefinite, and to be inscrutable to man." Though he distinguishes between spontaneity and chance, he says that both "are causes of effects which, though they might result from intelligence or nature, have in fact been caused by something *incidentally.*"

What happens by nature happens regularly, or for the most part, through causal necessity. This necessity results from the operation of essential causes, causes in the very nature of the moving things. When the regularity fails, it is due to the intervention of some accidental cause. What happens by chance, then, or contingently, is always due to an accidental (or better, incidental) cause. As indicated in the chapter on CAUSE, an accidental as opposed to an essential cause is, in Aristotle's theory, one which does not *by itself* produce the given effect. It does so only through the conjunction of other causes. But since it does not determine these other causes to operate, the effect—*contingent on their combined activity*—is produced by chance, that is, by the contingency of several incidental causes working coincidentally.

A world in which chance really exists is remarkably different from a world in which necessity prevails, in which everything is determined by causes and there are no uncaused coincidences. William James vividly epitomizes their difference by calling the world of absolute necessity or determinism—the world of Spinoza or Hegel—a "block universe" in contrast to what he describes as a "concatenated universe." Voltaire before him, in his *Philosophical Dictionary*, had used the phrase "the concatenation of events" to express the meaning of chance.

The phrase evokes the right image, the picture of a world in which many concurrent lines of causality, exercising no influence upon one another, may nevertheless concatenate or be joined together to produce a chance result. The block universe presents the contrasting picture of a world in which each motion or act determines and is determined by every other in the fixed structure of the whole.

Spinoza claims, for example, that "in nature there is nothing contingent, but all things are determined from the necessity of the divine nature to exist and act in a certain manner." Chance, in other words, does not exist in nature. A thing is said to be contingent, Spinoza writes, only "with reference to a deficiency in our knowledge. For if we do not know that the essence of a thing involves a contradiction, or if we actually know that it involves no contradiction, and nevertheless we can affirm nothing with certainty about its existence because the order of causes is concealed from us, that thing can never appear to us either as necessary or impossible, and therefore we call it either contingent or possible."

Hence, for Spinoza, contingency or chance is illusory rather than real—a projection of the mind's ignorance or of its inadequate knowledge of causes. The uncertainties involved in modern quantum mechanics would become for him indeterminabilities, not indeterminacies.

For a quite different reason, Calvin agrees that nothing happens fortuitously or by chance, saying that "if all success is blessing from God, and calamity and adversity are his curse, there is no place left in human affairs for Fortune and chance."

The issue between real indeterminism and absolute determinism—further discussed in the chapters on FATE and NECESSITY AND CONTINGENCY—inevitably raises theological questions. Just as the theologian must reconcile man's free will with God's predestination, so must he, if he accepts its reality, also reconcile chance with divine providence, apart from which nothing can happen either necessarily or contingently.

For Augustine it would seem that divine providence leaves no room for chance among natural things. After noting that causes are sometimes divided into a "fortuitous cause, a natural cause, and a voluntary cause," he dismisses "those causes which are called fortuitous" by saying that they "are not a mere name for the absence of causes, but are only latent, and we attribute them either to the will of the true God, or to that of spirits of some kind or other."

In certain places Aquinas seems to talk in much the same fashion—as though chance existed only for our limited intellects and not for God. "Nothing," he declares, "hinders certain things from happening by luck or chance, if compared to their proximate causes; but not if compared to divine providence, according to which 'nothing happens at random in the world,' as Augustine says." The example he uses to illustrate his point is that of two servants who have been sent by their master to the same place: "the meeting of the two servants, although to them it appears a chance circumstance, has been fully foreseen by their master, who has purposely sent them to meet at one place, in such a way that one has no knowledge of the other." In such a way also "all things must of necessity come under God's ordering," from which it follows that God directly causes the action of even accidental causes, and their coincidence. The chance event would then be necessitated by God. It would be determined by His will, however indeterminate it might appear to us.

Yet in other places Aquinas writes that "God wills some things to be done necessarily, some contingently . . . To some effects He has attached unfailing necessary causes, from which the effects follow necessarily; but to other defectible and contingent causes, from which effects arise contingently." For some minds this may only deepen the mystery rather than solve it. At least it leaves many questions unanswered.

Does Aquinas mean that coincidence of causes is not itself uncaused? Does he mean that God causes the concatenation of events, and that a sufficient reason for every contingency exists in God's will? If so, is chance an illusion, a function of our ignorance of divine providence? May chance be quite real on the level of nature where no natural causes determine the coincidence, while not real—at least not in the same sense—for God? Or does the statement that what "divine providence plans to happen contingently, happens contingently" mean that chance remains a real feature of the universe even for God?

One thing is clear. In one sense of the word, the Christian theologians completely deny chance. If "chance" means something which God does not foresee, something unplanned by His providence, then according to their faith nothing happens by chance. It is in this sense also that what happens by chance is opposed to what happens on purpose, or has a final as well as an efficient cause. As the chapter on CAUSE indicates, those who deny final causes in nature sometimes use the word "chance" to signify not lack of cause, nor even contingency, but only the blindness of causality—working to no end.

The controversy discussed in the chapter on WORLD—between those who see in the structure of the universe the grand design of a divine plan and those who attribute whatever order there is in nature to blind chance—further indicates the sense in which theologians like Augustine and Aquinas deny chance. But if "chance" means no more than *contingency,* then to affirm chance excludes, not providence, but fate, at least that sense of "fate" according to which everything is blindly necessitated. Here it is Spinoza's statement that "in nature there is nothing contingent, but all things are determined from the necessity of the divine nature" which opposes the statement of Aquinas that "the mode both of necessity and contingency falls under the foresight of God."

THE THEORY OF chance has obvious bearings on the theory of knowledge, especially with regard to the distinction between knowledge and opinion and between certainty and probability.

On any view of chance—whether it is real or illusory—when men call a future event contingent they mean that they cannot predict it with certitude. So far as human prediction goes, it makes no difference whether the future event is necessarily determined and we lack adequate knowledge of its causes, or the event has a genuine indeterminacy in the way it is caused or uncaused. Regardless of what the objective situation is, the assurance with which we predict anything reflects the state of our knowledge about it.

The ancients who, for the most part, regard chance as real and objective, treat probability as subjective. For them, the different degrees of probability which men attach to their statements measure the inadequacy of their knowledge and the consequent uncertainty of their opinions about matters which cannot be known but only guessed. Holding different theories of the distinction between knowledge and opinion, both Plato and Aristotle exclude the accidental and the contingent, along with the particular, from the objects of science. Since in their view certitude belongs to the essence of science—or of knowledge as contrasted with opinion—science for them deals not only with the universal but with the necessary.

In *The Republic* Socrates assigns opinion to the realm of becoming—the realm of changing and contingent particulars. Unlike Plato, Aristotle does not restrict knowledge to the realm of eternal and immutable being, but he does insist that physics, as a science of changing things, preserve the certitude of science by concerning itself only with the essential and the necessary. "That a science of the accidental is not even possible," he writes, "will be evident if we try to see what the accidental really is." It is a matter of chance that cold weather occurs during the dog days, for "this occurs neither always and of necessity, nor for the most part, though it might happen sometimes. The accidental, then, is what occurs, but not always nor of necessity, nor for the most part. Now . . . it is obvious why there is no science of such a thing."

Though he disagrees with Aristotle and Aquinas about the reality of chance or contingency, Spinoza agrees with them that knowledge—at least adequate knowledge—has the necessary for its object. Of individual things, he says, "we can have no adequate knowledge . . . and this is what is to be understood by us as their contingency." To be true to itself and to the nature of things, reason must "perceive things truly, that is to say, as they are in themselves, that is to say, not as contingent but as necessary."

The position of Aquinas is worth stating for comparison. To the question "whether our intellect can know contingent things," he replies that "the contingent, considered as such, is known directly by sense and indirectly by the intellect, while the universal and necessary principles of contingent things are known by the intellect. Hence," he goes on, "if we consider knowable things in their universal principles, then all science is of necessary things. But if we consider the things themselves, thus some sciences are of necessary things, some of contingent things."

Among the sciences of contingent things, Aquinas includes not only "the sciences of nature" but also "the moral sciences," because the latter, dealing with human action, must reach down to contingent particulars. In the sphere of morals as of nature, certainty can be achieved only on the level of universal principles. Deliberation about particular acts to be done moves on the level of probable opinion. In contrast to the moral scientist, the man of action must weigh chances and make decisions with regard to future contingencies. It would be as foolish, Aristotle says, to expect the certitude of scientific demonstration from an orator or a judge, as "to accept probable reasoning from a mathematician."

IT IS NOT SURPRISING that the modern theory of probability—or, as it was later called by George Boole, John Venn, and others, the "logic of chance"—should have its origin in the sphere of practical problems. Pascal's correspondence with Pierre de Fermat illustrates the early mathematical speculations concerning formulas for predicting the outcome in games of pure chance. For Pascal the logic of chance also has moral implications. If we are willing to risk money at the gaming table on the basis of calculated probabilities, how much more willing should we be to act decisively in the face of life's uncertainties, even to risking life itself on the chance of eternal salvation.

When we act "on an uncertainty, we act reasonably," Pascal writes, "for we ought to work for an uncertainty according to the doctrine of chance." If the chance of there being an after-life is equal to the chance of there being none—if the equiprobability reflects our equal ignorance of either alternative—then, Pascal argues, we ought to wager in favor of immortality and act accordingly. "There is here the infinity of an infinitely happy life to gain, a chance to gain against a finite number of chances of loss, and what you stake is finite."

Like Pascal, Hume thinks that we must be content with probability as a basis for action. "The great subverter of *Pyrrhonism* or the excessive principles of skepticism," he writes, "is action, and employment, and the occupations of common life." But unlike the ancients, Hume also thinks we should be content with probabilities in the sphere of the natural sciences. Certitude is attainable only by the mathematician who deals with the relations between ideas. Since the natural sciences deal with matters of fact or real existence, and since to know such things we must rely entirely upon our experience of cause and effect, we cannot reach better than probable conclusions.

The scientist, according to Hume, "weighs opposite experiments. He considers which side is supported by the greater number of experiments; to that side he inclines, with doubt and hesitation; and when at last he fixes his judgment, the evidence exceeds not what we properly call *probability*. All probability, then, supposes an opposition of experiments and observations . . . A hundred instances or experiments on one side, and fifty on another, afford a doubtful expectation of any event; though a hundred uniform experiments, with only one that is contradictory, reasonably beget a pretty strong degree of assurance."

Hume applies the logic of chance to weighing the evidence against and the testimony in favor of miracles, as well as to contrary hypotheses in science. As much as Spinoza, he denies the existence of chance or contingency in the order of nature. Chance is entirely subjective. It is identical with the probability of our opinions. In the throw of dice, the mind, he says, "considers the turning up of each particular side as alike probable; and this is the very nature of chance, to render all the particular events, comprehended in it, entirely equal." But there may also be "a probability, which arises from a superiority of chances on any side; and according as this superiority increases, and surpasses the opposite chances, the probability receives a proportionate increase . . . The case," Hume asserts, "is the same with the probability of causes, as with that of chance."

Since Hume's day, the theory of probability has become an essential ingredient of empirical science. The development of thermodynamics in the 19th century would have been impossible without it. This is also true of the quantum mechanics and atomic physics of our own time. But like the doctrine of chance, the theory of probability tends in one of two directions: *either* toward the subjective view that probability is only a quality of our judgments, measuring the degree of our ignorance of the real causes which leave nothing in nature undetermined; *or* toward the objective view that there is genuine indeterminism in nature and that mathematical calculations of probability estimate the real chance of an event's occurring.

THE ELEMENT OF chance also has a bearing on the general theory of art. The hypothesis of the melody which a kitten might compose by walking on the keyboard is obviously intended to contrast a product of chance with a work of art. The competent musician knows with certainty that he can do what the meandering kitten has only one chance in many millions of ever accomplishing.

In proportion as an art is developed, and to the degree that its rules represent a mastery of the medium in which the artist works, chance is excluded from its productions. This point is strikingly exemplified in the history of medicine. "If there had been no such thing as medicine," Hippocrates suggests, "and if nothing had been investigated or found out in it," all practitioners "would have been equally unskilled and ignorant of it, and everything concerning the sick would have been directed by chance." On the same principle, Galen distinguishes the physician from the empiric, who, "without knowing the cause," pretends that he is "able to rectify the failures of function." The empiric works by trial and error—the very opposite of art and science, for trial and error can succeed only by chance. The physician, learned and skilled in medicine, works from a

knowledge of causes and by rules of art which tend to eliminate chance.

Augustine reports a conversation with the proconsul concerning the relative merits of medicine and astrology. When the proconsul tells him that, as compared with medicine, astrology is a false art, Augustine, at this time himself "an enthusiast for books of astrology," asks how it can be explained that "the future was often correctly foretold by means of astrology." The proconsul answered, "it was all due to the power of chance, a force that must always be reckoned with in the natural order." Thus, Augustine says later, "when the astrologers were found to be right, it was due to luck or pure chance and not to their skill in reading the stars."

Neither art itself, nor skill in its practice, can ever be perfect enough to remove chance entirely, for the artist deals with particulars. Yet the measure of an art is the certainty which its rules have as directions for achieving the desired result; and the skill of the artist is measured by the extent to which he succeeds by rule and judgment rather than by chance.

When Aristotle quotes Agathon's remark that "art loves chance and chance loves art," he explains its sense to be that "chance and art are concerned with the same objects"— that which does not come to be by nature nor from necessity. Hence art sometimes fails, either from uncontrollable contingencies or from insufficient knowledge of causes. "All causes," says Hume, "are not conjoined to their usual effects with like uniformity. An artificer, who handles only dead matter, may be disappointed of his aim, as well as the politician, who directs the conduct of sensible and intelligent agents."

IN THE REALM OF human affairs—in morals, politics, and history—the factor of chance is usually discussed in terms of good and bad fortune. The word "fortune"—as may be seen in the root which it shares with "fortuitous"— has the same connotations as "chance." Aristotle treats fortune as the kind of chance that operates in the sphere of human action rather than natural change. Fortune, he thinks, can be attributed properly only to intelligent beings capable of deliberate choice. The sense of this distinction between chance and fortune seems to be borne out in history by the fact that fortune, unlike chance, receives personification in myth and legend. Fortune is a goddess, or, like the Fates whom she combats, a power with which even the gods must reckon.

The doctrine of chance or fortune occupies an important place in moral theory. Aristotle's classification of goods tends to identify external goods with goods of fortune—the goods which, unlike knowledge and virtue, we cannot obtain merely by the exercise of our will and faculties. Considering the elements of happiness, Aquinas groups together wealth, honor, fame, and power as goods of the same sort because they are "due to external causes and in most cases to fortune."

The goods of fortune, as well as its ills, consist in things beyond man's power to command and, in consequence, to deserve. Recognizing the unpredictable operation of fortune, Epictetus, the Stoic, argues that "we must make the best of those things that are in our power, and take the rest as nature gives it." We have "the power to deal rightly with our own impressions." Hence the Stoics advise us to control our reactions to things even though we cannot control the things themselves. Yet men will always ask, as Hamlet does, "Whether 'tis nobler in the mind to suffer the slings and arrows of outrageous fortune, or to take arms against a sea of troubles, and by opposing end them?"

The fact that the goods and ills of fortune are beyond our power to control raises the further question of man's responsibility regarding them. We can hardly be held responsible for everything that happens to us, but only for those things which are subject to our will. This traditional moral distinction between the good or evil which befalls us by fortune and that which we willfully obtain or accomplish

parallels the legal distinction between accidental and intentional wrongdoing.

What is true of the individual life seems to apply to history—the life of states and the development of civilization generally. For the most part, the historians—Herodotus and Thucydides, Plutarch, Tacitus, and Gibbon—find fortune a useful principle of interpretation. To Machiavelli history seems to be so full of accidents and contingencies—"great changes in affairs ... beyond all human conjecture"—that he tries to advise the prince how to make use of fortune in order to avoid being ruined by it. Such advice can be followed because, in his opinion, "fortune is the arbiter of one half of our actions, but still leaves us to direct the other half, or perhaps a little less."

Hegel, on the contrary, does not admit chance or fortune in his view of world history as a "necessary development out of the concept of the mind's freedom alone." For Tolstoy also, either necessity or freedom rules the affairs of men. Chance, he writes, does "not denote any really existing thing," but only "a certain stage of understanding of phenomena." Once we succeed in calculating the composition of forces involved in the mass movements of men, "we shall not be obliged to have recourse to chance for an explanation of those small events which made these people what they were, but it will be clear that all those small events were inevitable."

As the contingent is opposed to the necessary, as that which happens by chance is opposed to that which is fully determined by causes, so fortune is opposed to fate or destiny. This opposition is most evident in the great poems, especially the tragedies, which depict man's efforts to direct his own destiny, now pitting his freedom against both fate and fortune, now courting fortune in his struggle against fate.

10

Change

INTRODUCTION

From the pre-Socratic physicists and the ancient philosophers to Darwin, Marx, and James—and, later, Bergson, Dewey, and Whitehead—the fact of change has been a major focus of speculative and scientific inquiry.

In antiquity, for the pre-Socratic Heracleitus, nothing was permanent; flux or change was everywhere. This is as true for Bergson in the 20th century as it was for Heracleitus in antiquity. In his view, "reality is mobility . . . only changing states exist. Rest is never more than apparent, or, rather, relative." Similarly, for Whitehead, "Rest is merely a particular case" of "uniform rectilinear motion . . . when the velocity is and remains zero." Twentieth-century scientists confirm what is said by 20th-century philosophers. Heisenberg tells us that "modern physics is in some way extremely near to the doctrines of Heraclitus." While for Heracleitus, fire was at the heart of change, for us it is energy. "Energy may be called the fundamental cause for all change in the world."

Except by Parmenides and his school, the existence of change has never been denied. Nor can it be without rejecting all sense perception as illusory, which is precisely what Zeno's paradoxes seem to do, according to one interpretation of them. But if argument cannot refute the testimony of the senses, neither can reasoning support it. The fact of change, because it is evident to the senses, does not need proof.

That change is, is evident, but *what* change is, is neither evident nor easy to define. What principles or factors are common to every sort of change, how change or becoming is related to permanence or being, what sort of existence belongs to mutable things and to change itself—these are questions to which answers are not obtainable merely by observation. Nor will simple observation, without the aid of experiment, measurement, and mathematical calculation, discover the laws and properties of motion.

The analysis of change or motion has been a problem for the philosophers of nature. They have been concerned with the definition of change, its relation to being, the classification of the kinds of change. The measurement of motion, on the other hand, and the mathematical formulation of its laws have occupied the experimental natural scientists. Both natural philosophy and natural science share a common subject matter, though they approach it by different methods and with different interests. Both are entitled to use the name "physics" for their subject matter.

The Greek word *phüsis* from which "physics" comes has, as its Latin equivalent, the word *natura* from which "nature" comes. In their original significance, both words had reference to the sensible world of changing things, or to its underlying principle—to the ultimate source of change. The physics of the philosopher and the physics of the empirical scientist are alike inquiries concerning the nature of things, not in every respect but in regard to their change and motion. The conclusions of both inquiries have metaphysical implications for the nature of the physical world and for the character of physical existence.

The philosopher draws these implications for being from the study of becoming. The scientist, in turn, draws upon philosophical distinctions in order to define the objects of his study. Galileo, for example, in separating the problem of freely falling bodies from the motion of projectiles, employs the traditional philosophical distinction between natural and violent motion. The analysis of time and space (basic variables in Newtonian mechanics), the distinction between discontinuous and continuous change, and the problem of the divisibility of a continuous motion—these are philosophical considerations presupposed by the scientific measurement of motion.

WE HAVE SO FAR used the words "change" and "motion," as well as "becoming," as if all three were interchangeable in meaning. That is somewhat inaccurate, even for the ancients who regarded all kinds of change except one as motions; it is much less accurate for the moderns who have tended to restrict the meaning of "motion" to local motion or change of place. It is necessary, therefore, to examine briefly the kinds of change and to indicate the problems which arise with these distinctions.

In his physical treatises, Aristotle distinguishes four kinds of change. "When the change from contrary to contrary is *in quantity*," he writes, "it is 'growth and diminution'; when it is *in place,* it is 'motion'; when it is . . . *in quality,* it is 'alteration'; but when nothing persists of which the resultant is a property (or an 'accident' in any sense of the term), it is 'coming to be,' and the converse change is 'passing away.' " Aristotle also uses other pairs of words—"generation" and "corruption," "becoming" and "perishing"—to name the last kind of change.

Of the four kinds of change, only the last is not called "motion." But in the context of saying that "becoming cannot be a motion," Aristotle also remarks that "every motion is a kind of change." He does not restrict the meaning of motion to change in place, which is usually called "local motion" or "locomotion." There are, then, according to Aristotle's vocabulary, three kinds of motion: (1) local motion, in which bodies change from place to place; (2) alteration or qualitative motion, in which bodies change with respect to such attributes as color, texture, or temperature; (3) increase and decrease, or quantitative motion, in which bodies change in size. And, in addition, there is the one kind of change which is not motion—generation and corruption. This consists in the coming to be or passing away of a body which, while it has being, exists as an individual substance of a certain sort.

Becoming and perishing are most readily exemplified by the birth and death of living things, but Aristotle also includes the transformation of water into ice or vapor as examples of generation and corruption. One distinctive characteristic of generation and corruption, in Aristotle's conception of this type of change, is their instantaneity. He thinks that the other three kinds of change are continuous processes, taking time, whereas things come into being or pass away instantaneously. Aristotle thus applies the word "motion" only to the continuous changes which time can measure. He never says that time is the measure of change, but only of motion.

But the contrast between the one mode of change which is not motion and the three kinds of motion involves more than this difference with regard to time and continuity. Aristotle's analysis considers the subject of change—that which undergoes transformation—and the starting point and goal of motion. "Every motion," he says, "proceeds from something and to something, that which is directly in motion being distinct from that to which it is in motion and that from which it is in motion; for instance, we may take the three things 'wood,' 'hot,' and 'cold,' of which the first is that which is in motion, the second is that which to which the motion proceeds, and the third is that from which it proceeds."

In the alteration which occurs when the wood changes quality, just as in the increase or decrease which occurs with a body's change in quantity and in the local motion which occurs with a body's change of place, *that which changes* persists throughout the change as the same kind of substance. The wood does not cease to be wood when it becomes hot or cold; the stone does not cease to be a stone when it rolls from here to there, or the organism an animal of a certain kind when it grows in size. In all these cases, "the substratum"—that which is the subject of change—"persists and changes in its own properties . . . The body, although persisting as the same body, is now healthy and now ill; and the bronze is now spherical and at another time angular, and yet remains the same bronze."

Because the substance of the changing thing remains the same while changing in its properties—*i.e.*, in such attributes or accidents as quality, quantity, and place—Aristotle groups the three kinds of motion together as *accidental change*. The changing thing does not come to be or pass away absolutely, but only in a certain respect. In contrast, generation and corruption involve a change in the very substance of a thing. "When nothing perceptible persists in its identity as a substratum, and the thing changes as a whole," then, according to Aristotle, "it is a coming-to-be of one substance, and the passing-away of another."

In such becoming or perishing, it is matter itself rather than a body or a substance which is tranformed. Matter takes on or loses the form of a certain kind of substance. For example, when the nutriment is assimilated to the form of a living body, the bread or corn becomes the flesh and blood of a man. When an animal dies, its body decomposes into the elements of inorganic matter. Because it is a change of substance itself, Aristotle calls the one kind of change which is not motion *substantial change*, and speaks of it as "a coming-to-be or passing-away simply"—that is, not in a certain respect, but absolutely or "without qualification."

These distinctions are involved in a long tradition of discussion and controversy. They cannot be affirmed or denied without opposite sides being taken on the fundamental issues concerning substance and accident, matter and form, and the causes of change or motion. The adoption or rejection of these distinctions affects one's view of the difference between inorganic and organic change, and the difference between the motions of matter and the changes which take place in mind. The statement of certain problems is determined accordingly; as, for example, the problem of the transmutation of the elements, which persists in various forms from the physics of the ancients through medieval alchemy and the beginnings of modern chem-istry to present considerations of radioactivity and atomic fission.

SINCE THE 17TH CENTURY, motion has been identified with local motion. "I can conceive no other kind" of motion, Descartes writes, "and do not consider that we ought to conceive any other in nature." As it is expressed "in common parlance," motion, he says, "is nothing more than the *action by which any body passes from one place to another*."

This can hardly be taken to mean that change of place is the only observable type of change. That other kinds of change are observable cannot be denied. The science of mechanics or dynamics may be primarily or exclusively concerned with local motions, but other branches of natural science, certainly chemistry, deal with qualitative transformations; and the biological sciences study growth and decay, birth and death.

The emphasis on local motion as the only kind of motion, while it does not exclude apparent changes of other sorts, does raise a question about their reality. The question can be put in several ways. Are the various *apparently* different kinds of change *really* distinct, or can they all be reduced to aspects of one underlying mode of change which is local motion? Even supposing that the kinds of change are not reducible to one another, is local motion primary in the sense that it is involved in all the others?

When mechanics dominates the physical sciences (as has been so largely the case in modern times), there is a tendency to reduce all the observable diversity of change of various appearances of local motion. Newton, for example, explicitly expresses this desire to formulate all natural phenomena in terms of the mechanics of moving particles. In the Preface to the first edition of his *Mathematical Principles,* after recounting his success in dealing with celestial phenomena, he says, "I wish we could derive the rest of the phenomena of Nature by the same kind of reasoning from mechanical principles, for I am induced by many reasons to suspect that they may all depend upon certain forces by which the particles of bodies, by some causes hitherto unknown, are either mutually impelled towards one another, and cohere in regular figures, or are repelled and recede from one another."

The notion that all change can be reduced to the results of local motion is not, however, of modern origin. Lucretius expounds the theory of the Greek atomists that all the phenomena of change can be explained by reference to the local motion of indivisible particles coming together and separating. Change of place is the only change which occurs on the level of the ultimate physical reality. The atoms neither come to be nor pass away, nor change in quality or size.

But though we find the notion in ancient atomism, it is only in modern physics that the emphasis upon local motion tends to exclude all other kinds of change. It is characteristic of what William James calls "the modern mechanico-physical philosophy" to begin "by saying that the *only* facts are collocations and motions of primordial solids, and the only laws the changes of motion which changes in collocation bring." James quotes Hermann von Helmholtz to the effect that "the ultimate goal of theoretic physics is to find the last *unchanging* causes of the processes of Nature." If, to this end, "we imagine the world composed of elements with unalterable qualities," then, Helmholtz continues, "the only changes that can remain in such a world are spatial changes, *i.e.,* movements, and the only outer relations which can modify the action of the forces are spatial too, or, in other words, the forces are motor forces dependent for their effect on spatial relations."

In the history of physics, Aristotle represents the opposite view. No one of the four kinds of change which he distinguishes has for him greater physical reality than the others. Just as quality cannot be reduced to quantity, or either of these to place, so in his judgment the motions associated with these terms are irreducible to one another. Yet Aristotle does assign to local motion a certain primacy. "Motion in its most general and primary sense," he writes, "is change of place, which we call locomotion." He does not mean merely that this is the primary sense of the word, but rather that no other kind of motion can occur without local motion being somehow involved in the process. Showing how increase and decrease depends on alteration, and how that in turn depends on change of place, he says that "of the three kinds of motion . . . it is this last, which we call locomotion, that must be primary."

THE SHIFT IN MEANING of the word "motion" would not by itself mark a radical departure in the theory of change, but it is accompanied by a shift in thought which has the most radical consequences. At the same time that motion is identified with local motion, Descartes conceives motion as something completely actual and thoroughly intelligible. For the ancients, becoming of any sort had both less reality and less intelligibility than being.

Aristotle had defined motion as the actuality of that which is potential in a respect in which it is still potential to some degree. According to what Descartes calls its strict as opposed to its popular meaning, motion is "the transference of one part of matter or one body from the vicinity of those bodies that are in immediate contact with it, and which we regard as in repose, into the vicinity of others." This definition—contrasted with the Aristotelian conception which it generally supersedes in the subsequent tradition of natural science—is as revolutionary as the Cartesian analytic geometry is by comparison with the Euclidean. Nor is it an unconnected fact that analytic geometry prepares the way for the differential calculus that is needed to measure variable motions, their velocities, and their accelerations.

The central point on which the two definitions are opposed constitutes one of the most fundamental issues in the philosophy of nature. Does motion involve a transition from potential to actual existence, or only the substitution of one actual state for another—only a "transportation," as Descartes says, from one place to another?

While motion is going on, the moving thing, according to Aristotle's definition, must be partly potential and partly actual in the same respect. The leaf turning red, *while it is altering,* has not yet fully reddened. When it becomes as red as it can get, it can no longer change in that respect. Before it began to change, it was actually green; and since it could become red, it was potentially red. But while the change is in process, the potentiality of the leaf to become red is being actualized. This actualization progresses until the change is completed.

The same analysis would apply to a ball in motion. Until it comes to rest in a given place, its potentiality for being there is undergoing progressive actualization. In short, motion involves some departure from pure potentiality in a given respect, and never complete attainment of full actuality in that same respect. When there is no departure from potentiality, motion has not yet begun; when the attainment of actuality is complete, the motion has terminated.

The Aristotelian definition of motion is the object of much ridicule in the 17th century. Repeating the phrasing which had become traditional in the schools—"the actualization of what exists in potentiality, in so far as it is potential"—Descartes asks: "Now who understands these words? And who at the same time does not know what motion is? Will not everyone admit that those philosophers have been trying to find a knot in a bulrush?" Locke also finds it meaningless. "What more exquisite jargon could the wit of man invent than this definition . . . which would puzzle any rational man to whom it was not already known by its famous absurdity, to guess what word it could ever be supposed to be the explication of. If Tully, asking a Dutchman what *beweeginge* was," Locke continues, "should have received this explication in his own language, that it was *actus entis in potentia quatenus in potentia;* I ask whether any one can imagine he could thereby have guessed what the word *beweeginge* signified?"

Locke does not seem to be satisfied with any definition of motion. "The atomists, who define motion to be 'a passage from one place to another,' what do they more than put one synonymous word for another? For what is *passage* other than *motion*? . . . Nor will 'the successive application of the superficies of one body to those of another,' which the Carte-

sians give us, prove a much better definition of motion, when well examined." But though Locke rejects the definition of the atomists and the Cartesians on formal grounds, he accepts their idea of motion as simply change of place; whereas he dismisses the Aristotelian definition as sheer absurdity and rejects the idea that motion or change necessarily involves a potentiality capable of progressive fulfillment.

As we have already remarked, the omission of potentiality from the conception of motion is a theoretical shift of the deepest significance. It occurs not only in Descartes's *Principles of Philosophy* and in the atomism of Hobbes and Pierre Gassendi, but also in the mechanics of Galileo and Newton. According to these modern philosophers and scientists, a moving body is *always actually* somewhere. It occupies a different place at every moment in a continuous motion. The motion can be described as the successive occupation by the body of different places at different times. Though all the parts of the motion do not coexist, the moving particle is completely actual throughout. It loses no reality and gains none in the course of the motion, since the various positions the body occupies lie totally outside its material nature. It would, of course, be more difficult to analyze alteration in color or biological growth in these terms, but it must be remembered that efforts have been made to apply such an analysis through the reduction of all other modes of change to local motion.

The principle of inertia, first discerned by Galileo, is critically relevant to the issue between these two conceptions of motion. It is stated by Newton as the first of his "axioms or laws of motion." "Every body," he writes, "continues in its state of rest, or of uniform motion in a right line, unless it is compelled to change that state by forces impressed upon it." As applied to the motion of projectiles, the law declares that they "continue in their motions, so far as they are not retarded by the resistance of air, or impelled downwards by the force of gravity."

In his experimental reasoning concerning the acceleration of bodies moving down inclined planes, Galileo argues that a body which has achieved a certain velocity on the descent would, if it then proceeded along a horizontal plane, continue infinitely at the same velocity—except for the retardation of air resistance and friction. "Any velocity once imparted to a moving body," he maintains, "will be rigidly maintained as long as the external causes of acceleration or retardation are removed." So in the case of projectiles, they would retain the velocity and direction imparted to them by the cannon, were it not for the factors of gravity and air resistance. Bodies actually in motion possess their motion in themselves as a complete actuality. They need no causes acting on them to keep them in motion, but only to change their direction or bring them to rest.

The motion of projectiles presents a difficulty for the theory which describes all motion as a reduction of potency to act. "If everything that is in motion, with the exception of things that move themselves, is moved by something else, how is it," Aristotle asks, "that some things, *e.g.*, things thrown, continue to be in motion when their movent [moving cause] is no longer in contact with them?" This is a problem for Aristotle precisely because he supposes that the moving cause must act on the thing being moved throughout the period of the motion. For the potentiality to be progressively reduced to actuality, it must be continuously acted upon.

Aristotle's answer postulates a series of causes so that contact can be maintained between the projectile and the moving cause. "The original movent," he writes, "gives the power of being a movent either to air or to water or to something else of the kind, naturally adapted for imparting and undergoing motion . . . The motion begins to cease when the motive force produced in one member of the consecutive series is at each stage less than that possessed by the preceding member, and it finally ceases when one member no longer causes the next member to be a movent but only causes it to be in motion." It follows that inertia must be denied by those who hold that a moving body *always* requires a mover; or even that a body cannot sustain itself in motion beyond a point proportionate to the quantity of the impressed force which originally set it in motion.

FOR THE ANCIENTS, the basic contrast between being and becoming (or between the permanent and the changing) is a contrast between the intelligible and the sensible. This is most sharply expressed in Plato's distinction between the sensible realm of material things and the intelligible realm of ideas. "What is that which always is and has no becoming." Timaeus asks; "and what is that which is always becoming and never is?" He answers his own question by saying that "that which is apprehended by intelligence and reason is always in the same state; but that which is conceived by opinion with the help of sensations and without reason, is always in a process of becoming and perishing, and never really is."

Even though Aristotle differs from Plato in thinking that change and the changing can be objects of scientific knowledge, he, too, holds becoming to be less intelligible than being, precisely because change necessarily involves potentiality. Yet becoming can be understood to the extent that we can discover the principles of its being—the unchanging principles of change. "In pursuing the truth," Aristotle remarks—and this applies to the truth about change as well as everything else—"one must start from the things that are always in the same state and suffer no change."

For Aristotle, change is intelligible through the three elements of permanence which are its principles: (1) the enduring substratum of change, and the contraries—(2) that to which, and (3) that from which, the change takes place. The same principles are sometimes stated to be (1) matter, (2) form, and (3) privation; the matter or substratum being that which both lacks a certain form and has a definite potentiality for possessing it. Change occurs when the matter undergoes a transformation in which it comes to have the form of which it was deprived by the possession of a contrary form.

Neither of the contrary forms changes. Only the thing composite of matter and form changes with respect to the forms of its matter. Hence these principles of change are themselves unchanging. Change takes place *through,* not *in,* them. As constituents of the changing thing, they are the principles of its mutable being, principles of its *being* as well of its being *mutable.*

The explanation of change by reference to what does not change seems to be common to all theories of becoming. Lucretius, as we have already seen, explains the coming to be and passing away of all other things by the motions of atoms which neither come to be nor pass away. The eternity of the atoms underlies the mutability of everything else.

Yet the atoms are not completely immutable. They move forever through the void which, according to Lucretius, is required for their motion. Their local motion is, moreover, an actual property of the atoms. For them, *to be* is *to be in motion.* Here then, as in the Cartesian theory, no potentiality is involved, and motion is completely real and completely intelligible.

THE NOTIONS OF time and eternity are inseparable from the theory of change or motion. As the chapters on TIME and SCIENCE indicate, local motion involves the dimensions of space as well as time, but all change requires time, and time itself is inconceivable apart from change or motion. Furthermore, as appears in the chapters on TIME and ETERNITY, the two fundamentally opposed meanings of eternity differ according to whether they imply endless change or absolute changelessness.

Eternity is sometimes identified with infinite time. It is in this sense that Plato, in the *Timaeus,* refers to time as "the moving image of eternity" and implies that time, which belongs to the realm of ever-changing things, resembles the eternal only through its perpetual endurance. The other sense of the eternal is also implied—the sense in which eternity belongs to the realm of immutable being. The eternal in this sense, as Montaigne points out, is not merely "what never had birth, nor will ever have an end," but rather that "to which time never brings any change."

There are two great problems which use the word "eternity" in these opposite senses. One is the problem of the eternity of motion:

the question whether motion has or can have either a beginning or an end. The other is the problem of the existence of eternal objects—immutable things which have their being apart from time and change.

The two problems are connected in ancient thought. Aristotle, for example, argues that "it is impossible that movement should either have come into being or cease to be, for it must always have existed." Since "nothing is moved at random, but there must always be something present to move it," a cause is required to sustain the endless motions of nature. This cause, which Aristotle calls "the prime mover," must be "something which moves without being moved, being eternal, substance, and actuality."

Aristotle's theory of a prime mover sets up a hierarchy of causes to account for the different kinds of motion observable in the universe. The perfect circular motion of the heavens serves to mediate between the prime mover which is totally unmoved and the less regular cycles of terrestrial change. The "constant cycle" of movement in the stars differs from the irregular cycle of "generation and destruction" on earth. For the first, Aristotle asserts the necessity of "something which is always moved with an unceasing motion, which is motion in a circle." He calls this motion of the first heavenly sphere "the simple spatial movement of the universe" as a whole. Besides this "there are other spatial movements—those of the planets—which are eternal" but are "always acting in different ways" and so are able to account for the other cycle in nature—the irregular cycle of generation and corruption.

In addition, a kind of changelessness is attributed to all the celestial bodies which Aristotle calls "eternal." Eternally in motion, they are also eternally in being. Though not immovable, they are supposed to be incorruptible substances. They never begin to be and never perish.

The theory of a world eternally in motion is challenged by Jewish and Christian theologians who affirm, as an article of their religious faith, that "in the beginning God created heaven and earth." The world's motions, like its existence, have a beginning in the act of creation. Creation itself, Aquinas insists, is not change or motion of any sort, "except according to our way of understanding. For change means that the same thing should be different now from what it was previously . . . But in creation, by which the whole substance of a thing is produced, the same thing can be taken as different now and before, only according to our way of understanding, so that a thing is understood as first not existing at all, and afterwards as existing." Since creation is an absolute coming to be from nonbeing, no preexistent matter is acted upon as in generation, in artistic production, or in any of the forms of motion.

THE PHILOSOPHICAL and theological issues concerning creation and change, eternity and time, are further discussed in the chapters on CAUSE, ETERNITY, and WORLD. Other problems arising from the analysis of change must at least be briefly mentioned here.

Though less radical than the difference between creation and change, the difference between the motions of inert or nonliving things and the vital activities of plants and animals raises for any theory of change the question whether the same principles apply to both. The rolling stone and the running animal both move locally, but are both motions *locomotion* in the same sense? Augmentation occurs both in the growth of a crystal and the growth of a plant, but are both of them *growing* in the same sense? In addition, there seems to be one kind of change in living things which has no parallel in the movements of inert bodies. Animals and men learn. They acquire knowledge, form habits and change them. Can change of mind be explained in the same terms as change in matter?

The issues raised by the questions of this sort are more fully discussed in the chapters on ANIMAL, HABIT, and LIFE AND DEATH. Certain other issues must be entirely reserved for discussion elsewhere. The special problems of local motion—such as the properties of rectilinear and circular motion, the distinction between uniform and variable motion, and the uniform or variable acceleration of the latter—are problems which belong to the chapters on ASTRONOMY AND COSMOLOGY and MECHAN-

ICS. Change, furthermore, is a basic fact not only for the natural scientist, but for the historian—the natural historian or the historian of man and society. The considerations relevant to this aspect of change receive treatment in the chapters on EVOLUTION, HISTORY, and PROGRESS.

In his Preface to *Saint Joan,* Shaw writes, "Though all society is founded on intolerance, all improvement is founded on tolerance, or the recognition of the fact that the law of evolution is Ibsen's law of Change. And as the law of God in any sense of the word which can now command a faith proof against science is a law of evolution, it follows that the law of God is a law of change, and that when the Churches set themselves against change as such, they are setting themselves against the law of God."

Even these ramifications of discussion do not exhaust the significance of change. The cyclical course of the emotions and the alternation of pleasure and pain have been thought inexplicable without reference to change of state in regard to desire and aversion—the motion from want to satisfaction, or from possession to deprivation. Change is not only a factor in the analysis of emotion, but it is also itself an object of man's emotional attitudes. It is both loved and hated, sought and avoided.

According to Pascal, man tries desperately to avoid a state of rest. He does everything he can to keep things in flux. "Our nature consists in motion," he writes; "complete rest is death . . . Nothing is so insufferable to man," he continues, "as to be completely at rest, without passions, without business, without diversion, without study. He then feels his nothingness, his forlornness, his dependence, his weakness, his emptiness." Darwin does not think that the desire for change is peculiar to man. "The lower animals," he writes, "are . . . likewise capricious in their affections, aversions, and sense of beauty. There is also reason to suspect that they love novelty for its own sake."

But men also wish to avoid change. The old Prince Bolknoski, in *War and Peace,* "could not comprehend how anyone could wish to alter his life or introduce anything new into it." This is not merely an old man's view. For the most part, it is permanence rather than transiency, the enduring rather than the novel, which the poets celebrate when they express man's discontent with his own mutability. The withering and perishing of all mortal things, the assault of time and change upon all things familiar and loved, have moved them to elegy over the evanescent and the ephemeral. From Virgil's *Sunt lacrimae rerum et mentem mortalia tangunt* to Shakespeare's "Love is not love which alters when it alteration finds," the poets have mourned the inevitability of change.

11

Citizen

INTRODUCTION

"CITIZEN," like "comrade," has been and still is a revolutionary word. Both words have been titles proudly adopted by men to mark their liberation from the yoke of despotism or tyranny. Both titles are still sought by those who have not yet gained admission to the fraternity of the free and equal.

The rank and status of citizenship first appeared in the ancient world with the beginning of constitutional government in the city-states of Greece. The Greeks were conscious of this fact, and proud of it. In terms of it, they set themselves apart from the barbarians who were subjects of the Great King of Persia or the Egyptian Pharaoh. The Spartan heralds, according to Herodotus, thus address the Persian commander: "Thou hast experience of half the matter; but the other half is beyond thy knowledge. A slave's life thou understandest; but, never having tasted liberty, thou canst not tell whether it is sweet or no. Ah! hadst thou known what freedom is, thou wouldst have bidden us fight for it, not with the spear only, but with the battle-axe."

Not only Herodotus and Thucydides but also the great tragic poets, notably Aeschylus in *The Persians,* record this Hellenic sense of distinction from the surrounding peoples who lived in childlike submission to absolute rule. But the Greeks were also conscious that their political maturity as self-governing citizens was, as Aristotle intimates in the *Politics,* a recent development from the primitive condition in which tribal chieftains ruled despotically.

The basic distinction between *subjection* and *citizenship* is inseparable from the equally basic distinction between absolute and limited, or between despotic and constitutional, government. The difference between these two modes of government is treated in the chapter on CONSTITUTION. It is sufficient here to note that the difference in the authority and power possessed by rulers—according as it is absolute or limited—corresponds with a difference in the status, the degree of freedom, and the rights and privileges of the people ruled.

IN ORDER TO UNDERSTAND citizenship it is necessary to understand the several ways in which men can belong to or be parts of a political community. There are two divisions among men within a community which help us to define citizenship.

According to one of these divisions, the native-born are separated from aliens or foreigners. In the Greek city-states it was almost impossible for aliens to become citizens. Plutarch notes that Solon's law of naturalization, which he qualifies as "of doubtful character," would not allow strangers to become citizens unless "they were in perpetual exile from their own country, or came with their whole family to trade there." The *metics,* or aliens, who were allowed in the city were usually a class apart.

In Rome the situation was different; it was possible for outsiders to receive the high honor of Roman citizenship. "The aspiring genius of Rome," Gibbon writes, "sacrificed vanity to ambition, and deemed it more prudent, as well as honourable, to adopt virtue and merit for her own wheresoever they were found, among slaves or strangers, enemies or barbarians."

Most modern republics set up naturalization proceedings for the regular admission of some, if not all, immigrants to membership in the state. Yet a difference always remains between a citizen and a denizen, or mere resident. Accordingly, Rousseau criticizes Jean Bodin for confusing citizens with townsmen. "M. D'Alembert," he says, "has avoided this error, and in his article on Geneva, has clearly distinguished the four orders of men (or even five, counting mere foreigners) who dwell in our town, of which two only compose the Republic."

According to a second way in which men are divided within the political community, free men are separated from slaves. The latter, though they may be native-born, are not members of the political community, but merely part of its property. A slave, according to Aristotle, is one "who, being a human being, is also a possession." But, he says in another place, "property, even though living beings are included in it, is no part of a state; for a state is not a community of living beings only, but a community of equals."

On this principle, Aristotle excludes more than the chattel slave from the status and privilege of citizenship. "We cannot consider all those to be citizens," he writes, "who are necessary to the existence of the state; for example, children are not citizens equally with grown-up men . . . In ancient times, and among some nations," he continues, "the artisan class *were* slaves or foreigners, and therefore the majority of them are so now. The best form of state will not admit them to citizenship."

The "slaves who minister to the wants of individuals," and the "mechanics or laborers who are the servants of the community" are to be counted as its "necessary people" but not as members of the state. When he discusses the size and character of the population for an ideal state, Aristotle says, "we ought not to include everybody, for there must always be in cities a multitude of slaves and sojourners and foreigners; but we should include only those who are members of the state, and who form an essential part of it."

The exclusion of slaves and resident aliens from membership in the political community has a profound bearing on the meaning of the political concept expressed by the words "the people." The *people* is not the same as the *population*—all those human beings who

live within the state's borders. Even in societies which have abolished chattel slavery and in which suffrage tends to be unrestricted, infants and aliens remain outside the pale of political life. The *people* is always a part—the active political part—of the population.

THE DISTINCTION OF citizen from slave, infant, or alien does not complete the picture. The subjects of a king are not slaves, nor are they citizens of a republic. Yet like citizens, subjects have membership in the political community. They constitute the people the king serves as well as rules, unless he is a tyrant, for only if he is a tyrant does he treat them as if they were his property, to be used for his own pleasure or interest. Sometimes a distinction is made between first- and second-class citizens, and then the latter, who occupy an intermediate position between citizenship and slavery, are regarded as subjects. "Since there are many forms of government," Aristotle writes, "there must be many varieties of citizens, especially of citizens who are subjects; so that under some governments the mechanic and the laborer will be citizens, but not in others." The whole meaning of citizenship changes for Aristotle when the working classes are admitted to it.

From a somewhat different point of view, Aquinas holds that a man can be "said to be a citizen in two ways: first, absolutely; secondly, in a restricted sense. A man is a citizen absolutely if he has all the rights of citizenship; for instance, the right of debating or voting in the popular assembly. On the other hand, any man may be called citizen only in a restricted sense if he dwells within the state, even lowly people, or children, or old men, who are not fit to enjoy power in matters pertaining to the common welfare." Those who are thus disfranchised, but are not slaves, are subjects rather than citizens in the full sense.

It is possible, of course, for men to have the dual status of subject and citizen, as is the case now in England and the self-governing dominions of the British commonwealth. This double status does not blur the distinction between citizen and subject; rather it signifies the mixed nature of a form of government which is both royal—at least in its vestiges of

monarchy—and constitutional. In the time of
Locke, when a great constitutional victory had
been won against the despotism of the last
Stuart, the English people did not yet regard
themselves as citizens. Observing that the title
of citizen has never been given "to the subjects
of any prince, not even the ancient Macedo-
nians," Rousseau finds himself compelled to
add: "not even the English of today, though
they are nearer liberty than anyone else."

Unlike citizens, the subjects of a king, especially of one claiming absolute power, have
no voice in their own government, and no
legal means for protecting their natural rights
as men. So long as the absolute ruler does not
tyrannize, he governs for the welfare of his
people; and so, though a despot in the sense
of wielding absolute power over political inferiors, he is benevolent in the sense of serving
rather than using them. But if he ceases to
be benevolent and turns tyrannical, his subjects have no recourse except rebellion. They
must resort to violence in order to emancipate
themselves from a condition which amounts
to slavery.

A citizen, on the other hand, is safeguarded
in his legal as well as in his natural rights
and, in some modern republics at least, he is
provided with juridical means for rectifying
supposed injustices. For citizens, the right of
rebellion is the *last,* not the *only,* resort.

THE DISTINCT CONDITIONS of slavery, subjection, and citizenship can be summarized by
defining three ways in which rulers are related
to the persons they rule. These three relations
seem to have been first clearly differentiated
by Aristotle.

He finds all three relationships in the structure of the household, as that is constituted
in antiquity. Of household management, he
writes, "there are three parts—one is the rule
of a master over slaves . . . another of a father,
and a third of a husband." In each case, "the
kind of rule differs: the freeman rules over the
slave after another manner from that in which
the male rules over the female, or the man over
the child."

As we have already seen, Aristotle conceives
the slave as a piece of property. When he says

that the slave "wholly belongs to his master"
or that "he is a part of his master, a living
but separated part of his bodily frame," he is
obviously considering only the chattel slave.
There are, as the chapter on SLAVERY indicates,
other kinds or degrees of slavery less extreme
than this.

But chattel slavery, more clearly than the
attenuated forms of servitude, defines the nature of mastery. The master manages or uses
the slave as he manages and uses other instruments—inanimate tools or domesticated
animals. "The rule of a master," Aristotle declares, is "exercised primarily with a view to
the interest of the master." Yet it "accidentally
considers the slave, since, if the slave perish,
the rule of the master perishes with him."

Thus conceived, the slave lacks every vestige
of political liberty. He is treated as radically
inferior to his master—almost as if he were
something less than a man. He has no voice
in his own government, nor is his welfare the
paramount consideration of his ruler. In short,
we have slavery when one man governs another in the way in which a man manages his
property, using it for his own good.

When one man governs another in the way
in which good parents administer the affairs
of children as members of the household, we
have the type of rule which also appears in
the relation between absolute kings or benevolent despots and their subjects. "The rule of
a father over his children is royal," Aristotle
writes, "for he rules by virtue of both love and
of the respect due to age, exercising a kind
of royal power . . . A king," Aristotle adds, "is
the natural superior of his subjects, but he
should be of the same kin or kind with them,
and such is the relation of elder and younger,
father and son."

From the analogous type of rule in the
family, we see two differences between the
condition of a slave and that of a subject under absolute or despotic rule in the state. The
inferiority of children, unlike that of slaves, is
not their permanent condition. It is an aspect
of their immaturity. They are temporarily incapable of judging what is for their good, and
so need the direction of their superiors in age,
experience, and prudence. But children have

some equality with their parents, to the extent that their humanity is recognized as the reason why they should not be ruled as slaves, but governed for their own welfare.

The government of children, Aristotle declares, "is exercised in the first instance for the good of the governed, or for the common good of both parties, but essentially for the good of the governed." In the same way, the subjects of a benevolent despot, or of any absolute monarch who rules paternalistically, are said to be governed for their own good. They are served, not used, by their rulers; and to this extent they have a degree of political liberty. But they do not have the complete liberty which exists only with self-government.

That occurs only under constitutional rule, which for Aristotle has an imperfect analogue in the family in the relation of husband and wife. In the state, however, it is perfectly represented by the relation between the holders of public office and *other* citizens. "In the constitutional state," Aristotle says, "the citizens rule and are ruled by turns; for the idea of a constitutional state implies that the natures of the citizens are equal, and do not differ at all." The citizen, in other words, is one "who has the power to take part in the deliberative or judicial administration of the state." Rousseau seems to have a similar conception of the citizen as both ruling and ruled, though he uses the word "subject" to designate the citizen *as ruled*. "The people," he writes, "are called *citizens,* as sharing in the sovereign power, and *subjects,* as being under the laws of the State."

Because the man who holds office in a constitutional government is first of all a citizen himself, and only secondly an official vested with the authority of a political office, the citizen is a man ruled by his equals and ruled as an equal. Observing these facts, Aristotle describes citizenship as the one "*indefinite* office" set up by a constitution. It is indefinite both in tenure by comparison with the various magistracies or other offices which have more definitely assigned functions. Since a citizen is ruled only by other citizens, and since he has the opportunity of ruling others in turn, citizenship involves political liberty in the fullest sense. This does not mean freedom *from* government, but freedom through *self-government*—all the freedom a man can have in society, liberty under law and proportioned to justice.

Two of these three political conditions—slavery and subjection—naturally receive fuller treatment in the chapter on SLAVERY. The discussion of the third, citizenship, belongs not only to this chapter, but also to the chapter on CONSTITUTION, and to other chapters which deal with forms of constitutional government, such as ARISTOCRACY, DEMOCRACY, and OLIGARCHY.

FOR THE SAME REASON that the revolutionists against absolutism or despotism in the 18th century use the phrase "free government" for republican institutions, they also use "citizen" to designate a free man, a man who possesses the political liberty and equality which they regard as the natural right of men because they are men. In this respect they do not differ substantially from their Greek or Roman ancestors who prize constitutional government and citizenship as conditions of freedom and equality.

Furthermore, like the constitutionalists of antiquity, the republicans of the 18th century are, with few if any exceptions, *not* democrats in the sense of extending the rights and privileges of citizenship to *all* adults. In the 18th century slavery still exists; and a large part even of those who are not in economic bondage remains outside the pale of citizenship, disqualified by accidents of birth such as race or sex, and by the lack of sufficient wealth or property which makes it necessary for them to labor in order to live. It is not only an ancient oligarch like Aristotle who thinks that "the ruling class should be the owners of property, for they are citizens, and the citizens of a state should be in good circumstances; whereas mechanics" should have "no share in the state." In the 18th century, as well as in ancient Greece, extending the privileges of citizenship to indentured apprentices, day laborers, or journeymen, is a form of radicalism known as "extreme democracy."

Kant may be taken as representative of an enlightened point of view in the 18th century.

He finds that there are "three juridical attributes" that belong by right to the citizens: "1. constitutional freedom, as the right of every citizen to have to obey no other law than that to which he has given his consent or approval; 2. civil equality, as the right of the citizen to recognize no one as a superior among the people in relation to himself . . . and 3. political independence, as the right to owe his existence and continuance in society not to the arbitrary will of another, but to his own rights and powers as a member of the commonwealth."

The last attribute leads Kant to distinguish between "active and passive citizenship." Although he admits that this "appears to stand in contradiction to the definition of a citizen as such," he concludes that there are some in the community not entitled to the full privileges of citizenship. It is his contention, widely shared in the 18th century, that suffrage, which "properly constitutes the political qualification of a citizen," presupposes the "independence or self-sufficiency of the individual citizen among the people."

Consequently he denies suffrage to "everyone who is compelled to maintain himself not according to his own industry, but as it is arranged by others." Such a restriction, he says, includes "the apprentice of a merchant or tradesman, a servant who is not in the employ of the state, a minor" and "all women." They are "passive parts" of the state and do not have "the right to deal with the state as active members of it, to reorganize it, or to take action by way of introducing certain laws." Kant insists, however, that "it must be made possible for them to raise themselves from this passive condition in the State, to the condition of active citizenship."

THE FOREGOING DISCUSSION shows the connection between the idea of citizenship and the two revolutionary movements which J. S. Mill notes in the history of political thought and action. The first is the movement to obtain "recognition of certain immunities, called political liberties or rights, which it was to be regarded as a breach of duty in the ruler to infringe, and which if he did infringe, specific resistance, or general rebellion, was held to be justifiable." This is the revolutionary effort to overthrow despotism and to establish constitutional government, with the status of citizenship for at least some part of the population—frequently much less than half of the total.

The second revolutionary movement goes further. It presupposes the existence of government by law and aims to perfect it. It therefore seeks to obtain "the establishment of constitutional checks, by which the consent of the community, or of a body of some sort, supposed to represent its interests, is made a necessary condition to some of the more important acts of the governing power." Since, according to Mill, it aims to make the consent of the governed effective through an adequate representation of their wishes, this movement inevitably leads to the fight *against* franchise restrictions and *for* universal suffrage, which would admit every normal, adult human being to the freedom and equality of citizenship.

Commenting on the love for equality in democratic nations, Tocqueville writes, "It is possible to imagine an extreme point at which freedom and equality would meet and blend. Let us suppose that all the citizens take a part in the government and that each of them has an equal right to do so. Then, no man is different from his fellows, and nobody can wield tyrannical power; men will be perfectly free because they are entirely equal, and they will be perfectly equal because they are entirely free."

The first revolution has a long history. It begins with the Greek city-states which, having won this victory against the Persians, lost it to the Macedonian conquerors. It happens again with the establishment of the Roman republic after the expulsion of the Tarquins, and again it is undone when the Caesars assume absolute power. This part of the story is told with varying emotions by Plutarch and Polybius, Tacitus and Gibbon. During the Middle Ages the same struggle appears in the various efforts to establish the supremacy of law, particularly through the development of customary and canon law. The revolution still continues in the 17th and 18th centuries, and the new heights it reaches are reflected in the writings of a constitutionalist like Locke and republicans like Rousseau, Kant, and the American Federalists. The Declaration of Independence and the Constitution of the United States are perhaps the classic documents of this historical phase.

The second revolution, particularly as identified with the fight for universal suffrage, is a relatively recent event. Its roots may go back as far as Cromwell's time to the activity of the Levelers, and in the 18th century to the writings of John Cartwright. But what is, perhaps, its first full expression does not appear until Mill's *Representative Government*. In that book, Mill lays down the principles of the franchise reforms which began in the 19th century, but which, as in the case of woman suffrage or the repeal of the poll tax, were carried through only yesterday or are still in progress.

Yet the struggle for universal suffrage—or, as Mill would say, against treating any human being as a "political pariah"—does have an ancient parallel in the conflict between democratic and oligarchic constitutions in Greek political life and thought. These two types of constitution were opposed on the qualifications for citizenship and public office. The oligarchic constitution restricted both to men of considerable wealth. At the other extreme, as Aristotle observes, the most radical forms of Greek democracy granted citizenship to the working classes and gave no advantage to the rich in filling the magistracies, for they selected officials for the whole citizenry by lot.

The parallelism goes no further than that. Greek democracy, even when it denied special privileges to the propertied classes, never contemplated the abolition of slavery or the political emancipation of women.

THERE ARE OTHER differences between ancient and modern institutions which affect the character of citizenship. The problem of who shall be admitted to citizenship is fundamental in both epochs. Insofar as it connotes the condition of political liberty and equality, the status of citizenship remains essentially the same. But the rights and duties, the privileges and immunities, which belong to citizenship vary with the difference between ancient and modern constitutionalism.

Even if they had been written, the constitutions of the ancient world would not have declared the rights of man and the citizen, nor would they have had bills of rights appended to them. The significance of these modern innovations (which begin, perhaps, with Magna Carta) lies, not in a new conception of citizenship, but in the invention of juridical means to endow the primary office of citizenship with sufficient legal power to protect it from invasion by government. Commenting on the French Revolution and the *Declaration of the Rights of Man*, Tawney calls attention to "the difference between the universal and equal citizenship of France, with its five million peasant proprietors, and the organized inequality of England established solidly upon class traditions and class institutions."

In *The Federalist*, Hamilton maintains that "bills of rights are, in their origin, stipulations between kings and their subjects, abridgments of prerogative in favour of privilege, reservations of rights not surrendered to the prince." Defending the absence of a special bill of rights in the original Constitution, he insists that "the Constitution is itself, in every rational sense, and to every useful purpose, a bill of rights." It declares and specifies "the political privileges of the citizens in the structure and administration of the government," and "defines certain immunities and modes of proceeding, which are relative to personal and private concerns."

Nevertheless, the right of free speech and free assembly and the right to trial by a jury of peers, along with the immunity from unwarranted searches and seizures or from *ex post facto* laws and bills of attainder, provided by the early amendments to the Constitution, do give the citizen additional protection against interference in the performance of his civic duties, such as independent political thought and action, or in the exercise of his human privileges, such as freedom of religious worship. The invention of these constitutional devices sprang from the bitter experience of coercion and intimidation under Star Chamber proceedings, royal censorship, and unlimited police power. A citizen who can be coerced or intimidated by his government differs only in name from the subject of an absolute despot.

In addition to having these legal safeguards, modern differs from ancient citizenship in the way in which its rights and privileges are exercised. The machinery of suffrage is not the same when citizens act through elected representatives and when they participate directly in the deliberations and decisions of government, by voting in the public forum.

THE PROBLEM OF EDUCATION for citizenship is in some respects stated in almost identical terms by such different political philosophers as Plato and Mill.

In both *The Republic* and the *Laws,* Plato emphasizes that "education is the constraining and directing of youth towards that right reason which the law affirms." By this he means not only that education will affect the laws, but also that the laws themselves have an educational task to perform. The educational program is thus planned and conducted by the state. The guardians—the only citizens in *The Republic* in the full sense of the term—are trained for public life, first by the discipline of their passions, and second by the cultivation of their minds. Their passions are disciplined by music and gymnastics, their minds cultivated by the liberal arts and dialectic.

In the democracy which Mill contemplates as an ideal, "the most important point of excellence . . . is to promote the virtue and intelligence of the people themselves." He does not outline a specific curriculum for the training of citizens, but it is clear that he thinks their education cannot be accomplished in the schools alone. The superiority of democracy, according to Mill, lies in the fact that it calls upon the citizen "to weigh interests not his own; to be guided, in case of conflicting claims, by another rule than his private partialities; to apply at every turn, principles and maxims which have for their reason of existence the common good; and he usually finds associated with him in the same work minds more familiarized than his own with these ideas and operations, whose study it will be to supply reasons to his understanding, and stimulation to his feel-

ing for the general interest." In this "school of public spirit" a man becomes a citizen by doing the work of a citizen and so learning to act like one.

If the future citizen is to act like a free man, must he not also be trained in youth to think like one? Vocational training prepares a man to be an artisan, not a citizen. Only liberal education is adequate to the task of creating the free and critical intelligence required for citizenship. Hence in a state which rests on universal suffrage, the educational problem becomes greatly enlarged in scope, if not in intrinsic difficulty.

With the advent of universal suffrage, which Mill advocates, the state must face the responsibility for making liberal education available to every future citizen. To say that all normal children have enough intelligence to become citizens, but to regard the native endowment of a large number of them as incapable of liberal education, makes a travesty of citizenship. Will the child who cannot profit by liberal education be able to discharge the duties of the office to which he will be admitted upon coming of age?

THE TRAINING OF CHARACTER is always more difficult than the training of mind. In education for citizenship, the problem of moral training involves the question—discussed in the chapter on VIRTUE AND VICE—whether the good man and the good citizen are identical in virtue.

For Aristotle, and seemingly also for Mill, the virtue of the good man under an ideal constitution would be identical with that of the good citizen. As both ruling and being ruled, "the good citizen ought to be capable of both," Aristotle writes. "He should know how to govern like a freeman, and how to obey like a freeman—these are the virtues of a citizen. And although the temperance and justice of a ruler are distinct from those of a subject, the virtue of a good man will include both; for the virtue of the good man who is free and also a subject, *e.g.* his justice, will not be one but will comprise distinct kinds, the one qualifying him to rule, the other to obey."

The virtues of the citizen direct him primarily in the performance of his obligations to the state. But if the welfare of the state is not the ultimate end of man, if there are higher goods which command human loyalty, if man's common humanity takes precedence over his membership in a particular state, then civic virtue does not exhaust human excellence. More may be morally required of the good man than of the good citizen. The virtues of the saint and the patriot may be of a different order.

On this question, the great books reveal a fundamental disagreement among moralists and political philosophers, who differ as Plato and Hegel differ from Augustine and Aquinas, or from Locke and Mill, on the place of the state in human life.

The ancients frequently appeal to a law higher than that of the state. Socrates forever stands as the classic example of one who would rather die than disobey his inner voice—the command of his conscience. A Stoic like Marcus Aurelius is willing to give unqualified allegiance to the political community only when it is the ideal city of man, embracing the whole human brotherhood. "My city and my country, so far as I am Antoninus," he says, "is Rome, but so far as I am a man"—whose "nature is rational and social"—"it is the world."

For Christian theologians, membership in the city of God is a higher vocation than citizenship in any earthly community—even when that is the city of man at its best. The city of God demands a higher order of virtue than the city of man. Referring to the earthly city, Augustine says that "the things which this city desires cannot justly be said to be evil, for it is itself, in its own kind, better than all other human goods. For it desires earthly peace for the sake of enjoying earthly goods." It is all right for men to seek "these things" for they "are good things, and without doubt the gifts of God." But, Augustine goes on to say, "if they neglect the better things of the heavenly city, which are secured by eternal victory and peace never-ending, and so inordinately covet these present good things that they believe them to be the only desirable things," then, in Augustine's opinion, they are misdirected in their love.

In giving precedence to the commandments of God, the theologians do not deprecate the commands of the state or the obligations of citizenship. But those who belong to both cities may find themselves faced with a conflict between the law of the state and the divine law. In such circumstances, the faithful have no choice. They must obey God before man. "Laws that are contrary to the commandments of God," Aquinas holds, do not "bind a man in conscience" and "should not be obeyed."

THIS CONFLICT BETWEEN human and divine law finds expression in antiquity in the *Antigone* of Sophocles. Regarding the human law she disobeys, she tells the Theban King Creon,

It was not Zeus who made that order,
Nor did I think your orders were so strong
that you, a mortal man, could over-run
the gods' unwritten and unfailing laws.
Not now, nor yesterday's, they always live,
and no one knows their origin in time.

The problem which Antigone faces can occur in as many other ways as there are possibilities of tension between individual conscience or desire and political obligation. Whatever form this takes, the conflict confronts the political philosopher with all the questions that constitute the problem of the individual and society, or man and the state.

To what extent and in what respects is the individual's personality sacred and inviolable by the state? How much freedom from government has the individual a right to demand? How much individual sacrifice has the state a right to expect? Is the state merely a means in the individual's pursuit of happiness, or the end to which all other goods must be ordered? Is man made for the state, or the state for man?

To questions of this sort, the answers range from philosophical anarchism at one extreme to equally philosophical totalitarianism at the other, with all degrees of individualism and communism in between. The general problem of man and the state, with all its controversial issues, runs through many other chapters—such as CONSTITUTION, GOOD AND EVIL, LAW, LIBERTY, and STATE—but we have placed its principal formulation in this chapter because the concept of citizenship signifies the ideal condition of the human individual as a member of the political community.

12

Constitution

INTRODUCTION

THE idea of a constitution as establishing and organizing a political community; the principle of constitutionality as determining a generic form of government having many varieties; and the nature of constitutional government—these three problems are so intimately connected that they must be treated together. We have used the word "constitution" to express the root notion from which all other matters considered in this chapter are derived.

It is impossible to say precisely what a constitution is in a way that will fit the political reality of the Greek city-states, the Roman public and its transformation into the empire, medieval kingdoms and communes and their gradual metamorphosis into the limited monarchies and republics of modern times. No definition can adequately comprehend all the variations of meaning to be found in the great works of political theory and history. But there are a number of related points in the various meanings of "constitution" which indicate what is common to the understanding of such diverse thinkers as Plato and Locke, Aristotle and Rousseau, Kant and Mill, Montesquieu and Hegel, Aquinas, Hobbes, Tocqueville, and the American Federalists.

IT HAS BEEN SAID that the constitution is the form of the state. This can be interpreted to mean that the political, as opposed to the domestic, community requires a constitution in order to exist; just as a work of art has the very principle of its being in the form which the artist imposes upon matter. In the context of his general theory of political association, Aristotle's remark that "the man who first founded the state was the greatest of benefactors," may imply that the idea of a constitu-

tion is the creative principle by which the state was originally formed—or at least differentiated from the tribe and family.

Kant gives explicit expression to the notion that the invention of constitutions is coeval with the formation of states. "The act by which a People is represented as constituting itself into a State," he writes, "is termed the Original Contract" and this in turn signifies "the rightfulness of the process of organizing the Constitution."

In this sense, the constitution appears to be identical with the organization of a state. It would then seem to follow that every state, no matter what its form of government, is constitutional in character. But this would leave no basis for the fundamental distinction between constitutional and nonconstitutional—or what is usually called "absolute," "royal," or "despotic"—government.

That basic distinction among forms of government is as old as Plato and Aristotle. It is first made by Plato in the *Statesman* in terms of the role of law in government. It occurs at the very opening of Aristotle's *Politics* with his insistence on the difference between the king and the statesman, and between royal and political government. But Locke seems to go further than the ancients when he says that "absolute monarchy . . . is inconsistent with civil society, and so can be no form of civil government at all."

In addition to affirming the gravity of the distinction between constitutional government, he seems to be denying that the latter can constitute the form of a truly *civil* society, as opposed to a domestic society or the primitive patriarchate of a tribe. Yet Locke obviously does not deny the historical fact that there have been communities, which otherwise appear to be states, that have their character or form determined by absolute government. His point, therefore, seems to be that among types of government, absolute monarchy does not fit the nature of civil society.

If "constitution" is used merely as a synonym for "form" or "type," then even a state under absolute monarchy or despotic government can be said to have a constitution. Since every state is of some type, it can be said that it has a certain constitution, or that it is constituted in a certain way. If, however, we use the word "constitution" to conform to the distinction between constitutional and non-constitutional government, we are compelled to say that there are states which do not have constitutions.

With this distinction in mind, the statement that "the constitution is the form of the state" takes on a different and more radical meaning. It signifies that there are communities, larger than and distinct from the family or tribe, which cannot be called "states" in the strict sense because they do not have constitutions. Hegel, for instance, points out that "it would be contrary even to commonplace ideas to call patriarchal conditions a 'constitution' or a people under patriarchal government a 'state' or its independence 'sovereignty.' " In such conditions, what is lacking, he writes, is "the objectivity of possessing in its own eyes and in the eyes of others, a universal and universally valid embodiment in laws." Without such an "objective law and an explicitly established rational constitution, its autonomy is . . . not sovereignty."

From this it would appear that a despotically governed community, such as ancient Persia, is a political anomaly. It is intermediate between the family and the state, for it is like a state in its extent and in the size and character of its population, yet it is not a state in its political form. The truly political community is constitutionally organized and governed. In this sense, the English words "political" and "constitutional" become almost interchangeable, and we can understand how these two English words translate a single word in Greek political discourse.

As THE FORM of the state, the constitution is the principle of its organization. Whether written or unwritten, whether a product of custom or explicit enactment, a constitution, Aristotle writes, "is the organization of offices in a state, and determines what is to be the governing body, and what is the end of each community."

The idea of political office—of officials and official status—is inseparable from the idea of constitution. That is why the concept of citizenship is also inseparable from constitution. As the chapter on CITIZEN indicates, citizenship is the primary or *indefinite* office set up by a constitution. Citizenship is always the prerequisite for holding any other *more definite* office in a constitutional government, from juryman to chief magistrate. In specifying the qualifications for citizenship, a constitution sets the minimum qualifications for all other offices which usually, though not always, demand more than citizenship of the man who is to fill them.

A political office represents a share of political power and authority. "Those are to be called offices," Aristotle explains, "to which the duties are assigned of deliberating about certain measures and of judging and commanding, especially the last; for to command is the especial duty of a magistrate." As representing a share of political power and authority, a political office can be said to constitute a share of sovereignty. That would not seem to be true, however, for those who, like Rousseau, maintain that "sovereignty is indivisible." Yet Rousseau also admits that "each magistrate is almost always charged with some governmental function" and exercises a "function of sovereignty."

Since it is an arrangement of offices, a constitution is, therefore, also a division or partition of the whole sovereignty of government—or at least of the exercise of sovereignty—into units which have certain functions to perform, and which must be given the requisite power and authority to perform them. These units are political offices, defined according to their functions, and vested with a certain power and authority depending on their place and purpose within the whole.

Hamilton's maxim that "every power ought to be in proportion to its object" formulates the equation by which the function of an office, or its duties, determines its rights and powers, privileges and immunities. And except for the provision of a temporary dictatorship in the early Roman constitution, or its modern constitutional equivalent in emergency grants of power, political offices under constitutional government always represent limited amounts of power and authority—limited in that each is always only a part of the whole.

A CONSTITUTION defines and relates the various political offices. It determines the qualifications of officeholders. But it does not name the individuals who, from all those qualified, shall be selected for any office. Because its provisions have this sort of generality, a constitution has the character of law. This is equally true of written and unwritten constitutions, of those shaped by custom and those enacted by constituent assemblies.

Unlike all other man-made laws, a constitution is the law which creates and regulates government itself, rather than the law which a government creates and by which it regulates the conduct of men, their relation to one another and to the state. This is perhaps the basic distinction with regard to the laws of the state. "The fundamental law in every commonwealth," says Hobbes, "is that which being taken away the commonwealth faileth and is utterly dissolved." Montesquieu distinguishes what he calls "the law politic," which constitutes the state, from ordinary legislation; and Rousseau likewise divides the laws into "political" or "fundamental" laws and the "civil laws"—those "which determine the form of the government" and those which the government, once it is constituted, enacts and enforces.

In addition to being the source of all other positive laws of the state—for it sets up the very machinery of lawmaking—a constitution is fundamental law in that it establishes the standard of legality by which all subsequent laws are measured. Aristotle observes that "the justice or injustice of laws varies of necessity with constitutions." What may be a just enact-ment in one state may be unjust in another according to the difference of the constitutions.

In American practice and that modeled upon it, a law which violates the letter or spirit of the constitution is judged to be unconstitutional and is deprived thereby of the authority of law. "Every act of a delegated authority," Hamilton writes in *The Federalist,* "contrary to the tenor of the commission under which it is exercised, is void. No legislative act, therefore, contrary to the Constitution can be valid. To deny this would be to affirm that the deputy is greater than his principal; that the servant is above his master; that the representatives of the people are superior to the people themselves; that men acting by virtue of powers may do not only what their powers do not authorize, but what they forbid."

THE CONCEPTION of a constitution as a law or set of laws antecedent to all acts of government inevitably raises the question of how or by whom constitutions are made. If the provisions of a constitution were precepts of natural law, they would, according to the theory of natural law, be discovered by reason, not positively instituted. But though constitutions have the character of positive law, they cannot be made as other positive laws are made—by legislators, *i.e.,* men holding that office *under the constitution.*

The generally accepted answer is that a constitution is made by the people who form the political community. But, as Madison observes, some evidence exists to the contrary. "It is not a little remarkable," he writes, "that in every case reported by ancient history, in which government has been established with deliberation and consent, the task of framing it has not been committed to an assembly of men, but has been performed by some individual citizen of pre-eminent wisdom and approved integrity." He cites many examples from Plutarch to support this observation, but he adds the comment that it cannot be ascertained to what extent these lawgivers were "clothed with the legitimate authority of the people." In some cases, however, he claims that "the proceeding was strictly regular."

The writers of *The Federalist* are, of course,

primarily concerned with a constitution that is not the work of one man but the enactment of a constituent assembly or constitutional convention. From their knowledge of British law, they are also well aware that a constitution may sometimes be the product of custom, growing and altering with change of custom. But however it is exercised, the constitutive power is held by them to reside in the constituents of the state, the sovereign people. This power may be exercised through force of custom to produce an unwritten constitution, or through deliberative processes to draft a written one; but it can never be exercised by a government *except with popular consent,* since all the powers of a duly constituted government derive from its constitution. In the American if not the British practice, the amendment of the constitution also involves, at least indirectly, an appeal to the people.

Rousseau assigns the constitutive power to a mythical figure he calls "the legislator" or "the law-giver," describing him as the man who "sets up the Republic." Yet Rousseau says of this special office that it "nowhere enters into the constitution." He thus reaffirms the essential point that a constitution cannot create the office of constitution-making.

These remarks in *The Social Contract* have another significance. Rousseau tries to distinguish the formation of a government by the constitution (the political or fundamental law made by *the* legislator) from the formation of the state by the social contract entered into by the people in their original act of association. But is not the constitution also a formative contract or convention? If it is popular in origin, either through custom or enactment, is there more than a verbal difference between these two contracts—the one which establishes a political society and the one which establishes its government?

For Hobbes, and seemingly also for Locke, the compact by which men abandon the state of nature and establish a civil society results at the same time in the establishment of a government. It is, Hobbes writes, "as if every man should say to every man, I authorize and give my right of governing my self, to this Man or to this Assembly of men, on this condition,

that thou give up thy right to him, and authorize all his actions in like manner." According to Rousseau, "there is only one contract in the State, and that is the [original] act of association." For him, "the institution of government is not a contract."

The reality and significance of the difference between these three political philosophers would seem to depend on the precise historical meaning each gives to the hypothesis of men living in a state of nature prior to political association. If, prior to the state, men live in nonpolitical societies, and if the state, as opposed to the family or the despotically ruled community, begins to exist only when it is constituted, then the formation of the state and the formation of its government would seem to be the product of a single convention.

THE PRINCIPLE OF constitutionality is also necessary in order to understand the familiar distinction between government by laws and government by men. Except for the divine sort of government which is above both law and lawlessness, Plato employs "the distinction of ruling with law or without law" to divide the various forms of government into two groups. "The principle of law and the absence of law will bisect them all," the Eleatic Stranger says in the *Statesman.*

In the ordinary meaning of law as an instrument of government, it is difficult to conceive government by laws without men to make and administer them, or government by men who do not issue general directives which have the character of law. Government always involves both laws and men. But not all government rests upon the supremacy which consists in the equality of all before the law and the predominance of regular law as opposed to arbitrary decision. Nor is all government based upon a law that regulates the officials of government as well as the citizens and determines the legality of official acts, legislative, judicial, or executive. That law is, of course, the constitution.

Locke makes a distinction between governing by "absolute arbitrary power" and governing by "settled standing laws." It is his contention that "whatever form the commonwealth is under, the ruling power ought to govern by declared and received laws, and not by extempory dictates and undetermined resolutions, for then mankind will be in a far worse condition than in a state of Nature ... All the power the government has, being only for the good of the society, as it ought not to be arbitrary and at pleasure, so it ought to be exercised by established and promulgated laws, that both the people may know their duty, and be safe and secure within the limits of the law, and the rulers, too, kept within their due bounds."

As Locke states the distinction between government by laws and government by men, it seems to be identical with the distinction between constitutional and nonconstitutional government. In the latter, an individual man invests himself with sovereignty and, as sovereign, puts himself above all human law, being both its source and the arbiter of its legality. Such government is absolute, for nothing limits the power the sovereign man exercises as a prerogative vested in his person. In constitutional government, men are not sovereigns but officeholders, having only a share of the sovereignty. They rule not through *de facto* power, but through the juridical power which is vested in the office they hold. That power is both created and limited by the law of the constitution which defines the various offices of government.

ALTHOUGH ABSTRACTLY or in theory absolute and constitutional government are clearly distinct—more than that, opposed—political history contains the record of intermediate types. These can be regarded as imperfect embodiments of the principle of constitutionality, or as attenuations of absolute rule by constitutional encroachments. Despite their incompatibility in principle, historic circumstances have managed to combine absolute with constitutional government. It is this combination which medieval jurists and philosophers call "the mixed regime" or the *regimen regale et politicum,* "royal and political government."

It may be thought that a foreshadowing of the medieval mixed regime can be found in Plato's *Laws,* in the passage in which the Athenian Stranger says that monarchy and democracy are the "two mother forms of states from which the rest may be truly derived." He then asserts that, to combine liberty with wisdom, "you must have both these forms of government in a measure." Since the Persian despotism is cited as the "highest form" of monarchy and the Athenian constitution as the archetype of democracy, the combination proposed would seem to be a mixture of absolute with constitutional government. But the Athenian Stranger also says that "there ought to be no great and unmixed powers" if the arbitrary is to be avoided; and since the whole tenor of the book, as indicated by its title, is to uphold the supremacy of law, it is doubtful that a truly mixed regime is intended—a government which is *partly* absolute and *partly* constitutional.

Aristotle, furthermore, gives us reason to think that such a mixture would be unthinkable to a Greek. At least in his own vocabulary, the terms *royal* and *political* are as contradictory as *round* and *square.* Royal, or kingly, government for Aristotle is "absolute monarchy, or the arbitrary rule of a sovereign over all." In royal government, there are no political offices, and no citizens. The ruler is sovereign in his own person and the ruled are subject to his will, which is both the source of law and exempt from all legal limitations.

To Aristotle, political government means pure constitutionalism. It exists only where "the citizens rule and are ruled in turn," for "when the state is framed upon the principle of equality and likeness, the citizens think they ought to hold office by turns." To the generic form of constitutional government, Aristotle sometimes gives the name of "polity," though he also uses this name for the mixed constitution which combines democratic with oligarchic criteria for citizenship and public office. The mixed constitution is not to be confused with the mixed regime, for it is a mixture of different constitutional principles, not of constitutionalism itself with absolute government. When the word "polity" signifies constitutional government generally, it has the meaning which the Romans express by the word "republic" and which the constitutionalists of the 18th century call "free government."

The distinctive characteristics of such government—whether it is called political, republican, constitutional, or free—lie in the fact that the citizens are both rulers and ruled; that no man, not even the chief magistrate, is above the law; that all political power or authority is derived from and limited by the constitution which, being popular in origin, cannot be changed except by the people as a whole.

It is perhaps only in the Middle Ages that we find the mixed regime in actual existence. "That rule is called politic and royal," Aquinas writes, "by which a man rules over free subjects who, though subject to the government of the ruler, have nevertheless something of their own, by reason of which they can resist the orders of him who commands." These words seem to present an accurate picture of the peculiarly medieval political formation which resulted from the adaptation of Roman law (itself partly republican and partly imperial) to feudal conditions under the influence of local customs and the Christian religion.

The medieval mixed regime is not to be confused with modern forms of constitutional monarchy any more than with the mixed constitution or polity of the Greeks. "The so-called limited monarchy, or kingship according to law," Aristotle remarks, "is not a distinct form of government." The chapter on MONARCHY deals with the nature of constitutional monarchy and its difference from the mixed regime as well as its relation to purely republican government. The medieval king was not a constitutional monarch, but a sovereign person, in one sense above the law and in another limited by it.

To the extent that he had powers and prerogatives unlimited by law, the medieval king was an absolute ruler. He was, as Aquinas says, quoting the phrase of the Roman jurists, *legibus solutus*—exempt from the force of all man-made law. Aquinas also describes him as "above the law" insofar as "when it is expedient, he can change the law, and rule without it according to time and place." Yet he was also bound by his coronation oath to perform the duties of his office, first among which was the maintenance of the laws of the realm—the immemorial customs of the people which define their rights and liberties. The king's subjects could be released from their oath of allegiance by his malfeasance or dereliction in office.

To this extent, then, the medieval king was a responsible ruler, and the mixed regime was constitutional. Furthermore, the king did not have jurisdiction over customary law; yet where custom was silent, the king was free to govern absolutely, to decree what he willed, and even to innovate laws.

MEDIEVAL IN ORIGIN, the institution of a government both royal and political, or what Sir John Fortescue, describing England in the 15th century, called a "political kingdom," exerted great influence on modern constitutional developments. As late as the end of the 17th century, Locke's conception of the relation of king and parliament, royal prerogative and legal limitations, may emphasize the primacy of law, but it does not entirely divest the king of personal sovereignty. Locke quotes with approval the speech from the throne in 1609, in which James I said that "the king binds himself by a double oath, to the observation of the fundamental laws of his kingdom. Tacitly, as by being a king, and so bound to protect as well the people, as the laws of his kingdom, and expressly by his oath at his coronation." To this extent the British kingdom is, as Fortescue had said, "political." But the king also retains the prerogative to dispense with law and to govern in particular matters by decree apart from law, and to this extent the government still remains royal.

Locke recognizes the difficulty of combining the absolute power of the king in administration with the limitations on that power represented by Parliament's jurisdiction over the laws which bind the king. To the question, Who shall be judge of the right use of the royal prerogative? he replies that "between an executive power in being, with such prerogative, and a legislative that depends upon his will for their convening, there can be no judge on earth . . . The people have no other remedy . . . but to appeal to heaven."

Montesquieu as well as Locke can conceive monarchy, as distinct from despotism, in no other terms than those of the mixed regime.

He separates despotism as lawless, or arbitrary and absolute, government from all forms of government by law, and divides the latter into monarchies and republics. Montesquieu insists that the ancients had no notion of the kind of monarchy which, while it is legal government, is not purely constitutional in the sense of being republican. He calls this kind of monarchy "Gothic government," and, as Hegel later points out, it is clear that "by 'monarchy' he understands, not the patriarchal or any ancient type, nor on the other hand, the type organized into an objective constitution, but only feudal monarchy."

It is not until the 18th century that the slightest vestige of royal power comes to be regarded as inimical to law. For Rousseau "every legitimate government is republican"; for Kant, "the only rightful Constitution . . . is that of a Pure Republic," which, in his view, "can only be constituted by a *representative system* of the people." The writers of *The Federalist* take the same stand. They interpret the "aversion of the people to monarchy" as signifying their espousal of purely constitutional or republican government. In the tradition of the great books, only Hegel speaks thereafter in a contrary vein. Constitutional monarchy represents for him the essence of constitutionalism and the only perfect expression of the idea of the state.

Because modern republics, and even modern constitutional or limited monarchies, have developed gradually or by revolution out of mixed regimes; and because this development came as a reaction against the increasing absolutism or despotism of kings, the principle of constitutionality has been made more effective in modern practice than it was in the ancient world. In addition to asserting limitations upon governments, constitutions have also provided means of controlling them. They have been given the *force,* as well as the authority, of positive law. They have made officeholders accountable for their acts; and through such juridical processes as impeachment and such political devices as frequent elections and short terms of office, they have brought the administration of government within the purview of the law.

Following Montesquieu, the Federalists recommend the separation of powers, with checks and balances, as the essential means of enforcing constitutional limitations of office and of preventing one department of government from usurping the power of another. The citizens are further protected from the misuse of power by constitutional declarations of their rights and immunities; and constitutional government is itself safeguarded from revolutionary violence by such institutions as judicial review and by the availability of the amending power as a means of changing the constitution through due process of law.

Half a century later, it is Tocqueville who recognizes the great originality of the federal constitution of the United States as founded and adopted in 1787–1789. Of it, he writes:

This Constitution, which at first sight one is tempted to confuse with previous federal constitutions, in fact rests on an entirely new theory, a theory that should be hailed as one of the great discoveries of political science in our age.

In all confederations previous to that of 1789 in America, the peoples who allied themselves for a common purpose agreed to obey the injunctions of the federal government, but they kept the right to direct and supervise the execution of the union's laws in their territory.

The Americans who united in 1789 agreed not only that the federal government should dictate the laws but that it should itself see to their execution.

In both cases the right is the same, and only the application thereof different. But that one difference produces immense results . . .

In America the Union's subjects are not states but private citizens. When it wants to levy a tax, it does not turn to the government of Massachusetts, but to each inhabitant of Massachusetts. Former federal governments had to confront peoples, individuals of the Union. It does not borrow its power, but draws it from within. It has its own administrators, courts, officers of justice, and army.

IN THE HISTORY of political change, it is necessary to distinguish *change from* or *to* constitutional government and, within the sphere of constitutional government, the *change of* constitutions.

Republics are set up and constitutions established by the overthrow of despots or with their abdication. Republics are destroyed and constitutions overthrown by dictators who usurp the powers of government. Violence, or the threat of violence, usually attends these changes. Both of these changes occur, with the usual violence, in Orwell's satire of the Russian Revolution, *Animal Farm:* the animals overthrow Farmer Jones and set up a brief animal constitution, the first rule of which is that "Whatever goes upon two legs is an enemy"; this commandment is broken by the pigs, who, by the end, are indistinguishable from their human oppressors.

A change of constitutions may take place in two ways: either when one constitution replaces another, as frequently occurs in the revolutions of the Greek city-states; or when an enduring constitution is modified by amendment, as is customary in modern republics. Every constitutional change is in a sense revolutionary, but if it can be accomplished by due process of law, violence can be avoided.

All the changes in which constitutional government or constitutions are involved raise fundamental questions of justice. Is republican government always better than absolute monarchy and the mixed regime—better in the sense of being more just, better because it gives men the liberty and equality they justly deserve? Is it better relative to the nature and condition of certain peoples but not all, or of a people at a certain stage of their development, but not always? In what respects does one constitution embody more justice than another? What sorts of amendment or reform can rectify the injustice of a constitution? Without answering such questions, we cannot discriminate between progress and decline in the history of constitutionalism.

Divergent answers will, of course, be found in the great books. Among the political philosophers, there are the defenders of absolutism and those who think that royal government is most like the divine; the exponents of the supremacy of the mixed regime; the republicans who insist that nothing less than constitutional government is fit for free men and equals. And there are those who argue that the justice of any form of government must be considered relative to the condition of the people, so that republican government may be better only in some circumstances, not in all.

The issue arising from these conflicting views concerning constitutional and absolute government is treated in the chapters on CITIZEN, MONARCHY, and TYRANNY AND DESPOTISM. But one other issue remains to be discussed here. It concerns the comparative justice of diverse constitutions. Constitutions can differ from one another in the way in which they plan the operations of government, or in the qualifications they set for citizenship and public office. Usually only the second mode of difference seriously affects their justice.

In Greek political life, the issue of justice as between the democratic and the oligarchic constitution is a conflict between those who think that all free men deserve the equality of citizenship and the opportunity to hold office, and those who think it is unjust to treat the rich and the poor as equals. The latter insist that citizenship should be restricted to the wealthy and that the magistracies should be reserved for men of considerable means.

Finding justice and injustice on both sides, Aristotle favors what he calls "the mixed constitution." This unites the justice of treating free men alike so far as citizenship goes, with the justice of discriminating between rich and poor with respect to public office. Such a mixture, he writes, "may be described generally as a fusion of oligarchy and democracy," since it attempts "to unite the freedom of the poor and the wealth of the rich." The mixed constitution, especially if accompanied by a numerical predominance of the middle class, seems to him to have greater stability, as well as more justice, than either of the pure types of constitution which, oppressive to either poor or rich, provoke revolution.

In modern political life, the issue between oligarchy and democracy tends toward a different resolution. The last defenders of the oligarchic constitution were men like Edmund Burke, Alexander Hamilton, and John Adams in the 18th century. Since then, the great constitutional reforms have progressively extended the franchise almost to the point of universal suffrage. These matters are, of course, further treated in the chapters on DEMOCRACY and OLIGARCHY.

POLITICAL REPRESENTATION, with a system of periodic elections, seems to be indispensable to constitutional government under modern conditions. The territorial extent and populousness of the nation-state as compared with the ancient city-state makes impossible direct participation by the whole body of citizens in the major functions of government.

Considering the ancient republics of Sparta, Rome, and Carthage, the writers of *The Federalist* try to explain the sense in which the principle of representation differentiates the American republic from these ancient constitutional governments. "The principle of representation," they say, "was neither unknown to the ancients nor wholly overlooked in their political constitutions. The true distinction between these and the American government lies *in the total exclusion of the people, in their collective capacity,* from any share in the *latter,* and not in the *total exclusion of the representatives of the people* from the administration of the *former.*"

The Federalists then go on to say that "the distinction . . . thus qualified must be admitted to leave a most advantageous superiority in favor of the United States. But to insure to this advantage its full effect, we must be careful not to separate it from the other advantage of an extensive territory. For it cannot be believed that any form of representative government could have succeeded within the narrow limits occupied by the democracies of Greece."

In their opinion, representative government is not merely necessitated by the conditions of modern society, but also has the political advantage of safeguarding constitutional government from the masses. As pointed out in the chapter on ARISTOCRACY, where the theory of representation is discussed, the officers of government chosen by the whole body of citizens are supposed—at least on one conception of representatives—to be more competent in the business of government than their constituents. It is in these terms that the Federalists advocate what they call "republican goverment" as opposed to "pure democracy."

Like the idea of political offices, the principle of representation seems to be inseparable from constitutionalism and constitutional government. Though the principle appears to a certain extent in ancient republics—whether oligarchies or democracies—ancient political writing does not contain a formal discussion of the theory of representation. That begins in medieval treatises which recognize the consultative or advisory function of those who represent the nobles and the commons at the king's court. But it is only in recent centuries—when legislation has become the exclusive function of representative assemblies—that the idea of representation and the theory of its practice assume a place of such importance that a political philosopher like J. S. Mill does not hesitate to identify representative with constitutional government.

13

Courage

INTRODUCTION

THE heroes of history and poetry may be cruel, violent, self-seeking, ruthless, intemperate, and unjust, but they are never cowards. They do not falter or give way. They do not despair in the face of almost hopeless odds. They have the strength and stamina to achieve whatever they set their minds and wills to do. They would not be heroes if they were not men of courage.

This is the very meaning of heroism which gives the legendary heroes almost the stature of gods. In the Homeric age they do in fact contend with gods as well as men. The two Homeric epics, especially *The Iliad,* are peopled with men who cannot be dared or daunted. In Tennyson's poem, Ulysses, now restive in Ithaca, remembering the years at Troy and the long voyage home, says to his companions,

Some work of noble note may yet be done
Not unbecoming men that strove with Gods
. . . . and though
We are not now that strength which in old days
Moved earth and heaven; that which we are, we are:
One equal temper of heroic hearts,
Made weak by time and fate, but strong in will
To strive, to seek, to find, and not to yield.

In *The Iliad,* courage is the quality above all others which characterizes the great figures of Achilles and Hector, Ajax, Patroclus, and Diomedes, Agamemnon and Menelaus. The only other quality which seems to be equally prized, and made the subject of rivalry and boast, is cunning—the craft of Odysseus, that man of many devices, and the cleverness in speech of Nestor. Yet the best speech is only the prelude to action, and except for the night expedition of Odysseus and Diomedes into the Trojan camp, the great actions of *The Iliad* are unplanned deeds of prowess—stark, not stealthy.

The heroes have boundless passions, and fear is among them. When they are called fearless, it is not because nothing affrights them or turns their blood cold. Fear seizes them, as does anger, with all its bodily force. They are fearless only in the sense that they do not act afraid or fail to act. Their courage is always equal to the peril sensed or felt, so that they can perform what must be done as if they had no fear of pain or death. Such courage is exemplified by the title character of Hemingway's story *The Short Happy Life of Francis Macomber:*

"You know, I'd like to try another lion," Macomber said. "I'm not really afraid of them now. After all, what can they do to you?"

"That's it," said Wilson. "Worst one can do is kill you. How does it go? Shakespeare. Damned good. See if I can remember . . . 'By my troth, I care not; a man can die but once; we owe God a death and let it go which way it will, he that dies this year is quit for the next.' "

Yet brave men often speak of courage as if it were fearlessness and mark the coward as one who is undone by fear. An ambush, Idomeneus says in *The Iliad,* will show "who is cowardly and who is brave; the coward will change color at every touch and turn; he is full of fears, and keeps shifting his weight first on one knee and then on the other; his heart beats fast as he thinks of death, and one can hear the chattering of his teeth." The brave man, mastering fear, will appear to be fearless.

This is the courage of men of action, men in war, found not only in the heroes of Troy's siege, but in the stalwarts of all other battles—Leonidas at Thermopylae, Aeneas and Turnus engaged in single combat, the conquerors in Plutarch, the warrior-nobility in Shakespeare, the civilized Prince Andrew and young Rostov in *War and Peace*. It is the sort of courage which goes with physical strength, with feats of endurance; and, as signified by the root-meaning of "fortitude," which is a synonym for courage, it is a reservoir of moral or spiritual strength to sustain action even when flesh and blood can carry on no further. Such courage is a virtue in the primary sense of the Latin word *virtus*—manliness, the spirit, or strength of spirit, required to be a man.

THERE ARE OTHER sorts of courage. The courage of the tragic hero, of Oedipus and Antigone, goes with strength of mind, not body. This, perhaps even more than being lionhearted, is a specifically human strength. Courage does not consist only in conquering fear and in withholding the body from flight no matter what the risk of pain. It consists at least as much in steeling the will, reinforcing its resolutions, and turning the mind relentlessly to seek or face the truth.

Civil no less than martial action requires courage. Weary of empire, Marcus Aurelius summons courage each day for the performance of an endless round of duties. "In the morning when thou risest unwilling," he reminds himself, "let this thought be present— I am rising to the work of a human being." How he conceives the work of an emperor, he makes plain. "Let the deity which is in thee be the guardian of a living being, manly and of ripe age, and engaged in matter political, and a Roman, and a ruler, who has taken his post like a man waiting for the signal which summons him from life, and ready to go, having need neither of oath nor of any man's testimony." The burdens are heavy, the task difficult but not impossible, for a man "can live well even in a palace."

Civil courage is as necessary for the citizen as for the ruler. This virtue, in J. S. Mill's opinion, is especially necessary for citizens of a free government. "A people may prefer a free government," he writes, "but if, from indolence, or carelessness, or cowardice, or want of public spirit, they are unequal to the exertions necessary for preserving it; if they will not fight for it when it is directly attacked; if they can be deluded by the artifices used to cheat them out of it; if by momentary discouragement, or temporary panic, or a fit of enthusiasm for an individual, they can be induced to lay their liberties at the feet even of a great man, or trust him with powers which enable him to subvert their institutions; in all these cases they are more or less unfit for liberty: and though it may be for their good to have had it even for a short time, they are unlikely long to enjoy it."

The courage or pusillanimity of a people is sometimes regarded as the cause, and sometimes as the effect, of their political institutions. "The inhabitants of Europe," Hippocrates writes, are "more courageous than those of Asia; for a climate which is always the same induces indolence, but a changeable climate, laborious exertions, both of body and mind; and from rest and indolence cowardice is engendered, and from laborious exertions and pains, courage." This, according to Hippocrates, partly explains why the Asiatics readily submit to despotism and why the Europeans fight for political liberty. But the character of the Europeans, he adds, is also the result of "their institutions, because they are not governed by kings . . . for where men are governed by kings, there they must be very cowardly . . . and they will not readily undergo dangers in order to promote the power of another; but those that are free undertake dangers on their own account . . . and thus their institutions contribute not a little to their courage."

For Hegel, on the contrary, civic courage consists in undertaking dangers, even to the point of sacrifice, for the state. Moreover, for him true courage is entirely a civic virtue. "The intrinsic worth of courage as a disposition of the mind," he writes, "is to be found in the genuine, absolute, final end, the sovereignty of the state. The work of courage is to actualize this final end, and the means to this end is the sacrifice of personal actuality." Though he admits that courage "is multiform," he insists that "the mettle of an animal or a brigand, courage for the sake of honor, the courage of a knight, these are not true forms of courage.

The true courage of civilized nations is readiness for sacrifice in the service of the state, so that the individual counts as only one amongst many."

THE WORK OF MAN is learning as well as action. Man has a duty to the truth as well as to the state. The ability to face without flinching the hard questions reality can put constitutes the temper of a courageous mind. "The huge world that girdles us about," William James writes, "puts all sorts of questions to us, and tests us in all sorts of ways. Some of the tests we meet by actions that are easy, and some of the questions we answer in articulately formulated words. But the deepest question that is ever asked admits of no reply but the dumb turning of the will and tightening of our heart-strings as we say, 'Yes, I will even have it so!' When a dreadful object is presented, or when life as a whole turns up its dark abysses to our view, then the worthless ones among us lose their hold on the situation altogether . . . But the heroic mind does differently . . . It can face them if necessary, without for that losing its hold upon the rest of life. The world thus finds in the heroic man its worthy match and mate . . . He can *stand* this Universe."

Not only in answering questions, but in asking them, courage is required. The story which Saint Augustine tells in *The Confessions,* of his persistent questioning of doctrines and dogmas, his refusal to rest in any creed which did not wholly satisfy his mind, is a story of speculative courage, capped by the fortitude with which he bore the agony of irresolution and doubt.

Learning is never an easy enterprise, nor truth an easy master. The great scientists and philosophers have shown the patience and perseverance of courage in surmounting the social hardships of opposition and distrust, as well as the intellectual difficulties which might discourage men less resolved to seek and find the truth. The great religious martyrs, as indomitable in their humility as soldiers are in daring, have been as resolute—never yielding to a despair which would have dishonored their faith.

In all these types of fortitude, different motivations are apparent, as diverse as the forms which courage takes under the various demands of life. Not all the forms of courage may be equally admirable, partly because they are unequal in degree, but also partly because the courageous acts themselves, or the purposes for which fortitude is needed, are not of equal moral worth. Yet the essence of courage seems to be the same throughout. It sustains the honor of Don Quixote and in some sense even of Sir John Falstaff; it burnishes the fame of Alexander and Caesar; it fortifies Socrates and Galileo to withstand their trials. Whether in the discharge of duty or in the pursuit of happiness, courage confirms a man in the hard choices he has been forced to make.

AS THE CHAPTER ON VIRTUE AND VICE indicates, the traditional theory of the moral qualities places courage or fortitude among the four principal virtues. The other three are temperance, justice, and either wisdom or prudence, according to the enumeration of different writers.

Plato names these virtues when, in *The Republic,* he compares the parts of the state with the parts of the soul. "The same principles which exist in the State exist also in the individual," Socrates says, and "they are three in number." There is one "with which a man reasons . . . the rational part of the soul, another with which he loves and hungers and thirsts and feels the flutterings of any other desire—the irrational or appetitive, the ally of sundry pleasures and satisfactions." The third part is "passion or spirit" which "when not corrupted by bad education is the natural auxiliary of reason."

Corresponding to these three parts of the soul, there are, or should be, according to Plato, three classes in the state: the guardians or rulers, the husbandmen and artisans, or the workers, and the auxiliaries or the soldiers.

The virtues which belong to the several parts of the soul also belong to the corresponding parts of the state. Wise is the man, Socrates declares, "who has in him that little part which rules, and which proclaims commands, that part too being supposed to have a knowledge of what is for the interest of each of the three parts and of the whole." Courageous is he "whose spirit retains in pleasure and in pain the commands of reason about what he ought or ought not to fear."

Temperance, however, instead of being exclusively the perfection of one part, pervades the whole, and is found, according to Socrates, in the man "who has these same elements in friendly harmony, in which the one ruling principle of reason, and the two subject ones of spirit and desire are equally agreed that reason ought to rule." Justice—"the only virtue which remains ... when the other virtues of temperance and courage and wisdom are abstracted"—"is the ultimate cause and condition of the existence of all of them, and while remaining in them is also their preservative." It is the virtue which "does not permit the several elements within a man to interfere with one another, or any of them to do the work of others."

The political analogy finds justice in the well-ordered state, where wisdom rules, courage defends the laws and peace, and temperance balances the economy. Wisdom would belong most properly to the guardians, courage to the auxiliaries, while all three classes would need temperance. Hegel also associates courage with "the military class"—"that universal class which is charged with the defence of the state" and whose duty it is "to make real the ideality implicit within itself, *i.e.*, to sacrifice itself." But whereas for Hegel courage seems to be the foremost political virtue, Plato puts it last in the order of goods. "Wisdom is chief," the Athenian Stranger says in the *Laws;* "next follows temperance; and from the union of these two with courage springs justice, and fourth in the scale of virtue is courage."

In the context of a different psychological analysis, and a theory of the virtues which considers them primarily as habits, Aristotle's conception of courage differs from Plato's in a number of respects. It is most closely allied with temperance. These two virtues together belong to the irrational part of the soul—the passions or appetites—and are concerned with our attitude toward pleasure and pain. They discipline us, both in feeling and action, with

regard to the pleasurable objects of desire and the painful objects of fear or aversion. Aristotle seems to think courage more praiseworthy than temperance, "for it is harder to face what is painful than to abstain from what is pleasant."

Just as the temperate man is one who habitually forgoes certain pleasures and seeks other pleasures moderately for the sake of achieving some greater good, so the courageous man is one who can at any time endure pain and hardship, or overcome fear of danger and death, in order to achieve a paramount end. Since death is "the most terrible of all things," Aristotle declares that "properly, he will be called brave who is fearless in the face of a noble death, and of all emergencies that involve death." But it must be "for a noble end that the brave man endures and acts as courage directs."

The paramount end, the greatest good, which the moderation of temperance and the endurance of courage serve, is for Aristotle happiness. Yet through their relation to justice, which concerns the good of others and the welfare of the state, temperance and courage help a man to perform his social duties, whether as ruler or citizen, in peace or war. The man who acts lawfully will not only be just, but also courageous and temperate, for, in Aristotle's view, "the law bids us do both the acts of a brave man, *e.g.,* not to desert our post nor take flight nor throw away our arms, and those of a temperate man, *e.g.,* not to commit adultery nor to gratify one's lust." Not only may the law-abiding man be called upon to be courageous in the respects which Aristotle indicates, but it may sometimes take great courage to uphold the law itself against many temptations to the contrary. "After the death of Moses ... the Lord spake unto Joshua," and said unto him: "Be thou strong and very courageous, that thou mayest observe to do according to all the law which Moses my servant commanded thee: turn not from it to the right hand or to the left."

The fourth virtue with which courage, temperance, and justice are associated in the conduct of private or public life is prudence, or "practical wisdom." Though Aristotle classifies prudence as an intellectual virtue, consisting in the capacity for making a right judgment about things to be done, he also regards prudence as inseparable in origin and exercise from these other three virtues which he calls "moral" rather than "intellectual." Later writers call the four virtues taken together—courage, temperance, justice, and prudence—the "cardinal" virtues in order to signify, as Aquinas explains, that the whole of moral life "hinges" upon them.

The theory of the cardinal virtues, and of their connection with one another in such wise that none can be perfect in the absence of the others, is treated in the chapter on VIRTUE AND VICE. The chapters on JUSTICE, TEMPERANCE, and PRUDENCE discuss the doctrine that each of these virtues is only a part of virtue, which must be integrated with the other parts. The special role which prudence plays in relation to virtues like courage and temperance—at least according to Aristotle's view that "it is not possible to be good in the strict sense without practical wisdom, nor practically wise without moral virtue"—must be reserved for the chapter dealing with that virtue. Nevertheless, it is necessary to consider here how its dependence on prudence may qualify the meaning or nature of courage.

THE CONNECTION which some writers see between courage and prudence affects the definition of courage in two ways. The first involves the doctrine of the mean which enters into the consideration of all the moral virtues, but especially courage and temperance.

Aristotle originates the analysis of virtue as "a mean between two vices . . . because the vices respectively fall short of or exceed what is right in both passions and actions." It requires prudence to decide what things should be feared, when they should be feared, and how much; and so a prudent judgment is involved in fearing the right things at the right time and in the right manner—neither too much nor too little. "The coward, the rash man, and the brave man," Aristotle writes, "are concerned with the same objects but are differently disposed to them; for the first two exceed and fall short, while the third holds the middle, which is the right, position; and

rash men are precipitate and wish for dangers beforehand but draw back when they are in them, while brave men are keen in the moment of action, but quiet beforehand."

Aristotle is not the only one to define courage as a middle ground between contrary extremes. Most writers who devote any attention to the nature of courage come to somewhat the same conclusion. Epictetus, for example, in declaring that we should "combine confidence with caution in everything we do," seems also to make courage a mean. He points out that such a combination at first "may appear a paradox" since "caution seems to be contrary to confidence, and contraries are by no means compatible." But this, he says, is only due to "confusion." There would be a paradox "if we really called upon a man to use caution and confidence in regard to the same things . . . as uniting qualities which cannot be united." But, as Epictetus explains, caution and confidence can be united because they concern different objects.

The difference in objects which he has in mind becomes clear in the light of the Stoic maxim, "Be confident in all that lies beyond the will's control, be cautious in all that is dependent on the will." Sharply distinguishing between what does and does not lie within our control, Epictetus tells us to look with care and caution only to those things in which we can do evil by making an evil choice. "In such matters of will it is right to use caution." But in other matters, "in things outside the will's control, which do not depend on us . . . we should use confidence."

By uniting caution and confidence, we avoid the extremes of foolhardiness and cowardice and achieve the mean in which Aristotle says courage consists. Both are necessary. Cowardice is not the only vice opposed to courage. The man who acts without caution in the face of danger, recklessly disregarding what might be reasonably feared, is foolhardy rather than courageous; even as the coward is held back by fears which his reason tells him should be overcome.

Because he agrees that courage consists in avoiding both extremes, Spinoza writes that "flight at the proper time, just as well as fighting, is to be reckoned as showing strength of mind." These two acts are allied, since it is by "the same virtue of the mind" that a man "avoids danger . . . and seeks to overcome it."

To determine at a given moment whether to flee or to fight, so as to avoid either foolhardiness or cowardice, obviously involves a decision of reason. Such a decision, according to Spinoza, demands "strength of mind," by which he means "the desire by which each person endeavours from the dictates of reason alone to preserve his own being." Without rational direction or, as Aristotle would say, without prudence, one may be fearless but not courageous.

Those who, like Hobbes, do not include reason or prudence as an essential element in their conception of courage, treat courage as an emotion rather than a virtue, and tend to identify it with fearlessness, making its opposite the condition of being over-fearful. "Amongst the passions," writes Hobbes, "*courage* (by which I mean the contempt of wounds and violent death) inclines men to private revenges, and sometimes to endeavor the unsettling of the public peace; and *timorousness* many times disposes to the desertion of the public defense." As Hobbes describes courage, it may be of doubtful value to the individual or to the state. Melville seems to have this meaning of courage in mind when he says that "the most reliable and useful courage is that which arises from the fair estimation of the encountered peril"—the lack of which makes "an utterly fearless man . . . a far more dangerous companion than a coward." In the context of discussing dread—the existentialist's angst—Heidegger declares that "the dread felt by the courageous cannot be contrasted with the joy . . . of a peaceable life. It stands . . . in secret union with the serenity and gentleness of creative longing."

If apparent fearlessness were courage, then certain animals might be called "courageous," and men of sanguine temperament, extremely self-confident or at least free from fear, would be as courageous as those who succeed in mastering their fears in order to do what is expected of them. But, as Aristotle observes, drunken men often behave fearlessly and we do not praise them for their courage. Plato likewise presents a view of courage which requires forethought and a genuine concern for danger.

"I do not call animals . . . which have no fear of dangers, because they are ignorant of them, courageous," says Nicias in the *Laches*. They are "only fearless and senseless . . . There is a difference to my way of thinking," he goes on, "between fearlessness and courage. I am of the opinion that thoughtful courage is a quality possessed by very few, but that rashness and boldness, and fearlessness, which has no forethought, are very common qualities possessed by many men, many women, many children, and many animals." According to this conception of courage, "courageous actions," Nicias says, "are wise actions."

IN LINE WITH these considerations, the definition of courage would involve a reasonable, a wise or prudent, discrimination between what should be feared and what should be undertaken in spite of peril or pain. As the Parson declares, in his discourse on the Seven Deadly Sins in *The Canterbury Tales,* "this virtue is so mighty and so vigorous that it dares to withstand sturdily, and wisely to keep itself from dangers that are wicked, and to wrestle against the assaults of the Devil. For it enhances and strengthens the soul . . . It can endure, by long suffering, the toils that are fitting."

To be able to make decisions of this sort in particular cases, a man must have some view of the order of goods and the end of life. For a man to act habitually in a courageous manner, he must be generally disposed to value certain things as more important than others, so that he is willing to take risks and endure hardships for their sake.

Freud seems to be skeptical of what he calls "the rational explanation for heroism," according to which "it consists in the decision that the personal life cannot be so precious as certain abstract general ideals." More frequent, in his opinion, "is that instinctive and impulsive heroism which knows no such motivation and flouts danger in the spirit of Anzengruber's Hans the Road-Mender: 'Nothing can happen to *me.*'" But Aquinas, who emphasizes rational motivation as much as Freud discounts it, insists that courageous men "face the danger on account of the good of virtue, which is the abiding object of their will, however great the danger be."

Courage as Aquinas conceives it, though only a part of virtue in the sense of being one virtue among many, nevertheless represents the whole moral life from one point of view. The quality of courage, he points out, "overflows into the rest" of the virtues, as these in turn enter into courage. "Whoever can curb his desires for the pleasures of touch," Aquinas writes, "so that they keep within bounds, which is a very hard thing to do, for this very reason is more able to check his daring in dangers of death, so as not to go too far, which is much easier; and in this sense fortitude is said to be temperate.

"Again," he continues, "temperance is said to be brave because fortitude overflows into temperance. This is true in so far as he whose soul is strengthened by fortitude against dangers of death, which is a matter of very great difficulty, is more able to remain firm against the onslaught of pleasures, for, as Cicero says, *it would be inconsistent for a man to be unbroken by fear, and yet vanquished by cupidity, or that he should be conquered by lust, after showing himself to be unconquered by toil.*"

As the man who is temperate because he has rationally ordered his actions to a certain end can be expected to be courageous for the same reason, so, according to Aquinas, he will also be prudent, since both his temperance and his courage result from a prudent or rational choice of means to the end he pursues.

Writing as a theologian, Aquinas distinguishes what he calls "the perfecting virtues" of the religious life from "the social virtues" of the political life—the virtues with which the moral philosopher is concerned. He holds courage to be inseparable from the other virtues on either plane—whether directed to a natural or supernatural end—because it is the sameness of the end in each case which binds the virtues together. "Thus prudence by contemplating the things of God," he explains, "counts as nothing all the things of this world" and "temperance, so far as nature allows, neglects the needs of the body; fortitude prevents the soul from being afraid of neglecting the body and rising to heavenly things; and justice consists in the soul's giving a whole-hearted consent to follow the way thus proposed."

Kierkegaard also takes a theological view of courage in *Fear and Trembling,* in which he repeats the Genesis story of Abraham, the biblical patriarch whom Kierkegaard describes as a "knight of faith." Faith, according to Kierkegaard, is incomplete without some degree of courage: "A purely human courage is required to renounce the whole of the temporal to gain the eternal . . . But a paradoxical and humble courage is required to grasp the whole of the temporal by virtue of the absurd, and this is the courage of faith."

WE ARE THUS brought to the second qualification upon courage which arises from its connection with prudence, and through prudence with the other virtues. Does it make any difference whether the end for which a man strives valiantly is itself something commendable rather than despicable? If not, then the thief can have courage just as truly as the man who fears dishonor more than death; the tyrant can be courageous no less and no differently than the law-abiding citizen.

In his advice to the prince, Machiavelli seems to consider only the utility of courage. Referring to the end which he says "every man has before him, namely glory and riches," he points out that men proceed in various ways: "one with caution, another with haste; one by force, another by skill; one by patience, another by its opposite; and each one succeeds in reaching the goal by a different method." Fortune, he thinks, plays a large part in their success, and for that reason he holds no method certain. Any method requires us to use fortune to the best advantage. This demands courage and even audacity.

"It is better to be adventurous than cautious," he writes, "because fortune is a woman, and if you wish to keep her under it is necessary to beat and ill-use her; and it is seen that she allows herself to be mastered by the adventurous rather than by those who go to work more coldly. She is, therefore, always woman-like, a lover of young men, because they are less cautious, more violent, and with more audacity command her."

It would appear that Machiavelli recommends courage, or at least daring, to those who wish to succeed in great undertakings, whether the end in view is commendable or not. In either case, courage may improve the chances of success, and it is success that counts. According to their notions of courage as a virtue, Plato, Aristotle, and Aquinas sharply disagree with this, as we have already seen. So do Kant and Hegel.

"It is the positive aspect, the end and content," Hegel writes, which "gives significance to the spiritedness" of courageous actions. "Robbers and murderers bent on crime as their end, adventurers pursuing ends planned to suit their own whims, etc., these too have spirit enough to risk their lives." Because their ends are either malicious or unworthy, the mettle of a brigand and even the courage of a knight do not seem to Hegel to be true forms of courage.

According to Kant, "intelligence, wit, judgement, and other talents of the mind, however they be named, or courage, resolution, perseverance, as qualities of temperament, are undoubtedly good and desirable in many respects; but these gifts of nature may also become extremely bad and mischievous if the will which is to make use of them, and which, therefore, constitutes what is called *character,* is not good." If a good will is necessary to make courage virtuous, then the behavior of a scoundrel may look courageous, but it can only be a counterfeit. "Without the principles of a good will," such things as the ability to face dangers or to bear hardships, Kant thinks, "may become extremely bad . . . The coolness of a villain," he adds, "not only makes him far more dangerous, but also makes him more abominable in our eyes than he would have been without it."

It may still remain true that courage can take many forms according to the variety of objects which inspire fear, or according to the types of action which men find burdensome or painful. But if the truly courageous man must always be generally virtuous as well, then many of the appearances of courage do not spring from genuine virtue. The conception of virtue as a habit adds the criterion of a settled disposition: even the habitual coward may perform a single courageous act. Nor should courage be attributed to those who by freak of temperament are utterly fearless. The merit of virtue—overcoming fear—cannot be claimed by them.

IN THE GREAT political books, especially those of antiquity, the place of courage in the state and in the training of citizens receives particular attention. The constitutions of Crete and Sparta seem to make courage the only essential virtue for the citizen.

Plutarch, in his life of Lycurgus, shows how "the city was a sort of camp." The training and education of all was directed to military valor. "Their very songs had a life and spirit in them that inflamed and possessed men's minds with an enthusiasm and ardour for action . . . the subject always serious and moral; most usually, it was in praise of such men as had died in defence of their country, or in derision of those that had been cowards; the former they declared happy and glorified; the life of the latter they described as most miserable and abject." The result was, according to Plutarch, that "they were the only people in the world to whom war gave repose."

Both Plato and Aristotle criticize the constitutions of Crete and Sparta for making war the end of the state and exalting courage, which is only a part, above "the whole of virtue." Courage must be joined with the other virtues to make a man good, not only as a citizen but as a man. "Justice, temperance, and wisdom," says the Athenian Stranger in the *Laws,* "when united with courage are better than courage only."

Furthermore, military courage is not even the whole of courage. While recognizing the need for it, Plato thinks that a wise statesman would put it in its proper place, if men are to be trained to be good citizens, not merely good soldiers. Arguing that no sound legislator would order "peace for the sake of war, and not war for the sake of peace," the Athenian Stranger suggests that a broader conception of courage than the Cretans and Spartans seem to have would recognize its use, not only in external warfare, but in the tasks of peace—in the struggles to lead a good life and build a good society. "What is there," he asks Megillus the Spartan and Cleinias the Cretan, "which makes your citizens equally brave against pleasure and pain, conquering what they ought to conquer, and superior to the enemies who are most dangerous and nearest home?"

Nevertheless, through the centuries the type of courage which the poets and historians celebrate has been the bravery of men who put their very lives in jeopardy for their fellowmen—the courage of the citizen doing his duty, or, what is still more spectacular, of the soldier confronting his enemy. This fact among others is one reason why many writers, from the Greeks to Hegel, have found a moral stimulus in war; or, like James, have sought for its moral equivalent. On this point they are answered not merely by those who see only degradation in war, but also by the many expressions of the insight that peace can have its heroes too.

14

Custom and Convention

INTRODUCTION

THE contrast between the artificial and the natural is generally understood in terms of the contribution which man does or does not make to the origin or character of a thing. Works of art are man-made. The artificial is somehow humanly caused or contrived. The contrast between the natural and the conventional or customary involves the same point of difference. Though customs are not, in the strict sense, *made* by man, as are works of art, they do grow only as the result of the kind of acts which men perform voluntarily rather than instinctively. Similarly, conventions, like contracts, are social arrangements or agreements into which men enter voluntarily.

The fundamental notions with which this chapter deals are thus seen to be closely related to ideas and distinctions treated in the chapters on ART and NATURE. For example, the distinction between human action and production, or doing and making, helps us to understand how the conventional and the artificial differ from one another as opposites of the natural. Art involves voluntary making. Customs result from voluntary doing. In both cases, the distinction between the voluntary and the instinctive—the latter representing the natural—seems to be presupposed.

A third term—habit—is traditionally associated with the consideration of the voluntary and the instinctive. Like these others, it seems to have a critical bearing on the discussion of custom and art. Aristotle, for example, conceives art as an intellectual virtue, that is, a habit of mind, an acquired skill. For Hume the customary and the habitual are almost the same. Whether they are to be identified or only connected causally, the relation of habit to custom not only throws some light on the nature of custom but also calls our attention to the fact that the words "custom" and "convention" cannot be treated simply as synonyms.

In the tradition of the great books, the word "convention" has at least two meanings, in only one of which is it synonymous with "custom." When "convention" is used to signify habitual social practices, it is, for the most part, interchangeable with "custom." In this significance, the notion of convention, like that of custom, is an extension of the idea of habit. What habit is in the behavior of the individual, customary or conventional conduct is in the behavior of the social group.

The other meaning of "convention" does not connote the habitual in social behavior but stresses rather the voluntary as opposed to the instinctive origin of social institutions, arrangements, or practices. For example, different sorts of family organization are conventional in the sense that at different times or in different communities men have set up their domestic arrangements in different ways. In each case they tend to perpetuate the particular institutions which they or their ancestors originated. Whatever is conventional about social institutions might have been otherwise, if men had seen fit to invent and adopt different schemes for the organization of their social life. This indicates the connection between the two senses of the word "convention," for all customs are conventional in origin, and all conventions become customary when perpetuated.

THE FACT THAT men can depart from, as well as abide by, their conventions—that they can transgress as well as conform to custom—

seems to indicate that custom and convention belong to the sphere of human freedom. Yet there is also a sense in which custom is a constraining force, which reduces the tendency of individuals to differ from one another, and which has the effect of molding them alike and regimenting their lives. All the great novelists and playwrights in this set—notably Austen, George Eliot, Balzac, Cervantes, Dickens, Twain, Dostoevsky, Ibsen, Cather, Conrad, Chekhov, O'Neill—tell stories in which the leading characters are embroiled in conflicts with customs and conventions.

The repressive effect of custom can be seen, according to Freud, in the neurotic disorders from which men suffer when their instinctive impulses come into conflict with "accepted custom." Discussing the influence of custom upon the developing individual, he says that "its ordinances, frequently too stringent, exact a great deal from him, much self-restraint, much renunciation of instinctual gratification." It becomes, therefore, one of the aims of psychoanalytic therapy to release the individual from his bondage to custom, or at least to make him conscious of the way in which certain desires have been submerged or distorted, and his whole personality shaped, by the constraints which the mores and taboos of the tribe have imposed upon him.

Considered in relation to society, custom also seems to exercise a conservative, if not repressive effect. Established customs tend to resist change. They are sometimes thought to impede progress. But to the extent that they conserve the achievements of the past, they may be indispensable to progress because they provide the substance of what we call "tradition." A passage in Francis Bacon's *Advancement of Learning* illustrates these apparently contrary effects of custom.

Overemphasis upon either antiquity or novelty seems to Bacon a disease of learning, or an obstacle to its advancement. "Antiquity envieth there should be new additions," he writes, "and novelty cannot be content to add but it must deface." If custom tends to support antiquity against novelty, it may also encourage inventions or discoveries which genuinely enhance the tradition without defacing it. "Antiquity deserveth that reverence," Bacon says, "that men should make a stand thereupon and discover what is the best way; but when the discovery is well taken, then to make progression." As the preserver of antiquity, custom thus appears to afford a basis for progress.

One other fact about customs which most commentators from Herodotus to Montaigne, Freud, Weber, Frazer, and Lévi-Strauss, have observed is their variety and variability. Customs differ from time to time, and from place to place. But this diversity and variation in custom does not necessarily mean that no uniformity at all exists in the actions of men. "Were there no uniformity in human actions," Hume points out, it would be impossible "to collect any general observations concerning mankind." At least enough uniformity is found, in his opinion, for it to be "universally acknowledged that human nature remains still the same." To whatever extent human behavior is purely natural or instinctive, it is common to all members of the species, and does not, like customary conduct, vary remarkably from one part of the human race to another, or from generation to generation.

"The more we know about customs in different parts of the world," Dewey writes, "the more we learn how much manners differ from place to place and time to time . . . The particular form a convention takes has nothing fixed and absolute about it. But the existence of some form of convention is not itself a convention. It is a uniform attendant of all social relationships. At the very least, it is the oil which prevents or reduces friction."

The diversity and variation of customs seems therefore to be of their essence and to show that they are both man-made and voluntary in origin. "If they were not devices of men," Augustine writes, "they would not be different in different nations, and could not be changed among particular nations." The distinction between nature and convention can be formulated, therefore, partly in terms of the contrast between the constant and the variable, and partly in terms of the difference between the instinctive and the voluntary.

The early Greeks had an apt way of expressing this. As Aristotle phrases their insight, they referred to the natural as "that which everywhere has the same force and does not exist by people's thinking this or that," as, for example, "fire burns both here and in Persia." The conventional and those things which are "not by nature but by human enactment are not everywhere the same." The laws of Persia differ from the laws of Greece, and in Greece or in Persia, they change from time to time.

THE VARIABILITY of custom in contrast to the constancy or uniformity of nature puts the distinction between nature and convention at the service of the skeptic. One form of the skeptical attack upon natural law, universal moral standards, and the objectivity of truth or beauty consists in making custom the only measure of the acceptability of human actions or judgments. To say, for example, as Hume does, that the connection which the mind seems to make between cause and effect is based on custom rather than reason, has the skeptical effect which Hume intends. It substitutes the arbitrary for the rational. It dispossesses reason as a source of either the validity or the intelligibility of our conclusions concerning cause and effect.

As the chapters on KNOWLEDGE and OPINION indicate, the skeptical argument takes other forms. The reduction of all human judgments to opinion makes the differences between men, in either action or thought, unresolvable by argument or debate. One opinion can predominate over another only by force or by the weight of numbers. When it predominates by weight of numbers, it prevails by custom or convention. It is the opinion which the majority have agreed upon at a given time or place. To settle every controversy about what men should think or do by counting heads is to hold that everything is a matter of opinion and purely conventional.

Whether the skeptic reduces everything to opinion or to convention, he achieves the same effect. What he means by calling everything an "opinion" or a "convention" is equally inimical to reason. In either case, the willful or arbitrary is enthroned in reason's place and only force can be finally decisive. The two ideas—opinion and convention—

seem to be corollaries of one another. Both imply a kind of relativity. Opinion normally suggests relativity to the individual, custom or convention relativity to the social group. Either may be involved in the origin of the other. The individual may form his opinions under the pressure of prevailing customs of thought or action; the customary beliefs or practices of a society or culture may, and usually do, result from opinions which have come to prevail.

The Greek Sophists, we learn from the dialogues of Plato, appealed to the distinction between nature and convention and to the distinction between knowledge and opinion in exactly the same way. They used the notions of opinion and convention with equal force in their efforts to question absolute standards of conduct and the objectivity or universality of truth. The most familiar of all the sophistic sayings—the remark attributed to Protagoras that "man is the measure of all things"— is interpreted by both Plato and Aristotle to mean that what men wish to think or do determines *for them* what is true or right. Man's will governs his reason, and convention, or the agreement of individual wills, decides what is acceptable to the group.

In the *Gorgias*, which is named after another of the leading Sophists of the day, Plato puts into the mouth of Callicles the sophistic position that there is no law or standard of justice except the rule of the stronger. Insisting that "convention and nature are generally at variance with one another," Callicles attempts to show that all of Socrates' efforts to discover an absolute standard of justice come to naught, because he cannot help but resort "to the popular and vulgar notions of right, which are not natural, but conventional."

As they appear in Plato's dialogues, the Sophists are obviously impressed by the kind of information which fills *The History* of Herodotus—information about the great diversity of human beliefs and practices which anyone could discover for himself if he traveled, as Herodotus did, from people to people, observing their institutions and collecting their legends. Herodotus himself does not explicitly draw the skeptical conclusion, yet his own suspended judgment on many matters betokens a turn of mind made by the impact of contrary opinions and conflicting customs.

In the Hellenistic period when the main stream of Greek philosophy divides into a number of Roman schools of thought, the skeptical position receives what is perhaps its fullest and most explicit statement. But in the writings of Lucian and Pyrrhon, to take two examples, it is not so much the conflict of customs as it is what Lucian calls "the warfare of creeds," which occasions universal doubt. Yet whatever the source of doubt, Pyrrhonism states the traditional denials of the skeptic in their most extreme form. The senses are entirely untrustworthy. Reason is both impotent and self-deceiving. Men possess no knowledge or science. No truth is self-evident; none can be demonstrated.

THE CRITICAL TEMPER of the Greek Sophists, and of an observer of men and manners like Herodotus, reappears later in the questionings of Montaigne—sharpened somewhat, perhaps, by his acquaintance with the Roman skeptics. In his case, perhaps more than any other, it is the implications of custom which, everywhere expatiated on in his *Essays,* give them their skeptical tone. Not himself a traveler in distant parts, Montaigne traverses the world of time and space by reading. He becomes conversant with the strange customs of the aborigines and of the Orient through the reports of returned explorers. He culls from the historians and geographers of antiquity every difference in custom which their books set forth as fact or fable.

Montaigne's insatiable appetite for collecting and comparing customs is not an aimless fascination on his part with the spectacle of human variety. It steadfastly leads him to the conclusion which is for him the only one possible. Since every belief or practice can be paired with its opposite in the customs of some other time or place, no belief or practice can demand unqualified or universal assent. "There is nothing," he writes, "that custom will not or cannot do; and with reason Pindar calls her . . . the queen and empress of the world."

To say, as Montaigne does, that "the taste of good and evil depends in large part on the opinion we have of them" and that "each man is as well or as badly off as he thinks he is," amounts to saying that all moral judgments are matters of opinion, either individual or customary in origin. Beauty, too, is a matter of taste. "We imagine its forms to suit our fancy," according to Montaigne. As may be seen in the chapter on BEAUTY, Montaigne assembles an abundance of evidence to show that standards of beauty vary with different peoples. The tastes or preferences of one group are as unaccountable as they are frequently revolting to another.

Even in the field of speculative thought about the nature of things, Montaigne regards the things men hold to be true as nothing more than prevailing opinions—the cultural conventions of a time or place. "We have no other test of truth and reason," he declares, "than the example and pattern of the opinions and customs of the country we live in. *There* is always the perfect religion, the perfect government, the perfect and accomplished manners in all things."

Of all human deceptions or impostures, none is worse than that which flows from a man's unwillingness to qualify every remark with the admission that *this is the way it seems to me.* In Montaigne's eyes, "there is no more notable folly in the world" than the failure to recognize that we reduce truth and falsity "to the measure of our capacity and competence." When new ideas or the strange beliefs of others at first seem incredible simply because they are not our own, "we shall find that it is rather familiarity than knowledge that takes away their strangeness." For his own part, Montaigne makes his "motto" the question, "What do I know?" This, he says, sums up his Pyrrhonian philosophy.

ACCORDING TO the modern social scientist who claims that custom is the ultimate standard of conduct and that it provides the only criterion of moral judgment, no questions can be raised about the goodness or evil of particular customs. The customs of one people cannot be judged by another, at least not objectively or impartially, for those who judge must do so on the basis of their own customs. Since there is no arbiter above conflicting customs to say which is right, a particular custom has validity only for the group in which it prevails. Within that social group the character or conduct of its individual members is measured by conformity to the prevailing customs.

"Among most primitive peoples," writes Lévi-Strauss, "it is very difficult to obtain a moral justification or a rational explanation for any custom or institution . . . Even in our own society, table manners, social etiquette, fashions of dress, and many of our moral, political, and religious attitudes are scrupulously observed by everyone, although their real origin and function are not often critically examined."

The *descriptive* science of sociology or comparative ethnology thus tends to replace the *normative* science of ethics—or moral philosophy. The only scientifically answerable questions about human conduct take the form of "How *do* men behave?" or "How *have* they acted individually or in groups?" but not "How *should* they?" The study of morality, as in William Graham Sumner's *Folkways,* becomes a study of the mores—how the customs which measure conduct develop and dominate; or, as in the writings of Freud, it becomes a study of how the individual is psychologically formed or deformed by the mores of his tribe and culture, according to the way in which the growing child reacts to the pressures which the community imposes through parental discipline.

With these views, many philosophers and theologians, both ancient and modern, take issue. But their opposing doctrine seldom goes so far as to deny that morality has certain conventional aspects. In arguing that there are "no innate practical principles," Locke, for example, like Montaigne, cites instances of contradictory customs to show that "there is scarce that principle of morality to be named, or rule of virtue to be thought on . . . which is not, somewhere or other, slighted and condemned by the general fashion of whole societies of men, governed by practical opinions and rules of living quite opposite to others."

But Locke does not leave this observation of the diversity of customs unqualified. He goes on to assert that "though perhaps, by the different temper, education, fashion, maxims, or interest of different sorts of men, it fell out, that what was thought praiseworthy in one place, escaped not censure in another; and so in different societies, virtues and vices were changed: yet, as to the main, they for the most part kept the same everywhere. For, since nothing can be more natural than to encourage with esteem and reputation that wherein every one finds his advantage, and to blame and discountenance the contrary; it is no wonder that esteem and discredit, virtue and vice, should, in a great measure, everywhere correspond with the unchangeable rule of right and wrong, which the law of God hath established . . . Even in the corruption of manners, the true boundaries of the law of nature, which ought to be the rule of virtue and vice, were pretty well preferred."

For Locke, then, as for many others, there appear to be, underlying the variety of customs, moral principles of universal validity that draw their truth from the nature of man which represents a constant and common factor throughout the diversity of cultures. Accordingly, it would seem to follow that just as habits are modifications of instinct or developments of the individual's native capacities for action, so customs are conventional elaborations of what is natural to man as a social animal. On this theory, the conventional cannot be understood except by reference to the natural, *i.e.,* the nature of man or society.

THE VIEW THAT conventions have a natural basis is most readily exemplified by Aristotle's theory of natural and legal (or conventional) justice, and by the teaching of Aquinas concerning natural and positive law. For the Greeks the legal and the conventional are almost identical, so that it is a kind of justice rather than a kind of law which Aristotle calls "natural." Roman philosophers like Cicero, and Roman jurists like Gaius and Ulpian, make what seems to be an equivalent distinction in terms of law rather than justice. In his analysis, Aquinas follows the Latin, not the Greek vocabulary.

The Roman system of jurisprudence, Gibbon tells us, distinguished between those laws which are "positive institutions" and those which "reason prescribes, the laws of nature and nations." The former are man-made—the "result of custom and prejudice." This holds true of both written and unwritten laws, although only the unwritten precepts are now usually called "customary laws." These customary laws are *positive* in the sense that they are humanly instituted or enacted—posited by the will of the legislator rather than merely discovered by the reason of the philosopher. They are *conventional* in the sense that they represent some voluntary agreement on the part of the members of the community they govern, whether that consist in obeying the edicts of the emperor or in giving consent to the enactments of the senate.

So far as it is conventional, the law of one community differs from another; and within the history of a single community, the positive law changes from time to time. But such bodies of law, "however modified by accident or custom," the Roman jurists, Gibbon says, conceived as "drawn from the rule of right." The fact that "reason prescribes" this rule was their explanation of certain common elements which all bodies of positive law seem to contain.

The principles underlying all codes of civil law, whether discovered directly by reason or drawn inductively, as Grotius later suggests, from the comparative study of diverse legal systems, comprise the precepts of what the Romans, and later Aquinas, call "natural law." Thus these writers seem to reaffirm, though in somewhat different language, Aristotle's point that what is naturally just is the same for all men everywhere and always, while the laws of Greece and Persia represent diverse conventional determinations of the universal principles of justice.

The theory of natural right and natural law, as expressed in the writings of Hobbes, Locke, and Kant, as well as in the ancient and medieval tradition, is, of course, more fully treated in the chapters on JUSTICE and LAW. But one example of the distinction between natural and conventional justice may be instructive here.

Aquinas conceives positive rules as "determinations" of, rather than "deductions" from, natural law. He treats such precepts as "Thou shalt not kill" and "Thou shalt not steal" as conclusions that reason can draw deductively from the first principle of natural law, which is sometimes stated in the form of the command: *Do good, harm no one, and render to each his own.* Because these precepts are the prescriptions of reason rather than enactments of the state, they can be interpreted as declaring that murder and larceny are always and everywhere unjust. But what sort of killing and taking of what is not one's own shall be defined as murder and theft; and how offenders shall be tried, judged, and punished—these are matters which natural justice or the precepts of natural law leave open for determination by the positive laws of each community, according to its own constitution and its local customs.

The theory thus exemplified, of the relation between conventional and natural justice, or between positive and natural law, applies to moral rules and ethical standards generally. For the same reason that a positive law which violates natural justice cannot be called "just" even though it is harmonious with the customs of the community, so no rule of conduct, however much it represents prevailing custom, can be approved as morally right if it violates the right as reason sees it. The defenders of natural law, which is also sometimes called "the law of reason," proclaim the existence of an absolute standard, above the diversity and conflict of customs, by which their soundness is measured.

Conflicting ethical doctrines raise many issues concerning what it is right for men to do or good for them to seek; but the moralists at least agree that morality is based on reason or nature. For them the facts of human nature or the intuitions of reason will ultimately decide the points in issue. However far apart Plato and Aristotle, Aquinas and Hegel, Kant and J. S. Mill may be in their conceptions or analyses of the right and the good, they stand together, at least negatively, on the question of how their disputes can be resolved: *not* by appealing to the mores of the tribe, *not* by looking to the conventions of the community as a measure, *not* by letting the customs of the majority decide.

The deepest of all moral issues therefore exists between those who think that morality somehow derives from nature or reason and those who, like the ancient Sophists or Montaigne or Freud, find its source in custom and convention. According to the side a man takes on this issue, he does or does not believe it possible to discover standards independent of custom, thereby to judge whether customs are good, bad, or indifferent. On one belief, public manners are conventional determinations of moral principles or they are sometimes violations of them, just as positive laws are either determinations or violations of natural law. On the other belief, the individual may be approved or condemned for conforming to or transgressing the manners or mores of his group; but those manners or mores, whether they are liked or disliked by the individual, are above any tenable, objective criticism.

The controversy in jurisprudence and morality between the naturalists or rationalists who appeal to man's nature or reason, and the positivists who hold that human customs cannot be appealed from, parallels a controversy in the theory of knowledge or science. The parallel issue, considered at greater length in the chapters on HYPOTHESIS and PRINCIPLE, can be stated by the question whether the foundation of science—even of such sciences as logic and mathematics—consists of postulates or axioms.

Axioms, like the precepts of natural law, are supposed to have a universality derived from the nature of human reason. They are self-evident truths, compelling assent. Postulates, on the contrary, are like rules of positive law—voluntarily accepted assumptions which, when agreed upon by the experts in a certain science, become its conventional basis. In science as in law, the positivists recognize nothing beyond the agreement of men to determine what shall be *taken for granted* as true or just.

THE DIFFERENCE between nature and convention also enters into the traditional discussion of two of the most characteristic activities of man: speech and political association.

No one disputes whether the faculty of speech is natural to man. It is as natural for man to speak as for dogs to bark or birds to sing. But the question is whether any human language, having a certain vocabulary and syntax, is natural or conventional. The answer seems to be dictated at once by the facts of the matter.

Human languages exist or have existed in great number and diversity, and those which still endure have gradually developed and are undoubtedly subject to further change. Hence, according to the traditional understanding of the natural and the conventional, these various tongues must represent conventional languages—originally invented by this human group or that, perpetuated by custom, altered by the conventions of usage. In contrast, the expressive sounds instinctively made by other animals show themselves to be natural by the fact that they are common to all members of a species and do not change as long as the species endures.

Nevertheless, as the chapter on LANGUAGE indicates, the writers of the great books consider the hypothesis of a natural human language. The Old Testament story of the Tower of Babel is sometimes interpreted as implying the existence of one language for all men before God confounded their speech and diversified their tongues. The story of Adam's giving names to the various species of plants and animals in the Garden of Eden is also cited by those who think there can be natural as well as conventional signs. In Plato's *Cratylus* the attempt is made to discover the natural names for things, or at least to discern some natural basis for the words of a conventional language like Greek.

These who reject the hypothesis of a single human language from which all others have developed by diversification, or who regard a purely natural language as impossible in the very nature of the case, sometimes acknowledge the possibility of certain common elements—principles of syntax, if not words—present in all human languages. The discovery of the common rules of speech was the object of the speculative grammarians in the Middle Ages, and of those who, like Antoine Arnauld and others, later tried to formulate a "universal grammar." On their view, all languages, even if they are conventional as written or spoken, may have the same natural basis in the fact that they are all used to express what men can naturally perceive or think.

As in the case of language, so in the case of society, the question is whether the family and the state are wholly natural, wholly conventional, or partly one and partly the other—their institutions being erected by choice and custom upon a natural basis. And as in the case of language, here too the great books do not, for the most part, give either of the extreme answers. They do not say that the state is entirely natural, that it is the expression of human instinct as the beehive and the ant mound are instinctive formations. Nor do they say that the state is completely conventional, that it comes into existence *only* as the result of voluntary association on the part of men contracting to live together in a political community.

While Aristotle says that "man is by nature a political animal," and that the state is, therefore, "a creation of nature," he also distinguishes between the ways in which men and other animals are gregarious. Unlike the association of animals, which he attributes to instinct, the society of men rests on reason and speech. "Man is the only animal," he writes, "endowed with the gift of speech ... intended to set forth the expedient and the inexpedient, and therefore likewise the just and the unjust." Because of these things, cities differ from one another, as beehives or ant mounds do not.

The diversity of states represents for Aristotle a deliberate inventiveness on the part of reason and an exercise of free choice—certainly insofar as states are politically constituted, each with its own constitution. Aristotle's remark that while "a social impulse is implanted in all men by nature," yet "he who first founded the state was the greatest of benefactors," may look self-contradictory; but its two parts can be read as quite consistent with one another, if the first is taken as signifying the natural basis of the state (in a social impulse), and the second as saying that a certain convention (a constitution) is required to

shape that impulse before any state is actually established.

As Aristotle is sometimes interpreted to uphold the theory that the state is entirely natural, so Hobbes, Locke, and Rousseau are often read as maintaining the opposite extreme—that it is entirely conventional. The extreme interpretation is based on the sharpness with which each of them distinguishes between men living in a state of nature and in a state of civil society.

Though they differ among themselves in their exposition of these two conditions of man, they seem to agree that for men to pass from a state of nature, whether hypothetical or historical, in which men live in anarchy or at least in isolation, it is necessary for them to enter into a contract or compact with one another. Since this social contract is the original, or originating, convention by which the commonwealth or civil society is established, it would seem to follow that, on their view, the state is entirely a product of convention, and in no way natural.

Yet Hobbes, Locke, and Rousseau, each in his own way, add a qualification in favor of the naturalness of the state, just as Aristotle qualifies his remark that "the state is a creation of nature" by praising the man "who first founded the state." The exponents of the social contract theory of the state's origin find in the nature of man or in his reason an instinct, a need, or a law which impels or bids him to seek association with others for the sake of advantages which he cannot enjoy apart from civil society. This suffices to affirm the existence of a natural basis for the convention or contract which establishes the state.

These apparently opposed theories of what is natural and what conventional about the state thus appear to approach each other, though one starts from an emphasis on the state's naturalness, the other from its conventional origin. The whole problem is, of course, further treated in the chapters on FAMILY and STATE; but one point which the foregoing discussion suggests receives special consideration in still another chapter. The point concerns the relation between the idea of a constitution and the idea of a social contract. Both are conceived as the basic or primary convention which establishes the state. The question whether the two ideas are interchangeable or only analogous is examined in the chapter on CONSTITUTION.

CUSTOM IS BOTH a cause and an effect of habit. The habits of the individual certainly reflect the customs of the community in which he lives; and in turn, the living customs of any social group get their vitality from the habits of its members. A custom which does not command general compliance is as dead as a language no longer spoken or a law no longer observed. This general compliance consists in nothing more than a certain conformity among the habits of individuals.

The continuity between custom and statute as parts or phases of the positive law rests upon the relation of both to habit. "Custom," according to Aquinas, "has the force of a law, abolishes law, and is the interpreter of law" precisely because it operates through the habits of the people. "By repeated external actions," such as produce a custom, "the inward movement of the will and the conceptions of the reason are most revealingly declared," and, according to Aquinas, "all law proceeds from the reason and will of the lawgiver." The law which a prince or a people enacts, to become effective as social regulation, must develop a particular habit of conduct in many individuals. Then and only then does a new enactment obtain the full force of law. To remain effective it must continue to have the support of "the customs of the country."

Without that support it may be a law on the books but not in practice, for the authority of a law cannot long prevail against a contrary custom, except through a degree of coercion so oppressive as to produce rebellion. That is also why the customary or unwritten rule—usually the primitive form of positive law—is less flexible, less amenable to change or modification. Custom is a conservative factor. "There is nothing more difficult to take in hand," writes Machiavelli, nothing "more perilous to conduct, or more uncertain in its success, than to take the lead in the introduction of a new order of things. The innovator

has for enemies all those who have done well under the old conditions, and lukewarm defenders in those who may do well under the new."

Just as custom may either support the written law or render it ineffective, so custom works in opposite directions as a social force. It is both a factor of cohesion and of division among men—a cause of what is called "social solidarity" and a barrier separating peoples from one another. When the Athenians refuse to ally themselves with the Persians, they chide the Spartans, according to Herodotus, for fearing that they "might make terms with the barbarian." For all the gold on earth, they tell the Spartan envoys, they could not "take part with the Medes." To do so would betray "our common brotherhood with the Greeks, our common language, the altars and sacrifices of which we all partake, and the common character which we bear."

The barbarians or the gentiles—to use the traditional names for aliens or foreigners—are excluded by a social, not a geographic, boundary line, the line drawn between those who share a set of customs and all outsiders. When the stranger is assimilated, the group does not adopt him; he adopts the customs of the community. The very word "community" implies a multitude having much in common. More important than the land they occupy are the customs they share.

The Federalists, advocating the political union of the thirteen American states, could urge its feasibility on the ground that a social union already existed. "Providence has been pleased to give this one connected country," Jay writes, "to one united people—a people descended from the same ancestors, speaking the same language, professing the same religion, attached to the same principles of government, very similar in their manners and customs."

Those who today advocate world federal union cannot similarly point to a world society already in existence. They can only hope that if the separate states were to unite politically, the social cohesion of the world's people might subsequently develop as a result of the fostering of universal customs by universal law.

15

Definition

INTRODUCTION

DEFINITION has been variously defined in the tradition of the great books. These diverse conceptions of what a definition is raise many issues.

At one extreme, writers like Hobbes look upon definition as nothing more than an attempt to say what a word means—how it has been or is being used. At the other, writers like Aquinas regard definition as that act of the mind by which it expresses the nature of a thing or formulates its essence.

In one technical view associated with the name of Aristotle, to define is to state the genus and differentia by which the species of a thing is constituted. In another theory of definition advanced by Locke and others, any combination of traits which distinguishes one class or kind of thing from another defines the character common to all members of that class. In still another view, to be found in Spinoza, definition consists in giving the cause or genesis of a thing, in saying how the thing originated or was produced.

Sometimes definition through causes employs the final rather than the efficient or productive cause, and characterizes the thing by the end it naturally serves. And sometimes, as with William James, definitions simply express the purposes or interests which we have in mind when we classify things to suit ourselves.

In the tradition of the liberal arts of grammar, rhetoric, and logic, these various conceptions of definition are connected with controversies concerning the power and activity of the human mind, the relation of language to thought, the structure of science or, more generally, the nature of knowledge, and the constitution of reality, with particular reference to the existence of universals and individuals and their relation to one another.

These connections appear in the thought of Aristotle and Spinoza, Hobbes and Locke, Aquinas and James. Their views of the way in which definitions should be constructed or their conceptions of the function of definitions determine and reflect lines of agreement and opposition on many other matters. The use of definitions in the great works of mathematics and natural science—by Euclid, Descartes, Galileo, Newton, Lavoisier, and Darwin—tends to exemplify now one, now another, theory of definition. Modern discussions of the nature of science and mathematics, especially discussions influenced by the development of mathematical logic—from Whitehead, Russell, and Dewey—focus critical attention on the nature and role of definitions.

MANY OTHER chapters provide an illuminating context for topics discussed in this one, especially the chapters on LANGUAGE and LOGIC, IDEA, PRINCIPLE and REASONING, PHILOSOPHY and SCIENCE, and TRUTH. Though the issues concerning definition cannot be resolved apart from this larger context of controversy about the mind, reality, and knowledge, we can nevertheless formulate these issues in isolation. But in doing so we ought to bear in mind that they can be more readily understood in proportion as they are seen in the light of other relevant considerations.

There is, first of all, the question about the object of definition. What is being defined when men make or defend definitions? This question broadens into the problem of nominal as opposed to real definitions. That is a complex problem which raises a number of further questions. Are all definitions arbitrary, expressing the conventions of our speech or the particular purpose we have in mind when we classify things? Or do some, if not all, definitions express the real natures of the things defined? Do they classify things according to natural kinds which have reality apart from our mind and its interests?

These issues are in turn related to the issue concerning the limits of definitions and its ultimate principles—whether all things, or only some, are definable, and whether the indefinable terms, without which definition is itself impossible, can be arbitrarily chosen or must always be terms of a certain sort. The sense in which definitions may be true or false and the sense in which they cannot be either have a bearing on all these issues; and through them all run the divergent conceptions of how definitions can or should be constructed.

WHEN IN THE course of argument one man dismisses the opinion of another by saying, "That is just a matter of definition," the usual implication is that the rejected opinion has no truth apart from the way in which the man who proposed it uses words. He may even be accused of begging the question, of framing definitions which implicitly contain the conclusion he subsequently draws from them.

The underlying supposition here seems to be expressed by Pascal when, in his essay "On Geometrical Demonstration," he asserts that "there is great freedom of definition and definitions are never subject to contradiction, for nothing is more permissible than to give whatever name we please to a thing we have clearly pointed out." He calls "true definitions" those which are "arbitrary, permissible, and geometrical." The only restriction he would place upon our freedom to make definitions is that "we must be careful not to take advantage of our freedom to impose names by giving the same name to two different things." And even this case, he claims, is permissible "if we avoid confusion by not extending the consequences of one to the other."

If we are free to make whatever definitions we please, it would seem to follow that def-initions cannot be matters of argument; and differences of opinion which result from differences in definition would seem to be irreconcilable by any appeal to reason or to fact.

Such a conception of definition as verbal does not seem to prevent Hobbes from holding that definitions are first principles or foundations of science. "In Geometry (which is the only science that it hath pleased God hitherto to bestow on mankind), men begin," he writes, "at settling the signification of their words; which settling of significations, they call *Definitions;* and place them in the beginning of their reckoning." This shows, Hobbes thinks, "how necessary it is for any man that aspires to true knowledge to examine the definitions of former authors; and either to correct them, where they are negligently set down; or to make them himself. For the errors of definitions multiply themselves, according as the reckoning proceeds."

For Hobbes, then, definition is verbal; yet definitions can also be true or false, and on the truth of definitions depends the distinction between knowledge and opinion. "In the right definitions of names," he says, "lies the first use of speech; which is the acquisition of science." Only when discourse "begins with the definitions of words" can it reach conclusions that have the character of knowledge. "If the first ground of such discourse be not definitions . . . then the end or conclusion is opinion."

Hobbes accurately reports the nature of geometry when he says that in that science definitions serve as principles in reasoning or proof. The words "by definition" mark one of the steps in many Euclidean proofs. Descartes and Spinoza, proceeding in the geometrical manner, place definitions at the head of their works as ultimate principles to be used in validating their conclusions. But, unlike Hobbes, these writers do not seem to regard their definitions as merely verbal. Euclid goes further, as we shall presently see, and offers what amounts to proofs of his definitions, or at least of their geometrical reality. Aristotle and Aquinas certainly take the position not only that definitions are principles, but also that definitions themselves are capable of being demonstrated. But they complicate the matter by insisting that definitions are neither true nor false, since, as Aristotle says, they do not involve "the assertion of something concerning something."

At least two questions seem to be involved in this familiar dispute about the arguability of definitions and their role in argumentation. To avoid confusion, they should be kept distinct. One is the question of the truth and falsity of definitions. It should be separated from, even though it is related to, the other question about whether all definitions are nominal, *i.e.,* concerned only with assigning meanings to the words by which we name things. To understand what is involved in this second question, it may be helpful to consider the relation of words, thoughts, and things in the process of definition.

A DICTIONARY IS supposed to contain definitions. It does in part—insofar as the meaning of any words which are not synonyms for the word in question. The combined meanings of these other words determine the meanings of the word being defined.

For example, one definition of the word "brother" is "a male relative, the son of the same parents or parent." Another is "a male member of a religious order." These two definitions give different meanings for the same word. The dictionary is here recording two ways in which, as a matter of historical fact, the word has been used. It has been and can be used in still other ways. No one of these definitions can be called "right" and the others "wrong."

Dictionary definitions seem to be verbal and arbitrary in a number of ways. That the word "brother" should carry any of the meanings which the dictionary records is an accident of English usage. It is arbitrary that that particular sound or mark should be the name for a male relative who is the son of the same parents. It would be equally arbitrary to restrict the meaning of the word "brother" to any one of its definitions.

Nothing about a word limits the number of distinct meanings with which it can be used. As Locke says, "every man has so inviolable a liberty to make words stand for what ideas he pleases, that no one hath the power to make others have the same ideas in their minds that he has, when they use the same words that he does." A word is thus a conventional sound or mark, which can be given any meaning convention assigns to it. When that meaning is expressed *in other words,* we have a verbal definition, and such definitions are certainly nominal in this sense—that they state the meaning of a *name.*

But are they merely nominal? Are they entirely arbitrary? That this word should be used to name this thing is arbitrary, but that when it is so used a certain definition also applies may not be arbitrary. Among the several verbal definitions of a word, the one which applies in any particular case will depend upon the character of the thing which the word is used to name.

For example, if John and James are sons of the same parents, the name "brother" applies, but not with the same definition which is required for the application of the name to Mark and Matthew who, unrelated by blood, are members of the same monastic order. What the word "brother" is used to mean may be arbitrary, but when it is used now of John and James, and now of Mark and Matthew, it would be misapplied if it did not carry the appropriate definition. Which definition is appropriate in each case does not seem to be arbitrary, since that appropriateness depends not on our will but on the objective facts of the case—the actual relation of the persons called "brothers."

Precisely because the word is used to name a thing, the definition of the word *as so used* does more than state the meaning of the word. It states something about the character of the thing named. Definitions remain merely verbal only so long as the words they define are not actually used to name or to signify things in some way. Whenever a thing is named or signified, the definition which gives the meaning of the word must also signify something about the nature of the thing.

"In the natural order of ideas," writes Lavoisier, "the name of the class or genus is that which expresses a quality common to a great number of individuals; the names of the species, on the contrary, expresses a quality peculiar to certain individuals only. These distinctions are not, as some may imagine, merely metaphysical, but are established by Nature."

YET IT MAY BE said that the definition is still nominal, for it depends entirely on the meanings of the words which express it. For example, one definition of "brother" involves the meanings of such words as "male" and "relative," "son," "parent," and "same." If we were to look these words up in a dictionary, the definitions we found would involve the meanings of still other words, and so on in an endlessly circular fashion. Furthermore, we would find the account of certain words, such as "relative" and "same," somewhat unsatisfactory as definitions because the meaning of the defining words would immediately involve the meaning of the word to be defined. To say that "same" means "not other" or "not different" seems the same as saying "same" means "same." Yet we must know the meaning of "same," for otherwise we could not understand the meaning of "brother," in the definition of which the word "same" appears.

That some words seem to have indefinable meanings suggests that not all meanings are merely verbal or nominal, and that the meaning of every word cannot be found in the meanings of other words. In the Preface to his dictionary, Dr. Johnson observes that "as nothing can be proved but by supposing something intuitively known, and evident without proof, so nothing can be defined but by the use of words too plain to admit of definition." The circularity of the dictionary is thus avoided. When we trace meanings from one word to another, we finally come to words whose meanings we seem to understand immediately, or at least without reference to the meanings of other words.

Just as the arbitrary character of verbal definitions seems to be removed by the consideration of the things which words name or signify, so the purely nominal character of definitions seems to be removed by recourse to meanings which are understood without further verbal explanation—meanings which may in fact be incapable of such explanation.

NOT ALL WRITERS agree with Dr. Johnson. All of them would admit that some words must be left undefined in order to define others, but which shall be used as indefinable and which shall be defined is, in the opinion of some, a matter of choice. It is not something which can be determined by the order intrinsic to our ideas or meanings. The issue between the mathematical logicians who think that we are free to choose our primitive or indefinable terms, and those who, like Aquinas, think that certain terms, such as *being, same, one,* and *relation,* impose themselves upon our minds as principles, leaving us no choice, parallels the issue between the view that the principles of a science consist of postulates voluntarily assumed and the view that they are axiomatic or unavoidable.

Far from regarding such basic indefinable terms as clearest and most indisputable in meaning, Spinoza thinks that "these terms signify ideas in the highest degree confused." For him "the true definition of any one thing . . . expresses nothing but the nature of the thing defined." But to arrive at the true definition, it is necessary to discover the cause of the thing. For "every existing thing," he writes, "there is some certain cause by reason of which it exists." This cause "must either be contained in the nature itself and definition of the existing thing . . . or it must exist outside the thing." In the latter case, the definition of the thing always involves a statement of the external cause of its existence.

Accordingly, Spinoza rejects the traditional type of Aristotelian definition as purely subjective—a matter of individual memory and imagination. "Those who have more frequently looked with admiration upon the stature of men," he writes, "by the name *man* will understand an animal of erect stature, while those who have been in the habit of fixing their thoughts on something else will form another common image of men, describing man, for instance, as an animal capable of laughter, a biped without feathers, a rational animal, and so on; each person forming universal images of things according to the temperament of his own body."

However the issue between Spinoza and Aristotle is resolved, both seem to agree that more is involved in the process of definition than the statement of verbal equivalences. "We have a definition," Aristotle says, "not where we have a word and formula identical in meaning (for in that case all formulae or sets of words would be definitions)." The formula which is expressed in a phrase or combination of words must state the nature or essence of a thing, not just the meaning of a word. "The formula . . . in which the term itself is not present but its meaning is expressed, this," according to Aristotle, "is the formula of the essence of each thing" and, he adds, "there is an essence only of those things whose formula is a definition."

Even supposing the truth of these statements, which Hobbes or Locke certainly would question, the problem of real as opposed to nominal definition requires further examination. To explore the matter further, let us take two of the most famous definitions to be found in the great books. Both are definitions of man—"featherless biped" and "rational animal." As we have seen, these definitions must remain purely nominal—only stating the meaning of the word "man"—until that word is used to name some kind of thing. If, however, we apply the word "man" to existing entities which combine the characteristics of having two legs and lacking feathers, then "featherless biped" defines, not the word "man," but a class of real, that is, existing things. In addition to being nominal, the definition is now also real in the sense that the class or kind which it determines has existing members.

That animals exist may similarly be a fact of observation. But "animal" is only one of the two terms in the other nominal definition of "man." In order to make "rational animal" more than a nominal definition, it is necessary to verify the existence of animals which possess a certain characteristic, *rationality*, not possessed by all animals. If rationality in some degree belonged to all animals, then the word "man" (nominally defined by "rational ani-

mal") would be synonymous with "animal." But, unlike feathers, the presence or absence of which seems readily observable, the possession or lack of rationality is difficult to ascertain.

Here we face two possibilities. One is that we can never be sure that some existing animals are and some are not rational. Then the definition "rational animal" will never become real. It will always remain merely nominal, the statement of a possible meaning for "man," but one which we cannot employ when we apply the word to name any existing thing. The other possibility is that we can infer the existence of a special class of animals (distinguished by the possession of reason) from such evident facts as the activities of reading and writing, activities not performed by all animals. Then, members of the class defined having been found to exist, "rational animal" becomes a real definition of the beings to which we also arbitrarily assign the name "man."

THE PROCESS of verification by which a nominal is converted into a real definition can be regarded as a demonstration of a definition. Strictly speaking, it is not the definition which is thereby proved. It is rather a proposition in which the subject of the definition is affirmed to exist, or in which a subject already known to exist is said to have a certain definition. For example, it is not the definition "rational animal" which is proved, but the proposition "there exists an animal which differs from other animals in being rational," or the proposition "the real being which we call 'man' is both an animal and rational, and he alone is rational." If these propositions cannot be proved, "rational animal" remains a purely nominal definition.

That definitions are not as such either true or false is unaffected by the distinction between real and nominal definitions. The point is simply that a definition, which is always linguistically expressed by a phrase, never a sentence, neither affirms nor denies anything, and so cannot be either true or false. "Featherless biped" or "son of the same parents" makes no assertion about reality or existence.

Yet there is a special sense in which definitions can be true or false, which does have a bearing on the distinction between real and nominal definitions. Pascal suggests three alternatives with regard to the truth or falsity of definitions. "If we find it impossible," he writes, "it passes for false; if we demonstrate that it is true, it passes for a truth; and as long as it cannot be proved to be either possible or impossible, it is considered a fancy."

According to Aquinas, there are two ways in which a definition can be false. In one way, when the intellect applies "to one thing the definition proper to another; as that of a circle to a man. In another way, by composing a definition of parts which are mutually repugnant. A definition such as 'a four-footed rational animal' would be of this kind . . . for such a statement as 'some rational animals are four-footed' is false in itself."

But the truth or falsity of that statement can conceivably be argued, and therefore it is not so clear an example of a false definition as one which, in Pascal's terms, plainly represents an impossibility. Suppose someone offered "round square" as the nominal definition of "rectacycle." The phrase "round square" expresses a self-contradiction, and in consequence the definition is false. Its falsity is tantamount to the *impossibility* of there being any such figure as a *rectacycle* which has the definition proposed.

The truth of a definition—which is nothing more than its freedom from self-contradiction—is equivalent to the *possibility,* as opposed to the impossibility, of the thing defined. To call the definition "son of the same parents" or "featherless biped" *true* is to say that the words defined—"brother" or "man"—signify possible existences. In short, only those nominal definitions which are true can ever become real, and they become real only when the possibility they signify is actually known to be realized in existence.

Modern quantum mechanics introduces another consideration with regard to the truth and falsity of definitions. "The words 'position' and 'velocity' of an electron," Heisenberg tells us, "seemed perfectly well defined as to both their meaning and their possible connections, and in fact they were clearly defined concepts within the mathematical framework of Newtonian mechanics. But actually they were not well defined, as is seen from the relations of uncertainty. One may say that regarding their position in Newtonian mechanics they were well defined, but in their relation to nature they were not."

THE METHOD OF Euclid's *Elements* illustrates what is involved in the distinction between nominal and real definitions. Euclid defines certain geometrical figures, such as triangle, parallelogram, square. These definitions may appear to be free from contradiction, but that does not tell us whether they are more than nominal. The defined figures are possible, but the question is whether they exist in the space determined by Euclid's postulates.

To show that they do exist, Euclid undertakes to construct them according to his postulates which permit him the use of a straight edge and compass for purposes of construction. When in Proposition 1 Euclid proves that he can construct an equilateral triangle, he establishes the geometrical reality of the figure defined in Definition 20. A geometrical construction is thus seen to be what is called an "existence proof." It converts a nominal into a real definition. Figures which cannot be constructed must be postulated; as, for example, the straight line and the circle. Postulates 1 and 3 ask us to assume that a straight line can be drawn between any two points and that a circle can be described with any center and radius. These postulates give Definitions 4 and 15 their geometrical reality.

According to Poincaré, "*The axioms of geometry . . . are only definitions in disguise.* What, then, are we to think of the question: Is Euclidean geometry true? It has no meaning . . . One geometry cannot be more true than another; it can only be more convenient."

Though the method of construction is peculiar to geometry, the relation of definitions to proofs or postulates is the same for all sciences. Until a definition ceases to be nominal and becomes real, it cannot be used scientifically in the demonstration of other conclusions; to use a merely nominal definition in the proof begs the question.

If the existence of the thing defined is either directly observable or self-evident, no proof or postulation of existence is required. In theology, for example, there are those who think that the existence of God is immediately seen in the definition of God. Descartes and Spinoza seem to be of this opinion.

Descartes argues that "eternal existence" is necessarily included in the idea of God as "a supremely perfect Being." This is so evident, he declares, that "existence can no more be separated from the essence of God than can its having its three angles equal to two right angles be separated from the essence of a triangle, or the idea of a mountain from the idea of a valley." Concerning substance or God, Spinoza holds that, since it pertains to its nature to exist, "its definition must involve necessary existence, and consequently from its definition alone its existence must be concluded."

On the other hand, there are those who think that the existence of God must be proved by inference from effect to cause. Supposing that a man understands the meaning of the word "God," Aquinas maintains that it "does not therefore follow that he understands that what the name signifies exists actually, but only that it exists mentally." Hence, he declares, it is necessary to prove the existence of God, "accepting as a middle term the meaning of the name," but using an effect in "place of the definition of the cause in proving the cause's existence."

The difference between these two positions might be summed up by saying that Descartes and Spinoza, like Anselm before them, think the definition of God is intrinsically real, whereas Aquinas thinks we must begin with a nominal definition of God, which becomes real only with proof of God's existence. For some confirmed atheists, any definition of God is not only nominal, but false—the definition of an impossible being, incapable of existing.

THERE IS STILL another issue about nominal and real definitions. The point involved is the one raised by Locke's discussion of nominal and real essences. It is also raised by Aristotle's discrimination between essential and accidental unities, i.e., the difference between the unity signified by the phrase "featherless biped" and by the phrase "black man." Both phrases look like definitions. Each designates a possible class of individuals and sets up the conditions for membership in that class or exclusion from it.

The distinction between them does not rest, according to Aristotle, on the criterion of existence. Both of the objects defined may exist, but whereas the first is truly a species, the second is only, in Aristotle's opinion, an accidental variety within the species man. Man, being a species, can have a real essence, and so any definition of man—whether "featherless biped" or "rational animal"—can be a real definition, constituted by genus and differentia. But negro or aryan, not being a species, but only a race or variety, has no essence as such. The definitions—"black man" and "white man"—indicate this in that they are constituted by two terms which are related as substance and accident, not as genus and differentia.

Though Aristotle distinguishes these two types of formulas as essential and accidental definitions rather than as real and nominal definitions, the one principle of distinction is closely related to the other, for only essential definitions can have real essences for their objects. Accidental definitions do little more than state the meanings of words, or express what Locke calls the "nominal essences" of things. He doubts that the definition of anything except a mathematical object can ever grasp the real essence of a thing. For him all definitions are nominal, which is equivalent to saying that we never define by means of the true genus and differentia, but always by accidental and external signs, or by stating the component parts of a complex whole.

"Speaking of a man, or gold," Locke explains, "or any other species of natural substance, as supposed constituted by a precise and real essence which nature regularly imparts to every individual of that kind, whereby it is made to be of that species, we cannot be certain of the truth of any affirmation or negation made of it. For man or gold, taken in this sense, and used for species of things constituted by real essences, different from the complex idea in the mind of the speaker, stand for we know not what; and the extent of these species, with such boundaries, are so unknown and undetermined, that it is impossible with any certainty to affirm, that all men are rational, or that all gold is yellow."

THIS ISSUE HAS MANY ramifications. In one direction it leads into Aristotle's quarrel with Plato over the method of definition by division or dichotomy. In the *Sophist* and the *Statesman,* the search for definitions proceeds by the division of a class of things into two subclasses, one of which is then further subdivided, and so on until a class is reached which has the characteristics of the object to be defined. The attempt to define a Sophist, for example, starts with the notion that he is a man of art, and proceeds by dividing and subdividing the various kinds of art. At one point in the course of doing this, the Eleatic Stranger summarizes the process to that point.

"You and I," he says to Theaetetus, "have come to an understanding not only about the name of the angler's art, but about the definition of the thing itself. One half of all art was acquisitive—half of the acquisitive art was conquest or taking by force, half of this was hunting, and half of hunting was hunting animals, half of this was hunting water animals— of this again, the under half was fishing, half of fishing was striking; a part of striking was fishing with a barb, and one half of this again, being the kind which strikes with a hook and draws the fish from below upwards, is the art which we have been seeking, and which from the nature of the operation is denoted angling or drawing up . . . And now, following this pattern," he continues, "let us endeavour to find out what a Sophist is."

The pattern as illustrated indicates that, in the course of division, one of the two classes is discarded while the other is subject to further subdivision. Aristotle's criticism of this procedure turns partly on the fact that the division is always dichotomous, or into *two* subclasses, and partly on the fact that the terms which Plato uses in a succession of subdivisions do not seem to have any systematic relation to one another. If the class of animals, for example, is divided into those with and those without feet, it makes a difference, according to Aristotle, what terms are then used to differentiate footed animals into their proper subclasses.

"It is necessary," he insists, "that the division be by the differentia *of the differentia; e.g.,* 'endowed with feet' is a differentia of 'animal'; again the differentia of 'animal endowed with feet' must be of it *qua* endowed with feet. Therefore we must not say, if we are to speak rightly, that of that which is endowed with feet one part has feathers and one is featherless (if we do this we do it through incapacity); we must divide it into only cloven-footed and not-cloven; for these are differentiae in the foot; cloven-footedness is a form of footedness. And the process wants always to go on so till it reaches the species that contains no difference. And then there will be as many kinds of foot as there are differentiae, and the kinds of animals endowed with feet will be equal in number to the differentiae. If then this is so, clearly the *last* differentia will be the essence of the thing and its definition."

As Aristotle quarrels with Plato's method of division, so William James takes issue with Aristotle's theory that a real essence is defined when the right differentia is properly chosen within a certain genus of things. He tends to follow Locke's notion that definitions indicate no more than the nominal essences of things, but he gives this theory a special twist by adding the notion that all our definitions merely group things according to the interest or purpose, whether theoretical or practical, which motivates our classification of them. This has come to be known as the pragmatic theory of definition.

"My thinking," writes James, "is first and last and always for the sake of my doing." After pointing out that Locke "undermined the fallacy" of supposing that we can define the real essence of things, he goes on to say that "none of his successors, as far as I know, have radically escaped it, or seen that *the only meaning of essence is teleological, and that classification and conception are purely teleological weapons of the mind.* The essence of a thing is that one of its properties which is so *important for my interests* that in comparison with it I may neglect the rest . . . The properties which are important vary from man to man and from hour to hour."

In a footnote James adds: "A substance like oil has as many different essences as it has uses to different individuals." The classification of natural as well as artificial objects should therefore proceed according to the advice Mephistopheles gives to the student in Goethe's *Faust:* you will have more success, he says, if you learn "to systemize and then to classify." But if this is so, then no one scheme of classification, more than any other, represents the real structure or order of nature. Nature indifferently submits to any and all divisions which we wish to make among existing things. Some classifications may be more significant than others, but only by reference to our interests, not because they represent reality more accurately or adequately. It does not matter, therefore, whether we define by genus and differentia, by other characteristics in combination, or by reference to origins or functions.

Darwin's scheme of classification provides evidence relevant to this whole issue. As indicated in the chapters on ANIMAL and EVOLUTION, Darwin thinks that his genealogical classification of plants and animals comes nearer to the natural system of living organisms than the classifications proposed by his predecessors. "The Natural System," he writes, "is a genealogical arrangement, with the acquired grades of difference, marked by the terms, varieties, species, genera, families, etc.; and we have to discover the lines of descent by the most permanent characters whatever they may be and of however slight vital importance." Henceforth, following his method, "systematists will have only to decide . . . whether any form be sufficiently constant and distinct from other forms, to be capable of definition; and

if definable, whether the differences be sufficiently important to deserve a specific name."

But Darwin's statement reopens rather than resolves the great traditional questions. Are the various groupings made in classification divisions which the classifier finds useful to impose on nature, or do they represent lines of real distinction in the very nature of things? If the latter is the case, either wholly or in part, are we able to do more than approximate real distinction by whatever method of definition we employ? Can we discover real species, essentially distinct from one another, and can our definitions formulate the essence of each?

THE SEARCH FOR definitions basically belongs to the activity of the human mind in all its scientific or dialectical efforts to clarify discourse, to achieve precision of thought, to focus issues and to resolve them.

Men have no other way of coming to terms with one another than by defining the words they use to express their concepts or meanings. They make terms out of words by endowing words with exactness or precision of meaning. Definition does this and makes possible the meeting of minds either in agreement or in dispute. Definition also makes it possible for any mind to submit itself to the test of agreement with reality. Definition helps man to ask nature or experience the only sort of question to which answers can be found.

The search for definitions has, perhaps, its most dramatic exemplification in the dialogues of Plato. Socrates usually leads the conversation in quest of them; though it is only in certain dialogues, such as the *Sophist* and the *Statesman,* that the making of definitions is practiced in detail. Two other books in this set are largely concerned with ways of reaching and defending definitions—Aristotle's *Topics* (which should be considered together with the opening chapters of his *On the Parts of Animals*) and Francis Bacon's *Novum Organum.*

16

Democracy

INTRODUCTION

Of all the traditional names for forms of government, "democracy" has the liveliest currency today. Yet like all the others, it has a long history in the literature of political thought and a career of shifting meanings. How radically the various conceptions of democracy differ may be judged from the fact that, in one of its meanings, democracy flourished in the Greek city-states as early as the 5th century B.C.; while in another, democracy only began to exist in recent times or perhaps does not yet exist anywhere in the world.

In our minds democracy is inseparably connected with constitutional government. We tend to think of despotism or dictatorship as its only opposites or enemies. That is how the major political issue of our day is understood. But as recently as the 18th century, some of the American constitutionalists prefer a republican form of government to democracy; and at other times, both ancient and modern, oligarchy or aristocracy, rather than monarchy or despotism, is the major alternative. "Democracy" has even stood for the lawless rule of the mob—either itself a kind of tyranny or the immediate precursor of tyranny.

Throughout all these shifts in meaning and value, the word "democracy" preserves certain constant political connotations. Democracy exists, according to Montesquieu, "when the body of the people is possessed of the supreme power." As the root meaning of the word indicates, democracy is the "rule of the people." While there may be, and in fact often has been, a difference of opinion with respect to the meaning of "the people," this notion has been traditionally associated with the doctrine of popular sovereignty, which makes the political community as such the origin and basis of

political authority. In the development of the democratic tradition, particularly in modern times, this has been accompanied by the elaboration of safeguards for the rights of man to assure that government actually functions for the people, and not merely for one group of them.

Although they are essential parts of democracy, neither popular sovereignty nor the safeguarding of natural rights provides the specific characteristic of democracy, since both are compatible with any other just form of government. The specifically democratic element is apparent from the fact that throughout the many shifts of meaning which democracy has undergone, the common thread is the notion of political power in the hands of the many rather than the few or the one. Thus at the very beginning of democratic government, we find Pericles calling Athens a democracy because "its administration favours the many instead of the few." Close to our own day, J. S. Mill likewise holds that democracy is "the government of the whole people by the whole people" in which "the majority . . . will outvote and prevail."

According as the many exercise *legal* power as citizens or merely *actual* power as a mob, democracy is aligned with or against constitutional government. The quantitative meaning of "many" can vary from *more than the few* to *all* or something approximating all, and with this variance the same constitution may be at one time regarded as oligarchic or aristocratic, and at another as democratic. The way in which the many who are citizens exercise their power—either directly or through representatives—occasions the 18th-century distinction between a democracy and a republic, though this verbal ambiguity can be easily avoided by using the phrases "direct democracy" and "representative democracy," as was sometimes done by the writers of *The Federalist* and their American contemporaries.

These last two points—the extension of the franchise and a system of representation—mark the chief differences between ancient and contemporary institutions of democracy. Today constitutional democracy tends to be representative, and the grant of citizenship under a democratic constitution tends toward universal suffrage. That is why we no longer contrast democracy and republic. That is why even the most democratic Greek constitutions may seem undemocratic—oligarchic or aristocratic—to us.

To the extent that democracy, ancient or modern, is conceived as a lawful form of government, it has elements in common with other forms of lawful government which, for one reason or another, may not be democratic. The significance of these common elements—the principle of constitutionality and the status of citizenship—will be assumed here. They are discussed in the chapters on CONSTITUTION and CITIZEN. The general theory of the forms of government is treated in the chapter on GOVERNMENT, and the two forms most closely related to democracy, in the chapters on ARISTOCRACY and OLIGARCHY.

THE EVALUATIONS of democracy are even more various than its meanings. It has been denounced as an extreme perversion of government. It has been grouped with other good, or other bad, forms of government, and accorded the faint praise of being called either the most tolerable of bad governments or the least efficient among acceptable forms. It has been held up as the political ideal, the only perfectly just state—that paragon of justice which has always been, whether recognized or not, the goal of political progress.

Sometimes the same writer will express divergent views. Plato, for example, in the *Statesman,* claims that democracy has "a twofold meaning" according as it involves "ruling with law or without law." Finding it "in every respect weak and unable to do either any great

good or any great evil," he concludes that it is "the worst of all lawful governments, and the best of all lawless ones." The rule of the many is least efficient for either good or evil. But in *The Republic,* he places democracy at only one remove from tyranny. On the ground that "the excessive increase of anything often causes a reaction in the opposite direction," tyranny is said to "arise naturally out of democracy, and the most aggravated form of tyranny and slavery out of the most extreme form of liberty."

Similarly, Aristotle, in the *Politics,* calls democracy "the most tolerable" of the three perverted forms of government, in contrast to oligarchy, which he thinks is only "a little better" than tyranny, "the worst of governments." Yet he also notes that, among existing governments, "there are generally thought to be two principal forms—democracy and oligarchy . . . and the rest are only variations of these." His own treatment conforms with this observation. He devotes the central portion of his *Politics* to the analysis of oligarchy and democracy. In his view they are equal and opposite in their injustice, and to him both seem capable of degenerating into despotism and tyranny.

Among the political philosophers of modern times a certain uniformity of treatment seems to prevail in the context of otherwise divergent theories. Writers like Hobbes, Locke, and Rousseau, or Machiavelli, Montesquieu, and Kant differ in many and profound respects. But they classify the forms of government in much the same fashion. As Hobbes expresses it, "when the representative is one man, then is the commonwealth a monarchy; when an assembly of all that will come together, then it is a democracy, or popular commonwealth; when an assembly of a part only, then it is called an aristocracy." Though Hobbes favors monarchy and Montesquieu either aristocracy or democracy, these writers do not make the choice among the three traditional forms a significant expression of their own political theories. For them the more important choice is presented by other alternatives: for Hobbes between absolute and limited government; for Montesquieu and Locke, between government by law and despotism; for Rousseau and Kant, between a republic and a monarchy.

The authors of *The Federalist* definitely show their preference for "popular government" as opposed to monarchy, aristocracy, or oligarchy. They usually refer to it as a "republic," by which they mean "a government which derives all its powers directly or indirectly from the great body of the people, and is administered by persons holding their offices during pleasure, for a limited period, or during good behavior." Hamilton and others involved in the American constitutional debates, as for example James Wilson, occasionally call this system a "representative democracy," but in *The Federalist* a republic is sharply differentiated from a democracy. The "great points of difference," however, turn out to be only "the delegation of the government (in a republic) to a small number of citizens elected by the rest," and the "greater number of citizens, and greater sphere of country" to which a republic may extend. The difference, as already noted, is best expressed in the words "representative" and "direct" democracy.

In Mill's *Representative Government* we find democracy identified with the ideal state. "The ideally best form of government," he writes, "is that in which the sovereignty, or supreme controlling power in the last resort, is vested in the entire aggregate of the community, every citizen not only having a voice in the exercise of that ultimate sovereignty, but being, at least occasionally, called on to take an actual part in the government, by the personal discharge of some public function, local or general." Though Mill recognizes the infirmities of democracy and though he readily concedes that it may not be the best government for all peoples under all circumstances, his argument for its superiority to all other forms of government remains substantially unqualified.

Mill was greatly influenced by Tocqueville's *Democracy in America,* a book introduced by the statement, "No novelty in the United States struck me more vividly during my stay there than the equality of conditions."

For Tocqueville, equality, not liberty, lies at the heart of democracy. "Political liberty," he writes, "occasionally gives sublime pleasure to a few. Equality daily gives each man in the crowd a host of small enjoyments . . . Democratic peoples always like equality, but there are times when their passion for it turns to delirium." If given the choice between liberty and equality, they would always choose equality. But, unlike Tocqueville, Mill does not think that choice need ever occur.

IN MILL'S CONSTRUCTION of the democratic ideal as providing liberty and equality for all, the essential distinction from previous conceptions lies in the meaning of the word *all.* The republicans of the 18th century, in their doctrines of popular sovereignty and natural rights, understood citizenship in terms of equality of status and conceived liberty in terms of a man's having a voice in his own government. The ancients, seeing that men could be free and equal members of a political community only when they lived as citizens under the rule of law, recognized that the democratic constitution alone bestowed such equality upon all men not born slaves. But generally neither the ancients nor the 18th-century republicans understood liberty and equality *for all men* to require the abolition of slavery, the emancipation of women from political subjection, or the eradication of all constitutional discriminations based on wealth, race, or previous condition of servitude.

With Mill, *all* means every human person without regard to the accidents of birth or fortune. "There ought to be no pariahs in a full-grown and civilized nation," he writes, "no persons disqualified, except through their own default." Under the latter condition, he would withhold the franchise from infants, idiots, or criminals (including the criminally indigent), but with these exceptions he would make suffrage universal. He sums up his argument by claiming that "it is a personal injustice to withhold from any one, unless for the prevention of greater evils, the ordinary privilege of having his voice reckoned in the disposal of affairs in which he has the same interest as other people," and whoever "has no vote, and no prospect of obtaining it, will either be a permanent malcontent, or will feel as one whom the general affairs of society do not concern." But it should be added that for Mill the franchise is not merely a privilege or even a right; "it is," he says, "strictly a matter of duty." How the voter uses the ballot "has no more to do with his personal wishes than the verdict of a juryman . . . He is bound to give it according to his best and most conscientious opinion of the public good. Whoever has any other idea of it is unfit to have the suffrage."

The notion of universal suffrage raises at once the question of the economic conditions prerequisite to the perfection of political democracy. Can men exercise the political freedom of citizenship without freedom from economic dependence on the will of other men? It was commonly thought by 18th-century republicans that they could not. "A power over a man's subsistence," Hamilton declares, "amounts to a power over his will." On that basis it was urged by many during the Philadelphia convention that a property qualification was necessary for suffrage.

Kant also argues that suffrage "presupposes the independence or self-sufficiency of the individual citizen." Because apprentices, servants, minors, women, and the like do not maintain themselves, each "according to his own industry, but as it is arranged by others," he claims that they are "mere subsidiaries of the Commonwealth and not active independent members of it," being "of necessity commanded and protected by others." For this reason, he concludes, they are "passive," not "active," citizens and can be rightfully deprived of the franchise.

For political democracy to be realized in practice, more may be required than the abolition of poll taxes and other discriminations based on wealth. In the opinion of Marx, the "battle for democracy" will not be won, nor even the "first step" taken toward it, until "the working class raises the proletariat to the position of ruling class." Quite apart from the merits of the revolutionary political philosophy which Marx erects, his views, and those of other social reformers of the 19th century, have made it a central issue that democracy be conceived in social and economic terms as well as political. Otherwise, they insist, what is called "democracy" will permit, and may even try to condone, social inequalities and economic injustices which vitiate political liberty.

THERE IS ONE other condition of equality which the status of citizenship demands. This is equality of educational opportunity. According to Mill, it is "almost a self-evident axiom that the State should require and compel the education, up to a certain standard, of every human being who is born its citizen." All men may not be endowed with the same native abilities or talents, but all born with enough intelligence to become citizens deserve the sort of education which fits them for the life of political freedom. Quantitatively, this means a system of education as universal as the franchise; and as much for every individual as he can take, both in youth and adult life. Qualitatively, this means liberal education rather than vocational training, though in contemporary controversy this point is still disputed.

The way in which it recognizes and discharges its educational responsibility tests the sincerity of modern democracy. No other form of government has a comparable burden, for no other calls *all* men to citizenship. In such a government, Montesquieu declares, "the whole power of education is required." Whereas despotism may be preserved by fear and monarchy by a system of honor, a democracy depends on civic virtue. For where "government is intrusted to private citizens," it requires "love of the laws and of the country," and this, according to Montesquieu, is generally "conducive to purity of morals."

Universal schooling by itself is not sufficient for this purpose. Democracy also needs what Mill calls the "school of public spirit." It is only by participating in the functions of government that men can become competent as citizens. By engaging in civic activities, a man "is made to feel himself one of the public, and whatever is for their benefit to be for his benefit." The "moral part of the instruction afforded by the participation of the private citizen, if even rarely, in public functions," results, according to Mill, in a man's being able "to weigh interests not his own; to be guided, in case of conflicting claims, by another rule than his private partialities; to apply, at every turn, principles and maxims which have for their reason of existence the common good." If national affairs cannot afford an opportunity for every citizen to take an active part in government, then that must be achieved through local government, and it is for this reason that Mill advocates the revitalization of the latter.

"Bureaucracy," according to Weber, "inevitably accompanies modern *mass democracy* in contrast to the democratic self-government of small homogeneous units." Such bureaucratization of mass democracies stands in the way of active participation by individual citizens.

THERE ARE OTHER problems peculiar to modern democracy. Because of the size of the territory and population of the national state, democratic government has necessarily become representative. Representation, according to *The Federalist*, becomes almost indispensable when *the people* is too large and too dispersed for assembly or for continuous, as well as direct, participation in national affairs. The pure democracy which the Federalists attribute to the Greek city-states may still be appropriate for local government of the town-meeting variety, but for the operations of federal or national government, the Federalists think the republican institutions of Rome a better model to follow.

The Federalists have another reason for espousing representative government. The "mortal disease" of popular government, in their view, is the "violence of faction" which decides measures "not according to the rules of justice and the rights of the minority party, but by the superior force of an interested and overbearing majority." Believing the spirit of faction to be rooted in the nature of man in society, the American statesmen seek to cure its evil not by "removing its causes," but by "controlling its effects." The principle of representation, Madison claims, "promises the cure."

Representation, by delegating government to a small number of citizens elected by the rest, is said "to refine and enlarge the public views by passing them through the medium of a chosen body of citizens, whose wisdom may best discern the true interest of their country." From this it appears that representation provides a way of combining popular government with the aristocratic principle of government by the best men.

The assumption that representation would normally secure the advantages of aristocratic government is not unmixed with oligarchic prejudices. If, as the Federalists frankly suppose, the best men are also likely to be men of breeding and property, representative government would safeguard the interests of the gentry, as well as the safety of the republic, against the *demos*—in Hamilton's words, "that great beast." Their concern with the evil of factions seems to be colored by the fear of the dominant faction in any democracy—the always more numerous poor.

THE LEAVENING OF popular government by representative institutions in the formation of modern democracies raises the whole problem of the nature and function of representatives. To what extent does representation merely provide an instrument which the people employs to express its will in the process of self-government? To what extent is it a device whereby the great mass of the people select their betters to decide for them what is beyond their competence to decide for themselves?

According to the way these questions are answered, the conception of the representative's function—especially in legislative matters—will vary from that of serving as the mere messenger of his constituents to that of acting independently, exercising his own judgment, and representing his constituents not in the sense of doing their bidding, but only in the sense that he has been chosen by them to decide what is to be done for the common good.

At one extreme, the representative seems to be reduced to the ignominious role of a mouthpiece, a convenience required by the exigencies of time and space. Far from being a leader, or one of the best men, he need not even be a better man than his constituents. At the other extreme, it is not clear why the completely independent representative need even be popularly elected. In Edmund Burke's theory of *virtual* representation, occasioned by his argument against the extension of the franchise, even those who do not vote are adequately represented by men who have the welfare of the state at heart. They, no less than voting constituents, can expect the representative to consider what is for their interest, and to oppose their wishes if he thinks their local or special interest is inimical to the general welfare.

Between these two extremes, Mill tries to find a middle course, in order to achieve the "two great requisites of government: responsibility to those for whose benefit political power ought to be, and always professes to be, employed; and jointly therewith to obtain, in the greatest measure possible, for the function of government the benefits of superior intellect, trained by long meditation and practical discipline to that special task." Accordingly, Mill would preserve some measure of independent judgment for the representative and make him both responsive and responsible to his constituents, yet without directing or restraining him by the checks of initiative, referendum, and recall.

Mill's discussion of representation leaves few crucial question unasked, though it may not provide clearly satisfactory answers to all of them. It goes beyond the nature and function of the representative to the problem of securing representation for minorities by the now familiar method of proportional voting. It is concerned with the details of electoral procedure—the nomination of candidates, public and secret balloting, plural voting—as well as the more general question of the differences among the executive, judicial, and legislative departments of government with respect to representation, especially the difference of representatives in the upper and lower houses of a bicameral legislature. Like the writers of *The Federalist,* Mill seeks a leaven for the democratic mass in the leadership of men of talent or training. He would qualify the common sense of the many by the expertness or wisdom of the few.

THE ANCIENT ISSUE between the democratic and the oligarchic constitution turns primarily on a question of justice, not on the relative competence of the many and the few to rule. Either form of government may take on a more or less aristocratic cast according as men of eminent virtue or ability assume public office, but in neither case does the constitution itself guarantee their choice, except possibly on the oligarchic assumption that the possession of wealth signifies superior intelligence and virtue.

The justice peculiar to the democratic constitution, Aristotle thinks, "arises out of the notion that those who are equal in any respect are equal in all respects; because men are equally free, they claim to be absolutely equal." It does not seem to him inconsistent with democratic justice that slaves, women, and resident aliens should be excluded from citizenship and public office.

In the extreme form of Greek democracy, the qualifications for public office are no different from the qualifications for citizenship. Since they are equally eligible for almost every governmental post, the citizens can be chosen by lot rather than elected by vote. Rousseau agrees with Montesquieu's opinion of the Greek practice, that "election by lot is democratic in nature." He thinks it "would have few disadvantages in a real democracy, but," he adds, "I have already said that a real democracy is only an ideal."

The justice peculiar to the oligarchic constitution is, according to Aristotle, "based on the notion that those who are unequal in one respect are in all respects unequal; being unequal, that is, in property, they suppose themselves to be unequal absolutely." The oligarchic constitution consequently does not grant citizenship or open public office to all the freeborn, but in varying degrees sets a substantial property qualification for both.

Though he admits that the opposite claims of the oligarch and the democrat "have a kind of justice," Aristotle also points out the injustice of each. The democratic constitution, he thinks, does injustice to the rich by treating them as equal with the poor simply because both are freeborn, while the oligarchic constitution does injustice to the poor by failing to treat all freemen, regardless of wealth, as equals. "Tried by an absolute standard," Aristotle goes on to say, "they are faulty, and, therefore, both parties, whenever their share in the government does not accord with their preconceived ideas, stir up a revolution."

Plato, Thucydides, and Plutarch, as well as Aristotle, observe that this unstable situation permits demagogue or dynast to encourage lawless rule by the mob or by a coterie of the rich. Either paves the way to tyranny.

To stabilize the state and to remove injustice, Aristotle proposes a mixed constitution which, by a number of different methods, "attempts to unite the freedom of the poor and the wealth of the rich." In this way he hopes to satisfy the two requirements of good government. "One is the actual obedience of citizens to the laws, the other is the goodness of the laws which they obey." By participating in the making of laws, all freemen, the poor included, would be more inclined to obey them. But since the rich are also given a special function, there is, according to Aristotle, the possibility of also getting good laws passed, since "birth and education are commonly the accompaniments of wealth."

To Aristotle the mixed constitution is perfectly just, and with an aristocratic aspect added to the blend, it approaches the ideal polity. Relative to certain circumstances it has "a greater right than any other form of government, except the true and ideal, to the name of the government of the best."

Yet the true and the ideal, or what he sometimes calls the "divine form of government," seems to be monarchy for Aristotle, or rule by the one superior man; and in his own sketch of the best constitution at the end of the *Politics*—the best practicable, if not the ideal—Aristotle clearly opposes admitting all the laboring classes to citizenship.

As INDICATED IN the chapter on CONSTITUTION, Aristotle's mixed constitution should be distinguished from the medieval mixed regime, which was a combination of constitutional with nonconstitutional or absolute government, rather than a mixture of different constitutional principles. The mixed regime—or "royal and political government"—seems to

have come into being not as an attempt to reconcile conflicting principles of justice, but as the inevitable product of a decaying feudalism and a rising nationalism. Yet Aquinas claims that a mixed regime was established by divine law for the people of Israel; for it was "partly kingdom, since there is one at the head of all; partly aristocracy, in so far as a number of persons are set in authority; partly democracy, *i.e.*, government by the people, in so far as the rulers can be chosen from the people, and the people have the right to choose their rulers." In such a system, the monarchical principle is blended with aristocratic and democratic elements to whatever extent the nobles and the commons play a part in the government. But neither group functions politically as citizens do under purely constitutional government.

The question of constitutional justice can, however, be carried over from ancient to modern times. Modern democracy answers it differently, granting equality to all men on the basis of their being born human. It recognizes in wealth or breeding no basis for special political preferment or privilege. By these standards, the mixed constitution and even the most extreme form of Greek democracy must be regarded as oligarchic in character by a writer like Mill.

Yet Mill, no less than Aristotle, would agree with Montesquieu's theory that the rightness of any form of government must be considered with reference to the "humor and disposition of the people in whose favor it is established." The constitution and laws, Montesquieu writes, "should be adapted in such a manner to the people for whom they are framed that it would be a great chance if those of one nation suit another."

Mill makes the same point somewhat differently when he says, "the ideally best form of government . . . does not mean one which is practicable or eligible in all states of civilization." But although he is willing to consider the forms of government in relation to the historic conditions of a people, not simply by absolute standards, Mill differs sharply from Montesquieu and Aristotle in one very important respect. For him, as we have seen, representative democracy founded on universal suffrage is, absolutely speaking, the only truly just government—the only one perfectly suited to the nature of man. Peoples whose accidental circumstances temporarily justify less just or even unjust forms of government, such as oligarchy or despotism, must not be forever condemned to subjection or disfranchisement, but should rather be raised by education, experience, and economic reforms to a condition in which the ideal polity becomes appropriate for them.

THE BASIC PROBLEMS of democratic government—seen from the point of view of those who either attack or defend it—remain constant despite the altered conception of democracy in various epochs.

At all times, there is the question of leadership and the need for obtaining the political services of the best men without infringing on the political prerogatives of all men. The difference between the many and the few, between the equality of men as free or human and their individual inequality in virtue or talent, must always be given political recognition, if not by superiority in status, then by allocation of the technically difficult problems of statecraft to the expert or specially competent, with only certain broad general policies left to the determination of a majority vote. Jefferson and Mill alike hope that popular government may abolish privileged classes without losing the benefits of leadership by peculiarly gifted individuals. The realization of that hope, Jefferson writes Adams, depends on leaving "to the citizens the free election and separation of the *aristoi* from the *psuedo-aristoi,* of the wheat from the chaff."

At all times there is the danger of tyranny by the majority and, under the threat of revolution, the rise of a demagogue who uses mob rule to establish a dictatorship. Hobbes phrases this peculiar susceptibility of democracy to the mischief of demagogues by saying of popular assemblies that they "are as subject to evil counsel, and to be seduced by orators, as a monarch by flatterers," with the result that democracy tends to degenerate into government by the most powerful orator.

Tocqueville goes further than Hobbes and imagines the possibility of democratic totalitarianism that, in his view, is a form of tyranny worse than any known in antiquity and the Middle Ages. His insight on this point is more fully reported in the chapter on TYRANNY AND DESPOTISM.

The democratic state has seldom been tempted to undertake the burdens of empire without suffering from a discordance between its domestic and its foreign policy. Again and again, Thucydides describes the efforts of the Athenians to reconcile their imperialism abroad with democracy at home.

In his oration at the end of the first year of the Peloponnesian war, Pericles praises the democracy of Athens and at the same time celebrates the might of her empire. "It is only the Athenians," he says, "who, fearless of consequences, confer their benefits not from calculations of expediency, but in the confidence of liberality." But four years later, after the revolt of Mytilene, Cleon speaks in a different vein. Thucydides describes him as being "at that time by far the most powerful with the commons." He tells his fellow citizens of democratic Athens that he has "often before now been convinced that a democracy is incapable of empire," but "never more so than by your present change of mind in the matter of Mitylene [Mytilene]." He urges them to return to their earlier decision to punish the Mytilenians, for, he says, if they reverse that decision they will be "giving way to the three failings most fatal to empire—pity, sentiment, and indulgence."

Diodotus, who in this debate recommends a policy of leniency, does not do so in the "confidence of liberality" which Pericles had said was the attitude of a democratic state toward its dependencies. "The question is not of justice," Diodotus declares, "but how to make the Mitylenians useful to Athens . . . We must not," he continues, "sit as strict judges of the offenders to our own prejudice, but rather see how by moderate chastisements we may be enabled to benefit in the future by the revenue-producing powers of our dependencies . . . It is far more useful for the preservation of our empire," he concludes, "voluntarily to put up with injustice, than to put to death, however justly, those whom it is our interest to keep alive."

Twelve years later, Alcibiades, no democrat himself, urges the Athenians to undertake the Sicilian expedition by saying, "We cannot fix the exact point at which our empire shall stop; we have reached a position in which we must not be content with retaining but must scheme to extend it, for, if we cease to rule others, we are in danger of being ruled ourselves." In the diplomatic skirmishes which precede the invasion of Sicily, Hermocrates of Syracuse tries to unite the Sicilian cities so that they may escape "disgraceful submission to an Athenian master." The Athenian ambassador, Euphemus, finds himself compelled to speak at first of "our empire and of the good right we have to it"; but soon finds himself frankly confessing that "for tyrants and imperial cities nothing is unreasonable if expedient."

The denouement of the Peloponnesian war, and especially of the Syracusan expedition, is the collapse of democracy, not through the loss of empire but as a result of the moral sacrifices involved in trying to maintain or increase it. Tacitus, commenting on the decay of republican institutions with the extension of Rome's conquests, underlines the same theme. It is still the same theme when the problems of British imperialism appear in Mill's discussion of how a democracy should govern its colonies or dependencies.

The incompatibility of empire with democracy is on one side of the picture of the democratic state in external affairs. The other side is the tension between democratic institutions and military power or policy—in the form of standing armies and warlike maneuvers. The inefficiency traditionally attributed to democracy under peaceful conditions does not, from all the evidences of history, seem to render democracy weak or pusillanimous in the face of aggression.

The deeper peril for democracy seems to lie in the effect of war upon its institutions and on the morality of its people. As Hamilton writes in *The Federalist*: "The violent destruction of life and property incident to war, the continual effort and alarm attendant on a state of continual danger, will compel nations the most attached to liberty to resort for repose and security to institutions which have a tendency to destroy their civil and political rights. To be more safe, they at length become willing to run the risk of being less free."

17

Desire

INTRODUCTION

IN Darwin, J. S. Mill, William James, and Freud, at the modern end of the great tradition, the word "desire" primarily signifies a cause of animal and human behavior. It is one of the basic terms in psychological analysis, covering that whole range of phenomena which are also referred to by such terms as *wanting, needing, craving, wishing, willing,* all of which are discussed in connection with theories of instinct and emotion, libido and love, motivation and purpose.

"All of us have desires," Dewey declares, "all at least who have not become so pathological that they are completely apathetic. These desires are the ultimate moving springs of action . . . The intensity of the desire measures the strength of the efforts that will be put forth." The range and variety of desires is enormous; and in the great books, authors differ about whether the desire for sexual pleasure, wealth, power, or knowledge tends to predominate.

If we turn to traditional beginnings, to the writings of Plato, Aristotle, Galen, and Plotinus, we find that the psychological consideration of desire is part of a much larger context. The ancients are, of course, concerned with the role of desire in causing animal or human behavior, and with the causes of such desire, but they are also interested in cravings which seem to be present in plants as well as animals. Plato, for example, attributes to plants "feelings of pleasure and pain and the desires which accompany them." The vegetative activities of nutrition, growth, and reproduction seem to spring from basic appetites—or, in modern phraseology, "biological needs"—inherent in all living matter.

Because hunger and thirst so readily symbol-ize the essence of desire (or certainly represent its most general manifestation in living things), the words "appetite" and "desire" are frequently used as synonyms in the earlier phase of the tradition. As Hobbes observes, when he proposes to use "appetite" and "desire" as synonyms, desire is "the general name," and appetite is "oftentimes restrained to signify the desire for food, namely hunger and thirst." So, too, Spinoza says that "there is no difference between appetite and desire," yet he adds, "unless in this particular, that desire is generally related to men in so far as they are conscious of their appetites, and it may therefore be defined as appetite of which we are conscious."

Spinoza here seems to be reflecting the distinction made by earlier writers between natural appetite and conscious desire, which we today would, perhaps, express in terms of "need" and "wish." The ancient conception of tendencies inherent in all things—inanimate as well as living—which seek a natural fulfillment broadens the meaning of appetite or desire. When Aristotle says that "each thing seeks its own perfection" and that "nature does nothing in vain," he is thinking of nonliving as well as living bodies. Wherever in the physical world things seem to have a natural tendency to move in a certain direction or to change in a certain way, there appetite, belonging to the very nature of the moving thing, operates as a cause. Adopting this view, Dante declares that "neither Creator nor creature . . . was ever without love, either natural or of the mind"; and in his *Il convivio* he shows how each thing has its "specific love." The love, or desire, of the elements is their "innate affinity to their proper place"; minerals desire "the place where their generation is ordained" with the result that "the magnet ever receives power from the direction of its generation."

According to this view it is possible to speak of the natural desire of raindrops to fall or of smoke to rise. Such a manner of speaking may at first seem metaphorical—an expression of primitive animism or anthropomorphism—but the ancients, observing different natural tendencies in heavy and light bodies, mean this literally.

The sense of such statements is no different from what is meant when it is said that the sunflower, without consciousness, naturally tends to turn toward the sun, or that all men by nature desire to know.

FROM ITS NARROWEST meaning with reference to the behavior of animals and men, desire gains a wider connotation when it is conceived as covering the appetites found in living organisms. But in its broadest significance, it refers to the innate tendency inherent in matter itself. As we shall presently see, appetite, desire, or tendency is seated in matter according to that conception of matter which identifies it with potentiality or potential being. These considerations are more fully treated in the chapters on BEING, CHANGE, and MATTER, but their significance for the notion of desire can be briefly indicated here.

Plotinus suggests the basic insight when he describes matter as "in beggardom, striving as it were by violence to acquire, and always disappointed." Matter is that in natural things which is the reason for their motion and change. Considering natural change, Aristotle names what he thinks are its three principles. In addition to "something divine, good, and desirable," he writes, "we hold that there are two other principles, the one contrary to it, the other such as of its own nature to desire and yearn for it." These are respectively form, privation, and matter. The relation between matter and form is expressed by Aristotle in terms of desire. "The form cannot desire itself," he says, "for it is not defective; nor can the contrary desire it, for contraries are mutually destructive. The truth is that what desires the form is matter, as the female desires the male."

Conceived most generally as natural appetite or tendency, desire becomes a physical or metaphysical term. "*Natural appetite*," says Aquinas, "is that inclination which each thing has of its own nature." The significance of desire in this sense extends, far beyond psychological phenomena, to all things in motion under the impetus or inclination of their own natures, rather than moved violently by forces impressed on them from without.

In ancient physics every natural tendency has an end or fulfillment in which the motion governed by that tendency comes to rest. *Eros* and *telos*—desire and end—are complementary concepts, each implying the other as principles of physics, *i.e.*, as factors operating together throughout nature in the order of change. The *telos* of each thing is the perfection which satisfies the tendency of its nature. That nature does nothing in vain means simply that no natural desire—need or appetite—exists without the possibility of fulfillment.

CONSIDERING THE DESIGN of the universe and the relation of creatures to God, theologians like Augustine and Aquinas use the concept of desire in both its psychological and its metaphysical sense.

Considered metaphysically, desire can be present only in finite beings, for to be finite is to be in want of some perfection. Hence desire can in no way enter into the immutable, infinite, and perfect being of God. In desire, Aquinas points out, "a certain imperfection is implied," namely, the lack "of the good which we have not." Since God is perfect, desire cannot be attributed to Him, "except metaphorically." Love, however, implies perfection rather than imperfection, since it flows from the act of the will "to diffuse its own goodness among others." For that reason, although the infinite perfection of God precludes desire, it does not preclude love.

The theologian goes beyond the metaphysician or physicist when he carries the analysis of desire to the supernatural plane. As God is the supernatural efficient cause of all created things, so God is also the supernatural final cause—the end or ultimate good toward which all creatures tend. The metaphysical maxim that each thing seeks its own perfection is then transformed. "All things," Aquinas writes, "by desiring their own perfection, desire God Himself, inasmuch as the perfections of all things are so many similitudes of the divine being . . . Of those things which desire God, some know Him as He is Himself, and this is proper to the rational creature; others know some participation of His goodness, and this belongs also to sensible knowledge; others have a natural desire without knowledge, as being directed to their ends by a higher intelligence."

The existence in the creature of a desire for God raises difficult questions concerning the manner in which this desire is fulfilled. A supernatural end cannot be attained by purely natural means, *i.e.*, without God's help. The vision of God in which the souls of the blessed come to rest is, according to the theologian, the ultimate gift of grace. Hence, in man's case at least, it becomes necessary to ask whether he can have a purely natural desire to see God if the goal of such desire cannot be achieved by purely natural means.

The question is not whether men to whom God has revealed the promise of ultimate glory can *consciously* desire the beatific vision. Clearly that is possible, though to sustain such desire the theological virtue of hope, inseparable from faith and charity, may be required. Rather the question is whether the beatific vision which is man's supernatural end can be the object of natural desire. On this the theologians appear to be less clearly decided.

Aquinas holds that "neither man, nor any creature, can attain final happiness by his natural powers." Yet he also seems to maintain that man has a natural desire for the perfect happiness of eternal life. "The object of the will, *i.e.*, of man's appetite," he writes, "is the universal good, just as the object of the intellect is the universal truth." Man's natural desire to know the truth—not just some truths but the whole truth, the infinite truth—would seem to require the vision of God for its fulfillment. Aquinas argues similarly from the will's natural desire for the infinite good. "Naught can lull man's will," he writes, "save the universal good . . . to be found not in any creature, but in God alone." Some writers find this confirmed in the fact that whatever good a man sets his heart upon he pursues to infinity. No finite amount of pleasure or power or wealth seems to satisfy him. He always wants more. But there is no end to wanting more of such things. The infinity of such desires must result in frustration. Only God, says the theologian, only an infinite being, can satisfy man's infinite craving for all the good there is.

Seeing man's restlessness, no matter where he turns to find rest, Augustine declares to God: "You made us for yourself and our hearts find no peace until they rest in You." Pascal reaches the same conclusion when he considers the ennui of men which results from the desperation of their unending search. "Their error," he writes, "does not lie in seeking excitement, if they seek it only as a diversion; the evil is that they seek it as if the possession of the objects of their quest would make them really happy." With regard to the frantic pursuit of diversions, he claims that "both the censurers and the censured do not understand man's true nature" and the "misery of man without God." In such restlessness and vain seeking, the theologian sees evidence of man's natural desire to be *with* God.

Admitting the same facts, the skeptics interpret the infinity of man's desire as a craving to *be* God. If this is not every man's desire, it is certainly Satan's in *Paradise Lost*. Skeptic or believer, every man understands the question which Goethe and Dante among the great poets make their central theme. At what moment, amid man's striving and restlessness, will the soul gladly cry, "Remain, so fair thou art, remain!" Confident that there can be no such moment, Faust makes that the basis of his wager with Mephistopheles.

The two poets appear to give opposite answers to the question. Faust finds surcease in an earthly vision of progressive endeavor. Heavenly rest comes to the soul of Dante at the very moment it relinquishes its quest, winning peace through surrender.

IN THE BROADEST OR theological sense of the word, God alone does not desire. In the narrowest or psychological sense, only animals and men do. The contrast of meanings is useful. Natural appetite or tendency throws light on the nature of conscious desire.

In order to "determine the nature and seat of desire," Socrates in the *Philebus* considers such things as "hunger, thirst, and the like" as "in the class of desires." He points out that "when we say 'a man thirsts,' we mean to say that he 'is empty.'" It is not drink he desires, but replenishment by drink, which is a change of state. This insight Socrates generalizes by saying that "he who is empty desires . . . the opposite of what he experiences; for he is empty and desires to be full." In the *Symposium,* using the words "love" and "desire" as if they were interchangeable, Socrates declares that "he who desires something is in want of something" and "love is of something which a man wants and has not."

In the psychological sphere, desire and love are often identified—at least verbally. The one word is frequently substituted for the other. Here the fact already noted, that God loves but does not desire, suggests the root of the distinction between desire and love. Desire always involves some lack or privation to be remedied by a change; whereas love, certainly requited love, implies the kind of satisfaction which abhors change. Love and desire are, of course, frequently mixed, but this does not affect their essential difference as tendencies. They are as different as giving and getting. Love aims at the well-being of the beloved, while desire seeks to enjoy a pleasure or possess a good.

Not all writers, however, contrast the generosity of love with the acquisitiveness of desire. Locke, for example, finds self-interest and self-seeking in both. The meaning of love, he observes, is known to anyone who reflects "upon the thought he has of the delight which any present or absent thing is apt to produce in him . . . For when a man declares in autumn when he is eating them, or in spring when there are none, that he loves grapes, it is no more but that the taste of grapes delights him." The meaning of desire is, in Locke's opinion, closely related. It consists in "the uneasiness a man finds in himself upon the absence of anything whose present enjoyment carries the idea of delight with it." We desire, in short, the things we love but do not possess.

The distinction between love and desire, the question whether they are distinct in animals as well as in men, and their relation to one another when they are distinct, are matters more fully discussed in the chapter on LOVE. It is enough to observe here that when writers use the two words interchangeably, they use both words to signify wanting and seeking.

In the case of animals and men, the thing wanted is an object of conscious desire only if it is something known. In addition to being known as an object of science is known, it must also be deemed good or pleasant—in other words, worth having. For Locke, desire, as we have seen, is no more than "an uneasiness of the mind for want of some absent good," which is measured in terms of pleasure and pain. "What has an aptness to produce pleasure in us is that we call *good,* and what is apt to produce pain in us we call *evil.*" That which we consciously desire, that which we judge to be desirable, would thus be something we regard as good for us, while the "bad" or "evil" would be that which we seek to avoid as somehow injurious rather than beneficial to us.

There is no question that desire and aversion are psychologically connected with estimations of good and evil or pleasure and pain. This is the case no matter how we answer the moralist's question, Do we desire something because it is good, or do we call it "good" simply because we desire it? The ethical significance of the question, and of the opposite answers to it, is discussed in the chapter on GOOD AND EVIL.

THE METAPHYSICAL conception of natural desire provides terms for the psychological analysis of conscious desire and its object. Viewed as belonging to the very nature of a thing, appetite, according to Aristotle, consists in the tendency toward "something we do not have" and "which we need." Both factors are essential—the privation and the capacity, or potentiality, for having what is lacked. Privation in the strict sense is always correlative to potentiality.

The writers who use these terms would not speak of the sunflower being deprived of wisdom, even as they would not call a stone blind. Blindness is the deprivation of sight in things which have by nature a capacity to see. So when it is said that man by nature desires to know, or that certain animals, instinctively gregarious, naturally tend to associate with one another in herds or societies, the potentiality of knowledge or social life is indicated; and precisely because of these potentialities, ignorance and solitariness are considered privations.

We observe here two different conditions of appetite or desire. As the opposite of privation is possession—or of lacking, having— so the opposite states of appetite are the drive toward the unpossessed and satisfaction in possession. We do not strive for that which we have, unless it be to retain our possession of it against loss; and we do not feel satisfied until we get that which we have been seeking.

"If a man being strong desired to be strong," says Socrates in the *Symposium,* "or being swift desired to be swift, or being healthy desired to be healthy, he might be thought to desire something which he already has or is." This would be a misconception which we must avoid. To anyone who says "I desire to have simply what I have," Socrates thinks we should reply: "You, my friend, having wealth and health and strength, want to have the continuance of them . . . When you say, 'I desire that which I have and nothing else,' is not your meaning that you want to have in the future what you now have?" This "is equivalent to saying that a man desires something which is for him non-existent, and which he has not got"; from which Socrates draws the conclusion that everyone "desires that which he has not already, which is future and not present . . . and of which he is in want."

The object of desire—natural or conscious—thus seems to be an altered condition in the desirer, the result of union with the object desired. Man's natural desire to know impels him to learn. Every act of learning which satisfies this natural desire consists in a changed condition of his mind, a change which both Plato and Aristotle describe as a motion from ignorance to knowledge.

When we consciously desire food, it is not the edible thing as such we seek, but rather the eating of it. Only the eating of it will quiet our desire, with that change in our condition we call "nourishment." That the edible thing is only incidentally the object of our desire may be seen in the fact that no way in which we can possess food, *other than eating it,* satisfies hunger.

THE DISTINCTION between natural and conscious desire is complicated by other closely related distinctions which psychologists have made. Freud, for example, distinguishes between conscious and unconscious desire; Darwin separates instinctive from learned desires; and James observes how a conscious desire may become habitual and operate almost automatically, without our awareness of either its object or its action.

Part of the complication is verbal and can be removed by referring to natural desires as *non*-conscious rather than *un*-conscious. The word "conscious" literally means *with knowledge.* Creatures which lack the faculty of knowing cannot desire consciously. It does not follow, however, that sentient or conscious beings cannot have natural appetites. Man's natural desire to know is a case in point. That natural human tendency is not excluded by the fact that many men also consciously seek knowledge, knowing what knowledge is and considering it something worth having.

The instinctive desires of animals are not generally thought to operate apart from the perception of the object toward which the animal is emotionally impelled. The instinctive desire works consciously, both on the side of perception and on the side of the emotionally felt impulse. If, because it is innate rather than learned, or acquired through experience, we call the instinctive desire "natural," it is well to remember that we are not here using the word to signify lack of consciousness. Yet both instinctive and acquired desires may operate unconsciously.

What Freud means by a repressed desire

illustrates this point. The repressed desire, whether instinctual in origin or the result of some acquired fixation of the libido on object or ego, would be a conscious tendency *if it were not repressed*. Freud compares the process of repression to the efforts of a man to get from one room to another past the guard of a door-keeper. "The excitations in the unconscious . . . to begin with, remain unconscious. When they have pressed forward to the threshold and been turned back by the doorkeeper, they are 'incapable of becoming conscious'; we call them then repressed . . . Being repressed, when applied to any single impulse, means being unable to pass out of the unconscious system because of the door-keeper's refusal of admittance into the preconscious."

The repressed desire is made to operate unconsciously by being repressed, which does not prevent it from influencing our conduct or thought, but only from intruding its driving force and its goal upon our attention. In contrast, the desire which works habitually and therefore to some extent unconsciously, is not repressed, but merely one which no longer demands our full attention.

DESIRE AND EMOTION are often identified in our description of the behavior of animals and men. Sometimes, however, desire along with aversion is treated as just one of the emotions, and sometimes all the emotions are treated as manifestations of just one type of conscious appetite, namely, animal as opposed to rational desire.

The appetitive or driving aspect of emotions is indicated by James in his analysis of instinctive behavior. The functioning of an instinct may be viewed, according to James, as a train of psychological events of "general reflex type . . . called forth by determinate sensory stimuli in contact with the animal's body, or at a distance in his environment," arousing "emotional excitements which go with them." The emotional part of the instinctive behavior is at once an impulse to perform certain acts and the feeling which accompanies the acts performed. The sheep, instinctively recognizing the wolf as dangerous, fears and flees. It

runs away because it is afraid and feels fear in the act of flight. When, in his theory of the emotions, James goes so far as to say that the feeling of fear results from running away, he does not mean to deny that the emotion of fear involves the impulse to flee.

In its aspect as impulse—or tendency to act—an emotion is a desire, consciously aroused by sense perceptions and accompanied by conscious feelings. This conception of emotion has been variously expressed in the tradition of the great books. Aquinas, for example, calls all the emotions or passions "movements of the sensitive appetite." But he also uses the words "desire" and "aversion" along with "love" and "hate," "anger" and "fear" to name specific emotions.

Hobbes recognizes the appetitive tendency which is common to all the emotions when he finds at their root what he calls "endeavour"—"these small beginnings of motion within the body of man, before they appear in walking, speaking, striking, and other visible actions . . . This endeavour," he goes on to say, "when it is toward something which causes it, is called appetite, or desire." Spinoza makes the same point in somewhat different terms. "Desire," he writes, "is the essence itself or nature of a person in so far as this nature is conceived from its given constitution as determined towards any action . . . As his nature is constituted in this or that way, so must his desire vary and the nature of one desire differ from another, just as the affects from which each desire arises differ. There are as many kinds of desire, therefore, as there are kinds of joy, sorrow, love, etc., and in consequence . . . as there are kinds of objects by which we are affected."

Those psychologists who find in man two distinct faculties of knowledge—the senses and the reason or intellect—also find in him two distinct faculties of appetite or desire. The distinction is perhaps most sharply made by Aristotle and Aquinas, who claim that "there must be one appetite tending towards the universal good, which belongs to reason, and another with a tendency towards the particular good, which appetite belongs to sense."

The traditional name for the intellectual appetite, or the faculty of rational desire, is "will." In Spinoza's vocabulary, the effort of desire, "when it is related to the mind alone, is called *will,* but when it is related at the same time both to the mind and the body, is called *appetite.*"

Psychologists who attribute these diverse modes of desire, as they attribute sensation and thought, to a single faculty called "mind" or "understanding," nevertheless deal with the whole range of appetitive phenomena, including both the animal passions and acts of will. James, for example, treats the instinctive acts associated with the emotions as "automatic and reflex" movements, and separates them from "voluntary movements which, being desired and intended beforehand, are done with full prevision of what they are to be." In so doing, he draws a line between emotional impulses and acts of will, even though he does not distinguish two appetitive faculties.

With or without the distinction in faculties, almost all observers of human experience and conduct seem to agree upon a distinction in types of conscious desire, at least insofar as they recognize the ever-present conflict between the passions and the will. These matters are more fully considered in the chapters on EMOTION and WILL.

THE ROLE OF DESIRE in human life—especially emotional desire—is so intimately connected with problems of good and evil, virtue, duty, and happiness, that until quite recently the subject was discussed mainly in books on ethics, politics, rhetoric, or in works of imagination rather than psychology. Untempered desire leading to downfall is a theme repeated throughout the whole range of imaginative literature, from Homer to the present. Even attempts to repress desire are seen by some authors as paths to destruction, as Mann demonstrates with a quote from Plato in *Death in Venice:* "Detachment . . . and preoccupation with form lead to intoxication and desire, they may lead the noblest among us to frightful emotional excesses . . . So they too, they too, lead to the bottomless pit." Plato, Mann, and Joyce are among those writers who suggest that artists are more prone to such emotional excesses than other people.

Freud takes a similar view of the artist, who "is urged on by instinctual needs which are too clamorous; he longs to attain to honour, power, riches, fame, and the love of women . . . So, like any other with an unsatisfied longing, he turns away from reality and transfers all his interest . . . on to the creation of his wishes in the life of phantasy." For Freud, artists are only extreme cases of every "hungry soul," for "the intermediate world of phantasy is sanctioned by general human consent."

Freud tries to separate psychological description and explanation from moral principles or conclusions, but even he cannot avoid treating the effects of morality upon the dynamics of desire and the life of the passions. Many of the fundamental terms of psychoanalysis—conflict, repression, rationalization, sublimation, to name only some—carry the connotation of moral issues, even though they imply a purely psychological resolution of them.

Contrary to a popular misconception, Freud expressly declares that "it is out of the question that part of the analytic treatment should consist of advice to 'live freely.'" The conflict "between libidinal desires and sexual repression," he explains, is "not resolved by helping one side to win a victory over the other." Although Freud thinks that "what the world calls its code of morals demands more sacrifices than it is worth," he also declares that "we must beware of overestimating the importance of abstinence in effecting neurosis."

What Freud calls emotional infantilism resembles to some degree what a moralist like Aristotle calls self-indulgence or incontinence. To give vent to all the promptings of desire, without regard to the demands of society or reality is to revert to infancy—a state characterized, according to Freud, by "the irreconcilability of its wishes with reality." Because children "live at the beck and call of appetite, and it is in them that the desire for what is pleasant is strongest," Aristotle thinks it fitting that we should speak of self-indulgence when it occurs in an adult as a "childish fault."

Aristotle and Freud seem to be looking at

the same facts of human nature and seeing them in the same light. What Freud describes as the conflict between the "pleasure-principle" and the "reality-principle," Aristotle—and with him Spinoza—treats as a conflict between the passions and the reason, and Kant conceives in terms of the opposition between desire and duty. What Freud says of the reality-principle—that it "demands and enforces the postponement of satisfaction, the renunciation of manifold possibilities, and the temporary endurance of pain"—parallels traditional statements concerning the role of reason or of duty in the moral life. Where the moralists speak of the necessity for regulating or moderating emotional desires, Freud refers to the need of "domesticating" them, as one would train a beast to serve the ends of human life.

The implication, in Aristotle and Spinoza as well as in Freud, does not seem to be that man's animal appetites are in themselves bad, but that, if they are undisciplined or uncontrolled, they cause disorder in the individual life and in society. Some moralists, however, take an opposite view. For them desire is intrinsically evil, a factor of discontent, and fraught with pain.

"What we do not have," Lucretius writes, "seems better than everything else in all the world/But should we get it, we want something else." As often as a man gains something new, he discovers afresh that he is not better off. Either our desires are unsatisfied, and then we suffer the agony of frustration; or they are satiated and so are we—desperate with ennui. Hence, freedom from all desires, not just their moderation, seems to be recommended for peace of mind; as centuries later Schopenhauer recommended the negation of the will to live in order to avoid frustration or boredom.

Marcus Aurelius and the Stoics, and later Kant, similarly urge us "not to yield to the persuasions of the body . . . and never to be over-powered either by the motion of the senses or of the appetites." But whereas the Stoics would restrain desire "because it is animal" and in order to avoid pain, Kant argues that the renunciation of desire should be undertaken "not merely in accordance with duty . . . but from duty, which must be the true end of all moral cultivation."

The opposition between these two views of desire in the moral life represents one of the major issues in ethical theory, further discussed in the chapters on DUTY and VIRTUE AND VICE. The doctrine of natural appetite is crucially relevant to the issue. If the naturalist in ethics is right, he is so by virtue of the truth that natural tendencies are everywhere the measure of good and evil. If, however, there is no truth in the doctrine of natural desire, then the impulses which spring from man's animal passions can claim no authority in the court of reason.

18

Dialectic

INTRODUCTION

THE words "dialectical" and "dialectician" are currently used more often in a derogatory than in a descriptive sense. The person who criticizes an argument by saying, "It's just a matter of definition" is also apt to say, "That may be true dialectically, but . . . " or "You're just being dialectical." Implied in such remarks is dispraise of reasoning which, however excellent or skillful it may be as reasoning, stands condemned for being out of touch with fact or experience.

Still other complaints against dialectic are that it plays with words, begs the question, makes sport of contradictions. When the theologian Hippothadeus almost convinces Panurge that he "should rather choose to marry once, than to burn still in fires of concupiscence," Rabelais has Panurge raise one last doubt against the proposal. "Shall I be a cuckold, father," he asks, "yea or no?" Hippothadeus answers: "By no means . . . will you be a cuckold, if it please God." On receiving this reply Panurge cries out, "O the Lord help us now; whither are we driven to, good folks? To the conditionals, which, according to the rules and precepts of the dialectic faculty, admit of all contradictions and impossibilities. If my Transalpine mule had wings, my Transalpine mule would fly. If it please God, I shall not be a cuckold, but I shall be a cuckold if it please him."

As a term of disapproval, "dialectical" has been used by scientists against philosophers, by philosophers against theologians, and, with equal invective, by religious men against those who resort to argument concerning matters of faith.

The early Middle Ages witnessed a conflict between the mystical and the rational approaches to the truths of religion. Those for whom religious experience and revelation were the only avenue to God condemned the dialecticians—the philosophers or theologians who tried to use reason discursively rather than proceed by intuition and vision. With the Reformation and with the Renaissance, men like Martin Luther and Francis Bacon regarded dialectic as the bane of medieval learning. Because of its dialectical character, Luther dismissed all theological speculation as sophistry. Bacon, for the same reason, stigmatized scholastic philosophy as consisting in "no great quantity of matter and infinite agitation of wit."

On grounds which were common as well as opposite, both mystics and experimentalists attacked dialectic as a futile, if not vicious, use of the mind—as "hair-splitting" and "logic-chopping." Even when they admitted that it might have some virtue, they approved of it as a method of argument or proof, proper enough perhaps in forensic oratory or political debate, but entirely out of place in the pursuit of truth or in approaching reality.

A CERTAIN CONCEPTION of dialectic is implicit in all such criticisms. The dialectician is a man who argues rather than observes, who appeals to reason rather than experience, who draws implications from whatever is said or can be said, pushing a premise to its logical conclusion or reducing it to absurdity. This aspect of dialectic appears to be the object of Rabelais's satire in the famous dispute between Panurge and Thaumast, which is carried on "by signs only, without speaking, for the matters are so abstruse, hard, and arduous, that words proceeding from the mouth of man will never be sufficient for the unfolding of them."

In view of those who think that truth can be learned only by observation, by induction from particulars, or generalization from experience, the technique of dialectic, far from being a method of inquiry, seems to have virtue only for the purpose of disputation or criticism. "The human faculties," writes Gibbon, "are fortified by the art and practice of dialectics." It is "the keenest weapon of dispute," he adds, but "more effectual for the detection of error than for the investigation of truth."

J. S. Mill describes "the Socratic dialectics, so magnificently exemplified in the dialogues of Plato," as a "contrivance for making the difficulties of the question . . . present to the learner's consciousness . . . They were essentially a negative discussion of the great questions of philosophy and life," he continues, "directed with consummate skill to the purpose of convincing anyone who has merely adopted the commonplaces of received opinion that he did not understand the subject . . . The school disputations of the Middle Ages had a somewhat similar object." In Mill's opinion, "as a discipline to the mind, they were in every respect inferior to the powerful dialectics which formed the intellects of the 'Socratic viri'; but the modern mind," he says, "owes far more to both than it is generally willing to admit, and the present modes of education contain nothing which in the smallest degree supplies the place either of the one or of the other."

Disparaging comment on dialectic comes not only from those who contrast it unfavorably with the methods of experiment or empirical research. It is made also by writers who trust reason's power to grasp truths intuitively and to develop their consequences deductively. Sensitive to what may seem to be a paradox here, Descartes writes in his *Rules for the Direction of the Mind*: "It may perhaps strike some with surprise that here, where we are discussing how to improve our power of deducing one truth from another, we have omitted all the precepts of the dialecticians." The dialectician can proceed only after he has been given premises to work from. Since, in Descartes's view, dialectic provides no method for establishing premises or for discovering

first principles, it can "contribute nothing at all to the discovery of the truth . . . Its only possible use is to serve to explain at times more easily to others the truths we have already ascertained; hence it should be transferred from Philosophy to Rhetoric."

THE CONNECTION of dialectic with disputation and rhetoric has some foundation in the historical fact that many of the techniques of dialectic originated with the Greek Sophists who had primarily a rhetorical or forensic aim. Comparable to the Roman rhetoricians and to the law teachers of a later age, the Sophists taught young men how to plead a case, how to defend themselves against attack, how to persuade an audience. Skill in argument had for them a practical, not a theoretical, purpose; not truth or knowledge, but success in litigation or in political controversy. The familiar charge that the method they taught enabled men "to make the worse appear the better reason," probably exaggerates, but nonetheless reflects, the difference between the standards of probability in disputation and the standards of truth in scientific inquiry. This has some bearing on the disrepute of sophistry and the derogatory light cast on the *dialectical* when it is identified with the *sophistical*.

But there is another historical fact which places dialectic in a different light. In the tradition of the liberal arts, especially in their Roman and medieval development, "dialectic" and "logic" are interchangeable names for the discipline which, together with grammar and rhetoric, comprises the three liberal arts known as the "trivium." In his treatise *On Christian Doctrine* Augustine uses the word "dialectic" in this way. Whatever else it means, the identification of dialectic with logic implies its distinction from rhetoric and certainly from sophistry.

Yet Augustine does not fail to observe the misuse of dialectic which debases it to the level of sophistry. "In the use of it," he declares, "we must guard against the love of wrangling, and the childish vanity of entrapping an adversary. For there are many of what are called *sophisms*," he continues, "inferences in reasoning that are false, and yet so close an imitation of the true, as to deceive not only dull people, but clever men too, when they are not on their guard." He gives as an example the case of one man saying to another, "What I am, you are not." The other man may assent to this, thinking, as Augustine points out, that "the proposition is in part true, the one man being cunning, the other simple." But when "the first speaker adds: 'I am a man' " and "the other has given his assent to this also, the first draws his conclusion: 'Then you are not a man.' "

According to Augustine, "this sort of ensnaring argument" should not be called dialectical, but sophistical. He makes the same sort of observation about the abuse of rhetoric in speech which "only aims at verbal ornamentation more than is consistent with seriousness of purpose." That, too, he thinks, should be "called sophistical" in order to avoid attaching the name of rhetoric to misapplications of the art.

Dialectic for Augustine is the art which "deals with inferences, and definitions, and divisions" and "is of the greatest assistance in the discovery of meaning." Rhetoric, on the other hand, "is not to be used so much for ascertaining the meaning as for setting forth the meaning when it is ascertained." Dialectic, in other words, is divorced from the practical purpose of stating and winning an argument, and given theoretical status as a method of inquiry.

THIS CONCEPTION of dialectic originates in the dialogues of Plato. Not himself a Sophist, either by profession or in aim, Socrates found other uses for the analytical and argumentative devices invented by the Sophists. The same skills of mind which were practically useful in the public assembly and in the law courts could be used or adapted for clarification and precision in speculative discussions. They could also be used to find the truth implicitly in the commonly expressed convictions of men and to lay bare errors caused by lack of definition in discourse or lack of rigor in reasoning.

In the *Sophist* Plato separates the philosopher from the sophist, not by any distinction in method, but by the difference in the use each makes of the same technique. And in *The Republic,* one of the reasons Socrates gives for postponing the study of dialectic until the age of thirty is that youngsters, "when they first get the taste in their mouths, argue for amusement" and "like puppy-dogs, they rejoice in pulling and tearing at all who come near them." As a result of being vainly disputatious, they "get into the way of not believing anything which they believed before, and hence, not only they, but philosophy and all that relates to it is apt to have a bad name with the rest of the world . . . But when a man begins to get older, he will no longer be guilty of such insanity; he will imitate the dialectician who is seeking for truth, and not the sophist, who is contradicting for the sake of amusement."

In the hands of the philosopher, dialectic is an instrument of science. "There is," according to Socrates, "no other method of comprehending by any regular process all true existence or of ascertaining what each thing is in its own nature." It passes beyond the arts at the lowest level, "which are concerned with the desires or opinions of men, or are cultivated with a view to production and constructions." It likewise transcends the mathematical sciences, which, while they "have some apprehension of true being . . . leave the hypotheses which they use unexamined, and are unable to give an account of them." Using these as "handmaids and helpers," dialectic "goes directly to the first principle and is the only science which does away with hypotheses in order to make her ground more secure."

The dialectic of Plato has an upward and a downward path which somewhat resemble the inductive process of the mind from facts to principles, and the deductive process from principles to the conclusions they validate. Dialectic, says Socrates, ascends by using hypotheses "as steps and points of departure into a world which is above hypotheses, in order that she may soar beyond them to the first principle of the whole . . . By successive steps she descends again without the aid of any sensible object, from ideas, through ideas, and in ideas she ends."

As the disciplined search for truth, dialectic

includes all of logic. It is concerned with every phase of thought: with the establishment of definitions; the examination of hypotheses in the light of their presuppositions or consequences; the formulation of inferences and proofs; the resolution of dilemmas arising from opposition in thought.

WHEREAS FOR PLATO dialectic is more than the whole of logic, for Aristotle it is less. Dialectic is more than the process by which the mind goes from myth and fantasy, perception and opinion, to the highest truth. For Plato it is the ultimate fruit of intellectual labor— knowledge itself, and in its supreme form as a vision of being and unity. That is why Socrates makes it the ultimate study in the curriculum proposed for training the guardians to become philosopher kings. "Dialectic," he says, "is the coping-stone of the sciences, and is set over them; no other science can be placed higher— the nature of knowledge can go no further."

For Aristotle, dialectic, far from being at the summit of science and philosophy, lies at their base, and must be carefully distinguished from sophistry, which it resembles in method. "Dialecticians and sophists assume the same guise as the philosopher," Aristotle writes, "for sophistic is wisdom which exists only in semblance, and dialecticians embrace all things in their dialectic, and being is common to all things; but evidently their dialectic embraces these subjects because these are proper to philosophy. Sophistic and dialectic," he continues, "turn on the same class of things as philosophy, but philosophy differs from dialectic in the nature of the faculty required and from sophistic in respect of the purpose of the philosophic life. Dialectic is merely critical where philosophy claims to know, and sophistic is what appears to be philosophy but is not."

ACCORDING TO ARISTOTLE, dialectic is neither itself a science nor the method of science. It is that part of logic or method which he treats in the *Topics,* and it differs from the scientific method expounded in the *Posterior Analytics* as argument in the sphere of opinion and probabilities differs from scientific demonstration.

Unlike the conclusions of science, the conclusions of dialectical reasoning are only probable, because they are based on assumptions rather than self-evident truths. Since other and opposite assumptions cannot be excluded, one dialectical conclusion is usually opposed by another in an issue of competing probabilities.

Intermediate between science and rhetoric, dialectic can serve both. In addition to its practical employment in forensics, it is useful in the philosophical sciences because it develops skill in making and criticizing definitions, and in asking or answering questions. "The ability to raise searching difficulties on both sides of a subject," Aristotle says, "will make us detect more easily the truth and error about the several points that arise."

Though it is primarily a method of arguing from assumptions and of dealing with disputes arising from contrary assumptions, dialectic is also concerned with the starting points of argument. The *Topics* considers how assumptions are chosen, what makes them acceptable, what determines their probability. Here again Aristotle shows how the philosopher can make use of dialectic—as that "process of criticism wherein lies the path to the principles of all inquiries."

THERE ARE FOUR major expositions of dialectic in the tradition of the great books. It is as pivotal a conception in the thought of Kant and Hegel as it is in the philosophies of Plato and Aristotle. With differences which may be more important than the similarities, the Kantian treatment resembles the Aristotelian, the Hegelian the Platonic.

Like the division between the *Posterior Analytics* and the *Topics* in Aristotle's *Organon,* the transcendental logic of Kant's *The Critique of Pure Reason* falls into two parts—the analytic and the dialectic. The distinction between his transcendental logic and what Kant calls "general logic" is discussed in the chapter on LOGIC, but here it must be observed that for Kant "general logic, considered as an organon, must always be a logic of illusion, that is, be dialectical." He thinks that the ancients used the word "dialectic" in this sense, to signify "a sophistical art for giving ignorance, nay, even intentional sophistries, the coloring of truth, in which the thoroughness of procedure which logic requires was imitated." For his own purposes, however, he wishes "dialectic" to be understood "in the sense of a critique of dialectical illusion."

When he comes to his own transcendental logic, therefore, he divides it into two parts. The first part deals with "the elements of pure cognition of the understanding, and the principles without which no object at all can be thought." This is the "Transcendental Analytic, and at the same time a logic of truth"— a logic of science. Since in his view "it ought properly to be only a canon for judging of the empirical use of the understanding, this kind of logic is misused when we seek to employ it as an organon of the universal and unlimited exercise of the understanding."

When it is thus misused, "the exercise of the pure understanding becomes dialectical. The second part of our transcendental logic," Kant writes, "must therefore be a critique of dialectical illusion, and this critique we shall term Transcendental Dialectic—not meaning it as an art of producing dogmatically such illusion (an art which is unfortunately too current among the practitioners of metaphysical juggling), but as a critique of understanding and reason in regard to their hyperphysical use."

Kant goes further than Aristotle in separating dialectic from science. With regard to the sensible or phenomenal world of experience, science is possible; with regard to the mind's own structure, the supreme sort of science is possible. But when reason tries to use its ideas for other objects, and then regards them "as conceptions of actual things, their mode of application is *transcendent* and delusive." Kant explains that "an idea is employed transcendentally, when it is applied to an object falsely believed . . . to correspond to it; immanently, when it is applied solely to the employment of the *understanding* in the sphere of experience"; and he maintains that when ideas are used transcendentally, they do not give rise to science, but "assume a fallacious and dialectical character."

A conclusion of dialectical reasoning, according to Kant, is either opposed by a con-clusion equally acceptable to reason—"a perfectly natural antithetic"—as in the antinomies of pure reason; or, as in the paralogisms, the reasoning has specious cogency which can be shown to "conclude falsely, while the form is correct and unexceptionable." In this balance of reason against itself lies the illusory character of the transcendental dialectic.

Where Aristotle recognizes that reason can be employed on both sides of a question because it involves competing probabilities, Kant in calling dialectic "a logic of appearance" explicitly remarks that "this does not signify a doctrine of probability." He further distinguishes what he calls "transcendental illusory appearance" from "empirical illusory appearance" and ordinary "logical illusion." The latter two can be corrected and totally removed. But "transcendental illusion, on the contrary," he writes, "does not cease to exist even after it has been exposed and its nothingness has been clearly perceived by means of transcendental criticism."

The reason for this, Kant explains, is that "here we have to do with a *natural* and unavoidable illusion, which rests upon subjective principles, and imposes these upon us as objective . . . There is, therefore," he continues, "a natural and unavoidable dialectic of pure reason" which arises because the mind seeks to answer questions "well nigh impossible to answer," such as "how objects exist as things in themselves" or "how the nature of things is to be subordinated to principles." In its effort to transcend experience—"in disregard of all the warnings of criticism"—the mind cannot escape the frustration, the dialectical illusion, "which is an inseparable adjunct of human reason." It is not, Kant repeatedly insists, that "the ideas of pure reason" are "in their own nature dialectical; it is from their misemployment alone that fallacies and illusions arise."

FOR HEGEL AS for Plato dialectic moves in the realm of truth and ideas, not probabilities and illusions. But for Hegel dialectic is always the process of mind, or of the Idea, in interminable motion toward absolute truth—never resting in the intuition of that truth. The Idea, he writes, "is self-determined, it assumes successive forms which it successively transcends; and by this very process of transcending its earlier stages, gains an affirmative, and, in fact, a richer and more concrete shape."

The dialectical process is a motion in which contrary and defective truths are harmonized. The synthesis of *thesis and antithesis* results in a more complete truth. To illustrate his meaning, Hegel uses the example of building a house. For such a purpose, we must have "in the first instance, a subjective aim and design" and as means, "the several substances required for the work—iron, wood, stones." In rendering these materials suitable for our purpose, we make use of the elements: "fire to melt the iron, wind to blow the fire, water to set the wheels in motion, in order to cut the wood, etc."

Yet the house that we build is, according to Hegel, an opposite or antithesis of these elements. "The wind, which has helped to build the house, is shut out by the house; so also are the violence of rains and floods, and the destructive powers of fire, so far as the house is made fire-proof. The stones and beams obey the law of gravity—press downward—and so high walls are carried up." The result is that "the elements are made use of in accordance with their nature, and yet to cooperate for a product, by which their operation is limited." The initial opposition between the idea of a house and the elements is reconciled in the higher synthesis, which is the house itself.

While it shows the opposing theses and the resulting synthesis, this example does not fully exhibit the dynamic character of the Hegelian dialectic. If the resulting synthesis is not the whole truth, it too must be defective and require supplementation by a contrary which is defective in an opposite way. These two together then become the material for a higher synthesis, another step in that continuing dialectical process which is the life of mind— both the subjective dialectic of the human mind and the objective dialectic of the Absolute Mind or the Idea.

THE THREAD OF common meaning which runs through these four conceptions of dialectic is to be found in the principle of opposition. In each of them dialectic either begins or ends with some sort of intellectual conflict, or develops and then resolves such oppositions.

For Kant dialectical opposition takes the extreme form of irreducible contradictions from which the mind cannot escape. "It is a melancholy reflection," he declares, "that reason in its highest exercise, falls into an antithetic." This comes about because "all statements enunciated by pure reason transcend the conditions of possible experience, beyond the sphere of which we can discover no criterion of truth, while they are at the same time framed in accordance with the laws of the understanding, which are applicable only to experience; and thus it is the fact of all such speculative discussions, that while the one party attacks the weaker side of his opponent, he infallibly lays open his own weaknesses."

For Hegel the opposition takes the milder form of contrary theses and antitheses. They can be dialectically overcome by a synthesis which remedies the incompleteness of each half truth. "It is one of the most important discoveries of logic," Hegel says, "that a specific moment which, by standing in an opposition, has the position of an extreme, ceases to be such and is a moment in an organic whole by being at the same time a mean." The Hegelian opposition is thus also "mediation."

Dialectical opposition for Aristotle originates in the disagreements which occur in ordinary human discourse. But just as disagreement is reasonable only if there are two sides to the question in dispute, so reason can operate dialectically only with regard to genuinely arguable matters. The familiar topics concerning which men disagree represent the commonplace issues of dialectic, since for the most part they are formed from debatable propositions or questions. "Nobody in his senses," Aristotle believes, "would make a proposition of what no one holds; nor would he make a problem of what is obvious to everybody or to most people." Each of the conflicting opinions will therefore have some claim to probability. Here the dialectical process ends neither in a synthesis of incomplete opposites nor in a rejection of both as illusory; but, having "an eye to general opinion," it seeks to ascertain the more reasonable view—the more tenable or probable of the two.

In the Platonic theory of dialectic, the element of opposition appears in the tension between being and becoming, the one and many, or the intelligible and the sensible, which is found present in every stage of the mind's dialectical ascent to the contemplation of ideas. So fundamental is this tension that Socrates uses it to define the dialectician as one who is "able to see 'a One and Many' in Nature"—by comprehending "scattered particulars in one idea" and dividing it "into species according to their natural formation." Here as in the Hegelian theory the oppositions—*apparent* contradictions in discourse—can be resolved by dialectic, and through their resolution the mind then rises to a higher level.

It is only in the writings of Hegel or his followers that the meaning of dialectic is not limited to the activity of human thought. Hegel expressly warns that "the loftier dialectic . . . is not an activity of subjective thinking applied to some matter externally, but is rather the matter's very soul putting forth its branches and fruit organically." It is the "development of the Idea," which is "the proper activity of its rationality." If the whole world in its existence and development is the thought and thinking of an Absolute Mind, or the Idea, then the events of nature and of history are moments in a dialectical process of cosmic proportions. The principles of dialectic become the principles of change, and change itself is conceived as a progress or evolution from lower to higher, from part to whole, from the indeterminate to the determinate.

The dialectical pattern of history, conceived by Hegel as the progressive objectification of spirit, is reconstructed by Marx in terms of the conflict of material forces. Marx himself explicitly contrasts his dialectic with that of Hegel. "My dialectic method," he writes, "is not only different from the Hegelian, but is its direct opposite." Hegel, he claims, thinks that "the real world is only the external, phenomenal form of 'the Idea,'" whereas his own view is that "the ideal is nothing else than the material world reflected by the human mind, and translated into forms of thought."

Nevertheless, with respect to dialectic, Marx praises Hegel for being "the first to present its general form of working in a comprehensive and conscious manner." The only trouble is that with Hegel, dialectic "is standing on its head." It must therefore "be turned right side up again," a revolution which Marx thinks he accomplishes in his dialectical materialism.

Having put dialectic on its proper basis, Marx constructs the whole of history in terms of a conflict of material forces, or of social classes in economic strife, according to a dialectical pattern which provides "recognition of the existing state of things, at the same time also the recognition of the negation of that state, of its inevitable breaking up." History is thus viewed dialectically "as in fluid movement," yet it is also conceived as working toward a definite end—the revolution which has as its result the peace of the classless society. Bourgeois industry, by bringing about the concentration and association of the proletariat, produces "its own grave diggers; its fall and the victory of the proletariat" are "equally inevitable."

In Marx's vocabulary the phrases "historical materialism" and "dialectical materialism" are strictly synonymous. But Marx's protest to the contrary notwithstanding, a comparison of Marx and Hegel seems to show that a dialectic of history is equally capable of being conceived in terms of spirit or of matter.

The question whether there is a dialectic of nature as well as a dialectic of history remains a point of controversy in Marxist thought, despite the bearing which Hegel's *Science of Logic* and *The Phenomenology of Mind* might have upon the question. Engels tries in his *Dialectics of Nature* to give a fuller rendering of the Hegelian dialectic in strictly materialistic terms. Its universal scope, including all of nature as well as all of history, is also reflected in certain post-Darwinian doctrines of cosmic evolution.

Considerations relevant to the Hegelian or Marxist dialectic will be found in the chapters on HISTORY and PROGRESS. Without judging the issues which Hegel and Marx have raised in the thought of the last century, it may be permissible to report the almost violent intellectual aversion they have produced in certain quarters. Nietzsche is contemptuous of all dialecticians: "They pose as having discovered and attained their real opinions through the self-evolution of a cold, pure, divinely unperturbed dialectic . . . while what happens at bottom is that a prejudice, a notion, an 'inspiration,' generally a desire of the heart sifted and made abstract, is defended by them with reasons sought after the event—they are one and all advocates who do not want to be regarded as such." Freud is as unsympathetic in his criticism of Marx and as uncompromising in his rejection of dialectical materialism, as William James before him is extreme in the expression of his distaste for Hegel. Mocking "the Hegelizers" who think that "the glory and beauty of the psychic life is that in it all contradictions find their reconciliation," James declares: "With this intellectual temper I confess I cannot contend."

The Hegelian dialectic and what James calls "the pantomime-state of mind" are, in his opinion, "emotionally considered, one and the same thing. In the pantomime all common things are represented to happen in impossible ways, people jump down each other's throats, houses turn inside out, old women become young men, everything 'passes into its opposite' with inconceivable celerity and skill . . . And so in the Hegelian logic," James continues, "relations elsewhere recognized under the insipid name of distinctions (such as that between knower and object, many and one) must first be translated into impossibilities and contradictions, then 'transcended' and identified by miracle, ere the proper temper is induced for thoroughly enjoying the spectacle they show."

19

Duty

INTRODUCTION

LOCKE, discussing in the course of his essay *Concerning Human Understanding* "why a man must keep his word," notes that we meet with three different answers to this question. "If a Christian be asked, he will give as reason: Because God, who has the power of eternal life and death, requires it of us. But if a Hobbist be asked why? he will answer: Because the public requires it, and the Leviathan will punish you if you do not. And if one of the old philosophers had been asked, he would have answered: Because it was dishonest, below the dignity of a man, and opposite to virtue, the highest perfection of human nature, to do otherwise."

With these three answers Locke introduces us to some of the alternative views on what is perhaps the central problem concerning duty. All three acknowledge the existence of duty and the force of obligation. By accepting the question they affirm the proposition that a man *must* or *ought to* keep his word. But why? What creates the *ought* or obligation?

Two of the answers Locke cites—that of the Christian and that of the Hobbist—seem to derive duty from the commands of law, the law of God or of the state, in either case a law to be enforced by the sanctions of a superior power. Accordingly, the citizen has duties to the state, the religious man to God. Yet it does not seem to be entirely the case that such duties rest exclusively on the *superior power* of God or the state. Men who obey either divine or civil law from fear of punishment alone, are said to act not from duty but from expediency—in terms of a calculation of risks and consequences.

Obedience to law would appear to be acknowledged as a duty only by those who recognize the authority of the law or the right of the lawmaker to command. They would be willing to obey the law even if no external sanction could be enforced against them by a superior power. Those whom the law binds in conscience rather than by its coercive force obey the law because it is morally right to do so. The sense of the law's moral authority is for them the sense of duty from which the dictates of conscience flow.

Locke's third answer—that of the ancient philosophers—shows that duty is sometimes understood without reference to law, divine or human. We share this understanding whenever, having made a promise or contracted a debt, we feel an obligation to discharge it even if no superior commands the act. Here, furthermore, the obligation seems to be to another individual—to a person who may be our equal—rather than to the state or God.

As indicated by Locke's statement of this ancient view, it is the honest or just man who acknowledges such obligations apart from the law or his relation to any superior. Virtue may, of course, also direct a man to act for the common welfare and to obey the laws of the state or the commandments of God. But the immediate source of the obligation to act in a certain way toward one's fellowmen is placed by the ancients, according to Locke, in "virtue, the highest perfection of human nature." On this view, virtue alone provides the motivation. Without it men would act lawfully only because of the law's coercive force. Without it men would recognize no obligations to their fellowmen or to the state.

THESE TWO conceptions of duty—for the moment grouping the Christian and Hobbist answers together against the ancient view—may seem at first to be only verbally different. It seems certain that dutiful conduct would frequently be the same on either view. Yet they do conflict with one another, and each, if examined further, presents difficulties.

The theory that duty arises from a man's own virtue receives its classic expression, as Locke intimates, in the ancient philosophers, particularly Plato and Aristotle. It appears in *The Republic,* for example, when Socrates has to meet Glaucon's argument that men abide by moral rules, not simply because they ought to, but in order to avoid the pain of censure and punishment. Glaucon claims that, given the possession of Gyges' ring which can render a man invisible to others, "no man would keep his hands off what was not his own when he could safely take what he liked." He could "in all respects be like a God among men."

Against this Socrates sets his conception of the "just man" who does what he ought to do because it is just, and because justice is essential to the very life and health of the soul. According to Socrates' way of thinking, it is ridiculous to ask "which is the more profitable, to be just and act justly and practise virtue, whether seen or unseen of gods and men, or to be unjust . . . We know that, when the bodily constitution is gone, life is no longer endurable, though pampered with all kinds of meat and drinks, and having all wealth and all power; and shall we be told that when the very essence of the vital principle is undermined and corrupted, life is still worth having to a man, if only he be allowed to do whatever he likes with the single exception that he is not to acquire justice and virtue, or to escape from injustice and vice?"

On this view, it seems to be the virtue of justice which lies at the root of duty or obligation. But for Plato justice, though only one of the virtues, is inseparable from the other three—temperance, courage, and wisdom. It is almost indifferent therefore whether one attributes moral obligation to the particular virtue of justice or to virtue in general. As the chapters on JUSTICE and VIRTUE AND VICE indicate, Aristotle differs from Plato, both with respect to the virtues in general and to justice

in particular. For Aristotle it is justice alone, not virtue in general or any other particular virtue, which gives rise to duty or obligation.

Justice differs from the other virtues, according to Aristotle, in that it "alone of the virtues is thought to consider 'another's good' because it concerns the relation of a man to his neighbor." The other virtues, such as temperance and courage, do not give rise to obligations, *unless* they are somehow annexed to or united with justice. Whenever Aristotle speaks of duties he does so with reference to the obligations that follow from justice— "the duties of parents to children and those of brothers to each other . . . those of comrades and those of fellow-citizens."

Whereas for Aristotle justice always refers to the good of another, or to the common good of all, such virtues as temperance and courage, when they are isolated from justice, concern the well-being of the individual himself. That is why only justice entails duties, which are obligations to act in a certain way for the welfare of others. If the good of no other individual is involved, it seems that a man has no duty to be temperate or courageous, even when he possesses these virtues.

Precisely because of the essentially social character of justice, Aristotle raises the question "whether a man can treat himself unjustly or not." He is willing to admit that a man can do justice or injustice to himself only in a metaphorical sense. What he calls "metaphorical justice" is not a relation between a man and himself, but a relation between one part of himself and another.

Aquinas seems to follow Aristotle in connecting duty with justice and with no other virtue. "Justice alone of all the virtues," he writes, "implies the notion of duty." If he also intimates that duty may somehow enter into the acts of other virtues—as when he says that "it is not so patent in the other virtues as it is in justice"—his position still remains fundamentally Aristotelian. Referring to that "kind of metaphorical justice" to which Aristotle appeals in stating the sense in which a man can treat himself unjustly, Aquinas explains how "all the other virtues" can be said to "involve the duty of the lower powers to reason." Apart from this metaphorical duty of the passions to obey reason, duty in the strict sense comes, in the opinion of Aquinas, only from the precepts of justice, which concern the relation of one person to another.

ON THIS THEORY, duty is not coextensive with morality, the sense of duty is not identical with the moral sense, and specific duties obligate a man to other men even when no general law exists to be obeyed. Difficulty is found with this theory by those critics who think that the whole of morality, not simply one part of it, involves duties. Does not the sense of duty operate, they ask, in matters which do not affect any other individual or even the common good? Does a man, for example, have a duty to tell the truth only to others, but not to seek it for himself? Kant, as we shall see, holds that there are private as well as public duties, or, in his language, internal duties in the realm of ethics as well as external duties in the realm of jurisprudence.

The Hobbist theory of duty seems to face similar difficulties. The specific duties which are determined by the precepts of justice may, as we have seen, not always be the same as the specific duties imposed by civil law, though they will be identical whenever the law of the state is itself an expression or determination of justice. But when law rather than justice is the principle, duty seems to consist primarily in obedience to the law or rather to the lawgiver who has superior power and authority. Only secondarily, or in consequence, does it involve obligations to other men who are one's equals.

With Hobbes, for example, justice, and the obligation as well, begin only with the establishment of a constituted authority with the power of making laws. "Where there is no Commonwealth," he writes, "there is nothing unjust. So that the nature of justice consisteth in keeping of valid covenants; but the validity of covenants begins not but with the constitution of a civil power, sufficient to compel men to keep them." Duty and justice are both said to be "laws of nature," but, Hobbes adds, they "are not properly laws, but qualities that dispose men to peace, and to obedience," until "a Commonwealth is once settled," and then

they become "the commands of the Commonwealth." In other words, "it is the Sovereign power that obliges men to obey them," and obedience, which is said to be "part also of the law of nature," is its proper expression.

So far the two conceptions conflict or at least diverge. But if the legal theory of duty goes no further than the enactments of the state, the same question arises here as before. Does a man have no duties apart from his relation to the state? Can duty be coextensive with morality if the only rules of conduct to be obeyed are laws imposed from without—regulations which have authority simply because they come from one who has the right to command? Again, as we shall see, Kant would say no.

WE HAVE now stated the questions about duty which raise difficulties for Aristotle and Hobbes. Though they differ in their theories of law and justice, as well as in their conceptions of duty, they seem to concur in thinking that doing one's duty does not exhaustively solve all moral problems.

The same questions do not, however, seem to present difficulties to other moralists—to Kant and to the Stoics of antiquity, such as Marcus Aurelius and Epictetus. On the contrary, their moral philosophy, by making the sphere of duty coextensive with the whole of moral life, seems to prevent such questions from being raised.

As we turn to examine their conception of duty, we must observe that, in two respects, it alters Locke's threefold division of the answer to the question, Why must a man keep his word? In the first place, Locke's statement of the answer given by "the ancient philosophers" seems to have only Plato and Aristotle in mind, certainly not the Stoics. In the second place, Locke's statement of the Christian position seems to associate it with the Hobbist answer, against that of Plato and Aristotle. That association may be justified on the ground that duty to God, like duty to the state, involves obligation to a superior. But Aquinas, as we have seen, seems to agree with Aristotle about justice as a source of duty; and, as we shall see, he also seems to agree with Kant and the Stoics about the pervasiveness of duty in the realm of morals. Locke's statement of the Christian position, which selects one aspect of it only, may therefore be inadequate.

The point which unites Kant, the Stoics, and Aquinas is their agreement concerning the existence of a law which is neither enacted by the state nor proclaimed by God in his revealed commandments. This law the Stoics speak of as "the law of reason," Aquinas calls "the natural law," and Kant conceives to be "the moral law within." The common conception thus variously expressed is more fully treated in the chapter on Law; but that ampler discussion is not needed to perceive that the law of reason or of nature is a moral law, in that its general principles and detailed precepts govern the entire range of moral acts.

"Morality," according to Kant, "consists in the reference of all action to the legislation which alone can render a kingdom of ends possible." By this he means that "the will is never to act on any maxim which could not without contradiction be also a universal law." This law is also moral in the sense that it exercises only moral authority and should prevail even without the support of the external sanctions which accompany the positive commands of a superior. "The idea of duty," Kant declares, "would alone be sufficient as a spring [of action] even if the spring were absent which is connected by forensic legislation . . . namely external compulsion."

Making the natural or moral law the principle of duty introduces the element of obligation into every moral act. Whatever is right to do we are obliged to do in conformity to the law of nature or in obedience to the commands of the moral law. We need no external promulgation of this law—*i.e.,* no express formulation in words by a lawgiver—for this law is inherent in reason itself. Its various maxims or precepts can be deduced from what Aquinas calls the "first principle . . . of the practical reason" and Kant "the categorical imperative." Or, as the Stoics say, since reason is the "ruling principle" in man, man's duty consists in "holding fast" to it and "going straight on" so that it has "what is its own."

On this theory, we are obliged in con-

science to do whatever reason declares right, whether or not others are directly involved. The distinction between public and private morality—between the spheres of justice and the other virtues—is irrelevant to conscience. Conscience, according to Kant, functions equally in the spheres of internal and external duty. In both the realm of ethics and the realm of jurisprudence, conscience, applying the moral law, dictates our duty in the particular case. We stand in no different relation to ourselves and others, since the moral law is universally and equally binding on all persons. The obligation is in every case to obey the law. It is not a duty to persons, *except* as the moral law commands us to respect the dignity of the human person, ourselves and others alike.

The element of a superior commanding an inferior seems to be present in this conception of duty through the relation of reason to the will and appetites of man. Acting dutifully consists in the submission of the will to reason, and in overcoming all contrary inclinations or desires. But though Kant sometimes speaks in these terms, he also conceives duty as carrying with it an obligation to God. "The subjective principle of a responsibility for one's deeds before God," he says, is "contained, though it be only obscurely, in every moral self-consciousness."

Nevertheless, Kant insists that "the Christian principle of *morality* itself is not theological." It rests, in his opinion, on the "autonomy of pure practical reason, since it does not make the knowledge of God and his will the foundation of these laws, but only of the attainment of the *summum bonum,* on the condition of following these laws, and its does not even place the proper *spring* of this obedience in the desired results, but solely in the conception of duty, as that of which the faithful observance alone constitutes the worthiness to obtain those happy consequences."

It is "through the *summum bonum* as the object and final end of pure practical reason" that, in Kant's view of Christian morality, we pass from moral philosophy to "*religion,* that is, to the *recognition of all duties as divine commands.*" Christian theologians like Aquinas and Calvin, however, seem to go further than Kant in equating conformity to the moral law—or the natural law of reason—with religious obedience to God. Nor does he explain this equivalence by reference to the fact that God has made man's attainment of the *summum bonum*—or eternal happiness—depend on his free compliance with the moral law. Rather, for Aquinas, the natural law is "nothing else than the rational creature's participation in the eternal law" of God—the "imprint on us of the divine light." As God is the author of man's nature and reason, so is He the ultimate authority behind the commands of the natural law which He implanted in man's reason at creation.

For Christian theologians like Aquinas and Calvin, duty to God involves obedience to the moral law which reason can discover by itself, no less than obedience to those positive commandments which God has revealed to man. Aquinas seems to think that violation of the natural law is as much a sin as violation of the divine law. Both involve a rupture of that order laid down by God, the one "in relation to the rule of reason, in so far as all our actions and passions should be commensurate with the rule of reason," the other "in relation to the rule of the divine law." Thus, in all moral matters, it would appear that duty is, in William Wordsworth's phrase, "stern daughter of the voice of God." If the natural law commands us to use our faculties to the ends for which they were created, then the possession of a mind imposes upon us what Socrates in the *Apology* calls man's "duty to inquire." If we fail to seek the truth, we sin against God by sinning against our nature, even though "Thou shalt seek the truth" is nowhere explicitly prescribed in Holy Writ.

The mathematician G. H. Hardy tells us that "a man's first duty . . . is to be ambitious"; for in his opinion, "all substantial contributions to human happiness have been made by ambitious men."

ETHICAL DOCTRINES can be classified according to the role which they assign to duty as a moral principle. There is perhaps no more fundamental issue in moral philosophy than that between the ethics of duty and the ethics of pleasure or happiness. This issue obviously belongs to the chapters on HAPPINESS and PLEASURE AND PAIN as well as the present one. All three must be read together—and perhaps also the chapters on DESIRE, LAW, and VIRTUE AND VICE—to complete the picture.

According to the morality of duty, every act is to be judged for its obedience to law, and the basic moral distinction is between right and wrong. But where pleasure or happiness are central, the basic distinction is between good and evil, and desire rather than law sets the standard of appraisal. An analysis of means and ends and a theory of the virtues are usually found in the ethics of happiness, as a theory of conscience and sanctions is usually prominent in the ethics of duty.

At one extreme, there is the position which totally excludes the concept of duty. This fact more than any other characterizes the Epicureanism of Lucretius. The good life for him is one where man craves nothing "except that pain be absent from the body/And mind enjoy delight, with fear dispelled, /Anxiety gone." The life he describes—so disciplined and moderated that all but the simplest pleasures are relinquished in the effort to avoid pain—seems to leave no place for obligation or social responsibility.

In the much more elaborate moral philosophy of Aristotle, virtue entails moderation in the avoidance of pain as well as in the pursuit of pleasure. Though he admits that "most pleasures might perhaps be bad without qualification," Aristotle claims that "the chief good," which is happiness, "would involve some pleasure." But even as a good, pleasure is not the only good, for there are other objects of desire.

The happy man, according to Aristotle, is one who somehow succeeds in satisfying all his desires by seeking the various kinds of goods in some order and relation to one another. Happiness itself is something that "we choose always for itself and never for the sake of something else." Although we may also choose other things in some sense for themselves, such as "honor, pleasure, reason, and every virtue," still they are chosen "for the sake of happiness," since we judge them as "the means by which we shall be happy."

In Aristotle's ethics of happiness, duty is not entirely excluded, but neither is it given any independent significance. As we have seen, it is merely an aspect of the virtue of justice, and amounts to no more than the just man's acknowledgment of the debt he owes to others; or his recognition that he is under some obligation to avoid injuring other men and to serve the common good.

At the other extreme, there is the position which identifies the sense of duty with the moral sense. In the Stoicism of Marcus Aurelius and Epictetus, to live well is to do one's duty, and to set aside all contrary desires. "It is thy duty," the Emperor writes, "to order thy life well in every single act; and if every act does its duty, as far as is possible, be content; and no one is able to hinder thee so that each act shall not do its duty." Man is not destined to be happy; his happiness consists rather in doing what is required of him at his post of duty in the order of the universe. The only good is a good will, a dutiful will, a will which conforms itself to the law of nature.

Kant's much more elaborate moral philosophy presents the same fundamental teachings. This is indicated by the fact that he associates what he calls *eudaemonism* (*i.e.,* the ethics of happiness) with *hedonism* (*i.e.,* the ethics of pleasure). Happiness, he writes, is "a rational being's consciousness of the pleasantness of life uninterruptedly accompanying his whole existence," and its basis is "the principle of self-love." Therefore, according to Kant, both eudaemonism and hedonism commit the same error. Both "undermine morality and destroy its sublimity, since they put the motives to virtue and to vice in the same class, and only teach us to make a better calculation." Both admit desire as a moral criterion of good and evil. Both are utilitarian in that they are concerned with consequences, with means and ends. Both measure the moral act by reference to the end it serves.

For Kant, "an action done from duty derives its moral worth, not from the purpose which is to be attained by it, but from the maxim by which it is determined, and therefore does not depend on the realization of the object of the action, but merely on the principle of volition by which the action has taken place, without any regard to any object of desire . . . Duty," he goes on to say, "is the necessity of acting from respect for the law." From this he argues that duty, and consequently all moral action, must be done because it is right, because the law commands it, and for no other reason. The recommendation of any action solely on the ground that it will contribute to happiness as satisfying the inclination of the person and achieving the object of the will, is completely ruled out. That would be a judgment of pure expediency. Worse than *not* moral, it is, in the opinion of Kant, *immoral.*

"An action done from duty," Kant writes, "must wholly exclude the influence of inclination, and with it every object of the will, so that nothing remains which can determine the will except objectively the law, and subjectively pure respect for this practical law, and consequently the maxim that I should follow this law even to the thwarting of all my inclinations . . . The pre-eminent good which we call moral can therefore consist in nothing else than the conception of law in itself, which certainly is only possible in a rational being in so far as this conception, and not the expected effect, determines the will."

This law, which is the source of duty and of all moral action, is Kant's famous "categorical imperative"—or, in other words, reason's unconditional command. According to its decree, Kant declares, "I am never to act otherwise than so that I could also will that my maxim should become a universal law." By obeying the categorical imperative, we can know and do our duty and rest assured that our will is morally good. "I do not, therefore, need any far-reaching penetration to discern what I have to do," Kant writes, "in order that my will may be morally good. Inexperienced in the course of the world, incapable of being prepared for all its contingencies, I only ask myself: Canst thou also will that thy maxim should be a universal law? If not, then it must be rejected, and that not because of a disadvantage accruing from it to myself, or even to others, but because it cannot enter as a principle into a possible universal legislation."

To say that a man *ought to* do this or refrain

from doing that *in order to* achieve happiness is, for Kant, at best a conditional obligation, ultimately a specious one since he is not unconditionally obliged to be happy. Kant does not totally exclude happiness or the *summum bonum*. In fact he says that there is no need to maintain "an opposition" between them and morality. But he claims that "the moment duty is in question we should take no account of happiness." Just as Aristotle treats duty only in terms of justice, so Kant considers happiness to have a moral quality only insofar as to be worthy of it is an end set by the moral law.

TWO OTHER voices join in this great argument concerning duty and happiness. One is that of J. S. Mill, whose *Utilitarianism* recognizes Kant as the chief opponent of an ethics of happiness. Though Mill differs from Aristotle on many points, particularly in regard to the virtues as means to happiness, Mill's answer to Kant can be read as a defense of Aristotle as well as of his own theory.

From Kant's point of view, they are both utilitarians. They both argue in terms of means and ends. They both make purely pragmatic, not moral, judgments—judgments of expediency instead of judgments of right and wrong.

From Mill's point of view, Aristotle like himself needs no other principle of morality than happiness, an ultimate end which justifies every means that tends toward its realization. "The ultimate sanction of all morality, external motives apart," Mill writes, "is a subjective feeling in our own minds." He asserts that "when once the general happiness is recognized as the ethical standard," it will appeal to "a powerful natural sentiment." Man's nature as a social being, he holds, "tends to make him feel it one of his natural wants that there should be harmony between his feelings and aims and those of his fellow-creatures."

This conviction, in persons who have it, "does not present itself to their minds as a superstition of education, or a law despotically imposed by the power of society, but as an attribute which it would not be well for them to be without." This conviction, rather than an internal sense of obligation or fear of external sanctions imposed by a superior power, is

for Mill "the ultimate sanction of the greatest happiness morality"—which aims at the greatest happiness for the greatest number.

Where Mill answers Kant by excluding duty—even from considerations of justice—Aquinas seems to develop an analysis in which every moral act can be regarded as obeying or disobeying the natural law and yet, at the same time, be judged as a means which serves or fails to serve the ultimate end of man's natural desire. "The order of the precepts of the natural law is," in the words of Aquinas, "according to the order of natural inclinations." The dilemma set up by the opposition between duty and happiness seems to be denied, or at least avoided, by a theory which finds a perfect parallelism between the precepts of natural law and the objects of natural desire, a parallelism resulting from their common source in the creation of human nature by God.

THE TENSION between duty and desire—between obedience to rules of conduct and unrestrained indulgence—is one of the burdens which no other animal except man must bear. It is a constant theme in the great poems. It is pivotal to the plot of most of the great love stories. It is a theme of tragedy, for in whichever direction the tension is resolved—whether in the line of duty (as by Aeneas forsaking Dido) or in disobedience to law (as by Adam yielding to Eve in *Paradise Lost*)—ruin results.

The tragedy of being both rational and animal seems to consist in *having to choose* between duty and desire rather than in making any particular choice. It may be significant, however, that the tragic heroes of poetry more frequently abandon duty than desire or love, though seldom without mortal punishment, preceded by a deep sense of their transgression. Sometimes, however, they are self-deceived, and cloak desire in the guise of duty.

There is another source of tragic conflict in the sphere of duty. Men are torn by competing loyalties, obligations which pull them in opposite directions. In the basic relationships of the family, the duty a man owes to his parents often cannot be discharged without violating or neglecting obligations to his wife. When the moral law and the law of the state command contrary actions, duty is weighed against duty in an ordeal of conscience. Sometimes, however, one obligation seems to take clear precedence over another, as in the mind of Sophocles' Antigone, for whom the king's edict loses its authority when it runs counter to the law of God. Creon the king, not Antigone his subject, may be the play's more tragic personage. He sacrifices a dearly beloved son to uphold the authority he considers it his duty as a ruler to maintain.

If man is not a rational animal or if, whatever his nature, reason is not its ruling principle, then the sense of duty would appear to be an imposture that draws its driving force from the emotional energies with which certain man-made rules of conduct are invested. Rather than acting as a counterweight to desire, duty is itself the shape which certain desires take to combat others.

Weber cites with approval Nietzsche's theory of "resentment"—a theory that "regards the moral glorification of mercy and brotherliness as a 'slave revolt in morals' among those who are disadvantaged . . . The ethic of 'duty,' " he then goes on to say, "is thus considered a product of 'repressed' sentiments for vengeance on the part of banausic men who 'displace' their sentiments because they are powerless . . . They resent the way of life of the lordly stratum who live free of duties."

Conscience, or the *super-ego,* according to Freud, is born of the struggle between the *ego* and the *id.* Translated into "popular language," Freud tells us, "the ego stands for reason and circumspection, while the id stands for the untamed passions." What may originally have had a necessary function to perform in the psychic economy can grow to play too dominant a part. For the psychoanalyst, not tragedy but neurosis results from an overdeveloped sense of duty. When "the ego [is] forced to acknowledge its weakness," Freud explains, it "breaks out into anxiety: reality anxiety in face of the external world, normal anxiety in face of the super-ego, and neurotic anxiety in face of the strength of the passions in the id."

THE RELATION of ruler and ruled in the domestic or the political community may seem at first to impose duties or obligations only on the ruled. The ruler commands. His subjects are obliged to obey. Does the ruler in turn have no duties, no obligations to those whom he governs? If he has none, then neither have the persons he rules rights which he must respect. Such absolute rule—defined by a correlative absence of duties in the ruler and rights in the ruled—has been one conception of the relation between master and slave.

In the state rulers who are merely officeholders are obligated by the duties of their office as well as vested with its authority and power. The officeholder, duty-bound by the constitution, is not an absolute ruler. He is, in fact, a servant of the state, not its master. The medieval king who pledged himself in his coronation oath to discharge the duties of his office may not have been bound by human law, but so long as his conscience kept him loyal to his pledge, he recognized the supremacy of the natural law or of the law of God. The self-governing citizen of a republic is similarly duty-bound only when he recognizes the supremacy of the common good.

According to the theory of constitutional government, rights and duties are correlative. The acknowledgment of duties signifies that the holder of rights recognizes their limited or conditional character. To consider oneself entirely exempt from duties or obligations is to regard one's rights as absolute. Can anyone have absolute rights except on condition of being without a superior of any sort? One implied answer to this question is that neither despot nor state, but only God, is autonomous or without duty.

20

Education

THE great books assembled in this set are offered as means to a liberal or general education. The authors of these books were educated men; more than that, they typified the ideal of education in their various epochs. As their writings reveal, their minds were largely formed, or at least deeply impressed, by reading the works of their predecessors. Many of them were related as teacher and student, sometimes through personal contact, sometimes only through the written word. Many of them were related as divergent disciples of the same master, yet they often differed with him as well as with one another. There is scarcely one among them—except Homer—who was not acquainted with the minds of the others who came before him and, more often than not, profoundly conversant with their thought.

Yet with two exceptions, none of the writings in this set are specific treatises on education. The exceptions are Montaigne's essay "Of the Education of Children" and Dewey's *Experience and Education.* Some of these authors speak more or less fully of their own education, as does Marcus Aurelius in the opening book of his *Meditations,* Augustine in his *Confessions,* Descartes in his *Discourse on the Method,* and Boswell. Others refer to their educational experience in fictional guise, as does Aristophanes in the argument in *The Clouds* between the Just and Unjust Discourses; or Rabelais when he tells of Gargantua's schooling in Gargantua's letter to Pantagruel. Sometimes they report the way in which other men were trained to greatness, as does Plutarch; or, like Gibbon, Hegel, and J. S. Mill, they describe and comment on the historic systems of education.

In still other instances the great books contain sections or chapters devoted to the ends and means of education, the order of studies, the nature of learning and teaching, the training of statesmen and citizens; as for example, Plato's *The Republic,* Aristotle's *Politics,* Augustine's *On Christian Doctrine,* Francis Bacon's *Advancement of Learning,* Adam Smith's *The Wealth of Nations,* Hegel's *The Philosophy of Right,* the psychological writings of William James and Freud, an essay by Weber, and Whitehead's *Science and the Modern World.* But in no case is education the principal theme of these books, as it is for most of the works cited in the list of Additional Readings, among which will be found treatises on education by authors in this set.

EDUCATION IS not itself so much an idea or a subject matter as it is a theme to which the great ideas and the basic subject matters are relevant. It is one of the perennial practical problems which men cannot discuss without engaging in the deepest speculative considerations. It is a problem which carries discussion into and across a great many subject matters—the liberal arts of grammar, rhetoric, and logic; psychology, medicine, metaphysics, and theology; ethics, politics, and economics. It is a problem which draws into focus many of the great ideas—virtue and truth, knowledge and opinion, art and science; desire, will, sense, memory, mind, habit; change and progress; family and state; man, nature, and God.

This can be verified by noting the diverse contexts in which education is discussed in the great books. In each connection we shall find some of the special questions which together make up the complex problem of education. For example, the nature of teaching and learning is examined in the wider context of psychological considerations concerning man's abilities, the way in which knowledge is acquired, and how it is communicated by means of language or other symbols. Different conceptions of the nature of man and of the relation of his several capacities surround the question of the ends of education. In this context questions also arise concerning the parts of education—the training of man's body, the formation of his character, the cultivation of his mind—and how these are related to one another.

The whole theory of the virtues and of habit formation is involved in the question whether virtue can be taught or must be acquired in some other way, and in related questions about the influence of the family and the state on the growth of character. These questions are also asked in terms of general political theory. Different views of the state are involved in questions about the division of responsibility for education among various agencies. Questions about the purpose of education, and what sort of education shall be given to the diverse classes in the state, are differently raised and differently answered in the context of discussions of different forms of government.

Though they are far from exhaustive, these examples should nevertheless suffice to make the point that there can be no philosophy of education apart from philosophy as a whole. It may therefore not be a disadvantage to find the discussion of education in the great books almost always imbedded in the context of some more general theory or problem.

ONE OPINION FROM which there is hardly a dissenting voice in the great books is that education should aim to make men good as men and as citizens. "If you ask what is the good of education," Plato writes, "the answer is easy—that education makes good men, and that good men act nobly, and conquer their enemies in battle, because they are good." Men should enter upon learning, Bacon declares, in order "to give a true account of their gift of reason, to the benefit and use of men"; while James stresses the need for "a perfectly-

rounded development." Thus it would seem to be a common opinion in all ages that education should seek to develop the characteristic excellences of which men are capable and that its ultimate ends are human happiness and the welfare of society.

Within this area of general agreement there are, of course, differences which result from the different views that are taken of man's relation to the state or to God. If the good of the state takes precedence over individual happiness, then education must be directed to training men for the role they play as parts of a larger organism. Education then serves the purpose of preserving the state. Of all things, Aristotle says, "that which contributes most to the permanence of constitutions is the adaptation of education to the form of government . . . The best laws," he continues, "though sanctioned by every citizen of the state, will be of no avail unless the young are trained by habit and education in the spirit of the constitution."

Rousseau seems to take a similar view when he calls for a system of public education run by the state. Its object is to assure that the citizens are "early accustomed to regard their individuality only in its relation to the body of the state, and to be aware, so to speak, of their own existence merely as a part of that of the state." Taught in this way, the citizens, Rousseau claims, "might at length come to identify themselves in some degree with this greater whole, to feel themselves members of their country, and to love it with that exquisite feeling which no isolated person has save for himself."

If happiness cannot be fully achieved on earth, then whatever temporal ends education serves must themselves be ordered to eternal salvation, and the whole process of human development must be a direction of the soul to God. Nothing was learned, Augustine writes in his *Confessions*, when "I read and understood by myself all the books that I could find on the so-called liberal arts, for in those days I was a good-for-nothing and a slave to sordid ambitions . . . I had my back to the light and my face was turned towards the things which it illumined, so that my eyes, by which I saw the things which stood in the light, were themselves in darkness. Without great difficulty and without need of a teacher I understood all that I read on the arts of rhetoric and logic, on geometry, music, and mathematics. You know this, O Lord my God, because if a man is quick to understand and his perception is keen, he has these gifts from you. But since I made no offering of them to you," Augustine concludes, "it did me more harm than good." However, Augustine does not therefore conclude that, under no circumstances, can liberal education be put to good use. In his treatise *On Christian Doctrine,* he considers in detail how the liberal arts, which serve so well in the study of Sacred Scripture, may also serve to bring the soul to God.

SUCH DIFFERENCES DO NOT, however, annul one consequence of the general agreement, namely, the conception that education is concerned with the vocation of man, and prepares him in thought and action for his purpose and station in life. In these terms Smith argues for a minimum general education. He claims that "a man without the proper use of the intellectual faculties of a man, is, if possible, more contemptible than even a coward, and seems to be mutilated and deformed in a still more essential part of the character of human nature." He explicitly points out that this is the condition of "the great body of the people," who, by the division of labor, are confined in their employment "to a few very simple operations," in which the worker "has no occasion to exert his understanding, or to exercise his invention in finding out expedients for removing difficulties which never occur." The result, according to Smith, is that "the torpor of his mind renders him, not only incapable of relishing or bearing a part in any rational conversation, but of conceiving any generous, noble, or tender sentiment, and consequently of forming any just judgment concerning many even of the ordinary duties of private life."

When the vocation of man is thus understood, a general or liberal education is vocational in that it prepares each man for the common conditions and callings of human life. In this sense specialized training, which

by implication at least seems to be the object of Smith's criticism, is not vocational. It fits a man only for some specialized function, according to which he or his social class is differentiated from some other man or class.

In our day, the word "vocational" is used in the opposite sense to mean specialized training, whether it is preparation for the least skilled of trades or for the most learned of professions. Since all men are not called to the practice of law or medicine—any more than all are called to productive work in the various arts and crafts, or the tasks of commerce and industry—the training they may need to perform these functions does not fully develop their common humanity. It is not adequate to make them good as men, as citizens, or as children of God.

Twentieth-century writers, such as Whitehead and Weber, make much of the distinction between general education and training that is highly specialized. That is not surprising since specialization is a 20th-century phenomenon. Weber comments on the prevalence of highly specialized examinations at the university level in Europe; and Whitehead calls attention to the modern discovery "of the method of training professionals, who specialise in particular regions of thought"; and adds that "the dangers arising from this aspect of professionalism are great, particularly in our democratic societies . . . The leading intellects lack balance. They see this set of circumstances, or that set; but not both sets together." As a result, "the specialised functions of the community are performed better and more progressively, but the generalised direction lacks vision."

THE TRADITIONAL MEANING of the word "liberal" as applied to education entails a distinction between freemen and slaves. Slaves, like domesticated animals, are trained to perform special functions. They are not treated as ends, but as means, and so they are not educated for their own good, but for the use to which they are put. This is true not only of slaves in the strict sense of household chattel; it is also true of all the servile classes in any society which divides its human beings into those who work in order to live and those who live off the work of others and who therefore have the leisure in which to strive to live well.

In accordance with these distinctions, Aristotle divides education into "liberal" and "illiberal." Certain subjects are illiberal by nature, namely, "any occupation, art, or science, which makes the body or soul of the freeman less fit for the practice or exercise of virtue." In this category Aristotle includes "those arts which tend to deform the body, and likewise all paid employments, for they absorb and degrade the mind."

It is not only the nature of the subject, but also the end which education serves, that determines whether its character is liberal or illiberal. Even a liberal art becomes, in Aristotle's opinion, "menial and servile . . . if done for the sake of others." A man's education "will not appear illiberal" only so long as "he does or learns anything for his own sake or for the sake of his friends, or with a view to excellence." In other words, to be liberal, education must serve the use of leisure in the pursuit of excellence. It must treat man as an end, not as a means to be used by other men or by the state.

It follows that any society which abolishes the distinction of social classes and which calls all men to freedom, should conceive education as essentially liberal and for all men. It should, furthermore, direct education, in *all* its parts and phases, to the end of each man's living well rather than to the end of his earning a living for himself or others.

IN THE CLASSIFICATION of the kinds of education, the word "liberal" is frequently used in a more restricted sense to signify not all education designed for freemen, but only the improvement of the mind through the acquisition of knowledge and skill. In this sense liberal education is set apart from physical education which concerns bodily health and proficiency, and moral education which concerns excellence in action rather than in thought.

These divisions are clearly made, perhaps for the first time, in Plato's *The Republic*. The education described there begins in the early years with music and gymnastic. Gymnastic "presides over the growth and decay of the body." Music, which includes literature as well as the arts of harmony and rhythm, is said to educate its students "by the influence of habit, by harmony making them harmonious, by rhythm rhythmical," and its function is to develop moral as well as aesthetic sensibilities.

The second part of Plato's curriculum, "which leads naturally to reflection" and draws "the soul towards being," consists in the mathematical arts and sciences of arithmetic, geometry, music, and astronomy. The program is capped by the study of dialectic, to which all the rest is but "a prelude"; for "when a person starts on the discovery of the absolute by the light of reason only, and without any assistance of sense, and perseveres until by pure intelligence he arrives at the perception of the absolute good, he at last finds himself at the end of the intellectual world."

Up to this point, the program can be taken as liberal education in the narrow sense of learning how and what to think. The fifteen years of experience in civic affairs and the tasks of government, which Plato interposes at the age of thirty-five, seem to function as another phase of moral training. This period provides "an opportunity of trying whether, when they are drawn all manner of ways by temptation, they will stand firm or flinch."

To the extent that physical training aims, beyond health, at the acquirement of skill in a coordinated use of one's body, it can be annexed to liberal rather than moral education. Plato notes, for example, that gymnastic should not be too sharply distinguished from music as "the training of the body" from the "training of the soul." Gymnastic as well as music, he claims, has "in view chiefly the improvement of the soul," and he considers the two as balancing and tempering one another.

Whether they produce competence in gymnastic or athletic feats, or, like the manual arts, proficiency in productive work, all bodily skills, even the simplest, involve the senses and the mind as well as bones and muscles. They are arts no less than music or logic. Apart from their utility, they represent a certain type of human excellence, which will be denied only by those who can see no difference between the quality of a racehorse and the skill of his rider. Whether these skills as well as other useful arts are part of liberal education in the broader sense depends, as we have seen, on the end for which they are taught or learned. Even the arts which are traditionally called liberal, such as rhetoric or logic, can be degraded to servility if the sole motive for becoming skilled in them is wealth won by success in the law courts.

IN THE TWO traditional distinctions so far discussed, "liberal education" seems to have a somewhat different meaning when it signifies the opposite of servile training and when it signifies the opposite of moral cultivation. In the first case, the distinction is based upon the purpose of the education; in the second, it refers to the faculties or functions being cultivated. When the second is stated in terms of the distinction between the intellectual and the moral virtues, liberal (*i.e.,* intellectual) education is conceived as aiming at good habits of thinking and knowing, and moral education is thought of as aiming at good habits of will, desire, or emotion, along with their consequences in action.

Although he does not use these terms, Montaigne seems to have the contrast between moral and intellectual training in mind when he criticizes the education of his day for aiming "only at furnishing our heads with knowledge; of judgment and virtue, little news." It is, to him, "pedantic learning," which not only fails to achieve the highest educational purpose, but also results in a great evil, in that "any other knowledge is harmful to a man who has not the knowledge of goodness."

A too sharp separation of the intellectual and the moral may be questioned, or at least qualified, by those who, like Socrates, tend to identify knowledge and virtue. Yet they seldom go to the opposite extreme of supposing that no distinction can be made between the task of imparting knowledge to the mind and that of forming character. Socrates, for example, in the *Meno,* recognizes that a man cannot be made temperate, courageous, or just in the same way that he can be taught geometry.

From another point of view, the notion of moral training is questioned by those who, like Freud, think that the patterns of human desire or emotion can be beneficially changed apart from moral discipline. It is the object of psychoanalysis, he writes, "to strengthen the ego, to make it more independent of the super-ego, to widen its field of vision, and so to extend its organization that it can take over new portions of the id." To do this is radically to alter the individual's behavior-pattern. "It is reclamation work," Freud says, "like the draining of the Zuyder Zee." Emotional education, so conceived, is therapeutic—more like preventive and remedial medicine than moral training.

Religious education is usually regarded as both intellectual and moral, even as the science of theology is said to be both speculative and practical. Citing the admonition of Saint James, "Be ye doers of the word, and not hearers only," Aquinas holds that religious education is concerned with the knowledge not only of "divine things" but also of the "human acts" by which man comes to God. Since man is infinitely removed from God, he needs for this purpose the grace of God, which, according to Aquinas, "is nothing short of a partaking of the divine nature."

Both on the side of man's knowledge of God and on the side of his love and worship of God, religious education involves the operation of supernatural factors—revelation, grace, sacraments. Hence God is Himself the primary source of religious education. But as the dispenser of the sacraments whereby "grace is instrumentally caused," the church, according to Aquinas, functions instrumentally in the service of the divine teacher.

THE CONCEPTION OF THE means and ends of moral education will differ with different ethical theories of the good man and the good life, and according to differing enumerations and definitions of the virtues. It will differ even more fundamentally according to whether the primary emphasis is placed on pleasure and happiness or duty. The parties to this basic issue in philosophy, which is discussed in the chapters on DUTY and HAPPINESS, inevitably propose different ways of forming good character—by strengthening the will in obedience to law, or by habituating the appetites to be moderate or reasonable in their inclinations.

On either theory, the basic problem of moral education is whether morality can be taught and how. The Greeks formulated this question in terms of virtue, by asking whether such things as courage and temperance are *at all* teachable, as geometry and horsemanship plainly are. The problem remains essentially the same if the question is how the will can be trained. Can it be trained by the same methods as those which work in the improvement of the understanding?

The answer to the question, whichever way it is formulated, depends on the view that is taken of the relation between moral knowledge and moral conduct. Do those who understand the principles of ethics or who know the moral law necessarily act in accordance with their knowledge? Can a man know what is good or right to do in a particular case, and yet do the opposite? Saint Paul seems to suggest this when he says, "For the good that I would I do not: but the evil which I would not, that I do." If something more than knowledge or straight thinking is needed for good conduct, how is it acquired and how can one man help another to acquire it? Certainly not by learning and teaching in the ordinary sense which applies to the arts and sciences. Then how—by practice, by guidance or advice, by example, by rewards and punishments; or if by none of these, then by a gift of nature or by the grace of God?

These questions are necessarily prior to any discussion of the role of the family, the state, and the church in the process of moral training. They also provide the general background for the consideration of particular influences on character formation in men and children, such things as poetry and music, or laws and customs. All of these related problems of moral education have a political aspect, which appears in the issue concerning the state's right to censor or regulate the arts for morality's sake; in the question of the primacy of the family or the state in the moral guidance of the young; in the distinction between the good man and the good citizen or ruler, and the possible difference between

the training appropriate for the one and for the other.

THE MAIN PROBLEM of intellectual education seems to be the curriculum or course of study. The traditional attempts to construct an ideal curriculum turn on such questions as what studies shall be included, what their order shall be, and how they shall be taught or learned. A variety of answers results from a variety of views of man's faculties or capacities, the nature of knowledge itself, the classification and order of the arts and sciences. Especially important are the various conceptions of the nature and function of the liberal arts. Subordinate questions concern the place of the fine and useful arts in liberal education, and the role of experience and experiment—both in contrast to and in cooperation with the role of books and teachers.

In addition to the problem of the curriculum and its materials, the theory of intellectual education necessarily considers methods of teaching and learning. Here the various proposals derive from different views of the learning process—of the causes or factors at work in any acquisition of skill or knowledge.

The contribution of the teacher cannot be understood apart from a psychological analysis of learning, for the teacher is obviously only one among its many causes. It makes the greatest difference to the whole enterprise of learning whether the teacher is regarded as the principal cause of understanding on the part of the student; or whether the teacher is, as Socrates describes himself, merely a "midwife" assisting the labor of the mind in bringing knowledge and wisdom to birth, and "thoroughly examining whether the thought which the mind . . . brings forth is a false idol or a noble and true birth."

This Socratic insight is later reformulated in the comparison which Aquinas makes, in his tract *Concerning the Teacher,* between the art of teaching and the art of healing. Both are cooperative arts, arts which succeed only as "ministers of nature which is the principal actor," and not by acting, like the art of the cobbler or sculptor, to produce a result by shaping plastic but dead materials.

The comparison which Hippocrates makes of instruction in medicine with "the culture of the productions of the earth" exhibits the same conception of teaching. "Our natural disposition," he writes, "is, as it were, the soil; the tenets of our teacher are, as it were, the seed; instruction in youth is like the planting of the seed in the ground at the proper season; the place where the instruction is communicated is like the food imparted to vegetables by the atmosphere; diligent study is like the cultivation of the fields; and it is time which imparts strength to all things and brings them to maturity."

This conception of teaching as a cooperative art, analogous to medicine or to agriculture, underlies the principles of pedagogy in *The Great Didactic* of Comenius. It gives significance to the distinction that Aquinas makes between learning by discovery, or from experience, and learning by instruction, or from a teacher—even as a person is healed "in one way by the operation of nature alone, and in another by nature with the administration of medicine."

In addition to the technical considerations raised by the nature of the learning process, the discussion of teaching deals with the moral or emotional aspect of the relation between teacher and student. Without interest, learning seldom takes place, or if it does, it cannot rise above the level of rote memory. It is one thing to lay down a course of study; another to motivate the student. Though he does not hesitate to prescribe what is to be learned by the student, Plato adds the caution that there must be no "notion of forcing our system of education."

More than interest is required. Teaching, Augustine declares, is the greatest act of charity. Learning is facilitated by love. The courtesies between Dante and Virgil in *The Divine Comedy* present an eloquent picture of love between student and teacher, master and disciple. Not only love, but docility, is required on the part of the student; and respect for the student's mind on the part of the teacher. Intellectual education may not be directly concerned with the formation of character, yet the moral virtues seem to be factors in the pursuit of truth and in the discipline of the learning process.

Commenting on "the province and office of the teacher," Dewey maintains that, because the "development of experience comes about through interaction," it is "essentially a social process." The teacher, "as the most mature member of the group . . . has a peculiar responsibility for the conduct of the interactions and intercommunications which are the very life of the group as a community." Since for Dewey experience lies at the heart of the educative process, he declares that a sound philosophy of education depends on "a sound philosophy of experience."

WE HAVE ALREADY noted some of the political problems of education. Of these probably the chief question is whether the organization and institution of education shall be private or public. Any answer which assigns the control of education largely or wholly to the state must lead to a number of other determinations.

Who shall be educated, all or only some? Should the education of leaders be different from the education of others? If educational opportunity is to be equal for all, must the same kind as well as the same quantity of education be offered to all? And, in every case, to what end shall the state direct the education of its members—to its own welfare and security, or to the happiness of men and the greater glory of God? Should education always serve the status quo by preserving extant customs and perpetuating existing forms of government; or can and should it aim at a better society and a higher culture?

These are some of the questions with which statesmen and political philosophers have dealt, answering them differently according to the institutions of their time and in accordance with one or another theory of the state and its government. There are still other questions. Is freedom of expression, in teaching and discussion, indispensable to the pursuit of truth and the dissemination of knowledge? To what extent shall the state control the content and methods of education or leave such determination to the teaching profession? How shall public education be supported? Should it be carried beyond childhood and youth to all the ages of adult life; and if so, how should such education be organized outside of schools?

Mill, for example, holds it to be "almost a self-evident axiom that the State should require and compel the education, up to a certain standard, of every human being who is born its citizen." Yet he deprecates the idea of a "general state education" as a "mere contrivance for moulding people to be exactly like one another."

Discussing the pros and cons of this issue, Mill touches upon most, if not all, of the questions just raised. He believes that the difficulties could be avoided if the government would leave it "to parents to obtain the education where and how they pleased, and content itself with helping to pay the school fees of the poorer classes of children, and defraying the entire school expenses of those who have no one else to pay for them." Schools completely established and controlled by the state, he maintains, "should only exist, if they exist at all, as one among many competing experiments, carried on for the purpose of example and stimulus, to keep the others up to a certain standard of excellence."

So far as the problem of adult education concerns citizenship, Mill's answer, like Montesquieu's and Plato's before him, is that nothing can take the place of active participation in political life. Men become citizens by living and acting as citizens, under the tutelage of good laws and in an atmosphere of civic virtue. So far as the problem of adult education concerns the continued growth of the mind throughout the life of mature men and women, the answer is not to be found in the great books in the words of their authors. Yet the great books as a whole may constitute a solution to that problem.

The authors of these books, from Homer to Beckett, are the great original teachers in the tradition of our culture. They taught one another. They wrote for adults, not children, and in the main they wrote for the mass of men, not for scholars in this or that specialized field of learning.

The books exhibit these teachers at work in the process of teaching. They contain, moreover, expositions or exemplifications of the liberal arts as the arts of teaching and learning in every field of subject matter. To make these books and their authors work for us by working with them is, it seems to the editors and publishers of this set of books, a feasible and desirable program of adult education. To take advantage of them is to improve one's self, and as Dickens says, "no man of sense who has been generally improved, and has improved himself, can be called . . . uneducated."

There is a telling passage in Cather's *A Lost Lady*. It concerns the Bohn edition of the classics that "Judge Pommeroy had bought long ago when he was a student at the University of Virginia."

He had brought them West with him, not because he read them a great deal, but because, in his day, a gentleman had such books in his library, just as he had claret in his cellar. Among them was a set of Byron in three volumes, and last winter, apropos of a quotation which Niel didn't recognize, his uncle advised him to read Byron,—all except "Don Juan" . . . Niel, of course, began with "Don Juan." Then he read "Tom Jones" and "Wilhelm Meister" and raced on until he came to Montaigne and a complete translation of Ovid . . .
There were philosophical works in the collection, but he did no more than open and glance at them. He had no curiosity about what men had thought; but about what they had felt and lived, he had a great deal. If anyone had told him that these were classics and represented the wisdom of the ages, he would doubtless have let them alone. But ever since he had first found them for himself, he had been living a double life, with all its guilty enjoyments . . . If the Judge had left his Bohn library behind him in Kentucky, his nephew's life might have turned out differently.

21

Element

INTRODUCTION

THE words "atom" and "element" express basic notions in the analysis of matter. To some extent their meanings seem to be the same. Atoms or elements are usually understood to be ultimate units, the parts out of which other things are formed by combination. But as soon as further questions are asked—about the divisibility or indivisibility of these units, or about their number and variety—we are confronted with differing conceptions of the atom, and with a theory of the elements which is opposed to the atomic analysis of matter.

Even when the two notions are not opposed to one another, they are not interchangeable. "Atom" has a much narrower meaning. It usually designates a small particle of matter, whereas "element" signifies the least part into which anything at all can be divided. It is this broader meaning of "element" which permits Euclid to call his collection of the theorems in terms of which all geometric problems can be solved, the "elements" of geometry. According to Aristotle, this is true, not only of geometric proofs, but also "in general of the elements of demonstration; for the primary demonstrations, each of which is implied in many demonstrations," he says, "are called elements of demonstration." From this it follows that elements will be found in any subject matter or science in which analysis occurs, and not only in physics.

"An element," writes Nicomachus in his *Introduction to Arithmetic,* "is the smallest thing which enters into the composition of an object, and the least thing into which it can be analyzed. Letters, for example, are called the elements of literate speech, for out of them all articulate speech is composed and into them

finally it is resolved. Sounds are the elements of all melody; for they are the beginning of its composition and into them it is resolved. The so-called four elements of the universe in general are simple bodies, fire, water, air, and earth; for out of them in the first instance we account for the constitution of the universe, and into them finally we conceive of it as being resolved."

This explains why books in so many different fields have the word "element" in their titles. There are the elements of grammar or logic, the elements of language or music, the elements of psychology or economics. Elements in one subject matter or science are analogous to the elements in another because in each sphere they stand to everything else as the simple to the complex, the pure to the mixed, the parts to the whole. Thus the factors of price may be said to function as elements in economic analysis as do the parts of speech in grammatical analysis.

Another illustration comes from the theory of the four bodily humors in ancient physiology. In the traditional enumeration, which goes back to Hippocrates, they are blood, phlegm, yellow bile, and black bile, and they function analytically as do fire, water, air, and earth in ancient physics. They "make up the nature of the body of man," according to a Hippocratic treatise on the nature of man, "and through them he feels pain or enjoys health." Perfect health is enjoyed by a man "when these elements are duly proportioned to one another in respect of compounding, power, and bulk, and when they are perfectly mingled." Galen, in an analysis of temperaments, explains all varieties of temperament and all complexions of physique in terms of these humors, either by their mixture or by the predominance of one or another. Thus the sanguine, phlegmatic, choleric, or melancholic temperament is accounted for by the excess of one and a deficiency of the other humors.

Still another physiological application of the notion of element is to be found in the ancient division of tissue into flesh and bone, or in the more elaborate modern analysis of the types of cells which comprise all living matter.

THESE ILLUSTRATIONS indicate that the irreducibility of elements to anything simpler than themselves does not necessarily mean that they are absolutely indivisible. Cells can be further divided into nucleus, protoplasm, and membrane without ceasing to be the elements of tissue. The parts of speech—nouns, verbs, adjectives—can be further divided into syllables and letters without ceasing to be the elements of significant utterance. Letters, treated as the elements of language, can be physically divided. The fact that terms are sometimes regarded as the logical elements out of which propositions and syllogisms are formed does not prevent a distinction from being made between simple and complex terms. Nicomachus calls the triangle elementary among all plane figures, "for everything else is resolved into it, but it into nothing else"; yet the triangle is divisible into the lines which compose it and these lines in turn are divisible into points.

When Nicomachus says that the triangle is the element of all other figures "and has itself no element," he does not mean that the triangle is absolutely indivisible, but only relatively so. Relative to the analysis of plane figures, there is no simpler figure out of which the triangle can be formed. Similarly, relative to the analysis of significant speech, there is no simpler part than the word. Relative to the analysis of melody, there is no simpler part than the tone. Musical tones may be physically, but they are not musically, complex.

THE DEFINITION OF element can also be approached by comparing its meaning with that of principle and cause. All three terms are brought together by Aristotle in the beginning of his *Physics,* when he declares that we attain "scientific knowledge" through acquaintance with the "principles, causes, and elements" of things.

The word "principle" occurs almost as frequently as "element" in the titles of books which claim to be basic expositions or analyses. The two words are often used as synonyms. Lavoisier, for example, says that we can use "the term *elements,* or *principles of bodies,* to express our idea of the last point which analysis is capable of reaching."

To discover any difference in the meaning of "element" and "principle," it is necessary to specify their correlatives precisely. Out of elements, *compounds* or *mixtures* are formed. From principles, *consequences* are derived. In logic, for example, we say that terms are the elements of propositions (the proposition 'Socrates is a man' comprising the terms 'Socrates' and 'man'), but we say that axioms are the principles from which conclusions are derived. This does not prevent the same thing from being viewed in different connections as both element and principle—as an element because it is the simple part out of which a more complex whole is composed, and as a principle because it is the source from which something else is derived. The parts of speech in grammar are the elementary components of phrases and sentences; they are also the principles from which the rules of syntax are derived.

The third notion which belongs with element and principle is cause. Its correlative is *effect.* Again it can be said that that which is an element in one connection and a principle in another can be regarded as a cause from still a third point of view. In Aristotle's physical treatises, for example, matter is regarded in all three ways: it is an element of all bodies, for they are substances composed of matter and form; it is a principle of change, since from matter, form, and privation change is derived; it is a cause (*i.e.,* the material cause) of certain results.

But it must also be observed that everything which is any one of these three is not necessarily both of the others also. Since an element, according to Aristotle, is a "component immanent in a thing," anything that is an extrinsic principle or cause cannot be an element. Thus the action of one body upon another is a cause and a principle, but not an element. Referring to these distinctions, Aquinas declares that *"principle* is a wider term than *cause,* just as *cause* is more common than *element*." The chapters on CAUSE and PRINCIPLE tend to substantiate this observation about the scope of these ideas in the tradition of western thought.

THE BASIC ISSUES concerning elements occur in the analysis of matter. Before Plato and Aristotle, the early Greek physicists had asked such questions as, From what do all things come? Of what are all things made? A number of answers were given, ranging from one kind of ultimate, such as earth or fire, through a small set of ultimate kinds, to an infinite variety. The classical theory of the four elements is the middle answer, avoiding the extremes of unity and infinity.

According to Galen, it was Hippocrates who "first took in hand to demonstrate that there are, in all, four mutually interacting qualities" and who provided "at least the beginnings of the proofs to which Aristotle later set his hand" in developing the theory of the four elements. Galen also indicates that it was a subject of controversy among the ancients whether the "substances as well as the qualities" of the four elements "undergo this intimate mingling" from which results "the genesis and destruction of all things that come into and pass out of being."

Aristotle, in his treatise "On Generation and Corruption," enumerates the various senses in which the physicist considers elements. "We have to recognize three 'originative sources' (or elements)," he writes: "firstly, that which is potentially perceptible body; secondly, the contrarieties (*e.g.,* heat and cold); and thirdly, Fire, Water, and the like." The "potentially perceptible body" is identified with prime matter, and, since this "has no separate existence, but is always bound up with a contrariety," it can be ruled out from the usual notion of element. The elementary qualities, the "contrarieties" named secondly, are the hot and cold and dry and moist. The so-called elements, fire, air, water, and earth, are left to the last, and are mentioned "only thirdly," Aristotle says, because

they "change into one another . . . whereas the contrarieties do not change."

The elementary qualities "attach themselves" by couples to the "apparently 'simple' bodies." In consequence, Aristotle writes, "Fire is hot and dry, whereas Air is hot and moist . . . and Water is cold and moist, while Earth is cold and dry." Each of them, however, "is characterized *par excellence* by a single quality." In terms of these simple bodies and the elementary qualities all other material things can be explained.

In contrast to the elements stand the mixed, or compound, bodies, in the constitution of which two or more elements combine. There may be many kinds of mixed bodies, but none is irreducible in kind, as are the four elements; any mixed body can be divided into the different kinds of elementary bodies which compose it, whereas the elementary bodies cannot be divided into parts which are different in kind from themselves. A living body, for example, may contain parts of earth and water, but the parts of earth are earth, the parts of water, water.

It is precisely the mode of divisibility that Aristotle declares is "the fundamental question." In answering this question he opposes the theory of the four elements to another Greek account of the constitution of matter—the atomic theory, developed by Leucippus and Democritus, and expounded for us in Lucretius' poem *The Way Things Are.*

ACCORDING TO the Greek atomists, matter is not infinitely divisible. Lucretius writes,

. . . . . . if nature had not set a limit
To fragmentation, by this time all matter
Would have been so reduced by time's attrition
That not one thing could move from a beginning
To full, completed growth.

There must then be a "sure and certain limit" to the breaking of matter—a limit in physical division which ultimately reaches units of matter that are absolutely indivisible. Lucretius calls them "first beginnings" of "singleness/ Solid, coherent, not compound, but strong/In its eternal singleness"—the "seeds of things," or atoms. The Greek word from which "atom" comes literally means *uncuttable.*

From this it is evident that Aristotle can deny the existence of atoms while at the same time he affirms the existence of elementary bodies. The elements, unlike the atoms, are not conceived as indivisible in quantity, but only as incapable of division into diverse kinds of matter.

In the Greek conception of atom and element, the difference between them lies in this distinction between quantitative and qualitative indivisibility. The atom is the least quantity of matter. It cannot be broken into quantitative parts. The elementary body is not atomic. It is always capable of division into *smaller* units, but all of these units must be of the same kind as the elementary body undergoing division.

The element is indivisible only in the sense that it cannot be decomposed into other *kinds* of matter, as a mixed body can be decomposed into its diverse elements. The atom cannot be divided in any way. Only compound bodies can be divided into their constituent atoms, all of which are alike in kind, differing only quantitatively—in size, shape, or weight. Different kinds of matter occur only on the level of compounds and as the result of diverse combinations of atoms.

This last point indicates another contrast between atoms and elements in ancient physical theory. The elements are defined, as we have seen, by their qualitative differences from one another; or, more strictly, according to combinations of elementary sensible qualities—hot and cold, moist and dry. By virtue of the qualities peculiar to them, the four elements stand in a certain order to one another. Water and air, according to Plato, are "in the mean between fire and earth" and have "the same proportion so far as possible; as fire is to air so is air to water, and as air is to water so is water to earth." The quality which two of the elements have in common provides the mean. Thus fire and air are joined by the common quality of hot; air and water by moist; and water and earth by cold.

When their analysis reached its greatest refinement, the ancients recognized that the earth, air, fire, and water of common experience do not actually have the purity requisite for elements. They are "not simple, but blended," Aristotle writes, and while the elements "are indeed similar in nature to them, [they] are not identical with them." The element "corresponding to fire is 'such-as-fire,' not fire; that which corresponds to air is 'such-as-air,' and so on with the rest of them." Thus the four elements are only analogous to, for they are purer than, ordinary earth, air, fire, and water; yet their names continued to be used as symbols for the true elements, a connotation which is still retained when we speak of men struggling against or battling with "the elements."

Heisenberg's comment on Greek atomism is worth noting here. He writes: "In the philosophy of Democritus the atoms are eternal and indestructible units of matter, they can never be transformed into each other. With regard to this question modern physics takes a definite stand against the materialism of Democritus and for Plato and the Pythagoreans. The elementary particles are certainly not eternal and indestructible units of matter, they can actually be transformed into each other . . . But the resemblance of the modern views to those of Plato and the Pythagoreans can be carried somewhat further. The elementary particles in Plato's *Timaeus* are finally not substance but mathematical forms. 'All things are numbers' is a sentence attributed to Pythagoras. The only mathematical forms available at that time were such geometric forms as the regular solids or the triangles which form their surface. In modern quantum theory there can be no doubt that the elementary particles will finally also be mathematical."

"IT WILL NO DOUBT be a matter of surprise," Lavoisier writes in the Preface to his *Elements of Chemistry*, "that in a treatise upon the elements of chemistry, there should be no chapter on the constituent and elementary parts of matter; but I shall take occasion, in this place, to remark that the fondness for reducing all the bodies in nature to three or four elements, proceeds from a prejudice which has descended to us from the Greek philosophers. The notion of four elements, which, by the variety of their proportions, compose all the known substances in nature, is a mere hypothesis, assumed long before the first principles of experimental philosophy or of chemistry had any existence."

This does not mean that Lavoisier entirely rejects the notion of elements in chemical analysis. On the contrary, he says that "we must admit, as elements, all the substances into which we are capable, by any means, to reduce bodies by decomposition." His quarrel with the ancients chiefly concerns two points. The first is on the number of the elements, which he thinks experiment has shown to be much greater than the four of classical theory. The second is on the simplicity of the experimentally discovered elements. They can be called atoms or simple bodies only if we do not thereby imply that we know them to be absolutely indivisible—either qualitatively or quantitatively. We are not entitled "to affirm that these substances we consider as simple may not be compounded of two, or even of a greater number of principles" merely because we have not yet discovered "the means of separating them."

In 20th-century physics and chemistry, element is used in the sense of chemical element. Two quantities of matter are said to belong to the same chemical element if their chemical reactions are identical. Elements are made up of atoms, each of which consists of a massive, positively charged nucleus surrounded by a cloud of light, negatively charged electrons.

The chemistry of an atom—or several atoms bound together as a molecule—is determined by the associated electrons. Hence all of the atoms of a given element have the same number of electrons. In the usual usage, the atoms of a given element need not all have identical masses. Their nuclei can differ by the number of electrically neutral, massive particles—neutrons. For example, the hydrogen nucleus has a single positively charged, massive particle, the proton, while the heavy hydrogen nucleus has a proton and a neutron: both isotopes—hydrogen and heavy hydrogen—have the same chemistry and, as the term is now usually employed, would belong to the same element.

According to the ancient meaning of the terms, the molecule would seem to be both a mixture and a compound—*mixed,* in that

it can be broken up into other *kinds* of matter; *compound,* in that it can be divided into *smaller* units of matter. The combination of the elements to form molecular compounds is determined by the proportion of their weights or valences rather than by a fusion of their qualities.

The most radical change in theory is not this, however; nor is it the increase in the number of the elements from four to more than one hundred; nor the ordering of the elements by reference to their atomic weights rather than by the contrariety of their qualities. It results from the discovery that an atom is not uncuttable and that new elements can be produced by atomic fission and fusion. Fission refers to the splitting of a heavy nucleus, such as that of uranium, into lighter ones, and fusion refers to the conjoining of lighter nuclei into heavier ones.

Faraday's experimental work in ionization and in electrochemical decomposition lies at the beginning of the physical researches which have penetrated the interior structure of the atom and isolated smaller units of matter. Even before atoms were experimentally exploded, analysis had pictured them as constituted by positive and negative charges.

As the result of his researches, Faraday, for example, conceives of atoms as "mere centres of forces or powers, not particles of matter, in which the powers themselves reside." The atom thus ceases to be "a little unchangeable, impenetrable piece of matter," and "consists of the powers" it exercises. What was ordinarily referred to "under the term *shape*" becomes the "disposition and relative intensity of the forces" that are observed.

With Faraday it is evident that the meaning of "atom" has departed far from the sense in which Lucretius speaks of "single solid unity" or Newton of "solid, massy, hard, impenetrable, movable particles . . . incomparably harder than any porous bodies compounded of them; even so very hard as never to wear or break in pieces; no ordinary power being able to divide what God himself made one in the first creation." With the conception of the elements as different kinds of atoms; then, with the discovery of radioactive elements undergoing slow disintegration; finally, with the production of isotopes and new elements through atomic change; the meaning of "element" has moved equally far from its original sense.

Do THESE ALTERED meanings change the basic issues in the philosophy of nature? Are these issues resolved or rendered meaningless by experimental science?

The central point in the theory of elements is an irreducible qualitative diversity in kinds of matter. The elements of modern chemistry may no longer be *elementary* types of matter in the strict sense of the word; but the kind of difference which would be strictly elemental may be found in the distinction of the positive, the negative, and the neutral with respect to the electrical charge of subatomic particles.

Similarly, the central point in atomism as a philosophy of nature is the existence of absolutely indivisible units or quanta of matter; in other words, the denial that matter is infinitely divisible, that any particle, no matter how small, is capable of being broken into smaller parts. The strict conception of the atom is, therefore, not invalidated by the experimental discovery that the particles called "atoms" are not *atomic,* that they are themselves complex structures of moving particles, and that they can be physically divided.

It makes no difference to the philosophical atomist whether the particles which constitute molecules or the particles—the electrons and protons, the neutrons and mesons—which constitute "atoms," are *atomic*. Even if further experimental work should succeed in dividing these "subatomic" particles, the question could still be asked: Is matter infinitely divisible, regardless of our actual power to continue making divisions ad infinitum? Since the question, when thus formulated, cannot be put to experimental test, the issue concerning atoms would remain.

That issue would not refer to any particle of matter defined at a certain stage of physical analysis or experimental discovery. It would consist in the opposition of two views of the nature of matter and the constitution of the material universe: the affirmation, on the one hand, that truly atomic particles must exist;

and the denial, on the other, that no particle of matter can be atomic. The affirmative arguments of Lucretius and Newton make the constancy of nature and the indestructibility of matter depend on the absolute solidity and impenetrability of matter's ultimate parts. The negative arguments of Aristotle and Descartes proceed from the divisibility of whatever is continuous to the conclusion that any unit of matter must have parts.

The philosophical doctrine of atomism, in the form in which Lucretius adopts it from Epicurus, insists upon void as the other basic principle of the universe. "The nature of everything," he writes, "is dual—matter/And void; or particles and space, wherein/The former rest or move." Compound bodies are divisible because the atoms of which they are composed are not absolutely continuous with one another, but are separated by void or empty space. That is why they are not solid or impenetrable, as are the atomic particles which are composed of matter entirely without void. In Newton's language hardness must be "reckoned the property of all uncompounded matter," for if "compound bodies are so very hard as we find some of them to be, and yet are very porous," how much harder must be "simple particles which are void of pores."

The opponents of atomism tend to deny the existence not only of atoms, but of the void as well. Descartes, for example, denies that there can be "any atoms or parts of matter which are indivisible of their own nature . . . For however small the parts are supposed to be, yet because they are necessarily extended we are always able in thought to divide any one of them into two or more parts." For the same reason, he maintains, there cannot be "a space in which there is no substance . . . because the extension of space or internal place is not different from that of body." The physical world, on this view, is conceived as what the ancients called a plenum, continuously filled with matter. This controversy over void and plenum is elaborated in the chapter on SPACE.

Although he uses the language of the atomists, Faraday seems to agree with Descartes rather than with Newton. He pictures matter as "continuous throughout," with no distinction between "its atoms and any intervening space." Atoms, he thinks, instead of being absolutely hard, are "highly elastic," and they are all "mutually penetrable." He compares the combination and separation of two atoms with "the conjunction of two sea waves of different velocities into one, their perfect union for a time, and final separation into the constituent waves." Such a view of the constitution of matter, Faraday writes, leads to "the conclusion that matter fills all space, or at least all space to which gravitation extends."

The very continuity—the voidlessness or lack of pores—which the opponents of atomism insist is the source of matter's infinite divisibility, the atomists seem to give as the reason why the ultimate particles are without parts, hence simple, solid, and indivisible.

ON STILL OTHER POINTS, there is disagreement among the atomists themselves. Not all of them go to the extreme of denying existence or reality to anything immaterial; nor do all insist that whatever exists is either an atom or made up of atoms and void. In the tradition of the great books, the extreme doctrine is found in Lucretius alone. Though it is shared by Hobbes, and is reflected in the *Leviathan,* it is not expounded there. It is developed in his treatise *Concerning Body.*

For Lucretius, the atoms are eternal as well as indestructible. The "first beginnings" of all other things are themselves without beginning. "Atoms are moving," Lucretius writes, "in the same way now/As they have done forever, and will do/Forever," through an endless succession of worlds, each of which comes to be through a concourse of atoms, each in turn perishing as with decay that concourse is dissolved. Newton writes in what seems to be a contrary vein. "It seems probable to me," he says, "that God in the beginning formed matter in solid, massy, hard, impenetrable, movable particles." "All material things," he continues, "seem to have been composed of the hard and solid particles above mentioned, variously associated in the first Creation by the counsel of an intelligent Agent."

Nor does Newton appeal to the properties and motions of the ultimate particles except to explain the characteristics and laws of the physical world. Unlike Lucretius and Hobbes, he does not—and there seems to be some evidence in the *Optics* that he would not—reduce the soul of man to a flow of extremely mobile atoms, or attempt to account for all psychological phenomena (thought as well as sensation and memory) in terms of atom buffeting atom.

The atomic theory of the cause of sensation is not limited to the materialists. Writers like Locke, who conceive man as having a spiritual nature as well as a body, adopt an atomistic view of the material world. "The different motions and figures, bulk and number of such particles," he writes, "affecting the several organs of our senses, produce in us those different sensations which we have from the colours and smells of bodies." Furthermore, the distinction which is here implicit—between primary and secondary sense qualities—is not peculiar to atomism. It can also be found in a critic of atomism like Descartes.

The atomistic account of sensation is, nevertheless, of critical significance in the controversy concerning this type of materialism. Critics of atomism have contended that the truth of atomism as a materialistic philosophy can be no greater than the measure of its success in explaining sensation—the source upon which the atomist himself relies for his knowledge of nature—in terms of the properties and motions of particles themselves imperceptible.

The issues involving atomism have taken a remarkable new turn since the 1960s with the discovery of the quark. As the 20th century neared an end, the quark was believed to be the ultimate constituent of nuclear particles such as protons and neutrons. However, the theory of quarks predicts that it is impossible to break up a proton and neutron into its quark constituents. This means that, as a matter of principle, these atomic constituents are in a certain sense undetectable as free particles. This is quite unlike the situation with atoms and their nuclei, which can be broken up into their detectable constituents.

THE ULTIMATE QUESTION is asked by Heisenberg: "Why do the physicists claim that their elementary particles cannot be divided into smaller bits? The answer to this question clearly shows how much more abstract modern science is as compared to Greek philosophy. The argument runs like this: How could one divide an elementary particle? Certainly only by using extreme forces and very sharp tools. The only tools available are other elementary particles. Therefore, collisions between two elementary particles of extremely high energy would be the only processes by which the particles could eventually be divided. Actually they *can* be divided in such processes, sometimes into very many fragments; but the fragments are again elementary particles, not any smaller pieces of them, the masses of these fragments resulting from the very large kinetic energy of the two colliding particles. In other words, the transmutation of energy into matter makes it possible that the fragments of elementary particles are again the same elementary particles."

Writing almost a half century earlier than Heisenberg, Planck contrasts the naïveté of the atomism that prevailed from the Greeks to the 19th century with the present scientific account of subatomic elementary particles. "In our own day," Planck writes, "scientific research, fructified by the theory of relativity and the quantum theory, stands at the threshold of a higher stage of development, ready to mould a new world picture for itself . . . From today's point of view, therefore, we must regard the . . . classical world picture as naive. But nobody can tell whether some day in the future the same words will not be used in referring to our modern world picture, too."

22

Emotion

INTRODUCTION

THE emotions claim our attention in two ways. We experience them, sometimes in a manner which overwhelms us; and we analyze them by defining and classifying the several passions, and by studying their role in human life and society. We seldom do both at once, for analysis requires emotional detachment, and moments of passion do not permit study or reflection.

With regard to the emotions the great books are similarly divided into two sorts—those which are theoretical discussions and those which concretely describe the passions of particular men, exhibit their vigor, and induce in us a vicarious experience. Books of the first sort are scientific, philosophical, or theological treatises. Books of the second sort are the great epic and dramatic poems, the novels and plays, the literature of biography and history.

We customarily think of the emotions as belonging to the subject matter of psychology—proper to the science of animal and human behavior. It is worth noting therefore that this is largely a recent development, which appears in the works of Charles Darwin, William James, and Sigmund Freud. In earlier centuries the analysis of the passions occurs in other contexts: in treatments of rhetoric, as in certain dialogues of Plato and in Aristotle's *Rhetoric;* in the Greek discussions of virtue and vice; in the moral theology of Aquinas and in Spinoza's *Ethics;* and in books of political theory, such as Machiavelli's *The Prince* and Hobbes's *Leviathan.*

Descartes's treatise on *The Passions of the Soul* is probably one of the first discourses on the subject to be separated from the practical considerations of oratory, morals, and politics. Only subsequently do the emotions become an object of purely theoretic interest in psychology. But even then the interest of the psychiatrist or psychoanalyst—to the extent that it is medical or therapeutic—has a strong practical bent.

In the great works of poetry and history no similar shift takes place as one goes from Homer and Virgil to Tolstoy, Dostoevsky, and Proust, from Greek to Shakespearean tragedy, from Plutarch and Tacitus to Gibbon. What Wordsworth said of the lyric poem—that it is "emotion recollected in tranquillity"—may not apply to the narratives in an identical sense. Yet they too reenact the passions in all their vitality. Their pages are filled with the emotions of men in conflict with one another or suffering conflict within themselves.

This is no less true of historical narrative than of fiction. The memorable actions of men on the stage of history did not occur in calm and quiet. We would certainly not remember them as well if the historian failed to recreate for us the turbulence of crisis and catastrophe, or the biographer the storm and stress which accompanies the inward resolution of heroic lives.

It is impossible, of course, to cite *all* the relevant passages of poetry and history. In many instances, nothing less than a whole book would suffice. The particular references given in this chapter, which are far from exhaustive, have been selected for their peculiar exemplary significance in relation to a particular topic; but for the whole range of topics connected with emotion, the reader should certainly seek further in the realms of history and poetry for the raw materials which the scientists and philosophers have tried to analyze and understand.

To the student of the emotions, Francis Bacon recommends "the poets and writers of histories" as "the best doctors of this knowledge; where we may find painted forth with great life, how affections are kindled and incited; and how pacified and refrained; and how again contained from act and further degree; how they disclose themselves; how they work; how they vary; how they gather and fortify; how they are enwrapped one within another; and how they do fight and encounter one with another; and other like particularities."

FOUR WORDS—"passion," "affection" or "affect," and "emotion"—have been traditionally used to designate the same psychological fact. Of these, "affection" and "affect" have ceased to be generally current, although we do find them in Freud; and "passion" is now usually restricted to mean one of the emotions, or the more violent aspect of any emotional experience. But if we are to connect discussions collected from widely separated centuries, we must be able to use all these words interchangeably.

The psychological fact to which they all refer is one every human being has experienced in moments of great excitement, especially during intense seizure by rage or fear. In his treatise *On the Circulation of the Blood,* Harvey calls attention to "the fact that in almost every affection, appetite, hope, or fear, our body suffers, the countenance changes, and the blood appears to course hither and thither. In anger the eyes are fiery and the pupils contracted; in modesty the cheeks are suffused with blushes; in fear, and under a sense of infamy and of shame, the face is pale" and "in lust how quickly is the member distended with blood and erected!"

Emotional experience seems to involve an awareness of widespread bodily commotion, which includes changes in the tension of the blood vessels and the muscles, changes in heartbeat and breathing, changes in the condition of the skin and other tissues. Though some degree of bodily disturbance would seem to be an essential ingredient in all emotional experience, the intensity and extent of the physiological reverberation, or bodily commotion, is not the same or equal in all the emotions. Some emotions are much more violent than others. This leads James to distinguish what he calls the "coarser emotions . . . in which every one recognizes a strong organic reverberation" from the "subtler emotions" in which the "organic reverberation is less obvious and strong."

This fact is sometimes used to draw the line between what are truly emotions and what are only mild feelings of pleasure and pain or enduring sentiments. Nevertheless, sentiments may be emotional residues—stable attitudes which pervade a life even during moments of emotional detachment and calm—and pleasure and pain may color all the emotions. "Pleasure and pain," Locke suggests, are "the hinges on which our passions turn." Even though they may not be passions in the strict sense, they are obviously closely connected with them.

THAT THE EMOTIONS are organic disturbances, upsetting the normal course of the body's functioning, is sometimes thought to be a modern discovery, connected with the James-Lange theory that the emotional experience is nothing but the "feeling of . . . the bodily changes" which "follow directly the perception of the exciting fact." On this view, the explanation of emotion seems to be the very opposite of "common sense," which says, "we meet a bear, are frightened, and run." According to James, "this order of sequence is incorrect," and "the more rational statement is that we feel . . . afraid because we tremble." In other words, we do not run away because we are afraid, but are afraid because we run away.

This fact about the emotions was known to antiquity and the Middle Ages. Aristotle, for example, holds that mere awareness of an object does not induce flight unless "the heart is moved," and Aquinas declares that "passion is properly to be found where there is corporeal transmutation." He describes at some length the bodily changes which take place in anger and fear. Only very recently, however, have apparatus and techniques been devised for recording and, in some cases, measuring the physiological changes accompanying experimentally produced emotions—in both animals and men.

Modern theory also tries to throw some light on these organic changes by pointing out their adaptive utility in the struggle for existence. This type of explanation is advanced by Darwin in *The Expression of the Emotions in Man and Animals,* and is adopted by other evolutionists. "The snarl or sneer, the one-sided uncovering of the upper teeth," James writes, "is accounted for by Darwin as a survival from the time when our ancestors had large canines, and unfleshed them (as dogs now do) for attack . . . The distention of the nostrils in anger is interpreted by Spencer as an echo of the way in which our ancestors had to breathe when, during combat, their 'mouth was filled up by a part of the antagonist's body that had been seized' . . . The redding of the face and neck is called by Wundt a compensatory arrangement for relieving the brain of the blood-pressure which the simultaneous excitement of the heart brings with it. The effusion of tears is explained both by this author and by Darwin to be a blood-withdrawing agency of a similar sort."

Reviewing statements of this sort, James is willing to concede that "some movements of expression can be accounted for as *weakened repetitions of movements which formerly* (when they were stronger) *were of utility to the subject*"; but though we may thus "see the reason for a few emotional reactions," he thinks "others remain for which no plausible reason can even be conceived." The latter, James suggests, "may be reactions which are purely mechanical results of the way in which our nervous centres are framed, reactions which, although permanent in us now, may be called accidental as far as their origin goes."

Whether or not *all* the bodily changes which occur in such emotions as anger or fear serve the purpose of increasing the animal's efficiency in combat or flight—as, for example, the increase of sugar in the blood and the greater supply of blood to arms and legs seem to do—the basic emotions are generally thought to be connected with the instinctively determined patterns of behavior by which animals struggle to survive. "The actions we call

instinctive," James writes, "are expressions or manifestations of the emotions"; or, as other writers suggest, an emotion, whether in outward expression or in inner experience, is the central phase of an instinct in operation.

The observation of the close relation between instinct and emotion does not belong exclusively to modern, or post-Darwinian, thought. The ancients also recognize it, though in different terms. Following Aristotle's analysis of the various "interior senses," Aquinas, for example, speaks of the "estimative power" by which animals seem to be innately prepared to react to things useful or harmful.

"If an animal were moved by pleasing and disagreeable things only as affecting the sense"—that is, the exterior senses—"there would be no need to suppose," Aquinas writes, "that an animal has a power besides the apprehension of those forms which the senses perceive, and in which the animal takes pleasure, or from which it shrinks with horror." But animals need to seek or avoid certain things on account of their advantages or disadvantages, and such emotional reactions of approach or avoidance require, in his opinion, a sense of the useful and the dangerous, which is innate rather than learned. The estimative power thus seems to play a role which later writers assign to instinct. The relation of instinct to the emotions and to fundamental biological needs is further considered, from other points of view, in the chapters on DESIRE and HABIT.

LIKE DESIRE, emotion is neither knowledge nor action, but something intermediate between the one and the other. The various passions are usually aroused by objects perceived, imagined, or remembered, and once aroused they in turn originate impulses to act in certain ways. For example, fear arises with the perception of a threatening danger or with the imagination of some fancied peril. The thing feared is somehow recognized as capable of inflicting injury with consequent pain. The thing feared is also something from which one naturally tends to flee in order to avoid harm. Once the danger is known and until it is avoided by flight or in some other way, the characteristic feeling of fear pervades the whole experience. It is partly a result of what is known and what is done and partly the cause of how things seem and how one behaves.

Analytically isolated from its causes and effects, the emotion itself seems to be the feeling rather than the knowing or the doing. But it is not simply an awareness of a certain bodily condition. It also involves the felt impulse to do something about the object of the passion.

Those writers who, like Aquinas, identify emotion with the impulse by which "the soul is drawn to a thing," define the several passions as specifically different acts of appetite or desire—specific tendencies to action. Aquinas, for instance, adopts the definition given by Damascene: "Passion is a movement of the sensitive appetite when we imagine good or evil."

Other writers who, like Spinoza, find that "the order of the actions and passions of our body is coincident in nature with the order of the actions and passions of the mind," stress the cognitive rather than the impulsive aspect of emotion. They accordingly define the passions in terms of the characteristic feelings, pleasant and unpleasant, which flow from the estimation of certain objects as beneficial or harmful. Spinoza goes furthest in this direction when he says that "an affect or passion of the mind *is a confused idea . . . by which the mind affirms of its body, or any part of it, a greater or less power of existence than before.*"

There seems to be no serious issue here, for writers of both sorts acknowledge, though with different emphasis, the two sides of an emotion—the cognitive and the impulsive, that which faces toward the object and that which leads into action. On either view, the human passions are regarded as part of man's animal nature. It is generally admitted that disembodied spirits, if such exist, cannot have emotions. The angels, Augustine writes, "feel no anger while they punish those whom the eternal law of God consigns to punishment, no fellow-feeling with misery while they relieve the miserable, no fear while they aid those who are in danger." When we do ascribe emotions to spirits, it is, Augustine claims, because, "though they have none of our weakness, their acts resemble the actions to which these emotions move us."

In connection with the objects which arouse them, the emotions necessarily depend upon the senses and the imagination; and their perturbations and impulses require bodily organs for expression. That is why, as indicated in the chapter on DESIRE, some writers separate the passions from acts of the will, as belonging to the sensitive or animal appetite rather than to the rational or specifically human appetite. Even those writers who do not place so high an estimate on the role of reason, refer the emotions to the animal aspect of human behavior, or to what is sometimes called "man's lower nature." When this phrase is used, it usually signifies the passions as opposed to the reason, not the purely vegetative functions which man shares with plants as well as animals.

There seems to be no doubt that emotions are common to men and animals and that they are more closely related to instinct than to reason or intelligence. Darwin presents many instances which, he claims, prove that "the senses and intuitions, the various emotions and faculties, such as love, memory, attention, curiosity, imitation, reason, etc., of which man boasts, may be found in an incipient, or even sometimes in a well-developed, condition in the lower animals." Where Darwin remarks upon "the fewness and the comparative simplicity of the instincts in the higher animals . . . in contrast with those of the lower animals," James takes the position that man "is the animal richest in instinctive impulses." However that issue is decided, the emotions seem to be more elaborately developed in the higher animals, and man's emotional life would seem to be the most complex and varied of all. As Balzac observes, "the savage has only emotions. The civilized man has emotions plus ideas."

The question then arises whether particular passions are identical—or are only analogous—when they occur in men and animals. For example, is human anger, no matter how closely it resembles brute rage in its physiology and impulses, nevertheless peculiarly human? Do men alone experience righteous indignation because of some admixture in them of reason and passion? When similar questions are asked about the sexual passions of men and animals, the answers will determine the view one takes of the characteristically human aspects of love and hate. It may even be asked whether hate, as men suffer it, is ever experienced by brutes, or whether certain passions, such as hope and despair, are known to brutes at all?

IN THE TRADITIONAL theory of the emotions, the chief problem, after the definition of emotion, is the classification or grouping of the passions, and the ordering of particular passions. The vocabulary of common speech in all ages and cultures includes a large number of words for naming emotions, and it has been the task of analysts to decide which of these words designate distinct affects or affections. The precise character of the object and the direction of the impulse have been, for the most part, the criteria of definition. As previously noted, it is but recently that the experimental observation of bodily changes has contributed to the differentiation of emotions from one another.

Spinoza offers the longest listing of the passions. For him, the emotions, which are all "compounded of the three primary affects, desire, joy, and sorrow," develop into the following forms: astonishment, contempt, love, hatred, inclination, aversion, devotion, derision, hope, fear, confidence, despair, gladness, remorse, commiseration, favor, indignation, over-estimation, envy, compassion, self-satisfaction, humility, repentance, pride, despondency, self-exaltation, shame, regret, emulation, gratitude, benevolence, anger, vengeance, ferocity, audacity, consternation, courtesy, ambition, luxuriousness, drunkenness, avarice, lust.

Many of the foregoing are, for Hobbes, derived from what he calls "the simple passions," which include "appetite, desire, love, aversion, hate, joy, and grief." There are more emotions in Spinoza's list than either Aristotle or Locke or James mentions, but none which they include is omitted. Some of the items in Spinoza's enumeration are treated by other writers as virtues and vices rather than as passions.

The passions have been classified by reference to various criteria. As we have seen, James distinguishes emotions as "coarse" or "subtle" in terms of the violence or mildness of the accompanying physiological changes; and Spinoza distinguishes them according as "the mind passes to a greater perfection" or "to a less perfection." Spinoza's division would also seem to imply a distinction between the beneficial and the harmful in the objects causing these two types of emotion, or at least to involve the opposite components of pleasure and pain, for in his view the emotions which correspond to "a greater or less power of existence than before" are attended in the one case by "pleasurable excitement" and in the other by "pain."

Hobbes uses another principle of division. The passions differ basically according to the direction of their impulses—according as each is "a motion or endeavor . . . to or from the object moving." Aquinas adds still another criterion—"the difficulty or struggle . . . in acquiring certain goods or in avoiding certain evils" which, in contrast to those we "can easily acquire or avoid," makes them, therefore, "of an arduous or difficult nature." In these terms, he divides all the passions into the "concupiscible," which regard "good or evil simply" (i.e., love, hate, desire, aversion, joy, sorrow), and the "irascible," which "regard good or evil as arduous through being difficult to obtain or avoid" (i.e., fear, daring, hope, despair, anger).

Within each of these groups, Aquinas pairs particular passions as opposites, such as joy and sorrow, or hope and despair, either according to the "contrariety of object, i.e., of good and evil . . . or according to approach and withdrawal." Anger seems to be the only passion for which no opposite can be given, other than that "cessation from its movement" which Aristotle calls "calmness" and which Aquinas says is an opposite not by way of "contrariety but of negation or privation."

Using these distinctions, Aquinas also describes the order in which one passion leads to or generates another, beginning with love and hate, passing through hope, desire, and fear, with their opposites, and, after anger, ending in joy or despair. On one point, all observers and theorists from Plato to Freud seem to agree, namely, that love and hate lie at the root of all the other passions and generate hope or despair, fear and anger, according as the aspirations of love prosper or fail. Nor is the insight that even hate derives from love peculiarly modern, though Freud's theory of what he calls the "ambivalence" of love and hate toward the *same* object seems to be part of his own special contribution to our understanding of the passions.

Considering the wide variety of human feelings, moods, and emotions, Heidegger singles out one that he regards as having, one might say, metaphysical significance. That is angst or dread. "By 'dread' we do not mean 'anxiety,' which is common enough and is akin to nervousness"; he adds that dread also "differs absolutely from fear . . . We are always *afraid* of this or that definite thing, which threatens us in this or that definite way." But dread, according to Heidegger, "is pervaded by a peculiar kind of peace." It is "a mood so peculiarly revelatory in its import as to reveal Nothing itself." It is only in the "key-mood of dread" that we are "brought face to face with Nothing itself."

THE ROLE OF THE emotions or passions in human behavior has always raised two questions, one concerning the effect of conflict between diverse emotions, the other concerning the conflict between the passions and the reason or will. It is the latter question which has been of the greatest interest to moralists and statesmen.

Even though human emotions may have instinctive origin and be innately determined, man's emotional responses seem to be subject to voluntary control, so that men are able to form or change their emotional habits. If this were not so, there could be no moral problem of the regulation of the passions; nor, for that matter, could there be a medical problem of therapy for emotional disorders. The psychoanalytic treatment of neuroses seems, moreover, to assume the possibility of a voluntary, or even a rational, resolution of emotional conflicts—not perhaps without the aid of therapeutic efforts to uncover the sources of conflict and to remove the barriers between repressed emotion and rational decision.

The relation of the passions to the will, especially their antagonism, is relevant to the question whether the actions of men always conform to their judgments of good and evil, or right and wrong. As Socrates discusses the problem of knowledge and virtue, it would seem to be his view that a man who knows what is good for him will act accordingly. Men may "desire things which they imagine to be good," he says, "but which in reality are evil." Hence their misconduct will be due to a mistaken judgment, not to a discrepancy between action and thought. Eliminating the case of erroneous judgment, Socrates gets Meno to admit that "no man wills or chooses anything evil."

Aristotle criticizes the Socratic position which he summarizes in the statement that "no one . . . when he judges acts against what he judges best—people act badly only by reason of ignorance." According to Aristotle, "this view plainly contradicts the observed facts." Yet he admits that whatever a man does must at least *seem* good to him *at the moment;* and to that extent the judgment that something is good or bad would seem to determine action accordingly. In his analysis of incontinence, Aristotle tries to explain how a man may act against what is his better judgment and yet, at the moment of action, seek what he holds to be good.

Action may be caused either by a rational judgment concerning what is good or by an emotional estimate of the desirable. If these two factors are independent of one another—more than that, if they can tend in opposite directions—then a man may act under emotional persuasion at one moment in a manner contrary to his rational predilection at another. That a man may act either emotionally or rationally, Aristotle thinks, explains how, under strong emotional influences, a man can do the very opposite of what his reason would tell him is right or good. The point is that, while the emotions dominate his mind and action, he does not listen to reason.

These matters are further discussed in the chapter on TEMPERANCE. But it should be noted here that the passions and the reason, or the "lower" and the "higher" natures of man, are not always in conflict. Sometimes emotions or emotional attitudes serve reason by supporting voluntary decisions. They reinforce and make effective moral resolutions which might otherwise be too difficult to execute.

THE ANCIENTS DID not underestimate the force of the passions, nor were they too confident of the strength of reason in its struggle to control them, or to be free of them. They were acquainted with the violence of emotional excess which they called "madness" or "frenzy." So, too, were the theologians of the Middle Ages and modern philosophers like Spinoza and Hobbes. But not until Freud—and perhaps also James, though to a lesser extent—do we find in the tradition of the great books insight into the pathology of the passions, the origin of emotional disorders, and the general theory of the neuroses and neurotic character as the consequence of emotional repression.

For Freud, the primary fact is not the conflict between reason and emotion, or, in his language, between the *ego* and the *id*. It is rather the repression which results from such conflict. On the one side is the ego, which "stands for reason and circumspection" and has "the task of representing the external world," or expressing what Freud calls "the reality-principle." Associated with the ego is the superego—"the vehicle of the ego-ideal, by which the ego measures itself, towards which it strives, and whose demands for ever-increasing perfection it is always striving to fulfill." On the other side is the id, which "stands for the untamed passions" and is the source of instinctual life.

The ego, according to Freud, is constantly attempting "to mediate between the id and reality" and to measure up to the ideal set by the superego, so as to dethrone "the pleasure-principle, which exerts undisputed sway over the processes in the id, and substitute for it the reality-principle, which promises greater security and greater success." But sometimes it fails in this task. Sometimes, when no socially acceptable channels of behavior are available for expressing emotional drives in action, the ego, supported by the superego, represses the emotional or instinctual impulses, that is, prevents them from expressing themselves overtly.

Freud's great insight is that emotions repressed do not atrophy and disappear. On the contrary, their dammed-up energies accumulate and, like a sore, they fester inwardly. Together with related ideas, memories, and wishes, the repressed emotions form what Freud calls a "complex," which is not only the active nucleus of emotional disorder but also the cause of neurotic symptoms and behavior—phobias and anxieties, obsessions or compulsions, and the various physical manifestations of hysteria, such as a blindness or a paralysis that has no organic basis.

The line between the neurotic and the normal is shadowy, for repressed emotional complexes are, according to Freud, also responsible for the hidden or latent psychological significance of slips of speech, forgetting, the content of dreams, occupational or marital choices, and a wide variety of other phenomena usually regarded as accidental or as rationally determined. In fact, Freud sometimes goes to the extreme of insisting that all apparently rational processes—both of thought and decision—are themselves emotionally determined; and that most, or all, reasoning is nothing but the rationalization of emotionally fixed prejudices or beliefs. "The ego," he writes, "is after all only a part of the id, a part purposively modified by its proximity to the dangers of reality."

The ancient distinction between knowledge and opinion seems to be in essential agreement with the insight that emotions can control the course of thinking. But at the same time it denies that all thinking is necessarily dominated by the passions. The sort of thinking which is free from emotional bias or domination may result in knowledge, if reason itself is not defective in its processes. But the sort of thinking which is directed and determined by the passions *must* result in opinion. The former is reasoning; the latter what Freud calls "rationalization" or sometimes "wishful thinking."

BECAUSE THEY CAN be ordered when they get out of order, the emotions raise problems for both medicine and morals. Whether or not there is a fundamental opposition between the medical and the moral approaches to the problem, whether psychotherapy is needed only when morality has failed, whether morality is itself partly responsible for the disorders which psychotherapy must cure, the difference between the medical and the moral approaches is clear. Medically, emotional disorders call for diagnosis and therapy. Morally, they call for criticism and correction.

Human bondage, according to Spinoza, consists in "the impotence of man to govern or restrain the affects . . . for a man who is under their control is not his own master." A free man he describes as one "who lives according to the dictates of reason alone," and he tries to show "how much reason itself can control the affects" to achieve what he calls "freedom of mind or blessedness." While moralists tend to agree on this point, they do not all offer the same prescription for establishing the right relation between man's higher and lower natures.

The issue which arises here is also discussed in the chapters on DESIRE and DUTY. It exists between those who think that the passions are intrinsically evil, the natural enemies of a good will, lawless elements always in rebellion against duty; and those who think that the passions represent a natural desire for certain goods which belong to the happy life, or a natural aversion for certain evils.

Those who, like the Stoics and Kant, tend to adopt the former view recommend a policy of attrition toward the passions. Their force must be attenuated in order to emancipate reason from their influence and to protect the will from their seductions. Nothing is lost, according to this theory, if the passions atrophy and die. But if, according to the opposite doctrine, the passions have a natural place in the moral life, then the aim should be, not to dispossess them entirely, but to keep them in their place. Aristotle therefore recommends a policy of moderation. The passions can be made to serve reason's purposes by restraining them from excesses and by directing their energies to ends which reason approves.

As Aristotle conceives them, certain of the virtues—especially temperance and courage—are stable emotional attitudes, or *habits* of emotional response, which conform to reason and carry out its rule. The moral virtues require more than a momentary control or moderation of the passions; they require a discipline of them which has become habitual. What Aristotle calls continence, as opposed to virtue, consists in reason's effort to check emotions which are still unruly because they have not yet become habituated to reason's rule.

The fact of individual differences in temperament is of the utmost importance to the moralist who is willing to recognize that universal moral rules apply to individuals differently according to their temperaments. Both psychologists and moralists have classified men into temperamental types by reference to the dominance or deficiency of certain emotional predispositions in their inherited makeup. These temperamental differences also have a medical or physiological aspect insofar as certain elements in human physique—the four bodily humors of the ancients or the hormones of modern endocrinology—seem to be correlated with types of personality.

ONE OF THE GREAT issues in political theory concerns the role of the passions in human association. Have men banded together to form states because they feared the insecurity and the hazards of natural anarchy and universal war, or because they sought the benefits which only political life could provide? In the political community, once it is formed, do love and friendship or distrust and fear determine the relation of fellow citizens, or of rulers and ruled? Should the prince, or any other man who wishes to get and hold political power, try to inspire love or to instill fear in those whom he seeks to dominate? Or are each of these emotions useful for different political purposes and in the handling of different kinds of men?

Considering whether for the success of the prince it is "better to be loved than feared or feared than loved," Machiavelli says that "one should wish to be both, but, because it is difficult to unite them in one person, it is much safer to be feared than loved, when, of the two, either must be dispensed with . . . Nevertheless," he continues, "a prince ought to inspire fear in such a way that, if he does not win love, he avoids hatred; because he can endure very well being feared whilst he is not hated."

According to Hobbes, when men enter into a commonwealth so that they can live peacefully with one another, they are moved partly by reason and partly by their passions. "The passions that incline men to peace," he writes, "are fear of death; desire of such things as are necessary to commodious living; and a hope by their industry to obtain them." But once a commonwealth is formed, the one passion which seems to be the mainspring of all political activity is "a perpetual and restless desire of power after power, that ceaseth only in death"; for a man "cannot assure the power and means to live well, which he has present, without the acquisition of more."

Not all political thinkers agree with the answers which Machiavelli and Hobbes give on such matters; nor do all make such questions the pivots of their political theory. But there is general agreement that the passions are a force to be reckoned with in the government of men; that the ruler, whether he is despotic prince or constitutional officeholder, must move men through their emotions as well as by appeals to reason.

The two political instruments through which an influence over the emotions is exercised are oratory (now sometimes called propaganda) and law. Both may work persuasively. Laws, like other discourses, according to Plato, may have preludes or preambles, intended by the legislator "to create good-will in the persons whom he addresses, in order that, by reason of this good-will, they will more intelligently receive his command." But the law also carries with it the threat of coercive force. The threat of punishment for disobedience addresses itself entirely to fear, whereas the devices of the orator—or even of the legislator in his preamble—are not so restricted. The orator can play upon the whole scale of the emotions to obtain the actions or decisions at which he aims.

Finally, there is the problem of whether the statesman should exercise political control over other influences which affect the emotional life of a people, especially the arts and public spectacles. The earliest and perhaps the classic statement of this problem is to be found in Plato's *The Republic* and in his *Laws*. Considerations relevant to the question he raises, and the implications of diverse solutions of the problem, are discussed in the chapters on ART, LIBERTY, and POETRY.

23

Eternity

INTRODUCTION

THE notion of eternity, like that of infinity, has two meanings. One meaning may refer to something positive, yet both seem to be formulated by the human mind in a negative way. We grasp one meaning of eternity by saying that there is *no* beginning or end to time's process. The other sense of eternity we conceive by *denying* time itself and, with it, change or mutability.

Considering eternity as infinite duration, Locke says that we form this notion "by the same means and from the same original that we come to have the idea of time . . . *viz.,* having got the idea of succession and duration . . . we can in our thoughts add such lengths of duration to one another, as often as we please, and apply them, so added, to durations past or to come. And this we can continue to do, without bounds or limits, and proceed *in infinitum."*

The unimaginability of the infinite is no different in the sphere of time than in that of space or number. The difficulty, Locke points out, is the same in all three cases. "The idea of *so much* is positive and clear. The idea of *greater* is also clear." But these do not yet give us the idea of the infinite. That only comes with "the idea of *so much greater as cannot be comprehended,* and this is plainly negative, not positive . . . What lies beyond our positive idea *towards* infinity," Locke continues, "lies in obscurity, and has the indeterminate confusion of a negative idea, wherein I know I neither do nor can comprehend all I would, it being too large for a finite and narrow capacity."

In insisting that we can have no positive idea of infinity—whether of space, time, or number—Locke's point seems to be that it is beyond our finite capacity to form an image of an infinite object. But though our imaginations may be limited in this way, we do seem able to construct—in a negative manner—conceptions that go beyond experience, and have some meaning even if they lack imaginative content. Locke indicates this other aspect of the matter when he criticizes those who assert dogmatically that "the world is neither eternal nor infinite." It seems to him that the world's eternity or the world's infinity is "at least as conceivable as the contrary."

It may not be inconsistent, therefore, to say that infinite time, while unimaginable, remains quite conceivable; for to say that eternity is conceivable is simply to say that endless time is neither more nor less possible than time with a beginning and an end. The first conception is as meaningful as the second. It is in fact formed from the second by negation—by substituting the word "without" for "with" with respect to "a beginning and an end." But unlike our conceptions, our images cannot be formed by negation. When we imagine, as when we perceive, the object before us is positive and definite. We cannot imagine, as we cannot experience, a duration, or a span of time, without a beginning and an end.

WITH REGARD TO the other traditional meaning of "eternity," Locke takes a different position. It too might be defended as a negative conception, so far as human comprehension is concerned, since it involves the denial of time itself, *i.e.,* of a duration comprising a succession of moments. But here Locke says that there is "nothing more inconceivable to me than duration without succession . . . If our weak apprehensions," he continues, "cannot

separate succession from any duration whatsoever, our idea of eternity can be nothing but of
an infinite succession of moments of duration,
wherein anything does exist."

Nevertheless, Locke affirms that "we can
easily conceive in God infinite duration, and
we cannot avoid doing so." Whether he means
by this that God's eternity involves temporal
succession must be determined by an interpretation of the passage in which he maintains
that "God's infinite duration being accompanied with infinite knowledge and infinite
power, he sees all things past and to come; and
they are no more distant from his knowledge,
no farther removed from his sight, than the
present; they all lie under the same view."

If this passage means that time stands still
for God in a single moment in which all things
are copresent, then Locke may not be as resolute as Hobbes in rejecting the theologian's
conception of God's eternity. Criticizing the
Scholastics, Hobbes says that "for the meaning
of *Eternity,* they will not have it be an endless
succession of time." Instead, "they will teach
us that eternity is the standing still of the present time, a *Nunc-stans* (as the Schools call it)."
This, Hobbes thinks, "neither they nor anyone
else understands, no more than they would a
Hic-stans for an infinite greatness of place."

A theologian like Aquinas tries to avoid
the difficulty which Hobbes finds in this conception by distinguishing between the *now* of
eternity and the *now* of time. "The *now* of
time is the same," he writes, "as regards its
subject in the whole course of time, but it differs in aspect." Furthermore, "the flow of the
now, as altering in aspect, is time. But eternity
remains the same according to both subject
and aspect; and hence eternity is not the same
as the *now* of time."

The notion of the eternal as the timeless
and the immutable does not belong exclusively
to Christian theology. In the tradition of the
great books it is found, for example, in Plato
and Plotinus. Eternity, according to Plotinus,
is "a Life changelessly motionless and ever
holding the Universal content in actual presence; not this now and now that other, but
always all; not existing now in one mode and
now in another, but a consummation without

part or interval. All its content is in immediate
concentration as at one point; nothing in it
ever knows development: all remains identical
within itself, knowing nothing of change, for
ever in a Now since nothing of it has passed
away or will come into being; but what it is
now, that it is ever."

Eternity so conceived is perhaps even more
unimaginable than the eternity which is infinite time. We may feel that we have some
sense of an infinite duration when we talk, as
Ivan does in *The Brothers Karamazov,* about a
billion years or "a quadrillion of a quadrillion
raised to the quadrillionth power." Infinite
time is *like* that, *only longer.* But because
all our experience is temporal through and
through, it is more difficult to get any sense
of that which is both absolutely timeless and
endlessly enduring.

Poets, and sometimes philosophers turned
poets, have struggled to give this concept imaginative content by contrasting "the white radiance of eternity" with a "many-colored glass,"
or by speaking of time itself as "the moving
image of eternity." When Dimmler in *War and
Peace* tells Natasha that "it is hard for us to
imagine eternity," she replies that it does not
seem hard to her—that eternity "is now today,
and it will be tomorrow, and always, and was
there yesterday and the day before . . ."

These and similar attempts may not succeed
as much as the insight that if we could hold
the present moment still, or fix the fleeting
instant, we could draw an experience of the
eternal from the heart of time. "The *now* that
stands still," Aquinas writes, "is said to make
eternity according to our apprehension. For
just as the apprehension of time is caused in
us by the fact that we apprehend the flow
of the *now,* so the apprehension of eternity
is caused in us by our apprehending the *now*
standing still."

To UNDERSTAND the opposed views that constitute the major issues with regard to eternity,
it is necessary to hold quite separate the two
meanings of the word which have run side
by side in the tradition of western thought.
The first of these two senses, signifying interminable time, is the meaning of "eternity"

which has greatest currency in popular speech. This is the meaning which appears in the chapters on INFINITY and TIME. It is also the sense in which philosophers and theologians debate the problem of the eternity of the world—whether the world ever began or will ever end.

Since that which exists interminably is imperishable, the word "eternal" is also applied to substances which are thought to be everlasting. Thus Ptolemy, and the ancients generally, think of the heavenly bodies as "beings which are sensible and both moving and moved, but eternal and impassible." Aristotle calls the heavenly bodies "eternal and incorruptible." For Lucretius and the atomists, the atoms and the atoms alone are eternal. They are everlasting, he says: "Were this not true of matter, long ago/Everything would have crumbled into nothing." If the atomic particles "were to wear away, or break in pieces," Newton argues, "the nature of things depending on them, would be changed . . . And therefore, that nature may be lasting, the changes of corporeal things are to be placed only in the various separations and new associations and motions of these permanent particles."

The heavenly bodies and the atoms may be thought everlasting, but they are not immutable in all respects, for local motion is of their very essence. Imperishable in existence, they are also endlessly in motion. In Aristotle's view, local motion can be perpetual or eternal *only* if it is circular. Circular motion alone has neither beginning nor end.

The eternal circular motion of the heavens, according to Aristotle, in turn communicates an eternal cyclical movement to the rest of reality. "Since the sun revolves thus, the seasons in consequence come-to-be in a cycle . . . and since they come-to-be cyclically, so in their turn do the things whose coming-to-be the seasons initiate." Such an eternal return, it would seem, is also applied by Aristotle to human things, for he writes that "probably each art and each science has often been developed as far as possible and has again perished."

SINCE THE HEAVENS and the atoms are in motion, even though their motion is everlasting or eternal, they cannot be eternal in the second

meaning of "eternity," which is the very opposite of the first, not a variation or extension of it. In this meaning, the eternal is an existence absolutely immutable—a being which neither comes to be nor passes away, nor changes, nor moves in any respect whatsoever. Aquinas uses the word in this sense when he says that "the nature of eternity" consists in "the uniformity of what is absolutely outside of movement."

He also includes in this meaning of "eternity" the notion of interminability; for, he writes, "as whatever is wholly immutable can have no succession, so it has no beginning, and no end." Yet Aquinas preserves the sharp distinction between the two meanings when he differentiates the sense in which the world might be called eternal and the sense in which he would attribute eternity to God alone. "Even supposing that the world always was, it would not be equal to God in eternity," he writes; for "the divine being is all being simultaneously without succession, but with the world it is otherwise."

The conception of eternity as absolutely immutable existence is found in the ancient pagan writers. Plotinus, as we have already seen, makes immutability the mark of eternity. The unmoved prime mover of Aristotle and the Platonic Ideas or Forms also possess this characteristic. But it is the Jewish and Christian theologians who make eternity in this sense one of the prime attributes of God.

Augustine, for example, invokes God as "the splendour of eternity which is for ever still," and in which "nothing moves into the past: all is present." Since time is for him inconceivable apart from change or motion, that which exists immutably does not exist in time. Referring to God's eternity, he says, "Contrast it with time, which is never still, and see that it is not comparable . . . Your years neither go nor come, but our years pass and others come after them . . . Your years are one day, yet your day does not come daily but is always today . . . Your today is eternity."

Time and eternity are here conceived as two distinct orders of reality. The temporal order is the order of things in change or motion, the eternal the realm of the fixed or permanent, the immobile and immutable. "As eternity is the proper measure of being," Aquinas writes, "so time is the proper measure of movement."

The eternal and the temporal are similarly distinguished by Plato in terms of the realms of being and becoming—"the world of immutable being" and "the world of generation." In the one we find "the parts of time, and the past and the future," which do not apply to the other. "We unconsciously but wrongly transfer them," Plato declares, "to the eternal essence . . . but the truth is that 'is' alone is properly attributed to it, and 'was' and 'will be' are only to be spoken of becoming in time, for they are motions, but that which is immovably the same cannot become older or younger by time . . . nor is it subject at all to any of those states which affect moving and sensible things of which generation is the cause."

For Spinoza, the distinction consists in two ways of viewing the order of nature. "Things are conceived by us as actual in two ways," he writes; "either in so far as we conceive them to exist with relation to a fixed time and place, or in so far as we conceive them to be contained in God, and to follow from the necessity of the divine nature." Only in the second way do "we conceive things under the form of eternity." We can view things under the aspect of eternity only insofar as we know God and, through knowing God, are able to know all things according as "their ideas involve the eternal and infinite essence of God."

The separation of time and eternity into distinct spheres of reality, or even into distinct ways of conceiving the whole of being, is challenged by thinkers who find the eternal within the process of time. For both Jew and Christian, the eternal God intervenes directly in the temporal order. The most radical form which this fusion takes is perhaps exemplified in the doctrine of the Incarnation of Christ, when "the Word was made flesh, and dwelt among us." But, as Calvin reminds us, "the Word was eternally begotten by God," and it is this that establishes Christ's "true essence, his eternity, and divinity."

Whitehead challenges the sharpness of the separation from another point of view. He not only makes "eternal objects" ingredients in actual occasions or temporal events; but since the events which constitute the process of change are themselves unchangeable, they are for him eternal—even though they have their being within the sphere of change.

A similar point seems to be made in Aristotle's theory of change. When change is conceived as consisting in a transformation of matter, it is the thing composed of matter and form which changes, and neither the matter nor the form. Matter *as* matter, Aristotle writes, "does not cease to be in its own nature, but is necessarily outside the sphere of becoming and ceasing to be." The remark would seem to hold true as well of the form *as* form.

As indicated in the chapter on CHANGE, the Aristotelian analysis of motion finds in matter or the substratum of change, and in the contrary forms *from which* and *to which* a motion takes place, the elements of permanence underlying change. When a green leaf turns red, for instance, green has not changed into red; the leaf has changed from one color to another. The changing leaf is not eternal, but *red* and *green* are, since they are incapable of change. This is the sense of eternity in which the unchanging instant is eternal, or the past is eternal, even though both are somehow elements or aspects of time and the process of change.

The past may be eternal but it no longer exists. The passing moment may be eternal, but it has no duration. Lack of existence and lack of duration together distinguish that meaning of "eternal" in which it merely signifies the unchanging, from the meaning in which it signifies that which exists or endures forever without changing. It is only in the second of these two meanings that the eternal can be conceived as that which exists entirely outside the realm of time.

As WE HAVE ALREADY observed, the basic philosophical and theological issues concerning eternity cannot be intelligibly stated unless these meanings of "eternity" and "the eternal" are kept distinct.

The traditional problem of the eternity of the world asks, for example, not whether the order of nature is free from change or succession, but whether the changing physical universe ever had a beginning or ever will end. As indicated in the chapters on CHANGE, TIME, and WORLD, it is a question of the infinity of time; or, in another formulation, a question of the interminability of change or motion.

Aristotle appears to answer these questions affirmatively, especially in the last book of his *Physics* where he claims to demonstrate the impossibility of there having been a beginning to motion. Aquinas, on the other hand, does not think that the eternity of the world can be demonstrated; and of Aristotle's arguments he says that they are not "absolutely demonstrative, but only relatively so—*viz.*, as against the arguments of some of the ancients who asserted that the world began to be in some actually impossible ways." In support of this contention, he cites a remark made by Aristotle in the *Topics,* that among "dialectical problems which we cannot solve demonstratively," one is "*whether the world is eternal.*"

For Kant the problem is typically dialectical. It occurs as part of the first antinomy in the Transcendental Dialectic, the thesis of which asserts that "the world has a beginning in time" and the antithesis that "the world has no beginning, but is infinite in respect both to time and space." The fact that *apparently* cogent arguments can be marshaled for both of these contradictory propositions shows, in Kant's opinion, that the reasoning on either side is not demonstrative, but only dialectical and, as he says, "illusory."

The Jewish and Christian doctrine of the world's creation by God might seem to require the denial of the world's eternity. But in fact the theologians find either alternative compatible with divine creation, which they conceive as the cause of the world's *being,* not necessarily of its *beginning.* Augustine, for example, examines the sense in which the world is held by some to be coeternal with God, even though made or created by God. "As if a foot," he interprets them to say, "had been always from eternity in dust, there would always have been a print underneath it; and yet no one would doubt that this print was made by the pressure of the foot, nor that, though the one was made by the other, neither was prior

to the other." So, he goes on, it might also be said that the world has always existed and yet is always, throughout eternity, created, *i.e., caused to exist,* by God.

Commenting on this passage, Aquinas adds the observation that if an "action is instantaneous and not successive, it is not necessary for the maker to be prior in duration to the thing made." Hence it does not follow necessarily, he writes, "that if God is the active cause of the world, He must be prior to the world in duration; because creation, by which He produced the world, is not a successive change"—but an instantaneous act.

Writing both as a philosopher and as a theologian, Maimonides—many centuries before Kant stated his antinomy—thinks he is able to show that the question of infinite time and endless motion "cannot be decided by proof, neither in the affirmative nor in the negative." Just as for Augustine and Aquinas, so for him it is indifferent—from a *philosophical* point of view—whether the created world and its Creator are coeternal or whether, as Genesis says, "in the beginning God created heaven and earth."

But both alternatives are not equally acceptable to the theologian. Since there is no proof on either side "sufficient to convince us," Maimonides writes, "we take the text of the Bible literally, and say that it teaches us a truth which we cannot prove"—namely, that the world had a beginning in time. Aquinas comes to the same conclusion. "That the world did not always exist," he writes, "we hold by faith alone." It is not "an object . . . of demonstration or science." For Christian and Jew alike, the religious dogma that the world is not only created by God, in the sense of depending for its existence upon God as cause, but was also initiated by God, or caused to begin to exist and move, is based on the revealed word of God in Holy Writ.

Those who, on philosophical grounds, deny creation ex nihilo also deny the world's beginning. Pursuant to his theory of the world as a necessary and perpetual emanation from the One, Plotinus, for example, declares that "the Kosmos has had no beginning . . . and this is warrant for its continued existence. Why should there be in the future a change that has not yet occurred?" For Spinoza likewise, "all things which follow from the absolute nature of any attribute of God must for ever exist"; and to this extent at least, the world is eternal and uncreated.

The man of faith, however, believes in a God who is free to create or not to create, not one from whom the world emanates as a necessary effect from its source. When, therefore, he affirms that God freely chose to produce the world out of nothing, he seems to meet the question, "What was God doing before he made heaven and earth?" To the questioner Augustine refrains from the "frivolous retort . . . made before now, so we are told, in order to evade the point of the question" that " 'He was preparing Hell for people who pry into mysteries.' "

Instead he points out that the question itself is illicit for it assumes a time before time began. "If there was no time before heaven and earth were created," he writes, "how can anyone ask what you were doing 'then'? If there was no time, there was no 'then.' " In the phrase "before creation" the word "before" has no temporal significance. It signifies a different kind of priority—the sense in which eternity precedes time, the sense in which Augustine says of God that "it is not in time that you precede it . . . It is in eternity, which is supreme over time because it is a never-ending present, that you are at once before all past time and after all future time."

TURNING FROM eternity in the sense of infinite time to the eternal in the sense of the timeless and unchanging, the great question is whether anything eternal exists. The atoms of Lucretius are not eternal in this sense, nor are the supposedly imperishable heavenly bodies. Nor is it sufficient to point out that change itself involves aspects or elements of permanence; for the question, strictly interpreted, asks whether anything exists in and of itself which, having no beginning or end, also has no past, present, or future—no temporal phases in its continued endurance. Only such a thing would be utterly nontemporal or changeless.

Since nothing made of matter is exempt from motion, it is generally supposed that no material thing is eternal in this sense. Not even God is eternal unless God is absolutely immutable as well as spiritual. The angels are spiritual beings, yet, according to Christian theology, they cannot be called "eternal" because, in the first place, they are creatures and had an origin; and, in the second place, they are subject to spiritual change even if they are not involved in the sorts of motion to which bodies are susceptible. The theologians, therefore, use the word "aeviternal" to signify the mode of angelic existence in that it is "a mean between eternity and time." Aeviternity, Aquinas explains, has "a beginning but no end," while "eternity has neither beginning nor end . . . and time both beginning and end."

THE QUESTION ABOUT the eternal as timeless and immutable existence has two parts: Does an immutable God exist? Does anything else exist which is immutable?

To the first question, it does not suffice to reply by affirming the existence of God. Some modern theologians deny God's absolute immutability, and so deny the eternality of His being in the precise sense under consideration.

With regard to the second question, we must observe that, in the tradition of the great books, eternality has been claimed for two things other than God, namely, for truth and ideas. Whatever "is produced by reasoning aright," Hobbes says, is "general, eternal, and immutable truth." On somewhat different grounds William James declares, "there is no denying the fact that the mind is filled with necessary and eternal relations which it finds between certain of its ideal conceptions, and which form a determinate system, independent of the order of frequency in which experience may have associated the conception's originals in time and space." He quotes Locke to the effect that "truths belonging to the essences of things . . . are eternal, and are to be found out only by the contemplation of those essences."

The common phrase—"the eternal verities"—which James uses testifies to the prevalence of the notion that truth itself cannot change, and that when men speak of a new truth or the growth of truth, the change they refer to is only a change of mind with respect to what men think is true or false, not a change in the truth itself. Whatever is true now, always was true and always will be. Time and change make no difference to the truth of *two plus two equals four*.

But even so it can still be asked how the truth exists, for the attribution of eternity to anything also requires us to consider its mode of being. If, for example, the truth exists only in the mind, then it exists unchangingly only in the mind of an absolutely infallible knower, a mind which neither learns nor forgets, nor changes in any respect with regard to what it knows. If God is such a knower, eternal truth can have existence in God's mind.

The theologians sometimes go further and identify absolute truth, as they identify absolute goodness, with God. Aquinas writes, for example, that "if we speak of truth as it is in things, then all things are true by one primary truth; to which each one is assimilated according to its entity, and thus, although the essences or forms of things are many, yet the truth of the divine intellect is one, in conformity to which all things are said to be true." On this view, it would appear that there are not two eternal beings, but only one.

James finds immutability not only in the truth, but also in the concepts of the human mind. "Each conception," he writes, "eternally remains what it is, and never can become another. The mind may change its states, and its meanings, at different times; may drop one conception and take up another, but the dropped conception can in no intelligible sense be said to *change into* its successor . . . Thus, amid the flux of opinions and of physical things, the world of conceptions, or things intended to be thought about, stands stiff and immutable, like Plato's Realm of Ideas."

In the case of ideas, however, the problem is complicated by the question whether ideas exist in and by themselves, outside the mind of God or man. If, according to a doctrine attributed to Plato and the Platonists, the Ideas or Forms exist separately, then they constitute a realm of eternal beings, for their immutability is unquestionable. If, from an opposite point of view, the realm of unchanging ideas is identical with the divine intellect, then no eternal being or beings exist apart from God.

THE PROPOSITION that God is the only eternal being, the only uncreated and immutable existence, is inextricably connected with the proposition that God is the only actually infinite being, the *ens realissimum* having all perfections. "Eternity is the very essence of God," Spinoza writes, "in so far as that essence involves necessary existence." In saying this he appeals to his definition of eternity, by which we are to understand "existence itself, so far as it is conceived necessarily to follow from the definition alone of the eternal thing." For Spinoza, as well as for Aquinas, the same fact which makes God eternal—namely, the identity of his essence and existence—also constitutes his infinity and uniqueness. It is impossible, Spinoza argues, for there to be two infinite substances. For the same reason, there cannot be two eternal beings.

As indicated in the chapter on INFINITY, when the word "infinite" is applied to God, the theologians give it a positive rather than a negative significance. They mean by it the actual infinity of perfect being and absolute power, in sharp distinction from the potential infinity by which the mathematicians signify the *lack* of a limit in addition or division.

These two meanings of "infinity" seem to parallel the two meanings of "eternity" which we have dealt with throughout this chapter—one the negative sense in which it means the *lack* of a beginning or an end to time, the other the positive sense in which God's eternity consists in that fullness of being which can exist apart from time and change. Because our intellects are finite, we may apprehend eternal being in a negative manner by calling it "timeless" or by conceiving it as infinite duration, but Spinoza cautions us against supposing that it can be "explained by duration or time, even if the duration be conceived without beginning or end."

One other theological discussion raises issues which involve in a unique way the two meanings of eternity. It deals with the revealed doctrine of perdition and salvation as eternal death and eternal life. Is the eternality of hell and heaven equivalent to a period of *endless* duration or does it mean—more fundamentally—the *unchanging* state of souls after the Last Judgment?

It is the eternity of hell that Pascal puts into scales against the temporal brevity of earthly pleasures in his formulation of the wager between temporary earthly pleasures and eternal life. As Joyce observes, "To bear even the sting of an insect for all eternity would be a dreadful torment."

According to Augustine and Aquinas, the eternity of heaven and hell means the moral immutability of the immortal soul as well as the interminability of the beatitude it enjoys or the punishment it suffers. Only in purgatory does a change of moral state occur, but the process of purification which takes place there is always limited in period. Purgatory is, therefore, not eternal in either sense.

As Kant sees it, however, the afterlife must not only be interminable, or of infinite duration, but it must also permit a progressive moral development without end. Man is justified, according to Kant, "in hoping for an endless duration of his existence" only on the ground that "the holiness which the Christian law requires . . . leaves the creature nothing but a progress *in infinitum*." From still another point of view, Dr. Johnson questions the traditional Christian dogma that the souls of the blessed are secure in a perpetual state of rectitude—in this respect like the good angels who are confirmed in their goodness from the first instant of creation.

Boswell had "ventured to ask him whether, although the words of some texts of Scripture seemed strong in support of the dreadful doctrine of an eternity of punishment, we might not hope that the denunciation was figurative, and would not be literally executed." To this, Dr. Johnson replied: "Sir, you are to consider the intention of punishment in a future state. We have no reason to be sure that we shall then be no longer able to offend against God. We do not know that even the angels are quite in a state of security . . . It may, therefore, perhaps be necessary, in order to preserve both men and angels in a state of rectitude, that they should have continually before them the punishment of those who have deviated from it."

On Dr. Johnson's theory, the moral condition of the damned seems to be immutable. It is irremediable even by the punishments which, according to him, may exercise some deterrent effect upon the blessed who, he seems to think, are not as unalterably set in the path of righteousness as the wicked are in their iniquity.

On any of these conceptions of heaven and hell, and of the state of the soul in the afterlife, the meaning of "eternity" is somewhat altered; for eternal life or eternal death is conceived as having a beginning, if not an end, for the individual soul. As in the case of all fundamental religious dogmas, the truth asserted remains obscure and mysterious. It is not only beyond imagination, but also beyond any adequate rational conception, analysis, or demonstration.

24

Evolution

INTRODUCTION

THIS chapter belongs to Darwin. Not that his writings, which are cited under almost all headings, stand alone in the various places they appear. The point is rather that many of the topics are dictated by and draw their meaning from his thought, and that he figures in all the major issues connected with the origin of species, the theory of evolution, and the place of man in the order of nature. With respect to the matters under consideration in this chapter, the other writers in the tradition of the great books cannot escape from being classified as coming before or after Darwin, or as being with or against him.

Darwin's influence on later writers may be variously estimated, but it is plainly marked by their use of his language and their reference to his fundamental notions. William James's *The Principles of Psychology,* especially in its chapters on instinct and emotion, views the behavior of men and animals and the phenomena of intelligence or mind in evolutionary terms. The writings of Freud are similarly dominated by the genetic approach and by an appeal to man's animal ancestry in order to explain the inherited constitution of his psyche in conformity with the doctrine of evolution.

Outside psychology the concept of evolution is reflected in theories of progress or of a dialectical development in history; as, for example, in the dialectical or historical materialism of Marx and Engels, which is set forth in the latter's *Dialectics of Nature.* An even more general reorientation of philosophy, which stems from an evolutionary way of thinking, is to be found in the writings of Bergson and Dewey, such as *Creative Evolution* and *The Influence of Darwin on Philosophy.* These give some measure of the influence of Darwin on philosophical thought. In the biological sciences, Darwin's ideas have guided the direction of virtually all later research. Later works on biological evolution, such as Dobzhansky's *Genetics and the Origin of Species,* continue to support the broad outlines of Darwin's theory while offering refinements in understanding of the mechanisms of evolution, particularly the processes of heredity, mutation, and the genetics of populations.

WITH REGARD TO Darwin's predecessors the question is not so much one of their influence upon him as of their anticipation, in one way or another, of his discoveries, his conceptions, and his theory.

The observation made in antiquity concerning a hillside deposit of marine fossils is sometimes taken as implying an early recognition of the evolution of terrestrial life. More apposite perhaps is the statement by Lucretius that "the new earth began with grass and brush,/ And then produced the mortal animals/Many and various." Lucretius also speaks of strange monsters which nature did not permit to survive:

. . . this weird assortment earth produced
In vain, since nature would not let them grow.
They could not reach to any flourishing,
Find nourishment, be joined in acts of love . . .
Many attempts were failures; many a kind
Could not survive; whatever we see today
Enjoying the breath of life must from the first
Have found protection in its character.

Apparently susceptible to similar interpretation are Aristotle's statements that "nature proceeds little by little from things lifeless to animal life"; that "there is observed in plants a continuous scale of ascent toward the animal";

and that "throughout the entire animal scale there is a graduated differentiation in amount of vitality and in capacity for motion." Augustine's commentary on the first chapter of Genesis seems even more explicitly to contemplate the successive appearance of the various forms of life. Plants and animals did not actually exist when the world began. Though their causes were created by God and existed from the beginning, the actual production of plants and animals in their various kinds is, as Aquinas tells us while summarizing Augustine's view, "the work of propagation"—not of creation.

Like Aristotle, both Aquinas and Locke represent the world of living organisms as a graduated scale ascending from less to more perfect forms of life. But where Aquinas tends to conceive that graduated scale as a hierarchy involving essential differences, Locke sees an almost perfect continuity involving only differences in degree. "In all the visible world," he writes, "we see no chasms or gaps." To illustrate this, he points out that "there are fishes that have wings, and are not strangers to the airy region; and there are some birds that are inhabitants of the water, whose blood is cold as fishes . . . There are animals so near of kin to both birds and beasts that they are in the middle between both: amphibious animals link the terrestrial and aquatic together . . . and the animal and vegetable kingdoms are so nearly joined, that, if you will take the lowest of one and the highest of the other, there will scarce be perceived any great difference between them: and so on, till we come to the lowest and the most inorganic parts of matter, we shall find everywhere that the several species are linked together, and differ but in almost insensible degrees."

But for the theory of evolution the observation of a hierarchy in nature, or even of a continuity in which the species differ by "almost insensible degrees," constitutes only background. What the theory of evolution brings to the fore is the notion of a developmental or genetic relation among the various forms of life. Because it seems to contain this insight, the anticipation of Darwin to be found in Kant's *The Critique of Judgement* is perhaps

the most remarkable; even though, in a closely related passage in which Kant discusses epigenesis, he uses the word "evolution" in a sense quite contrary to Darwin's conception.

"It is praiseworthy," Kant writes, "to employ a comparative anatomy and go through the vast creation of organized beings in order to see if there is not discoverable in it some trace of a system, and indeed of a system following a genetic principle . . . When we consider the agreement of so many genera of animals in a certain common schema, which apparently underlies not only the structure of their bones, but also the disposition of their remaining parts, and when we find here the wonderful simplicity of the original plan, which has been able to produce such an immense variety of species by the shortening of one member and the lengthening of another, by the involution of this part and the evolution of that, there gleams upon the mind a ray of hope, however faint, that the principle of the mechanism of nature, apart from which there can be no natural science at all, may yet enable us to arrive at some explanation in the case of organic life. This analogy of forms, which in all their differences seem to be produced in accordance with a common type, strengthens the suspicion that they have an actual kinship due to descent from a common parent. This we might trace in the gradual approximation of one animal species to another, from that in which the principle of ends seems best authenticated, namely from man, back to the polyp, and from this back even to mosses and lichens, and finally to the lowest perceivable stage of nature."

FINDING ANTICIPATIONS of Darwin involves judgments much more subject to controversy than tracing his influences. It is questionable, for example, whether the suggestive passages in Lucretius and Locke bear more than a superficial resemblance to Darwin's thought. The matter is further complicated by Darwin's own sense of his divergence from and disagreement with his predecessors—both immediate precursors like Buffon and Linnaeus and earlier philosophers and theologians.

Darwin tells us himself of his quarrel with

the theologians. His followers elaborate on the opposition between his conception of species and that of Aristotle, an opposition which Darwin intimates by the great stress he lays on the difference between a static taxonomy and a dynamic or genealogical classification of living things.

We must therefore try to locate the central points of Darwin's theory in order to judge comparable views for their agreement or disagreement.

As the title of his major work indicates, it is not evolution as a grand scheme of biological, or cosmic, history, but the origin of species with which Darwin seems to be principally concerned. He is concerned with establishing the fact that new species do originate in the course of time, against those who suppose the species of living things to be fixed in number and immutable in type throughout the ages. He is concerned with describing the circumstances under which new species arise and other forms cease to have the status of species or become extinct. He is concerned with formulating the various factors in the differentiation of species, and with showing, against those who think a new species requires a special act of creation, that the origin of species, like their extinction, is entirely a natural process which requires no factors other than those at work every day in the life, death, and breeding of plants and animals. Only as a consequence of these primary considerations does he engage in speculations about the moving panorama of life on earth from its beginnings to its present and its future.

Darwin looks upon the term "species" as "arbitrarily given," and for that reason does not attempt any strict definition of it. He uses it, moreover, like his predecessors in systematic biological classification, to signify "a set of individuals closely resembling each other"—a class of plants or animals having certain common characteristics. Darwin would probably agree with Locke's criticism of those who suppose that our definitions of species grasp the real essences or relate to the substantial forms inherent in things. As indicated in the chapter on DEFINITION, Locke insists that our notion of a species expresses only what he calls the "nominal essence"—a set of characteristics we attach to the name we give things of a sort when we group them and separate them in our classifications. "The boundaries of species, whereby man sorts [things], are made by men," he writes; "the essences of the species, distinguished by different names, are . . . of man's making." Advancements in the science of genetics, however, may lend support to the opposite position. Dobzhansky argues that species represent real genetic discontinuities in nature—arrays of genes which are preserved because of barriers to interbreeding. They are, in fact, "natural units."

Species is not the only term of classification. A *genus,* for example, is a more inclusive group than a *species*. Groups which differ specifically belong to the same genus if their difference is accompanied by the possession of common traits. As species differ from one another within a generic group, so genera are in turn sub-classes of more inclusive groupings, such as phyla, families, and orders. But there are also smaller groupings within a species. There are races or varieties and subvarieties, the members of which share the characteristics of the species but differ from one another in other respects. Ultimately, of course, within the smallest class the systematist bothers to define, each individual differs from every other in the same group with whom, at the same time, it shares certain characteristics of the race, the species, the genus, and all the larger classes to which they belong.

This general plan of botanical or zoological classification does not seem to give *species* peculiar status in the hierarchy of classes or groupings or to distinguish it from other classes except as these are more or less inclusive than itself. Why then should attention be focused on the origin of species, rather than of varieties or of genera?

One part of the answer comes from the facts of generation or reproduction. Offspring tend to differ from their parents, as well as from each other, but they also tend to resemble one another. "A given germ," Aristotle writes, "does not give rise to any chance living being, nor spring from any chance one; but each germ springs from a definite parent and gives rise to a definite progeny." This is an early formulation of the insight that in the process of reproduction, the law of like generating like always holds for those characteristics which identify the species of ancestors and progeny.

In other words, a species always breeds true; its members always generate organisms which can be classified as belonging to the *same* species, however much they vary among themselves as individuals within the group. Furthermore, the subgroups—the races or varieties—of a species are able to breed with one another, but diverse species cannot interbreed. Organisms different in species either cannot mate productively at all, or if crossbred, like the horse and the ass, they produce a sterile hybrid like the mule. From the viewpoint of genetics, this reproductive isolation is the defining characteristic of species. According to Dobzhansky, species differ from races or varieties only by virtue of the existence of isolating mechanisms which prevent interbreeding.

In the hierarchy of classes, then, species would seem to be distinguished from all smaller groupings by their *stability* from generation to generation. If species are thus self-perpetuating, they in turn give stability to all the larger groupings—the genera, phyla, families—which remain as fixed from generation to generation as the species which constitute them. Hence the question of origin applies peculiarly to species rather than to varieties or to genera.

On the supposition stated, no origin of species would seem to be possible except by a special act of creation. Either all the existing species of organisms have always existed from the beginning of life on earth; or, if in the course of ages new species have arisen, their appearance cannot be accounted for by natural generation. By the law of natural generation, offspring will always be of the same species as the parent organisms.

Spontaneous generation, of course, remains a possibility. A new species of organism might come to be without being generated by other living organisms. But apart from the question of fact (*i.e.,* whether spontaneous generation ever does occur), such origin of a form of life seems to lie outside the operation of natural causes and to imply the intervention of supernatural power.

The possibility of spontaneous generation was entertained in antiquity and the Middle Ages, and was even thought to be supported by observation, such as that of maggots emerging from putrefying matter. But modern science tends to affirm the biogenetic law that living organisms are generated only by living organisms. To Kant, the notion that "life could have sprung up from the nature of what is void of life," seems not only contrary to fact, but absurd or unreasonable. Yet, while affirming the principle that like produces like by insisting upon "the generation of something organic from something else that is also organic," Kant does not carry that principle to the point where it would make the generation of a *new* species impossible. "Within the class of organic beings," he writes, it is possible for one organism to generate another "differing specifically from it."

AGAINST THE BACKGROUND of these various suppositions, Darwin is moved to a new insight by the conjunction of certain types of fact: the results of breeding under domestication which exhibit the great range of variation within a species and the tendency of *inbred* varieties to breed true; his own observations of the geographical distribution of species of flora and fauna, especially those separated from one another by impassable barriers; the facts of comparative anatomy and embryology which reveal affinities in organic structure and development between organisms distinct in species; and the geological record which indicates the great antiquity of life upon the earth, which gives evidence of the cataclysmic changes in the earth's surface (with consequences for the survival of life), and which above all contains the fossil remains of forms of life now extinct but not dissimilar from species alive in the present age.

Briefly stated, Darwin's insight is that new species arise when, among the varieties of an existing species, certain intermediate forms become extinct, and the other circumstances are such that the surviving varieties, now become more sharply separated from one another in type, are able to reproduce their kind, and, in the course of many generations of inbreeding, also tend to breed true. They thus perpetuate their type until each in turn ceases to be a species and becomes a genus when its own extreme varieties, separated by the extinction of intermediates, become new species, as they themselves did at an earlier stage of history. For the very same reason that Darwin says "a well-marked variety may be called an incipient species," a species may be called an incipient genus.

The point is misunderstood if it is supposed that when new species originate from old, both the new and the old continue to survive as species. On the contrary, when in the course of thousands of generations some of the varieties of a species achieve the status of species, the species from which they originated by variation ceases to be a species and becomes a genus.

"The only distinction between species and well-marked varieties," Darwin writes, "is that the latter are known, or believed, to be connected at the present day with intermediate gradations, whereas species were formerly thus connected . . . It is quite possible that forms now generally acknowledged to be merely varieties may hereafter be thought worthy of specific names; and in this case scientific and common language will come into accordance. In short, we shall have to treat species in the same manner as those naturalists treat genera who admit that genera are merely artificial combinations made for convenience . . . Our classifications will come to be, as far as they can be so made, genealogies."

The *origin of species* thus seems to be identical with the *extinction of intermediate varieties,* combined with the survival of one or more of the extreme varieties. These seem to be simply two ways of looking at the same thing. Still another way of seeing the point may be achieved by supposing, contrary to fact, the survival of all the varieties ever produced through the breeding of organisms.

"If my theory be true," Darwin writes, "numberless intermediate varieties, linking closely together all the species of the same group, must assuredly have existed; but the very process of natural selection constantly tends, as has been so often remarked, to exterminate the parent-forms and the intermediate links." If one were to suppose the simultaneous coexistence of *all* intermediate varieties in the present day, the groups now called "species" would be continuously connected by slight differences among their members and would not, therefore, be divided into distinct species, as they now are because certain links are missing.

In *The Critique of Pure Reason,* Kant states the principle of continuity in the following manner. "This principle," he writes, "indicates that all differences of species limit each other, and do not admit of transition from one to another by a *saltus,* but only through smaller degrees of the difference between the one species and the other. In one word, there are no species or sub-species which . . . are the nearest possible to each other; intermediate species or sub-species being always possible, the difference of which from each of the former is always smaller than the difference existing between these." But, Kant adds, "it is plain that this continuity of forms is a mere idea, to which no adequate object can be discovered in experience," partly because "the species in nature are really divided . . . and if the gradual progression through their affinity were continuous, the intermediate members lying between two given species must be infinite in number, which is impossible."

Dobzhansky differs from both Kant and Darwin in his interpretation of continuity in nature. Since the differences among organisms represent differences in one or more genes, complete continuity would require the existence of every possible combination of genes. If we suppose such an extreme case, the result would not be an infinite number of species, but no species and genera at all. The array of plants and animals would approach a perfectly continuous series in which there would only be individual differences. In fact, existing species represent "only an infinitesimal fraction of the possible gene combinations," while most of the possible combinations intermediate between existing species would produce ill-adapted monstrosities, incapable of survival.

Species are groups of population the gene exchange between which is "prevented through one, or a combination of several, physiological isolating mechanisms." Only by means of such barriers to interbreeding can adaptive "constellations of genes" be preserved. Thus, from the viewpoint of genetics, biological species reflect real discontinuities in nature—not arbitrarily drawn categories. It is in this sense that Dobzhansky speaks of species as "natural units."

ON DARWIN'S conception of the origin of species, its causes divide into two sets of factors: first, those which determine the extinction or survival of organisms and, with their survival, their opportunities for mating and reproduction; second, those which determine the transmission of characteristics from one generation to another and the variation of offspring from their ancestors and from each other. Without genetic variation there would be no range of differences within a group on which the factors of selection could operate. Without the inheritance of ancestral traits there would be no perpetuation of group characteristics in the organisms which manage to survive and reproduce.

For Darwin the operation of the first set of factors constitutes the process of natural selection whereby "variations, however slight and from whatever cause proceeding, if they be in any degree profitable to the individuals of a species . . . will tend to the preservation of such individuals, and will generally be inherited by the offspring." Darwin's understanding of natural selection is grounded in Malthusian principles: all organisms tend to produce more offspring than can survive without outrunning the food supply. By means of high rates of mortality, nature "selects" those organisms best equipped to survive and reproduce. This process takes place in many ways: through geological catastrophes which make certain areas of the earth's surface uninhabitable for all organisms, or for those types which cannot adapt themselves to the radically changed environment; through the competition among organisms for the limited food supply available in their habitat; through the struggle for

existence in which organisms not only compete for food but also prey upon one another; and through the sexual selection which operates within a group when some organisms are prevented by others from mating and reproducing.

For Darwin's immediate followers the essence of selection was thought to be captured in the notion that "the fittest survives." But whether survival is of the fittest alone, or whether the multiplication of inferior organisms also gives evolution another direction, has been disputed. According to Darwin, "natural selection works solely by and for the good of each being; all corporeal and mental endowments will tend to progress toward perfection . . . Thus, from the war of nature, from famine and death . . . the production of the higher animals directly follows." But Dobzhansky is more cautious. The process of natural selection is indeed creative, he argues, for it "gives rise to previously nonexistent coherent entities, new organisms fit to perpetuate themselves in certain habitats." But selection is also opportunistic, favors variants with immediate value, and possesses no foresight. It thus "involves risk of failure and miscreation." There is danger, he points out, in any application of our own notions of fitness to the products of natural selection. Organisms which appear to us monstrosities nevertheless survive and reproduce in nature. Waddington and Dobzhansky agree that any serious attempt to define fitness leads to a truism: Those organisms are considered fit which survive to reproduce. "The essence of selection," Dobzhansky writes, "is that the carriers of different genotypes in a population contribute differentially to the gene pool of the succeeding generations." Darwinian fitness is nothing more than the reproductive efficiency of a given genotype.

With respect to the factors of heredity and variation, tremendous advances since Darwin in the experimental science of genetics require revisions in this part of his theory of evolution. Writing before Mendel's classic experiments in hybridization, Darwin seems to suppose a blending of hereditary factors; whereas, according to Mendel, inheritance is particulate.

Distinct genetic factors combine to produce a certain somatic result without losing their separate identities. They can therefore be re-assorted and enter into new genetic combinations in the next generation. With regard to the origin of variations Darwin was also in error. First, his theory of the effects of the use and disuse of parts, which in most respects follows Lamarck's ideas on the inheritance of acquired characteristics, was shown to be false. The researches of August Weismann, as James recounts, proved it "*a priori* impossible that any peculiarity acquired during the lifetime by the parent should be transmitted to the germ." Second, he made the error of assuming that the natural variation which occurs among all organisms because of the differential effects of the environment on development could be passed on to succeeding generations. His ignorance of the processes of heredity left him unable to distinguish, in other words, between variations caused by *genotype* and those produced by *phenotype,* the interaction of the genotype with the environment.

Darwin was cognizant of the occurrence of mutations, but they seemed to occur at much too slow a rate to account for the great variation in nature. The discovery that random mutations of genes are sufficient to account for all hereditary variation removed, according to Dobzhansky, the greatest difficulty in Darwin's theory. The discovery of abrupt mutations causing dramatic changes in a single generation seemed, for a time, to support the supposition that such mutations could act on their own as agents of evolutionary change. This has been proved not to be the case except in instances, found mostly in plants, where a multiplication of the number of chromosomes (polyploidy) can bring about the origin of an entirely new species in a single generation. For the majority of species, Darwin's maxim *natura non facit saltum*—"nature does nothing by jumps"—has been upheld. Because species differ in numerous genes, slowly acquired changes in what Dobzhansky calls "constellations of genes" have been shown to be much more important for the origin of species than isolated mutations. Spontaneous mutations of numerous genes in a single generation are unknown.

Advances in genetics since Darwin's day do not alter the main outlines of his theory. The mechanisms of heredity may be much more complicated than Darwin knew, and involve much of which he was ignorant, such as the structure of genetic materials, the nature of rates of mutation, or the various types, causes, and effects of hybridization. But that merely leads to a more elaborate or different explanation of genetic variation in offspring and the transmission of ancestral traits. No matter how these are explained, their occurrence is all that is needed to permit new species to originate through natural processes of heredity and selection. "Our present theory of evolution," writes Waddington, "can indeed be regarded as for the most part no more than a restatement of Darwinism in terms of Mendelian genetics." The achievement of 20th-century evolutionary theory has been in increasing our understanding of the interrelationship among various mechanisms that guide the evolutionary process. The relative contributions of mutation, genetic drift, geographical isolation, population size, rate of reproduction, migration, and natural selection to the evolutionary process and to the origin of species can now be understood in far greater depth than was possible in Darwin's day. "If Darwin were alive today," Julian Huxley writes, "the title of his book would have to be not the 'origin' but the 'Origins of Species.' For perhaps the most salient single fact that has emerged from recent studies is that species may arise in a number of quite distinct ways."

THE READER MUST judge for himself to what extent Darwin's theory of evolution was anticipated by those who, like Augustine, affirm the appearance of new species of life on earth at various stages in its history, or even by a writer like Kant, who seems to possess the germ of its insight.

The critical test in every case is whether those who affirm the occurrence of *new* species by natural processes rather than by special creation, think of them as simply *added* to the organic forms already in existence without any change in the status as species of the preexisting forms. Those who think in this way do not have Darwin's idea of the origin of species; for in conceiving an increase in the number of species as merely a matter of addition, they necessarily attribute stability to each species, new as well as old. By this test, not even Kant seems to be near the center of Darwin's hypothesis of the origin of species by the extinction of intermediate varieties.

In comparing Darwin with certain of his predecessors, notably Aristotle and Aquinas, it seems necessary to apply another kind of test. Here the problem is not so much one of discovering affinities or disagreements, as one of determining whether they are talking about the same thing and therefore, when they appear to disagree, whether the issue between them is genuine. They do not seem to conceive a species in the same way. Certainly they use the word differently. This affects the way in which the whole problem of origins is understood. The controversies concerning the fixity or mutability of species, concerning evolution and creation, and concerning the origin of man involve genuine issues only if those who seem to disagree do not use the word "species" in widely different senses.

It is *possible* that certain forms of life do not originate by descent from a common ancestor and do not derive their status as quite distinct types from the mere absence of intermediate varieties—varieties which once must have existed but are now extinct. If such forms were to be called "species," the word would have a different meaning from the meaning it has when applied to types of pigeons, beetles, or rats.

The first of these two meanings may express the philosophical conception of a living species as a class of organisms having the same essential nature, according to which conception there never could have been intermediate varieties. The second meaning may be that of the scientific taxonomist in botany or zoology who constructs a system of classification, genealogical or otherwise. On this meaning, one million and a half would be a conservative estimate of the number of plant and animal types classified by the systematist as "species." In contrast, the number of species, in the philosophical sense of distinct essences, would be extremely small.

Darwin, for example, says, "I cannot doubt that the theory of descent with modification embraces all the members of the same great class or kingdom. I believe that animals are descended from at most only four or five progenitors, and plants from an equal or lesser number. Analogy would lead me one step farther, namely, to the belief that all animals and plants are descended from some one prototype. But analogy may be a deceitful guide." It is immaterial to the theory of evolution, he adds, whether this inference, "chiefly grounded on analogy . . . be accepted."

The issue between Darwin and the theologians may or may not be genuine according to the interpretation of this passage, and according to the possibility of a double use of the word "species"—for both the small number of progenitors from which all the extant types of plants and animals have evolved, *and* for a very large number of those extant types. If the theologians use the word "species" in the first sense, and Darwin in the second, they need not be in disagreement. The "view of life" which Darwin attributes to certain eminent authorities, he himself does not flatly reject, namely, that life, "with its several powers [has] been originally breathed by the Creator into a few forms or into one."

Is there common ground here in the admitted possibility that life may have been originally created in a small number of distinct forms and that these are to be regarded as species in one conception, though not in another? If so, the affirmation of a certain fixity to species would apply only to a few primordial forms. Concerning forms which have appeared with the passage of time, two questions would have to be answered. First, are they species in the philosopher's sense of distinct and immutable essences, or species in the scheme of systematic biological classification? Second, is their first appearance at a historical moment due to a special act of creation, to spontaneous generation, or to evolution from already existing organic forms by "descent with modification"?

To join issue with Darwin, it would seem to be necessary for the person answering these questions to use the word "species" in the biologist's sense and at the same time to account for the historical origin of the new species by special creation or spontaneous generation. But in the tradition of the great books, theologians like Augustine and Aquinas do not attribute to God any special acts of creation after the original production of the world, except to explain the origin of individual human souls.

"Nothing entirely new was afterwards made by God," Aquinas writes, "but all things subsequently made had in a sense been made before in the work of the six days ... Some existed not only in matter, but also in their causes, as those individual creatures that are now generated existed in the first of their kind. Species also that are new, if any such appear, existed beforehand in various active powers; so that animals, and perhaps even new species of animals, are produced by putrefaction by the power which the stars and elements received at the beginning. Again, animals of new kinds arise occasionally from the connection of individuals belonging to different species, as the mule is the offspring of an ass and a mare, but even these existed previously in their causes, in the work of the six days."

WHETHER OR NOT the theologian's conception of a historical development of the forms of life conforms to the evolutionist's hypothesis, even though it does not offer the same type of explanation, is a matter which the reader of the texts must decide. But one issue, which still remains to be discussed, can leave little doubt of a basic controversy between Darwin and some of his predecessors, especially the theologians.

It concerns the origin and nature of man. It can be stated in terms of two views of human nature. One is that man is a species in the philosophical sense, essentially and abruptly distinct from brute animals; the other, that man is a species in the biologist's sense, and differs from other animals only by continuous variation.

On the first view, *either* man would have to be created, in body as well as soul; *or* if the human species has an origin which in part or whole involves the operation of natural causes,

it must be conceived as *emerging* from a lower form of life. The rational soul, Aquinas maintains, "cannot come to be except by creation." But it is not only man's soul which, according to Aquinas, "cannot be produced save immediately by God." He also insists that "the first formation of the human body could not be by the instrumentality of any created power, but was immediately from God." He does not reject the suggestion of Augustine that the human body may have preexisted in other creatures *as an effect preexists in its causes*. But he adds the qualification that it preexists in its causes only in the manner of a "passive potentiality," so that "it can be produced out of pre-existing matter only by God." A Christian theologian like Aquinas might entertain the hypothesis of emergent evolution as applied to the human organism, but only with the qualification that natural causes by themselves do not suffice for the production of man.

On the second view, which is Darwin's, man and the anthropoid apes have descended from a common ancestral form which is now extinct, as are also many of the intermediate varieties in the chain of development—unless, as it is sometimes thought, certain fossil remains supply some of the missing links. "The great break in the organic chain between man and his nearest allies, which cannot be bridged over by any extinct or living species, has often been advanced," Darwin admits, "as a grave objection to the belief that man is descended from some lower form; but this objection," he continues, "will not appear of much weight to those who, from general reasons, believe in the general principle of evolution. Breaks often occur in all parts of the series, some being wide, sharp and defined, others less so in various degrees, as between the orang and its nearest allies—between the Tarsius and the other Lemuridae—between the elephant, and in a more striking manner between the Ornithorhynchus or Echidna, and all other mammals." Furthermore, Darwin insists, no one who has read Lyell's *The Geological Evidence of the Antiquity of Man* will lay much stress ... on the absence of fossil remains"; for Lyell has shown "that in all the vertebrate classes the discovery of fossil remains has been a very slow and fortuitous process. Nor should it be forgotten that those regions which are the most likely to afford remains connecting man with some extinct ape-like creature, have not as yet been searched by geologists."

On either of these two conflicting views, the organic affinities between man and the most highly developed mammals would be equally intelligible, though they would be differently interpreted by Aquinas and Darwin. But according to the doctrine of man's creation by God, or even on the hypothesis of emergent evolution, there need not be—strictly speaking, there *cannot* be—a missing link between ape and man, for the emergent species is a whole step upward in the scale of life. Man is thus not one of several organic types which have become species through the extinction of intermediate varieties, and hence he differs from other animals not in an accidental, but rather in an essential manner—that is, he differs in kind rather than degree.

This issue concerning human nature is discussed from other points of view in the chapters on ANIMAL and MAN. Here the issue, stated in terms of man's origin, seems to involve three possibilities: special creation, evolution by descent from a common ancestor, and emergent evolution. But these three possibilities apply not only to man, but to the origin of every species which did not exist at the first moment of life on earth.

The hypothesis of special creation does not seem to be held by the theologians, at least not in the tradition of the great books. The hypothesis of emergent evolution raises questions concerning the factors—natural or supernatural—which must be operative to cause the emergence of higher from lower forms of organic matter. Whether or not Aristotle and Aquinas can supply an answer to these questions in terms of their theory of matter's potentiality for a variety of forms, Darwin's theory of descent with modification seems to be definitely opposed to the hypothesis of emergent evolution. Speaking as a Darwinian, James says that "the point which as evolutionists we are bound to hold fast to is that all the new forms of being that make their appearance are really nothing more than results of the redistribution of the original and unchanging materials . . . No new *natures,* no factors not present at the beginning, are introduced at any later stage."

In this dispute between two theories of evolution, does not the solution depend in every case upon a prior question concerning the relation of the species under consideration—whether or not it is possible for them to be or to have been developmentally connected by intermediate varieties? If, for example, the evidence were to prove that man and ape, as they now exist in the world, are essentially distinct—different in kind—then no intermediate varieties could ever have existed to account for their descent from a common ancestor. If, on the other hand, the evidence were to prove that they differ only in degree, then no difficulty stands in the way of the Darwinian hypothesis. The ultimate issue concerning the origin of species would thus seem to reduce to the problem of which meaning of "species" applies to the organic types in question.

25

Experience

INTRODUCTION

EXPERIENCE is regarded as a source of knowledge. It is also spoken of as containing what is known.

Sometimes it is identified with sense perception; sometimes it involves more—memory and the activity of the imagination. Sometimes it includes thoughts, feelings, and desires as well, all the contents of consciousness, every phase of mental or psychic life. The temporal flow of experience is then identified with the stream of consciousness.

Experience may connote something which is private or public, subjective or objective—something which no man can share with another or something which is common to all men who live in the same world and who are acquainted with the same objects.

There are still other divisions of experience: intuitive or aesthetic experience, religious experience, and mystical experience.

Experience is said to be that which makes a man expert in an art or in a sphere of practical activity. A man is better able to do or make that which he has much experience in doing or making. He is also better able to judge what should be undertaken or what has been accomplished by others as well as by himself. In this connection experience is called practical, both because it is the result of practice and because it is a means to be used in directing action. But it is also praised for the opposite reason—as something to be enjoyed for its own sake, serving no end beyond itself unless it be the enrichment of life by the widest variety of experiences.

THESE ARE SOME of the myriad meanings of "experience"—not all, but those which occur with major emphasis in the tradition of the great books. No author uses the word in all these senses. Some of these senses are contradictory. According to the context of the discussion or the subject matter under consideration, the same author will shift from one meaning to another.

For example, in his account of the origin of science, Aristotle says that "out of sense-perception comes to be what we call memory, and out of frequently repeated memories of the same thing develops experience; for a number of memories constitute a single experience." The further product of experience—"the universal stabilized in its entirety within the soul"—is obtained by abstraction and the related act of induction or generalization. Art or science arises, Aristotle writes, "when from many notions gained by experience, one universal judgment about a class of objects is produced." Hence it can be said, he thinks, that from experience "originate the skill of the craftsman, the knowledge of the man of science, skill in the sphere of coming to be and science in the sphere of being."

In the study of nature, experience, according to Aristotle, is essential for "taking a comprehensive view of the admitted facts" which can come only from dwelling "in intimate association with nature and its phenomena." In the context of ethical or political problems, he treats experience as the basis for a prudent judgment, which is not "concerned with universals only," but "must also recognize the particulars." This fact, Aristotle writes, explains "why some who do not know," but who "have experience, are more practical than others who know." In the field of poetry, as in moral matters, it is the man of experience, according to Aristotle, who can best judge what is good or bad; he can "judge rightly the works produced . . . and understand by what means or how they are achieved, and what harmonizes with what," whereas "the inexperienced must be content if they do not fail to see whether the work has been well or ill made."

Hobbes and William James also use the word for the possession of expertness or sound judgment in practical affairs, as well as in connection with the origin or nature of knowledge. Hobbes, like Aristotle, says that "much memory, or memory of many things, is called *Experience*." He connects it with prudence. It is that knowledge, he writes, which "is not attained by reasoning, but found as well in brute beasts as in man; and is but a memory of successions of events in times past, wherein the omission of every little circumstance altering the effect, frustrates the expectation of the most prudent."

For James, however, experience is usually identified with the stream of consciousness. "Experience moulds us every hour," he writes, "and makes of our minds a mirror of the time-and-space-connections between the things in the world." He distinguishes it from conception, reasoning, or thought, and associates it with sensation and feeling. "The way of 'experience' proper is the front door," he writes, "the door of the five senses."

For the most part, experience is a term in psychological analysis, with implications for the development of theoretical knowledge or practical wisdom. That is the way it is chiefly used by Aquinas, Francis Bacon, Descartes, Spinoza, Locke, and Hume, as well as the authors already mentioned. It is still a term in the dimension of psychology when it is used by Plotinus and by the theologians to discuss the mystical union of the soul with God.

But with Hume experience also is reality or, in his phrase, the realm of "matters of fact and existence," as opposed to "relations of ideas." He tends to identify the order of nature with the succession of events in experience, though he also seems to conceive a "pre-established harmony between the course of nature and the succession of our ideas." Nature, he goes on to say, "has implanted in us an instinct, which carries forward the thought in a correspon-dent course to that which she has established among external objects."

Hume's difficulty or indecision with regard to the objectivity of experience does not appear in Kant, for whom experience ceases to be psychological in any subjective sense of that word. The order of nature—the object of the theoretical sciences—*is* the order of experience. In Kant's technical sense of *mögliche Erfahrung*, nature is the realm of all possible experience. His distinction between judgments of perception and judgments of experience differentiates what for other writers is subjective sense-experience, from knowledge of reality or of objects shared by many minds.

Experience is the domain of such public objects precisely because its sense materials are formed and ordered by the structure of the mind itself—by the forms of intuition and the categories of the understanding in a synthesis which Kant calls the "transcendental unity of apperception." Without this synthesis, experience "would be merely a rhapsody of perceptions, never fitting together into any connected text, according to rules of a thoroughly united (possible) consciousness, and therefore never subjected to the transcendental and necessary unity of apperception."

Though it may not seem possible, James goes further than Kant in the conception of experience as a realm of being. Kant does not think that *all possible experience* circumscribes reality. "That which is not phenomenon," he writes, "cannot be an object of experience; it can never overstep the limits of sensibility, within which alone objects are presented to us." In contrast to this phenomenal reality with which he identifies experience, Kant posits a noumenal world—a world of intelligible or supra-sensible beings. To this realm, Kant writes, belong those "possible things which are not objects of our senses, but are cogitated by the understanding alone." Since the things Kant calls *Ding-an-sich* are unconditioned, that is, not subject as they are in themselves to the forms of intuition or the categories of the understanding, they cannot have an empirical or sensible reality, but only an intelligible existence.

James goes further in his *Essays in Radi-*

cal Empiricism, when he takes experience as equivalent to the whole of reality, including the actual and the possible or imaginary, the concrete and the abstract, the objective and the subjective. All differentiations must be made within experience, and experience itself is neutral with respect to all distinctions—receptive of all. There can be no meaningful distinction between experience and some other realm of existence. It is in this all-inclusive sense that experience is said to be the central term in the philosophy of Dewey when it functions as *mind* does for Hegel, *substance* for Spinoza, or *being* for Aquinas and Aristotle.

For Dewey, although education depends upon experience, "experience and education cannot be directly equated to each other. For some experiences are mis-educative," because they have "the effect of arresting or distorting the growth of further experience." We must therefore "discriminate between experiences which are educative and those which are mis-educative."

WE HAVE GONE from one extreme to another in passing from a purely psychological to something like a metaphysical conception of experience. These are opposite in a way which suggests the contrast between the practical and the aesthetic values of experience—the actively useful and the intrinsically enjoyable. At least the metaphysical identification of experience with all existence seems analogous to the aesthetic ideal of a life which embraces every variety of experience.

There is some intimation of this ideal in the lust for adventure which motivates Odysseus and his men. Dante, in fact, finds the secret of his character in the ardor of Odysseus "to gain experience of the world, and of human vice and worth," which leads him "to pursue virtue and knowledge," even to the point of his "mad flight."

There is some suggestion of this ideal of experience in the unbounded vitality of Gargantua and Pantagruel, and in the enterprise of the Wife of Bath, in Chaucer's tale. But the great poetic expression of this ideal is written in *Faust*—in the worlds of experience Mephistopheles opens to the man who has wagered his soul for one ultimately satisfying moment.

My heart, from learning's tyranny set free,
Shall no more shun distress, but take its toll
Of all the hazards of humanity,
And nourish mortal sadness in my soul.
I'll sound the heights and depths that men can
  know,
Their very souls shall be with mine entwined,
I'll load my bosom with their weal and woe,
And share with them the shipwreck of mankind.

THE BASIC ISSUE concerning the role of experience in the origin of knowledge, especially the organized knowledge of the arts and sciences, turns on whether it is *the* source or only *a* source. It is rarely if ever supposed that nothing can be learned from experience, or that everything worth learning can come to be known entirely apart from experience. During the early centuries of Christianity, devoutly religious men preached that God has revealed to man all he needs to know in order to live well and be saved. But this extreme position rejects the constructions of reason as well as the materials of experience.

Among philosophers and scientists, concerned with what man can learn by the exercise of his own powers, the controversy over experience usually involves a distinction between the senses and the reason or intellect. As indicated in the chapters on IDEA, MIND, and SENSE, whether this distinction can be validly made is itself a major issue in the tradition of the great books. Those who make it, however, tend to regard experience as something which results from the activity of the senses. For them the problem is whether our ideas—the general notions or concepts that enter into our scientific judgments and reasoning—come from sense-experience, which either is or originates from the perception of particulars. The contrast between the particular and the universal, between percept, sense impression, or concrete image on the one hand, and concept or abstract idea, on the other, lies at the heart of the problem.

One possibility is that the mind, by processes of abstraction or induction, somehow draws all its concepts and generalizations from experience. Aquinas is representative of this view. He adopts Aristotle's notion that the intellect is "like a tablet on which nothing is written." This tabula rasa depends upon the senses and the imagination for the materials out of which concepts are formed. "For the intellect to understand actually," Aquinas writes, "not only when it acquires new knowledge, but also when it uses knowledge already acquired, there is need for the act of the imagination and of the other powers."

Without experience the mind would remain empty, but experience itself does not fill the intellect with ideas. The activity of the sensitive faculty is not by itself the cause of knowledge. The perceptions and images furnished by sense-experience, Aquinas writes, "need to be made actually intelligible," and this requires the activity of the intellect, not merely its passivity in receiving impressions from experience. For this reason, he concludes, "it cannot be said that sensitive knowledge is the total and perfect cause of intellectual knowledge, but rather that it is in a way the material cause." Although experience is the indispensable source of the materials on which the intellect actively works, knowledge worthy of the name of science or of art does not come from experience alone.

Thus we see that those who, like Aquinas, affirm that there is nothing in the intellect which was not previously in the senses do not mean to imply that the materials of sense-experience reach the intellect untransformed. On the contrary, the primary contribution of the intellect is the translation of experienced particulars into universal notions. Nor do those who, like Bacon, affirm that the principles of knowledge are obtained by induction from experience necessarily imply that all knowledge is *directly* drawn from experience. To the extent that deductive reasoning is a way of learning new truths, the truths thus learned derive from experience only indirectly. Their direct source is truths already known, which must in turn have come from experience by induction.

Harvey criticizes those who misconceive the part which reason should play in relation to the senses. In the field of his own inquiries, "some weak and inexperienced persons," he writes, "vainly seek by dialectics and far-fetched arguments, either to upset or establish things that are only to be founded on anatomical demonstration, and believed on the evidence of the senses . . . How difficult it is," he continues, "to teach those who have no experience, the things of which they have not any knowledge by their senses!"

As in geometry, so in all the sciences, according to Harvey, it is the business of reason "from things sensible to make rational demonstration of the things that are not sensible; to render credible or certain things abstruse and beyond sense from things more manifest and better known." Science depends upon both reason and sense; but sense, not reason, is the ultimate arbiter of what can be accepted as true. "To test whether anything has been well or ill advanced, to ascertain whether some falsehood does not lurk under a proposition, it is imperative on us," Harvey declares, "to bring it to the proof of sense, and to admit or reject it on the decision of sense."

THE FOREGOING views are not a necessary consequence of the distinction between the faculties of sense and reason. The theory of innate ideas presents another possibility. As expressed by Descartes, for example, this theory holds that there are "purely intellectual [ideas] which our understanding apprehends by means of a certain inborn light." Hence it would seem that experience can be dispensed with, except for its value in dealing with particulars. But for most of the writers who take this view, experience, in addition to providing acquaintance with particulars, acts as the stimulus or the occasion for the development of the seeds of knowledge implanted in the mind at birth. Although he rests his metaphysics on the innate ideas of self and God, Descartes also appeals to experimental knowledge in the sphere of natural science. To answer such a question as, "what is the nature of the magnet?" the inquirer must "first collect all the observations with which experience can supply him about this stone, and from these he will next try to deduce its character."

The extreme position which denies any role to experience can be taken only by those who think that the growth of actual knowledge from innate ideas requires no outside impetus; and perhaps also by those who make ideas the objects of the mind's intuitive apprehension. It is questionable whether anyone goes to this extreme without the qualification that, for particulars at least, sense-experience is knowledge.

The other extreme—that experience is the *only* source of knowledge—is approached by those who deny the distinction in faculties, and substitute for the duality of sense and reason, each with its characteristic contribution to human knowledge, a distinction between the function of perceiving and that of reworking the received materials. Though in different ways, Hobbes, Locke, Berkeley, and Hume all appear to take this position.

They represent, according to James, "the empirical school in psychology." He tries to summarize their view by saying that "if *all* the connections among ideas in the mind could be interpreted as so many combinations of sense-data wrought into fixity . . . then experience in the common and legitimate sense of the word would be the sole fashioner of the mind." If, in other words, all that is done with the sensations, impressions, or ideas—whatever term is used for the original data of experience—consists in their reproduction by memory and imagination, and their comparison, combination, and connection in various ways to produce complex ideas, judgments, and trains of reasoning, then the entire content of human knowledge can be reduced to elements derived exclusively from experience.

Whether this position is taken *with* or *without* qualification depends on the disposition that is made of the problem of universals or abstractions, which is more fully discussed in the chapters on IDEA, SENSE, and UNIVERSAL AND PARTICULAR. Locke's treatment of abstract ideas and the special consideration given by Hume to the concepts of mathematics suggest that there are kinds or aspects of knowledge which cannot be accounted for by reduction to experience. Both men introduce a certain qualification upon their empiricism. However slight that may be, it does not appear in Hobbes and Berkeley, for they completely deny the existence of abstract or universal no-

tions in the mind. If "abstract," "universal," or "general" applies to names alone, then the mind or understanding adds nothing to, and does not radically transform, the materials of experience.

THE CONTROVERSY concerning experience and knowledge can also be stated in terms of the opposition between the *a priori* and the *a posteriori*. These terms are sometimes used to signify what is possessed before and what comes after or from experience, and sometimes they are used to indicate, without reference to the time order, what is independent of and what is dependent upon experience.

The distinction between the *a priori* and the *a posteriori* is not made in the same way with respect to propositions or judgments and with respect to reasoning or inference. The distinction and its significance for science and philosophy are discussed in the chapters on JUDGMENT and REASONING. It is sufficient here to point out that an *a priori* judgment is not determined by experience nor does it need empirical verification.

It might at first be supposed that those who agree in thinking that experience is just one—not the only—source of knowledge would also agree that some judgments, especially the basic propositions of science, are *a priori*. But this does not appear to be the case. Bacon, for example, like Aristotle, holds that the principles of the various sciences are derived by induction from experience. "There are and can exist," he writes, "but two ways of investigating and discovering truth. The one hurries on rapidly from the senses and particulars to the most general axioms, and from them, as principles and their supposed indisputable truth, derives and discovers the intermediate axioms . . . The other constructs its axioms from the senses and particulars, by ascending continually and gradually, till it finally arrives at the most general axioms." All axioms, on this view, are *a posteriori* propositions.

Descartes and Kant, while differing in the terms of their analysis, think, as we have seen, that the mind itself provides the ground for certain judgments which are therefore *a priori*. It does not even seem to be the case that those who make experience the only source of knowledge regard all propositions as *a posteriori*. Hume's treatment of mathematical propositions and James's treatment of axioms or necessary truths seem to be the exceptions here.

There is still another way in which the issue can be stated. The question is whether human knowledge extends to objects beyond experience, to things or beings which are not sensible and which transcend all possible experience.

Again it might be supposed that those who take an *a posteriori* view of the origin of knowledge would also limit apprehension to things experienceable. But Aristotle and Aquinas seem to say that the origin of knowledge from experience does not restrict the knowable to things capable of being experienced. Aquinas cites Aristotle's work on the heavens to show that "we may have a scientific knowledge" of things we cannot experience, "by way of negation and by their relation to material things." He would hold what is true of astronomy to be even more the case in metaphysics and theology. Even though all our concepts are abstracted from experience, we can by means of them reach beyond the sensible world to purely intelligible realities—to immaterial and nonsensible beings or aspects of being. Locke, who may be thought even more emphatic than Aristotle or Aquinas in his insistence on the empirical origin of knowledge, goes as far as they do in affirming man's knowledge of God and the soul.

Hume, in contrast, holds that knowledge may go beyond experience only if it is knowledge of the relation of our ideas, as exemplified in the science of mathematics. Precisely because mathematics is not knowledge of matters of fact or real existence, its propositions are, according to Hume, "discoverable by the mere operation of thought, without dependence on what is anywhere existent in the universe." But with regard to "matters of fact," Hume thinks that "experience is our only guide." Russell adds another *caveat:* "Nothing can be known to exist except by the help of experience ... If we wish to prove that something of which we have no direct experience exists, we must have among our premises

the existence of one or more things of which we have direct experience." Accordingly, all proofs of existence are *a posteriori*.

Any science which claims to be knowledge of reality or existence rather than of the relations between ideas, is thus limited to the realm of experienceable objects. According as the objects of a science fall within experience, so also must its conclusions be verified by reference to experience. Experience is the ultimate test of what truth there is in the propositions of natural science. Only the propositions of mathematics can have a validity which does not require empirical verification.

By these criteria Hume challenges the validity of metaphysics or natural theology. Such disciplines claim to be knowledge of real existences, but their objects are not experienceable and their conclusions cannot be empirically verified. The existence of God and the immortality of the soul may be objects of faith, but they are not verifiable conclusions of science; nor for that matter can metaphysics give us scientific knowledge of the ultimate constitution of the physical world if that involves knowledge of substances and causes which lie behind the phenomena and outside of experience. "All the philosophy in the world," Hume writes, "and all the religion . . . will never be able to carry us beyond the usual course of experience."

Kant, like Hume, limits theoretical knowledge to mathematics and the study of nature. A metaphysics which pretends to know objects outside the phenomenal order cannot be defended. "The understanding has no power to decide," he writes, "whether other perceptions besides those which belong to the total of our possible experience [exist], and consequently whether some other sphere of matter exists." What transcends all possible experience, in other words, cannot be known, at least not in the manner of the speculative sciences; only the moral sciences, proceeding in a different fashion, have access to the realm of the supra-sensible.

Kant's position seems to resemble Hume's. But it involves a quite different conception of mathematics and natural science, especially the latter, which Kant divides into pure and empirical physics. Kant identifies "pure physic" with the "metaphysic of nature" in distinction from the "metaphysic of morals," the one a theoretical, the other a practical science. For Kant the principles of both mathematics and pure physics are *a priori* rather than *a posteriori;* the objects of both are objects of actual or possible experience.

IN THE CLASSIFICATION of sciences, the natural sciences are usually set apart from mathematics, as well as from metaphysics, by being called "empirical" or "experimental." These names signify not merely the inductive method by which the knowledge is obtained from experience; they also imply that hypotheses, however formulated, and conclusions, however reached, must be verified by the facts of experience. Newton states it as a rule of reasoning "in experimental philosophy [that] we are to look upon propositions inferred by general induction from phenomena as accurately or very nearly true, notwithstanding any contrary hypotheses that may be imagined, till such time as other phenomena occur, by which they may either be made more accurate, or liable to exceptions." In similar tenor, Lavoisier says that "we ought, in every instance, to submit our reasoning to the test of experiment, and never to search for truth but by the natural road of experiment and observation." According to Planck, "Experimenters are the shocktroops of science. They perform the decisive experiments, carry out the all-important work of measurement."

The two words "empirical" and "experimental" should not, however, be used interchangeably. No science can be experimental without being empirical, but, as the chapter on ASTRONOMY AND COSMOLOGY indicates, the converse does not appear to be true.

There seem to be three different types of experience from which knowledge can be derived: (1) the ordinary everyday experiences which men accumulate without making any special effort to investigate, explore, or test; (2) the special data of experience which men collect by undertaking methodical research and making systematic observations, with or without apparatus; and (3) experiences artificially produced by men who exercise control over the phenomena and with respect to which the observer himself determines the conditions of his experience. "Those experiences which are used to prove a scientific truth," James writes, "are for the most part artificial experiences of the laboratory, gained after the truth itself has been conjectured."

Of these three only the last is an experimental experience. The first type of experience may be employed by the scientist, but it is seldom sufficient or reliable enough for his purposes. The distinction between the empirical sciences which are and those which are not experimental turns on the difference between the second and third types.

It is not always possible for the scientist to perform experiments, as, for example, in astronomy, where the phenomena can be methodically observed and exactly recorded, but cannot be manipulated or controlled. Among the great books of natural science, the biological writings of Hippocrates, Aristotle, Galen, and Darwin, the astronomical works of Ptolemy, Copernicus, Kepler, and Newton, and the clinical studies of Freud are examples of scientific works which are more or less empirical, but not experimental. In contrast, Galileo's *Concerning Two New Sciences,* Newton's *Optics,* Harvey's *On the Motion of the Heart and Blood in Animals,* Lavoisier's *Elements of Chemistry,* and Faraday's *Researches in Electricity* represent empirical science which has recourse to experimentation at crucial points.

ON THE SIDE OF their production, experiments are like inventions. They do not happen by chance or without the intervention of art. They are usually performed under carefully controlled conditions and by means of apparatus artfully contrived. This explains the interplay between technology and experimental science. Progress in each occasions progress in the other.

On the side of their utility, experiments seem to serve three different though related purposes in scientific work. In those branches of physics which are both mathematical and experimental, the experiment enables the scientist to make exact measurements of the phenomena and so to determine whether one or another mathematical formulation fits the observable facts of nature. Investigating accelerated motion, Galileo seeks not only to demonstrate its definition and its properties, but also to show that "experimental results . . . agree with and exactly correspond with those properties which have been, one after another, demonstrated by us."

The experiment of the inclined plane yields measurements which exemplify those ratios between space and time that are determined by one rather than by another mathematical definition of the acceleration of a freely falling body. The experiment is thus used to decide between two competing mathematical theories, choosing that one "best fitting natural phenomena." In those sciences, Galileo writes, "in which mathematical demonstrations are applied to natural phenomena . . . the principles, once established by well-chosen experiments, become the foundation of the entire super-structure."

Concerned with the phenomena of heat, Joseph Fourier makes the same point concerning the relation of mathematics and experiments. "Mathematical analysis," he says, "can deduce from general and simple phenomena the expression of the laws of nature; but the special application of these laws to very complex effects demands a long series of exact observations" for which experiments are needed.

In addition to testing hypotheses and providing measurements whereby mathematical formulations can be applied to nature, experiments function as the source of inductions. A crucial experiment constitutes a single clear case from which a generalization can be drawn that is applicable to all cases. Newton's optical experiments are of this sort. He calls this use of experiments "the method of analysis." It consists in "making experiments and observations, and in drawing general conclusions from them by induction . . . And although the arguing from experiments and observations by induction be no demonstration of general conclusions, yet it is the best way of arguing which the nature of things admits of."

A third use for experiments is in the explo-ration of new fields of phenomena, for purposes of discovery rather than of induction or verification. Hypotheses may result from such explorations, but in the first instance, the experimentation may be undertaken without the guidance of hypotheses. This employment of experimental technique is illustrated by Faraday's remark that "the science of electricity is in that state in which every part of it requires experimental investigation, not merely for the discovery of new effects, but what is just now of far more importance, the development of the means by which the old effects are produced."

Experimental exploration, apart from the direction of hypotheses, seems to be a procedure of trial and error. Experimentation in this sense reflects what Hippocrates had in mind when he spoke of "the experiment perilous." In the work of Hippocrates at the very beginning of empirical science, recourse to experiment, far from being the most prized technique, signified a lack of scientific knowledge. Only the physician who could not cure the patient by art based on science took the risk of experimenting—of proceeding by trial and error.

REVIEWING MODERN THOUGHT, Whitehead deals with the peculiarly modern conflict between realism and idealism. There were no epistemological idealists in antiquity or the Middle Ages. "The distinction between realism and idealism," he points out, "does not coincide with that between objectivism and subjectivism. Both realists and idealists can start from an objective standpoint. They may both agree that the world disclosed in sense-perception is a common world, transcending the individual recipient. But the objective idealist, when he comes to analyse what the reality of this world involves, finds that cognitive mentality is in some way inextricably concerned in every detail. This position the realist denies."

Another voice on this distinction between the objective and the subjective is that of Heisenberg. "In the description of atomic events, since the measuring device has been constructed by the observer," he cautions us "to remember that what we observe is not nature in itself but nature exposed to our method of questioning . . . In this way quantum theory reminds us, as Bohr has put it . . . that in the drama of existence we are ourselves both players and spectators."

26

Family

INTRODUCTION

THE human family, according to Rousseau, is "the most ancient of all societies and the only one that is natural." On the naturalness of the family there seems to be general agreement in the great books, although not all would claim, like Rousseau, that it is the *only* natural society. The state is sometimes also regarded as a natural community, but its naturalness is not as obvious and has often been disputed.

The word "natural" applied to a community or association of men can mean either that men *instinctively* associate with one another as do bees and buffalo; or that the association in question, while voluntary and to that extent conventional, is also *necessary* for human welfare. It is in this sense of necessity or need that Rousseau speaks of family ties as natural. "The children remain attached to the father only so long as they need him for their preservation," he writes. "As soon as this need ceases, the natural bond is dissolved." If after that "they remain united, they continue so no longer naturally, but voluntarily; and the family itself is then maintained only by convention."

Locke appears to attribute the existence of the human family to the same sort of instinctive determination which establishes familial ties among other animals, though he recognizes that the protracted infancy of human offspring make "the conjugal bonds . . . more firm and lasting in man than the other species of animals." Since with other animals as well as in the human species, "the end of conjunction between male and female [is] not barely procreation, but the continuation of the species," it ought to last, in Locke's opinion, "even after procreation, so long as is necessary to the nourishment and support of the young ones,

who are to be sustained by those who got them till they are able to shift and support for themselves. This rule," he adds, "which the infinite wise Maker hath set to the works of His hands, we find the inferior creatures steadily obey."

Yet Locke does not reduce the association of father, mother, and children entirely to a divinely implanted instinct for the perpetuation of the species. "Conjugal society," he writes, "is made by a voluntary compact between man and woman, and though it consists chiefly in such a communion and right in one another's bodies as is necessary to its chief end, procreation, yet it draws with it mutual support and assistance, and a communion of interests, too."

If the human family were *entirely* an instinctively formed society, we should expect to find the pattern or structure of the domestic community the same at all times and everywhere. But since the time of Herodotus, historians and, later, anthropologists have observed the great diversity in the institutions of the family in different tribes or cultures, or even at different times in the same culture. From his own travels among different peoples, Herodotus reports a wide variety of customs with respect to marriage and the family. From the travels of other men, Montaigne culls a similar collection of stories about the diversity of the mores with respect to sex, especially in relation to the rules or customs which hedge the community of man and wife. Lévi-Strauss goes even further when he says, "the biological family is ubiquitous in human society. But what confers upon kinship its socio-cultural character is not what it retains from nature, but, rather, the essential way in which it diverges from nature. A kinship system does not consist in the objective ties of descent or consanguinity between individuals. It exists only in human consciousness; it is an arbitrary system of representations, not the spontaneous development of a real situation."

Such facts raise the question whether the pattern of monogamy pictured by Locke represents anything more than one type of human family—the type which predominates in western civilization or, even more narrowly, in Christendom. Marx, for instance, holds that the structure of the family depends on the character of its "economical foundation," and insists that "it is of course just as absurd to hold the Teutonic-Christian form of the family to be absolute and final as it would be to apply that character to the ancient Roman, the ancient Greek, or the Eastern forms which, moreover, taken together form a series in historic development."

Though the observation of the various forms which the human family takes has led some writers to deny the naturalness of the family—at least so far as its "naturalness" would mean a purely instinctive formation— it has seldom been disputed that the family fulfills a natural human need. Conventional in structure, the family remains natural as a means indispensable to an end which all men *naturally* desire. "There must be a union of those who cannot exist without each other," Aristotle writes, "namely, of male and female, that the race may continue"; and he goes on to say that this union is formed "not of deliberate purpose, but because, in common with other animals and with plants, mankind have a natural desire to leave behind them an image of themselves."

The human infant, as Locke observes, requires years of care in order to survive. If the family did not exist as a relatively stable organization to serve this purpose, some other social agency would have to provide sustained care for children. But wherever we find any other social units, such as tribes or cities, there we also find some form of the family in existence, not only performing the function of rearing children, but also being the primitive social group out of which all larger groupings seem to grow or to be formed. Aristotle, for example, describes the village or tribe as growing out of an association of families, just as later the city or state comes from a union of villages.

We have seen that the naturalness of the family—as answering a natural need—is not incompatible with its also being a product of custom or convention. The facts reported by Herodotus, Montaigne, Darwin, and Lévi-Strauss, which show the variability of families in size and membership, in form and government, do not exclude, but on the contrary emphasize, the further fact that wherever men live together at all, they also live in families.

Whether or not the political community is also a natural society, and if so, whether it is natural in the same way as the family, are questions reserved for the chapter on STATE. But it should be noted here that for some writers, for Aristotle particularly and to a lesser extent for Locke, the naturalness of the family not only points to a natural development of the state, but also helps to explain how, in the transition from the family to the state, paternal government gives rise to royal rule or absolute monarchy. Even Rousseau, who thinks that the family is the *only* natural society, finds, in the correspondence between a political ruler and a father, reason for saying that "the family . . . may be called the first model of political societies."

IN WESTERN CIVILIZATION, a family normally consists of a husband and wife and their offspring. If the procreation and rearing of offspring is *the* function, or even *a* function, which the family naturally exists to perform, then a childless family cannot be considered normal. Hegel suggests another reason for offspring. He sees in children the bond of union which makes the family a community.

"The relation of love between husband and wife," he writes, "is in itself not objective, because even if their feeling is their substantial unity, still this unity has no objectivity. Such an objectivity parents first acquire in their children, in whom they can see objectified the entirety of their union. In the child, a mother loves its father and he its mother. Both have their love objectified for them in the child. While in their goods their unity is embodied only in an external thing, in their children it is embodied in a spiritual one in which the parents are loved and which they love."

Until recent times when it has been affected by urban, industrial conditions, the family tended to be a much larger unit, not only with regard to the number of children, but also with respect to other members and relationships. The household included servants, if not slaves; it included blood-relatives in various degrees of consanguinity; its range extended over three or even four generations. Sancho Panza's wife, for instance, pictures the ideal marriage for her daughter as one in which "we'll be able to keep an eye on her, and we'll all be together, parents and children, grandchildren, sons-in-law and daughters-in-law, and peace and God's blessing will be upon us." Even though they belong to the 19th century, the families in *War and Peace* indicate how different is the domestic establishment under agrarian and semifeudal conditions.

But even when it comprised a larger and more varied membership, the family differed from other social units, such as tribe or state, in both size and function. Its membership, determined by consanguinity, was usually more restricted than that of other groups, although blood-relationships, often more remote, may also operate to limit the membership of the tribe or the state. Its function, according to Aristotle, at least in origin, was to "supply men's everyday wants," whereas the state went beyond this in aiming at other conditions "of a good life."

In an agricultural society of the sort we find among the ancients, the household rather than the city is occupied with the problems of wealth. In addition to the breeding and rearing of children, and probably because of this in part, the family as a unit seems to have been concerned with the means of subsistence, on the side of both production and consumption. Its members shared in a division of labor and in a division of the fruits thereof.

Apart from those industries manned solely by slave labor in the service of the state, the production of goods largely depended on the industry of the family. In modern times this system of production came to be called the "domestic" as opposed to the "factory" system. It seems to persist even after the industrial revolution. But, according to Marx, "this modern so-called domestic industry has nothing, except the name, in common with the old-fashioned domestic industry, the existence of which presupposes independent urban handicrafts, independent peasant farming, and above all, a dwelling house for the laborer and his family."

In effect, the industrial revolution produced an economy in which not only agriculture but the family ceased to be central. The problem shifts from the wealth of families to the wealth of nations, even as production shifts from the family to the factory. "Modern industry," according to Marx, "by assigning an important part in the process of production, outside the domestic sphere, to women, to young persons, and to children of both sexes, creates a new economical foundation."

The family was for centuries what the factory and the storehouse have only recently become in an era of industrialism. For the ancients, the problems of wealth—its acquisition, accumulation, and use—were domestic, not political. "The so-called art of getting wealth," Aristotle writes, is "according to some . . . identical with household management, according to others, a principal part of it." In his own judgment, "property is a part of the household, and the art of acquiring property is a part of the art of managing the household"—but a *part only,* because the household includes human beings as well as property, and is concerned with the government of persons as well as the management of things.

The foregoing throws light on the extraordinary shift in the meaning of the word "economics" from ancient to modern times. In the significance of their Greek roots, the word "polity" signifies a state, the word "economy" a family; and as "politics" referred to the art of governing the political community, so "economics" referred to the art of governing the domestic community. Only in part was it concerned with the art of getting wealth. As the chapter on WEALTH indicates, Rousseau tries to preserve the broader meaning when he uses the phrase "political economy" for the general problems of government; but for the most part in modern usage "economics" refers to a science or art concerned with wealth, and it is "political" in the sense that the management of wealth, and of men with respect to wealth, has become the problem of the state rather than the family. Not only has the industrial economy become more and more a political affair, but the character of the family as a social institution has also changed with its altered economic status and function.

THE CHIEF QUESTION about the family in relation to the state has been, in ancient as well as in modern times, whether the family has natural rights which the state cannot justly invade or transgress.

The proposal in Plato's *The Republic*—"that the wives of our guardians are to be common, and their children are to be common, and no parent is to know his own child, nor any child his parent"—was as radical in the 5th century B.C. as its counterpart would be today. When Socrates proposes this, Glaucon suggests that "the possibility as well as the utility of such a law" may be subject to "a good many doubts." But Socrates does not think that "there can be any dispute about the very great utility of having wives and children in common; the possibility," he adds, "is quite another matter, and will be very much disputed."

Aristotle questions both the desirability and possibility. "The premise from which the argument of Socrates proceeds," he says, is " 'the greater the unity of the state the better.' " He denies this premise. "Is it not obvious," he asks, "that a state may at length attain such a degree of unity as to be no longer a state?—since the nature of a state is to be a plurality, and in tending to a greater unity, from being a state, it becomes a family, and from being a family, an individual." Hence "we ought not to attain this greatest unity even if we could, for it would be the destruction of the state." In addition, "the scheme, taken literally, is impracticable."

It is significant that Aristotle's main argument against Plato's "communism" (which includes the community of property as well as the community of women and children) is based upon the nature of the state rather than on the rights of the family. It seems to have been a prevalent view in antiquity, at least among philosophers, that the children should be "regarded as belonging to the state rather than to their parents." Antigone's example shows, however, that this view was by no means without exception. Her defiance of Creon, based on "the gods' unwritten and unfailing laws," is also undertaken for the honor of kindred blood. In this sense, it constitutes an affirmation of the rights and duties of the family.

In the Christian tradition the rights of the family as against the state are also defended by reference to divine law. The point is not that the state is less a natural community than the family in the eyes of a theologian like Aquinas; but in addition to having a certain priority in the order of nature, the family, more directly than the state, is of divine origin. Not only is it founded on the sacrament of matrimony, but the express commandments of God dictate the duties of care and obedience which bind its members together. For the state to interfere in those relationships between parents and children or between husband and wife which fall under the regulation of divine law would be to exceed its authority, and hence to act without right and in violation of rights founded upon a higher authority.

In the Christian tradition philosophers like Hobbes and Kant state the rights of the family in terms of natural law or defend them as natural rights. "Because the first instruction of children," writes Hobbes, "depends on the care of their parents, it is necessary that they should be obedient to them while they are under their tuition . . . Originally the father of every man was also his sovereign lord, with power over him of life and death." When the fathers of families relinquished such absolute power in order to form a commonwealth or state, they did not lose, nor did they have to give up, according to Hobbes, all control of their children. "Nor would there be any reason," he goes on, "why any man should desire to have children, or take the care to nourish and instruct them, if they were afterwards to have no other benefit from them than from other men. And this," he says, "accords with the Fifth Commandment."

In the section of his *The Science of Right* devoted to the "rights of the family as a domestic society," Kant argues that "from the fact of procreation there follows the duty of preserving and rearing children." From this duty he derives "the right of parents to the management and training of the child, so long as it is itself incapable of making proper use of its body as an organism, and of its mind as an understanding. This includes its nourishment and the care of its education." It also "includes, in general, the function of forming and developing it practically, that it may be able in the future to maintain and advance itself, and also its moral culture and development, the guilt of neglecting it falling upon the parents."

As is evident from Hobbes and Kant, the rights of the family can be vindicated without denying that the family, like the individual, owes obedience to the state. In modern terms, at least, the problem is partly stated by the question, To what extent can parents justly claim exemption from political interference in the control of their own children? But this is only part of the problem. It must also be asked whether, in addition to regulating the family for the general welfare of the whole community, the state is also entitled to interfere in the affairs of the household in order to protect children from parental mismanagement or neglect. Both questions call for a consideration of the form and principles of domestic government.

THE KINDS OF RULE and the relation between ruler and ruled in the domestic community have a profound bearing on the theory of government in the larger community of the state. Many of the chapters on the forms of government—especially CONSTITUTION, MONARCHY, and TYRANNY AND DESPOTISM—indicate that the great books of political theory, from Plato and Aristotle to Locke and Rousseau, derive critical points from the comparison of domestic and political government.

We shall pass over the master-slave relationship, both because that is considered in the chapter on SLAVERY, and because not all households include human chattel. Omitting this, two fundamental relationships which domestic government involves remain to be examined: the relation of husband and wife, and of parents and children.

With regard to the first, there are questions of equality and administrative supremacy. Even when the wife is regarded as the complete equal of her husband, the administrative question remains, for there must either be a division of authority, or unanimity must prevail, or one—either the husband or the wife—must have the last word when disagreement must be overcome to get any practical matter decided. So far as husband and wife are concerned, should the family be an absolute monarchy, or a kind of constitutional government?

Both an ancient and a modern writer appear to answer this question in the same way. "A husband and father," Aristotle says, "rules over wife and children, both free, but the rule differs, the rule over his children being a royal, over his wife a constitutional rule." Yet the relation between husband and wife, in Aristotle's view, is not perfectly constitutional. In the state "the citizens rule and are ruled in turn" on the supposition that their "natures . . . are equal and do not differ at all." In the family, however, Aristotle thinks that "although there may be exceptions to the order of nature, the male is by nature fitter for command than the female."

According to Locke, "the husband and wife, though they have but one common concern, yet having different understandings, will unavoidably sometimes have different wills too. It therefore being necessary that the last determination (*i.e.,* the rule) should be placed somewhere, it naturally falls to the man's share as the abler and the stronger." But this, Locke thinks, "leaves the wife in the full and true possession of what by contract is her peculiar right, and at least gives the husband no more power over her than she has over his life; the power of the husband being so far from that of an absolute monarch that the wife has, in many cases, a liberty to separate from him where natural right or their contract allows it."

In the so-called Marriage Group of the *The Canterbury Tales,* Chaucer gives voice to all of the possible positions that have ever been taken concerning the relation of husband and wife. The Wife of Bath, for example, argues for the rule of the wife. She claims that nothing will satisfy a wife until she has "the self-same sovereignty/Over her husband as over her lover,/And master him; he must not be above her." The Clerk of Oxford, in his tale of patient Griselda, presents the wife who says to her husband, "at my father's doors/I left my clothing. Was it not the same/To leave my will and freedom when I came?" The Franklin in his tale allows the mastery to neither wife nor husband, "save that his sovereignty in name upon her/He should preserve." He dares to say,

Lovers must each be ready to obey
The other, if they would long keep company.
Love will not be constrained by mastery; . . .
Women by nature long for liberty
And not to be constrained or made a thrall,
And so do men, if I may speak for all . . .
Thus in this humble, wise accord
She took a servant when she took a lord,
A lord in marriage in a love renewed
By service, lordship set in servitude.

In Molière's *The School for Wives,* we find this passage:

Marriage, my dear, is not a laughing matter.
The status of wife binds one to solemn duties,
And you will not ascend to that position
In order to live a free and easy life . . .
Although mankind's divided in two halves,
Nevertheless these halves are far from equal.
One is the major half, the other minor.

WHILE THERE MAY be disagreement regarding the relation between husband and wife, there is none regarding the inequality between parents and children during the offspring's immaturity. Although every man may enjoy "equal right . . . to his natural freedom, without being subjected to the will or authority of any other men," children, according to Locke, "are not born in this full state of equality, though they are born to it."

Paternal power, even absolute rule, over children arises from this fact. So long as the child "is in an estate wherein he has no understanding of his own to direct his will," Locke

thinks he "is not to have any will of his own to follow. He that understands for him must will for him too; he must prescribe to his will, and regulate his actions." But Locke adds the important qualification that when the son "comes to the estate which made his father a free man, the son is a free man too."

Because children are truly inferior in competence, there would seem to be no injustice in their being ruled by their parents; or in the rule being absolute in the sense that children are precluded from exercising a decisive voice in the conduct of their own or their family's affairs. Those who think that kings cannot claim the absolute authority of parental rule frequently use the word "despotic" to signify unjustified paternalism—a transference to the state of a type of dominion which can be justified only in the family.

The nature of despotism as absolute rule is discussed in the chapters on MONARCHY and TYRANNY AND DESPOTISM, but its relevance here makes it worth repeating that the Greek word from which "despot" comes, like its Latin equivalent *paterfamilias,* signifies the ruler of a household and carries the connotation of absolute rule—the complete mastery of the father over the children and the servants, if not over the wife. Accordingly there would seem to be nothing invidious in referring to domestic government as despotic, at least not to the extent that, in the case of the children, absolute rule is justified by their immaturity. The problem arises only with respect to despotism in the state, when one man rules another mature man as absolutely as a parent rules a child.

The great defender of the doctrine that the sovereign must be absolute, "or else there is no sovereignty at all," sees no difference between the rights of the ruler of a state—the "sovereign by institution"—and those of a father as the natural master of his family. "The rights and consequences of both paternal and despotical dominion," Hobbes maintains, "are the very same with those of a sovereign by institution." On the other hand, Rousseau, an equally staunch opponent of absolute rule, uses the word "despotism" only in an invidious sense for what he regards as illegitimate government—absolute monarchy. "Even if there were as close an analogy as many authors maintain between the State and the family," he writes, "it would not follow that the rules of conduct proper for one of these societies would be also proper for the other."

Rousseau even goes so far as to deny that parental rule is despotic in his sense of that term. "With regard to paternal authority, from which some writers have derived absolute government," he remarks that "nothing can be further from the ferocious spirit of despotism than the mildness of that authority which looks more to the advantage of him who obeys than to that of him who commands." He agrees with Locke in the observation that, unlike the political despot, "the father is the child's master no longer than his help is necessary." When both are equal, the son is perfectly independent of the father, and owes him "only respect and not obedience." As Tocqueville observes, "among democratic nations every word a son addresses to his father has a tang of freedom, familiarity, and tenderness all at once, which gives an immediate impression of the new relationship prevailing in the family."

Misrule in the family, then, would seem to occur when these conditions or limits are violated. Parents may try to continue their absolute control past the point at which the children have become mature and are competent to take care of their own affairs. A parent who does not relinquish his absolutism at this point can be called "despotic" in the derogatory sense of that word.

Applying a distinction made by some political writers, the parent is tyrannical rather than despotic when he uses the children for his own good, treats them as property to exploit, even at a time when his absolute direction of their affairs would be justified if it were for the children's welfare. The existence of parental tyranny raises in its sharpest form the question of the state's right to intervene in the family for the good of its members.

THE CENTRAL ELEMENT in the domestic establishment is, of course, the institution of marriage. The discussion of marriage in the great books deals with most of the moral and psychological, if not all of the sociological and economic, aspects of the institution. The most profound question, perhaps, is whether marriage is merely a human institution to be regulated solely by custom and civil law, *or* a contract under the sanctions of natural law, *or* a religious sacrament signifying and imparting God's grace. The last two of these alternatives may not exclude one another, but those who insist upon the first usually reject the other two.

Some, like the Parson in *The Canterbury Tales*, consider marriage not only a natural but also a divine institution—a "sacrament . . . ordained by God Himself in Paradise, and confirmed by Jesus Christ, as witness St. Matthew in the gospel: 'For this cause shall a man leave father and mother, and shall cleave to his wife; and they twain shall be one flesh,' which betokens the knitting together of Christ and of Holy Church."

Others, like Kant, seem to stress the character of marriage as an institution sanctioned by natural law. The "natural union of the sexes," he writes, "proceeds either according to the mere animal nature (*vaga libido, venus vulgivaga, fornicatio*), or according to law. The latter is marriage (*matrimonium*), which is the union of two persons of different sex for life-long reciprocal possession of their sexual faculties." Kant considers offspring as a natural end of marriage, but not the exclusive end, for then "the marriage would be dissolved of itself when the production of the children ceased . . . Even assuming," he declares, "that enjoyment in the reciprocal use of the sexual endowments is an end of marriage, yet the contract of marriage is not on that account a matter of arbitrary will, but is a contract necessary in its nature by the Law of Humanity. In other words, if a man and a woman have the will to enter on reciprocal enjoyment in accordance with their sexual natures, they *must* necessarily marry each other."

Still others see marriage primarily as a civil contract. Freud, for example, considers the view that "sexual relations are permitted only on the basis of a final, indissoluble bond between a man and woman" as purely a convention of "present-day civilization." Marriage, as a set of taboos restricting the sexual life, varies from culture to culture; but in Freud's opinion the "high-water mark in this type of development has been reached in our Western European civilization."

The conception of marriage—whether it is merely a civil, or a natural, and even a divine institution—obviously affects the position to be taken on monogamy, on divorce, on chastity and adultery, and on the comparative merits of the married and the celibate condition. The pagans, for the most part, regard celibacy as a misfortune, especially for women, as witness the tragedy of the unwedded Electra. Christianity, on the other hand, celebrates the heroism of virginity and encourages the formation of monastic communities for celibates. Within the Judeo-Christian tradition there are striking differences. Not only were the patriarchs of the Old Testament polygamous, but orthodox Judaism and orthodox Christianity also differ on divorce.

Augustine explains how a Christian should interpret those passages in the Old Testament which describe the polygamous practices of the patriarchs. "The saints of ancient times," he writes, "were under the form of an earthly kingdom, foreshadowing and foretelling the kingdom of heaven. And on account of the necessity for a numerous offspring, the custom of one man having several wives was at that time blameless; and for the same reason it was not proper for one woman to have several husbands, because a woman does not in that way become more fruitful . . . In regard to matters of this sort," he concludes, "whatever the holy men of those times did without lust, Scripture passes over without blame, although they did things which could not be done at the present time except through lust."

On similar grounds Aquinas holds that "it was allowable to give a bill of divorce," under the law of the Old Testament, but it is not allowable under the Christian dispensation because divorce "is contrary to the nature of a sacrament." The greatest familiarity between man and wife requires the staunchest fidelity which "is impossible if the marriage bond can be sundered." Within the Christian tradition

Locke takes an opposite view of divorce. He can see good reason why "the society of man and wife should be more lasting than that of male and female amongst other creatures," but he does not see "why this compact, where procreation and education are secured, and inheritance taken care for, may not be made determinable either by consent, or at a certain time, or upon certain conditions, as well as any other voluntary compact, there being no necessity in the nature of the thing . . . that it should always be for life." Against Locke, Dr. Johnson would argue that "to the contract of marriage, besides the man and wife, there is a third party—Society; and if it be considered as a vow—God; and therefore it cannot be dissolved by their consent alone."

Laws and customs, however, represent only the external or social aspect of marriage. The discussion of these externals cannot give any impression of the inwardness and depth of the problem which marriage is for the individual person. Only the great poems, the great novels and plays, the great books of history and biography can adequately present the psychological and emotional aspects of marriage in the life of individuals. Heightened in narration, they give more eloquent testimony than the case histories of Freud to support the proposition that marriage is at all times—in every culture and under the widest variety of circumstances—one of the supreme tests of human character.

The relation between men and women in and out of marriage, the relation of husband and wife before and after marriage, the relation of parents and children—these create crises and tensions, conflicts between love and duty, between reason and the passions, from which no individual can entirely escape. Marriage is not only a typically human problem, but it is the one problem which, both psychologically and morally, touches every man, woman, and child. Sometimes the resolution is tragic, sometimes the outcome seems to be happy, almost blessed; but whether a human life is built on this foundation or broken against these rocks, it is violently shaken in the process and forever shaped.

To some degree each reader of the great

books has, in imagination if not in action, participated in the trials of Odysseus, Penelope, and Telemachus; in the affections of Hector and Andromache, Alcestis and Admetus, Natasha and Pierre Bezúkhov; in the jealousy of Othello, the anguish of Lear, the decision of Aeneas or the indecision of Hamlet; in the rebellion of the adolescent Huck Finn; and certainly in the reasoning of Panurge about whether to marry or not. In each of these cases, everyone finds some aspect of love in relation to marriage, some phase of parenthood or childhood which has colored his own life or that of his family; and he can find somewhere in his own experience the grounds for sympathetic understanding of the extraordinary relation between Electra and her mother, Clytemnestra, between Augustine and Monica his mother, between Oedipus and Jocasta, Prince Hamlet and Queen Gertrude, Pierre Bezúkhov and his wife, or what is perhaps the most extraordinary case of all—Adam and Eve in *Paradise Lost*.

On one point the universality of the problem of marriage and family life seems to require qualification. The conflict between conjugal and illicit love exists in all ages. The entanglement of the bond between man and wife with the ties—of both love and blood—which unite parents and children, is equally universal. But the difficulties which arise in marriage as a result of the ideals or the illusions of romantic love seem to constitute a peculiarly modern problem. It is folly to suppose, says Erasmus, that "many marriages would ever be made if the bridegroom made prudent inquiries about the tricks that little virgin . . . was up to long before the wedding."

The ancients distinguished between sexual love and the love of friendship, and they understood the necessity for both in the conjugal relationship if marriage is to prosper. But not until the later Middle Ages did men think of matrimony as a way to perpetuate throughout all the years the ardor of that moment in a romantic attachment when the lovers find each other without flaw and beyond reproach.

Matters relevant to this modern problem are discussed in the chapter on LOVE. As is there indicated, romantic love, though it seems to be of Christian origin, may also be a distortion—even a heretical perversion—of the kind of Christian love which is pledged in the reciprocal vows of holy matrimony.

WE HAVE ALREADY considered some of the problems of the family which relate to children and youth—the immature members of the human race—such as whether the child *belongs* to the family or the state, and whether the family is solely responsible for the care and training of children, or a share of this responsibility falls to the state or the church.

There are other problems. Why do men and women want offspring and what satisfactions do they get from rearing children? For the most part in Christendom, and certainly in antiquity, the lot of the childless is looked upon as a grievous frustration. To be childless is not merely contrary to nature, but for pagan as well as Christian it constitutes the deprivation of a blessing which should grace the declining years of married life. The opposite view, so rarely taken, is voiced by the chorus of women in *The Medea* of Euripides.

"Those who have never/Had children, who know nothing of it,/In happiness have the advantage/Over those who are parents," the women chant in response to Medea's tragic leave-taking from her own babes.

The childless, who never discover
Whether children turn out as a good thing
Or as something to cause pain, are spared
Many troubles in lacking this knowledge.
And those who have in their homes
The sweet presence of children, I see that their lives
Are all wasted away by their worries.
First they must think how to bring them up well and
How to leave them something to live on.
And then after this whether all their toil
Is for those who will turn out good or bad,
Is still an unanswered question.

Still other questions arise concerning children, quite apart from the attitude of parents toward having and rearing them. What is the economic position of the child, both with respect to ownership of property and with respect to a part in the division of labor? How has the economic status of children been affected by industrialism? What are the mental and moral characteristics of the immature which exclude them from participation in political life, and which require adult regulation of their affairs? What are the criteria—emotional and mental as well as chronological—which determine the classification of individuals as children or adults, and how is the transition from childhood to manhood effected economically, politically, and above all emotionally?

The authors of the great books discuss most of these questions, but among them only Freud sees in the relation of children to their parents the basic emotional determination of human life. The fundamental triangle of love and hate, devotion and rivalry, consists of father, mother, and child. For Freud all the intricacies and perversions of love, the qualitative distinctions of romantic, conjugal, and illicit love, the factors which determine the choice of a mate and success or failure in marriage, and the conditions which determine the emergence from emotional infantilism—all these can be understood only by reference to the emotional life of the child in the vortex of the family.

The child's "great task," according to Freud, is that of "freeing himself from the parents," for "only after this detachment is accomplished can he cease to be a child and so become a member of the social community . . . These tasks are laid down for every man" but, Freud writes, "it is noteworthy how seldom they are carried through ideally, that is, how seldom they are solved in a manner psychologically as well as socially satisfactory. In neurotics, however," he adds, "this detachment from the parents is not accomplished at all."

In one sense, it is never fully accomplished by anyone. What Freud calls the "ego-ideal"—which represents our higher nature and which, in the name of the reality-principle, resists instinctual compliance with the pleasure-principle—is said to have its origin in "the identification with the father, which takes place in the prehistory of every person." Even after an individual has achieved detachment from the family, this ego-ideal acts as "a substitute for the longing for a father"; and in the form of conscience it "continues . . . to exercise the censorship of morals."

ONE OTHER GROUP of questions which involve the family—at least as background—concerns the position or role of women. We have already considered their relation to their husbands in the government of the family itself. The way in which that relation is conceived affects the status and activity of women in the larger community of the state, in relation to citizenship and the opportunities for education, to the possession of property and the production of wealth (for example, the role of female labor in an industrial economy).

Again it is Euripides who gives voice to the plight of women in a man's world in two of his great tragedies, *The Trojan Women* and *The Medea*. In the one, they cry out under the brunt of the suffering which men leave them to bear in the backwash of war. In the other, Medea passionately berates the ignominy and bondage which women must accept in being wives:

Of all things which are living and can form
  a judgment
We women are the most unfortunate creatures.
Firstly, with an excess of wealth it is required
For us to buy a husband and take for our bodies
A master; for not to take one is even worse.

The ancient world contains another feminist who goes further than Euripides in speaking for the right of women to be educated like men, to share in property with them, and to enjoy the privileges as well as to discharge the tasks of citizenship. In the tradition of the great books, the striking fact is that after Plato the next great declaration of the rights of women should be written by one who is as far removed from him in time and temper as J. S. Mill.

In Plato's *The Republic,* Socrates argues that if the difference between men and women "consists only in women bearing and men begetting children, this does not amount to proof that a woman differs from a man in respect to the sort of education she should receive." For the same reason, he says, "the guardians and their wives ought to have the same pursuits." Since he thinks that "the gifts of nature are alike diffused in both," Socrates insists that "there is no special faculty of administration in a state which a woman has because she is a woman, or which a man has by virtue of his sex. All the pursuits of men are the pursuits of women also." Yet he adds that "in all of them a woman is inferior to a man." Therefore when he proposes to let women "share in the toils of war and the defence of their country," Socrates suggests that "in the distribution of labors the lighter are to be assigned to the women, who are the weaker natures."

In the 19th century, Nietzsche and Mill express dramatically opposed views on the relation between men and women. "Woman wants to be independent," writes Nietzsche, "and to that end she is beginning to enlighten men about 'woman as such'—*this* is one of the worst developments in the general *uglification* of Europe. For what must these clumsy attempts on the part of female scientificality and self-exposure not bring to light! Woman has so much reason for shame; in woman there is concealed so much pedanticism, superficiality, schoolmarmishness, petty presumption, petty unbridledness and petty immodesty—one needs only to study her behaviour with children!—which has fundamentally been most effectively controlled and repressed hitherto by *fear* of man . . . To blunder over the fundamental problem of 'man and woman', to deny here the most abysmal antagonism and the necessity of an eternally hostile tension, perhaps to dream here of equal rights, equal education, equal claims and duties: this is a *typical* sign of shallow-mindedness . . . Since the French Revolution the influence of woman in Europe has grown *less* in the same proportion as her rights and claims have grown greater; and the 'emancipation of woman', in so far as it has been demanded and advanced by women themselves (and not only by male shallow-pates), is thus revealed as a noteworthy symptom of the growing enfeeblement and blunting of the most feminine instincts."

Ibsen's play *A Doll's House* dramatically portrays a wife leaving home and seeking emancipation from household duties. Her husband tells her she is "betraying [her] most sacred duty"—"duty to your husband and your children." Nora replies that she has "another duty equally sacred"—duty to herself. Shaw, in many ways a disciple of Ibsen, expresses the same sentiments in his Preface to *Saint Joan*. He writes, "it is not necessary to wear trousers and smoke big cigars to live a man's life any more than it is necessary to wear petticoats to live a woman's. There are plenty of gowned and bodiced women in ordinary civil life who manage their own affairs and other people's, including those of their menfolk, and are entirely masculine in their tastes and pursuits. There always were such women, even in the Victorian days when women had fewer legal rights than men, and our modern women magistrates, mayors, and members of Parliament were unknown. In reactionary Russia in our own century a woman soldier organized an effective regiment of amazons, which disappeared only because it was Aldershottian enough to be against the Revolution. The exemption of women from military service is founded, not on any natural inaptitude that men do not share, but on the fact that communities cannot reproduce themselves without plenty of women. Men are more largely dispensable, and are sacrificed accordingly."

Mill's tract *On the Subjection of Women* is his fullest statement of the case for social, economic, and political equality between the sexes. In *Representative Government,* his defense of women's rights deals primarily with the question of extending the franchise to them. Difference of sex, he contends, is "as entirely irrelevant to political rights, as difference in height, or in the color of the hair. All human beings have the same interest in good government . . . Mankind have long since abandoned the only premises which will support the conclusion that women ought not to have votes. No one now holds that women should be in personal servitude; that they should have no thought, wish, or occupation, but to be the domestic drudges of husbands, fathers, or brothers. It is allowed to unmarried, and wants but little of being conceded to married women to hold property, and have pecuniary and business interests, in the same manner as men. It is considered suitable and proper that women should think, and write, and be teachers. As soon as these things are admitted," Mill concludes, "the political disqualification has no principle to rest on." On all of these points, Veblen, writing at the beginning of the 20th century, reports the failure of the "new-woman movement" to achieve the emancipation of women either in the family or the state.

Though Mill is the only author who speaks so directly for the emancipation of women from domestic and political subjection, many of the great books do consider the differences between men and women in relation to war and love, pleasure and pain, virtue and vice, duty and honor. Some are concerned explicitly with the pivotal question—whether men and women are more alike than different, whether they are essentially equal in their humanity or unequal. Since these are matters pertinent to human nature itself, as it is affected by gender, the relevant passages are collected in the chapter on MAN.

27

Fate

INTRODUCTION

FATE—sometimes personified, sometimes abstractly conceived—is the antagonist of freedom in the drama of human life and history. So at least it seems to the poets of antiquity. In many of the Greek tragedies, fate sets the stage. Some curse must be fulfilled. A doom impends and is inexorable. But the actors on the stage are far from puppets. Within the framework of the inevitable the tragic hero works out his own destiny, making the choices from which his personal catastrophe ensues. Oedipus, doomed to kill his father and marry his mother, is not fated to inquire into his past and to discover the sins which, when he sees, he wills to see no more. The curse on the house of Atreus does not require Agamemnon to bring Cassandra back from Troy or to step on the purple carpet. The furies which pursue Orestes he has himself awakened by murdering his mother, Clytemnestra, a deed not fated but freely undertaken to avenge his father's death.

The idea of cheating fate—which Oedipus attempts by leaving his place of birth—is an actual practice among the primitive tribes described by Frazer in *The Golden Bough*. "Imitative magic is called in to annul an evil omen by accomplishing it in mimicry. The effect is to circumvent destiny by substituting a mock calamity for a real one. In Madagascar . . . every man's fortune is determined by the day or hour of his birth, and if that happens to be an unlucky one his fate is sealed, unless the mischief can be extracted, as the phrase goes, by means of a substitute."

The ancients did not doubt that men could choose and, through choice, exercise some control over the disposition of their lives. Tacitus, for example, while admitting that "most men . . . cannot part with the belief that each person's future is fixed from his very birth," claims that "the wisest of the ancients . . . leave us the capacity of choosing our life." At the same time he recognizes an order of events beyond man's power to control, although he finds no agreement regarding its cause—whether it depends "on wandering stars" or "primary elements, and on a combination of natural causes." For his own part, Tacitus declares, "I suspend my judgment" on the question "whether it is fate and unchangeable necessity or chance which governs the revolutions of human affairs." In so doing, he grants the possibility that not everything which lies beyond man's control is fated. Some of the things which happen without man's willing them may happen by chance or fortune.

It is sometimes supposed that "fate" and "fortune" are synonyms, or that one has a tragic and the other a happy connotation. It is as if fortune were always good and fate always malevolent. But either may be good or evil from the point of view of man's desires. Although fate and fortune are hardly the same, there is some reason for associating them. Each imposes a limitation on man's freedom. A man cannot compel fortune to smile upon him any more than he can avoid his fate. Though alike in this respect, fate and fortune are also opposed to one another. Fate represents the inexorable march of events. There is no room for fortune unless some things are exempt from necessity. Only that which can happen by chance is in the lap of fortune.

It would seem that fate stands to fortune as the necessary to the contingent. If everything were necessitated, fate alone would reign. Contingency would be excluded from nature. Chance or the fortuitous in the order of nature and freedom in human life would be reduced to illusions men cherish only through ignorance of the inevitable.

In a sense fortune is the ally of freedom in the struggle against fate. Good fortune seems to aid and abet human desires. But even misfortune signifies the element of chance which is more congenial than fate, if not more amenable, to man's conceit that he can freely plan his life.

THE TERMS *necessity* and *contingency* cannot be substituted for *fate* and *fortune* without loss of significance. As the chapter on NECESSITY AND CONTINGENCY indicates, they are terms in the philosophical analysis of the order of nature and causality. They may have, but they need not have, theological implications. Necessity and contingency can be explained without any reference to the supernatural, as is evident from the discussion of these matters in the chapter on CHANCE. But fate and fortune, in their origin at least, are theological terms.

In ancient poetry and mythology, both inevitability and chance were personified as deities or supernatural forces. There were the goddess of Fortune and the three Fates, as well as their three evil sisters or counterparts, the Furies. The Latin word from which "fate" comes means an oracle, and so signifies what is divinely ordained. What happens by fate is *fated*—something destined and decreed in the councils of the gods on Olympus; or it may be the decision of Zeus, to whose rule all the other divinities are subject; or, as we shall see presently, it may be a supernatural destiny which even Zeus cannot set aside.

In any case, the notion of fate implies a supernatural will, even as destiny implies predestination by an intelligence able not only to plan the future but also to carry out that plan. The inevitability of fate and destiny is thus distinguished from that of merely natural necessity which determines the future only insofar as it may be the inevitable consequence of causes working naturally.

But the ancients do not seem to be fatalists in the extreme sense of the term. To the extent that men can propitiate the gods or provoke divine jealousy and anger, the attitudes and deeds of men seem to be a determining factor in the actions of the gods. To the extent that the gods align themselves on opposite sides of a human conflict (as in *The Iliad*), or oppose each other (as in *The Odyssey*), it may be thought that what happens on earth merely reflects the shifting balance of power among the gods.

But human planning and willing do not seem to be excluded by the divine will and plan which are forged out of the quarrels of the gods. On the contrary, polytheism seems to make fortune itself contingent on the outcome of the Olympian conflict, and so permits men a certain latitude of self-determination. Men can struggle against the gods precisely because the gods may be with them as well as against them.

The ultimate power of Zeus to decide the issue may, however, place the accent on fate rather than on freedom. This is certainly so if Zeus is not the master of even his own fate, much less the omnipotent ruler among the gods or the arbiter of human destiny. In *Prometheus Bound,* the Chorus asks, "Who then is the steersman of necessity?" Prometheus answers, "The triple-formed Fates and the remembering Furies." The Chorus then asks, "Is Zeus weaker than these?" To which Prometheus replies, "Yes, for he, too, cannot escape what is fated." When they ask what this doom is, Prometheus tells them to inquire no more, for they verge on mysteries. Later Zeus himself sends Hermes to wrest from Prometheus the secret of what has been ordained for him by "all consummating Fate" or "Fate's resistless law." Prometheus refuses, saying that "me he shall not bend by all this to tell him who is fated to drive him from his tyranny."

The question Aeschylus leaves unanswered is whether Zeus would be able to escape his doom if he could foresee what Fate holds in store for him. The suggestion seems to be that without omniscience the omnipotence of Zeus cannot break the chains of Fate.

IN THE TRADITION of Judeo-Christian theology the problem of fate is in part verbal and in part real. The verbal aspect of the problem concerns the meaning of the word "fate" in relation to the divine will, providence, and predestination. With the verbal matter settled, there remains the real problem of God's will and human freedom. The strictly monotheistic conception of an omnipotent and omniscient God deepens the mystery and makes it more difficult than the problem of fate and freedom in pagan thought.

If anyone "calls the will or the power of God itself by the name of fate," Augustine says, "let him keep his opinion, but correct his language . . . For when men hear that word, according to the ordinary use of language, they simply understand by it the virtue of that particular position of the stars which may exist at the time when anyone is born or conceived, which some separate altogether from the will of God, whilst others affirm that this also is dependent on that will. But those who are of the opinion that, apart from the will of God, the stars determine what we shall do, or what good things we shall possess, or what evils we shall suffer, must be refused a hearing by all, not only by those who hold the true religion, but by those who wish to be the worshippers of any gods whatsoever, even false gods. For what does this opinion really amount to but this, that no god whatsoever is to be worshipped or prayed to?"

Since the word "fate" has been used for those things which are determined apart from the will of God or man, Augustine thinks it would be better for Christians not to use it, but to substitute "providence" or "predestination" when they wish to refer to what God wills. Aquinas, however, retains the word "fate" but restricts its meaning to the "ordering . . . of mediate causes" by which God wills "the production of certain effects."

According to the definition given by Boethius which Aquinas quotes, "Fate is a disposition inherent to changeable things, by which providence connects each one with its proper order." Thus fate is not identified with providence but made subordinate to it. The distinction, Aquinas explains, depends on the way we consider "the ordering of effects" by God. "As being in God Himself . . . the ordering of the effects is called Providence." But "as

being in the mediate causes ordered by God," it is called fate. While admitting that "the divine power or will can be called fate, as being the cause of fate," he declares that "essentially fate is the very disposition or *series, i.e.,* order, of second causes."

The position Lucretius takes seems to be exactly opposite to that of Augustine and Aquinas. Lucretius condemns the fatalism of those who believe that the gods control the order of nature and who therefore attribute whatever befalls them to divine ordination. For him, "nature has no tyrants over her,/ But always acts of her own will; she has/No part of any godhead whatsoever." He tries to teach men that everything happens according to the laws of nature, *other than which there is no fate.* The decrees of fate lie in the laws by which "a new motion always has to come/ Out of an old one, by fixed law." If man by his free will can "cause new moves which break/ The laws of fate," in order that cause does not follow cause, it is because in the atoms of his makeup "there has to be some other cause for motion," which Lucretius believes to be the "ever-so-slight atomic swerve/At no fixed time, at no fixed place whatever."

Nevertheless, according to Augustine, Lucretius is a fatalist who disbelieves in providence, *other than which there is no fate.* Each of them uses the word "fate," the one to deny, the other to affirm, the power of God.

But even if a Christian avoids the superstitions of astrology, or some similar belief in a natural necessity which does not depend on God, he may still commit the sin of fatalism which follows from the denial of man's free will. Understanding fate as identical with providence, the Christian is a fatalist if, in the belief that every human act is foreordained by God, he resigns himself to his fate, making no moral effort and taking no moral responsibility for his soul's welfare. To do that is to argue like Chaucer's Troilus:

"Since all that comes, comes by necessity,
Thus to be lost is but my destiny.
And certainly, I know it well," he cried,
"That, in His foresight, Providence Divine
Forever has seen me losing my Criseyde,
(Since God sees everything) and things combine
As He disposes them in His design

According to their merits, and their station
Is as it shall be, by predestination."

Troilus sees no way of avoiding the conclusion that free choice is an illusion.

THE CHRISTIAN THEOLOGIANS, including Calvin as well as Augustine and Aquinas, recognize the difficulty of reconciling providence and free will. The truth must lie somewhere between two heresies. If it is heresy to deny God's omnipotence and omniscience, then nothing remains outside the all-encompassing scope of divine providence, nothing happens contrary to the divine will, no future contingency is or can be unforeseen by God. If, on the other hand, to deny that man sins freely means that God must be responsible for the evil that man does, then it is a heresy to deny free will, for that imputes evil to God.

This is the problem with which Milton deals in *Paradise Lost,* announcing that he will try "to justify the ways of God to man." In a conversation in heaven, the Father tells the Son that though He knows Adam will disobey his rule, Adam remains quite free to sin or not to sin, and the fault is his own, just as the rebellious angels acted on their own free will. The angels, God says,

So were created, nor can justly accuse
Thir maker, or thir making, or thir Fate;
As if Predestination over-rul'd
Thir will, dispos'd by absolute Decree
Or high foreknowledge; they themselves decreed
Thir own revolt, not I: if I foreknew,
Foreknowledge had no influence on their fault,
Which had no less prov'd certain unforeknown.
So without least impulse or shadow of Fate,
Or aught by me immutablie foreseen,
They trespass, Authors to themselves in all,
Both what they judge and what they choose; for so
I formed them free, and free they must remain,
Till they enthrall themselves: I else must change
Thir nature, and revoke the high Decree
Unchangeable, Eternal, which ordain'd
Thir freedom, they themselves ordain'd their fall.

A solution of the problem is sometimes developed from the distinction between God's foreknowledge and God's foreordination. God foreordained the freedom of man, but only foreknew his fall; man ordained that himself. Strictly speaking, however, the word "foreknowledge" would seem to carry a false connotation, since nothing is future to God. Everything that has ever happened or ever will is simultaneously together in the eternal present of the divine vision.

During his ascent through Paradise, Dante, wishing to learn about his immediate future, asks his ancestor Cacciaguida to foretell his fortune, for he, "gazing upon the Point to which all times are present," can see "contingent things before they exist in themselves." Cacciaguida prefaces his prediction of Dante's exile from Florence by telling him that the contingency of material things "is all depicted in the Eternal Vision. Yet thence it takes not necessity, any more than from the eyes in which it is mirrored does a ship which is going down the stream." The difference between time and eternity is conceived as permitting the temporal future to be contingent even though God knows its content with certitude.

But, it may still be asked, does not God's knowledge imply the absolute predestination of future events by providence, since what God knows with certitude cannot happen otherwise than as He knows it? In a discussion of divine grace and man's free will, Dr. Johnson remarks, "I can judge with great probability how a man will act in any case, without his being restrained by my judging. God may have this probability increased to certainty." To which Boswell replies that "when it is increased to *certainty,* freedom ceases, because that cannot be certainly foreknown, which is not certain at the time; but if it be certain at the time, it is a contradiction to maintain that there can be afterwards any contingency dependent upon the exercise of will or anything else."

Against such difficulties Aquinas insists that divine providence is compatible, not only with natural necessity, but also with contingency in nature and free will in human acts. Providence, he writes, "has prepared for some things necessary causes so that they happen of necessity; for others contingent causes, that they may happen by contingency." Human liberty does not imply that the will's acts are not caused by God who, being the first cause, "moves causes both natural and voluntary. Just as by moving natural causes, He does not prevent their acts being natural, so by moving voluntary causes, He does not deprive their actions of being voluntary." God causes man to choose freely and freely to execute his choice.

THE UNCOMPROMISING conception of fate is that which leaves no place for chance or freedom anywhere in the universe, neither in the acts of God, nor in the order of nature, nor in the course of history. The doctrine of absolute determinism, whether in theology, science, or history, is thus fatalism unqualified.

The ancient historians are not fatalists in this sense. Herodotus, for example, finds much that can be explained by the contingencies of fortune or by the choices of men. The crucial decision, for example, in the defense of Athens is presented as an act of man's choice. Upon receiving the prophecy that "safe shall the wooden wall continue for thee and thy children," the Athenians exercise their freedom by disagreeing about its meaning. "Certain of the old men," Herodotus writes, "were of the opinion that the god meant to tell them the citadel would escape; for this was anciently defended by a palisade . . . Others maintained that the fleet was what the god pointed at; and their advice was that nothing should be thought of except the ships." The eloquence of Themistocles carried the latter view. To stress its importance, the historian observes that "the saving of Greece" lay in the decision that led Athens to "become a maritime power."

In presenting a comparable decision by the Persians, Herodotus seems to be contrasting their fatalism with the freedom of the Greeks. At first Xerxes accepts the council of Artabanus not to go to war against the Greeks. But after a series of visions, which appear to both the king and his councillor, that decision is reversed, for, according to the dream, the war "is fated to happen."

The conception of fate and freedom in *The Aeneid* seems closer to the Greek than to the Persian view. Even though the consummation of history, which will come with the founding of the Roman empire, is projected as a divinely appointed destiny, the hero who brings that great event to pass acts as if he were free to accept or evade his responsibilities.

The Christian understanding of historical destiny in terms of providence permits—more than that, requires—men to exercise free choice at every turn. "The cause of the greatness of the Roman empire," writes Augustine, "is neither fortuitous nor fatal, according to the judgment or opinion of those who call those things *fortuitous* which either have no causes or such causes as do not proceed from some intelligible order, and those things *fatal* which happen independently of the will of God and man, by the necessity of a certain *order* . . . Human kingdoms are established by divine providence." The fatalism which Augustine here condemns involves independence not only of the will of God, but of man's will also.

It is only in modern times, with Hegel and Marx, that necessity reigns supreme in the philosophy of history. Hegel spurns the notion that history is "a superficial play of casual, so-called 'merely human' strivings and passions." He also condemns those who "speak of Providence and the plan of Providence" in a way that is "empty" of ideas since "for them the plan of Providence is inscrutable and incomprehensible." For Hegel, history is "the necessary development, out of the concept of the mind's freedom alone." But this development and this freedom are entirely matters of necessity as far as individuals and their works are concerned. "They are all the time the unconscious tools and organs of the world mind at work within them."

For Marx, history seems likewise to have the same necessity. He deals with individuals, he writes in the preface to *Capital,* "only in so far as they are the personifications of economic categories, embodiments of particular class-relations and class-interests. My standpoint," he says, is one from which "the evolution of the economic formation of society is viewed as a process of natural history," and within which the individual cannot be "responsible for relations whose creature he socially remains, however much he may subjectively raise himself above them." Here it is a question only "of these laws themselves, of these tendencies working with iron necessity towards inevitable results."

According to the historical determinism of Hegel and Marx, which is further considered in the chapter on HISTORY, men play a part which is already written for them in the scroll of history. Human liberty apparently depends on man's knowledge of and acquiescence in the unfolding necessities.

HISTORICAL DETERMINISM is merely a part of the doctrine of a causal necessity which governs all things. Causality seems to be understood by moderns like Spinoza, Hume, and Freud as excluding the possibility of chance or free will. Among the ancients, Plotinus alone seems to go as far as Spinoza in affirming the universal reign of natural necessity. What Spinoza says of God or Nature, Plotinus says of the All-One, namely, that for the first principle which is the cause of everything else, freedom consists in being *causa sui,* or cause of itself—self-determined rather than determined by external causes.

"God does not act from freedom of the will," Spinoza writes. Yet "God alone is a free cause, for God alone exists . . . and acts from the necessity of his own nature." As for everything else in the universe, Spinoza maintains that "there is nothing contingent, but all things are determined from the necessity of the divine nature to exist and act in a certain manner." This applies to man, who, according to Spinoza, does "everything by the will of God alone."

From quite different premises, Hume seems to reach much the same conclusion concerning chance and liberty. "Chance," he writes, "when strictly examined, is a mere negative word, and means not any real power which has anywhere a being in nature." But he also thinks that liberty, "when opposed to necessity, not to constraint, is the same thing with chance."

Hume embraces the consequences of such a position. "If voluntary action be subjected to the same laws of necessity with the operations of matter, there is a continued chain of necessary causes, pre-ordained and pre-determined, reaching from the original cause of all to every single volition of every human creature. No contingency anywhere in the universe; no indifference; no liberty."

When confronted with the objection that it then becomes impossible "to explain distinctly, how the Deity can be the mediate cause of all the actions of men, without being the author of sin and moral turpitude," Hume replies that "these are mysteries, which natural and unassisted reason is very unfit to handle . . . To defend absolute decrees, and yet free the Deity from being the author of sin, has been found hitherto to exceed all the power of philosophy."

Unlike Spinoza and Hume, Freud does not deal with the theological implications or presuppositions of determinism. For him, determinism is an essential postulate of science and even to some extent a scientifically discoverable fact. The "deeply rooted belief in psychic freedom and choice," he writes, is "quite unscientific, and it must give ground before the claims of a determinism which governs even mental life." He thinks it can be shown on the basis of clinical experience that every psychic association "will be strictly determined by important inner attitudes of mind, which are unknown to us at the moment when they operate, just as much unknown as are the disturbing tendencies which cause errors, and those tendencies which bring about so-called 'chance' actions."

The fatalism of what is often called "scientific determinism" is that of blind necessity. It not only eliminates liberty and chance but also purpose and the operation of final causes. Every future event, in nature, history, or human behavior, is completely predetermined by efficient causes—predetermined, but not predestined, for there is no guiding intelligence at work, no purpose to be fulfilled. "The system of *fatality,* of which Spinoza is the accredited author," Kant writes, is one which "eliminates all *trace of design,* and leaves the original ground of the things of nature divested of all intelligence."

Whether such complete fatalism is the only doctrine compatible with the principles and findings of natural science has been questioned by philosophers like William James. It is certainly not the only doctrine compatible with the view that nothing happens without a cause. As the chapters on CHANCE and WILL

show, ancient and medieval thinkers who affirm contingency in nature or freedom in human acts do so without denying the universal
reign of causation.

28

Form

INTRODUCTION

THE great philosophical issues concerning form and matter have never been resolved. But the terms in which these issues were stated, from their first formulation in antiquity to the 17th or 18th centuries, have disappeared or at least do not have general currency in contemporary discourse. Kant is perhaps the last great philosopher to include these terms in his basic vocabulary. The conceptions of matter and form, he writes, "lie at the foundation of all other reflection, so inseparably are they connected with every mode of exercising the understanding. The former denotes the determinable in general, the second its determination."

The word "form" is no longer a pivotal term in the analysis of change or motion, nor in the distinction between being and becoming, nor in the consideration of the modes of being and the conditions of knowledge. The word "matter" is now used without reference to form, where earlier in the tradition all of its principal meanings involved "form" as a correlative or an opposite. Other words, such as "participation" and "imitation," have also fallen into disuse or lost the meanings which derived from their relation to form and matter.

The problems which these words were used to state and discuss remain active in contemporary thought. There is, for instance, the problem of the universal and the particular, the problem of the immutable and the mutable, the problem of the one and the many, or of sameness and diversity. These problems appear in the writings of William James and Bergson, Dewey and Santayana, Whitehead and Russell. Sometimes there is even a verbal approximation to the traditional formulation, as in Whitehead's doctrine of "eternal ob-jects" or in Santayana's consideration of the "realm of essence" and the "realm of matter." Whatever expressions they use, these thinkers find themselves opposed on issues which represent part, if not the whole, of the great traditional controversy between Plato and Aristotle concerning form.

THERE IS A TENDENCY AMONG the historians of thought to use the names of Plato and Aristotle to symbolize a basic opposition in philosophical perspectives and methods, or even in what James calls "intellectual temperaments." Later writers are called "Platonists" or "Aristotelians" and doctrines or theories are classified as Platonic or Aristotelian. It almost seems to be assumed at times that these names exhaust the typical possibilities: that minds or theories must be one or the other, or some sort of mixture or confusion of the two.

If this tendency is ever justified, it seems to be warranted with regard to the problems of form. Here, if anywhere, there may be poetic truth in Whitehead's remark that the history of western thought can be read as a series of footnotes to Plato; though perhaps the observation should be added that Aristotle, the first to comment on Plato, wrote many of the principal footnotes. In Plotinus the two strains seem to be intermingled. The issue between Plato and Aristotle concerning form dominates the great metaphysical and theological controversies of the later Middle Ages, and, with some alterations in language and thought, it appears in the writings of Hobbes, Francis Bacon, Descartes, Spinoza, and Locke, where it is partly a continuation of, and partly a reaction against, the medieval versions of Platonic and Aristotelian doctrine.

The most extreme reaction is, of course, to be found in those who completely reject the term *form* or its equivalents as being without significance for the problems of motion, existence, or knowledge. Bacon retains the term, but radically changes its meaning. "None should suppose from the great part assigned by us to forms," Bacon writes, "that we mean such forms as the meditations and thoughts of men have hitherto been accustomed to." He does not mean either "the concrete forms" or "any abstract forms of ideas," but rather "the laws and regulations of simple action . . . The form of heat or form of light, therefore, means no more than the law of heat or the law of light." But Hobbes and Locke tend to reject the term itself—especially when it occurs in the notion of substantial form—as meaningless or misleading.

"We are told," says Hobbes, "there be in the world certain essences, separated from bodies, which they call *abstract essences, and substantial forms* . . . Being once fallen into this error of *separated essences,* [men] are thereby necessarily involved in many other absurdities that follow it. For seeing they will have these forms to be real, they are obliged to assign them *some place*"; which they cannot succeed in doing, according to Hobbes, "because they hold them incorporeal, without all dimension of quantity, and all men know that place is dimension, and not to be filled but by that which is corporeal."

With regard to *substantial form,* Locke declares, "I confess I have no idea at all, but only of the sound 'form.' " Those "who have been taught . . . that it was those *forms* which made the distinction of substances into their true species and genera, were led yet further out of the way by having their minds set upon fruitless inquiries after 'substantial forms' "—a subject which Locke regards as "wholly unintelligible."

Since form and matter are supposed to be correlative, the denial to form of meaning or reality leads to materialism, as in the case of Hobbes—the affirmation of matter alone as a principle or cause. Materialists of one sort or another are the opponents of both Plato and Aristotle, and of Platonists and Aristotelians.

That part of the controversy is discussed in the chapter on MATTER. Here we are concerned with the issues arising from different views of form and its relation to matter.

THE POPULAR meaning of "form" affords an approach to the subtleties of the subject. As ordinarily used, "form" connotes figure or shape. That connotation expresses one aspect of the technical significance of "form." A great variety of things, differing materially and in other respects, can have the *same* figure or shape. The same form can be embodied in an indefinite number of otherwise different individuals. But figures or shapes are sensible forms, forms perceptible to vision and touch. To identify form with figure or shape would put an improper limitation on the meaning of form. This is popularly recognized in the consideration of the form of a work of art—the structure of an epic poem or a symphony—which seems to be more a matter of understanding than of direct sense-perception.

Russell's definition of the form of a proposition effectively illustrates the point involved. The form of a proposition, he says, is that which remains the same in a statement when everything else is changed. For example, these two statements have the same grammatical and logical form: (1) *John followed James,* and (2) *Paul accompanied Peter.* What might be called the matter or subject matter of the two statements is completely different, but both have the same form, as may an indefinite number of other statements.

This illustration helps us to grasp the meaning of form, and the distinction between form and matter, or the formal and the material aspects of anything. It is thus that we understand the phrase "formal logic" to signify a study of the forms of thought or discourse, separated from the subject matter being thought about or discussed. Similarly, abstractionism or surrealism is a kind of formalism in painting which tries to separate visible patterns or structures from their representative significance or their reference to familiar objects.

Kant's doctrine of space and time as transcendental forms of intuition exemplifies the meaning of form as pure order or structure divorced from sensuous content. "That which in the phenomenon corresponds to the sensation, I term its *matter*," he writes; "that which effects that the content of the phenomenon can be arranged under certain relations, I call its *form*." Sometimes the consideration of form emphasizes not its separation from, but its union with matter. The form dwells in the thing, constituting its nature. The sensible or intelligible characteristics of a thing result from the various ways in which its matter has been formed.

It is impossible to say more about the meaning of *form* without facing at once the great controversy between Plato and Aristotle and the difficulties which their theories confront.

PLATO DOES NOT deny that things—the sensible, material, changing things of experience—have something like form. Nor does he deny that the ideas by which we understand the natures of things are like forms. Rather he asks us to consider that which they are *like*.

In the *Phaedo*—only one of the many dialogues in which the doctrine of forms is discussed—Socrates argues that "there is such a thing as equality, not of one piece of wood or stone with another, but that, over and above this, there is absolute equality." Socrates gets Simmias to admit that "we know the nature of this absolute essence," and then asks, "Whence did we obtain our knowledge?" It could not have been obtained from the pieces of wood or stone, Socrates tries to show, because they "appear at one time equal, and at another time unequal," whereas the idea of equality is never the same as that of inequality. Hence he thinks "we must have known equality previously to the time when we first saw the material equals . . . Before we began to see or hear or perceive in any way, we must have had a knowledge of absolute equality, or we could not have referred to that standard the equals which are derived from the senses." The equality which supplies the "standard" by which material equals are measured is the Form or Idea of equality.

What is true in this one case Socrates thinks is true in every other. Whether we consider the "essence of equality, beauty, or anything else,"

Socrates holds, the "Ideas or essences, which in the dialectical process we define as . . . true existences . . . are each of them always what they are, having the same simple self-existent and unchanging forms, not admitting of variation at all, or in any way or at any time." Apart from the perishable things of the sensible world, and apart from the ideas which are involved in our process of learning and thinking, there exist the Forms or the Ideas themselves—the immutable objects of our highest knowledge.

Because the same English words are employed in these quite distinct senses, it is useful to follow the convention of translators who capitalize the initial letter when "Form" or "Idea" refers to that which is separate from the characteristics of material things and from the ideas in our mind. The words "Form" and "Idea" are interchangeable, but the words "Idea" and "idea" are not. The latter refers to a notion in the human mind, by which it knows; whereas "Idea"—as Plato uses the word—signifies the object of knowledge, *i.e.,* that which is known. These differences are further discussed in the chapter on IDEA.

By imitating the Forms, sensible things, according to Plato, have the characteristics we apprehend in them. The ideas we have when we apprehend the resemblance between sensible things and their Forms (which sensible things exhibit) would seem to be indirect apprehensions of the Forms themselves. When in *The Republic* Socrates discusses knowledge and opinion, he distinguishes them from one another according to a division of their objects—the realm of intelligible being on the one hand, and the realm of sensible becoming on the other. The latter stands to the former as image or copy to reality, and Socrates finds this relationship repeating itself when he further divides each of the two parts. The realm of becoming divides into images or shadows and into that "of which this is only the resemblance," namely, "the animals which we see, and everything that grows or is made." The realm of intelligible being he also subdivides into two parts, of which the first is as an image or reflection of the second, namely, the hypotheses we form in our minds and the Ideas or Forms themselves.

From this it appears that just as we should regard the form of the thing as an imitation of, or participation in, the separate Form, so should we regard the idea we have (that is, our understanding of the thing) as an approximation of the Idea. The Ideas are outside the human mind even as the Forms are separate from their sensible, material imitations. When we apprehend things by reason we know the Forms they imitate; when we apprehend them by our senses we know them as imitations, or as images of the Ideas.

THE PLATONIC THEORY changes the ordinary meaning of the word "imitation." We ordinarily think of imitation as involving a relation of resemblance between two sensible things, both of which we are able to perceive; for example, we say that a child imitates his father's manner, or that a portrait resembles the person who posed for it. The painter, according to Socrates in *The Republic,* is not the only "creator of appearances." He compares the painter who pictures a bed with the carpenter who makes one.

Like the bed in the painting, the bed made by the carpenter is not the real bed. It is not, says Socrates, the Idea "which, according to our view, is the essence of the bed." The carpenter "cannot make true existence, but only some semblance of existence." As the bed in the picture is an imitation of the particular bed made by the carpenter, so the latter is an imitation of the Idea—the essential *bed-ness* which is the model or archetype of all particular beds.

Shifting to another example, we can say that a statue, which resembles a particular man, is the imitation of an imitation, for the primary imitation lies in the resemblance between the particular man portrayed and the Form or Idea, Man. Just as the statue derives its distinctive character from the particular man it imitates, so that particular man, or any other, derives his manhood or humanity from Man. Just as the particular man imitates Man, so our idea of Man is also an imitation of that Idea. Knowledge, according to Plato, consists in the imitation of Ideas, even as sensible, material things have whatever being they have by imitation of the true beings, the Forms.

Another name for the primary type of imitation is "participation." To participate in is to partake of. In the dialogue in which Plato has the young Socrates inquiring into the relation between sensible particulars and the Ideas or Forms, Parmenides tells him that "there are certain ideas of which all other things partake, and from which they derive their names; that similars, for example, become similar, because they partake of similarity; and great things become great, because they partake of greatness; and that just and beautiful things become just and beautiful, because they partake of justice and beauty." The Forms or Ideas are, Parmenides suggests, "patterns fixed in nature, and other things are like them, and resemblances of them—what is meant by the participation of other things in the ideas, is really assimilation to them."

The fact of particularity and multiplicity seems to be inseparable from the fact of participation. That in which the many particulars participate must, on the other hand, have universality and unity. The Forms or Ideas are universals in the sense that each is a one which is somehow capable of being in a many—by resemblance or participation. Parmenides asks Socrates whether he thinks that "the whole idea is one, and yet, being one, is in each one of the many." When Socrates unhesitatingly says Yes, Parmenides points out to him that we then confront the difficulty that "one and the same thing will exist as a whole at the same time in many separate individuals" and that "the ideas themselves will be divisible, and things which participate in them will have a part of them only and not the whole idea existing in each of them." Nor can we say, Socrates is made to realize, that "the one idea is really divisible and yet remains one."

THIS DIFFICULTY concerning the relation of particulars to the Ideas they participate in, is discussed in the chapter on UNIVERSAL AND PARTICULAR. It is not the only difficulty which Plato himself finds in the theory of Ideas. Another concerns the individuality of each of the indefinite number of particulars which copy a single model or archetype. What makes the various copies of the same model different from one another?

Plato meets this problem by adding a third principle. To the intelligible patterns or archetypes and their sensible imitations, he adds, in the *Timaeus,* the principle which is variously named, sometimes "the receptacle," sometimes "space," sometimes "matter." However named, it is the absolutely formless, for "that which is to receive all Forms should have no form . . . The mother and receptacle of all visible and in any way sensible things . . . is an invisible and formless being which receives all things and in some mysterious way partakes of the intelligible, and is most incomprehensible."

It is this material or receiving principle which somehow accounts for the numerical plurality and the particularization of the many copies of the one absolute model. When a number of replicas of the same pattern are produced by impressing a die on a sheet of plastic material at different places, it is the difference in the material at the several places which accounts for the plurality and particularity of the replicas. Yet the one die is responsible for the character common to them all.

The sensible things of any one sort are not only *particular* because the Form they imitate is somehow received in matter; they are also *perishable* because of that fact. The receptacle is the principle of generation or of change. It is, Timaeus says, "the natural recipient of all impressions," which is "stirred and informed by them, and appears different from time to time by reason of them, but the forms which enter into and go out of her are the likenesses of real existences modelled after their patterns in a wonderful and inexplicable manner."

Matter, as Plato here suggests, is the mother of changing things, things which, between coming to be and passing away, are what they are because of the unchanging Forms. The Form which is received in matter for a time makes the changing thing an *imitation,* as the matter in which the Form is received makes the changing thing a *participation.*

The admittedly mysterious partaking of the Forms by the formless receptacle constitutes the realm of becoming, in which being and nonbeing are mixed. But the Forms or Ideas themselves, existing apart from their sensible imitations, are "uncreated and indestructible, never receiving anything from without, nor going out to any other, but invisible and imperceptible by any sense." They constitute the realm of pure being. They are the intelligible reality.

What Plato calls the eternal Forms and treats as the modes of actual being rather than becoming, Whitehead calls eternal objects and treats as modes of possible being. "The metaphysical status of an eternal object," he writes, "is that of a possibility for an actuality. Every actual occasion is defined as to its character by how these possibilities are actualised for that occasion. Thus actualisation is a selection among possibilities."

THE CRITICISM OF the Forms or Ideas which we find in the writings of Aristotle is primarily directed against their separate existence. "Plato was not far wrong," Aristotle says, "when he said that there are as many Forms as there are kinds of natural object"; but he immediately adds the qualification: "if there *are* Forms distinct from the things of this earth." It is precisely that supposition which Aristotle challenges.

Aristotle's criticism of Plato stems from his own notion of substance, and especially from his conception of sensible substances as composed of matter and form. He uses the word "substance" to signify that which exists in and of itself; or, in other words, that which exists separately from other things. Hence, when he says that, in addition to sensible substances, "Plato posited two kinds of substances—the Forms and the objects of mathematics," he is translating the affirmation that the Forms have being separately from the sensible world of changing things, into an assertion that they are substances.

"Socrates did not make the universals or the definitions exist apart," Aristotle writes; but referring to the Platonists, he says, "*they,* however, gave them separate existence, and this was the kind of thing they called Ideas." What proof is there, he repeatedly asks, for the separate existence of the Forms, or universals, or the objects of mathematics? "Of the various ways in which it is proved that the

Forms exist," he declares, "none is convincing." Furthermore, he objects to the statement that "all other things come from the Forms"; for "to say that they are patterns and the other things share in them is to use empty words and poetical metaphors." There is the additional difficulty, he thinks, that "there will be several patterns of the same thing, and therefore several Forms; *e.g.,* 'animal' and 'two-footed' and also 'man himself' will be Forms of man."

Aristotle's denial of separate existence, or substantiality, to the Ideas or universals stands side by side with his affirmation of the place of forms in the being of substances and the role of universals in the order of knowledge. Furthermore, he limits his denial of the substantiality of Ideas to those Forms which seem to be the archetypes or models of sensible things. Particular physical things—familiar sensible substances, such as the stone, the tree, or the man—are not, in his opinion, imitations of or participations in universal models which exist apart from these things. He leaves it an open question whether there are self-subsistent Forms or Ideas—that is, purely intelligible substances—which do not function as the models for sensible things to imitate.

Stated positively, the Aristotelian theory consists in two affirmations. The first is that the characteristics of things are determined by "indwelling forms," which have their being not apart from but in the things themselves. To illustrate his meaning he turns to the realm of art. When we make a brass sphere, he writes, "we bring the form," which is a sphere, "into this particular matter," the brass, and "the result is a brazen sphere." There is no "sphere apart from the individual spheres," and no brass apart from the particular lumps of metal that are brass. "The 'form' means the 'such,' and is not a 'this'—a definite thing," such as *this* individual brazen sphere.

Aristotle analyzes natural things in the same manner. It is from "the indwelling form and the matter," he says, that "the concrete substance is derived." Men such as Callias or Socrates, for example, consist of "such and such a form in this flesh and in these bones," and "they are different in virtue of their matter (for that is different) but the same in form."

The flesh and bones of Callias are not the flesh and bones of Socrates; but though different as *individual* men, they are the same as *men* because they have the same form.

The second point is that our understanding of things involves the forms of things, but now somehow in the intellect rather than in the things themselves. In order to know things, Aristotle says, we must have within us "either the things themselves or their forms. The former alternative is of course impossible: it is not the stone which is present in the soul," he maintains, "but its form."

The form in the thing is as individual as the thing itself. But in the mind, as the result of the intellect's power to abstract this form from its matter, the form becomes a universal; it is then called by Aristotle an "idea," "abstraction," or "concept." Forms are universals in the mind alone. If there were a form existing apart from both matter and mind, it would be neither an individual form nor an abstract universal.

The indwelling forms, according to Aristotle, are not universals. Except for the possibility of Forms which dwell apart and bear *no resemblance at all* to sensible things, all forms are either in matter or, abstracted from matter, in the human mind. These are often called "material forms" because they are the forms which matter takes or can take, and which the mind abstracts from matter. Their being consists in informing or determining matter, just as the being of matter consists in the capacity to receive these forms and to be determined by them.

THE FOREGOING helps to explain Aristotle's use of the word "composite" as a synonym for "substance" when he is considering particular sensible things. The independently existing, individual physical things which Aristotle calls "substances" are all composite of form and matter. He sometimes also calls form and matter "substances," but when he uses the word "substance" strictly and in its primary sense, he applies it only to the concrete individual. Form and matter are only principles or constituents of the concrete thing—the composite substance.

The union of form and matter to constitute physical substances also explains the Aristotelian identification of form with actuality and of matter with potentiality; and the relation of form and matter to a third term in the analysis of change, namely, *privation.* As a physical thing changes, its matter gives up one form to take on another. Its matter thus represents its capacity or *potentiality* for form. Matter is the *formable* aspect of changing things. What things are *actually* at any moment is due to the forms they possess. But they may have the potentiality for acquiring other forms, with respect to which they are in *privation.*

"Mutability," Augustine writes, "which belongs to all things that are subject to change, comprehends all the forms which those things take when changes occur in them." Change consists in a *transformation* of *matter,* which is another way of saying that it consists in the *actualization* of a thing's *potentialities.* The Aristotelian theory of form and matter is a theory of becoming as well as an analysis of the being changing things. Illustrative applications of this theory will be found in the chapters on ART, CAUSE, and CHANGE.

Some forms are sensible. Some are shapes, some are qualities, some are quantities. But not all forms are perceptible by the senses; as, for example, the form which matter takes when a plant or animal is generated and which gives the generated thing its specific nature. This type of form came to be called a "substantial form" because it determines the kind of substance which the thing is. In contrast, the forms which determine the properties or attributes of a thing are called its "accidents" or "accidental forms." For example, size and shape, color and weight, are accidental forms of a man; whereas that by virtue of which this thing (*having* a certain size, shape, and color) is a *man,* is its substantial form.

Aristotle's distinction between substantial and accidental form affects his analysis of change and his conception of matter. Generation and corruption are for him substantial change, change in which matter undergoes transformation with respect to its substantial form. The various types of motion—alter-ation, increase or decrease, and local motion—are changes which take place in enduring substances, and with respect to their accidental forms.

The substratum of accidental change is not formless matter, but matter having a certain substantial form; whereas in the coming to be or passing away of substances, the substratum would seem to be a primary sort of matter, devoid of all form. As indicated in the chapter on MATTER, this, according to Aristotle, is "the primary substratum of each thing, from which it comes to be without qualification, and which persists in the result." He tries to help us grasp prime matter by using an analogy. "As the bronze is to the statue, the wood to the bed," he writes, "so is the underlying nature to substance"—matter absolutely formless to substantial form.

Aristotle sometimes speaks of the substantial form as a first act or actuality, and of accidental forms as second actualities. Accordingly he also distinguishes between a primary and secondary kind of matter—the one absolutely potential, and underlying substantial change; the other partly actualized and partly potential, and involved in accidental change. "Primary matter," Aquinas explains, "has substantial being through its form ... But when once it exists under one form it is in potentiality to others."

Perhaps one more distinction should be mentioned because of its significance for later discussions of form. Regarding living and non-living things as essentially distinct, Aristotle differentiates between the forms constituting these two kinds of substances. As appears in the chapter on SOUL, he uses the word "soul" to name the substantial form of plants, animals, and men.

BOTH THE PLATONIC theory of the separate Forms and the Aristotelian theory of the composition of form and matter raise difficulties which their authors consider and which become the subject of intense controversy among Platonists and Aristotelians in the Hellenistic and medieval periods.

The Platonic theory faces a question which arises from supposing the existence of an eternal and immutable Form for every appearance in the sensible world of becoming. If the Idea and the individual are alike, then "some further idea of likeness will always be coming to light," Parmenides says to Socrates; "and if that be like anything else, then another; and new ideas will be always arising, if the idea resembles that which partakes of it." Because of this difficulty with the doctrine of participation, Parmenides suggests that it may be necessary to conclude that "the Idea cannot be like the individual or the individual like the Idea." In addition, the relationships of the Forms to one another presents a difficulty. Is the relation of one Form to another, Parmenides asks, determined by the essence of each Form, or by the relationships among the sensible particulars that imitate the Forms in question? Either solution seems to be unsatisfactory because of the further difficulties which both raise.

Yet, after propounding questions of this sort, and multiplying difficulties, Parmenides concludes by telling Socrates why the theory of Ideas cannot be given up. "If a man, fixing his attention on these and like difficulties," he says, "does away with the Forms of things and will not admit that every individual thing has its own determinate Idea which is always one and the same, he will have nothing on which his mind can rest; and so he will utterly destroy the power of reasoning."

The Aristotelian theory has difficulties of its own with respect to the ultimate character of matter apart from all forms. Completely formless matter would be pure potentiality and would therefore have no actual being. It would be completely unintelligible, since form is the principle of anything's intelligibility. Nevertheless, something like formless matter seems to be involved in substantial change, in contrast to the substantially formed matter which is the substratum of accidental change.

The problem of prime matter is related in later speculations to the problem of the number and order of the various forms which matter can take. The question is whether matter must have a substantial form before it can have any accidental form; and whether it can have a second substantial form in addition to a first, or is limited to having a single substantial

form, all subsequent forms necessarily being accidental.

Aquinas plainly argues in favor of the unity of substantial form. "Nothing is absolutely one" he maintains, "except by one form, by which a thing has being; because a thing has both being and unity from the same source, and therefore things which are denominated by various forms are not absolutely one; as, for instance, a white man. If, therefore," Aquinas continues, "man were *living* by one form, the vegetative soul, and *animal* by another form, the sensitive soul, and *man* by another form, the intellectual soul, it would follow that man is not absolutely one ... We must, therefore, conclude," he says, "that the intellectual soul, the sensitive soul, and the nutritive soul are in man numerically one and the same soul." In other words, "of one thing there is but one substantial form." It is not only "impossible that there be in man another substantial form besides the intellectual soul," but there is also no need of any other, because "the intellectual soul contains virtually whatever belongs to the sensitive soul of brute animals and the nutritive soul of plants."

The Aristotelian theory also has difficulties with respect to substantial forms as objects of knowledge and definition. The definition which the mind formulates attempts to state the essence of the thing defined. The formulable essence of a thing would seem to be identical with its form. But Aristotle raises the question and his followers debate at length whether the essence of a composite substance is identical with its substantial form or includes its matter as well.

Among his followers Aquinas maintains that, in defining the essence or species of a composite substance, the genus is used to signify the matter and the differentia the form. "Some held," he writes, "that the form alone belongs to the species, while the matter is part of the individual, and not of the species. This cannot be true, for to the nature of the species belongs what the definition signifies, and in natural things the definition does not signify the form only, but the form and the matter. Hence in natural things the matter is part of the species; not, indeed, signate matter, which is the principle of individuation, but common matter." He explains in another place that "matter is twofold; common and *signate,* or individual: common, such as flesh and bone; individual, such as this flesh and these bones." In forming the universal concept *man,* for example, the intellect abstracts the notion of the species "from *this flesh and these bones,* which do not belong to the species as such, but to the individual . . . But the species of *man* cannot be abstracted by the intellect from *flesh and bones.*"

As will be seen in the chapters on ONE AND MANY and UNIVERSAL AND PARTICULAR, the Platonic and the Aristotelian theories of form are equally involved in the great problem of the universal and the individual. Even though they seem to be diametrically opposed on the existence of universals—whether apart from or only in minds—both Plato and Aristotle face the necessity of explaining individuality. What makes the particular that imitates a universal Form the unique individual it is? What makes the indwelling form of a composite substance an individual form, as unique as the individual substance of which it is the form?

We have already noted that both Platonists and Aristotelians appeal to matter as somehow responsible for individuation or individuality, but that only raises further questions. The Platonists conceive matter as the receptacle of all Forms, and so in itself absolutely formless. How, then, can it cause the particularizations which must be accounted for? Since prime matter, like the receptacle, is formless, the Aristotelians resort to what they call "signate matter" or "individual matter" to explain the individuality of forms and substances; but it has been argued that this only begs the question rather than solves it.

THE CORRELATIVE terms *form* and *matter* seem to occur in modern thought under the guise of certain equivalents; as, for example, the distinct substances which Descartes calls "thought" and "extension"—*res cogitans* and *res extensa*—or the infinite attributes of substance which Spinoza calls "mind" and "body." They appear more explicitly in Kant's analysis of knowledge, related as the *a priori* and the *a posteriori* elements of experience. But it is in the great theological speculations of the Middle Ages that the most explicit and extended use of these terms is made, often with new interpretations placed on ancient theories.

The doctrine of spiritual substances, for example, has a bearing on the theory of self-subsistent Forms. The angels are sometimes called "separate forms" by the theologians. They are conceived as immaterial substances, and hence as simple rather than composite. But though Plotinus identifies the order of purely intelligible beings with the pure intelligences, the Christian theologian does not identify the Platonic Ideas with the angels. He regards the angels as intelligences. They exist as pure forms, and therefore are intelligible as well as intellectual substances. But they are in no sense the archetypes or models which sensible things resemble.

Nevertheless, Christian theology does include that aspect of the Platonic theory which looks upon the Ideas as the eternal models or patterns. But, as Aquinas points out, the separately existing Forms are replaced by what Augustine calls "the exemplars existing in the divine mind."

Aquinas remarks on the fact that "whenever Augustine, who was imbued with the doctrines of the Platonists, found in their teaching anything consistent with faith, he adopted it; and those things which he found contrary to faith he amended." He then goes on to say that Augustine could not adopt, but had to amend, the teaching of the Platonists that "the forms of things subsist of themselves apart from matter." He did this, not by denying the ideas, "according to which all things are formed," but by denying that they could exist outside the divine mind. The divine ideas are the eternal exemplars and the eternal types—*types,* Aquinas explains, insofar as they are the likenesses of things and so the principles of God's knowledge; *exemplars* insofar as they are "the principles of the making of things" in God's act of creation.

The profound mystery of the creative act which projects the divine ideas into substantial or material being replaces the older problem of how physical things derive their natures by participation in the Forms. According to the Aristotelian theory, both natural generation and artistic production involve the transformation of a preexistent matter. According to the Platonic myth of the world's origin, only changing things are created, neither the receptacle nor the Ideas. But the Christian dogma of creation excludes everything from eternity except God.

Ideas are eternal only as inseparable from the divine mind. Being spiritual *creatures,* the angels, or self-subsistent forms, are not eternal. And in the world of corporeal creatures, matter as well as its forms must begin to be with the creation of things. Since matter and its forms cannot exist in separation from one another, the theologians hold that God cannot create them separately. It cannot be supposed, Augustine says, "that God first created matter without form and then gave it form." He goes on to explain this point by the analogy of sound and song. "Song is ordered sound, and although a thing may very well exist without order, order cannot be given to a thing which does not exist . . . We do not first emit formless sounds, which do not constitute song, and then adapt them and fashion them in the form of song." Thus, God must be understood to have made the world of formless matter, but to have created the world simultaneously. God "concreates" form and matter, Augustine holds, giving form to matter's formlessness without any interval of time.

Defending Augustine's interpretation of the passage in Genesis which says that the earth, which God in the beginning created, "was unformed and void," Aquinas argues that "if formless matter preceded in duration, it already existed; for this is implied by duration . . . To say, then, that matter preceded, but without form, is to say that being existed actually, yet without actuality, which is a contradiction in terms . . . Hence we must assert that primary matter was not created altogether formless." But neither, according to Aquinas, can the form of any material thing be created apart from its matter. "Forms and other non-subsisting things, which are said to co-exist rather than to exist," he declares, "ought to be called *concreated* rather than *created* things."

Aristotle's theory of physical substances as composite of form and matter raises certain special difficulties for Christian theology. Those who, like Aquinas, adopt his theory must also adapt it to supernatural conditions when they deal with the problems of substance involved in the mystery of the Incarnation of the second person of the Trinity and the mystery of transubstantiation in the Eucharist.

Furthermore, Aristotle's identification of soul with the substantial form of a living thing makes it difficult to conceive the separate existence of the individual human soul. Again an adaptation is required. As indicated in the chapters on IMMORTALITY and SOUL, the Christian doctrine of personal survival is given an Aristotelian rendering by regarding the human soul as a form which is not completely material. Hence it is conceived as capable of self-subsistence when, with death and the dissolution of the composite nature, it is separated from the body.

29

God

INTRODUCTION

WITH the exception of certain mathematicians and physicists, almost all the authors of the great books are represented in this chapter. In sheer quantity of references, as well as in variety, it is the largest chapter. The reason is obvious. More consequences for thought and action follow from the affirmation or denial of God than from answering any other basic question. They follow for those who regard the question as answerable only by faith or only by reason, and even for those who insist upon suspending judgment entirely.

In addition to the primary question of God's existence, there are all the problems of the divine nature and of the relation of the world and man to the gods or God. The solutions of these problems cannot help influencing man's conception of the world in which he lives, the position that he occupies in it, and the life to which he is called.

The whole tenor of human life is certainly affected by whether men regard themselves as the supreme beings in the universe or acknowledge a superior—a superhuman being whom they conceive as an object of fear or love, a force to be defied or a Lord to be obeyed. Among those who acknowledge a divinity, it matters greatly whether the divine is represented merely by the concept of God— the object of philosophical speculation—or by the living God whom men worship in all the acts of piety which comprise the rituals of religion.

The most radical differences in man's conception of his own nature follow from the exclusion of divinity as its source or model on the one hand, and from the various ways in which man is seen as participating in divinity on the other. Many fundamental themes and issues are therefore common to this chapter and to the chapter on MAN.

SOME OF THE TOPICS IN this chapter are primarily philosophical. They belong to the subject matter of rational speculation or poetic imagination in all the great epochs of our culture, regardless of differences in religious belief. Other topics, however, are peculiarly restricted to matters of faith or religion. With respect to such matters, dogmatic differences, or differences in articles of faith, must be explicitly recognized.

The materials here assembled must therefore, in some instances, be divided according to their origin from pagan or from Jewish and Christian sources. Though no great books from the Muslim tradition are included in this set, the fact that Gibbon discusses the Muslim faith and compares its teachings with those of Judaism and Christianity explains the inclusion of Islam in one group of topics. That is the group which deals with the doctrines common to these three religions, as distinguished from the tenets on which Judaism and Christianity differ dogmatically. The existence of certain common beliefs in the western tradition enables us to begin, as it seems advisable to do, with the conception of God that is shared by the living religions of western culture today.

Calvin is, perhaps, more extreme than earlier Christian theologians in maintaining that the idea of God is implanted in the minds of all men everywhere. Early in his *Institutes of the Christian Religion,* he writes:

That there exists in the human mind, and indeed by natural instinct, some sense of Deity, we hold to be beyond dispute, since God himself, to prevent any man from pretending ignorance, has endued all men with some idea of his Godhead, the memory of which he constantly renews and occasionally enlarges, that all to a man, being aware that there is a God, and that he is their Maker, may be condemned by their own conscience when they neither worship him nor consecrate their lives to his service. Certainly, if there is any quarter where it may be supposed that God is unknown, the most likely for such an instance to exist is among the dullest tribes farthest removed from civilisation. But, as a heathen [Cicero] tells us, there is no nation so barbarous, no race so brutish, as not to be imbued with the conviction that there is a God. Even those who, in other respects, seem to differ least from the lower animals, constantly retain some sense of religion; so thoroughly has this common conviction possessed the mind, so firmly is it stamped on the breasts of all men. Since, then, there never has been, from the very first, any quarter of the globe, any city, any household even, without religion, this amounts to a tacit confession, that a sense of Deity is inscribed on every heart.

IN OUR CIVILIZATION, what is denied by an atheist who says there is no God? Not idols or images which men may seek to placate. Not philosophical constructions or mythological figures. Certainly not the universe itself, either as an infinite and everlasting whole, or as finite and temporal, but equally mysterious in its ultimate incomprehensibility to the human mind. In our civilization the atheist denies the existence of a supernatural being, the object of religious belief and worship among Jews, Christians, and Muslims. He denies the single, personal God Who created the world out of nothing, Who transcends this created universe and sustains it by His immanent power, Who has made laws for the government of all things and cares for each particular by His providence, and Who created man in His own image, revealed Himself and His will to men, and metes out eternal rewards and punishments to the children of Adam, whom He also helps by His grace.

In this sense of atheism, Nietzsche is the outstanding modern atheist among the authors of the great books. He is the source of the proposition that God is dead. He discusses the Bible that Jews and Christians regard as God's self-revelation, by saying that if God is its author, "he seems incapable of making himself clearly understood." Nietzsche concedes that in the west, "the religious instinct is [still] in vigorous growth"; but adds that theism is rejected "with profound mistrust."

In the religious conception of God, one term must be saved from misinterpretation. The word "personal" should not be read with anthropomorphic imagery, though its meaning does entitle man as well as God to be called a person rather than a thing. "Although the term *person* is not found applied to God in Scripture, either in the Old or New Testament," Aquinas writes, "nevertheless what the term signifies is found to be affirmed of God in many places of Scripture; as that He is the supreme self-subsisting being, and the most perfectly intelligent being."

Boethius had defined a person as "an individual substance of a rational nature," or, as Locke later said, "a thinking intelligent being." In applying the term *person* to God, in the meaning which Boethius had given it, Aquinas comments on the difference in its meaning when it is applied to men. God can be said to have a *rational nature*, he writes, only "if reason be taken to mean, not discursive thought, but, in a general sense, an intelligent nature . . . God cannot be called an *individual*" in the sense in which physical things are, but only in the sense of uniqueness. "*Substance* can be applied to God [only] in the sense of signifying self-subsistence." Aquinas does not conclude from this that "person" is said improperly of God, but rather that when God is called "personal" the meaning is applied "in a more excellent way," for God does not *possess*, God *is*, an intelligence.

We shall use this idea of a personal God, the reality of which the contemporary atheist denies, in order to distinguish divergent conceptions in other doctrines. Then we shall examine more closely what is involved in this idea itself.

IN THE WESTERN tradition, the various pagan religions—reflected especially in the poems and histories of Greek and Roman antiquity—were all polytheistic. The number of their gods, Montaigne estimates, "amounts to thirty-six thousand." Augustine offers one explanation of why there were so many. "The ancients," he writes, "being deceived either by their own conjectures or by demons, supposed that many gods must be invited to take an interest in human affairs, and assigned to each a separate function and a separate department—to one the body, to another the soul; and in the body itself, to one the head, to another the neck, and each of the other members to one of the gods; and in like manner, in the soul, to one god the natural capacity was assigned, to another education, to another anger, to another lust; and so the various affairs of life were assigned—cattle to one, corn to another, wine to another, oil to another, the woods to another, money to another, navigation to another, wars and victories to another, marriages to another, births and fecundity to another, and other things to other gods."

That polytheism, no less than monotheism, conceives the divine as personal, appears in Plato's *Apology*. When Socrates is accused of atheism, he asks whether the indictment means that he does not "acknowledge the gods which the state acknowledges, but some other new divinities or spiritual agencies in their stead." Meletus answers that he thinks Socrates is a complete atheist who recognizes no gods at all. To this Socrates replies by suggesting that his enemies must be confusing him with Anaxagoras, who had blasphemed against Apollo by calling the sun "a red hot stone." As for himself, he offers evidence to show that he believes in divine or spiritual agencies "new or old, no matter"; and "if I believe in divine beings," he asks, "how can I help believing in spirits or demigods?"

Like the one God of Judaism and Christianity, the many gods of pagan antiquity have immortal life, but they are not without origin. Zeus is the son of Kronos, and he has many offspring, both gods and demigods, who perform different functions and are not of equal station in the Olympian hierarchy. The realm of the divine includes such figures as the Titans and the Cyclops, who are neither gods nor men; and demigods, like Heracles, who are offspring of divine and human mating. These deities exercise superhuman powers, but none is completely omnipotent or omniscient, not even Kronos or Zeus who cannot escape the decrees of Fate. Moreover, with the excep-

tion, perhaps, of that of Zeus, the power of one divinity is often challenged and thwarted by another. This aspect of polytheism and its bearing on the intervention of the gods in the affairs of men are discussed in the chapter on FATE.

The extent to which we think of the pagans as idolatrous because they made graven images of their gods in human form, or regard the pagan conceptions of the gods as anthropomorphic, depends on our interpretation of religious symbolism. Plato for one thinks that many of the poets' descriptions of the gods and their activities should be dismissed as unworthy, precisely because they debase the gods to the human level.

According to Gibbon, a Greek or Roman philosopher "who considered the system of polytheism as a composition of human fraud and error, could disguise a smile of contempt under the mask of devotion, without apprehending that either the mockery or the compliance would expose him to the resentment of any invisible, or, as he conceived them, imaginary powers." But the early Christians, he points out, saw the many gods of antiquity "in a much more odious and formidable light" and held them to be "the authors, the patrons, and the objects of idolatry."

Those who take symbols with flat literalism might also attack Christianity as anthropomorphic and idolatrous; in fact they have. The defense of Christianity against this charge does not avail in the case of Roman emperor-worship, which consisted not in the humanization of the divine for the sake of symbolic representation, but in the deification of the merely human for political purposes.

Although there are radical differences, there are also certain fundamental agreements between paganism and Judeo-Christianity regarding the nature of the divine. As we have already noted, the deities are conceived personally, not in terms of impersonal, brute forces. Conceived as beings with intelligence and will, the gods concern themselves with earthly society; they aid or oppose man's plans and efforts; they reward men for fidelity and virtue or punish them for impiety and sin.

Despite all other differences between paganism and Christianity, these agreements are substantial enough to provide many common threads of theological speculation throughout our tradition, especially with regard to the abiding practical problems of how man shall view himself and his destiny in relation to the divine or the supernatural. We have therefore attempted to place passages from the great books of pagan antiquity under every heading except those which are specifically restricted to the dogmas of Judaism and Christianity—even under headings which are worded monotheistically, since even here there is continuity of thought and expression from Homer and Virgil to Dante and Milton; from Plato, Aristotle, and Plotinus to Augustine, Aquinas, Calvin, Erasmus, Descartes, and Kant; from Lucretius to Newton and Darwin.

THE DOCTRINES known as deism and pantheism, like unqualified atheism, are as much opposed to the religious beliefs of polytheism as to the faith of Judaism and Christianity.

Of these two, pantheism is much nearer atheism, for it denies the existence of a transcendent supernatural being or beings. God is Nature. God is immanent in the world and, in the extreme form of pantheism, not transcendent in any way. Certain historic doctrines which are often regarded as forms or kinds of pantheism seem to be less extreme than this, for they do not conceive the physical universe as exhausting the infinite being of God. The world, for all its vastness and variety, may only represent an aspect of the divine nature.

According to Spinoza, the attributes of extension and thought, in terms of which we understand the world or nature as being of the divine substance, are merely those aspects of God which are known to us, for the divine substance consists "of infinite attributes, each one of which expresses eternal and infinite essence." In the conception of Plotinus, the whole world represents only a partial emanation from the divine source. Yet thinkers like Plotinus and Spinoza so conceive the relation of the world to God that—as in the strictest pantheism—the religious doctrines of creation, providence, and salvation are either rejected or profoundly altered.

In the ancient world the teaching of the Stoic philosophers expresses a kind of pantheism. "There is one universe made up of all things," Marcus Aurelius writes, "and one God who pervades all things, and one substance, and one law, one common reason in all intelligent animals, and one truth." He speaks of the "common nature," which is apparently divine, and of which "every particular nature is a part, as the nature of the leaf is a part of the nature of the plant." But, although he stresses the oneness and divinity of all things, Aurelius also at times uses language which seems to refer to a god who dwells apart from as well as in the world, as, for example, when he debates whether the gods have any concern with human affairs.

Another type of ancient pantheism appears in the thought of Plotinus, for whom all things have being only insofar as they participate in, even as they emanate from, the power of The One, or Primal Source. "God is sovranly present through all," he writes. "We cannot think of something of God here and something else there, nor of all of God gathered at some one spot: there is an instantaneous presence everywhere, nothing containing and nothing left void, everything therefore fully held by the divine." The relation between The One and every other thing is compared to the number series. "Just as there is, primarily or secondarily, some form or idea from the monad in each of the successive numbers—the latter still participating, though unequally, in the unit—so the series of beings following upon The First bear, each, some form or idea derived from that source. In Number the participation establishes Quantity; in the realm of Being, the trace of The One establishes reality: existence is a trace of The One."

But although The One is in all things, and all things depend upon it for their very existence, The One itself has no need of them. It is in this sense that Plotinus says that "The One is all things and no one of them . . . Holding all—though itself nowhere held—it is omnipresent, for where its presence failed something would elude its hold. At the same time, in the sense that it is nowhere held, it is not present: thus it is both present and not present; not present as not being circumscribed by anything; yet as being utterly unattached, not inhibited from presence at any point." Thus all things partake of The One in absolute dependence. But The One, *considered in itself,* is absolutely transcendent. Plotinus even denies it the name of God or Good or Being, saying it is beyond these.

Whether or not Spinoza is a pantheist, has long been debated by his commentators. An explicit, even an extreme form of pantheism would seem to be expressed in the proposition that "whatever is, is in God, and nothing can be or be conceived without God." But while the one and only substance which exists is at once nature and God, Spinoza identifies God only with the nature he calls "*natura naturans.*" God is not reduced to the nature that falls within man's limited experience or understanding—the nature he calls "*natura naturata.*"

"By *natura naturans,*" he explains, "we are to understand that which is in itself and is conceived through itself, or those attributes of substance which express eternal and infinite essence, that is to say, God in so far as He is considered as a free cause. But by *natura naturata* I understand everything which follows from the necessity of the nature of God, or of any one of God's attributes, that is to say, all the modes of God's attributes in so far as they are considered as things which are in God and which without God can neither be nor can be conceived."

God is the infinite and eternal substance of all finite existences, an absolute and unchanging *one* underlying the finite modes in which it variably manifests itself. Though God for Spinoza is transcendent in the sense of vastly exceeding the world known to man, in no sense does God exist apart from the whole of nature. Spinoza's view thus sharply departs from that of an orthodox Jewish or Christian theologian. When the latter says that God is transcendent, he means that God exists apart, infinitely removed from the whole created universe. When the latter speaks of God as being immanent in that universe, he carefully specifies that it is not by His substance, but by the power of His action and knowledge. But Spinoza calls God "the immanent, and not the transitive, cause of all things," for the reason that "outside God there can be no substance, that is to say, outside Him nothing can exist which is in itself."

These divergent conceptions of God's immanence and transcendence—so relevant to the question of who is or is not a pantheist—are further discussed in the chapters on NATURE and WORLD.

UNLIKE PANTHEISM, deism affirms gods or a God, personal intelligences existing apart from this world; but, as in the teaching of Lucretius, deism sometimes goes to the extreme of believing in absentee gods who neither intervene in the order of nature nor concern themselves with human affairs.

"The gods," writes Lucretius,

Must, by their nature, take delight in peace,
Forever calm, serene, forever far
From our affairs, beyond all pain, beyond
All danger, in their own resources strong,
Having no need of us at all, above
Wrath or propitiation.

Such gods neither create the world nor govern it; above all they do not reward or punish man, and so they do not have to be feared or propitiated. According to Lucretius, we should not be

So foolish as to say that for men's sake
The gods were more than willing to prepare
The gorgeous structure of the universe,
Which therefore, as the work of gods, must be
Considered laudable, and as their work
Immortal also—what a sinful thing
(We think) for such a world, established by
The ancient planning of the gods for men,
To be subverted, ever, from its base
By any violence, subject to storms
Of sacrilegious verbiage, overthrown,
Brought low, brought down, destroyed, annihilated,
And so forth, and so on. All nonsense . . .
What could the blessèd, the immortal, gain
From any such munificence as ours? . . .

Divinity seems to have moral significance to Lucretius only insofar as the gods exemplify the happy life; and religion is immoral because its superstitions concerning divine motives and meddling make men servile and miserable.

When the deism of Lucretius is contrasted with the more familiar modern forms of that doctrine, the influence of Christianity is seen. The modern deist affirms the supremacy of one God, the infinite and eternal Creator of this world, Whose laws are the laws of nature which are laid down from the beginning and which govern all created things. Rousseau speaks of this as "the religion of man" and even identifies it with Christianity—"not the Christianity of today, but that of the Gospel, which is entirely different." He describes this religion as that "which has neither temples, nor altars, nor rites, and is confined to the purely internal cult of the supreme God and the eternal obligations of morality."

Not all deists, certainly not those of the 17th and early 18th centuries, go to the Lucretian extreme of picturing an uninterested and morally neutral God. Many of them believe in an afterlife. But modern deism did tend toward this extreme. By Kant's time it had even ceased to look upon God as a personal intelligence. Kant therefore takes great pains to distinguish deism from theism.

The deist, according to Kant, "admits that we can cognize by pure reason alone the existence of a supreme being, but at the same time maintains that our conception of this being is purely transcendental, and that all we can say of it is, that it possesses all reality, without being able to define it more closely." The theist, on the other hand, "asserts that reason is capable of presenting us, from the analogy with nature, with a more definite conception of this being, and that its operations, as the cause of all things, are the results of intelligence and free will."

Kant even maintains that "we might, in strict rigor, deny to the deist any belief in God at all, and regard him merely as a maintainer of the existence of a primal being or thing—the supreme cause of all other things." In any case, deism seems to be an essentially un-Jewish and un-Christian or anti-Jewish and anti-Christian doctrine, for it denies God's supernatural revelation of Himself; it denies miracles and every other manifestation of supernatural agency in the course of nature or the life of man; it denies the efficacy of prayer and sacrament. In short, it rejects the institutions and practices, as well as the faith and hope, of any religion which claims supernatural foundation and supernatural warrant for its dogmas and rituals. Deism, which "consists simply in the worship of a God considered as great, powerful, and eternal," is, in Pascal's opinion, "almost as far removed from the Christian religion as atheism, which is its exact opposite." Like Pascal, Calvin asks: "What avails it, in short, to know a God with whom we have nothing to do?"

What Pascal and Kant call "deism" and Rousseau "the religion of man," others like Hume call "natural religion." His *Dialogues Concerning Natural Religion* provide a classic statement of rationalism, which is the same as naturalism, in religion; though, as the chapter on RELIGION indicates, it may be questioned whether the word "religion" can be meaningfully used for a doctrine which claims no knowledge beyond that of the philosopher, and no guidance for human life beyond the precepts of the moralist.

THE SYSTEMATIC exposition of man's knowledge of God is the science of theology. In addition to considering all things—the whole world and human life—in relation to God, theology treats especially of God's existence, essence, and attributes. Throughout the range of its subject matter and problems, theology may be of two sorts: it may be either natural knowledge, obtained by ordinary processes of observation and reasoning; or knowledge which is supernatural in the sense of being based on divine revelation. This is the traditional distinction between natural and sacred or, as it is sometimes called, dogmatic theology. The one belongs to the domain of reason; it is the work of the philosopher. The other belongs to the domain of faith, and is the work of the theologian who seeks to understand his faith.

These distinctions are discussed in the chapters on THEOLOGY, METAPHYSICS, and WISDOM. Here we are concerned with different attitudes toward the problem of man's knowledge of God. The deist, as we have seen, rejects supernatural revelation and faith; theology, like religion, is held to be entirely natural, a work of reason. The agnostic makes the opposite denial. He denies that anything supernatural can be known by reason. It cannot be proved or, for that matter, disproved. The evidences of nature and the light of reason do not permit valid inferences or arguments concerning God or creation, providence or immortality.

It is usually with respect to God's existence that the agnostic most emphatically declares reason's incompetence to demonstrate. He often accompanies the declaration with elaborate criticisms of the arguments which may be offered by others. This is not always the case, however. For example, the great Jewish theologian Moses Maimonides thinks that God's existence can be proved by reason entirely apart from faith; but with regard to the essence or attributes of God, his position seems to be one which might be called agnostic.

When men "ascribe essential attributes to God," Maimonides declares, "these so-called essential attributes should not have any similarity to the attributes of other things, just as there is no similarity between the essence of God and that of other beings." Since the meaning of such positive attributes as *good* or *wise* is derived from our knowledge of things, they do not provide us with any knowledge of God's essence, for no comparison obtains between things and God. Hence Maimonides asserts that "the negative attributes of God are the true attributes." They tell us not what God is, but what God is not.

Even though Maimonides holds that "existence and essence are perfectly identical" in God, he also insists that "we comprehend only the fact that He exists, not His essence . . . All we understand," he goes on to say, in addition to "the fact that He exists," is the fact that "He is a Being to whom none of his creatures is similar." This fact is confirmed in all the negative attributes such as eternal (meaning nontemporal), infinite, or incorporeal; even as it is falsified by all the positive attributes, expressed by such names as "good" or "living" or "knowing," insofar as they imply a comparison between God and creatures. When they cannot be interpreted negatively, they can be tolerated as metaphors, but they must not be taken as expressing an understanding "of the true essence of God," concerning which Mai-

monides maintains, "there is no possibility of obtaining a knowledge."

Aquinas takes issue with such agnosticism about the divine nature in his discussion of the names of God. Although he says that "we cannot know what God is, but rather what He is not," Aquinas disagrees with Maimonides that all names which express some knowledge of God's essence must be interpreted negatively or treated as metaphors. He denies that "when we say God lives, we mean merely that God is not like an inanimate thing" as "was taught by Rabbi Moses." On the contrary, he holds that "these names signify the divine substance . . . although they fall short of representing Him . . . For these names express God, so far as our intellects know Him. Now since our intellect knows God from creatures, it knows Him as far as creatures represent Him." Therefore, Aquinas concludes, "when we say, *God is good,* the meaning is not, *God is the cause of goodness,* or, *God is not evil:* but the meaning is, *Whatever good we attribute to creatures pre-exists in God,* and in a higher way."

IF MAIMONIDES were right that the names which are said positively of both God and creatures are "applied . . . in a purely equivocal sense" (*e.g.,* having literal meaning when said of creatures but being only metaphoric when said of God), then, according to Aquinas, it would follow that "from creatures nothing at all could be known or demonstrated about God." Those who say, on the other hand, that "the things attributed to God and creatures are univocal" (*i.e.,* are said in exactly the same sense), claim to comprehend more than man can know of the divine essence. When the term *wise* "is applied to God," Aquinas writes, "it leaves the thing signified as uncomprehended and as exceeding the signification of the name." Aquinas does not go as far as Erasmus in saying that only God is wise. Instead he declares that "this term *wise* is not applied in the same way to God and to man. The same applies to other terms. Hence no name is predicated univocally of God and creatures" but rather all positive names "are said of God and creatures in an analogous sense."

A further discussion of the names of God

will be found in the chapter on SIGN AND SYMBOL; and the consideration of the analogical, the univocal, and the equivocal will also be found there as well as in the chapter on SAME AND OTHER. We have dealt with these matters here only for the sake of describing that degree of agnosticism, according to which Maimonides, by contrast with Aquinas, is an agnostic. But agnosticism usually goes further and denies that man can have any natural knowledge of God—either of His existence or of His essence.

So understood, agnosticism need not be incompatible with religion, unless a given religion holds, as an article of faith itself, that the existence of God can be *proved by reason.* In fact, the agnostic may be a religious man who accepts divine revelation and regards faith as divinely inspired.

Montaigne's *Apology for Raymond Sebond* illustrates this position. Sebond had written a treatise on natural theology, which to Montaigne seems "bold and courageous, for he undertakes by human and natural reasons to establish and prove against the atheists all the articles of the Christian religion." Though Montaigne says of Sebond's work, "I do not think it is possible to do better in that argument," and though he entertains the conjecture that it may have been "from Saint Thomas Aquinas; for in truth that mind, full of infinite erudition and admirable subtlety, was alone capable of such ideas"; nevertheless, Montaigne does "not think that purely human means are at all capable of this."

According to Montaigne, "it is faith alone that embraces vividly and surely the high mysteries of our religion." In his view, reason by itself is incapable of proving *anything,* much less *anything about God.* "Our human reasons and arguments," he writes, are "the heavy and barren matter; the grace of God is their form; it is that which gives them shape and value." The light and value in Sebond's arguments come from the fact that faith supervenes "to color and illumine" them, and "makes them firm and solid."

Such arguments, Montaigne says, may serve as "a first guide to an apprentice" and may even "make him capable of the grace of God";

but for himself, skeptical of all arguments, the way of faith alone can provide "a certain constancy of opinions . . . Thus I have, by the grace of God, kept myself intact, without agitation or disturbance of conscience, in the ancient beliefs of our religion, in the midst of so many sects and divisions that our century has produced."

Kierkegaard's view of religion also precludes reason. For him, faith is the realm of the absurd, a paradox that says "the individual is higher than the universal" and thereby allows a more personal relationship with God. "The paradox can also be expressed by saying that there is an absolute duty toward God; for in this relationship of duty the individual as an individual stands related absolutely to the absolute."

Far from being religious as Montaigne and Kierkegaard were, the agnostic may be a skeptic about faith as well as reason. He may look upon faith either as superstition or as the exercise of the will to believe with regard to the unknowable and the unintelligible—almost wishful thinking. He may even go so far as to treat religion as if it were pathological.

Freud, for example, regards religion as an illusion to be explained in terms of man's need to create gods in his own image—to find a surrogate for the father, on whom his infantile dependence can be projected. Freud finds confirmation for this in the fact that in the religions of the west, God "is openly called Father. Psychoanalysis," he goes on, "concludes that he really is the father, clothed in the grandeur in which he once appeared to the small child."

Though the grown man "has long ago realized that his father is a being with strictly limited powers and by no means endowed with every desirable attribute," Freud thinks that he nevertheless "looks back to the memory-image of the overrated father of his childhood, exalts it into a Deity, and brings it into the present and into reality. The emotional strength of this memory-image and the lasting nature of his need for protection"—for, as Freud explains, "in relation to the external world he is still a child"—"are the two supports of his belief in God." In this sense, Freud might agree with

Voltaire's remark that "If God did not exist, it would be necessary to invent him."

AT THE OTHER extreme from agnosticism is, as the name implies, gnosticism. Like deism, it dispenses with faith, but it exceeds traditional deism in the claims it makes for reason's power to penetrate the divine mysteries. Between exclusive reliance on faith and an exaltation of reason to the point where there is no need for God to reveal anything, a middle ground is held by those who acknowledge the contributions of both faith and reason. Those who try to harmonize the two usually distinguish between the spheres proper to each, and formulate some principle according to which they are related to each other in an orderly fashion.

Whatever is purely a matter of faith, Aquinas says, is assented to solely because "it is revealed by God." The articles of Christian faith are typified by "the Trinity of Persons in Almighty God, the mystery of Christ's Incarnation, and the like." With regard to such matters, which Aquinas thinks belong primarily to faith, some auxiliary use can be made of reason, "not, indeed, to prove faith," he explains, but to make clear the things that follow from it. Certain matters, such as God's existence and attributes, he classifies as belonging to "the preambles to faith" because they fall, in his view, within reason's power to demonstrate, unaided by faith. Yet even here he does not assign the affirmation of the truth to reason alone.

Just as "it was necessary for the salvation of man that certain truths which exceed human reason should be made known to him by divine revelation," so even with regard to "those truths about God which human reason can investigate," Aquinas thinks it was also necessary that "man be taught by a divine revelation. For the truth about God, such as reason can know it, would only be known by a few, and that after a long time, and with the admixture of many errors." Because "human reason is very deficient in things concerning God"—"a sign of which is that philosophers . . . have fallen into many errors and have disagreed among themselves"—men would have no knowledge of God "free from doubt and uncertainty" un-

less all divine truths were "delivered to them by the way of faith, being told to them, as it were, by God Himself Who cannot lie."

In different ways faith supports reason and reason helps faith. On matters which belong to both reason and faith, faith provides a greater certitude. On matters strictly of faith, reason provides some understanding, however remote and inadequate, of the mysteries of religion. "The use of human reason in religion," Francis Bacon writes, "is of two sorts: the former, in the conception and apprehension of the mysteries of God to us revealed; the other, in the inferring and deriving of doctrine and direction thereupon . . . In the former we see God vouchsafeth to descend to our capacity, in the expressing of his mysteries in sort as may be sensible unto us; and doth grift his revelations and holy doctrine upon the notions of our reason and applieth his inspiration to open our understanding, as the form of the key to the ward of the lock. For the latter, there is allowed us an use of reason and argument, secondary and respective, although not original and absolute. For after the articles and principles of religion are placed and exempted from examination of reason, it is then permitted unto us to make derivations and inferences from and according to the analogy of them, for our better direction."

In addition to all discursive knowledge of God, whether it be by faith or by reason, there is the totally incommunicable and intimate acquaintance with the supernatural which the mystic claims for his vision in moments of religious ecstasy or which is promised to the blessed as their heavenly beatitude. When, at the culmination of *Paradiso,* Dante sees God, "my vision," he declares, "was greater than speech can show."

Knowing that his speech will "fall more short . . . than that of an infant who still bathes his tongue at the breast," he tries nevertheless to communicate in words "a single spark of Thy glory for the folk to come." In the presence of God, he writes, his mind, "all rapt, was gazing, fixed, motionless and intent, ever enkindled by its gazing. In that Light one becomes such that it is impossible he should ever consent to turn himself from it for other sight; for the good, which is the object of the will, is all gathered in it, and outside of it that is defective which is perfect there."

THE ARGUMENTS FOR the existence of the gods or of one God constitute one of the greatest attempts of the human mind to go beyond the sensible or phenomenal world of experience. The attempt has been made in every age and by minds of quite different persuasions in religious belief or philosophical outlook. It is possible, nevertheless, to classify the arguments into two or three main types.

Within the domain of pure or speculative reason there seem to be two ways of approaching the problem of God's existence.

One is in terms of the conception of God as an infinite, perfect, and necessary being, whose nonexistence is therefore inconceivable. According to Anselm, God cannot be conceived in any other way than as "a being than which nothing greater can be conceived." But since "the fool hath said in his heart, there is no God," how shall he be made to know that the God, which exists in his understanding at the moment when he denies His real existence, also really exists outside his understanding? "For it is one thing for an object to be in the understanding, and another to understand that the object exists." Hence Anselm considers the consequence of supposing that God exists in the understanding alone.

"If that, than which nothing greater can be conceived," he argues, "exists in the understanding alone, the very being, than which nothing greater can be conceived, is one than which a greater can be conceived"—for to exist in reality as well as in the understanding is to have *more* being. But this leads to "an irreconcilable contradiction," since "if that, than which nothing greater can be conceived, can be conceived not to exist, it is not that than which nothing greater can be conceived." Therefore Anselm concludes that a being "than which nothing greater can be conceived" must exist "both in the understanding and reality."

Anselm summarizes his argument by saying that "no one who understands what God is, can conceive that God does not exist." Since the nonexistence of God is inconceivable, God must exist. Descartes gives the same argument a slightly different statement in terms of the inseparability of God's essence from God's existence.

"Being accustomed," he writes, "in all other things to make a distinction between existence and essence, I easily persuade myself that the existence can be separated from the essence of God, and that we can thus conceive God as not actually existing. But, nevertheless, when I think of it with more attention, I clearly see that existence can no more be separated from the essence of God than can its having its three angles equal to two right angles be separated from the essence of a rectilinear triangle, or the idea of a mountain from the idea of a valley; and so there is not any less repugnance to our conceiving a God (that is, a Being supremely perfect) to whom existence is lacking (that is to say, to whom a certain perfection is lacking), than to conceive of a mountain which has no valley."

Spinoza defines a "cause of itself" as "that whose essence involves existence; or that whose nature cannot be conceived unless existing." Since in his conception of substance, substance is necessarily infinite, it is also cause of itself. Hence he concludes that "God or substance . . . necessarily exists"; for "if this be denied, conceive if it be possible that God does not exist. Then it follows that His essence does not involve existence. But this is absurd. Therefore God necessarily exists."

This mode of argument, which takes still other forms, is traditionally called the "ontological argument" or the "*a priori* proof" of God's existence. Its critics sometimes deny that it is an argument or proof in any sense at all. Aquinas, for example, interprets Anselm not as providing God's existence, but rather as asserting that God's existence is self-evident. Those who say that the proposition "God does not exist" is self-contradictory, are saying that the opposite proposition "God exists" must be self-evident.

Aquinas does not deny that the proposition "God exists" is intrinsically self-evident. On this point he goes further than Anselm, Descartes, and Spinoza. Where they say God's essence *involves* His existence, Aquinas asserts that in God essence and existence are *identical*. When Moses asks God, "If they should say to me, What is His name? what shall I say to them?" the Lord says unto Moses, "I AM THAT I AM," and adds, "Say to the children of Israel: HE WHO IS hath sent me to you." This name—HE WHO IS—Aquinas holds to be "the most proper name of God" because it signifies that "the being of God is His very essence."

For this reason he thinks that the proposition "God exists" is self-evident in itself. Its subject and predicate are immediately related. Nevertheless, Aquinas holds that the proposition is not self-evident to us "because we do not know the essence of God." Even supposing, he writes, "that everyone understands this name *God* as signifying something than which nothing greater can be thought, nevertheless, it does not therefore follow that he understands that what the name signifies exists actually, but only that it exists mentally. Nor can it be argued that it actually exists, unless it be admitted that there actually exists something than which nothing greater can be thought; and this precisely is not admitted by those who hold that God does not exist."

The writer of "The First Set of Objections" to Descartes's *Meditations on First Philosophy* maintains that the criticism advanced by Aquinas applies to Descartes as well as to Anselm. Whether stated in terms of the conception of an absolutely perfect being or in terms of essence and existence, the argument is invalid, he thinks, which asserts that God actually exists because His nonexistence is inconceivable. Kant's later criticism of the ontological argument takes a similar course. A proposition may be logically necessary without being true in fact.

"The conception of an absolutely necessary being," he writes, "is a mere idea, the objective reality of which is far from being established by the mere fact that it is a need of reason . . . The unconditioned necessity of a judgment does not form the absolute necessity of a thing." From the fact that "existence belongs necessarily to the object of the conception," we cannot conclude that "the existence of the thing . . . is therefore absolutely necessary—merely," Kant says, "because its existence has been cogitated in the conception . . . Whatever be the content of our conception of an object, it is necessary to go beyond it, if we wish to predicate existence of the object . . . The celebrated ontological or Cartesian argument for the existence of a supreme being is therefore insufficient."

THE SECOND MAIN approach to the problem of God's existence lies in the sort of proof which, Locke thinks, "our own existence and the sensible parts of the universe offer so clearly and cogently to our thoughts." He refrains from criticizing the argument from "the *idea* of a most perfect being," but he does insist that we should not "take some men's having that idea of God in their minds . . . for the only proof of a Deity." He for one prefers to follow the counsel of Saint Paul, that "the invisible things of God are clearly seen from the creation of the world, being understood by the things that are made, even his eternal power and Godhead."

We have, according to Locke, an intuitive knowledge of our own existence. We know, he says, that "nonentity cannot produce any real being"; and so "from the consideration of ourselves, and what we infallibly find in our constitution, our reason leads us to the knowledge of this certain and evident truth—*That there is an eternal, most powerful, and most knowing Being.*"

Without labeling it a proof of God's existence, Augustine in his *Confessions* presents a similar argument—from the visible creation. "Earth and the heavens," he says, "are before our eyes. The very fact that they are there proclaims that they were created, for they are subject to change and variation . . . Earth and the heavens also proclaim that they did not create themselves. 'We exist,' they tell us, 'because we were made. And this is proof that we did not make ourselves. For to make ourselves, we should have had to exist before our existence began' . . . It was you, then, O Lord, who made them."

This second approach to the existence of God by reasoning from the facts of experience or the evidences of nature is called the "*a posteriori* proof." In the tradition of the great books, it has been formulated in many different ways. What is common to all of them is the principle of causality, in terms of which the known existence of certain effects is made the basis for inferring the existence of a unique cause—a first cause, a highest cause, an uncaused cause.

Aristotle, for example, in the last book of his *Physics,* argues from the fact of motion or change to the existence of an unmoved mover. He sums up his elaborate reasoning on this point in the following statement. "We established the fact that everything that is in motion is moved by something, and that the movent [moving cause] is either unmoved or in motion, and that, if it is in motion, it is moved either by itself or by something else and so on throughout the series: and so we proceeded to the position that the first principle that directly causes things that are in motion to be moved is that which moves itself, and the first principle of the whole series is the unmoved." Jumping from the 4th century B.C. to the 20th century, we find Whitehead saying that "in the place of Aristotle's God as Prime Mover, we require God as the Principle of Concretion." Nothing could be more evocative of Whitehead's anti-Aristotelianism.

Aristotle's argument, unlike that of Augustine or Locke, does not presuppose the creation of the world, at least not in the sense of the world's having a beginning. On the contrary, he holds the world and its motions to be as eternal as their unmoved mover. "It is impossible," he writes in the *Metaphysics,* "that movement should either have come into being or cease to be." Precisely because he thinks the world's motions are eternal, Aristotle holds that the prime mover, in addition to being everlasting, must be immutable. This for him means "a principle whose very essence is actuality." Only a substance without any potency, only one which is *purely actual,* can be an absolutely immutable, eternal being.

Whatever has any potentiality in its nature is capable of not existing. If everything were of this sort, nothing that now is "need be, for it is possible for all things to be capable of

existing, but not yet to exist." Hence, in still another way, Aristotle seems to reach the conclusion that a purely actual being must exist; and, furthermore, he seems to identify this being with a living and thinking God. "Life also belongs to God," he writes; "for the actuality of thought is life, and God is that actuality; and God's self-dependent actuality is life most good and eternal."

Where Aristotle argues from motion and potentiality to a prime mover and a pure actuality, Newton gives the *a posteriori* proof another statement by arguing from the design of the universe to God as its designer or architect. "The most wise and excellent contrivances of things, and final causes" seem to him the best way of knowing God. "Blind metaphysical necessity, which is certainly the same always and everywhere, could produce no variety in things. All that diversity of natural things which we find suited to different times and places could arise from nothing but the ideas and will of a Being necessarily existing."

In similar fashion Berkeley maintains that "if we attentively consider the constant regularity, order, and concatenation of natural things, the surprising magnificence, beauty, and perfection of the larger, and the exquisite contrivance of the smaller parts of the creation, together with the exact harmony and correspondence of the whole, but, above all, the never enough admired laws of pain and pleasure, and the instincts or natural inclinations, appetites, and passions of animals; I say if we consider all these things, and at the same time attend to the meaning and import of the attributes, one, eternal, infinitely wise, good, and perfect, we shall clearly perceive that they belong to the . . . Spirit, who 'works all in all,' and 'by whom all things consist.'" This seems to him so certain that he adds, "we may even assert that the existence of God is far more evidently perceived than the existence of men."

But, according to Berkeley, all the visible things of nature exist only as ideas in our minds, ideas which, unlike our own memories or imaginations, we do not ourselves produce. "Everything we see, hear, feel, or anywise perceive by sense," he writes, must have some other cause than our own will, and is therefore "a sign or effect of the power of God." To the "unthinking herd" who claim that "they cannot *see* God," Berkeley replies that "God . . . is intimately present to our minds, producing in them all that variety of ideas or sensations which continually affect us."

The existence of any idea in us is for Berkeley ground for asserting God's existence and power as its cause. But for Descartes *one* idea alone becomes the basis of such an inference. He supplements his *a priori* or ontological argument with what he calls an "*a posteriori* demonstration of God's existence from the mere fact that the idea of God exists in us."

That he is himself imperfect, Descartes knows from the fact that he doubts. Even when doubting leads to knowledge, his knowledge is imperfect, "an infallible token" of which, he says, is the fact that "my knowledge increases little by little." But the idea which he has of God, he declares, is that of an absolutely perfect being, "in whom there is nothing merely potential, but in whom all is present really and actually." On the principle that there cannot be more reality or perfection in the effect than in the cause, Descartes concludes that his own imperfect mind cannot be the cause of the idea of a perfect being. "The idea that I possess of a being more perfect than I," he writes, "must necessarily have been placed in me by a being which is really more perfect."

The radical imperfection of man, and indeed of all creation, offers Augustine still another proof for God's existence, which he attributes to the "Platonists." "They have seen," he writes, "that whatever is changeable is not the most high God, and therefore they have transcended every soul and all changeable spirits in seeking the supreme. They have seen also that, in every changeable thing, the form which makes it that which it is, whatever be its mode or nature, can only *be* through Him who truly *is,* because He is unchangeable. And therefore, whether we consider the whole body of the world, its figure, qualities, and orderly movement, and also all the bodies which are in it; or whether we consider all life, either that which nourishes and maintains, as the life of trees; or that which, besides this, has also sensation, as the life of beasts; or

that which adds to all these intelligence, as the life of man; or that which does not need the support of nutriment, but only maintains, feels, understands, as the life of angels—all can only *be* through Him who absolutely *is.* For to Him it is not one thing to *be,* and another to live, as though He could *be,* not living; nor is it to Him one thing to live, and another to understand, as though He could live, not understanding; nor is it to Him one thing to understand, another to be blessed, as though He could understand and not be blessed. But to Him to live, to understand, to be blessed, are to *be.* They have understood, from this unchangeableness and this simplicity, that all things must have been made by Him, and that He could Himself have been made by none."

The variety of arguments we have so far examined seems to fit the "five ways" in which, according to Aquinas, the existence of God can be proved *a posteriori.* "The first and most manifest way is the argument from motion," which Aquinas attributes to Aristotle. "The second way is from the nature of an efficient cause." Berkeley's argument or Locke's would seem, in some respects, to offer a version of this mode of reasoning. "The third way is taken from possibility and necessity," and seems to develop the argument from potentiality in Aristotle's *Metaphysics,* and to contain the inference from mutability and contingency which is implicit in the argument attributed to the Platonists by Augustine. "The fourth way is taken from the gradation to be found in things." Proceeding from the existence of the imperfect to absolute perfection, it resembles in principle the reasoning of Descartes concerning the perfection in the cause relative to the perfection in the effect. "The fifth way is taken from the governance of the world"— from the fact that everything acts for an end— and so is like the argument which Newton offers from final causes and the existence of order in the universe.

These "five ways" may or may not be regarded as an exhaustive list of the *a posteriori* proofs. It may even be questioned whether the five ways are logically distinct and independent. Aquinas himself says that "in speculative matters the medium of demonstration, which demonstrates the conclusion perfectly, is only one; whereas probable means of proof are many." Since he considers the argument for God's existence to be a certain, not a probable proof, it would seem to follow that, in strict logic, only one principle can be involved in that proof.

As already suggested, the principle—common to all the various ways in which such *a posteriori* reasoning is expressed—seems to be the principle of causality. This appears in the argument from the existence of contingent beings, which cannot cause their own being, to the existence of a being which needs no cause of its being, because its very essence is to exist. This may be the one argument for God's existence or, if one among many, it may be the core of all the others. It has the distinction at least of conceiving God as the cause of being, rather than of motion or of hierarchy and order in the world.

According to the statement of Aquinas that "being is the proper effect of God," it establishes God as the *unique* and *direct* cause of the being possessed by every finite thing. This formulation of the proof is more fully examined in the chapter on NECESSITY AND CONTINGENCY; and its relation to the question of whether the world had a beginning or is eternal, and if eternal, whether it is created or uncreated, will be seen in the chapters on CAUSE, ETERNITY, and WORLD.

THE VALIDITY OF the *a posteriori* argument for God's existence—in one form or another—is questioned by those who think that the causal principle cannot be applied beyond experience, or who think that our knowledge of cause and effect is not sufficient to warrant such inferences.

"The existence of any being can only be proved by arguments from its cause or its effect," Hume writes; "and these arguments are founded entirely on experience ... It is only experience which teaches us the nature and bounds of cause and effect, and enables us to infer the existence of one object from that of another." But Hume doubts "whether it be possible for a cause to be known only by its effect ... or to be of so singular and particular

a nature as to have no parallel and no similarity with any other cause or object, that has ever fallen under our observation ... If experience and observation and analogy be, indeed, the only guides which we can reasonably follow in inferences of this nature," as Hume thinks is the case, then it follows that "both the effect and the cause must bear a similarity and resemblance to other effects and causes which we know.

"I leave it to your own reflection," he adds, "to pursue the consequences of this principle." One seems obvious enough; namely, that God—a unique and unparalleled cause—cannot be proved by reasoning from our experience of effects and their causes. Hume himself draws this conclusion when he declares that theology, insofar as it is concerned with the existence of a Deity, has "its best and most solid foundation," not in reason or experience, but in "*faith* and divine revelation."

Like Hume, Kant thinks that our notions of cause and effect cannot be applied outside experience or to anything beyond the realm of sensible nature. But he offers an additional reason for denying validity to all *a posteriori* reasoning concerning God's existence. "It imposes upon us," he says, "an old argument in a new dress, and appeals to the agreement of two witnesses, the one with the credentials of pure reason, and the other with those of empiricism; while, in fact, it is only the former who has changed his dress and voice."

The principle of the argument from the contingency of the world or its parts Kant states as follows: "If something exists, an absolutely necessary being must likewise exist." One premise in the argument, namely, that contingent things exist, has its foundation in experience and therefore Kant admits that the reasoning "is not completely *a priori* or ontological." But in order to complete the proof, he thinks it must be shown that an *ens realissimum,* or most perfect being, is the same as an absolutely necessary being, in order for the obtained conclusion (*a necessary being exists*) to be translated into the conclusion desired (*God exists*).

That "an *ens realissimum* must possess the additional attribute of absolute necessity"—

or, in other words, that a perfect being is identical with one which necessarily exists— is, according to Kant, "exactly what was maintained in the ontological argument." Hence he maintains that the argument from contingency is invalid because it cannot avoid including what is for Kant the invalid premise of the ontological argument as "the real ground of its disguised and illusory reasoning."

THE CONTROVERSY concerning the proof of God's existence raises issues in logic, in metaphysics and physics, and in the theory of knowledge. Philosophers are opposed on the question whether a valid demonstration is possible. Those who think it possible differ from one another on the way in which the proof should be constructed. Those who think it impossible do not always go to the opposite extreme of making the affirmation of God's existence a matter of faith; or of denying with the skeptic that we can have any light on the question at all. Pascal and Kant, for example, reject the theoretical arguments as inconclusive or untenable, but they do not think the problem is totally insoluble. They offer instead *practical* grounds or reasons for accepting God's existence.

"The metaphysical proofs of God are so remote from the reasoning of men," Pascal asserts, "and so complicated, that they make little impression." He will "not undertake," he tells us in his *Pensées,* "to prove by natural reasons . . . the existence of God." In his view "there are only three kinds of persons: those who serve God, having found Him; others who are occupied in seeking Him, not having found Him; while the remainder live without seeking Him, and without having found Him." Since he regards the first as "reasonable and happy," the last as "foolish and unhappy," he addresses himself to the middle group whom he regards as "unhappy and reasonable."

He asks them to consider whether God is or is not. "Reason can decide nothing here," he says. If a choice is to be made by reason, it must be in the form of a wager. "Which will you choose then? Let us see. Since you must choose, let us see which interests you least. You have two things to lose, the true and the good; and two things to stake, your reason and your will, your knowledge and your happiness; and your nature has two things to shun, error and misery. Your reason is no more shocked in choosing one rather than another, since you must of necessity choose. This is one point settled. But your happiness? Let us weigh the gain and the loss in wagering that God is. Let us estimate these two chances. If you gain, you gain all, if you lose, you lose nothing. Wager then, without hesitation, that He is."

We are incapable of knowing either that God is or what God is, according to Pascal, because "if there is a God, He is infinitely incomprehensible" and "has no affinity to us." Nevertheless, proceeding on the practical level of the wager, reason may lead to Christian faith, yet not in such a way as to give adequate reasons for that belief, since Christians "profess a religion for which they cannot give a reason."

Kant also makes the affirmation of God a matter of faith, but for him it is a "purely rational faith, since pure reason . . . is the sole source from which it springs." He defines a *matter of faith* as any object which cannot be known through the speculative use of reason, but which "must be thought *a priori,* either as consequences or as grounds, if pure practical reason is to be used as duty commands . . . Such is the *summum bonum,*" he says, "which has to be realized in the world through freedom . . . This effect which is commanded, *together with the only conditions on which its possibility is conceivable by us,* namely, the existence of God and the immortality of the soul, are *matters of faith* and are of all objects the only ones that can be so called."

For Kant, then, the existence of God is a "postulate of pure practical reason . . . as the necessary condition of the possibility of the *summum bonum.*" The moral law commands us to seek the highest good, with perfect happiness as its concomitant; but Kant thinks that "there is not the slightest ground in the moral law for a necessary connexion between morality and proportionate happiness in a being that belongs to the world as a part of it." Since man is a part of the world or nature, and dependent on it, "he cannot by his will be a cause of this nature, nor by his own power make it thoroughly harmonize, as far as his happiness is concerned, with his practical principles." The only possible solution lies in "the existence of a cause of all nature, distinct from nature itself, and containing the principle of this connexion, namely, of the exact harmony of happiness with morality." That is why, Kant explains, "it is morally necessary to assume the existence of God."

IN THE TRADITION of the great books, the common ground shared by reason and faith is marked by the convergence of the contributions made by pagan, Jew, and Christian— and by poets, philosophers, and theologians— to the problem of God's existence and the understanding of the divine nature, the essence of God and His attributes.

In the 20th century Barth dissents from traditional discourse about God, as the following quotation from *The Word of God and the Word of Man* reveals:

God is the new, incomparable, unattainable, not only heavenly but more than heavenly interest, who has drawn the regard of the men of the Bible to himself. He desires their *complete* attention, their *entire* obedience. For he must be true to himself; he must be and remain holy. He cannot be grasped, brought under management, and put to use; he cannot serve. He must rule. He must himself grasp, seize, manage, use. He can satisfy no other needs than his own. He is not in another world over against this one; he submerges all of this in the other. He is not a thing among other things, but the *Wholly Other,* the infinite aggregate of all merely relative others. He is not the form of religious history but is the Lord of our life, the eternal Lord of the world. *He* it is of whom the Bible speaks.

Certain attributes of God, such as simplicity, immateriality, eternity, infinity, perfection, and glory, are usually regarded as so many different ways in which the human understanding apprehends the divine nature in itself. Other attributes, such as the divine causality, omnipotence, omnipresence, omniscience, love, justice, and mercy, are usually taken as ways of considering God's nature in relation to the world or to creatures. But to divide the attributes in this way, as is done in the Outline of Topics, is to make a division which cannot be fully justified except in terms of convenience

for our understanding. God's will, for example, no less than God's intellect, can be considered in relation to Himself. God's intellect, no less than God's will, can have the world for its object. So, too, the divine goodness can be considered with reference to things, even as God's love can be considered with reference to Himself.

The difficulties we meet in classifying or ordering the attributes of God confirm the opinion of almost all theologians, that our understanding is inadequate to comprehend the essence of God. The fact that we employ a multiplicity of attributes to represent to ourselves what in itself is an absolute unity is another indication of the same point. The one attribute of *simplicity* would seem to deny us the right to name others, unless we take the plurality of attributes to signify something about man's understanding of God rather than a real complexity in the divine nature.

"He that will attribute to God," Hobbes writes, "nothing but what is warranted by natural reason, must either use such negative attributes, as *infinite, eternal, incomprehensible;* or superlatives, as *most high, most great,* and the like; or indefinite, as *good, just, holy, creator;* and in such sense, as if he meant not to declare what He is (for that were to circumscribe Him within the limits of our fancy), but how much we admire Him, and how ready we would be to obey Him; which is a sign of humility and of a will to honor Him as much as we can: for there is but one name to signify our conception of His nature, and that is, I AM: and but one name of His relation to us, and that is GOD; in which is contained Father, King, and Lord."

Even when they are discussed by the philosophers and reflected on by the poets, certain matters belong especially to theology because they constitute the dogmas of religion—articles of religious faith based solely on divine revelation, not discovered by human inquiry or speculation. That God created the world out of nothing and of His free will; that the world had a beginning and will have an end are, for example, dogmas of traditional Judaism and Christianity. Philosophers may argue about the freedom or necessity of the creative act, or about the possibility of a beginning or an end to time and the world, but Jewish and Christian theologians find in Sacred Scripture the warrant for believing that which may not be thoroughly intelligible to reason, much less demonstrable by it. What is true of creation applies generally to the religious belief in divine providence and the positive commandments of God, to the gift of grace which God bestows upon men, and to the performance of miracles.

Judaism and Christianity share certain dogmas, though the degree to which Jewish and Christian theologians commonly understand what is apparently the same dogma varies from great similarity of interpretation (as in the case of creation and providence) to differences so great (as, for example, with regard to grace) that there may be some doubt whether the dogma in question is really the same. The line of demarcation between these faiths would seem to be more easily determined than their common ground; yet even here such matters as the resurrection of the body—even when we take differences of interpretation into account—may be regarded as a dogma shared by both.

The basic differences between Jewish and Christian theology center, of course, on the issue between a unitarian and a trinitarian conception of the Godhead, with immediate consequences for disbelief or belief in Christ as the incarnate second person of the Trinity—the Word become flesh. This in turn has consequences for doctrines of salvation, and of the nature and mission of the church, its rituals and its sacraments. Even within Christianity, however, there have been and still are serious doctrinal differences on all these matters. The most fundamental heresies and schisms of early Christianity concerned the understanding of the Trinity and the Incarnation. The great modern schism which divided Christendom arose from issues about the sacraments, the organization and practices of the church, and the conditions of salvation.

It would seem to be just as easy to say what beliefs are common to religious Jews and Christians, as to articulate the faith common to all sects of Christianity. If all varieties of Protestant doctrine are included, little remains in common except belief in the God of Abraham, Isaac, and Jacob—creator and provider, governor and judge, dispenser of rewards and punishments.

ONE BOOK STANDS OUT from all the rest because, in our tradition, it is—as the use of "Bible" for its proper name implies—*the* book about God and man. For those who have faith, Holy Writ or Sacred Scripture is the revealed Word of God. Its division into Old and New Testaments represents the historic relation of the Jewish and Christian religions.

Without prejudice to the issue between belief and unbelief, or between Jewish and Christian faith, we have attempted to organize the references to specifically religious doctrines concerning God and His creatures according to their origin and foundation in either the Old or in the New Testament, or in both. On certain points, as we have already seen, the line of distinction can be clearly drawn. For example, the doctrines of God's covenant with Israel, of the Chosen People, of the Temple and the Torah, are indisputably drawn from the Old Testament; and from the New Testament come such dogmas as those concerning Christ's divinity and humanity, the Virgin Birth, the Church as the mystical body of Christ, and the seven sacraments.

Under all these topics we have assembled passages from the Bible, interpretations of them by the theologians, and materials from the great books of poetry and history, philosophy and science. Since the criterion of relevance here is the reflection of sacred or religious doctrine in secular literature, the writings of pagan antiquity are necessarily excluded, though they are included in the more philosophical topics of theology, such as the existence and nature of one God.

Despite its length, this chapter by no means exhausts the discussion of God in the great books. The long list of Cross-References, which follows the Reference section of this chapter, indicates the various ways in which the idea of God occurs in the topics of other chapters. The reader will find that list useful not only as an indication of the topics in other chapters which elaborate on or extend the discussion of matters treated here, but also as a guide to other Introductions in which he is likely to find the conception of God a relevant part of the examination of some other great idea.

30

Good and Evil

INTRODUCTION

THE theory of good and evil crosses the boundaries of many sciences or subject matters. It occupies a place in metaphysics. It is of fundamental importance in all the moral sciences—ethics, economics, politics, jurisprudence. It appears in all the descriptive sciences of human behavior, such as psychology and sociology, though there it is of less importance and is differently treated.

The relation of good and evil to truth and falsity, beauty and ugliness, carries the discussion into logic, aesthetics, and the philosophy of art. The true, it has been said, is the good in the sphere of our thinking. So it may be said of the beautiful that it is a quality which things have when they are good as objects of contemplation and love, or good as productions. It is no less possible to understand goodness and beauty in terms of truth, or truth and goodness in terms of beauty.

One aim of analysis, with respect to the true, the good, and the beautiful, is to preserve their distinctness without rendering each less universal. This has been attempted by writers who treat these three terms as having a kind of parallelism in their application to everything, but who also insist that each of the three notions conceives things under a different aspect or in a different relation. "As good adds to being the notion of the desirable," Aquinas writes, "so the true adds a relation to the intellect"; and it is also said that the end "of the appetite, namely good, is in the desirable thing," whereas the end "of the intellect, namely the true, is in the intellect itself."

In that part of theology which goes beyond metaphysics and moral philosophy, we meet with the concept of infinite goodness—the goodness of an infinite being—and we then face the problem of how God's goodness is to be understood by man. The basic terms of moral theology—righteousness and sin, salvation and damnation—are, like virtue and vice, happiness and misery, conceptions of good and evil in the condition of man. (Their special theological significance comes from the fact that they consider the goodness or evil of man in terms of his relation to God.) But the theological problem which is traditionally called "the problem of evil" concerns the whole universe in its relation to the divine perfection. According to Barth, "The problem of ethics contains the secret that man as we know him in this life is an impossibility. *This* man, in God's sight, can only perish."

That problem, which is further discussed in the chapter on WORLD, can be formulated in a number of ways. How are we to understand the existence of evil in a world created by a God who is omnipotent and perfectly good? Since God is good and since everything which happens is within God's power, how can we account for the sin of Satan or the fall of man, with all the evil consequent thereupon, without limiting God's power or absolving the erring creature from responsibility? Can it be said, as Voltaire's Dr. Pangloss over and over again attributes to Leibniz, that this is the best of all possible worlds, if it is also true that this world is far from perfectly good, and if, as certain theologians hold, "God could make other things, or add something to the present creation, and then there would be another and a better universe"?

THE CONTEMPORARY discussion of good and evil draws its terminology from economics rather than theology. The word "value" has almost replaced "good" and "evil." What in other centuries were the various moral sciences are now treated as parts of the general theory of value. The substitution of "value" for "good" or of "value judgment" for "moral judgment" reflects the influence of economics.

According to Marx, Aristotle "was the first to analyse . . . the form of value." As indicated in the chapter on WEALTH, economics at its origin was treated by Aristotle, along with ethics and politics, as a moral discipline. But he made it subordinate to them because it dealt not with the whole of human welfare, but only with wealth—one of the goods.

In the modern development of economics, the word "goods" comes to have a special significance. It refers to commodities or utilities, as in the phrase "goods and services." More generally, anything which is useful or exchangeable has the character of an economic good. This general sense is usually conveyed by the economist's use of the word "value." According to Adam Smith, "the word *value* . . . has two different meanings, and sometimes expresses the utility of some particular object, and sometimes the power of purchasing other goods which the possessor of that object conveys." These two meanings are distinguished as "value in use" and "value in exchange." Marx accepts this distinction, but thinks that there is a more fundamental notion of value. He thinks it is possible to abstract from both use-value and exchange-value, and to discover the underlying property which gives value to all exchangeable things, namely, that they are products of labor.

With Smith and Marx, as with Aristotle, the theory of value does not deal with every type of good, but only with that type which earlier moralists called "external goods" or "goods of fortune." But more recently the concept of value has been extended, by economists and others, to the evaluation of everything which men think of as desirable in any way. In consequence, the age-old controversy about the objectivity or subjectivity of good and evil is now stated in terms of the difference between facts and values, or between judgments of fact and judgments of value.

The issue, as currently stated, is whether questions of value can be answered in the same way as questions of fact. One position maintains that, unlike questions of fact which can be answered by scientific investigation and can be objectively solved, questions of value elicit no more than expressions of opinion, relative to the individual's subjective response or to the conventions of his society at a given time. The other side of the issue is held by those who insist that the norms of value are as objective and as scientifically determinable as the criteria of fact or existence.

THE WORD "VALUE" does not change the problem in any way; for what does evaluating anything mean except judging it as good or bad, better or worse? The problem, which has a history as long as the tradition of the great books, is the problem of how we can defend such judgments and what they signify about the things judged. Are good and evil determined by nature or convention? Are they objects of knowledge or opinion?

The title of an essay by Montaigne—"That the taste of good and evil depends in large part on the opinion we have of them"—indicates one set of answers to these questions. "If evils have no entry into us but by our judgment," he writes, "it seems to be in our power to disdain them or turn them to good use . . . If what we call evil and torment is neither evil nor torment in itself, if it is merely our fancy that gives it this quality, it is in us to change it." Echoing Montaigne, Hamlet remarks that "there is nothing either good or bad but thinking makes it so." The Greek Sophists, centuries earlier, appear to take the same view. The statement of Protagoras that "man is the measure of all things," Plato thinks, does not significantly apply to *all* things, but only to such things as the good or the right, the true or the beautiful. In the *Theaetetus*, Protagoras is made to say that as "to the sick man his food appears to be bitter, and to the healthy man the opposite of bitter," so in general men estimate or judge all things according to their own condition and the way things affect them. This theory of good and evil necessarily denies the possibility of moral science. Socrates calls it "a high argument in which all things are said to be relative."

Plato and Aristotle respond to the Sophists by arguing in the opposite vein. For Plato, the good is not a matter of opinion, but an object of knowledge. Knowledge of good and evil is the best fruit of the tree of knowledge. "Let each one of us leave every other kind of knowledge," Socrates says at the end of *The Republic*, "and seek and follow one thing only," that is, "to learn and discern between good and evil."

Aristotle does not think that ethics, or any science which deals with good and evil, can have as much precision as mathematics. "Our discussion will be adequate," he writes, "if it has as much clearness as the subject matter admits of, for precision is not to be sought for alike in all discussions." This, however, does not exclude the possibility of our knowing with great exactitude the first principles of moral science, such as the nature of happiness and virtue. Indefiniteness and even a certain kind of relativity occur only when these principles are applied to particular cases. Hence, in Aristotle's view, the moral sciences, such as ethics and politics, can have objective and universal validity no less than physics or mathematics, at least on the level of principles.

In modern times, Locke and Kant also affirm the scientific character of ethics, but without the qualification which Aristotle insists upon when we go from principles to practice. Locke explains the grounds on which he is "bold to think that morality is capable of demonstration, as well as mathematics"; for, he says, "the precise real essence of the things moral words stand for may be perfectly known, and so the congruity and incongruity of the things themselves may be certainly discovered; in which consists perfect knowledge." He is confident that "from self-evident propositions, by necessary consequences, as incontestible as those in mathematics, the measures of right and wrong might be made out, to any one that will apply himself with the same indifference and attention to the one as he does to the other of these sciences." But Locke adds, "this is not to be expected, whilst the desire of esteem, riches, or power makes men espouse the well-endowed opinions in fashion." He himself seems to tend in the opposite direction when he identifies the good with the pleasant and makes it relative to individual desires.

For Kant the two major parts of philosophy—physics and ethics—are on equal footing, the one concerned with the "laws of *nature*," the other with the "laws of *freedom*." In each case there is both empirical and *a priori* knowledge. Kant calls the latter in each case "metaphysics" and speaks of "a *metaphysic of nature* and a *metaphysic of morals*." The nature of science, he thinks, requires us to "separate the empirical from the rational part, and prefix to physics proper (or empirical physics) a metaphysic of nature, and to practical anthropology a metaphysic of morals, which must be carefully cleared of everything empirical."

This partial inventory of thinkers who stand against skepticism or relativism in the field of morals indicates that agreement on this point is accompanied by some disagreement about the reasons for holding what appears to be the same view. The opposite view seems also to be shared by thinkers of quite different cast, such as Spinoza and J. S. Mill, who differ from each other as well as from Montaigne and the ancient Sophists.

The terms "good and evil," Spinoza writes, "indicate nothing positive in things considered in themselves, nor are they anything else than modes of thought . . . One and the same thing may at the same time be both good and evil or indifferent"—according to the person who makes the judgment of it. Spinoza therefore defines "good" as "that which we certainly know is useful to us." Apart from society, he says, "there is nothing which by universal consent is good or evil, since everyone in a natural state consults only his own profit." Only when men live together in a civil society under law can it be "decided by universal consent what is good and what is evil."

Holding that all men seek happiness and that they determine what is good and evil in particular cases by reference to this end, Mill seems to offer the standard of utility as an objective principle of morality. But insofar as he identifies happiness with a sum total of pleasures or satisfactions, it tends to become relative to the individual or the group. If competent judges disagree concerning which of two pleasures is the greater or higher, there can be no appeal, Mill says, except to the verdict of the majority. To this extent at least, judgments of value are expressions of opinion, not determinations of science. Nor does Mill hesitate to say that "the ultimate sanction of all morality" is "a subjective feeling in our minds."

As Nietzsche represents the epitome of atheism in theology, so he also represents the most extreme rejection of all the traditional doctrines of morality in the western tradition. In *Beyond Good and Evil,* he declares that, in reviewing all the "finer and coarser moralities which have ruled or still rule on earth I found certain traits regularly recurring together and bound up with one another . . . There is *master morality* and *slave morality*—I add at once that in all higher and mixed cultures attempts at mediation between the two are apparent and more frequently confusion and mutual misunderstanding between them, indeed sometimes their harsh juxtaposition—even within the same man, within *one* soul . . . Slave morality is essentially the morality of utility. Here is the source of the famous antithesis 'good' and '*evil*'—power and danger were felt to exist in evil, a certain dreadfulness, subtlety and strength which could not admit of contempt. Thus, according to slave morality the 'evil' inspire fear; according to master morality it is precisely the 'good' who inspire fear and want to inspire it, while the 'bad' man is judged contemptible. The antithesis reaches its height when, consistently with slave morality, a breath of disdain finally also comes to be attached to the 'good' of this morality—it may be a slight and benevolent disdain—because within the slaves' way of thinking the good man has in any event to be a *harmless* man: he is good-natured, easy to deceive, perhaps a bit stupid, *un bonhomme.* Wherever slave morality comes to predominate, language exhibits a tendency to bring the words 'good' and 'stupid' closer to each other."

IN ORDER TO clarify this basic issue it is necessary to take note of other terms which are usually involved in the discussion of good and evil—such terms as pleasure and pain, desire and aversion, being, nature, and reason. In the course of doing this, we will perceive the relevance of the chapters which deal with those ideas.

It has been said, for example, that the good is identical with the pleasant; that the good is what men desire; that the good is a property of being or existence; that the good is that which conforms to the nature of a thing; that the good is that which is approved by reason. It is possible to see some truth in each of these statements. But each, taken by itself, may be too great a simplification. Searching questions can be asked by those who refuse to equate the good with the pleasant or the desirable, the real, the natural, or the reasonable. Are there no pleasures in any way bad, no pains in any way good? Are all desires themselves good, or are all equally good? How does calling a thing "good" add anything to its being or existence? Does not evil exist or qualify existence? By what standards can the natural and the rational be judged good, if the good is that which conforms to nature and reason?

These questions call for more analysis of each of these factors in the discussion of good and evil and suggest that no one of these factors *by itself* is sufficient to solve the problem of defining good and evil or formulating their criteria. Of the five things mentioned, two particularly—pleasure and desire—seem to leave open the question whether good and evil are objective or subjective. They require us to decide whether things please us *because they are good* or are good *because they please us;* whether we desire things because they are good or simply call them "good" when we desire them. On this issue Spinoza flatly declares that "we do not desire a thing because we adjudge it good, but, on the contrary, we call it good because we desire it." In saying that "a thing is good so far as it is desirable," Aquinas takes the opposite position, for according to him "a thing is desirable only in so far as it is perfect." It can be desirable, therefore, without being actually desired by this or that individual.

The other three terms—unlike pleasure and desire—seem to favor the objectivity of good and evil, at least for those who regard the order of existence, the nature of things, and the laws of reason as independent of our desires or preferences. Thus for Spinoza the *nature* of man and his *reason* seem to provide an objective standard for determining what is good alike for all men. Nothing, he writes, "can be good except in so far as it agrees with our nature, and therefore the more an object agrees with our nature the more profitable it will be." And in another place he says, "by *good* I understand . . . everything which we are certain is a means by which we may approach nearer and nearer to the model of human nature we set before us." That model, he tells us, is the man of reason, the man who always acts "according to the dictates of reason," for "those desires which are determined by man's power or reason are always good."

Nevertheless, if desire and pleasure cannot be eliminated from the consideration of good and evil—at least not the good and evil which enter into human life—then the problem of finding a purely objective foundation for our moral judgments is not solved simply by an appeal to being, nature, and reason.

Some help toward a solution may be found in one often reiterated fact about the relation between the good and human desire. The ancients insist that no man desires anything but what at the time *seems* good to him in some way. "No man," Socrates observes, "voluntarily pursues evil, or that which he thinks to be evil. To prefer evil to good is not in human nature; and when a man is compelled to choose one of two evils, no one will choose the greater when he may have the less." This, however, does not prevent men from desiring "what they suppose to be goods although they are really evils." Since they are mistaken in their judgment "and suppose the evils to be goods, they really desire goods."

The object consciously desired is always at least *apparently* good. When men are mistaken in their estimate of things as beneficial or injurious to themselves, the apparent good—the good actually desired—will be really an evil, that is, something actually undesirable. An object which is really good may not appear to be so, and so it will not be desired although it is desirable. The deception of appearances, Socrates says, tricks us into taking "at one time the things of which we repent at another, both in our actions and in our choice of things great and small."

THE DISTINCTION between the *real* and the *apparent* good is, of course, connected with the problem of the objective and the subjective good. The apparent good varies from individual to individual and from time to time. If there were a real good, it would be free from such relativity and variability. Unless there are real, as distinct from merely apparent, goods, moralists cannot distinguish between what men *should* desire and what in fact they *do* desire.

Since moral science deals with human behavior, its province can be separated from that of other sciences which treat the same subject matter—such as psychology and sociology—only in terms of a different treatment of that subject matter. Moral science must be normative or prescriptive rather than descriptive. It must determine what men *should* seek, not what they *do* seek. The very existence of normative sciences, as well as their validity, would thus seem to depend on the establishment of a real, as opposed to a merely apparent, good.

This creates no special difficulty for moralists who think that man knows what is really good for him, both in general and in particular, by intuition or rational deduction, through the commandments of the divine law, or through the precepts of the law of reason. But for those who insist that the good is always somehow relative to desire and always involves pleasure, the distinction between the real and the apparent good raises an extremely difficult problem.

To say that an apparent good is not really good suggests, as we have seen, that what is called "good" may not be in itself desirable. That something which is really good may not in fact appear to be so, seems to imply that the word "good" can be significantly applied to something which is not actually desired—at least not consciously. How, then, is the good always relative to desire? The traditional answer to this question must appeal to the distinction between natural and conscious desire, which is discussed in the chapter on DE-SIRE. It is by reference to natural desire that the good is said to be in itself always desirable—even when the really good thing is not consciously desired.

The relation of good and evil to pleasure and pain can also be clarified by a basic distinction between the pleasure which is an object of desire and pleasure conceived as the satisfaction of desire. This is discussed in the chapter on PLEASURE AND PAIN. If obtaining a desired good is satisfying, then there is certainly a sense in which the good and the pleasant (or the satisfying) are always associated; but it may also be true that pleasure is only one kind of good among various objects of desire and that certain pleasures which men desire appear to be, but are not really, good.

THE FOREGOING considerations apply to the good in the sphere of human conduct. But the human good, the practicable good, the good for man, does not exhaust the meaning of the term *good*. The idea of the good is, for Plato, the measure of perfection in all things; it is "not only the author of knowledge to all things known, but of their being and essence, and yet the good is not essence, but far exceeds essence in dignity and power."

The absolute good is also, as in *The Divine Comedy,* the final cause or ultimate end of the motions of the universe. It is the "Alpha and Omega," Dante says, "of all the scripture which Love reads to me . . . that Essence wherein is such supremacy that whatsoever good be found outside of It is naught else save a beam of Its own radiance . . . the Love which moves the sun and the other stars."

So too, in Aristotle's cosmology, the circular motions of the celestial spheres, and through them all other cycles of natural change, are sustained eternally by the prime mover, which moves all things by the attraction of its perfect being. It therefore "moves without being moved," for it "produces motion through being loved."

Though desire and love enter into the conception of the good as a cosmic final cause, they are not *human* desire or love. Though the goodness which inheres in things according to

the degree of their perfection may make them desirable, it is not dependent on their being consciously desired by men.

In Jewish and Christian theology, for example, the goodness of God is in no way measured by human desires, purposes, or pleasures; nor is the goodness of created things which, according to Genesis, God surveyed and found "very good." The order of creation, moreover, involves a hierarchy of inequalities in being and goodness. Even when each thing is perfect in its kind, all things are not equally good, for according to the differences in their natures, diverse kinds are capable of greater or less perfection.

In the metaphysical conception of goodness, that which has more actuality either in existence or power has more perfection. God's infinite goodness is therefore said to follow from the fact that he is completely actual—infinite in being and power. Things "which have life," Augustine writes, "are ranked above those which have none . . . And among those that have life, the sentient are higher than those which have no sensation . . . and among the sentient, the intelligent above those that have no intelligence."

Augustine contrasts these gradations of perfection which are "according to the order of nature" with the "standards of value" which are "according to the utility each man finds in a thing." That which is less good in a metaphysical sense may be preferred on moral grounds as being better for man. "Who," he asks, "would not rather have bread in his house than mice, gold than fleas?" Is it not true that "more is often given for a horse than for a slave, for a jewel than for a maid"?

According to Augustine, as well as to Aquinas later, metaphysical goodness consists in "the value a thing has in itself in the scale of creation," while moral goodness depends upon the relation in which a thing stands to human need or desire, and according to the estimation placed upon it by human reason. It is in the moral, not the metaphysical sense that we speak of a good man, a good will, a good life, and a good society; or of all the things, such as health, wealth, pleasure, virtue, or knowledge, which it may be good for man to seek and possess. Only in the metaphysical sense can things be thought of as good entirely apart from man; only then can we find a hierarchy of perfections in the world which accords with a hierarchy of beings. Thus Spinoza declares that "the perfection of things is to be judged by their nature and power alone; nor are they more or less perfect because they delight or offend the human senses, or because they are beneficial or prejudicial to human nature."

THE METAPHYSICAL conception of goodness raises peculiarly difficult problems. Are there as many meanings of "good" as there are of "being"? When we say God is good, are we making a moral or a metaphysical judgment? Are we attributing perfection of being or goodness of will to God? If goodness is a property of being, then must not all evil become a privation of being? Conceiving evil in this way, Augustine points out that if things "are deprived of all good, they cease altogether to be," so that "evil does not exist" in itself; and Aquinas maintains that "no being is said to be evil, considered as being, but only so far as it lacks being."

If to understand what the notion of goodness adds to the notion of being it is necessary to say that being has goodness in relation to appetite, the question inevitably arises, "Whose appetite?" Not man's certainly, for then the moral and the metaphysical good become identical. If God's, then not appetite in the form of desire, but in the form of love, for the divine perfection is usually thought to preclude desire.

Problems of this sort confront those who, conceiving the good both *apart from* and also *relative to* man, are obligated to connect the metaphysical and the moral meanings of good and to say whether they have a common thread. Some writers, however, limit their consideration to the strictly moral good, and deny, as do the Stoics, goodness or evil to anything but man's free acts of will.

We should, says Marcus Aurelius, "judge only those things which are in our power, to be good or bad." In this we are entirely free, for "things themselves have no natural power to form our judgments . . . If thou art pained by any external thing, it is not this thing which disturbs thee, but thy own judgment about it. And it is in thy power to wipe out this judgment now . . . Suppose that men kill thee, cut thee in pieces, curse thee. What then can these things do to prevent thy mind from remaining pure, wise, sober, just?"

Though Kant develops what he calls a "metaphysic of ethics," he does not seem to have a metaphysical as opposed to a moral conception of the good; unless in some analogous form it lies in his distinction between "value" and "dignity," according to which "whatever has reference to the general inclinations and wants of mankind has a *market value*," whereas "whatever . . . is above all value, and therefore admits of no equivalent, has a dignity"—"not a merely relative worth, but an intrinsic worth."

But since Kant thinks that only men, or rational beings, can have intrinsic worth, he finds goodness only in the moral order. He agrees with the Stoics that good and evil occur only in the realm of freedom, not at all in the realm of existence or nature. "Good or evil," he writes, "always implies a reference to the *will*, as determined by the *law of reason*" which is the law of freedom. According to Kant, "nothing can possibly be conceived in the world, or even out of it, which can be called good without qualification, except a Good Will"; and in another place he says, "If anything is to be good or evil absolutely . . . it can only be the manner of acting, the maxim of the will." In this sense, the free will complying with or resisting the imperatives of duty is either the seat or the source of all the goodness or evil that there is. "Men may laugh," Kant says, "at the Stoic, who in the severest paroxysms of gout cried out: Pain, however thou tormentest me, I will never admit that thou art an evil: he was right . . . for pain did not in the least diminish the worth of his person, but only that of his condition."

IN THE SPHERE of moral conduct, and especially for those who make desire or pleasure rather than duty the principle, there seems to be a plurality of goods which require classification and order.

Some things, it would appear, are not desired for themselves, but for the sake of something else. They are good only as means to be used. Some things are desired for their own sake, and are good as ends, to be possessed or enjoyed. This division of goods into means and ends—the useful and the enjoyable or pleasant—permits a third type of good which is an end in one respect, and a means in another. Analysis of this sort leads to the concept of a *summum bonum*—that good which is not a means in any respect, but entirely an end, the supreme or highest good for which all else is sought.

The chief question with respect to the *summum bonum* is whether it is *a* good or *the* good—whether it is merely one type of good, more desirable than any other, or the sum of all good things which, when possessed, leaves nothing to be desired. Aristotle and Mill seem to take the latter view in their conception of happiness as the *summum bonum*. "Human nature," Mill says, "is so constituted as to desire nothing which is not either a part of happiness or a means of happiness." Happiness, he insists, is "not an abstract idea, but a concrete whole" including all other goods within itself. It is the only good which is desired entirely for its own sake. Aristotle treats virtue and knowledge as intrinsic goods, but he also regards them as means to happiness. In Mill's terms, their goodness remains subject to the criterion of utility, from which happiness alone is exempt since it measures the utility of all other goods.

If the evaluation of all things by reference to their contribution to happiness as the ultimate good constitutes utilitarianism in ethics, then Aristotle no less than Mill is a utilitarian, even though Aristotle does not refer to the principle of utility, does not identify the good with pleasure, and conceives the virtues as intrinsically good, not merely as means. Kant would regard them as in fundamental agreement despite all their differences—or at least he would regard them as committing the same fundamental error. For a quite different reason, Weber dismisses an "ethic of ultimate ends," on the ground that "the problem of the justification of means by ends . . . has only the

possibility of rejecting all action that employs morally dangerous means." Weber goes on to say that "it is not possible to bring an ethic of ultimate ends and an ethic of responsibility under one roof."

To Kant any discussion of human conduct which involves the calculation of means to ends is pragmatic or utilitarian, even when the controlling end is the *summum bonum* or happiness. Kant makes a sharp distinction between what he calls "pragmatical rules" of conduct which consider what should be done by one who wishes to be happy, and what he regards as the strictly "moral or ethical law" which "has no other motive than the *worthiness of being happy*." Morality, he says in another place, "is not properly the doctrine of how we should *make* ourselves happy, but how we should become *worthy* of happiness"—through doing our duty.

Kant's criticism of Aristotle's ethics of happiness is therefore applicable to the utilitarianism of Mill; and Mill's rejoinder to Kant serves as a defense of Aristotle. This basic issue concerning the primacy of happiness or duty—of desire or law—is discussed in the chapters on DUTY and HAPPINESS, where it is suggested that in an ethics of duty, right and wrong supplant good and evil as the fundamental terms, and the *summum bonum* becomes a derivative notion rather than the first principle of morality.

At the other extreme are those who deny duty entirely, and with it any meaning to right and wrong as distinct from good and evil. A middle ground is held by those who employ right and wrong as subordinate terms in the analysis of good and evil, finding their special significance in the consideration of the good of others or the social good. To do right is to do good to others; to do wrong is to injure them. The question which Plato so insistently raises, whether it is better to do injustice or to suffer it, can also be stated in terms of good and evil, or right and wrong. Is it better to suffer evil or to do it? Is it better to be wronged by others or to wrong them? As justice for Aristotle is that one among the virtues which concerns the good of others and the common good, and as it is the one virtue which is thought to involve duty or obligation, so the criteria of right and wrong measure the goodness or evil of human acts by reference to law and society.

THE DIVISION of goods into means and ends is not the only distinction made by moralists who recognize the plurality and inequality of goods.

Goods have been divided into the limited and the unlimited with respect to quantity; the pure and the mixed with respect to quality; sensible and intelligible goods or particular goods and the good in general; external goods, goods of the body, and goods of the soul; the pleasant, the useful, and the virtuous. More specific enumerations of the variety of goods list wealth, health, strength, beauty, longevity, pleasure, honor (or fame), virtue, knowledge, friendship.

All of the foregoing classifications can be combined with one another, but there is one distinction which stands by itself, although it affects all the others. That is the distinction between the individual and the common good, or between private and public good, the good for this one man and the good of all others and of the whole community. In the language of modern utilitarianism, it is the distinction between individual happiness and what Jeremy Bentham called "the greatest good for the greatest number."

The phrase "common good" has several meanings in the tradition of the great books. One sense, which some think is the least significant, refers to that which can be shared or used by many, as, for example, land held in common and worked by a number of persons or families. Thus we speak of the "commons" of a town or village. This meaning applies particularly to economic goods which may either belong to the community as a whole or be divided into parcels of private property.

Another sense of common good is that in which the welfare of a community is a common good participated in by its members. The welfare of the family or the state is a good which belongs to a multitude organized for some common purpose. If the individual members of the group derive some benefit from their association with one another, then the prosperity of the community is not only a common good viewed collectively, but also a common good viewed distributively, for it is the good of each member of the group as well as of the whole.

With this in mind, perhaps, Mill speaks of "an indissoluble association between [the individual's] happiness and the practice of such mode of conduct, negative and positive, as regard for the universal happiness prescribes; so that not only he may be unable to conceive the possibility of happiness to himself, consistently with conduct opposed to the general good, but also that a direct impulse to promote the general good may be in every individual one of the habitual modes of action." If this statement by Mill is used to interpret Bentham's phrase—"the greatest good for the greatest number"—then the greatest number cannot be taken to mean a majority, for the good of nothing less than the whole collectively or of all distributively can be taken as the common or general good.

Still another conception of the common good is possible. A good may be common in the sense in which a specific nature is common to the members of the species—not as organized socially in any way, but simply as so many *like* individuals. If all men seek happiness, for example, then happiness is a common good, even though each individual seeks his own happiness. In a deeper sense it is a common good if the happiness each seeks is the same for all men because they are all of the same nature; but, most strictly, it is a common good if the happiness of each individual cannot be separated from the happiness of all.

Aquinas seems to be using this meaning of *common good* when, in defining law as a rule of conduct "directed to the common good," he refers not merely to the good of the community or body politic, but beyond that to "the last end of human life," which is "happiness or beatitude." Law, he says, "must needs concern itself properly with the order directed to universal happiness." Mill also seems to conceive happiness as a common good in this sense. "What the assailants of utilitarianism seldom have the justice to acknowledge," he writes, is "that the happiness which forms the utilitarian standard of what is right in conduct, is not the agent's own happiness, but that of all concerned."

The several meanings of the common good create a fundamental issue. Some writers use it in one sense only, rejecting the others. Some not only use the term in all its meanings, but also develop a hierarchy of common goods. They regard universal happiness, for example, as a common good of a higher order than the welfare of the political community. Yet in every order they insist upon the primacy of the common over the individual good. In the political order, for example, they think the welfare of the community takes precedence over individual happiness. They would regard Smith's statement of the way in which individuals accidentally serve the common good while seeking their private interests, as a perversion of the relationship. To say that an individual considering only his own gain is "led by an invisible hand to promote an end which was no part of his intention" (*i.e.*, the general prosperity of society) does not excuse the individual's failure to aim at the common good.

The several meanings of the common good also complicate the statement of the issue between those who seem to say that the welfare of the community always takes precedence over individual well-being or happiness—that

the good of the whole is always greater than the good of its parts—and those who seem to say that the state is made for man, not man for the state, or that the prosperity of the society in which men live is good primarily because it enables each of them to live well. This issue, which runs through all the great books of political theory from Plato and Aristotle to Hegel and Mill, is discussed in the chapters on CITIZEN and STATE.

The opposition between collectivism and individualism in economics and politics does not exhaust the issue which, stated in its broadest moral terms, is a conflict between self-interest and altruism. The primary problem to consider here is whether the issue is itself genuine, or only an opposition between false extremes which needlessly exclude the half-truth that each contains.

The collective aspect of the common good may not need to be emphasized at the expense of its distributive aspect. The good of each man and the good of mankind may be inseparable. It may be the same good which, in different respects, is individual and common. It may be that no good can be supreme which is not both immanent and transcendent—at once the highest perfection of the individual and a good greater than his whole being and his life.

31

Government

INTRODUCTION

THE usual connotation of "government" is political. The word is often used interchangeably with "state." But there is government in a university, in an economic corporation, in the church, in any organization of men associated for a common purpose. The theologian speaks of the divine government of the universe, and the moralist speaks of reason as the ruling power in the soul which governs the appetites or passions.

In all these contexts, the notion of government involves the fundamental relations of ruling and being ruled, of command and obedience. Though the character of these relationships varies somewhat with the terms related, there is enough common meaning throughout to permit a general consideration of the nature of government. But that is not the way in which government is discussed in the great books. For the most part, government is considered in one or another of its special settings—as it functions in the family or the state, in the soul or the universe. The common thread of meaning is noted only indirectly, by the way in which comparisons are made or analogies are drawn between the various modes of government.

In view of this, we have found it convenient to restrict this chapter to government in the political sense, treating domestic and ecclesiastical government under FAMILY and RELIGION, economic government under WEALTH, divine government in the chapters on GOD and WORLD, and government in the soul in the several chapters which consider the relation of reason to the passions, such as DESIRE and EMOTION.

Government and *state* are often used as if they were interchangeable terms. Some writers differentiate their meaning by using "state" to signify the political community itself, and "government" to refer to the way in which it is politically organized. Yet the two concepts tend to fuse in traditional political theory. The kinds of states, for example, are usually named according to their forms of government. The great books speak of monarchical and republican states, as we today speak of the fascist or the democratic state.

Nevertheless, we recognize the distinction between a state and its government when we observe that the state can maintain its historic identity while it undergoes fundamental changes in its form of government. The state is not dissolved by a revolution which replaces a monarchy by a republic, or conversely. There is a sense in which Rome is the same state under the Tarquins, under the Republic, and under the Caesars. In contrast, some rebellions, such as the War of Secession in American history, threaten to dissolve the state itself.

Despite the fact that government involves a relation between rulers and ruled, the word is often used to designate one term in that relationship, namely, the rulers. When the citizens of a republic speak of "the government," they usually refer to the officialdom—not the body of citizens as a whole, but only those who for a time hold public office. But government cannot consist of governors alone, any more than education can consist of teachers alone. The different forms of government can be distinguished as readily by looking to the condition of the ruled as to the powers of the rulers. Furthermore, the same individuals may both "rule and be ruled by turns," as Aristotle observes of constitutional government.

Though the notion of government includes

both rulers and ruled, the word usually appears in political literature with the more restricted meaning. When writers refer to the branches or departments of government, or when they speak of the sovereignty of a government, they direct attention to the ruling power, and to the division of that power into related parts.

THE GREAT BOOKS OF political theory ask a number of basic questions about government. What is the origin of government, its nature and necessity? What ends does government serve and how do these ends define its scope and limits? What is the distinction between good and bad government, between legitimate and illegitimate, or just and unjust, government? What are the forms of government, of good government, of bad government? What are the various departments or branches of government, and how should they function with respect to one another?

These questions are related. The origin, nature, and necessity of government have a bearing on its ends and limits. These same considerations enter into the discussion of the legitimacy and justice of governments. They also have a bearing on the classification of the forms of government, and on the evaluation of diverse forms. The way in which the several branches of government should be related is affected by the way in which the various forms of government differ.

These questions are not always approached in the same order. Some of the great political theorists—for example, Hobbes, Locke, and Rousseau—find their fundamental principles in the consideration of the origin of government. They start with such questions as, What makes it legitimate for one man to govern another? Is the exercise of political power both justified and limited by the end it serves? In answering these questions, they imply or make a distinction between good and bad government and indicate the abuses or corruptions to which government is subject. Though they enumerate the various forms of government in a manner which reflects the traditional classifications, they do not seem to regard that problem as of central importance.

Other eminent political thinkers make the classification and comparison of diverse forms the central problem in the theory of government. Plato and Aristotle, Montesquieu and J. S. Mill, are primarily concerned with the criteria by which the justice or goodness of a government shall be judged. They compare various forms of government as more or less desirable, nearer to the ideal or nearer to the opposite extreme of corruption. In the course of these considerations they answer questions about the necessity, the legitimacy, and the ends of government in general.

THERE SEEMS TO BE considerable agreement on one point, namely, that government is necessary for the life of the state. It is generally held by the authors of the great books that no community can dispense with government, for without government men cannot live together in peace. None is an anarchist, like Thoreau or Kropotkin, although Kropotkin claims that *War and Peace* and even Mill's essay *On Liberty* contain "anarchist ideas." Marx and Engels may be the other possible exception to the rule.

As Weber sees it, Trotsky was correct in saying that "every state is founded on force." In his view, without the use of force, "the concept of 'state' would be eliminated, and a condition would emerge that could be designated as 'anarchy,' in the specific sense of this word." But Weber fails to distinguish between violence and a legitimate use of coercive force by government. The error here is corrected by defining legitimate government as exercising a monopoly of authorized force. All unauthorized force is violence.

Marx and Engels appear to take the opposite view, a view that is expounded in Lenin's *The State and Revolution*. They do so on the ground that with the advent of a classless society after the communist revolution, the class war will come to an end and there will no longer be any need for government. The state can quietly wither away. But, according to Aquinas, even if society were free from all injustice and iniquity, even if men lived together in a state of innocence and with the moral perfection they would possess if Adam had not sinned, even then government would be necessary. "A social life," he thinks, "cannot exist among a number of people unless government is set up to look after the common good."

The great books do not agree about the naturalness of the state. They do not agree about the way in which government originates historically or about the functions it should and should not perform. They do not all reflect in the same way on the good and evil in government. Nor do they all give the same reasons for the necessity of government. In consequence they set different limits to the scope of government and assign it different functions, which range from the merely negative function of preventing violence to the duty to provide positively for human welfare in a variety of ways.

On all these things they differ, but with the exceptions noted they do concur in thinking that anarchy—the total absence of government—is unsuitable to the nature of man. Man being what he is, "any form of government," in Darwin's opinion, "is better than none." Some, like Hobbes and Kant, identify anarchy with the state of nature which is for them a state of war. Some, like Locke, think that the state of nature is not a state of war, yet find great advantages to living in civil society precisely because government remedies the inconveniences and ills which anarchy breeds. But though they often write as if men could choose between living in a state of nature or in a civil society, they do not think man has any option with respect to government if he wishes the benefits of the civilized life. They cannot conceive civil society as existing for a moment without government.

THE GENERAL AGREEMENT about the necessity of government tends to include an agreement about the two basic elements of government— authority and power. No government at all is possible, not even the most attenuated, unless men obey its directions or regulations. But one man may obey another either *voluntarily* or *involuntarily*—either because he recognizes the right vested in that other to give him commands or because he fears the consequences which he may suffer if he disobeys.

These two modes of obedience correspond to the authority and power of government. Authority elicits voluntary compliance. Power either actually coerces or, by threatening coercion, compels involuntarily obedience. Authority and power are the right and might of government. Either can exist and may operate apart from the other; but, as Rousseau points out, when right is lacking, government is illegitimate; and as Hamilton points out, when might is lacking, it is ineffective.

In a famous passage, the Federalists explain that rule by authority alone might work in a society of angels. But since men are men, not angels, their obedience must be assured by the threat of force. In any society in which some men are good, some bad, and all may be either at one time or another, force is the only expedient to get the unwilling to do what they should do for the common good. Even when the institutions of government have their authority from the consent of the governed, they cannot function effectively without the use of power or force. For this reason Hamilton dismisses "the idea of governing at all times by the simple force of law" as having "no place but in the reveries of those political doctors whose sagacity disdains the admonitions of experimental instruction."

If authority without force is ineffective for the purposes of government, might without right is tyrannical. "Wherever law ends, tyranny begins," Locke writes, "and whosoever in authority exceeds the power given him by the law, and makes use of the force he has under his command to compass that upon the subject which the law allows not, ceases in that to be a magistrate." The use of unauthorized force may take the form of either usurpation or tyranny. If it is "the exercise of power which another hath a right to," Locke declares it is usurpation; if it is "the exercise of power beyond right, which nobody can have a right to," it is tyranny.

The distinction between legitimate rule and all dominations by force rests not on the use of power, but on whether the power which must be employed is or is not legally authorized.

THE NOTION OF sovereignty involves considerations of authority and power. The word itself is medieval and feudal in origin. It signifies the supremacy of an overlord who owes allegiance to no one and to whom fealty is due from all who hold fiefdoms under him. Since the supremacy of the sovereign lord is clothed with legal rights, according to the customs of feudal tenure, sovereignty seems to imply the union of power with authority, not the use of naked force.

The political philosophers of antiquity do not use the term *sovereignty*. But their discussion of the distribution of political power is certainly concerned with the possession of authority as well as the control of force. Aristotle's question, for example, about "what is to be the supreme power in the state—the multitude? or the wealthy? or the good? or the one best man?" deals with the same problem which modern writers express by asking where sovereignty resides. As Aristotle sees the conflict between the oligarchic and the democratic constitutions, the issue concerns the legal definition of the ruling class: whether the constitution puts all the political power in the hands of the rich or in the hands of the freeborn, rich and poor alike. It does not seem to be too violent an interpretation for modern translators to use the word "sovereignty" here, for sovereignty can be said to belong to whatever person or class holds the supreme power by law.

Within this meaning of sovereignty the basic difference between absolute and limited government, or between the despotic and the constitutional regime, leads to a distinction between the sovereign man and the sovereign office.

The ruler who holds sovereignty in his person is an absolute sovereign if his power and authority are in no way limited by positive law. According to some political philosophers, sovereignty must be absolute. In the opinion of Hobbes, for example, the notion of a limited sovereignty seems to be as self-contradictory as that of a supremacy which is not supreme.

After discussing the absolute rights which constitute sovereignty, Hobbes goes on to say that "this great authority being indivisible . . . there is little ground for the opinion of them that say of sovereign kings, though they be *singulis majores,* of greater power than every one of their subjects, yet they be *universis minores,* of less power than them all together. For if by *all together* they mean not the collective body as one person, then *all together* and *every one* signify the same, and the speech is absurd. But if by *all together* they understand them as one person (which person the sovereign bears), then the power of all together is the same as the sovereign's power, and so again the speech is absurd."

It makes no difference, Hobbes argues, whether the sovereignty is held by one man or by an assembly. In either case "the sovereign of a commonwealth . . . is not subject to the civil laws. For having the power to make and repeal laws, he may when he pleases, free himself from that subjection by repealing those laws that trouble him." The sovereign therefore has absolute power, which consists in the absolute right or liberty to do as he pleases, for "he that is bound to himself only is not bound" at all.

Aquinas seems to be taking the same view when he admits that "the sovereign is . . . *exempt from the law* as to its coercive power, since, properly speaking, no man is coerced by himself, and law has no coercive power save from the authority of the sovereign." But Aquinas differs from Hobbes in thinking that the authority, if not the power, of the prince is limited by the constitutional character of the kingly office. In the medieval conception of monarchy, the king is bound not to himself alone, as Hobbes insists, but to his subjects. Their oath of allegiance to him is reciprocated by his coronation oath, in which he assumes the obligation to uphold the customs of the realm.

WHERE AQUINAS CONCEIVES the sovereign prince as one element—the other being established law—in a government which is therefore both absolute and constitutional, Hobbes conceives the sovereign as identical with a government which is wholly absolute. The distinction here implied—between a mixed regime and one that is purely absolute—is more fully discussed in the chapters on CONSTITUTION and MONARCHY. In contrast to both, a republic, or purely constitutional government, substitutes the sovereign office for the sovereign man. It denies the possession of sovereignty to men *except* in their capacity as officeholders.

According to the republican notions of Rousseau, not even government itself has sovereignty except as representing the political community as a whole, which is the sovereign. Sovereignty, he writes, is vested in the government "simply and solely as a commission, an employment in which the rulers, mere officials of the Sovereign, exercise in their own name the power of which it makes them depositaries." Since this power is not theirs except by delegation, it can be limited, modified, or recovered at pleasure, "for the alienation of such a right is incompatible with the nature of the social body, and contrary to the end of association."

The unity of sovereignty is not impaired by the fact that a number of men may share in the exercise of sovereign power, any more than the unity of government is destroyed by its division into separate departments or branches, such as the legislative, executive, and judicial. Since in a republic the government (in all its branches or offices) derives its power and authority from the constitution (or what Rousseau calls "the fundamental law"), and since it is the people as a whole, not the officials of government, who have the constitutive power, the people are in a sense supreme or sovereign.

Popular sovereignty may mean that the people as a whole govern themselves without the services of magistrates of any sort; but this would be possible only in a very small community. It is questionable whether a people has ever exercised sovereignty in this way in any state of historic importance. Popular sovereignty more usually means what is implied by Aquinas when he conceives the magistrate or ruler as merely the vicegerent of the people. "To order anything to the common good," he writes, "belongs either to the whole people, or to someone who is the vicegerent of the whole people. Hence the making of a law belongs either to the whole people or to a public personage who has the care of the whole people." Similarly, the exercise of coer-

cive force "is vested in the whole people or in some public personage, to whom it belongs to inflict penalties."

The notion of a *public personage,* as Aquinas uses it in these passages, is clearly that of a surrogate for or representative of the whole people. The people as a whole have, in the first instance, the authority and power to perform all the functions of government. Only if for convenience or some other reason they constitute one or more public personages to act in their stead, do individual men exercise sovereignty, and then only as representatives.

Locke's fundamental principle—that "men being . . . by nature all free, equal, and independent, no one can be put out of this estate and subjected to the political power of another without his own consent"—is another expression of the idea of popular sovereignty. It reappears in the Declaration of Independence in the statement that since governments are instituted by men to secure their fundamental rights, they must derive "their just powers from the consent of the governed."

Hegel objects to the sense "in which men have recently begun to speak of the 'sovereignty of the people' " as "something opposed to the sovereignty existent in the monarch. So opposed to the sovereignty of the monarch," he writes, "the sovereignty of the people is one of the confused notions based on the wild idea of the 'people.' " If the sovereignty of the people means nothing more than the sovereignty of the whole state, then, he says, the sovereignty which "is there as the personality of the whole . . . is there, in the real existence adequate to its concept, as the person of the monarch."

But republican writers would reply that the sense in which they speak of the sovereignty of the people cannot be opposed to the sovereignty of government, so long as that government is constitutional, not absolute. When the sovereignty of the people is conceived as the source or basis, not as the actual exercise, of the legitimate powers of government, there is no conflict between these two locations of sovereignty in the state. Yet the supremacy of the government always remains limited by the fact that all its powers are delegated and can be withdrawn or changed at the people's will.

THE QUESTION OF absolute or limited sovereignty and the connected question of unified or divided sovereignty have a different meaning in the case of the relation of governments to one another.

The theory of federal government, discussed in *The Federalist* and in Mill's *Representative Government,* contemplates a division of sovereignty, not as between the people and their government, but as between two distinct governments, to each of which the people grant certain powers. Distinguishing between the government of a national state and the government of a federal union, Madison writes: "Among a people consolidated into one nation . . . supremacy is completely vested in the national legislature. Among communities united for particular purposes, it is vested partly in the general and partly in the municipal legislatures. In the former case, all local authorities are subordinate to the supreme; and may be controlled, directed, or abolished by it at pleasure. In the latter, the local or municipal authorities form distinct and independent portions of the supremacy, no more subject, within their respective spheres, to the general authority than the general authority is subject to them within its own sphere." The federal or general and the state or local governments draw on the same reservoir of popular sovereignty, but the sovereignty which each derives from that source is limited by the definition of matters reserved to the jurisdiction of the other.

The fundamental difference between the condition of states in a federation and the condition of colonial dependencies or subject peoples is that imperial government, unlike federal government, claims an unlimited sovereignty. The issues of imperialism which arise from the exercise of such power are discussed in the chapters on TYRANNY AND DESPOTISM and SLAVERY.

The one remaining situation is that of independent governments, the governments of separate states associated with one another only by treaties or alliances, or at most in the kind of loose hegemony or league represented by the Greek confederacies or the American *Articles of Confederation.* In this situation, the word "sovereignty" applied to independent governments signifies supremacy, not in the sense of their having the authority and power to command, but in the opposite sense of *not being subject to any political superior.*

This radical difference in meaning is explicitly formulated in Hegel's distinction between internal and external sovereignty.

After stating the conditions of the sovereignty of the state in relation to its own people, Hegel says, "This is the sovereignty of the state at home. Sovereignty has another side, *i.e.,* sovereignty *vis-à-vis* foreign states." The state's individuality resides in its awareness of its own existence "as a unit in sharp distinction from others"; and in this individuality Hegel finds the state's autonomy, which he thinks is "the most fundamental freedom which a people possesses as well as its highest dignity."

But from the fact that "every state is sovereign and autonomous against its neighbors," it also follows, according to Hegel, that such sovereigns "are in a state of nature in relation to each other." It is this state of nature which Hobbes had earlier described as a state of war. Precisely because independent states have absolute sovereignty in relation to one another, "they live in the condition of perpetual war, and upon the confines of battle, with their frontiers armed, and cannons planted against their neighbors round about."

In their relation to one another they are, writes Kant, like "lawless savages." Following Rousseau, he thinks it is fitting that the state "viewed in relation to other peoples" should be called "a power." Unlike sovereign governments which unite authority with power in their domestic jurisdiction, sovereign states in their external relations can exert force alone upon each other. When their interests conflict, each yields only to superior force or to the threat of it. A fuller discussion of these matters will be found in the chapters on LAW, STATE, and WAR AND PEACE.

As ALREADY INDICATED in several places, the materials covered in this chapter necessarily demand a study of many related chapters dealing with political topics. This is peculiarly true of the problems concerning the forms of government. Separate chapters are devoted to each of the traditionally recognized forms, *viz.*, ARISTOCRACY, DEMOCRACY, MONARCHY, OLIGARCHY, TYRANNY AND DESPOTISM. Each of these chapters defines a particular form, distinguishes it from others, and compares their merits. In addition, the chapter on CONSTITUTION deals with what is perhaps the most fundamental of all distinctions in forms of government, that between a republic and a despotism, or between government by laws and government by men.

Here, then, it is necessary only to treat generally of the issues raised by the classification and comparison of diverse forms of government. They can be summarized in the following questions.

What are the criteria or marks of good government? Is the goodness of government determined by the end it serves, by the way in which it is instituted, by its efficiency in promoting whatever end it serves? Are such criteria of good government as justice, legitimacy, and efficiency, independent or interchangeable?

What is the nature of bad government? Can a distinction be made between the abuses or weakness to which good government is subject in actual operation, and government which is essentially bad because perverse or corrupt in principle as well as practice?

Are there several forms of good government? Of bad government? How are they differentiated from one another? Are all good forms equally good, all bad forms equally bad? If not, what is the principle in terms of which some order of desirability or undesirability is established? For example, is one good form of government better than another, one bad form worse than another, in terms of degrees of justice and injustice, or in terms of efficiency and inefficiency? To put this question in another way, is one form of good government better than another because it achieves a better result or merely because it achieves the same result more completely?

If there are several distinct forms of good government, are there one or more ways in which these can be combined to effect a composite or mixed form? If a mixed form is comparable with the pure forms it unites, is it superior to all, to some, to none of them? On what grounds? In what circumstances?

While proposing what they consider to be the ideal form of government, some political philosophers admit that the ideal may not be realizable under existing circumstances or with men as they are. Plato, for example, recognizes that the state he outlines in *The Republic* may not be practicable; and in the *Laws* he proposes institutions of government which represent for him something less than the ideal but which may be more achievable. The Athenian Stranger says of the state described in *The Republic* that, "whether it is possible or not, no man, acting upon any other principle, will ever constitute a state which will be truer or better or more exalted in virtue." The state which he is discussing in the *Laws* "takes the second place." He refers to "a third best" which, far from being even the practicable ideal, may be merely the best form of government which now actually exists.

Aristotle also sets down the various ways in which forms of government can be judged and compared. We may consider, he writes, "of what sort a government must be to be most in accordance with our aspirations, if there were no external impediment," but we must also consider "what kind of government is adapted to particular states." In addition, Aristotle thinks it is necessary "to know the form of government which is best suited to states in general" as well as "to say how a state may be constituted under any given conditions."

Most important of all, it is necessary to know "not only what form of government is best, but also what is possible." Though "political writers have excellent ideas," Aristotle thinks they "are often impractical." Since "the best is often unattainable," the true legislator "ought to be acquainted not only with what is best in the abstract, but also with what is best relative to circumstances."

Both Montesquieu and Mill later apply this basic distinction between the best form of government considered absolutely or in the abstract, and the best form relative to particular historic circumstances. Among these are a people's economic condition, level of culture, political experience, geography, climate, and racial characteristics. Montesquieu, for example, thinks that government by law, absolutely considered, is better than despotic government, yet he also holds that despotic government is better for certain peoples. Mill thinks that the institutions of a representative democracy represent the ideal form of government, but he acknowledges that absolute monarchy may be better for a rude or uncivilized people who have not yet advanced far from barbarism.

The great question here is whether the circumstances themselves can be improved so that a people may become fit or ready for a better form of government, and ultimately for the best that is attainable, that is, the form relative to the best possible conditions. Since Montesquieu emphasizes what he considers to be fixed racial characteristics, such as the servility of the Asiatics, whereas Mill stresses conditions which are remediable by education, economic progress, and social reforms, these two writers tend to give opposite answers. The issue is more fully discussed in the chapters on DEMOCRACY, MONARCHY, and PROGRESS.

Still other questions remain and should be mentioned here. Are the ideal state and the ideal form of government inseparable, or can one be conceived apart from the other? How shall the ideal government be conceived—in terms of the best that is practicably attainable, given man as he is or can be; or in terms of a perfection which exceeds human attainment and which men can imitate only remotely or imperfectly, if at all? Does divine government, for example, set a model which human government should aim to approximate? Is that human government ideal which is most like the divine; or, on the contrary, is the perfection of human government measured by standards drawn from the nature of man and the difficulties involved in the rule of men over men?

THE TRADITIONAL enumeration of the functions of government is threefold: the legislative, the judicial, and the executive. Locke adds what he calls "the federative power," the power of making treaties or alliances, and in general of conducting foreign affairs. It may be questioned whether this function is strictly coordinate with the other three, since foreign, like domestic, affairs may fall within the province of the executive or the legislature, or both, as in the case of the Constitution of the United States.

In our own day, the multiplication of administrative agencies and the development of planning boards have been thought to add a new dimension to the activities of government, but again it may be questioned whether these are not merely supplemental to the functions of making law, applying law to particular cases, and regulating by administrative decree those matters which fall outside the domain of enforceable law. The executive branch of government seems the most difficult to define, because it involves both law enforcement and the administration of matters not covered by legislative enactment or judicial decision.

If the threefold division of the functions of government is exhaustive, the question remains how these distinct activities shall be related to one another, and by whom they shall be performed. In an absolute monarchy, in which the king *is* the government, all powers are in the hands of one man. Though he may delegate his powers to others, they act only as his deputies or agents, not as independent officials. This does not obliterate the theoretical distinction between legislation, adjudication, and execution, but in this situation there can be no practical separation of the three powers, certainly no legal system of checks and balances.

It is the separation of powers, according to Montesquieu, that is the basis of political liberty. "Power should be a check to power," he writes. In a system of separated powers, "the legislative body being composed of two parts, they check one another by the mutual privilege of rejecting. They are both restrained by the executive power, as the executive is by the legislative."

Whether or not Montesquieu is right in attributing this aspect of constitutionalism to the limited monarchy of England in his own day, his argument can be examined apart from history, for it raises the general question whether government by law can be preserved from degenerating into despotic government except by the separation of powers.

For the American Federalists, the system of checks and balances, written into the Constitution, so contrives "the interior structure of the government that its several constituent parts may, by their mutual relations, be the means of keeping each other in their proper places." This they consider the prime advantage to be gained from Montesquieu's principle of the separation of powers. The principle itself they hold to be "the sacred maxim of free government."

32

Habit

INTRODUCTION

THE familiar word "habit" has a tremendous range of meaning. Some of its meanings in technical discourse are so divergent from one another—as well as from the popular understanding of the term—that it is difficult to find a common thread of derivation whereby to pass from one meaning to another.

We can eliminate at once the use of the word to designate apparel, as when we speak of a "riding habit." Yet even this sense contains a root of meaning which cannot be dismissed. Augustine points out that "the term 'habit' is derived from the verb 'to have,'" and Aristotle, considering the meanings of "to have," includes the sense in which a man may be said "to have a coat or tunic" along with the sense in which a man may be said to have a habit—"a piece of knowledge or a virtue." Just as clothes are something a person *has* or *possesses* in a manner more or less fitting to the body, so habits in the psychological sense are qualities which a person has or possesses, and they too can be judged for their fitness.

This understanding of habit is conveyed in the ancient remark which has become a common expression—that "habit is second nature." Habit is not *original* nature, but something added thereto as clothes are added to the body. But unlike clothes, which are added externally and merely by contact, habits as second nature are nature itself transformed or developed. In the words of an ancient poet, whom Aristotle quotes with approval, "habit's but long practice, and this becomes men's nature in the end."

Not all, as we shall see, would grant that practice is essential to habit. Nevertheless the word "practice" suggests one notion that is common to all theories of acquired habit, namely, that habit is a *retained effect*—the result of something done or experienced. Within this common understanding, there are opposite views. According to one view, the acquisition of habits depends on activity. According to another, habits are modifications, passively, not actively, acquired.

The word "habit" is also used in a sense diametrically opposite to the meanings so far considered. It is the sense in which Aristotle, in the *History of Animals,* discusses the habits of animals, and differentiates species according to the differences in their habits. Here the word "habit" is used to signify not an acquired pattern of behavior, but an innate predisposition to act or react in a certain way. The difference between acquired habits and "the habits to which there is an innate tendency," William James tells us, is marked by the fact that the latter generally "are called instincts."

The opposition between these two meanings of "habit" is clear. On the one hand, habits represent what, in the case of living things at least, is added by nurture to nature—the results of experience, training, or activity. On the other hand, habits which are identical with instincts belong to original nature itself—part of the native endowment of the animal. Is there any common thread of meaning in the notions of acquired and innate habit which may explain the use of the word in such opposite senses?

The familiar statement that a person does what he is in the habit of doing indicates that a habit is a tendency to a particular sort of behavior. Knowledge of a person's habits enables us to predict what he is likely to do in any situation which elicits habitual conduct on his part. So, too, an animal's behavior in a particular situation may be predicted from a knowl-edge of its instincts. Instinct and habit—or innate and acquired habits—seem to have this common character, that they are tendencies to behavior of a specific or determinate sort. They are definitely not random behavior. In the one case, the tendency is preformed, a part of the inherited nature of the organism. In the other, the tendency is somehow a product of experience and learning. In neither case does "habit" refer to mere capacity for action, un-formed and indeterminate, nor does it refer to the action, but rather to the tendency to act.

THE MODIFIABILITY OF instincts by experience indicates another and more dynamic con-nection between innate and acquired habits. James conceives innately determined behavior as if it were a plastic material out of which new patterns of conduct can be formed. The process of animal learning he thinks can be generally described as the replacement of in-stincts by habits. "Most instincts," he writes, "are implanted for the sake of giving rise to habits, and this purpose once accomplished, the instincts themselves, as such, have no *rai-son d'être* in the psychical economy, and con-sequently fade away."

Some years before the Russian physiologists Vladimir Bekhterev and Ivan Pavlov experi-mentally studied the conditioning of reflexes, James described animal learning in terms of the substitution of new for old responses to stimuli which had previously called forth an instinc-tive reaction, or in terms of the attachment of instinctive responses to new stimuli. "The actions we call instinctive," James writes, "all conform to the general reflex type" and "are called forth by determinate sensory stimuli." For example, a predatory animal, instinctively responsive to various perceptible signs of the whereabouts of its prey, may learn to hunt for its food in a particular locality, at a particular time, and in a particular way. Or, to take the example James gives, "if a child, in his first at-tempts to pat a dog, gets snapped at or bitten, so that the impulse of fear is strongly aroused, it may be that for years to come no dog will excite in him the impulse to fondle again." Similarly, an animal which has no instinctive

fear of man may acquire a habitual tendency to flee at man's approach, as the result of experiences in which the appearance of man is associated with instinctively recognized signs of danger.

In the classification of animals, from Aris-totle on, the instincts peculiar to each species have been used in their differentiation. In ad-dition, the degree to which the instincts of an animal are either relatively inflexible at one extreme or easily modifiable at the other has been thought to indicate that animal's rank in the scale of intelligence. The higher ani-mals seem to have a greater capacity to form habits and to be capable, therefore, of modi-fying their instinctive patterns of behavior as the result of experience. In consequence, their behavior is both more adaptive and more vari-able than that of animals which always follow the lines of action laid down by instinct.

Species whose instincts are largely unmod-ifiable are at a disadvantage in a changing environment or in one to which they are not innately adapted. In the struggle for existence, Darwin observes, it is the organism that "varies ever so little, either in habits or structure" which "gains an advantage over some other inhabitant of the same country." Though for the most part instincts seem to be directed to-ward the animal's survival, intelligence, or the power of modifying instincts by learning, may sometimes be needed to save the animal from his own instincts.

If the lower animals are most dependent on their instincts and least able to modify them, that would seem to indicate a kind of oppo-sition between instinct and intelligence. Dar-win quotes Georges Cuvier to the effect that "instinct and intelligence stand in an inverse ratio to each other," but he himself does not wholly accept this view. He thinks that the behavior of beavers, for example, or of certain classes of insects, shows that "a high degree of intelligence is certainly compatible with com-plex instincts." Yet he admits that "it is not improbable that there is a certain amount of interference between the development of free intelligence and of instinct."

On this subject of instinct in relation to intelligence or reason, James seems to take a less equivocal position. According to him, "man possesses all the impulses that [animals] have, and a great many more besides." After enumerating what he considers to be the instinctive tendencies of the human species, he concludes by saying that "no other mammal, not even the monkey, shows so large an array." But since James also thinks that man has the keenest intelligence and may even be the only reasoning animal, he cannot believe that there is any "material antagonism between instinct and reason." On the contrary, a high development of the faculties of memory, of associating ideas, and of making inferences implies not the absence of instinct, but the modifiability of instinct by experience and learning. "Though the animal richest in reason might be also the animal richest in the instinctive impulses too," James writes, "he would never seem the fatal automaton which a *merely* instinctive animal would be."

The opposite position is taken by those who, like Cuvier, hold that the more adequate an animal's instinctive equipment is for its survival, the less it needs free intelligence for adaptive purposes, and the less important is the role of learning and habit formation. Some writers, like Aquinas, go further than this and maintain that in the case of man, the power of reason as an instrument of learning and of solving life's problems supplants instinct almost entirely, or needs to be supplemented by instinctive impulses of an extremely rudimentary sort—hardly more complex than simple reflexes.

What other animals do by instinct man does by reason. "Brute animals," Aquinas writes, "do not act at the command of reason," but "if they are left to themselves, such animals act from natural instinct." Since in his opinion habits can be formed only by acts which involve reason as a factor, he does not think that, strictly speaking, habits are to be found in brutes. But, he adds, to the extent that man's reason may influence brutes "by a sort of conditioning to do things in this or that way, so in this sense to a certain extent we can admit the existence of habits in brute animals."

THE MODIFICATION of instincts in the course of individual life raises a question about their modifiability from generation to generation. The question has obvious significance for the theory of evolution.

It is thought by some that an animal's instincts represent the past experience of the race. In a passage quoted by James, Herbert Spencer, for example, maintains that "reflex actions and instincts . . . result from the registration of experience continued for numberless generations." Freud appears to hold much the same opinion. "All organic instincts are conservative," he writes. They are "historically acquired, and are directed towards regressions, towards reinstatement of something earlier." Indeed, he claims that the instincts of living things revert back *beyond* ancestral history to the inorganic. They go back to "an ancient starting point, which the living being left long ago." They are an "imprint" left upon the development of the organism by the "evolution of our earth and its relation to the sun."

James, on the other hand, claims that there is "perhaps not one single unequivocal item of positive proof" in favor of the view that "adaptive changes are inherited." He thinks the variability of instincts from generation to generation must be accounted for by some other means than the inheritance of acquired characteristics, according to which the habits *acquired* by earlier generations gradually become, through hereditary transmission, the *innate* habits of later generations.

The question of their origin aside, what is the structure of instincts? In the chapter on EMOTION, where this matter is considered, instinctive behavior is described as having three components. It involves, first, an innate ability to recognize certain objects; second, an emotional reaction to them which includes an impulse to act in a certain way; and, third, the ability to execute that impulse without benefit of learning.

James covers two of these three points when he defines an instinct as "the faculty of acting in such a way as to produce certain ends, without foresight of the ends, and without previous education in the performance"; and he touches on the remaining one when he declares that "instinctive reactions and emotional expressions shade imperceptibly into each other. Every object that excites an instinct," he goes on to say, "excites an emotion as well," but emotions "fall short of instincts in that the emotional reaction usually terminates in the subject's own body, whilst the instinctive reaction is apt to go further and enter into practical relations with the exciting object."

In the discussion of instincts from Aristotle to Freud, the emphasis on one or another of these components has varied from time to time. Medieval psychologists, if we take Aquinas as an example, seem to stress the cognitive aspect. He speaks of the sheep running away "when it sees the wolf, not because of its color or shape, but as a natural enemy." The point which he thinks notable here is not the fact that the sheep runs away, but rather the fact that without any previous experience of wolves, the sheep recognizes the wolf as dangerous. "The sheep, seeing the wolf, judges it a thing to be shunned . . . not from deliberation, but from natural instinct." This instinctive power of recognizing what is to the animal's advantage or peril Aquinas calls "the estimative power" and assigns it, along with memory and imagination, to the sensitive faculty.

Later writers stress the emotional and conative aspects of instinct—feeling and impulse. James, for example, indicates this emphasis when he says that "every instinct is an impulse"; and Freud makes desire central rather than perception or action. An instinct, he says, may be described as a stimulus, but it would be more exact to speak of "a stimulus of instinctual origin" as a "need." The instincts are the basic cravings or needs, and these instinctual needs are the primary unconscious determinants of behavior and thought.

What Freud calls "instinctual needs" seem to be the counterpart of what, in an earlier phase of the tradition, are called "natural desires." These two notions are far from being strictly interchangeable, but they do have a certain similarity in their reference to desires which are not conscious or acquired through experience. This matter is further discussed in the chapter on DESIRE.

IF WE TURN NOW to the consideration of habit as something acquired by the individual, we find two major issues. The first of these has already been mentioned in connection with the conception of habit as a *retained effect*.

According to James, the capacity for habit formation is a general property of nature, found in inanimate matter as well as in living things. "The moment one tries to define what habit is," he writes, "one is led to the fundamental properties of matter." He regards the laws of nature, for example, as "nothing but the immutable habits which the different elementary sorts of matter follow in their actions and reactions upon each other. In the organic world, however, the habits are more variable than this."

James attributes this universal capacity for habit formation to what he calls the "plasticity" of matter, which consists in "the possession of a structure weak enough to yield to an influence, but strong enough not to yield all at once. Each relatively stable phase of equilibrium in such a structure is marked by what we may call a new set of habits." He cites as examples of habit formation in inorganic matter such things as the magnetizing of an iron bar, the setting of plaster, scratches on a polished surface or creases in a piece of cloth. The matter in each of these cases is not only plastic and yielding, but retentive through its inertia. "When the structure has yielded," he writes, "the same inertia becomes the condition of its comparative permanence in the new form, and of the new habits the body then manifests."

The habits of living things or of the human mind are to be regarded only as special cases of nature's general plasticity and retentiveness. James does not fail to observe the difference between the magnetized bar, the scratched surface, or the creased cloth, and the habits of a trained animal or a skilled workman. The latter are acquired by activity—by practicing the same act repeatedly. Furthermore, they are not merely passive relics of a past impression, but are themselves tendencies to action. They erupt into action almost spontaneously when the occasion for performance arises.

It may be questioned whether the word "habit" should be used so broadly. Unlike James, most writers restrict its application to living things, and even there they limit habit formation to the sphere of learning. If the capacity to learn from experience is not a property of plant life, then plants cannot form habits. The same may be said of certain species of animals whose activity is entirely and inflexibly instinctive. Habits are possessed only by those organisms—animals or men—whose future conduct can be determined by their own past behavior. Aquinas, as we have seen, goes further than this, and limits habit formation in a strict sense to man alone.

This leads at once to the second issue. For those who believe that man is not specifically different from all other animals, man's habits and his habit formation require no special distinction or analysis. They hold that human intelligence differs from animal intelligence only in degree, not in kind. No other factors, they think, are present in human learning than those which operate when animals somehow profit from experience or acquire new models of behavior. In the great books there is to be found, however, a very special theory of habit which is part of the doctrine that man is specifically different from all other animals in that he alone is rational and has free will.

The issue about man's nature is discussed in other chapters (ANIMAL, EVOLUTION, MAN, MIND). Here we must examine the consequences for the theory of habit of these opposing views. Do animals and men form habits *in the same sense* of that term? The use of the word is not at stake, for "habit" may be used in a different sense for the acquired dispositions of animals. Those who hold that brute animals and men do not have habits in the same sense acknowledge that men may have, in addition to their specifically human habits, the sort of modified instincts or conditioned reflexes which are typical of animal habit formation. Furthermore, it is recognized that human and animal habits are alike in certain respects. Both are acquired by activity and both are tendencies to activity of a determinate sort.

The question, therefore, is simply this: Does one conception of habit apply to men and animals, or does human nature require a special conception applicable to man alone? To clarify this issue, it is necessary to summarize the analysis of human habits which Aristotle and Aquinas develop more fully than other writers, even than those who share their view of the rationality and freedom of man.

THAT ARISTOTLE and Aquinas should be the authors of an elaborate theory of human habits becomes intelligible in terms of two facts.

In the first place, they consider habit in the context of moral theory. For them the virtues, moral or intellectual, are habits, and so necessarily are the opposite vices. Virtues are good habits, vices bad habits; hence, good or bad, human habits must be so formed and constituted that they can have the moral quality connoted by virtue or vice. Since virtue is praiseworthy and vice blameworthy only if their possessor is responsible, human habit is conceived as arising from freely chosen acts.

In the second place, their understanding of habit is affected by their psychological doctrine of faculties, and especially by their analysis of the powers and activities which they think belong peculiarly to man. This in turn gives a metaphysical meaning to habit, for they treat human powers and human acts as special cases of potentiality and actualization.

Aquinas bases much of his discussion of habit on Aristotle's definition of it as "a disposition whereby that which is disposed is disposed well or ill, and this, either in regard to itself or in regard to another." In calling a habit a disposition, Aristotle goes on to say that all "dispositions are not necessarily habits," for while dispositions are unstable or ephemeral, habits "are permanent" or at least "difficult to alter."

For a disposition to be a habit, certain other conditions must be present, according to Aquinas. "That which is disposed should be distinct from that to which it is disposed," he writes, and hence "should be related to it as potentiality is to act." If there is a being which lacks all potentiality, he points out, "we can find no room in such a thing for habit . . . as is clearly the case in God."

It is also necessary that "that which is in a state of potentiality in regard to something else be capable of determination in several ways and to various things." If there were a potentiality which could be actualized in one way and one way only, then such a power of operation could not be determined by habits. Some of man's powers seem to be of this sort. His faculty of sensation, for example, functions perfectly when the sense organs have normally matured. A man does not learn to *see* colors or to *hear* tones, and so the simple use of his senses—apart from aesthetic perceptions and trained discriminations—does not lead to sensory habits. "The exterior apprehensive powers, as sight, hearing, and the like," Aquinas maintains, "are not susceptive of habits but are ordained to their fixed acts, according to the disposition of their nature."

In contrast, man's faculty of thinking and knowing can be improved or perfected by activity and exercise. The words "improved" and "perfected" are misleading if they are thought to exclude bad habits, for a bad habit is no less a habit than a good one. The definition of habit, Aquinas points out, includes dispositions which "dispose the subject well or ill to its form or to its operation." Hence when we say that a power of operation is "improved" or "perfected" by being exercised, we must mean only that after a number of particular acts, the individual has a *more determinate* capacity for definite operation than he had before.

A man may have at birth the mere capacity for knowing grammar or geometry, but after he has learned these subjects he has the habit of such knowledge. This, according to Aristotle and Aquinas, means that his original capacity has been rendered more determinate in its activity. It would be so even if he had learned errors, that is, even if the intellectual habits he had formed disposed his mind in a manner which would be called "ill" rather than "well."

The difference between a man who has learned grammar and one who has not is a difference in their capacity for a certain intellectual performance, a difference resulting from the intellectual work which has been done by the man who has learned grammar. That difference is an intellectual habit. The man who has not learned grammar has the same unde-

veloped capacity for knowing grammar with which he was born. The man who has learned grammar has had his native capacity for grammatical knowledge developed. That developed capacity is a habit of knowledge or skill which manifests itself in the way in which he writes and speaks. But even when he is not actually exercising his grammatical skill, the fact that he has formed this particular habit means that he will be able, whenever the occasion arises, to do correctly with speed and facility what the man who does not have the habit cannot do readily or easily if he can do it at all.

It may be helpful to illustrate the same points by reference to a bodily habit, such as a gymnastic or athletic skill which, being an art, is a habit not of body alone, but of mind as well. If two men are born with normal bodies equally capable of certain muscular coordinations, they stand in the same relation to performing on the tennis court. Both are equally able to learn the game. But when one of them has learned to play, his acquired skill consists in the trained capacity for the required acts or motions. The other man may be able to perform all these acts or go through all these motions, but not with the same facility and grace, or as pleasantly, as the man whose mastery of the game lies in a habit formed by much practice in doing what is required. As the habit gradually grows, awkwardness is overcome, speed increases, and pleasure in performance replaces pain or difficulty.

Clearly, then, the habit exists even when it is not in operation. It may even develop during periods of inactivity. As James remarks, there is a sense in which "we learn to swim during the winter and to skate during the summer" when we are not actually engaging in these sports. This would seem to be inconsistent with the general insight, common to all observers, that habits are strengthened by exercise and weakened or broken by disuse or by the performance of contrary acts. But James explains that his point, stated less paradoxically, means only that during periods of rest the effects of prior activity seem to consolidate and build up a habit.

The dynamism of habit formation and habitual activity is summarized, in the language of Aristotle and Aquinas, by the statement that "habit is a kind of medium between mere power and mere act." On the one hand, a habit is like a power or capacity, for though it is an improvement on native ability, it is still only an ability to perform certain acts; it is *not* the actual performance of them. On the other hand, habit is like operation or activity, for it represents an actualization or development of capacity, even as a particular operation is an actualization of the power to act. That is why habit is sometimes called a second grade of potentiality (compared to natural capacity as first potentiality) and also "a first grade of actuality" (compared to operation as complete act).

ACCORDING TO THE theory of specifically human habits, habits are situated only in man's powers of reason and will. Habits are formed in the other powers only to the extent that they are subject to direction by his reason and will. Specifically human habits can be formed only in that area of activity in which men are free to act or not to act; and, when they act, free to act this way or that. Habit, the product of freedom, is not thought of as abolishing freedom. However difficult it may be to exert a free choice against a strong habit, even the strongest habit is not conceived as unbreakable; and if it is breakable, it must permit action contrary to itself. Habitual behavior only seems to lack freedom because a man does habitually, without conscious attention to details, what he would be forced to do by conscious choice at every step if he lacked the habit.

In the theory under consideration habits are classified according to the faculty which they determine or perfect, on the ground that "every power which may be variously directed to act needs a habit whereby it is well disposed to its act." Consequently there are intellectual habits, or habits of thinking and knowing; and appetitive habits, or habits of desire which involve the emotions and the will, and usually entail specific types of conduct. Within a single faculty, such as the intellect, habits are further differentiated by reference to their objects or to the end to which their characteristic operation is directed. For example, the habit of knowing which consists in a science like geometry and the habit of artistic performance such as skill in grammar both belong to the intellect, but they are distinct habits according to their objects or ends.

All of these distinctions have moral as well as psychological significance. They are used in formulating the criteria of *good* and *bad* habits which are more appropriately discussed in the chapter on VIRTUE AND VICE. But here one further psychological distinction deserves comment. Some of man's acquired habits are regarded as natural in a special sense—not in the sense in which instincts are called "natural" or "innate" habits. The distinction is drawn from the supposition that certain habits develop in *all* men because, since human nature is the same for all, men will inevitably form these habits if they act at all. This word "natural" here applied to a habit simply means that it is common to all having the same nature.

For example, the understanding of the law of contradiction—that *the same thing cannot be affirmed and denied at the same time*—and other simple axioms of theoretical knowledge are said to be possessed by the human mind as a matter of natural habit. If a man thinks at all he will come to know these truths. "It is owing to the very nature of the intellectual soul," Aquinas writes, "that man, having once grasped what is a whole and what is a part, should at once perceive that every whole is larger than its part."

The sense in which Aquinas says that "*the understanding of first principles* is called a natural habit" applies to the first principles of the practical reason as well as to the axioms of theoretical knowledge. Just as no man who makes theoretical judgments about the true and the false can be, in his opinion, without habitual knowledge of the principle of contradiction, so he thinks no man who makes practical judgments about good and evil can be without habitual knowledge of the natural moral law, the first principle of which is that *the good is to be sought and evil avoided.* "Since the precepts of the natural law are sometimes considered by reason actually," Aquinas writes, "while sometimes they are in the reason only habitually, in this way the natural law may be called a habit."

In a different phase of the tradition Hume regards it as an inevitable tendency of the human mind to interpret any repeated sequence of events in terms of cause and effect. If one thing has preceded another a certain number of times in our experience, we are likely to infer that if the first occurs, the second will follow. The principle which determines us "to form such a conclusion" is, Hume says, "Custom or Habit." All our inferences from experience are "effects of custom, not of reasoning"; and since the habit of inferring a future connection between things which have been customarily conjoined in the past is, in his opinion, universally present in human nature, Hume refers to it as "a species of natural instinct which no reasoning or process of thought and understanding is able either to produce or prevent."

Even Kant's synthetic judgments *a priori* have a certain similarity to the thing called "natural habit." They comprise judgments the mind will make because of its own nature or, in Kant's terms, its transcendental structure. Though *a priori,* the judgment itself is not innate, for it arises only when actual experience provides its subject matter. So, too, the natural habit of first principles, of which Aquinas speaks, is not innate, but a result of experience.

THERE IS STILL ONE other traditional meaning of the phrase "natural habit." It occurs in Christian theology. Habits are there distinguished according as they are acquired by man's own efforts or are a gift of God's grace, which adds to or elevates human nature. The former are natural, the latter supernatural.

In the sphere of supernatural habits the theologian makes a distinction between grace itself and the special habits which accompany grace. Aquinas, for example, writes that "just as the natural light of reason is something different from the acquired virtues, which are ordained to this natural light, so also the light of grace, which is a participation of the divine nature, is something different from the infused virtues which are derived from and are or-

dained to this light." These "infused virtues," like the natural virtues, are good habits—principles of operation, determining acts of thought or desire. They are either the specifically theological virtues of faith, hope, and charity, or the supernatural counterparts of the acquired intellectual and moral virtues—the habits which are called "the infused virtues" and "the moral and intellectual gifts."

Grace, taken in itself rather than in its consequences, is not an *operative* habit, that is, it is not a habit of performing certain acts. Nevertheless, regarded as something added to and perfecting nature, it is considered under the aspect of habit. But rather than "a habit whereby power is inclined to an act," Aquinas includes it among those habits by which "the nature is well or ill disposed to something, and chiefly when such a disposition has become a sort of nature." Through the habit of grace, man's nature is elevated by becoming "a partaker . . . of the divine nature."

To distinguish this kind of habit from those in the operative order, it is sometimes called an "entitative habit"—a habit of the very *being* of man's personality. On the purely natural plane, health may be thought of in the same way as a habit which is entitative rather than operative. It is a habit not of thought, desire, or conduct, but of man's physical being.

THE WORD "CUSTOM" is sometimes a synonym for "habit" and sometimes a variant with special connotations. What a man does habitually is customary for him to do. So far as the single individual is concerned, there seems to be no difference between habit and custom. But we usually think of customs in terms of the group or community rather than the individual. As indicated in the chapter on CUSTOM AND CONVENTION, the prevailing modes of behavior in a society and its widely shared beliefs represent common habits of thought and action on the part of its members. Apart from the habits of individuals social customs have no existence whatsoever. But social customs and individual habits cannot be equated because, with respect to any customary practice or opinion, there may be nonconforming individuals—men of divergent habit. The prevalent or predominant customs are the habits of the majority. It is in this sense that Veblen regards an accepted standard of living as customary or habitual.

No society endures for long or functions peacefully unless common habits generate the ties of custom. To perpetuate itself, the state necessarily attempts to mold the habits of each growing generation—by every means of education, by tradition, by law. So important is the stability of custom in the life of society, according to Montaigne, that it is "very iniquitious . . . to subject public and immutable institutions and observances to the instability of a private fancy." He doubts "whether there can be such evident profit in changing an accepted law, of whatever sort it be, as there is harm in disturbing it." His extreme caution with regard to changing the law comes from a preference for the stability of settled customs and from the recognition that "government is like a structure of different parts joined together in such a relation that it is impossible to budge one without the whole body feeling it."

Without habits of action, at least, neither the individual nor society can avoid chaos. Habits bind day to day in a continuity which would be lost if the recurring problems of conduct or thought had to be solved anew each time they arose. Without habits life would become unbearably burdensome; it would bog down under the weight of making decisions. Without habits men could not live with themselves, much less with one another. Habits are, as James remarks, "the fly-wheel of society." As Dewey observes, habit "covers the formation of attitudes . . . our basic sensitivities and ways of meeting and responding to all the conditions which we meet in living." In this view, "the principle of continuity of experience" rests upon "the fact of habit."

33

Happiness

INTRODUCTION

THE great questions about happiness are concerned with its definition and its attainability. In what does happiness consist? Is it the same for all men, or do different men seek different things in the name of happiness? Can happiness be achieved on earth, or only hereafter? And if the pursuit of happiness is not a futile quest, by what means or steps should it be undertaken?

On all these questions, the great books set forth the fundamental inquiries and speculations, as well as the controversies to which they have given rise, in the tradition of western thought. There seems to be no question that men want happiness. "Man wishes to be happy," Pascal writes, "and only wishes to be happy, and cannot wish not to be so." To the question, what moves desire? Locke thinks only one answer is possible: "happiness, and that alone."

But this fact, even if it goes undisputed, does not settle the issue whether men are right in governing their lives with a view to being or becoming happy. There is therefore one further question. *Should* men make happiness their goal and direct their acts accordingly?

According to Kant, "the principle of *private* happiness" is "the direct opposite of the principle of morality." He understands happiness to consist in "the satisfaction of all our desires: *extensive,* in regard to their multiplicity; *intensive,* in regard to their degree; *protensive,* in regard to their duration." What Kant calls the "pragmatic" rule of life, which aims at happiness, "tells us what we have to do, if we wish to become possessed of happiness."

Unlike the moral law, it is a hypothetical, not a categorical, imperative. Furthermore, Kant points out that such a pragmatic or utilitarian ethics (which is for him the same as an "ethics of happiness") cannot help being empirical, "for it is only by experience," he says, "that I can learn either what inclinations exist which desire satisfaction, or what are the natural means of satisfying them." Such empirical knowledge "is available for each individual in his own way." Hence there can be no universal solution in terms of desire of the problem of how to be happy. To reduce moral philosophy to "a theory of happiness" must result, therefore, in giving up the search for ethical principles which are both universal and *a priori*.

In sharp opposition to the pragmatic rule, Kant sets the "moral or ethical law," the motive of which is not simply to be happy, but rather to be *worthy* of happiness. In addition to being a categorical imperative which imposes an absolute obligation upon us, this law, he says, "takes no account of our desires or the means of satisfying them." Rather it "dictates how we ought to act in order to deserve happiness." It is drawn from pure reason, not from experience, and therefore has the universality of an *a priori* principle, without which, in Kant's opinion, a genuine science of ethics—or metaphysic of morals—is impossible.

With the idea of moral worth—that which alone deserves happiness—taken away, "happiness alone is," according to Kant, "far from being the complete good. Reason does not approve of it (however much inclination may desire it) except as united with desert. On the other hand," Kant admits, "morality alone, and, with it, mere *desert,* is likewise far from being the complete good." These two things must be united to constitute the true *summum bonum* which, according to Kant, means both the *supreme* and the *complete* good. The man "who conducts himself in a manner not unworthy of happiness, must be able to hope for the possession of happiness."

But even if happiness combined with moral worth does constitute the supreme good, Kant still refuses to admit that happiness, as a practical objective, can function as a moral principle. Though a man can hope to be happy only if under the moral law he does his duty, he should not do his duty with the hope of thereby becoming happy. "A disposition," he writes, "which should require the prospect of happiness as its necessary condition, would not be moral, and hence also would not be worthy of complete happiness." The moral law commands the performance of duty *unconditionally*. Happiness should be a consequence, but it cannot be a condition, of moral action.

In other words, happiness fails for Kant to impose any moral obligation or to provide a standard of right and wrong in human conduct. No more than pleasure can happiness be used as a first principle in ethics, if morality must avoid all calculations of utility or expediency whereby things are done or left undone for the sake of happiness, or any other end to be enjoyed.

THIS ISSUE BETWEEN an ethics of duty and an ethics of happiness, as well as the conflict it involves between law and desire as sources of morality, are considered, from other points of view, in the chapters on DESIRE and DUTY, and again in GOOD AND EVIL where the problem of the *summum bonum* is raised. In this chapter, we shall be concerned with happiness as an ethical principle, and therefore with the problems to be faced by those who, in one way or another, accept happiness as the supreme good and the end of life. They may see no reason to reject moral principles which work through desire rather than duty. They may find nothing repugnant in appealing to happiness as the ultimate end which justifies the means and determines the order of all other goods. But they cannot make happiness the first principle of ethics without having to face many questions concerning the nature of happiness and its relation to virtue.

Discussion begins rather than ends with the fact that happiness is what all men desire. Once they have asserted that fact, once they have made happiness the most fundamental of all ethical terms, writers like Aristotle or Locke, Aquinas or J. S. Mill, cannot escape the question whether *all* who seek happiness look for it or find it in the *same* things.

Holding that a definite conception of happiness cannot be formulated, Kant thinks that happiness fails even as a pragmatic principle of conduct. "The notion of happiness is so indefinite," he writes, "that although every man wishes to attain it, yet he never can say definitely and consistently what it is that he really wishes." He cannot "determine with certainty what would make him truly happy; because to do so he would need to be omniscient." If this is true of the individual, how various must be the notions of happiness which prevail among men in general.

Locke plainly asserts what is here implied, namely, the fact that "everyone does not place his happiness in the same thing, or choose the same way to it." But admitting this fact does not prevent Locke from inquiring how "in matters of happiness and misery . . . men come often to prefer the worse to the better; and to choose that which, by their own confession, has made them miserable." Even though he declares that "the same thing is not good to every man alike," Locke thinks it is possible to account "for the misery that men often bring on themselves" by explaining how the individual may make errors in judgment—"how things come to be represented to our desires under deceitful appearances . . . by the judgment pronouncing wrongly concerning them."

But this applies to the individual only. Locke does not think it is possible to show that when two men differ in their notions of happiness, one is right and the other wrong. "Though all men's desires tend to happiness, yet they are not moved by the same object. Men may choose different things, and yet all choose right." He does not quarrel with the theologians who, on the basis of divine revelation, describe the eternal happiness in the life hereafter which is to be enjoyed *alike* by all who are saved. But revelation is one thing, and reason another.

With respect to temporal happiness on earth, reason cannot achieve a definition of the end that has the certainty of faith concerning salvation. Hence Locke quarrels with "the philosophers of old" who, in his opinion, vainly sought to define the *summum bonum* or happiness in such a way that all men would agree on what happiness is; or, if they failed to, some would be in error and misled in their pursuit of happiness.

It may be wondered, therefore, what Locke means by saying that there is a science of what man ought to do "as a rational and voluntary agent for the attainment of . . . happiness." He describes ethics as the science of the "rules and measures of human actions, which lead to happiness" and he places "morality amongst the sciences capable of demonstration, wherein . . . from self-evident propositions, by necessary consequences, as incontestable as those in mathematics, the measures of right and wrong might be made out, to any one that will apply himself with the same indifferency and attention to the one, as he does to the other of these sciences."

THE ANCIENT philosophers with whom Locke disagrees insist that a science of ethics depends on a first principle which is self-evident in the same way to all men. Happiness is not that principle if the content of happiness is what each man thinks it to be; for if no universally applicable definition of happiness can be given—if when men differ in their conception of what constitutes happiness, one man may be as right as another—then the fact that all men agree upon giving the name "happiness" to what they ultimately want amounts to no more than a nominal agreement. Such nominal agreement, in the opinion of Aristotle and Aquinas, does not suffice to establish a science of ethics, with rules for the pursuit of happiness which shall apply universally to all men.

On their view, what is truly human happiness must be the same for all men. The reason, in the words of Aquinas, is that "all men agree in their specific nature." It is in terms of their specific or common nature that happiness can be objectively defined. Happiness so conceived is a common end for all, "since nature tends to one thing only."

It may be granted that there are in fact many different opinions about what constitutes happiness, but it cannot be admitted that all are equally sound without admitting a complete relativism in moral matters. Erasmus, in *Praise of Folly,* has Folly argue for such relativism: "What difference is there, do you think, between those in Plato's cave who can only marvel at the shadows and images of various objects, provided they are content and don't know what they miss, and the philosopher who has emerged from the cave and sees the real things? If Mycillus in Lucian had been allowed to go on dreaming that golden dream of riches for evermore, he'd have had no reason to desire any other state of happiness." It is clear from this passage that Erasmus is using the word "happiness" in its psychological sense, in which it means contentment, not in its ethical sense, in which it means a whole life well lived.

That men do *in fact* seek different things under the name of happiness does not, according to Aristotle and Aquinas, alter the truth that the happiness they *should* seek must be something appropriate to the humanity which is common to them all, rather than something determined by their individually differing needs or temperaments. If it were the latter, then Aristotle and Aquinas would admit that questions about what men should do to achieve happiness would be answerable only by individual opinion or personal preference, not by scientific analysis or demonstration.

With the exception of Locke and perhaps to a less extent Mill, those who think that a science of ethics can be founded on happiness as the first principle tend to maintain that there can be only one right conception of human happiness. That right conception consists in the cumulative possession of *all* real goods in the course of a lifetime, leaving nothing more to be desired. That is why happiness, thus conceived, should be called the *totum bonum,* not the *summum bonum.* Other notions are misconceptions that may appear to be, but are not really, the *totum bonum.* The various definitions of happiness which men have given thus present the problem of the real and the apparent good, the significance of which is considered in the chapter on GOOD AND EVIL.

IN THE EVERYDAY discourse of men there seems to be a core of agreement about the meaning of the words "happy" and "happiness." This common understanding has been used by philosophers like Aristotle and Mill to test the adequacy of any definition of happiness.

When a man says "I feel happy" he is saying that he feels pleased or satisfied—that he has what he wants. When men contrast tragedy and happiness, they have in mind the quality a life takes from its end. A tragedy on the stage, in fiction, or in life is popularly characterized as "a story without a happy ending." This expresses the general sense that happiness is the quality of a life which comes out well on the whole despite difficulties and vicissitudes along the way. Only ultimate defeat or frustration is tragic.

There appears to be some conflict here between *feeling* happy at a given moment and *being* happy for a lifetime, that is, living happily. It may be necessary to choose between having a good time and leading a good life. Nevertheless, in both uses of the word "happy" there is the connotation of satisfaction. When men say that what they want is happiness, they imply that, having it, they would ask for nothing more. If they are asked why they want to be happy, they find it difficult to give any reason except "for its own sake." They can think of nothing beyond happiness for which happiness serves as a means or a preparation. This aspect of ultimacy or finality appears without qualification in the sense of happiness as belonging to a whole life. There is quiescence, too, in the momentary feeling of happiness, but precisely because it does not last, it leaves another and another such moment to be desired.

Observing these facts, Aristotle takes the word "happiness" from popular discourse and gives it the technical significance of ultimate good, last end, or *summum bonum*. "The chief good," he writes, "is evidently something final . . . Now we call that which is in itself worthy of pursuit more final than that which

is worthy of pursuit for the sake of something else, and that which is never desirable for the sake of something else more final than the things that are desirable both in themselves and for the sake of that other thing. Therefore, we call final without qualification that which is always desirable in itself and never for the sake of something else. Such a thing happiness, above all else, is held to be; for this we choose always for itself and never for the sake of something else."

The ultimacy of happiness can also be expressed in terms of its completeness or sufficiency. It would not be true that happiness is desired for its own sake and everything else for the sake of happiness, if the happy man wanted something more. The most obvious mark of the happy man, according to Aristotle, is that he wants for nothing. The happy life leaves nothing to be desired. It is this insight which Boethius later expresses in an oft-repeated characterization of happiness as "a life made perfect by the possession in aggregate of all good things." So conceived, happiness is not a particular good itself, but the sum of goods. "If happiness were to be counted as one good among others," Aristotle argues, "it would clearly be made more desirable by the addition of even the least of goods." But then there would be something left for the happy man to desire, and happiness would not be "something final and self-sufficient and the end of action."

Like Aristotle, Mill appeals to the common sense of mankind for the ultimacy of happiness. "The utilitarian doctrine," he writes, "is that happiness is desirable, and the only thing desirable as an end; all other things being only desirable as means." No reason can or need be given why this is so, "except that each person, so far as he believes it to be attainable, desires his own happiness." This is enough to prove that happiness is *a* good. To show that it is *the* good, it is "necessary to show, not only that people desire happiness, but that they never desire anything else."

Here Mill's answer, like Aristotle's, presupposes the rightness of the prevailing sense that when a man is happy, he has everything he desires. Many things, Mill admits, may be desired for their own sake, but if the possession of any one of these leaves something else to be desired, then it is desired only as a part of happiness. Happiness is "a concrete whole, and these are some of its parts . . . Whatever is desired otherwise than as a means to some end beyond itself, and ultimately to happiness, is desired as itself a part of happiness, and is not desired for itself until it has become so."

THERE ARE OTHER conceptions of happiness. It is not always approached in terms of means and ends, utility and enjoyment or satisfaction. Plato, for example, identifies happiness with spiritual well-being—a harmony in the soul, an inner peace which results from the proper order of all the soul's parts.

Early in *The Republic*, Socrates is challenged to show that the just man will be happier than the unjust man, even if in all externals he seems to be at a disadvantage. He cannot answer this question until he prepares Glaucon for the insight that justice is "concerned not with the outward man, but with the inward." He can then explain that "the just man does not permit the several elements within him to interfere with one another . . . He sets in order his own inner life, and is his own master and his own law, and is at peace with himself."

In the same spirit Plotinus asks us to think of "two wise men, one of them possessing all that is supposed to be naturally welcome, while the other meets only with the very reverse." He wants to know whether we would "assert that they have an equal happiness." His own answer is that we should, "if they are equally wise . . . [even] though the one be favored in body and in all else that does not help towards wisdom." We are likely to misconceive happiness, Plotinus thinks, if we consider the happy man in terms of our own feebleness. "We count alarming and grave what his felicity takes lightly; he would be neither wise nor in the state of happiness if he had not quitted all trifling with such things."

According to Plotinus, "Plato rightly taught that he who is to be wise and to possess happiness draws his good from the Supreme, fixing his gaze on That, becoming like to That, living by That . . . All else he will attend to

only as he might change his residence, not in expectation of any increase in his settled felicity, but simply in a reasonable attention to the differing conditions surrounding him as he lives here or there." If he "meets some turn of fortune that he would not have chosen, there is not the slightest lessening of his happiness for that." Like Plato, Plotinus holds that nothing external can separate a virtuous man from happiness—that no one can injure a man except himself.

The opposite view is more frequently held. In his argument with Callicles in the *Gorgias*, Socrates meets with the proposition that it is better to injure others than to be injured by them. This can be refuted, he thinks, only if Callicles can be made to understand that the unjust or vicious man is miserable in himself, regardless of his external gains. The fundamental principle, he says, is that "the happy are made happy by the possession of justice and temperance and the miserable miserable by the possession of vice." Happiness is one with justice because justice or virtue in general is "the health and beauty and well-being of the soul."

This association of happiness with health— the one a harmony in the soul as the other is a harmony in the body—appears also in Freud's consideration of human well-being. For Freud, the ideal of health, not merely bodily health but the health of the whole man, seems to identify happiness with peace of mind. "Anyone who is born with a specially unfavorable instinctual constitution," he writes, "and whose libido-components do not go through the transformation and modification necessary for successful achievement in later life, will find it hard to obtain happiness." The opposite of happiness is not tragedy but neurosis. In contrast to the neurotic, the happy man has found a way to master his inner conflicts and to become well-adjusted to his environment.

The theory of happiness as mental health or spiritual peace may be another way of seeing the self-sufficiency of happiness, in which all striving comes to rest because all desires are fulfilled or quieted. The suggestion of this point is found in the fact that the theologians conceive beatitude, or supernatural happiness, in both ways. For them it is both an ultimate end which satisfies all desires and also a state of peace or heavenly rest.

The ultimate good, Augustine writes, "is that for the sake of which other things are to be desired, while it is to be desired for its own sake"; and, he adds, it is that by which the good "is finished, so that it becomes complete"—all-satisfying. But what is this "final blessedness, the ultimate consummation, the unending end"? It is peace. "Indeed," Augustine says, "we are said to be blessed when we have such peace as can be enjoyed in this life; but such blessedness is mere misery compared to that final felicity," which can be described as "either peace in eternal life or eternal life in peace."

THERE MAY BE differences of another kind among those who regard happiness as their ultimate end. Some men identify happiness with the possession of one particular type of good—wealth or health, pleasure or power, knowledge or virtue, honor or friendship—or, if they do not make one or another of these things the only component of happiness, they make it supreme. The question of which is chief among the various goods that constitute the happy life is the problem of the order of goods, to which we shall return presently. But the identification of happiness with some one good, to the exclusion or neglect of the others, seems to violate the meaning of happiness on which there is such general agreement. Happiness cannot be that which leaves nothing to be desired if any good—anything which is in any way desirable—is overlooked.

But it may be said that the miser desires nothing but gold, and considers himself happy when he possesses a hoard. That he may consider himself happy cannot be denied. Yet this does not prevent the moralist from considering him deluded and in reality among the unhappiest of men. The difference between such illusory happiness and the reality seems to depend on the distinction between conscious and natural desire. According to that distinction, considered in the chapter on DESIRE, the miser may have all that he consciously desires, but lack many of the things toward which his nature tends and which are therefore objects of natural desire. He may be the unhappiest of men if, with all the wealth in the world, yet self-deprived of friends or knowledge, virtue or even health, his exclusive interest in one type of good leads to the frustration of many other desires. He may not consciously recognize these, but they nevertheless represent needs of his nature demanding fulfillment.

As suggested in the chapter on DESIRE, the relation of natural law to natural desire may provide the beginning, at least, of an answer to Kant's objection to the ethics of happiness on the ground that its principles lack universality or the element of obligation. The natural moral law may command obedience at the same time that it directs men to happiness as the satisfaction of all desires which represent the innate tendencies of man's nature. The theory of natural desire thus also has a bearing on the issue whether the content of happiness must really be the same for all men, regardless of how it may appear to them.

Even if men do not identify happiness with one type of good, but see it as the possession of every sort of good, can there be a reasonable difference of opinion concerning the types of good which must be included or the order in which these several goods should be sought? A negative answer seems to be required by the view that real as opposed to apparent goods are the objects of natural desire.

Aquinas, for example, admits that "*happy is the man who has all he desires,* or *whose every wish is fulfilled,* is a good and adequate definition" only "if it be understood in a certain way." It is "an inadequate definition if understood in another. For if we understand it simply of all that man desires by his natural appetite, then it is true that he who has all that he desires is happy; since nothing satisfies man's natural desire, except the perfect good which is Happiness. But if we understand it of those things that man desires according to the apprehension of reason," Aquinas continues, then "it does not belong to Happiness to have certain things that man desires; rather does it belong to unhappiness, in so far as the possession of such things hinders a man from having all that he desires naturally." For this reason, Aquinas points out, when Augustine approved the statement that "*happy is he who has all he desires,*" he added the words "provided he *desires nothing amiss.*"

As men have the same complex nature, so they have the same set of natural desires. As they have the same natural desires, so the real goods which can fulfill their needs comprise the same variety for all. As different natural desires represent different parts of human nature—lower and higher—so the several kinds of good are not equally good. And, according to Aquinas, if the natural object of the human will "is the universal good," it follows that "naught can satisfy man's will save the universal good." This, he holds, "is to be found, not in any created thing, but in God alone."

We shall return later to the theologian's conception of perfect happiness as consisting in the vision of God in the life hereafter. The happiness of this earthly life (which the philosopher considers) may be imperfect by comparison, but such temporal felicity as men can attain is no less determined by natural desire. If a man's undue craving for one type of good can interfere with his possession of another sort of good, then the various goods must be ordered according to their worth; and this order, since it reflects natural desire, must be the same for all men. In such terms Aristotle seems to think it possible to argue that the reality of happiness can be defined by reference to human nature and that the rules for achieving happiness can have a certain universality—despite the fact that the rules must be applied by individuals differently to the circumstances of their own lives. No particular good should be sought excessively or out of proportion to others, for the penalty of having too much of one good thing is deprivation or disorder with respect to other goods.

THE RELATION OF happiness to particular goods raises a whole series of questions, each peculiar to the type of good under consideration. Of these, the most insistent problems concern pleasure, knowledge, virtue, and the goods of fortune.

With regard to pleasure, the difficulty seems to arise from two meanings of the term which are more fully discussed in the chapter on PLEASURE AND PAIN. In one of these meanings pleasure is an object of desire, and in the other it is the feeling of satisfaction which accompanies the possession of objects desired. It is in the latter meaning that pleasure can be identified with happiness or, at least, be regarded as its correlate, for if happiness consists in the possession of all good things it is also the sum total of attainable satisfactions or pleasures. Where pleasure means satisfaction, pain means frustration, not the sensed pain of injured flesh. Happiness, Locke can therefore say, "is the utmost pleasure we are capable of"; and Mill can define it as "an existence exempt as far as possible from pain, and as rich as possible in enjoyments." Nor does Aristotle object to saying that the happy life "is also in itself pleasant."

But unlike Locke and Mill, Aristotle raises the question whether all pleasures are good, and all pains evil. Sensuous pleasure as an object often conflicts with other objects of desire. And if "pleasure" means satisfaction, there can be conflict among pleasures, for the satisfaction of one desire may lead to the frustration of another. At this point Aristotle finds it necessary to introduce the principle of virtue. The virtuous man is one who finds pleasure "in the things that are by nature pleasant." The virtuous man takes pleasure *only* in the right things, and is willing to suffer pain for the right end. If pleasures, or desires and their satisfaction, can be better or worse, there must be a choice among them for the sake of happiness. Mill makes this choice depend on a discrimination between lower and higher pleasures, not on virtue. He regards virtue merely as one of the parts of happiness, in no way different from the others. But Aristotle seems to think that virtue is the principal means to happiness because it regulates the choices which must be rightly made in order to obtain all good things; hence his definition of happiness as "activity in accordance with virtue." ·

This definition raises difficulties of still another order. As the chapter on VIRTUE AND VICE indicates, there are for Aristotle two kinds of virtue, moral and intellectual, the one concerned with desire and social conduct, the other with thought and knowledge. There are also two modes of life, sometimes called the active and the contemplative, differing as a life devoted to political activity or practical tasks differs from a life occupied largely with theoretical problems in the pursuit of truth or in the consideration of what is known. Are there two kinds of happiness then, belonging respectively to the political and the speculative life? Is one a better kind of happiness than another? Does the practical sort of happiness require intellectual as well as moral virtue? Does the speculative sort require both also?

In trying to answer these questions, and generally in shaping his definition of happiness, Aristotle considers the role of the goods of fortune, such things as health, wealth, auspicious birth, native endowments of body or mind, and length of life. These gifts condition virtuous activity or may present problems which virtue is needed to solve. But to the extent that having or not having them is a matter of fortune, they are not within a man's control—to get, keep, or give up. If they are indispensable, happiness is precarious, or even unattainable by those who are unfortunate. In addition, if the goods of fortune are indispensable, the definition of happiness must itself be qualified. More is required for happiness than activity in accordance with virtue.

"Should we not say," Aristotle asks, "that he is happy who is active in accordance with complete virtue and is sufficiently equipped with external goods, not for some chance period but throughout a complete life? Or must we add 'and who is destined to live thus and die as befits his life'? . . . If so, we shall call happy those among living men in whom these conditions are, and are to be, fulfilled—but happy *men*."

THE CONSIDERATION of the goods of fortune has led to diverse views about the attainability of happiness in this life. For one thing, they may act as an obstacle to happiness. Pierre Bezúkhov in *War and Peace* learned, during his period of captivity, that "man is created for happiness; that happiness lies in himself, in the satisfaction of his natural human cravings; that all unhappiness arises not from privation but from superfluity."

The vicissitudes of fortune seem to be what Solon has in mind when, as reported by Herodotus, he tells Croesus, the king of Lydia, that he will not call him happy "until I hear that thou has closed thy life happily . . . for oftentimes God gives men a gleam of happiness, and then plunges them into ruin." For this reason, in judging of happiness, as "in every matter, it behoves us to mark well the end."

Even if it is possible to call a man happy while he is alive—on the ground that virtue, which is within his power, may be able to withstand anything but the most outrageous fortune—it is still necessary to define happiness by reference to a complete life. Children cannot be called happy, Aristotle holds, because their characters have not yet matured and their lives are still too far from completion. To call them happy, or to call happy men of any age who still may suffer great misfortune, is merely to voice the hopes we have for them. "The most prosperous," Aristotle writes, "may fall into great misfortunes in old age, as is told of Priam in the Trojan cycle; and one who has experienced such chances and has ended wretchedly no one calls happy."

Among the goods of fortune which seem to have a bearing on the attainment of happiness, those which constitute the *individual* nature of a human being at birth—physical traits, temperament, degree of intelligence—may be unalterable in the course of life. If certain inherited conditions either limit the capacity for happiness or make it completely unattainable, then happiness, which is defined as the end of man, is not the *summum bonum* for all, or not for all in the same way.

In the Aristotelian view, for example, women cannot be happy to the same degree or in the same manner as men; and natural slaves, like beasts, have no capacity for happiness at all, though they may participate in the happiness of the masters they serve. The theory is that through serving him, the slave gives the master the leisure necessary for the political or speculative life open to those of auspicious birth. Even as the man who is a slave belongs wholly to another man, so the highest good of his life lies in his contribution to the happiness of that other.

The question whether happiness can be achieved by all normal human beings or only by those gifted with very special talents, depends for its answer in part on the conception of happiness itself. Like Aristotle, Spinoza places happiness in intellectual activity of so high an order that the happy man is almost godlike; and, at the very end of his *Ethics,* he finds it necessary to say that the way to happiness "must indeed be difficult since it is so seldom discovered." Nevertheless, "true peace of soul" can be found by the rare individual. "All noble things are as difficult as they are rare." In contrast, a statement like Tawney's— that "if a man has important work to do, and enough leisure and income to enable him to do it properly, he is in possession of as much happiness as is good for any of the children of Adam"—seems to make happiness available to more than the gifted few.

Whether happiness is attainable by all men, even on Tawney's definition, may also depend on the economic system and the political constitution, to the extent that they determine whether all men will be granted the opportunity and the leisure to use whatever talents they have for leading a decent human life. There seems to be a profound connection between conceiving happiness in such a way that all normal men are capable of it and insisting that all normal men deserve political status and economic liberty. Mill, for example, differs from Aristotle on both scores.

DIFFERING FROM the position of both Aristotle and Mill is the view that happiness is an illusory goal—that the besetting ills of human life as well as the frailty of men lead inevitably to tragedy. The great tragic poems and the great tragedies of history may, of course, be read as if they dealt with the exceptional case, but another interpretation is possible. Here writ large in the life of the hero, the great or famous man, is the tragic pattern of human life which is the lot of all men.

Sophocles seems to be saying this, when he writes in *Oedipus at Colonus:* "Not to be born surpasses thought and speech. / The second best is to have seen the light / And then to go back quickly whence we came. / The feathery

follies of his youth once over, / What trouble is beyond the range of man? / What heavy burden will he not endure? / Jealousy, faction, quarreling, and battle— / The bloodiness of war, the grief of war. / And in the end he comes to strengthless age, / Abhorred by all men, without company, / Unfriended in that uttermost twilight / Where he must live with every bitter thing."

Death is sometimes regarded as the symbol of tragic frustration. Sometimes it is not death, but the fear of death which overshadows life, so that for Montaigne, learning how to face death well seems indispensable to living well. The happiness of life, he writes, "which depends on the tranquillity and contentment of a well-born spirit and the resolution and assurance of a well-ordered soul, should never be attributed to a man until he has been seen to play the last act of his comedy, and beyond doubt the hardest. In everything else there may be sham . . . But in the last scene, between death and ourselves, there is no more pretending; we must talk plain . . . we must show what there is that is good and clean at the bottom of the pot."

So, too, for Lucretius, what happiness men can have depends on their being rid of the fear of death through knowing the causes of things. But neither death nor the fear of death may be the crucial flaw. It may be the temporal character of life itself.

It is said that happiness consists in the possession of all good things. It is said that happiness is the quality of a whole life, not the feeling of satisfaction for a moment. If this is so, then Solon's remark to Croesus can be given another meaning, namely, that happiness is not something actually enjoyed by a man at any moment of his life. Man can come to possess all good things only in the succession of his days, not simultaneously; and so happiness is never actually achieved but is always in the process of being achieved. When that process is completed, the man is dead, his life is done.

It may still be true that to live well or virtuously—with the help of fortune—is to live happily, but so long as life goes on, happiness is pursued rather than enjoyed. On earth and in time, man does not seem able to come to rest in any final satisfaction, with all his desires quieted at once and forever by that vision of perfection which would deserve Faust's cry: "Remain, so fair thou art, remain!"

As ALREADY INTIMATED, the problem of human happiness takes on another dimension when it is treated by the Christian theologians. Any happiness which men can have on earth and in time is, according to Augustine, "rather the solace of our misery than the positive enjoyment of felicity."

"Our very righteousness," he goes on to say, "though true in so far as it has respect to the true good, is yet in this life of such a kind that it consists rather in the remission of sins than in the perfecting of virtues . . . For as reason, though subjected to God, is yet 'pressed down by the corruptible body,' so long as it is in this mortal condition, it has not perfect authority over vice . . . For though it exercises authority, the vices do not submit without a struggle. For however well one maintains the conflict, and however thoroughly he has subdued these enemies, there steals in some evil thing, which, if it do not find ready expression in act, slips out by the lips, or insinuates itself into the thought; and therefore his peace is not full so long as he is at war with his vices."

Accepting the definition of happiness as the possession of all good things and the satisfaction of all desires, the theologians compare the successive accumulation of finite goods with the unchanging enjoyment of an infinite good. An endless prolongation of the days of our mortal life would not increase the chances of becoming perfectly happy, because time and change permit no rest, no finality. Earthly happiness is therefore intrinsically imperfect.

Perfect happiness belongs to the eternal life of the immortal soul, completely at rest in the beatific vision, for in the vision of God the soul is united to the infinite good by knowledge and love. In the divine presence and glory all the natural desires of the human spirit are simultaneously satisfied—the intellect's search for truth and the will's yearning for the good. "That final peace to which all our righteousness has reference, and for the sake of which it is maintained," Augustine describes as "the fe-

licity of a life which is done with bondage"— to vice or conflict, to time and change. In contrast, the best human life on earth is miserable with frustrations and an ennui that human nature cannot escape.

The doctrine of immortality is obviously presupposed in the theological consideration of happiness. For Kant immortality is a necessary condition of the soul's infinite progress toward the moral perfection, the holiness, which alone deserves perfect happiness. But for theologians like Augustine and Aquinas, neither change nor progress play any part in immortal life. On the contrary, the immortal soul finds its salvation in eternal rest. The difference between motion and rest, between time and eternity, belongs to the very essence of the theologian's distinction between imperfect happiness on earth and perfect happiness hereafter.

These matters, of relevance to the theory of happiness, are discussed in the chapters on ETERNITY and IMMORTALITY; and in the chapter on SIN we find another religious dogma, that of original sin, which has an obvious bearing on earthly happiness as well as on eternal salvation. Fallen human nature, according to Christian teaching, is incompetent to achieve even the natural end of imperfect temporal happiness without God's help. Milton expounds this doctrine of indispensable grace in *Paradise Lost,* in words which God the Father addresses to His Son:

Man shall not quite be lost, but sav'd who will,
Yet not of will in him, but grace in me
Freely voutsaft; once more I will renew
His lapsed powers, though forfeit and enthrall'd
By sin to foul exorbitant desires;
Upheld by me, yet once more he shall stand
On even ground against his mortal foe,
By me upheld, that he may know how frail
His fall'n condition is, and to me owe
All his deliv'rance, and to none but me.

God's grace is needed for men to lead a good life on earth as well as for eternal blessedness. On earth, man's efforts to be virtuous require the reinforcement of supernatural gifts—faith, hope, and charity, and the infused moral virtues. The beatific vision in heaven totally exceeds the natural powers of the soul and comes with the gift of added supernatural light. It seems, in short, that there is no purely natural happiness according to the strict tenets of Christian doctrine.

Aquinas employs the conception of eternal beatitude not only to measure the imperfection of earthly life, but also to insist that temporal happiness is happiness at all only to the extent that it is a remote participation of true and perfect happiness. It cannot be said of temporal happiness that it "excludes every evil and fulfills every desire. In this life every evil cannot be excluded. For this present life is subject to many unavoidable evils: to ignorance on the part of the intellect; to inordinate affection on the part of the appetite; and to many penalties on the part of the body . . . Likewise," Aquinas continues, "neither can the desire for good be satiated in this life. For man naturally desires the good which he has to be abiding. Now the goods of the present life pass away, since life itself passes away . . . Wherefore it is impossible to have true happiness in this life."

If perfect happiness consists in "the vision of the Divine Essence, which men cannot obtain in this life," then, according to Aquinas, only the earthly life which somehow partakes of God has a measure of happiness in it. Earthly happiness, imperfect because of its temporal and bodily conditions, consists in a life devoted to God—a kind of inchoate participation here and now of the beatific vision hereafter. On earth there can be only a beginning "in respect of that operation whereby man is united to God . . . In the present life, in as far as we fall short of the unity and continuity of that operation, so do we fall short of perfect happiness. Nevertheless it is a participation of happiness; and so much the greater, as the operation can be more continuous and more one. Consequently the active life which is busy with many things, has less of happiness than the contemplative life, which is busied with one thing, *i.e.*, the contemplation of truth."

When the theologians consider the modes of life on earth in terms of the fundamental distinction between the secular and the religious, or the active and the contemplative, they seem to admit the possibility of imperfect happiness in either mode. In either, a devout Christian dedicates every act to the glory of God, and through such dedication embraces the divine in the passing moments of his earthly pilgrimage.

34

History

IN our language the term *History*," Hegel observes, "unites the objective with the subjective side ... It comprehends not less what has *happened* than the *narration* of what has happened. This union of the two meanings we must regard as of a higher order than mere outward accident; we must suppose historical narrations to have appeared contemporaneously with historical deeds and events."

Our daily speech confirms Hegel's observation that "history" refers to that which has happened as well as to the record of it. We speak of the history of a people or a nation, or of the great events and epochs of history; and we also call a history the book which gives a narrative account of these matters.

It is as if we used the word "physics" to name both the object of study and the science of that object; whereas normally we tend to use "physics" for the science and refer to its subject matter as the physical world. We do not say that matter in motion is physics, but that it is the object of physics, one of the things a physicist studies. We might similarly have adopted the convention of using "history" in a restricted sense to signify a kind of knowledge or a kind of writing, and then called the phenomena written about or studied "historical" but not "history."

That, however, is not the prevailing usage. The word "history" seems to have at least four distinct meanings. It refers to a kind of knowledge. It refers to a type of literature. It means an actual sequence of events in time, which constitutes a process of irreversible change. This can be *either* change in the structure of the world or any part of nature, *or* change in human affairs, in society or civilization.

Historical knowledge and historical writing can be about natural history or human history. In his classification of the kinds of knowledge, Francis Bacon makes this distinction when he divides history into "natural, civil, ecclesiastical, and literary." Whereas the last three deal with human things, the first is concerned with the nonhuman part of the natural world. At the same time, this natural history is not, in Bacon's judgment, the same thing as "natural philosophy," or what we would now call "natural science."

In this set of great books, natural history, even cosmic history, makes its appearance in works which we ordinarily classify as science or philosophy; for example, Darwin's *The Origin of Species*, Lucretius' *The Way Things Are*, or Plato's *Timaeus*. The great books of history deal with man and society, not nature or the universe. For the most part this is true also of the great philosophies of history. They, too, are primarily concerned with human civilization, not the physical world.

IN ITS ORIGINAL Greek root, the word "history" means research, and implies the act of judging the evidences in order to separate fact from fiction. The opening line of Herodotus is sometimes translated not "these are the histories of Herodotus of Halicarnassus," but "these are the researches ..."

The word "research" can, of course, mean any sort of inquiry—into what is the case as well as into what has happened. The title of one of Aristotle's biological works, the *History of Animals*, suggests that it is concerned with researches about animals. The book does not deal with natural history; it is not a history of animals in the sense of giving the stages of their development in the course of time.

The redundancy of "historical research" can therefore be excused on the ground that it is necessary to distinguish between two kinds of inquiry or research—scientific and historical.

Originally, research set the historian apart from the poet and the maker of myths or legends. They told stories, too; but only the historian restricted himself to telling a story based on the facts ascertained by inquiry or research. Herodotus deserves the title "father of history" for having originated a style of writing which differs from poetry in this extraordinary respect. He tries to win the reader's belief not by the plausibility of his narrative, but rather by giving the reader some indication of the sources of information and the reliability of the evidence on which the narrative is based.

The poet tries to tell a likely story, but the historian tries to make credible statements about particular past events. He makes an explicit effort to weigh the evidence himself or, as Herodotus so frequently does, to submit conflicting testimony to the reader's own judgment. "Such is the account which the Persians give of these matters," he writes, "but the Phoenicians vary from the Persian statements"; or "this much I know from information given me by the Delphians; the remainder of the story the Milesians add"; or "that these were the real facts I learnt at Memphis from the priests of Vulcan"; or "such is the truth of this matter; I have also heard another account which I do not at all believe"; or again, "thus far I have spoken of Egypt from my own observation, relating what I myself saw, the ideas that I formed, and the results of my own researches. What follows rests on accounts given me by the Egyptians, which I shall now repeat, adding thereto some particulars which fell under my own notice."

Herodotus seems quite conscious of the difference between himself and Homer, especially on those matters treated by the poet which fall within his purview as a historian. The Trojan War lies in the background of the conflict with which Herodotus is directly concerned—the Persian invasion of Greece— for the Persians "trace to the attack upon Troy their ancient enmity towards the Greeks."

Herodotus does not doubt that the siege of Troy took place as Homer relates, but he learns from the Egyptians a legend about the landing of Paris and Helen on Egyptian soil and the detention of Helen by Proteus, king of Memphis. "Such is the tale told me by the priests concerning the arrival of Helen at the court of Proteus. It seems to me that Homer was acquainted with this story, and while discarding it, because he thought it less adapted for epic poetry than the version which he followed, showed that it was not unknown to him."

Herodotus cites passages in *The Iliad* and *The Odyssey* to corroborate this point. He is willing to use the Homeric poems as one source of information, but not without checking them against conflicting accounts. "I made inquiry," he writes, "whether the story which the Greeks tell about Troy is a fable or not." When he comes to the conclusion that Helen was never within the walls of the city to which the Greeks laid siege for ten years, he tells the reader his reasons for thinking so. Homer, however, when he narrates Helen's actions during the siege, does not bother to establish the facts of the matter or to give the reader contrary versions of what took place. That is not the poet's task, as Herodotus recognizes. It belongs to the historian, not the poet. The story which may have greater probability in fact may not be the better story for the poet.

SINCE HE IS BOTH an investigator and a storyteller, the historian stands comparison with the scientist in one respect and with the poet in another. The special character of history as a kind of knowledge distinct from science or philosophy seems clear from its object— the singular or unique events of the past. The scientist or philosopher is not concerned with what has happened, but with the nature of things. Particular events may serve as evidences for him, but his conclusions go beyond statements of particular fact to generalizations about the way things are or happen at any time and place. In contrast, the historian's research begins and ends with particulars. He uses particulars directly observed by himself or testified to by others as the basis for circumstantial inference to matters which cannot be established by direct evidence. The method of investigation developed by the early historians may be the precursor of scientific method, but the kind of evidence and the mode of argument which we find in Hippocrates or Plato indicate the divergence of the scientist and philosopher from the procedure of the historian.

The contrast between history and science—or what for the purpose of comparison may be the same, philosophy—is formulated in Aristotle's statement concerning poetry, that it is "more philosophical than history, because poetry tends to express the universal, history the particular." History deals with what has actually happened, whereas poetry, like philosophy, may be concerned with whatever is or can be.

One comparison leads to another. Unlike poetry, history and science are alike in that they both attempt to prove what they say. But in distinction from science or philosophy, history resembles poetry, especially the great epic and dramatic poems, in being narrative literature. The historian and the poet both tell stories.

If the poet and the historian—including, of course, a biographer like Plutarch—are also moralists, they are moralists in the same way. Their works do not contain expositions of ethical or political doctrine, but rather concrete exemplifications of theories concerning the conduct of human life and social practices. That fact explains why much of the content of the great historical books is cited in other chapters dealing with moral and political, even psychological, topics. But in this chapter we are concerned with history itself rather than with the particulars of history. We are concerned with the methods and aims of history as a kind of knowledge and literature; and we are concerned with the historical process as a whole, the consideration of which belongs to the philosophy of history.

THE AIMS AND methods of writing history are discussed by the historian himself, as well as by the philosopher. Philosophers like Hobbes, Bacon, or Descartes consider history largely from the point of view of the kind of knowledge it is and the contribution it makes to the whole of human learning. Historians like Herodotus, Thucydides, Tacitus, and Gibbon state more specifically the objectives of their work, the standards of reliability or authenticity by which they determine what is fact, and the principles of interpretation by which they select the most important facts, ordering them according to some hypothesis concerning the meaning of the events reported.

Herodotus writes, he tells us, "in the hope of preserving from decay the remembrance of what men have done, and of preventing the great and wonderful actions of the Greeks and the barbarians from losing their due meed of glory." Thucydides proceeds in the belief that the war between the Peloponnesians and the Athenians "was the greatest movement yet known in history, not only of the Hellenes, but of a large part of the barbarian world—I had almost said of mankind." Not very different is the declaration of Tacitus: "My purpose is not to relate at length every motion, but only such as were conspicuous for excellence or notorious for infamy. This I regard as history's highest function, to let no worthy action be uncommemorated, and to hold out the reprobation of posterity as a terror to evil words and deeds."

But though there seems to be a striking similarity in the purpose of these historians, Tacitus alone of the three avows a moral purpose. Furthermore, each of the three is conscious of the individual way in which he has put his intention into effect. Thucydides, for example, seems to have Herodotus in mind when he fears that "the absence of romance in my history will detract somewhat from its interest; but if it be judged useful by those inquirers who desire an exact knowledge of the past . . . I shall be content." Like Thucydides, Tacitus is a historian of contemporary events and he fears comparison with the historian of antiquity who can "enchain and refresh a reader's mind" with "descriptions of countries, the various incidents of battle, glorious deaths of great generals." His own work may be instructive, he thinks, but it may also give very little pleasure because he has "to present in succession the merciless biddings of a tyrant, incessant prosecutions, faithless friendships, the ruin of innocence, the same causes issuing in the same results, and [he is] everywhere confronted with a wearisome monotony in [his] subject-matter."

As we have already noted, Herodotus seems satisfied to let the reader decide between conflicting accounts. Only occasionally does he indicate which is more likely in his own judgment. Thucydides claims that he has made a greater effort to determine the facts. "I did not even trust my own impressions," he writes; the narrative "rests partly on what I saw myself, partly on what others saw for me, the accuracy of the report being always tried by the most severe and detailed tests possible. My conclusions have cost me some labor from the want of coincidence between the accounts of the same occurrences by different eye-witnesses." But he thinks that his conclusions "may safely be relied on," undisturbed "either by the lays of a poet displaying the exaggeration of his craft, or by the compositions of the chroniclers which are attractive at truth's expense."

The historians are aware of the difficulty of combining truth telling with storytelling. Most men, Thucydides remarks, are unwilling to take enough pains "in the investigation of truth, accepting readily the first story that comes to hand." The difficulty, according to Tacitus, is the obscurity of the greatest events, "so that some take for granted any hearsay, whatever its source, others turn truth into falsehood, and both errors find encouragement with posterity."

Reviewing the enormous scope of his work, Gibbon at the very end concludes that "the historian may applaud the importance and variety of his subject; but, while he is conscious of his own imperfections, he must often accuse the deficiency of his materials." Because of the scarcity of authentic memorials, he tells us in another place, the historian finds it hard "to preserve a clear and unbroken thread of narration. Surrounded with imperfect fragments, always concise, often obscure, and sometimes contradictory, he is reduced to collect, to compare, and to conjecture; and though he ought never to place his conjectures in the rank of facts, yet the knowledge of

human nature, and of the sure operation of its fierce and unrestrained passions, might, on some occasions, supply the want of historical materials."

Clearly, the historians have different criteria of relevance in determining the selection and rejection of materials and different principles of interpretation in assigning the causes which explain what happened. These differences are reflected in the way each historian constructs from the facts a grand story, conceives the line of its plot and the characterization of its chief actors. Herodotus, for example, has been compared with Homer as writing in an epic manner; Thucydides, with the dramatic writers of tragedy. Even if they all agreed on the ascertainment of fact, the great historians would differ from one another as the great poets do; each has a style and a vision as personal and poetic as Homer or Virgil, Melville or Tolstoy.

ONLY ONE OF THE great books is, by title and design, devoted entirely to the philosophy of history—to the formulation of a theory which embraces the whole of man's career on earth. This is Hegel's *The Philosophy of History*. Augustine's *The City of God* presents an equally comprehensive vision, but a comparison of the two suggests that they differ from one another as philosophy from theology.

The point of this comparison is not that God and His providence are omitted from the philosopher's view. On the contrary, Hegel regards the history of the world as a "process of development and the realization of Spirit— this is the true theodicy, the justification of God in History. Only this insight can reconcile Spirit with the History of the World— *viz.*, that what has happened and is happening every day is not only not 'without God' but is essentially His Work."

The difference is rather to be found in the ultimate source of insight concerning human development and destiny. Augustine sees everything in the light of God's revelation of His plan in Holy Writ; Hegel and other philosophers of history from Giambattista Vico to Arnold Toynbee seek and sometimes claim to find in the records of history itself the laws which govern and the pattern which inheres in the procession of events from the beginning to the end of human time.

For Augustine, the great epochs of history are defined religiously. They are stages in the development of the city of God on earth, not the city of man. Man is viewed as dwelling on earth under four distinct dispensations from God: (1) in Paradise before the Fall; (2) in the world after expulsion from Eden and before the Promise and the Law were given to the Jews; (3) under the Law and before the coming of Christ; (4) between the first and second coming under the dispensation of grace.

Augustine sometimes makes other divisions of history, but they are always primarily religious. For example, he divides all of time into seven ages, corresponding to the seven days of creation. "The first age, as the first day, extends from Adam to the deluge; the second from the deluge to Abraham . . . From Abraham to the advent of Christ there are, as the evangelist Matthew calculates, three periods, in each of which are fourteen generations— one period from Abraham to David, a second from David to the captivity, a third from the captivity to the birth of Christ in the flesh. There are thus five ages in all. The sixth is now passing, and cannot be measured by any number of generations . . . After this period God shall rest as on the seventh day, when He shall give us (who shall be the seventh day) rest in Himself . . . The seventh shall be our Sabbath, which shall be brought to a close, not by an evening, but by the Lord's day, as an eighth and eternal day, consecrated by the resurrection of Christ, and prefiguring the eternal repose not only of the spirit, but also of the body . . . This is what shall be in the end without end."

This same projection of history—in all essentials, at least—is laid before Adam by the archangel Michael in Milton's *Paradise Lost,* just before Adam leaves the Garden of Eden.

Unlike the four major dispensations of which Augustine and Milton speak, Hegel's four stages of the world are epochs in the development of Spirit as manifested in the State. They are secularly defined as the Oriental, the Greek, the Roman, and the German world and

are seen as a "progress of the consciousness of Freedom." The "various grades in the consciousness of Freedom," Hegel writes, "supply us with the natural division of universal History . . . The Orientals have not attained the knowledge that Spirit—Man *as such*— is free; and because they do not know this, they are not free. They only know that *one is free* . . . that *one* is therefore only a Despot; not a *free man*. The consciousness of Freedom first arose among the Greeks, and therefore they were free; but they, and the Romans likewise, knew only that *some* are free—not man as such . . . The Greeks, therefore, had slaves and their whole life and the maintenance of their splendid liberty, was implicated with the institution of slavery . . . The German nations, under the influence of Christianity, were the first to attain the consciousness that man, as man, is free."

With the complete emancipation of man in the German-Christian world, history is consummated for Hegel. "The grand principle of being is realized," he declares; "consequently the end of days is fully come." Another sign of the finality of the German-Christian world seems to be its reconciliation of Church and State: "European history is the exhibition of the growth of each of these principles severally . . . then of an antithesis on the part of both . . . lastly, of the harmonizing of the antithesis." In the German-Christian world, the secular and the religious modes of life are ultimately harmonized, fused in a single order of "rational Freedom."

APART FROM THE opposition between the philosophical and theological approaches, here represented by Hegel and Augustine, there seem to be two main issues in the general theory of human history. The first concerns the pattern of change; the second, the character of the causes at work.

The pattern most familiar because of its prevalence in modern speculations is that of progress or evolution. The progress may be conceived as a dialectical motion in the realm of Spirit, contrasted by Hegel with the realm of Matter or Nature, according as "the essence of Matter is Gravity . . . and the essence of

Spirit is Freedom." But it may also be thought to occur, as in the dialectical materialism of Marx and Engels, through the resolution of conflicting material or economic forces.

"The whole history of mankind," Engels writes in his preface to the *Manifesto of the Communist Party,* "since the dissolution of primitive tribal society, holding land in common ownership, has been a history of class struggles, contests between exploiting and exploited, ruling and oppressed classes; the history of these class struggles forms a series of evolutions in which, now-a-days, a stage has been reached where the exploited and oppressed class, the proletariat, cannot attain its emancipation from the sway of the exploiting and ruling class, the bourgeoisie, without, at the same time, and once for all, emancipating society at large from all exploitation, oppression, class-distinction and class-struggle." The four great economic systems—the systems of slave labor, feudal serfdom, industrial capitalism, and the communistic or classless society—are thus seen as the stages of progress toward an ultimate perfection in which history comes to rest because it has at last fully realized its controlling tendency. Veblen in his *The Theory of the Leisure Class* also contributes to this discussion of cultural history in economic terms.

The pattern of progress may be conceived not as a dialectical motion involving conflict and synthesis, but rather, as by Kant, in terms of an increasing actualization of the potentialities for good in human life. Giving the name of *culture* to "the production in a rational being of an aptitude for any ends whatever of his own choosing," Kant declares, "it is only culture that can be the ultimate end which we have cause to attribute to nature in respect of the human race." The progressive realization of culture consists in "the liberation of the will from the despotism of desires whereby, in our attachment to certain natural things, we are rendered incapable of exercising a choice of our own." In these terms history moves toward a perfection which can never be fully achieved on earth, for man's "own nature is not so constituted as to rest or be satisfied in any possession or enjoyment whatever."

As conceived by the evolutionist, progress may or may not attain its limit, but in either case its manifestation in human history appears to be analogous to as well as an extension of the line of development along which the world or all of living nature has gradually advanced.

THESE VIEWS ARE given further discussion in the chapters on EVOLUTION, PROGRESS, and WORLD. Whether or not the same pattern of change obtains in the historical order of nature as in the history of man and society, is a question to be answered by those who deny as well as by those who affirm progress. There is cyclical change in nature, the same pattern of birth, growth, decay, and death repeating itself generation after generation. That history too repeats itself with the rise and decline of cities and civilizations seems to be the ancient view. It reappears in our day with Oswald Spengler and, somewhat qualified by the possibility of progress, with Toynbee.

"The cities which were formerly great," Herodotus observes, "have most of them become insignificant; and such as are at present powerful were weak in olden time. I shall, therefore, discourse equally of both, convinced that prosperity never continues long in one stay." Lucretius finds the cyclical pattern both in the succession of worlds and in the succession of civilizations. The myth of the golden age of Kronos and the earthbound age of Zeus, which Plato tells in the *Statesman,* also applies both to nature and society.

According to the myth, "there is a time when God himself guides and helps to roll the world in its course; and there is a time, on the completion of a certain cycle, when he lets go, and the world being a living creature, and having originally received intelligence from its author and creator, turns about and by an inherent necessity revolves in the opposite direction." Thus the history of the world runs through "infinite cycles of years," and one age succeeds another in an endless round.

There is still a third view which sees history as neither cyclical nor simply progressive. Virgil reverses the order of the Platonic myth by placing the golden age in the future. It dawns with Rome, where, in the words of the fourth *Eclogue,*

...... a great new cycle of centuries
Begins. Justice returns to earth, the Golden Age
Returns, and its first-born comes down from heaven
   above.
Look kindly ... upon this infant's birth,
For with him shall hearts of iron cease, and hearts
   of gold
Inherit the whole earth.

Rome for Virgil is not only the beginning of the golden age; it is also the consummation of history. In *The Aeneid* Jupiter himself declares that he has given the Romans "un-limited power"—that he has set for them "no bounds, either in space or time." The "togaed people" of Rome shall be "the lords of cre-ation ... whose fame shall end in the stars"; then "shall the age of violence be mellowing into peace." The perpetuity of Rome seems to leave little room for any further essential progress and no chance for another cycle of decay and regeneration.

The Christian dogma of the fall of man from grace and his return through divine mediation to grace and salvation seems to give history a pattern that is partly Platonic in the sequence which makes the loss of a golden age the occa-sion for striving to regain it. But it also seems to be Virgilian in part. The epochal transitions of history happen only once. The coming of Christ is an absolutely singular event, after which there is no essential progress in man's condition until the Last Judgment at the end of the world.

COMMON TO THESE diverse conceptions of the pattern of history is the problem concerning the causes which are at work as history un-folds. Whatever the factors, they will operate in the future as they have in past, unless the millennium is already upon us or about to dawn. From the knowledge of their own past or from their dim perception of divine prov-idence, men derive a sense of the future; but they look forward to that future differently according as some part of it will stem from choices freely made, or according as all of it is inexorably determined by causes beyond their control.

The basic alternatives of fate and freedom, of necessity and contingency, God's will and man's choice, are considered in the chapters on CHANCE, FATE, and NECESSITY AND CON-TINGENCY. Sometimes the issue is resolved in the same way for the course of nature and the course of history: necessity reigns in both; as there is contingency in the events of nature, so there is freedom in the acts of history. Some-times the processes of nature and history are distinguished: the motions of matter are gov-erned by inviolable laws; whereas the motions of men are directed by laws which leave them free to work out a destiny which is determined by, rather than determines, the human spirit.

Those who do not deny freedom entirely in the realm of history seldom give it unlimited scope. What men can do is conditioned from below by the operation of material forces, and from above by what Hegel calls "God's pur-pose with the world." The vast "arras-web of Universal History" is woven by the interaction between God's will (the Absolute Idea) and human purposes or interests, which Hegel calls "the complex of human passions."

History for him is "the union of Freedom and Necessity," where "the latent abstract process of Spirit is regarded as Necessity, while that which exhibits itself in the conscious will of men, as their interest, belongs to the domain of freedom." But this freedom which coheres with necessity seems to belong more to the human race as a whole than to individual men. The individual man is tossed aside if he tries to obstruct the path of history. He is powerless to change its course.

Not even great men can make or determine history. They are great only because, sensing the next phase of the historical process, they identify themselves with the wave of the fu-ture and conform their purposes to the march of events—the dialectical development of the Absolute Idea. A few men thus become "world-historical individuals" because their own "par-ticular aims involve those large issues which are the will of the World-Spirit." They have "an insight into the requirements of the time— what was ripe for development ... the very Truth for their age, for their world; the spe-cies next in order, so to speak, and which was already formed in the womb of time."

Like Hegel and unlike the ancient historians, Tolstoy also regards the leadership of great men as illusory. To believe in the efficacy of heroes or great men, he thinks, is to commit the fallacy of the man "who, watching the movements of a herd of cattle and paying no attention to the varying quality of the pasturage in different parts of the field, or to the driving of the herdsman, attributes the direction the herd takes to the animal which happens to be at its head."

Great men are only celebrated puppets, pushed ahead on the moving front of history. The motion of history derives its force and direction from the individual acts of the innumerable nameless men who comprise the human mass. The act of the individual counts little. The mass motion is a complex resultant of slight impulses tending in many directions. But however slight the impulse each man gives, his contribution to history is a free act, conditioned only by the circumstances under which he makes a choice and by the divine providence which grants him the freedom to choose. Like "every human action," history, according to Tolstoy, thus "appears to us as a certain combination of freedom and inevitability."

In the 20th century, with the rise of the social sciences, the separation of history from anthropology is questioned. "We are no longer satisfied with political history," writes Lévi-Strauss, "which chronologically strings dynasties and wars on the thread of secondary rationalizations and reinterpretations. Economic history is, by and large, the history of unconscious processes. Thus any good history book . . . is saturated with anthropology."

According to Lévi-Strauss, we go "on the road toward the understanding of man . . . from the study of conscious content to that of unconscious forms." The historian and the anthropologist "both go the same way. The fact that their journey together appears to each of them in a different light . . . does not in the least alter the identical character of their fundamental approach."

DIFFERENT FROM speculations on a grand scale concerning the whole historical process is that type of philosophizing about history which considers its place in education—the light it affords to the mind, and the lessons it teaches for the guidance of conduct.

Montaigne, for example, makes the reading of history and biography the window through which a man looks out upon the world. "This great world," he writes, "is the mirror in which we must look at ourselves to recognize ourselves from the proper angle." Only against the large scene history reveals and amid the variety of human nature it exhibits can a man truly know himself and his own time. In a similar vein, Gibbon declares that "the experience of history exalts and enlarges the horizon of our intellectual view." Hegel, on the other hand, insists that "what experience and history teach is that peoples and governments never have learned anything from history, or acted on principles deduced from it."

Shaw takes a much more skeptical view of history in his preface to *Saint Joan.* For him, history is "always out of date." That is "why children are never taught contemporary history. Their history books deal with periods of which the thinking has passed out of fashion, and the circumstances no longer apply to active life. For example, they are taught history about Washington, and told lies about Lenin. In Washington's time they were told lies (the same lies) about Washington, and taught history about Cromwell. In the fifteenth and sixteenth centuries they were told lies about Joan, and by this time might very well be told the truth about her. Unfortunately the lies did not cease when the political circumstances became obsolete. The Reformation, which Joan had unconsciously anticipated, kept the questions which arose in her case burning up to our own day (you can see plenty of the burnt houses still in Ireland), with the result that Joan has remained the subject of anti-Clerical lies, of specifically Protestant lies, and of Roman Catholic evasions of her unconscious Protestantism. The truth sticks in our throats with all the sauces it is served with: it will never go down until we take it without any sauce at all."

On the practical side, political writers like Machiavelli, Montesquieu, and the Federalists use history to exemplify or confirm their generalizations. They agree with Thucydides that "an exact knowledge of the past is an aid to the interpretation of the future, which in the course of human things must resemble if it does not reflect it." Most men, adds Tacitus, "learn wisdom from the fortunes of others."

It is on these grounds that the great books of history belong with treatises on morals and politics and in the company of philosophical and theological speculations concerning the nature and destiny of man. Liberal education needs the particular as well as the universal, and these are combined in the great historical narratives. Apart from their utility, they have the originality of conception, the poetic quality, the imaginative scope which rank them with the great creations of the human mind.

35

Honor

INTRODUCTION

THE notions of honor and fame are sometimes used as if their meanings were interchangeable, and sometimes as if each had a distinct connotation. In the tradition of the great books, both usages will be found. It is seldom just a matter of words. The authors who see no difference between a man's honor and his fame are opposed on fundamental issues of morality to those who think the standards of honor are independent of the causes of fame. This opposition will usually extend to psychological issues concerning human motivation and to political issues concerning power and justice. It entails contrary views of the role of rewards and punishments in the life of the individual and of society.

Praise and blame seem to be common elements in the significance of fame and honor. The meaning of honor seems to involve in addition the notion of worth or dignity. But whether a man is virtuous or not, whether he *deserves* the good opinion of his fellowmen, does not seem to be the indispensable condition on which his fame or infamy rests. Nor does his good or ill repute in the community necessarily signify that he is a man of honor or an honorable man. Where others consider what it means for a person to be honorable, Nietzsche substitutes the notion of nobility. Nietzsche's hero, the superman, is noble.

The connection and distinction of these terms would therefore appear to be the initial problem of this chapter. Any solution of the problem must consider the relation of the individual to the community, and the standards by which the individual is appraised— by himself and his fellowmen. Honor and fame both seem to imply public approval, but

the question is whether both presuppose the same causes or the same occasions for social esteem.

"The manifestation of the value we set on one another," writes Hobbes, "is that which is commonly called Honoring and Dishonoring. To value a man at a high rate, is to *honor* him; at a low rate, is to *dishonor* him. But high and low, in this case, is to be understood by comparison to the rate that each man setteth on himself." Does Hobbes mean that the value a man sets on himself is the true standard of his worth? Apparently not. Let men, he says, "rate themselves at the highest value they can; yet their true value is no more than it is esteemed by others." What, then, is the measure of such esteem? "The *value*, or worth of a man," answers Hobbes, "is as of all other things, his price; that is to say, so much as would be given for the use of his power; and therefore, is not absolute but a thing dependent on the need and judgment of another."

Here, then, honor is not what a man has in himself, but what he receives from others. Honor is paid him. He may think himself dishonored if others do not pay him the respect which accords with his self-respect, but their evaluation of him is somehow independent of the standard by which he measures himself. It depends on the relation in which he stands to them, in terms of his power and their need. Virtue and duty—considerations of good and evil, right and wrong—do not enter into this conception of honor. The distinction between honor and fame tends to disappear when honor reflects the opinion of the community, based on the political utility rather than the moral worth of a man.

THERE IS ANOTHER conception of honor which not only separates it from fame, but also makes it independent of public approbation. This is not an unfamiliar meaning of the term. The man who says "on my honor" or "my word of honor" may not be an honest man, but if he is, he pledges himself by these expressions to fulfill a promise or to live up to certain expectations. He is saying that he needs no external check or sanction. A man who had to be compelled by threat or force to honor his obligations would not be acting from a sense of honor.

"It is not for show that our soul must play its part," Montaigne writes. "It is at home, within us, where no eyes penetrate but our own. There it protects us from the fear of death, of pain, and even of shame; there it makes us secure against the loss of our children, of our friends, and of our fortunes; and, when the opportunity presents itself, it also leads us on to the hazards of war." Montaigne quotes Cicero, who claims that all such ventures are *"not for any profit, but for the beauty of merit itself."*

A sense of honor thus seems to function like a sense of duty. Both reflect the light of conscience. Both operate through an inner determination of the will to do what reason judges to be right in the particular case. If there is a difference between them, it is not so much in their effects as in their causes.

Duty usually involves obligations to others, but a man's sense of honor may lead him to act in a certain way though the good of no other is involved. To maintain his self-respect he must respect a standard of conduct which he has set for himself. Accordingly, a man can be ashamed of himself for doing or thinking what neither injures anyone else nor ever comes to the notice of others. A sense of shame—the reflex of his sense of honor—torments him for having fallen short of his own ideal, for being disloyal to his own conceptions of what is good or right; and his shame may be even more intense in proportion as the standard he has violated is not one shared by others, but is his own measure of what a man should be or do.

Dmitri Karamazov exhibits these mixed feelings of honor and shame when he declares at the preliminary legal investigation: "You have to deal with a man of honor, a man of the highest honor; above all—don't lose sight of it—a man who's done a lot of nasty things, but has always been, and still is, honorable at bottom, in his inner being . . . That's just what's made me wretched all my life, that I yearned to be honorable, that I was, so to say, a martyr to a sense of honor, seeking for it with a lantern, with the lantern of Diogenes, and yet all my life I've been doing filthy things."

The sense of honor and the sense of duty differ in still another respect. Duty presupposes law. The essence of law is its universality. A sense of duty, therefore, leads a man to do what is expected of him, but not of him alone, for he is no different from others in relation to what the law commands. In contrast, a sense of honor presupposes *self-consciousness* of virtue in the individual. It binds him in conscience to live up to the image of his own character, insofar as it has lineaments which seem admirable to him.

Without some self-respect, a man can have no sense of honor. In the great tragic poems, the hero who dishonors himself in his own eyes dies spiritually with the loss of his self-respect. To live on in the flesh thereafter would be almost a worse fate than the physical demise which usually symbolizes the tragic ending. Racine, using the tragic poets as a model, portrays ancient Rome as a place where the striving for honor prohibits Emperor Titus from taking Berenice as his wife; in Racine's world, honor can be as tragic as dishonor. Two centuries later, and under quite different circumstances, honor plays an equally important role in the career of William Dorrit, in the novel by Dickens entitled *Little Dorrit*. In that novel, William Dorrit is not a hero, but he tries to preserve his honor in a debtor's prison. True honor, as displayed by Little Dorrit and Arthur Clennam, is the anonymous performance of one's duty.

THE SENSE IN WHICH a man can honor or dishonor himself is closely akin to the sense in which he can be honored or dishonored by others. Both involve a recognition of virtue or its violation. But they differ in this: that a man's personal honor is an internal consequence of virtue and inseparable from it, whereas public honor bestowed upon a man is an external reward of virtue. It is not always won by those who deserve it. When it is, "it is given to a man," as Aquinas points out, "on account of some excellence in him, and is a sign and testimony of the excellence that is in the person honored."

When "wealth becomes the foundation of public esteem," Tawney observes, "the mass of men who labor, but who do not acquire wealth, are thought to be vulgar and meaningless and insignificant compared with the few who acquire wealth."

There can be no separation between what a community considers honorable and what it considers virtuous or excellent in mind or character. But it does not necessarily follow that the man who is actually virtuous will always receive the honor which is due him. Public honor can be misplaced—either undeservedly given or unjustly withheld. The virtuous should be prepared for this, in the judgment of Aquinas, since honor is not "the reward for which the virtuous work, but they receive honor from men by way of reward, *as from those who have nothing greater to offer.*" Happiness, he goes on to say, is the "true reward . . . for which the virtuous work; for if they worked for honor, it would no longer be virtue, but ambition."

Tolstoy, however, deplores the injustice of the honor given Napoleon and the dishonor in which Kutuzov was held. "Napoleon," he writes, "that most insignificant tool of history who never anywhere, even in exile, showed human dignity—Napoleon is the object of adulation and enthusiasm; he is *grand*. But Kutuzov—the man who from the beginning to the end of his activity in 1812, never once swerving by word or deed from Borodino to Vilna, presented an example exceptional in history of self-sacrifice and a present consciousness of the future importance of what was happening—Kutuzov seems to them

something indefinite and pitiful, and when speaking of him and of the year 1812 they always seem a little ashamed."

Kutuzov later received some measure of honor when he was presented with the rarely awarded Order of St. George. But what is perhaps a much higher honor came to him after his death when Tolstoy enshrined him as one of the heroes of *War and Peace*. Sometimes the virtuous or truly honorable man, living in a bad society, goes without honor in his own time to be honored only by posterity. He may even be dishonored by a society which has contempt for virtue. Sometimes a man of indifferent character and achievement, or even one who is actually base and ignoble, wins honor through cleverly simulating the possession of admirable traits.

It seems appropriate to consider the proportion between a man's intrinsic worth and the honor he receives. The distribution of honors raises questions of justice—in fact, it is thought to be one of the chief problems of distributive justice. For those who hold that honor and fame are utterly distinct in principle, this is the clear mark of their difference. Justice does not require that fame be proportionate to virtue. Though there is a sense in which fame may not be deserved, the qualities in a person which justify fame are of a different order from those which honor should reward. Fame belongs to the great, the outstanding, the exceptional, without regard to virtue or vice. Infamy is fame no less than good repute. The great scoundrel can be as famous as the great hero. Existing in the reputation a man has regardless of his character or accomplishments, fame does not tarnish, as honor does, when it is unmerited. But for the same reason, fame is often lost as fortuitously as it is acquired. "Fame has no stability," Aquinas observes; "it is easily ruined by false report. And if it sometimes endures, this is by accident."

Woolf asks the question, "Fame lasts how long?" She goes on to say, "It is permissible even for a dying hero to think before he dies how men will speak of him hereafter. His fame lasts perhaps two thousand years. And what are two thousand years? . . . What, indeed, if you look from a mountain top down the long wastes of the ages? The very stone one kicks with one's boot will outlast Shakespeare."

THE DISTINCTION between honor and fame is not acknowledged by those who ignore merit as a condition of praise. Machiavelli, for example, places fame—or, as he sometimes calls it, glory—in that triad of worldly goods which men want without limit and without relation to justice. If the aim of life is to get ahead in the world, money, fame, and power are the chief marks of success. A man is deemed no less successful if he acquires power by usurping it, or gains it by foul means rather than fair; so, too, if he becomes famous through chicanery or deception and counterfeits whatever form of greatness men are prone to praise.

Along with riches, fame, says Machiavelli, is "the end which every man has before him." This men seek to obtain by various methods: "one with caution, another with haste; one by force, another by skill; one by patience, another by its opposite; and each one succeeds in reaching the goal by a different method." Some methods, he admits in another place, "may gain empire, but not glory," such as "to slay fellow-citizens, to deceive friends, to be without faith, without mercy, without religion." Nevertheless, he declares: "Let a prince have the credit of conquering and holding a state, the means will always be considered honest, and he will be praised by everybody."

Because fame seems to be morally neutral, it replaces honor in the discussions of those who measure men in terms of success instead of virtue, duty, or happiness. Because it is morally neutral, it is the term used by those who wish to judge, not men, but the impression they make. What counts is the magnitude of that impression, not its correspondence with reality.

To be famous is to be widely, not necessarily well, spoken of by one's fellowmen, now or hereafter. The man who stands above the herd, whose outlines are clear and whose deeds are memorable, takes his place among the famous of his time or of all times. Plutarch the moralist certainly does not regard the men whose lives he writes as paragons of virtue. On the contrary, he plainly indicates that many of them are examples of extraordinary depravity. But Plutarch the biographer treats them all as famous. He takes that as a matter of historic fact, not of moral judgment. Good or bad, they were acknowledged to be great men, leaders, figures of eminent proportions, engaged in momentous exploits. They were not all victorious. Few if any were successful in all that they attempted or were able to preserve what successes they achieved. But each ventured beyond the pale of ordinary men; and each succeeded at least in becoming a symbol of great deeds, a monument in human memory.

The opposite of fame is anonymity. In Dante's moral universe, only the Trimmers on the rim of Hell are totally anonymous; neither good nor bad, they lack name and fame. Because they "lived without infamy and without praise," Hell will not receive them, "lest the wicked have some glory over them." To them alone no fame can be allowed. Honor and glory belong only to the blessed, but the damned in the pits of Hell, by the record they left for men to revile, are as well remembered, and hence as famous, as the saints in Heaven.

THAT MEN NORMALLY desire the esteem of their fellowmen seems to be undisputed. "He must be of a strange and unusual constitution," Locke writes, "who can content himself to live in constant disgrace and disrepute with his own particular society. Solitude many men have sought, and been reconciled to; but nobody that has the least thought or sense of a man about him, can live in society under the constant dislike and ill opinion of his familiars, and those he converses with. This is a burden too heavy for human sufferance."

A society of misanthropes, despising each other, is as unthinkable as an economy of misers. The social nature of man requires sympathy and fellow feeling, love and friendship, and all of these involve some measure of approval based on knowledge or understanding. According to one theory, the highest type of friendship springs from mutual admiration, the respect which men have for one another. The old saying that "there is honor among thieves" suggests that even among bad men there is a desire to hold the approbation of those who share a common life. With this in mind apparently, William James describes fame and honor as a man's "image in the eyes of his own 'set,' which exalts or condemns him as he conforms or not to certain requirements that may not be made of one in another walk of life."

Molière takes a much narrower view of honor. Chrysalde in *The School for Wives* declares:

Equating happiness with security,
And making honor lie in one point only!
Cruelty, greed, baseness and double-dealing
Are unimportant, in comparison;
Regardless of one's life and character,
Honor consists in dodging cuckoldry!

Though Pascal regards "the pursuit of glory" as "the greatest baseness of man," he must admit that "it is also the greatest mark of his excellence; for whatever possessions he may have on earth, whatever health and essential comfort, he is not satisfied if he has not the esteem of men. He values human reason so highly that, whatever advantages he may have on earth, he is not content if he is not also ranked highly in the judgment of man . . . Those who most despise men, and put them on a level with brutes, yet wish to be admired and believed by men, and contradict themselves by their own feelings."

But is this universal wish for the esteem of others a desire for honor or a desire for fame? Does it make any difference to our conception of happiness whether we say that men cannot be happy without honor or that they cannot be happy unless they are famous?

Even those who do not distinguish between honor and fame are led by these questions to discriminate between fame and infamy. As we have already noted, fame and infamy are alike, since both involve the notoriety enjoyed by the outstanding, the exceptional, the great, whether good or bad. If what men desire is simply to be known by others, and to have a kind of immortality through living on in the memory of later generations, then evil will serve as well as good repute. All that matters is the size of the reputation, and its vitality. But

if the desire is for approbation or praise, good opinion alone will satisfy, and then the question becomes whether the object is fame or honor. Which does Iago have in mind when he says, "Good name in man and woman, dear my Lord, is the immediate jewel of their souls"?

Opposite answers seem to be determined by opposite views of human nature and human happiness. Those who, like Plato, think that virtue is an indispensable ingredient of happiness, include honor among the "good things" which the virtuous man will seek in the right way. Possession of good things by itself is not sufficient, Socrates says in the *Euthydemus*. A man must also use them and use them well, for "the wrong use of a thing is far worse than the non-use." Applied to honor, this would seem to mean that the virtuous man will not seek praise for the wrong reasons—either for that which is not praiseworthy in himself or from others whose lack of virtue disqualifies them from giving praise with honesty. The virtuous man will not seek fame or be unhappy lacking it, for fame, like pleasure or wealth, can be enjoyed by bad men as well as good and be sought for wrong as well as right reasons or in the wrong as well as the right way. Virtue, according to the moralists, protects a man from the seductions of money, fame, and power— the things for which men undisciplined by virtue seem to have an inordinate desire.

In the theory of virtue, honor, unlike fame, belongs only to the good and is always a good object, worthy of pursuit. Honor is, in fact, the object of two virtues which Aristotle defines in the *Nicomachean Ethics*. One of these virtues he calls "ambition," and the Greek name for the other, which is literally rendered by "high-mindedness," is sometimes translated by the English word "magnanimity" and sometimes by "pride." The Christian connotation of "pride" makes it a difficult word to use as the name for a virtue, but it can nevertheless be so used when it is understood to mean a justifiable degree of self-respect—not conceit but a middle ground between undue self-esteem and inordinate self-deprecation. When the Aristotelian names for these two vices are translated in English by "vanity" and "humility," it is again necessary to point out that "humility" must be understood, not in its Christian significance as meaning the virtue of the truly religious man, but rather as signifying an exaggerated meekness or pusillanimity.

The difference between pride and ambition lies in the magnitude of the other virtues they accompany and the scale of honor with which they are concerned. Both are concerned with honor, which Aristotle calls "the greatest of external goods." In both cases, "honor is the prize of virtue, and it is to the good that it is rendered." The proud man is one "who, being truly worthy of great things, also thinks himself worthy of them; for he who does so beyond his deserts is a fool, but no virtuous man is foolish or silly." The proud man will be pleased "only by honors that are great and that are conferred by good men . . . Honor from casual people and on trifling grounds, he will utterly despise, since it is not this that he deserves."

Humility and vanity are, according to Aristotle, the vices of defect and excess which occur when a man fails to be proud. The unduly humble man, underestimating his worth, does not seek the honor he deserves. The vain man, at the other extreme, overestimates himself and wants honor out of proportion to his qualities. Honor, like any other external good, "may be desired more than is right, or less, or from the right sources and in the right way. We blame both the over-ambitious man as aiming at honor more than is right and from the wrong sources, and the unambitious man as not willing to be honored even for noble reasons."

However words are used, the point seems to be clear. It is possible for men to desire honor more than they should and less. It is also possible for honor to be rightly desired. Honor desired to excess or in the wrong way may be called "fame," even as the excessive desire for honor is sometimes regarded as the vice of ambition or an aspect of the sin of pride. The word "pride" seems to have both a good and a bad connotation. But the point remains that the difference between these two meanings of "pride," like the difference between honor and fame, is understood by moralists in terms of virtue, and it is discounted by those who reject the relevance of virtue.

Sociologists, and philosophers who are sociological in their approach, such as Nietzsche, take a different view. According to Weber, "the place of 'status groups' is within the social order, that is, within the sphere of the distribution of 'honor.' " In his view a "status situation" is one "that is determined by a specific, positive or negative, social estimation of *honor*. This honor may be connected with any quality shared by a plurality, and, of course, it can be knit to a class situation." In another place, Weber explains that by "status situation" he means "the probability of certain social groups' receiving positive or negative social *honor*. The chances of attaining social honor are primarily determined by differences in the *styles of life* of these groups, hence chiefly by differences of *education*."

THOUGH HONOR MAY be regarded as inseparable from virtue in moral theory, certain political philosophers make its separation from virtue the principle of a type of government.

In Plato's *The Republic*, monarchy and aristocracy are defined in terms of the virtue of the rulers—either of the one wise man or of the excellent few. Government by the few is oligarchy rather than aristocracy when wealth rather than virtue is the principle of their selection. Plato sees the possibility of an intermediate between these two which occurs as a kind of transitional form when aristocracy tends to degenerate into oligarchy. He calls that intermediate "timocracy" and describes it as "a mixture of good and evil" in which the ruler is "a lover of power and a lover of honor, claiming to be a ruler, not because he is eloquent, or on any ground of that sort, but because he is a soldier and has performed feats of arms." In such a state, he claims, "one thing, and one thing only, is predominantly seen—the spirit of contention and ambition; and these are due to the prevalence of the passionate or spirited element." In a timocracy, in other words, honor is divorced from virtue and wisdom and becomes the only qualification for public office.

With Montesquieu, the situation is quite reversed. For him, virtue is absolutely requisite in popular government or democracy, and to a less extent in that other form of republic which he calls "aristocracy." As virtue is necessary in a republic, so is honor in a monarchy. "Honor—that is, the prejudice of every person and rank—supplies the place of political virtue. A monarchical government supposes pre-eminences and ranks, as likewise a noble descent. Since it is the nature of honor to aspire to preferments and titles, it properly placed in this government."

Though Montesquieu and Plato differ in their classification of the forms of government, they seem to agree that honor divorced from virtue is a counterfeit. Honor identified with ranks and titles, honor which moves individuals to serve the public good in order to promote their own interests, Montesquieu admits is a false honor, "but even this false honor is as useful to the public as true honor could possibly be to private persons." Considering the laws of education characteristic of monarchical governments, Montesquieu points out that it is not in colleges or academies, but in the world itself, which is the school of honor, that the subjects of monarchy are chiefly trained. "Here the actions of men are judged, not as virtuous, but as shining; not as just, but as great; not as reasonable, but extraordinary."

HEROISM IS DISCUSSED in the chapter on COURAGE, and the role of the hero—the leader or great man—in the chapter on HISTORY. Here we are concerned with the hero in the esteem of his fellowmen, the symbol of human greatness and the object of human admiration.

Honor, fame, and glory combine in various proportions to constitute the heroic figures of classical antiquity: honor, to the extent that none is without some virtue and each possesses certain virtues at least to a remarkable degree; fame, because they are the great among men, outstanding and well-known, godlike in their preeminence; and glory, almost in the theological sense, inasmuch as the heroes celebrated by Homer and Virgil are beloved by the gods.

It is not accidental that the central figure in the Greek tragedies is called a "hero," since in the ancient view the tragic character must necessarily belong to a great man, a man of noble proportions, one who is "better than the ordinary man," says Aristotle. If he also has some fault or flaw, it is a consequence of strength misused, not a mark of individual weakness. Such weakness as he has is the common frailty of man.

In the modern world heroism and the heroic are more difficult to identify or define. We tend to substitute the notion of genius in considering the exceptionally gifted among men. Glory is dimly recognized and honor takes second place to fame. That portion of modern poetry which deals in heroes—as, for example, the tragedies and historical plays of Shakespeare—borrows them from, or models them on, legendary figures. The great modern novels, counterparts of the epic poems of antiquity, portray exceptional men and women without idealizing them to heroic stature. One of these novels, Tolstoy's *War and Peace,* seeks to deflate the fame of great men. They do not deserve even their reputation for great deeds, much less the honor owed the truly great.

"If we assume as historians do that great men lead humanity to the attainment of certain ends . . . then it is impossible," Tolstoy declares, "to explain the facts of history without introducing the conceptions of *chance* and *genius*." But in Tolstoy's opinion "the words *chance* and *genius* do not denote any really existing thing and therefore cannot be defined." We can dispense with these meaningless words, he thinks, if we are willing to renounce "our claim to discern a purpose immediately intelligible to us" and admit "the ultimate purpose to be beyond our ken." Then "not only shall we have no need to see exceptional ability in Napoleon and Alexander, but we shall be unable to consider them to be anything but like ordinary men, and we shall not be obliged to have recourse to *chance* for an explanation of those small events which made these people what they were, but it will be clear that all those small events were inevitable."

This view of history, with its emphasis on impersonal forces, finds another expression in Marxist theory. The machine and the proletariat mass are the heroes of history, or of the revolution. Yet the modern period is not without an opposite strain of thought. Machiavelli calls for a great man, a hero, to become the "liberator" of Italy, "who shall yet heal her wounds and put an end to the ravaging and plundering of Lombardy, to the swindling and taxing of the kingdom and of Tuscany, and cleanse those sores that for long have festered." His maxims for the prince may be read, not merely as advice for getting and holding power, but as preparing for a heroic effort in which the prince's power and fame will be used for liberty. The great man has the historic mission of a pioneer, not the role of a puppet.

Even in the Renaissance, however, Machiavelli is answered by Montaigne, who prizes moderation too much to praise heroism more than a little. Comparing Socrates and Alexander, Montaigne places all of the latter's actions under the maxim, "Subdue the world," whereas Socrates, he says, acts on the principle that it is wise to "lead the life of man in conformity with its natural condition." To Montaigne, "The value of the soul consists not in flying high, but in an orderly pace. Its greatness is exercised not in greatness, but in mediocrity."

The medieval Christian conception of heroism centers on the practice of heroic virtue, by which the theologian defines sanctity. In the calendar of saints, there is every type of spiritual excellence, but all alike—martyrs, virgins, confessors, doctors—are regarded as having, with God's grace, superhuman strength. The saints not only perform acts of exemplary perfection; they are godlike men in their exemption from the frailties of human flesh.

The heroes of antiquity also wear an aspect of divinity, but, like Achilles, each has a weakness in his armor. Moreover, the heroes of *The Iliad, The Odyssey,* and *The Aeneid* are men of overweening pride. They are relentlessly jealous of their honor. They strive not so much for victory as for the due meed of honor which is its fruit. Nothing grieves them so much as to have their deeds go unrequited by abundant praise. In the contribution made by this love of praise to the growth of the Roman empire, Augustine sees the providential working of God. In order that that empire "might overcome the grievous evils which ex-

isted among other nations," he writes, God "purposely granted it to such men as, for the sake of honor, and praise, and glory, consulted well for their country, in whose glory they sought their own, and whose safety they did not hesitate to prefer to their own, suppressing the desire of wealth and many other vices for this one vice, namely, the love of praise."

To Augustine, however, this glory found in human praise is far removed from the true glory. It is, in fact, a sin. "So hostile is this vice to pious faith," he writes, "if the love of glory be greater in the heart than the fear or love of God, that the Lord said, 'How can ye believe, who look for glory from one another, and do not seek the glory which is from God alone?'"

The Christian hero, consequently, seeks not his own glory, but the glory of God, and in contrast to the pagan hero, he is great, not in pride, but in humility. His model is seen in the Apostles, who, according to Augustine, "amidst maledictions and reproaches, and most grievous persecutions and cruel punishments, were not deterred from the preaching of human salvation. And when . . . great glory followed them in the church of Christ, they did not rest in that as in the end of their virtue, but referred that glory itself to the glory of God . . . For their Master had taught them not to seek to be good for the sake of human glory, saying, 'Take heed that ye do not your righteousness before men to be seen of them' . . . but 'Let your works shine before men, that they may see your good deeds, and glorify your Father who is in heaven.'"

The word "glory" in its theological connotation thus has a meaning distinct from, and even opposed to, the sense in which it is sometimes used as a synonym for "fame." In the liturgy of the church, the psalms and hymns (especially those of the doxology which sing the *gloria Patri* and the *gloria in excelsis Deo*) render unto God the homage which is due His infinite goodness, the reflexive splendor of which is the divine glory. As in the strict moral sense honor on the human plane is due to virtue alone, so in a strict theological sense glory belongs only to God.

Strictly, God's glory cannot be increased by human recognition. Yet every act of religious devotion is said to redound to the greater glory of God and to diffuse His glory among creatures through the divinity they acquire when they love God and are beloved by Him. God is "all fullness and the acme of all perfection"; nevertheless, Montaigne writes, "his name may grow and increase by the blessing and praise we give to his external works."

According to Dante, "The glory of the All-Mover penetrates through the universe and re-glows in one part more, and in another less." In his journey through Paradise, he beholds the saints whom God loves especially, each with a distinct degree of glory according to the proximity with which he approaches the presence of God. Their halos and aureoles, in the imagery of Christian art, are the symbols of the glory in which they are bathed as in reflected light.

36

Hypothesis

INTRODUCTION

A COMPARISON of their Greek and Latin roots shows that the English words "hypothesis" and "supposition" are synonymous. To hypothesize or to suppose is *to place under*—to make one thing the basis of another in the process of thought.

The word "hypothesis" is today often popularly misapplied to mean a guess or hunch. The sleuth in a detective story speaks of having a hypothesis about who committed the crime. The popular notion of what it means to suppose something, or to entertain a supposition, more accurately reflects the meaning of hypothesis in logic, mathematics, and scientific or philosophical method.

A supposition is generally understood to be something taken for granted, something assumed for the purpose of drawing implications or making inferences. What is supposed is not known to be true; it may be true or false. When we make a supposition, our first concern is to see what follows from it, and only then to consider its truth in the light of its consequences. We cannot reverse this order, when we employ suppositions, and ask first about their truth.

The word "if" expresses the essence of supposing. The word "then" or the phrase "it follows that" introduces the consequences for the consideration of which we make the supposition. We are not interested in the "if" for its own sake, but for the sake of what it may lead to. In any statement of the "if . . . then . . ." sort, it is the if-clause which formulates the supposition or the hypothesis; the other part of the statement, the then-clause, formulates the consequences or implications. The whole complex statement, which makes an *if* the logical basis for a *then,* is not

a hypothesis. Rather it is what is traditionally called in logic a hypothetical proposition.

THERE IS ONE USE of the word "hypothesis" in mathematics which seems at odds with the foregoing summary. In Euclid's *Elements,* for example, a hypothesis is that which is given, not as the basis from which the conclusion is drawn or proved, but as a condition of solving the geometric problem under consideration. Let us take Proposition 6 of Book I. It reads: "*If* in a triangle two angles be equal to one another, *then* the sides which subtend the equal angles will also be equal to one another." In the demonstration of this theorem, a triangle having two equal angles is regarded as *given* or *granted.* That figure or geometric condition is a fact obtained by *hypothesis.* It is the fact stated in the hypothesis, or the if-clause, of the theorem.

If the geometric reality of that fact itself is questioned, the answer would have to be obtained by a prior proof that such a figure, conforming to the definition of an isosceles triangle, can be constructed by the use of no other instruments than a straight edge and a compass. The construction is not made, however, as part of the proof of Theorem 6, any more than is the demonstration of an antecedent theorem, which may have to be used in the proof of Theorem 6. In the proof of Theorem 6, the first line, beginning with the word "let," declares that the constructibility of the figure is to be taken for granted as a matter of hypothesis.

The whole problem of Theorem 6 is to prove that the then-clause follows from the if-clause. Euclid appears to accomplish this by introducing other propositions—drawn from his axioms, definitions, postulates, or theorems previously demonstrated—which establish this connection and so certify the conclusion as following from the hypothesis. Two points about this procedure should be noted.

First, the conclusion does not follow from the hypothesis directly, for if that were so, the "if-then" proposition would be self-evident and would need no proof. The mind which sees immediately that the sides opposite to the equal angles in an isosceles triangle are necessarily equal does not need any demonstration of the connection between equal angles and equal sides. The Euclidean demonstration consists in making this connection, which is not *immediately* evident, *mediately* evident; that is, evident through the mediation of other propositions. It is not the hypothesis alone which proves the conclusion, but the hypothesis in the company of other propositions which serve to take the mind step by step from the hypothesis granted to the conclusion implied.

Second, the proposition with the truth of which the reasoning seems to end is not the proposition to be proved. The Q.E.D. at the end of a Euclidean demonstration does not apply to the last proposition in the line of proof, but to the theorem itself, for that is the proposition to be proved. The last proposition in the reasoning is merely the consequent which, according to the theorem, is proposed as following from the hypothesis. When he is able to verify the proposed connection between the hypothesis and its conclusion or consequent, Euclid says Q.E.D. to the theorem as a whole—*the whole if-then statement.*

The process of proof seems to be the same when the theorem is stated categorically rather than hypothetically. For example, Theorem 6 might have been stated, as other Euclidean theorems are, in the following manner: "The sides subtended by equal angles in a triangle are also equal to one another." This variation in mode of statement raises a question, not about the meaning of "by hypothesis" in Euclidean proof, but about the difference between hypothetical and categorical propositions, which we will consider later.

THE EUCLIDEAN USE of a given (that is, a constructible) figure as a hypothesis does not seem

to be a method of making a supposition in order to discover its implications. Nor does it seem to be a way of testing the truth of a hypothesis by reference to its consequences. Both of these aspects of hypothetical reasoning do appear, however, in Plato's dialogues.

In the *Meno,* for example, Socrates proposes, at a certain turn in the conversation about virtue and knowledge, that he and Meno entertain the hypothesis that virtue *is* knowledge. Socrates immediately inquires about the consequences. "If virtue is knowledge," he asks, "will it be taught?" Since Meno already understands that knowledge is teachable, he answers the question affirmatively. The utility of advancing the hypothesis that virtue is knowledge gradually appears in the next phase of the dialogue, wherein it is discovered that virtue is not teachable at all, or at least not in the way in which the arts and sciences are teachable. The discovery throws some doubt on the truth of the hypothesis that virtue is knowledge; at least it does not seem to be knowledge in the same sense as science or art.

This mode of reasoning exemplifies the use of a hypothesis to test its truth in terms of its consequences. The underlying logical principle is that the denial of the consequences requires a denial of the antecedent hypothesis, just as an affirmation of the antecedent would require an affirmation of the consequent. Nothing follows logically from a denial of the hypothesis, or from an affirmation of its consequences.

This example from the *Meno* also illustrates the difference between Euclid's and Plato's use of hypotheses. Socrates is not here trying to prove that *if* virtue is knowledge, *then* virtue is teachable. The validity of the foregoing if-then statement is already understood in terms of the fact that *knowledge is teachable*. With the if-then statement accepted as valid, Socrates uses it for the purpose of ascertaining whether or in what sense virtue is knowledge. It is not the hypothetical or if-then statement which is proved, but the hypothesis—the antecedent in that statement—which is tested.

The same general method of employing hypotheses and testing them is found in the empirical sciences. In medical practice the physician, according to Hippocrates, "must be able to form a judgment from having made himself acquainted with all the symptoms, and estimating their powers in comparison with one another"; he should then "cultivate prognosis," since "he will manage the cure best who has foreseen what is to happen from the present state of matters."

The preliminary diagnosis states a hypothesis (what the disease may be) and the prognosis foresees a set of consequences (what is likely to happen if the diagnosis is correct). Observation of the course of the symptoms and the patient's changing condition will either confirm or invalidate the prognosis. Confirmation leaves the diagnosis a lucky guess, but fails to prove it. If the disease does not run the predicted course, however, the diagnosis on which the prognosis was based can be dismissed as a false hypothesis.

WHEN A HYPOTHESIS takes the form of a prediction of what should happen if the hypothesis is true, the failure of the consequences to occur refutes the hypothesis. Though discussions of scientific method frequently speak of "prediction and verification," it would seem as though prediction can only lead to the refutation of a hypothesis rather than to its verification. A hypothesis is overthrown when its prediction fails, but it is not verified when its prediction comes true. To think that it can be verified in this way is to commit the logical fallacy of arguing from the truth of a conclusion to the truth of its premises. How, then, do empirical scientists prove a hypothesis to be true? What do they mean by prediction and verification in relation to the use of hypothesis?

There seem to be two possible ways in which a hypothesis can be proved by empirical or experimental research. One way can be used when we know that the consequences implied follow *only* from the truth of the hypothesis. Should the consequences implied be impossible *unless* the supposed condition exists, then the confirmation of the prediction verifies the hypothesis.

The other possible method of verification has come to be called "the method of multiple working hypotheses." The validity of this method depends on our knowing that the several hypotheses being entertained *exhaust* all the relevant possibilities. Each hypothesis generates a prediction; and if upon investigation the observed facts negate every prediction except one, then that one remaining hypothesis is verified. If negative instances have eliminated the false hypotheses, the hypothesis remaining must be true, on the condition, of course, that it is the *only* possibility which is left. That is why Poincaré cautions scientists "not to multiply hypotheses indefinitely."

Both of these methods seem to be valid only if a prerequisite condition is fulfilled. To verify one of a series of multiple hypotheses through the elimination of the others, the scientist must know that the hypotheses enumerated are truly *exhaustive*. In the verification of a single hypothesis by the confirmation of its prediction, the scientist must know that the observed consequences can follow from no other supposition. Since such knowledge is often unavailable, probability rather than complete proof results from the testing of hypotheses by observation or experiment.

In his *Treatise on the Vacuum*, Pascal offers a summary of the logical situation by distinguishing the true, the false, and the doubtful or probable hypothesis. "Sometimes its negation brings a conclusion of obvious absurdity, and then the hypothesis is true and invariable. Or else one deduces an obvious error from its affirmation, and then the hypothesis is held to be false. And when one has not been able to find any mistake either in its negation or its affirmation, then the hypothesis remains doubtful, so that, in order that the hypothesis may be demonstrable, it is not enough that all the phenomena result from it, but rather it is necessary, if there ensues something contrary to a single one of the expected phenomena, that this suffice to establish its falsity."

IN POINCARÉ'S VIEW, "every generalisation is a hypothesis." Therefore, in science, hypothesis "plays a necessary rôle, which no one has ever contested." But science requires that hypotheses "should always be as soon as possible submitted to verification." According to Poincaré, "some hypotheses are dangerous,—

first and foremost those which are tacit and unconscious. And since we make them without knowing them, we cannot get rid of them."

Both the use of hypotheses and the method of verifying them vary from science to science, according as the character of the science happens to be purely empirical (*e.g.*, the work of Hippocrates, Darwin, Freud), or experimental (*e.g.*, the work of Harvey and Faraday), or a combination of experimentation with mathematical reasoning (*e.g.*, the work of Galileo, Newton, Poincaré, Planck, Einstein, Bohr, Dobzhansky). Not all scientific work is directed or controlled by hypotheses, but in the absence of well-formulated hypotheses, the research can hardly be better than exploration.

A well-constructed experiment, especially what Francis Bacon calls an *experimentum crucis,* derives its demonstrative character from the hypothetical reasoning which formulates the problem to be solved. The value of such a crucial experiment appears in Bacon's reasoning about the rise and fall of the tides. "If it be found," he writes, "that during the ebb the surface of the waters at sea is more curved and round, from the waters rising in the middle, and sinking at the sides or coast, and if, during a flood, it be more even and level, from the waters returning to their former position, then assuredly, by this decisive instance, the raising of them by a magnetic force can be admitted; if otherwise, it must be entirely rejected."

In the field of mathematical physics, and particularly in astronomy, the meaning of hypothesis is both enlarged and altered. So far we have considered hypotheses which are single propositions implying certain consequences. But in mathematical physics, a whole theory—a complex system of propositions—comes to be regarded as a single hypothesis.

In his preface to the work of Copernicus, Andreas Osiander says that the task of the astronomer is "to use painstaking and skilled observation in gathering together the history of the celestial movements; and then—since he cannot by any line of reasoning reach the true causes of these movements—to think up or construct whatever causes or hypothe-

ses he pleases, such that, by the assumption of these causes, those same movements can be calculated from the principles of geometry, for the past and for the future too." The elaborate system constructed by Copernicus and the system constructed by Ptolemy which Copernicus hopes to replace are sometimes called "the Copernican hypothesis" and "the Ptolemaic hypothesis"; and sometimes these two theories are referred to as "the heliocentric hypothesis" and "the geocentric hypothesis."

A whole theory, regarded as a hypothesis, must be tested in a different way from a single proposition whose implication generates a prediction. As rival hypotheses, one theory may be superior to another in internal consistency or in mathematical simplicity and elegance. Kepler is thus able to argue against Ptolemy by appealing to criteria which Ptolemy accepts, pointing out that Ptolemy himself wishes "to construct hypotheses which are as simple as possible, if that can be done. And so if anyone constructs simpler hypotheses than he—understanding simplicity geometrically—he, on the contrary, will not defend his composite hypotheses."

But even if the Copernican hypothesis is superior on the grounds of being geometrically simpler, it must meet another test. As indicated in the chapter on ASTRONOMY AND COSMOLOGY, mathematical theories about physical phenomena must be more than ideal constructions of possible universes. They must try to account for this one real world and are therefore subject to the test of their applicability to reality. However elegant it may be mathematically, a hypothesis—when considered from the point of view of physics—is satisfactory only if it accounts for the phenomena it was invented to explain. In the words of Simplicius of Cilicia, it must "save the appearances."

A hypothesis can therefore be tested for its application to reality by the way in which it fits the observed facts. "In those sciences where mathematical demonstrations are applied to natural phenomena," Galileo writes, "the principles" which are "the foundations of the entire superstructure" must be "established by well-chosen experiments." By such means Galileo chooses between the hypothesis that the uniform acceleration of a freely falling body is proportional to the units of space traversed and the hypothesis that it is proportional to the units of time elapsed.

According to Dewey, "There is no such thing as experiment in the scientific sense unless action is directed by some leading idea. The fact that the ideas employed are hypotheses, not final truths, is the reason why ideas are more jealously guarded and tested in science than anywhere else . . . as hypotheses, they must be continuously tested and revised, a requirement that demands they be accurately formulated."

To borrow Plato's expression in the *Timaeus,* the mathematical consistency of a theory makes it "a likely story." The theoretical integrity of the hypothesis makes it credible. But when competing credible hypotheses exist, each saving the relevant appearances equally well, which is to be believed? The fact that one of them, as in the case of the Copernican-Ptolemaic controversy, is mathematically superior cannot decide the question, since the question is, Which is true of reality?

Sometimes a single fact, such as the phenomenon of the Foucault pendulum, may exercise a decisive influence, if one of the two competing theories finds that fact congenial and the other leaves it inexplicable. Sometimes, as appears in the discussion of the Copernican hypothesis in the chapter on Astronomy and Cosmology, of two hypotheses which are equally satisfactory so far as purely astronomical phenomena are concerned, one may have the additional virtue of covering other fields of phenomena which that hypothesis was not originally designed to explain.

As interpreted by Kepler and as developed in Newton's theory of universal gravitation, the Copernican hypothesis brings the terrestrial phenomena of the tides and of falling bodies under the same set of laws which applies to the celestial motions. The hypothesis then has the amazing quality of consilience—a bringing together under one formulation of phenomena not previously thought to be related. This seems to be what Huygens has in mind when he considers the degree of probability that is attainable through experimental research. We have "scarcely less than complete proof," he writes, when "things which have been demonstrated by the principles assumed, correspond perfectly to the phenomena which experiment has brought under observation; and further, principally, when one can imagine and foresee new phenomena which ought to follow from the hypotheses which one employs, and when one finds that therein the fact corresponds to our prevision."

Then, in common parlance, we say that it is no longer a theory, but has become a fact. Yet the question remains whether the empirical tests which eliminate the less satisfactory hypothesis can ever make the more satisfactory hypothesis more than a likely story.

In the *Mathematical Principles of Natural Philosophy,* Newton says, "I have not been able to discover the cause of those properties of gravity from phenomena, and I frame no hypotheses; for whatever is not deduced from the phenomena is to be called an hypothesis; and hypotheses, whether metaphysical or physical, whether of occult qualities or mechanical, have no place in experimental philosophy." The context of this passage, and of a similar statement at the end of the *Optics,* as well as the association in Newton's mind of hypotheses with occult qualities, substantial forms, and hidden causes, seems to indicate a special meaning of "hypothesis."

Newton criticizes the vortices in the physics of Descartes on the ground that it is unnecessary to appeal to occult or unobservable *entities* in order to explain natural phenomena. The Cartesian vortices, like the substantial forms of Aristotle, are, for Newton, hypotheses in a very special sense. They are *hypothetical entities.* They are not inferred from the phenomena. Although treated as if they were realities underlying the phenomena, they are, as Gilbert says of the *primum mobile,* a "fiction, something not comprehensible by any reasoning and evidenced by no visible star, but purely a product of imagination and mathematical hypothesis."

There is almost a play on words in this identification of hypotheses with imaginary entities to which reality is attributed; for in their Greek and Latin roots, the words "hypothesis" and "hypostasis," "supposition" and "substance," are closely related. The first word in each of these pairs refers to a *proposition* which underlies reasoning, the second to a *reality* which underlies observable qualities or phenomena. To make hypotheses, in the sense in which Newton excludes them from experimental philosophy, is to *hypostatize* or to *reify*, that is, to make a thing out of, or to give reality to, a fiction or construction of the mind.

It has seemed to some critics that, no less than the Cartesian vortices, the ether in Newton's theory of light is a hypothesis in precisely this sense—an imaginary entity. For many centuries, the atoms and molecules postulated to explain chemical combinations and changes were attacked as fictions and defended as useful hypotheses. On the one hand, there is an issue concerning the theoretical usefulness of such constructions; on the other, a question concerning their counterparts in reality.

It is sometimes thought that fictions are useful for purposes of explanation even when their unreality is admitted. Rousseau, for example, explicitly denies any historical reality to the idea of man living in a state of nature prior to the formation of society by the social contract. In this matter, he says, we can lay "facts aside, as they do not affect the question." These related notions—the state of nature and the social contract—are "rather calculated to explain the nature of things, than to ascertain their actual origin; just like the hypotheses which our physicists daily form respecting the formation of the world."

Similarly Lavoisier posits the existence of "caloric" for its explanatory value. "It is difficult," he writes, "to comprehend these phenomena, without admitting them as the effects of a real and material substance, or very subtile fluid, which, insinuating itself between the particles of bodies, separates them from each other; and, even allowing the existence of this fluid to be hypothetical, we shall see in the sequel, that it explains the phenomena of nature in a very satisfactory manner."

ONE OTHER MEANING of hypothesis remains to be considered. It is the sense in which postulates or assumptions are distinguished from axioms in the foundations of a science. In Euclid's geometry, as in Descartes's, both sorts of principles appear. The axioms or common notions are those propositions which are immediately seen to be true without proof. The postulates or assumptions are hypotheses in the sense that their truth is taken for granted without proof.

Both sorts of propositions serve as principles or starting points for the demonstration of theorems, or the conclusions of the science. Both are principles of demonstration in that they are used to demonstrate other propositions without themselves being demonstrated. But axioms are traditionally regarded as intrinsically indemonstrable, whereas hypotheses—postulates or assumptions—may not be indemonstrable. They are simply asserted without demonstration.

The possibility of demonstrating a hypothesis gives it the character of a provisional assumption. In the *Discourse on the Method*, Descartes refers to certain matters assumed in his *Dioptrics* and *Meteors,* and expresses his concern lest the reader should take "offence because I call them hypotheses and do not appear to care about their proof." He goes on to say: "I have not named them hypotheses with any other object than that it may be known that while I consider myself able to deduce them from the primary truths which I explained above, yet I particularly desired not to do so, in order that certain persons may not for this reason take occasion to build up some extravagant philosophical system on what they take to be my principles."

The distinction between axioms and postulates or hypotheses raises two issues. The first concerns the genuineness of the distinction itself. Axioms, self-evident propositions, or what William James calls "necessary truths," have been denied entirely or dismissed as tautologies. The only principles of science must then be hypotheses—assumptions voluntarily made or conventionally agreed upon. This issue is more fully discussed in the chapter on PRINCIPLE. The other issue presupposes the reality of the distinction but is concerned with different applications of it in the analysis of science.

Aristotle, for example, defines scientific knowledge in terms of three elements, one of which consists of the primary premises upon which demonstrations rest. The principles of a particular science may be axioms in the strict sense of being self-evident truths and hence absolutely indemonstrable; or they may be provisional assumptions which, though not proved in this science, can nevertheless be proved by a higher science, as in "the application of geometrical demonstrations to theorems in mechanics or optics, or of arithmetical demonstrations to those of harmonics." The latter are not axioms because they are demonstrable; yet in a particular science they may play the role of axioms insofar as they are used, without being demonstrated, to demonstrate other propositions.

Reasoning which rests either on axioms or on demonstrable principles Aristotle calls *scientific,* but reasoning which rests only on hypotheses he regards as *dialectical.* Reasoning results in scientific demonstration, according to Aristotle, "when the premises from which the reasoning starts are true and primary, or are such that our knowledge of them has originally come through premises which are primary and true." In contrast, reasoning is dialectical "if it reasons from opinions that are generally accepted," and, Aristotle explains, "those opinions are 'generally accepted' which are accepted by everyone or by the majority or by the philosophers—*i.e.,* by all, or by a majority, or by the most notable and illustrious of them." In another place, he adds one important qualification. In defining a dialectical proposition as one that is "held by all men or by most men or by the philosophers," he adds: "provided it be not contrary to the general opinion; for a man would assent to the view of the philosophers, only if it were not contrary to the opinions of most men."

For Aristotle, dialectical reasoning or argument moves entirely within the sphere of opinion. Even an opinion generally accepted, not only by the philosophers but also by most men, remains an opinion. The best opinions are probabilities—propositions which are not self-evident and which cannot be proved. They are not merely *provisional* assumptions. Resting on assumptions which cannot ever be more than probable, the conclusions of dialectical reasoning are also never more than probable. Since they lack the certain foundation which axioms give, they cannot have the certitude of science.

Plato, on the other hand, seems to think that the mathematical sciences are hypothetical in their foundation, and that only in the science of dialectic, which he considers the highest science, does the mind rise from mere hypotheses to the ultimate principles of knowledge. "The students of geometry, arithmetic, and the kindred sciences," Socrates says in *The Republic,* "assume the odd and the even, and the figures and the three kinds of angle and the like in their several branches of science; these are their hypotheses, which they and everybody are supposed to know, and therefore they do not deign to give an account of them either to themselves or others." There is a higher sort of knowledge, he goes on, "which reason herself attains by the power of dialectic, using the hypotheses not as first principles, but only as hypotheses—that is to say, as steps and points of departure into a world which is above hypotheses, in order that she may soar beyond them to first principles."

The issue between Plato and Aristotle may be only verbal—a difference in the use of such words as "science" and "dialectic." Whether it is verbal or real is considered in the chapters on DIALECTIC and METAPHYSICS. In any case, the issue throws light on the difference between a hypothesis as a merely provisional assumption, susceptible to proof by higher principles, and a hypothesis as a probability taken for granted for the purposes of argument, which is itself incapable of being proved.

FINALLY WE COME to the meaning of "hypothetical" in the analysis of propositions and syllogisms. The distinction between the categorical and the hypothetical proposition or syllogism, briefly touched on in Aristotle's *Organon,* is developed in the tradition of logic which begins with that book.

In his work *On Interpretation* he distinguishes between simple and compound propositions. The compound proposition consists of several simple propositions in some logical relation to one another. In the tradition of logical analysis, three basic types of relation have been defined as constituting three different kinds of compound proposition. One type of relation is the *conjunctive;* it is signified by the word "and." Another is the *disjunctive;* it is signified by the words "either . . . or . . ." The third type is the *hypothetical* and is signified by the words "if . . . then . . ."

To take an example we have already used, "virtue is knowledge" and "virtue is teachable" are simple propositions. In contrast, the statement, *"if* virtue is knowledge, *then* virtue is teachable," is a compound proposition, hypothetical in form. If the proposition were stated in the sentence, *"either* virtue is knowledge *or* it is not teachable," it would be disjunctive in form; if stated in the sentence "virtue is knowledge *and* virtue is teachable," it would be conjunctive in form. In each of these three cases, the compound proposition consists of the two simple propositions with which we began, though in each case they appear to be differently related.

Whereas Aristotle divides propositions into simple and compound, Kant divides all judgments into the categorical, the hypothetical, and the disjunctive. In the categorical judgment, he says, "we consider two concepts"; in the hypothetical, "two judgements"; in the disjunctive, "several judgements in their relation to one another." As an example of the hypothetical proposition, he offers the statement, "If perfect justice exists, the obstinately wicked are punished." As an example of the disjunctive judgment, "we may say . . . [that] the world exists either by blind chance, or by internal necessity, or by an external cause." Each of these three alternatives, Kant points out, "occupies a part of the sphere of all possible knowledge with regard to the existence of the world, while all together occupy the whole sphere." The hypothetical judgment does no more than state "the relation of two propositions . . . Whether both these propositions are true remains unsettled. It is only the conse-

quence," Kant says, "which is laid down by this judgement."

In the *Prior Analytics,* Aristotle distinguishes between the categorical and the hypothetical syllogism. The following reasoning is categorical in form: "Knowledge is teachable, virtue is knowledge; therefore, virtue is teachable." The following reasoning is hypothetical in form: *"If* virtue is knowledge, it is teachable; *but* virtue is knowledge; *therefore* it is teachable"; or *"If* virtue is knowledge, it is teachable; *but* virtue is not teachable; *therefore* is not knowledge."

The basic issue with respect to the distinction between categorical and hypothetical syllogisms is whether the latter are always reducible to the former. One thing seems to be clear. The rules for the hypothetical syllogism formally parallel the rules for the categorical syllogism. In hypothetical reasoning, the consequent must be affirmed if the antecedent is affirmed; the antecedent must be denied if the consequent is denied. In categorical reasoning, the affirmation of the premises requires an affirmation of the conclusion, and a denial of the conclusion requires a denial of the premises.

With respect to the distinction between the categorical and hypothetical proposition, there is also an issue whether propositions stated in one form can always be converted into propositions having the other form of statement. In modern mathematical logic, for example, general propositions, such as "All men are mortal," are sometimes expressed in hypothetical form: "If anything is a man, it is mortal." Logicians like Russell think that the hypothetical form is more exact because it explicitly refrains from suggesting that men exist; it merely states that if the class 'man' should have any existent members, they will also belong to the class 'mortal.'

Apart from the question whether a universal proposition should or should not be interpreted as asserting the existence of anything, there seems to be a formal difference between the categorical and hypothetical proposition. This is manifest only when the hypothetical is truly a compound proposition, not when it is the statement of a simple proposition in hypothetical form, as, for example, the simple proposition "All men are mortal," is stated in hypothetical form by "If anything is a man, it is mortal." Because it is truly a compound proposition, and not merely the hypothetical statement of a general proposition, the proposition, "If virtue is knowledge, then virtue is teachable," cannot be restated in the form of a simple categorical proposition.

A simple proposition, whether stated categorically or hypothetically, may be the conclusion of either a categorical or a hypothetical syllogism. But the hypothetical statement which is really a compound proposition can never be the conclusion of any sort of syllogism, though it may be one of the premises in hypothetical reasoning.

37

Idea

INTRODUCTION

As the topical analysis or outline in each chapter indicates, the great ideas are not simple objects of thought. Each of the great ideas seems to have a complex interior structure—an order of parts involving related meanings and diverse positions which, when they are opposed to one another, determine the basic issues in that area of thought.

The great ideas are also the conceptions by which we think about things. They are the terms in which we state fundamental problems; they are the notions we employ in defining issues and discussing them. They represent the principal content of our thought. They are *what* we think as well as what we think *about.*

If, in addition to its objects and content, we wish to think about thought itself—its acts or processes—we shall find in the tradition of the great books a number of related terms which indicate the scope of such inquiry. Some of them are: idea, judgment, understanding, and reasoning; perception, memory, and imagination; sense and mind. Here we are concerned with one of these—the idea IDEA. It is probably the most elementary of all these related terms, for according to different conceptions of the nature and origin of ideas, the analysis of thought and knowledge will vary. Different positions will be taken concerning the faculties by which men know, the acts and processes of thinking, and the limits of human understanding.

DOES THE WORD "idea," when it is used in the technical discourse of metaphysics or psychology, signify that which is known or understood? Does it signify, not the object of thought, but the thought itself? Or both? Certainly in popular speech the word is used both ways, for men speak of understanding an idea and note differences in their understanding of the same idea; and they also say that they have different ideas about the same thing, meaning that they understand the same thing differently.

The word "idea" has many other oppositions of meaning in its tremendous range of ambiguity. It is sometimes used exclusively for the eternal types in the divine mind or the intelligible forms that exist apart from material things which are their copies; sometimes for concepts in the human mind, abstracted from sense-experience; sometimes for the seeds of understanding which belong innately to the intellect and so do not need to be derived from sense. Sometimes "idea" means a sensation or a perception as well as an abstract thought, and then its connotation extends to almost every type of mental content; sometimes it is denied that there are any abstract or general ideas; and sometimes "idea" has the extremely restricted meaning of an image which is the memory of a sense impression.

Kant vigorously protests against what he thinks is a needless abuse of the term *idea.* "I beg those who really have philosophy at heart," he writes, "to exert themselves to preserve to the expression *idea* its original signification." There is, he insists, "no want of words to denominate adequately every mode of representation without encroaching upon terms which are proper to others."

Kant proposes a "graduated list" of such terms. He begins with *perception,* which he divides into *sensation* and *cognition,* according as it is subjective or objective. A cognition, he then goes on, "is either an *intuition* or a *conception,*" according as it has either an immediate or a mediate relation to its object. Dividing conceptions into the *empirical* and the *pure,* Kant finally reaches the term *idea* as one subdivision of pure conceptions. If the pure conception "has its origin in the understanding alone, and is not the conception of a pure sensuous image," it is a *notio* or notion; and "a conception formed from notions, which transcends the possibility of experience, is an *idea,* or a conception of reason."

According to Kant, anyone "who has accustomed himself to these distinctions," will find it "quite intolerable to hear the representation of the color red called an idea." Tolerable or intolerable, the word "idea" has been used quite persistently with the very meaning that Kant abominates, as well as with a variety of others. The reader of the great books must be prepared for all these shifts in meaning and, with them, shifts in doctrine; for according to these differences in meaning, there are different analyses of the nature or being of ideas, different accounts of their origin or their coming to be in the human mind, and different classifications of ideas. These three questions—what ideas are, how ideas are obtained, and of what sorts they are—are so connected that the answer given to one of them tends to circumscribe the answers which can be given to the other two.

THE UNITY OF EACH chapter in this guide to the great books depends on some continuity of meaning in its central term, some common thread of meaning, however thin or tenuous, which unites and makes intelligible the discussions of various authors about the same thing. Without this, they would not move in the same universe of discourse at all. Nor could they even disagree with one another, if the words they used were utterly equivocal, as for example the word "pen" is equivocal when it designates a writing instrument and an enclosure for pigs.

The extraordinary ambiguity of the word "idea" as it is used in the great books puts this principle to the test. Are Plato and Hume talking about the same thing *at all,* when the one discusses ideas as the only intelligible reality and the other treats ideas as the images derived through memory from the original impressions of sense-experience? Is there any common ground between Aristotle and Berkeley—between the identification of human ideas with abstract or general conceptions, quite distinct from the perceptions or images of sense, and the identification of ideas with particular perceptions, accompanied by a denial of abstract or general notions?

Do writers like Locke or William James, for whom ideas of sensation and abstract ideas (or percepts and concepts) belong to the one faculty of understanding or to the single stream of consciousness, communicate with writers like Plotinus, Descartes, and Spinoza, for whom ideas belong to the intellect or to the thinking being, separate from matter and from sensations which are only bodily reactions? Or with writers like Aristotle and Aquinas, for whom there is a sharp distinction between the faculties of sense and intellect? Can Aristotle and Aquinas in turn explain the origin of concepts or intelligible species by reference to the intellect's power of abstracting them from experience or sensible species, and still carry on discussion with Plato, Augustine, and Descartes, who regard the intellect as in some way innately endowed with ideas, with the principles or seeds of understanding? Which of these have anything in common with Poincaré, Whitehead, and G. H. Hardy when they talk about mathematical ideas? Hardy, for example, writes: "A mathematician . . . has no material to work with but ideas, and so his patterns are likely to last longer, since ideas wear less with time than words."

The foregoing is by no means an exhaustive inventory. It fails, for example, to ask about the sense in which the theologians speak of ideas in the mind of God and of the illumination of the angelic or the human intellect by ideas divinely infused. (What is the common thread of meaning between such discourse and that concerned with the formation of abstract concepts or with the revival of sense impressions in images?) It fails also to question the meaning of idea in Kant's tripartite analysis of the faculties of intuition, judgment, and reasoning; or in Hegel's ultimate synthesis of all nature and history in the dialectical life of the Absolute Idea. (What do these meanings of "idea" have in common with the sense in which Freud distinguishes between conscious and unconscious ideas?)

The inventory is also incomplete in that it does not indicate the many divergent routes taken by authors who seem to share a common starting point. Even those who, on certain points, seem to talk the same language, appear to have no basis for communication on other points in the theory of ideas. But the questions which have been asked suffice for the purpose at hand. However great the ambiguity of "idea," it does not reach that limit of equivocation which would destroy the universe of discourse. There is a slender thread of meaning which ties all the elements of the tradition together—not in a unity of truth or agreement, but in an intelligible joining of issues.

This unity can be seen in two ways. It appears first in the fact that any consideration of ideas—whether as objects or contents of the mind—involves a theory of knowledge. This much is common to all meanings of "idea."

Those, like Plato and Berkeley, for whom ideas constitute a realm of intelligible or sensible being, make knowledge of reality consist in the apprehension or understanding of ideas. Those, like Aristotle and James, for whom ideas have no being except as perceptions or thoughts, make them the instruments whereby reality is known. On either view, knowledge involves a relationship between a knower and a known, or between a knowing faculty and a knowable entity; but on one view ideas are the reality which is known, and on the other they are the representations by which is known a reality that does not include ideas among its constituents. These two views do not exhaust the possibilities.

Ideas are sometimes regarded both as objects of knowledge and as representations of reality. Some writers (as, for example, Plato) distinguish two orders of reality—the sensible and the intelligible—and two modes of apprehension—sensing and understanding; and they use the word "idea" for both the intelligible object and the understanding of it. Locke, begging the reader's pardon for his frequent use of the word "idea," says that it is the term "which serves best to stand for whatsoever is the object of the understanding when a man thinks." But Locke also distinguishes between knowledge of real existences through ideas "that the mind has of things as they are in themselves," and knowledge of the relations among our own ideas, which the mind "gets from their comparison with one another." For Hume, too, ideas as well as impressions are involved in our knowledge of matters of fact, but relations between ideas may also be objects of knowledge, as in "the sciences of geometry, algebra, and arithmetic."

This double use of "idea" is sometimes accompanied, as in Aquinas, by an explicit acknowledgment and ordering of the two senses. For Aquinas, concepts are primarily the means of knowledge, not the objects of knowledge. A concept, Aquinas writes, "is not *what* is actually understood, but *that by which* the intellect understands"—that by which something else is known. Secondarily, however, concepts become *that which* we know when we reflexively turn our attention to the contents of our own mind. Using the phrase "intelligible species" to signify concepts, Aquinas explains that "since the intellect reflects upon itself, by such reflection it understands not only its own act of intelligence but also the species by which it understands. Thus the intelligible species is that which is understood secondarily; but that which is primarily understood is the object, of which the species is the likeness."

It is possible, therefore, to have ideas about things or ideas about ideas. In the vocabulary of this analysis by Aquinas, the ideas or concepts whereby real things are understood are sometimes called the "first intentions" of the mind. The ideas whereby we understand these ideas or first intentions are called the mind's "second intentions." An idea is always a mental intention, an awareness or representation, never an independent reality for the mind to know.

Locke's differentiation between ideas of sensation and ideas of reflection seems to parallel the medieval distinction between first and second intentions; but whereas second intentions are ideas engaged in a reflexive understanding of ideas as objects to be understood, Locke's ideas of reflection comprise "the perception of the operations of our own mind within us, as it is employed about the ideas it has got." A closer parallel, perhaps, is to be found in Locke's distinction between our knowledge of reality or of real existences and our knowledge of the relations existing between our own ideas.

THE SECOND WAY of seeing a connection among meanings of "idea" depends on recognizing what is common to contrary views.

The word "pen" is utterly equivocal, as we have noted, when it names a writing instrument and an animal enclosure. Hence men cannot contradict one another no matter what opposite things they may say about *pens* in one sense and *pens* in the other. The two meanings of "pen" are not even connected by being opposed to one another. But all the meanings of "idea" do seem to be connected by opposition at least, so that writers who use the word in its different senses and have different theories of idea cannot avoid facing the issues raised by their conflicting analyses.

The root of this opposition lies in the positive and negative views of the relation of ideas to sensations—or, more generally, to sense and the sensible. Though there are different analyses of sensation, one or both of two points seems to be agreed upon: that sensations are particular perceptions and that sensations result from the impingement of physical stimuli upon the sense organs of a living body.

Berkeley insists upon the first point while emphatically denying the second. Ideas or sensations are always particulars; but, he says, "the various sensations or ideas imprinted on the sense, however blended or combined together (that is, whatever objects they compose), cannot exist otherwise than in a mind perceiving them," and their cause is neither physical matter nor the perceiving mind, but "some other will or spirit that produces them." Others, like Lucretius and Hobbes, who regard sensations as particular perceptions, do not use the word "idea," as Berkeley does, for perceptions of external origin, but restrict it to inner productions of the mind itself in its acts of memory or imagination.

The various theories of idea thus range from those which identify an idea with a sensation or perception or with the derivatives of sensation, to those which deny the identity or even any relationship between ideas and sensations or images of sense.

THE FIRST POSITION is taken by writers who conceive mind or understanding, in men or animals, as the only faculty of knowledge. It performs all the functions of knowing and thinking. It is sensitive as well as reflective. It perceives and remembers as well as imagines and reasons.

Within this group of writers there are differences. Berkeley, for example, thinks "the *objects* of human knowledge" include "either ideas actually imprinted on the senses; or else such as are perceived by attending to the passions and operations of the mind; or lastly ideas formed by the help of memory and imagination—either compounding, dividing, or barely representing those originally perceived in the aforesaid ways." Hume, on the other hand, divides "all the perceptions of the mind into two classes or species, which are distinguished by their different degrees of force or vivacity. The less forcible and lively are commonly denominated *Thoughts* or *Ideas*. The other species want a name in our language and in most others . . . Let us, therefore, use a little freedom and call them *Impressions*." By this term, Hume explains, "I mean all our more lively perceptions, when we hear, or see, or feel, or love, or hate, or desire, or will."

Another use of terms is represented by Locke, who distinguishes between ideas of sensation and reflection, simple and complex ideas, particular and general ideas, and uses the word "idea" both for the original elements of sense-experience and for all the derivatives produced by the mind's activity in reworking these given materials, whether by acts of memory, imaginative construction, or abstraction. Still another variation is to be found in James. Despite the authority of Locke, he thinks that the word " 'idea' has not domesticated itself in the language so as to cover bodily sensations."

Accordingly, he restricts the word "idea" to concepts, and never uses it for sensations or perceptions. Nevertheless, like Locke, he does not think that the development of concept from percept needs the activity of a special faculty. Both concept and percept belong to the single "stream of thought" and are "states of consciousness."

THE SECOND POSITION is taken by writers who in one way or another distinguish between sense and intellect and regard them as quite separate faculties of knowing. The one is supposed to perform the functions of perception, imagination, and memory; the other, the functions of thought—conception, judgment, and reasoning, or if not these, then acts of intellectual vision or intuition. Here, too, there are differences within the group.

Just as the extreme version of the first position is taken by those who identify ideas with perceptions, so here the opposite extreme consists in the denial of any connection between ideas and all the elements of sense-experience. The ideas in the divine mind, or the ideas infused by God into the angelic intellects, have no origin in experience, nor any need for the perceptions, memories, or images of sense. They are not abstract ideas, that is, they are not concepts abstracted from sense-materials.

"Our intellect," Aquinas writes, "abstracts the intelligible species from the individuating principles"—the material conditions of sense and imagination. "But the intelligible species in the divine intellect," he continues, "is immaterial, not by abstraction, but of itself." The divine ideas, Aquinas quotes Augustine as saying, "are certain original forms or permanent and immutable models of things which are contained in the divine intelligence." Following Augustine's statement that "each thing was created by God according to the idea proper to it," Aquinas restricts the word "idea" to the "exemplars existing in the divine mind" and to the species of things with which God informs the angelic intellects. He uses the word "concept" where others speak of "ideas" in the human mind.

Descartes, on the other hand, endows the human mind with ideas—not concepts abstracted from and dependent on sense, but intuitive apprehensions which, since they cannot be drawn in any way from sense-experience, must be an innate property of the human mind. He does not, however, always use the word "idea" in this strict sense. Some ideas, he says, "appear to be innate, some adventitious, and others to be formed or invented by myself." The ideas called "adventitious" are those which seem to come from the outside, as when "I hear some sound, or see the sun, or feel heat." Those which we form or invent ourselves are "constructions of the imagination." Only innate ideas, in Descartes's view, are truly ideas in the sense of being the elements of certain knowledge and the sources of intellectual intuition. "By intuition," he says, "I understand, not the fluctuating testimony of the senses, nor the misleading judgment that proceeds from the blundering constructions of the imagination," but "the undoubting conception of an unclouded and attentive mind" which "springs from the light of reason alone."

As mind and body are separate substances for Descartes—mind being conceived by him as a *res cogitans* or thinking substance, quite separate from a *res extensa* or the extended matter of a bodily substance—so ideas and sensations are independent in origin and function. Like infused ideas in the angelic intellect, innate ideas in the human mind are not abstract, for they are not abstracted. But unlike the angelic intellect, the human mind, even when it employs innate ideas, is discursive or cogitative. It is never conceived as entirely free from the activities of judgment and reasoning, even when its power is also supposed to be intuitive—that is, able to apprehend intelligible objects without analysis or without recourse to the representations of sense.

The doctrine of innate ideas does not always go as far as this in separating intellectual knowledge—or knowledge by means of ideas—from sense-experience. In the theories of Plato and Augustine, for example, sense-experience serves to awaken the understanding to apprehend the intelligible objects for the intuition of which it is innately equipped.

Learning those things "which do not reach our minds as images by means of the senses but are recognized by us in our minds, without images," is, according to Augustine, "simply a process of thought by which we gather together things which, although they are muddled and confused, are already contained in the memory." Moreover, the memory contains not only "images imprinted on the memory by the senses of the body, but also the ideas of the emotions themselves," which are not received "through any of the body's gateways to the mind."

This process of learning by remembering appears to be similar to the process which Plato also calls "recollection" or "reminiscence." In the *Meno* Socrates demonstrates that a slave boy, who thinks he knows no geometry, can be led simply by questioning to discover that he knew all the while the solution of a geometric problem. "There have always been true thoughts in him," Socrates tells Meno, thoughts "which only needed to be awakened into knowledge by putting questions to him." Hence "his soul must always have possessed this knowledge." Learning, according to this doctrine of innate ideas, must therefore be described as an attempt "to recollect," not "what you do not know," but "rather what you do not remember."

Learning by recollection or reminiscence seems to be a process in which latent ideas (whether they are retained by the soul from a previous life or are part of the soul's endowment at its creation) become active either through the questioning of a teacher or through being awakened by the perceptions of the bodily senses. Though such bodily stimulation of thought implies a functional connection between body and soul, nevertheless both Plato and Augustine hold that ideas are independent in origin. They are not derived from sense, though their appearance may be occasioned by events in the world of sense.

ONE OTHER VIEW still remains to be considered. It denies that ideas are innate in the human mind at the same time that it distinguishes between the intellect and the senses as separate faculties of knowing. Having to explain whence the intellect gets its ideas, writers like Aristotle and Aquinas attribute to the hu-

man intellect an abstractive power by which it draws "the intelligible species" from sensory images, which Aquinas calls "phantasms."

The concepts by which "our intellect understands material things," we obtain "by abstracting the form from the individual matter which is represented by the phantasms." Through the universal concept thus abstracted, we are able, Aquinas holds, "to consider the nature of the species apart from its individual principles." It should be added here that abstractions are not vehicles of intuitive apprehension. Conception, which is the first act of the mind, yields knowledge only when concepts are used in subsequent acts of judgment and reasoning.

Abstract or universal concepts are as different from the ideas which belong to intellects separate from bodies—the divine or angelic intellects—as they are different from the particular perceptions or images of sense. They occupy an intermediate position between the two, just as, according to Aquinas, "the human intellect holds a middle place" between angelic intelligence and corporeal sense. On the one hand, the human intellect is for Aquinas an incorporeal power; on the other hand, it functions only in cooperation with the corporeal powers of sense and imagination. So the concepts which the human intellect forms, being universal, are immaterial; but they are also dependent, in origin and function, on the materials of sense. Not only are universal concepts abstracted from the phantasms, but for the intellect to understand physical things, "it must of necessity," Aquinas writes, "turn to the phantasms in order to perceive the universal nature existing in the individual."

This theory of abstract ideas seems not far removed from the position of Locke, who distinguishes between particular and general ideas (which he calls "abstract") or that of James, who distinguishes between universal concepts and sense perceptions. Yet on one question the difference between them is radical, namely, whether particular sensations and universal ideas belong to the same faculty of mind or to the quite distinct faculties of sense and intellect.

This difference seems to have considerable

bearing on the way in which these writers explain the process of abstraction or generalization, with consequences for certain subtleties, acknowledged or ignored, in the analysis of the grades of abstraction. Nevertheless, the resemblance between the positions of Locke and Aquinas, or those of James and Aristotle, each affirming in his own way that the mind contains nothing not rooted in the senses, serves to mediate between the more extreme positions.

THE DISPUTE ABOUT innate ideas and the controversy over abstract ideas are issues in psychology inseparable from fundamental differences concerning the nature and operation of the faculty *or* faculties of knowing. There are other issues which concern the being or the truth of ideas. Here the first question is not whether ideas are objects of knowledge, but whether the existence of ideas is real or mental—outside the mind or in it.

One aspect of this controversy is considered in the chapter on FORM, *viz.,* the argument between Aristotle and Plato about the being of the Ideas or Forms apart from both matter and mind. It is in the context of this argument that the traditional epithet "realism" gets one of its meanings, when it signifies the view that ideas or universals have an independent reality of their own. The various opponents of this view are not called "idealists." If they deny any existence to universal ideas outside the mind, they are usually called "conceptualists"; if they deny the presence of universals even in the mind, they are called "nominalists." These doctrines are more fully discussed in the chapters on SAME AND OTHER, UNIVERSAL AND PARTICULAR.

The controversy about the being of ideas has another phase that has already been noted in this chapter; and it is in this connection that the epithet "idealism" gets one of its traditional meanings. The doctrine is not that ideas have real existence outside the mind. On the contrary, it is that the only realities are mental—either minds or the ideas in them.

Berkeley's famous proposition—*esse est percipi,* to be is to be perceived—seems intended to permit only one exception. The perceiving mind has being without being perceived, but nothing else has. Everything else which exists is an idea, a being of and in the mind. According to this doctrine (which takes different forms in Berkeley and in Hegel, for example) the phrase "idea of" is meaningless. Nothing exists of which an idea can be a representation. There is no meaning to the distinction between thing and idea. The real and the ideal are identical.

Plato is sometimes called an "idealist" but not in this sense. He has never been interpreted as completely denying reality to the changing material things which imitate or copy the eternal ideas, the immutable archetypes or Forms. Applied to Plato or to Plotinus, "idealism" seems to signify the superior reality of ideal (as opposed to material or physical) existence. Just as "idealism" has these widely divergent meanings, so does "realism" when it designates, on the one hand, those who attribute independent reality to ideas and, on the other hand, those who affirm the existence of an order of real existences independent of the ideas which represent them in the mind.

Writers who distinguish between things and ideas, or between the order of reality and the mind's conception of it, face the problem of differentiating between these two modes of being. To say that ideas or concepts exist only in the mind is not to say that they do not exist at all, but only that they do not exist in the same way as things outside the mind.

Does an entity in its real existence apart from knowledge have the same character that it has when, as an object known, it somehow belongs to the knowing mind? Is there a kind of neutral essence which can assume both modes of existence—real existence, independent of mind, and ideal existence, or existence in the mind, as an object conceived or known? Is an idea or concept in the mind nothing but the real thing objectified, or transformed into an object of knowledge; or is the real thing, the thing in itself, utterly different from the objects of experience or knowledge—neither knowable nor capable of representation by concepts?

These questions, relevant to the consideration of ideas as representations of reality, are of course, also relevant to problems considered in the chapters on Being, Experience, and Knowledge. The issues indicated are there discussed.

Intimately connected with them are questions about the truth of ideas. Can ideas or concepts be true or false in the sense in which truth and falsity are attributed to propositions or judgments? Under what conditions is an idea true? In what does its truth consist, and what are the signs or marks of its truth? These matters are discussed in the chapter on Truth. Here it is sufficient to point out that the traditional distinction between adequate and inadequate ideas, and the comparison of clear and distinct with obscure and confused ideas, are used to determine the criteria of truth. It may be the truth of a concept taken by itself or of the judgment into which several concepts enter. To the extent that ideas are regarded as representative, their truth (or the truth of the judgments they form) seems to consist in some mode of agreement or correspondence with the reality they represent, or, as Spinoza says, its *ideatum*.

Within the conceptual or mental order itself, there is a further distinction between ideas which do not perform a representative function and those which do. The former are treated as fantasies, fictions, or chimeras; the latter are called, by contrast, "real ideas," or ideas having some reference to reality. The question of the reality of ideas takes precedence over the question of their truth, at least for those who regard the division into true and false as applicable only to representations. Yet the criteria of the distinction between the real and the imaginary are difficult to separate from the criteria of true and false. The separation is made most readily by those who use "idea" to mean memory image. They can test the reality of an idea by tracing it back to the impression from which it originated.

Another sort of test is applied by those who measure the reality of abstract ideas by their fidelity to the sense perceptions from which they were abstracted. Still another criterion, proposed by James, is that of freedom from contradiction. An idea has truth and its object has reality if it "remains uncontradicted." The idea of a winged horse illustrates the point.

"If I merely dream of a horse with wings," James writes, "my horse interferes with nothing else and has not to be contradicted ... But if with this horse I make an inroad into the world otherwise known, and say, for example, 'That is my old mare Maggie, having grown a pair of wings where she stands in her stall,' the whole case is altered; for now the horse and place are identified with a horse and place otherwise known, and what is known of the latter objects is incompatible with what is perceived with the former."

The consideration of ideas or concepts belongs to logic as well as to psychology and metaphysics. The logician sometimes deals with concepts directly and with the judgments into which they enter; sometimes he deals with them only as they find verbal expression in terms and propositions.

The distinction between concepts and judgments (or between terms and propositions) is discussed in the chapter on Judgment. There also we see that the classification of judgments or propositions depends in part on the acceptance or rejection of the notions of subject and predicate in the analysis of concepts or terms; and, if they are accepted, on the way in which terms are distinguished both as subjects and as predicates.

This in turn depends upon certain traditional divisions which are applicable to terms, if not always to concepts, such as the familiar distinctions between concrete and abstract, and particular and universal, terms. When the concept, which is sometimes called the "mental word," is regarded as by its very nature abstract and universal, these distinctions are applicable only to the physical words which are terms. Concrete and particular terms are then treated as verbal expressions of sense perceptions or images; abstract and universal terms, as verbal expressions of ideas or concepts. But when ideas are identified with sense perceptions or images, and abstract concepts are denied, the existence of general names in ordinary discourse suffices for the distinction between particular and universal terms, even though the latter do not express any actual content of the mind.

Unlike the foregoing, other divisions of terms, as, for example, the distinction between the univocal and the analogical, or between species and genera, do not occur throughout the tradition of logic. They tend to be characteristic of the logic of Aristotle and its medieval development. Of these two distinctions, that between univocal and analogical terms or concepts appears explicitly, so far as this set of great books is concerned, only in the *Summa Theologica*. Nevertheless, Aquinas does have some background for his special theory of analogical terms in Aristotle's treatment of univocal and equivocal names, and in his separation of terms which predicate a sameness in species or genus from those which predicate a sameness by analogy. The analysis of these distinctions is undertaken in the chapters on SAME AND OTHER and SIGN AND SYMBOL.

Other writers, in dealing with universal terms, recognize that they have different degrees of generality. They sometimes formulate this as an order of more and less inclusive classes. Sometimes they refer to the intension and extension, or connotation and denotation, of terms. The more general terms have a less restricted connotation and hence represent more extensive or inclusive classes. The more specific terms have a more determinate meaning and so also have a narrower denotation and represent less inclusive classes. What seems to be peculiar to Aristotle's analysis of species and genera is the setting of upper and lower limits to the hierarchy of universal terms, with a small number of irreducible categories (or *summa genera*) under which all species fall, and, at the other extreme, with a finite number

of lowest (or *infimae*) species which are incapable of subsuming other species.

The terms which fall under the lowest species must either be particulars or accidental classes. Those which seem to be predicable of the categories themselves, such as *being* or *one*, cannot be genera. These are the terms which Aristotle's medieval followers call "transcendental" and "analogical." Using the word "transcendental" in a different sense, Kant enumerates a set of concepts which bear some resemblance to Aristotle's *summa genera,* but which he treats as transcendental categories.

The difference among concepts with respect to generality is of interest to the psychologist as well as the logician, for it raises the problem of whether the more or the less general takes precedence in the order of learning. The order and relation of ideas is even more the common ground of both logic and psychology. Both, for example, deal with the position and sequence of terms or concepts in reasoning, though the logician aims to *prescribe* the forms which reasoning must take in order to be valid, whereas the psychologist tries to *describe* the steps by which thinking actually goes on.

Only the logician, however, is concerned with the way in which terms are ordered to one another as positive and negative, or as contraries; just as from Aristotle to Freud, only the psychologist deals with the association of ideas in the stream of thought by relationships of contiguity and succession, similarity and difference. According as the logical connection of ideas or their psychological association is made the primary fact, radically divergent interpretations are given of the nature of mind, the life of reason, and the process of thought.

38

Immortality

INTRODUCTION

THE mortality of man defines by contrast the immortality which some men hope for, some men fear, some men scoff at, but no man ever fails sooner or later to consider. The life of man, like that of other animals, moves through a normal span of years between birth and death. Legend tells of certain heroes upon whom the immortal gods bestowed immortal life, gracing them with an aspect of their own divinity. Jewish and Christian faith holds that Adam, with all his posterity, would never have suffered disease or death if he had refrained from sin. But according to the theologians, the imperishability of the bodily frame of man in a state of grace is a preternatural condition. Except, then, for the miraculous or the supernatural, death follows birth and life, that which comes to be passes away, all things of flesh and blood perish.

The proposition "All men are mortal" has been repeated during centuries of lessons in logic. Its truth has never been seriously challenged even by those who have criticized the syllogism which reaches the conclusion that since he is a man, Socrates is mortal. But throughout the same period, the great books of poetry and religion, of philosophy and theology, have recorded the qualifications which men have placed upon this truth.

Man dies in the flesh to be reborn in the spirit. Man, composite of soul and body, perishes as do all things which are subject to dissolution; but the soul itself, a simple spiritual substance, is immortal, living on after its union with the body is dissolved. The immortal soul is sometimes conceived as having many incarnations, inhabiting now this body, now that, in an endless pilgrimage through endless time; and sometimes, as in the Christian faith, each soul has only one embodiment on earth. It is specially created by God to inform the body of a human being. It is destined to be his immortal spirit in a future which belongs to eternity rather than to time.

Except for the form it takes in the doctrine of reincarnation, or the transmigration of souls, the idea of immortality is usually attended by conceptions of an afterlife in another world—the life of the shades in the Elysian Fields or in Hades, the life of the blessed in heaven or of the damned in hell. The afterlife is never merely a continuation of the life begun on earth. The other world is not just an abode for the disembodied soul. It is a place of judgment, of rewards and punishments, in which the soul realizes the good, or pays the penalty for the evil, toward which its earthly career inclined. The connection of immortality with rewards and punishments appears even in the theory of reincarnation, for as the soul passes from one embodiment to another, it enjoys or suffers the consequences befitting its previous existence.

STATED AS A speculative problem, the question of immortality is traditionally formulated as a question about the soul or the spirit of man: whether it exists by itself either before or after its conjunction with a human body; and if so, in what manner it subsists. For those who affirm the soul's separate existence, there seems to be no question about its everlasting endurance, either without beginning at all or from the moment of its creation. But the manner of the soul's subsistence leads to speculation concerning an afterlife or an other-life in a world of spirits, or in realms as far apart as heaven and hell.

We shall presently consider to what extent such speculations have been submitted to argument and to what extent they have been matters of religious belief. But in both these modes of consideration, the theme of immortality is never merely a matter of speculative interest, never merely a question of spiritual substances and their subsistence. It is always a problem for the moralist.

Is this earthly life and its brief temporal span enough for the aspirations of the human spirit, and for its striving toward a perfection of knowledge, of love, and of repose? If external sanctions are needed to support the voice of conscience, are earthly rewards and punishments—either humanly dispensed, or capriciously distributed by chance or fortune—sufficient sanction for the moral law? Can perfect justice be done unless there is a divine law and a divine judge, a judge who can see beyond the acts of men into their hearts, from whose judgment no one escapes, and whose rewards and punishments are supernaturally established states of blessedness and misery for the soul?

Whether or not God, freedom, and immortality are, as Kant suggests, the three great objects of speculative thought, they do seem to form the basic triad of religious beliefs. In the religions of the west, these beliefs take various forms, but the belief in immortality is seldom if ever found separate from belief in a supernatural order, in gods or a God to whom man owes certain duties and before whom man stands to be judged as a responsible moral agent who was free to obey or disobey the divine commands. But, this fact admitted, the question remains whether the principles of morality can be adequately stated, or made effective in the regulation of human conduct, without a religious foundation, or at least without reference to God and immortality.

On this the moralists disagree. The argument in Plato's *Gorgias*, for example, about whether it is better to do or suffer injustice, ends with a myth which tells of the soul standing naked before its divine judge after a man's death, showing no marks of the evil the individual has suffered during his life, but only of the evil he has done. The reader who

thinks the myth is necessary to complete the argument concerning justice and punishment takes one position on the question. He adopts the view that without the judgment of souls in an afterlife justice cannot be done.

The preoccupation with immortality in a great many of Plato's dialogues is not always based upon moral considerations. It appears as frequently in discussions of the relation between the soul and the objects of its knowledge. If, to be proper objects of knowledge, the Ideas must be eternal, the soul which knows them must also be immortal. But when the discussion of immortality involves a comparison of this life and the life to come, it usually turns on considerations of goodness rather than of knowledge and truth. For Kant, if not for Plato, immortality is almost entirely a moral matter; and where the Platonic myth deals with just rewards and punishments in an afterlife, the Kantian argument is concerned with the achievement of moral perfection.

In his *The Critique of Practical Reason,* Kant affirms immortality, along with the existence of God and the freedom of the will, as necessary practical postulates—indispensable conditions of the moral life. "The perfect accordance of the will with the moral law," Kant writes, "is *holiness,* a perfection of which no rational being of the sensible world is capable at any moment of his existence ... It can only be found in a progress *in infinitum* towards that perfect accordance ... It is necessary to assume such a practical progress as the real object of our will." The realization of happiness, or the *summum bonum,* Kant concludes, "is only possible practically on the supposition of the immortality of the soul."

The opposite view appears to be taken in Aristotle's *Nicomachean Ethics* and J. S. Mill's *Utilitarianism.* The *summum bonum* is a temporal happiness, a perfection attainable on earth and by purely natural means. In those passages in which Aristotle defines happiness in terms of contemplative activity, he also speaks of it as a godlike life and therefore one which has a touch of immortality. Man is able to lead such a life, he writes, only "in so far as something divine is present in him." To lead the life of reason, which is divine in comparison with any other mode of human life, we must, he says, "so far as we can, make ourselves immortal, and strain every nerve to live in accordance with the best thing in us."

But to be immortal in this way seems to mean the possession of a godlike quality in this life rather than the promise of a life hereafter. Aristotle demands only "a complete term of life" as a necessary condition for "the complete happiness of man." He passes lightly over the question whether "the dead share in any good or evil." So far as he considers a *blessedness* which the gods can add to human happiness, it does not belong to an afterlife, but consists rather in the good fortune which the gods grant to some men and which increases and secures their happiness beyond that which is attainable by virtue alone.

The moral issue concerning immortality is more explicitly faced by Mill in his examination of the need for religious or supernatural sanctions. While he does not admit their indispensability, neither does he deny their utility. "There is evidently no reason," he declares, "why all these motives for observance should not attach themselves to the utilitarian morality, as completely and as powerfully as to any other." Yet he himself stresses "the possibility of giving to the service of humanity, even without the aid of belief in a Providence, both the psychological power and the social efficacy of a religion."

Mill does not go as far as Lucretius in regarding the belief in immortality, with the attendant possibility of everlasting torment for the soul, as itself an immoral doctrine. For Lucretius it is a nightmare which haunts the waking hours of men, filling them with false fears and putting future pains in the way of present pleasures. "The fear of Acheron/Must, first and foremost, be dismissed," he writes. "This fear/Troubles the life of man from its lowest depths,/Stains everything with death's black darkness, leaves/No pleasure pure and clear."

Where others see in man's fear of death his natural desire for immortality, Lucretius thinks it is the dread of immortality which causes man's fear of death. "In our death we have no cause for fear," he says, if death is the end. "We cannot be wretched in non-existence."

IN THE GREAT POEMS of antiquity we find the imagery and detail of the pagan conception of the life hereafter. Both Odysseus and Aeneas visit the underworld. They see the shades of the departed heroes; all that is visible to the bodily eye are shimmering wraiths. They talk with the departed, listen to their memories, or hear them speak prophetically of the future. From Anchises, his dead father, Aeneas learns his destiny; and Ulysses hears in Hades what has befallen his companions at Troy and his family at home during his years of wandering.

Yet there is a striking difference between Virgil's poem and Homer's with respect to the afterlife. The division which Virgil makes between Elysium and Tartarus corresponds much more closely than anything in Homer— or for that matter in the other Greek poets— to the Christian distinction between heaven and hell. Though Elysium and Tartarus both belong to the underworld, one is the abode of the blessed, the other a place of torment for sinners.

In the sixth book of *The Aeneid,* the Sibyl explains the topography of the underworld to Aeneas. There is a place "where the way forks," she says:

The right-hand leads beneath the battlements of
    great Dis,
And is our route to Elysium; the left-hand takes the
    wicked
To Tartarus, their own place, and punishment
    condign.

Tartarus, the abode of the condemned, is surrounded by "a flaming torrent—Hell's river of fire," and is filled with the noise of punishment. Elysium, on the other hand, is

The Happy Place, the green and genial
Glades where the fortunate live, the home of the
    blessed spirits.
What largesse of bright air, clothing the vales in
    dazzling
Light, is here! This land has a sun and stars of
    its own.

Its inhabitants, in sharp contrast with the unfortunates in Tartarus, seem to pass their time in peace and pleasure.

Homer makes no such sharp division between the realm of the blessed and the realm of the condemned. Plutarch speaks of "the isles of the blessed celebrated by Homer," but the reference cannot be substantiated. In one passage in *The Odyssey* Menelaus is promised that he will be taken "to the Elysian Field," which is at "the limits of the earth, where fair-haired Rhadamanthys [Rhadamanthus] is, and where there is made the easiest life for mortals, for there is no snow, nor much winter there, nor is there ever rain." But even this seems to describe a different life rather than an afterlife.

So far as the underworld is described on the occasion of Ulysses' descent into "the house of Hades and of revered Persephone," we are told that the Theban prophet Teiresias alone has his "senses stay unshaken." Persephone "has granted intelligence ... after death" to Teiresias alone, while all other souls in Hades are "flittering shadows." The shades of good men and bad alike languish in the domain of darkness. Tityus, Tantalus, and Sisyphus are subjected to special punishments for their grievous sins and transgressions, but all the shades—even of those men whom the gods loved and honored—seem to be in a state of misery. Though they are not all beset with torments and agonies, none seems to be overcome with joy or to have reached contentment.

Those whom the gods love do not join the deities on Mount Olympus. When they enter the somber realm of Pluto—the deity of the underworld—they, like all the other shades whom Charon ferries across the river Styx, are more remote from the gods than are mortal men on earth. The only exception perhaps is Heracles, whom Odysseus meets in Hades, or rather "his image, that is ... he himself among the immortal gods enjoys their festivals, married to sweet-stepping Hebe, child of great Zeus and Hera."

The general attitude of all who dwell in the underworld is summed up by Achilles when he tells Odysseus: "never try to console me for dying. I would rather follow the plow as thrall to another man, one with no land allotted him and not much to live on, than be a king over all the perished dead." And the mother of Odysseus describes the condition of the dead in Hades as one in which "the sinews no longer hold the flesh and the bones together, and once the spirit has left the white bones,

all the rest of the body is made subject to the fire's strong fury, but the soul flitters out like a dream and flies away."

Among other ancient peoples such as the Egyptians, the Babylonians, and the Persians, Herodotus found other views of immortality than those which prevailed in Greece. He reports, for example, the doctrine of transmigration or reincarnation—a doctrine which also appears in the myth of Er at the end of Plato's *The Republic* and is alluded to elsewhere in the Platonic dialogues. "The Egyptians," Herodotus writes, "were the first to broach the opinion that the soul of man is immortal, and that, when the body dies, it enters into the form of an animal which is born at the moment, thence passing on from one animal into another, until it has circled through the forms of all creatures which tenant the earth, the water, and the air, after which it enters again into a human frame and is born anew."

Herodotus, however, seems more interested in the effect of such beliefs on the practices of the living, especially their funeral rites and other devotions, than he is with the truth of conflicting theories of immortality.

"The doctrine of a future state," according to Gibbon, "was scarcely considered among the devout polytheists of Greece and Rome as a fundamental article of faith." Before the time of Christ, "the description of the infernal regions had been abandoned to the fancy of painters and of poets, who peopled them with so many phantoms and monsters who dispensed their rewards and punishments with so little equity, that a solemn truth, the most congenial to the human heart, was oppressed and disgraced by the absurd mixture of the wildest fictions." Lacking an acceptable or satisfying belief, yet inclined to believe in, as men are inclined to hope for, a better life, the pagan world, Gibbon thinks, could not long resist the appeal of Christian teaching. "When the promise of eternal happiness was proposed to mankind on condition of adopting the faith, and of observing the precepts of the Gospel, it is no wonder," he declares, "that so advantageous an offer should have been accepted by great numbers of every religion, of every rank, and of every province in the Roman empire."

THE ARGUMENTS for personal immortality which Christian theologians draw from the nature of the human soul do not differ essentially from the proofs offered by philosophers without recourse to religious faith. This applies to arguments advanced before and after Christianity by Plato and Plotinus as well as to those developed by philosophers like Descartes and Locke who belong to the Christian community. The exclusively theological aspects of the Christian doctrine of immortality are those matters which, since they are beyond the reach of reason, belong to faith alone.

The doctrine that the individual soul is created and that it has a unique affiliation with one human body, is not capable of being proved or defended by reason against the quite opposite theory that the soul has always existed and inhabits any number of bodies in the course of many reincarnations. The existence of hell, purgatory, and heaven as supernatural states of the soul; the time, place, and manner of the Last Judgment; the resurrection of the body and the difference between the bodies reunited with the souls of the blessed and the damned; the joy of eternal happiness and the misery of eternal damnation—these dogmas of Christian orthodoxy go far beyond all merely philosophical attempts to prove the soul's immortality or to consider its life apart from the body.

The great theologians undertake to do more than expound these articles of faith. Reason asks questions which the man of faith must try to answer, defending his faith, not by proof, but by overcoming doubts, by answering objections, by making dogmas intelligible. Yet the great theologians admit an irreducible core of mystery. The joy of the soul united to God in the beatific vision surpasses temporal understanding. The mysteries of hell are perhaps even greater.

The preacher in Joyce's *A Portrait of the Artist as a Young Man,* dwelling on the spiritual torments of hell, declares that "of all these spiritual pains by far the greatest is the pain of loss . . . a torment greater than all the others. Saint Thomas, the greatest doctor of the church . . . says that the worst damnation consists in this, that the understanding of man is totally deprived of divine light and his affection obstinately turned away from the goodness of God." The accompanying spiritual pains are "the pain of conscience" and "the pain of extension," but the "last and crowning torture of all the tortures of that awful place," the preacher concludes, "is the eternity of hell."

The deprivation of God's love and exclusion from His presence constitute a spiritual misery comparable to the beatitude of beholding God and being within the circle of the divine light. One is an infinite anguish of frustration and loss; the other, an infinite rest of peace and fulfillment. But the theologians also teach that the damned suffer the pains of sense in hell, as well as the pains of deprivation. "That hell, which also is called a lake of fire and brimstone," Augustine says, "will be material fire and will torment the bodies of the damned." When hellfire and the expiatory punishments of purgatory are not merely symbols for the imagination, they raise extraordinarily difficult questions, as both Augustine and Aquinas admit.

Dante asks us to read the descriptions he gives of hell, purgatory, and paradise in *The Divine Comedy* in a strictly literal sense as well as in several symbolic meanings, such as the moral and the allegorical. But he explains in his own commentary on the poem that the literal meaning also involves symbolism, insofar as the things that the words refer to when taken in their literal sense are themselves the symbols of other things. In any case, the poet may be more successful than the theologian in making intelligible through symbol and metaphor what in its literal significance is strictly unimaginable. The imagery of darkness, sultriness, noise, and heaviness, which grows more intense as the descent proceeds in the *Inferno,* does more than the anguished outcries of the damned to convey the reality of hell.

The metaphors of music and agility express the harmony of heaven. But it is especially the symbolism of light which captures the invisible in terms of vision, except perhaps when it reaches a climax in the blinding effulgence at the end of the *Paradiso.* As Dante moves upward in the realm of love, where courtesy prevails in every speech and charity suffuses every will, he sees the mystic rose of heaven entirely through reflected light. The saints, and especially those glorious spirits who instruct his progress, become pale mirrors of the ineffable vision which they themselves behold.

Milton too pictures heaven and hell, but in *Paradise Lost* the destiny of the immortal soul remains a prophecy, a consequence of the earthly immortality which Adam lost. Except for the Prologue, hell and heaven are offstage in Goethe's *Faust,* though they are the main implications of the wager Faust makes with Mephistopheles, which puts his immortal soul in the balance.

THE PHILOSOPHICAL issue concerning immortality cannot be separated from issues concerning the existence and nature of man's soul. The various arguments for immortality seem to rest not merely on the reality of the distinction between soul and body, but more precisely on the immateriality of the soul. Lucretius, for example, does not deny the existence of soul, nor does he fail to differentiate the soul from the body wherein it is located. The soul, according to Lucretius, like everything else in the universe, consists of atoms. These differ from those of the body by their roundness, smoothness, and mobility. They are "much smaller than those which form the body's substance,/ But they are also fewer, here and there/At wider intervals throughout the framework."

On this view of the soul as material in nature and as constituted of many quite separable parts, the soul is necessarily as perishable as the rest of the body. Lucretius writes,

When time's dominion shakes the body,
When limbs react with dull ungainliness,
Then the mind limps, tongue is a babbler, mind
Is palsied, all is failure, all is loss.
So spirit's quality must dissolve like smoke
Into the air aloft . . .
Its birth, its growth, its aging, and its death
Are one with ours.

It should be observed, however, that it is not the materiality of the soul, but rather its divisibility into parts, which accounts for its mortality. The atoms after all are material, but since as the ultimate units of matter they are simple bodies and so are absolutely indivisible, they cannot perish. Only the simple is imperishable.

The *imperishability of the simple* (*i.e.,* of that which has no parts) occurs as a premise in one of the great arguments for the immortality of the soul. In Plato's *Phaedo,* which formulates this argument as immortality is discussed in the prison cell where Socrates awaits his execution, two assumptions seem to be made: first, that the soul is the principle of life in animate bodies, for, as Socrates says, "whatever the soul possesses, to that she comes bearing life"; and second, that as an immaterial being, the soul must be simple, for only bodies are "composite" and "changing."

From the first of these assumptions, the argument proceeds in terms of what it means for bodies to be alive or dead. Socrates argues from examples. "If any one asks you," he says, "what that is, of which the inherence makes the body hot, you will reply not heat . . . but fire . . . Or if any one asks you why a body is diseased, you will not say from disease, but from fever." So if any one asks, "what is that of which the inherence will render the body alive?" the answer is not life but "the soul." As the principle of life itself, the soul "will never receive the opposite of what she brings," namely, death. Therefore the soul is immortal.

On the second assumption, the endless duration of the soul follows from its simplicity as an immaterial and immutable being. "The compound or composite," Socrates says, "may be supposed to be naturally capable, as of being compounded, so also of being dissolved; but that which is uncompounded, and that only, must be, if anything is, indissoluble." When the soul leaves the body, for which it has been both motor and pilot, the body ceases to be alive and perishes in the manner of material things; the soul lives on, freed from temporary bondage to the body, its prison house. It "departs to the invisible world—to the divine and immortal and rational."

The argument from simplicity, as repeated in Moses Mendelssohn's *Phädon,* is criticized by Kant. Admitting that a truly "simple being cannot cease to exist," Kant contends that the *knowable* soul—which is for him the empirical ego or consciousness—may have intensive, though it lacks extensive, quantity. It would therefore be capable of diminution in reality; and so it "can become less and less through an infinite series of smaller degrees."

With regard to the soul as an immaterial and simple substance (*i.e.,* the transcendental ego), Kant is willing to affirm that immortality necessarily belongs to such a nature. But he denies that we can have any knowledge of the soul except as a phenomenon of experience. There can be no valid theoretical argument for immortality precisely because there can be no scientific knowledge of the nature of transcendental objects—beings beyond all possible experience. What Kant calls "the paralogisms of rational psychology" are offered to show the dialectical futility of proofs or disproofs of immortality, in the same way that "the cosmological antinomies" attempt to expose the untenability of arguments for or against the infinity of time and space, the infinite divisibility of matter, the existence of a free will and of God.

Without deciding whether Kant's theory of experience and knowledge is true, this much we can learn from him about the issue of immortality. Those philosophers who, like Descartes and Locke, think they have grounds for affirming the existence of the soul (or mind or spirit) as an immaterial substance, also have grounds for affirming its immortality. Those who, like Lucretius and Hobbes, think they have grounds for denying the existence of anything except material particles, also have grounds for denying either the existence of the soul or its having a permanence not possessed by other material wholes. And those who, like Hume, think there are no grounds for affirming the existence of any kind of enduring substance, material or spiritual—even to the point of doubting personal identity from moment to moment—can admit no grounds for affirming a substantial, much less an immortal, soul.

ONE OTHER POSITION remains to be considered. Though it does not fall outside the foregoing alternatives, Aristotle's theory represents an important variation on one of them. As against Hume or Kant, Aristotle holds that substances exist and are knowable. The sensible, material things of experience are such substances. But, according to Aristotle, these substances are not *exclusively* material. They are composed of two principles, matter and form, neither of which is a substance capable of existing by itself. As the exposition of this theory (in the chapters on FORM and MATTER) tries to make plain, form and matter exist only in union with one another. It is the composite substance resulting from their union which exists in and of itself.

The form which enters into the composition of a substance can be called its "substantial form." In relation to the matter with which it is united, the substantial form is the actualization of the potentiality in matter to exist as a substance of a certain kind. Not all substances are of the same kind. Some are alive; some inanimate and inert. In the case of living substances, the substantial form, according to Aristotle, confers upon matter not only the act of existing as a substance, but also the act of being alive. Because it thus differs from the form of an inanimate substance, Aristotle gives a special name to the substantial form of a living thing. Because the word "soul" has long been used to designate "the principle of life in living things," Aristotle feels justified in using it as the name for the substantial forms of plants and animals as well as men.

This theory and its principal opposite (which regards the human soul as a complete substance, not a substantial form) are more fully discussed in the chapter on SOUL. Here we are concerned only with the consequences of Aristotle's theory for human immortality. If, as he seems to hold, substantial forms exist only insofar as they exist in the substances of which they are the forms, then when a composite substance perishes through the decomposition of its matter and form, the form perishes also. Souls—the substantial forms of living things—would seem to be no exception. "The soul," Aristotle writes, "is inseparable from its body, or at any rate certain parts of it are (if it has parts)—for the actuality of some of them is nothing but the actualities of their bodily parts. Yet some may be separable because they are not the actualities of any body at all."

The exception which Aristotle seems to have in mind is that part of the human soul which is the intellect. It differs from other powers of the soul, he suggests, as the eternal from the perishable. "It alone," he says, "is capable of existence in isolation from all other psychic powers." He argues that "in so far as the realities it knows"—or at least some of them—"are capable of being separated from their matter, so is it also with the power of the mind."

What is the significance, for the immortality of the human soul, of the supposed ability of the intellect to act independently of the body? Aristotle answers in terms of the principle that "if there is any way of acting or being acted upon proper to soul, soul will be capable of separate existence; if there is none, its separate existence is impossible." If we consider nutrition, sensation, and emotion, there seems to be, he admits, "no case in which the soul can act or be acted upon without involving the body." The one possible exception may be thinking, but Aristotle adds at once that "if this too proves to be a form of imagination or to be impossible without imagination, it too requires a body as a condition of its existence."

Later, when he is discussing the power of thought, Aristotle flatly insists that "the soul never thinks without an image" and that "no one can learn or understand anything in the absence of sense," for "when the mind is actively aware of anything it is necessarily aware of it along with an image." According to his own principles it would seem to follow that since thinking proves "to be impossible without imagination, it too requires a body as a condition of its existence." Hence the intellect is not separable from matter, nor is the human soul, of which the intellect is the highest power.

Nevertheless, Aristotle declares, in a passage which has become famous, that mind as the active power of thinking "is separable, impassible, unmixed"; and with this declaration of the intellect's separability from matter, he seems to affirm immortality, at least for the intellectual part of the soul. "When mind is set free from its present conditions," he writes,

"it appears as just what it is and nothing more: this alone is immortal and eternal."

THE PASSAGES QUOTED have been subject to conflicting interpretations. The Arabic commentators on Aristotle, notably Averroës, find in them no basis for the immortality of the individual human soul. The texts, according to their view, support the theory of a *single* active intellect which exists apart from the minds of individual men—almost a divine principle in the universe which, acting on the rational souls of individual men, enables them to think and understand. Aquinas argues against them to the opposite conclusion.

Against the Averroists Aquinas contends that if the individual man, Socrates, can be said to think, then whatever powers are required for thinking must belong to his individual nature. The powers required for thinking are, according to Aquinas, twofold: an active intellect, able to abstract the intelligible forms of things from their material representation in sensory images; and a possible or potential intellect, capable of receiving these forms when separated from matter by the act of abstraction.

The theory of knowledge and thought which this involves is discussed in the chapters on FORM, IDEA, MIND, and UNIVERSAL AND PARTICULAR. Here we are concerned only with the point which Aquinas makes, that since thinking involves universal notions, and since forms can be universal only apart from matter, the intellect which abstracts and receives abstractions must itself be immaterial. The intellectual powers do not operate through a bodily organ, as the power of nutrition operates through the alimentary system or the power of vision through the eye. The brain, in other words, is not the organ of understanding or thought, but rather, along with the external sense organs, it is the material organ of perception, memory, and imagination.

The argument for the immortality of the human soul then proceeds on the premise that that which can *act* apart from matter can also *exist* apart from matter. "The intellectual principle which we call the mind or the intellect has an operation *per se* apart from the body. Now only that which subsists can have an operation *per se,* for nothing can operate but what is actual; wherefore a thing operates according as it is." Hence Aquinas concludes that "the human soul, which is called the intellect or mind, is something incorporeal and subsistent." The attribution of subsistence to the human soul means that although it is the substantial form of the human body, it is also capable of existing in and of itself as if it were a simple substance.

Unlike angels, which as spiritual substances are by their very nature *separate* forms, not forms of matter, human souls are substantial forms which, having a certain degree of immateriality, are also to that degree separable from matter. But the reverse is also true. To the extent that the soul's powers, such as sensation and imagination, require corporeal organs, the soul is inseparable from the body. Since, furthermore, Aquinas agrees with Aristotle that every act of understanding or thought involves imagination, he faces the difficulty of explaining how the soul can function in any way when separated from the body after death.

"To solve this difficulty," he says, "we must consider that as nothing acts except as it is actual, the mode of action in every agent follows from its mode of existence. Now the soul has one mode of being when in the body, and another when apart from it . . . The soul, therefore, when united to the body, has consistently with that mode of existence, a mode of understanding by turning to corporeal images, which are in corporeal organs; but when it is separated from the body, it has a mode of understanding by turning to simply intelligible objects, as is proper to other separate substances." Nevertheless, Aquinas adds, it is not natural for the soul to understand in the latter way, for it is not by nature a separate substance. Therefore, "to be separated from the body is not in accordance with its nature."

THIS LAST POINT has both philosophical and theological significance. Philosophically, it may be easier to prove the immortality of the soul if one starts, as the Platonists do, with the proposition that the soul is a purely spiritual principle or substance which does not depend upon the body. But then, according to Aquinas, you prove the immortality of the soul at the expense of destroying the unity of man, for if the soul is a substance rather than a form, the individual man, composed of body and soul, consists of two distinct substances.

Theologically, Christian faith believes in the resurrection of the body after the Last Judgment and the end of the world, as well as in the soul's separate existence immediately after death. From the point of view of a theologian like Aquinas, a philosophical proof of immortality must corroborate both of these dogmas. In his judgment a proof which rests upon the proposition that the soul has a nature akin to that of an angel (*i.e.,* a purely spiritual substance), makes the Christian dogma of the resurrected body unintelligible or even abhorrent.

If the immortal soul were a complete and separate substance, it would have no need for its body in the life hereafter. It has that need only if its nature is that of a substantial form, partly immersed in matter and partly separate therefrom. Then, because of these two aspects of its nature, it can be said, not only that "the human soul retains its proper existence when separated from the body," but also that it has "an aptitude and a natural inclination to be united to the body."

The incompleteness of the soul without the body and, even more, the dependence of man's mind upon his bodily senses and imagination raise, as we have seen, the difficult problem of how the soul exists and operates when separated from the body by death and before it is reunited to a resurrected body. It may even raise the question whether the reasoning of Aquinas constitutes a valid philosophical argument for the actual existence of the soul in separation from the body, or merely suggests the possibility of such existence. But the facts which create these difficulties are the very facts to which Aquinas appeals in his "Treatise on the Resurrection," in order to explain the basis in nature for the miraculous reunion of the body with the soul.

THE ARGUMENTS FOR and against immortality so far considered are couched in the form of proofs or disproofs which aim at certainty. All except one are, moreover, theoretical or speculative in the sense that they proceed in terms of observations, assumptions, and inferences about the nature of things—about atoms and substances, matter and form, extension and thought, inert bodies and living organisms. The one exception, already mentioned, is Kant's practical argument based on the moral necessity of an immortal life.

There is still another argument, both speculative and practical in character, which does not aim at certainty nor take the form of a proof. It is the proposal of a wager concerning the equally unknown alternatives of oblivion after death and eternal life. Supposing no rational evidence to favor the truth of either alternative, Pascal weighs the probability of gain and loss which is consequent upon living according to each hypothesis. The probability, he thinks, vastly preponderates on the side of those who choose to forego the worldly life because, to take the chance of gaining the whole world during the short term of earthly life, they would risk the loss of eternal happiness for their immortal souls.

Locke engages in the same type of calculation. "When infinite happiness is put into one scale, against infinite misery in the other; if the worst that comes to the pious man, if he mistakes, be the best that the wicked can attain to, if he be right, who," Locke asks, "can without madness run the venture? Who in his wits would choose to come within the possibility of infinite misery; which if he miss, there is yet nothing to be got by that hazard? Whereas, on the other side, the sober man ventures nothing against infinite happiness to be got, if his expectation comes to pass." If, wagering on immortal life, "the good man be right, he is eternally happy"; but "if he mistakes"—if death ends all—"he is not miserable, he feels nothing."

ALL THESE THEORIES, including Kant's postulate and the wager proposed by Pascal and Locke, are clearly concerned with arguing for personal immortality or individual survival. Among those who deny the survival of the individual human spirit, some—Hegel and Spinoza, for example—conceive an impersonal type of immortality.

For Hegel it is Spirit itself which is immortal. "The successive phases of Spirit that animate the Nations in a necessitated gradation," he writes, "are themselves only steps in the development of the one Universal Spirit, which through them elevates and completes itself to a self-comprehending totality." In considering the history of the world, he regards everything as the manifestation of Spirit; and because of this, even when we traverse the past, we have, he says, "only to do with what is *present;* for philosophy, as occupying itself with the True, has to do with the *eternally present.* Nothing in the past is lost for it, for the Idea is ever present; Spirit is immortal; with it there is no past, no future, but an essential now. This necessarily implies that the present form of Spirit comprehends within it all earlier steps . . . The grades which Spirit seems to have left behind it, it still possesses in the depths of its present."

What Spirit is for Hegel, Nature is for Spinoza. Spinoza, however, conceives a kind of immortality for the individual man, which is achieved through his participation in the eternity of Nature. The body of the individual man, according to Spinoza, belongs to the infinite matter of Nature. It is "a certain mode of extension actually existing." The individual human mind is similarly "a part of the infinite intellect of God." In one sense, both the body and the mind are temporal things which, like all other finite modes of God or Nature, have a fixed and limited duration. Furthermore, the personal memories and thoughts of the individual man depend on the coexistence of his mind and body. "The mind can imagine nothing, nor can it recollect anything that is past," Spinoza writes, "except while the body exists."

But Spinoza also maintains that "only in so far as it involves the actual existence of the body, can the mind be said to possess duration, and its existence be limited by a fixed time." Of every individual thing—whether it is a finite mind or a finite body—there exists in the infinite and eternal essence of God a conception or idea. "To conceive things under the form of eternity," Spinoza writes, "is to conceive them in so far as they are conceived through the essence of God." Because he holds that the human mind can have adequate knowledge of God, he holds that the mind can conceive "itself and its body under the form of eternity." Hence through knowing God, or the eternal truth about temporal things, the mind participates in eternity.

Imagination and memory may belong to time, but not the intellect, which is capable of knowing God. To explain why we feel "that we are eternal," Spinoza points out that "the mind is no less sensible of those things which it conceives through intelligence than of those which it remembers." Although we cannot *imagine* or *remember* that "we existed before the body," we can *know intellectually* something about mind and body which belongs to eternity; because, in addition to conceiving them as "existing with relation to a fixed time and place," we can conceive them as "contained in God" and as following "from the necessity of the divine nature." Since it "pertains to the nature of the mind to conceive the essence of the body under the form of eternity," Spinoza concludes that "the human mind cannot be absolutely destroyed with the body, but something of it remains which is eternal."

Such immortality is, in a way, enjoyed in this life, for it is a present participation in eternity through the mind's knowledge of God. There is also the impersonal immortality which men enjoy through contemplating the perpetuation of the species, or more particularly the persistence of an image of themselves in their offspring. In the *Symposium,* Socrates reports a conversation with Diotima in which she explains to him that in procreation "the mortal nature is seeking as far as is possible to be everlasting and immortal." Men hope that offspring "will preserve their memory and give them the blessedness and immortality which they desire in the future." But if procreation through the pregnancy of the body is a

way of achieving immortality, artistic creation through a kind of pregnancy in the soul, Diotima argues, is even more so. "Who, when he thinks of Homer and Hesiod and other great poets," she asks, "would not rather have their children than ordinary ones? Who would not emulate them in the creation of children such as theirs, which have preserved their memory and given them everlasting glory?"

Such impersonal immortality belongs to the leading characters in the great works of fiction—to Shakespeare's Hamlet and to Cervantes' Don Quixote and Sancho Panza. As Pirandello says in *Six Characters in Search of an Author,* "The man, the writer . . . will die, but his creation does not die."

One need think "only of the ambition of men" and what they will do "for the sake of leaving behind them a name which shall be eternal," to realize how deeply "they are stirred by the love of an immortality of fame." Even deeper, according to Diotima, is their love of the good, or more precisely, their desire for "the everlasting possession of the good" which leads all men necessarily to "desire immortality together with the good."

Whether it is to be attained through the perpetuation of the species, through survival in the memory of mankind, through knowledge of God, or through the subsistence of the soul, the desire for immortality seems to express man's dread of disappearance into utter nothingness. Yet, facing death, Socrates faces the alternatives with equanimity. "Either death," he declares, "is a state of nothingness and utter unconsciousness, or, as men say, there is a change and migration of the soul from this world to another." Either it is like a dreamless and undisturbed sleep or it opens a new world to which the good man can look forward with hope. On either alternative we can be of good cheer, he tells his friends, if we believe that "no evil can happen to a good man, either in life or after death."

39

Induction

As the list of Additional Readings indicates, the theory of induction falls within the province of logic and is part of the logician's concern with the methods of inference or reasoning employed in the sciences. The great controversies about induction seem to be of relatively recent origin in the history of logic, beginning perhaps with the argument between William Whewell and J. S. Mill over the contributions of reason and experience to the inductive process. Later in the 19th century and in our own time, writers like W. E. Johnson and John Maynard Keynes, Bertrand Russell and Jean Nicod, who present different formulations of inductive inference, call attention to the unsolved problems with which any theory is left. They underline the assumptions that seem to be unavoidable in any statement of the formal conditions which validate the so-called "inductive leap"—the jump from observed particulars to general truths, truths having a wider generality than the particular evidences from which they are drawn or on which they are based.

The problem of induction, in anyone's version of it, is the problem of generalization. This may involve psychological questions about how the mind generalizes from experience. But however they are answered, the basic logical questions remain substantially unaltered. By what criteria is valid distinguished from fallacious induction? Can induction be secured from error by rules of inference? Is induction indispensable in the development of scientific knowledge, or is there, as Whewell, for example, suggests, a sharp distinction between the inductive and the deductive sciences?

What is the relation of induction to deduction? Is it the relation of a method of discovery to a method of demonstration or proof? Is it a relation between two modes of reasoning, both of which can be formulated as processes of proof? Is there both an inductive and a deductive type of syllogism, or is induction the very opposite of all forms of reasoning and proof?

It is with these last questions that the discussion of induction begins in the great books, especially in Aristotle's *Organon* and Francis Bacon's *Novum Organum,* but also in the writings of Descartes and Locke, and in observations on scientific method by Newton, Harvey, and Pascal. Though many of the controversies and problems which become central in the 19th century do not appear explicitly in the earlier tradition, they are anticipated by the fundamental distinctions and issues which can be found in the earlier writers.

Bacon's dissatisfaction with Aristotle, for example, leads him to formulate specific rules for induction. Going further in the same general direction, Mill later develops his elaborate theory of inductive inference. We move in the opposite direction if we are guided by Aristotle's distinction between scientific and dialectical induction and by his way of setting induction off as the very opposite of reasoning. The question then arises whether Bacon and Mill are treating induction in all or in only one of several quite distinct senses.

As THE CHAPTER on LOGIC indicates, the names of Aristotle and Bacon are sometimes used as the symbols of opposed tendencies in logic. The one is supposed to represent an almost exclusive emphasis on deduction, the other the primacy and importance of induction. An opposition between Aristotle and Bacon is also implied in the current use of such phrases as "inductive logic" and "deductive logic." These phrases are sometimes used to suggest that the inductive or the deductive process can be favored to the exclusion, or at least the subordination, of the other. Such understanding of the matter usually includes the popular notion that induction is always reasoning from particulars to universals and deduction always reasoning from universals to particulars.

But none of these things seems to be true, or at least not without serious qualification. Neither Aristotle nor Bacon emphasizes deduction or induction to the exclusion of the other. On the contrary, both appear to insist on the absolute priority of induction, since, according to them, it provides deductive reasoning with its ultimate premises. Far from conflicting, induction and deduction complement each other. "The consilience of the results of both these processes," Mill writes, "each corroborating and verifying the other, is requisite to give to any general proposition the kind and degree of evidence which constitutes scientific proof."

Until principles are established, the deduction of their implications or consequences cannot begin. Unless principles, once they are obtained, are then used in the proof of other truths, or are otherwise rationally employed, the purpose of inductive generalization is not fully realized. In this understanding of the relationship between induction and reasoning, Aristotle and Bacon do not seem to disagree, nor does either of them conceive induction as a process of *reasoning* from particulars to universals.

There is no question that the direction of induction is from particulars; but in the precise sense in which induction precedes deduction—the sense in which both Bacon and Aristotle regard it as the source of axioms—they do not think it is a process of reasoning or a form of proof. As for deduction, it is questionable, at least for Aristotle, whether its direction can be described as from the universal to the particular.

Aristotle seldom uses the word "deduction" as the name for that phase of thought which is complementary to induction. He speaks rather of demonstration. Demonstration takes place through the various forms of reasoning which he calls "syllogisms." As the chapter on REASONING explains, these are collections of premises each of which yields a conclusion by valid inference. In the most perfect forms of reasoning, the conclusion is as universal as its premises, and though there are syllogisms in which a particular proposition can be demonstrated from a universal and a particular premise, it is seldom the case that from exclusively universal premises a particular conclusion can be validly drawn. The statement that deduction is reasoning from universals to particulars certainly does not seem to fit Aristotle's theory of the syllogism, and even less his conception of scientific demonstration, the aim of which is to prove universal, not particular, propositions.

"WE LEARN EITHER by induction or by demonstration," Aristotle writes in the *Prior Analytics*. "Demonstration develops from universals, induction from particulars." In the *Posterior Analytics* he says that the ultimate premises of demonstration must be primary or basic truths. A basic truth is an immediate proposition—what is sometimes called a "first principle" or an "axiom." Since in his view "an immediate proposition is one which has no other proposition prior to it," the basic premises cannot be demonstrated.

Whence come these primary premises which are indispensable to demonstration but which demonstration cannot establish? Aristotle's answer is that "we know the primary premises by induction." In another place he says, "it is by intuition that we obtain the primary premises."

The word "intuition" indicates an essential characteristic of the sort of induction which, because it is not itself a form of reasoning, can be prior to all reasoning and *must be,* in order to supply the premises from which reasoning proceeds. Reasoning is discursive. It is a process involving steps. One proposition is drawn from another by the mediation of a third. Intuition, in contrast, is immediate. Like an act of seeing, it apprehends its object at once and directly. When Aristotle speaks of induction as a kind of intuition, he implies, therefore, that it consists in the immediate grasp of a universal truth. The proposition thus held he calls "immediate" precisely because it can be known intuitively and in no other way. Intuitive induction, as opposed to what may be called "inductive reasoning," consists in seeing the universal in the particular. When what is seen is expressed in the form of a proposition, the universal implicit in the known particulars is made explicit.

Induction and intuition are, however, not identical for Aristotle. In one passage in the *Prior Analytics* he considers syllogistic induction, which can hardly be called "intuitive." And in the *Nicomachean Ethics,* where he discusses intuitive reason, he distinguishes between two sorts of primary truth that can be known by intuition.

"Intuitive reason," he writes, "is concerned with the ultimates in both directions; for both the first terms and the last are objects of intuitive reason and not of argument, and the intuitive reason which is presupposed by demonstrations grasps the unchangeable and first terms, while the intuitive reason involved in practical reasoning grasps the last and variable fact, *i.e.,* the minor premise. For these variable facts are the starting-points for the apprehension of the end, since the universals are reached from the particulars; of these therefore we must have perception, and this perception is intuitive reason."

This applies to theoretical as well as practical knowledge. By intuitive reason, it seems, we grasp both the universal principles or axioms and the particular facts of sense perception. As perception is intuition on the part of the sensitive faculty, so induction is an intuitive use of the intellect (though Aristotle attributes both to "intuitive reason").

These two forms of intuition are functionally related. The induction of universal truths from particulars is impossible without sense perception, "for it is sense-perception alone which is able to grasp the particulars." But, according to Aristotle, a single isolated perception does not give rise to an intuitive induction. Repeated perceptions of things of a certain sort—particulars of a certain class— are formed by memory into what he calls "an experience." Because the experience refers, not to a single individual, but to a class of similar individuals, it provides the material for the mind's intuitive act of induction.

This theory of the role of experience in induction is more fully discussed in the chapter on EXPERIENCE. For our present purposes, the main point is that the universal, lying implicitly in the experience, is ready, as it were, to be extracted therefrom and made explicit. "Though the act of sense-perception is of the particular, its content is universal," Aristotle writes. With the help of memory and experience, induction makes the latent universal manifest.

BACON'S CRITICISM of the logic of Aristotle seems to rest on two counts: first, he complains of Aristotle's overemphasis on syllogisms, whether they are used dialectically or demonstratively; and second, he charges Aristotle with a superficial understanding of induction. One of the chief efforts of the *Novum Organum* is to correct the latter mistake.

"There are and can exist," says Bacon, "but two ways of investigating and discovering truth. The one hurries on rapidly from the senses and particulars to the most general axioms, and from them, as principles, and from their supposed indisputable truth, deduces the intermediate axioms. This is the way now in use. The other constructs its axioms from the senses and particulars, by ascending continually and gradually, until it finally arrives at the most general axioms, which is the true but unattempted way."

Where Aristotle proposes that only the primary truths or first principles be established by induction, while all the others (which Bacon calls "intermediate axioms") are to be derived from them by demonstration, Bacon urges a method of induction which shall mount gradually from the least general to the most universal propositions. We should not "suffer the understanding to jump and fly from particulars to remote and most general axioms." We should "proceed by a true scale and successive steps, without interruption or breach, from particulars to the lesser axioms, thence to the intermediate (rising one above the other), and lastly, to the most general."

According to this theory, induction can intuitively draw more general from less general truths, as well as the least general truths from the particulars of perception. It might seem at first as if there were no place for deduction in the development of science. But Bacon divides the study of nature into two phases: "the first regards the eliciting or creating of axioms from experiments, the second the deducing or deriving of new experiments from axioms." Here too there seems to be a crucial difference between Bacon and Aristotle. This difference is indicated by Bacon's emphasis upon *experiments* both as the source of inductive generalization and also as that which is ultimately derived by deduction from axioms.

The difference between *experience* (which Aristotle makes the source of induction) and *experiment* is more than verbal. "The axioms now in use," Bacon contends, "are derived from a scanty handful, as it were, of experience, and a few particulars of frequent occurrence." There has been too little attention given to negative instances, that is, of cases which seem to run counter to the generalization being formed. "In establishing any true axiom," Bacon insists, "the negative instance is the most powerful."

The chapter on EXPERIENCE dwells on the difference between ordinary experience and planned experiments. Where Aristotle seems to be satisfied with the ordinary experience which arises from the perceptions of men in the course of daily life, Bacon thinks it does not suffice. Because it is haphazard, it fails to collect the variety of instances, both positive and negative, upon which genuine and solid inductions can be founded. Unusual and special experiences must be sought out, and the effort must be made to invent experiences which do not arise spontaneously. For this, experiment—or the production of experiences—is necessary. Bacon thinks we must, "by every kind of experiment, elicit the discovery of causes and true axioms."

TWO CONSEQUENCES FOLLOW from the several differences we have noted between Aristotle's and Bacon's theories of induction.

In the first place, Aristotle does not seem to think that induction can be methodically prescribed by logical rules. It is a natural act of intelligence to draw universals from experience. Though men may differ in the readiness of their native wit, the induction of the primary truths, which are the axioms or first principles of science, does not require special genius nor can it be improved or rendered more certain by following rules. Precisely because it is intuitive rather than discursive, induction, unlike reasoning, cannot be regulated by rules of inference such as those which govern the syllogism.

Without disagreeing that it is intuitive rather than argumentative, Bacon seems to think that induction requires the practice of the most detailed and precise method. Not only must the various ascending stages of induction be regulated by observance of an order of generality, but the making of experiments and the collection and arrangement of particulars, "forming tables and coordinations of instances," must be governed by a complex set of rules. The twenty-seven tables of instances, set forth in the second book of the *Novum Organum*, constitute the heart of Bacon's method of induction. This new method "of discovering the sciences," he observes, "levels men's wits and leaves but little of their superiority, since it achieves everything by the most certain rules."

In the second place, since genuine induction depends for Bacon upon ample experiments, it belongs primarily to the method of the experimental sciences—the physical or natural sciences in which experimentation is possible. Though the first principles or axioms of arithmetic and geometry may be learned by induction, the method of gradual ascent from experiments through intermediate generalizations does not apply to mathematics. Here we may have the beginning of the notion that only the experimental sciences are primarily inductive, whereas other sciences, like mathematics, are primarily deductive.

But such a division of the sciences does not accord with Aristotle's theory of induction. He thinks mathematics and metaphysics require induction for their foundation no less than physics and in no different way; if anything, induction is of the greatest importance for metaphysics, because all its principles are indemonstrable, whereas some of the principles needed in mathematics and physics can be demonstrated in metaphysics. Yet no science is peculiarly inductive, just as none stands in a special relation to experience. All depend equally upon experience for the induction of the primary truths on which their demonstrations rest.

Descartes seems to fall somewhere between Aristotle and Bacon. He regards arithmetic and geometry as more certain than the physical sciences, because mathematics is largely developed by deduction, whereas the study of nature depends upon induction from experiments. In this lies the superiority of mathematics. "While our inferences from experience are frequently fallacious," Descartes writes, "deduction, or the pure illation of one thing from another . . . cannot be erroneous when performed by an understanding that is in the least degree rational."

Nevertheless, Descartes does not exclude induction as the source of the axioms of mathematics or, for that matter, of metaphysics; he only excludes the kind of induction which depends upon experiments. Such axioms as *when equals are taken from equals the remainders are equal* or *the whole is greater than any of its parts* are products of induction, as may be seen, he points out, from the fact that a child can be taught these general truths only "by showing him examples in particular cases." Similarly, the metaphysical truth in the proposition *I think; therefore, I exist* cannot be learned by deduction or syllogistic reasoning. The axiom that *to think is to exist* has to be learned by induction "from the experience of the individual—that unless he exists he cannot think. For our mind is so constituted by nature that general propositions are formed out of the knowledge of particulars."

FROM THE FOREGOING we can gather that different theories of induction may be, in large part, theories about different kinds of induction. Common to induction of every sort is the motion of the mind from particulars, apprehended by sense, to general propositions or universal notions. But the character of the induction, or its conditions and method, may differ according to the precise character of its source: (1) whether it arises from ordinary sense-experience or from planned experiments; and (2) whether it is based upon a single experiment or upon an enumeration of instances. There remains the most radical distinction in type of induction: (3) whether it is intuitive or discursive—accomplished by an act of immediate insight or by a process of reasoning from premises to a conclusion.

These three divisions cross one another to some extent. Descartes, for example, seems to regard the complete enumeration of a series of connected facts as a way of drawing a general conclusion about their connection. That he has inductive reasoning rather than intuitive induction in mind, we learn from his statement that "by adequate enumeration or induction is meant that method by which we attain surer conclusions than by any other type of proof, with the exception of simple intuition."

Pascal seems to be making the same point when he says that "in all matters whose proof is by experiment and not by demonstration, no universal assertion can be made except by the general enumeration of all the parts and all the different cases." Bacon, on the other hand, always thinks of induction as intuitive generalization, and therefore maintains that "induction which proceeds by simple enumeration is puerile, leads to uncertain conclusions, and is exposed to danger from one contradictory instance."

The elaborate procedure which Bacon proposes for collating instances stresses, not completeness of enumeration, but an examination of their relation to one another and, in the light thereof, an interpretation of their significance. Mill's four or five methods of induction bear a close resemblance to Bacon's more numerous tables of instances; but Mill's methods are attempts to formulate the rules of inference for inductive reasoning, whereas Bacon's rules are rules, not of reasoning, but of tabulating the particulars from which intuitive generalizations can be formed.

On Mill's view of induction, it may be questioned whether induction from an exhaustive enumeration is induction at all, for it seems to result in a *summary* of the facts enumerated rather than a *generalization* from particulars. Where there is no inductive leap, there is no induction. Where the inductive leap does occur, however, it seems easier to understand it as an intuitive act—a seeing of the universal in the particular—rather than as a process of reasoning. Each of Mill's methods requires a rule of inference which is itself a universal proposition. His critics have asked, Whence come these universal propositions about the relations of cause and effect or about the order and uniformity of nature? They point out that he cannot answer that these propositions are themselves conclusions of inductive reasoning without begging the question.

The uniformity of nature, according to Russell, is the controlling principle of induction from repeated instances of the same natural occurrence or natural association of cause and effect. "A sufficient number of cases of association will make the probability of a fresh association nearly a certainty." Russell goes on to say this principle is "not capable of being *disproved* by an appeal to experience," and he adds that it is "equally incapable of being *proved* by an appeal to experience."

In Whitehead's view, "induction presupposes metaphysics . . . it rests upon an antecedent rationalism. You cannot have a rational justification for your appeal to history till your metaphysics has assured you that there *is* a history to appeal to." Without this, "you have made nonsense of induction." Whitehead also tells us that he does "not hold Induction to be in its essence the derivation of general laws. It is the divination of some characteristics of a particular future from the known characteristics of a particular past."

SUCH CRITICISM of inductive reasoning does not seem to apply to Aristotle's conception of it, for with him it is not, as with Mill, distinct in form from the syllogism. It is simply a distinct type of syllogism, which consists in reasoning from effect to cause rather than from cause to effect. Nor does the observation that an inductive inference cannot be more than probable apply to what Aristotle means by an inductive syllogism. What Poincaré calls

"mathematical induction" or "reasoning by recurrence" is not, strictly speaking, induction at all, but a form of demonstration.

The certainty or probability of non-syllogistic induction depends on the source of the inference—whether it derives from a single specially constructed experiment or from an enumeration of particular instances, with or without a statistical calculation based on their frequency. The conception of a perfect experiment implies that the operation of a universal law can be exhibited in a single case. It is almost as if the controlling aim of the experiment were to make the universal manifest in the particular.

Newton's experiments on reflection and refraction seem to be of this sort. From them certain laws of optics are directly induced, even as, according to Aristotle and Descartes, the axioms of mathematics or metaphysics can be directly induced from simple experiences, available to a child or familiar to all men. Yet Newton does not think that the inductive establishment of such laws is as certain as demonstration.

The analytic method, he writes, "consists in making experiments and observations and in drawing general conclusions from them by induction. And although the arguing from experiments and observations by induction be no demonstration of general conclusions; yet it is the best way of arguing which the nature of things admits of, and may be looked upon as so much stronger, by how much the induction is more general. If no exception occur from phenomena, the conclusion may be pronounced generally; but if at any time afterwards any exception shall occur from experiments, it may then begin to be pronounced with such exceptions as occur."

Because it must depend on inductive generalizations from experience which, in his view, can never be certain, Locke doubts that physics can ever become a science. "I deny not," he writes, "that a man, accustomed to rational and regular experiments, shall be able to see further into the nature of bodies and guess righter at their yet unknown properties, than one that is a stranger to them; but yet, as I have said, this is but judgment and opinion, not knowledge and certainty. This way of *getting and improving our knowledge in substances only by experience and history,* which is all that the weakness of our faculties in this state of mediocrity . . . can attain to, makes me suspect," Locke concludes, "that *natural philosophy is not capable of being made a science.*"

Hume offers two reasons for the inconclusiveness and uncertainty which he thinks qualify all our generalizations or inductions from experience. The first calls attention to the fact that, unlike mathematical reasoning, inferences from experience in the realm of physical matters depend on the number of cases observed. "The conclusions which [reason] draws from considering one circle," he says, "are the same it would form upon surveying all the circles in the universe. But no man, having seen only one body move, after being impelled by another, could infer that every other body will move after a like impulse."

The principle "which determines him to form such a conclusion" is, according to Hume, "Custom or Habit"; and precisely because inductive generalization is an effect of custom rather than of reasoning in the strict sense, the strength of the induction—or the force of custom—varies with the number of cases from which it arises. "After the constant conjunction of two objects—heat and flame, for instance, weight and solidity—we are determined by custom alone to expect the one from the appearance of the other. This hypothesis," Hume maintains, "seems . . . the only one which explains the difficulty, why we draw, from a thousand instances, an inference which we are not able to draw from one instance, that is in no respect different from them. Reason is incapable of any such variation."

Since *all* the relevant cases can never be exhaustively observed, the inference from a customary conjunction must always remain uncertain, no matter how high a probability it derives from the multiplication of like instances. To this first point, concerning the dependence of the probability of generalizations from experience upon the frequency of the observed instances, Hume adds a second point about the similarity of the cases under observation. Analogy, he says, "leads us to expect from any cause the same events, which we have observed to result from similar causes. Where the causes are entirely similar, the analogy is perfect, and the inference drawn from it is regarded as certain and conclusive . . . But where the objects have not so exact a similarity, the analogy is less perfect, and the inference is less conclusive; though still it has some force, in proportion to the degree of similarity and resemblance." The absence of perfect similarity is Hume's second reason for the inconclusiveness or uncertainty of inductive generalizations.

The contrary supposition—that one case can be perfectly representative of an infinite number of similar cases—may explain why Aristotle seems to think that induction is able to produce the primary truths or principles of science with a certitude which gives certainty to all the demonstrations founded on these axioms. Another explanation of Aristotle's view may be found in his distinction between scientific and dialectical induction. He regards the former as based on the kind of common experience which, unlike even the best experiment, admits of no exceptions. In contrast, dialectical induction, or the still weaker form of induction which he calls "rhetorical," is based on an enumeration of cases (which may not be complete) or upon a single example (which provides no safeguard against possible exceptions).

In its dialectical form, the inductive argument proceeds from a number of particulars taken for granted. Aristotle offers this example of dialectical induction: "Supposing the skilled pilot is the most effective, and likewise the skilled charioteer, then, in general, the skilled man is the best at his particular task." In its rhetorical form, no more than a single example may be used, as when the orator generalizes that honesty is the best policy from the story of a particular individual who was finally rewarded for his virtue.

In both forms, the inductive generalization is at best probable; and it is more or less probable according to the soundness of the suppositions or the examples from which it originates—to be tested only by extending the enumeration of particulars. But if an induction is merely probable in the first place, it can only be made more probable, it can never be made certain, by multiplying cases or by increasing their variety.

Aristotle's theory of dialectical induction thus seems to have a bearing on the probability of induction from limited experiments (or from a single experiment whose perfection is not assured) and of induction from the frequency or variety of observed instances. The other point to be noted is that Bacon's basic rule of gradual ascent from particular cases through less general to more general propositions seems to be relevant to dialectical induction, but not, on Aristotle's view, to that kind of induction which produces the axioms or principles of science.

40

Infinity

INTRODUCTION

ONE of the persistent questions concerning infinity is whether we can know or comprehend it. Another is whether the infinite exists, and if so, to what kind of thing infinity belongs. It is not surprising, therefore, that the discussion of infinity often borders on the unintelligible.

The idea of infinity, like the idea of eternity, lacks the support of the imagination or of sense-experience. The fact that the infinite cannot be perceived or imagined seems sufficient to lead Hobbes and Berkeley to deny its reality. "Whatsoever we imagine is *finite*," writes Hobbes. "Therefore there is no idea, or conception of anything we call *infinite* . . . When we say anything is infinite, we signify only that we are not able to conceive the ends and bounds of the thing named, having no conception of the thing, but of our own inability."

On similar grounds Berkeley rejects the possibility of infinite division. "If I cannot perceive innumerable parts in any infinite extension," he writes, "it is certain that they are not contained in it: but it is evident, that I cannot distinguish innumerable parts in any particular line, surface, or solid, which I either perceive by sense, or figure to myself in my mind; wherefore I conclude that they are not contained in it."

But for most of the great writers on the subject, the impossibility of representing infinity and eternity to the imagination does not render them inconceivable or meaningless. Yet it does account for the difficulty of grasping their meaning, a difficulty further increased by the fact that, whatever their meaning, *infinity* and *eternity* are indefinable. To define the infinite would be to limit—even in thought—the unlimited.

The notion of infinity involves greater perplexities than that of eternity. The meaning of eternity is weighted with the mystery of God, the world, and time. All these affect the conception of infinity; but for the infinite there are also the mysteries of number and of space, of matter and motion. In the sphere of quantity, or of things subject to quantity, infinity is itself the source of mystery, or at least the root of difficulty in analysis. It is the central term in the discussion of the continuous and the indivisible, the nature of series and of limits.

As INDICATED in the chapter on ETERNITY, that idea in each of its applications seems to have one or the other of two meanings—(1) the meaning in which it signifies infinite time, time without beginning or end, and (2) the meaning in which it signifies the timelessness or immutability of being. Both meanings are negative, so far as our understanding is concerned. Yet what is signified by the second is in itself something positive, at least in the opinion of those who think that to be exempt from change entails having every perfection or being lacking in nothing.

This split in meaning also occurs in the idea of infinity. As applied to being, the term *infinite* signifies something positive, even though our understanding of what is signified remains negative or, at best, analogical. An infinite being is one which lacks no attribute that can belong to a being. This is the positive condition of absolute perfection. The infinite here still means the unlimited, but that which is unlimited in being has no defect. To lack deficiencies is to be perfect.

It is in this sense that Spinoza defines God as "Being absolutely infinite, that is to say, substance consisting of infinite attributes, each one of which expresses eternal and infinite essence." Like Spinoza, Aquinas maintains that "besides God nothing can be infinite." But he distinguishes the absolute or positive sense in which God alone is infinite from the sense of the word in which it can be said that "things other than God can be relatively infinite, but not absolutely infinite." This other meaning, according to Aquinas, is not only relative but negative, for it connotes "something imperfect." It signifies indeterminacy or lack of perfection in being.

What Aquinas calls the relative or potential infinite, he attributes to matter and to quantities—to bodies, to the magnitudes of space and time, and to number. This sense of "infinite" corresponds to that meaning of "eternal," according to which time consists of an endless series of moments, each having a predecessor, each a successor, no matter how far one counts them back into the past or ahead into the future.

But in the field of quantities other than time, the meanings of infinite and eternal part company. There is, of course, some parallelism between infinite space and infinite time, insofar as an infinite extension is one which does not begin at any point or end at any; but the consideration of space and number leads to an aspect of infinity which has no parallel in the consideration of eternity.

"In sizes or numbers," Pascal writes, "nature has set before man two marvelous infinities . . . For, from the fact that they can always be increased, it follows absolutely that they can always be decreased . . . If we can multiply a number up to 100,000 times, say, we can also take a hundred thousandth part of it by dividing it by the same number we multiply it with, and thus every term of increase will become a term of division by changing the integer into a fraction. So that infinite increase includes necessarily infinite division." As endless addition produces the infinitely large, so endless division produces the infinitesimal or the infinitely small.

A trillion trillion is a finite number, because the addition of a single unit creates a larger number. The fact that the addition of another unit produces a different number indicates that a trillion trillion has a determinate size, which is the same as saying that it is a finite number. An infinite number cannot be increased by addition, for it is constituted—in thought at least—as a number larger than the sum of any two finite numbers; which is another way of saying that it is approached by carrying on the process of addition endlessly.

What Galileo points out about two infinite quantities seems to hold for an infinite and a finite quantity. He asks us to consider the totality of all integers (which is infinite) and the totality of their squares (which is also infinite). On the one hand, there appear to be as many squares as there are integers; on the other hand, the totality of integers includes all the squares. Precisely because "the number of squares is not less than the totality of all numbers, nor the latter *greater than* the former," Galileo insists that "the attributes 'equal,' 'greater,' and 'less' are not applicable to infinite, but only to finite quantities." Nor does the sense in which one finite quantity can be greater or less than another—that is, by a determinate difference between them—apply in the comparison of a finite and an infinite quantity. The latter, being indeterminately large, is indeterminately larger than any finite quantity.

These remarks apply to the infinitely small as well. The infinitesimal is immeasurably small or indeterminately less than any finite fraction, no matter how small, because its own size is indeterminate. The finite fraction, itself a product of division, can be divided again, but if an infinitesimal quantity were capable of further division, it would permit a smaller, and since that smaller quantity would be a determinate fraction of itself, the infinitesimal would have to be determinate in size. Since that is not so, the infinitesimal must be conceived as the indivisible or as the limit approached by carrying on division endlessly.

"Because the hypothesis of indivisibles seems somewhat harsh," Newton proposes an analysis in terms of what he calls "nascent and evanescent quantities," or quantities just *beginning* to be more than nothing or just at the point at which they *vanish* into nothing. "As there is a limit which the velocity at the end of a motion may attain, but not exceed . . . there is a like limit in all quantities and proportions that begin or cease to be." Newton warns his reader, therefore, that if he "should happen to mention quantities as least, or evanescent, or ultimate," the reader is "not to suppose that quantities of any determinate magnitude are meant, but such as are conceived to be always diminished without end."

Later, speaking of quantities which are "variable and indetermined, and increasing or decreasing, as it were, by a continual motion or flux," he adds: "Take care not to look upon finite quantities as such." The method of fluxions provides an infinitesimal calculus on the hypothesis of limits rather than of indivisibles.

THROUGH ALL THESE conceptions of infinity—metaphysical, mathematical, and physical—run the paired notions of the unlimited and of limits approached but not attained. The finite is neither unlimited nor does it insensibly approach a limit. There are also the opposite notions of the perfect and the indeterminate. The finite is neither, for it is determinate without being a totality or complete.

Though they have a common thread of meaning, and though each raises similar difficulties for the understanding, the conception of infinity in being or power, and the conception of infinite (or infinitesimal) quantity require separate consideration. The same questions may be asked of each, questions about the existence of the infinite and about our knowledge of it, but the same answers will not be given in each case. There are those who deny the existence of an actually infinite body or an actually infinite number, yet affirm the infinite existence of God. There are those who declare the infinity of matter to be intrinsically unintelligible, but maintain that God, Who is infinite, is intrinsically the most intelligible object. They add, of course, that the infinite being of God cannot be comprehended by our finite intellects.

On each of these points, an opposite view has been taken, but the dispute concerning the infinity of God involves issues other than those which occur in the controversy over the infinite divisibility of matter or the infinity of space and time. It seems advisable, therefore, to deal separately with the problems of infinity as they arise with respect to different objects or occur in different subject matters.

THE CONCEPTION of God, in the words of Anselm, as a being "than which a greater cannot be conceived"—or, in the words of Kant, as an *ens realissimum,* a most real being—expresses the plenitude of the divine nature and existence. The medieval thesis, defended by Descartes, that God's essence and existence are identical, implies that neither is contracted or determined by the other. The still earlier notion of Aristotle, repeated by Aquinas, that God is pure actuality, carries with it the attributes of completeness or perfection, which are the positive aspects of immutability or incapacity for change. Spinoza's definition of substance as that which exists, not only in itself, but through itself and by its very nature, entails the autonomy or utter independence of the divine being.

These are so many different ways of stating that God is an infinite being. Both Aquinas and Spinoza make infinity the basis for proving that there can be only one God. When Spinoza argues that "a plurality of substances possessing the same nature is absurd," he has in mind the identification of infinite substance with God. "If many gods existed," Aquinas writes, "they would necessarily differ from each other. Something would therefore belong to one, which did not belong to another. And if this were a privation, one of them would not be absolutely perfect; but if it were a perfection, one of them would be without it. So it is impossible for many gods to exist"—that is, of course, if infinity is a property of the divine nature. Aquinas makes this condition clear when he goes on to say that "the ancient philosophers, constrained as it were by the truth, when they asserted an infinite principle, asserted likewise that there was only one such principle."

But while it is impossible for there to be two infinities of being, it is not impossible for there to be two, or more, infinite quantities. One explanation of this difference seems to be the actuality or existence of an infinite being, in contrast to the conceptual character of the infinite objects of mathematics, which are sometimes called "potential infinites" because they are conceived as in an endless process of becoming, or as approaching a limit that is never reached.

When the physical existence of infinite quantities is asserted, as, for example, a universe of infinite extent or an infinite number of atoms, the uniqueness of these actual totalities seems to follow. Two infinite worlds cannot coexist, though the one world can be infinite in several distinct respects—in space or duration, or in the number of its constituents—even as the infinity of God, according to Spinoza, involves "infinite attributes, each one of which expresses eternal and infinite essence."

Spinoza's argument against two actual infinities seems to find confirmation in the position taken by Aquinas that God's omnipotence does not include the power to create an infinite world. God's infinity, as we have already noted, follows from the identity of God's essence and existence. Since a created being has existence added to its essence, Aquinas asserts that "it is against the nature of a created thing to be absolutely infinite. Therefore," he continues, "as God, although He has infinite power, cannot make a thing to be not made (for this would imply that two contradictories are true at the same time), so likewise He cannot make anything to be absolutely infinite."

On this view, an infinite world cannot coexist with an infinite God, if, in their separate existence, one is dependent on the other, as creature upon creator. The infinity of the world or of nature, in Spinoza's conception, is not separate from the infinity of God, but consists in the infinity of two of God's attributes—extension and thought.

In our time there has arisen the conception of a finite God—a God who, while the most perfect being, yet is not without capacity for growth or change, a God who is eternal without being immutable. This conception, which in the light of traditional theology appears to be as self-contradictory as *round square,* has

arisen in response to the difficulties certain critics have found in the traditional doctrine of an infinite being. They point to the difficulty of understanding how finite beings can exist separate from, yet in addition to, an infinite being; they also cite difficulties in the notions of infinite knowledge, infinite power, and infinite goodness.

The infinity of the divine omniscience extends to the possible as well as to the actual. But the possible includes things which are incompatible with one another, things which, in the language of Leibniz, are not *compossible.* The *incompossible* would thus seem to be embraced in the infinite scope of divine thought or knowledge. In the view of one theologian, Nicholas of Cusa, the mystery of God's infinity is best expressed by affirming that in God all contradictions are somehow reconciled.

The infinity of God's power, or the divine omnipotence, also raises questions about the possible and the impossible. Is nothing impossible to God or must it be said that there are certain things which not even God can do, such as reverse the order of time or create a world which shall be as infinite and perfect as himself? In the assertion that God cannot do the impossible, Aquinas sees no limitation on God's power. The impossible, he writes, does not "come under the divine omnipotence, not because of any defect in the power of God, but because it has not the nature of a feasible or possible thing." For this reason, he claims, "it is better to say that such things cannot be done, than that God cannot do them." The inability to do the *undoable* constitutes no violation of infinite power, even as the lack of nothing does not deprive infinite being of anything.

The infinite goodness of God is sometimes set against the fact of evil, or the existence of imperfections, in the created world. This aspect of the problem of evil, like that which concerns man's freedom to obey or disobey the divine will, cannot be separated from the fundamental mystery of God's infinity—in power and knowledge as well as in goodness. The problem is considered in the chapter on GOOD AND EVIL. The point there mentioned, that evil is essentially nonbeing or deprivation of being, leads to one solution of the problem. It accepts the finitude, and consequently the imperfection, of creatures as a necessary consequence of God's infinity. The best of all possible worlds cannot be infinitely good.

TO MAN ALONE, among all admittedly finite things, has infinity been attributed and even made a distinctive mark of his nature. Does this introduce a new meaning of infinity, neither quantitative nor divine?

It has seldom if ever been questioned that man is finite in being and power. The limits of human capacity for knowledge or achievement are a perennial theme in man's study of man. Yet it is precisely with regard to *capacity* that certain writers have intimated man's infinity.

Pascal, for example, finds the apparent contradictions in human nature intelligible only when man is understood as yearning for or impelled toward the infinite. "We burn with desire," he says, "to find solid ground and an ultimate sure foundation whereon to build a tower reaching to the Infinite. But our whole groundwork cracks and the earth opens to abysses." In this fact lies both the grandeur and the misery of man. He aspires to the infinite, yet he is a finite being dissatisfied with his own finitude and frustrated by it.

It is sometimes said that the touch of infinity in man—with the suggestion that it is a touch of madness—consists in his wanting to be God. Those who regard such desire as abnormal or perverse interpret it as a misdirection of man's natural desire to know God face to face and to be filled with the love of God in the divine presence. But, according to the theory of natural desire, the tendency of each nature is somehow proportionate to its capacity. If man's restless search for knowledge and happiness can be quieted only by the possession of the infinite truth and goodness which is God, then man's intellect and will must somehow be as infinite in nature as they are in tendency. Yet that is not an unqualified infinity, for the same theologians who teach that man naturally seeks God also hold that man's finite intellect cannot *comprehend* the infinite being of God as God knows Himself. Nor do they think that man's capacity for know-

ing and loving God can be fulfilled except in the beatific vision, which is a supernatural gift rather than a natural achievement.

These and related matters are discussed in the chapters on DESIRE and KNOWLEDGE. The great books speak of other objects than God as objects of man's infinite desire. The appetite for money, for pleasure, or for power seems to be an infinite craving which no finite quantity of these goods ever satisfies. Two comments are made upon this fact, which is so amply evidenced in the human record. One is that man's infinite lust for worldly goods expresses even as it conceals his natural desire for a truly infinite good. The other is that these worldly goods are seductive objects precisely because they are infinite.

Here the word "infinite" is used, not in the sense which signifies perfection, but in the quantitative sense which has the meaning of indetermination. Plato's division, in the *Philebus*, of goods into the finite and the infinite separates measured and definite goods from those which need some limitation in quantity. Socrates exemplifies the distinction by reference to the fact that "into the hotter and the colder there enters a more and a less" and since "there is never any end of them . . . they must also be infinite." In contrast, "when definite quantity is once admitted, there can be no longer a 'hotter' or a 'colder.' " Such things, he says, "which do not admit of more or less" belong "in the class of the limited or finite."

Following the line of this example, Socrates later distinguishes between infinite and finite pleasures, or pleasures without limit and those which have some intrinsic measure. "Pleasures which are in excess," he says, "have no measure, but those which are not in excess have measure; the great, the excessive . . . we shall be right in referring to the class of the infinite, and of the more and less," and "the others we shall refer to the class which has measure." The fact that the goodness of wealth or of certain pleasures is indeterminate or indefinite makes it necessary to determine or measure the amount of wealth it is good to possess, or the quantity of such pleasure it is good to enjoy.

As in the case of desire, so the human intellect is also said to be infinite in the sense of reaching to an indefinite quantity. On the theory which he holds that the intellect knows by means of universal concepts, Aquinas attributes to the human mind "an infinite power; for it apprehends the universal, which can extend itself to an infinitude of singular things." Each universal signifies what is common to an indefinitely large class of particular instances.

There is still another sense in which the intellect is said to be infinite, namely, by reason of its having the potentiality to apprehend *all* knowable things. But this is a relative infinity, as is the corresponding infinity of prime matter, which is conceived as the potentiality for taking on all forms. In both cases, the infinite is qualified by a restriction—on the kind of things knowable to the intellect and the type of forms receivable in matter. The infinity of prime matter—matter totally devoid of form—is also comparable to the infinity of God in a contrast of extreme opposites: the absolute indeterminacy of pure potentiality on the one hand, the absolute perfection of pure actuality on the other.

THE INFINITY OF matter involves different considerations when the problem concerns, not prime matter, but material things—bodies. The question is twofold. Can there be a body of infinite magnitude? Is there an infinite number of bodies? To both questions Aristotle gives the negative answer, while Spinoza seems to answer the first, and Lucretius the second, affirmatively.

Spinoza's affirmation may be qualified, of course, by his conception of infinite body as an attribute of God. But there is no qualification on Lucretius' assertion that "there must be an infinite supply of matter," unless it is his statement that "atoms have a finite number of differing shapes." It is only the number of atoms which is infinite, not their variety.

Aristotle presents many arguments against the existence of an infinite body or an infinite number of things, all of which ultimately rest on his distinction between an actual and a potential infinite. It is not that infinity in magnitude or multitude is impossible—for he affirms the infinity of time and he insists upon

the infinite divisibility of matter—but rather that if an infinite body existed its infinity would have to be actual. Its actuality would necessarily involve certain determinations, especially those of dimension and place, which would be inconsistent with the indeterminacy of the infinite. Similarly, a multitude of coexisting things—unlike the moments of time which do not coexist—cannot be infinite, because their coexistence implies that they can be actually numbered, whereas their infinity implies that they are numberless.

The potential infinite, Aristotle writes, "exhibits itself in different ways—in time, in the generations of man, and in the division of magnitudes. For generally," he says, "the infinite has this mode of existence: one thing is always being taken after another, and each thing that is taken is always finite, but always different." When this takes place in the division of spatial magnitudes, "what is taken persists, while in the succession of times and of men, it takes place by the passing away of these in such a way that the source of supply never gives out."

The opposition between Lucretius and Aristotle with regard to the divisibility of matter is discussed in the chapter on ELEMENT. The notions of infinity and continuity are differently employed on the two sides of the argument. Where Aristotle makes the continuity of matter the condition of its infinite divisibility, Lucretius makes the atom's continuity—its solidity or lack of void—the cause of its indivisibility. Where Aristotle asserts that at any moment there can be only a finite number of particles in the world because the partition of matter cannot be infinitely carried out short of infinite time, Lucretius, on the contrary, thinks that the division of matter into smaller and smaller parts finds an end in the atomic particles; and yet he also asserts an infinite number of atoms.

To contain an infinite number of atoms, an infinite space is required, according to Lucretius. This presents no greater difficulty for him than an infinite time. Aristotle, on the other hand, differentiates between space and time with respect to infinity. Time can be potentially infinite by way of addition because "each part that is taken passes in succession out of existence." But though space may be infinitely divisible, it cannot be infinitely extended, for all its parts, unlike those of time, must coexist. It would therefore have to be an *actually*, rather than a *potentially*, infinite quantity, and this Aristotle thinks is impossible.

These and other conflicting views concerning the infinity of space and time appear in Kant's statement of the first cosmological antinomy. His intention is not to resolve the issues, but to show that they cannot be resolved by proof or argument. To do this, Kant sets up what seems to him to be equally strong—or equally inconclusive—arguments for and against the infinity of space and time.

Suppose it be granted, Kant argues on the one hand, that "the world has no beginning in time." Then it would follow that "up to every given moment in time, an eternity must have elapsed, and therewith passed away an infinite series of successive conditions or states of things in the world." But since "the infinity of a series consists in the fact that it can never be completed by means of a successive synthesis," it also "follows that an infinite series already elapsed is impossible, and that consequently a beginning of the world is a necessary condition of its existence."

On the other hand, Kant argues with what he thinks is equal force, "let it be granted that [the world] has a beginning. A beginning," he explains, "is an existence which is preceded by a time in which the thing does not exist." Then, Kant continues, "on the above supposition, it follows that there must have been a time in which the world did not exist, that is, a void time. But in a void time, the origination of a thing is impossible; because no part of any such time contains a distinctive condition of being in preference to that of non-being . . . Consequently, many series of things may have a beginning in the world, but the world itself cannot have a beginning, and is, therefore, in relation to past time, infinite."

With regard to the infinity or finitude of space, Kant proceeds similarly. If we suppose space to be infinite, then "the world must be an infinite given total of co-existent things." But in order to "cogitate the world, which fills all space as a whole, the successive synthesis of the parts of an infinite world must be looked upon as completed; that is to say; an infinite time must be regarded as having elapsed in the enumeration of all co-existing things." This, Kant argues, "is impossible," and therefore "an infinite aggregate of actual things cannot be considered as a given whole." Hence it follows that "the world is, as regards extension in space, *not infinite*, but enclosed in limits."

If, however, we suppose "that the world is finite and limited in space, it follows," according to Kant, "that it must exist in a void space, which is not limited. We should, therefore, meet not only with a relation of things *in space*, but also a relation of things *to space*." But the "relation of the world to a void space is merely a relation to *no object*" and "such a relation, and consequently the limitation of the world by void space, is nothing." It follows, therefore, Kant concludes, that "the world, as regards space, is not limited; that is, it is infinite in regard to extension."

The way in which these opposite arguments nullify each other reveals more than our inability to prove or disprove the infinity of space and time. It shows, in Kant's theory of human knowledge, that we are "not entitled to make any assertion at all respecting the whole object of experience—the world of sense."

"Space and time," Russell writes, "appear to be infinitely divisible. But as against these apparent facts—infinite extent and infinite divisibility—philosophers have advanced arguments tending to show that there could be no infinite collections of things, and that therefore the number of points in space, or of instants in time, must be finite. Thus a contradiction emerged between the apparent nature of space and time and the supposed impossibility of infinite collections."

ONE OTHER PROBLEM of infinity in the sphere of physics receives its initial formulation in one of the great books—in the part of the *Dialogues Concerning the Two New Sciences* where Galileo discusses the uniform acceleration of a freely falling body. The body which is said to accumulate equal increments of velocity in equal intervals of time is also said to start "from infinite slowness, *i.e.*, from rest." One of the persons in the dialogue challenges this, saying that "as the instant of starting is more and more nearly approached, the body moves so slowly that, if it kept on moving at this rate, it would not traverse a mile in an hour, or in a day, or in a year, or in a thousand years; indeed, it would not traverse a span in an even greater time; a phenomenon which baffles the imagination, while our senses show us that a heavy falling body suddenly acquires great speed."

What our senses *seem* to show us is corrected by an experiment which refines the observation. But this still leaves a purely analytical question. Against the statement that the "velocity can be increased or diminished without limit," Simplicio points out in the dialogue that "if the number of degrees of greater and greater slowness is limitless, they will never be all exhausted," and therefore the body will never come to rest when it is slowing down or be able to start to move when it is at rest.

"This would happen," Salviati answers, "if the moving body were to maintain its speed for any length of time at each degree of velocity, but it merely passes each point without delaying more than an instant, and since each time interval, however small, may be divided into an infinite number of instants, these will always be sufficient to correspond to the infinite degrees of diminished velocity."

The problem of the infinitesimal velocity provides another illustration of the difference between infinity in the physical and the mathematical orders. Unlike parallel lines in Euclidean geometry, which are lines that remain equidistant from one another when both are prolonged to infinity, an asymptote is a straight line which a curved line continuously approaches but never meets, even when both are infinitely extended. The distance between the curve and its asymptote diminishes to smaller and smaller intervals, but no matter how small they become, the two lines never coincide. The diminishing intervals between the curve and its asymptote are like the diminishing degrees of velocity in a body starting from or coming to rest. But we know that the body does begin or cease to move, and so there

is the mysterious jumping of the gap between rest and motion in the physical order, whereas in the mathematical order the limiting point can be forever approached and never reached.

THERE IS ONE other context in which infinity is discussed in the great books.

The logicians treat certain terms and judgments as infinite. Aristotle, for example, regards the negative term—such as *not-man* or *not-white*—as indefinite. The indefiniteness of its signification may be seen when such terms are used as subjects of discourse. What is being talked about? The answer must be given, in part at least, in positive terms: *not-man* represents the *whole universe* leaving man out, or the *totality of everything* except man. Thus, in its positive signification, the negative term has a kind of infinity—the infinite totality of subjects diminished by one, the one that is negated.

In his classification of judgments, Kant makes a threefold division of judgments according to quality: the affirmative, the negative, and the infinite. The infinite judgment involves a negative in its construction, but when that negative is given an affirmative interpretation, the infinite significance of the proposition becomes apparent. An example will make this clear.

The proposition *this animal is-not white* is negative; it simply denies a certain quality of a certain thing. But the proposition *this animal is not-white* is infinite, for it affirms the negated term, and so places the subject in the infinite class or totality which includes everything except white things. (The position of the hyphen serves to indicate whether the statement shall be construed negatively or affirmatively *and* infinitely.)

The problems of definition and demonstration are differently solved by logicians according to the way in which they propose to avoid infinite regressions in analysis or reasoning. There would be no end to the process of defining if every term had to be defined before it could be used in the definition of another term. There would be no beginning to the process of proof if, before a proposition could be used as a premise to demonstrate some conclusion, it had itself to be demonstrated as a conclusion from prior premises.

In his essay "On Geometrical Demonstration," Pascal refers to the proposal of a plan for defining and proving everything. "Certainly this method would be beautiful," he says, "but it is absolutely impossible; for it is evident that the first terms we wished to define would presuppose others for their explication, and that similarly the first propositions we wished to prove would suppose others that preceded them, and it is thus clear we should never arrive at the first propositions."

The chapter on DEFINITION considers the character and choice of the indefinable terms by which an infinite regression is avoided in the elucidation of meanings. The chapters on INDUCTION and PRINCIPLE consider the various sorts of primary propositions—axioms, postulates, assumptions—by which a similar regression is avoided in the process of proof. The chapter on CAUSE deals with the problem of an infinite regression in causes and effects. Here it is appropriate to consider the difference between an infinite series of reasons and an infinite series of causes.

To the extent that both are truly series—the succession of one thing after another—neither seems to be impossible, *given infinite time.* Those who deny the possibility of an infinite number of causes distinguish between essential and accidental causes, that is, between causes which must coexist with their effects and causes which can precede their effects, and cease to be before their effects occur. If there were an infinite time, there could be an infinite series of accidental causes. But it may be questioned whether, even granted an infinite time, the relation between the premises and conclusion of reasoning permits an infinite regression. If the truth of a conclusion cannot be known until the truth of its premises is known, then the pursuit of truth may be vitiated by a search *ad infinitum.*

AT THE END OF THE 19th century, especially with the work of Georg Cantor, new insights into the nature of infinity in mathematics emerged. The number of objects in a set of objects is equal to the number of objects in a second set if the objects in each set can be paired off with each other in a one-to-one correspondence. Hence the fingers on the left hand and the fingers on the right hand can be so paired, meaning that each hand has an identical number of fingers.

By definition, a set with an infinite number of elements is a set that has the same number of elements as one of its subsets. Thus the number of positive integers is infinite because the positive integers can be paired off in a one-to-one correspondence with, for example, the even integers. This number is, in the notation of Cantor, designated as "aleph naught." The great discovery of Cantor was that this is the smallest of the infinite numbers.

A larger infinite number is the number of points on a line—a number which is called "C," for the number of points in a continuum. Indeed, there is an entire hierarchy of transfinite numbers. When this discovery was first made, it was considered extremely paradoxical. Now, it is a standard part of contemporary mathematics.

41

Judgment

INTRODUCTION

The word "judgment" has a range of meanings which includes three principal variants referring to (1) *a quality of the mind*, (2) *a faculty of the mind*, and (3) *an act of the mind*. Of these three meanings, it is the third which is extensively considered in this chapter; and it is this meaning of "judgment" which many writers use the word "proposition" to express. They sometimes substitute the one word entirely for the other; sometimes they use both words, not as strict synonyms, but to express distinct yet closely related aspects of the same fundamental phenomenon.

The sense in which judgment is *a quality of the mind* is the sense in which we ordinarily speak of a person as having sound judgment or poor judgment. "We credit the same people," Aristotle says, "with possessing judgment and having reached years of reason and with having practical wisdom and understanding." To be "a man of understanding and of good or sympathetic judgment," he continues, is to be "able to judge about the things with which practical wisdom is concerned."

The capacity to judge well concerning what is to be done is often connected with the capacity to deliberate about the advantages and disadvantages or other circumstances relevant to the action in question. It may or may not be accompanied by a capacity to resolve thought into action, to carry into execution the decision which judgment has formed. These three qualities of mind—deliberateness, judgment, and decisiveness—are conceived by Aristotle and Aquinas as belonging together as parts of the intellectual virtue they call "prudence" or "practical wisdom." The qualities may occur separately, but the prudent man will possess all three.

This meaning of "judgment" is reserved for discussion in the chapter on PRUDENCE; and in the chapter on LAW will be found the consideration of the judgment which a court renders—the judgment which is the decision of a judge when he applies the law to the particular case. In the legal sense of a judicial decision, judgment reflects not so much the quality of the judge's mind as his duty and authority to dispose of the case and to have his decision executed by the appropriate officers of the law. The legal significance of judgment is not primarily psychological or logical; and, just as the moral consideration of judgment falls under prudence, the legal consideration is also more appropriately developed in the context of other ideas.

We are left with the meanings which belong to psychology, logic, and the theory of knowledge. The sense in which "judgment" designates *a faculty or function of the mind*—a distinct sphere of mental operation—is much more special than the sense in which "judgment" or "proposition" signifies *a particular act of the mind* in the process of knowing or in the verbal expression of that process. Many authors discuss the kinds of judgment which the mind makes, and the kinds of propositions it forms and asserts or denies, but only a few—notably Locke and Kant—use the word "judgment" to name a mental faculty.

Locke, for example, says that "the mind has two faculties conversant about truth and falsehood." One is the faculty of knowing; the other of judging. "The faculty which God has given man to supply the want of clear and certain knowledge, in cases where that cannot be had, is *judgment*: whereby the mind takes its ideas to agree and disagree, or, which is the same, any proposition to be true or false, without perceiving a demonstrative evidence in the proofs." The way in which Locke distinguishes between knowing and judging and the fact that he relates this distinction to the difference between certainty and probability suggest the parallel distinction between knowledge and opinion. The faculty of judgment for Locke is the equivalent of what other writers treat as the forming of opinions.

Kant also makes judgment a faculty. Along with understanding and reason, judgment is one of the three faculties of cognition. It has a distinct function of its own and is coordinate with the other two. As the laws of nature are the work of the understanding in the sphere of speculative reason; as the rules of the moral law are the work of the reason in the practical sphere, wherein it is related to the faculty of desire; so the purposiveness of nature comes under the faculty of judgment which operates in relation to the faculty of pleasure and pain.

Kant divides all the faculties of the soul into "three which cannot be any further derived from one common ground: the *faculty of knowledge,* the *feeling of pleasure and pain* and the *faculty of desire.*" He sees each of the three cognitive functions (of understanding, judgment, and reason) as standing in a peculiar relation to these three primary faculties. The faculty of judgment functions with respect to pleasure and pain, which is connected with the faculty of desire. Yet the aesthetic judgment of beauty and the theological judgment of purposiveness in nature are of a speculative rather than a practical character. Because of these two related facts, Kant holds that "the judgement in the order of our cognitive faculties, forms a mediating link between Understanding and Reason."

Kant, perhaps more than any other thinker, makes judgment—both as a faculty and as an act—one of the central terms in his philosophy. It is pivotal in each of the three critiques, but it is *The Critique of Judgement* which serves to connect *The Critique of Pure Reason* and *The Critique of Practical Reason.* "The Understanding legislates *a priori* for nature as an object of sense—for theoretical knowledge of it in a possible experience. Reason legislates

a priori for freedom and its peculiar causality; as the supersensible in the subject, for an unconditioned practical knowledge. The realm of the natural concept under one legislation, and that of the concept of freedom under the other, are entirely removed from all mutual influence which they might have upon one another (each according to its fundamental laws) by the great gulf that separates the supersensible from phenomena." It is the judgment, according to Kant, which "furnishes the mediating concept between the concept of nature and that of freedom."

KANT'S THEORY of the faculties of understanding, judgment, and reason is so complex a doctrine that it cannot be readily compared with other analyses of the capacities or functions of mind. His threefold division bears a superficial—perhaps only a verbal—resemblance to Aquinas' division of mental acts into conception, judgment, and reasoning.

According to Aquinas, judgment is the second of the three acts of a single cognitive faculty variously called "mind" or "intellect" or "reason." This faculty, he writes, "first apprehends something about a thing, such as its essence, and this is its first and proper object; and then it understands the properties, accidents, and various dispositions affecting the essence. Thus it necessarily relates one thing with another by composition or division; and from one composition and division it necessarily proceeds to another, and this is *reasoning.*"

The first act of the mind is conception, *i.e.,* the simple apprehension of the essence and properties of a thing. Judgment, the second act, unites or separates concepts by affirming or denying one or another. As in the Kantian analysis, judgment is a kind of mediating link; for after the judgment is formed by what Aquinas calls the "composition or division" of concepts, it in turn serves as the unit of the mind's third act, which is reasoning. Reasoning is the process of going from judgment to judgment.

The act of judgment is that act of the mind, and the only act, which can have the quality of truth or falsity. "Truth," Aquinas writes, "resides in the intellect composing and dividing"; for when the intellect "judges that a thing corresponds to the form which it apprehends about that thing, then it first knows and expresses truth . . . In every proposition," the mind "either applies to, or removes from, the thing signified by the subject some form signified by the predicate." Moreover, the judgment involves assertion or denial as the concept does not. Whatever truth there is implicitly in concepts must be explicated in judgments and the truth of the conclusion in reasoning depends upon the truth of the judgments which are the premises. The judgment, therefore, is the basic unit of knowledge.

On this last point Kant seems to be in agreement with earlier writers. It is possible, therefore, to compare Kant's classification of judgments or propositions with the classifications of Aristotle, Descartes, or Locke. But it is necessary, first, to consider the relation between judgment and proposition. After that we can examine the difference between theoretical and practical judgments. With respect to the theoretical judgment (or proposition), we shall be able to state opposite views of the nature of the judgment and diverse views of the formal structure of judgments, their material content, their relation to one another and to the whole process of knowing.

THE SENTENCE "all men are mortal" can be interpreted as expressing a judgment or a proposition. From certain points of view, the choice of interpretation makes no difference; for example, it does not matter whether, in a consideration of "all men are mortal" and "some men are not mortal," the comparison is expressed in terms of universal and particular, affirmative and negative, judgments *or* propositions, or whether it is said that these are contradictory judgments *or* contradictory propositions. The basic problems of logic seem to be conceived in the same way by writers like Aristotle and Locke, who tend to use "proposition" in place of "judgment," and by writers like Aquinas, Descartes, and Kant, who tend to use both words with some difference in meaning.

What is the difference? It is sometimes understood as a difference between an act of the mind, asserting or denying, and the subject matter being asserted or denied. The proposition is that which may be either asserted or denied; or in the third alternative stressed by Descartes, the mind may suspend judgment and merely entertain the proposition. It may decline to judge it true or false, and so refuse to assert or deny it. The fact that the proposition is itself either affirmative or negative does not signify its assertion or denial by a judgment of the mind, for an affirmative proposition can be denied and a negative can be affirmed.

Judgment adds to the proposition in question the mind's decision with respect to its truth or falsity. That decision may be right or wrong. A proposition which is in fact true may be denied. The truth of the proposition is unaffected by the falsity of the judgment, or if the mind suspends judgment on a proposition which is true, the truth of the proposition has failed to elicit a judgment. This seems to confirm the separation between the proposition and the judgment.

According to Russell, "in every act of judgement there is a mind which judges, and there are terms concerning which it judges." These terms are the constituent elements of the proposition judged to be true or false—affirmed or denied.

Sometimes the difference between the judgment and the proposition is found in the difference between the mind's act of "composing" or "dividing" concepts and the formulation of that act in words. On this view, the proposition is related to the judgment as the term to the concept, as the physical to the mental word, as language to thought. In consequence, there is no separation for either the judgment or the proposition between that which can be asserted or denied and the assertion or denial of it. The affirmative judgment *is* an assertion, the negative a denial; and the same holds for the affirmative and the negative proposition.

But on either theory of the difference, it is thought necessary to distinguish between the sentence and the proposition, especially when the proposition is also regarded as a verbal formulation—a statement of thought in words. This is particularly important in a logical treatise like Aristotle's, which analyzes *terms, propositions,* and *syllogisms* rather than *concepts, judgments,* and *reasonings.*

In both the "Categories," which deals with terms, and the treatise "On Interpretation," which deals with propositions, Aristotle differentiates between a grammatical and a logical handling of the units of language. His distinction, for example, between simple and composite expressions (words and phrases on the one hand, and sentences on the other) is related to, but it is not identical with, his distinction between terms and propositions. Not every simple expression can be used as a term. For example, prepositions and conjunctions cannot be used as terms, as nouns and verbs can be. Nor can every sentence be used as a proposition.

"A sentence is a significant portion of speech," Aristotle writes, "some parts of which have an independent meaning, that is to say, as an utterance, though not as the expression of any positive judgment . . . Every sentence has meaning," he goes on, "by convention. Yet every sentence is not a proposition; only such are propositions as have in them truth or falsity. Thus a prayer is a sentence, but is neither true nor false. Let us therefore dismiss all other types of sentence but the proposition, for this last concerns our present inquiry, whereas the investigation of the others belongs rather to the study of rhetoric or of poetry."

It seems possible to relate the two separate distinctions we have been considering—that between sentence and proposition and that between proposition and judgment. As the proposition can be regarded as a sentence logically (rather than grammatically) construed, so it can also be regarded as the linguistic expression of a judgment of the mind. The proposition thus appears to be a kind of middle ground between language and thought, for when a sentence is used for the purpose of stating a proposition it can also express a judgment. When a judgment is expressed in words, the verbal statement is also a proposition. The proposition is thus the logical aspect of a sentence and the verbal aspect of a judgment. A similar consideration of terms in relation to words and concepts occurs in the chapter on IDEA.

WHAT IS PERHAPS the most fundamental division in the sphere of judgments—the separation of the practical from the theoretical or speculative—can be initially explained by reference to the forms of language. Aristotle's remark about sentences and propositions tends to identify propositions with declarative sentences. Sentences in the subjunctive mood state prayers or wishes, not propositions. An interrogative sentence asks a question to which the answers may be propositions, or they may be hopes and desires. The imperative sentence issues a command to act in a certain way, whether the command is a direction for others or a decision for one's self. This last type of sentence represents the practical mood of thought as well as speech—thought concerned with actions to be done or not done, rather than with what does or does not exist.

The imperative sentence is not the only kind of practical statement. It is merely the most terse and emphatic. It is also the expression of that type of practical judgment which most immediately precedes action itself, or the execution of a command. There are other sentences which, because they are apparently declarative in form, conceal their imperative mood. Yet upon examination their essentially practical rather than theoretical significance can be discovered.

Sentences which contain the words "ought" or "should" are of this sort, *e.g.,* "Men ought to seek the truth," "You should work for peace," "I ought to make this clear." By omitting "should" or "ought," these sentences can be changed into the strictly declarative mood of theoretical propositions, *e.g.,* "Men do seek the truth," "You will work for peace," "I shall make this clear." They can also be made plainly imperative, *e.g.,* "Seek the truth," etc. The chief difference between the blunt form of the imperative and its indicative expression using "ought" or "should" is that the latter indicates the person to whom the command is addressed.

The contrast in significance between a declarative and an imperative statement does, therefore, convey the distinction between a theoretical and a practical proposition or judgment. Kant's further division of practical judgments into the hypothetical and the categorical simply differentiates commands or "oughts" which involve no preamble from those which propose that action be taken to achieve a certain end, or which base a direction to employ this or that means on the supposition that a certain end is desired or sought. Examples of hypothetical or conditional imperatives would be such judgments as "If you want to be happy, seek the truth" or "Seek the truth in order to be happy."

The distinction between theoretical and practical judgments is currently made in terms of the contrast between statements of fact and statements of value or, as in judicial procedure, between statements of fact and rules of law. A rule of law has the form of a general practical statement, usually a conditional rather than a categorical imperative; whereas the decision of a court applying the rule to a case is a particular practical judgment.

Beginning with Francis Bacon, the distinction between the theoretical and the practical is also made in terms of the difference between the pure sciences and their applications in technology. Technical judgments, prescribing the way to make something or produce a certain effect, are traditionally associated, under the head of the practical, with moral judgments concerning the good to be sought and the ways of seeking it. Both are prescriptive of conduct rather than descriptive of existence or nature in the manner of theoretical statements.

Thinkers like Aristotle, Aquinas, and Kant, who divide science or philosophy into the theoretical disciplines (*e.g.*, physics, mathematics, metaphysics) and the practical or moral disciplines (*e.g.*, ethics, economics, politics), place the discussion of the difference between theoretical and practical judgments in the context of other distinctions; as, for example, between the speculative and the practical reason, or between theoretical and practical knowledge; or in the context of considering the kinds of truth appropriate to each, and the modes of inference or demonstration in each. These related distinctions and considerations are treated in the chapters on KNOWLEDGE, MIND, REASONING, and TRUTH.

For the most part, however, the great books in the tradition of logic itself do not give an analysis of practical judgments or reasoning in any way comparable to their treatment of the theoretical forms of thought and statement. The logical problems concerning propositions or judgments, now to be considered, apply only to the theoretical forms.

TWO BASIC ISSUES in the theory of propositions or judgments have their origin in the tradition of the great books, but for their explicit and full development other works must be consulted—the special treatises on logic, of relatively recent date, listed in the Additional Readings. One of these two issues has already been briefly commented on, but for the full implications of the distinction between propositions and judgments one must go to such writers as G. W. F. Hegel, F. H. Bradley, Bernard Bosanquet, John Cook Wilson, W. E. Johnson, and John Dewey, who make this distinction the crux of a controversy over the scope of formal logic.

The other basic issue lies in the opposition between what has come to be called "subject-predicate logic" and "relational logic." Here one side is fully represented by the *Organon* of Aristotle and by the later books which adopt the Aristotelian logic of predication. The other logical theory is intimated but not fully developed by such writers as Locke, Hume, Kant, and William James who, though they sometimes employ the subject-predicate formulation, tend to construct the unit of knowledge—the proposition or judgment—as a relation between ideas or concepts.

The fact that Kant places substance and accident under the category of relation can be taken as exemplifying this tendency, as can Locke's emphasis on the connection of, and agreement or disagreement between, our ideas. Nevertheless, these are at most intimations of the theory that the proposition is a relation of two or more terms, not the application of a predicate to a subject. As indicated in the chapter on LOGIC, the relational theory does not receive an adequate exposition until the modern development of symbolic or mathematical logic, beginning with the writings of George Boole, William Stanley Jevons, and John Venn, and culminating in such works as the *Principia Mathematica* of Russell and Whitehead.

In the Aristotelian logic, simple propositions consist of a subject and a predicate—what is being talked about and what is said of it. The copula "is" is the sign of predication; it also signifies an affirmation of the unity of subject and predicate. For example, in "Socrates is a man" the predicate *man* is applied to the subject *Socrates,* and the unity of *being Socrates* and *being a man* is affirmed. All the terms of discourse can be classified according to their character as subjects and predicates; so, too, can propositions be classified by reference to the type of subject-term and the type of predicate-term which comprise them. The formal structure not only of the proposition, but also of the syllogism, is determined by the order of subjects and predicates. "When one term is predicated of another," Aristotle writes, "any term which is predicable of the predicate will also be predicable of its subject."

According to the theory of the proposition as a relation of terms or of classes, predication represents merely one type of relationship—the membership of an individual in a class, or the inclusion of one class in another. There are many other types of relation which, it is held, cannot be reduced to class-membership or class-inclusion; as, for example, the relationship stated by the proposition "John hit James," or the proposition "January comes before February." Propositions can be classified according to the number of terms involved in a single relationship, or by reference to the type of relation which organizes them, whether it is symmetrical or asymmetrical, transitive or intransitive, reflexive or irreflexive. In this theory it is the character of the relationship, not the character of the terms, which is the fundamental element in logical analysis, and this determines the formal structure of inference as well as of propositions.

It has been claimed for each of these logical theories that it is the more general analysis and that it is able to reduce the formulations of the opposite theory to its own terms or subsume them as a special case. Certainly it is verbally possible to convert all predications into statements of relationship, or all relational statements into subject-predicate propositions. But this by itself does not seem to resolve the issue to the satisfaction of either theory; each side contends that such reductions violate its fundamental principles. Stated in its most drastic form, the unresolved question is whether there is one logic or two—or perhaps more.

WITHIN THE tradition of Aristotelian logic, there are divergent schemes for classifying propositions or judgments. So far as the great books are concerned, this can be best illustrated by mentioning Kant's departures in analysis.

Aristotle distinguishes between simple and composite propositions, the former consisting of a single subject and predicate, the latter "compounded of several propositions." For example, since the two predicates in the proposition "This man is good and a shoemaker" do not form a unity, the sentence expresses a conjunction of two simple propositions: "This man is good" and "This man is a shoemaker." Other types of compound propositions are the hypothetical and the disjunctive, *e.g.,* "If Socrates is a man, Socrates is mortal," and "Either all men are mortal or no men are mortal." Kant treats these distinctions under the head of *relation*. He calls the proposition which is a "relation of the predicate to the subject, categorical" and he regards the hypothetical or disjunctive judgment (based on relations of cause and effect or of the parts of a whole) as concerned with propositions "in relation to each other."

Aristotle classifies simple propositions by reference to their quantity and quality. In regard to quantity he distinguishes between the universal (*e.g.,* "All men are mortal") and the particular (*e.g.,* "Some men are mortal"). To these he adds the indefinite proposition which leaves the quantity (*all* or *some*) undetermined. Under the head of quantity, Kant makes a threefold division according to unity, plurality, and totality. He adds the singular proposition "Socrates is mortal" to Aristotle's particular and universal. The difference between the singular on the one hand, and the particular and the universal on the other, seems to be represented in Aristotle's thought by the distinction between propositions about an individual subject and propositions about a universal subject.

The quality of categorical propositions, according to Aristotle, is either affirmative (*i.e.*, positive) or negative, *e.g.*, "All men are mortal" and "Some men are *not* mortal." To these two Kant adds a third type of judgment under the head of *quality*—the infinite judgment which affirms a negative predicate of a subject, *e.g.*, "The soul is non-mortal." Though Aristotle recognizes the special character of a term like "non-mortal," since it is both negative and indefinite, he does not seem to think that the use of such terms affects the quality of a proposition.

Finally, Aristotle divides propositions according to whether they are simple assertions of fact or are assertions qualified by the notions of necessity or contingency (*i.e.*, possibility). Every proposition, he says, "states that something either is or must be or may be the attribute of something else." The distinction between the necessary and contingent modes of statement has come to be called a difference in "modality," and statements which have one or another modality are called "modal propositions."

It is sometimes thought that the Aristotelian classification treats only necessary and contingent propositions, with their several opposites, as modal propositions, and separates the simple or pure assertion from them as nonmodal. In contrast to this, Kant makes a threefold division of judgments under the head of modality: the "problematical" (*i.e.*, the possible, what *may be*), the "assertoric" (*i.e.*, the existent, what *is*), and the "apodictic" (*i.e.*, the necessary, what *must be*).

THE CLASSIFICATION of the types of judgment or proposition is usually preliminary in logical analysis to a consideration of their order and connection.

The formal pattern of what is traditionally called "the square of opposition" is deter-

mined by the quality and quantity of the simple propositions which are therein related as contradictory, contrary, and subcontrary. Two propositions are contradictory if they are opposite in both quality and quantity (*e.g.*, "All men are mortal" is contradicted by "Some men are not mortal"). Two universal propositions are contrary if one is affirmative and the other negative (*e.g.*, "All men are mortal" is contrary to "No men are mortal"); and an affirmative and a negative particular proposition are related as subcontraries (*e.g.*, "Some men are mortal" and "Some men are not mortal"). The significance of these three basic relationships for the truth and falsity of the opposed propositions is discussed in the chapter on OPPOSITION; and in the chapter on NECESSITY AND CONTINGENCY the special problems of opposition among modal propositions are examined.

Other than their opposition, the only formal relationship of propositions or judgments occurs in the structure of inference or reasoning. According to the traditional analysis, the implication of one proposition by another—insofar as that is determined by the form of each—is immediate inference. In contrast, the pattern of *mediated* inference or reasoning always involves at least three propositions, ordered not only with respect to the sequence from premises to conclusion, but also by the relation of the premises to one another. These matters are discussed in the chapter on REASONING.

With respect to their origin, status, or import, judgments or propositions are subject to further distinctions in type. The certainty or probability with which propositions are asserted or judgments are made is connected by some writers with the distinction between knowledge and opinion, by others with the difference between science and dialectic, and by others with the difference between knowing the relation of ideas and knowing matters of fact or real existence. Propositions which express certain knowledge are, furthermore, divided by some analysts into those which are axiomatic, self-evident, or immediate and those which are known only by mediated inference, reasoning, or demonstration, not by intuition or induction. The former are also sometimes called "principles," the latter "conclusions."

Locke's distinction between "trifling" and "instructive" propositions, like Kant's distinction between "analytic" and "synthetic" judgments, is made in the general context of an examination of how we learn or know.

Trifling propositions, according to Locke, "are universal propositions which, though they be certainly true, yet they add no light to our understanding; bring no increase to our knowledge." All "purely identical propositions" are of this sort—propositions such as "body is body" or "a vacuum is a vacuum." Such propositions "teach nothing but what every one who is capable of discourse knows without being told, *viz.,* that the same term is the same term, and the same idea the same idea." They are all instances of the law of identity; or, as Locke expresses it, they are all "equivalent to this proposition, *viz., what is, is.*" If the trifling proposition, the analytic judgment, or what in our day is called a "tautology," goes beyond the statement of an identity between subject and predicate, it goes no further than the explication of a definition. It predicates, Locke says, "a part of the definition of the word defined," as, for example, in the proposition "Lead is a metal."

Analytic or explicative judgments, Kant says in the *Prolegomena,* "express nothing in the predicate but what has already been actually thought in the concept of the subject ... When I say, 'all bodies are extended,' I have not amplified in the least my concept of body, but have only analyzed it ... On the contrary, this judgment, 'All bodies have weight,' contains in its predicate something not actually thought in the general concept of body; it amplifies my knowledge, by adding something to my concept, and must therefore be called synthetical."

For Locke not all axioms or self-evident propositions are trifling or tautological, for some go beyond statements of identity or the explication of definitions, as, for example, that the whole is greater than the part. Nor are they all useless. Some which Locke distinguishes from the rest by calling them "maxims," are of

use, he maintains, "in the ordinary methods of teaching sciences as far as they are advanced, but of little or none in advancing them further. They are of use in disputes, for the silencing of obstinate wranglers, and bringing those contests to some conclusion."

For Kant there is a further division of judgments into the *a posteriori* and the *a priori,* according as their truth is or is not grounded in the data of experience. The former are empirical in origin, the latter transcendental, that is, they have a foundation which transcends experience. These two types of judgment express two corresponding types of knowledge—*a priori* knowledge by which Kant understands "not such as is independent of this or that kind of experience, but such as is absolutely so of *all* experience. Opposed to this is empirical knowledge, or that which is possible only *a posteriori,* that is, through experience."

In Kant's view, there is no problem about the truth of analytic judgments, for these have an *a priori* foundation in the principle of contradiction. (The contradictory of an analytic judgment is always self-contradictory.) Nor do synthetic judgments which are empirical or *a posteriori* raise any special difficulties. The central question in the theory of knowledge concerns the possibility and validity of synthetic judgments *a priori.*

"If I go out of and beyond the conception A, in order to recognize another, B, as connected with it, what foundation have I to rest on," Kant asks, "whereby to render the synthesis possible? I have here no longer the advantage of looking out in the sphere of experience for what I want. Let us take, for example, the proposition, 'everything that happens has a cause.' In the conception of *something that happens,* I indeed think an existence which a certain time antecedes, and from this I can derive analytical judgments. But the conception of a cause lies quite outside the above conception, and indicates something entirely different from 'that which happens,' and is consequently not contained in that conception. How then am I able to assert concerning the general conception—'that which happens'—something entirely different from that conception, and to recognize the conception of cause although not contained in it, yet as belonging to it, and even necessarily? What is here the unknown X, upon which the understanding rests when it believes it has found, outside the conception A, a foreign predicate B, which it nevertheless considers to be connected with it?" It is the discovery and solution of this problem which Kant believes to be the signal contribution of his transcendental logic of the judgment.

It may be wondered whether this problem can be stated in terms other than those peculiar to Kant's analytic vocabulary. Other writers admit that propositions which are particular and contingent have "existential import." Their truth concerns real existences, and so whether they are true or not can and must be learned from experience. These are like Kant's synthetic judgments *a posteriori*. Universal and necessary propositions, on the other hand, are sometimes interpreted as having no existential significance. Instead of being read as asserting that anything exists, they are taken simply as statements of the relation between our own ideas. These, for Locke and Hume, are like Kant's *a priori* analytic judgments.

What remains is to discover a parallel for Kant's synthetic judgments *a priori*. In terms other than Kant's, the most likely parallel seems to be the universal and necessary proposition conceived as a statement about reality rather than about relations in the realm of our own concepts. When universal propositions are so interpreted, two questions arise. How do we establish that the subjects of such propositions really exist? What is the ultimate ground for the truth of such propositions, the unlimited universality of which outruns experience? In these two questions we find a problem which is at least analogous to Kant's problem of the possibility of synthetic judgments *a priori*.

42

Justice

INTRODUCTION

THE discussion of justice is the central theme in two dialogues of Plato—*The Republic* and the *Gorgias*. The dispute between Socrates and Thrasymachus in the one and between Socrates and Callicles in the other is of such universal scope and fundamental character that it recurs again and again in the great books with little change except in the personalities and vocabularies of the disputants.

It is a conflict of such polar opposites that all other differences of opinion about justice become arguable only after one or the other of the two extreme positions is abandoned. It is the conflict between the exponents of might and the exponents of right—between those who think that might *makes* right and that justice *is* expediency, and those who think that power can be wrongly as well as rightly exercised and that justice, the measure of men and states, cannot be measured by utility.

Though Plato gives us the first full-fashioned statement of this issue, he does not fashion it out of whole cloth. The issue runs through the fabric of Greek life and thought in the age of the imperialistic city-states which played the game of power politics culminating in the Peloponnesian War. In his history of that war, Thucydides highlights the Melian episode by dramatically constructing a conversation between the Athenian envoys and the representatives of Melos, a little island colony of Sparta which had refused to knuckle under to Athenian aggression.

Recognizing the superior force of the aggressors, the Melians enter the conference with a sense of its futility, for, as they point out, if they insist upon their rights and refuse to submit, they can expect nothing from these negotiations except war and, in the end, slav-ery. The Athenians reply with a frankness that is seldom found in the diplomatic exchanges of our own day, though in their real contentions the conferences which have preceded or followed the world wars of our century repeat what happened, if not what was said, at Melos.

The Athenians tell the Melians that they will not waste time with specious pretences "either of how we have a right to our empire . . . or are now attacking you because of a wrong you have done us." Why make a long speech, they say, which would not be believed? Instead they come directly to the point and put the matter simply or, as we now say, realistically. "You know as well as we do," they tell the Melians, "that right, as the world goes, is only in question between equals in power, whereas the stronger do whatever they can and the weaker suffer whatever they must." There is nothing left for the Melians except an appeal to expediency. "You debar us from talking about justice and invite us to obey your interest," they reply to the Athenians, before trying to persuade them that their policy will end in disaster for Athens.

The language of Thrasymachus in *The Republic* resembles that of the Athenian envoys. "I proclaim," he says, "that justice is nothing else than the interest of the stronger . . . The different forms of government make laws democratical, aristocratical, tyrannical, with a view to their several interests; and these laws, which are made by them for their own interests, are the justice which they deliver to their subjects, and him who transgresses them they punish as a breaker of the law, and unjust. And this is what I mean when I say that in all states there is the same principle of justice which is the interest of the government; and as the government must be supposed to have power, the only reasonable conclusion is that everywhere there is one principle of justice which is the interest of the stronger."

The thesis seems to have two applications. For the stronger, it means that they have the right, as far as they have the might, to exact from the weaker whatever serves their interests. Their laws or demands cannot be unjust. They cannot do injustice. They can only fail to exert sufficient might to hold on to the power which can secure them, not from the charge of injustice, but from reprisals by those whom they have oppressed or injured.

The thesis also means, for the weaker, that they can only do injustice but not suffer it. Injustice on their part consists in disobeying the law of their rulers. Hence for them, too, justice is expediency, only now in the sense that they are likely to suffer if they try to follow their own interests rather than the interests of the stronger.

This thesis appears to be repeated in somewhat different language by Hobbes and Spinoza. To men living in a purely natural condition, the notions of justice and injustice do not apply. They apply only to men living in civil society. "Where there is no Commonwealth," Hobbes writes, "there is nothing unjust. So that the nature of justice consists in the keeping of valid covenants; but the validity of covenants begins not but with the constitution of a civil power sufficient to compel men to keep them." The breach of civil laws or covenants "may be called injustice, and the observance of them justice."

It is Spinoza's opinion that "everything has by nature as much right as it has power to exist and operate." It follows, therefore, that "in a natural state there is nothing which can be called just or unjust, but only in a civil state." Here as before justice consists in obedience, injustice in disobedience, to whatever laws the state has the power to enforce, the laws themselves being formulated not by reference to justice, but to the interests of the state which must seek its own preservation and has the right to do so, so long as it has the power.

THOSE WHO TAKE the opposite view agree that justice is political in the sense that the state, in organization and operation, is a work of justice. Wisdom is the virtue of the rulers in *The Republic,* but justice is the organizing principle of Plato's ideal state.

Aristotle maintains that man is a political animal, whereas other animals are merely gregarious. He cites the fact that man alone has a power of speech able to communicate opinions about the expedient and the just. "Justice is the bond of men in states, for the administration of justice, which is the determination of what is just, is the principle of order in political society." Aristotle describes man "when separated from law and justice" as the worst of animals. "Justice being taken away," Augustine asks, "what are kingdoms but great robberies?"

Those who agree that political institutions involve justice are confronted by these alternatives: *either* the principle of justice is antecedent to the state, its constitution, covenants, and laws, *or* the determination of what is just and unjust is entirely relative to the constitution of a state, dependent upon its power, and consequent to its laws.

When the second alternative is chosen, the proposition that justice is political is seriously qualified. It is *merely* political. There is no natural justice, no justice apart from man-made laws, nothing that is just or unjust in the very nature of the case and without reference to civil institutions. On this theory, only the individual who is subject to government can be judged just or unjust. The government itself cannot be so judged, nor can its constitution, its laws, or its acts; for, since these determine what is just and unjust, they cannot themselves be judged for their justice.

The opposite answer conceives political justice as a determination of natural justice. "Political justice," Aristotle remarks, "is partly natural and partly conventional or legal." The fact that there is a sense in which just action on the part of a citizen consists in law-abiding conduct, does not exclude another sense in which the laws themselves can be called just or unjust, not only the laws, but the constitution of the state itself. Though the justice of civil laws is partly relative to the constitution under which they are made and administered, there are some enactments which, since they violate natural justice, cannot be justified under any constitution. The constitution, moreover, cannot be regarded as the ultimate standard of justice by those who compare the justice of different forms of government or diverse constitutions. On their view, the ultimate measure of justice in all human institutions and acts, as well as in the characters of men, is not itself a man-made standard, but rather a natural principle of justice, holding for all men at all times everywhere.

THE ISSUE JOINED BY these two theories of justice extends by implication into many related matters. The opposition, for example, between those who affirm the reality of natural law as the source of legality in all civil regulations and those who derive the legality of positive laws from the will of the sovereign alone, is considered in the chapter on LAW, but its parallelism with the issue of natural and conventional justice should be noted here.

Those who deny natural justice and natural law also tend to deny natural rights, which, unlike civil rights, are not conferred on the individual by the state, but are inherent in his human personality. They are, according to the Declaration of Independence, "unalienable" in the sense that the state cannot rescind them. What the state does not create, it cannot destroy. If a government transgresses natural rights, it negates its own reason for being, since it is "to secure these rights [that] governments are instituted among men."

According to Tocqueville, it is by reference to natural rights that "men have defined the nature of license and of tyranny." No nation, in his view, can be "great without respect for rights; one might almost say that without it there can be no society."

Those who deny natural rights, among which the right to liberty is usually included, do not have a standard for judging when governments violate the rights and invade the liberties of men. When men are thought to have no rights except those granted by their rulers, the absolute power which the rulers exercise cannot be criticized as tyrannical or despotic.

Considering the situation of men in what he calls "a state of perfect freedom"—apart from government and civil institutions—Locke says of this state of nature that it "has a law of nature to govern it, which obliges everyone; and reason, which is that law, teaches all mankind who will but consult it, that, being all equal and independent, no one ought to harm another in his life, health, liberty, or possessions . . . Everyone, as he is bound to preserve himself, and not quit his station willfully, so, by the like reason, when his own preservation comes not in competition, ought he, as much as he can, to preserve the rest of mankind, and not, unless it be to do justice on an offender, take away or impair the life, or what tends to the preservation of the life, the liberty, health, limb, or goods of another." Since this law of nature, and its implied principle of just dealing between men, is not abolished when men associate in the common life of a civil society, natural justice and natural rights remain, according to Locke and others, to limit the powers of government and to measure the justice of its laws.

The principle of natural justice is sometimes not accompanied by a doctrine of natural law and natural rights, as for example in Greek thought. Their connection first seems to occur in Roman jurisprudence and medieval theory. Not all the opponents of natural justice avoid the use of the words "natural law" and "natural rights." Using these words in a different sense, Hobbes, for example, speaks of men living under natural law in a state of nature, which is "a condition of war of every one against every one," and "in such condition every man has a right to everything, even to another's body." Only when men *abandon* this unlimited right in order to form a commonwealth, do they acquire in recompense certain civil rights or, as Hobbes says, "proprieties." Then, and only then, can there be any meaning to justice, conceived according to the ancient maxim which Hobbes accepts, that justice is "the constant will to render to each man what is his due."

Both Spinoza and Hume make the same point. Where there is no recognized title to property, or *legally established* right, there can be no justice—no respecting of what is a man's own or giving him what belongs to him. The difference between Locke and these others seems to lie in his conception of *property* as the natural right which a man has to the preservation of his life, liberty, and estate. There can be justice, therefore, between men in a state of nature, for even then each has some property that the others are bound to respect.

THE MEANING of natural justice can be examined apart from these different interpretations of the so-called "state of nature." Those who, like Aristotle and Aquinas, do not conceive the origin of political society as a transition from the "state of nature" do, nevertheless, appeal to a principle of natural justice. For Aquinas, this principle seems to be an integral part of the natural law. Sometimes the statement of the first precept of the natural law is "Seek the good; avoid evil." Sometimes it is "Do good to others, injure no one, and render to every man his own." In this second formulation, the natural law seems to be identical with the precept of justice. The essential content of this precept seems to be present—separate from any doctrine of natural law—in Aristotle's analysis of the nature of justice both as a virtue and as a quality of human acts.

"The just," Aristotle says, "is the lawful and the fair." What he means by the word "lawful" in this context does not seem to be simply the law-abiding, in the sense of conforming to the actual laws of a particular society. He thinks of law as aiming "at the common advantage . . . We call those acts just," he writes, "that tend to produce and preserve happiness and its components for the political society." Lawful (or just) actions thus are those which are for the common good or the good of others; unlawful (or unjust) actions, those which do injury to others or despoil the society.

It is in this sense of justice that both Plato and Aristotle lay down the primary criterion for differentiating between good and bad governments. Those which are lawful and serve the common good are just; those which are lawless and serve the private interests of the rulers are unjust. This meaning of justice ap-

plies as readily to all citizens—to all members of a society—as it does to those who have the special duties or occupy the special offices of government.

Whether it is stated in terms of the good of other individuals or in terms of the common good of a community (domestic or political), this understanding of justice seems to consider the actions of a man as they affect the well-being, not of himself, but of others. "Justice, alone of the virtues," says Aristotle, "is thought to be 'another's good,' because it is related to our neighbor." Concerned with what is due another, justice involves the element of duty or obligation. "To each one," Aquinas writes, "is due what is his own," and "it evidently pertains to justice," he adds, "that a man give another his due." That is why "justice alone, of all the virtues, implies the notion of duty." Doing good to others or not injuring them, when undertaken as a matter of strict justice, goes no further than to discharge the debt which each man owes every other.

In consequence, a difference of opinion arises concerning the adequacy of justice to establish the peace and harmony of a society. Some writers, like Kant, seem to think that if perfect justice obtained, a multitude of individual wills would be perfectly harmonized in free action. Others, like Aquinas, think justice necessary but insufficient precisely because it is a matter of duty and debt. "Peace," he writes, "is the *work of justice* indirectly, in so far as justice removes the obstacles to peace; but it is the *work of charity* directly, since charity, according to its very nature, causes peace; for love is *a unitive force.*" The bonds of love and friendship unite men where justice merely governs their interaction. What men do for one another out of the generosity of love far exceeds the commands of justice. That is why mercy and charity are called upon to qualify justice or even to set it aside. "Earthly power," Portia declares in *The Merchant of Venice,* "doth then show likest God's when mercy seasons justice."

THE PRECEPT "to render unto others what is their due" is read in a different light when the other aspect of justice is considered. When the just is conceived as the fair, the fairness which is due ourselves or others applies, not to benefit and injury generally, but to the exchange and distribution of goods or burdens. What is the principle of a fair exchange or a fair distribution? Aristotle's answer to this question is in terms of equality.

In the transactions of commerce, fairness seems to require the exchange of things equivalent in value. The rule of an eye for an eye, a tooth for a tooth, is another expression of the principle of equality as the criterion of a fair penalty or a just compensation. If honors or rewards are to be distributed, equals should in fairness be treated equally, and those who are unequal in merit should receive unequal shares. For all to share alike is not a just distribution of deserts if all do not deserve alike. "Awards should be 'according to merit,' " Aristotle writes. He claims that "all men agree" with this, "though they do not all specify the same sort of merit, but democrats identify it with the status of freeman, supporters of oligarchy with wealth or with noble birth, and supporters of aristocracy with excellence." The unequal treatment of unequals, however, still derives its fairness from the principle of equality, for there is an equivalence of ratios in the proportion of giving more to the more deserving and less to the less.

Aristotle employs the distinction between these modes of equality—arithmetic and geometric, or simple and proportional, equality— to define the difference between fairness in exchange and fairness in distribution. The one is the type of justice which is traditionally called "commutative," "corrective," or "remedial," the other "distributive."

The type of justice "which plays a rectifying part in transactions between man and man," Aristotle further divides into two kinds. "Of transactions," he writes, "(1) some are voluntary and (2) others involuntary—voluntary such transactions as sale, purchase, loan for consumption, pledging, loan for use, depositing, letting . . . while of the involuntary (a) some are clandestine, such as theft, adultery, poisoning, procuring, enticement of slaves, assassination, false witness, and (b) others are violent, such as assault, imprisonment, mur-

der, robbery with violence, mutilation, abuse, insult." The sphere which Aristotle assigns to commutative or corrective justice thus appears to cover both criminal acts and civil injuries. But, as applied to civil injuries, the principle of fairness in exchange usually involves a payment for damages, restitution, or compensation in kind; whereas the principle of commutative justice as applied to criminal wrongdoing usually calls for a punishment somehow equalized in severity to the gravity of the offense. This last is the principle of the *lex talionis*—an eye for an eye, a life for a life. The problems of justice which it raises are considered in the chapter on PUNISHMENT.

JUSTICE IS SOMETIMES divided into economic and political according as, on the one hand, fairness or equalization concerns the kind of goods which originate with the expenditure of labor, or as, on the other hand, it involves the status of men in the state. The difference between these two modes of justice seems to be largely dependent upon the kind of transaction to which the principle of justice is applied. The forms of justice—the two modes of equality or fairness—appear to remain the same. The special problems of economic justice are more fully examined in the chapters on LABOR and WEALTH, as the special problems of political justice are treated in greater detail in all the chapters dealing with the state, government, and the several forms of government. Here we shall consider only the generalities, and especially those which touch the main issues in the theory of justice.

Though Marx does not engage in the controversy over natural justice, he seems to take the side which looks upon justice as a universal standard that does not derive from, but rather measures, human institutions. Something like "from each according to his ability, to each according to his needs"—or, in another variant of the maxim, "to each according to his deserts"—seems to be for Marx the maxim of a just economy, stated without argument as if a principle self-evident in the very nature of the case. So, too, in his consideration of the exploitation of labor in its various historic forms—chattel slavery, feudal serfdom or agrarian peonage, and what he calls "wage slavery" under industrial capitalism— Marx assumes that a clear and unquestionable principle of justice is being violated when the goods produced by the labor of one man enrich another disproportionately to that other's contribution or desert. Such basic words in *Capital* as "expropriation," "exploitation," and "unearned increment" seem never to be simply terms of description, but of evaluation. Each implies a specific injustice.

The labor theory of value, the origin of which he attributes to Adam Smith, Marx conceives as solving a problem in justice which Aristotle stated but did not solve. He refers to the chapter in the book on justice in Aristotle's *Nicomachean Ethics,* in which Aristotle discusses money as a medium to facilitate the exchange of commodities. Money permits so many units of one commodity to be equated with so many units of another. But the problem is how to determine equivalents in the exchange of unlike things, apparently incommensurable in value. How can the value of a house be commensurated with the value of a bed, so that an equality in value can be set up between a house and a certain number of beds? Abstracting entirely from considerations of supply and demand, the determination of a just exchange or a fair price requires an equation of comparable quantities.

Aristotle tells us, Marx points out, why he found the problem insoluble. "It was the absence of any concept of value. What is that equal something, that common substance, which admits of the value of beds being expressed by a house? Such a thing, in truth, cannot exist, says Aristotle. And why not? Compared with beds, the house does represent something equal to them, in so far as it represents what is really equal, both in the beds and the house. And that is—human labor . . . The brilliancy of Aristotle's genius is shown by this alone, that he discovered, in the expression of the value of commodities, a relation of equality. The peculiar conditions of the society in which he lived alone prevented him from discovering what, 'in truth,' was at the bottom of this equality."

We cannot help noting the character of the labor theory of value as an analysis not only of justice in exchange, but also of just compensation to labor for its productivity. The principle of justice here employed seems to be the same as that underlying the medieval condemnation of interest as unjust or usurious, or the later effort to discriminate between just and unjust interest rates. The principle even seems to be implicitly involved in Smith's distinction between real or natural price and the market price which fluctuates with variations in supply and demand.

When the economic problem is one of distribution rather than exchange, another standard of fairness—the proportional equality of distributive justice—becomes relevant.

The assumption of a primitive possession of all things in common, especially land and its resources, is the background against which such thinkers as Aquinas and Hobbes, Locke and Rousseau, Montesquieu and Hegel, Smith and Marx consider the origin or justification of private property. Insofar as the question is one of justification, rather than of actual historic origin, the division of common holdings into privately held shares is a matter of justice in distribution. In the opinion of many, a just distribution would recognize that labor alone entitles a man to claim possession of the raw materials improved by his work and of the finished products of that work.

The other face of the problem assumes an existing inequitable distribution. It is then asked how this can be rectified by some method of redistributing wealth more justly; or it is proposed that the whole system of private property be reformed in the direction of public ownership of the means of production, as the basis for a just distribution of the fruits of human productivity.

THE CONNECTION which has become evident between justice and both liberty and equality does not imply that these three basic notions are simply coordinate with one another. On the contrary, equality seems to be the root of justice, at least insofar as it is identified with fairness in exchange or distribution; and justice in turn seems to be the foundation, not the consequence of liberty.

The condemnation of slavery confirms this observation. If slavery were not unjust, the slave would have no right to be free. The injustice of treating a man as a chattel ultimately rests on the equality between him and his master as human beings. His right to the same liberty which his master enjoys stems from that equality. The justice of equal treatment for equals recognizes that right and sets him free. Aristotle's theory of natural slavery is based on a supposition of natural inequality which is thought to justify the enslavement of some men and the freedom of others. Whenever slavery is justified or a criminal is justly imprisoned, neither the slave nor the criminal is regarded as deprived of any liberty to which he has a right.

It would seem to follow that if a man is justly treated, he has all the liberty which he deserves. From the opposite angle, J. S. Mill argues that a man is entitled to all the liberty that he can use justly, that is, use without injuring his fellowman or the common good. More liberty than this would be license. When one man encroaches on the rights of others, or inflicts on them "any loss or damage not justified by his own rights," he is overstepping the bounds of liberty and is, according to Mill, a fit object "of moral reprobation, and, in grave cases, of moral retribution and punishment."

The various relations of liberty to justice, and of both to law, are considered in the chapters on LIBERTY and LAW. All the writers who make the distinction between government by law and government by men fundamental in their political theory also plainly express a preference for the former on grounds both of justice and liberty.

Absolute government, which violates the equality of men, unjustly subjects them, even when it does not through tyranny enslave them. The benevolence of the despot ruling for the common good has one aspect of justice, but there are other aspects of political justice which can be achieved, as Mill points out, only if "despotism consents not to be despotism . . . and allows the general business of government to go on as if the people really governed themselves." The greater justice of constitutional government consists in its

granting to men who deserve the equal freedom of equals, the equality of citizenship—an equality under the law which levels those citizens who happen to hold public office with those in private life.

The major controversy over the several forms of constitutional government turns on a third point of justice. The defenders of democracy and oligarchy each contend that equalities or inequalities in birth or wealth justify a broader or a narrower franchise. It is Mill again who insists that nothing less than universal suffrage provides a just distribution of the political status of citizenship, and that "it is a personal injustice to withhold from anyone, unless for the prevention of greater evils, the ordinary privilege of having his voice reckoned in the disposal of affairs in which he has the same interest as other people."

Of the three points of justice which seem to be involved in the comparison of forms of government, only the first (concerned with whether political power is exercised for the common good or the ruler's private interests) is not recognizable as a matter of distributive justice. Yet even here the requirement that the ruler should treat the ruled as ends rather than as means derives from a fundamental equality between ruler and ruled. The injustice of tyranny lies in a violation of this equality.

ONE MEANING of justice remains to be considered. It is related to all the foregoing considerations of economic and political justice, of just constitutions, just laws, and just acts. It is that meaning of justice in which a man is said to be just—to possess a just will, to be just in character, to have the virtue of justice. Here difference in theory reflects the difference between those moralists for whom virtue is the basic conception, and those who, like Kant, emphasize duty or who, like Mill, reduce the propensity for justice to a moral sentiment. But even among those who treat justice as a virtue, there seems to be a profound difference in analysis.

For Aristotle, the virtue of justice, like other moral virtues, is a habit of conduct. It differs from courage and temperance in that it is a habit of action, not of the passions. It is not a rationally moderated tendency of the emotions with regard to things pleasant and painful. It is that settled inclination of the will "in virtue of which the just man is said to be a doer, by choice, of that which is just, and one who will distribute either between himself and another or between two others not so as to give more of what is desirable to himself and less to his neighbor (and conversely with what is harmful), but so as to give what is equal in accordance with proportion."

Another difference between justice and the other moral virtues is that courageous and temperate acts are performed only by courageous and temperate men, whereas an act which is outwardly just can be done by an unjust man as well as by a just one.

Fair dealing in the exchange or distribution of goods, determined by objective relations of equality, is the substance of justice as a special virtue; but there is in addition what Aristotle calls "general" as opposed to "special" justice. Aristotle calls the general virtue of justice "complete virtue," because "he who possesses it can exercise his virtue not only in himself but towards his neighbor also." It embraces all the moral virtues insofar as their acts are directed to the good of others.

"Justice in this sense," he goes on to say, "is not a part of virtue, but virtue entire"; whereas special justice—the justice of distributions and exchanges—is merely a part of moral virtue, merely one particular virtue. Yet special justice, no less than general justice, is a social virtue. The difference between the way each directs actions toward the good of others seems to be like the difference between the lawful and the fair, or the difference between the common good of society as a whole and the good of other individuals.

The thoroughly social conception of justice in Aristotle may have some parallel in the meaning of justice in Plato's *Gorgias* (where the question is whether it is better to suffer than to do injustice), but the definition of justice as a virtue in *The Republic* does not express or develop the social reference. In the state as in the soul, justice is a fitting disposition or harmonious order—of the several classes of men in the state, of the several virtues in the soul. The just state is not described as acting justly toward other states, nor is the just man pictured as a doer of good deeds. Rather the picture of the soul in which justice resides is one of interior peace or spiritual health—the well-being of happiness.

"Justice," Socrates declares, is concerned "not with the outward man, but with the inward, which is the true self and concernment of man: for the just man does not permit the several elements within him to interfere with one another, or any of them to do the work of others—he sets in order his own inner life, and is his own master and his own law, and at peace with himself." His is "one entirely temperate and perfectly adjusted nature."

This conception of justice bears a certain resemblance to what the Christian theologians mean by "original justice." The perfect disposition of Adam's soul in a state of supernatural grace consisted, according to Aquinas, in "his reason being subject to God, the lower powers to reason, and the body to the soul—the first subjection being the cause of both the second and the third, since while reason was subject to God, the lower powers remained subject to reason." The justice of man's obedience to God seems to be inseparable from the injustice internal to his own members.

The way in which justice is discussed in the *Gorgias* may similarly be inseparable from the way it is defined in *The Republic*. Certainly Callicles will never understand why it is always better to suffer injustice than to do it, unless Socrates succeeds in explaining to him that the man who is wronged suffers injury in body or in external things, while the man who does wrong injures his own soul by destroying what, to Socrates, is its greatest good—that equable temper from which all fitting actions flow.

43

Knowledge

INTRODUCTION

KNOWLEDGE, like being, is a term of comprehensive scope. Its comprehensiveness is, in a way, correlative with that of being. The only thing which cannot be an object of knowledge or opinion, which cannot be thought about in any way except negatively, is that which has no being of any sort—in short, *nothing*. Not all things may be knowable to us, but even the skeptic who severely limits or completely doubts man's power to know is usually willing to admit that things beyond man's knowledge are in themselves knowable. Everyone except Berkeley would agree that the surfaces of bodies which we cannot see are not, for that reason, in themselves invisible.

The consideration of knowledge extends, therefore, to all things knowable, to all kinds of knowers, to all the modes of knowledge, and all the methods of knowing. So extensive an array of topics exceeds the possibility of treatment in a single chapter and requires this chapter to be related to many others.

The Cross-References which follow the References indicate the other chapters which deal with particulars we cannot consider here. For example, the nature of history, science, philosophy, and theology, and their distinction from one another, are treated in the chapters devoted to those subjects. So, too, the chapters on metaphysics, mathematics, physics, mechanics, and medicine deal with the characteristics and relations of these special sciences. The psychological factors in knowing—the faculties of sense and mind, of memory and imagination, the nature of experience and reasoning—also have their own chapters. Still other chapters deal with the logical elements of knowledge, such as idea and judgment, definition, hypothesis, principle, induction, and reasoning, logic and dialectic.

THE PROGRAM which Locke sets himself in his essay *Concerning Human Understanding* is often taken to include the basic questions about knowledge. His purpose, he tells us, is "to inquire into the original, certainty, and extent of human knowledge, together with the grounds and degrees of belief, opinion, and assent." Two other matters, not explicitly mentioned by Locke in his opening pages, assume central importance in the fourth book of his essay. One is the question about the nature of knowledge itself. The other concerns the kinds of knowledge.

It may be thought that certain questions are prior to these and all others. Is knowledge possible? Can we know anything? The man the skeptic challenges is one who thinks that knowledge is attainable and who may even claim to possess knowledge of some sort. But the issue between the skeptic and his adversaries cannot be simply formulated. Its formulation depends in part upon the meaning given knowledge and the various things with which it is sometimes contrasted, such as belief and opinion, or ignorance and error. It also depends in part on the meaning of truth and probability. It would seem, therefore, that some consideration of the nature of knowledge should precede the examination of the claims concerning knowledge which provoke skeptical denials.

The theory of knowledge is a field of many disputes. Most of the major varieties of doctrine or analysis are represented in the tradition of the great books. But the fact that knowledge involves a relationship between a knower and a known seems to go unquestioned. William James expresses this insight, perhaps more dogmatically than some would allow, in the statement that knowledge "is a thoroughgoing dualism. It supposes two elements, mind knowing and thing known ... Neither gets out of itself or into the other, neither in any way *is* the other, neither *makes* the other. They just stand face to face in a common world, and one simply knows, or is known unto, its counterpart." This remains true even when attention is turned to the special case of knowledge about knowledge or the knower knowing himself. The mind's examination of itself simply makes the mind an object to be known as well as a knower.

This suggests a second point about the nature of knowledge which seems to be undisputed. If knowledge relates a knower to a known, then what is somehow possessed when a person claims to have knowledge, is the object known. It does not seem possible for anyone to say that he knows something without meaning that he *has* that thing *in mind*. "Some sort of signal," James writes, "must be given by the thing to the mind's brain, or the knowing will not occur—we find as a matter of fact that the mere *existence* of a thing outside the brain is not a sufficient cause for our knowing it: it must strike the brain in some way, as well as be there, to be known." What is not in any way present to or represented in the mind is not known in any of the various senses of the word "know." What the mind cannot reach to and somehow grasp cannot be known. The words which are common synonyms for knowing—"apprehending" and "comprehending"—convey this sense that knowledge somehow takes hold of and surrounds its object.

That knowledge is a kind of possession occasions the comparisons which have been made between knowledge and love. The ancients observed that likeness and union are involved in both. Plato, for example, suggests in the *Symposium* that both the knower and the lover strive to become one with their object. "Love is also a philosopher," Diotima tells Socrates, and, as "a lover of wisdom," the philosopher is also a lover.

With regard to some objects, love and knowledge are almost inseparable. To know them is to love them. But this does not hold for all objects, nor does the inseparability of knowledge and love in certain cases prevent their analytic distinction in all. Like is known by like, but unlikes attract each other. Furthermore, according to one theory of knowledge, expounded by Aquinas, the knower is satisfied to possess an image of the thing to be known. This image provides the likeness through which knowledge occurs; and thus, Aquinas writes, "the idea of the thing understood is in the one who understands." The lover, on the other hand, is "inclined to the thing itself, as existing in itself." He seeks to be united with it directly. The nobility or baseness of the object known does not affect the knower as the character of the object loved affects the lover. This understanding of the difference between knowledge and love leads Aquinas to say that "to love God is better than to know God; but, on the contrary, to know corporeal things is better than to love them."

The principle of likeness between knower and known does not go undisputed. On the contrary, the opposite views here form one of the basic issues about the nature of knowledge. The issue is whether the thing known is actually present to the knower, existing in the mind or consciousness exactly as it exists in itself; or whether the thing is represented in the mind by a likeness of itself, through which the mind knows it. In this view, the mode of existence of the thing outside the mind is different from the way in which its representative exists in the mind.

Berkeley, at one extreme, identifies being and being known. "As to what is said of the absolute existence of unthinking things without any relation to their being perceived, that seems perfectly unintelligible," he writes. "Their *esse* is *percipi,* nor is it possible they should have any existence, out of the minds or thinking things which perceive them."

At the other extreme are those like Kant for whom the thing in itself is unknowable precisely because there can be no resemblance between the phenomenal order of objects represented under the conditions of experience and the noumenal order of the unconditioned. "All conceptions of things in themselves," he writes, "must be referred to intuitions, and with us men these can never be other than sensible, and hence can never enable us to know objects as things in themselves but only as appearances . . . The unconditioned," he adds, "can never be found in this chain of appearances."

In between these extremes there are those who agree that things exist apart from being known without ceasing to be knowable, but who nevertheless differ with respect to whether the thing exists in reality in the same way that it exists in the mind. The several forms of idealism and realism, distinguished in the chapter on IDEA, mark the range of traditional differences in the discussion of this difficult problem.

FOR ANY THEORY of what knowledge is there is a distinction between knowledge and ignorance—between having or not having something in mind. Nor does anyone confuse ignorance and error. The mind in error claims to know that of which, in fact, it is ignorant. This, as Socrates points out in the *Meno*, makes it easier to teach a person aware of his ignorance than a person in error; for the latter, supposing himself to know, resists the teacher. Hence getting a person to acknowledge ignorance is often the indispensable first step in teaching.

But though the difference between knowledge and ignorance and that between ignorance and error seems to be commonly understood, it does not follow that everybody similarly agrees upon the difference between knowledge and error. This much is agreed, that to know is to possess the truth about something, whereas to err is to be deceived by falsity mistaken for truth. The disagreement of the philosophers begins, however, when the meaning of truth and falsity is examined.

Truth is one thing for those who insist upon some similarity between the thing known and that by which it is known or represented in the mind. It is another for those who think that knowledge can be gained without the media-

tion of images or representations. In the first case, truth will consist in some kind of correspondence between what the mind thinks or understands and the reality it tries to know. In the other, truth will be equivalent to consistency among the mind's own ideas.

The examination of this fundamental disagreement is reserved for the chapter on TRUTH. Here the identification of knowing with having the truth calls for the consideration of another distinction, first made by Plato. In his language, as in that of Aristotle and others, it is the difference between knowledge and opinion. Sometimes, as with Locke, a similar distinction is made in terms of knowledge and judgment; sometimes it is made in terms of knowledge and belief; sometimes in terms of adequate and inadequate, or certain and probable, knowledge.

The difference between these opposites, unlike that between knowledge and error, is not a matter of truth and falsity. There is such a thing as "right opinion," according to Socrates, and it is "not less useful than knowledge." Considering the truth so far as it affects action, Socrates claims that the man with right opinion "will be just as good a guide if he thinks the truth, as he who knows the truth." The difference between right opinion and knowledge is here expressed by the contrast between the words "thinks" and "knows." It does not consist in the truth of the conclusion, but in the way that conclusion has been reached or is held by the mind.

The trouble with right opinion as compared with knowledge, Socrates explains, is that it lacks stability and permanence. Right opinions are useful "while they abide with us . . . but they run away out of the human soul and do not remain long, and therefore they are not of much value until they are fastened by the tie of the cause"—or, in other words, until they are fixed in the mind by the reasons on which they are grounded. "When they are bound," Socrates declares, "they have the nature of knowledge and . . . they are abiding."

At this point in his conversation with Meno, Socrates makes the unusual confession that "there are not many things which I profess to know, but this is most certainly one of them," namely, that "knowledge differs from true opinion." It may be that Socrates claims to know so little because he regards knowledge as involving so much more than simply having the truth, as the man of right opinion has it. In addition to having the truth, knowledge consists in seeing the reason why it is true.

This criterion can be interpreted to mean that a proposition which is neither self-evident nor demonstrated expresses opinion rather than knowledge. Even when it happens to be true, the opinion is qualified by some degree of doubt or some estimate of probability and counterprobability. In contrast, when the mind has adequate grounds for its judgment, when it knows that it knows and why, it has the certainty of knowledge.

For some writers, such as Plato, certitude is as inseparable from knowledge as truth is. To speak of "a false knowledge as well as a true" seems to him impossible; and "uncertain knowledge" is as self-contradictory a phrase as "false knowledge."

Others use the word "knowledge" more loosely to cover both adequate and inadequate knowledge, the probable as well as the certain. They make a distinction within the sphere of knowledge that is equivalent to the distinction between knowledge and opinion.

Spinoza, for example, distinguishes three kinds of knowledge. He groups the perception of individual things through the bodily senses, which he calls "knowledge from vague experience," with knowledge "from signs" which depends on ideas formed by the memory and imagination. "These two ways of looking at things," he writes, "I shall hereafter call knowledge of the first kind—opinion or imagination." In contrast, that which is derived "from our possessing common notions and adequate ideas of the properties of things," he calls "reason and knowledge of the second kind."

The third kind, which he calls "intuitive science," is that sort of knowing which "advances from an adequate idea of certain attributes of God to the adequate knowledge of the essence of things." Knowledge of the second and third kinds, he maintains, "is necessarily true." That there can be falsity in the first kind, and only there, indicates that it is not genuinely knowledge at all, but what other writers would insist upon calling "opinion."

The several meanings of the word "belief" are determined by these distinctions. Sometimes belief is associated with opinion, sometimes with knowledge, and sometimes it is regarded as an intermediate state of mind. But in any of these meanings belief stands in contrast to make-believe, and this contrast has a bearing on knowledge and opinion as well. To know or to opine puts the mind in some relation to the real or actual rather than the merely possible, and subjects it to the criteria of truth and falsity. The fanciful or imaginary belongs to the realm of the possible (or even the impossible) and the mind in imagining is fancy-free—free from the restraints and restrictions of truth and reality.

SKEPTICISM IN ITS most extreme form takes the position that there is nothing true or false. But even those who, like Montaigne, deny certitude with respect to everything except matters of religious faith, do not go this far.

In his *Apology for Raymond Sebond* he concedes that if opinions are weighed as more or less probable, their truth or falsity is implied— at least as being the limit which an increasing probability or improbability approaches. Referring to ancient skeptics of the Academic school, he comments on the fact that they acknowledged "some things were more probable than others"—as, for example, that snow is white rather than black. The more extreme skeptics, the Pyrrhonians, he points out, were bolder and also more consistent. They refused to incline toward one proposition more than toward another, for to do so, Montaigne declares, is to recognize "some more apparent truth in this one than in that." How can men "let themselves be inclined toward the likeness of truth," he asks, "if they know not the truth? How do they know the semblance of that whose essence they do not know?"

In this respect Montaigne's own skepticism tends to be of the more moderate variety, since, in the realm of action at least, he would admit the need for judgments of probability. But in all other respects, he takes a firm skeptical stand that nothing is self-evident, nothing has been proved. The contradictory of every-thing has been asserted or argued by someone. "There cannot be first principles for men," he writes, "unless the Divinity has revealed them; all the rest—beginning, middle, and end—is nothing but dreams and smoke . . . every hu-man presupposition and every enunciation has as much authority as another . . . The impres-sion of certainty is a certain token of folly and extreme uncertainty."

The skeptical extreme is represented in the great books only through references to it for the purpose of refutation. Aristotle in the *Metaphysics,* for example, reports the position of those who say that all propositions are true or that all propositions are false, and who therefore deny the principle of contradiction and with it the distinction between true and false. But if all propositions are true, then the proposition "Some propositions are false" is also true; if all propositions are false, the proposition "All propositions are false" is also false. The skeptic may reply, of course, that he is not checked by arguments which try to make him contradict himself, for he does not mind contradicting himself. To this there is only one answer, which is not to argue with the skeptic any further.

From the skeptic's point of view his po-sition is irrefutable so long as he does not allow himself to accept any of the standards by which refutation can be effected. From his opponent's point of view, complete skepticism is self-refuting because if the skeptic says any-thing definite at all, he appears to have some knowledge or at least to hold one opinion in preference to another. His only choice is to remain silent. If he insists upon making state-ments in defiance of self-contradiction, his opponent can do nothing but walk away.

"It may seem a very extravagant attempt of the skeptics to destroy *reason* by argument and ratiocination," Hume writes, "yet this is the grand scope of all their enquiries and disputes." He has in mind the excessive skep-ticism, or *Pyrrhonism,* from which he tries to distinguish a mitigated and beneficial form of skepticism. Referring to Berkeley's arguments against the independent reality of matter or bodies, Hume says their effect is skeptical,

despite Berkeley's professed intention to the contrary. That his arguments are skeptical "ap-pears from this, *that they admit of no answer and produce no conviction.* Their only effect is to cause that momentary amazement and irresolution and confusion, which is the result of skepticism."

Here and elsewhere, as in his comment on Descartes's skeptical method of doubting ev-erything which can be doubted, Hume does not seem to think that excessive skepticism is refutable or even false. But it is impractical. "The great subverter of *Pyrrhonism* or the ex-cessive principles of skepticism," he says, "is action, and employment, and the occupations of life." Extreme skepticism becomes unten-able in thought the moment thought must face the choices of life and take some responsibility for action.

There is, however, "a more *mitigated* skep-ticism or *academical* philosophy which may be both durable and useful." This, according to Hume, consists in becoming "sensible of the strange infirmities of human understanding," and consequently in "the limitation of our en-quiries to such subjects as are best adapted to the narrow capacity of human understanding."

His own view of the extent and certainty of human knowledge seems to him to exemplify such mitigated skepticism in operation. The only objects with respect to which demon-stration is possible are quantity and number. Mathematics has the certitude of knowledge, but it deals only with relations between ideas, not with what Hume calls "matters of fact and existence." Such matters "are evidently inca-pable of demonstration." This is the sphere of "moral certainty," which is not a genuine certainty, but only a degree of probability *sufficient for action.* Probabilities are the best that experimental reasoning or inquiry about matters of fact can achieve. If probability is characteristic of opinion rather than knowl-edge, then we can have nothing better than opinion concerning real existences.

G. H. Hardy seems to agree with Hume on the distinction between mathematical knowl-edge and knowledge of reality when he notes that "a chair may be a collection of whirling electrons, or an idea in the mind of God: each of these accounts of it may have its merits, but neither conforms at all closely to the suggestions of common sense."

THE DIAMETRICAL opposite to the extreme of skepticism would have to be a dogmatism which placed no objects beyond the reach of human knowledge, which made no distinction between degrees of knowability and admitted equal certitude in all matters. Like excessive skepticism this extreme is not a position actually held in the great books. All the great thinkers who have considered the problem of human knowledge have set limits to man's capacity for knowledge. They have placed certain objects beyond man's power to apprehend at all, or have distinguished between those which he can apprehend in some inadequate fashion, but cannot comprehend. They have indicated other objects concerning which his grasp is adequate and certain.

They all adopt a "mitigated skepticism"—to use Hume's phrase—if this can be taken to mean avoiding the extremes of saying that nothing is knowable at all and that everything is equally knowable. But they differ in the criteria they employ to set the limits of knowledge and to distinguish between the areas of certainty and probability. Consequently they differ in their determination of the knowability of certain types of objects, such as God or the infinite, substance or cause, matter or spirit, the real or the ideal, the self or the thing in itself.

For example, Plato and Aristotle agree that knowledge must be separated from opinion and even appeal to certain common principles in making that separation; but they do not define the scope of knowledge in the same way, as is indicated by their disagreement about the knowability of sensible things. Nor do Descartes and Locke, Francis Bacon and Spinoza, Hume and Kant agree about the knowability of God or of the soul or about the conditions any object must meet in order to be knowable. All alike proceed from a desire to be critical. Each criticizes what other men have proposed as knowledge and each proposes a new method by which the pursuit of knowledge will be safeguarded from illusory hopes or endless controversy.

In this last respect the moderns depart most radically from their medieval and ancient predecessors. At all times men have been interested in examining knowledge itself as well as in exercising their powers to know. But in the earlier phase of the tradition knowledge about knowledge does not seem to take precedence over all other inquiries or to be prerequisite to them. On the contrary, the ancients proceed as if the study of knowledge necessarily presupposed the existence of knowledge. With them the examination takes place because the mind is essentially reflexive rather than for reasons of self-criticism. But beginning with Descartes's *Discourse on the Method,* in which a method of universal doubt is proposed to clear the ground before the foundations of the sciences can be laid, the consideration of knowing is put before any attempt to know.

Sometimes, as with Descartes and Bacon, the emphasis is upon a new method which will at last establish knowledge on a firm footing or advance learning. Sometimes, as with Locke and Hume, attention is given first of all to the faculty of understanding itself.

"If we can find out," says Locke, "how far the understanding can extend its views, how far it has faculties to attain certainty, and in what cases it can only judge and guess, we may learn to content ourselves with what is attainable by us in this state . . . When we know our own strength, we shall the better know what to undertake with hopes of success; and when we have well surveyed the powers of our own minds, and made some estimate of what we may expect from them, we shall not be inclined either to sit still, and not set our thoughts to work at all, in despair of knowing anything; nor, on the other side, question everything, and disclaim all knowledge, because some things are not to be understood."

Hume also proposes that a study of human understanding precede everything else, to "show from an exact analysis of its powers and capacity" what subjects it is or is not fitted to investigate. "There is a truth and falsehood in all propositions on this subject which lie not beyond the compass of human understanding." No one can doubt that a science of the mind—or knowledge about knowing—is possible unless he entertains "such a skepticism as is entirely subversive of all speculations, and even action."

Disagreeing with the principles of Locke and Hume, as well as with their conclusions, Kant does approve the priority they give to the question of the possibility of knowing certain objects. To proceed otherwise, as Kant charges most other philosophers with doing, is dogmatism. The use of the word "critique" in the title of Kant's three major works signifies his intention to construct a critical philosophy which does not presume that "it is possible to achieve anything in metaphysic without a previous criticism of pure reason." He does not object to what he calls "the dogmatical procedure of reason" in the development of science, but only after reason's self-criticism has determined just how far reason can go. For Kant, as for Bacon, dogmatism and skepticism are the opposite excesses which only a critical method can avoid. Russell attributes to Kant his "having made evident the philosophical importance of the theory of knowledge"; and also his "having perceived that we have *a priori* knowledge which is not purely 'analytic', i.e. such that the opposite would be self-contradictory."

These two different approaches to the theory of knowledge seem to result in different conclusions concerning the nature and scope of human knowledge. Those who begin with the established sciences and merely inquire into their foundations and methods appear to end with unqualified confidence in man's ability to know. Those who make the inquiry into the foundations and methods of science a necessary preparation for the development of the sciences tend for the most part to set narrower boundaries to the area of valid knowledge. The two approaches also affect the way in which the various kinds of knowledge are distinguished and compared.

There are two sorts of comparison involved in the classification of kinds of knowledge. One is a comparison of human knowledge with divine, or with angelic knowledge and the knowledge of brute animals. The other is a comparison of the parts or modes of human knowledge according to such criteria as the objects to be known, the faculties engaged in the process of knowing, and the manner of their operation. Though made separately, those two comparisons are seldom independent of one another. As the nature of man is conceived in relation to other beings, superior or inferior to himself, his faculties will be rated accordingly, and his power as a knower will suggest the methods or means available to him for knowing.

Aquinas, for example, attributes to man the kind of knowledge appropriate to his station in the hierarchy of beings. Man is superior to the brutes because he has a faculty of reason in addition to the faculties of sense and imagination which he shares with them. Man is inferior to purely spiritual beings—the angels and God—because, since he is corporeal, his intellect cannot function independently of his bodily senses and imagination. Unlike the angels and God, he is not a purely intellectual being.

Accordingly, the essential characteristics of human knowledge are, first, that it is always both sensitive and intellectual, never merely sense perception as with the brutes or pure intellectual intuition as with the angels; second, that its appropriate object is the physical world of sensible, material things, with respect to which the senses enable man to know the existence of individuals, while the intellect apprehends their universal natures; and, finally, that the way in which the human mind knows the natures of things is abstractive and discursive, for the intellect draws its concepts from sense and imagination and proceeds therefrom by means of judgment and reasoning.

This analysis denies innate ideas. It denies man's power to apprehend ideas intuitively or to use them intuitively in the apprehension of things. It can find no place for a distinction between *a priori* and *a posteriori* knowledge, since sense perception and rational activity contribute elements to every act of knowing. It affirms that knowledge is primarily of real existence, not of the relations between ideas; but it does not limit human knowledge to the changing temporal things of the material universe. Though these are the objects man is able to know with greatest adequacy, he can also know something of the existence and nature of immaterial and eternal beings.

Yet, according to Aquinas, even when man's knowledge rises above the realm of experienceable things, it is obtained by the same natural processes and involves the cooperation of the senses with reason. The theologian does, however, distinguish sharply between knowledge gained through man's own efforts and knowledge received through divine revelation. In addition to all knowledge acquired by the natural exercise of his faculties, man may be elevated by the supernatural gift of knowledge—the wisdom of a faith surpassing reason.

The foregoing summary illustrates, in the case of one great doctrine, the connection between an analysis of the kinds of knowledge and a theory of the nature and faculties of man in relation to all other things. There is no point in this analysis which is not disputed by someone—by Plato or Augustine, Descartes, Spinoza, or Locke, by Hume, Kant, or James. There are many points on which others agree—not only Aristotle and Bacon, but even Augustine, Descartes, and Locke.

These agreements or disagreements about the kinds of knowledge, or the scope of human knowledge, its faculties, and its methods, seldom occur or are intelligible except in the wider context of agreements and disagreements in theology and metaphysics, psychology and logic. Hence most of the matters considered under the heading "kinds of knowledge" receive special consideration in other chapters. The Cross-References should enable the reader to examine the presuppositions or context of the materials assembled here.

THE CULT OF IGNORANCE receives little or no attention in the tradition of the great books. Even those who, like Rousseau, glorify the innocence of the primitives, or who, like Erasmus, satirize the folly so often admixed with human wisdom and the foibles attending the advance of learning, do not seriously question the ancient saying that all men by nature desire to know. Nor is it generally doubted that knowledge is good; that its possession

contributes to the happiness of men and the welfare of the state; that its pursuit by the individual and its dissemination in a society should be facilitated by education, by the support and freedom of scholars and scientists, and by every device which can assist men in communicating what they know to one another.

But knowledge is not valued by all for the same reason. That knowledge is useful to the productive artist, to the statesman, to the legislator, and to the individual in the conduct of his life, seems to be assumed in discussions of the applications of science in the various arts, in the consideration of statecraft, and in the analysis of virtue. In this last connection, the problem is not whether knowledge is morally useful, but whether knowledge of good and evil is identical with virtue so that sin and vice result from error or ignorance.

If there is a negative opinion here, it consists in saying that knowledge is not enough. To know is not to do. Something more than knowledge is required for acting well.

The more radical dispute about the value of knowledge concerns the goodness of knowledge for its own sake, without any regard to its technical or moral utility. Is the contemplation of the truth an ultimate end, or does the goodness of knowledge always consist in its power to effect results in the mastery of nature and the guidance of conduct? The utility of knowledge is seldom denied by those who make speculative wisdom and theoretical science good in themselves, even the highest goods, quite apart from any use to which they may be put. The contrary position, however, does not admit the special value of contemplation or the separation of truth from utility. To those who say that "the contemplation of truth is more dignified and exalted than any utility or extent of effects," Bacon replies that "truth and utility are perfectly identical, and the effects are more of value as pledges of truth than from the benefit they confer on men."

How knowledge and action are related is one question; how knowledge itself is divided into the speculative and practical is quite another. Bacon, for example, insists upon the necessity of distinguishing the speculative and

practical branches of natural philosophy—
concerned with "the search after causes and
the production of effects." Unlike Aristotle
and Kant he does not use the word "practical"
for the kind of knowledge which is contained
in such sciences as ethics or politics, but only
for the applied sciences or technology. Ethics
and politics fall under what he calls "civil
philosophy."

Despite these differences in language, the
way in which Bacon divides the whole sphere
of knowledge closely resembles Aristotle's tripartite classification of the sciences as theoretical, productive (or technical), and practical
(or moral); and, no less, a similar threefold division by Kant. But Kant and Aristotle (and, it
should be added, Aquinas) give a more elaborate analysis of these three types of knowledge,
especially with regard to the principles appropriate to each, the nature of the judgments and
reasoning by which they are developed, and
the character and criteria of their truth.

We owe to Russell an important distinction
that, surprisingly, was not made by any of
his predecessors. It is the distinction between
knowledge by acquaintance and knowledge by
description. "When, for example, we make a
statement about Julius Caesar," Russell points
out, "it is plain that Julius Caesar himself is not
before our minds, since we are not acquainted
with him. We have in mind some *description*
of Julius Caesar: 'the man who was assassi-
nated on the Ides of March', 'the founder of
the Roman Empire'. " Russell goes on to say
that "the chief importance of knowledge by
description is that it enables us to pass beyond
the limits of our private experience." Nevertheless, "what is known by description is
ultimately reducible to knowledge concerning
what is known by acquaintance."

44

Labor

INTRODUCTION

MEN have dreamed of a golden age in the past when the world was young and everything needed for the support of life existed in profusion. Earth, Lucretius writes, once brought forth

Vineyards and shining harvests, pastures, arbors,
And all this now our very utmost toil
Can hardly care for, we wear down our strength
Whether in oxen or in men, we dull
The edges of our ploughshares, and in return
Our fields turn mean and stingy, underfed.

When the aged plowman "compares the present to the past," Lucretius adds, he realizes that "the past was better, infinitely so,/His father's lot was fortunate," for he lived in the time of earth's plenty.

This ancient myth of a golden age has sometimes taken the form, as with Rousseau, of an idealization of primitive society, uncorrupted by civilization, in which an easy, almost effortless, existence corresponded to the simplicity of man's needs. Rousseau pictures a situation in which "the produce of the earth furnished [man] with all he needed, and instinct told him how to use it," so that "singing and dancing, the true offspring of love and leisure, became the amusement, or rather the occupation of men and women assembled together with nothing else to do."

In our own day, industrial utopias have been projected into a future made free from toil by the adequacy of machines or the efficiency of atomic energy. Long before the industrial era, Aristotle envisioned, as a supposition contrary to fact, a society built upon labor-saving machines. "If every instrument could accomplish its own work," he writes, if it could obey or anticipate commands, if "the shuttle would weave . . . without a hand to guide it, the chief

workmen would not want servants, nor masters slaves."

In all these conceptions of a better life, labor is eliminated or reduced. The implication seems to be that the labor required for the maintenance of all historic societies is an affliction, a drudgery, a crushing burden which deforms the lives of many, if not all. The pains of toil do not belong to human life by any necessity of human nature, but rather through the accident of external circumstances which might be other than they are. "Work became indispensable," according to Rousseau, only when "property was introduced," and then "vast forests became smiling fields, which man had to water with the sweat of his brow." It was the result of "some fatal accident, which, for the public good, should never have happened." Man might have realized his nature more surely and richly if, like the lilies of the field, he neither toiled nor spun.

The contrary view would maintain that work is not a curse but a blessing, filling man's hours usefully, turning to service energies which would otherwise be wasted or misspent in idleness or mischief. The sinfulness of sloth implies the virtue of work. The principle of activity, according to Hegel, whereby "the workman has to perform for his subsistence," gives man a dignity which "consists in his depending entirely on his diligence, conduct, and intelligence for the supply of his wants. In direct contravention of this principle" are "pauperism, laziness, inactivity."

It is even suggested that useful occupations save men from a boredom they fear more than the pain of labor, as evidenced by the variety of amusements and diversions they invent or frantically pursue to occupy themselves when work is finished. The satisfactions of labor are as peculiarly human as its burdens. Not merely to keep alive, but to keep his self-respect, man is obliged to work.

"In the morning when thou risest unwilling," the emperor Marcus Aurelius tells himself, "let this thought be present—I am rising to the work of a human being. Why, then, am I dissatisfied if I am going to do the things for which I exist and for which I was brought into the world? Or have I been made for this, to lie in the bed-clothes and keep myself warm? But this is more pleasant. Dost thou exist, then, to take thy pleasure, and not at all for action and exertion?"

The perspectives of theology give still another view of labor. It is not an accidental misfortune which men may some day be able to correct. But neither is it a blessing nor the thing for which man was created. When the golden age of Saturn came to an end, and Jupiter replaced him on the throne of heaven, then, as Virgil tells the story, labor was first introduced into the world. "Before Jove's time,

No settlers brought the land under subjection;
Not lawful even to divide the plain with landmarks
    and boundaries:
All produce went to a common pool, and earth
    unprompted
Was free with all her fruits.
Jove put the wicked poison in the black ser-
    pent's tooth,
Jove told the wolf to ravin, the sea to be
    restive always,
He shook from the leaves their honey, he had all
    fire removed,
And stopped the wine that ran in rivers everywhere,
So thought and experiment might forge man's
    various crafts
Little by little, asking the furrow to yield the
    corn-blade,
Striking the hidden fire that lies in the veins of flint.

Here, while labor may in some sense be a punishment, or at least a fall from the golden age, it still does result in benefits. "The Father of agriculture . . . sent worries to sharpen our mortal wits/And would not allow his realm to grow listless from lethargy"; as a result, "numerous arts arose." But although "labor and harsh necessity's hand will master anything," it is still "unremitting labor."

According to Judeo-Christian doctrine, la-

bor is an inevitable consequence of man's fall from grace, a punishment for Adam's disobedience like disease and death. In the earthly paradise of Eden, the children of Adam would have lived without labor or servitude of any sort. But when Adam sinned, the Lord God said unto him: "Cursed is the ground for thy sake; in toil shalt thou eat of it all the days of thy life . . . In the sweat of thy face, shalt thou eat bread, till thou return into the ground."

That work should be painful belongs to its very essence. Otherwise it would not serve as a penalty or a penance. But, in the Christian as in the Virgilian view, labor also contributes to such happiness as man can enjoy on earth. The distinction between temporal and eternal happiness is a distinction between a life of work on earth and the activity of contemplation in heaven. This does not mean the elimination of leisure and enjoyment from earthly life, but it does make labor their antecedent and indispensable condition. It also means that even in his highest activities—in the development of his arts and sciences—man must be perpetually at work. His achievement of truth or beauty is never so perfect and lasting that he can rest in it.

IN THESE DIVERSE conceptions of the relation of labor to human life, work seems to have several different meanings. It always involves activity or exertion. Its clearest opposite is sleep. But other things are also opposed to work—play or amusement, leisure, idleness. When leisure is not identified with idleness, it involves activity no less than work. So, too, many of the forms of play require intense exertion of body or mind. The difference, therefore, must lie in the nature or purpose of the activity.

Aristotle suggests what the difference is when he puts play, work, and leisure in an ordered relationship to one another. Nature, he writes, "requires that we should be able, not only to work well, but to use leisure well." Leisure is "the first principle of all action" and so "leisure is better than work and is its end." As play and with it rest (i.e., sleep) are for the sake of work, so work in turn is for the sake of leisure.

The characteristics of work as the middle term here seem to be, first, that work is activity directed to an end beyond itself and, second, that it is productive of the necessities which sustain life rather than of the goods by which life is perfected. The political or speculative activity which Aristotle considers the proper occupation of leisure is intrinsically good or enjoyable. For participation in such activities leisure—in the sense of time free from labor—is required; but since the good life cannot be lived unless life itself is sustained, labor also is a prerequisite.

Work is thus defined by wealth as its immediate end—the production of the external, economic, or consumable goods which support life. Though play has the immediately enjoyable character of an activity performed for its own sake, Aristotle subordinates it to work, assigning to it the same utility which rest has. Both refresh men from the fatigues of labor and recreate the energies needed for work. "Amusement," he writes, "is needed more amid serious occupations than at other times, for he who is hard at work has need for relaxation, and amusement gives relaxation."

The economic sense which connects work and labor with wealth seems to be the primary but not the only sense in which these terms are used in the great books. There is the more general sense of human work as any productive activity in which men exercise some art or skill. The familiar distinction between skilled and unskilled labor may be only a distinction in degree if there is truth in the theory that some degree of skill—some rudimentary art at least—is required for the performance of the simplest tasks of hand and eye.

Kinds of work, according to this theory, can be differentiated by reference to the type of art involved. The ancient distinction between the servile and the liberal arts also divides workers into those who manipulate and transform physical materials and those who employ the symbols of poetry, music, or science to produce things for the mind. This distinction between manual and mental work, based on the character of the work itself, is not to be identified with the distinction between slave and free labor. The latter is based

on the status of the worker. Even in the slave economies of the ancient world, some freemen were artisans, farmers, or sailors, and some slaves were philosophers. Nor is mental as opposed to manual work necessarily directed to the production of the goods of the mind. The white-collar workers of an industrial economy, employed with the symbols of finance, accounting, or management, do mental work which has its ultimate end in the production or exchange of material goods.

There are still other traditional distinctions among kinds of work and types of workers, all of which cannot be put together into a single scheme of classification without much overlapping. Some distinctions, like that between handwork and machine labor or between healthful and unhealthful occupations, turn on the characteristics of the work itself. Some depend on the social conditions under which the work is done or on the relationship between the individual worker and other men. The work to be done may be accomplished by an individual working alone, or by the cooperative labor of many; and, in the latter case, the social organization of the laboring group may involve the ranking of men according to the functions they perform.

Here we get the division into the master craftsmen, who plan and superintend, and all grades of helpers who execute their directions. One meaning of the word "menial" as applied to work signifies the inferior tasks in the hierarchy of functions; but it is also used to express society's opinion of those who perform certain tasks, such as that of the domestic servant. The distinction between what is menial and what is dignified work varies, of course, from society to society and from one age to another.

The characterization of labor as productive or nonproductive, and of work as useful or wasteful, is based on strictly economic criteria and on considerations of social welfare. The sense in which work cannot be divorced from the production of some extrinsic effect is not violated by the conception of nonproductive labor as work which in no way increases the wealth of nations.

"There is one sort of labor which adds to the subject upon which it is bestowed; there is another which has no such effect. The former," writes Adam Smith, "may be called productive; the latter, unproductive labor . . . The labor of some of the most respectable orders in society is . . . unproductive of any value . . . The sovereign, for example, with all the officers both of justice and war who serve under him, the whole army and navy, are unproductive laborers . . . Like the declamation of the actor, the harangue of the orator, or the tune of the musician, the work of all of them perishes in the very instant of its production."

The standard by which Marx judges the usefulness of labor also implies the economic notion of a commodity. "Nothing can have value," he says, "without being an object of utility. If the thing is useless, so is the labor contained in it." But Marx also adds a criterion of social utility. "Whoever directly satisfies his own wants with the produce of his labor, creates, indeed, use-values, but not commodities. In order to produce the latter, he must not only produce use-values, but use-values for others, social use-values." It is by this last criterion that Marx criticizes the capitalist economy for its "most outrageous squandering of labor power" in superfluous or socially useless production. These distinctions, it should perhaps be said, have largely disappeared from modern economic literature and usage.

THE PRINCIPLE OF the division of labor does not depend upon any particular classification of work or workers according to type. Nor does it belong to one system of economy rather than another. But the ancients, concerned as they were with its bearing on the origin and development of the state, saw the division of labor as primarily of political significance; whereas the moderns are more concerned with its economic causes and consequences.

Thucydides compares the poverty and crude life of the early Hellenic tribes with the wealth, the power, and the civilization of Athens, Sparta, Corinth, and other city-states at the opening of the Peloponnesian War. The difference is not to be accounted for in terms of the invention of new tools, but rather in terms of the greater efficiency in production which is obtained by a division of labor. This is both an effect and a cause of the enlargement of the community, and its increasing population. The greater the number of men associated in a common life, the greater the number of specialized tasks which can be assigned to different members of the community.

This observation is formulated by Plato and Aristotle in their accounts of the origin of the state. The advantages which the state confers upon its members are in part won by the division of labor in which they participate.

The isolated family, Aristotle remarks, is barely able to supply the "everyday wants" of its members. The tribe or village, which is an association of families, can achieve a little more than bare subsistence; but not until several tribes unite to form a city does a truly self-sufficing community come into existence, and one with an adequate division of labor. Some men, if not all, can then acquire the leisure to engage in the arts and sciences and politics— the pursuits of civilization which have their material basis in sufficient wealth.

The effect of the division of labor on the social structure of the state seems to be generally agreed upon by all observers, ancient and modern. Men are divided into social classes according to the kind of work they do—not only by reference to the type of economically productive labor, but also in terms of the distinction between labor and leisure, or between economic and other functions in society.

All do not agree, however, that such class distinctions are as beneficial to society as the increase of wealth or opulence which the division of labor affords. They not only threaten the unity and peace of the society, but tend to degrade the condition of labor by reducing the individual worker to a cog in the machine. The division of labor frequently restricts him to a slight and insignificant task, repetitively performed, and so makes it impossible for him to develop his skill or to enjoy any pride of workmanship. From a purely economic point of view, Smith advocates the greatest intensification of the division of labor. Each more minute subdivision of tasks augments efficiency in production. But from the human point of view, he sees that this method of maximizing wealth by dividing men into functional groups—one man, one task—leads to the mental impoverishment of the men, who require a multiplicity of functions for their development.

"In the progress of the division of labor," Smith writes, "the employment of the far greater part of those who live by labor . . . comes to be confined to a few very simple operations, frequently one or two . . . The man whose whole life is spent in performing a few simple operations . . . has no occasion to exert his understanding or to exercise his invention . . . He naturally loses, therefore, the habit of such exertion, and generally becomes as stupid and ignorant as it is possible for a human creature to become." The situation seems even worse to Marx. The industrial system, revolutionizing the mode of work, "converts the laborer into a crippled monstrosity, by forcing his detailed dexterity at the expense of a world of productive capabilities and instincts." Marx's phrase "crippled monstrosity" can be read into the character of Kafka's Gregor Samsa in *The Metamorphosis,* in which the reader senses that the monotony of Samsa's job has contributed to his transformation into a cockroach. The degradation of labor in the modern world is a large part of Kafka's metaphor of angst.

THE GREAT ISSUES concerning labor seem to be moral and political rather than economic. The consideration of the division of labor from the point of view of efficiency in production remains purely economic only when it is abstracted from any concern about the effect upon the laborer. The analysis of factors affecting the productivity of labor ceases to be merely economic when the hours, conditions, and organization of work are viewed in terms of the workingmen.

The determination of wages by the buying and selling of labor (or, as Marx insists, of labor-power) as a commodity subject to market conditions of supply and demand; the difference between real and nominal wages as determined by the level of wages in relation to the price of other commodities; the so-called "iron law of wages" according to which wages will be established at the minimum of bare subsistence for the laborer and his family—these are matters which the economist may deal with in a descriptive or historical manner, calculating rates and ratios without regard to questions of justice. But in terms of such formulations questions of justice are raised and become the great issues concerning the rights of workmen to the fruits of their labor, to the security of full employment and other forms of protection, to collective bargaining, to a voice in the management of industry or business.

These are the problems of a capitalist economy, to which the earlier partisans of capital and of labor proposed different solutions. Yet the principles of justice to which the parties in conflict appeal seem to be no less applicable to even earlier conflicts in other economic systems—between master and slave or between feudal lord and serf. All the institutional differences among these three economies should not, according to Marx, conceal from us the profound analogy which obtains in the relation between owners and workers, whether the workers are chattel slaves, peons bound to the land, or industrial proletarians selling their labor-power.

"Wherever a part of society possesses a monopoly of the means of production," he writes, "the laborer, free or not free, must add to the working time necessary for his own maintenance an extra working time in order to produce the means of subsistence for the owners of the means of production, whether this proprietor be the Athenian gentleman, Etruscan theocrat, civis Romanus, Norman baron, American slave-owner, Wallachian Boyard, modern landlord or capitalist."

Marx undertakes to explain how the surface difference between slave labor and wage labor conceals the analogy. "In slave labor, even that part of the working-day in which the slave is only replacing the value of his own means of existence, in which, therefore, he works for himself alone, appears as labor for his master. All the slave's labor appears as unpaid labor. In wage-labor, on the contrary, even surplus labor, or unpaid labor, appears as paid. There the property-relation conceals the labor of the slave for himself; here the money-relation conceals the unrequited labor of the wage laborer."

Two phrases here—"unpaid labor" and "unrequited labor"—indicate that Marx is thinking in terms of justice. Elsewhere he calls the industrial proletariat "wage-slaves" to emphasize the presence in an apparently free economy of the same unjust exploitation which the word "slave" connotes when it refers to the use of men as chattel. The essential similarity in all forms of economic exploitation—which makes all forms of economic slavery essentially similar—is seen by Marx in terms of the production of a surplus value by the laborer; that is, he produces a greater value in commodities than he needs to support his own subsistence. This surplus value, when appropriated by the owner of the materials and the tools on and with which the propertyless laborer works, becomes an unearned increment, or, in other words, an unjust profit from the work of another man.

In *Animal Farm,* Orwell illustrates how such exploitation of workers is analogous to the abuse of animals by men. Old Major, the prophesying pig who symbolizes Marx, attacks man as Marx attacked the owners of the means of production: "Man is the only creature that consumes without producing . . . Yet he is lord of all the animals. He sets them to work, he gives back to them the bare minimum that will prevent them from starving, and the rest he keeps for himself."

THE NOTION OF VALUE—the value of commodities and the value of labor itself—is obviously of central importance. As indicated in the chapter on JUSTICE, the formulas of equality, which determine fair exchanges or distributions, require some measure of equivalents in value. What determines the intrinsic value of a commodity according to which it can be compared with another commodity, without reference to the price of each in the market-place? Smith's answer to this question is *labor.* It is the answer given before him by Locke, and after him by Marx.

"Equal quantities of labor, at all times and places," Smith declares, "may be said to be of equal value to the laborer. In his ordinary state of health, strength and spirits; in the ordinary degree of his skill and dexterity, he must always lay down the same portion of his ease, his liberty, and his happiness. The price which he pays must always be the same, whatever may be the quantity of goods which he receives in return for it. Of these, indeed, it may sometimes purchase a greater and sometimes a smaller quantity; but it is their value which varies, not that of the labor which purchases them." From this Smith concludes that "labor alone, therefore, never varying in its own value, is alone the ultimate and real standard by which the value of all commodities can at all times and places be estimated and compared. It is their real price; money is their nominal price only."

This labor theory of value raises the further question of the value of labor itself. What determines its natural or real price, as opposed to its market or nominal price? On this Marx and Smith appear to part company, which may account for their further divergence when Marx declares that "the real value of labor is the cost of its production, not the average price it can command in the market"; and then goes on to explain how a surplus value is derived by the capitalist who pays for labor-power on a basis of the cost of producing and sustaining the laborer, but uses his labor-power to produce a real value in commodities which exceeds the real price of labor itself.

Smith, on the other hand, holds that "the whole produce of labor belongs to the laborer" only "in that original state of things, which precedes both the appropriation of land and the accumulation of stock." When "land becomes private property," the landlord "makes the first deduction" in the form of *rent;* and the capitalist, or the person who invests some part of his stock accumulation, "makes a second deduction" in the form of *profit.* After rent and profit are taken, the laborer's *wage* represents what is left of "the whole produce of labor."

Yet Smith also says of the landlords that "as soon as the land of any country has all become private property," they, "like all other men, love to reap where they never sowed." The implication of unearned increment in this remark suggests that Smith is neither disinclined to mix moral judgment with economic description, nor is he at variance with Marx on the principle of economic justice. That Smith regards profit as the price properly paid for the use of capital and that he does not see reaping without sowing as an essential element in profit making may perhaps be read as a challenge to Marx's development of the labor theory of value into a theory of surplus value and unearned increment.

IT IS POSSIBLE, of course, that the difference in the conclusions of Smith and Marx from a common premise can be explained by the different directions their analyses take. It may not represent a direct opposition on a point of fact. The proposition that value derives from labor seems to yield a number of theoretical consequences.

Locke, for example, holding that it is labor which "puts the difference of value on everything," makes this the basis for the right to private property, certainly in its original appropriation from the common domain which is God's gift to mankind. "Though the earth and all inferior creatures be common to all men, yet every man has a property in his own person. The labor of his body and the work of his hands we may say are properly his. Whatsoever, then, he removes out of the state that nature hath provided and left it in, he hath mixed his labor with, and joined to it something that is his own, and thereby makes it his property."

This view is shared by Rousseau. "It is impossible to conceive," he says, "how property can come from anything but manual labor; for what else can a man add to things which he does not originally create, so as to make them his own property?" In the same vein, Smith declares that "the property which every man has in his own labor, as it is the original foundation of all other property, so it is the most sacred and inviolable."

What further conclusions follow from this justification of private property as a right founded upon labor? How is the original right to property extended into a right of inheritance? How does this conception of the origin of property bear on the Marxist conception of the origin of the proletariat—the propertyless workers who have nothing but their labor-power to sell? Denying the charge that communists desire to abolish "the right of personally acquiring property as the fruit of a man's own labor," Marx and Engels make the countercharge that the development of industrial capitalism "has to a great extent already destroyed it and is still destroying it daily." They propose public ownership of the means of production to protect the property rights of labor; they seek to abolish only "the bourgeois form of private property" which, in their view, is a use of property to exploit labor.

The rights of labor seem to be central in any formulation of the problem of a just distribution of wealth. But when other rights are taken into consideration, the problem of economic justice becomes more complex; and different solutions result from differences in emphasis. Even with regard to one group of solutions, J. S. Mill observes that "some communists consider it unjust that the produce of the labor of the community should be shared on any other principle than that of exact equality; others think it just that those should receive most whose wants are greatest." To weigh the merits of competing solutions, as well as to reach an adequate statement of the problem, the discussion of labor must be connected with the discussion of related considerations in the chapters on JUSTICE, REVOLUTION, and WEALTH.

THERE ARE ISSUES of justice concerning labor other than the strictly economic problem of income distribution. In the ancient world, for example, not only chattel slaves but also free artisans were frequently regarded as incapable of participation in political life. Only men of independent wealth had enough leisure for the activities of citizenship which, in the Greek city-states, was almost a full-time occupation. This, according to Aristotle, is one reason for the disfranchisement of the laboring classes who must devote a great part of their energy to earning a living and who have neither the time nor training for liberal pursuits. "Since leisure is necessary both for the development of virtue and the performance of political duties," citizens, he maintains, cannot "lead the life of mechanics or tradesmen."

Against this oligarchic view (which also involves the notion that wealth deserves special political privileges), the Greek democrats take the position that all freemen should be citizens on an equal footing, regardless of the amount of their property or their conditions of labor and leisure. But the oligarchic principle still tends to prevail among republicans in the 18th century. Kant, for example, holds that citizenship "presupposes the independence or self-sufficiency of the individual citizen among the people." On this basis he excludes from the suffrage, as only "passive" citizens, "the apprentice of a merchant or tradesman, a servant who is not in the employ of the state, a minor (*naturaliter vel civiliter*), all women, and, generally, everyone who is compelled to maintain himself not according to his own industry, but as it is arranged by others (the state excepted)." They are "without civil personality, and their existence is only, as it were, incidentally included in the state."

The preference shown by the writers of *The Federalist* for a republican as opposed to a democratic form of government—or representative government as opposed to direct democracy—rests partly on their fear of the political incompetence, as well as the factional interests, of wage earners and day laborers. While expressing "disapprobation" of poll taxes, they still defend the right of the government to exact them, in the belief that "there may exist certain critical and tempestuous conjunctures of the State, in which a poll-tax may become an inestimable resource." Yet such a tax would seem to be primarily a device for disfranchising workingmen of no property and small income, and in the opinion of a later day along with the disfranchisement of minorities it has been so regarded.

The democratic revolution does not begin until the middle of the 19th century. But even then, Mill, who advocates universal suffrage, argues for the disqualification of paupers or those on the dole, without raising the question whether the right to work—to avoid poverty and involuntary indigence—is not a democratic right inseparable from the right to citizenship. It is "required by first principles," Mill writes, "that the receipt of parish relief should be a peremptory disqualification for the franchise. He who cannot by his labor suffice for his own support has no claim to the privilege of helping himself to the money of others. By becoming dependent on the remaining members of the community for actual subsistence, he abdicates his claim to equal rights with them in other respects."

The historic connection of democracy with a movement toward political justice for the laboring classes strongly suggests that political democracy must be accompanied by economic democracy in order to attain its full realization.

IN MORE RECENT times, notably in the 20th century, the discussion of fairness or justice and of the factors determining the wage level has greatly receded. Writing at the very end of the 19th century, Veblen did distinguish, in *The Theory of the Leisure Class,* between two broad classes of employment—what he called "exploit" and "drudgery." "Those employments which are to be classed as exploit are worthy, honorable, noble; other employments, which do not contain this element of exploit, and especially those which imply subservience or submission, are unworthy, debasing, ignoble." But Veblen did not pursue this distinction to any operative conclusion; reform, let alone revolution, was not part of his interest or system. Here, as elsewhere, Veblen writes as much to infuriate as to instruct. And, partly for this reason, it is the rich—the leisured class—not the workers, that attract his attention. For more on this, see the chapter on WEALTH.

There is from Veblen's writings, however, one comment of enduring value on labor: his identification of, as he terms it, "the instinct of workmanship," otherwise described as "a taste for effective work." This is something that anyone who has read Veblen notices thereafter almost every day. It is the inner-directed desire of the worker, whatever his or her station or occupation, to be a master of the task and its requirements—to show that he or she, whatever the work, can do it well and with the particular skill and competence that serve the satisfaction of the observer, the employer, and most of all, the worker himself.

A second, more recent view of labor emphasizes not the employment but the social context of the worker and its relation to well-being and personal fulfillment. Tawney deals with this at a level of no slight modern relevance; modern capitalism, as presented in *The Acquisitive Society* (and Tawney's other writings), places a heavy burden of proof on work that contributes to the public components of the common living standard, that is to say productive activity devoted to education, public recreation facilities, health care, libraries, the provision of law and order, and much else. And it accords a moral premium to private effort serving the market economy. This, in turn, penalizes those who depend on public services, such as schools or libraries, and favors those who can afford a private alternative.

More generally, Tawney sees the ruling ideas of the time as sanctioning social indifference and even cruelty on a larger scale with, inevitably, a special impact on those who toil. "Since England first revealed the possibilities of industrialism, it has gone from strength to strength ... The secret of its triumph is obvious. It is an invitation to men to use the powers with which they have been endowed by nature or society, by skill or energy or relentless egotism, or mere good fortune, without inquiring whether there is any principle by which their exercise should be limited." Central to Tawney's system, as it is to the British Fabian movement of which he was much a part, is a sense of balance. On the one hand is the energy and, needless to say, the will to expression which is to be welcomed; on the other are the restraints that enlarge the liberty and well-being of others, especially those who, lacking the skill, energy, relentless egotism, or good fortune, toil or live otherwise at the mercy of the more favored. Marx saw a solution in revolution and the euthanasia of the ruling power; Tawney, however, sees the solution in a humanized social and political context. His community or state can be civilized and improved; Marx's must be overturned.

A different view of the position of labor comes from Weber. This view emphasizes the emerging role of bureaucracy—the passage from individual to group or organizational authority. He sees this movement as a broad and immutable trend; he identifies it initially with public service and, in a notable account, reminds the reader that "the bureaucratization of organized warfare may be carried through in the form of private capitalist enterprise, just like any other business." Until the 18th century the regiment was a managerial unit with the colonel, who supplied the uniforms and arms, the entrepreneur. Army procurement is one of "private capitalism's first giant enterprises of a far-going bureaucratic character."

Although the approved ideology still resists it—as did Weber to some extent—he opens the way for recognition of the role of the worker in the modern industrial enterprise. This worker in the characteristic great corporation responds not to the orders and interests of an entrepreneur or capitalist, but to those of a large and complex bureaucracy, where the line between the director and the directed is often indistinct.

WITH THE YEARS of the Great Depression there came a large, even massive, change in the discussion of the position of labor in the modern industrial society. In the United States power as affected by collective bargaining and the role of the trade union in politics—old issues in Europe—was still on stage. But the matters heretofore mentioned receded into the background. In the industrial world the overwhelmingly important issue regarding labor was now its employment. Life might be less than perfect when one was on a payroll, but life was markedly imperfect if one had no job at all. In Britain this had been a problem of some urgency in the 1920s. In the 1930s unemployment became the nearly universal problem of capitalism.

Of the many who spoke to the issue, the most heard voice was that of Keynes. His *General Theory of Employment, Interest and*

Money, published in 1936, not only made employment the major topic of economic discussion, but, for the time, removed nearly all other questions concerning labor.

Prior to Keynes, the accepted, and in some economic thought the all-but-compelled, assumption was of a full-employment equilibrium. Were there, indeed, unemployment, some short-run cyclical problems apart, those so suffering could always get a job by lowering their wage claim. Then it would be worthwhile—profitable—for some employer to hire them. Admittedly unions might negate this remedy; not surprisingly, they were, in consequence, blamed for unemployment.

Keynes identified unemployment with failure of effective demand to carry off the supply of goods and services being produced or rendered. Since the time of the noted French economist and near contemporary of Smith, Jean-Baptiste Say, it had been an economic axiom—Malthus was one of the few dissenters—that production, in the rent, interest, profit, and wages that it paid out, created an equivalent and wholly adequate demand. This was Say's law. From Keynes came the denial of this proposition; from undue savings there could be a shortfall in demand uncorrected by lower interest rates and a greater flow of investment. Correction would come when production and employment spiraled down, eliminating the excess of saving and establishing a new underemployment or unemployment equilibrium.

From this analysis came the great, at the time even revolutionary, remedy of Keynes. The state should intervene, and through borrowing and spending—running a deliberate deficit in the public budget—offset the deficiency of demand in the private or market economy. So it followed: deliberate deficit spending to increase employment, a nearly unheard-of thing in its day. From this came the yet larger conclusion, which entered fully on public policy in the years following World War II: the state would now assume responsibility for the level of economic activity in the economy and for its rate of expansion. The rate of economic growth would become a prime measure of the success of public policy.

Keynes's *General Theory* is not a book that is always clear as to contention. Like the Bible or Marx's *Capital,* it lends itself to sharp differences in interpretation. As with the Bible or Marx's *Capital,* the resulting debate as to meaning and intent confirmed many as disciples, for having invested time and effort in defending an interpretation, one is thereafter a disciple. As regards employment, labor, and the resulting public attitudes and policy, *The General Theory* remains the most influential economic work of the 20th century.

45

Language

THE liberal arts of grammar, rhetoric, and logic are all concerned with language. Each of these disciplines establishes its own rules for the use of language, each by reference to a special standard of excellence or correctness which measures language as an instrument of thought or communication. Together these three arts regulate discourse as a whole. Their relation to one another represents the relation of the various aspects of discourse—the emotional, the social, and the intellectual.

The tradition of the great books is the tradition of the liberal arts. Their greatness consists not only in the magnitude of the ideas or problems with which they deal, but also in their formal excellence as products of liberal art. Some of the great books are expositions of logic or rhetoric. None is a treatise on grammar. But they all plainly exemplify, even where they do not expound, the special refinements of the arts of language; and many of them, especially the works of science, philosophy, and theology, and even some of the poetical works, deal explicitly with the difficulties of discourse, and the devices that have been used to overcome them. Language is their instrument, and they are consciously critical in its use.

One of the great books—Augustine's treatise *On Christian Doctrine*—is directly and explicitly concerned with grammar in the broad sense of the art of reading. Wittgenstein, in his own discussion of language, comments on Augustine's treatise, criticizing it for its emphasis on the use of nouns rather than verbs. But he fails to recognize the special interest in reading that is focal in Augustine's treatise. Addressed to "earnest students of the word," *On Christian Doctrine* attempts to "lay down

rules for interpretation," and, in so doing, it is compared by Augustine to "one who teaches reading, that is, shows others how to read for themselves." It is not reading in general, however, but the reading of one book—the Bible—with which Augustine is concerned. We shall return later to this special problem of interpreting the word of God, or language which is thought to be inspired.

In our day, there is a lively interest in the problems of language. This is partly because of the development of historical and comparative studies of the various human languages, and the scientific formulation of what is common to all languages in origin, structure, and change. But it also results in part from the claims of a discipline popularly called "semantics" to have discovered the properties of language as a medium of expression, and especially to have discovered its limitations. The claims of semantics often go so far as to find in the misuse of language the origin of many human ills. The novelty of semantics is supposed to lie both in the diagnosis and in the remedies proposed.

Of these two sources of interest in language, the second calls attention to the vitality of the liberal arts, of which semantics is a contemporary formulation. It might almost be said that there is nothing new about semantics except the name. Hobbes, Francis Bacon, and Locke, for example, deal explicitly with the abuses of language and the treachery of words. Each makes recommendations for the correction of these faults. Plato and Aristotle, Augustine and Aquinas, Berkeley and Hume are similarly concerned with ambiguity in speech, with the multiple senses in which discourse of every sort can be interpreted, and with the methods by which men can approximate precision in the use of language.

The other interest in language is also represented in the great books. Though the science of linguistics and the history of languages are researches of recent origin, speculation about the origin of language and, in that context, consideration of the natural and conventional aspects of language extend throughout the tradition. At all times the discussion of the nature of man and society considers language as one of the principal characteristics of the specifically human world or compares the language of men with the speech of brutes.

In addition there is the broad philosophical inquiry into the nature of signs and symbols in general. This is not limited to the problem of how written or spoken words get their meaning. The general question calls for an examination of every type of signifying and every sort of symbol, verbal and nonverbal, natural and artificial, human and divine. Though these matters are closely related to the problems of language and may therefore be touched upon here, their main treatment is reserved for the chapter on SIGN AND SYMBOL.

THE TREATMENT OF language seems to have a different tenor in ancient and modern times. It is only in modern times that we can find a philosopher, such as Heidegger, saying that "one of the essential theatres of speechlessness is dread in the sense of the terror into which the abyss of Nothing plunges us." Only in modern times do we find a physicist, such as Heisenberg, pointing out that in quantum theory "the most difficult problem" concerns "the use of the language." We have "no simple guide for correlating the mathematical symbols with concepts of ordinary language."

The philosophers of antiquity appreciate the need to safeguard discourse from the aberrations of speech. Plato and Aristotle usually preface their discussion of a subject with an examination of the relevant words in current use. Discovering the variety of meanings attached to common words, they take pains to enumerate the various senses of a word, and to put these meanings in some order. They pursue definitions or construct them to con-trol the ambiguity that is latent in the language anyone must use to express or communicate ideas. But they do not expect to remove ambiguity entirely. They tend to accept the fact that the same word will have to be used in a number of senses; and they discriminate between the occasions when it is desirable to be precise about a word's meaning and those times when the purpose of discourse is better served by permitting a word to carry a whole range of meanings. They see no special difficulty in abstract as opposed to concrete words, or in general names as distinguished from the proper names which designate individuals, or in words which refer to purely intelligible objects like ideas rather than to the objects of sense-experience.

The mood of the ancients, which also prevails for the most part among the philosophers and theologians of the Middle Ages, seems to express a certain tolerance of the imperfections of language. If men do not think clearly, if they do not reason cogently or argue honestly, the fault is primarily the result of the misuse of their faculties, not of the betrayal of their intentions by the intractable character of language as an instrument. Even when men misunderstand one another, the inadequacy of language as a medium of communication is not solely responsible for the failure of minds to meet through the interchange of words. With greater effort, with a more assiduous application of the liberal arts, men can succeed even if language works against them.

Some things are inexpressible in human speech even as they are incapable of being fully grasped by human thought. "My vision," Dante says when he reaches the mystic rose of Paradise, "was greater than speech can show." Such knowledge as we can have of "the highest matters and the first principles of things" Plato thinks "does not admit of exposition like other branches of knowledge." In his *The Seventh Letter,* he even goes so far as to say that "no man of intelligence will venture to express his philosophical views in language."

With these exceptions the ancients seem to adopt a mood of tolerance toward language. This does not imply an underestimation of the difficulties of using language well. It simply does not make of language an insidious enemy of clarity and truth. The deficiencies of language are like the weaknesses of the flesh. As man can in large part overcome them through the discipline of the moral virtues, so through the discipline of the liberal arts—by skill in grammar, rhetoric, and logic—he can make language express almost as much truth as he can acquire, and communicate it almost as clearly as he can think it. Men need not succumb to the tyranny of words if they will make the requisite effort to master language to serve their purpose.

But the liberal arts do not guarantee purity of purpose. Obscurantism, obfuscation, deception, and falsification are sometimes the aim. Men try to persuade others at all costs, or to win the argument regardless of where the truth lies. They try to confuse their opponents or mislead their audience. The use of language for such ends requires as much skill as its employment in the service of truth. If such use is a misuse, then language is equally available for use or misuse.

It is an ancient saying that only the competent in grammar can make grammatical errors intentionally. So, as Plato recognizes, the difference between the sophist and the philosopher is not one of skill but of purpose. When he criticizes the trickery of sophistic argument, he also acknowledges the cleverness with which the sophists juggle words and propound absurdities under the cover of superficially significant speech. The sophistic fallacies which Aristotle enumerates are seldom accidental errors. Far from being the result of the impediments which language places in the way of thought, they are in large measure artfully contrived equivocations. They are ways of using language against logic. According to Aristotle, they represent "foul fighting in disputation" and are resorted to only by "those who are resolved to win at all costs."

IN THE MODERN treatment of language there is more of an imputation that words cause men unwittingly to deceive themselves as often as they enable one man intentionally to deceive another. Men are duped or tricked by the tendency of words to counterfeit a reality which does not exist. This, in the view of Hobbes or Locke, Berkeley or Hume, is particularly true of general or universal names—or words that signify nothing which can be perceived or imagined.

We cannot imagine anything infinite, says Hobbes. Hence a word like "infinite" is a form of absurd speech "taken upon credit (without any signification at all) from deceived philosophers and deceived, or deceiving, Schoolmen." In addition to the deceptions of ordinary ambiguity and of metaphoric speech, Hobbes pays particular attention to the absurd, insignificant, or nonsensical use of words "whereby we conceive nothing but the sound"; he gives as examples, not merely "round quadrangle," but "infused virtue," "free will," and "immaterial substance."

In the light of the examples, this theory of insignificant or meaningless speech explains what Hobbes means when he says that "words are wise men's counters, they do but reckon by them; but they are the money of fools." It also indicates how Hobbes uses the susceptibility of men to self-deception through language as a way of explaining the errors—he calls them "absurdities"—into which his predecessors have fallen. What is novel here is not that he disagrees with earlier thinkers on points of psychology and metaphysics or theology, but that he reduces what might be supposed to be an issue between true and false opinions to a difference between significant and absurd speech. His opponents might reply that unless his own views about matter and mind are true, his semantic criticism of them does not hold. They have been seduced by language into talking nonsense only if Hobbes is right in his metaphysics and psychology.

The criticism of arguments which seem to rely on metaphors is not peculiarly modern. In his attack on the Platonic theory of ideas, Aristotle dismisses the statement that the Forms "are patterns and other things share in them" as a use of "empty words and poetical metaphors." But Hobbes carries this method of criticism much further. He frequently rests his case against other philosophers entirely on the ground that they are talking nonsense. Though he himself catches the imagination,

almost as often as Plato does, by his skillfully wrought metaphors, he would insist that
what he says can always be rendered literally,
whereas the metaphors of others conceal the
insignificance of their speech.

Bacon provides another illustration of the
modern attitude which ascribes a diabolic
character to language. "There arises from a
bad and unapt formation of words," he writes,
"a wonderful obstruction to the mind. Nor
can the definitions and explanations with
which learned men are wont to guard and
protect themselves in some instances afford a
complete remedy—words still manifestly force
the understanding, throw everything into confusion, and lead mankind into vain and innumerable controversies and fallacies." He goes
on to say that "the idols imposed upon the understanding by words are of two kinds. They
are either names of things which have no existence . . . or they are names of actual objects,
but confused, badly defined, and hastily or
irregularly abstracted from things."

Here, as in the case of Hobbes, a theory of
reality and of the way in which the mind draws
its ideas from experience seems to underlie the
charge that language tangles the mind in a web
of words, so that it deals with words rather
than with things. In the same spirit, though not
from the same premises, Locke tells his reader
why he found it necessary to include in his
essay *Concerning Human Understanding* the
long third book on language, which examines
in detail the imperfections as well as the abuses
of words, and the remedies therefor.

"Vague and insignificant forms of speech,
and abuse of language," he says, "have so long
passed for mysteries of science; and hard or
misapplied words with little or no meaning
have, by prescription, such a right to be mistaken for deep learning and height of speculation, that it will not be easy to persuade either
those who speak, or those who hear them,
that they are but the covers of ignorance, and
hinderance of true knowledge . . . So few are
apt to think they deceive, or are deceived in
the use of words or that the language of the
sect they are of has any faults in it."

Without judging the fundamental issues involved concerning the nature of things and of
man and his mind, one point seems to be clear.
According as men hold different conceptions
of the relation of language to thought (and
in consequence assume different attitudes toward the imperfections or misuse of language),
they inevitably take opposite sides on these
issues. Whether the discipline of language is
called semantics or the liberal arts, the standards by which one man criticizes the language
of another seem to depend upon what he
holds to be true.

The present work on the great ideas aims,
in part, to record the agreements and disagreements among the great minds of the western
tradition. It also records how those minds
have used the same word in different senses
or have used quite distinct words for the same
thing. It could not do either unless it did both.
This indicates the basic relationship between
language and thought which the great books
exemplify, even when they do not explicitly
make it the basis of their discussion of the
relation between language and thought.

THE IDEAL OF A perfect and universal language
seems to arise in modern times from dissatisfaction with the inadequacy of ordinary
language for the analytic refinement and precision of mathematics or science. As Descartes
holds up the method of mathematics as the
procedure to be followed in all other inquiries
and subject matters, so his conception of a
"universal mathesis" calls for a language which
shall be the perfect instrument of analysis and
demonstration.

It is sometimes supposed that the symbolism
of mathematics is itself that perfect language.
Lavoisier quotes Étienne Bonnot de Condillac
to the effect that algebra, "in the most simple,
most exact, and best manner, is at the same
time a language and an analytical method." Of
the analytic equations "which Descartes was
the first to introduce into the study of curves
and surfaces," Joseph Fourier remarks that
"they extend to all general phenomena. There
cannot be a language more universal and more
simple, more free from errors and obscurities,
that is to say, more worthy to express the invariable relations of natural things . . . Its chief
attribute is clearness; it has no marks to ex-

press confused notions . . . It follows the same course in the study of all phenomena; it interprets them by the same language."

This praise of mathematical symbolism indicates that one feature of the ideal is an exact correspondence between words and ideas. "Like three impressions of the same seal," Lavoisier says, "the word ought to produce the idea, and the idea to be a picture of the fact." If there were a perfect one-to-one correspondence between physical symbols and mental concepts, there would never be any failures of communication. Men would be able to understand each other as well as if they could see directly into each other's minds. Though they still used external signs as a medium of communication, they would approximate the immediate communication which the theologians attribute to angels. In addition, the process of thinking itself, quite apart from communication, could be perfectly regulated by the rules of grammar—the rules for manipulating symbols.

In the sense in which Lavoisier says that "the art of reasoning is nothing more than a language well arranged," the rules of thought might be reduced to the rules of syntax if there were a perfect language. If the symbols of mathematics lack the universality to express every sort of concept, then it may be necessary, as Leibniz proposes, to construct a "universal characteristic" which would make possible a symbolic calculus for the performance of all the operations of thought. This conception seems to contain the principle and the motivation for the various logistic schemes which accompany the modern development of symbolic or mathematical logic, from George Boole and John Venn to Giuseppe Peano, Gottlob Frege, Louis-Alexandre Couturat, Bertrand Russell, and Ludwig Wittgenstein. The hopes to be realized by an algebra of logic find expression in William Stanley Jevons' plan for a logical abacus which, like an adding machine or comptometer, would be a thinking machine able to solve all problems that can be put in suitable terms.

Is THE IDEAL of a perfect and universal language a genuine hope or a utopian dream?

Not all modern scientists seem to agree with Lavoisier's point that the improvement of a science and the improvement of its language are inseparable. Faraday, for example, apologizing for the invention of new words to name electrical phenomena, says that he is "fully aware that names are one thing and science another." The utopian character of the ideal seems to be implied in Swift's satirization of a universal language. On his voyage to the cloudland of the scientists in Laputa, Gulliver learns of a project which is being considered by the professors of language. "Since words are only names for things, it would be more convenient for all men to carry about them such things as were necessary to express the particular business they are to discourse on." The substitution of things for words would thus provide a "universal language to be understood in all civilized nations."

In the ancient world the imperfection of ordinary speech gives rise, not to the conception of a perfect language which man should try to construct, but to the consideration of the distinction between a hypothetical natural language and the existing conventional languages actually in use. If there were a natural language, it would not only be the same for all men everywhere, but its words would also be perfect images or imitations of things. That human language is conventional rather than natural may be seen not only in the plurality of tongues, but also in the fact that existing languages embody contradictory principles of symbolization.

This fact, Plato suggests in the *Cratylus,* indicates that human language does not originate as a gift from the gods, for if the gods had given men the names they use, signs would be perfectly and consistently adapted to things signified. The hypothesis of a natural or god-given language is not proposed as an ideal to inspire men to try to invent a perfect language for themselves. It functions rather as a norm for the criticism of man-made language and for discovering the natural elements common to all conventional languages.

Like human society, human language seems to be partly natural, partly conventional. As there are certain political principles, such as that of natural justice, common to all societies despite the diversity of their customs and institutions, so all conventional languages have certain common characteristics of structure which indicate their natural basis in the physical and mental constitution of man. In the tradition of the liberal arts, the search for a universal grammar, applicable to all conventional languages, represents not the hope to create a universal or perfect language, but the conviction that all languages have a common, natural basis.

THE HYPOTHESIS OF a natural language takes another form and has another implication in the Judeo-Christian tradition, where it is discussed in the light of certain portions of revelation. Yet it retains the same fundamental relevance to the problem of the origin and characteristics of the many conventional languages which now exist.

Genesis relates how, after God formed every beast of the field and every fowl of the air, He "brought them to Adam to see what he would call them; and whatsoever Adam called every living creature, that was the name thereof." The names which Adam devised constituted a natural language, at least insofar as, according to Augustine's interpretation, it is the one "common language of the race" both before the flood and for some time after. But there is the further question whether the names which Adam gave to things were their rightful or proper names—whether they were natural signs in the sense of true representations of the natures of the things signified.

Hobbes suggests one answer when he says that "the first author of speech was God himself, who instructed Adam how to name such creatures as he presented to his sight"; Augustine suggests another answer by identifying the original language of man with Hebrew, and by affirming the continuity of the Hebrew spoken after Babel with the language all men spoke before the confusion of tongues.

At the time when men began to build "a tower whose top may reach unto heaven," Genesis tells us that "the whole earth was of one language and one speech . . . And the Lord said, Behold, the people is one, and they have all one language; and this they begin to do; and now nothing will be restrained from them, which they have imagined to do. Go to, let us go down, and there confound their language, that they may not understand one another's speech."

This, according to Hobbes, means that the language "gotten and augmented by Adam and his posterity, was again lost at the tower of Babel, when by the hand of God every man was stricken for his rebellion, with an oblivion of his former language." If the further implication is that the lost language was unlike any of the conventional languages in the historical record, then it may be supposed to have been that natural form of speech in which each thing is named according to its nature. The modern ideal of a perfect and universal language may even be looked upon as an impious wish to achieve what God took away from men at Babel.

THE PROBLEM OF the origin of human language is not an easy one for the theologian. It is more difficult still for those who speculate about it in purely naturalistic terms. Rousseau tries to expose some of the perplexities in such speculations.

If speech did not become a social necessity until men passed from isolation in a state of nature to living together in society, how, he asks, could societies have been formed before languages had been invented? "If men need speech to learn to think," he remarks, "they must have stood in much greater need of the art of thinking, to be able to invent that of speaking." The development of languages already in existence, or the way in which the child learns to speak through living in an environment where speech exists, "by no means explains how languages were originally formed."

Rousseau imagines a primitive condition in which men uttered instinctive cries "to implore assistance in case of danger, or relief in case of suffering"; he supposes that to such cries, men may have added gestures to signify visible and movable objects, and imitative sounds to signify audible ones. Such methods of expression being insufficient to convey ideas about absent or future things, men had at last to invent "the articulate sounds of the voice" and to institute these as conventional signs. But, as he observes, "such an institution could only be made by common consent . . . itself still more difficult to conceive, since such a common agreement must have had motives, and speech, therefore, seems to have been highly necessary in order to establish the use of it."

The problem of the origin of human language is not only connected with the problem of the origin of human society, but also with the problem of the origin of man himself. The faculty of articulate speech does not, according to Darwin, "offer any insuperable objection to the belief that man has been developed from some lower form." Though the habitual use of articulate language is peculiar to man, "he uses, in common with the lower animals, inarticulate cries to express his meaning, aided by gestures and the movements of the muscles of the face." The songs of birds and the speech of parrots show that animals can learn to make and repeat certain definite sounds, and even to connect words with things. It seems to Darwin quite credible that man's articulate language "owes its origin to the imitation and modification of various natural sounds, the voices of other animals, and man's own instinctive cries, aided by signs and gestures."

Such an account of the origin of human speech is not credible, however, to those who disagree with Darwin's statement that "the lower animals differ from man solely in his almost infinitely larger power of associating together the most diversified sounds and ideas." Those who hold that human rationality differs in kind, rather than degree, from animal intelligence tend to find a corresponding difference in kind between human language and the sounds of brutes. Aristotle, for example, says that man is the only animal whom nature "has endowed with the gift of speech. Mere vocalization is only an indication of pleasure and pain and is therefore found in other animals," but men alone have the power to discuss the expedient and the just, and this fact distinguishes human association from the companionship of gregarious animals.

Human speech is, for Descartes, one of the two criteria by which we can "recognize the difference that exists between men and brutes. For it is a very remarkable fact that there are none so depraved and stupid, without even excepting idiots, that they cannot arrange different words together, forming of them a statement by which they can make known their thoughts; while, on the other hand, there is no other animal . . . which can do the same. It is not the want of organs that brings this to pass, for it is evident that magpies and parrots can utter words just like ourselves, and yet they cannot speak as we do, that is, so as to give evidence that they think of what they say . . . This does not merely show that the brutes have less reason than men, but that they have none at all."

The difference between men and other animals is more fully discussed in the chapter on MAN. Here we are concerned with opposite opinions on that subject only in relation to opposite views of human language and its origin. When, as in Descartes's view, human language is distinguished by syntax and grammar or, as in Locke's, by man's special power to use sounds "as signs of internal conceptions, and to make them stand as marks for ideas within his own mind," the origin of human speech does not seem explicable in evolutionary terms.

The relation of grammar to the other liberal arts and to the various uses of language is considered in the chapters on LOGIC, POETRY, and RHETORIC. Isolated from these others, grammar is primarily concerned with the distinction of the parts of speech, such as noun and verb, or particle and adjective.

"By a noun," says Aristotle, "we mean a sound significant by convention, which has no reference to time, and of which no part is significant apart from the rest." In contrast to the noun, the verb is defined by Aristotle as the sort of word which, "in addition to its proper meaning, carries with it the notion of time . . . Moreover," he continues, "a verb is always a sign of something said of something else." The grammatical function of nouns and verbs is, in Locke's opinion, more generally recognized and better defined than that of particles, prepositions, and conjunctions. Such words, Locke writes, "show what connexion, restriction, distinction, opposition, emphasis, etc. [a man] gives to each respective *part* of his discourse . . . He who would show the right use of particles, and what significancy and force they have, must take a little more pains, enter into his own thoughts, and observe nicely the several postures of his mind in discoursing."

Grammar is also concerned with the difference between words (or phrases) and sentences, or, in Aristotle's terms, between simple and composite expressions; and with the rules of syntax which govern the order and agreement of words according to their function as parts of speech. By reference to these rules the grammarian criticizes the misuse of language and classifies a great variety of common errors.

One test of whether grammar is a universal art applicable to all languages—not just a set of rules for using a particular conventional language correctly—is the naturalness of its theoretical distinctions. Does Aristotle's distinction between noun and verb, for example, respond to something natural in all discourse, or is it peculiar to the Greek or to the Indo-European languages?

THERE IS A MEANING of language which includes more than the speech of men and brutes. From Hippocrates on, the physician regards the symptoms of disease as if they were a connected system of signs, a language for which his diagnostic art provides a grammar of interpretation. This is particularly true in the psychological realm where, in the psychoanalysis of the neuroses and especially in Freud's interpretation of dreams, both symptom and dream-symbol are treated as an elaborate language. That language serves to express the unconscious thoughts and desires which cannot be expressed in the ordinary language of social intercourse over which consciousness exercises some control.

These medical examples represent a conception of language according to which the whole of nature is a book to be read by the scientist.

He penetrates the mysteries of nature by learning the grammar of natural signs. To know the relation of natural things as cause and effect or whole and part is to discover nature's syntax. According to another conception, expressed by Galileo, the book of nature "is written in mathematical language, its symbols being triangles, circles, and other geometrical figures, without whose help it is impossible to comprehend a single word of it."

The book of nature may also be read as the language of God. Prophecy or divination is such a reading of dreams or of other events as omens and portents which bespeak the divine purpose. When he reaches the highest heaven Dante finds in the vision of the Trinity, "bound by love in one single volume, that which is dispersed in leaves throughout the universe." Berkeley goes further than this. All of the ideas which man gets by sense perception are words in a divine vocabulary. The uniform appearances of nature "may not unfitly be styled the Language of its Author, whereby He discovers His attributes to our view and directs us how to act for the convenience and felicity of life."

God speaks to man in still another way. Within the Judeo-Christian tradition at least, God is believed to have revealed himself to man through the vehicle of human language. Written by men under divine inspiration, Sacred Scripture is the word of God. Because it is at once human and divine, this language is the most difficult for man to interpret.

The art of interpreting the Bible involves the most elaborate theory of signs, and of the types and levels of meaning. It involves special rules of reading. The development of this theory and these rules by Augustine and Aquinas, Maimonides and Spinoza, Hobbes and Pascal, has deepened the liberal arts and enlarged the scope of man's understanding of other languages—his own or nature's. Since the heart of this larger consideration of language lies in the analysis of meaning and the modes of signification, the discussion of the symbolism of nature and the word of God belongs to the chapter on SIGN AND SYMBOL; and, in its theological aspects, to the chapters on PROPHECY and RELIGION.

THE DISCUSSION OF language, as we have seen, cannot be separated from the consideration of human nature and human society. "Linguistics," Lévi-Strauss maintains, "occupies a special place among the social sciences, to whose ranks it unquestionably belongs."

Because He "designed man for a sociable creature," God, according to Locke, "made him not only with an inclination, and under a necessity to have fellowship with those of his own kind, but furnished him also with language, which was to be the great instrument and common tie of society."

It is not merely that the fellowship of men depends upon speech. According to Locke, men cannot enjoy "the comfort and advantage of society . . . without the communication of thoughts." The fact that "man had by nature his organs so fashioned as to be fit to frame articulate sounds . . . was not enough to produce language"—at least not human language, "for parrots, and several other birds, can be taught to make articulate sounds distinct enough," and yet, Locke writes, they are "by no means capable of language. Besides articulate sounds, therefore, it was further necessary," he insists, that the sounds men formed should be the instrument whereby "the thoughts of men's minds [are] conveyed from one to another."

Rousseau, on the other hand, seems to think that under the primitive circumstances surrounding the origin of both society and language, the association of men "would not require a language much more refined than that of rooks or monkeys, who associate together for much the same purpose. Inarticulate cries, plenty of gestures and some imitative sounds, must have been for a long time the universal language," he writes; "and by the addition, in every country, of some conventional articulate sounds . . . particular languages were produced; but these were rude and imperfect, and nearly such as are now to be found among some savage nations."

The plurality of conventional, historic languages seems to parallel the plurality of the nations or societies into which mankind is divided. But underlying the diversity of tongues there is also a unity which implies the possibility of mankind's unification. To the extent that language expresses thought, diverse languages are but different mediums for the same thing. "All men [may] not have the same speech sounds," Aristotle declares, "but the mental experiences, which these directly symbolize, are the same for all."

The human community conceived in terms of the communication of thought extends as far as the bounds of such communication among men. It is not limited by political boundaries. It overcomes by translation the barriers set up by a diversity of tongues. It includes the living and the dead and extends to those as yet unborn. In this sense, human civilization can be described as the civilization of the dialogue, and the tradition of the great books can be conceived as the great conversation in which all men can participate. The extent of this conversation measures the range of western thought. The vocabulary of its language is the stock of ideas with which each individual can begin to think for himself when he turns from dialogue to soliloquy; for, as Plato observes, "thought and speech are the same, with this exception, that what is called thought is the unuttered conversation of the soul with itself."

46

Law

INTRODUCTION

THE notion of law is associated with a diversity of subject matters, and its meaning undergoes many variations as the discussion shifts from one context to another. The most radical difference separates the way in which natural scientists use the term *law* from the way in which it is used in the arts and in morals or politics.

We ordinarily think of law as a rule—a command or a prohibition—which should be obeyed and can be disobeyed. Both alternatives are usually present. Though the duty or obligation which a law creates is one of obedience, there would be no moral significance to discharging this duty if the law could not be violated. But the laws of nature which the scientist tries to discover do not have this characteristic. They are inviolable. The so-called law of gravitation, for example, or Newton's three laws of motion, cannot be disobeyed. Scientists may disagree about the truth of any formulation of a natural law, but if the formulation is valid, then the general rule of behavior is supposed to obtain without exception; and if exceptions are found, they are not interpreted as instances of disobedience, but rather as cases to which the law does not apply.

"Magic," writes Frazer, "is a spurious system of natural law as well as a fallacious guide of conduct . . . Regarded as a system of natural law . . . it may be called Theoretical Magic."

The rules of an art may be violated, either unwittingly or intentionally. For example, grammatical errors can be made by those ignorant of the rules or by those who wish to disregard them. The so-called "law of contradiction" in the art of logic seems to be like the rules of grammar or of any other art. Men certainly contradict themselves in spite of the rule which places the penalty of error on those who make contradictory statements.

But according to another conception of the law of contradiction, which belongs to the science of metaphysics rather than to the art of logic, nothing can both be and not be at the same time in the same respect. This law of being, like the laws of motion, is regarded as inviolable by those who think it true. In this it has the aspect of a scientific or natural law. The law of contradiction, conceived as a rule of logic, may also be natural in the sense of *not being man-made*. In the opinion of certain philosophers, man does not invent either the metaphysical rule which all existences *must* observe or the logical rule which the human mind *should* always obey. He discovers both.

There still remains that other class of rules to which the word "law" is most commonly applied. These are rules of moral action or social conduct which, like rules of art, are essentially violable. "Laws, in their most general signification," Montesquieu writes, "are the necessary relations arising from the nature of things. In this sense all beings have their laws." But he points out that law operates differently in the realm of physical nature and in the realm of intelligent beings like man. The latter, he says, "does not conform to [its laws] so exactly as the physical world. This is because, on the one hand, particular intelligent beings are of a finite nature, and consequently liable to error; and on the other, their nature requires them to be free agents." Hence, even the laws "of their own instituting, they frequently infringe."

The profound division between laws of nature and laws of human conduct thus seems to involve two points: (1) the former may apply to all things, the latter are addressed to man alone; (2) the former, being inviolable, state the necessities of behavior, the latter, precisely because they are violable, imply freedom in those to whom they are addressed.

These two kinds of law have this much in common. Both the laws of nature discovered by the scientist and the rules of conduct instituted by the legislator are general rather than particular. Their generality has been made, in the tradition of jurisprudence, the basis for differentiating rules of law from particular decisions or decrees. On theological grounds, however, the two kinds of law can be said to have a more significant characteristic in common.

Aquinas conceives the laws of nature which the scientist discovers as laws implanted in the very nature of things at their creation by God. The laws which God implants in human nature do not differ in their eternal origin in the divine intellect and will, or in their manifestation of the divine government of the world. They differ only in that it is part of man's nature to be free and therefore able to disobey even the rules of his own nature. Thus both sorts of law are directions of behavior. Only if the laws which science discovers are not attributed to God, will they seem to be merely descriptive rather than prescriptive.

In this chapter we shall be primarily concerned with law as a direction of human conduct or, as Kant would say, law in the sphere of freedom. But within the one meaning of law which concerns us here, there are still many important distinctions of type. The division of law into divine and human, natural and positive, private and public, moral and political— to name only some of the traditional distinctions—determines the outlines of the diverse philosophies of law which the great books contain, and underlies the great issues concerning the origin, the properties, and the authority of law.

DIFFERENT WRITERS use different criteria to set up their classification of the kinds of law. It is nevertheless possible to perceive certain parallels in analysis and classification. The opposite of natural law is sometimes called "human law," "positive law," or "written law," sometimes "civil law" or "municipal law." Sometimes, as with Kant, for whom the analysis of law derives from an analysis of rights, the differentiation between natural and positive right is also expressed in terms of innate and acquired right, public and private right.

Thus, for Kant, "natural right rests upon pure rational principles *a priori;* positive or statutory right is what proceeds from the will of a legislator . . . Innate right is that right which belongs to everyone by nature, independent of all juridical acts of experience. Acquired right is that right which is founded upon such juridical acts." From natural or innate right develops "the system of those laws which require no external promulgation" and which therefore belong to the sphere of private right. Positive or civil rights are the acquired rights of men living in a state of civil society under "the system of those laws which require public promulgation" and which therefore belong to the sphere of public right. The source of differentiation here seems threefold: whether the right is inherent in human nature or acquired from the state; whether men are viewed as living in a state of nature or as living in a civil society; whether the laws do or do not need to be publicly promulgated.

The distinction between the state of nature and the state of civil society is used by many other writers in differentiating between natural and positive (or civil) law, *e.g.,* by Hobbes, Spinoza, Locke, Montesquieu, Rousseau. They also recognize that the law which governs men living in a state of nature is natural in the sense of being instinctive, or a rule of conduct which man's reason is innately competent to prescribe; whereas the civil law originates with specific acts of legislation by a political power, vested in a sovereign person, in a representative assembly, or in the whole body of the people.

Dividing all laws into two kinds—"laws of nature and laws of the land"—Hegel holds that "the laws of nature are simply what they are and are valid as they are." In contrast, positive law is "valid in a particular state, and this legal authority is the guiding principle for the knowledge of right in this positive form, *i.e.,* for the science of positive law." Our manner of knowing their content further distinguishes between these two kinds of law. "To know the law of nature," Hegel explains, "we must learn to know nature, since its laws are rigid, and it is only our ideas about them that can be false . . . Knowledge of the laws of the land is in one way similar, but in another way not. These laws too we learn to know just as they exist . . . But the difference in the case of laws of the land is that they arouse the spirit of reflection, and their diversity at once draws attention to the fact that they are not absolute."

This leads us to the heart of the distinction. The law of the land, or civil law, is "something posited, something originated by men." It is positive law in the sense that it must be *posited* (*i.e.,* officially instituted) in order to exist. The civil law is not something *discovered* by examining man's nature. It is *made,* and must be externally promulgated so that those who are subject to it can learn its provisions. Anyone who will inquire can learn the natural law for himself; or he can be helped to discover it by a teacher who instructs him in this matter as he would instruct him in geometry, not as a lawyer informs clients concerning the prevailing laws of the state.

AQUINAS BOTH subtracts from and adds to this analysis of the difference between natural and positive law. On the one hand, he does not appeal to the condition of man in a state of nature as contrasted with civil society. On the other hand, he finds the chief difference between the natural and the positive law in their originating sources. The one is made by God, the other by man. "The natural law," Aquinas writes, "is nothing else than the rational creature's participation in the eternal law." It is God's eternal law with respect to man as that is received and exists in human nature. It exists in man as the first principle of his practical reason and includes all the precepts which can be discovered by reasoning therefrom.

Hence, for Aquinas as for Locke, the law of nature is not only the law of reason but the law of nature's God. But Aquinas distinguishes between the law of nature generally, or the eternal law, and the natural law in man. The latter is a *moral* law, both in the sense that it is a law governing free acts, and also in the sense that it directs man with regard to good and evil in the sphere of his private life, not merely with regard to the political common good.

Natural and positive law are alike in the very respects in which they differ. Both share in the nature of law which, according to Aquinas, "is nothing else than an ordinance of reason for the common good, made by him who has care of the community, and promulgated." Each has a maker, God or man; each proceeds in a certain way from the reason and will of its maker; each must be promulgated, though not in the same manner; and each is concerned with a common good—human happiness or the welfare of the state.

The further additions which Aquinas makes consist of distinctions with respect to divine and human law. With respect to the divine law he distinguishes between God's eternal ordinances and His positive commandments. The eternal part of the divine law, as we have seen, is that which, at the moment of creation, "God imprints on the whole of nature," to instill in each created species "the principles of its proper actions." "If man were ordained to no other end than that which is proportionate to his natural faculties," Aquinas writes, "there would be no need for man to have any further direction . . . besides the natural law and the human law which is derived from it." But "man is ordained to the end of eternal happiness"; and since salvation is a supernatural end which exceeds man's power to achieve without God's help, "it was necessary that . . . man should be directed to this end by a law given by God."

God gave such a body of law to man, not at creation, but at a certain moment in history. He did not implant it in his nature but promulgated it, in the manner appropriate to positive law, through verbal declaration—through His revealed word in the Old and the New Testaments, *e.g.,* the Ten Commandments and the two precepts of charity.

Where for Aquinas the divine law, both old and new, functions by giving us directions of the paths to follow in order to achieve salvation, for Calvin, God's law is an instrument for measuring our sinfulness. It is, he writes, "a kind of mirror. As in a mirror we discover any stains upon our face, so in the Law we behold, first, our impotence; then . . . our iniquity; and, finally, the curse, as the consequence of both."

The human law Aquinas divides "into the *law of nations* [or the *ius gentium*] and *civil law*." The civil law is that which is instituted by a community for its own members. With regard to the *ius gentium* Aquinas follows the tradition of the Roman jurists. What he has in mind in using this term should, therefore, not be confused with what later writers, such as Hugo Grotius, treat as the *ius inter gentes* or international law. Yet applicable to both the law of nations and international law is the question whether such law belongs more properly to the sphere of natural or to the sphere of positive law.

International law concerns the relations between autonomous states which, as Hegel points out, are "in a state of nature in relation to one another," since "the sovereignty of a state is the principle of its relations to others." Laws cannot be applied to sovereign states with the coercive force of positive law. "It follows," says Hegel, "that if states disagree and their particular wills cannot be harmonized, the matter can only be settled by war." His statement that international law "does not go beyond an ought-to-be" separates it from positive law. On similar grounds Aquinas separates the *ius gentium* from positive law. He recognizes, as will presently appear, that it does not result from legislative enactment. Furthermore, he points out that it is discovered by reason and derives its rules by way of deduction from natural law. The law of nations is, therefore, not positively instituted.

That the law of nations lacks some of the properties of civil law does not make it, for Aquinas, less essentially a body of law; but for Hegel it falls short of the essence of law, which consists in a determinate and universal rule of right posited by a sovereign will. The great legal positivists of the 19th century, such as John Austin, go further and deny that anything is truly law except the positive enactments of a government which has the power to enforce its ordinances. The laws of nature are laws only in a metaphoric sense.

The Greeks also appear to regard law as primarily a creation of the state. Aristotle conceives political justice as "part natural, part legal—natural, that which everywhere has the same force and does not exist by people's thinking this or that; legal, that which is originally indifferent, but when it has been laid down is not indifferent." This tends to identify the legal aspect of justice with the conventional. The threefold division of law into civil law, law of nations, and natural law is not Greek but Roman in origin.

Yet the Greeks do not hold that all law is of human institution or merely a matter of local convention. The fundamental opposition between the divine law and the man-made law of the state occurs frequently in the Greek tragedies, and with particular force in the *Antigone* of Sophocles. In burying her brother, Antigone violates the king's edict, but, in her view, not to have done so would have been to violate "the gods' unwritten and unfailing laws," which, she declares, are "not now, nor yesterday's, they always live, / and no one knows their origin in time. / So not through fear of any man's proud spirit," she says, "would I be likely to neglect these laws" and "draw on myself the gods' sure punishment."

Aristotle cites this passage from Sophocles when, in his *Rhetoric*, he advises the forensic orator (or trial lawyer) "to appeal to the universal law, and insist on its greater equity and justice," *if* "the written law tells against our case." Under such circumstances, he thinks it is wise to "urge that the principles of equity are permanent and changeless, and that the universal law does not change either, for it is the law of nature, whereas written laws often do change." Under the opposite circumstances, that is, when "the written law supports our case," he prescribes an opposite course—to cite the laws of the state and to urge that they be upheld.

Though Aristotle here speaks of "the law of nature," he seems to have in mind the notion of "a universal law," or a body of law that is *common* to all peoples. For the most part, he speaks of natural justice rather than natural law. Whether or not the two notions are equivalent, his principle of natural justice stands in the same relation to political enactments as, for later writers, the natural law stands to the positive law. Plato's conception of law as "a disposition of reason" which orders things according to their natures, even more explicitly recognizes that law neither depends upon nor derives its authority from the power of the state. The phrase "natural law" may be infrequent in the Greek books, but its meaning is not unrepresented in Greek thought.

OTHER DISTINCTIONS in kinds of law—written and unwritten, statutory and customary, constitutional law and the various particular bodies of law, such as the law of contracts, of crimes, or of torts—are for the most part subdivisions of positive law. The one exception, perhaps, is the unwritten law, which, when not identified with customary law, stands for the natural law or the law of reason. With respect to these parts of law, the chief problems concern constitutions and customs. The difference between a constitution as law and all other laws obtaining in a state is considered in the chapter on CONSTITUTION; and the legal force of custom, both in itself and also in relation to legislative enactments, is discussed in the chapter on CUSTOM AND CONVENTION.

Here our major concern is with positive law as a whole, with its properties and defects, but above all with its relation to natural law. Some of the properties of positive law are agreed upon even by those who sharply disagree concerning its relation to natural law.

It is generally agreed, for example, that a rule of positive law cannot be made by *any* man, but only by him who exercises the legislative authority and has the power to enforce the rule. Agreement also prevails concerning the mutability of positive law, though not all would go as far as Montaigne in holding that "there is nothing subject to more continual agitation than the laws." Yet it is generally recognized that the content of positive law continually undergoes change with the nullification or amendment of old rules and the addition of new ones, and that positive regulations on any particular matter may vary from state to state.

No less common is the understanding of the indispensability of courts and judges. "Laws are a dead letter without courts to expound and define their true meaning and operation," Hamilton writes. Though rules of law, in distinction from decrees, are formulated to cover an indefinite number of like cases, the cases to which they must be applied by the judicial process are far from uniform. Courts and judges have the task of deciding whether the facts of the particular case bring that case under the specific provisions of the law. This is the field of judicial discretion and the battleground of litigants and lawyers.

The propensities of men of law, on the bench and at the bar, to protract and complicate the procedures of a trial, to multiply and divide the issues, to separate themselves from laymen by a heavy curtain of language, have been satirically noted in the great diatribes against the legal profession, from Aristophanes to Chaucer, Rabelais, Montaigne, and Swift.

Rabelais, for example, has Pantagruel undertake to arbitrate in the litigation between "Lord Kissbreech, plaintiff of one side, and ... Lord Suckfist, defendant of the other, whose controversy was so high and difficult in law that the court of parliament could make nothing of it." Pantagruel conducts the proceedings in an unusual style. When the counselors and attorneys "delivered into his hands the bags wherein were the writs and pancarts concerning that suit, which for bulk and weight were almost enough to load four great couillard or stoned asses, Pantagruel said unto them, Are the two lords, between whom this debate and process is, yet living?" Upon being told they are alive, "to what a devil, then, said he, serve so many paltry heaps and bundles of papers and copies which you give me? Is it not better to hear their controversy from their own mouths, whilst they are face to face before us, than to read these vile fopperies, which are nothing but trumperies, deceits, diabolical cozenages of Cepola, pernicious slights and subversions of equity."

Furthermore, Pantagruel continues, "seeing

the laws are excerpted out of the middle of moral and natural philosophy, how should these fools have understood it, that have, by G—, studied less in philosophy than my mule? In respect of human learning, and the knowledge of antiquities and history, they are truly laden with these faculties as a toad is with feathers. And yet of all this the laws are so full, that without it they cannot be understood ... Therefore, if you will that I make any meddling in this process, first, cause all these papers to be burned; secondly, make the two gentlemen come personally before me, and, afterwards, when I shall have heard them, I will tell you my opinion freely, without any feignedness or dissimulation whatsoever." The trial which Pantagruel then conducts, in which the two lords are forced to plead without benefit of counsel, is a choice and proper piece of litigation.

THE PROBLEMS of casuistry, with which Pascal deals at length in his *The Provincial Letters*, are sometimes thought of as peculiar to the canon law, but casuistry, in the sense of distinguishing cases and examining them in relation to general rules, necessarily occurs in the judicial application of any body of law. The most difficult cases are those which may fall under the letter of a law but seem to be inconsistent with its spirit. The reverse also happens; cases fall outside the letter of the law but the purpose of the law seems to cover them. All such cases indicate an unavoidable defect in rules of law.

The defect is unavoidable, Aristotle says. Law aims at universality "but about some things it is not possible to make a universal statement which shall be correct." To remedy this defect, the intention of the lawmaker should be consulted. The particular case should be treated as he would have treated it if he had had it in mind when he framed the general rule. Such handling of the difficult case is what Aristotle means by the equitable—"a correction of the law where it is defective owing to its universality."

The law which equity is called upon to correct may be a just rule, but that does not prevent its being unjustly applied. Equity prevents the injustice of misapplication by dispensing justice in the particular case according to the spirit, not the letter, of the law. It is a kind of justice, Aristotle says; "not legal justice but a correction of legal justice ... not better than absolute justice but better than the error which arises from the absoluteness of the rule."

Those who share Aristotle's theory of equity acknowledge a standard of justice by which not only the law's application, but also the law itself, is to be measured. In his terms, natural justice provides this standard. The justice of laws made by the state is not only relative to the constitution of the state, but since the constitution itself can be more or less just, there is a standard of justice prior to and independent of the state—in this sense, *natural*.

Essentially the same point is made by those who, like Montesquieu and Locke, appeal to the natural law, both as a measure of constitutions and as a criterion for distinguishing good from bad law. "Before laws were made," Montesquieu writes, "there were relations of possible justice. To say that there is nothing just or unjust but what is commanded or forbidden by positive laws, is the same as saying that before the describing of a circle all the radii were not equal."

The law of nature, according to Locke, does not apply only to the conduct of men living in a state of nature. The law of nature which Locke describes as a rule "of common reason and equity which is that measure God has set to the actions of men for their mutual security," is not abolished when men enter into civil society. "The obligations of the law of nature cease not in society, but only in many cases are drawn closer, and have by human laws known penalties annexed to them, to enforce their observation. Thus the law of nature stands as an eternal rule to all men, legislators as well as others." The rules of positive law, writes Locke, must "be conformable to the law of nature, *i.e.,* to the will of God, of which that is the declaration." The municipal laws of any particular state "are only so far right as they are founded on the law of nature, by which they are to be regulated and interpreted."

THE POSITION of Locke and Aquinas makes natural law the source as well as the standard of positive law. As a source, natural law gives rise to positive law in a way which, for Aquinas at least, differentiates it from the law of nations or the *ius gentium*.

"Something may be derived from the natural law in two ways," he writes. "First, as a conclusion from premises; secondly, by way of determination of certain generalities. The first way," he explains, "is like to that by which, in sciences, demonstrated conclusions are drawn from the principles; while the second mode is likened to that whereby, in the arts, general forms are particularized as to details: thus the craftsman needs to determine the general form of a house to some particular shape." Now "to the law of nations belong those things which are derived from the law of nature, as conclusions from premises, *e.g.,* just buyings and sellings, and the like, without which men cannot live together, which is a point of the law of nature, since man is by nature a social animal . . . But those things which are derived from the law of nature by way of particular determination, belong to the civil law, according as each state decides on what is best for itself."

Aquinas exemplifies the determinations of positive law by pointing out that "the law of nature has it that the evildoer should be punished; but that he be punished in this way or that, is a determination of the law of nature," which the positive law must institute. He might also have used as an example the fact that the universal prohibition of killing is a conclusion from the principle of natural law that "*one should do harm to no man,*" whereas the various kinds and degrees of murder are differently defined in different countries according to the determination of the natural law made by the positive law of homicide in each country.

The rules of positive law cannot be arrived at deductively. They do not follow necessarily from principles. They are only determinations which particularize the precepts of natural law in a manner which fits the contingent circumstances of a particular society. Whatever is made determinate by positive law is something which the natural law leaves indeterminate because no point of justice or right is involved. Other determinations could have been made. An element of choice is involved in the making of positive laws. In addition to being formulated by the reason, they must be posited by the will of whoever has the authority to make laws.

Rules of positive law are the work of reason to the extent that reason is called upon to propose various *possible* determinations of the natural law, *e.g.,* one or another definition of murder in the first degree, one or another definition of the penalty for it. Since a definite rule of positive law cannot be instituted until a choice is made among the alternative possibilities, the positive law cannot be solely the work of reason. Choice, according to Aquinas, is always an act of the will.

Though he recognizes the role of choice, and hence of the will, in the enactment of positive law, Aquinas does not go to the other extreme of making the will the sole arbiter of what is law. The legality of the state's ordinances does not depend entirely on their being posited by the will of a sovereign authority. If a positive regulation is not derived from the natural law, it cannot be a just rule. Quoting Augustine's remark that "a law which is not just is a law in name only," Aquinas goes on to say: "Every human law has just so much of the nature of law as it is derived from the law of nature. But if in any point it departs from the law of nature, it is no longer a law but a perversion of law."

An ordinance which had no other foundation than the will of a sovereign prince or government might have the coercive force of law, but it would lack the moral authority of law. It would bind men, not through conscience, but only through their fear of punishment for disobedience. "That force and tyranny may be an element in law," writes Hegel, "is accidental to law, and has nothing to do with its nature."

A COMPLETELY opposite view is taken by those who deny natural law or principles of innate right and natural justice. There is, in addition, a theory of natural law which leads to an opposite view of the legal and the just, though the opposition in this case is qualified to some extent.

According to Hobbes, "civil and natural law are not different kinds, but different parts of law." The law of nature and the civil law, he says, "contain each other and are of equal extent." But he also says that "the laws of nature ... are not properly laws, but qualities that dispose men to peace and to obedience."

Before the formation of a commonwealth, by the contract or covenant whereby men transfer the rights and liberties which they possess in a state of nature, the natural law directs men, first, to preserve their lives in the war "of every man against every man"; and second, to seek the security of peace by leaving the natural state of war to join with their fellowmen in the order of a civil society. The nineteen precepts of natural law which Hobbes enumerates seem to set forth reason's recognition of the advantages of civil society over the state of nature and also reason's understanding of the conditions indispensable to a firm foundation of the commonwealth.

These rules of reason "are the laws of nature, dictating peace, for a means of the conservation of men in multitudes, and which only concern the doctrine of civil society." But until the commonwealth exists, the laws of nature bind in conscience only, and they are therefore not effective in achieving their end, which is security. "When a commonwealth is settled, then they are actually laws and not before; as being then the commands of the commonwealth, and therefore also civil laws. For it is the sovereign power which obliges men to obey them."

The distinction between natural and civil law then becomes a distinction between unwritten and written rules; but the test of whether any rule is actually a law is the same, namely, whether it is adopted and enforced by the sovereign. "All laws, written and unwritten, have their authority and force from the will of the commonwealth," Hobbes writes.

The difference between the Hobbesian theory and that of Locke or Aquinas reveals itself in its consequences. Under what circumstances can a subject or citizen refuse obedience to the laws of the state? On the ground that they

are unjust or tyrannical? By the criterion that they violate precepts of natural law or the positive commandments of God? Is the individual bound in conscience to obey every command of the civil law, because the civil law includes the natural law, interprets it, and gives it the authority and force of law; and because the natural law itself commands obedience to the civil law once a commonwealth has been instituted? Or, on the contrary, is an individual in conscience free to disobey those positive enactments which lack the authority of law because they are not in conformity to the natural law or the divine law?

TO QUESTIONS OF THIS SORT, and to the whole problem of the right of rebellion, different answers seem to be given in terms of different views of the nature of law, the sources of its authority, and its sanctions.

At one extreme there is the doctrine that rebellion is never justified, that the security of peace, which the maintenance of law and order provides, is always better than the anarchy and war which result from rebellion. Hobbes, for example, holds that "nothing the sovereign representative can do to a subject, on what pretence soever, can properly be called injustice, or injury." The rebel would, therefore, always be a criminal, a man who takes the law into his own hands, and uses force to gain his ends. A man may be justified in using force, according to Hobbes, only to repel force used against him, and then only in defense of his life. So much the law of nature permits or requires. But it does not permit or require him to decide which laws enacted by his sovereign he shall obey or disobey.

At the other extreme there is the doctrine of civil disobedience as expounded by Henry David Thoreau, Mohandas K. Gandhi, and Martin Luther King, Jr. Unjust laws, or laws which violate a man's conscience, may have the force of the state behind them. But they exert no authority over him. The just man is called upon to break them and to submit gladly to the consequences of breaking them, by suffering whatever penalties may be attached to their breach. It is not enough for the individual citizen to satisfy his conscience by criticizing the government and joining with like-minded fellow citizens in an effort to get unjust laws abolished or reformed. He is obliged in conscience not to await help from others or to be patient in the use of gradual means. He is obliged to act alone and at once—by disobeying the unjust law.

Kant seems to go this far when he interprets the precept "Do wrong to no one" as meaning "Do no wrong to anyone, even if thou shouldst be under the necessity, in observing this duty, to cease from all connection with others and to avoid all society." But he qualifies this somewhat by the precept: "Enter, if wrong cannot be avoided, into a society with others in which everyone may have *secured* to him what is his own."

Another sort of qualification limits disobedience, rebellion, or secession from society—even when the individual conscience recoils from the injustice or illegality of a civil ordinance. The principle, as stated by Aquinas, seems to be that the common good may, under certain circumstances, be better served by acquiescence than by disobedience. Unless what the law commands involves a transgression of God's commandments, an unjust law may be obeyed "in order to avoid scandal or disturbance."

Even with regard to reforming law by legal means Aquinas recommends that the disadvantages resulting from the change of law be weighed against the advantages. The effectiveness of law depends upon the habits of obedience it forms and upon the customary behavior it establishes. "Consequently," Aquinas says, "when a law is changed, the binding power of law is diminished, in so far as custom is abolished." This harm to the common welfare may, of course, be compensated either by "the benefit conferred by the new enactment" or by the fact that "the existing law is clearly unjust, or its observance extremely harmful."

Locke states the principle somewhat differently. So long as due process of law is available to remedy unjust ordinances or illegal acts, the individual is not justified in disobedience, for such action would "unhinge and overturn all polities, and, instead of government and order, leave nothing but anarchy and confusion." Nor is it effective for the individual to act alone in using force to resist tyranny or injustice. But if these illegal acts have extended to the majority of the people "and they are persuaded in their consciences, that their laws, and with them their estates, liberties, and lives are in danger, and perhaps, their religion too, how they will be hindered from resisting illegal force used against them, I cannot tell. This is an inconvenience, I confess, that attends all governments." There is no alternative then but rebellion—"properly a state of war wherein the appeal lies only to heaven."

As the foregoing discussion indicates, the basic issues in the philosophy of law are inseparable from questions about justice and liberty, the rights of the individual and the authority of the state, the powers of government, and the fundamental alternatives of crime and punishment, war and peace. These matters are considered in the chapters appropriate to the terms mentioned above. More particular consequences of the theory of law, especially natural law, are found in such chapters as REVOLUTION, SLAVERY, and TYRANNY AND DESPOTISM, CITIZEN, CONSTITUTION, and WEALTH.

47

Liberty

INTRODUCTION

LIBERTY and law, liberty and justice, liberty and equality—the familiar connection of these terms breeds neglect of the meaning they confer upon one another through association. A few simple questions may help to restore the significance of these relationships. Are men free when their actions are regulated by law or coercion? Does liberty consist in doing whatever one pleases or whatever one has the power to do, or is one required by justice to abstain from injury to others? Do considerations of justice draw the line between liberty and license? Can there be liberty apart from equality and perhaps also fraternity?

Other questions immediately suggest themselves. Does not the rule of law secure liberty to the governed? Is not slavery the condition of those who are ruled tyrannically or lawlessly? Does it make a difference to freedom whether the law or the constitution is just? Or is that indifferent because government itself is the impediment to liberty? Does liberty increase as the scope of government dwindles and reach fullness only with anarchy or when men live in a state of nature?

Yet are not some forms of government said to be fitting and some uncongenial to free men? Do all men have a right to freedom, or only some? Are some men by nature free and some slave? Does such a differentiation imply both equality and inequality in human nature with, as a consequence, equality and inequality in status or treatment? What implications for law, justice, and equality has the distinction between free societies and dependent or subject communities?

As Tolstoy points out, the variety of questions which can be asked about liberty indicates the variety of subject matters or sciences in which the problems of freedom are differently raised. "What is sin, the conception of which arises from the consciousness of man's freedom? That is a question for theology ... What is man's responsibility to society, the conception of which results from the conception of freedom? That is a question for jurisprudence ... What is conscience and the perception of right and wrong in actions that follow from the consciousness of freedom? That is a question for ethics ... How should the past life of nations and of humanity be regarded—as the result of the free, or as the result of the constrained, activity of man? That is a question for history."

The great traditional issues of liberty seem to be stated by these questions. From the fact that most, perhaps all, of these questions elicit opposite answers from the great books, it might be supposed that there are as many basic issues as there are questions of this sort. But the answers to certain questions presuppose answers to others. Furthermore, the meaning of liberty or freedom or independence is not the same throughout the questions we have considered. Answers which appear to be inconsistent may not be so when the meanings involved in their formulation are distinguished. We must, therefore, find the roots of the several distinct doctrines of liberty in order to separate real issues from verbal conflicts.

THE HISTORIANS report the age-old struggle on the part of men and of states for liberty or independence. History as a development of the spirit does not begin, according to Hegel, until this struggle first appears. "The History of the world," he writes, "is none other than the progress of the consciousness of Freedom," which does not reach its climax until freedom is universally achieved. But though freedom is its product, history, in Hegel's view, is not a work of freedom, but "involves an absolute necessity." Each stage of its development occurs inevitably.

Other historians see man as free to work out his destiny, and look upon the great crises of civilization as turning points at which freemen, that is, men having free will, exercise a free choice for better or for worse. "Whether we speak of the migration of the peoples and the incursions of the barbarians, or of the decrees of Napoleon III, or of someone's action an hour ago in choosing one direction out of several for his walk, we are unconscious of any contradiction," Tolstoy declares, between freedom and necessity. "Our conception of the degree of freedom," he goes on to say, "often varies according to differences in the point of view from which we regard the event, but every human action appears to us as a certain combination of freedom and inevitability. In every action we examine we see a certain measure of freedom and a certain measure of inevitability. And always the more freedom we see in any action the less inevitability do we perceive, and the more inevitability the less freedom."

Accordingly, neither necessity which flows from the laws of matter or of spirit, nor overhanging and indomitable fate determines the direction of events. If the theologians say that nothing happens which God does not foresee, they also say that divine providence leaves the world full of contingencies and man a free agent to operate among them. "Though there is for God a certain order of all causes," it does not follow, Augustine says, that nothing depends "on the free exercise of our own wills, for our wills themselves are included in that order of causes which is certain to God, and is embraced by His foreknowledge, for human wills are also causes of human actions."

These matters are further discussed in the chapters on FATE, HISTORY, and NECESSITY AND CONTINGENCY. The mention of them here suggests another meaning of liberty—that of free choice or free will—and with it issues other than those involved in the relation of the individual to the state or to his fellowmen. The metaphysical problems about free will and freedom of choice are treated in the chapter on WILL. Yet the metaphysical questions about liberty and necessity, or freedom and causality, and the theological questions about man's freedom under God, are not without bearing on the political problems of man's freedom in society, or his rights and powers. The fundamental doctrines of civil liberty certainly seem to differ according to the conception of natural freedom on which they are based. Freedom may be natural in the sense that free will is a part of human nature; or in the sense that freedom is a birthright, an innate and inalienable right. It may be natural in the sense in which freedom in a state of nature is distinguished from political liberty, or liberty under civil law and government.

THE EFFORT TO clarify meanings requires us to look at the three words which we have used as if they were interchangeable—"liberty," "freedom," and "independence." For the most part, "liberty" and "freedom" are synonyms. Both words are used in English versions of the great books. Though authors or translators sometimes prefer one, sometimes the other, their preference does not seem to reflect a variation in meaning.

In English the word "freedom" has a little greater range in that it permits the formation of the adjective "free." It is also adapted to speaking of freedom *from* certain restraints or undesirable conditions, as well as of freedom *to* act in accordance with desire or to exercise certain privileges. In consequence, the word "freedom" is more frequently employed in the discussion of free will. Though the traditional enumeration of civil liberties may use the phrasing "liberty of conscience or worship" as frequently as "freedom of conscience or worship," "freedom of speech" is more usual, and "freedom from fear or want or economic dependence" does not seem to have an alternative phrasing.

The word "independence" has special connotations which make it equivalent to only part of the meaning of "freedom" or "liberty." Negatively, independence is a freedom from limitation or from being subject to determination by another. Positively, independence implies self-sufficiency and adequate power. When we speak of a man of independent means, we refer not only to his freedom from want or economic dependence on others, but also to his having sufficient wealth to suit his tastes or purposes. A moment's reflection will show that this is a relative matter. It is doubtful whether absolute economic independence is possible for men or even for nations.

The real question here seems to be a metaphysical one. Can any finite thing be absolutely independent? The traditional answer is No. As appears in the chapter on INFINITY, only a being infinite in perfection and power—only the Supreme One of Plotinus, the uncreated God of Aquinas, or the self-caused God of Spinoza—has complete independence. God has the freedom of autonomy which cannot belong to finite things. There is, however, another sense of divine freedom which Aquinas affirms and both Plotinus and Spinoza deny. That is freedom of choice.

"God does not act from freedom of will," Spinoza writes; yet God alone acts as a free cause, for God alone "exists from the necessity of his own nature and is determined to action by himself alone." The divine freedom consists in God's self-determination which, for Spinoza, does not exclude necessity. The opposite view is most clearly expressed in the Christian doctrine of creation. The created world does not follow necessarily from the divine nature. "Since the goodness of God is perfect," Aquinas writes, "and can exist without other things, inasmuch as no perfection can accrue to Him from them, it follows that for Him to will things other than Himself is not absolutely necessary." This issue of freedom or necessity with regard to God's will and action is more fully discussed in the chapters on WILL and WORLD.

The metaphysical identification of independence with infinity does not carry over into the sphere of political freedom. Yet in one respect there is an analogy. The autonomous is that which is a law unto itself. It admits no superior authority. When in the tradition of political thought states are called "free and independent," their autonomy or sovereignty means that by virtue of which, in the words of the Declaration of Independence, "they have full power to levy war, conclude peace, contract alliances, establish commerce, and to do all other acts and things which independent states may of right do."

Free and independent states do not have infinite power. There is always the possibility of their being subjugated by another state and reduced to the condition of a dependency. But though their power is not infinite, they acknowledge no superior. To be a sovereign is to accept commands from no one.

Since autonomy or sovereignty is incompatible with living under human law or government, the independence of sovereign princes or states must be an anarchic freedom—a freedom from law and government. This seems to be the view of Hobbes, Locke, Kant, and Hegel, all of whom refer to the anarchy of independent states or sovereign princes to explain what they mean by the "state of nature." Sovereigns are, in the words of Kant, "like lawless savages."

Applying this conception to individual men, Hobbes and Locke define natural as opposed to civil liberty in terms of man's independence in a state of nature. In a state of nature man had a limited independence, since each man might be coerced by a superior force; but it was an absolute independence in the sense that he was subject to no human government or man-made law.

THE NATURAL FREEDOM of man, according to Hobbes, is not free will. Since "every act of man's will, and every desire and inclination, proceed from some cause, and that from another cause, in a continual chain (whose first link is in the hand of God, the first of all causes), they proceed from *necessity*." Liberty is not of the will, but of the man, consisting in this: "that he finds no stop in doing what he has the will, desire, or inclination to do." The proper application of the word "free" is to bodies in motion, and the liberty it signifies when so applied is merely "the absence of external impediments."

The natural right of every man is "the liberty

each man has to use his own power ... for the preservation of his own nature, that is to say, of his own life ... and consequently of doing anything which in his own judgment and reason he shall conceive to be the aptest means thereunto." This liberty or natural right belongs to man only in a state of nature. When men leave the state of nature and enter the commonwealth, they surrender this natural liberty in exchange for a civil liberty which, according to Hobbes, consists in nothing more than their freedom to do what the law of the state does not prohibit, or to omit doing what the law does not command.

Locke agrees that man's natural liberty is not the freedom of his will in choosing, but the freedom to do what he wills without constraint or impediment. He differs from Hobbes, however, in his conception of natural liberty because he differs in his conception of the state of nature.

For Hobbes the state of nature is a state of war; the notions of right and wrong, justice and injustice, can have no place in it. "Where there is no common power, there is no law: where no law, no injustice." The liberty which sovereign states now have is the same as "that which every man should have if there were no civil laws, nor commonwealth at all. And the effects of it also are the same. For as amongst masterless men, there is perpetual war of every man against his neighbor ... so in states and commonwealths not dependent on one another, every commonwealth has an absolute liberty to do what it shall judge ... most conducing to its benefit."

For Locke the state of nature is not a state of war, but a natural as opposed to a civil society, that is, a society in which men live together under natural rather than under civil law. Men who live in this condition are "in a state of perfect freedom to order their actions and dispose of their possessions as they think fit, within the bounds of the law of nature." This is a limited, not an absolute freedom; or, as Locke says, "though this be a state of liberty, yet it is not a state of license." The line between liberty and license is drawn by the precepts of the natural law. The difference, then, between natural and civil liberty

lies in this. Natural liberty consists in being "free from any superior power on earth," or not being "under the will or legislative authority of man." Only the rules of natural law limit freedom of action. Civil liberty, or liberty under civil law, consists in being "under no other legislative power but that established by consent." It is a freedom for the individual to follow his own will in all matters not prescribed by the law of the state.

IN THE ARGUMENTS for and against free will, one view regards free will as incompatible with the principle of causality, natural necessity, or God's omnipotence; the other conceives free choice as falling within the order of nature or causality and under God's providence. We shall not consider these alternatives in this chapter, since this issue is reserved for the chapter on WILL.

Yet one thing is clear for the present consideration of political liberty. If the statement that men are born free means that it is a property of their rational natures to possess a free will, then they do not lose their innate freedom when they live in civil society. Government may interfere with a man's actions, but it cannot coerce his will. Government can go no further than to regulate the expression of man's freedom in external actions.

Nor is the range of free will limited by law. As indicated in the chapter on LAW, any law—moral or civil, natural or positive—which directs human conduct can be violated. It leaves man free to disobey it and take the consequences. But if the rule is good or just, then the act which transgresses it must have the opposite quality. The freedom of a free will is therefore morally indifferent. It can be exercised to do either good or evil. We use our freedom properly, says Augustine, when we act virtuously; we misuse it when we choose to act viciously. "The will," he writes, "is then truly free, when it is not the slave of vices and sins."

Those who conceive the natural moral law as stating the precepts of virtue or the commands of duty and who, in addition, regard every concrete act which proceeds from a free choice of the will as either good or bad—

never indifferent—find that the distinction between liberty and license applies to every free act. The meaning of this distinction is the same as that between freedom properly used and freedom misused. Furthermore, since there is no good act which is not prescribed by the moral law, the whole of liberty, as opposed to license, consists in doing what that moral law commands.

These considerations affect the problem of political liberty, especially on the question whether the spheres of law and liberty are separate, or even opposed. One view, as we have seen, is that the area of civil liberty lies outside the realm of acts regulated by law. To break the law may be criminal license, but to obey it is not to be free. The sphere of liberty increases as the scope or stringency of law diminishes.

The opposite view does not regard freedom as freedom *from* law. "Freedom," Hegel maintains, "is nothing but the recognition and adoption of such universal substantial objects as Right and Law." All that matters in the relation between liberty and law is whether the law is just and whether a man is virtuous. If the law is just, then it does not *compel* a just man to do what he would *freely* elect to do even if the law did not exist. Only the criminal is coerced or restrained by good laws. To say that such impediment to action destroys freedom would be to deny the distinction between liberty and license.

Nevertheless, liberty can be abridged by law. That is precisely the problem of the good man living under unjust laws. If, as Montesquieu says, "liberty can consist only in the power of doing what we ought to will, and in not being constrained to do what we ought not to will," then governments and laws interfere with liberty when they command or prohibit acts contrary to the free choice of a good man.

The conception of freedom as the condition of those who are rightly governed—who are commanded to do only what they would do anyway—seems to be analogically present in Spinoza's theory of human bondage and human freedom. It is there accompanied by a denial of the will's freedom of choice.

According to Spinoza human action is causally determined by one of two factors in man's nature—the passions or reason. When man is governed by his passions, he is in "bondage, for a man under their control is not his own master, but is mastered by fortune, in whose power he is, so that he is often forced to follow the worse, although he sees the better before him." When man is governed by reason he is free, for he "does the will of no one but himself, and does those things only which he knows are of greatest importance in life, and which he therefore desires above all things." The man who acts under the influence of the passions acts in terms of inadequate ideas and in the shadow of error or ignorance. When reason rules, man acts with adequate knowledge and in the light of truth.

Like Spinoza, Dewey holds that "the only freedom that is of enduring importance is freedom of intelligence, that is to say, freedom of observation and of judgment exercised in behalf of purposes that are intrinsically worth while."

So, too, in the theory of Augustine and Aquinas, the virtuous man is morally or spiritually free because human reason has triumphed in its conflict with the passions to influence the free judgment of his will. The rule of reason does not annul the will's freedom. Nor is the will less free when it is moved by the promptings of the passions. "A passion," writes Aquinas, "cannot draw or move the will directly." It does so indirectly, as, for example, "when those who are in some kind of passion do not easily turn their imagination away from the object of their affections." But though the will is not altered in its freedom by whether reason or emotion dominates, the situation is not the same with the human person as a whole. The theologians see him as a moral agent and a spiritual being who gains or loses freedom according as the will submits to the guidance of reason or follows the passions.

On the supernatural level, the theologians teach that God's grace assists reason to conform human acts to the divine law, but also that grace does not abolish free choice on the part of the will. "The first freedom of the will," Augustine says, "which man received when he was created upright, consisted in an ability not to sin, but also in an ability to sin." So long as man lives on earth, he remains free to sin. But supernatural grace, added to nature, raises man to a higher level of spiritual freedom than he can ever achieve by the discipline of the acquired virtues.

Still higher is the ultimate freedom of beatitude itself. Augustine calls this "the last freedom of will" which, by the gift of God, leaves man "not able to sin." It is worth noting that this ultimate liberty consists in freedom from choice or the need to choose, not in freedom from love or law. Man cannot be more free than when he succeeds, with God's help, in submitting himself through love to the rule of God.

THE POLITICAL significance of these moral and theological doctrines of freedom would seem to be that man *can be* as free in civil society as in a state of nature. Whether in fact he *is* depends upon the justice of the laws which govern him, not upon their number or the matters with which they deal. He is, of course, not free to do whatever he pleases regardless of the well-being of other men or the welfare of the community, but that, in the moral conception of liberty, is not a loss of freedom. He loses freedom in society only when he is mistreated or misgoverned—when, being the equal of other men, he is not treated as their equal; or when, being capable of ruling himself, he is denied a voice in his own government.

The meaning of tyranny and slavery seems to confirm this conception of political liberty. To be a slave is not merely to be ruled by another; it consists in being subject to the mastery of another, *i.e.,* to be ruled as a means to that other's good and without any voice in one's own government. This implies, in contrast, that to be ruled as a freeman is to be ruled for one's own good and with some degree of participation in the government under which one lives.

According to Aristotle's doctrine of the natural slave—examined in the chapter on SLAVERY—some men do not have the nature of freemen, and so should not be governed as freemen. Men who are by nature slaves are not

unjustly treated when they are enslaved. "It is better for them as for all inferiors," Aristotle maintains, "that they should be under the rule of a master." Though they do not in fact have the liberty of freemen, they are not deprived thereby of any freedom which properly belongs to them, any more than a man who is justly imprisoned is deprived of a freedom which is no longer his by right.

The root of this distinction between freemen and slaves by nature lies in the supposition of a natural inequality. The principle of equality is also relevant to the injustice of tyranny and the difference between absolute and constitutional government. In *The Republic* Plato compares the tyrant to an owner of slaves. "The only difference," he writes, "is that the tyrant has more slaves" and enforces "the harshest and bitterest form of slavery." The tyrannical ruler enslaves those who are his equals by nature and who should be ruled as freemen. Throughout the whole tradition of political thought the name of tyranny signifies the abolition of liberty. But absolute or despotic government is not uniformly regarded as the enemy of liberty.

The issue concerning the legitimacy or justice of absolute government is examined in the chapters on MONARCHY and TYRANNY AND DESPOTISM. But we can take it as generally agreed that the subjects of a despot, unlike the citizens of a republic, do not enjoy any measure of self-government. To the extent that political liberty consists in some degree of self-government, the subjects of absolute rule lack the sort of freedom possessed by citizens under constitutional government. For this reason the supremacy of law is frequently said to be the basic principle of political liberty.

"Wherever law ends, tyranny begins," Locke writes. In going beyond the law, a ruler goes beyond the grant of authority vested in him by the consent of the people, which alone makes man "subject to the laws of any government." Furthermore, law for Locke is itself a principle of freedom. "In its true notion," he writes, it "is not so much the limitation as the direction of a free and intelligent agent to his proper interest, and prescribes no farther than is for the general good of those under that law.

Could they be happier without it, the law, as a useless thing, would of itself vanish, and that ill deserves the name of confinement which hedges us in only from bogs and precipices. So that however it may be mistaken, the end of law is not to abolish or restrain, but to preserve and enlarge freedom."

A constitution gives the ruled the status of citizenship and a share in their own government. It may also give them legal means with which to defend their liberties when officers of government invade their rights in violation of the constitution. According to Montesquieu, for whom political liberty exists only under government by law, never under despotism or the rule of men, the freedom of government itself demands "from the very nature of things that power should be a check to power." This is accomplished by a separation of powers. A system of checks and balances limits the power of each branch of the government and permits the law of the constitution to be applied by one department against another when its officials usurp powers not granted by the constitution or otherwise act unconstitutionally.

Yet, unlike tyranny, absolute government has been defended. The ancients raise the question whether, if a truly superior or almost godlike man existed, it would not be proper for him to govern his inferiors in an absolute manner. "Mankind will not say that such a one is to be expelled and exiled," Aristotle writes; "on the other hand, he ought not to be a subject—that would be as if mankind should claim to rule over Zeus, dividing his offices among them. The only alternative," he concludes, "is that all should joyfully obey such a ruler, according to what seems to be the order of nature, and that men like him should be kings in their state for life." Those subject to his government would be free only in the sense that they would be ruled for their own good, perhaps better than they could rule themselves. But they would lose that portion of political freedom which consists in self-government. Faced with this alternative to constitutional government—which Aristotle describes as the government of freemen and equals—what should be the choice of men who are by nature free?

Freedom, as Tocqueville sees it in the United States, is not enough to avoid tyranny. While earlier writers show tyranny extending from a fault in the rulers, Tocqueville shows how modern tyranny—what we might call totalitarianism—results, in part, from a fault in the ruled. He envisions a world in which men are "circling around in pursuit of the petty and banal pleasures" while their government "extends its embrace to include the whole of society." The irony here is that freedom is the driving force behind revolutions, as well as the numbing factor leading to tyranny. Orwell shows this to be the case in *Animal Farm,* in which, after revolting against the humans, most of the animals forget why the revolution ever took place, thus leaving themselves open for oppression by the pigs.

THE ANCIENT ANSWER is not decisively in one direction. There are many passages in both Plato and Aristotle in which the absolute rule of a wise king (superior to his subjects as a father is to children, or a god to men) seems to be pictured as the political ideal. The fact that freemen would be no freer than children in a well-administered household does not seem to Plato and Aristotle to be a flaw in the picture. They do not seem to hold that the fullness of liberty is the primary measure of the goodness of government.

On the contrary, justice is more important. As Aristotle suggests, it would be unjust for the superior man to be treated as an equal and given the status of one self-governing citizen among others. But he also points out that "democratic states have instituted ostracism" as a means of dealing with such superior men. "Equality is above all things their aim, and therefore they ostracized and banished from the city for a time those who seemed to predominate too much." Because it saves the superior man from injustice and leaves the rest free to practice self-government, "the argument for ostracism," Aristotle claims, "is based upon a kind of political justice," in that it preserves the balance within the state, and perhaps also because it leaves men free to practice self-government among themselves.

Since the 18th century, a strong tendency in

the opposite direction appears in the political thought of Locke, Montesquieu, Rousseau, Kant, the American constitutionalists, and J. S. Mill. Self-government is regarded as the essence of good government. It is certainly the mark of what the 18th-century writers call "free government." Men who are born to be free, it is thought, cannot be satisfied with less civil liberty than this.

"Freedom," says Kant, "is independence of the compulsory will of another; and in so far as it can co-exist with the freedom of all according to a universal law, it is the one sole, original inborn right belonging to every man in virtue of his humanity. There is, indeed, an innate equality belonging to every man which consists in his right to be independent of being bound by others to anything more than that to which he may also reciprocally bind them." The fundamental equality of men thus appears to be founded in their equal right to freedom; and that, for Kant at least, rests on the freedom of will with which all men are born. The criterion of the good society is the realization of freedom.

Kant's conception of human society as a realm of ends, in which no free person should be degraded to the ignominy of being a means, expresses one aspect of political freedom. The other is found in his principle of the harmonization of individual wills which results in the freedom of each being consistent with the freedom of all. In institutional terms, republican government, founded on popular sovereignty and with a system of representation, is the political ideal precisely because it gives its citizens the dignity of freemen and enables them to realize their freedom in self-government.

Citizenship, according to Kant, has three inseparable attributes: "1. constitutional freedom, as the right of every citizen to have to obey no other law than that to which he has given his consent or approval; 2. civil equality, as the right of the citizen to recognize no one as a superior among the people in relation to himself, except in so far as such a one is as subject to *his* moral power to impose obligations, as that other has power to impose obligations upon him; and 3. political independence, as

the right to owe his existence and continuance in society not to the arbitrary will of another, but to his own rights and powers as a member of the commonwealth, and, consequently, the possession of a civil personality, which cannot be represented by any other than himself."

Kant leans heavily on Rousseau's conclusions with regard to political liberty. Rousseau, however, approaches the problem of freedom somewhat differently. "Man is born free," he begins, "and everywhere he is in chains." He next considers two questions. What makes government legitimate, "since no man has a natural authority over his fellow, and force creates no right"? Answering this first question in terms of a convention freely entered into, Rousseau then poses the second problem— how to form an association "in which each, while uniting himself with all, may still obey himself alone, and remain as free as before." This, he says, is "the fundamental problem of which the *Social Contract* provides the solution."

The solution involves more than republican government, popular sovereignty, and a participation of the individual through voting and representation. It introduces the conception of the general will, through which alone the freedom of each individual is to be ultimately preserved. Like Kant's universal law of freedom, the general will ordains what each man would freely will for himself if he adequately conceived the conditions of his freedom. "In fact," says Rousseau, "each individual, as a man, may have a particular will contrary or dissimilar to the general will which he has as a citizen. His particular interest may speak to him quite differently from the common interest." Nevertheless, under conditions of majority rule, the members of the minority remain free even though they appear to be ruled against their particular wills.

When a measure is submitted to the people, the question is "whether it is in conformity with the general will, which is their will. Each man, in giving his vote, states his opinion on that point; and the general will is found by counting votes. When, therefore, the opinion that is contrary to my own prevails, this proves neither more nor less than that I was mistaken, and that what I thought to be the general will was not so. If my particular opinion had carried the day, I should have achieved the opposite of what was my will; and it is in that case that I should not have been free. This presupposes, indeed, that all the qualities of the general will still reside in the majority; when they cease to do so, whatever side a man may take, liberty is no longer possible."

TOCQUEVILLE, WHOSE BOOK *Democracy in America* greatly influenced Mill, thinks "that democratic communities have a natural taste for freedom; left to themselves, they will seek it, cherish it, and view any privation of it with regret. But for equality," Tocqueville adds, "their passion is ardent, insatiable, incessant, invincible; they call for equality in freedom; and if they cannot obtain that, they still call for equality in slavery."

Mill sees the same problem from the opposite side. Constitutional government and representative institutions are indispensable conditions of political liberty. Where Aristotle regards democracy as the type of constitution most favorable to freedom because it gives the equality of citizenship to all *freeborn* men, Mill argues for universal suffrage to give equal freedom to *all* men, for all are born equal. But neither representative government nor democratic suffrage is sufficient to guarantee the liberty of the individual and his freedom of thought or action.

Such phrases as "self-government" and "the power of the people over themselves" are deceptive. "The 'people' who exercise the power," Mill writes, "are not always the same people with those over whom it is exercised; and the 'self-government' spoken of is not the government of each by himself, but of each by all the rest. The will of the people, moreover, practically means the will of the most numerous or the most active part of the people; the majority, or those who succeed in making themselves accepted as the majority."

To safeguard individual liberty from the tyranny of the majority, Mill proposes a single criterion for social control over the individual, whether by the physical force of law or the moral force of public opinion. "The sole end for which mankind are warranted, individually or collectively, in interfering with the liberty of action of any of their number, is self-protection . . . The only part of the conduct of anyone, for which he is amenable to society, is that which concerns others. In the part which merely concerns himself, his independence is, of right, absolute. Over himself, over his own body and mind, the individual is sovereign."

Mill's conception of individual liberty at first appears to be negative—to be freedom *from* externally imposed regulations or coercions. Liberty increases as the sphere of government diminishes; and, for the sake of liberty, that government governs best which governs least, or governs no more than is necessary for the public safety. "There is a sphere of action," Mill writes, "in which society, as distinguished from the individual, has, if any, only an indirect interest; comprehending all that portion of a person's life and conduct which affects only himself, or if it also affects others, only with their free, voluntary, and undeceived consent and participation. When I say only himself," Mill continues, "I mean directly and in the first instance; for whatever affects himself, may affect others through himself . . . This, then, is the appropriate region of human liberty."

But it is the positive aspect of freedom from governmental interference or social pressures on which Mill wishes to place emphasis. Freedom *from* government or social coercion is freedom *for* the maximum development of individuality—freedom to be as different from all others as one's personal inclinations, talents, and tastes dispose one and enable one to be.

"It is desirable," Mill writes, "that in things which do not primarily concern others, individuality should assert itself." Liberty is undervalued as long as the free development of individuality is not regarded as one of the principal ingredients of human happiness and indispensable to the welfare of society. "The only freedom which deserves the name," Mill thinks, "is that of pursuing our own good in our own way, so long as we do not attempt to deprive others of theirs, or impede their efforts to obtain it"; for, "in proportion to the development of his individuality, each person becomes more valuable to himself, and is therefore capable of being more valuable to others. There is a greater fullness of life about his own existence, and when there is more life in the units there is more in the mass which is composed of them."

Mill's praise of liberty as an ultimate good, both for the individual and for the state, finds a clearly antiphonal voice in the tradition of the great books. Plato, in *The Republic* advocates political regulation of the arts, where Mill, even more than Milton before him, argues against censorship or any control of the avenues of human expression. But the most striking opposition to Mill occurs in those passages in which Socrates deprecates the spirit of democracy because of its insatiable desire for freedom. That spirit, Socrates says, creates a city "full of freedom and frankness, in which a man may do and say what he likes . . . Where such freedom exists, the individual is clearly able to order for himself his own life as he pleases."

The democratic state is described by Socrates as approaching anarchy through relaxation of the laws or through utter lawlessness. Under such circumstances there will be the greatest variety of individual differences. It will seem "the fairest of states, being like an embroidered robe which is spangled with every sort of flower." But it is a state in which liberty has been allowed to grow without limit at the expense of justice and order. It is "full of variety and disorder, and dispensing a sort of equality to equals and unequals alike."

48

Life and Death

INTRODUCTION

MEN have divided the totality of things in various ways. The three most fundamental divisions rest on the distinction between the natural and the supernatural, between the material and the spiritual, and between the lifeless and the living.

The same kind of basic question is raised by each of these divisions, and given opposite answers in the tradition of the great books. The question is not always formulated in the same way. It may be a question about the existence of the supernatural order or of incorporeal beings. It may be a problem of whether the terms of the division represent a real duality or merely different aspects of one and the same whole. Are God and nature one or are they radically distinct? Is spirituality merely one expression of bodily existence, or are there two worlds, a world of bodies and a world of spirits?

These issues are considered in the chapters on GOD, NATURE, ANGEL, and MATTER, as well as in the chapter on BEING. The issue raised by the third great division is one of the central topics in this chapter. That issue concerns the difference between the living and the nonliving. There is no question here about whether, in the order of nature, living things exist. The fact of life is not denied, at least not as a matter of observation. On the surface there certainly appears to be a striking difference between the living tree and the stone, or between the animal which a moment ago was alive and is now dead.

But how this difference is to be understood is the question. Does it signify an absolute break, a discontinuity, between the world of living bodies and the domain of inanimate things? Or is the continuity of nature pre-served across the line which divides inorganic and organic matter? Is the difference between the nonliving and the living (or the living and the dead) one of kind or of degree?

Those who answer that it is a difference in kind usually formulate a definition of life which draws a sharp line, on one side of which are the things that have the indispensable properties of life, while on the other side are things totally lacking in these properties. The critical point here turns on whether vitality is present in some degree or totally absent. The definition of life may not always be the same. It may not always, for example, postulate the soul as the principle in all living things, or involve the same conception of soul in relation to living organisms. But when life is defined as an essential characteristic of some natures, the definition implies the existence of natures which are totally lacking in the properties essential to life. It also implies the impossibility of intermediate links between the lowest form of life and the most complex of the inorganic substances.

The opposite answer that there is only a difference in degree between the inanimate and the animate, affirms the continuity of nature across the gap between things which appear lifeless and those which seem to be alive. All bodies have the same fundamental properties, though not in the same magnitude. But here there is a further question. It can be asked whether those properties are the powers or functions commonly associated with the appearance of being alive, such as growth, reproduction, sensitivity, desire, locomotion; or whether they are the mechanical properties of matter in motion—properties which vary only with the degrees of complexity in the organization of matter.

According to the doctrine which is sometimes called "animism" and sometimes "panpsychism," everything is alive, every body is besouled, though at the lower end of the scale the signs of vitality remain hidden from ordinary observation. Although this theory is usually attributed to a primitive view of nature, it appears in a subtle form in certain philosophical developments which make soul or mind a principle as universal as matter. "There is one common substance," says Marcus Aurelius, "though it is distributed among countless bodies which have their several qualities. There is one soul, though it is distributed among infinite natures and individual circumscriptions."

Whitehead's organic theory of matter may be viewed as a more recent incarnation of this philosophy. According to this theory, the elementary particles of matter—electrons, atoms, and molecules—share many of the qualities often thought to be distinctive of living organisms. Like living organisms, they are not merely influenced by their environment; they also influence it and adapt to it. "Science," Whitehead writes, "is becoming the study of organisms. Biology is the study of the larger organisms; whereas physics is the study of the smaller organisms."

The doctrine which in modern times is called "mechanism" conceives the continuity of nature in terms of the universality of purely mechanical principles. It reduces all phenomena to the interaction of moving parts or particles. No new principle is needed to explain the phenomena of life. The laws of physics and chemistry suffice. Biophysics and biochemistry simply deal with the mechanics of more complex material systems. The apparent differences in function between "living" and "nonliving" things represent the same functions. They are altered only in *appearance* by the more complex organization of the matter which is called "living."

THE CONTROVERSY over mechanistic principles in the analysis of life arose with great explicitness in the latter part of the 19th century and continues to our own day. The chief opponents of the mechanists are those who at one time called themselves "vitalists" to signify their insistence upon an essential difference between vital and mechanical phenomena. The work of Jacques Loeb can be taken to represent the mechanistic side of this controversy; the writings of Bergson, J. S. Haldane, Whitehead, the vitalist position.

Those who regard the realm of living things as a distinct domain in nature also think that the study of living things has special concepts, principles, and methods as different from those of physics and chemistry as the objects studied are distinct.

Biology is a science of ancient origin. The Hippocratic collection of writings on health and disease, the extensive biological researches of Aristotle, the work of Galen, represent more than a bare beginning of the science. The ancient classification of vital functions establishes the terms of biological analysis. Ideas which have come to seem obvious because of traditional acceptance were once great discoveries; for example, that all living bodies nourish themselves, grow, and reproduce; that these are the minimal, not the maximal, functions of organic matter; that there is a regular cycle of growth and decay in the normal life span which is itself different for different types of organisms; that in the dynamic equilibrium between the living organism and its physical environment, the organism actively maintains itself through a certain balance of exchanges in the biological economy, of which breathing is a prime example.

The great books of biological science from Aristotle to Harvey seem to be of one mind on the point that living matter possesses distinctive powers and performs functions which are not present *in any degree* in the realm of the inert or inorganic. For the most part they reflect the theory that the living body possesses a soul which is the principle of its vitality and the source of the vital powers embodied in its various organs.

In ancient and medieval theory, the soul is not conceived as belonging peculiarly to man; it is not identified with mind or with the intellectual faculties. The word "animal" derives from the Latin name for soul—the principle of animation. It is true that Galen distinguishes between what he calls the "natural" and the "psychic" faculties. The latter for him are the powers of sensitivity, desire, and locomotion. Yet his analysis of the vegetative powers of nutrition, growth, and reproduction which are common to plants and animals squares with Aristotle's conception of the vegetative soul.

"What has soul in it," Aristotle writes, "differs from what has not, in that the former displays life. Now this word has more than one sense . . . Living, that is, may mean thinking or perception or local movement and rest, or movement in the sense of nutrition, decay, and growth. Hence we think of plants also as living, for they are observed to possess in themselves an originative power through which they increase and decrease in all spatial directions. This power of self-nutrition . . . is the originative power, the possession of which leads us to speak of things as *living*."

IN THE GREAT BOOKS the opposite position with respect to the living and nonliving seems to appear for the first time with Descartes. It might be supposed that Lucretius, since he denies the soul as an immaterial principle, would also tend to reject anything except a difference in degree between animate and inanimate bodies. But this is not the case. According to Lucretius, living things are not merely more complex combinations of atoms and void. Their constitution includes a special type of soul-atom, whose round, smooth shape and speed of movement through all parts of the living body accounts for the powers and activities which are peculiar to that body. Lucretius is recognized as a materialist and a mechanist, yet he sharply separates living from nonliving bodies and appeals to a special principle—the soul-atom—to explain this difference in kind.

As appears in the chapters on MIND and SOUL, Descartes is at variance not only with Lucretius but also with Aristotle, Galen, and Plotinus in his conception of the soul and of life. The soul is not a body or composed of bodies. Neither, in his opinion, is it an immaterial principle conjoined with organic matter to constitute the living body. It is itself an immaterial substance, quite separate from the human body to which it is allied.

Descartes tells us how he passed from "a description of inanimate bodies and plants . . . to that of animals, and particularly to that of men." He asks us to consider the supposition that "God formed the body of man altogether like one of ours . . . without making use of any matter other than that which I have described and without at first placing in it a rational soul or any other thing which might serve as a vegetative or sensitive soul." He then goes on to say that "examining the functions which might in accordance with this supposition exist in this body, I found precisely all those which might exist in us without our having the power of thought, and consequently without our soul—that is to say, this part of us, distinct from the body, of which it has been said that its nature is to think."

The mechanistic implications of his supposition are explicitly developed by Descartes in his consideration of Harvey's discovery of the motions of the heart and blood. These movements, he says, follow "as necessarily from the very disposition of the organs . . . as does that of a clock from the power, the situation, and the form, of its counterpoise and of its wheels." In these motions, as well as in the actions of the nerves, brain, and muscles, it is not necessary to suppose any other cause than those operating according "to the laws of Mechanics which are identical with those of nature."

This will not seem strange, Descartes adds, to those who know "how many different automata or moving machines can be made by the industry of man, without employing in so doing more than a very few parts in comparison with the great multitude of bones, muscles, nerves, arteries, veins or other parts that are found in the body of each animal. From this aspect, the body is regarded as a machine, which, having been made by the hands of God, is incomparably better arranged, and possesses in itself movements which are much more admirable, than any of those which can be invented by man." Only the functions of reason, only the acts of thinking—not those of living—operate under other than the mechanical laws of corporeal nature. Whether living or not, all bodies without reason or a rational soul are automata or machines. Whatever they do can be explained as a kind of clock-work—by the disposition and interaction of their parts.

THE CARTESIAN VIEWPOINT has been extraordinarily fruitful in guiding the direction of research in the biological sciences, and 20th-century writers on the subject must be considered mechanists insofar as they assert that living things are formed of the same atoms as inanimate things, that the laws of physics are the same for both, and that no vital force is necessary to explain life. But they seem to reject the notion that the activities and properties of living matter differ only in degree of complexity from those of inanimate things. In other words, they hold that there is a fundamental discontinuity between living and nonliving things, based not on material composition or some postulated "life-force," but on structure or organization.

The peculiar structure of living matter causes new laws to come to light which are not observed among inanimate things. Waddington suggests the analogy of a computer: "Who, seeing a few pieces of glass, metal, plastic and so on, would suspect that they could beat him at chess? Yet we know that, assembled into a computer, they could wipe the floor with any but the world champions. The secret of their performance in this way is architecture, or, to use the Aristotelian term, form." In similar fashion, the distinctive characteristic of living matter—namely, its ability to avoid decay, to preserve and reproduce "orderliness"—is due to the unique molecular structure of chromosome fiber which is described by Schrödinger as an *aperiodic solid*. "The arrangements of atoms in the most vital parts of an organism," he writes, "differ in a fundamental way from all those arrangements of atoms which physicists and chemists have hitherto made the object of their experimental and theoretical research."

The purely mechanistic interpretation of life was shaken by quantum theory, for, as Waddington points out, the assertion that living things behave as though they were nothing but machines constructed of material compo-nents "presupposes that one knows what mere material components are, and what kind of mechanisms they can be built into." Cartesian theory is built on a high degree of confidence in our knowledge of matter and the mechanical principles governing its motions; the substitution of quantum for classical mechanics destroyed the basis for this confidence. It is of no use to describe the workings of a complicated machine as reducible to the movement of individual cogs if one is unsure of how and why the cogs move. "It is not the case," writes Waddington, "that we begin by knowing all about the ultimate constituents of the inorganic world, and can then ask whether they can account for the observable phenomena of biology. Always, whether in physics or in biology, it is from observable phenomena that we have to start."

ANOTHER SOURCE and another version of the view that the continuity of nature is uninterrupted, comes from the theory of evolution. Darwin himself, in his brief consideration of the origin of life, deals mainly with the alternative hypotheses of the divine creation of a *single* original form or of *several* primitive forms from which the whole of the plant and animal kingdoms has developed by the natural steps of evolution. He rejects the division of the animate world into more than the two great kingdoms of plant and animal life, and holds that man differs from other animals only in degree, not in kind.

As indicated in the chapters on ANIMAL and EVOLUTION, Darwin questions the discontinuity between plants and animals. He refers to the intermediate forms which seem to belong to both kingdoms. He suggests the possibility that the lowest forms of animal life may have developed by natural evolutionary descent from plant organisms. But he does not *seriously* consider the hypothesis of an evolutionary transition from inorganic matter to living organisms. Here, on the contrary, he seems to recognize a difference in kind. "The most humble organism," he writes, "is something much higher than the inorganic dust under our feet; and no one with an unbiased mind can study any living creature, however humble, without being struck with enthusiasm at its marvellous structure and properties." He questions the notion that living organisms might have originated from inorganic matter by spontaneous generation. "Science has not as yet proved the truth of this belief," he says, "whatever the future may reveal."

Nevertheless, with the extension of Darwin's theory of the origin of species into a doctrine of cosmic evolution, what William James calls "the evolutionary afflatus" leads writers like John Tyndall and Herbert Spencer to "talk as if mind grew out of body in a continuous way . . . So strong a postulate is continuity," James writes, that the evolutionists try to "leap over the breach" between inorganic matter and consciousness.

"In a general theory of evolution," he explains, "the inorganic comes first, then the lowest forms of animal and vegetable life, then forms of life that possess mentality, and finally those like ourselves that possess it in a high degree . . . We are dealing all the time with matter and its aggregations and separations; and although our treatment must perforce be hypothetical, this does not prevent it from being *continuous*. The point which as evolutionists we are bound to hold fast is that all the new forms of being that make their appearance are nothing more than results of the redistribution of the original and unchanging materials. The self-same atoms which, chaotically dispersed, made the nebula, now, jammed and temporarily caught in peculiar position, form our brains; and the 'evolution' of the brains, if understood, would be simply the account of how the atoms came to be so caught and jammed. In this story no new *natures,* no factors not present at the beginning, are introduced at any later stage."

James is here presenting a theory which he himself rejects. He recognizes the strength of the "postulate of continuity" in the theories of Spencer, Tyndall, and other evolutionists, but he thinks the evident "contrasts between living and inanimate performances" favor the division of nature into two realms. Yet he also seems to regard some degree of intelligence or mentality as an accompaniment of life. Hence his criterion of the difference in

kind "between an intelligent and a mechanical performance"—namely, purposiveness or "the pursuance of future ends and the choice of means"—also serves as the mark of distinction between the animate and the inanimate.

Whitehead offers a third approach to the problem. Like James, he rejects a mechanical and materialist explanation of life. "Evolution, on the materialistic theory," he says, "is reduced to the role of being another word for the description of the changes of the external relations between portions of matter. There is nothing to evolve, because one set of external relations is as good as any other set of external relations." But whereas James views purposiveness as a mark of distinction between animate and inanimate matter, Whitehead seems to attribute this quality in some degree to all things, whether we call them animate or inanimate. "The whole point of the modern doctrine," he writes, "is the evolution of complex organisms from antecedent states of less complex organisms. The doctrine thus cries aloud for a conception of organism as fundamental for nature."

IT IS WORTH remarking that this criterion is one of the tests Descartes proposes for differentiating man from all the rest of nature, man alone having reason or thought. It is also worth noting that in associating different degrees of mentality or consciousness with life at all levels of development, James himself affirms a continuity in the realm of all living things. He therefore does not go as far in the direction of discontinuity as do those in the tradition of the great books who find an essential difference between the inanimate and the living, between plant and animal, and between brute and human life.

The issues raised by these last two distinctions are further considered in the chapters on ANIMAL, MAN, and MIND. Here we are concerned only with the fact that those who find genuine differences in kind in the world of animate things also tend to distinguish between the living and the nonliving by reference to the most generic properties of corporeal life, that is, the powers or functions shared by plants, animals, and men. The question of origins does not seem to be relevant to the problem of differences. Aquinas, for example, does not seem to regard the hypothesis of the spontaneous generation of living organisms from putrefying organic matter as inconsistent with his assertion that the vegetative functions of plants and animals are not performed—*in any degree*—by inanimate bodies.

When Aristotle says of natural bodies that "some have life in them, others not; and by life we mean self-nutrition and growth," he is aware that the word "growth" occurs in the description of a certain type of change in inanimate bodies. Other than living things increase in size. To avoid an equivocal use of the word "growth," he assigns three distinguishing characteristics to the quantitative change or increase in living things: "(1) Any and every part of the growing magnitude is made bigger, (2) by the accession of something, and (3) in such a way that the growing thing is preserved and persists."

To exemplify this difference, Galen compares the growth of an organism with the expansion of a dried bladder when children blow air into it. The expanding bladder seems to grow, but not as it did when it was a part of a living animal and when the growth of the whole involved the growth of each part. "In these doings of the children," Galen writes, "the more the interior cavity of the bladder increases in size, the thinner, necessarily, does its substance become. But, if the children were able to bring nourishment to this thin part, then they would make the bladder big in the same way that Nature does . . . To be distended in all directions belongs only to bodies whose growth is directed by Nature; for those which are distended by us undergo this distension in one direction but grow less in the others; it is impossible to find a body which will remain entire and not be torn through whilst we stretch it in the three dimensions. Thus Nature alone has the power to expand a body in all directions so that it remains unruptured and preserves completely its previous form."

Modern biologists sometimes compare the growth of crystals in solution with living growth and reproduction. Or, making the point that "other systems in dynamic equi-librium show in essence all the properties of living things," they say that "it is almost impossible to distinguish a candle flame from a living organism." Aristotle considers the latter comparison and rejects it. He observes that "the growth of fire goes on without limit so long as there is a supply of fuel"; but no amount of nutriment can increase the size of living things without limit. "There is a limit or ratio which determines their size and increase, and the limit and ratio are marks of the soul, but not of fire."

The flame is a lively thing, but to say that it is alive, that it grows or dies, is in Aristotle's view a poetic metaphor, not a scientific statement. "When I have plucked the rose," Othello says, "I cannot give it vital growth again, it needs must wither." But to the candle burning beside Desdemona's bed, he says: "If I quench thee, thou flaming minister, I can again thy former light restore." The flame is lit or extinguished by motions from without; but the birth and death, the nourishing and growth of the living thing is self-movement.

According to Aristotle and Aquinas self-movement is the essential mark of being alive. "All things are said to be alive," Aquinas writes, "which determine themselves to movement or operation of any kind; whereas those things which cannot by their own nature do so, cannot be called living except by a similitude." He further defines the meaning of self-movement by distinguishing between the *transitive* action of one inert body upon another and the *immanent* activity of a living thing, whereby the agent itself is perfected. Growing, sensing, and understanding are immanent actions because they are activities which affect the growing, sensing, or understanding thing. The result of such actions *remains in the agent*. In contrast, heating is a transitive action. In heating, one thing acts upon another, and the hot thing loses its own heat in the process.

As vital operations differ thus from the actions of inanimate bodies, so do vital powers differ from the capacities of inert matter, through which bodies can act upon or react to other bodies. The power of self-movement (or immanent activity) enables living things alone to change from a less perfect to a more perfect state of being, as measured by the thing's nature, rather than simply to change from contrary to contrary, as a body changes when it moves locally from this place to that, or alters from hot to cold, or cold to hot.

Schrödinger, like Aristotle and Aquinas, views self-movement as the essential quality which sets apart living from inanimate things. A piece of matter is said to be alive, he says, "when it goes on 'doing something,' moving, exchanging material with its environment, and so forth." By contrast, "when a system that is not alive is isolated or placed in a uniform environment, all motion usually comes to a standstill very soon as a result of various kinds of friction . . . A permanent state is reached, in which no observable events occur." He proceeds to define life according to the principles of thermodynamics: a living system is one that counteracts the tendency, common to all systems, to fall into disorder by drawing nourishment from its environment. Living things survive, Schrödinger says, by feeding on "negative entropy," or, to use a different phrase, by "sucking orderliness" from their environment.

FOR THE THEOLOGIAN, there is an additional aspect to the problem of defining life. If the realm of corporeal substances is divided into inert and living bodies, what is to be said about incorporeal substances (*i.e.,* the angels) and about God? It is easier to think of the angels as *not being* than to conceive them as *not being alive.* More than "infinite" or "omnipotent" or "eternal," "the ever-living God" is the phrase which, in the language of religious worship, expresses positively the divine nature. But the fundamental activities which distinguish living from nonliving bodies (such as nutrition, growth, reproduction) are essentially corporeal in nature. So, too, are sensing and locomotion. What common meaning of life, then, can apply to material and spiritual beings?

Aquinas answers by saying that "since a thing is said to live in so far as it operates of itself and not as moved by another, the more perfectly this power is found in anything, the more perfect is the life of that thing." By this criterion, plants are less perfectly alive than animals, in whom self-movement is found to a higher degree because of their sensitive faculties; and among animals, there are grades of life according to degrees of sensitivity, and according to the possession of mobility, a power which certain animals seem to lack. In both the higher animals and in man, there is purposive behavior, but man alone, through his intellect and will, can freely determine his own ends and choose the means to them; hence these faculties give human life an even greater degree of self-movement.

But the action of the human intellect is not perfectly self-determined, for it depends in part upon external causes. Wherefore Aquinas concludes that life in the highest degree belongs properly to God—"that being whose act of understanding is its very nature and which, in what it naturally possesses, is not determined by another." He quotes Aristotle's remark that the perfection of God's life is proportionate to the perfection of the divine intellect, which is purely actual and eternally in act. And he goes on to remark that, in the sense in which understanding is movement, and that which understands itself moves itself, "Plato also taught that God moves Himself."

Nourishment, growth, and reproduction are indispensable features of corporeal life precisely because corporeal things are perishable. They need "reproduction to preserve the species," Aquinas writes, "and nourishment to preserve the individual." Hence the higher powers of life, such as sensing and understanding, are never found in corporeal things apart from the vegetative powers. This does not hold, however, for spiritual beings which are by nature imperishable. Spiritual life is essentially immortal life.

Subject to the ravages of time, corporeal life at every moment betrays its mortality— in its need for sleep, in the enfeeblement of its powers, in disease, decay, or degeneration. Death is the correlative of life for those who sharply divide the living from the nonliving. Rocks may crumble into dust, bodies may disintegrate, and atoms explode—but they do not die. Death is a change which only living matter undergoes.

The transition from life to death accentuates the mystery of life. The notion of spontaneous generation aside, life always seems to come from life. Whether by cell division or by germination, the living thing that is generated comes from the living substance of another thing. But when a living thing dies, it crosses the gap between the living and the nonliving. As the organic matter of the corpse decomposes, nothing is left but the familiar inorganic elements and compounds. This seems to be a change more radical than generation or birth. All the metaphysical problems of form and substance, of matter and the soul, of continuity and discontinuity in nature, which appear in the analysis of life, become more intense in the understanding of death.

As APPEARS IN the chapter on IMMORTALITY, the living are preoccupied with death, not predominantly with analyzing it, but with facing and fearing it, struggling against or embracing it. Death, as the great poems reveal, is the object of soliloquy in moments of greatest introspection or self-appraisal. To die well, Montaigne points out, requires greater moral stamina than to live well. For him the essence of the philosophical temper, as for others the meaning of heroism or martyrdom, consists in facing death with an equanimity which reflects the highest qualities of a well-resolved life.

Montaigne devotes a long essay to the subject that "to philosophize is to learn to die," and he begins it by quoting Cicero's statement that to study philosophy "is nothing else but to prepare for death." Socrates then is the prototype of the philosopher, for in conversation with his friends in prison while awaiting death, he tells them that "the true votary of philosophy . . . is always pursuing death, and dying." He tries to prove to them, by his actions as well as by his words, that "the real philosopher has reason to be of good cheer when he is about to die."

While the ideal of the philosopher may be to face death with equanimity, the poet uses the specter of death to convey lessons to the living: the frailty of life, the fleetingness of earthly glory, and the grim equality of fate shared by all men. These themes received particular emphasis during the Middle Ages, as

Huizinga recounts, but they have recurred in art and literature throughout history. Religion in particular has sought to use the fear of death—and what waits after it—to arouse the conscience of the living. "Ever to suffer, never to enjoy; ever to be damned, never to be saved; ever, never; ever, never," warns the preacher in Joyce's *A Portrait of the Artist as a Young Man*. "Such is the terrible punishment decreed for those who die in mortal sin by an almighty and a just God."

Not only death but the dead exercise a profound effect upon the living. The historians describe the various forms which the ceremonials of death take in every society. Whether the rituals are secular or sacred, they are among the most significant customs of any culture, for they reveal the value placed upon life and the conception of life's meaning and man's destiny. No deeper differences exist among the great religions than those which appear in the practices or sacraments in preparation for death and in the services for the dead.

The moral, social, and religious aspects of death appear to be peculiarly human. Yet on the biological level, the same fundamental instincts and emotions seem to prevail in animals and men. The struggle to remain alive may be presumed to occur in plants. But it is not there as plainly discernible as in the specific patterns of behavior manifested by the animal instinct of self-preservation. Almost in proportion to the degree of vitality, the instinct of self-preservation operates with a strength and pertinacity as vigorous as the love for life and arouses as an emotional corollary an equally devouring fear of death.

The instinct of self-preservation is the life instinct. Directed toward the related ends of maintaining and increasing life are the reproductive impulses and the erotic instincts. But, according to Freud, there is in all living matter a more primitive instinct than these, and one which aims in the opposite direction. That is the death instinct—the impulse of the living to return to lifelessness.

"It would be contrary to the conservative nature of instinct," Freud writes, "if the goal of life were a state never hitherto reached. It must rather be an ancient starting point, which the living being left long ago, and to which it harks back again . . . If we may assume as an experience admitting of no exception that everything dies from causes within itself, and returns to the inorganic, we can only say 'The goal of all life is death.' "

The death instinct, according to Freud, originates with life itself. "At one time or another, by some operation of force which completely baffles conjecture, the properties of life were awakened in lifeless matter . . . The tension then aroused in the previously inanimate matter strove to attain an equilibrium; the first instinct was present, that to return to lifelessness." The death instinct acts against the tendency of the erotic instincts, "which are always trying to collect living substances together into ever larger unities . . . The co-operation and opposition of these two forces produce the phenomena of life to which death puts an end."

Freud's hypothesis of the death instinct has a bearing on the impulse to commit suicide and on the question whether it is natural or perverse for men to choose this escape from the tensions and difficulties of life. The psychological problem here, especially with regard to the unconscious forms of the suicidal impulse, is not the same as the moral problem. The question whether animals other than men ever commit suicide, like the question whether the killing of one animal by another can be called "murder," indicates the difference between psychological description and moral judgment.

FOR THE MORALIST the condemnation of suicide seems to rest on the same grounds as the condemnation of murder. With Kant, for example, it represents the same type of violation of the universal moral law. The categorical imperative requires us to act always as if the maxim of our individual action could be universalized as a rule for all men to follow. But, in the case of suicide as in the case of murder, the maxim of the action cannot be universalized without accomplishing a result which no one intends. Furthermore, suicide is not consistent with the idea of the human person as an end in itself. The man, says Kant, who destroys himself "in order to escape from painful circumstances uses a person merely as a means to maintain a tolerable condition up to the end of life."

Suicide is also condemned by the theologians as a contravention of the divine as well as of the natural law. Men are God's handiwork and, therefore, as Locke puts it, "they are His property . . . made to last during His, not one another's, pleasure." Under the natural law, a man is not at liberty to destroy himself, nor consequently is he at liberty to sell himself into slavery. Everyone "is bound to preserve himself and not quit his station willfully." If, furthermore, there is an afterlife of rewards and punishments, suicide is no escape. "Death so snatched," Adam tells Eve in *Paradise Lost,* "will not exempt us from the pain we are by doom to pay."

There is similar reasoning in pagan antiquity. Suicide is an act of violence and, says Plotinus, "if there be a period allotted to all by fate, to anticipate the hour could not be a happy act . . . If everyone is to hold in the other world a standing determined by the state in which he quitted this, there must be no withdrawal as long as there is any hope of progress." A Christian would add that to relinquish hope as long as life persists is the sin of despair.

But the pagan tradition also speaks with an opposite voice. For the Stoics, suicide does not seem to be as reprehensible as murder. To those who complain of life's pains and the fetters of the body, Epictetus says, "The door is open." In a doctrine in which all things that affect only the body are indifferent to the soul's well-being, death too is indifferent. "Death is the harbor for all; this is the place of refuge; as soon as you choose, you may be out of the house."

49

Logic

INTRODUCTION

IN this set of great books, the *Organon* of Aristotle, the *Novum Organum* of Francis Bacon, Descartes's *Discourse on the Method* and his *Rules for the Direction of the Mind,* and Kant's *The Critique of Pure Reason* indicate or discuss the nature, scope, and divisions of the discipline which has come to be called "logic." Though of all the works mentioned the *Organon* is perhaps the most extensive treatment of the subject, Aristotle does not use the word "logic" to name the science or art of which he seems to be the inventor—certainly the first systematic expounder—in the tradition of western thought.

Here as elsewhere Aristotle is indebted to his predecessors for providing him with materials to develop or criticize: to the Sophists for the construction of arguments, for the formulation of methods of disputation, and for the discovery of fallacies; to Plato for the theory of classification and definition, for the root notion of the syllogism and a conception of proof or demonstration, for the general outlines of an intellectual method to which Plato gives the name "dialectic."

As indicated in the chapter on DIALECTIC, Aristotle uses Plato's name for the whole method of the mind in the pursuit of truth, in order to designate just one part of his method, the part concerned with probability rather than truth. Yet in the Roman and medieval tradition, the words "logic" and "dialectic" come to be used interchangeably. This is exemplified by the Stoic division of the sciences into physics, ethics, and logic *or* dialectic, and by the medieval enumeration of the liberal arts of the *trivium* as grammar, rhetoric, and logic *or* dialectic. So used, these names designate the whole range of discussion to be found in Aristotle's *Organon.*

In their opposition to Aristotelian or what they sometimes call "scholastic" logic, modern inventors of new methods, like Bacon or Descartes, tend to restrict the meaning of logic. For them logic is little more than the doctrine of the syllogism. And this they judge to be no part of genuinely fruitful method, or they hold it to be of use mainly as a critical instrument in disputation rather than discovery. Their identification of logic with dialectic (like their association of both with rhetoric) seems to have an intentionally invidious significance.

But with Kant, who was influenced by the scholasticism of Christian Wolff, "logic" is generally restored as the name for the whole range of materials in Aristotle's *Organon,* of which dialectic again becomes a part. In his own *Introduction to Logic,* Kant speaks of Aristotle as "the father of Logic." Though "logic has not gained much in extent since Aristotle's time," he says, "there are two amongst more recent philosophers who have again brought general logic into vogue, Leibnitz and Wolff." Since their day, and certainly since Kant's, as may be seen from the titles listed under Additional Readings, "logic" prevails as the name for treatises which discuss, in whole or part, the matters treated in Aristotle's *Organon.*

"Logic" is also used in modern times as the name for an inquiry or study which bears little resemblance to the discipline expounded in Aristotle's *Organon.* What is called "modern logic" to distinguish it from the traditional Aristotelian or scholastic logic, is purely a science, and in no sense an organon, methodology, instrument, or art. It does not restrict itself to stating the laws of thought or formulating the rules of inference. In the words of Josiah Royce, it is "the science of order" and it is applicable to the order of things as well as the order of thought. So conceived, the science of logic is sometimes regarded as having the kind of generality which is traditionally assigned to metaphysics; as, for example, by Russell in his essay, "Logic as the Essence of Philosophy."

But it is mathematics rather than metaphysics with which logic is identified by its modern exponents. "Logistic or mathematical logic," writes Russell, "is mathematical in two different senses: it is itself a branch of mathematics, and it is the logic which is specially applicable to other more traditional branches of mathematics." Since George Boole's *Laws of Thought,* which, according to Russell, initiates the modern development of mathematical logic, "logic has become more mathematical and mathematics has become more logical. The consequence," he says, "is that it has now become wholly impossible to draw a line between the two; in fact, the two are one."

"In what sense," Wittgenstein asks, "is logic something sublime?" His answer stresses the universal significance of logic and the fact that it lies "at the bottom of all the sciences . . . It seeks to see to the bottom of things and is not meant to concern itself whether what actually happens is this or that . . . It takes its rise . . . from an urge to understand the basis, or essence, of everything empirical." In sharp contrast, the existentialist Heidegger asserts that logic "is only *one* exposition of the nature of thinking, and one which . . . is based on the experience of Being as attained in Greek thought."

ARISTOTLE's *Organon* stands to the tradition of logic as Euclid's *Elements* stands to the tradition of geometry. In both cases the work of later minds may alter considerably the structure and content of the discipline. In both cases there are modern departures from the earlier tradition. As in the one case we have Descartes's analytic geometry and the various non-Euclidean geometries, so in the other we have Kant's transcendental logic and the various non-Aristotelian logics.

But all these innovations, even when they might be described as anti-Aristotelian rather than simply as non-Aristotelian, bear the marks of their traditional origin. Kant, for example, takes pains everywhere to indicate the parallelism between the formulations of his transcendental logic and those of Aristotle's logic. Even the various systems of relational and mathematical logic usually attempt to show that the Aristotelian logic of subject and predicate, of particular and universal propositions, and of syllogisms can be treated as a special case under their own formulations. The proposals of Bacon or J. S. Mill with respect to induction and the method of Descartes, though accompanied in each case by a critique of the syllogism, are less radical departures, for they do not apparently reject Aristotle's basic doctrines of predication and proof.

Many of these issues in logical theory are dealt with in other chapters, *e.g.,* in DIALECTIC, INDUCTION, and HYPOTHESIS, in IDEA, JUDGMENT, and REASONING. Here we are principally concerned with the conception of logic itself, not with the detailed content of the science as much as with its character as an art or science, its relation to other arts and sciences, its major divisions, and its leading principles. Though such considerations are more explicitly treated by Kant than by Aristotle, the formative influence of the *Organon* warrants examining it first.

THE PARTS OF LOGIC, as Aristotle conceives them, seem to be indicated by the subject matter of the various books which comprise the collection of writings assembled under the title of *Organon*. That title has a bearing on the question whether logic is a science or an art and on its difference from other sciences and arts. The word "organon" has the meaning of instrument or method. That in turn suggests something to be used as rules of art are used—as directions to be followed to produce a certain result.

Aristotle's own differentiation of the speculative sciences, the practical sciences, and the arts throws light on this view of logic as an art. "The end of theoretical knowledge," he writes, "is truth, while that of practical knowledge is action." In other words, the theoretical, or speculative, sciences differ from the practical sciences in that they are knowledge for its own sake as opposed to knowledge for an ulterior end. According as the ulterior end is the production or "making" of something, as distinct from human action or conduct, art is distinct from the other practical sciences. "Making and acting are different," Aristotle says; "the reasoned state of capacity to act is different from the reasoned state of capacity to make. Hence, too, they are not included one in the other; for neither is acting making nor is making acting." Logic, then, if it is an art, will be concerned with the "making" of something, with producing a work or an effect.

The way in which Aristotle himself refers to the *Organon* seems to confirm this view. He regards it as a preparation for work in the theoretical sciences. "Due to a want of training in logic," he writes, some men attempt to discuss the criteria of truth in mathematics or physics at the same time that they are considering the subject matter of these sciences. "They should know these things already when they come to a special study, and not be inquiring into them while they are listening to lectures on it." Logic, in Aristotle's view, trains the mind in the ways of science. Its productive goal as an art is the making of science itself. For this reason, in the medieval period, logic comes to be called a "speculative art" or, with grammar and rhetoric, a liberal art.

"Even in speculative matters," Aquinas says, "there is something by way of work, *e.g.,* the making of a syllogism, or of a fitting speech, or the work of counting or measuring. Hence whatever habits are ordained to such works of the speculative reason are, by a kind of comparison, called arts indeed, but *liberal* arts, in order to distinguish them from those arts that are ordained to works done by the body . . . On the other hand, those sciences which are not ordained to any such work are called sciences absolutely and not arts."

But though it may not be a science, *absolutely speaking,* because it is an instrument of intellectual work, logic, in addition to being an art, may also have some of the characteristics of a science. If it is a science, what is the object of its knowledge?

Aristotle's division of the speculative sciences, which he seems to present as exhaustive, leaves no place for logic. "There are three kinds of theoretical sciences," he writes, "physics, mathematics, theology" or metaphysics, as the last came to be called. Each of these sciences, furthermore, seems to have a distinctive subject matter which is some aspect of reality, such as change, or quantity, or being. But insofar as logic is concerned with the study of terms, propositions, and syllogisms, it deals with elements common to all sciences.

This suggests that whereas reality is the object of the other sciences, the object of logic as a science is science itself, or more generally the whole of discourse. It considers the elements or patterns of discourse in a formal manner; that is, it considers them apart from their reference to reality or their real significance as the terms, propositions, and syllogisms of particular subject matters or sciences. Because it separates the forms which discursive thought takes from the matter or content it may have, logic is traditionally called a "formal science."

WHERE ARISTOTLE makes his object the elements of discourse (or thought expressed in language), later logicians treat the formal aspect of thought itself. They deal with concepts, judgments, and reasoning instead of with terms, propositions, and syllogisms. This difference results in a definition of logic as the science of thought; the basic formulations of logic are the laws of thought. Thus, for example, Kant says that logic "treats of nothing but the mere forms of thought." Its limits "are definitely fixed by the fact that it is a science which has nothing to do but fully to exhibit and strictly to prove all formal rules of thought."

The logical principles of identity, excluded middle, and contradiction, as well as the principles of inference, are said to be "laws of thought." William James proposes as the most "fundamental principle of inference" what he calls the "axiom of skipped intermediaries," which states that "*skipping intermediary terms leaves relations the same.*" That "equals of equals are equal" is a special application of this principle in the sphere of quantities. Because it applies to all subject matters equally, James regards the principle as "on the whole the broadest and deepest law of man's thought."

In either conception of logic as a formal science, questions arise concerning the relation of logic to other sciences. For Aristotle the question is about logic and metaphysics, because both seem to have an unrestricted scope. Metaphysics considers the being of *everything* which is; logic, the formal components of discourse about *anything*. Aristotle says of philosophy in relation to dialectic, that both "embrace all things" but that "dialectic is merely critical where philosophy claims to know." The same comparison could apply to metaphysics and logic. Both "embrace all things" but not from the same point of view.

Aristotle also asks whether it belongs to metaphysics as well as to logic to inquire "into the truths which are called axioms"—especially those which are the first principles of all knowledge or demonstration, not merely the foundations of knowledge about some limited subject matter. "Since these truths clearly hold good for all things *qua* being," the science which studies being *qua* being (*i.e.*, metaphysics) must be concerned with them. It also belongs to metaphysics as well as to logic "to inquire into the principles of the syllogism."

The principles of identity, excluded middle, and contradiction belong to both sciences—to the one as the most universal truths about existence, to the other as the basic rules of discourse or the laws of thought. This sharing of a common ground does not seem to Aristotle to violate their separateness; but Bacon charges him with having "corrupted natural philosophy by logic." Of Aristotle's physics, he says that it is built of "mere logical terms," and, Bacon adds, Aristotle "remodelled the same subject in his metaphysics under a more imposing title."

Whereas Aristotle considers the relation of logic to metaphysics, Kant considers its relation to psychology. Both logic and psychology are concerned with thinking and knowing.

Distinguishing between pure and applied logic, Kant says that pure logic "has nothing to do with empirical principles and borrows nothing from psychology." Applied logic depends on psychology. In fact, says Kant in his *Introduction to Logic,* it is "a psychology in which we consider what is the usual process in our thought, not what is the right one." Applied logic ought not to be called logic at all, for "logic is the science of the right use of the understanding and the reason generally, not subjectively, that is, not according to empirical (psychological) principles, as to how the understanding actually thinks, but objectively, that is, according to *a priori* principles, as to how it ought to think."

James also insists upon the distinction between psychology and logic. He even uses Kant's terms in calling logic an *a priori* and psychology an empirical science. What the psychologist calls "laws of thought," such as the laws of the association of ideas, describe the actual flow of thought and connections which depend upon similarity and succession. The laws of logic, in contrast, state reason's perception of the rational structure of thought itself and the relations which must obtain if thought is to be rational.

RETURNING NOW to the indication of the parts of logic which may be found in the structure of the *Organon,* we can see two orders in the books. The first three books—the *Categories, On Interpretation,* and the *Prior Analytics*—deal with terms, propositions, and syllogisms: with the classification of terms and their relation to one another; with the classification of propositions and their opposition to one another; with the analysis of the various types of syllogisms and the formulation of the rules of valid inference. Terms are the elements of propositions; terms and propositions are the elements of the syllogism. This seems to determine the order of the first three books.

The first three books as a whole stand in a certain order to the remaining books. Taking the latter as a group, their differentiation from what precedes them seems to lie in the fact that they deal with terms, propositions, and syllogisms, not abstracted from all considerations of knowledge and truth about reality, but rather with primary emphasis upon the logic of actual knowledge, or on the processes of knowing and arguing about what is true or probable. In the traditional development of Aristotelian logic, this division between the first three and the remaining books of the *Organon* is sometimes characterized as a distinction between *formal* and *material* logic.

In the *Posterior Analytics* and the *Topics* Aristotle considers the discovery and establishment of either the true or the probable. He distinguishes between induction and syllogism (or reasoning) as modes of learning and arguing. The later division of logic into deductive and inductive—sometimes confused with the distinction between formal and material logic—does not seem to correspond to the difference between the *Prior* and the *Posterior Analytics*. In the *Advancement of Learning,* for example, Bacon divides the art of judgment, "which treats of the nature of proof or demonstration," into that which concludes by induction and that which concludes by syllogism; whereas Aristotle appears to treat induction as that upon which syllogistic demonstration depends for its primary and indemonstrable premises.

The distinction between truth and probability, or between knowledge and opinion, does not affect the formal character of either induction or syllogism. A syllogism may be scientific (*i.e.,* demonstratively certain) or dialectical (*i.e.,* merely probable) according to the character of its premises. In either case its formal structure remains the same. Similarly, the difference between scientific and dialectical induction appears only in its result, *i.e.,* whether it is knowledge or opinion. The *Posterior Analytics* and the *Topics* consider the employment of both syllogism and induction. The *Posterior Analytics* treats them in relation to the development and structure of scientific knowledge. The *Topics* discusses them in relation to the dialectical procedures of argument and discovery.

The last book of the *Organon,* which is concerned with exposing the fallacies in sophistical proofs or refutations, serves to protect both scientific and dialectical reasoning from such sophistry. Unlike the philosopher or the dialectician, the sophist does not aim at the truth. Sophistry misuses the weapons of logic—the same weapons used by the scientist or dialectician—to produce a counterfeit of wisdom or, as Aristotle says, "a wisdom which exists only in semblance." Though the dialectician cannot claim to know, he does, nevertheless, deal with opinions critically and respects the canons of logic as much as the philosopher.

The art of logic seems to have three main employments. To its use by the scientist and the dialectician, Aristotle adds its utilization by the orator for the purposes of persuasion. The rhetorician and the dialectician are most closely allied because both deal with probabilities and disputable matters concerning which opposite conclusions can be drawn. "As in dialectic, there is induction on the one hand and syllogism . . . on the other, so it is in rhetoric." Aristotle says that "the enthymeme is a rhetorical syllogism, and the example a rhetorical induction."

The foregoing suggests that a certain order obtains between two of the three arts traditionally called the *trivium.* The elements and principles of logic are, in a sense, prior to the rules of rhetoric. The art of rhetoric depends on and uses logic. The third art, that of grammar, seems to serve both logic and rhetoric. It serves the logician in his task of forming terms and propositions out of words, phrases, and sentences. It serves the rhetorician in his effort to make a forceful use of language. This conception of the uses of grammar appears in Aristotle's *Rhetoric* in his consideration of style, and in the opening books of the *Organon* in his discussion of univocal and equivocal names, the parts of speech, simple and composite expressions, and the different types of sentences.

KANT SEEMS TO diverge from Aristotle both with regard to the unity of logic and with regard to the nature and relation of its parts. Formal or elementary logic, Kant thinks, is not the same as an organon of the sciences. He explains, in his *Introduction to Logic,* that an organon gives instructions as to "how some particular branch of knowledge is to be attained . . . An organon of the sciences is therefore not a mere logic, since it presupposes the accurate knowledge of the objects and sources of the sciences . . . Logic, on the contrary, being the general propaedeutic of every use of the understanding and of the reason, cannot meddle with the sciences and anticipate their matter." Conceding that it may be called an organon so far as it serves, "not for the *enlargement,* but only for the *criticism* and *correction* of our knowledge," Kant insists that "logic is not a general art of discovery, nor an organon of truth; it is not an algebra by the help of which hidden truths may be discovered."

Aristotle, according to Kant, treats the whole of his logic as an organon, dividing it into an analytic and a dialectical part. As Kant sees it, the dialectical part arises from a misuse of the analytic part. This occurs, he says in *The Critique of Pure Reason,* when general or elementary logic (*i.e.,* the analytic part) "which is meant to be a mere canon of criticism, is employed as if it were an organon, for the real production of at least the semblance of objective assertions . . . This general logic," says Kant, "which assumes the semblance of an organon, is called dialectic."

Kant here seems to identify dialectic with what Aristotle calls sophistry. He says of dialectic that "different as are the significations in which the ancients use this name of a science or art, it is easy to gather from its actual employment that with them it was nothing but a logic of semblance. It was a sophistic art of giving to one's ignorance, nay, to one's intentional casuistry, the outward appearance of truth, by imitating the accurate method which logic always requires." When logic is treated as an organon, it "is always an illusive logic, that is, dialectical. For as logic teaches nothing with regard to the contents of knowledge . . . any attempt at using it as an organon in order to extend and enlarge our knowledge, at least in appearance, can end in nothing but mere talk, by asserting with a certain plausibility anything one likes, or, if one likes, denying it."

Yet Kant himself retains Analytic and Dialectic as the major divisions of his own transcendental logic, explaining that he employs the title of dialectic, not for the misuse of logic, but rather to signify that portion of logic which is the critique of "dialectical semblance" or sophistry. General or ordinary logic takes no account of the content of knowledge and applies to all objects universally because "it treats of the form of thought in general." Transcendental logic does not entirely ignore the content of knowledge, but only the content of that knowledge which is empirical in origin. If there are transcendental or *a priori* concepts which do not originate from experience, then there can be a science which treats "of that knowledge which belongs to the pure understanding, and by which we may think objects entirely *a priori.*"

That is the science Kant calls "*transcendental Logic.*" It deals, he writes, "with the laws of the understanding and reason in so far only as they refer *a priori* to objects." That part of it "which teaches the elements of the pure knowledge of the understanding, and the principles without which no object can be thought, is the transcendental Analytic." The second part of it is the transcendental Dialectic—"a critique of the understanding and reason with regard to their hyperphysical employment, in order thus to lay bare the false semblance of its groundless pretensions . . . serving as a protection of the pure understanding against all sophistical illusions."

THE ISSUE BETWEEN Kant and Aristotle cannot be understood if it is read simply as a dispute about the nature and divisions of logic. Their diverse views of logic must be seen against the larger background of their philosophical differences with regard to the nature of the mind, the nature of reality, the origin of knowledge, and the character of its objects. Controversies about logic (and even within logic, about this or that theory of judgment or reasoning) usually reflect fundamental issues in psychology and metaphysics. The attack made by some modern logicians, for example, against the subject-predicate logic of Aristotle cannot be separated from their rejection of his doctrine of substance and accident in physics and metaphysics; even as their own relational logic represents a different view of the structure of reality or the constituents of experience.

On the other hand, the criticism of Aristotelian logic by Bacon and Descartes seems to be motivated primarily by considerations of method. They do not have a different logic to propose, as do Kant and later symbolic or mathematical logicians. Rather for them logic itself—by which they mean Aristotle's logic and particularly his doctrine of the syllogism—appears useless for the purposes of enlarging knowledge, discovering new truths, and developing the sciences. Where Kant criticizes Aristotle for regarding logic as an organon or method for acquiring knowledge, Bacon and Descartes complain that logic does not serve that purpose at all, and therefore a *novum organum*—not a new logic, but a new method—is needed.

"The present system of logic is useless for the discovery of the sciences," Bacon writes. It "rather assists in confirming and rendering inveterate the errors founded on vulgar notions than in searching after truth, and is therefore more hurtful than useful." The syllogism, for example, "is unequal to the subtlety of nature . . . Our only hope is in genuine induction." Induction is the key to an art of discovery, and the rules of induction the heart of a fruitful method of inquiry.

The relation of induction to demonstration in Aristotle's logic, and the difference between Aristotle's and Bacon's theories of induction, are discussed in the chapter on that subject. In Bacon's view, the *Novum Organum* departs radically from the old *Organon*. The new can be substituted for the old in its entirety. It may be asked, he says, "whether we talk of perfecting natural philosophy alone according to our method, or the other sciences also, such as logic, ethics, politics." His answer is that "as common logic, which regulates matters by syllogisms, is applied not only to natural, but also to every other science, so our inductive method likewise comprehends them all."

Demonstration is opposed not only to induction, but to discovery. Accordingly, logic conceived as concerned only with the rules of demonstration is opposed to other methods which aim at directing scientific inquiry and research. The basic contrast is between criticism and construction, or between examining what is offered as knowledge for its validity and developing techniques for adding new knowledge to old. In his *Concerning Two New Sciences* Galileo says that logic "teaches us how to test the conclusiveness of any argument or demonstration already discovered and completed" but not "to discover correct arguments and demonstrations." It does not, "as regards stimulation to discovery, compare with the power of sharp distinction which belongs to geometry."

In the same vein Descartes says of logic that "the syllogisms and the great part of the other teaching serve better in explaining to others those things that one knows . . . than in learning what is new . . . This made me feel that some other method must be found." The four rules of the method he then states, which codify the steps he himself has taken to make discoveries in geometry and physics, seem to him a general procedure for insuring the advancement of all fields of learning.

As his *Rules for the Direction of the Mind* indicates, Descartes's method does not omit the intuition of principles and the deduction of conclusions therefrom—the apparent equivalents of induction and demonstration in Aristotle's *Organon*. But he explains why he has "omitted all the precepts of the dialecticians" even though he is himself concerned with improving "our power of deducing one truth from another." Their style of argument, he says, "contributes nothing at all to the discovery of the truth . . . Its only possible use is to serve to explain at times more easily to others the truths we have already ascertained; hence it should be transferred from Philosophy to Rhetoric."

Furthermore, the forms of the traditional syllogism do not seem able to accommodate the connections in mathematical reasoning or the structure of mathematical proof. "Everyone will perceive in mathematical demonstrations," Locke writes, "that the knowledge gained thereby, comes shortest and clearest without syllogisms." Locke identifies logic with the doctrine of the syllogism and, even more explicitly than Descartes, rejects it as an aid to reasoning.

THE QUESTION whether logic is itself a methodology, or includes rules for the discovery as well as the demonstration of truth, is answered in terms of broader and narrower conceptions of the science or art. Those who regard the rules of logic as primarily a canon of criticism, which test the validity of intellectual work, look elsewhere for a method whose rules are productive rather than critical. The question then usually arises whether there is one methodology applicable to *all* fields of inquiry, or as many distinct methods as there are different disciplines or subject matters.

The difference between the traditional Aristotelian and the modern mathematical logic suggests that there may be a plurality of logics. The attempts made by the exponents of each to subsume the other as a special case do not seem to be entirely successful. Though Aristotelian logic appears to give a satisfactory account of the forms of judgment and reasoning in certain types of discourse, it cannot, in the opinion of symbolic logicians, be applied to mathematics. "Mathematics consists of deductions, and yet," according to Russell, "the orthodox accounts of deduction are largely or wholly inapplicable to existing mathematics." Symbolic logic, on the other hand, may succeed in formulating the relational structure of modern mathematics, but it does not, in the opinion of its critics, hold for metaphysics— at least not the sort of metaphysics which treats relation as a category subordinate to substance.

As Heisenberg points out, "the mathematical scheme of quantum theory can be interpreted as an extension or modification of classical logic . . . In classical logic it is assumed that, if a statement has any meaning at all, either the statement or the negation of the statement must be correct." That logical principle must be modified in quantum mechanics to accommodate the principle of indeterminacy.

THE DIFFERENCE BETWEEN the kind of thinking that men do in science and in law suggests another type of diversity among logics. The practical or moral judgment seems to involve a special type of predicate. What Aristotle calls the "practical syllogism" and what Aquinas describes as the process of "determination"— quite distinct from deduction—by which positive laws are derived from natural law, seem to call for a logic of practical thinking, quite distinct from the logic of all the theoretical sciences.

Using the word "logic" in its broadest sense, we must ask whether there is one logic common to all the sciences; or a logic which fits mathematics but not physics or metaphysics, a logic appropriate to speculative philosophy but not to experimental or empirical research, a logic peculiar to the nature of the practical or moral sciences, such as ethics and politics, or to the work of jurisprudence.

There is evidence in the great books that sciences as different as mathematics and physics, or as metaphysics and politics, differ in their methods of discovery and demonstration. This may mean that they differ in their logics as well. Yet it also appears to be the case that the principle of contradiction applies in all, that fallacious inference is detected by the same criteria in all, and to this extent all share a common logic. Where alternative methods have been proposed within a single major field—notably in the case of philosophy—this may reflect different conceptions of philosophy itself rather than alternative routes to the same end.

Because of their relevance to the basic issues about logic (and especially those concerning its scope and unity), the rules of methodology in general and the various methods proposed for particular disciplines are included in this chapter. They are also considered, of course, in chapters devoted to the special disciplines or subject matters, *e.g.*, ASTRONOMY AND COSMOLOGY, HISTORY, MATHEMATICS, METAPHYSICS, PHYSICS, THEOLOGY; and in the chapters on SCIENCE and PHILOSOPHY. What is distinctive about each of these methods is discussed in those chapters in relation to the type of knowledge or inquiry which seems to require a method of its own.

50

Love

INTRODUCTION

HERE, as in the chapters on GOD and MAN, almost all the great books are represented except those in mathematics and the physical sciences. Even those exceptions do not limit the sphere of love. As the theologian understands it, love is not limited to things divine and human, nor to those creatures less than man which have conscious desires. Natural love, Aquinas writes, is not only "in all the soul's powers, but also in all the parts of the body, and universally in all things: because, as Dionysius says, 'Beauty and goodness are beloved by all things.' "

Love is everywhere in the universe—in all things which have their being from the bounty and generosity of God's creative love and which in return obey the law of love in seeking God or in whatever they do to magnify God's glory. Love sometimes even takes the place of other gods in the government of nature. Though he thinks the motions of the world are without direction from the gods, Lucretius opens his poem *The Way Things Are* with an invocation to Venus, the "Creatress": "without you no thing has ever come / Into the radiant boundaries of light ... without you nothing is ever glad, / And nothing ever lovable."

Nor is it only the poet who speaks metaphorically of love as the creative force which engenders things and renews them, or as the power which draws all things together into a unity of peace, preserving nature itself against the disruptive forces of war and hate. The imagery of love appears even in the language of science. The description of magnetic attraction and repulsion borrows some of its fundamental terms from the vocabulary of the passions; Gilbert, for example, refers to "the love of the iron for the loadstone."

On the other hand, the impulsions of love are often compared with the pull of magnetism. But such metaphors or comparisons are seldom intended to conceal the ambiguity of the word "love" when it is used as a term of universal application. "Romeo wants Juliet as the filings want the magnet," writes William James, "and if no obstacles intervene he moves toward her by as straight a line as they. But Romeo and Juliet, if a wall be built between them, do not remain idiotically pressing their faces against its opposite sides"—like iron filings separated from the magnet by a card.

THE LOVE BETWEEN man and woman makes all the great poems contemporaneous with each other and with ourselves. There is a sense in which each great love affair is unique—a world in itself, incomparable, unconditioned by space and time. That, at least, is the way it feels to the romantic lovers, but to the dispassionate observer there seems to be a world of difference between the relationship of Paris and Helen in *The Iliad* and that of Prince Andrew and Natasha in *War and Peace,* or Swann and Odette, Troilus and Criseyde, Gatsby and Daisy, Don Quixote and Dulcinea, Jason and Medea, Aeneas and Dido, Othello and Desdemona, Dante and Beatrice, Hippolytus and Phaedra, Faust and Margaret, Henry V and Catherine, Paolo and Francesca, Samson and Delilah, Antony and Cleopatra, Admetus and Alcestis, Orlando and Rosalind, Haemon and Antigone, Ulysses and Penelope, and Adam and Eve.

The analyst can make distinctions here. He can classify these loves as the conjugal and the illicit, the normal and the perverse, the sexual and the idyllic, the infantile and the adult, the romantic and the Christian. He can, in addition, group all these loves together despite their apparent variety and set them apart from still other categories of love: the friendships between human beings without regard to gender; the familial ties—parental, filial, fraternal; the love of a man for himself, for his fellowmen, for his country, for God. All these other loves are, no less than the love between man and woman, the materials of great poetry even as they are omnipresent in every human life.

The friendship of Achilles and Patroclus dominates the action of *The Iliad* even more, perhaps, than the passion of Paris for Helen. The love of Hamlet for his father and, in another mood, for his mother overshadows his evanescent tenderness for Ophelia. Prince Hal and Falstaff, Don Quixote and Sancho Panza, Pantagruel and Panurge seem to be bound more closely by companionship than any of them is ever tied by Cupid's knot. The love of Cordelia for Lear surpasses, though it does not defeat, the lusts of Goneril and Regan. The vision of Rome effaces the image of Dido from the heart of Aeneas. Brutus lays down his life for Rome as readily as Antony gives up his life for Cleopatra. And the love of a young boy keeps Aschenbach in Venice during a plague in Mann's *Death in Venice*.

Richard III, aware that he "wants love's majesty," implies that he cannot love anyone because he is unable to love himself. Why should "I love myself," he asks, "for any good that I myself have done unto myself"? This element of self-love which, in varying degrees, prompts the actions of Achilles, Ulysses, Oedipus, Macbeth, Faust, and Captain Ahab, finds its prototype in the almost infinite *amour-propre* of Lucifer in *Paradise Lost*. This self-love, which in its extreme form the psychoanalyst calls "narcissism," competes with every other love in human life. Sometimes it qualifies these other loves; when, for example, it enters into Pierre Bezúkhov's meditations about freeing his serfs and turns his sentiment of brotherly love into a piece of sentimentality which is never confirmed by action.

Yet self-love, like sexual love, can be overcome by the love which is charity toward or compassion for others. True self-love, according to Locke, necessarily leads to love of neighbor; and, in Dante's view of the hierarchy of love, men ascend from loving their neighbors as themselves to loving God. Through the love he bears Virgil and Beatrice for the goodness they represent, Dante mounts to the highest heaven where he is given the Good itself to love.

The panorama of human love is not confined to the great works of poetry or fiction. The same drama, with the same types of plot and character, the same lines of action, the same complications and catastrophes, appears in the great works of history and biography. The stories of love told by Herodotus, Thucydides, Plutarch, Tacitus, and Gibbon run the same gamut of the passions, the affections, the tender feeling and the sacrificial devotion, in the attachments of the great figures of history.

Here the loves of a few men move the lives of many. History itself seems to turn in one direction rather than another with the turning of an emperor's heart. Historic institutions seem to draw their strength from the ardor of a single patriot's zeal; and the invincible sacrifices of the martyrs, whether to the cause of church or state, seem to perpetuate with love what neither might of arms nor skill of mind could long sustain. History's blackest as well as brightest pages tell of the lengths to which men have gone for their love's sake, and as often as not the story of the inner turbulence lies half untold between the lines which relate the consequences in acts of violence or heroism.

A very special mode of love originated in the Middle Ages, and has an heir in the romantic love so characteristic of modern times. "When in the twelfth century," Huizinga tells us, "unsatisfied desire was placed by the troubadours of Provence in the centre of the poetic conception of love, an important turn in the history of civilization was effected . . . Love now became the field where all moral and cultural perfection flowered. Because of his love, the courtly lover is pure and virtuous. The spiritual element dominates more and more, till towards the end of the thirteenth century, the *dolce stil nuovo* of Dante and his friends ends by attributing to love the gift of bringing about a state of piety and holy intuition. Here an extreme had been reached."

STILL OTHER OF THE great books deal with love's exhibition of its power. A few of the early dialogues of Plato discuss love and friendship, but more of them dramatically set forth the love his disciples bear Socrates, and Socrates' love of wisdom and the truth. Montaigne can be skeptical and detached in all matters. He can suspend judgment about everything and moderate every feeling by the balance of its opposite, except in the one case of his friendship with Etienne de La Boétie, where love asserts its claims above dispute and doubt. The princely examples with which Machiavelli documents his manual of worldly success are lovers of riches, fame, and power—that triad of seducers which alienates the affections of men for truth, beauty, and goodness.

The whole of Pascal's meditations, insofar as they are addressed to himself, seems to express one thought, itself a feeling. "The heart has its reasons, which the reason does not know. We feel it in a thousand things. I say that the heart naturally loves the Universal Being, and also itself, according as it gives itself to them; and it hardens itself against one or the other at its will. You have rejected the one, and kept the other. Is it by reason that you love yourself?"

In *The Confessions* of Augustine, a man who finally resolved the conflict of his loves lets his memory dwell on the torment of their disorder in order to repent each particular sin against the love of God. "I cared for nothing," he writes, "but to love and be loved. But my love went beyond the affection of one mind for another, beyond the arc of the bright beam of friendship. Bodily desire, like a morass, and adolescent sex welling up within me exuded mists which clouded over and obscured my heart, so that I could not distinguish the clear light of true love from the murk of lust."

Augustine shows us the myriad forms of concupiscence and avarice in the lusting of the flesh and of the eyes, and in the self-love which is pride of person. In no other book except perhaps the Bible are so many loves ar-rayed against one another. Here, in the life of one man, as tempestuous in passion as he was strong of will, their war and peace produce his bondage and his freedom, his anguish and his serenity.

In the Bible the history of mankind itself is told in terms of love, or rather the multiplicity of loves. Every love is here—of God and Mammon, perverse and pure, the idolatry and vanity of love misplaced, every unnatural lust, every ecstasy of the spirit, every tie of friendship and fraternity, and all the hates which love engenders.

THESE BOOKS of poetry and history, of meditation, confession, and revelation, teach us the facts of love even when they do not go beyond that to definition and doctrine. Before we turn to the theory of love as it is expounded by the philosophers and theologians, or to the psychological analysis of love, we may find it useful to summarize the facts of which any theory must take account. And on the level of the facts we also meet the inescapable problems which underlie the theoretical issues formed by conflicting analyses.

First and foremost seems to be the fact of the plurality of loves. There are many different kinds of love—different in object, different in tendency and expression—and as they occur in the individual life, they raise the problem of unity and order. Does one love swallow up or subordinate all the others? Can more than one love rule the heart? Is there a hierarchy of loves which can harmonize all their diversity? These are the questions with which the most comprehensive theories of love find it necessary to begin.

Plato's ladder of love in the *Symposium* has different loves for its rungs. Diotima, whom Socrates describes as his "instructress in the art of love," tells him that if a youth begins by loving a visibly beautiful form, "he will soon of himself perceive that the beauty of one form is akin to the beauty of another," and, therefore, "how foolish would he be not to recognize that the beauty in every form is one and the same." He will then "abate his violent love of the one," and will pass from being "a lover of beautiful forms" to the realization that "the beauty of the mind is more honorable than the beauty of the outward form." Thence he will be led to love "the beauty of laws and institutions . . . and after laws and institutions, he will go on to the sciences, that he may see their beauty." As Diotima summarizes it, the true order of love "begins with the beauties of earth and mounts upwards . . . from fair forms to fair practices, and from fair practices to fair notions, until from fair notions [we] arrive at the notion of absolute beauty."

Aristotle classifies different kinds of love in his analysis of the types of friendship. Since the lovable consists of "the good, pleasant, or useful," he writes, "there are three kinds of friendship, equal in number to the things that are lovable; for with respect to each there is a mutual and recognized love, and those who love each other wish well to each other in that respect in which they love one another." Later in the *Nicomachean Ethics* he also considers the relation of self-love to all love of others, and asks "whether a man should love himself most, or someone else."

Aquinas distinguishes between love in the sphere of the passions and love as an act of will. The former he assigns to what he calls the "concupiscible faculty" of the sensitive appetite; the latter, to the "rational or intellectual appetite." The other basic distinction which Aquinas makes is that between love as a natural tendency and as a supernatural habit. Natural love is that "whereby things seek what is suitable to them according to their nature." When love exceeds the inclinations of nature, it does so by "some habitual form superadded to the natural power," and this habit of love is the virtue of charity.

Freud's theory places the origin of love in the sexual instincts, and so for him the many varieties of love are simply the forms which love takes as the libido fixes upon various objects. "The nucleus of what we mean by love," he writes, "naturally consists . . . in sexual love with sexual union as its aim. We do not separate from this," he goes on to say, "on the one hand, self-love, and on the other, love for parents and children, friendship and love for humanity in general, and also devotion to concrete objects and to abstract ideas . . . All these tendencies are an expression of the same instinctive activities." They differ from sexual love only because "they are diverted from its aim or are prevented from reaching it, though they always preserve enough of their original nature to keep their identity recognizable." Sexual love undergoes these transformations according as it is repressed or sublimated, infantile or adult in its pattern, degraded to the level of brutal sexuality or humanized by inhibitions and mixed with tenderness.

All of these classifications and distinctions belong to the theory of human love. But the fact of love's diversity extends the theory of love to other creatures and to God. In the tradition of biology from Aristotle to Darwin, the mating of animals and the care of their young is thought to exhibit an emotion of love which is either sharply contrasted with or regarded as the root of human love. Darwin, for example, maintains, "it is certain that associated animals have a feeling of love for each other, which is not felt by non-social adult animals."

At the opposite pole, the theologians identify God with love and see in God's love for Himself and for His creatures the principle not only of creation, and of providence and salvation, but also the measure of all other loves by which created things, and men especially, turn toward or away from God. "Beloved, let us love one another," Saint John writes, "for love is of God; and everyone that loveth is born of God, and knoweth God. He that loveth not knoweth not God; for God is love. In this was manifested the love of God toward us, because that God sent his only begotten Son into the world, that we might live through him. Herein is love, not that we loved God, but that he loved us . . . And we have known and believed the love that God hath to us. God is love; and he that dwelleth in love dwelleth in God, and God in him."

In the moral universe of *The Divine Comedy,* heaven is the realm of love, "pure light," Beatrice says, "light intellectual full of love, love of true good full of joy, joy that transcends every sweetness." There courtesy prevails among the blessed, and charity alone of the theological virtues remains. The beatitude of those who see God dispenses with faith and hope, but the vision of God is inseparable from the fruition of love. "The good, which is the object of the will," Dante writes, "is all gathered in it, and outside of it that is defective which is perfect there." Desire and will are "revolved, like a wheel that is evenly moved, by the Love which moves the sun and the other stars." Hell is made by the absence of God's love—the punishment of those who on earth loved other things more than God.

THERE IS A second fact about love to which poetry and history bear testimony. Love frequently turns into its opposite, hate. Sometimes there is love and hate of the same object; sometimes love inspires hate, as it occasions jealousy, of the things which threaten it. Anger and fear, too, follow in the wake of love. Love seems to be the primal passion, generating all the others according to the oppositions of pleasure and pain and by relations of cause and effect. Yet not all the analysts of love as a passion seem to agree upon this point, or at least they do not give the fact the same weight in their theories.

Hobbes, for example, gives primacy to fear, and Spinoza to desire, joy, and sorrow. Spinoza defines love as "joy with the accompanying idea of an external cause," and he defines hatred similarly in terms of sorrow. Nevertheless, Spinoza, like Aquinas and Freud, deals more extensively with love and hate than with any of the other passions. He, like them, observes how their fundamental opposition runs through the whole emotional life of man. But he does not, like Aquinas, regard love as the root of all the other passions. Treating the combination of love and hate toward the same object as a mere "vacillation of the mind," he does not, like Freud, develop an elaborate theory of emotional ambivalence which tries to explain why the deepest affections of men are usually mixtures of love and hate.

A THIRD FACT which appears in almost every one of the great love stories points to another aspect of love's contrariness. There seems to be no happiness more perfect than that which love confirms. But there is also no misery more profound, no depth of despair greater, than that into which lovers are plunged when they are bereft, disappointed, unrequited. Can the pleasures of love be had without its pains? Is it better to have loved and suffered than never to have loved at all? Is it wiser not to love than to love not wisely but too well? Is the world well lost for love?

These questions paraphrase the soliloquies of lovers in the great tragedies and comedies of love. For every praise of love there is, in Shakespearean speech or sonnet, an answering complaint. "All creatures in the world through love exist, and lacking love, lack all that may persist." But "thou blind fool, love, what does thou to mine eyes, that they behold and see not what they see?" "The greater castle of the world is lost," says Antony to Cleopatra; "we have kissed away kingdoms and provinces." But in Juliet's words to Romeo, "My bounty is as boundless as the sea, my love as deep; the more I give to thee, the more I have, for both are infinite."

In *To the Lighthouse,* Woolf writes, "if you asked nine people out of ten they would say they wanted nothing but this—love; while the women . . . would all the time be feeling, This is not what we want; there is nothing more tedious, puerile, and inhumane than this; yet it is also beautiful and necessary."

Love is all opposites—the only reality, the great illusion; the giver of life and its consumer; the benign goddess whose benefactions men beseech, and—to such as Hippolytus or Dido—the dread Cyprian who wreaks havoc and devastation. She is a divinity to be feared when not propitiated, her potions are poison, her darts are shafts of destruction. Love is itself an object of love and hate. Men fall in love with love and fight against it. *Omnia vincit amor,* Virgil writes—"love conquers all."

In the dispassionate language of the moralist, the question is simply whether love is good or bad, a component of happiness or an obstacle thereto. How the question is answered depends upon the kind of love in question. The love which consists in the best type of friendship seems indispensable to the happy life and, more than that, to the fabric of any society, domestic or political.

Such love, Aristotle writes, "is a virtue or

implies virtue, and is besides most necessary with a view to living. For without friends no one would choose to live though he had all other goods . . . Friendship seems too to hold states together, and lawgivers care more for it than for justice." When it is founded on virtue, it goes further than justice, for it binds men together through benevolence and generosity. "When men are friends," Aristotle says, "they have no need of justice."

But Aristotle does not forget that there are other types of friendship, based on utility or pleasure-seeking rather than upon the mutual admiration of virtuous men. Here, as in the case of other passions, the love may be good or bad. It is virtuous only when it is moderated by reason and restrained from violating the true order of goods, in conformity to which man's various loves should themselves be ordered.

When the love in question is the passion of the sexual instinct, some moralists think that temperance is an inadequate restraint. Neither reason nor law is adequate to the task of subduing—or, as Freud would say, of domesticating—the beast. To the question Socrates asks, whether life is harder toward the end, the old man Cephalus replies in the words of Sophocles, when he was asked how love suits with age, "I feel as if I had escaped from a mad and furious master."

In the most passionate diatribe against love's passion, Lucretius condemns the sensual pleasures which are so embittered with pain. Venus should be entirely shunned, for once her darts have wounded men, "the sore / Takes on new life, persists and thrives; the madness / Worsens from day to day, its weight of pain / More burdensome . . .

Nothing else
Inflames us, once we have it, with desire
Of more and more and more . . . for a little time,
The furious fire subsides. But it will blaze,
Break out again in madness, and they'll seek
Again whatever it is they want to reach,
Find no prescription, no device to stop
This rank infection, so they peak and pine,
Confused and troubled by their secret wound . . .
Griefs like these
Are common enough when things are going well
And happily, as we say. When things are rough,
Griefs multiply to such infinities

Your eyes, tight shut, can see them. Be on guard,
As I have taught you, don't be taken in.
It's easier to avoid the snares of love
Than to escape once you are in that net.

This doctrine by the poet Lucretius is echoed by the novelist Proust. "There can be no peace of mind in love," he writes, "since what one has obtained is never anything but a new starting-point for further desires."

In the doctrines of most moralists, however, the sexual passion calls for no special treatment different from other appetites and passions. Because it is more complex in its manifestations, perhaps, and more imperious in its urges, more effort on the part of reason may be required to regulate it, to direct or restrain it. Yet no special principles of virtue or duty apply to sexual love. Even the religious vow of chastity is matched by the vow of poverty. The love of money is as serious a deflection from loving God as the lust of the flesh.

Sex is treated differently by the sociologist. Weber writes of "the tension between religion and sex," through which sex has been sublimated into "eroticism"; and this has "consisted precisely in a gradual turning away from the naive naturalism of sex." Weber also comments on the intellectual quality of this sexually sublimated eroticism. "As the knowing love of the mature man stands to the passionate enthusiasm of the youth, so," he writes, "stands the deadly earnestness of this eroticism of intellectualism to chivalrous love . . . [It] reaffirms the natural quality of the sexual sphere, but it does so consciously, as an embodied creative power."

WHAT IS COMMON to all these matters is discussed in the chapters on DUTY, EMOTION, VIRTUE AND VICE, and SIN. But here one more fact remains to be considered—the last fact about love which the poets and the historians seem to lay before the moralists and theologians.

When greed violates the precepts of justice, or gluttony those of temperance, the vice or sin appears to have no redeeming features. These are weaknesses of character incompatible with heroic stature. But many of the great heroes of literature are otherwise noble men or women who have, for love's sake, deserted their duty or transgressed the rules of God and man, acknowledging their claims and yet choosing to risk the condemnation of society even to the point of banishment, or to put their immortal souls in peril. The fact seems to be that only love retains some honor when it defies morality; not that moralists excuse the illicit act, but that in the opinion of mankind, as evidenced by its poetry at least, love has some privileged status. Its waywardness and even its madness are extenuated.

The poets suggest the reason for this. Unlike the other passions which man shares with the animals, characteristically human love is a thing of the spirit as well as the body. A man is piggish when he is a glutton, a jackal when he is craven, but when his emotional excess in the sphere of love lifts him to acts of devotion and sacrifice, he is incomparably human. That is why the great lovers, as the poets depict them, seem admirable in spite of their transgressions. They almost seem to be justified—poetically, at least, if not morally—in acting as if love exempted them from ordinary laws; as if their love could be a law unto itself. "Who ever bound a lover by a law?" Arcite asks in Chaucer's "The Knight's Tale." "Love is law unto itself," he says. "What earthly man can have more law than that?"

To a psychologist like Freud, the conflict between the erotic impulses and morality is the central conflict in the psychic life of the individual and between the individual and society. There seems to be no happy resolution unless each is somehow accommodated to the other. At one extreme of repression, "the claims of our civilization," according to Freud, "make life too hard for the greater part of humanity, and so further the aversion to reality and the origin of neuroses"; the individual suffers neurotic disorders which result from the failure of the repressed energies to find outlets acceptable to the moral censor. At the other extreme of expression, the erotic instinct "would break all bounds and the laboriously erected structure of civilization would be swept away." Integration would seem to be achieved in the individual personality and society would seem to prosper only when sexuality is transformed into those types of love which reinforce laws and duties with emotional loyalty to moral ideals and invest ideal objects with their energies, creating the highest goods of civilization.

To the theologian, the conflict between love and morality remains insoluble—not in principle, but in practice—until love itself supplants all other rules of conduct. The "good man," according to Augustine, is not he "who knows what is good, but who loves it. Is it not then obvious," he goes on to say, "that we love in ourselves the very love wherewith we love whatever we love? For there is also a love wherewith we love that which we ought not to love; and this love is hated by him who loves that wherewith he loves what ought to be loved. For it is quite possible for both to exist in one man. And this co-existence is good for a man, to the end that this love which conduces to our living well may grow, and the other, which leads us to evil may decrease, until our whole life be perfectly healed and transmuted into good." Only a better love, a love that is wholly virtuous and right, has the power requisite to overcome love's errors. With this perfect love goes only one rule, Augustine says: *Dilige, et quod vis fac*— "love, and do what you will."

This perfect love, which alone deserves to be a law unto itself, is more than fallen human nature can come by without God's grace. It is, according to Christian theology, the supernatural virtue of charity whereby men participate in God's love of Himself and His creatures—loving God with their whole heart and soul and mind, and their neighbors as themselves. On these two precepts of charity, according to the teaching of Christ, "depends the whole law and the prophets."

The questions which Aquinas considers in his treatise on charity indicate that the theological resolution of the conflict between love and morality is, in essence, the resolution of a conflict between diverse loves, a resolution accomplished by the perfection of love itself. Concerning the objects and order of charity, he asks, for example, "whether we should love charity out of charity," "whether irrational creatures also ought to be loved out of charity," "whether a man ought to love his body out of charity," "whether we ought to love sinners out of charity," "whether charity requires that we should love our enemies," "whether God ought to be loved more than our neighbors," "whether, out of charity, man is bound to love God more than himself," "whether, out of charity, man ought to love himself more than his neighbor," "whether a man ought to love his neighbor more than his own body," "whether we ought to love one neighbor more than another," "whether we ought to love those who are better more than those who are more closely united to us," "whether a man ought, out of charity, to love his children more than his father," "whether a man ought to love his wife more than his father and mother," "whether a man ought to love his benefactor more than one he has benefited."

THE DIVERSITY of love seems to be both the basic fact and the basic problem for the psychologist, the moralist, the theologian. The ancient languages have three distinct words for the main types of love: *eros, philia, agape* in Greek; *amor, amicitia* (or *dilectio*), and *caritas* in Latin. Because English has no such distinct words, it seems necessary to use such phrases as "sexual love," "love of friendship," and "love of charity" in order to indicate plainly that love is common to all three, and to distinguish the three meanings. Yet we must observe what Augustine points out, namely, that the Scriptures "make no distinction between *amor, dilectio,* and *caritas,*" and that in the Bible "*amor* is used in a good connection."

The problem of the kinds of love seems further to be complicated by the need to differentiate and relate love and desire. Some writers use the words "love" and "desire" interchangeably, as does Lucretius who, in speaking of the pleasures of Venus, says that "Cupid [*i.e.,* desire] is the Latin name of love." Some, like Spinoza, use the word "desire" as the more general word and "love" to name a special mode of desire. Still others use "love" as the more general word and "desire" to signify an aspect of love. "Love," Aquinas writes, "is naturally the first act of the will and appetite; for which reason all the other appetitive movements presuppose love, as their root and ori-gin. For nobody desires anything nor rejoices in anything, except as a good that is loved."

One thing seems to be clear, namely, that both love and desire belong to the appetitive faculty—to the sphere of the emotions and the will rather than to the sphere of perception and knowledge. When a distinction is made between desire and love as two states of appetite, it seems to be based on their difference in tendency. As indicated in the chapter of DESIRE, the tendency of desire is acquisitive. The object of desire is a good to be possessed, and the drive of desire continues until, with possession, it is satisfied. Love equated with desire does not differ from any other hunger.

But there seems to be another tendency which impels one not to possess the object loved, but to benefit it. The lover wishes the well-being of the beloved, and reflexively wishes himself well through being united with the object of his love. Where desire devoid of love is selfish in the sense of one's seeking goods or pleasures for oneself without any regard for the good of the other, be it thing or person, love seeks to give rather than to get, or to get only as the result of giving. Whereas nothing short of physical possession satisfies desire, love can be satisfied in the contemplation of its object's beauty or goodness. It has more affinity with knowledge than with action, though it goes beyond knowledge in its wish to act for the good of the beloved, as well as in its wish to be loved in return.

Those who distinguish love and desire in such terms usually repeat the distinction in differentiating kinds of love. The difference between sexual love and the love which is pure friendship, for example, is said to rest on the predominance of selfish desires in the one and the predominance of altruistic motives in the other. Sexual love is sometimes called the "love of desire" to signify that it is a love born of desire; whereas in friendship love is thought to precede desire and to determine its wishes.

In contrast to the love of desire, the love of friendship makes few demands. "In true friendship, in which I am expert," Montaigne declares, "I give myself to my friend more than I draw him to me. I not only like doing him good better than having him do me good, but also would rather have him do good to himself than to me; he does me most good when he does himself good. And if absence is pleasant or useful to him, it is much sweeter to me than his presence."

These two loves appear in most of the great analyses of love, though under different names: concupiscent love and fraternal love; the friendship based on pleasure or utility and the friendship based on virtue; animal and human love; sexuality and tenderness. Sometimes they are assigned to different faculties: the love of desire to the sensitive appetite or the sphere of instinct and emotion; the love of friendship to the will or faculty of intellectual desire, capable of what Spinoza calls the *amor intellectualis Dei*—"the intellectual love of God." Sometimes the two kinds of love are thought able to exist in complete separation from one another as well as in varying degrees of mixture, as in romantic and conjugal love; and sometimes the erotic or sexual component is thought to be present to some degree in all love. Though he asserts this, Freud does not hold the converse, that sexuality is always accompanied by the tenderness which character-

izes human love. The opposite positions here seem to be correlated with opposed views of the relation of man to other animals, or with opposed theories of human nature, especially in regard to the relation of instinct and reason, the senses and the intellect, the emotions and the will.

As suggested above, romantic love is usually conceived as involving both possessive and altruistic motives, the latter magnified by what its critics regard as an exaggerated idealization of the beloved. The theological virtue of charity, on the other hand, is purely a love of friendship, its purity made perfect by its supernatural foundation. One of the great issues here is whether the romantic is compatible with the Christian conception of love, whether the adoration accorded a beloved human being does not amount to deification—as much a violation of the precepts of charity as the pride of unbounded self-love. Which view is taken affects the conception of conjugal love and the relation of love in courtship to love in marriage. These matters and, in general, the forms of love in the domestic community are discussed in the chapter on FAMILY.

51

Man

INTRODUCTION

Whether or not the proper study of mankind is man, it is the only study in which the knower and the known are one, in which the object of the science is the nature of the scientist. If we consider every effort men have made in response to the ancient injunction "know thyself," then psychology has perhaps a longer tradition than any other science. But by a stricter conception of science, more is required than individual insight or self-consciousness. Definitions, principles, analyses applicable to all men must be established, and it has been questioned whether the method of introspection suffices for this purpose. What methods should be used by the psychologist depends in part upon the precise object and scope of his inquiry. According as different subject matters and different methods define psychology, there seem to be several disciplines bearing that name, each with its own tradition in western thought.

In one conception, psychology begins with the dialogues of Plato and with Aristotle's treatise *On the Soul*. As Aristotle's title indicates, and as the Greek roots of the word "psychology" connote, the soul rather than man is the object of the science. Anthropology, Kant later suggests, would be a more appropriate name for the science of man. The Greek inquiry into the soul extends, beyond man, to all living things. It is because "the soul is in some sense the principle of animal life," Aristotle writes, that "the knowledge of the soul admittedly contributes greatly to the advance of truth in general, and, above all, to our understanding of Nature."

Nevertheless, psychology for the Greeks is principally concerned with the study of man. The analysis of the parts or faculties of the human soul is an analysis of the properties of human nature—the powers which man has and the characteristically human acts or functions he can perform. The methods by which this analysis is developed are, for the most part, the same methods which the Greek philosophers use in physics. "The study of the soul," Aristotle writes, "falls within the science of Nature." The definitions of the psychologist, like those of the physicist, give "a certain mode of movement of such and such a body (or part or faculty of a body) by this or that cause and for this or that end." In the case of the human soul, however, the psychologist can employ a method not applicable to other things. The human intellect is able to examine itself. Mind can thus know things about mind which are not otherwise observable.

The subject matter of psychology narrows somewhat when, at a later moment in the tradition, the study of mind tends to replace the study of man. This narrowing takes place gradually. Though Descartes identifies soul with mind or intellect, he treats of the passions and the will as well as thought and knowledge. Differing from Descartes with regard to body and soul, Hobbes and Spinoza also give as much attention to the emotions as to ideas and reasoning. But with Locke, Berkeley, and Hume there is an increasing tendency to analyze the contents of consciousness and the acts of the understanding, treated exclusively as a faculty of thinking or knowing. Where in the earlier tradition the observation of human behavior and the behavior of other animals appears to be useful in psychology, here the main source of psychological knowledge seems to be introspection.

The Principles of Psychology by William

James and the writings of Sigmund Freud represent a return to the broader conception of the science. According to James, "it is better . . . to let the science be as vague as its subject . . . if by so doing we can throw any light on the main business in hand." If psychology "takes into account the fact that minds inhabit environments which act on them and on which they in turn react" and "takes mind in the midst of all its concrete relations, it is immensely more fertile than the old-fashioned 'rational psychology,' which treated the soul as a detached existent, sufficient unto itself, and assumed to consider only its nature and properties. I shall therefore feel free," James goes on to say, "to make any sallies into zoology or into pure nerve-physiology which may seem instructive for our purposes."

Though in the hands of James and Freud the scope of psychology extends no further than the range of topics Aquinas covers in his treatise on man and his treatise on human acts and passions, their return to the study of man as a whole is accompanied by an interest in or invention of new methods, experimental and clinical. "As a science," Freud writes, "psychoanalysis is characterized by the methods with which it works, not by the subject matter with which it deals." Those who distinguish between science and philosophy in terms of empirical research date the beginning of psychology from the inception of these new methods. They regard most psychological writings earlier than James and Freud as works of speculation or philosophy.

Controversy over the validity of conclusions in psychology sometimes turns on the conflicting claims of rival methods to be the *only* way of arriving at the truth; and sometimes, as with Kant, the issue of method seems to be subordinate to the issue of subject matter. Kant admits the possibility of an empirical psychology which would confine its inquiries to the phenomenal processes of thought and feeling, because with respect to such an object "we could call in aid observations on the play of our thoughts," and thence derive "natural laws of the thinking self." But, he goes on to say, "it could never be available for discover-

ing those properties which do not belong to possible experience."

What Kant calls "rational psychology" aims at what is for him impossible, namely, knowledge of the reality or substance of the soul itself. It is impossible, he says, to make "any dogmatical affirmation concerning an object of experience beyond the boundaries of experience." Kant's critique of rational psychology thus appears to be based on the same principles which underlie his critique of metaphysical assertions concerning God's existence and the freedom of the will.

Those principles are in turn based on an elaborate theory of the human faculties, such as sense, understanding, and reason, and the role they play in the constitution of experience and knowledge. But Kant does not regard his own theory of the faculties as psychology. Writers like Locke and Hume, on the other hand, seem to make their psychology—certainly in its principal concern with how the content of the mind is acquired and formed—the basis for appraising the validity of all other knowledge. They do not question the validity of psychology itself. They seem to assume that self-knowledge has unique advantages over all other inquiries.

THESE ISSUES of the scope and validity of psychology are in one sense more relevant to the chapters on KNOWLEDGE, MIND, and SOUL than to this one. Their relevance here is limited by their connection with the main issues about the nature of man. Not merely the tradition of psychology, but the whole tradition of western thought seems to divide on the question of man's essence.

The question can be put in a number of ways. Is man a rational animal, and does that definition imply that only man has reason? Does it imply that man has free will, and that only man has free will? Like the question about the distinction between living and nonliving things or the similar question about the difference between plants and animals, this question can also be asked in terms of the contrast between difference in kind and difference in degree. Does man differ essentially or in kind from other animals, or do all animals possess the same fundamental properties? Does man differ from the others only in the degree to which he possesses some of these shared qualities?

Some, like Darwin, think that "the difference in mind between man and the higher animals, great as it is, certainly is one of degree and not of kind. We have seen," he writes, "that the senses and intuitions, the various emotions and faculties, such as love, memory, attention, curiosity, imitation, reason, etc., of which man boasts, may be found in an incipient, or even sometimes in a well-developed condition, in the lower animals. They are also capable of some inherited improvement, as we see in the domestic dog compared with the wolf or jackal. If it could be proved that certain high mental powers, such as the formation of general concepts, self-consciousness, etc., were absolutely peculiar to man, which seems extremely doubtful, it is not improbable that these qualities are merely the incidental results of other highly-advanced intellectual faculties; and these again mainly the result of the continued use of a perfect language." Such a view clearly takes the position that man varies from other animals in the same way that one species of animal varies from another.

Those who take the opposite position do not always agree on the precise nature of the difference in kind. For the most part, they attribute rationality to man alone and use the word "brute" to signify that all other animals totally lack reason, no matter how acute their intelligence or the apparent sagacity of their instinctive reactions. Milton, for example, in common with many others, describes man as

. . . a creature who not prone
And brute as other creatures, but endued
With sanctity of reason, might erect
His stature, and upright with front serene
Govern the rest, self-knowing, and from thence
Magnanimous to correspond with heaven.

Those who find a difference in kind between man and other animals also tend to think that human society and human language are essentially different from the beehive or the ant mound, from bird calls, jungle cries, or parroting, because they are the work or expression of reason. Unlike Darwin, some of them find

in human speech not the cause of man's *apparent* difference in kind from other animals, but the consequence of his *real* difference in kind—his distinctive rationality. The fact that man does certain things that no other animal does at all means to them that man possesses certain powers which no other animal shares to any degree, even the slightest. They would therefore interpret Darwin's admission that an anthropoid ape could not fashion "a stone into a tool" or "follow a train of metaphysical reasoning, or solve a mathematical problem, or reflect on God, or admire a grand natural scene," as an indication that the ape totally lacked human reason or intellect, however acute his animal intelligence. But the writers who agree that man is radically different from the brutes do not all agree in the account they give of human reason; nor do they all affirm free will as the natural accompaniment of rationality.

Locke, for example, begins his essay *Concerning Human Understanding* with the remark that "the understanding . . . sets man above the rest of sensible beings." Men and other animals alike have the powers of sense, memory, and imagination, but, he says, "brutes abstract not . . . The power of abstracting is not at all in them." This power of having "general ideas is that which puts a perfect distinction betwixt man and brutes, and is an excellency which the faculties of brutes do by no means attain to." But Locke denies that man has free will in the sense of a free choice among alternatives. Rousseau, on the other hand, declares that "every animal has ideas . . . and it is only in degree that man differs, in this respect, from the brute . . . It is not, therefore, so much the understanding that constitutes the specific difference between the man and the brute, as the human quality of free agency . . . and it is particularly in his consciousness of this liberty that the spirituality of his soul is displayed."

James agrees with Locke that "it is probable that brutes neither attend to abstract characters nor have associations by similarity," but it is the latter fact which James himself makes the principal distinction between man and brute. "We may," he asserts, "consider it proven that the most elementary single difference between the human mind and that of brutes lies in this deficiency on the brute's part to associate ideas by similarity." James enumerates "other classical *differentiae* of man besides that of being the only reasoning animal." Man has been called, he says, "the laughing animal" and "the talking animal," but these distinctive traits, like human reasoning, James regards as "consequences of his unrivalled powers . . . to associate ideas by similarity."

Reason and speech are for James the effects, where for Adam Smith they are the cause, of man's peculiarly human attributes. "The propensity to truck, barter, and exchange one thing for another," Smith writes, is "common to all men, and to be found in no other race of animals." This seems to him to be a "necessary consequence of the faculties of reason and speech" which are peculiar to man. Hobbes, as we shall see presently, takes still another position, since he explains man's reasoning power in terms of his faculty of speech, a faculty which is possessed by no other animal. Tocqueville remarks that "Though man resembles the animals in many respects, one characteristic is peculiar to him alone: he improves himself, and they do not."

Discussions of the difference between man and other animals are not only the province of philosophers and social theorists, but also of writers of fiction, who are often not as quick to praise man over beasts. In Swift's *Gulliver's Travels,* the horselike Houyhnhnms criticize the human race as lacking reason and virtue, and in *Moby Dick,* Melville demonstrates how the whale is far more sublime than man. In *Animal Farm,* Orwell gives new meaning to Aristotle's statement that "man is a political animal" by comparing man to such creatures as pigs and sheep—political epithets that are still in vogue. Certainly the most shocking of fictional comparisons between men and animals appears in Kafka's *The Metamorphosis,* where the opening line tells the reader that the main character has been transformed into a cockroach—a symbol of lowly existence as Kafka sees it.

Despite all these variations in theory or explanation, writers like Locke, Rousseau, James,

Smith, and perhaps Hobbes seem to agree that man and brute differ in kind. On that point they agree even with writers like Plato, Aristotle, Augustine, Aquinas, Descartes, Spinoza, Kant, and Hegel who hold, as they most definitely do not, that man has a special faculty of mind, reason, or intellect. The contradictory position is, therefore, not to be found in the denial of some particular theory of reason, but rather in the denial that any faculty or attribute which man possesses warrants our calling him "rational" and other animals "brute."

THE ISSUE IS sharply drawn between these contradictory positions. Yet it is avoided by those who go no further than to see in human civilization certain distinctive features, such as the arts and sciences, or law, government, and religion. J. S. Mill, for example, discussing the sentiment of justice, finds its root in the natural impulse "to resent, and to repel or retaliate, any harm done or attempted against ourselves, or against those with whom we sympathise . . . common to all animal nature." Man differs from other animals, he writes, "first, in being capable of sympathising, not solely with their offspring, or, like some of the more noble animals, with some superior animal who is kind to them, but with all human and even with all sentient beings. Secondly, in having a more developed intelligence, which gives a wider range to the whole of their sentiments, whether self-regarding or sympathetic. By virtue of his superior intelligence, even apart from his superior range of sympathy, a human being is capable of apprehending a community of interest between himself and the human society of which he forms a part."

A view of this sort would seem to leave open the question whether such typically human developments signify the possession by man of special powers which set him apart as *different in kind*. While admitting extraordinary differences between the behavior or accomplishments of men and other animals, this view does not reject the possibility that such accomplishments may represent merely wide differences in degree of power, which give the *appearance* of differences in kind.

As we have already observed, the issue about man and brute cannot be separated from the controversy about the so-called "higher faculties" of man. Except for the view that man is a purely spiritual being, who merely inhabits or uses a physical body, no theory of human nature doubts that man, as a living organism, possesses in common with plants and animals certain bodily powers or functions. The vegetative functions which Galen calls "the natural faculties" are indispensable to human as to all other forms of corporeal life. Similarly, the powers of sensitivity and appetite or desire are obviously present in man as in other animals. To the observer, who sees only the externals of human and animal behavior, men and the higher animals appear to react to the physical stimulation of their sense organs with a similar repertoire of bodily movements, which vary only as their skeletal structure and their organs of locomotion differ. They also manifest outward signs of inner emotional disturbance sufficiently similar to warrant treating emotions like fear and rage as common to men and other animals.

On all this there seems to be little dispute in the tradition of the great books. But difficult questions arise when the inner significance of these external movements is considered. Both men and animals have the familiar sense organs and such powers as touch, taste, smell, hearing, and vision. But do sensations give rise to knowledge in the same way for both men and animals? Do the powers of memory and imagination extend an animal's range of apprehension as they do man's? Do these powers affect the perception of present objects in the same way for men and animals?

Such questions are not readily answered by observation of external behavior alone. What seems to be called for—a comparison of human and animal experience—cannot be obtained. The difficulty of the problem becomes most intense when a special faculty of knowledge or thought is attributed to man, for animal and human sense perception, imagination, or even emotion may be incommensurable if a special factor of understanding or reason enters into all human experience and is totally absent from that of animals.

In the ancient and medieval periods, the sensitive faculty, including the interior sensitive powers of memory and imagination, is generally distinguished from another faculty, variously called "intellect," "reason," or "mind." Writers like Plato, Aristotle, Plotinus, Lucretius, Augustine, and Aquinas have different conceptions of intellect or mind, in itself and in its relation to sense and imagination, but they do not question its existence as a separate faculty. The range of the sensitive powers does not extend to ideas or intelligible objects, nor is sensitive memory or imagination for them the same as rational thought.

Not only does it seem unquestionable in the ancient and medieval tradition that man has these two distinct faculties of knowledge, but it is generally assumed that other animals have to a greater or less degree, the power of the senses alone. Only men can understand as well as perceive; only men can know the universal as well as the particular; only men can think about objects which are neither sensible nor, strictly, imaginable—objects such as atoms and God, the infinite and the eternal, or the intellect itself. The affirmation of an essential difference between reason and sense seems to be inseparable from the affirmation of an essential difference between men and brutes.

DOUBTS OR DENIALS with regard to both affirmations achieve considerable prevalence in modern times. But though the two affirmations appear inseparable, they are not always denied together. Montaigne, for example, does not so much doubt that men have reason as he does that other animals lack it. He considers the matter in the light of external evidences, in terms of the comparable performances of men and animals. The light of reason seems to shine in both.

He repeats many stories from Plutarch, Pliny, and Chrysippus that supposedly reveal the comparable mentality of animals and men. One is the story of the hound who, following the scent, comes to a triple parting of the ways. After sniffing along the first and second paths and discovering no trace of the scent, the hound, without a moment's hesitation or sniffing, takes up the pursuit along the third trail. This, Montaigne suggests, is a kind of syllogizing; as if the dog reasoned thus with himself: "I have traced my master to this crossroad; he must necessarily be going by one of these three roads; it is not by this one or that one; so he must infallibly be going by this other."

It is noteworthy that Aquinas tells exactly the same story in order to make the point that such *appearances* of reasoning in animals can be explained as instinctively determined conduct. "In the works of irrational animals," he writes, "we notice certain marks of sagacity, in so far as they have a natural inclination to set about their actions in a most orderly manner through being ordained by the supreme art. For which reason, too, certain animals are called prudent or sagacious; and not because they reason or exercise any choice about things." That such behavior is not the work of reason, he claims, "is clear from the fact that all that share in one nature invariably act in the same way."

Unlike Montaigne, Machiavelli seems to imply that men and brutes are alike not in having reason, but in lacking it. The passions control behavior. Intelligence exhibits itself largely as craft or cunning in gaining ends set by the passions. Man is no less the brute in essence because in the jungle of society he often succeeds by cunning rather than by force. He may have more cunning than the fox, but without armor he also has less strength than the lion. The prince, Machiavelli remarks, "being compelled knowingly to adopt the beast, ought to choose the lion and the fox, because the lion cannot defend himself against snares and the fox cannot defend himself against wolves."

For the most part, however, the modern dissent from the ancient and medieval view takes the form of denying that reason and sense are distinct powers. In its most characteristic expression, this denial is accompanied by a denial of abstract ideas as in the writings of Hobbes, Berkeley, and Hume. Their position, discussed more fully in the chapter on UNIVERSAL AND PARTICULAR, is that men only give the appearance of having abstract or general ideas because they employ common names which have general significance.

Language, according to Hobbes, is the root of all other differences between man and brute. Sense and imagination are "common to man and beast." Reasoning, or the "train of thoughts," can take place in any animal which has memory and imagination. But that type of understanding which Hobbes describes as "conception caused by speech" is peculiar to man. His statement that "by the help of speech and method, the same faculties" which belong to both men and beasts "may be improved to such a height as to distinguish men from all other living creatures," would seem to imply that Hobbes regards man as superior to other animals only in degree. Yet, on the other hand, he enumerates a variety of institutions peculiar to human life, such as religion, law, and science, which imply a difference in kind.

Like Hobbes, Berkeley thinks that men use general names but do not have general or abstract ideas. But he seems much less willing than Hobbes to assert man's clear superiority, even on the basis of man's attainments through the power of speech. If the fact that "brutes abstract not," he says in reply to Locke, "be made the distinguishing property of that sort of animals, I fear a great many of those that pass for men must be reckoned into their number." Hume goes further than either Berkeley or Hobbes. Agreeing with them that man has no faculty above sense and imagination, and hence no faculty which animals do not also possess, he alone explicitly draws the conclusion which that implies.

"Animals as well as men," he writes, "learn many things from experience and infer that the same events will always follow from the same causes." Such inferences, in animals or men, are not "founded on any process of argument or reasoning." They are the result of the operation of custom and instinct. "Were this doubtful with regard to men, it seems to admit of no question with regard to the brute creation; and the conclusion being once firmly established in the one, we have a strong presumption, from all the rules of analogy, that it ought to be universally admitted, without any exception or reserve."

But if custom and instinct underlie the appearance of reasoning in both men and animals, it may be asked, says Hume, "how it happens that men so much surpass animals in reasoning, and one man so much surpasses another?" His answer seems to be entirely in terms of degree of the same factors. The same sort of difference which obtains between a superior and an inferior intelligence among men obtains between men and other animals.

All the evidence which Darwin later assembles on the characteristics of human mentality is offered by him in proof of the same point. But to those who think that man alone has an intellect or a rational faculty, over and above all his sensitive powers, such evidence remains inconclusive. As in the case of the dog, whose behavior Aquinas and Montaigne interpret differently, the same observed facts seem to be capable of quite opposite explanation by those who hold opposite theories of human and animal intelligence.

Is THERE INTERNAL evidence, obtained from man's introspective experience of his own thought, which can resolve the controversy? As Descartes sees it, the interpretation of such evidence also seems to depend on the prior assumption one makes about the sameness or difference of men and brutes.

"We cannot help at every moment experiencing within us that we think," he writes; "nor can anyone infer from the fact that it has been shown that the animate brutes can discharge all these operations entirely without thought, that he therefore does not think; unless it be that having previously persuaded himself that his actions are entirely like those of the brutes, just because he has ascribed thought to them, he were to adhere so pertinaciously to these very words, 'men and brutes operate in the same way,' that when it was shown to him that the brutes did not think, he preferred to divest himself of that thought of his of which he could not fail to have an inner consciousness, rather than to alter his opinion that he acted in the same way as the brutes."

On the other hand, Descartes continues, those who hold "that thought is not to be distinguished from bodily motion, will with much better reason conclude that it is the same thing in us and in them, since they notice in them all corporeal movements as in us; they will add that a difference merely of greater and less makes no difference to the essence, and will infer that, though perchance they think that there is less reason in the beasts than in us, our minds are of exactly the same species."

THE ISSUE concerning the senses and the reason is more fully discussed in the chapters on MIND and SENSE, and also in the chapters on IDEA and UNIVERSAL AND PARTICULAR, where the problem of abstract ideas or universal notions is considered. The issue concerning soul in general and the human soul in particular belongs primarily to the chapter on SOUL, and also to the chapter on MIND. But like the issue about sense and intellect, its bearing on the problem of man's nature deserves brief comment here.

The question is not whether man has a soul, but whether only man has a soul; a rational soul; a soul which is, in whole or in part, immaterial; a soul capable of separate existence from the body; an immortal soul. If soul is conceived as the principle of life in all living organisms—as Aristotle conceives it—then having a soul does not distinguish man from plants or animals. If, furthermore, the rational soul is distinguished from the sensitive and vegetative soul in the same way that men are distinguished from brute animals and plants, namely, by reference to certain powers, such as intellect and will, then the statement that men alone have rational souls would seem to add nothing to the statement that men alone are rational.

But if the human soul, through being rational, confers a mode of immaterial, or spiritual, being upon man, then man's possession of such a soul sets him apart from all other physical things, even further than the special power of reason separates him from the brutes. The position of Lucretius illustrates this distinction in reverse. He does not deny that man has a soul. Unlike other living things which also have souls, man's soul includes a special part which Lucretius calls "mind" or "intellect." He describes it as "the force that gives direction to a life / As well as understanding," and "a part

/ Of a man's make-up, every bit as much / As are his hands and feet and seeing eyes."

So far as his having this special faculty is concerned, man is set apart. But for Lucretius nothing exists except atoms and void. Consequently, "mind . . . must have a bodily nature," which consists of "particles very round and smooth indeed, / And very small indeed, to be so stirred . . . in motion by the slightest urge." In his physical constitution man does not differ in any fundamental respect from any other composite thing. The materiality of his soul, furthermore, means that it is as perishable as any composite body.

At the other extreme from Lucretius, Descartes conceives man as a union of two substances. "I possess a body," he writes, "with which I am very intimately conjoined, yet because, on the one side, I have a clear and distinct idea of myself inasmuch as I am only a thinking and unextended thing, and as, on the other, I possess a distinct idea of body as it is only an extended and unthinking thing, it is certain that this I (that is to say, my soul by which I am what I am), is entirely and absolutely distinct from my body and can exist without it." Nevertheless, "sensations of pain, hunger, thirst, etc." lead Descartes to add: "I am not only lodged in my body as a pilot in a vessel, but . . . I am very closely united to it, and so to speak so intermingled with it that I seem to compose with it one whole."

Only man has a dual nature, thus compounded. Other living things, Descartes seems to hold, are merely bodies, having the structure and operation of complex machines. If, like the "*automata* or moving machines . . . made by the industry of man," there were "such machines, possessing the organs and outward form of a monkey, or some other animal without reason, we should not have . . . any means of ascertaining that they were not of the same nature as those animals."

It is indifferent to Descartes whether other animals are conceived as automata or whether, because they have life, sensation, and imagination, they are granted souls. "I have neither denied to the brutes," he writes, "what is vulgarly called life, nor a corporeal soul, or organic sense." What he has denied is thought, and it is this one factor which makes it impossible for a machine to imitate human speech and action. It is this one factor which also requires man's soul, unlike that of the brute, to be an incorporeal substance.

Unlike sensations and passions, acts of thought and will, according to Descartes, cannot be functions of bodily organs. "Even though I were to grant," he says, "that thought existed" in dogs and apes, "it would in nowise follow that the human mind was not to be distinguished from the body, but on the contrary rather that in other animals also there was a mind distinct from their body." When Descartes affirms man's uniqueness, he is therefore affirming more than that man alone has reason and free will. He is affirming that of all things man alone is "formed of body and soul"—not a corporeal soul, but a spiritual substance. The angels, in contrast, are simply spirits.

The remark of Plotinus, that "humanity is poised midway between the gods and the beasts," applies with somewhat altered significance to the Cartesian view. But there are other conceptions of the human constitution which, though they preserve the sense of man's dual nature, do not make him a union of two separate substances.

Spinoza, for example, gives man special status in the order of nature by conferring on him alone participation in the divine mind. "The human mind," he writes, "is a part of the infinite intellect of God." The human body, on the other hand, is "a mode which expresses in a certain and determinate manner the essence of God in so far as He is considered as the thing extended." Man is thus "composed of mind and body," but for Spinoza this duality in human nature is a duality of aspects, not a duality of substances.

There is still another way in which a certain immateriality is attributed to man. In Aristotle's theory, the soul is not a substance in its own right, but the substantial form of an organic body. This is true of all kinds of souls—whether of plants, animals, or men. But when Aristotle enumerates the various powers which living things possess—such as "the nutritive, the appetitive, the sensory, the locomotive, and the power of thinking"—he assigns to man alone, or "possibly another order like man or superior to him, the power of thinking, *i.e.,* mind." Furthermore, of all the parts or powers of the soul, thinking seems to Aristotle to afford "the most probable exception" to the rule that "all the affections of soul involve body."

Apart from thinking, "there seems to be no case," he says, "in which the soul can act or be acted upon without involving body." Whereas the sensitive powers are seated in bodily organs and cannot act except as bodily functions, the intellect is immaterial. It has no bodily organ which is comparable to the eye as the organ of vision and the brain as the organ of memory and imagination. The act of understanding is not a function of physical matter.

According to this theory, man as a whole is a single substance, composite of correlative principles of being—matter and form, or body and soul. But man differs from all other physical substances which are similarly composite in that he has a faculty and mode of activity separate from matter. In the later development of this theory by Aquinas, the immateriality of the intellect becomes the basis for arguing that the rational soul of man can exist apart from matter when the composite human substance is disintegrated by death.

As indicated in the chapters on IMMORTALITY and SOUL, this is not the only argument for the immortality of the soul. We are not here concerned, however, with the various arguments and their merits, but only with the fact that certain conceptions of man's constitution attribute to man something more than the power of rationality, namely, the distinction of having a spiritual and immortal life.

HIS FUTURE AND his past color the present life of man and alter the aspect under which he conceives his place in the general scheme of things. Immortality promises release from mutability as well as salvation from death. With an immortal soul, man belongs to eternity as well as to time. He is not merely a transient character in the universe. His stature and his dignity are not the same when man regards himself as completely dissolvable into dust.

The question of man's past or origin is, perhaps, even more critical in its bearing on man's present status. Ancient poetry and history contain many myths of man's kinship with the gods. The heroes trace their lineage back to the gods. Through them or through the progenitors of the race, man conceives himself as of divine descent or, at least, as having more affinity with the immortal gods than with all other earthbound things.

In *The Descent of Man,* Darwin paints a different picture of human origin. Two propositions determine its general outlines. The first, already stated, is that man belongs to the animal kingdom without any differentiation except in degree. Not only in anatomy, physiology, and embryology are there marks of man's affinity with the mammals; man's behavior and mentality also show, according to Darwin, that man possesses no attribute so peculiarly human that some trace of it cannot be found in the higher forms of animal life.

The second proposition is that man's origin on earth has come about by a process of natural variation from an ancestral type, exactly as other new species of plants or animals have originated by descent with variation from a common ancestor. This theory of the origin of species is discussed in the chapter on EVOLUTION. Its special application to the human species involves the notion of a common ancestor for both man and the anthropoid apes, and the disappearance not only of the ancestral form, but of the intermediate varieties—the so-called "missing links" in the chain of variation.

These two propositions are logically interdependent. If the proposition is false that man differs from other animals only in degree, the proposition cannot be true that man originated along with the anthropoid apes by descent from a common ancestor. Conversely, if the Darwinian theory of man's origin is true, it cannot be true that men and brutes differ in kind. But though the truth of each of these two propositions implies the truth of the other, the problem of the difference between man and other animals has a certain logical priority over the problem of man's origin, simply because more evidence is available to solve it.

That question calls for an examination of man as he is today in comparison with other extant species; whereas the other question necessarily requires the collection and interpretation of historical evidence, which may have some bearing on hypothetical missing links.

It should be added that if, in regard to the first question, the evidence favored the affirmation of a difference in kind, that would not entail the denial of biological evolution, though it would necessarily challenge the Darwinian theory of how such evolution took place. One alternative to the Darwinian hypothesis is the theory of emergent evolution, according to which lower forms of life may give rise to new organic forms which are not only higher but are distinct in kind.

Whether or not Christian theology and some theory of biological evolution can be reconciled, there seems to be an inescapable contradiction between Darwin's view of man's origin and the Judeo-Christian conception of man as a special creation, special above all in the sense that "God created man in his own image."

As God is in essence a perfect intelligence and a spiritual being, man, according to Aquinas, "is said to be to the image of God by reason of his intellectual nature." In all creatures "there is some kind of likeness to God," but it is only in man that that likeness is an image. Man's finitude, imperfection, and corporeal existence make the image a remote resemblance; yet, according to the theologians, it is precisely that likeness which separates man from all other earthly creatures and places him in the company of the angels.

But man is no more an angel than he is a brute. He is separated from the one by his body as from the other by his reason. Nor does he in the present life have the spiritual existence of a disembodied and immortal soul. To these three negatives in the definition of man—*not* an angel, *not* a brute, *not* a soul—the Christian theologian adds a fourth, drawn from man's past. Man is of the race begotten by Adam, but he does not have the attributes which Adam possessed before the fall.

The dogma of man's fall from grace is discussed in the chapter on SIN. Here we are concerned only with its implications for the understanding of man's present nature, as not only being deprived of the extraordinary gifts of life and knowledge which Adam lost through disobedience, but as also being wounded in perpetuity by Adam's sin. Weakness, ignorance, malice, and concupiscence, Aquinas declares, "are the four wounds inflicted on the whole of human nature as a result of our first parent's sin." Man in the world is not only disinherited from Adam's gifts, but with the loss of grace, he also suffers, according to Aquinas, a diminution in "his natural inclination to virtue."

THERE ARE OTHER divisions in the realm of man, but none so radical as that between Eden and the world thereafter. As retold by Plato, the ancient myths of a golden age when men lived under the immediate benevolence of the gods also imply a condition of mankind quite different from the observable reality, but they do not imply a decline in human nature itself with the transition from the golden age to the present. The modern distinction between man living in a state of nature and man living in civil society considers only the external circumstances of human life and does not divide man according to two conditions of his soul. Other dichotomies—such as that between prehistoric and historic man, or between primitive and civilized man—are even less radical, for they deal even more in gradations or degrees of the same external conditions.

These considerations lead us to another phase of man's thinking about man. Where the previous problem was how man differs from everything else in the universe, here the question is how man is divided from man. If men are not equal as individuals, to what extent are their individual differences the result of the unequal endowment of the natures with which they are born, and to what extent are they the result of individual acquirement in the course of life?

The range of human differences, whether innate or acquired, may itself become the basis for a division of men into the normal and the abnormal, a division which separates the feebleminded and the insane from the competent and sane. From a moral and political point of view, this is perhaps the most fundamental of all classifications. It must be admitted, however, that traditionally the problem of the difference between men and women and the problem of the difference between the ages of man from the extreme of infancy to the extreme of senility seem to have exercised more influence on the determination of political status and moral responsibility.

One other differentiation of man from man seems to have significance for the theory of human society and the history of civilization. That is the division of men into groups, sometimes by reference to physical and mental traits which separate one race from another—whether these traits are supposed to be determined biologically as inheritable racial characteristics or are attributed to environmental influences; sometimes by reference to the customs and ideals of a culture. Both sets of criteria appear to be used in the traditional discussion of the opposition between Greek and barbarian, Jew and gentile, European and Asiatic. But it is only in the 20th century that racial differences within the human species are scientifically treated in physical anthropology and in the handling of the problem in a book such as Dobzhansky's *Genetics and the Origin of Species*.

It is also only in the 20th century that the problem of gender—the problem of male and female in the human species—comes to the fore. Throughout the great books from Homer to the end of the 19th century, the word "man" is used as signifying all members of the human species, never as signifying only males. And with the possible exceptions of Plato in antiquity and Mill in the 19th century, almost all the authors of the great books from Aristotle to Nietzsche regard males as superior to females. Nietzsche is most emphatic on this point. For him, it is a "sign of shallow-mindedness" to deny the antagonism and hostile tension between men and women and "to dream here of equal rights, equal education, equal claims and duties." Even in the early 20th century, Veblen describes the status of women in American society as "that of a drudge . . . fairly contented with her lot."

The woman's suffrage movement, of which Mill was a leading progenitor, achieved success in the first quarter of the 20th century, but the feminist movement did not erupt until the third quarter. Yet earlier than that, we find in Shaw's Preface to *Saint Joan* an extraordinary anticipation of its credo. To understand Saint Joan properly, he writes, it is necessary to throw off "sex partialities and their romance," and to regard "woman as the female of the human species."

THE ULTIMATE questions which man asks about himself are partly answered by the very fact of their being asked. The answer may be that man is the measure of all things; that he is sufficient unto himself or at least sufficient for the station he occupies and the part he plays in the structure of the universe. The answer may be that man is not a god overlooking the rest of nature, or even at home in the environment of time and space, but rather that he is a finite and dependent creature aware of his insufficiency, a lonely wanderer seeking something greater than himself and this whole world. Whatever answer is given, man's asking what sort of thing he is, whence he comes, and whither he is destined symbolizes the two strains in human nature—man's knowledge and his ignorance, man's greatness and his misery.

Man, writes Pascal, is "a nothing in comparison with the Infinite, an All in comparison with the Nothing, a mean between nothing and everything. Since he is infinitely removed from comprehending the extremes, the end of things and their beginning are hopelessly hidden from him in an impenetrable secret; he is equally incapable of seeing the Nothing from which he was made, and the Infinite in which he is swallowed up.

"Man," Pascal goes on, "must not think that he is on a level either with the brutes or with the angels, nor must he be ignorant of both sides of his nature; but he must know both." In recognizing both lies his wretchedness and grandeur. "Man knows that he is wretched. He is therefore wretched, because he is so; but he is really greater because he knows it."

52

Mathematics

INTRODUCTION

IT is necessary for us to observe the difference between problems *in* mathematics and
the problem of the truth *about* mathematics.
In the case of any science—in physics, logic, or
metaphysics, as well as mathematics—it is one
thing to examine the discourses or treatises
of the scientists on the special subject matter
of their field, and quite another to examine
discussions of the science itself, its scope,
branches, and unity, its objects, its methods,
and its relation to other disciplines. The chapter on QUANTITY deals with the subject matter
of arithmetic, geometry, and other branches of
mathematics; here we are primarily concerned
with the nature of mathematical science itself.

Sometimes reflections on the nature of a
science are expressed by experts who comment on the scientific enterprises in which
they are engaged, in prefaces or interspersed
remarks. Sometimes such reflections are the
commentary on a particular science by those
who may claim to speak with competence on
the processes of the human mind, the nature
of knowledge or of science in general, but who
claim no special competence in the particular
science under consideration. This is usually
the commentary of philosophers who may assert their right to make all knowledge, as well
as all reality, their province. The same man
may, of course, be both a mathematician and a
philosopher; as, for example, Plato, Descartes,
Pascal, and Whitehead.

In the case of mathematics, the disparity between discourse *in* and *about* the science could
hardly escape notice. Even if no preliminary
rule of caution were laid down, we should
be struck by the contrast between the agreement mathematicians have been able to reach
in the solution of their problems and the dis-

agreement of the commentators on basic questions about mathematics. To this there may
be one significant exception. Mathematics is
honored for the precision of its concepts, the
rigor of its demonstrations, the certitude of its
truth. Even its detractors—like Swift or Berkeley—concede the exactitude and brilliance of
mathematics while questioning its utility; or
they admit its intellectual austerity while chal-
lenging some application of its method. Its
"clearness and certainty of demonstration,"
Berkeley writes, "is hardly anywhere else to
be found."

This general agreement about the quality
of mathematical thought may explain why in
all epochs mathematics has been looked upon
as the type of certain and exact knowledge.
Sometimes it is taken as more than a model
for other sciences; it is regarded as the method
of pure science itself or as the universal science. Sometimes its excellences are thought to
be qualified by the limited or special character
of its objects; or it is contrasted with other
disciplines which, employing different methods, deal with more fundamental matters no
less scientifically. But always the conclusions
of mathematics serve to exemplify rational
truth; always the method of mathematics represents the spirit of dispassionate thought; always mathematical knowledge symbolizes the
power of the human mind to rise above sensible particulars and contingent events to universal and necessary relationships.

Mathematics means this not only to mathematicians and philosophers, but also to
moralists and statesmen. "The objects of geometrical inquiry," writes Alexander Hamilton,
"are so entirely abstracted from those pursuits which stir and put in motion the unruly

passions of the human heart, that mankind, without difficulty, adopt not only the more simple theorems of the science, but even those abstruse paradoxes which, however they may appear susceptible of demonstration, are at variance with the natural conceptions which the mind, without the aid of philosophy, would be led to entertain upon the subject . . . But in the sciences of morals and politics, men are found far less tractable." This, Hamilton points out, is not due merely to the passionate interest in their problems. "It cannot be pretended," he says, "that the principles of moral and political knowledge have, in general, the same degree of certainty with those of mathematics."

ADMIRATION FOR MATHEMATICS often extends beyond enthusiasm for its exemplary virtues or delight in its intellectual beauty to the recognition of its influence on the whole history of thought. Yet here differences of opinion begin to appear.

In the ancient world Plato and Aristotle represent opposite estimates of the importance of mathematics for the rest of philosophy. For the Platonists, Aristotle says, "mathematics has come to be identical with philosophy, though they say that it should be studied for the sake of other things." He complains of those students of science who "do not listen to a lecturer unless he speaks mathematically." They make the error of supposing that "the minute accuracy of mathematics is . . . to be demanded in all cases," whereas, according to Aristotle's own view, "its method is not that of natural science."

In the modern world, thinkers who are both mathematicians and philosophers, like Descartes and Whitehead, represent a return to the Platonic point of view; while Kant, even more than Aristotle, insists that the philosopher is grievously misled if he tries to follow the method of mathematics in his own inquiries. Whitehead charges Aristotle with having deposed mathematics from its high role "as a formative element in the development of philosophy"—a demotion which lasted until, with Descartes and others in the 17th century, mathematics recovered the importance it had for Plato.

Attempting to qualify his own enthusiasm, Whitehead admits that he would not "go so far as to say that to construct a history of thought without a profound study of the mathematical ideas of successive epochs is like omitting Hamlet from the play which is named after him. That would be claiming too much. But it is certainly analogous to cutting out the part of Ophelia. This simile is singularly exact. For Ophelia is quite essential to the play, she is very charming—and a little mad. Let us grant that the pursuit of mathematics is a divine madness of the human spirit, a refuge from the goading urgency of contingent happenings."

For Kant the madness lies not in the pursuit of mathematics itself, but in the delusion of the philosopher that he can proceed in the same way. "The science of mathematics," Kant writes, "presents the most brilliant example of how pure reason may successfully enlarge its domain without the aid of experience. Such examples are always contagious, particularly when the faculty is the same, which naturally flatters itself that it will meet with the same success in other cases which it has had in one." The expectation naturally arises that the method of mathematics "would have the same success outside the field of quantities." But philosophers who understand their own task, Kant thinks, should not be infected by the "confidence . . . of those who are masters in the art of mathematics . . . as to their ability of achieving such success" by applying its method in other fields.

"The exactness of mathematics," Kant holds, "depends on definitions, axioms, and demonstrations . . . None of these can be achieved or imitated by the philosopher in the sense in which they are understood by the mathematician," because, according to Kant, the validity of the mathematician's definitions and demonstrations ultimately depends on the fact that he is able to *construct* the concepts he uses. The point is not that mathematics obtains its objects from reason rather than experience, but rather that it obtains them from reason by construction; as, for example, Euclid begins by constructing a triangle which corresponds with his definition of that figure.

Hence, Kant maintains, "we must not try

in philosophy to imitate mathematics by beginning with definitions, except it be by the way of experiment . . . In philosophy, in fact, the definition in its complete clearness ought to conclude rather than begin our work"; whereas in mathematics we cannot begin until we have constructed the objects corresponding to our definitions. "It follows from all this," Kant concludes, "that it is not in accordance with the very nature of philosophy to boast of its dogmatical character, particularly in the field of pure reason, and to deck itself with the titles and ribands of mathematics."

DIFFERENCES OF opinion about mathematics represent, for the most part, philosophical controversy concerning the nature of science or the objects of its knowledge. Mathematicians who engage in such controversy assume the role of philosophers in doing so, for mathematics itself is not concerned with questions of this sort. But there are some questions about mathematics which seem to call for a close study of the science itself and even for proficiency in its subject matter and operations. These are questions about the scope of mathematics and about the divisions of the science, in relation to one another and to its unity. On these issues mathematicians disagree not only with philosophers but among themselves and in their capacity as mathematicians.

These issues usually involve different interpretations of the history of mathematics. The problem is not one of the origin of mathematics.

The ancient opinion, found in Herodotus, Plato, and Aristotle, that the mathematical arts, especially geometry, were first developed by the Egyptians, is of interest because of the questions it raises about the circumstances of the origin of mathematics. Herodotus seems to suggest that geometry arose as an aid in the practice of surveying land. The word "geometry" means earth-measurement. "From this practice," he says, "geometry first came to be known in Egypt, whence it passed into Greece." Aristotle, on the other hand, separating from the useful arts those which "do not aim at utility," thinks the latter arose "first in the places where men first began to have

leisure. That is why the mathematical arts were founded in Egypt, for there the priestly caste was allowed to be at leisure."

The Greek development of mathematics very early distinguishes between the pure sciences of arithmetic and geometry and their useful applications in the arts of measurement. The Greeks conceived mathematics as essentially speculative rather than practical or productive. They also divorced it from empirical investigation of the sensible world. As arithmetic is concerned with numbers, not with numbered things, and geometry with figures, not with physical shapes, areas, or volumes, so Plato points out that music and astronomy belong to the mathematical sciences when they deal not with audible harmonies but with their numerical ratios, not with visible celestial motions but with their geometrical configurations.

Provoked by Glaucon's interest in the usefulness of the mathematical arts, Socrates excludes their utility as being of no interest to the philosopher. He recommends arithmetic and its sister disciplines only insofar as these sciences entirely ignore the world of sensible things. The reason why the philosopher "who has to rise out of the sea of change and lay hold of true being . . . must be an arithmetician," he explains, is that arithmetic can have "a very great and elevating effect," when it compels "the soul to reason about abstract number" and rebels "against the introduction of visible or tangible objects into the argument." In the same way, only when it concerns itself with "knowledge of the eternal," not with measuring earthly distances, will geometry "draw the soul towards truth, and create the spirit of philosophy." The astronomer, like the geometer, "should employ problems, and let the heavens alone, if he would approach the subject in the right way"; and, like the astronomer, the student of harmony will work in vain, if he compares "the sounds and consonances which are heard only" and so fails to "reach the natural harmonies of number."

About the nonempirical or nonexperimental character of mathematics there has been little dispute. It is seldom suggested that the growth of mathematical knowledge depends upon improvement in methods of observation. But on the relation of mathematics to physics, which raises the whole problem of pure and applied mathematics, or of mathematical and experimental physics, there has been much controversy, especially in modern times.

Bacon, for example, adopts the ancient division of mathematics into pure and mixed, the former "wholly abstracted from matter and physical axioms." Though he regards mathematics as a useful instrument in physics— "the investigation of nature" being "best conducted when mathematics are applied to physics"—he also insists upon the primacy of physics and upon its essentially experimental character. Physics has been corrupted, he says, by logic and by mathematics when these seek to dominate instead of to serve it. "It is a strange fatality that mathematics and logic, which ought to be but handmaids to physics, should boast their certainty before it, and even exercise dominion against it."

The certainty and clarity which Hume is willing to attribute to mathematics cannot, in his opinion, be extended to mathematical physics. "The most perfect philosophy of the natural kind," he thinks, "only staves off our ignorance a little longer . . . Nor is geometry, when taken into the assistance of natural philosophy, ever able to remedy this defect, or lead us into the knowledge of ultimate causes, by all that accuracy of reasoning for which it is so justly celebrated. Every part of mixed mathematics," Hume continues, "proceeds upon the assumption that certain laws are established by nature in her operations; and abstract reasonings are employed, either to assist experience in the discovery of these laws, or to determine their influence in particular instances, where it depends upon any precise degree of distance or quantity." When mixed with physics, mathematics remains subordinate—at best an aid in the formulation and the discovery of the laws of nature.

A different view seems to be taken by the great mathematicians and physicists of the 17th century. Galileo, Descartes, and Newton tend to make mathematical analysis an integral part of physics. As the structure of the world is mathematical, so, too, must the science of nature be mathematical. Geometry, says Descartes, is "the science which furnishes a general knowledge of the measurement of all bodies." If we retain the ancient distinction between geometry and mechanics, it can only be in terms of the assumption, "confirmed by the usage" of these names, that "geometry is precise and exact, while mechanics is not."

In the preface to his *Mathematical Principles of Natural Philosophy,* Newton also says that "geometry is founded in mechanical practice, and is nothing but that part of universal mechanics which accurately proposes and demonstrates the art of measuring." What is called "rational mechanics" must not be confused with the manual arts of measurement which are imperfect and inexact; and it is therefore wrong to distinguish geometry from mechanics as that which is perfectly accurate from that which is less so. "But since the manual arts are chiefly employed in the moving of bodies, it happens that geometry is commonly referred to their magnitude, and mechanics to their motion."

Newton himself does not abide by this distinction. His aim is to subject all the phenomena of nature "to the laws of mathematics" and to cultivate mathematics as far as it relates to natural philosophy. "I offer this work as the mathematical principles of philosophy, for the whole burden of philosophy consists in this— from the phenomena of motions to investigate the forces of nature and from these forces to demonstrate the other phenomena." He regrets that he has not been able to deduce *all* the phenomena of nature "by the same kind of reasoning from mechanical principles."

Joseph Fourier goes even further. "Mathematical analysis," he says, is "as extensive as nature itself." Mathematical analysis has "necessary relations with sensible phenomena." In laying hold "of the laws of these phenomena," mathematics "interprets them by the same language as if to attest the unity and simplicity of the plan of the universe, and to make still more evident that unchangeable order which presides over all natural causes." This much had been said or implied by Descartes and Newton. But in addition to all this, Fourier, from his own experience in developing a mathematical theory of heat, comes to the conclusion that "profound study of nature is the most fertile source of mathematical discoveries." Mathematics itself benefits from its alliance with physics; it increases in analytic power and in the generality of its formulations as physical inquiries extend the range of phenomena to be analyzed and formulated.

THE RELATIONS OF mathematics to physics are considered in the chapters on ASTRONOMY AND COSMOLOGY, MECHANICS, and PHYSICS. Mathematical physics must be examined in the light of the opinion that mathematics and physics are separate sciences, distinct in object and method. Furthermore, whereas some of the major contributions to mathematics appear in the great books of physics or natural philosophy (*e.g.,* Archimedes, Kepler, Newton, Poincaré, Einstein, Bohr, and Heisenberg), even more fundamental formulations of the science occur in great books devoted exclusively to mathematics: Euclid's *Elements* (on geometry), Nicomachus' *Introduction to Arithmetic,* Descartes's *The Geometry,* Pascal's mathematical papers, Whitehead's *Introduction to Mathematics,* and G. H. Hardy's *A Mathematician's Apology.* Others belonging to this latter group are listed in the Additional Readings. The great modern advances in mathematics are exemplified by the works of Carl Friedrich Gauss, N. I. Lobachevsky, William Rowan Hamilton, Bernhard Riemann, George Boole, Richard Dedekind, Giuseppe Peano, Gottlob Frege, Georg Cantor, David Hilbert, and Kurt Gödel.

It would be both natural and reasonable to inquire about the relation between the great works of mathematics included in this set and the equally great treatises or monographs, listed in the Additional Readings, which represent for the most part the contributions of the 19th century. But since the major question which immediately confronts us in such an inquiry concerns the relation of modern to ancient mathematics, we can examine the problem in terms of the works included in this set, for they represent both the continuity and the discontinuity in the tradition of mathematical science.

Galileo and Newton are disciples of Euclid and Archimedes. But Descartes is the great innovator. He seems to be quite self-conscious of his radical departure from the ancients and from the state of mathematics as he found it in his own day. Yet the truth and power of his mathematical discoveries seem so evident to him that he cannot doubt the ancients must have had some inkling of it.

"I am quite ready to believe," he writes, "that the greater minds of former ages had some knowledge of it, nature even conducting them to it. We have sufficient evidence that the ancient Geometricians made use of a certain analysis which they extended to the resolution of all problems, though they grudged the secret to posterity. At the present day also there flourishes a certain kind of Arithmetic, called Algebra, which designs to effect, when dealing with numbers, what the ancients achieved in the matter of figures. These two methods," he claims, "are nothing else than the spontaneous fruit sprung from the inborn principles of the discipline here in question."

Descartes does not regard his success as consisting in the advance of mathematical truth through discoveries based upon principles or conclusions already established. Nor would he even be satisfied to say that his use of algebra in developing analytic geometry created a new branch of mathematics. Rather, in his own view, it tended to unify all existing branches and to form a single universal method of analysis. In effect, it revolutionized the whole character of mathematics and laid the foundation for the characteristically modern development of that science since his day. "To speak freely," he writes, "I am convinced that it is a more powerful instrument of knowledge than any other that has been bequeathed to us by human agency, as being the source of all others."

One need not quite agree with Russell that pure mathematics was not discovered until the 19th century in order to perceive that the discoveries made in that century carry out the spirit of the Cartesian revolution. If one understands the difference between the universal mathematics of Descartes and the separate sciences of arithmetic and geometry as developed by the ancients; if one understands the difference between the theory of equations in Descartes and the theory of proportions in Euclid; if one understands how algebraic symbolism, replacing numbers by letters, frees both arithmetic and geometry from definite quantities, then the profound discontinuity between modern and ancient mathematics begins to be discernible. It is especially in the 19th and 20th centuries that the distinction between pure and applied mathematics is thoroughly discussed; but, as Hardy points out, that distinction "hardly affects their utility."

There are other differences contributing to the discontinuity of modern and ancient mathematics, such as the modern treatment of the infinite, the invention of the calculus, and the theory of functions. But what is of prime importance for the purpose of understanding the nature of mathematics, its objects, and its methods, is the perception of the discontinuity in any one or another of its manifestations. Here is a fundamental disagreement about the nature of mathematics which is not an issue between philosophers disputing the definition of the science, but rather an issue made by the actual work of mathematicians in ancient and modern times.

In his "The Battle of the Books"—ancient and modern—Swift sees only the great poets and philosophers of the two epochs set against one another. The battle between the ancient and the modern books of mathematics might be as dramatically represented. In such affairs there is a natural tendency to prejudge the issue in favor of the modern contender. That prejudice has reason on its side in certain fields of knowledge where the perfection of new instruments and the discovery of new facts work to the advantage of the latecomer. But it is questionable whether in this dispute over the nature of mathematics the same advantage prevails.

When the issue is fairly explored by an examination of the differences between the great masterpieces of ancient and modern mathematics, it may be found impossible to say that truth lies more on one side than on the other, or that one conception of mathematics is more fruitful than another, because the two versions of the science may seem to be incommensurable in their aims, methods, and standards of accomplishment.

ONE EXAMPLE WILL illustrate this incommensurability. The ancient notion of number, as may be seen in Nicomachus' *Introduction to Arithmetic,* limits the variety of numbers. A number always numbers a number of things, even though we can deal with the number itself apart from any set of numbered things. It is always a positive and integral quantity which, excepting unity itself, "the natural starting point of all numbers" contains a multitude of discrete units.

Numbers are classified according to the way in which they are constituted of parts and according to the constitution of these parts. The primary division of numbers is into even and odd. "The even is that which can be divided into two equal parts without a unit intervening in the middle; and the odd is that which cannot be divided into two equal parts because of the aforesaid intervention of a unit."

According to Nicomachus, the even numbers are capable of subdivision into the even-times-even, the odd-times-even, and the even-times-odd; and the odd into the prime and incomposite, the secondary and composite, and the number which, in itself, is secondary and composite, but relatively is prime and incomposite. The peculiarities of these types of number are explained in the chapter on QUANTITY. There are still further classifications of numbers into superabundant, deficient, and perfect; and of the parts of numbers in relation to the numbers of which they are parts.

Finally, numbers are considered in terms of their geometrical properties, to be observed when their units are disposed discretely in spatial patterns, and in one, two, or three dimensions. There are linear, plane, and solid numbers, and among plane numbers, for example, there are triangular, square, pentagonal, hexagonal numbers, and so on.

As Nicomachus views them, the arithmetic operations of addition, subtraction, multiplication, and division are performed in the production of numbers or in the resolution of numbers into their parts. But though any

two numbers can be added together or multiplied, the inverse operations cannot always
be performed. A greater number cannot be
subtracted from a less, for subtraction consists in taking a part from the whole, and
leaving a positive remainder. Since division is
the decomposition of a number into its parts,
a number cannot be divided by one greater
than itself, for the greater cannot be a part
of the less.

In short, in Nicomachus' theory of numbers what later came to be treated as negative numbers and fractions can have no place.
Nicomachus will not carry out arithmetical
operations in all possible directions without
regard to the result obtained. He refuses to
perform these operations when the results
which would be obtained do not have for him
the requisite mathematical reality. He does not
find it repugnant to reason that subtraction
and division, unlike addition and multiplication, are not possible for any two numbers;
as, for example, subtracting a larger from
a smaller number, or using a divisor which
does not go into the dividend evenly, and so
leaves a fractional remainder. On the contrary,
Nicomachus finds it repugnant to reason to
perform these operations in violation of their
proper meaning, and to produce thereby results, such as negative quantities and fractions,
which are for him not numbers, *i.e.*, which
cannot number any real thing.

Understanding the nature of square numbers, Nicomachus would be able to understand a square root, but he would not see why
the operation of extracting the square root
should be applied to numbers which are not
square. Hence another kind of modern number, the irrational fraction which is generated
by such operations as the extraction of the
square of positive integers which are not perfect squares, would never appear in Nicomachus' set of numbers; nor would the imaginary
number, which is the result of applying the
same operation to negative quantities.

When the arithmetical operations are performed algebraically, with unknowns as well
as definite quantities, the solution of equations requires the employment of terms which
Nicomachus would not admit to be num-

bers—negatives, fractions (both rational and
irrational), imaginaries, and complex numbers,
which are partly real and partly imaginary.
Descartes finds nothing repugnant in these
novel quantities. On the contrary, he would
find it repugnant not to be able to perform the
basic arithmetical operations without restriction. Algebra would be impossible, and with it
the general method of analysis that proceeds in
terms of the purely formal structure of equations from which all definite quantities have
been excluded. It would also be impossible to
do what Descartes thinks essential to the unity
of mathematics, namely, to represent geometric operations algebraically and to perform
most algebraic operations geometrically.

Geometric loci cannot be expressed by algebraic formulae or equations, unless there are
as many numbers as there are points on a line.
The number series for Nicomachus, without
fractions and irrationals, is neither dense nor
continuous. There are fewer numbers than
there are points on a line. And without the
use of zero, negative numbers, and fractions—
none of which would be regarded as numbers
by Nicomachus—it would be impossible for
Descartes to construct a set of coordinates
for the geometric representation of equations,
whereby all the points in a plane have their
unique numerical equivalents.

The Cartesian synthesis of algebra and geometry, which in his view vastly increases the
power of each, violates the ancient distinction
between continuous and discontinuous quantities—magnitudes (like lines and planes) and
multitudes (or numbers). Euclid, for example,
treats the irrational or the incommensurable
always as a relation of magnitudes, never of
multitudes, or numbers; for him certain geometric relationships cannot be expressed numerically. Arithmetic and geometry are not
even coordinate, much less coextensive sciences. Arithmetic is the simpler, the more
elementary science, and is presupposed by
geometry.

Other examples arising from the innovations
of Descartes might be employed to show the
chasm between the arithmetic and geometry
of the ancients and that of modern mathematics—such as the treatment of infinite magni-

tudes and numbers, the theory of functions, and the method of the calculus. But the multiplication of examples does not seem necessary to suggest that there may be no answer to the question, Is Descartes right, and Nicomachus and Euclid wrong? or to the question, Are the modern innovations improvements or corruptions of the mathematical arts and sciences?

These questions are not like questions concerning the truth or falsity of a proposition in mathematics or the validity of a proof. A given theorem in Euclid must, in the light of his definitions, axioms, and postulates, be either true or false; and accordingly Euclid's demonstrations or constructions are either cogent or fallacious. The same rules apply to Descartes. But whether Euclid's or Descartes's conception of the whole mathematical enterprise is right seems to present a choice between disparate worlds, a choice to be made by reference to principles and purposes which are themselves not mathematical.

Modern mathematics may be much more useful in its physical applications, especially in the analysis and calculation of variable notions or quantities. It may have a special elegance and simplicity, as well as greater unity and even systematic rigor. But it may also purchase these qualities at the expense of the kind of intelligibility which seems to characterize ancient mathematics as a result of the insistence that its objects have an immediately recognizable reality. Ancient mathematics never occasioned such an extreme remark as that made by Russell about modern mathematics—that it is "the science in which we never know what we are talking about, nor whether what we are saying is true." Though modern mathematics has proved more useful than the mathematics of antiquity, it is a modern mathematician, Hardy, who discounts its usefulness. He writes: "If useful knowledge is . . . knowledge which is likely, now or in the comparatively near future, to contribute to the material comfort of mankind, so that mere intellectual satisfaction is irrelevant, then the great bulk of higher mathematics is useless. Modern geometry and algebra, the theory of numbers, the theory of aggregates and functions, relativity, quantum mechanics—no one of them stands

the test much better than another." As for the great modern mathematicians, Hardy claims, "the world would have been as happy a place without them."

THE QUESTION OF the reality of the objects of mathematics is in part a problem for the mathematician and in part a question for the philosopher. The problem for the mathematician seems to be one of establishing the existence of the objects he defines. This can be illustrated by reference to Euclid's *Elements*.

The basic principles, as Euclid expounds the science, seem to be threefold: definitions, postulates, and axioms or common notions. The axioms are called "common notions" because they are truths common to other branches of mathematics as well as to geometry. The common notions are called "axioms" because their truth is supposed to be self-evident. In contrast, the postulates are peculiar to geometry, for they are written as rules of construction. They demand that certain operations be *assumed* possible, such as the drawing of a straight line or a circle, or the transposition of a figure from one portion of space to another without alteration of its form or quantity.

Euclid's definitions include the definition of a straight line and a circle. His first two postulates, therefore, seem to ask us to assume that space is such that these defined geometric objects exist in it as they are defined; or, in other words, that objects corresponding to the definitions have geometric reality. But there are many definitions—of a triangle, of an equilateral triangle, of a parallelogram—for which Euclid states no postulate demanding that we assume the geometric reality of the object defined. Hence before he undertakes to demonstrate the properties of these figures, he finds it necessary to prove that they can be constructed. Until they are constructed, and the construction demonstrated, the definitions state only possibilities to which no geometric realities are *known* to correspond in the space determined by Euclid's postulates.

In his first constructions, Euclid can employ only the definition of the figure itself, his axioms, and those postulates which permit him to use certain mechanical devices—the straight edge and the compass, which are the mechanical equivalents of his postulates that a straight line can be drawn between any two points and a circle described with any radius from any point upon a plane. When, for example, in the first proposition of Book I, Euclid thus demonstrates the construction of an equilateral triangle, he has proved the geometric existence of that figure, or, in other words, its reality in the space of his postulates.

A number of questions can be asked about this and many other similar demonstrations. The postulates being assumptions, their truth can be questioned and an effort made to prove or disprove them. This type of questioning led to the development of the non-Euclidean geometries. After centuries of trying unsuccessfully to prove Euclid's postulate about parallel lines, geometers like Lobachevsky and Riemann postulated other conditions concerning parallels, with consequences for the properties of other geometric figures.

The interior angles of a Euclidean triangle, for example, equal the sum of two right angles; in certain non-Euclidean triangles, they add up to more or less than two rights. One interpretation of this situation is that the truth of conclusions in geometry is entirely dependent on arbitrary assumptions. Another is that the several variants of the parallel postulate indicate the selection of different spaces in which to construct figures; and under each set of spatial conditions postulated, there is only one body of geometric truths concerning the properties of the figures therein constructed.

THE PRECISE CHARACTER of our geometric knowledge, Euclidean and non-Euclidean, especially of its axioms, is the subject of controversy among 20th-century mathematicians. On the one hand, Poincaré declares that "*the geometrical axioms are . . . neither synthetic à priori intuitions nor experimental facts.* They are conventions. Our choice among all possible conventions is *guided* by experimental facts; but it remains *free,* and is only limited by the necessity of avoiding every contradiction, and thus it is that postulates may remain rigorously true even when the experimental laws which have determined their adoption are only

approximate. In other words, *the axioms of geometry* (I do not speak of those of arithmetic) *are only definitions in disguise.* What, then, are we to think of the question: Is Euclidean geometry true? It has no meaning. We might as well ask if the metric system is true, and if the old weights and measures are false; if Cartesian co-ordinates are true and polar co-ordinates false. One geometry cannot be more true than another; it can only be more convenient. Now, Euclidean geometry is, and will remain, the most convenient."

On the other hand, we find Hardy saying, "There is the science of pure geometry, in which there are many geometries, projective geometry, Euclidean geometry, non-Euclidean geometry, and so forth. Each of these geometries is a *model,* a pattern of ideas, and is to be judged by the interest and beauty of its particular pattern. It is a *map* or *picture,* the joint product of many hands, a partial and imperfect copy (yet exact so far as it extends) of a section of mathematical reality. But the point which is important to us now is this, that there is one thing at any rate of which pure geometries are *not* pictures, and that is the spatio-temporal reality of the physical world."

Another type of question concerns the logical, as opposed to the geometric, conditions of geometric proof. In his essay "On Geometrical Demonstration," Pascal declares the geometric method to be the most perfect available to men, for it "consists not in defining or in proving everything, nor in defining or proving nothing, but in maintaining itself in the middleground of not defining things which are clear to all men and in defining all others; and not proving everything known to men, but in proving all the other things." This method, it seems, is not restricted to the subject matter of geometry; to Descartes and Spinoza, at least, it seems to be the method for demonstrating any theoretical truth. Descartes presents "arguments demonstrating the existence of God and the distinction between soul and body, drawn up in geometrical fashion"; and as its title page indicates, the whole of Spinoza's *Ethics* is set forth "in geometrical order."

It may be questioned whether the postulates which Descartes adds to his definitions and axioms, or those which Spinoza introduces beginning with Proposition 13 of Book II, function as postulates do in geometry, *i.e.,* as rules of construction; it may similarly be questioned whether Spinoza is following the geometric method in Book I where he proceeds without any postulates at all. But the more general question concerns the criteria for testing the consistency and the adequacy of the primitive propositions—the definitions, axioms, postulates—laid down as the foundation for all that is to be demonstrated. The investigation of this problem calls for an examination of the whole process of proof, from which has developed the modern theory of mathematical logic that challenges the universality and adequacy of the traditional logic of Aristotle, and asserts that mathematics and logic are inseparable from one another. They are essentially the same discipline.

THE ISSUES RAISED by mathematical logic or the logic of mathematics are considered in the chapters on HYPOTHESIS, LOGIC, and REASONING. Here we must turn finally to one other question which is of interest principally to the philosopher rather than the mathematician. It concerns the objects of mathematics. It is a question about their reality or mode of existence which cannot be answered by the mathematical proof of a construction.

When, for example, Euclid constructs an equilateral triangle, the figure established cannot be the one imperfectly drawn upon paper. The postulated permission to use a ruler and compass does not remove the imperfection of these mechanical instruments or the inaccuracy in their physical use. The triangle whose properties the geometer tries to demonstrate must be perfect, as no actually drawn figure can be. The philosophical question, therefore, concerns the reality or existence of this ideal, perfect figure. The same question can be asked about pure numbers—numbers apart from all numbered things.

Are the objects of mathematics purely intelligible beings existing apart from the sensible world of material things? Or are they ideal entities—not in the sense of existing outside the mind, but in the sense of being ideas in the mind itself rather than perceptible particulars? As indicated in the chapters on BEING, FORM, and IDEA, Plato and Aristotle seem to answer these questions differently. But there are further differences among those who regard mathematical objects as having being only in the mind.

Aristotle, Aquinas, Locke, and William James, for example, think of the objects of mathematics as universals formed by abstraction from the particulars of sense and imagination. "The mathematicals," such as numbers and figures, Aquinas writes, "do not subsist as separate beings." Apart from numbered things and physical configurations, numbers and figures "have a separate existence only in the reason, in so far as they are abstracted from motion and matter." Hobbes, Berkeley, and Hume, on the other hand, deny abstract ideas or universal concepts. "Let any man try to conceive a triangle in general," Hume declares, "which is neither *isosceles* nor *scalenum,* nor has any particular length or proportion of sides; and he will soon perceive the absurdity of all the scholastic notions with regard to abstraction and general ideas."

Despite these differences, there seems to be general agreement in the tradition of the great books that the truths of mathematics are rational rather than empirical; or, in the language of Kant and James, *a priori* rather than *a posteriori.* But the meaning of this agreement is not the same for those who think that truth in mathematics does not differ from truth in other sciences and those who think that mathematical truths stand alone precisely because they are not about matters of fact or real existence.

Plato, for whom all science is knowledge of purely intelligible objects, regards the mathematical sciences as inferior to dialectic in the knowledge of such objects "because they start from hypotheses and do not ascend to principles." The students of such sciences, Plato writes, "assume the odd and the even and the figures and three kinds of angles and the like in their several branches of science; these are their hypotheses, which they and everybody are supposed to know, and therefore they do not deign to give any account of them either to themselves or others; but they begin with them, and go on until they arrive at last, and in a consistent manner, at their conclusion."

For Aristotle, what differentiates mathematics from physics and metaphysics is the special character of its objects. Physics and metaphysics both deal with substances as they exist outside the mind, whereas the objects of mathematics are abstractions. Though figures and numbers "are inseparable in fact" from material substances, they are "separable from any particular kind of body by an effort of abstraction." This does not deny, for example, that physical things have perceptible figures. It merely insists that the geometer does not treat figures *as* sensible, but *as* intelligible, that is, as abstracted from matter. Nevertheless, the truths of mathematics, no less than those of physics and metaphysics, apply to reality. All three sciences are further alike in demonstrating their conclusions rationally rather than by experiment. All three employ induction to obtain their principles, though metaphysics alone attains to the first principles of all science.

For Kant, "mathematical cognition is cognition by means of the *construction* of conceptions." To explain this he cites the example of the construction of a triangle. "I construct a triangle, by the presentation of the object which corresponds to this conception, either by mere imagination (in pure intuition) or upon paper (in empirical intuition); in both cases completely *a priori* without borrowing the type of that figure from any experience . . . We keep our eye merely on the act of the construction of the conception, and pay no attention to the various modes of determining it, for example, its size, the length of its sides, the size of its angles." The *a priori* character of such intuitions, on which rests the *a priori* character of mathematical truths, does not mean that mathematics has no relevance to experience. Arithmetic and geometry are like physics, according to Kant; they are sciences of experience or nature but like pure (as opposed to empirical) physics, they are *a priori* sciences. Since Kant holds that experience itself is constituted by *a priori* forms of perception, he can ascribe the validity which mathematics has for all possible experience to the "*a priori* intuition of the pure forms of phenomena—space and time."

Russell rejects this "Kantian view which [asserts] that mathematical reasoning is not strictly formal, but always uses intuitions, *i.e.,* the *a priori* knowledge of space and time. Thanks to the progress of Symbolic Logic . . . this part of the Kantian philosophy," Russell holds, "is now capable of a final and irrevocable refutation." Leibniz, before Kant, had advocated "the general doctrine that all mathematics is a deduction from logical principles," but, according to Russell, he had failed to substantiate this insight, partly because of his "belief in the logical necessity of Euclidean geometry." The same belief is, in Russell's opinion, the cause of Kant's error. "The actual propositions of Euclid . . . do not follow from the principles of logic alone; and the perception of this fact," he thinks, "led Kant to his innovations in the theory of knowledge. But since the growth of non-Euclidean geometry, it has appeared that pure mathematics has no concern with the question whether the axioms and propositions of Euclid hold of actual space or not."

Russell asserts that "by the help of ten principles of deduction and ten other premises of a general logical nature (*e.g.,* 'implication is a relation'), all mathematics can be strictly and formally deduced." He regards "the fact that all Mathematics is Symbolic Logic" as "one of the greatest discoveries of our age; and when this fact has been established, the remainder of the principles of Mathematics consists in the analysis of Symbolic Logic itself." Though this view of mathematics may not be worked out in detail except in such treatises as Russell's *The Principles of Mathematics* and in the *Principia Mathematica,* on which he collaborated with Whitehead, the conception of mathematics as a purely formal science, analogous to (if not identical with) logic, does have some anticipations in the great books. For James, as for Locke and Hume, mathematics is strictly a science of the relations between ideas, not of real existences. "As regards mathematical judgments," James writes, "they are all 'rational propositions' . . . for they express results of comparison and nothing more.

The mathematical sciences deal with similarities and equalities exclusively, and not with coexistences and sequences." Both James and Locke, however, differ from Hume in thinking that there are sciences other than those of number and quantity which can demonstrate their conclusions with certitude.

The foregoing discussion indicates *some* of the differences among philosophers concerning the objects of mathematics, the conditions of its truth, and its relation to other sciences. These disagreements do not seem to take the form of an opposition between ancient and modern thought, like that between ancient and modern mathematicians concerning the nature of their science. The two oppositions do not run parallel to one another.

On the contrary, the objections which modern philosophers, especially Berkeley, Hume, and Kant, raise against the notion of infinite quantities seem to favor the ancient rather than the modern tenor of mathematical thought. Though the reasons they give do not derive from the same principles as those to which Plato and Aristotle appeal, they, like the ancients, appear to insist upon a certain type of intelligibility in the objects of mathematics, which seems to have been sacrificed in the mathematical development initiated by Descartes.

THE NOTION THAT ALL mathematical truths "can be strictly and formally deduced," as stated by Russell and Whitehead, was widely accepted by mathematicians until the work of Gödel in the early 1930s. Gödel posed the problem of whether arithmetic, for example, was a consistent, logical system. Could one prove that it was impossible to deduce at the same time two incompatible arithmetical propositions? Gödel's answer was no, it was not impossible. He discovered that in a logical system as rich as arithmetic, propositions would occur that were *undecidable*. No formal proof could be found for both of them in the system. In addition, one of the undecidable statements in any system was the proposition that asserted the logical consistency of the system itself.

In other words, Gödel showed that within the formal structure of arithmetic itself, there was no way of proving that arithmetic was internally consistent. One possible way out is to elevate the discussion of the consistency of arithmetic to a higher system—a system of *meta*-arithmetic. But then one could not show that this *meta*-arithmetic was consistent in terms of its own language; and if one were to repeat this process by a still further elevation to a higher system, one would find oneself in the grip of an infinite regress.

Many mathematicians now accept the fact that there are mathematical truths that cannot be proved formally. This demolishes the program set forth by Russell and Whitehead in their *Principia Mathematica,* a program shared by other mathematicians and logicians at the beginning of the 20th century, such as Hilbert, Peano, and Frege. Gödel's contribution was to deflate their exaggerated claim for logical rigor in mathematics; but with the deflation of that excessive claim the fact still remains that pure mathematics is logically rigorous in a way that is not to be found in the nonmathematical, purely empirical sciences.

53

Matter

INTRODUCTION

"AFTER we came out of the church," says Boswell in his *Life of Samuel Johnson,* "we stood talking for some time together of Bishop Berkeley's ingenious sophistry to prove the non-existence of matter, and that everything in the universe is merely ideal. I observed that though we are satisfied his doctrine is not true, it is impossible to refute it. I shall never forget the alacrity with which Johnson answered, striking his foot with mighty force against a large stone, till he rebounded from it, 'I refute it thus.' "

But Berkeley's argument anticipated Dr. Johnson's style of refutation. "I do not argue," he says, "against the existence of any one thing that we can apprehend either by sense or reflexion. That the things I see with my eyes and touch with my hands do exist, really exist, I make not the least question. The only thing whose existence I deny is that which *philosophers* call Matter or corporeal substance. And in doing this there is no damage done to the rest of mankind, who, I dare say, will never miss it."

The rest of mankind does need to be instructed, however, that when they use the word "matter," they speak of *nothing.* They may from careless habit suppose they are referring to the most obvious something there is in the world—the solid, massy, concrete stuff of which tangible, visible, movable, and moving things are made. Of them, Berkeley would ask how they know such stuff exists. It is not itself perceptible.

We perceive a variety of qualities—colors, shapes, temperatures, textures, sizes, or extensions—but these, Berkeley argues, have their being *in being perceived.* Even if certain of these sensible qualities, sometimes called "pri-

mary," such as figure, size, or weight, are supposed to belong to bodies when they are not actually being sensed, they are not matter, but only its properties. Matter itself is not sensible. Those who assert its existence postulate it as a substratum or support for the sensible qualities they perceive.

The question, therefore, is whether such a substratum is a necessary or an unnecessary hypothesis. Berkeley does not deny the existence of beings which cannot be directly sensed. He affirms the existence of the human spirit or mind, of minds other than his own, and the spiritual being of God. These must be inferred to exist in order to explain the phenomena of our sensible experience and the experience of our own activities in thinking, imagining, willing. If, in addition, the existence of matter or a material substance were necessary to explain the phenomena, Berkeley would not object to affirming its existence by inference, even if it could in no way be directly perceived.

His argument therefore involves, first, a denial of Locke's distinction between primary and secondary qualities. Supposing it to be generally agreed that colors, sounds, odors have no actual existence except in the perceiving mind, he denies that perceptible figure, size, or motion can exist otherwise. "It having been shown that none even of these can possibly exist otherwise than in a Spirit or Mind which perceives them, it follows that we have no longer any reason to suppose the being of Matter."

Matter is not needed as a substratum or support for the qualities we perceive. This is the second main point in Berkeley's argument. "Though we give the materialists their external bodies, they by their own confession are never the nearer knowing how our ideas are produced; since they own themselves unable to comprehend in what manner body can act upon spirit, or how it is possible it should imprint any idea in the mind. Hence it is evident that the production of ideas or sensations in our minds can be no reason why we should suppose Matter or corporeal substances, since that is acknowledged to remain equally inexplicable with or without this supposition."

Russell regards Berkeley's argument as fallacious. "But whether valid or not," he writes, "the argument has been very widely advanced in one form or another; and very many philosophers, perhaps a majority, have held that there is nothing real except minds and their ideas. Such philosophers are called 'idealists.' When they come to explaining matter, they either say, like Berkeley, that matter is really nothing but a collection of ideas, or they say, like Leibniz, that what appears as matter is really a collection of more or less rudimentary minds."

BERKELEY'S ARGUMENTS against matter, which occupy the greater part of his *The Principles of Human Knowledge,* may not have the same force when they are applied against different theories of matter. Berkeley seems to regard his attack on materialism as the refutation of an error at the root of skepticism, atheism, and irreligion. He also thinks materialism creates difficulties for the sciences. But are all affirmations of matter to be lumped together as materialism *in the same sense?* Are Aristotle, Plotinus, Descartes, Spinoza, and Locke materialists in the same sense as Lucretius, Hobbes, and perhaps Marx? Does it make no difference whether bodies are said to be the only real existences, or whether, in addition to bodies, immaterial substances or spiritual beings are also said to exist?

Does it make no difference how matter is conceived—whether as a self-subsistent substance in its own right, capable of existing apart from any qualities except extension and motion which belong to its very essence, or merely as one factor in the constitution of bodies, the factor of potentiality which, as

will be presently explained, has no existence apart from the forms which actualize it? Are skepticism, atheism, and irreligion to be associated with all affirmations of matter, in view of the fact that theologians like Augustine and Aquinas seem to think that a sound view of matter supports the truths of religion against the errors of the materialists?

There seem to be, in short, three distinct positions to which Berkeley's blanket denial of matter stands opposed. The diametrically opposite view seems to be the blanket denial of anything except bodies, or of anything which cannot be reduced to a property or function of matter. The atomism of Lucretius, discussed in the chapter on ELEMENT, may be taken as representative of this view, though Engels would insist that materialism can be dialectical rather than atomistic or mechanical.

Between the two extremes, there appear to be two middle positions which are alike insofar as both affirm the immaterial as well as the material. Although they are alike in asserting the existence of spiritual substances, they may, of course, define the nature of these immaterial things differently, and differently interpret their relation to the realm of matter. But, as theories of matter, their principal difference consists in the way in which they conceive the being of bodies, material substances, or the bodily mode of substance.

In the conceptions of Descartes and Locke, for example, it is matter which gives actuality to sensible bodies. We have "no other idea or notion of matter," Locke writes, "but something wherein those many sensible qualities, which affect our sense, do subsist." The entire substance of sensible bodies consists of matter. All their properties derive from the essence or nature of matter. But in the conceptions of Aristotle and Plotinus, bodies would not exist at all if they were composed only of matter, for matter is no more than a capacity for being, not something which by itself actually is. Sensible bodies derive their being and all their attributes from the forms which matter assumes when its potentialities are actualized. Matter totally devoid of form is not the *nothing* Berkeley calls it, but it is so near to nothing that Plotinus says it is "more plausibly called a nonbeing . . . a bare aspiration towards substantial existence."

These theories of matter or corporeal being seem to be as contrary to one another as together they are contrary to Berkeley's doctrine. Yet each of the two middle positions leans toward one of the opposite extremes.

The conception of matter seems to be very much the same in the complete materialism of Lucretius and Hobbes and in the view of Descartes, Spinoza, and Locke. In the former, only bodies exist. In the latter, bodies do not comprise the whole of existence, but matter is the whole substance of bodies. The separation of body and mind, or matter and spirit, into distinct substances, or modes of substance, leaves matter the same kind of stuff that it is in a world which admits of no other reality. Atomism, furthermore, may be common to both theories, at least to the extent that it is held that the complex bodies we perceive are composed of minute and insensible particles. Unlike Lucretius, Locke may not insist upon the absolute indivisibility of the particles, or upon the eternity of the uncreated atoms of matter; but he, like Hobbes and Newton, carries the division of the familiar bodies of sense-experience down to parts which cannot be perceived and yet have, in a way, a more ultimate reality as units of matter than the complex bodies they constitute.

"Had we senses acute enough to discern the minute particles of bodies, and the real constitution on which their sensible qualities depend," Locke writes, "I doubt not but that would produce quite different ideas in us; and that which is now the yellow color of gold, would then disappear, and instead of it we should see an admirable texture of parts, of a certain size and figure."

At the other extreme, Berkeley's complete denial of matter has less in common with the view of Aristotle, Plotinus, Augustine, and Aquinas than the theory of Descartes, Spinoza, and Locke has with the materialism of Lucretius and Hobbes. They would appear to be close enough, for one seems to hold that matter is almost nonbeing and the other that matter is simply nothing at all. But where Berkeley denies any role to matter, Aristotle

and those who take his view affirm matter to be an indispensable factor in the constitution of physical things. They do not question the reality of bodies or their existence apart from mind. On both of these points they are as opposed to Berkeley as they would be if they were complete materialists. Nevertheless they lean toward Berkeley rather than toward the other extreme in one respect. Where Berkeley denies the existence of matter, they deny its substantiality. Where Berkeley says matter has no being, they say it has the lowest grade of being—on the very verge of not being!

IN SPITE OF ALL the differences noted, the idea of matter has a certain constant meaning throughout the tradition of the great books.

It is generally associated with the idea of quantity, and especially the basic magnitudes, such as time, space, and mass. Sometimes it is said that the essence of matter itself is extension; sometimes that bodies—not matter itself—have the property of tridimensionality. But in either case that which *is* or *has* matter in it necessarily occupies space.

The manner of that occupation is also generally agreed upon. Two bodies or two distinct quantities of matter cannot occupy the same place at the same time. A body may not be impenetrable in the sense of being indivisible, but so long as it remains the whole that it is, it offers resistance to other bodies tending to move into the place it occupies.

It is in terms of its occupation of definite quantities of space and time that Whitehead defines matter. In his view, matter, or the material, the corporeal, has "the property of simple location in space and time, or, if you adopt the more modern ideas, in space-time . . . The characteristic common both to space and time is that material can be said to be *here* in space and *here* in time, or *here* in space-time, in a perfectly definite sense which does not require for its explanation any reference to other regions of space-time."

There is another connection between matter and quantity. To those who ask what makes two otherwise identical things two in number—or what is involved in the merely numerical difference of things alike in every other respect—the usual answer is in terms of matter. Matter is traditionally spoken of as "the principle of individuation." Aquinas, for example, holds that angels, unlike physical substances, cannot differ from one another as do numerically distinct individuals. Because they are immaterial, they can differ only as do species or kinds. "Such things as agree in species," he writes, "but differ in number, agree in form, but are distinguished materially. If, therefore, the angels be not composed of matter and form, it follows that it is impossible for two angels to be of one species; just as it would be impossible for there to be several whitenesses apart, or several humanities, since whitenesses are not several, except in so far as they are in several substances."

The way in which matter is related to individual differences can be exemplified in works of art. Two coins, stamped out of the same kind of matter by the impression of the same die, may differ in no other discernible respect than that they are *two* of the same kind. Their *twoness* seems to be somehow related to the fact that each consists of a distinct quantity of matter. But it may be asked how two units of matter have the distinction of being two while they differ in no other respect. One answer to this difficult question is that their distinction consists in their occupying different places. In the Platonic theory of the origin of many particulars all participating in the same form, diversity of place seems to play the role which matter plays for Aristotle and Aquinas.

Plato's doctrine of the receptacle, which is discussed in the chapter on FORM, is sometimes interpreted by conceiving the receptacle as space, and sometimes by conceiving it as matter. The receptacle, it is said in the *Timaeus,* is that which, "while receiving all things, never departs at all from her own nature and never in any way, or at any time, assumes a form like that of any of the things which enter into her." This, according to Plotinus, means that "its one form is an invincible formlessness."

But Plotinus, who combines Plato's doctrine of the receptacle and the forms with Aristotle's theory of potentiality and actuality, holds that it is matter, not space, which is "the recepta-

cle and nurse of all generation." He says that "recipient and nurse" is a better description of matter than the term "mother," for that term "is used by those who think of a mother as matter to the offspring, as a container only, giving nothing to them." In his own view, matter is more than space or mere receptivity. He is willing to admit the "parallel with motherhood" only to the extent that "matter is sterile, not female to full effect, female in receptivity only, not in pregnancy."

TRADITIONALLY, the distinction between universal and particular is understood as a distinction between the intelligible and the sensible. This indicates another traditional meaning of matter or the material. The realm of sensible things is the realm of bodies. But the atoms which are the elementary bodies are also usually called "insensible particles of matter." This, however, can be interpreted to mean, not that a definite material mass or bulk is in itself absolutely *intangible* or *imponderable,* but that, because of the limitation in our senses, it is imperceptible to us. On this interpretation it would then seem possible to say that *all* bodily existence is sensible existence.

But if we ask about the sensibility of matter itself, rather than of bodies large or small, questions arise which are more difficult to solve. On one theory of matter, matter devoid of form is as insensible as it is unintelligible, yet forms which are not material, that is, not in matter, are also insensible but not unintelligible. On the contrary, they are regarded as more perfectly intelligible than embodied forms. How, then, does matter which is itself insensible cause the forms which it assumes to become sensible when they are materialized?

The theory of matter which does not regard it as a co-principle with form seems to be confronted with a different problem of sensibility. It is supposed that some of the qualities which we sense in bodies are actually in them whether we sense them or not—such properties as size, figure, weight, motion. Other sensible qualities, such as colors, odors, temperatures, or sounds, are supposed to be effects produced by the motions of material particles acting on the sensitive apparatus of animals. This distinction between what Locke calls "primary and secondary qualities"—found also in Lucretius and Descartes—is more fully considered in the chapters on QUALITY and SENSE, but here it calls attention to the problem of how matter, devoid of certain sensible qualities, causes these qualities to arise.

For Lucretius the peculiar difficulty of the problem seems to lie in the fact that the sensitive animal is itself nothing but a material system. All its powers and acts are conceived as functions of matter in motion. How, then, does moving matter within the organism generate certain qualities which do not belong to moving matter outside the organism? For Locke the problem raises a difficulty of still another sort. Secondary qualities, such as colors, sounds, odors, exist only as sensations in the mind. In corporeal substances, or bodies, such qualities, he writes, "are nothing but the powers those substances have to produce several ideas in us by our senses; which ideas are not in the things themselves, otherwise than as anything is in its cause." Though they result from the impact of moving particles on the bodily sense organs, they do not belong to the world of matter at all, but to the realm of spirit. How, then, do the motions of matter cause effects which exist only in the immaterial domain of mind?

These questions indicate some of the problems of matter as an object, condition, or cause of knowledge. They also show how the nature of the problem varies with different conceptions of matter, both in itself and in its relation to mind. There are still other problems which confront those theories of mind which separate reason or intellect from the sensitive faculty.

In such theories the consideration of matter's relation to mind goes beyond the question of the origin of sensations. It takes sensations and images as somehow the functions of living matter—the acts of the various sense organs and the brain. But sensations and images, because they are acts of corporeal organs, have the same limitation which belongs to everything material. As matter is said to cause the individuality or numerical diversity of bodies, so is it said to make sensations and images "particular intentions of the mind"— that is, capable of representing only particular objects, not general kinds or classes. Hence such theories face the problem of the relation of sensations and images to the "universal intentions of the mind," its general concepts or abstract ideas.

ONE MORE TRADITIONAL meaning of matter remains to be mentioned. The sciences of physics or mechanics are concerned with change or motion. They are not concerned with mutability in general, but with the kind of mutability that is manifested by material things. Material things are never conceived as unmovable or unchangeable.

The question whether matter itself is immutable has different meanings for different theories of matter. On the theory (discussed in the chapter on CHANGE) that matter and form are together principles of change in changing substance, it is neither matter nor form but the substance composite of matter and form which changes. Those who think that the motions of the physical world are without beginning and end, attribute a similar eternity to matter and conceive it as imperishable. The theologians who think that God can annihilate whatever He creates, do not hold that matter is indestructible, but they nevertheless attribute everlasting endurance to matter in God's plan. Aquinas, for example, in his treatise on the end of the world, describes the final conflagration which will purge the material universe but leave its matter in existence under the forms of the elements and the heavenly bodies. "The world will be renewed," he writes, "in such a way as to throw off all corruption and remain forever at rest." Hence nothing can be "the subject of that renewal, unless it be a subject of incorruption," such as "the heavenly bodies, the elements, and man."

On other theories of matter the fact that motion is regarded as an intrinsic property of bodies seems to be similarly consistent with the notion that matter itself is immutable or indestructible. This indestructibility may be conceived in terms of the absolute indivisibility of the atoms, as in Lucretius and Newton; or, as in Spinoza, it may be established by the uncreated and eternal nature of God. "By body," Spinoza writes, "I understand a mode which expresses in a certain and determinate manner the essence of God in so far as He is considered as the thing extended."

In the modern development of the science of mechanics the law of the conservation of matter seems to be another expression of the same insight. "We may lay it down as an incontestable axiom," Lavoisier writes, "that in all the operations of art and nature, nothing is created; an equal quantity of matter exists both before and after the experiment." What appears to be the destruction of a body is merely the transformation of its matter into another physical condition without loss of mass unless there is an equivalent gain in energy. The total quantity of matter and energy remains constant throughout all physical changes.

But though change or motion seems to be inherent in the material world, the mutability of bodies, as well as the immutability of matter, seems to be differently conceived according to different conceptions of matter. The difference between the physics of Aristotle and the physics of Descartes can be expressed in terms of contrary definitions of motion, or divergent notions of causality, but neither of these differences is fully intelligible apart from the variance of these theories from one another on the nature of matter.

When matter is an actual substance, whose essence is extension and whose chief property is local motion, the principles of physics are mechanical. The laws of mechanics, with time, space, and mass as their fundamental variables, were adequate for physics until the middle of the 19th century. At this time, through the work of Faraday and Maxwell, the notion of a field of force entered physics. The first field to be considered was the electromagnetic field, of which the electron was considered the source. Emanating from an electron, this field in turn influences the motions of other electrons and causes the fields emanating from them to change in space and time. Like the electron, all electrically charged particles generate electromagnetic fields. There is also the gravitational field generated by all massive objects as well as other fields that influence the behavior of subatomic particles. In modern physics, prior to the introduction of the notion of fields, changes in material things were either the local motions of bodies or the result of the local motions of their parts. Motions are determined in their magnitude and direction by the impressed force which one body exerts upon another via the fields generated and the resistance of that other. Motion is itself completely actual, as matter is; and the only type of cause to which physics need appeal is the efficient cause, that is, the push or pull of one body upon another through the mediation of the fields.

Physicists who share this conception of matter may not agree, as Descartes and Newton do not, in their mechanical formulations. They may or may not be atomists. They may, like Lucretius, think that local motion is an absolutely intrinsic property of the eternal particles; or, like Descartes and Newton, they may think that God first imparted motion to matter at the world's creation. They may hold that all subsequent motions issue therefrom in a continuous chain of cause and effect. But when matter is the only factor in the constitution of bodies, and one body differs from another only in its quantitative determinations, the consequence for physical theory seems to be one or another sort of mechanical formulation.

When matter is nothing more than a body's potentiality for change, and when neither what the body is nor how it changes can be explained by reference to its matter alone, physical theory seems to be constructed in other than mechanical terms. Its concepts and principles resemble those of biology. It finds natural tendencies or desires, and ends or final causes, in the motion of inert as well as animate bodies.

Central to Aristotle's physics are his theory of the four causes, discussed in the chapter on CAUSE, and his theory of the four types of change, discussed in the chapter on CHANGE. But even more fundamental is his definition of motion as the actualization of that which is potential in a respect in which it is potential. With motion so defined, the principles of physics must include the correlative factors of potentiality and actuality which Aristotle conceives in terms of matter and form.

REMOVE MATTER entirely from a thing and, according to Aristotle, you remove its capacity for physical change. Remove form, and you remove its existence, for nothing can exist without being actual or determinate in certain respects. When a thing changes physically, it loses certain determinate characteristics and acquires others. The determinations it acquires it had previously lacked, yet all the while it must have had a capacity for acquiring them. The thing is "capable both of being and of not being," Aristotle says, "and this capacity," he goes on to say, "is the matter in each." The matter of an existing substance is thus conceived as that which has certain forms (the respects in which the substance is actually determinate), and lacks certain forms which it can assume (the respects in which the substance is both indeterminate and potential).

As the chapter on ART indicates, Aristotle frequently uses artistic production to afford a simple illustration of his theory of matter and form as principles of change. When a man sets out to make a bed, he chooses material, such as wood, which can be shaped in a certain way. The same wood could have been made into a chair or a table. With respect to these various possible determinations in structure, the wood is itself indeterminate and determinable.

Before the artist has worked on it productively, the wood is in a state of both privation and potentiality with regard to the form of a bed, a chair, or a table. The transformation which the artist effects consists in his actualizing certain potentialities in the material for forms or determinations which the material at the moment lacks. When the bed is made, the wood or matter which is now actually in the form of a bed may still have the potentiality for being *remade* into a chair or table.

The wood, of course, remains actually wood throughout these artificial changes, as it does not when it suffers the natural change of combustion. This indicates that though the wood may be called matter or material by the artist, it is not matter, but a substance, a thing composite of matter and form; for when the wood is reduced to ashes by fire, the matter which had the form of wood assumes another form.

In the analysis of accidental change, which artistic production illustrates, it suffices to treat a composite substance, like wood or iron or bronze, as the material principle. But in the analysis of substantial change, when matter itself changes from being one kind of matter to being another in the coming to be or perishing of composite substances, the material principle must be pure matter—matter totally devoid of form. Where a whole substance can be regarded as the matter or substratum of accidental change (in quality, quantity, or place) the substratum of substantial change, which Aristotle calls "generation and corruption," must be matter in condition of absolute indeterminacy and pure potentiality.

Referring to this ultimate substratum as "the underlying nature," Aristotle says that it "is an object of scientific knowledge by analogy. For as the bronze is to the statue, the wood to the bed, so is the matter and the formless before receiving form to anything which has form, and so also is the underlying nature to substance, *i.e.*, the actually existing."

ARISTOTLE'S DEFINITION of matter as "the primary substratum of each thing, from which it comes to be without qualification, and which persists in the result" not only signifies an object which the physicist must apprehend analogically (*i.e.*, by comparison with substantially formed matter like wood and bronze), but also indicates that matter, by definition, must be in itself both unintelligible and nonexistent. What Aristotle calls "the primary substratum" is later called by Plotinus "primal matter," by Augustine "formless matter," and by Aquinas "prime matter." Since they all agree that that which is without form lacks all determination and actuality, they deny that it can have existence by itself or be an object of knowledge, either by sense or reason.

Augustine and Aquinas go further. They deny even to God's omnipotence the power of creating matter without form. They speak of matter not as created, but as *concreated,* that is, united at the very instant of its creation with the forms it must assume in order to exist. God "made formless matter of absolutely nothing, and the form of the world from this formless matter," Augustine writes. Yet He "created both simultaneously, so that form came upon matter with no space of time intervening."

IN THE TRADITION of Aristotle's physics and metaphysics, especially as developed by Aquinas, matter and form become basic analytic terms, often having a significance remote from their original meaning in the analysis of change. The conception of prime (or formless) matter as the substratum of substantial change leads to the designation of the formed matter underlying accidental change as "second matter." This, in turn, is called "signate matter" when, considered as the matter of an individual substance, it is viewed as having the limiting determinations of individuality.

"Matter is twofold," Aquinas writes, "common, and signate or individual; common, such as flesh and bones; and individual, as this flesh and these bones." When the intellect forms concepts of different kinds of physical substances, it abstracts "from the individual sensible matter, but not from the common sensible matter." In defining the nature of man, for example, we abstract, Aquinas says, from "this flesh and these bones, which do not belong to the species as such, but to the individual"; but we do not abstract from the fact that man, consisting of body and soul, is a thing of flesh and bones.

To say that man consists of body and soul is to indicate that common matter enters into the definition of man as a physical substance. But in distinction from definitions of this type, which are proper to physics, mathematical and metaphysical definitions carry the abstraction from matter still further. In mathematics, Aquinas declares, the intellect abstracts "not only from individual sensible matter, but also from common sensible matter." In conceiving numbers and figures, the intellect does not, however, abstract from matter entirely, but only from individual intelligible matter. The common intelligible matter which is represented by "substance as subject to quantity"

underlies all mathematical notions. "But some things," Aquinas maintains, "can be abstracted even from common intelligible matter, such as *being, unity, potency, act,* and the like, all of which can exist without matter." Such abstraction characterizes the concepts of metaphysics. Aquinas thus differentiates the three speculative sciences of physics, mathematics, and metaphysics in terms of three grades of abstraction, each distinguished by the type of matter from which the concepts of the science are abstracted.

With one exception physical matter is not said to be of different kinds when it exists under different forms. The one exception for both Aristotle and Aquinas is the matter of terrestrial and celestial bodies.

Basing his inference on the observations available to him, Aristotle holds that the heavenly bodies are eternal—"not subject to increase or diminution, but unaging and unalterable and unmodified." Immutable in every other way, they are, however, subject to local motion. Since they are eternal, both their matter and their motion must be different from that of perishable terrestrial bodies. "All things that change have matter," Aristotle writes, "but matter of different sorts; of eternal things those which are not generable but are movable in space have matter—not matter for generation, however, but for motion from one place to another." That motion from place to place is, unlike terrestrial motion, circular; it has the appropriate characteristic of endlessness.

Kepler challenges this theory of a radical difference between celestial and terrestrial matter or motion, and as the chapter on ASTRONOMY AND COSMOLOGY shows, by so doing he not only gives impetus to the Copernican system, but also paves the way for Newton to frame laws of motion applicable to matter everywhere in the universe. Because their matter is the same, it is possible, Kepler insists, to explain the motion of the heavenly bodies by the same principles which account for the motion of bodies on earth.

In contemporary cosmology, the possibility is raised that the universe could continue expanding indefinitely. One may then ask what the ultimate state of matter would resemble.

Until recently one would have imagined it would be material objects such as protons and electrons along with massless objects such as neutrinos and electromagnetic radiation. However, some contemporary theories suggest that the proton decays into other particles which, in turn, decay into massless objects and electrons. Some cosmologies are cyclical in character with alternating phases of expansion and contraction. A fascinating question is whether our present universe would then contain any traces of its ancestors.

54

Mechanics

INTRODUCTION

MECHANICS, taken as the name for just one of the physical sciences, would merit no place on a small list of basic, focal terms. But the word "mechanics" means more than that. In the tradition of western thought it signifies a whole philosophy of nature, and it connotes a set of fundamental principles under which, it has been thought, all the physical sciences can be unified.

The principles of mechanics have been applied not only in statics and dynamics, which are concerned with the action and reaction of bodies at rest or in motion, but also in acoustics and optics and the sciences of heat, magnetism, and electricity. They have been extended to astronomical phenomena to constitute what is called "celestial mechanics." They have been thought to govern the action or motion of invisible particles or waves as well as the familiar bodies of ordinary experience. In the range and variety of the phenomena it covers, mechanics would seem to be coextensive with physics. Such at least appears to be its scope at one stage in the development of natural science.

We shall presently consider the dissatisfaction with the mechanical point of view which causes scientists in our own day to hail the replacement of "classical mechanics" by the "new physics" as a great advance in science. The intellectual significance of this change can be compared with that earlier revolution in the 17th century when the new natural science founded on the achievements of Galileo, Huygens, and Newton replaced the physics of Aristotle, which had long reigned as the traditional philosophy of nature. What Einstein calls "the rise and decline of the mechanical point of view" thus seems to provide an apt title for the story of three stages in the history of science, in only one of which does the whole of physics appear to be dominated by mechanics.

One way, then, of understanding the importance of mechanics is in terms of that story. Other chapters, such as ASTRONOMY AND COSMOLOGY, CHANGE, ELEMENT, MATTER, PHYSICS, SPACE, and TIME—and perhaps also CAUSE and HYPOTHESIS—tell part of that story, especially the part which turns on the differences between Aristotle's physics (which is neither experimental nor mathematical) and modern physics (which is both). This chapter focuses on issues which fall largely within modern physics—issues belonging to that part of the story which, in the great books, begins with Galileo, Huygens, and Newton and runs to Faraday. The story itself does not end there, but the point to which Faraday carries it suggests the sequel in James Clerk Maxwell and Einstein, just as Galileo's point of departure reflects antecedents in Aristotle. The great books state the issues sufficiently well, though they do not tell the whole story. That can be fully documented only by a host of supplementary scientific classics in various fields, such as the works listed in the Additional Readings.

IN MODERN TIMES it is accepted that physics should be both experimental and mathematical. No one questions the ideal of unifying the physical sciences and finding the unity in nature's laws. But the question is whether that unification can be achieved under the aegis of mechanics; and the issue is whether physics should gather its experimental findings together under purely mathematical formulations or should also try to give those mathematical formulas a mechanical interpretation.

The issue involves more than a question of scientific method. It concerns the ultimate aim of natural science and the kind of concepts it should employ to fulfill this aim. Should the scientist seek to do no more than describe the phenomena of nature in terms of the simplest and most universal mathematical relations? Or should he go beyond description to an explanation of the phenomena in terms of their causes?

When the issue is thus stated as a choice between being content with description or striving for explanation, it appears to be broader than the question whether physics should or should not be mechanical. Even granted that explanation is desirable, does it necessarily follow that physical explanation must employ the principles and concepts of mechanics? Aristotle's physics, it can be argued, provides a negative answer. His various physical treatises represent a natural science which tries to explain the phenomena without doing so mechanically, just as it tries to describe the phenomena without doing so mathematically.

That the connection of these two features of Aristotle's physics is not accidental seems to be indicated by the conjunction of their opposites in modern physics. When in the 17th century the physicist describes natural phenomena in mathematical terms, he explains them—if he tries to explain them at all—in mechanical terms. "The laws of Mechanics," writes Descartes, "are the laws of Nature." Huygens opens his *Treatise on Light* by referring to optics as the kind of science "in which Geometry is applied to matter"; but he at once expresses the desire to advance this branch of mathematical physics by investigating "the origin and the causes" of the truths already known, in order to provide "better and more satisfactory explanations." Such explanations, he thinks, will be found only if we conceive "the causes of all natural effects in terms of mechanical motions." He declares it his opinion that "we must necessarily do this, or else renounce all hopes of ever comprehending anything in Physics."

Galileo and Newton, as will be noted, do not unqualifiedly share Huygens' view that it is proper for the mathematical physicist to inquire about causes. But they would agree that if any explanation is to be given for laws of nature expressed in mathematical form, one or another type of mechanical hypothesis would be required to state the causes. Postponing for the moment the consideration of whether the investigation of causes belongs to mathematical physics, let us examine what is involved in giving a mechanical explanation of anything and why this type of explanation tends to occur in the causal interpretation of mathematically formulated laws of nature.

Two points seem to constitute the essence of mechanical theory. Both are fundamental notions and both are philosophical in the sense that they do not seem to result from the findings of experimental research. The first point is an exclusive emphasis upon efficient causes, which means the exclusion of other types of causes, especially final and formal causes, from mechanical explanation. As the chapter on CAUSE indicates, efficient causality consists in *one thing acting on another*. But not every sort of action by which one thing affects another is mechanical. According to the doctrine, an efficient cause is mechanical only if it consists in a moving body acting on another by impact, or if it consists in a force exerted by one body to cause motion in another or to change its quantity or direction. The notion of a force which does not work through the impact of one moving thing upon another raises the problem of action-at-a-distance to which we shall return subsequently.

The second fundamental point is an exclusive emphasis upon quantities. Mechanical explanation makes no references to qualities or other attributes of things. Paradoxically this point is sometimes expressed in terms of a distinction between primary and secondary *qualities;* but, as the chapters on QUANTITY and QUALITY point out, the primary qualities are all quantities. According to Locke, they are "solidity, extension, figure, motion or rest, and number"; according to Newton, "the universal qualities of all bodies whatsoever" are "extension, hardness, impenetrability, mobility, and inertia." Others, like Galileo and Descartes, give still different enumerations, but the point remains that the only attributes of bodies which have mechanical significance are measurable quantities. Such secondary qualities, for example, as colors and tones belong to the physical world (as it is mechanically conceived) only by reduction to the local motion of particles or waves having certain velocities, lengths, or other quantitative attributes.

We need not be concerned here with what sort of reality is assigned to secondary qualities, or how their presence in experience is accounted for. These problems are discussed in other chapters, such as QUALITY and SENSE. However they are solved, the philosophy of mechanism excludes from the physical world whatever does not consist in, or cannot be reduced to, quantities of matter (or mass), motion, or force, and such related quantities as those of time and space (or distance).

The two points of mechanical theory are obviously connected, for the kind of cause which mechanical explanation employs to the exclusion of all others consists in a quantity of motion or of force. Just as obviously, mechanical explanation, dealing only in quantities and in causes which are quantitatively measurable, is precisely the type of explanation which would seem to be appropriate if one felt called upon to give an interpretation of the mathematical relationships which the mathematical physicist formulates as laws of nature. These mathematical laws are, after all, statements of the relations among physical quantities which have been subjected to experimental determination or measurement.

AS A PHILOSOPHICAL theory the mechanical view of nature antedates modern physical science. The atomistic conception of the world, which Lucretius expounds, contains both of the fundamental points of mechanism—the doctrine of primary and secondary qualities and the doctrine that all effects in nature are produced by efficient moving causes.

The controversy over mechanism is also ancient. Aristotle denies both points of doctrine in his criticism of the Greek atomists, Democritus and Leucippus; and in the exposition of his own physical theories he states an opposite view. To qualities and qualitative change he assigns physical reality. He explains change in terms of four types of causes, not one. He does not exclude the mechanical type of cause in his explanation of local motion. On the contrary, with respect to local motion his theory that a body in motion must be directly acted upon by a moving cause throughout the period of its motion seems to be more mechanical than the modern theory that no cause need be assigned for the continuing uniform motion of a body along a straight line but only for a change in its direction or velocity.

What is new in modern times is not the philosophical doctrine of mechanism, but the introduction of mechanical explanation into experimental and mathematical physics, and the controversy about whether it belongs there or can be defended as useful. The so-called rise and decline of the mechanical view in modern physics is connected with experimental discoveries and mathematical formulations. It is not an alternation between success and failure on the level of philosophical argument concerning the ultimate truth of mechanical conceptions. When these conceptions are rejected, it is not for the sake of returning to opposite notions in physical theory, such as those of Aristotle, but rather because, as Einstein says, "science did not succeed in carrying out the mechanical program convincingly, and today no physicist believes in the possibility of its fulfillment."

There is a touch of prophecy in the conversation Swift imagines taking place between Aristotle and the physicists of the 17th century. According to Swift, when Aristotle was confronted with René Descartes and Pierre Gassendi, he "freely acknowledged his own mistakes in natural philosophy, because he proceeded in many things upon conjecture, as all men must do; and he found that Gassendi, who had made the doctrine of Epicurus as palatable as he could, and the *vortices* of Descartes, were equally exploded. He predicted the same fate to *attraction,* whereof the present learned are such zealous asserters. He said that new systems of nature were but new fashions, which would vary in every age; and even those who pretend to demonstrate them from mathematical principles, would flourish but a short period of time, and be out of vogue when that was determined."

BOTH GALILEO and Descartes restate the philosophical doctrine which first appears in ancient atomism, but both restate it in a way that suggests its utility for an experimental investigation of nature. It is significant that Galileo's statement occurs in the context of his concern with the nature and causes of heat. He wishes to explain, he writes in *Saggiatore,* why he thinks that "motion is the cause of heat." To do this he finds it necessary to question a prevalent notion "which is very remote from the truth"—the belief that "there is a true accident, affection, or quality, really inherent in the substance by which we feel ourselves heated." He denies the physical reality of heat as an inherent quality of bodies on the same ground that he denies the physical reality of other qualities. "I do not believe," he declares, "that there exists anything in external bodies for exciting tastes, smells, and sounds, but size, shape, quantity, and motion, swift or slow; and if ears, tongues, and noses were removed, I am of the opinion that shape, quantity, and motion would remain, but there would be an end of smells, tastes, and sounds, which, apart from the living creature, I regard as mere words."

Descartes's statement of the doctrine is bolder, perhaps, in its suggestion of a mechanical program for physical research. "Colors, odors, savors, and the rest of such things," he writes, are "merely sensations existing in my thought." They differ from the real properties of bodies just as much as "pain differs from the shape and motion of the instrument which inflicts it." The true physical properties, such as "gravity, hardness, the power of heating, of attracting and purging" consist, in Descartes's opinion, "solely in motion or its absence, and in the configuration and situation of [bodily] parts."

As a philosophical doctrine, the mechanical view is not necessarily tied to atomism. Descartes opposes atomism as plainly as does Aristotle. Furthermore, Newton, who is an atomist, disagrees with both Descartes and the Greek atomists on one fundamental point in mechanical theory. The ancient atomists make the actual motion of one particle in collision with another the indispensable cause of a change of motion in the latter. Descartes likewise requires one motion to be the cause of another and explains gravity in terms of actual bodily motions. Newton rejects Descartes's mechanical hypothesis of material vortices as the cause of gravitation. He seems to have this in mind, and to put Descartes in the same class with Aristotle, when he says that "hypotheses, whether metaphysical or physical, whether of occult qualities or mechanical, have no place in experimental philosophy."

The force of gravity, according to Newton, is a power of attraction which one body exercises on another without the first being in motion or coming into contact with the second. Newton acknowledges the problem of action-at-a-distance which his theory raises. For the most part he lets it stand as a problem which does not affect the mathematical results of his work. But in the Queries he attaches to his *Optics* he suggests, by way of solution, the hypothesis of an ether as the continuous medium through which gravitational force is exerted. In the opinion of later physicists, Newton's hypothesis is no less mechanical than Descartes's. Nor does there seem to be any philosophical ground for preferring one hypothesis to the other.

But Newton's quarrel with Descartes is not on a philosophical issue. It turns on which mechanical conception, if any at all is to be offered, fits best with the mathematical laws of terrestrial and celestial motion which Newton had succeeded in formulating as universal laws of nature. Those mathematical laws, moreover, had the merit of fitting the observed phenomena and so, of realizing the scientific ideal of accurate description stated in the most generalized form. Newton's triumph over Descartes, then, is a triumph in mathematical and experimental physics, not a triumph in philosophy.

Alexander Pope's couplet

Nature and Nature's Laws lay hid in Night,
God said, Let Newton be, and all was light

records that triumph, and celebrates the illumination of nature by the mechanical as well as the mathematical principles of Newton's physics. Newton's picture of the world dominates the mind of a century and controls its science. Locke speaks of "the incomparable Mr. Newton" and of "his never enough to be admired book"; Hume refers to him as the philosopher who, "from the happiest reasoning . . . determined the laws and forces, by which the revolutions of the planets are governed and directed"; and even Berkeley, who challenges his theories of space, time, and attraction, regrets that he must take issue with "the authority of so great a man," a man "whom all the world admires" as the author of "a treatise on Mechanics, demonstrated and applied to nature."

NEWTON'S ACHIEVEMENT is to have accomplished an extraordinary synthesis of all that was good in previous scientific work, and a sweeping criticism of all that was considered stultifying. That so many and such varied phenomena should be organized mathematically by a theory as simple as Newton's, is altogether impressive. Equally astonishing is the predictive power of Newton's laws and the explanatory power of his mechanics, not to mention the technological fruits of the latter in mechanical engineering and the invention of machinery of all sorts. Whatever difficulties are implicit in the Newtonian mechanics—subsequently to become, with new discoveries, more and more perplexing—the scope and grandeur of Newton's book gives mechanics a commanding position with respect to the future of science for at least two centuries.

In the century between the publication of Newton's *Mathematical Principles of Natural Philosophy* and the publication in 1787 of Joseph-Louis Lagrange's *Mécanique analytique,* "the notion of the mechanical explanation of all the processes of nature," writes Whitehead, "finally hardened into a dogma of science." In the next century, the mechanical dogma spreads from physics and chemistry throughout the whole domain of natural science—into biology and psychology—and even beyond that, into economics and sociology. Books bear such titles as *The Mechanistic*

Conception of Life, The Mechanism of Human Behavior, Social Statics, Social Dynamics. At the end of the 19th century, William James notes the conquests which are being made on all sides by the mechanical idea. "Once the possibility of *some* kind of mechanical interpretation is established," he writes, "Mechanical Science, in her present mood, will not hesitate to set her brand of ownership upon the matter."

James himself testifies to the persuasiveness and success of the mechanical dogma, though not without some resentment. "The modern mechanico-physical philosophy, of which we are so proud," he says, "because it includes the nebular cosmogony, the conservation of energy, the kinetic theory of heat and gases, etc., etc., begins by saying that the *only* facts are collocations and motions of primordial solids, and the only laws the changes in motion which changes in collocation bring. The ideal which this philosophy strives after," he continues, "is a mathematical world-formula, by which, if all the collocations and motions at a given moment were known, it would be possible to reckon those of any wished-for future moment, by simply considering the necessary geometrical, arithmetical, and logical implications."

Pierre-Simon Laplace had in fact pictured a lightning calculator who, given the total configuration of the world at one instant, would be able to bring the whole future "present to his eyes." And James quotes Hermann von Helmholtz to the effect that the whole problem of physical science is "to refer natural phenomena back to unchangeable attractive and repulsive forces whose intensity depends wholly upon distance. The solubility of this problem is the condition of the complete comprehensibility of nature."

In commenting on this, James admits that "the world grows more orderly and rational to the mind, which passes from one feature of it to another by deductive necessity, as soon as it conceives it as made up of so few and so simple phenomena as bodies with no properties but number and movement to and fro." But he also insists that it is "a world with a very minimum of rational *stuff.* The sentimental facts and relations," he complains, "are butchered at a blow. But the rationality yielded is so superbly complete in *form* that to many minds this atones for the loss, and reconciles the thinker to the notion of a purposeless universe, in which all the things and qualities men love . . . are but illusions of our fancy attached to accidental clouds of dust which will be dissipated by the eternal cosmic weather as careless as they were formed."

WITH THE END OF the 19th and beginning of the 20th century, great changes in the dogma of mechanism start to occur. By the middle of the 19th century, with the work of Maxwell and Faraday, the notion of a field of force entered physics. All electrically charged particles, they discovered, influence each other through the mediation of a long-range field of force. (This had also been implicit in Newtonian physics, where massive particles influence each other through the mediation of the gravitational field.)

However, in the beginning of field theory, mechanism remained a feature of the field of description since the fields were thought of as a disturbance in an esoteric medium called the ether. This ether was described mechanically, although its mechanical properties became more and more bizarre as the description developed.

Moreover, despite heroic efforts, no experiment was ever able to detect the ether directly. In 1905, in his paper on the special theory of relativity, Einstein dismissed the entire ether concept with the statement: "The introduction of a 'luminous ether' will prove to be superfluous in as much as the view here to be developed will not require an absolutely stationary space," by which he means a frame of reference that is absolutely at rest. Although many of Einstein's contemporaries could not, at first, accept his rejection of the ether, the success of the theory of relativity eventually convinced most physicists that the ether really was a superfluous concept. In a certain sense, the ether was the last bastion of classical mechanism.

In commenting on this, Einstein quotes the passage from Helmholtz that James had cited,

in which Helmholtz goes on to say that the vocation of physics "will be ended as soon as the reduction of natural phenomena to simple forces is complete." This "*mechanical view,* most clearly formulated by Helmholtz," Einstein concedes, "played an important role in its time"; but, he adds, it "appears dull and naive to a twentieth century physicist." The rejection of the ether is a wonderful example of Ockham's rule that no hypothetical entity should be posited as really existing unless it is needed to explain the observed phenomena.

Einstein reviews the assumptions which physicists had to make in order to construct a mechanical theory of light, gravitation, and electricity. "The artificial character of all these assumptions," he says, "and the necessity for introducing so many of them all quite independent of each other, was enough to shatter the belief in the mechanical point of view . . . In the attempt to understand the phenomena of nature from the mechanical point of view," he continues, "throughout the whole development of science up to the twentieth century, it was necessary to introduce artificial substances like electric and magnetic fluids, light corpuscles, or ether." According to Einstein, "attempts to construct an ether in some simple way" have been "fruitless"; but what is more important in his opinion, such failures "indicate that the fault lies in the fundamental assumption that it is possible to explain all events in nature from a mechanical point of view."

Does this mean that the contemporary physicist has found another and better way of explaining nature? Is there a nonmechanical way of explaining the phenomena, which fits the mathematical laws of experimental physics; or does discarding mechanics mean relinquishing all efforts to explain nature?

Eddington suggests an answer. "One of the greatest changes in physics between the nineteenth century and the present day," he writes, "has been the change in our ideal of scientific explanation. It was the boast of the Victorian scientist that he would not claim to understand a thing until he could make a model of it; and by a model he meant something constructed of levers, geared wheels, squirts, and other appliances familiar to the engineer. Nature in building the universe was supposed to be dependent on just the same kind of resources as any human mechanic . . . The man who could make gravitation out of cogwheels would have been a hero in the Victorian age." Today, however, Eddington continues, "we do not encourage the engineer to build the world for us out of his material, but we turn to the mathematician to build it out of his material."

We may turn to the mathematician's construction of the world in his terms; but in the tradition of western thought, mathematically formulated laws of nature are not, with the single exception perhaps of the Pythagoreans, regarded as explanations of why things behave as they do or how they work. The change from the 19th to the 20th century with respect to "our ideal of scientific explanation" cannot, then, be the substitution of the mathematical for the mechanical account of why and how. The shift from mechanics to mathematics is rather a shift from explanation as the scientific ideal to the statement of laws which, while having maximum generality, remain purely descriptive. What Eddington means by building the world out of the material of mathematics seems to be the same as what Galileo means, four centuries earlier, when he says that the book of nature "is written in mathematical language." The materials are such symbols as "triangles, circles, and other geometrical figures." Without the help of these, Galileo writes to Kepler, nature "is impossible to comprehend."

But does the mathematical comprehension of nature mean a causal explanation of it? More explicitly than Eddington, Galileo insists that explanation—at least in the sense of stating the causes—is not the business of the mathematical physicist. In a passage which cannot be read too often or examined too closely, he names three opinions which the philosophers have expressed about "the cause of the acceleration of natural motion." Some, he says, "explain it by attraction to the center, others to repulsion between the very small parts of the body, while still others attribute it to a certain stress in the surrounding

medium which closes in behind the falling body and drives it from one of its positions to another. Now all of these fantasies," he continues, "and others too, ought to be examined, but it is not really worthwhile."

They ought to be examined by philosophers, perhaps, but debating them is not worthwhile in "those sciences where mathematical demonstrations are applied to natural phenomena." Perfectly defining the program of mathematical physics, Galileo sets himself a limited task: "merely to investigate and to demonstrate some of the properties of accelerated motion (whatever the cause of this acceleration may be)." It should be noted that of the three opinions about causes which Galileo mentions, the first, which anticipates Newtonian attraction, is no less summarily dismissed than the third, which summarizes the Aristotelian theory.

"What I call Attraction," Newton later writes, "may be performed by impulse or by some other means unknown to me. I use that word here to signify only in general any force by which bodies tend towards one another, whatsoever be the cause." It is well known, he asserts in the same passage of the *Optics,* "that bodies act one upon another by the attractions of gravity, magnetism, and electricity"; but, he goes on, "how these attractions may be performed I do not here consider."

Newton's attitude toward causes and explanation would seem to be identical with Galileo's. Galileo calls opinions about causes "fantasies" and dismisses them; Newton calls them "hypotheses" and seems to banish them as resolutely. "Hypotheses are not to be regarded in experimental philosophy," he declares in one place; and in another, having just referred to predecessors who feigned hypotheses "for explaining all things mechanically," he says that, on the contrary, "the main business of natural philosophy is to argue from phenomena without feigning hypotheses."

The task of the physicist who is both experimental and mathematical in his method, Newton plainly states, is "to derive two or three general principles of motion from phenomena, and afterwards to tell us how the properties and actions of all corporeal things follow from those manifest principles. [This] would be a very great step in philosophy, though the causes of those principles were not yet discovered. And therefore," he says of his own work, "I scruple not to propose the principles of motion above mentioned, they being of very general extent, and leave their causes to be found out."

The two or three principles of motion mentioned in this passage from the *Optics* are the foundation of Newton's other great work, the *Mathematical Principles of Natural Philosophy*. Its title indicates the clearly conceived intention of its author to limit himself to the program of mathematical physics on which both he and Galileo seem to agree. He will not try to define "the species or physical qualities of forces"; he will only investigate "the quantities and mathematical proportions of them." In the General Scholium with which the *Mathematical Principles* concludes, Newton disavows once more any knowledge of the cause of gravity. "To us it is enough," he says, "that gravity does really exist, and acts according to the laws which we have explained, and abundantly serves to account for all the motions of the celestial bodies, and of our sea." Admitting that he has "not been able to discover the causes . . . of gravity from phenomena," Newton flatly reiterates his policy: "I frame no hypotheses."

IN VIEW OF THIS policy, how does the name of Newton come to be associated with the triumph of the mechanical point of view in physics? Why do contemporary scientists like Einstein identify Newtonian physics with classical mechanics? If a mathematical physicist, like Newton or Galileo, refrains from guessing at or asserting causes, how can he be charged with having indulged in the impurity of a mechanical explanation of the phenomena, and with having foisted a mechanical conception of the universe upon mankind?

The answer to these questions, so far as Newton is concerned, may be partly found in his own writings. He did not, it seems, entirely disavow an inquiry into the cause of attractive force, as in itself either misguided or irrelevant to science. "We must learn from the phenomena of nature," he tells us, "what bodies attract one another, and what are the laws and properties of the attraction, before we enquire the cause by which the attraction is performed." This statement postpones, but does not exclude, an inquiry into causes. In another statement, Newton even gives us a reason for the postponement. "In mathematics," he says, "we are to investigate the quantities of force with their proportions consequent upon any conditions supposed; then, when we enter upon physics, we compare those proportions with the phenomena of nature, that we may know the several kinds of attractive bodies. And this preparation being made, we argue more safely concerning the physical species, causes, and proportions of the forces."

These remarks of Newton do not give the whole answer. For the other and perhaps more important part of it, we must go to the actual development of physical science in the 17th century. The steps in this development—largely discoveries and formulations made by Galileo, Huygens, and Newton—lead to crises from which the scientists could not extricate themselves without discussing causes—the causes of gravity and of the propagation of light. We may thus be able to understand why Newton could not abandon the search for causes; and why, in the Queries he appended to the *Optics,* he proposes a mechanical hypothesis in order to explain how the attractive force of gravity exerts itself across great distances, and also defends his mechanical theory of light against the equally mechanical but different hypothesis of Huygens.

It might well be argued that, though Galileo's pure position initiated modern mathematical physics, it was the persistence of impurity in the worrying about causes, or even the inescapability of such concern, which caused great scientific advances to be made. The concern about causes seems to provide, time and time again, the pivot for new discoveries. The causes are not found, but new hypotheses are made, and these, when employed, lead to wider, more general results in the form of more inclusive, unifying laws. We see this happen not only in the study of gravitation and light, but also in the investigation of heat and electricity. The concern of Faraday, for example, to explain electrical attraction and repulsion in terms of the action of contiguous particles, and to establish the existence of physical lines of force, leads to Maxwell's theory of the electromagnetic field; and his field equations, combined with Faraday's speculations concerning the relation between electrical and gravitational attraction, lead to the attempt, on the part of contemporary physics, to construct a unified field theory covering all physical phenomena.

Physics may return in the 20th century to the purely mathematical character it had at the beginning of its modern development. But as may be seen in any introduction to recent physics written for the layman, it is necessary to mark the influence of mechanical conceptions upon scientific discovery and thought, in order to understand the difference between the unifying mathematical laws of the 17th and the 20th centuries. As we retrace the steps we see how fertile is the interplay between mathematical insights and mechanical hypotheses.

As JOSEPH FOURIER tells the story of "rational mechanics," the "discoveries of Archimedes" begin the science. "This great geometer," he says, "explained the mathematical principles of the equilibrium of solids and fluids. About eighteen centuries elapsed before Galileo, the originator of dynamical theories, discovered the laws of motion of heavy bodies." Statics and dynamics are related as the two parts of mechanics when that is conceived narrowly as the science which treats of the local motions of inert or inanimate bodies. The rest or equilibrium of bodies, which is the subject of statics, can be thought of as a limiting case of their motions, to which the principles of dynamics apply.

In the eighteen centuries between Archimedes and Galileo, little progress is made in mechanics. So far as statics is concerned, Archimedes, according to Galileo, by the "rigor of his demonstration" established the science in all its essentials; "since upon a single proposition in his book on Equilibrium depends not only the law of the lever but also those of most other mechanical devices." Pascal may later enlarge statics, by showing in his *Treatise on the Equilibrium of Liquids* that "a vessel full of water is a new principle of Mechanics, a new machine which will multiply force to any degree we choose"; in other works Pascal extends these conceptions further, as in his treatment of the pressure of air. But at the time of Galileo, it could be said that although Archimedes had offered an exemplary model of mathematical physics, no progress was made until the work of Galileo's immediate predecessors.

Not without assistance from certain predecessors like Simon Stevin, Galileo founded the science of dynamics. It may be wondered why, with the start made by Archimedes, no earlier application of his principles and method had been made. The answer may be found in the physics of Aristotle. His theory of the four elements carried with it a doctrine of natural motions to different natural places, drawn from the observation of fire rising, stones dropping, air bubbling up through water. Such a doctrine would prevent the search for laws of motion applicable to all bodies; and the general character of Aristotle's physics, treating qualities as well as quantities, seems to have discouraged the application of mathematics even to the study of local motions.

In Aristotle's mechanics, it was necessary to apply a force to maintain a constant velocity. There was no law of inertia. That Aristotle should have formulated this particular mechanical construct is quite understandable. This mechanical law is obeyed when a body is confronted by friction. It requires an applied opposing force to make an object move when the object encounters friction. One needs an enormous leap of imagination to envision the situation in an idealized frictionless world.

This is the leap of imagination that was made by Galileo and Newton. In a frictionless world, a body will continue its motion indefinitely unless an opposing force intervenes. Force is proportional to acceleration, not velocity.

The mathematical expression of the laws of motion is Galileo's objective. His interest in the new astronomy which affirmed the motion of the earth led him, he told Hobbes, to the careful study of movements on the earth. His aim was simply to describe with precision the motions to be found in a child's play—stones dropped and stones thrown, the one the natural motion of free fall, the other the violent motion of a projectile. It is clear to observation that the motion of a freely falling body is accelerated. But though, as a mathematical physicist, Galileo refrains from asking why this is so, he is not satisfied to know simply that it is so. He wants to know the properties of such acceleration. What is the relation of the rate of increase in velocity to the durations and distances of the fall? How much increase in velocity is acquired and how fast? What is the body's velocity at any given point in the fall? Similarly, when Galileo turns to projectiles, he wants to know, not merely that their trajectory is consistently curvilinear, but precisely what curve the path of the projectile describes.

Galileo succeeds in answering all these questions without being perturbed by any of the philosophical perplexities connected with space and time; nor does he allow questions about the forces involved in these motions to distract him from his purpose to "demonstrate everything by mathematical methods." With mathematical demonstration he combines observation and experiment and uses the latter to determine which mathematical conclusions can be applied to nature—which principles can be empirically verified as well as mathematically deduced.

ONE OF GALILEO's principles, however, seems to outrun ordinary experience and to defy experimental verification. In the interpretation of his experiments on inclined planes, Galileo expresses an insight which Newton later formulates as the first law of motion, sometimes called the "law of inertia." It declares that "every body continues in its state of rest, or of uniform motion in a right line, unless it is compelled to change that state by forces impressed upon it." Though Newton describes his method as one of "making experiments and observations, and in drawing general conclusions from them by induction," the law of inertia seems to be an exception; for it is

difficult to say, as Hume does, that "we find by experience that a body at rest or in motion continues forever in its present state"—that is, *unless* it is acted on by some new force.

The condition introduced by "unless" raises Poincaré's question: "Have there ever been experiments on bodies acted on by no forces?" If not, and if they are impossible, then James may be right in saying that "the elementary laws of mechanics" are "never matters of experience at all, but have to be disengaged from under experience by a process of elimination, that is, by ignoring conditions which are always present." Because "the idealized experiment [which it calls for] can never be performed," the law of inertia, according to Einstein, can be derived "only by speculative thinking consistent with observation."

In any case, the first law of motion initiates a new departure in physics. So far as local motion is concerned, Aristotle and his followers look for the cause which keeps a moving body in motion or a stationary body at rest. According to Galileo and Newton, uniform motion continues naturally without cause. Only a change in the velocity or direction of that motion requires a cause, such as a force impressed upon it.

How radical this innovation is may be judged from its consequences in celestial mechanics, which in turn lead to a completely unified dynamics for both celestial and terrestrial motions. These advances are the work of Newton's mathematical genius, but the ground for them had been laid by the investigations of Galileo. Galileo had resolved the curvilinear motion of a projectile into the imparted rectilinear motion and the deflecting pull of gravity. This composition of forces—sometimes called the "parallelogram law"—explains why the path of the projectile is a parabola. The path of the planets in their orbits, Kepler had previously shown, is another conical curve—an ellipse. But Kepler, lacking the first law of motion, could theorize physically about the cause of the planetary orbits only by looking for a force, projected outward from the sun, which would sweep around to keep the planets moving in their paths. On the other hand, a follower of Galileo, as Whitehead points out, would seek "for normal forces to deflect the direction of motion along the curved orbit." He would look for a force pulling the planet off its own rectilinear course inward toward the sun.

That is precisely what Newton did. When the problem, which others had been able to formulate, was put to Newton, he simply went to his study for the solution. He had solved that problem some years before. He had found the law of the force which, attracting the planets to the sun, would produce their elliptical paths and the other proportionalities stated in Kepler's purely descriptive laws.

With that single discovery, Galileo's terrestrial dynamics becomes a celestial one, too; and the traditional separation of the heavens from the earth is overcome. Newton goes even further. He guesses, and then shows by mathematical reasoning, that the force deflecting the planets around the sun and the moon around the earth, is the same force which makes apples fall and stones heavy in the hand. He generalizes this insight in his famous inverse-square law: "Every particle of matter attracts every other particle of matter with a force proportional to the mass of each and to the inverse square of the distance between them."

Accordingly, the world can be pictured as one in which material particles each have position in absolute space and a determinate velocity. The velocity of each particle causes the change of its position, and changes in velocity are caused by forces, the amounts of which are determined by positions. From his laws of motion and this simple law of force Newton is able, by mathematical deduction, to account for the perturbations of the moon, the oblateness of the earth, the precession of the equinoxes, the solar and lunar tides, and the paths of the comets.

But is Newton's law of force as simple as it appears to be at first? Its mathematical meaning is plain enough, and its application to measured phenomena reveals its descriptive scope. When we ask, however, about its physical significance, we raise difficult questions concerning the nature of this attractive force and how it operates. To call it the "force of gravity" and to point out that this is a familiar force which everyone experiences in his own person hardly answers the question.

GALILEO WOULD NOT have tried to answer it. In his *Dialogue Concerning the Two Chief World Systems,* one of the characters, Simplicio, refers to that manifest cause which "everyone knows is gravity." To this Salviati replies: "You should say that everyone knows it is *called* gravity. I do not question you about the name," he continues, "but about the essence of the thing"; and that, he concludes, is precisely what cannot be defined.

A physicist like Huygens, who expects the explanation of natural effects to be expressed in the familiar mechanical terms of bodily impact, has other objections. "I am not at all pleased," he writes to Leibniz about Newton, "with any theories which he builds on his principle of attraction, which seems to me absurd." What shocks Huygens is a scandal that Newton himself cannot avoid facing. It is the scandal of action-at-a-distance—of the force of gravity being propagated instantaneously across great distances and producing effects at some remote place but no effects along the way. Newton recognizes the strangeness of such a force. In a letter to Richard Bentley, he echoes Huygens' protest to Leibniz. "That gravity should be innate, inherent and essential to matter," he says, "so that one body may act on another at a distance through a vacuum, without the mediation of anything else, by and through which their action and force may be conveyed from one to another, is to me so great an absurdity, that I believe no man who has in philosophical matters a competent faculty of thinking, can ever fall into it."

The absurdity of action-at-a-distance seems to be recognized by common sense and philosophy alike. "No action of an agent," Aquinas remarks, "however powerful it may be, acts at a distance except through a medium"; and Kant, who regards Newtonian physics as the model of a rational science of nature, speaks of "*a force of attraction without contact*" as a "chimerical fancy" which "we have no right to assume." How can Newton avoid this absurdity without violating his rule of method in mathematical physics—not to frame hypotheses?

Newton's dilemma can perhaps be stated in the following alternatives: *either* the inverse-square law of gravitational attraction is to be treated as a purely mathematical, and hence a purely descriptive, proposition of great simplicity and generality; *or* it must be given physical meaning by a causal explanation of how gravitational force operates. On the first alternative, Newton can avoid framing hypotheses, but the physical meaning of the concepts he employs to state the mathematical law is then left dark. On the second alternative, he can solve the mechanical problem created by such words in his law as "attracts" and "force," but only by going beyond mathematical physics into the realm of mechanical hypotheses.

Newton seems to take the first alternative in his *Mathematical Principles of Natural Philosophy,* and the second in his *Optics.* There he proposes the hypothesis of an ethereal medium to explain the attractive force of gravity. "Is not this medium," he asks, "much rarer within the dense bodies of the sun, stars, planets, and comets, than in the empty celestial spaces between them? And in passing from them to great distances, doth it not grow denser and denser perpetually, and thereby cause the gravity of those great bodies towards one another, and of their parts towards the bodies; every body endeavoring to go from the denser parts of the medium towards the rare? . . . And though this increase of density may at great distances be exceeding slow, yet if the elastic force of this medium be exceeding great, it may suffice to impel bodies from the denser parts of the medium towards the rarer, with all that power which we call gravity."

The hypothesis fits the law of gravitation if, as Maxwell points out, "the diminution of pressure [in the ether] is inversely as the distance from the dense body." Newton recognized, according to Maxwell, that it then becomes necessary "to account for this inequality of pressure in this medium; and as he was not able to do this, he left the explanation of the cause of gravity as a problem for succeeding ages . . . The progress made towards the solution of the problem since the time

of Newton," Maxwell adds, "has been almost imperceptible."

THE PROBLEM OF the mechanical properties of an ethereal medium occurs in another form in the field of optics. Here it is complicated by the rivalry between two theories of light—Newton's corpuscular theory and Huygens' undulatory or wave theory. Each involves a mechanical hypothesis—one concerning the motion of particles emitted from the light source, and one concerning the wavelike propagation of the light impulse through a medium. Both theories involve the motion of particles. In their explanation of the oar which appears bent in the water, both appeal to the action of the particles in the refracting medium on the light corpuscles or the light waves.

Both theories, furthermore, are expressed by their authors in a mathematical form which permits the deduction of quantitative facts like the equality of the angles of incidence and of reflection, the bending of the light ray in refraction according to the law of sines, and the recently discovered fact of the finite velocity of light. Huygens' book gives prominence to the explanation of the strange phenomena of double refraction found in "a certain kind of crystal brought from Iceland"—Iceland spar. But both theories seem to be equally competent in dealing with the established facts of reflection and refraction, and the new facts about dispersion.

For a century at least, their rivalry resembles that between the Ptolemaic and Copernican theories at a time when they seemed equally tenable so far as accounting for the phenomena was concerned. Later, new discoveries, such as those by Thomas Young and Augustin-Jean Fresnel, tend to favor the wave theory of light. At present, light is regarded as having the potentiality for revealing either particle or wave aspects depending on the observational arrangement. In this sense, light is neither a particle nor a wave. Eddington, in reviewing this matter, suggested the invention of the word "wavicle" to signify the complementary use of both particles and waves in the modern theory of radiation.

Unlike the rivalry between the Ptolemaic

and Copernican systems, which seemed for a while to be entirely a matter of different mathematical descriptions of the same phenomena, the conflict between these two theories of light involves from the very beginning an issue between diverse mechanical hypotheses to explain the phenomena. That issue is argued not only with respect to the adequacy of either theory to explain such phenomena as the rectilinear propagation of light and its different behavior in different mediums, but it is also debated in terms of the underlying mechanical conceptions. As gravitational force acting at a distance raises a mechanical problem which Newton's ether is not finally able to solve, so Huygens' ether as the medium through which light is propagated in waves raises mechanical problems which, if insoluble (as they seem to be), contribute even more heavily to the general scientific scandal of mechanics.

The two authors take different attitudes toward hypotheses and mechanical explanation. Huygens, as we have seen, begins his book with the express intention to "investigate . . . the causes" and to express them "in terms of mechanical motions." Newton, on the other hand, begins his with a reiteration of his disavowal of hypotheses. "My design in this book," he writes, "is not to explain the properties of light by hypotheses, but to propose and prove them by reason and experiments." Nevertheless, Newton's explanation of how the prism produces from white light the band of colors in the spectrum seems to require the assumption of a distinct kind of light corpuscle for each color; and, in addition, the assumption that, although all light particles have the same velocity when they travel together making white light, separate particles for different colors are differently refrangible, that is, differently susceptible to the action of the particles in the refracting medium of the glass.

Perhaps only in Newton's somewhat artificially restricted sense of the word "hypothesis" could these assumptions escape that denomination. In any case, the existence of Huygens' rival theory prevented his escaping a controversy about hypotheses. In the Queries attached to his *Optics*, he engages in that controversy with an acumen which shows another side of his genius.

HUYGENS' WAVE THEORY requires what anybody would have to call a hypothesis and requires it from the very start. "It is inconceivable," he writes, "to doubt that light consists in the motion of some sort of matter." He immediately rejects the notion that light rays consist in the "transport of matter coming to us from the [luminous] object, in the way in which a shot or an arrow traverse the air"—if for no other reason, because "the rays traverse one another without hindrance." The similarity between the phenomena of light and the phenomena of sound suggests to him the "way that light spreads," and causes him to extend the mechanics of sound—conceived as a wave motion—to light.

"We know that by means of air, which is an invisible and impalpable body," Huygens argues, "sound spreads around the spot where it has been produced, by a movement which is passed on successively from one part of air to another; and that the spreading of this movement, taking place equally on all sides, ought to form spherical surfaces ever enlarging and which strike our ears. Now there is no doubt at all that light also comes from the luminous body to our eyes by some movement impressed on the matter which is between the two . . . If, in addition, light takes time for its passage . . . it will follow that this movement, impressed on the intervening matter, is successive; and consequently it spreads, as sound does, by spherical surfaces and waves; for I call them waves from their resemblance to those which are seen to be formed in water when a stone is thrown into it."

Huygens is aware, however, that the analogy between light and sound is far from perfect. "If one examines," he says, "what this matter may be in which the movement coming from the luminous body is propagated, one will see that it is not the same that serves for the propagation of sound . . . This may be proved," he goes on, "by shutting up a sounding body in a glass vessel from which the air is withdrawn." An alarm clock beating its bell in a jar without air makes no sound, but a jar without air is no less transparent than one with air. Since when "the air is removed from the vessel the light does not cease to traverse it as before," and since waves have to be waves of something, and light waves cannot be waves of air, they must be waves of a substance, says Huygens, "which I call ethereal matter."

This ether, a transparent medium permeating the whole universe, proves to be what Einstein calls the *enfant terrible* in the family of hypothetical physical substances. Postulated by Huygens in order to explain light mechanically, it in turn calls for a mechanical account of its own extraordinary properties. Huygens does not avoid this new problem, but neither does he undertake to solve it completely.

Suppose "one takes a number of spheres of equal size, made of some very hard substance, and arranges them in a straight line, so that they touch one another." Then, says Huygens, "one finds, on striking with a similar sphere against the first of these spheres, that the motion passes as in an instant to the last of them, which separates itself from the row, without one's being able to perceive that the others have been stirred." This type of motion in the ether would account for "the extreme velocity of light" and yet "this progression of motion is not instantaneous," as the motion of light also is not.

"Now in applying this kind of movement to that which produces light," Huygens continues, "there is nothing to hinder us from estimating the particles of the ether to be of a substance as nearly approaching to perfect hardness and possessing a springiness as prompt as we choose." Beyond this Huygens does not go. "It is not necessary to examine here," he says, "the causes of this hardness, or of that springiness . . . Though we shall ignore the true cause of springiness we still see that there are many bodies which possess this property; and thus there is nothing strange in supposing that it exists also in little invisible bodies like the particles of the ether."

But difficulties which Huygens did not foresee make his ether more than a strange supposition—almost a mechanical impossibility. Huygens had thought that light waves are transmitted in the ether in the way that sound waves are in the air, that is, longitudinally, the direction in which the individual particles vibrate being the same as the direction of the wave motion itself. But when, in the 19th century, it was found that the phenomena of the polarization of light could not be explained by the corpuscular theory, but only by the wave theory (thus shifting the scales decisively in favor of the latter), it was also found that the wave theory could explain polarization *only* on the assumption that the motion of the ether particles which produce the light waves is not longitudinal, but transverse, that is, in a direction perpendicular to the waves produced by the vibration of the particles.

As Fresnel pointed out at the time, "the supposition that the vibrations were transverse was contrary to the received ideas on the nature of the vibration of elastic fluids." They had all involved, as in the case of air as the medium for sound, a longitudinal transmission. The character of the ether is changed by the requirement that its particles vibrate transversely. It ceases to be an airlike ether and must be imagined as a jellylike ether.

The task which Huygens had postponed—that of giving a mechanical explanation of the ether he had posited in order to state the mechanics of light—becomes in consequence far more difficult, if not impossible. In their efforts to construct "the ether as a jellylike mechanical substance, physicists," according to Einstein, had to make so many "highly artificial and unnatural assumptions," that they finally decided to abandon the whole program of mechanical explanation.

OF NEWTON'S TWO objections to the wave theory of light, the second by itself seems to create an insuperable difficulty for Huygens' ether, even before the realization that it must be a jellylike medium.

Newton's first objection is that any wave theory is inconsistent with the fact of the rectilinear propagation of light. "If light consisted in pression or motion, propagated either in an instant or in time, it would bend into the shadow; for," he points out, "pression or motion cannot be propagated in a fluid in right lines, beyond an obstacle which stops part of the motion, but will bend and spread every way into the quiescent medium which lies beyond the obstacle . . . The waves, pulses or vibrations of the air, wherein sound consists, bend manifestly, even though not so much as the waves of water."

This objection loses its force when, in the 19th century, light's bending is experimentally discovered. But Newton's other objection gains force when, two centuries after he made it, a jellylike density is imposed upon the ether by the experimental facts of polarization. This second objection does not point to the inadequacy of the wave theory with respect to the phenomena which must be described, but rather calls attention to its inconsistency with celestial mechanics.

Light travels through interstellar space. But so also do the planets. Newton's astronomy accounts for the motion of the planets with great precision, *only on the supposition of no resistance from a medium.* "To make way for the regular and lasting motions of the planets and comets," he writes, "it is necessary to empty the heavens of all matter, except perhaps . . . such an exceedingly rare ethereal medium as we described above." Here he refers to the ether he himself had posited as a possible cause of gravitational attraction. Its resistance, he thinks, is "so small as to be inconsiderable." The "planets and comets and all gross bodies [can] perform their motions more freely in this ethereal medium than in any fluid, which fills all space adequately without leaving any pores." Such "a dense fluid . . . serves only to disturb and retard the motions of those great bodies, and make the frame of nature languish." Since it "hinders the operations of nature," and since "there is no evidence for its existence," Newton concludes that "it ought to be rejected."

The next conclusion follows immediately. "If it be rejected, the hypotheses that light consists in pression or motion, propagated through such a medium, are rejected with it." Newton would seem entitled to draw these conclusions because, no matter how slight the density of ethereal matter, the use of the ether in the wave theory of light involves some interaction between the particles of ether and

the particles of matter. Unless such interaction takes place, no explanation can be given of the change in the velocity of light when it enters a medium like glass or water. Since in Newton's universe there is no difference between terrestrial and celestial matter, Newton cannot accept an ether which interacts with the matter of glass or water, but does not interact with the matter of the planets.

This objection of Newton's, pointing to an inconsistency between the kind of ether required by the wave theory of light and the unretarded motion of the heavenly bodies, appears not to have been answered, but only waived, at the time of the wave theory's ascendancy. The famous Michelson-Morley experiment on ether drift later reopens Newton's penetrating query about the ether. But this occurs at a time when physicists are prepared to give up not only the ether, but also with it the mechanical explanations of gravity and light which it had brought into conflict with one another.

BEFORE THE MECHANICAL dogma runs its course, it has a career in other fields of physical inquiry. The phenomena of heat, magnetism, and electricity are explored and explained under its inspiration. The history of these subjects is marked by a very rash of hypotheses. Each time mechanical explanation is attempted for a new domain of phenomena, new substances are added.

The postulated entities—calorific, magnetical, and electric fluids—are unobservable and without weight. In Newton's terms, they are "occult"; though, it must be added, they are no more occult than the ether Newton himself postulated to explain gravity or the ether Huygens postulated to explain light. In fact, each of these new substances seems to resemble the aeriform or fluid ether, just as each is conceived, as the gravitational or optical ether was earlier conceived, in the context of the issue of action-at-a-distance as opposed to action-by-contact. They would seem to be unavoidable in a mechanical account of the radiations of heat, magnetism, and electricity.

The phenomena of heat, Lavoisier writes, are "difficult to comprehend . . . without admitting them as the effects of a real and material substance, or very subtle fluid . . . Wherefore," he continues, "we have distinguished the cause of heat, or that exquisitely elastic fluid which produces it, by the term of caloric." Lavoisier declares himself "unable to determine whether light be a modification of caloric, or if caloric be, on the contrary, a modification of light." But in terms of observed effects he does attribute etherlike properties to caloric. "This subtle matter," he says, "penetrates through the pores of all known substances"; for "there are no vessels through which it cannot escape."

The theory of caloric serves its purpose before it gives way to the theory of heat as molecular motion, a conception which can be integrated with the molecular, or kinetic, theory of gases. "The development of the kinetic theory of matter," writes Einstein, "is one of the greatest achievements directly influenced by the mechanical view." It is all the more striking, therefore, that in the opening pages of Fourier's *The Analytical Theory of Heat*—wherein he reviews the triumphs of explanation achieved by Newton and his successors—Fourier should so flatly assert: "But whatever may be the range of mechanical theories, they do not apply to the effects of heat. These make up a special order of phenomena which cannot be explained by the principles of motion and equilibrium."

It is equally striking that Lavoisier seems to have anticipated not only the mechanical theory of heat, but the possibility of a purely mathematical treatment of the phenomena. "We are not obliged to suppose [caloric] to be a real substance," he writes; it is sufficient "that it be considered as the repulsive cause, whatever that may be, which separates the particles of matter from each other, so that we are still at liberty to investigate its effects in an abstract and mathematical manner."

The second of these two things is precisely what Fourier proposes to undertake, but he disavows any interest in the first, namely, the explanation of heat in terms of the mechanical separation of particles by repulsion. In language which resembles Newton's disavowal of concern with the cause of attraction, Fourier declares that "primary causes are unknown to us, but are subject to simple and constant laws, which may be discovered by observation."

In another place he writes: "Of the nature of heat only uncertain hypotheses could be formed, but the knowledge of the mathematical laws to which its effects are subject is independent of all hypothesis." Fourier's aim, therefore, with respect to "the very extensive class of phenomena, not produced by mechanical forces, but resulting simply from the presence and accumulation of heat," is "to reduce the physical questions to problems of pure analysis" and "to express the most general conditions of the propagation of heat in differential equations." He expresses his indebtedness to Descartes for "the analytical equations" which that mathematician "was the first to introduce into the study of curves and surfaces," but "which are not restricted to the properties of figures, and those properties which are the object of rational mechanics." These equations, he insists, "extend to all general phenomena," and "from this point of view, mathematical analysis is as extensive as nature itself."

This strongly worded statement affirms the mathematical character of nature as the support and justification for a purely mathematical physics. If Fourier's remarks about causes and hypotheses are reminiscent of Newton in his mathematical mood, how much more is Fourier's faith in pure mathematical analysis reminiscent of Galileo. Like Galileo, and unlike Newton, Fourier never deviates from his indifference to causes and never softens his judgment of the incompetence and irrelevance of mechanics to the subject he is investigating. His trust in mathematical analysis, which is able by itself to yield and organize physical discoveries, not only revives the spirit of Galileo, but also seems to have inspired Maxwell to turn from a mechanical to a mathematical theory of electricity.

Certain of Fourier's mathematical achievements, such as his theory of dimensions, prove useful to Maxwell. More important, perhaps, is the fact that Maxwell's predictions about the propagation of electromagnetic waves, later experimentally verified by

Heinrich Hertz, are the result of mathematical analysis. With such a demonstration of the power of mathematics to work fruitfully with experiment, *and without any aid from mechanical hypotheses,* Maxwell gives up the attempt to formulate a mechanics for his equations describing the electromagnetic field. He is quite content to let his field theory state the mathematical structure of the phenomena.

BETWEEN FOURIER and Maxwell comes Faraday. One of the greatest experimenters in the whole tradition of science, Faraday discovers the phenomena whose mathematical structure Maxwell later develops. He prepares the way for Maxwell's application to electricity and magnetism of the method Fourier had practiced. His speculations concerning the relation of electrical and gravitational force point ahead, beyond Maxwell, to the possibility of a field theory which might unify all physical phenomena under a single set of mathematical laws.

Faraday sees no incompatibility between experimentation and speculation. On the contrary he says that "as an experimentalist I feel bound to let experiment guide me into any train of thought which it may justify; being satisfied that experiment, like analysis, must lead to strict truth, if rightly interpreted; and believing also that it is in its nature far more suggestive of new trains of thought and new conditions of natural power." Faraday's faith seems to have been amply justified. His experiments not only discovered a stunning number of new facts, but the speculations to which they led transformed the whole mode of thinking about electricity and magnetism, and, to some extent, the whole of physics.

The Elizabethan Gilbert, with his bold and brilliantly handled thesis that the earth is a magnet, had made magnetism appear something more than a random phenomenon occasionally met with in nature. But not until Faraday's discovery of diamagnetism, announced in a memoir *On the Magnetic Condition of All Matter,* would anyone have dared to say that "all matter appears to be subject to the magnetic force as universally as it is to the gravitating, the electric and the chemical or cohesive forces." Of electricity, he can only predict, as the result of his protracted experimental investigations, that "it is probable that every effect depending upon the powers of inorganic matter ... will ultimately be found subordinate to it."

These remarks indicate the controlling theme of Faraday's researches, namely, the convertibility and unity of natural forces. It seems to have been suggested to him by the discovery that both electrical and magnetic forces obey the same simple inverse-square law as the force of gravitational attraction. The fact that certain forces obey the same law or that their action can be described by the same equations, would not of itself reveal whether one of these forces is primary or all are derivative from some other primary force. But it would suggest questions to be asked by experiment.

Gilbert compares magnetism and electricity, but he is not able to convert one into the other. Hans Christian Ørsted, before Faraday, is the first to establish one aspect of their convertibility. He shows that an electric current has a magnetic effect. Faraday succeeds in showing the reverse—that a magnetic current has electrical power. He expresses his fascination with such reversibilities in his remarks on the electrical torpedo fish. "Seeback," he writes, "taught us how to commute heat into electricity; and Peltier has more lately given us the strict converse of this, and shown us how to convert electricity into heat ... Oersted showed how we were to convert electric into magnetic forces, and I had the delight of adding the other member of the full relation, by reacting back again and converting magnetic into electrical forces. So perhaps in these organs, where nature has provided the apparatus by means of which the fish can exert and convert nervous into electric force, we may be able, possessing in that point of view a power far beyond that of the fish itself, to reconvert the electric into the nervous force."

Faraday demonstrates still another such reversibility in nature. The nature of his discovery is indicated by the titles of the papers in which he announces it: *On the Magnetization of Light and the Illumination of Magnetic Lines of Force* and *Action of Electric Currents on Light.* These papers, in his opinion, "established for the first time, a true, direct relation and dependence between light and the magnetic and electric forces"; and he concludes them with an explicit statement of the central theme of all his researches and speculations.

"Thus a great addition is made," he writes, "to the facts and considerations which tend to prove that all natural forces are tied together and have one common origin. It is no doubt difficult in the present state of our knowledge to express our expectation in exact terms; and, though I have said that another of the powers of nature is, in these experiments, directly related to the rest, I ought, perhaps, rather to say that another form of the great power is distinctly and directly related to the other forms."

ONE FORM OF the "great power" remained to be connected with such "other forms" as those of light, heat, electricity, and magnetism. That was the power of gravitational force. Faraday comes to this last stage of his speculations concerning the unity of nature's powers in terms of his conception of "lines of force" and of what later came to be called "the field of force."

The earliest theories of electricity and magnetism, in an orthodox atomistic vein, had conceived them as exerting an influence by means of the effluvia which they emitted. Newton, for example, speculates on "how the effluvia of a magnet can be so rare and subtle, as to pass through a plate of glass without any resistance or diminution of their force, and yet so potent as to turn a magnetic needle beyond the glass." When electrical conduction is later discovered, effluvia are replaced by fluids, on the analogy of caloric as the fluid conductor of heat. But when Faraday finds that he can induce from one current to another, he becomes interested in the dielectric, nonconducting medium around the circuits. He is strongly averse to any theory which involves action-at-a-distance, and so he argues that induction takes place by the action of contiguous particles. To support that argument he

shows experimentally that electrical induction can "turn a corner."

From his study of all the phenomena of magnetism, Faraday forms the conception of "lines of force" and concludes that there is "a centre of power surrounded by lines of force which are physical lines essential both to the existence of force within the magnet and to its conveyance to, and exertion upon, magnetic bodies at a distance." He says of this "idea of lines of force" that "all the points which are experimentally established with regard to [magnetic] action, *i.e.,* all that is not hypothetical, appear to be well and truly represented by it"; and he adds: "Whatever idea we employ to represent the power ought ultimately to include electric forces, for the two are so related that one expression ought to serve for both."

Subsequently Faraday satisfies himself as to the physical reality of electrical lines of force in addition to the magnetic lines. The compulsion of his interest in the unity of nature then drives him to speculate about gravitational force. He begins by admitting that, "in the case of gravitation, no effect sustaining the idea of an independent or physical line of force is presented to us; as far as we at present know, the line of gravitation is merely an ideal line representing the direction in which the power is exerted." But encouraged, perhaps, by Newton's repeated references to "the attractions of gravity, magnetism, and electricity," and by Newton's letter to Bentley which he interprets as showing Newton to be "an unhesitating believer in physical lines of gravitating force," Faraday goes to work experimentally.

The report of these researches *On the Possible Relation of Gravity to Electricity* opens with the restatement of Faraday's central theme. "The long and constant persuasion that all the forces of nature are mutually dependent, having one common origin, or rather being different manifestations of one fundamental power, has made me often think upon the possibility of establishing, by experiment, a connexion between gravity and electricity, and so introducing the former into the group, the chain of which, including also magnetism, chemical force and heat, binds so many and such varied exhibitions of force together by common relations." His experiments, he tells us, unfortunately "produced only negative results," but that does not shake his "strong feeling of the existence of a relation between gravity and electricity."

THOUGH FARADAY FAILS to prove "that such a relation exists," he does bequeath, as a legacy to 20th-century physics, the problem of a field theory which would embrace both gravitational and electrical force. But whereas Faraday conceives the problem mechanically in terms of the physical reality, as well as unity, of all lines of force, in which contiguous particles act on one another, those who inherit the problem from him cease to concern themselves with the physical existence of "lines of force" and their mechanical basis in the action and reaction of bodies. Influenced by the amazing generality implicit in Maxwell's field equations, they proceed to search for a purely mathematical statement of nature's structure.

In the judgment of the 20th-century physicist mathematics may at last succeed in doing precisely what mechanics, from Newton to Faraday, kept promising but forever failing to do. If the unity of nature can be expressed in a single set of laws, they will be, according to Einstein, laws of a type radically different from the laws of mechanics. Taking the form of Maxwell's equation, a form which appears "in all other equations of modern physics," they will be, he writes, "laws representing the *structure* of the field."

In saying that "Maxwell's equations are structure laws" and that they provide "a new pattern for the laws of nature," Einstein means to emphasize their nonmechanical character. "In Maxwell's theory," he writes, "there are no material actors"; whereas "Newton's gravitational laws connect the motion of a body here and now with the action of a body at the same time in the far distance." Maxwell's equations "connect events which happen now and here with events which will happen a little later in the immediate vicinity." Like the equations which describe "the changes of the electromagnetic field, our new gravitational laws are," according to Einstein, "also structure laws describing the changes of the gravitational field."

The heart of the difference between a "structure law" and a mechanical law seems to be contained in Einstein's statement that "all space is the scene of these laws and not, as for mechanical laws, only points in which matter or changes are present." This contrast between matter and space brings to mind the difference between physics and geometry. Yet Einstein's repeated reference to "changes" in these space-structures also reminds us that the electrical and gravitational fields are not purely geometric, but physical as well.

The structure laws of the new physics may be geometric in form, but if they are to have any physical meaning, can they entirely avoid some coloring by the mechanical conceptions which have been traditionally associated with the consideration of matter and motion? At least one 20th-century physicist appears to think that mechanics survives to bury its undertakers. After describing the development in which geometry progressively "swallowed up the whole of mechanics," Eddington observes that "mechanics in becoming geometry remains none the less mechanics. The partition between mechanics and geometry," he continues, "has broken down and the nature of each of them has diffused through the whole"; so that "besides the geometrisation of mechanics, there has been a mechanisation of geometry."

WE ARE LEFT with a number of questions. Is the story of mechanics the story of its rise and decline or the story of its changing role—now dominant, now subordinate; now more manifest, now more concealed—at all stages in the development of a physics which is committed to being both mathematical and experimental? Do the status and character of mechanical conceptions change with changes in the form of the mathematical laws which describe the phenomena? Can physics be totally devoid of mechanical insight and yet perform experiments which somehow require the scientist to act on bodies and to make them act on one another? Could a pure mathematical physics have yielded productive applications in mechanical engineering without the intermediation of mechanical notions of cause and effect?

In the light of these questions, we should ponder the point made by Heisenberg in his statement of the paradox found in the Copenhagen interpretation of quantum theory. "Any experiment in physics," Heisenberg writes, "whether it refers to the phenomena of daily life or to atomic events, is to be described in the terms of classical physics. The concepts of classical physics form the language by which we describe the arrangement of our experiments and state the results. We cannot and should not replace these concepts by any others. Still the application of these concepts is limited by the relations of uncertainty. We must keep in mind this limited range of applicability of the classical concepts while using them, but we cannot and should not try to improve them."

Whichever way the foregoing questions are answered, we face alternatives that seem to be equally unsatisfactory. *Either* experimental physics is purely mathematical and proclaims its disinterest in as well as its ignorance of causes; *or* physics cannot be experimental and mathematical without also being mechanical, and without being involved in a search for causes which are never found.

To the layman there is something mysterious about all this. He stands in awe of the physicist's practical mastery of matter and its motions, which he naively supposes to depend upon a scientific knowledge of the causes, while all the time the scientists protest that the causes remain unknown to an experimental and mathematical physics. Mechanical explanations may be offered from time to time, but the various "forces" they appeal to can be understood only from their effects, and are nothing more than verbal shorthand for the formulas or equations which express the mathematical laws. Yet they remain cause-names, and seem to stimulate advances in science—both experimental and mathematical—almost as a consequence of the exasperating elusiveness of these hidden causes.

Certain philosophers hold a view which suggests that the clue to the mystery may lie in the word "hidden." Causes exist and we can control them to build machines and explode bombs, but we cannot with our senses catch them in the very act of causing, or perceive the inwardness of their operation. If the fact that they are thus unobservable means that they are occult, then all causes are occult—not least of all the mechanical type of cause which consists in the impact of one body upon another. In the century in which physicists tried to avoid the scandal of forces acting at a distance by postulating mechanical mediums through which one body acted directly on another, philosophers like Locke and Hume express their doubts that such causal action is any less occult than Newton had said Aristotle's causes were.

"The passing of motion out of one body into another," Locke thinks, "is as obscure and unconceivable, as how our minds move or stop our bodies by thought . . . The increase of motion by impulse, which is observed or believed sometimes to happen, is yet harder to understand. We have by daily experience, clear evidence of motion produced both by impulse and by thought; but the manner how, hardly comes within our comprehension; we are equally at a loss in both." In Locke's judgment we will always remain "ignorant of the several powers, efficacies, and ways of operation, whereby the effects, which we daily see, are produced." If scientific knowledge is knowledge of causes, then "how far soever human industry may advance useful and experimental philosophy in physical things, scientifical will still be out of our reach."

When we try to observe efficient causes at work, what do we see? Hume answers that we only see one thing happening after another. "The impulse of one billiard-ball is attended with motion in the second. This is the whole that appears to the *outward* senses." Nor can we form any "*inward* impression" of what takes place at the moment of impact. "We are ignorant," he writes, "of the manner in which bodies operate on each other"; and we shall always remain so, for "their force or energy is entirely incomprehensible."

As the chapter on CAUSE indicates, Aristotle holds an opposite view of the matter. What takes place in efficient causation may be imperceptible, but it is not incomprehensible.

All causes may be occult so far as the senses are concerned, but they are not obscure to the intellect. But Aristotle would also insist that the action of efficient causes cannot be understood if they are totally isolated from other causes—material, formal, final. A purely mechanical physics, in his opinion, defeats itself by its basic philosophical tenets, which exclude all properties that are not quantitative and all causes except the efficient. Only a different metaphysics—one which conceives physical substances in terms of matter and form, or potentiality and actuality—can yield a physics which is able to deal with causes and explain the phenomena; but such an Aristotelian physics, from the modern point of view, stands condemned on other grounds. It is not experimental. It is not productive of useful applications. It is not mathematical; nor is it capable of comprehending all the phenomena of nature under a few simple, universal laws.

THE TRUE REVOLUTION in mechanics begins early in the 20th century with the discovery of the quantum theory. Of his three great papers of 1905, including the one on relativity, the only one that Einstein himself characterized as revolutionary was the paper in which the light quantum made its first appearance. What is counterintuitive in the special relativity paper is the consequence of the unique features of light propagation.

For example, no material object can move faster than the speed of light. This means that no influence of one object upon another that is caused by the propagation of a field can take place instantaneously. In this sense, there is no action-at-a-distance in which objects influence each other instantaneously. Influences on the present that propagate to us from the past always take a finite amount of time in the process. That these influences can propagate in a vacuum is not regarded as a paradox, but rather as a fact.

Quantum mechanics, on the other hand, is, from the point of view of the classical physics that preceded it, truly revolutionary. The so-called "old quantum theory" began with the work of Bohr, who attempted to account for the spectral light emitted by atoms when they are excited by such forces as electrical discharges. Bohr imagined the electrons circulating in well-defined orbits around the atomic nucleus. Light, he argued, was emitted when an electron made a quantum jump to the nucleus. This theory was an amalgam of classical mechanics—orbits—and quantum effects. It failed to account for the details of the atomic spectra.

In the mid-1920s, the "old quantum theory" was replaced by quantum mechanics—the work of men such as Heisenberg, Schrödinger, Wolfgang Pauli, and P. A. M. Dirac. In quantum mechanics, strictly speaking, there are no orbits. The fundamental quantity in the theory is the so-called wave function. Using this function, one can compute the probability of finding, say, an electron at some point in space at a given time. The classical orbits of Newton and Einstein are positions in space where, on the average, electrons are most likely to be found.

What people like Einstein found so disturbing about this theory was not so much its probability aspect, but rather its apparent rejection of classical objective reality. An electron, for example, has, according to the usual interpretation of quantum mechanics, neither a position nor a momentum, but rather the potentiality to exhibit positions and momenta, if observed by a suitable experimental apparatus. (This situation is like the particle-wave duality for light.)

There are limitations to the degree of accuracy that any experiment can measure positions and momenta; these are formalized in the Heisenberg uncertainty principle. Einstein thought that this inability of quantum theory to give a complete objective account of the individual subatomic particle was a weakness of the theory, and this meant for him that it was, at best, transitional. He did, however, accept those predictions that were confirmed by experiment.

Most physicists now accept the fact that the objective reality of classical mechanics does not apply to subatomic phenomena. There is, however, the puzzling question of where to draw the line between the classical and quantum worlds. Some physicists believe there is no classical world at all, and some, like Bohr, believe that there must be a classical world for us to be able to describe our experiments in classical terms, involving pointers and meter sticks.

While these questions are far from settled, the quantum theory itself has proved to be, in terms of its predictive and explanatory power, the greatest scientific theory so far discovered.

55

Medicine

INTRODUCTION

MEDICINE is the name of an art, of a science or group of sciences, and of a learned profession whose members are proficient in these sciences and experienced in the practice of the art. By derivation it is also the name for curative drugs, physics, or other remedies prescribed by the physician. The archaic usage of the English word "physic" as the name for the art, practice, and profession of what is now generally called "medicine" suggests what the word's Greek root signifies, namely, that the physician, no less than the physicist, is a student of nature.

There is one other historic use of "medicine" which indicates its scope and connections in the western tradition. When medieval institutions first shaped the university, the basic divisions of learning then embodied in its structure reflected different uses of learning as well as differences in subject matter. The three faculties of medicine, law, and theology not only disciplined their students in different branches of knowledge, but also trained them for distinct applications of knowledge to practice.

The faculty of medicine represented all the natural sciences, especially those which have come to be called "biological sciences," just as the faculty of law or jurisprudence represented all the moral sciences and their later offshoots, now called "social sciences." The doctor of medicine was concerned with knowledge bearing on the relation of man to nature, as the doctor of laws was concerned with knowledge bearing on the relation of man to man, and the doctor of theology with knowledge bearing on the relation of man to God.

It is a curious accident that the word "doctor," which in origin signified the competence

to teach others who might practice in each of these great fields of learning, has come in popular usage to designate, not the teacher, but the practitioner, and chiefly the practitioner in only one of the learned professions. Medicine may not deserve the implied emphasis upon the learning of its practitioners, but there would be some truth in granting it the distinction of being the oldest of the professions in the sense that it comprises a group of men who not only share a common training in the relevant sciences and arts, but who also have adopted a code of practice and obligated themselves to perform a service to their fellowmen.

The Hippocratic Oath, sworn to in the name of "Apollo the physician and Aesculapius, and Health . . . and all the gods and goddesses," is the first explicit formulation of a professional ideal. In the collection of writings attributed to Hippocrates, *The Law* explicitly indicates, as *The Oath* implies, that there are intellectual as well as moral conditions to be fulfilled by those who would dedicate themselves to the service of health. Only those who have satisfied all requisites for the study of medicine and by diligent application have acquired a true knowledge of it shall be "esteemed physicians not only in name but in reality."

The same high conception of medicine appears in the Bible. We read in Ecclesiasticus: "Honor the physician for the need thou hast of him: for the most High hath created him. For all the healing is from God, and he shall receive gifts of the king. The skill of the physician shall lift up his head, and in the sight of great men he shall be praised. The most High hath created medicines out of the earth, and a wise man will not abhor them . . . The virtue

515

of these things is come to the knowledge of men, and the most High hath given knowledge to men, that he may be honored in his wonders. By these he shall cure and shall allay their pains, and of these the apothecary shall make sweet confections, and shall make up ointments of health, and of his works there shall be no end. For the peace of God is over all the face of the earth."

FIVE OF THE authors of the great books—Hippocrates, Galen, Gilbert, Harvey, and Freud—belonged to the profession of medicine. They were major figures in its history. Practitioners of its arts, they were also contributors to the sciences concerned with health and disease. Three others combined medicine with other pursuits. Copernicus studied medicine at Padua and devoted considerable time to its practice; Locke was Lord Shaftesbury's personal physician; William James took a medical degree at Harvard after years spent in the biological sciences. Still another, Rabelais, not only studied and practiced medicine, but also edited the *Aphorisms* of Hippocrates and Galen's little treatise on the medical art. His knowledge of medicine and his observation of its contemporary practices can be readily discerned in his comic exaggerations of anatomic and physiological detail, and of regimens of diet or exercise.

The discussion of medicine in the great books is not limited to its professors or practitioners. Montaigne has many doubts about medical diagnosis and the possibility of charting the causes of disease or the remedies which cure. The patient's ignorance permits the physician to claim credit for his successes and to blame fortune for his failures.

Montaigne, characteristically, delights in observing that the doctors disagree. He offers, as "an example of the ancient controversy in medicine," the following: "Hierophilus lodges the original cause of diseases in the humors; Erasistratus, in the blood of the arteries; Asclepiades, in the invisible atoms flowing in our pores; Alcmaeon, in the exuberance or deficiency of our bodily powers; Diocles, in the inequality of the elements of the body and in the quality of the air we breathe; Strato, in

the abundance, crudity, and corruption of the nourishment we take; Hippocrates lodges it in the spirits." There is no great danger, he adds, "in our miscalculating the height of the sun or the fraction of some astronomical computation; but here, where our whole being is at stake, it is not wisdom to abandon ourselves to the mercy and the agitation of so many conflicting winds." Molière writes in a similar vein. A doctor means no ill in anything that he does: "it's with the best faith in the world that he will finish you off, and in killing you he will do just what he has done to his wife and children, and what, if the occasion should arise, he will do to himself."

Such commentary as this bears more on the history of medicine than on the abiding problems of its science or art, which, from Hippocrates to Freud, have been more generally agreed upon than the theories proposed for their solution. Of similar historical significance are the passages in the great works of history which describe the phenomena of disease as they appeared to contemporary observers, the plagues which ravaged Athens, Rome, and London, or the maladies which afflicted eminent individuals. Poetry, as well as history and biography, contributes to this record. The novels of Tolstoy, Mann, and Proust, the plays of Shakespeare and Molière, the tales of Cervantes and Chaucer, the Greek tragedies, and the Homeric epics furnish evidence of both the constant and the changing elements in the conception of disease, the vocation of medicine, and the social acceptance of the physician.

The history of medicine is an epitome of the history of the natural sciences. The researches of the Hippocratic school initiate specific methods of empirical investigation, such as the systematic collection and comparison of observations and the painstaking record of individual case histories. The fundamental concepts of medical theory reflect the philosophy of nature and of man. Conflicting notions of the causes of disease focus major issues in biology, such as the controversy in which Galen engages with Asclepiades and Erasistratus in the defense of what he supposes to be Hippocrates' and Aristotle's organic view of nature against mechanism and atomism.

Medicine, moreover, provides some of the clearest examples of the interdependence of theory and practice, for the rules of the healing art put theories to work and to the test; and as the rules are refined or altered by the accumulated experience of particular cases, inductive insight leads to new theoretical generalizations. As the work of Harvey illustrates, biological science is both the source and the reflection of medical knowledge. Medicine also affords Bacon and Descartes the prime example of a useful application of the knowledge gained by the new methods they propose.

More than engineering or the invention of mechanical utilities, medicine represents for them knowledge in the service of mankind. That science shall bear fruit in technology "is not merely to be desired," writes Descartes, "with a view to the invention of an infinity of arts and crafts ... but principally because it brings about the preservation of health, which is without doubt the chief blessing and the foundation of all other blessings in this life ... It is true that the medicine which is now in vogue contains little of which the utility is remarkable; but, without any intention of decrying it, I am sure that there is no one, even among those who make its study a profession, who does not confess that all that men know is almost nothing in comparison with what remains to be known."

The subsequent history of medicine, some of the great documents of which are cited in the list of Additional Readings under the names of Jenner, Bichat, Virchow, Bernard, and Koch, seems to substantiate Descartes's prophecy. But it also seems to be true that the major problems of medical practice are not greatly altered or diminished by the tremendous increase in our knowledge of the causes of specific diseases and our vast store of well-tested remedies.

What sort of art medicine is; to what extent the physician should let nature run its course; with what restraint or prudence the physician should apply general rules to particular cases; whether health is better served by the general practitioner treating the whole man or by a specialist treating a special organ; how the relation of the physician to his patient is itself a therapeutic factor and underlies the effectiveness of his skill in all other respects; to what extent mind and body interact both in the origin and in the cure of disease—these are the problems of medicine concerning which Hippocrates and Galen can converse with William Osler and Freud almost as contemporaries.

THE DISTINCTION made in the chapter on ART between the simply productive and the cooperative arts associates medicine with agriculture and teaching, and separates these arts, which merely help a natural result to come about, from the arts which produce an effect that would never occur without the work of the artist. Plants grow and reproduce without the help of farmers. The mind can discover some truth without the aid of teachers. Animals and men can preserve and regain their health without the care of physicians. But without shoemakers or house builders, shoes and houses would not be produced.

The art of medicine does not produce health in the sense in which the shoemaker produces a shoe, or the sculptor a statue. These other arts imitate nature by embodying natural forms or functions in materials wherein they do not naturally arise. An art like medicine seems to imitate nature by cooperating with natural processes. It follows the course of nature itself and, by working with it, enables the natural result to eventuate more surely than it might if art made no attempt to overcome the factors of chance.

Socrates expresses this understanding of the physician's art when he uses the metaphor of midwifery to characterize his own method of teaching. As it is the mother who labors and gives birth, so it is the student who is primarily active in the process of learning. The teacher, like the midwife, merely assists in a natural process which might be more painful, and might possibly fail, without such help. "The teacher," writes Aquinas, "only brings exterior help as does the physician who heals; just as the interior nature is the principal cause of the healing, so the interior light of the intellect is the principal cause of knowledge.

"Health," he continues, "is caused in a sick man, sometimes by an exterior principle, namely, by the medical art; sometimes by an interior principle, as when a man is healed by the force of nature . . . Just as nature heals a man by alteration, digestion, rejection of the matter that caused the sickness, so does art . . . The exterior principle, art, acts not as a primary agent, but as helping the primary agent, which is the interior principle, and by furnishing it with instruments and assistance, of which the interior principle makes use in producing the effect. Thus the physician strengthens nature, and employs food and medicine, of which nature makes use for the intended end."

Medicine as practiced by primitive tribes seems to take the contrary view: the art of healing is a process of subverting nature. The tribal medicine man or shaman, as described by Lévi-Strauss, proceeds from the belief that a sick person has lost his "spiritual double or, more correctly, one of the specific doubles which together constitute . . . vital strength." During meditation, the shaman "undertakes a journey to the supernatural world in order to snatch the double from the malevolent spirit who has captured it; by restoring it to its owner, he achieves the cure." Shamanism consists of "a curious mixture of pantomime, prestidigitation, and empirical knowledge," and in Lévi-Strauss's accounts, it often makes the art of healing look like the art of drama.

The subordination of the medical art to nature seems to be the keystone of the whole structure of Hippocratic medicine. It is implied in the emphasis which Hippocrates places on the control of the patient's regimen, especially the elements of his diet, the exercise of his body, and the general circumstances of his life. Even in the treatment of acute diseases, Hippocrates looks to the regimen first, prescribing changes or special articles of diet.

Medicines or drugs perform an auxiliary function. Surgery is always a last resort, to be used primarily in the treatment of injuries, and not to be employed in diseases which will yield to a course of regimen and medication. There is an element of violence in surgery which puts it last among the means of an art which should work by cooperating with nature rather than by operating on it. And among medicines, those are preferable which, like ptisan, a special preparation of barley water, derive their efficacy from properties similar to those of normal nutriment.

According to Hippocrates, the control of regimen is not only the primary factor in therapy, but also the original principle of medicine. In the treatise *On Ancient Medicine,* he points out that "the art of medicine would not have been invented at first, nor would it have been made the subject of investigation (for there would have been no need for it), if when men are indisposed, the same food and other articles of regimen which they eat and drink when in good health were proper for them, and if no other were preferable to these . . . The diet and food which people in health now use would not have been discovered, provided it suited man to eat and drink in like manner as the ox, the horse, and all other animals . . . What other object, then, has he in view who is called a physician, and is admitted to be a practitioner of the art, who found out the regimen and diet befitting the sick, than he who originally found out and prepared for all mankind that kind of food which we all now use, in place of the former savage and brutish mode of living?"

THE SAME CONCEPTION of medicine's relation to nature seems to be fundamental in Galen's thought. He attributes to Hippocrates his own reformulation of the insight that the art of healing consists in imitating the health-giving and healing powers of nature itself. The medical doctrines which he criticizes were based on the atomism of Epicurus. They regarded the body as a complex piece of machinery. When it gets out of order, it needs a mechanic and mechanical remedies to fix it. On the contrary, it seems to him, the living body is an organic unity, not an aggregation of atoms, or a system of interlocking parts.

"Nature is not posterior to the corpuscles, but a long way prior to them," Galen writes. "Therefore it is nature which puts together the bodies both of plants and animals; and this she does by virtue of certain faculties which she possesses—these being, on the one hand, attractive and assimilative of what is appropriate, and, on the other, expulsive of what is foreign. Further, she skillfully moulds everything during the stage of genesis; and she also provides for the creatures after birth, employing here other faculties again."

Nature, according to Galen, works not by the external impact of part upon part, but by its faculties or powers for the performance of natural functions and the production of natural effects. Galen's polemic against the mechanists thus leads him to reverse the usual statement. Where Hippocrates looks upon nature as the model for art to follow, Galen calls Nature the artist, in order to set his view in sharp contrast to all mechanical conceptions. "Instead of admiring Nature's artistic skill," he declares, "they even go so far as to scoff and maintain that . . . things have been made by Nature for no purpose!" Nature, Galen holds, produces effects according to its powers and in conformity to its needs. It seems to work with intelligence and for an end, not blindly and by chance. The true art of medicine, therefore, borrows its method from "Nature's art."

The conception of nature as an artist may be taken metaphorically or literally, but the insight controlling the practice of medicine remains the same. The physician is a servant, not a master, of nature. Aristotle's doctrine of final causes, summarized in the maxim Galen so often repeats—that "nothing is done by Nature in vain"—furnishes a principle for physiological research, as well as the rules of medical art. Whether because of faulty observation on his part, or because of a failure to apply his own principle, Galen leaves to Harvey one of the great discoveries which can be credited to close attention to final causes. Always observant of the relation between structure and function, always questioning the purpose which bodily organs serve, Harvey establishes the fact that the blood circulates, and finds therein the reason for the structure of the heart, its motions, and its relation to the lungs.

It may also be possible for a principle to be carried to excess. Montaigne, for example, expresses his distrust of medical theory and the physician's remedies by an unqualified trust in nature's own resourcefulness. Drugs, especially purgatives, do violence to nature. "We disturb and arouse a disease by attacking it head on. It is by our mode of life that we should weaken it, by gentle degrees, and bring it to its end. The violent struggles between the drug and the disease are always at our expense, since the combat is fought out within us and the drug is an untrustworthy assistant, by its nature an enemy to our health, and having access to our constitution only through disturbance . . . Let us let things take their course: the scheme of things that takes care of fleas and moles also takes care of men who have the same patience to let themselves be governed as fleas and moles."

Nor is there any need for an art of medicine when nature can do better by herself. "We should give free passage to diseases . . . I find that they do not stay so long with me, who let them go ahead; and some of those that are considered most stubborn and tenacious, I have shaken off by their own decadence, without help and without art, and against the rules of medicine. Let us give Nature a chance; she knows her business better than we do." Molière seems to be of the same mind. When sick, we best do nothing, Béralde advises his hypochondriac brother in *The Would-Be Invalid*. "Just stay quiet. When we let nature alone, she recovers by herself from the disorder she's fallen into. It's our disquiet, our impatience which upsets everything; and most men die of their remedies, and not of their illnesses." The Hippocratic doctrine seems to occupy a middle ground between this view of nature as an unerring artist and the opposite extreme which permits all sorts of tampering and tinkering with the machinery of the body.

THE ART OF MEDICINE "consists in three things," writes Hippocrates: "the disease, the patient, and the physician. The physician is the servant of the art, and the patient must combat the disease along with the physician." With regard to diseases, the physician must "have two special objects in view . . . to do good, and to do no harm."

This celebrated summary indicates the two kinds of knowledge which the physician should possess. He should know about disease in general, so that he can classify diseases according to their special causes, their symptoms, and the typical course each seems to take. Such knowledge underlies the doctor's diagnosis of the patient's malady. That in turn determines his prognosis of the stages through which the illness will run, from its onset through various crises or turning points to its *sequelae* or consequences. Upon the accuracy of his diagnosis and the certainty of his prognosis may depend the effectiveness of any remedy the physician prescribes in the individual case.

But individual cases are seldom completely alike. The physician must therefore know the patient as an individual, and all the relevant circumstances of his life as well as the particular characteristics of this instance of the disease; even though its general characteristics are familiar to him from much experience in the treatment of similar cases. *The Book of Prognostics* and the treatise *Of the Epidemics* in the Hippocratic collection seem to combine both these kinds of knowledge. They enumerate the symptoms by which diseases can be recognized and their future foretold. They also set forth individual case histories from which such generalizations can be drawn.

The practice of medicine thus appears to require more than scientific knowledge of health and disease in general, and more than general rules of art. It requires the sort of experience which can be gained only from actual practice. Without prudence born of experience, general rules can be misapplied, for no general rule, in medicine as in law, fits all cases alike. The most famous of Hippocratic aphorisms conveys a sense of the hazards of medical practice: "Life is short, and Art long; the crisis fleeting; experiment perilous, and decision difficult. The physician must not only be prepared to do what is right himself, but also to make the patient, the attendants, and the externals cooperate."

To persuade the patient to cooperate is the first maxim governing the physician's relation to his patient. Plato contrasts the right and wrong relation between doctor and patient by comparing the practice of the physicians who treated slaves and those who treated freemen. "The slave-doctor," he says, "prescribes what mere experience suggests, as if he had exact

knowledge, and when he has given his orders, like a tyrant, he rushes off with equal assurance to some other servant who is ill . . . But the other doctor, who is a freeman, attends and practices upon freemen; and he carries his enquiries far back, and goes into the nature of the disorder; he enters into discourse with the patient and with his friends, and is at once getting information from the sick man, and also instructing him as far as he is able, and he will not prescribe for him until he has first convinced him; at last, when he has brought the patient more and more under his persuasive influences and set him on the road to health, he attempts to effect a cure."

In the treatment of mental diseases, as Freud points out, the proper development and management of the relationship between patient and physician is itself a major factor in psychotherapy. "It presupposes a profound interest for psychological incidents, as well as a personal sympathy for the patient," he writes. "It requires the full consent and the attention of the patients, but above all, their confidence, for the analysis regularly leads to the inmost and most secretly guarded psychic processes." Since fears, anxieties, or other temperamental dispositions on the part of the patient may affect the course of an organic ailment, the patient's confidence in the physician and, even more generally, his emotional response to the physician's character play an important role in the successful treatment of bodily ills as well as of mental or functional disorders.

Hippocrates recommends that the physician cultivate prognosis, not only for the guidance of his own actions, but also for the sake of the patient. "By foreseeing and foretelling, in the presence of the sick, the present, the past, and the future, and explaining the omissions which patients have been guilty of, he will be the more readily believed to be acquainted with the circumstances of the sick; so that men will have confidence to entrust themselves to such a physician."

Certain issues surrounding the ethics of the physician-patient relationship seem to be peculiar to the 20th-century practice of medicine. The right of the mortally ill to die is an issue the significance of which is a measure of the advances in medical technology; the issue would never have arisen if doctors had not been able to preserve the life of a patient far longer than could be expected naturally. According to Weber, medicine falls into difficulties by aiming both to preserve life and to reduce suffering to the greatest extent possible. "This is problematical," writes Weber. "By his means the medical man preserves the life of the mortally ill man, even if the patient implores us to relieve him of life . . . Whether life is worth while living and when—this question is not asked by medicine."

THE RELATION OF physician and patient raises a question about the organization of the practice of medicine, to which opposite answers have been given in both ancient and modern times. Herodotus reports a high degree of medical specialization in Egypt. "Medicine is practised among them on a plan of separation," he writes; "each physician treats a single disorder, and no more: thus the country swarms with medical practitioners, some undertaking to cure diseases of the eye, others of the hand, others again of the teeth, others of the intestines, and some those which are not local." The fact that the next paragraph begins a discussion of funerals can hardly be taken as revealing the attitude of Herodotus toward specialization, though his comment on the Egyptian practice does imply a contrast to Greek medicine.

One sentence in the Hippocratic Oath—"I will not cut persons laboring under the stone, but will leave this to be done by men who are practitioners of this work"—indicates some division of labor in the organization of Greek medicine. But apart from the special tasks and skills of surgery, the Hippocratic conception of the physician's work favors the practice of general medicine rather than specialization. The man, not the disease, is to be treated, and to treat him well the physician must examine the man as a whole, not merely the organ or bodily part in which the disorder seems to be located. The Hippocratic formula for getting a case history calls for an inquiry into the background of the individual's life, his antecedents, his occupation, his temperament,

"the patient's habits, regimen, and pursuits; his conversation, manners, taciturnity, thoughts, sleep, or absence of sleep, and sometimes his dreams, what they are and when they occur; his picking and scratching; his tears." From these as well as from the symptoms, says Hippocrates, "we must form our judgment."

The defense of general practice against specialization is part of Galen's argument with his adversaries. Treatment of the disordered part as if it could be isolated from the living unity of the whole man is, to Galen, one of the deplorable consequences in medical practice of atomism or mechanism in medical theory.

This issue is argued again and again in the history of medicine, with each side pressing the advantages in its favor. Montaigne, for example, states the case for the specialist by analogy with the advantages of specialization in other arts. "As we have doublet makers and breeches makers to clothe us, and are served all the better by them because each one performs only his own specialty and needs a more restricted and limited skill than a tailor who undertakes everything; and as, in the matter of food, the great find it preferable to have separate functions for soup cooks and roasting cooks . . . so, for curing us, the Egyptians were right to reject the general practice of medicine and to subdivide this profession." With Freud and the development of a greater awareness of the psychological origin of many bodily disorders, a new factor enters into the argument. It tends to favor the general practitioner who, from his acquaintance with the patient as a person, may be better able than the specialist to detect hidden psychological causes.

THE CONCEPTION of disease is usually determined by the conception of health. The abnormality is judged and measured as a deviation from the norm. Hippocrates uses the outward appearance of man in a healthy condition as the standard for discerning the visible signs of illness. The physician, he says, "should observe . . . first the countenance of the patient, if it be like those of persons in health, and more so, if like itself, for this is the best of all; whereas the most opposite to it is the worst." He should also take note when he finds the patient reclining in a posture which resembles the normal disposition of the healthy body. "To find the whole body lying in a relaxed state" is a more favorable sign than to find him "upon his back, with the hands, neck, and the legs extended."

The history of medicine, especially on the side of its science and theory, if not so much with regard to its art and practice, can be told in terms of refinements in the classification of diseases and progressive discovery of their specific causes, both internal and external, predisposing and exciting. But the analysis of diseases according to their etiology and by reference to the typical picture of the disease process leaves unanswered the general question about the nature of disease as a loss of health.

Apart from its causes and its symptoms, its modes and its patterns, what is disease? This is the question of major speculative interest in the tradition of the great books. The answers given have a certain uniformity in spite of the varying terms in which they are expressed.

The humoral hypothesis of ancient medical theory, for example, conceives health as that condition of the body in which the physiological elements are in a proper proportion or balance, and in which the various parts or powers function harmoniously with one another. As health is harmony or good order in the body, so disease consists in imbalance and disharmony—an excess or defect with consequent disproportion of the elements, or the disorder of conflicting bodily processes.

In the *Timaeus*, Plato first states this theory in terms of the four physical elements. "There are four natures out of which the body is compacted, earth and fire and water and air, and the unnatural excess or defect of these, or the change of any of them from its own natural place into another . . . produces disorders and diseases." He then considers the diseases which result from excess or defect of one or another of the four humors—blood, phlegm, black and yellow bile.

The humoral hypothesis, which Hippocrates and Galen share with Plato and Aristotle, undergoes many transformations in the history of medicine. The four elements or humors are replaced by other physiological factors, such as the hormones or internal secretions, or the elements of modern biochemistry. But constant throughout these changing formulations is the conception of health as an equilibrium, and of disease as its loss through disorder and disproportion.

This broad conception of health and disease seems to apply to mental as well as bodily ills. There is not only a basic continuity between Plato's and Freud's discussion of the bodily origin of mental disorders and the psychic origin of physical ailments; but the Freudian emphasis upon conflict and disintegration in the neurotic character—milder forms of the schizophrenia or "split personality" which characterizes insanity—also appeals to harmony as the principle of health. The language of modern psychiatry which refers to "the integrated personality" or "the well-balanced and adjusted individual" defines the norm or the ideal of mental health.

The various kinds and degrees of mental disorder, especially those which seem to be entirely functional rather than organic, represent abnormalities which, though they differ in cause, symptom, and tendency, have in common some excess or defect in the psychic structure or some unresolved conflict in the nature of man. Freud's psychoanalytic method in the treatment of mental ills places psychotherapy in the main tradition of medical practice; for in addition to insisting that the patient shall help to cure himself, it is directed toward the resolution of conflict, restoring the harmony which is health.

56

Memory and Imagination

INTRODUCTION

CONCERNING memory and imagination, the tradition of western thought seems to be involved in less dispute than it is on other aspects of human and animal life. There are, as we shall see, points of difficulty and debatable theories. But these arise only within the framework of certain fundamental insights which are widely, if not universally, shared. Here at least we can begin without having to deal with verbal ambiguities. Unlike many of the words which are the traditional bearers of the great ideas, "memory" and "imagination" have a constant core of meaning in almost everyone's discourse.

It is understood that memory and imagination depend upon sense perception or upon previous experience. Except for illusions of memory, we do not remember objects we have never perceived or events in our own life, such as emotions or desires, that we have not experienced. The imagination is not limited in the same way by prior experience, for we can imagine things we have never perceived and may never be able to.

Yet even when imagination outruns perception, it draws upon experience for the materials it uses in its constructions. It is possible to imagine a golden mountain or a purple cow, though no such object has ever presented itself to perception. But, as Hume suggests, the possibility of combining a familiar color and a familiar shape depends upon the availability of the separate images to be combined.

"When we think of a golden mountain," Hume writes, "we only join two consistent ideas, *gold* and *mountain*, with which we were formerly acquainted . . . All this creative power of the mind amounts to no more than the faculty of compounding, transposing, augment-ing, or diminishing the materials afforded us by the senses and experience." A congenitally color-blind man who lived entirely in a world of grays would not be able to imagine a golden mountain or a purple cow, though he might be able to imagine things as unreal as these.

Because of their dependence on sense perception, memory and imagination are usually regarded as belonging to the same general faculty as the external senses. Not all writers, however, conceive of a generic power of sense, which they then divide into the exterior senses such as sight, hearing, and touch, and the interior senses such as memory and imagination. Some, like Hobbes, treat imagination as "nothing but decaying sense," and use the word "memory" to "express the decay, and signify that the sense is fading, old, and past."

The image, whether it is a memory-image or fancy-free, *re-produces* or *re-presents* sensory material. It may be less vivid, less sharp in outline, and less definite in detail than the sensation or perception from which it is derived. But in one important respect the image does not differ from the original sense impression. That is the respect in which ideas or concepts do differ from sense impressions—at least according to those who hold that ideas or concepts have a certain universality and abstractness which is not found in sensations and sensory images. Those who, like Berkeley and Hume, call sensations or images "ideas" deny the existence of abstract ideas or universal notions precisely because they, too, agree that sense impressions or sensory images are always particular in their content and meaning.

THE FUNDAMENTAL controversy about what an idea is and the verbal confusion occasioned by the ambiguity of the word (which appears in the chapter on IDEA) do not seem to affect the understanding of the nature of images or their role in the activities of memory and imagination. As William James points out, in discussing the "blended" or "generic" image which is somehow associated with abstract or universal meaning, "a blurred thing is just as particular as a sharp thing, and the generic character of either sharp image or blurred image depends on its being felt *with its representative function.*" He speaks of this function as "the mysterious *plus,* the understood meaning," but he denies the possibility of universal or abstract *images,* whatever may be the truth about ideas which are not images at all. Certainly those who deny the presence of anything abstract or universal in the understanding do so on the ground that the content of the mind is basically sensory, whether the mind is perceiving or remembering, imagining or thinking.

The controversy about the nature of the mind does not seem to affect the conception of memory or imagination. As neither is confused with sense perception, so neither is confused with rational thought. This remains the case whether the theory of mind looks upon the intellect as a faculty separate from the sensitive faculty (including memory and imagination), or conceives the understanding as a single faculty which is active in judgment and reasoning as well as in perceiving, remembering, and imagining.

Russell makes an important observation of the special contribution made by imagination and memory to human knowledge. "The essence of memory," he writes, "is not constituted by the image, but by having immediately before the mind an object which is recognized as past." Without such memory images, "we should not know that there ever was a past at all, nor should we be able to understand the word 'past,' any more than a man born blind can understand the word 'light.' Thus there must be intuitive judgements of memory," judgments that Russell calls self-evident, "and it is upon them, ultimately, that all our knowledge of the past depends."

THIS AND RELATED issues are considered in the chapter on MIND. Except for one point, perhaps, such issues can be ignored here. Sensation is attributed to both animals and men—to all organisms which give evidence of having sense organs or some sort of sensitive apparatus. Whether all animals, even those which have the most rudimentary sensorium, also have memory and imagination may be disputed; but no one doubts that the higher animals, with central nervous systems and brain structures resembling those of men, can remember and imagine as well as perceive.

All agree, furthermore, that memory and imagination require bodily organs, though the assignment of these two functions to the brain as their organic seat is more uniformly a tenet of modern than of ancient physiology, and can be more clearly expounded as the result of modern researches in neurology. But the question whether the memory or imagination of men and other animals differs more than their bodies do, elicits opposite answers from those who affirm that man alone has reason and those who deny that man has powers of knowing or thinking not possessed by other animals to some degree.

Nevertheless, if man alone is considered, the nature of memory and imagination is clear. The object remembered or imagined need not be physically present to the senses like the object perceived. The object imagined need not be located in the past like the object remembered; nor, for that matter, need it have any definite location in time and space. It need have no actual existence. It may be a mere possibility, unlike the object which cannot be known without being known to exist. As the object of memory is an event which no longer exists, so the object of imagination may be something which has never existed and never will.

Thus memory and imagination greatly enlarge the world of human experience, as novelists such as Henry James, James Joyce, and Virginia Woolf vividly illustrate. Memory is both form and subject matter of Proust's *Remembrance of Things Past.* "It is a labour in vain to attempt to recapture" the past, he writes. "All the efforts of our intellect must prove futile. The past is hidden somewhere outside the realm, beyond the reach of intellect, in some material object . . . of which we have no inkling. And it depends on chance whether or not we come upon this object before we ourselves must die." This chance comes for Proust's narrator in the form of a sensory association. After tasting the "petites madeleines," the little cakes he used to eat as a child, his memories are lifted out of his unconscious as though he were drugged. "When from a long-distant past nothing subsists," Proust writes, "after the people are dead, after the things are broken and scattered, taste and smell alone, more fragile but more enduring, more unsubstantial, more persistent, more faithful, remain poised a long time, like souls, remembering, waiting, hoping, amid the ruins of all the rest; and bear unflinchingly, in the tiny and almost impalpable drop of their essence, the vast structure of recollection."

Regardless of Proust's difficulty of recapturing the past, even he would agree that without memory and imagination, man would live in a confined and narrow present, lacking past and future, restricted to what happens to be actual out of the almost infinite possibilities of being. Without memory and imagination, man could be neither a poet nor a historian; and unless he had an angelic sort of intellect which in no way depended on sense-experience, he would be impeded in all the work of science, if memory and imagination did not extend the reach of his senses.

In religious mysticism, imagination makes the effort to transcend sense-experience. It tries "in vain," writes Huizinga, "to express the ineffable by giving it shape and figure." For example, "The mystic imagination found a very impressive concept in adding to the image of the desert, that is to say, extension of surface—that of the abyss, or extension of depth. The sensation of giddiness is added to the feeling of infinite space." Huizinga comments on "the hopeless attempt to dispense with images and to attain 'the state of void, that is mere absence of images,' which only God can give."

THE PSYCHOLOGICAL analysis of memory usually divides it into a number of separate acts or phases. Recollection presupposes the retention of the material to be recalled. The ingenious experiments of Hermann Ebbinghaus that William James reports—using the memorization of nonsense syllables to isolate the factors influencing memory—seem to show that retention is affected by the strength of the original associations. But retention is also affected by the interval between the time of learning and the time of revival. The amount of forgetting seems to be a function of two separate factors: the force with which the material to be recalled is originally committed to memory, and the lapse of time.

That retention is not the same as recall may be seen from Ebbinghaus' experimental discovery of the fact that forgetting is never complete. Material which lies below the threshold of recall is nevertheless retained, and manifests its presence by its effect on attempts to relearn the material which *appears* to have been forgotten.

Nothing can be utterly forgotten if, as Augustine suggests, what seems to be forgotten remains in the memory. He considers the effort men make to remember a forgotten name. How can we remember a name, he asks, "unless we bring it out from the memory? For even if we recognize it because someone else prompts us, it is still by our own memory that we do so, because we do not accept it as a fresh piece of knowledge but agree that it is the right name, since we can now remember it. If the name were completely obliterated from our minds," Augustine argues, "we could not remember it even if we were prompted. For we do not entirely forget what we remember that we have forgotten. If we had completely forgotten it, we should not even be able to look for what was lost."

Freud considers forgetting from another point of view. He describes the psychoanalytic method at its inception as a "talking cure" involving efforts in reminiscence. The things which we have put out of mind, he claims, are "hindered from becoming conscious, and forced to remain in the unconscious by some sort of force." He calls this "repression." Freud observed that it occurred when "a wish had been aroused, which was in sharp opposition to the other desires of the individual, and was not capable of being reconciled with the ethical, aesthetic, and personal pretensions of the patient's personality . . . The end of this inner struggle was the repression of the idea which presented itself to consciousness as the bearer of this irreconcilable wish. This was repressed from consciousness and forgotten."

On this view things which have been put out of mind because we find them unpleasant to contemplate, things which are repressed in order to avoid conflict, are not forgotten when they cannot be consciously remembered. Nor are they below the threshold of recall in the sense that our retention of them has been so weakened by time that no effort at recollection can revive them. On the contrary, they may be capable of quite vivid revival when the emotional obstacles to recollection are removed. Freud applies his theory of the "obliviscence of the disagreeable" to such everyday occurrences as the forgetting of familiar names as well as to the repression of memories connected with the emotional traumas of early life.

Recollection is distinct not only from retention, but also from recognition. The illusion known as déjà vu consists in the experience of intense familiarity with a place or scene that, so far as one can recall, has never been witnessed before. In contrast, normal recognition depends upon previous acquaintance with the object being cognized again, i.e., re-cognized. The fact, noted by many observers, that recognition may or may not be accompanied by recollection of the previous circumstances, indicates the separation of recall and recognition as acts of memory. Whereas recollection is remembering through the recall of images, recognition consists in remembering at the very moment of perceiving. Both, however, depend upon what seems to be memory's fundamental act—retention.

WITH REGARD TO retention, there are two problems which have been the subject of inquiry throughout the whole tradition. The first concerns what is usually called "the association of ideas." From Aristotle through Hobbes and Hume to James and Freud, there have been various formulations of the laws of association and various interpretations of what such laws signify about the mind. Ebbinghaus, for example, used nonsense syllables in order to measure the effect upon retention of the associations formed by repetition of a series of sounds. All meaning had been removed in order to avoid the influence upon recollection of associations resulting from meaningful connections of the sort which exists among ordinary words. The repetition of nonsense syllables in pairs or series illustrates association by contiguity or succession. According to most writers, the elements of experience become associated through other modes of relation also, such as their similarity or contrast with one another in any significant respect.

It is not the association itself which is remembered. Rather it is through the association of one part of experience with another that memory seems to work, one particular tending to recall others with which it has been associated in one or more ways. Recollection seems to occur through activating connections which have been formed and retained. The modern differentiation of controlled and free association indicates two ways in which this can happen—either by a purposeful pursuit of the past or by the apparently chance recall of one thing by another. The ancients make a parallel distinction between reminiscence and reverie. The former is a process in which recollection resembles reasoning in proceeding step by step through a series of related terms; the latter is more like daydreaming or spontaneous fantasy.

The second problem can be stated, perhaps, as the mystery of retention itself. In describing the capacity of the memory to hold the innumerable things which are not now in mind but can be recalled, the ancients speak of memory as "the storehouse of images." Every variety of thing which can be perceived can be "stored in the vast capacity of memory," says Augustine. "I may say to myself 'If only this or that would happen!' or 'God forbid that this or that should be!' No sooner do I say this than the images of all the things of which I speak spring forward from the same great treasure-house of the memory. And, in fact,

I could not even mention them at all if the images were lacking ... the things themselves do not penetrate into the memory. It is simply that the memory captures their images with astonishing speed and stores them away in its wonderful system of compartments, ready to produce them again in just as wonderful a way when we remember them."

The marvel of memory deepens into a mystery when we ask what the metaphor of the storehouse literally means. Where actually are the images when they are not actually in mind? If an image is by its nature an act of consciousness, whereby we apprehend objects not immediately present to our senses, how do images exist outside of consciousness during intervals when they do not function in remembering, imagining, or other acts of knowing? Their return to consciousness seems to imply that they have been retained, but where and how is the problem not solved by the metaphor of things stored away in a capacious barn.

The physical storehouse does not require any fundamental transformation in the being of the things it holds between periods when they are actually in use. The memory does. This problem of the nature and causes of retention James seems to think can be solved only in terms of the retentive power of nervous tissue—what he calls "physiological retentiveness"—though in the view of others the problem becomes no easier (and may even be more complicated) when it is transferred from mind to matter. On either view, there seems to be no question that changes in the brain are somehow causally connected with the activity of memory and imagination, especially retention and recall. Aquinas, for example, observes that the imagination and memory may be "hindered by a lesion of the corporeal organ ... or by lethargy," an observation many times extended by more recent investigations of the brain pathology underlying amnesia and aphasia.

JAMES'S TREATMENT of retention as somehow based on pathways traced in the brain, with recall the result of a retracing of these paths, tends to emphasize the affinity between mem-

ory and habit. His theory, discussed in the chapter on HABIT, that the plasticity of matter, certainly living matter, underlies learning or habit formation, while the inertia or retentiveness of matter, especially the neural matter of the brain, explains memory or the persistence of habits during periods of disuse, seems almost to identify habit and memory. Ice skating after many years of absence from the sport is as much remembering how to ice-skate as reciting a poem committed to memory in youth is the exercise of an old habit.

Not all conceptions of habit and memory permit this fusion of the two—or even their affinity as related aspects of the same phenomenon. Aquinas, for example, restricts memory to an act of knowledge. The performance popularly called "reciting from memory" would not be for him an act of memory, though it might involve memory if the recitation were accompanied by knowledge of the time or place and occasion when the poem was first learned. Such knowledge would be a memory, but the recitation itself would not be, any more than ice skating is. These performances represent the exercise of habits of skill or art.

In view of this, Aquinas raises the question whether the act of knowledge, of the sort involved in reconsidering a geometric proof learned at some earlier moment and now recalled to mind, is an act of memory. The knowledge of the proof which is retained by the intellect during periods when it is not actually exercised, he would call an intellectual habit or habit of knowledge. But should the recollection of this retained knowledge, or the activation of this intellectual habit, also be called an act of memory? Aquinas answers No, on the ground that no reference to the past need be involved in reworking a geometric problem solved at some earlier time. But if the individual also happens to recall *when* he first solved the problem, that is another matter. Even so, Aquinas claims that "if in the notion of memory we include its object as something past, then the memory is not in the intellectual, but only in the sensitive part." The intellect is said to remember only in the sense of recalling a truth retained by habit, and "not in the sense that it understands the past as something here and now."

Memory is considered in still another way in relation to speculative truths about scientific or philosophical matters. The question is one of the origin of such knowledge. In the usual conception of memory as knowledge of past particulars, one traditional view, found in Aristotle, holds that "out of sense-perception comes to be what we call memory, and out of frequently repeated memories of the same thing develops experience"—the generalized experience which gives rise to induction and the apprehension of the universal. But in the tradition of the great books we also find a more radical and, perhaps, less familiar conception of memory as the chief source of knowledge.

This is Plato's doctrine of reminiscence, in which all learning is a kind of remembering of knowledge already present in the soul. All teaching takes the form of helping the learner to recollect things he may not be aware he knows, by reminding him through a process of questioning which awakens the knowledge already latent in him.

In the *Meno,* Meno asks Socrates, "What do you mean by saying that we do not learn, and that what we call learning is only a process of recollection?" Socrates undertakes to show Meno what he means by taking a slave boy who appears not to know the solution of a certain geometric problem and merely by questioning him, without ever giving him a single answer, getting the slave boy to find the right solution for himself. Meno assures Socrates that the slave boy had never been taught geometry. Since the boy was not told the answer, he must have always known it, and needed only some reminding to remember what he knew. Socrates suggests the explanation that the boy's soul always possessed this knowledge, bringing it from another life.

Before he undertook the demonstration with the slave boy, Socrates had proposed this hypothesis. "The soul, being immortal, and having been born again many times, and having seen all things that exist . . . has knowledge of them all; and it is no wonder that it should be able to call to remembrance all that it ever knew about virtue, and about everything; for as all nature is akin, and the soul has learned all things, there is no difficulty in her eliciting, or as men say learning, out of a single recollection all the rest, if a man is strenuous and does not faint; for all enquiry and all learning is but recollection."

Though he differs from Plato in his conception of the soul and the origin of the knowledge which it innately possesses, Augustine seems to hold a similar view. As he examines his own memory, it appears to contain much that has not been implanted there by sense experience. Certain things, referred to by words he understands, he says, "have not reached me through any of my bodily senses. I could not see them at all except in my mind, and it is not their images that I store in my memory but the facts themselves. But they must themselves tell me, if they can, by what means they entered my mind. For I can run through all the organs of sense, which are the body's gateways to the mind, but I cannot find any by which these facts could have entered." If the seeds of learning are in the soul at its creation, memory can draw from these "seminal reasons" the full fruit of knowledge.

THE DOCTRINE OF reminiscence changes the meaning of both learning and memory at the same time. When learning consists in remembering knowledge not acquired in this life, then the activity of memory cannot be, as it is usually conceived, a recollection of knowledge previously acquired in this life by learning. In order to understand a doctrine in which familiar meanings are so profoundly altered, it is perhaps necessary to understand the problem it tries to solve.

That problem exists only for those who make an absolute distinction between particular sensory images and universal ideas or abstract concepts. Those who, like Hobbes, Berkeley, or Hume, deny universals or abstractions as any part of the mind's content, see no special problem in the origin of that part of the mind's content which is not received as sense impressions. The original impressions are somehow externally caused, and all the rest of the mind's content—its images and memories and all constructions of the sort Locke calls "complex ideas"—then arise by natural derivation from the original sense impressions.

But those who, on the contrary, maintain that ideas or concepts are *not* images of any sort, cannot avoid the problem of how the mind comes by its ideas. One solution of this problem attributes existence to ideas as intelligible objects, and attributes to the mind the power to apprehend them by direct intuition, just as the senses directly apprehend sensible objects. But if ideas, whether or not they exist outside the mind, cannot be apprehended intuitively, then what is the origin of the ideas whereby the mind understands intelligible objects?

To this question, the doctrine of reminiscence is one answer. Another answer is the doctrine of abstraction, as formulated by Aristotle and Aquinas. Locke and James also seem to recognize a distinction in kind between abstractions and other mental content, but they do not appear to find any need for a special power to perform the act of abstracting general ideas or universal concepts from the sensory particulars of perception and imagination. Aquinas, however, thinks that a special faculty called "the active intellect" must be postulated to account for the mind's possession of the ideas or concepts whereby it actually understands what it cannot perceive or imagine.

THESE THEORIES are considered in the chapters on IDEA and MIND. But just as the doctrine of reminiscence is relevant here for its bearing on the discussion of memory, so the doctrine of abstraction which posits an active intellect is relevant to the discussion of imagination.

"Imagination," writes Aristotle, "is different from either perceiving or discursive thinking, though it is not found apart from sensation or judgment without it. That this activity is not the same kind of thinking as judgment is obvious. For imagining lies within our own power whenever we wish (*e.g.*, we can call up a picture, as in the practice of mnemonics by the use of mental images), but in forming opinions we are not free; we cannot escape the alternatives of falsehood or truth."

The point is not that images cannot be false. They frequently are, as (according to Aristotle) sensations never are. But the falsity of our imaginations involves a judgment that things really are as we imagine them to be. If imagination is not accompanied by judgment, the question of truth or falsity does not arise, for in pure imagination we are not concerned with the way things actually exist, but with the possible, *i.e.*, the imaginary rather than the real. "Everyone knows the difference," says James, "between imagining a thing and believing in its existence."

Conceiving imagination as an activity depending upon the prior activity of the senses, Aristotle holds that imagination is "incapable of existing apart from sensation." In this he does not differ from other psychologists. But he also holds that rational thought, which for him is quite distinct from imagination, cannot exist apart from imagination. "To the thinking soul images serve as if they were the contents of perception . . . That is why the soul never thinks without an image."

Aristotle is here saying more than that a special faculty of mind or intellect abstracts the universal form—or what Aquinas calls "the intelligible species"—from the sensory matter of the image, or what Aquinas calls "the phantasm." Aristotle is, in addition, insisting that the act of understanding is always accompanied by imaginative activity. The kind of thinking which depends upon the abstraction of ideas from imagery also depends upon the presence of images when the thinking takes place. "The faculty of thinking," says Aristotle, "thinks the forms in the images"; or, as Aquinas expresses it, "for the intellect to understand actually, not only when it acquires new knowledge, but also when it uses knowledge already acquired, there is need for the act of imagination . . . It must of necessity turn to the phantasms in order to perceive the universal nature existing in the individual." The cooperation of the imagination with the intellect is shown, furthermore, by the fact that "when the act of imagination is hindered by a lesion of the corporeal organ . . . we see that a man is hindered from understanding actually even those things of which he had a previous knowledge."

Augustine, on the contrary, refers to things which "are recognized by us in our minds, without images." When we consider numbers, for example, "it is not their images" that we store in memory, "but the facts themselves." The question of imageless thought—of thinking abstractly without the use of images—seems to be peculiarly insistent in sciences like mathematics, metaphysics, and theology, in which the conceivable may not be imaginable. The objects peculiar to these sciences seem to require the scientist to do without imagery, or, as Aquinas says, "to rise above his imagination."

This may be true even in physics. Atoms, according to Lucretius, are conceivable, but they are no more imaginable than they are perceptible. If we need images to think of them, we must use imagery in a metaphoric way, picturing the atom as the smallest particle imaginable—only more so! To the objection that there must be imageless thought if we can think of incorporeal beings, of which there can be no images or phantasms, Aquinas replies that we do so "by comparison with sensible bodies of which there are phantasms."

ARISTOTLE'S THEORY that the operations of thinking are always dependent on (though not reducible to) acts of imagination, does not imply that imagination is always accompanied by abstract or rational thought. Normally, human thinking and knowing is a work which combines both sense and intellect, both reason and imagination, but sometimes even in man imagination may be active without judgment or reasoning. Brute animals, according to Aristotle, are largely guided by their imaginations "because of the non-existence in them of mind." But when imagination takes the place of thought in men, it is "because of the temporary eclipse of their minds by passion or disease or sleep."

Dreaming seems to be the striking case of imagination divorced from reason's judgment or control. It has long been suspected that animals also dream, but the question whether they can distinguish their dreams from their waking perceptions may prove forever unanswerable. Philosophers and psychologists have, however, asked themselves whether there is any way of being certain of the difference between waking thought and the phantasmagoria of dreams.

Descartes, for example, asks, "How do we know that the thoughts that come in dreams are more false than those that we have when we are awake, seeing that often enough the former are not less lively and vivid than the latter?" It seems to him that "there are no certain indications by which we may clearly distinguish wakefulness from sleep." Even as he writes these words, he can almost persuade himself that he is dreaming. Yet he does find one probable sign whereby to tell dreaming from waking. "Our memory," he observes, "can never connect our dreams with one another, or with the whole course of our lives, as it unites events which happen to us while we are awake."

Aquinas finds other evidences of the difference. When a man is fully asleep, he does not dream at all, for his imagination is inactive as well as his senses and his mind. But as sleep passes gradually into waking, his faculties begin to act again, not merely the imagination, but the reason also, so that "a man may judge that what he sees is a dream, discerning, as it were, between things and their images. Nevertheless, the common sense remains partly suspended, and therefore, although it discriminates some images from reality, yet it is always deceived in some particular. Even while a man is asleep, his sense and imagination may be to some extent free, and similarly the judgment of his intellect may be unfettered, though not entirely. Consequently, if a man syllogizes while asleep, when he wakes up he invariably recognizes a flaw in some respect."

APART FROM QUESTIONS of truth and falsity, or reality and illusion, the nature and causes of dreaming are perennial themes in the tradition of western thought. As different suppositions are made concerning the cause of dreams, so different interpretations are given of their content.

When it is supposed that the dream is inspired by the gods or is a divine visitation, it becomes a medium of divination or prophecy—a way of foretelling the future, or of knowing what the gods intend in general, or for the guidance of some particular man. In the great books of ancient poetry and history, and in the Old Testament as well, dreams, like oracles, are interpreted as supernatural portents, and figure as one of the major sources of prophecy. Aristotle discounts both the fulfillment of dreams and their nonfulfillment, "for coincidences do not occur according to any universal or general law." Regarding prophetic dreams as mere coincidences, he does not find it surprising that "many dreams have no fulfillment." From the fact that "certain of the lower animals also dream," he thinks "it may be concluded that dreams are not sent by God, nor are they designed for the purpose of revealing the future."

Instead, Aristotle proposes natural causes for the origin of dreams. Slight stimulations of the sense organs awaken the dream process and determine its content. "Dreamers fancy that they are affected by thunder and lightning, when in fact there are only faint ringings in their ears . . . or that they are walking through fire and feeling intense heat, when there is only a slight warmth affecting certain parts of the body." Lucretius similarly explains dreams by natural causes, but attributes their content to events which have dominated the thought of waking life.

In dreams, Lucretius writes, "we find,

Each one of us, whatever our desires
Seize and hang onto in our waking hours.
The lawyers plead in court or draw up briefs,
The generals wage wars, the mariners
Fight with their ancient enemy the wind.

This is true even of animals:

Some day, in fact, you'll see a thoroughbred,
Asleep in a stall, break out in a sudden sweat,
His breath come faster and faster, and his sides
Heave as he seems to pass the winning post
Or break as the starting-gate flies open. Hounds
Twitch in their sleep, or try their best to run,
Give tongue, and sniff the air, as if they caught
Scent of their quarry.

IN THE TRADITION of the great books, modern writers like their ancient forebears appeal thus to sensation and memory as the natural causes of the origin and content of dreams. But, ex-

cept for daydreams or waking fantasy, they do not observe that dreaming may be even more profoundly a product of desire. If Freud's extraordinary insight on this point is supported by all the evidences he assembles in his great work, *The Interpretation of Dreams,* then the lateness of this discovery may be thought even more extraordinary than the theory itself.

The theory is not simply that the content of dreams is determined by desires. When Oedipus tells Jocasta of his fear that in taking her to wife he has unwittingly married his mother, she tells him to fear not, for "many men ere now have so fared in dreams also." If that is so, then such dreams do not call for the interpretation which Freud gives. If there are men who suffer from what Freud calls "the Oedipus complex," involving repressed incestuous desires, then the expression of those desires in dreaming will not take the form of imagining them to be actually fulfilled.

On the contrary, Freud's theory of dream symbolism holds that "the dream as remembered is not the real thing at all, but a distorted substitute." Beneath what he calls "the manifest dream-content"—the actual moving images which occupy the dreaming consciousness—lie "the latent dream-thoughts" which are distorted in the actual dream. This distortion "is due to the activities of censorship, directed against the unacceptable unconscious wish-impulses . . . invariably of an objectionable nature, offensive from the ethical, aesthetic, or social point of view, things about which we do not dare to think at all, or think of only with abhorrence." The repressed desires or wishes, the loves or fears, which the dreamer refuses to acknowledge consciously must, therefore, appear in dreams in a disguised form. The imagery of dreams seems to Freud to be a kind of language in which the repressed materials of thought and feeling employ a special symbolism to express what the moral censor will not permit us to express in the ordinary language of our conscious thought or social conversation.

As ordinary language contains symbols conventionally agreed upon, so Freud finds that the recurrence again and again of certain images in the dreams of neurotic patients, and of normal persons as well, gives them the character of conventional symbols. "The number of things which are represented symbolically in dreams is," according to Freud, "not great." They are, he says, "the human body as a whole, parents, children, brothers and sisters, birth, death, nakedness—and one thing more. The only typical, that is to say, regularly occurring, representation of the human form as a whole is that of a *house* . . . When the walls are quite smooth, the house means a man; when there are ledges and balconies which can be caught hold of, a woman. Parents appear in dreams as *emperor* and *empress, king* and *queen,* or other exalted personages . . . Children and brothers are less tenderly treated, being symbolized by little *animals* or *vermin.* Birth is almost invariably represented by some reference to *water* . . . For dying we have setting out upon a *journey* or *travelling* by train. *Clothes* and *uniforms* stand for nakedness." The one thing more, which Freud mentions in

his enumeration, comprises the sexual organs and acts. In contrast to all the others, these, he says, "are represented by a remarkably rich symbolism . . . An overwhelming majority of symbols in dreams are sexual symbols."

Freud points out why it would be a mistake to treat dream symbols like the words of an ordinary language. "Their object is not to tell anyone anything; they are not a means of communication; on the contrary, it is important to them not to be understood." Wresting their secret from such symbols is a remarkable achievement. Aristotle's remark, which Freud quotes, that "the most skilful interpreter of dreams is he who has the faculty of observing resemblances," seems to be borne out in the Freudian method of discovering the latent content of the dream symbolism. But Freud's therapeutic use of what can thus be discovered makes the psychoanalytic method a thing totally unanticipated by any of his predecessors.

57

Metaphysics

INTRODUCTION

In this chapter, as in MATHEMATICS, we must distinguish controversies about the science we are considering from controversies in it. But here the situation is complicated by many ambiguities. In the tradition of western thought, the name of science has never been denied to mathematics, no matter how its subject matter has been defined or what conception of science has prevailed. But controversies about metaphysics often begin, in modern times at least, by questioning our right to use the word "science" when we speak of metaphysical inquiry or speculation. The challenge usually implies that metaphysics cannot be regarded as a body of valid knowledge because the peculiar objects it has chosen to investigate are not susceptible to scientific inquiry.

If experimentation were the *sine qua non* of scientific knowledge, it would follow, of course, that a discipline which could not perform experiments or even less rigorous types of empirical research could not be called a science. But by that standard mathematics would also be ruled out. It does not seem to be the case, however, that mathematics and metaphysics stand or fall together.

Hume, for example, admits the one and excludes the other. If we are persuaded of his principles concerning science, what havoc, he says, must we make when we run over our libraries. "If we take in our hand any volume; of divinity or school metaphysics, for instance; let us ask, *Does it contain any abstract reasoning concerning quantity or number?* No. *Does it contain any experimental reasoning concerning matter of fact and existence?* No. Commit it then to the flames; for it can contain nothing but sophistry and illusion."

Nor does Kant make experimentation or empirical research indispensable to valid and certain knowledge. On the contrary, pure, as opposed to empirical, physics is for him like mathematics in having the superior status of *a priori* knowledge. They are both sciences in the highest sense of the term because they consist of valid synthetic judgments *a priori*. Kant, therefore, does not exclude metaphysics from the ranks of science because he thinks that "metaphysic, according to its proper aim, consists merely of synthetic propositions *a priori*." Not the method of metaphysics, nor the form of its propositions, but the character of its objects seems to be the cause of its frustration, reducing it to what Kant calls an "illusory dialectic" rather than a valid science.

It might be supposed that those who take the opposite view—that metaphysics is a science, even, perhaps, the highest of the sciences—would agree in defining its objects or the scope of its inquiry. This does not seem to be the case, any more than it seems to be true that all those who criticize metaphysics conceive its subject matter in the same way.

Following what he takes to be the traditional conception of metaphysics in the medieval schools, which appears to him to be continued in the writings of René Descartes, Gottfried Wilhelm Leibniz, and Christian Wolff, Kant says that "metaphysic has for the proper object of its inquiries only three grand ideas: God, Freedom, and Immortality." This also seems to be at least part of what Hume has in mind when he refers to "school metaphysics" and associates it with "divinity," by which he means theology, natural or sacred. Yet we find William James saying that "Hume is at bottom as much of a metaphysician as Thomas Aquinas," because he is engaged in speculations concerning the relation or lack of relation, the identity or lack of identity, in the discrete elements of immediate experience. Here the question seems to be not about God, freedom, and immortality, but about the existence of enduring substances underlying all perceptible qualities, or about a fixed order of reality behind the sequence of phenomena in experience. According to James, "the whole question of interaction and influence between things is a metaphysical question, and cannot be discussed at all by those who are unwilling to go into matters thoroughly."

In the Preface to his *The Principles of Psychology*, James declares his plan to limit his own inquiries to what can be known by the empirical methods of the natural sciences. Psychology, like physics, must assume certain data. The discussion of these assumptions, he says, "is called metaphysics and falls outside the province of this book . . . The data assumed by psychology, just like those assumed by physics and the other natural sciences, must sometime be overhauled. The effort to overhaul them clearly and thoroughly is metaphysics; but metaphysics can only perform her task well when distinctly conscious of its great extent." The implication seems to be not that metaphysics is impossible but rather that metaphysics, as James conceives it, does not yet exist in any mature or satisfactory development. "Only a metaphysics alive to the weight of her task," he writes, can hope to be successful. "That will perhaps be centuries hence."

JAMES COULD NOT have fully foreseen the departures in the name of metaphysics that were to occur in the 20th century, though he did have a sympathetic understanding of the direction taken by Bergson. According to Bergson, "Science and metaphysics . . . come together in intuition. A truly intuitive philosophy would realize the much-desired union of science and metaphysics . . . It would put more science into metaphysics, and more metaphysics into science." But we also find Bergson saying that "positive science works . . . with symbols," whereas "*metaphysics . . . is the science which claims to dispense with symbols.*"

The volume in this set that contains 20th-century contributions to philosophy contains two treatises on metaphysics—one by Bergson and one by Heidegger. In the latter, we find a totally different approach to the subject. Heidegger defines metaphysics as the history of the truth about what-is. "If indeed the question of Being as such is the all-embracing question of metaphysics, then the question of Nothing proves to be such as to span the whole metaphysical field"; adding that "because the truth of metaphysics is so unfathomable there is always the lurking danger of profoundest error. Hence no scientific discipline can hope to equal the seriousness of metaphysics. Philosophy can never be measured with the yard-stick of the idea of science."

Physicists and mathematicians in the 20th century also venture into the discussion of metaphysics. Planck remarks that "metaphysical reality does not stand spatially *behind* what is given in experience, but lies fully *within* it . . . The essential point is that the world of sensation is not the only world which may conceivably exist, but that there is still another world. To be sure, this other world is not directly accessible to us, but its existence is indicated, time and again, with compelling clarity . . . by the labors of science." Planck maintains that "scientists have learned that the starting point of their investigations does not lie solely in the perceptions of the senses, and that science cannot exist without some small portion of metaphysics."

The mathematician G. H. Hardy first distinguishes between physical and mathematical reality. He then maintains that "a man who could give a convincing account of mathematical reality would have solved very many of the most difficult problems of metaphysics. If he could include physical reality in his account, he would have solved them all."

As Russell sees it, "Most of the great ambitious attempts of metaphysicians have proceeded by the attempt to prove that such and such apparent features of the actual world were self-contradictory, and therefore could not be real. The whole tendency of modern thought, however, is more and more in the direction of showing that the supposed contradictions were illusory, and that very little can be proved *a priori* from considerations of what *must* be."

WE CANNOT FULLY explore the issue concerning the objects of metaphysics without observing that other names are used in the tradition of the great books to designate the discipline which, rightly or wrongly, claims to be the highest human science. The Greeks initiated the conception of a discipline which should be preeminent because it deals with first principles and highest causes. It not only searches for wisdom about the ultimate realities; it also lays the foundations for all other sciences. But the Greeks do not have one name for this discipline, nor is "metaphysics" even among the various names they use.

Aristotle, whose *Metaphysics* is the first great book to have this word in its title, never uses the word to refer to the science which he is trying to define and establish. In the opening chapters, he speaks of it under the name of wisdom, for "all men suppose what is called Wisdom to deal with the first causes and the principles of all things." There are other theoretical sciences, such as physics and mathematics, which investigate causes or deal with principles, but they do not reach to the highest causes or first principles, nor do they take all things in their most universal aspect as the object of their inquiry.

Though "physics also is a kind of Wisdom," says Aristotle, "it is not the first kind"; and elsewhere he says that "both physics and mathematics must be classed as *parts* of Wisdom." Physics deals only with material things in motion; and "the mathematician investigates abstractions"—objects which, except as abstracted, cannot exist apart from matter and motion. "If there is something which is eternal and immovable and separated from matter, clearly the knowledge of it belongs to a theoretical science—not, however, to physics nor to mathematics, but to a science prior to both." It is that science which is the highest part of wisdom.

Aristotle gives two names to the supreme form of human wisdom or the highest of the theoretical sciences. He denominates it both from the position it occupies in relation to all other disciplines and also in terms of the kind of substance which it alone investigates. If there is "no substance other than those which are formed by nature, natural science (*i.e.*, physics) will be the first science, but if there is an immovable substance, the science of this must be prior and must be first philosophy." But this highest science also deserves to be called "theology" as well as "first philosophy." There are, Aristotle says, "three theoretical philosophies, mathematics, physics, and what we may call theology, since it is obvious that if the divine is present anywhere, it is present in things of this sort," *i.e.*, the eternal, immutable, immaterial.

THERE IS STILL another name for the highest speculative discipline in the Greek conception of the order of the sciences. "Dialectic" is the name which Plato gives to the search for first principles and for the knowledge of the most intelligible realities. As appears in the chapter on DIALECTIC, Aristotle contrasts the dialectician and the philosopher as respectively concerned with opinion and knowledge, but Plato regards the dialectician as preeminently the philosopher. Not only does dialectic belong to the realm of knowledge rather than opinion, but in the realm of knowledge, mathematics occupies the lower, dialectic the upper part. The mathematical sciences build upon hypotheses which they do not and cannot establish. Dialectic uses hypotheses only "as steps and points of departure into a world which is above hypotheses, in order that she may soar beyond them to the first principle of the whole; and . . . by successive steps she descends again without the aid of any sensible object from ideas, through ideas, and in ideas she ends."

Despite all the relevant differences between Plato and Aristotle concerning being and becoming, reason and sense, the intelligible and the sensible, it seems possible to compare the knowledge which Plato calls "dialectic" with what Aristotle calls "first philosophy" or "theology."

Both, for example, proceed from first principles and establish the foundations of the inferior sciences. On its downward path, dialectic, according to Plato, brings the light of reason to bear on the understanding of the hypotheses which are the principles of mathematics. Though Aristotle thinks that mathematics rests on axioms or self-evident truths, he also says that "it must be the business of first philosophy to examine the principles of mathematics" because the mathematician only uses them in a special application without investigating their general truth. Furthermore, the question concerning how the objects of mathematics exist is a question for the first philosopher, not the mathematician.

In the *Sophist,* Plato, to illustrate the difference between the sophist and the dialectician or philosopher, develops an analysis of such terms as being and nonbeing, true and false, same and other, one and many, rest and motion. These, it seems, are the fundamental concepts in the philosopher's knowledge of the ultimate reality. But these are also the fundamental concepts in Aristotle's *Metaphysics.* In the medieval period when "metaphysics" generally replaces "dialectic" as the name for the first philosophy, the so-called transcendental terms—such as *being, essence, other, one, true, good*—are treated as the basic metaphysical concepts; and what is characteristic of them as abstractions helps to characterize the nature of metaphysics as a science.

The word "metaphysics" comes into use as a result of the title supposedly given by the Alexandrian librarians to the work in which Aristotle treats the problems of the first philosophy. The word is short for "the books which come after the books on physics." Plotinus uses the word and connects it with the Platonic meaning of "dialectic." In the training of the metaphysician he says, dialectic is the ultimate study.

Dialectic, according to Plotinus, "is the method, or discipline, that brings with it the power of pronouncing with final truth upon the nature and relation of things—what each is, how it differs from others, what common quality all have, to what kind each belongs and in what rank each stands in its kind and whether its being is real-being, and how many beings there are, and how many non-beings to

be distinguished from beings." But we must not think of dialectic, Plotinus declares, "as the mere tool of the metaphysician." It goes beyond metaphysics as vision or contemplative wisdom goes beyond discursive reasoning and demonstration. "It leaves to another science all that coil of premises and conclusions called the art of reasoning."

THE QUESTION which Plotinus raises—whether there is a higher science or form of knowledge than metaphysics—is naturally considered by the great Christian theologians. In part their answer resembles that of Plotinus; in part it differs. Where Plotinus speaks of dialectic as "the most precious part of philosophy" because it transcends reasoning and argument and reaches the sort of immediate apprehension of reality which cannot be expressed in words, theologians recognize the supremacy of mystical knowledge—a foretaste in this life of what the vision of God will be like in the life to come. But, unlike Plotinus, they do not think such knowledge, here or hereafter, is natural wisdom. Rather it is supernatural knowledge, the divine gift to man of a contemplative wisdom to which his nature cannot attain by its own unaided powers.

The subordination of metaphysical science to knowledge which is both supernatural and nonscientific (*i.e.,* neither discursive nor analytic nor demonstrative) is considered in the chapters on THEOLOGY and WISDOM. Another subordination of metaphysics, considered there also, must be mentioned here as well. That is the subordination of metaphysics to theology. Both metaphysics and theology may be conceived as sciences which are engaged in reasoning and argument and in trying to demonstrate conclusions from principles. But one is merely a human science working with the principles of reason, whereas the other is what Aquinas calls "sacred doctrine," in order to signify that its principles are articles of religious faith.

In the hierarchy of human sciences, metaphysics remains supreme—the first philosophy. It suffers only by comparison with theology insofar as the latter rests upon divine revelation and, since it enjoys the certainty of faith, escapes the insecurity of reason. Though metaphysics and theology differ in their principles and somewhat in their methods, they do not differ entirely in their subject matter. Both, for example, may treat of God and of the existence of immaterial and imperishable beings. Aquinas, therefore, must face the objection that there is no need for any knowledge in addition to metaphysics because "everything that is, is treated of in philosophical science—even God Himself, in that part of philosophy called theology, or the divine science, by Aristotle." To this he replies by giving two reasons for sacred theology.

It is necessary, he says, "for the salvation of man that certain truths which exceed human reason should be made known to him by divine revelation. Even as regards those truths about God which human reason could have discovered, it was necessary that man should be taught by a divine revelation; because the truth about God such as reason could discover, would only be known by a few, and that after a long time, and with the admixture of many errors." Furthermore, he continues, there is no reason "why those things which may be learnt from philosophical science, so far as they can be known by natural reason, may not also be taught us by another science so far as they fall within revelation. Hence the theology included in sacred doctrine differs in kind from that theology which is a part of philosophy."

These two kinds of theology are traditionally distinguished as natural and sacred. When Francis Bacon divides the sciences "into theology and philosophy," he adds that "in the former we do not include natural theology." Natural theology is the divine part of philosophy, yet it is clearly distinct from sacred theology or what Bacon calls "inspired divinity."

This distinction, in whatever language it is made, raises two problems. The first concerns the relation of natural to sacred theology, especially with regard to the scope of natural theology and the precise nature of its independence of sacred doctrine. On this question there seems to be considerable difference between such writers as Augustine and Aquinas, or Bacon and Descartes. As already noted, the various issues involved are reserved for discussion in the chapter on THEOLOGY. The second problem is directly pertinent to metaphysics alone. The question is whether metaphysics and natural theology are identical in subject matter or scope, or whether natural theology is only a part of metaphysics.

Aristotle seems to answer this question when he suggests that "first philosophy" and "theology" are interchangeable designations for the highest branch of speculative knowledge. To the extent that he declares this science to be an inquiry concerning the existence and nature of immaterial and imperishable substances, his definition of the object of metaphysics would seem to justify the title of theology.

Descartes, who also separates metaphysics from physics by reference to the immateriality and materiality of the substances which are their objects, even more explicitly seems to give the whole of metaphysics a theological character. In the Preface to his *Meditations on First Philosophy,* he says that he is concerned to treat of "God and the human soul"; for, as he explains to the professors of Sacred Theology of the Sorbonne, "I have always considered that the two questions respecting God and the soul were the chief of those that ought to be demonstrated by philosophical rather than theological argument."

Though he adds the freedom of the human will to the existence of God and the immortality of the soul, Kant's definition of the objects of metaphysical speculation similarly makes metaphysics an inquiry into things which lie outside the realm of physics and associates it with the traditional subject matter of theology, at least in the sense that here reason tries to prove propositions which are the main tenets of religious faith. In his Preface to the first edition of *The Critique of Pure Reason,* Kant remarks that when reason "finds itself compelled to have recourse to principles which transcend the region of experience," it "falls into confusion and contradictions . . . The arena of these endless contests is called Metaphysic."

IF NOTHING IMMATERIAL exists, if there are no beings apart from the changing things of sense-experience, or if, although such things exist, they cannot be known by reason proceeding in the manner of speculative science, does it follow that metaphysics must also be denied existence, at least as a speculative science? The answer seems to be clear. If the declared objects of a science do not exist, or if those objects are unknowable by the methods which that science proposes to follow, then it seems difficult to defend its claims to be a valid science against those who challenge them. The controversy over the validity of metaphysics would thus appear to turn on the truth or falsity of the two "ifs" just mentioned.

But the matter cannot be so resolved if natural theology does not exhaust the whole of metaphysics; that is, if metaphysics considers objects other than the immaterial, and if it inquires into their nature rather than their existence. Aristotle's definition of the subject matter of the first philosophy seems to contain an alternative conception of metaphysics, one which may be quite consistent with the conception of it as theology, but which, however, gives it problems to solve in the realm of physical things.

"There is a science," Aristotle writes, "which investigates being as being and the attributes which belong to being in virtue of its own nature." This definition of the first philosophy seems to differentiate it from mathematics and physics as sharply as the other definition in terms of immaterial and imperishable substances. The other sciences, according to Aristotle, do not treat of "being *qua* being universally." The properties of anything which is "in so far as it has being, and the contraries in it *qua* being, it is the business of no other science to investigate; for to physics one would assign the study of things not *qua* being, but rather *qua* sharing in movement"; and mathematics is concerned with the attributes of things insofar as they are "quantitative and continuous." These sciences "mark off some particular kind of being, some genus, and inquire into this, but not being simply, nor *qua* being . . . Similarly, these sciences omit the question whether the genus with which they deal exists or does not exist, because it belongs to the same kind of thinking to show what it is and that it is."

Only the first philosophy "does not inquire about particular subjects in so far as each has some attribute or other, but speculates about being, in so far as each particular thing is." Its subject matter, then, includes *all* existing things as existing, and involves not only the question how anything which exists exists (*i.e.*, the properties of being), but also the question whether certain things, whose existence can be questioned, do in fact exist. Whatever truths hold good for all things *qua* being—such as the principle that the same thing cannot both be and not be in the same respect at the same time—belong to the first philosophy, even though, as in this case Aristotle points out, the law of contradiction may also belong to logic as the principle of demonstration.

THIS BROADER CONCEPTION of the first philosophy explains, as its restriction to natural theology could not explain, why the central books in Aristotle's *Metaphysics* treat of sensible, physical substances; their nature as substances; the distinction between substance and accident, form and matter, potentiality and actuality, as principles of the composite nature of changing substances; and the properties of such existences in virtue of their having being, *e.g.,* their unity and divisibility, their sameness and otherness.

Aristotle does not inquire whether such substances exist. He seems to take their existence as unquestionable, for he frequently refers to physical things as "the readily recognized substances." But in addition to the question "how sensible substances exist," there are such questions as "whether there are or are not any besides sensible substances . . . and whether there is a substance capable of separate existence, apart from sensible substances, and if so why and how." These latter questions lead to the concluding books of the *Metaphysics* which inquire into the existence of the non-sensible, the immaterial, the immutable. If Aristotle's theology begins here, then theology is only a part—the crowning part, perhaps—of a larger science whose object is not a special realm of being, but all of being.

Hobbes and Bacon go further than Aristotle in the direction of opposing the identification of metaphysics with theology. Where Aristotle seems to admit theological subject matter as a part of the first philosophy, they exclude it entirely.

Hobbes does not use the word "metaphysics" in his own classification of the sciences; he employs it only as a term of derogation to refer to scholastic doctrines which he repudiates. His own classification makes *philosophia prima* that branch of natural philosophy which is prior to the mathematical and mechanical sciences. The latter deal with determinate quantity and motion. The antecedent science deals with "quantity and motion *indeterminate*." These "being the principles or first foundation of philosophy," the science which deals with them "is called *Philosophia Prima*."

Bacon distinguishes between first philosophy and metaphysics and between metaphysics and natural theology. First philosophy, he says, is "the common parent of sciences." It is concerned with "axioms, not peculiar to any science, but common to a number of them" and also with "the adventitious or transcendental condition of things, such as little, much, like, different, possible, impossible, entity, nonentity, etc." Natural theology, which is the divine part of philosophy because it inquires about "God, unity, goodness, angels, and spirits," is separate from the rest of natural philosophy.

"But to assign the proper office of metaphysics, as contra-distinguished from primary philosophy and natural theology," Bacon writes, "we must note that as physics regards the things which are wholly immersed in matter and movable, so metaphysics regards what is more abstracted and fixed; that physics supposes only existence, motion, and natural necessity, whilst metaphysics supposes also mind and idea . . . As we have divided natural philosophy into the investigation of causes and the production of effects, and referred the investigation of causes to theory, which we again divide into physical and metaphysical, it is necessary that the real difference of these two be drawn from the nature of the causes they inquire into." Physics, according to Bacon, inquires into efficient and material causes; metaphysics, into formal and final causes; and as

mechanics is the practical application of physical theory, so what Bacon calls "magic" is the practical doctrine that corresponds to the metaphysical theory of forms.

AGREEMENT OR disagreement concerning the subject matter and problems of that which claims to be the highest human science, however named, does not seem to be uniformly accompanied by agreement or disagreement concerning the status and development of the discipline in question.

There seems to be some similarity, for example, between Plato's dialectic as an inquiry into forms and Bacon's notion of metaphysics as concerned with formal causes—a similarity which Bacon himself observes. But where Plato seems to think that dialectic exists, to be taught and learned, Bacon's judgment is that this part of metaphysics, if not the part dealing with final causes, has not yet been developed because the right method has not been employed.

Again, Aristotle's conception of metaphysics as concerned with the primary axioms, the universal principles applicable to all existence, and the transcendental properties of being, seems to bear some resemblance to Bacon's primary philosophy. But Bacon writes as if Aristotle's *Metaphysics* had not been written, or at least as if it had not succeeded, as Aristotle might have supposed it had, in establishing the science which Bacon finds for the most part in a defective or undeveloped condition.

If we turn to natural theology, either as a part of metaphysics (with Aristotle), or as separate from metaphysics (with Bacon), or as identical with metaphysics (with Descartes), we find the same situation. Aside from some verbal and some real differences concerning the objects of the inquiry, Aristotle, Bacon, and Descartes think that the existence of beings apart from the sensible world of matter and change can be demonstrated and that something can be known of their nature—whether they are called immaterial substances, spirits, and intelligences, or God, angels, and souls.

With some alterations in language and thought, Plato and Plotinus, Augustine and Aquinas, Spinoza and Locke can be added to this company. They are theologians in that sense of "theology" which implies a rational knowledge—without religious faith, and either by intuition or demonstration—of beings which really exist, yet are not sensible or material or mutable or finite. Spinoza, for example, does not use the word "metaphysics," but he holds that "the human mind possesses an adequate knowledge of the eternal and infinite essence of God." Although Locke's use of the word "metaphysics" is derogatory, and though the purpose of his essay *Concerning Human Understanding* is to prevent human inquiries from extending beyond man's capacities, he attributes greater certainty to our knowledge of God and the soul than to our knowledge of bodies, and finds no greater difficulty in our speculations about spirits than about particles of matter.

"Experimenting and discovering in ourselves knowledge, and the power of voluntary motion, as certainly as we experiment, or discover in things without us, the cohesion and separation of solid parts, which is the extension and motion of bodies," Locke writes, "we have as much reason to be satisfied with our notion of immaterial spirit, as with our notion of body, and the existence of the one as well as the other . . . But whichever of these complex ideas be clearest, that of body, or immaterial spirit, this is evident, that the simple ideas that make them up are no other than what we have received from sensation or reflection; and so is it of all our other ideas of substances, even of God himself."

As we have already seen, Hume and Kant deny metaphysics (so far as it is identified with what is traditionally natural theology) the status of a valid theoretical science. For them it is incapable of taking its place beside physics and mathematics. Hume, in addition, denies validity to metaphysical speculation concerning causes and substances in the natural order. Unlike Hume, who simply removes metaphysical problems from the realm of questions worth thinking about, Kant does not reject the problems but rather offers alternative methods of stating and solving them. He hopes thereby to accomplish a reformation rather than an abolition of metaphysical inquiry.

The existence of God, freedom, and immortality must be affirmed, Kant thinks, in the order of practical, not speculative reason. They are indispensable "conditions of the necessary object of our will . . . that is to say, conditions of the practical use of pure reason." Yet, he adds, "we cannot affirm that we *know* and *understand,* I will not say the actuality, but even the possibility, of them."

Furthermore, by redefining metaphysics to mean "any system of knowledge *a priori* that consists of pure conceptions," Kant not only gives his fundamental treatises in morals and ethics a metaphysical character, but sees the possibility of a genuine metaphysic emerging from *The Critique of Pure Reason.* Once "the dogmatism of metaphysic" has been removed, "that is, the presumption that it is possible to achieve anything in metaphysic without a previous criticism of pure reason . . . it may not be too difficult to leave a bequest to posterity in the shape of a systematical metaphysic, carried out according to the critique of pure reason."

Kant's transcendental philosophy, and especially what he calls "the architectonic of pure reason," is in a sense that metaphysic already begun. In subject matter, if not in its method or conclusions, it resembles the traditional inquiry concerning the universal principles and transcendental properties of being. The objects of natural theology are, of course, excluded as being beyond the power of reason to know in a speculative manner.

Metaphysics as a possible science is for Kant "nothing more than the inventory of all that is given us by *pure reason,* systematically arranged . . . Such a system of pure speculative reason," he says in his original preface to the *Critique,* "I hope to be able to publish under the title of *Metaphysic of Nature.*" And in the last pages of the *Critique,* wherein he criticizes all speculative efforts in the sphere of natural theology, Kant reaffirms "the speculative and the practical use of pure reason" to constitute "a Metaphysic of Nature and a Metaphysic of Ethics." The former, he says, is "what is commonly called Metaphysic in the more limited sense." Both together "form properly that department of knowledge which may be termed, in the truest sense of the word, philosophy.

The path which it pursues is that of science, which, when it has once been discovered, is never lost, and never misleads."

CONTROVERSIES ABOUT metaphysics can be distinguished from metaphysical controversies—that is, disputes within the field of metaphysical thought. We have confined our attention to the former throughout this chapter. But it may not be possible to judge, much less to resolve, the issues about the scope, methods, and validity of metaphysics without engaging in, or at least facing, issues which are themselves metaphysical.

The only way to escape this would be to suppose that psychology (as an analysis of the powers of the mind) or epistemology (as a theory of the criteria of valid knowledge) could determine in advance of any examination of metaphysical discussion whether the matters to be discussed fall within the range of questions concerning which the human mind has the power to find and validate answers. But if this supposition is untenable in itself; or if it is untenable because psychology and epistemology, when they are treated as the first philosophy, themselves presuppose a metaphysics or conceal their metaphysical presuppositions; then no alternative remains but to judge metaphysics directly by its fruits.

In that case, the issues surveyed in this chapter require an examination of the metaphysical discussions to be found in such chapters as GOD, ANGEL, IDEA, SOUL, IMMORTALITY, WILL (which are relevant particularly to the problems of natural theology); and (as relevant to other parts or problems of metaphysics) such chapters as BEING, CAUSE, FORM, MATTER, ONE AND MANY, RELATION, SAME AND OTHER.

58

Mind

INTRODUCTION

IN the tradition of the great books, the word "mind" is used less frequently than "reason," "intellect," "understanding," or "soul." There are still other words, like "intelligence," "consciousness," and even "spirit" or "psyche," which often carry some part of the connotation of the word "mind." Certain authors use "mind" as a synonym for one or another of these words, and give it the meaning which other writers express exclusively in terms of "reason" or "understanding." Some discuss mind without reference to soul, some identify mind with soul or spirit, and some conceive mind as only a part of soul or spirit.

For the purpose of assembling in a single chapter references to all discussions which fall within the area of meaning common to all these terms, it was necessary to adopt some single covering word. Our choice of "mind" is partly the result of its present currency, partly the result of the fact that it is somewhat more neutral than the others and therefore less prejudicial to the conflicting theories which are juxtaposed in this chapter.

Words like "reason" or "intellect" usually imply a sharper distinction between the functions or faculties of sensation and thought than does the word "mind." Imagination and memory, for example, are attributed to the understanding in the writings of Locke and Hume, whereas, in the analytic vocabulary of Aristotle and Aquinas, imagination and memory belong to sense, not to reason or intellect. Similarly, words like "soul" or "spirit" usually connote a substantial as well as an immaterial mode of being, whereas "mind" can have the meaning of a faculty or a power to be found in living organisms.

The adoption of the word "mind" is purely a matter of convenience. It begs no questions and decides no issues. The relations between what is here discussed and the matters considered in the chapters on SOUL, SENSE, MEMORY AND IMAGINATION, remain the same as they would be if "reason" or "intellect" were used in place of "mind." Different formulations of these relationships are not affected by the words used, but by different theories of what the mind is, however it is named.

Before we consider the diverse conceptions of the human mind which are enumerated under the seven main divisions of the first section in the Outline of Topics, it may be useful to examine the elements of meaning more or less common to the connotation of all the words which "mind" here represents. Even here we must avoid begging the question whether mind is a peculiarly human possession. Other animals may have minds. Mind may be, as it is on one theory, a universal property of matter. According to another theory, there may be superhuman minds or intelligences, or a single absolute mind, a transcendent intelligence.

What, then, does the universe contain because there is mind in it, which would be lacking if everything else could remain the same with mind removed? The facts we are compelled to mention in answering this question should give us some indication of the elements of meaning common to "mind" and all its synonyms.

FIRST IS THE FACT of thought or thinking. If there were no evidence of thought in the world, mind would have little or no meaning. The recognition of this fact throughout the tradition accounts for the development of diverse theories of mind. None of the great writers denies the phenomenon of thought, however differently each may describe or explain it; none, therefore, is without some conception of mind.

It may be supposed that such words as "thought" or "thinking" cannot, because of their own ambiguity, help us to define the sphere of mind. But whatever the relation of thinking to sensing, thinking seems to involve more—for almost all observers—than a mere reception of impressions from without. This seems to be the opinion of those who make thinking a consequence of sensing, as well as of those who regard thought as independent of sense. For both, thinking goes beyond sensing, either as an elaboration of the materials of sense or as an apprehension of objects which are totally beyond the reach of the senses. To the extent that this insight is true, the elements or aspects of thought discussed in the chapters on IDEA, JUDGMENT, and REASONING have an obvious relevance to the various theories of mind discussed in this chapter.

THE SECOND FACT which seems to be a root common to all conceptions of mind is that of knowledge or knowing. This may be questioned on the ground that if there were sensation without any form of thought, judgment, or reasoning, there would be at least a rudimentary form of knowledge—some degree of consciousness or awareness by one thing of another. Granting the point of this objection, it nevertheless seems to be true that the distinction between truth and falsity, and the difference between knowledge, error, and ignorance, or knowledge, belief, and opinion, do not apply to sensations in the total absence of thought. The chapter on KNOWLEDGE reports formulations of these distinctions or differences. Any understanding of knowledge which involves them seems to imply mind for the same reason that it implies thought.

"The faculty of being acquainted with things other than itself," Russell writes, "is the main characteristic of a mind ... it is this that constitutes the mind's power of knowing things. If we say that the things known must be in the mind, we are either unduly limiting the mind's power of knowing, or we are utter-

ing a mere tautology." The tautology becomes apparent when "we mean by '*in* the mind' the same as by '*before* the mind,' i.e. if we mean merely being apprehended by the mind."

There is a further implication of mind in the fact of self-knowledge. Sensing may be awareness of an object and to this extent it may be a kind of knowing, but it has never been observed that the senses can sense or be aware of themselves. Take, for example, definitions of sense, or theories of sensation and the objects of sense. Such definitions and theories must be regarded as works of reflective thought; they are not products of sensation.

Thought seems to be not only reflective, but reflexive, that is, able to consider itself, to define the nature of thinking and to develop theories of mind. This fact about thought—its reflexivity—also seems to be a common element in all the meanings of "mind." It is sometimes referred to as "the reflexivity of the intellect" or as "the reflexive power of the understanding" or as "the ability of the understanding to reflect upon its own acts" or as "self-consciousness." Whatever the phrasing, a world without self-consciousness or self-knowledge would be a world in which the traditional conception of mind would probably not have arisen.

THE THIRD FACT is the fact of purpose or intention, of planning a course of action with foreknowledge of its goal, or working in any other way toward a desired and foreseen objective. As in the case of sensitivity, the phenomena of desire do not, without further qualification, indicate the realm of mind. According to the theory of natural desire, for example, the natural tendencies of even inanimate and insensitive things are expressions of desire. But it is not in that sense of desire that the fact of purpose or intention is here taken as evidence of mind.

It is rather on the level of the behavior of living things that purpose seems to require a factor over and above the senses, limited as they are to present appearances. It cannot be found in the passions which have the same limitation as the senses, for unless they are checked they tend toward immediate emotional discharge. That factor, called for by the direction of conduct to future ends, is either an element common to all meanings of "mind" or is at least an element associated with mind.

It is sometimes called the faculty of will—rational desire or the intellectual appetite. Sometimes it is treated as the act of willing which, along with thinking, is one of the two major activities of mind or understanding; and sometimes purposiveness is regarded as the very essense of mentality. Considerations relevant to this aspect of mind are discussed in the chapter on WILL. The understanding of will as intellectual appetite is to be found not only in Aquinas but also in Calvin. Both treat these two faculties of man as conjoined—one a power of reasoning and understanding, the other a power of intention and choice.

THESE THREE OR FOUR FACTS—thought, knowledge or self-knowledge, and purpose—seem to be common to all theories of mind. More than that, they seem to be facts which require the development of the conception. They are, for the most part, not questioned in the tradition of the great books; but they are not always seen in the same light. They are not always related in the same way to one another and to other relevant considerations. From such differences in interpretation and analysis arise the various conflicting conceptions of the human mind.

The conflict of theories concerning *what* the human mind is, what *structure* it has, what *parts* belong to it or what *whole* it belongs to, does not comprise the entire range of controversy on the subject. Yet enough is common to all theories of mind to permit certain other questions to be formulated.

How does the human mind operate? How does it do whatever is its work, and with what intrinsic excellences or defects? What is the relation of mind to matter, to bodily organs, to material conditions? Is mind a common possession of men and animals, or is whatever might be called mind in animals distinctly different from the human mind? Are there minds or a mind in existence apart from man and the whole world of corporeal life?

Such questions constitute the major topics of this chapter. Other topics which appear here, such as the moral and political aspects of mind, are reserved for discussion in the many other chapters devoted to the great ideas of moral and political thought. Still others, like the problem of insanity—the loss or derangement of mind—are obviously relevant here even though the more general consideration of psychopathology belongs elsewhere, *e.g.,* in the chapter on MEDICINE.

The intelligibility of the positions taken in the dispute of the issues which are here our major concern depends to some degree on the divergent conceptions of the human mind from which they stem. It seems necessary, therefore, to examine the seven notions of mind which appear in the great books. This will at least provide the general context for the reader's further explorations, even if it is not possible to trace the implications each of these notions may have for the great controversial issues.

Seven is, of course, a fiction of analysis. There are, from one point of view, more—perhaps as many as there are, among the great authors, thinkers who have dwelt at length on the subject. From another point of view, there may be fewer than seven, for when the lines are drawn according to certain basic differences, several of these theories appear to be variants of a single doctrine.

"THAT IN THE SOUL which is called mind," Aristotle writes, is "that whereby the soul thinks and judges." For him, as for Plato, the human intellect or reason is a part or power of the soul of man, distinct from other parts or faculties, such as the senses and the imagination, desire and the passions. Though the human soul is distinguished from the souls of other living things by virtue of its having this part or power, and is therefore called by Aristotle a "rational soul," these writers do not identify mind and soul. As soul is the principle of life and all vital activities, so mind is the subordinate principle of knowledge and the activities of thinking, deliberating, deciding.

Within the general framework of this theory, many differences exist between Plato and Aristotle and between them and others who share their views. These differences arise not only with respect to the soul of which the intellect is a part, but also with respect to the power or activity of the intellect itself. For example, the distinction which Aristotle initiates, between mind as an active and as a passive power, is more explicitly formulated by Aquinas in his theory of the active intellect and the intellect as potential.

The human intellect, Aquinas writes, "is in potentiality to things intelligible, and is at first *like a clean tablet on which nothing is written*, as the Philosopher says. This is made clear from the fact that at first we are only in potentiality towards understanding, and afterwards we are made to understand actually. And so it is evident that with us to understand is *in a way to be passive*." But the forms of things, or what Aquinas calls their "intelligible species," are not actually intelligible as they exist in material things. He therefore argues that in addition to the "power receptive of such species, which is called the *possible intellect* by reason of its being in potentiality to such species," there must also be another intellectual power, which he calls the active or "agent" intellect. Nothing, he says, can be "reduced from potentiality to act except by something in act" or already actual. "We must therefore assign on the part of the intellect some power to make things actually intelligible, by the abstraction of the species from material conditions. Such is the necessity for positing an agent intellect."

The more explicit formulation which Aquinas gives of the distinction between the active and the possible intellects as distinct powers has further consequences for the analysis of three states of the passive or possible intellect distinguished by Aristotle. The intellectual power which is receptive of the intelligible species may either be in complete potentiality to them, as it is when it has not yet come to understand certain things. Or it may be described as in habitual possession of the intelligible species when it has previously acquired the understanding of certain things, but is not now actually engaged in understanding them. In the third place, the potential intellect may also be actual or in act whenever it is actually exercising its habit of

understanding or is for the first time actually understanding something.

In this traditional theory of mind, many other distinctions are made in the sphere of mental activity, but none is thought to require a division of the mind into two distinct powers, or even to require the discrimination of several states of the same power. Just as Plato regards the intuition or direct apprehension of intelligible objects as an activity of the same intelligence which is able to reason discursively about the ideas it can contemplate, so Aristotle and Aquinas assign three different activities to the intellectual power which apprehends intelligible objects, not by intuition, but only as the result of the abstraction of forms from matter by the active intellect.

Once the possible intellect is actualized by the reception of the abstracted species, it can act in three ways. It can express in concepts the species which have been impressed upon it. This—the first act of the intellect— is conception. Its second and third acts—of judgment and of reasoning—consist in forming propositions out of concepts and in seeing how one proposition follows from others in inference or proof.

Unlike abstraction and conception, which Aquinas assigns to the active and the possible intellect respectively, conception, judgment, and reasoning do not, in his opinion, require distinct powers. Nor do the two kinds of thought or reasoning which Aquinas calls "speculative" and "practical." The speculative and practical intellects, he maintains, "are not distinct powers," for they differ only in their ends. The speculative intellect "directs what it apprehends, not to operation, but to the sole consideration of truth"; the practical intellect "directs what it apprehends to operation" or action. But to the nature of intellect as a power of apprehension, "it is accidental whether it be directed to operation or not."

NOT ALL THE foregoing distinctions are made, or made in the same way, by Plato, Aristotle and other authors like Plotinus, Augustine, or Aquinas, who stand together in regarding mind as only a part of the human soul. Lucretius belongs with them on this point, though he differs radically from them on the issue of mind and matter. Mind, for him, is only "the force that gives direction" to the soul, "the lord and master / Holding dominion over all the body." It is only the thinking or deciding part of the soul. But Plato, Aristotle, and their followers make a distinction in kind between sensations or images and universal ideas or abstract concepts. Sense and intellect are for them distinct faculties of knowing and have distinct objects of knowledge. For Lucretius, on the other hand, thinking is merely a re-working of the images received by the senses. In this one respect at least, Lucretius is more closely associated with the theory of mind to be found in Hobbes, Locke, and Hume.

In the consideration of mind, agreement on one point seems everywhere to be accompanied by disagreement on another. Locke does not agree with Lucretius or Hobbes about the materiality of mind; and though he agrees with Berkeley that mind is a spiritual entity, he does not agree with him, any more than he agrees with Hobbes and Hume, about the abstraction of general concepts from particular sense-impressions. Plato and Aristotle agree that the senses and the intellect or reason are quite distinct, but they do not agree about the relation of these faculties, especially not on the extent to which the mind can act independently of sense and imagination. Augustine seems to share Plato's doctrine of reminiscence as an account of how the senses recall actively to mind ideas it has always somehow possessed. Aquinas adopts Aristotle's doctrine of abstraction as the quite contrary account of the role the senses play in providing the materials on which the mind works to obtain ideas. But Augustine and Aquinas come together on another point in which they depart alike from Aristotle and Plato. They distinguish with precision between the intellect and will as separate faculties of the soul, whereas Plato and Aristotle treat thinking and willing (or knowing and loving) as merely diverse aspects of mental life.

THE SAME SITUATION prevails with respect to the other theories of mind which we must now consider in their own terms. Descartes, for example, resembles Plato and Augustine on the point on which we have seen that they together differ from Aristotle and Aquinas, namely, the relation of mind or reason to the senses or imagination. Yet he is also closer to Aristotle and Plato in a respect in which they together differ from Augustine and Aquinas, namely, in regarding thinking and willing as acts of the mind rather than as belonging to completely separate faculties.

These agreements and differences occur in the context of a basic opposition between Descartes and all the other writers so far mentioned. Unlike all of them, he *identifies* the human mind with the rational soul of man. In the dual nature of man, he says, "there are certain activities, which we call corporeal, *e.g.,* magnitude, figure, motion, and all those that cannot be thought of apart from extension in space; and the substance in which they exist is called *body* . . . Further, there are other activities, which we call *thinking* activities, *e.g.,* understanding, willing, imagining, feeling, etc., which agree in falling under the description of thought, perception, or consciousness. The substance in which they reside we call a *thinking thing* or *the mind,* or any other name we care, provided only we do not confound it with corporeal substance, since thinking activities have no affinity with corporeal activities, and thought, which is the common nature in which the former agree, is totally different from extension, the common term for describing the latter." Descartes denies that brutes possess thought, but "even though I were to grant," he says, "that thought existed in them, it would in nowise follow that the human mind was not to be distinguished from the body, but on the contrary that in other animals also there was a mind distinct from their body."

The two components of human nature are, according to Descartes, each of them substances—a *res cogitans* or a thinking substance and a *res extensa* or an extended substance. Descartes uses the phrases "rational soul" and "mind" interchangeably. Reason or intellect—the capacity to think—is not a power of the soul. Nor is thinking an act which the soul sometimes performs, sometimes does not. It is the very essence of the soul itself, even as extension is the essence of body. Just as bodies cannot exist without actually having three dimensions, so the mind cannot exist without thinking.

Though it is literally translated into English by "I think, therefore I am," Descartes's *cogito, ergo sum* can be rendered by "Thinking is; therefore, the mind is," or by the strictly equivalent statement, "The mind exists; therefore, there is thinking." It is precisely this equation of the mind's existence with the activity of thought which Locke challenges. "We know certainly, by experience," he writes, "that we sometimes think, and thence draw this infallible consequence, that there is something in us that has the power to think; but whether that substance perpetually thinks or not, we can be no farther assured than experience informs us . . . I grant that the soul in a waking man is never without thought, because it is the condition of being awake: but whether sleeping, without dreaming, be not an affection of the whole man, mind as well as body, may be worth a waking man's consideration . . . Methinks every drowsy nod shakes their doctrine, who teach that the soul is always thinking."

What is striking about this disagreement is that Locke and Descartes agree in their conception of man as a union of two distinct substances—the union of a material substance or body with a spiritual substance, a mind or soul. It is not surprising, however, that Berkeley should hold the Cartesian view against Locke. Considering the flow of time in terms of the succession of ideas, Berkeley affirms it to be "a plain consequence that the soul always thinks." To try to "abstract the *existence* of a spirit from its cogitation" is, he adds modestly, "no easy task." He might have said it is impossible, for since he holds that bodies do not exist and that man consists of mind or spirit alone, he need not hesitate to assert that the mind cannot cease to think without ceasing to be. Neither he nor Descartes is, in William James's opinion, "free to take the appearances for what they seem to be, and to admit that the mind, as well as the body, may go to sleep."

Despite these differences, Descartes, Locke, and Berkeley seem to agree on the range of activities within the sphere of mind. The mind is a thinking substance for Descartes, yet it also senses and imagines, suffers passions, and exercises acts of will. What Descartes says in terms of acts, Locke says in terms of powers. Mind has many distinct powers, among which Locke includes all the cognitive faculties (not only the powers of abstract thought and reasoning, but also those of sense and imagination), and such voluntary faculties as choosing and willing. Berkeley also includes the whole range of psychological phenomena—sensation, imagination, memory, the passions, reasoning, and choice.

Hume takes a similar view, though in his case one basic qualification must be added. He does not conceive the mind as a soul or a spirit or any other sort of substance. He even has some difficulty with the notion of its continuity or identity from moment to moment in the flow of experience. Yet, he says, "it cannot be doubted that the mind is endowed with several powers and faculties, that these powers are distinct from each other . . . There are many obvious distinctions of this kind, such as those between will and understanding, the imagination and the passions, which fall within the comprehension of every human creature." What the mind is or how it exists, we may not be able to say; but Hume thinks that "if we can go no farther than this mental geography, or delineation of the distinct parts and powers of the mind, it is at least a satisfaction to go so far."

Descartes's theory of mind seems to serve as a point of departure in another direction from that taken by Locke. Spinoza agrees that the mind is a thinking thing. He agrees that man consists of an individual body united with an individual mind. But he differs from Descartes on the meaning of substance. By its very nature, substance is infinite; and because it is infinite, there can be only one substance, which is God. Finite individual things, whether bodies or minds, do not exist as substances, but as modes of the divine attributes.

"The human mind is a part of the infinite intellect of God, and therefore," Spinoza declares, "when we say that the human mind perceives this or that thing, we say nothing less than that God has this or that idea." He includes love and desire, as well as perception and imagination, among the affections of the mind, even calling them "modes of thought." He adds, however, that these do not exist apart from the idea of the thing loved or desired, "though the idea may exist although no other mode of thinking exist."

OF THE REMAINING three of the seven conceptions of mind here being considered, two bear certain resemblances to theories already mentioned. Bergson's conception of mind does not seem to be covered by any of the seven mentioned. For him, mind is continually in a state of flux. "There is no state of mind, however simple," he writes, "which does not change every moment."

Hegel's view of the human mind as a phase or dialectical moment of the Absolute Mind or Spirit seems comparable to Spinoza's conception of the human mind as a part of God's infinite intellect. The Hegelian theory of mind, developed in such works as *The Phenomenology of Mind* and *The Philosophy of Mind,* is reflected in his *The Philosophy of History* and in his *The Philosophy of Right*. The expression of his view of mind appears, therefore, in the chapters on HISTORY and STATE, as well as here.

There seems to be similar justification for associating the views of James with those of Locke and Hume. Willing to posit a soul "influenced in some mysterious way by the brain states and responding to them by conscious affections of its own," James goes on to say that "the bare phenomenon, however, the immediately known thing which on the mental side is in apposition with the entire brain-process is the state of consciousness and not the soul itself."

What the soul is and whether it exists belong to metaphysics. So far as psychological observation and analysis are concerned, the phenomena of mind are to be found in the stream of thought or consciousness. States of mind are states of consciousness. James uses the words "feeling" or "thought" to cover every type of mental operation, every state of mind, every form of consciousness, including sensations and emotions, desires and wishes, as well as conception and reasoning.

Locke and Hume distinguish powers of the mind according to different types of mental operation. James tends rather to analyze the mind in terms of its diverse states according to different types of mental content. But he also lays great stress on the dynamic interconnection of the various elements of consciousness in the continuous flow of the stream of thought.

Freud too presents an analysis of different types of mental content and accompanies it by a theory of the different layers of mind—or psychic structure. He holds, for example, that "we have two kinds of unconscious—that which is latent but capable of becoming conscious, and that which is repressed and not capable of becoming conscious in the ordinary way . . . That which is latent, and only unconscious in the descriptive and not in the dynamic sense, we call *preconscious;* the term unconscious we reserve for the dynamically unconscious repressed, so that we have three terms, conscious (Cs), preconscious (Pcs), and unconscious (Ucs)."

Like James, Freud is concerned with the dynamic interaction of various mental operations or contents. In addition, a further point of similarity exists between them. James says that "the pursuance of future ends and the choice of means for their attainment are . . . the mark and criterion of the presence of mentality . . . No actions but such as are done for an end, and show a choice of means, can be called indubitable expressions of Mind." Freud goes further in the same direction. By identifying "psychic energy in general" with what he calls "libido," he implies that mind in its most primitive form has entirely the aspect of desire or seeking. It expresses itself in "two fundamentally different kinds of instincts, the sexual instincts in the widest sense of the word . . . and the aggressive instincts, whose aim is destruction."

FINALLY, THERE IS the theory in which mind is neither one of the faculties of the soul, nor itself a thinking substance; nor is it a soul or spirit with a diversity of powers. "All our knowledge," Kant writes, "begins with sense, proceeds thence to understanding, and ends with reason beyond which nothing higher can be discovered in the human mind for elaborating the matter of intuition and subjecting it to the highest unity of thought." These three faculties have distinct functions for Kant. The sensitive faculty is a faculty of intuition. The faculty of understanding is a faculty of judgment and scientific knowledge. The faculty of reason, when properly employed, performs a critical and regulative function in the realm of thought, but when employed beyond the province of its power leads thought into blind alleys or dialectical frustrations.

Mind is not one of these faculties, nor is it the being in which these faculties inhere. The notion of mind seems to have significance, for Kant, primarily in a collective sense. It represents the unity and order of the triad of cognitive faculties. The faculties of feeling and will—which Kant adds to these in his enumeration of "the higher faculties"—belong to the "transcendental ego," but they do not fall within that part of the transcendental structure which is mind. Kant's distinction between the speculative and the practical use of reason, and his distinction between the moral and the aesthetic judgment, involve different relationships between mind—or its triad of faculties—and these other faculties.

THE FOREGOING SURVEY of conceptions of the human mind gives some indication of the way in which other questions about mind are answered.

With regard to the relation of mind and matter, for example, the theories of Descartes, Spinoza, Locke, and James seem to affirm a duality of substances, or of modes of substance, or at least of realms—the physical and the mental. They are confronted by the problem of the relation which obtains between the two—their independence or interaction.

"Mental and physical events," writes James, "are, on all hands, admitted to present the strongest contrast in the entire field of being. The chasm which yawns between them is less easily bridged over by the mind than any inter-

val we know. Why, then, not call it an absolute chasm," he asks, "and say not only that the two worlds are different, but that they are independent?"

James thinks that to urge this theory of the complete independence of mind and body "is an *unwarrantable impertinence in the present state of psychology.*" He prefers the common-sense theory that each acts on the other somehow. But earlier writers who consider body and mind as distinct substances, find grave difficulties in the way of conceiving their interaction. "How our minds move or stop our bodies by thought, which we every moment find they do," is, according to Locke, "obscure and inconceivable." According to Hume, there is no "principle in all nature more mysterious than the union of soul with body." He interprets one consequence of the union to be that "a supposed spiritual substance acquires such an influence over a material one, that the most refined thought is able to actuate the grossest matter. Were we empowered by a secret wish, to remove mountains, or control planets in their orbit; this extensive authority," Hume thinks, "would not be more extraordinary, nor more beyond our comprehension."

Denying that bodies exist, Berkeley nevertheless argues that even if they did, they could exert no influence upon mind. "Though we give the materialists their external bodies," he says, "they by their own confession are never the nearer knowing how our ideas are produced; since they own themselves unable to comprehend in what manner body can act upon spirit, or how it is possible that it should imprint any idea in the mind. Hence it is evident that the production of ideas or sensations in our minds can be no reason why we should suppose matter or corporeal substances, since that is acknowledged to remain equally inexplicable with or without this supposition."

Those who deny the existence of matter, like Berkeley, or the existence of anything immaterial, like Lucretius or Hobbes, are confronted by problems of their own. Berkeley must explain the mind's perception of bodies or why the mind thinks of matter. Lucretius must explain perception, thought, and choice as functions of material particles in motion.

The reduction of mind to matter raises a question which leads in the opposite direction. Why may it not be supposed that thought and feeling are present in the universe wherever matter is—an atom of mind inseparably conjoined with every atom of matter, as in the "mind-stuff" or "mind-dust" theory which James considers and criticizes? Still another formulation of the relation of mind to matter is found in the theory of Aristotle and Aquinas, according to whom the rational soul is "the substantial form of an organic body," but the intellect—one of its powers—is not united to matter in any way. Mind is said to be immaterial in that understanding or thought does not require a bodily organ.

The angelic intellect, according to Aquinas, is a "cognitive power which is neither the act of a corporeal organ, nor in any way connected with corporeal matter." The human mind is not so completely divorced from matter, for, though man's intellect "is not the act of an organ, yet it is a power of the soul, which is the form of the body." Among all bodily forms, the human soul alone has the distinction of possessing "an operation and a power in which corporeal matter has no share whatever." But Aquinas also maintains that "the body is necessary for the action of the intellect, not as its organ of action, but on the part of the object"—the phantasm or image produced by the sensitive faculty. He conceives this dependence in the following manner. "For the intellect to understand actually . . . there is need for the act of the imagination and of the other powers" that are acts of bodily organs. "When the act of the imagination is hindered by a lesion of the corporeal organ, for instance, in a case of frenzy, or when the act of the memory is hindered, as in ·the case of lethargy, we see that a man is hindered from understanding actually even those things of which he had a previous knowledge."

The problem of body and mind is discussed more fully in the chapter on MATTER. Other problems involved in the theory of mind similarly occur in other chapters as well as in this one, e.g., the problem of mind in animals and men (in the chapters on ANIMAL and MAN); the problem of the existence of minds superior to that of man (in the chapters on ANGEL and GOD); the problem of the origin of ideas in the human mind (in the chapters on IDEA and MEMORY AND IMAGINATION). It should be noted, however, that agreement or disagreement on the nature of the human mind does not always determine agreement or disagreement with respect to these other questions.

Sharing the view that the mind is a spiritual substance, Locke and Descartes do not agree about innate ideas or principles. Locke tends to agree with Aristotle when he says that the mind is a *tabula rasa,* "void of all characters, without any ideas. How comes it to be furnished?" he asks. "Whence has it all the *materials* of reason and knowledge? To this I answer in one word, from *Experience.* In that all our knowledge is founded; and from that it ultimately derives itself. Our observation employed either about external sensible objects, or about the internal operations of our own minds, is that which supplies our understandings with all the *materials* of thinking."

But Locke does not accept Aristotle's sharp distinction between the faculties of sense and reason, nor does he find it necessary to adopt Aristotle's notion of an active intellect to explain how the mind abstracts general ideas from the particulars of sense perception. So far as his theory attributes to mind the power of sense, Locke has more affinity with Berkeley and Hume than with Aristotle; yet on the question of abstract ideas or the distinction between men and brutes, he is as much opposed to them as they are to Aristotle.

These few observations may be taken as a sample of the many intricately crossing lines of thought which make the complex pattern of the traditional discussion of mind. With few exceptions, almost any other choice of authors and topics would provide similar examples. That fact, combined with the fact that almost every major topic in this chapter leads into the discussion of other great ideas, tends to make the chapter on MIND a kind of focal point for perspective on the whole world of thought. It is not surprising that this should be the case, for on any theory, mind is somehow the place of ideas or, as Aristotle says, "the form of forms."

59

Monarchy

INTRODUCTION

Of all the traditionally recognized forms of government, monarchy is the easiest to define and to identify. As the word indicates, it is government by one man. It is indifferent whether that man is called king or prince, Caesar or Czar. Of all such titles, "king" is the most frequent; and in consequence monarchy is often called kingship or referred to as the royal form of government.

When monarchy is thus defined in terms of the principle of *unity,* other forms of government, such as aristocracy or oligarchy and democracy, tend to be characterized as government by the few or the many. But the numerical criterion by itself is obviously inadequate. To those who distinguish between aristocracy and oligarchy, it makes a difference whether the few who rule are selected for their pre-eminence in virtue or in wealth. A tyranny, like a monarchy, may be government by one man. Hence those who wish to use the word "monarch" or "king" eulogistically cannot be satisfied with a definition that fails to distinguish between king and tyrant.

It has been said—by Aristotle, for example—that the perversion of, or "deviation from, monarchy is tyranny; for both are forms of one-man rule. But," he adds, "there is the greatest difference between them; the tyrant looks to his own advantage, the king to that of his subjects." Both Aristotle and Plato also say that as tyranny is the worst form of government, so monarchy at the opposite extreme is the best. But though in their opinion tyranny is *always* the worst form of government, Aristotle at least does not seem to think that monarchy is always—*under all conditions*—best.

Further complications appear when other views are taken into consideration. The chapters on Citizen, Constitution, and Government discuss the basic opposition between absolute and limited government in the various terms in which that opposition is traditionally expressed: royal as opposed to political, despotic as opposed to constitutional government; or government by men as opposed to government by law. That opposition seems to be relevant to the theory of monarchy, certainly to any conception of monarchy which tends to identify it with absolute rule, or which sees some affinity between royal and despotic government.

The word "despotic" is, of course, sometimes used in a purely descriptive rather than a disparaging sense. Used descriptively, it designates the absolute rule exercised by the head of a household over children and slaves, neither of whom have any voice in their own government. Aristotle sometimes characterizes the royal government of a political community as despotic to signify its resemblance to the absolute rule of the father or master. He expresses the same comparison in reverse when he says that "the rule of a father over his children is royal."

The derogatory sense of "despotic" would seem to apply to those cases in which grown men are ruled as if they were children, or freemen as if they were slaves. The great issue concerning monarchy, therefore, is whether royal government is despotic in this sense. Always, or only under certain conditions? And if despotic, is it also tyrannical? Is monarchy in principle the foe of human liberties? To all these questions there are opposite answers in the great books of political theory. Where Hegel says that "public freedom in general and an hereditary monarchy guarantee each other," others, like Rousseau and J. S. Mill, identify the freedom of citizenship with republican or representative government.

This central issue is complicated not only by the various meanings of "despotism" (discussed in the chapter on TYRANNY AND DESPOTISM), but also by variations in the meaning of the word "monarchy" as it is used by different writers. The word is even used by the same writer in a number of senses. Rousseau, for example, says in one place that "every legitimate government is republican," and in another that "monarchical always ranks below republican government." But he also treats monarchy or royal rule as one form of legitimate government. He describes the king, in whose hands all political power is concentrated, as only having "the right to dispose of it in accordance with the laws." He distinguishes not only between king and tyrant, but also between king and despot.

To avoid what may be only verbal difficulties here, Kant suggests the use of the word "autocrat" to signify "one who has *all* power" and who in his own person "*is* the Sovereign." In contradistinction "monarch" should signify the king or chief magistrate (sometimes called "president") who "merely represents the sovereignty" or the people who "are themselves sovereign."

SOME POLITICAL theorists distinguish between absolute and limited (or constitutional) monarchy. This in turn raises new problems of definition and evaluation.

Is absolute government always monarchical in form, so that absolute government and absolute monarchy can be treated as identical? Hobbes, who seems to think that government by its very nature must be absolute, nevertheless treats aristocracy and democracy along with monarchy as forms of absolute government. Furthermore, as Rousseau points out, "the Roman Empire saw as many as eight emperors at once, without it being possible to say that the Empire was split up." The absolutism of the government was not diminished by the fact that two or more Caesars often held power at the same time. The triumvirates were also absolute dictatorships.

It would seem, therefore, that the principle of absolute government can be separated from the principle of monarchy. But can monarchy as a form of government be separated from absolute rule?

The question is not whether, in a republic, the monarchical principle is present in the sense that *one* man may hold the office of chief executive. On the issue of a single as opposed to a plural executive, Hamilton and Madison—and with them Jefferson—emphatically favor the principle of unity in the executive branch of the government. "Energy in government," according to *The Federalist,* "requires not only a certain duration of power, but the execution of it by a single hand." The qualities essential to a good executive, such as "decision, activity, secrecy, and dispatch," Hamilton says, "will generally characterize the proceedings of one man in a much more eminent degree than the proceedings of any greater number; and in proportion as the number is increased, these qualities will be diminished."

Yet the authors of *The Federalist,* and Jefferson too, are equally emphatic in insisting upon the difference in kind, not degree, between the power granted the president of the United States and that enjoyed by the king of Great Britain. For them, monarchies and republics are fundamentally opposed in the spirit of their institutions. Despotism is inherent in the nature of monarchy—not only absolute, but even limited monarchy.

According to Weber, "a president elected according to fixed rules can formally legitimize the governmental actions of the respective victorious party as 'lawful,' just as well as a parliamentary monarch. But the monarch, in addition to such legitimation, can perform a function which an elected president can not fulfil: a parliamentary monarch formally delimits the politicians' quest for power, because the highest position in the state is occupied once and for all." For Weber, "this essentially negative function . . . is of the greatest practical importance."

If the Constitution of the United States does not set up a constitutional monarchy, even though it provides for one man as chief executive, then a constitutional monarchy must have some other principle in it which distinguishes it from a republic. That may be hereditary succession to the throne; or it may be a certain symbolic identification of the king with the state. But in a monarchy, no matter how attenuated, so long as it does not become purely and simply constitutional government, the king also seems to retain some degree of despotic power—the absolute power exercised by a sovereign person who is free from the supervision of law.

Aristotle takes a similar view. Enumerating five types of kingly rule, he sets one form apart from all the rest—the form in which one man "has the disposal of everything . . . This form corresponds to the control of a household. For as household management is the kingly rule of a family, so kingly rule is the household management of a city or of a nation." The other forms are all, in one way or another, kingships according to law. Of these, most clearly exemplified in the Spartan constitution, Aristotle says that "the so-called limited monarchy, or kingship according to law . . . is not a distinct form of government, for under all governments, as for example, in a democracy or aristocracy, there may be a general holding office for life, and one person is often made supreme over the administration of a state."

Whether or not there is a supreme commander or a chief magistrate, elected or hereditary, the government is not distinctively royal if the man called "king" is subject to the laws and if the other men in the state are not his subjects but his fellow citizens. For somewhat different reasons, Hobbes agrees with the view that only absolute monarchy is monarchy. When the king is limited in power, he says, the sovereignty is always "in that assembly which had the right to limit him; and by consequence the government is not monarchy, but either democracy or aristocracy; as of old time in Sparta, where the kings had a privilege to lead their armies, but the sovereignty was in the *Ephori*." Hobbes uses the government of one people over another people—the mother country over colonies, or the conqueror over a subjugated nation—to illustrate what he

means by absolute monarchy. This suggests a significant parallelism between the problems of monarchy and the problems of empire.

IF THERE WERE universal agreement on the point that only absolute monarchy is truly monarchy, the issue concerning monarchy could be readily translated into the basic opposition between rule by men and rule by law. But such agreement seems to be wanting, and the problems of monarchy are, in consequence, further complicated.

Plato, for example, distinguishes in the *Statesman* between three forms of government according to established laws, of which one is monarchy. Monarchy is better than aristocracy and democracy, obviously not with respect to the principle of the supremacy of law, but simply because government by one seems to be more efficient than government by a few or many; just as tyranny is the worst form of government because, in violating or overthrowing the laws, one man can succeed in going further than a multitude, which is "unable to do either any great good or any great evil."

But all these forms of government, good and bad, better and worse, are compared by Plato with a form of government which he says "excels them all, and is among States what God is among men." It seems to be monarchical in type, but, though not lawless like tyranny, it is entirely above the need of written or customary rules of law. "The best thing of all," Plato writes, "is not that the law should rule, but that a man should rule, supposing him to have wisdom and royal power." Whether such government can ever exist apart from divine rule, or perhaps the advent of the "philosopher king," the point remains that Plato seems to conceive monarchy in two quite distinct ways—both as an absolute rule and also as one of the legally limited forms of government.

Montesquieu separates monarchy from absolute government entirely. At the same time, he distinguishes it from republics, whether aristocracies or democracies. According to him, monarchy is as much a government by law, as much opposed to despotism or absolute government, as are republics. Monarchies and republics are the two main kinds of constitutional government, just as aristocracies and democracies are the two main kinds of republic.

Where Aristotle holds that constitutional monarchy is not a distinct type of government, Montesquieu holds that absolute monarchy does not deserve the name of "monarchy," but should be called "despotism" instead. He criticizes Aristotle's fivefold classification of kingships, saying that "among the number of monarchies, he [Aristotle] ranks the Persian empire and the kingdom of Sparta. But is it not evident," he asks, "that the one was a despotic state and the other a republic?" Since Montesquieu's own view of monarchy involves, in addition to a king, a body of nobles in whom intermediate and subordinate powers are vested, he thinks no true notion of monarchy can be found in the ancient world.

Hegel agrees with Montesquieu that constitutional monarchy is the very opposite of despotism, but he goes much further than Montesquieu in the direction of identifying monarchy with constitutional government. For him constitutional monarchy is the ultimately true form of government. "The development of the state to constitutional monarchy is the achievement of the modern world." He thinks Montesquieu was right in recognizing that the ancient world knew only the patriarchal type of monarchy, a kind of transference of familial government to larger communities still organized on the domestic pattern. But according to Hegel, Montesquieu himself, in stressing the role of the nobility, shows that he understands, not the type of monarchy which is "organized into an objective constitution" and in which "the monarch is the absolute apex of an organically developed state," but only "feudal monarchy, the type in which the relationships recognized in its constitutional law are crystallized into the rights of private property and the privileges of individuals and corporations."

It may be questioned, however, whether Hegel's theory of constitutional monarchy avoids the issue raised by republicans who think that monarchy is inseparable from some form of absolutism, or that monarchy, if entirely devoid of absolutism, has no special character as a form of government. In spite of his acceptance of the traditional distinction between constitutional government and despotism, Hegel seems to regard the sovereignty of the state as absolute in relation to its own subjects at home—no less absolute than is its sovereignty in external affairs vis-à-vis foreign states. The crown is the personification of the absolute sovereignty of the state at home. The absolute power of the state comes into existence only in the person of a monarch who has the final decision in all matters.

"The sovereignty of the people," writes Hegel, "is one of the confused notions based on the wild idea of the 'people.' Taken without its monarchy and the articulation of the whole which is the indispensable and direct concomitant of monarchy, the people is a formless mass and no longer a state." Hegel thus dismisses the notion of popular sovereignty (which to Rousseau, Kant, and the Federalists is of the essence of republican government) as inconsistent with "the Idea of the state in its full development." A profound opposition, therefore, exists between Hegel's theory of constitutional monarchy and republican theories of constitutional government. Even though the issue cannot be stated in terms of government by men versus government by laws, a monarchy as opposed to a republic still seems to represent the principle of absolutism in government.

THERE IS STILL another conception of a type of government which is neither a pure republic nor an absolute monarchy. What the medieval writers call a "mixed regime" is not a constitutional monarchy in the Hegelian sense, nor is it what Aristotle means when he uses that term. The medieval mixed regime is a combination of two distinct principles of government—the *royal principle,* according to which absolute power is vested in the sovereign personality of an individual man; and the *political principle,* according to which the supremacy of law reflects the sovereignty of the people, who have the power of making laws either directly or through their representatives.

This conception of a mixed regime—of government which is *both royal and political*—appears at first to be self-contradictory. In Aristotle's terms, it would seem impossible to combine the supremacy of law, which is the essence of constitutional government, with the supremacy of a sovereign person, which is the essence of royal government. The mixed regime would also seem to be impossible in terms of Hobbes's theory of the indivisibility of sovereignty. Impossible in theory, the mixed regime nevertheless existed as a matter of historic fact in the typical medieval kingdom, which derived its character from the feudal conditions under which it developed.

Does not the fact of its historic existence refute the incompatibility of the principles which the mixed regime combines? The answer may be that, like a mixture of oil and water, royal and political government can only exist as a mixture in unstable equilibrium. Originating under feudal conditions, the mixed regime tends toward dissolution as these conditions disappear with the rise of the modern nation-state. It first tends to be supplanted by a movement toward absolute monarchy. Then, in the course of reaction and revolution, it tends toward constitutional monarchies or republics through added limitations on the power of the throne.

These historic developments seem to indicate that the principles of the mixed regime are ultimately as irreconcilable in fact as they are in theory.

Montesquieu's remark that the ancients "had not a clear idea of monarchy" can be interpreted to mean that they did not have the conception of a mixed regime. Before the accidents of history brought it into existence, it is unlikely that anyone would have conceived of a government both royal and political. Montesquieu does not adopt the medieval description of a mixed regime, which, as stated by Aquinas, is "partly kingdom, since there is one at the head of all; partly aristocracy, in so far as a number of persons are set in authority; and partly democracy, *i.e.,* government by the people, in so far as the rulers can be chosen by the people, and the people have the right to choose their rulers." Yet Montesquieu's theory of monarchy seems to be determined by characteristics peculiar to the medieval kingdom.

This seems to be the point of Hegel's observation, already quoted, that Montesquieu's theory of monarchy identifies it with the feudal kingdom. The point is confirmed in another way by the fact that Montesquieu's ideal of monarchy is the government of England at the end of the 17th century, which, he says, "may be justly called a republic, disguised under the form of a monarchy." Locke's conception of the English government in his own day tends to clarify this point.

The form of a government, says Locke, "depends upon the placing of the supreme power, which is the legislative." When the power of making laws is placed in the hands of one man, then it is a monarchy. But, according to Locke, "the legislative and executive power are in distinct hands . . . in all moderated monarchies and well-framed governments."

What Locke here calls a "moderated monarchy" (intending to describe the government of England), seems to be the mixed regime, the form of government which John Fortescue had earlier called a "political kingdom," and Henry de Bracton a *regimen regale et politicum.* The legislative power is in the hands of the people or their representatives. If it belonged exclusively to the king as a right vested in his sovereign person, and not merely as the people's representative—or, in the language of Aquinas, their vicegerent—the government would be in form an absolute monarchy. If, on the other hand, the king were merely a representative, the government would be a republic.

The sovereign character of the king in a mixed regime seems to stem from his unique relation to the laws of the land. In one way, he is above the laws, and has certain powers not limited by law; in another way, his whole power is limited by the fact that he does not have the power to make laws in his own right or authority. When a people are free and able to make their own laws, Aquinas writes, "the consent of the whole people expressed by custom counts far more in favor of a particular observance, than does the authority of the sovereign, who has not the power to frame laws, except as representing the people." But

Aquinas also says that the sovereign is "*exempt from the law*, as to its coercive power; since, properly speaking, no man is coerced by himself, and law has no coercive power save from the authority of the sovereign."

The coercive power of the law belongs to the sovereign as executive, not legislator. Admitting the king to a share in legislative power, Locke conceives his essential function—that which belongs to him alone—as executive. The absoluteness of this executive power Locke defines in terms of the royal prerogative, that "being nothing but a power in the hands of the prince to provide for the public good in such cases which, depending upon unforeseen and uncertain occurrences, certain and unalterable laws could not safely direct." Prerogative, he then goes on to say, is the power "to act according to discretion for the public good without the prescription of law, and sometimes even against it."

Locke thus gives us a picture of the mixed regime in which the king's sovereign power is limited to the exercise of an absolute prerogative in performing the executive functions of government. In the executive sphere, the king's power is absolute, yet his sovereignty is not absolute; for in the legislative sphere, he either has no voice at all where ancient customs prevail, or, in the making of new laws, he can count himself merely as one representative of the people among others.

The extent of the prerogative permitted the king depends upon the extent to which matters are explicitly regulated by law. When in the infancy of governments the laws were few in number, "the government was almost all prerogative," as Locke sees it. He thinks that "they have a very wrong notion of government who say that the people have encroached upon the prerogative when they have got any part of it to be defined by positive laws. For in so doing they have not pulled from the prince anything that of right belonged to him, but only declared that that power which they indefinitely left in his or his ancestors' hands, to be exercised for their good, was not a thing they intended him, when he used it otherwise."

Here we see the seed of conflict between sovereign king and sovereign people in the combination of incompatible principles that constitute a mixed regime. As the king, jealous of his prerogative, tries to maintain or even extend his power, royal and political government tends toward absolute monarchy. As the people, jealous of their sovereignty, try to safeguard their legislative power from royal usurpations, the mixed regime tends to dissolve in the other direction. This happens as it moves toward republican government through various stages of limited or constitutional monarchy in which the sovereignty of the king becomes more and more attenuated.

When the king's prerogative includes the power of calling parliament into session, nothing short of revolution may resolve the issue; for, as Locke observes, "between an executive power in being, with such a prerogative, and a legislative that depends upon his will for their convening, there can be no judge on earth."

IN THE DISCUSSION of monarchy, as in the discussion of democracy or other forms of government, the fundamental terms and issues do not have the same meaning in the various epochs of western thought. The continuity of discussion in the tradition of the great books must be qualified, especially in the field of political theory, by reference to the differing historic institutions with which their authors are acquainted and concerned. Ancient and modern controversies over the merits of monarchy in relation to other forms of government seem to be comparing institutions of government as different as the ancient and modern forms of the democratic constitution.

In the ancient world, the choice between purely royal and purely political government underlies the meaning and evaluation of monarchy. In the modern world, with its heritage from the feudal institutions of the Middle Ages, either the mixed regime or constitutional monarchy is thought to offer a third alternative. The praise of monarchy may therefore be the corollary of a justification of absolute government or the absolute state, as with Hobbes and Hegel; it may be accompanied by an attack on absolute or despotic power, as with Locke and Montesquieu; or in defense of purely republican principles, monarchy may be attacked, as by Rousseau and the Federalists, without differentiation between its absolute and limited forms.

This does not mean that there is no continuity between ancient and modern discussion. It seems to exist with respect to both elements in the idea of monarchy—the unification of government through its having one head, and the rightness of absolute power. On the point of unity, Plato's argument that monarchy is the most efficient of the several forms of government which are otherwise equally just, seems to be paralleled by modern arguments for a unified executive in the constitution of a republic. It is also reflected in the reasoning of Montesquieu and Rousseau concerning the greater competence of monarchies to govern extensive territories. On the point of absolute power, there is some continuity between ancient and modern discussions of government by men versus government by law. But here there seems to be greater similarity between ancient and modern arguments against giving sovereignty to an individual human being than there is between the modern defense of monarchy and ancient speculations concerning royal government.

Taking different shape in Hobbes and Hegel, the argument for the *necessity* of absolute government seems to be peculiarly modern. It is not simply the point made by the ancients, that under certain circumstances it may be right for the man of superior wisdom to govern his inferiors in an absolute manner, as a father governs children, or a god men. The point is rather that the very nature of government and the state requires a unified repository of absolute power. Hobbes does not ask whether the monarch in whose hands such power is placed deserves this by reason of personal superiority to his subjects. Hegel explicitly repudiates the relevance of any consideration of the monarch's particular character. Neither Hobbes nor Hegel argues for the divine right of kings, or their divine appointment; though Hegel does insist that the constitution itself, which establishes the supremacy of the crown, is not something made by man, but "divine and constant, and exalted above the sphere of things that are made."

That kings have absolute power by divine right is another peculiarly modern argument for absolute monarchy. "Not all the water from the rough rude sea," says Shakespeare's Richard II, "can wash the balm off from an anointed king. The breath of worldly men cannot depose the deputy elected by the Lord." According to the theory of divine right, the king is God's vicar, not, as Aquinas thinks, the vicegerent of the people. The theory of the divine right of kings does not seem to be a medieval doctrine. It appears later in such tracts as those by William Barclay and Robert Filmer, which Locke undertakes to answer.

The controversy involves its adversaries in dispute over the interpretation of Holy Writ. The anointing of Christian kings is supposed to draw its significance from the establishment of this practice among the ancient Hebrews. But the story of the origin of the Hebrew kingship can be given an opposite interpretation.

The people of Israel, after the leadership of Moses and Aaron, first submitted their affairs to the government of judges, and "there was no king in Israel, but every one did that which seemed right to himself." Later they went to Samuel, their judge, saying: "Make us a king to judge us like all the nations." This displeased Samuel. Samuel prayed unto the Lord, and the Lord said unto Samuel: "Hearken to the voice of the people in all that they say unto thee; for they have not rejected thee, but they have rejected me, that I should not reign over them." The Lord then describes the tribulations the people will suffer at the hands of an earthly ruler with absolute power, a punishment they deserve for wanting to be ruled by a king, instead of by God and God's law, administered for them by judges.

THE GREAT POEMS and histories of ancient Greece and Rome would seem to indicate that the divinity of kings is not a modern notion. The deification of emperors and kings certainly appears to be a common practice. But the assumption of divinity by kings is not supposed to signify divine appointment, or election by the gods; nor do the rulers of the ancient world justify their absolute power as a god-given right.

Furthermore, in the political theory of Plato and Aristotle, the analogy between royal rule and divine government works in the opposite direction. According to their view, the right to absolute government depends upon a radical inequality between ruler and ruled. If a god were to rule men on earth, as in the myth retold in Plato's *Statesman,* he would govern them absolutely, deciding everything by his wisdom and without recourse to written laws or established customs. If there were a godlike man, or if a true philosopher were to become king, he too would deserve to be an absolute monarch. It would be unjust, says Aristotle, to treat the godlike man merely as a citizen, and so to treat him as no more than "the equal of those who are so far inferior to him in virtue and in political capacity." It would also seem to be unjust for a man who does not have great superiority over his fellowmen to rule them like a king, instead of being merely a citizen entitled to hold public office for a time.

Aristotle frequently refers to royal government as the divine sort of government, but he does not justify its existence except when one man stands to others as a god to men. Though some of the historic kingships which Aristotle classifies are absolute monarchies, none is royal government of the divine sort. That seems to remain for Aristotle, as for Plato, a purely hypothetical construction.

Actual royal government has a patriarchal rather than a divine origin. It is the kind of government which is appropriate to the village community rather than to the city-state. The kingly form of government prevails in the village because it is an outgrowth of the family. That is why, says Aristotle, "the Hellenic states were originally governed by kings; the Hellenes were under royal rule before they came together, as the barbarians still are."

In thinking that absolute or despotic government befits the servile Asiatics, but not the freemen of the Greek city-states, Aristotle takes a position which has a certain counterpart in the views of Montesquieu and Mill. These modern opponents of absolute monarchy do not assert that constitutional government is unconditionally better than despotism.

For certain peoples, under certain conditions, self-government may not be possible or advantageous. "A rude people," Mill writes, "though in some degree alive to the benefits of civilized society, may be unable to practice the forbearance which it demands: their passions may be too violent, or their personal pride too exacting, to forego private conflict, and leave to the laws the avenging of their real or supposed wrongs. In such a case, a civilized government, to be really advantageous to them, will require to be in a considerable degree despotic; to be one over which they do not themselves exercise control, and which imposes a great amount of forcible restraint upon their actions." Montesquieu seems further to suppose that different races—largely as a result of the climate in which they live—are by nature inclined toward freedom or servitude. The Asiatics are for him a people whose spirit perpetually dooms them to live under despotism.

In contrast, Mill's conditional justification of absolute government demands that despotism serve only a temporary purpose. It must seek not merely to keep order, but by gradual steps to prepare the people it rules for self-government. "Leading-strings are only admissible," he says, "as a means of gradually training the people to walk alone." When they have reached that stage of development where they are able to govern themselves, the despotic ruler must either abdicate or be overthrown.

There is a deeper contrast between Mill on the one hand, and Aristotle and Plato on the other, one which goes to the very heart of the issue concerning royal and political government. Both Aristotle and Plato seem to be saying that if the superior or godlike man existed, then royal government would be better than the best republic, even for the civilized Greeks. In calling royal rule the divine form of government, they imply that it is the ideal, even if it can never be realized. This Mill most emphatically denies.

The notion that "if a good despot could be ensured, despotic monarchy would be the best form of government, I look upon," he writes, "as a radical and most pernicious conception of what good government is." The point at issue is not whether the good despot—the godlike ruler or philosopher king—can be found. Suppose him to exist. The point then to be made is that the people ruled by "one man of superhuman mental activity" would of necessity have to be entirely passive. "Their passivity is implied in the very idea of absolute power . . . What sort of human beings," Mill asks, "can be formed under such a regimen?" Men must actually engage in self-government in order to pass from political infancy to maturity. Whenever it is possible, representative or constitutional government is therefore better than absolute monarchy.

60

Nature

INTRODUCTION

NATURE is a term which draws its meaning from the other terms with which it is associated by implication or contrast. Yet it is not one of a fixed pair of terms, like necessity and contingency, one and many, universal and particular, war and peace. When things are divided into the natural and the artificial, or into the natural and the conventional, the opposite of the natural does not represent a loss or violation of nature, but rather a transformation of nature through the addition of a new factor. The unnatural, on the other hand, seems to be merely a deviation, a falling away from, or sometimes a transgression of nature.

Most of the terms which stand in opposition to nature represent the activity or being of man or God. As appears in the chapter on MEDICINE, Galen thinks of nature as an artist. Harvey later develops this notion. But with these two exceptions, the traditional theory of art conceives it not as the work of nature, but of man. Despite other differences in the great books on the theory of art, especially with regard to art's imitation of nature, there seems to be a common understanding that works of art are distinguished from productions of nature by the fact that man has added something to nature. A world which man left exactly as he found it would be a world without art or any trace of the artificial in it.

The ancient authors who contrast the natural and the conventional and the modern authors who distinguish man's life in a state of nature from his life in civil society seem to imply that without something done by man there would be nothing conventional or political. Locke appears to be an exception here. He thinks that there is a natural as well as a civil, or political, society. Natural society is the society of "men living together according to reason without a common superior on earth, with authority to judge between them." Unlike Hobbes or Kant or Hegel, Locke does not think that the state of nature is necessarily a state of war. But this difference between Locke and others does not affect the point that the political institutions of civil society are things of man's own devising.

There may be, among the social insects, natural organizations such as the beehive and the ant mound. It may even be, as Locke supposes, that in a state of nature, "men living together according to reason" would constitute a society. But in neither case does the society we call "a state" result. States differ from one another in many features of their political organization. In this sense the state or political community is conventional rather than natural; its institutions are humanly contrived.

The social contract theory of the origin of the state is not necessarily involved in the recognition that the state is partly conventional. Aristotle, for example, who regards the state as natural—he speaks of it as "a creation of nature"—does not think of the political community as natural in the sense in which a beehive is natural. That men should form political communities is, in his view, the result of a natural desire, a tendency inherent in the nature of man as a political animal. But what form the political community will take is at least partly determined by the particular arrangements men voluntarily institute. Man-made laws are conventional, but so also are other institutions which vary from state to state or change from time to time.

THE ISSUES IN political theory raised by any consideration of what is and is not natural about society or the state are discussed in other chapters, *e.g.,* FAMILY and STATE. What is true in this connection is likely to be true of each of the other fundamental oppositions in which the notion of nature is involved. The issues raised by the relation of art to nature are, for example, considered in the chapter on ART; those raised by the distinction between nature and nurture are considered in the chapter on HABIT, and so on. Here we are concerned not with the theoretical consequences of different conceptions of nature, but with the various meanings of the term itself as it is used in different contexts.

Common to all meanings is the notion that the natural is that which man's doing or making has not altered or enlarged. The distinction between nature and nurture confirms this. Man's activities are the source of modifications in his own nature as well as in the nature of other things. The human nature man is born with undergoes transformations in the course of life: the acquirement of knowledge, the formation of habits (which are often called "second nature"), the modification of instincts. The sum of these changes represents what nurture adds to nature.

When changes of this sort are looked at collectively they give rise to the notions of culture or civilization—two more terms which present a contrast to nature. In Rousseau and others we meet the feeling that man may have lost, not gained, by exchanging the natural for the civilized life. The ideal of a return to nature involves more than a return to the soil, or an exodus from the city to the country. In its most radical form, this ideal calls upon man to divest himself of all the artifices and conceits with which he has thought to improve on nature—"by renouncing its advances," Rousseau says, "in order to renounce its vices."

But why, it may be asked, is the whole world which man creates not as natural as the materials which man finds to work with—the resources of physical nature and the native equipment which is man's nature at birth? If man himself is a natural entity, and if all human activities are somehow determined by human nature, then why are not the works of art and science, the development of political institutions, the cultivation of human beings by education and experience, and all other features of civilization—why are not all these just as natural as the falling stone, the flourishing forest, or the beehive? Why, in short, should there by any contrast between the works of nature and the works of man?

THIS QUESTION points to one of the fundamental issues in the traditional discussion of nature. Those who uphold the validity of the contrast defend its significance in terms of something quite special about human nature. If man were entirely a creature of instinct—if everything man did were determined by his nature so that no choices were open to him and no deviation from the course of nature possible—then the human world would seem to fade into the rest of nature. Only on the supposition that man is by nature rational and free do those human works which are the products of reason or the consequences of free choice seem to stand in sharp contrast to all other natural existences or effects of natural causes.

Of these two factors—rationality and freedom—the element of freedom is usually the one most emphasized. The line is drawn between that which natural causes determine and that which man determines by his own free choice. The laws of nature are often conceived as expressing an inherent rationality in nature itself, but they also state the uniformity of nature's operations. Such maxims of nature as "nature does nothing in vain," "nature abhors a vacuum," or "nature does nothing by jumps" are usually interpreted as describing nature's invariable way of doing things. Aristotle's distinction between things which happen naturally and those which happen by chance turns on the regularity of the events which result from causes in the very nature of things. The natural is that which happens either always or for the most part.

Hence, even if there is rationality of some sort in the structure of nature, that supposition does not seem to affect the position of those who connect human reason with human freedom and who, in consequence, divide the things which happen as a result of man's free choice from everything else which happens in the course of nature. This may be exemplified by the Greek understanding of the difference between nature and convention. The laws of Persia vary from the laws of Greece, the political institutions of the city-states vary from those of the Homeric age, customs and constitutions differ from city to city. Unlike such conventions, "that which is by nature," Aristotle writes, "is unchangeable and has everywhere the same force, as fire burns both here and in Persia." The conventional is the variable, the natural the uniform. The variability of conventions, moreover, seems to suggest that they are products of freedom or choice.

The difference between the beehive and the human city is that one is *entirely* a creation of nature, a social organization entirely determined by the instincts of the bees, so that wherever bees form a hive, it is formed in the same way; whereas the human city involves something more than a natural desire of men, since when these political animals associate in different places, they set up different forms of government and different kinds of law. The same comparison can be made between the spider's web or the beaver's dam and such products of human art as cloth and houses. The variability of the works of reason, as opposed to the uniformity of instinctive productions of all sorts, implies the factor of choice in reason's work.

THE CONCEPTION OF nature which tries to separate the natural from what man contributes thus seems to depend upon the conception of man. Controversies concerning man's difference from other animals, especially the dispute about human freedom (considered in such chapters as MAN and WILL), bear directly on the issue of the naturalness of the things which result from man's doing and making.

Spinoza, for example, in holding that human actions constitute no exception to the reign of necessity throughout nature, removes any ground for distinguishing the effects of human operation from other effects. Man exercises no freedom of choice; nor does man in any other way introduce a new principle into the order or process of nature. Hobbes and Locke concur in the denial of free will, but they separate the inventions of man's mind or his social institutions from what happens without human contrivance in the realm of thought or action. The difference between simple and complex ideas for Locke seems to parallel the ancient distinction between nature and art.

At the other extreme from Spinoza, Kant separates the order of nature and the order of freedom into worlds as radically asunder as the Cartesian realms of matter and mind. The world of nature is the system or order of the objects of sense—"the sum total of phenomena insofar as they . . . are connected with each other throughout." For Kant this means two things which are strictly correlative. Nature is the object of the theoretical sciences and it is also the realm of time, space, and causality. Like Spinoza, Kant identifies the order of nature with the order of causal necessity. But, unlike Spinoza, Kant places the moral and political life of man in an order unconditioned by time, space, and causality. This realm of freedom is the sphere of the moral or practical sciences. The natural or theoretical sciences do not extend to what Kant calls the "supersensible" or the "noumenal" order— the world of things lying outside the range of sense-experience.

There is an alternative to Spinoza's location of all events within the order of nature and to Kant's separation of the realm of nature from the domain of freedom. It takes the form of Aristotle's or Aquinas' distinction between the natural and the voluntary. The voluntary is in one sense natural, in another not. It is natural in the sense that what happens voluntarily in the realm of animal and human motions proceeds from causes as natural as those responsible for the motions of inert bodies. A voluntary act, according to Aquinas, comes from "an intrinsic principle," just as the falling of a stone proceeds from "a principle of movement in the stone." But among the factors responsible for voluntary acts is "knowledge of the end"—knowledge of the object being sought. The sphere of the voluntary can therefore be equated with the sphere of conscious desire, *i.e.*, with desire aroused by an object known, whether known by sense or reason. The natural in the sense in which it is distinguished from the voluntary is the sphere of motions in line with natural desire, *i.e.*, with tendencies founded in the very nature of a body or organism and unaccompanied by any awareness of the goal toward which it is thus inclined to move.

Aristotle's distinction between natural and violent motion (which Galileo and other physicists adopt) seems to throw light on a double use of the term 'natural' here. Galileo treats the motion of a freely falling body as natural, in contrast to the motion of a projectile. In the former case, it is the nature of heavy bodies to gravitate toward the earth; whereas in the latter case, in addition to the motion of gravitation, another motion is imparted to the body when it is shot from a gun—a motion which does not proceed from the body's own nature but is caused by the motions of other bodies. In terms of this distinction, voluntary motions are natural rather than violent. In fact, the violent is sometimes thought to be even more opposed to the voluntary than to the natural, in the sense that a man acting contrary to his will under external coercion suffers violence. When he does what he wishes, his conduct is not only voluntary but natural, *i.e.*, free from the violence of external forces.

It is necessary to consider the additional distinction between the voluntary and the free. Animals acting from desires caused by the perception of certain objects act voluntarily, but, in the theory of Aristotle and Aquinas, only men freely choose among alternative objects of desire or between means for accomplishing an end. The effects of voluntary action differ from other natural events only because knowledge enters into their determination. But that which happens as the result of man's free choice is determined neither by his nature nor by his knowledge. Hence whatever comes into existence through man's choice stands apart from all that is naturally determined to exist.

One other matter bears on this consideration of the natural in relation to the voluntary and the free. Spinoza excludes the operation of final causes, as well as free choice, from the order of nature. Purposes or ends are not

principles of nature. Aristotle, on the other hand, thinks that final causes are operative in every part of nature. He finds them in the sphere of inert bodies which naturally tend toward certain results. He finds them in the sphere of animal and human motions, where the final cause or end may be an object of conscious desire.

So far as the search for causes is concerned, nature presents the same kind of problems to the physicist as to the biologist or psychologist. In only one sense are final causes peculiarly present in human conduct; that is the sense in which the change effected is not the ultimate end, but only a means to some further end desired. Here there is an extrinsic final cause as well as a final cause intrinsic to the change itself. It may be with regard to this special sense that Francis Bacon says of final causes that they are "more allied to man's own nature than to the system of the universe." Yet Bacon, far from denying their presence in the scheme of things, assigns the investigation of final causes to metaphysics (as a branch of natural philosophy) rather than to physics. For him the ascertainment of final causes does not discover a purpose in the nature of things. Rather it looks to God's plan and providence.

WE HAVE SO FAR dealt with that consideration of nature which opposes the natural to the works of man. The discussion of nature also moves on a theological plane. Here, on one traditional view, the natural is not opposed to, but rather identified with the work of God. "Things which are said to be made by nature," Plato writes, "are the work of divine art." Those who conceive the universe as God's creation, and think of God alone as uncreated being, tend to use the word "nature" collectively for the whole world of creatures and distributively for each type of thing which has its being from God.

The distinction between the supernatural and the natural has many interpretations in Christian theology, but none more basic than that which divides all being into the uncreated and the created. On this view, the order of nature includes more than the world of physical, sensible things. It includes the spiritual creation—angels and souls—as well. Immaterial beings are no more supernatural than bodies. They, too, are created natures. Only God is uncreated being.

Those who do not have or who deny a doctrine of creation use the word "nature" in a *less* and in a *more* comprehensive sense. The Greek philosophers, for example, seem to restrict the natural to the physical, *i.e.,* to the realm of material, sensible, changing things. Change is an element in the connotation of the Greek word *phüsis,* of which *natura* is the Latin equivalent. As Greek scientists conceive the study of nature, it is the business of physics to investigate the principles, causes, and elements of change.

Things which are thought to be untouched by change, such as the objects of mathematics, self-subsistent ideas, or separate forms; or things which are thought to be eternal and immutable, such as immaterial substances or intelligences, do not belong to the realm of physics or *natural* science. In Aristotle's classification of the sciences such beings are the objects of mathematics and metaphysics, or theology. Since, for him, whatever is both sensible and mutable is also material, the realm of nature includes no more than the whole material universe, celestial as well as terrestrial.

The *more* comprehensive sense of nature appears in Spinoza's identification of nature with the infinite and eternal substance of God. "Besides God," says Spinoza, "no substance can be nor be conceived ... Whatever is, is in God, and nothing can either be or be conceived without God." All finite things are modes of the divine substance or, more precisely, of the attributes of God, such as extension and thought. Nature, therefore, is the totality of finite things, both material and immaterial. But nature exceeds even this totality, for the infinite substance of God is greater than the sum of its parts.

To make this clear, Spinoza employs the distinction between *natura naturans* and *natura naturata.* "By *natura naturans* we are to understand that which is in itself and is conceived through itself, or those attributes of substance which express eternal and infinite essence; that is to say, God in so far as He is considered as a free cause. But by *natura naturata* I understand everything which follows from the necessity of the nature of God, or of any one of God's attributes in so far as they are considered as things which are in God, and which without God can neither be nor be conceived."

Viewed under the aspect of time rather than eternity, the order of nature (*i.e., natura naturata*) is as much an order of ideas as it is an order of things. "The order and connection of ideas is the same as the order and connection of things," Spinoza writes. "Whether we think of nature under the attribute of extension or under the attribute of thought, or under any other attribute whatever, we shall discover one and the same order, or one and the same connection of causes."

Except perhaps for the Stoics, like Marcus Aurelius and Epictetus, Spinoza seems to stand alone in this conception of nature as all-embracing. The Stoics too regard nature as the system of the universe, with man a part of its cosmic structure, and with God or divinity inherent in nature as the rational principle governing all things. But with or without reference to God and creation, thinkers like Descartes and Hume tend to identify nature not with the totality of finite things, but with the world of bodies in motion or changing sensible things.

For Descartes, nature does not include the realm of thought or thinking substances, though these, like bodies, are finite and dependent creatures of God. For Hume, nature seems to be that which lies outside experience—in a way, the reality which underlies appearances. Where Spinoza thinks that the system of ideas is as much a part of nature as the system of bodies in motion, Hume speaks of "a kind of pre-established harmony between the course of nature and the succession of our ideas."

Hume's distinction between knowledge of the relation between our own ideas and knowledge of matters of fact or real existence seems furthermore to imply that nature is the reality known (however inadequately) when we assert certain things to be matters of fact. Here we perceive another meaning of nature, defined by another basic opposition, this time between the real and the ideal or the imaginary. It is in this sense that medieval writers oppose *entia naturae, i.e.,* natural or real beings, to *entia rationis,* or things which have their being in the mind.

THIS DISTINCTION, like most of the others in which nature is concerned, does not have universal acceptance. Kant, as we have seen, far from making nature the reality which exists independently of our experience or knowledge, conceives the realm of nature as identical with all possible experience. "We possess two expressions," Kant writes, "*world* and *nature,* which are generally interchanged. The first denotes the mathematical total of all phenomena and the totality of their synthesis . . . And the world is termed nature, when it is regarded as a dynamical whole—when our attention is not directed to the aggregation in space and time . . . but to the unity in the *existence* of phenomena."

On quite different principles of analysis, Berkeley also treats as natural things the ideas or sensations which "are not produced by, or dependent on, the wills of men." Natural beings do not exist apart from the mind, but unlike imaginary ones, natural beings are those ideas which are not subject to our will or the human mind's own constructive activities. Such ideas are produced in our minds immediately by God.

To the question whether "Nature hath no share in the production of natural things," Berkeley answers: "If by *Nature* is meant the visible series of effects or sensations imprinted on our minds, according to certain fixed and general laws, then it is plain that Nature, taken in this sense, cannot produce anything at all. But, if by *Nature* is meant some being distinct from God, as well as from the laws of nature, and things perceived by sense, I must confess that word is to me an empty sound without any intelligible meaning annexed to it. Nature, in this acceptation, is a vain chimera, introduced by those heathens who had not just notions of the omnipresence and infinite perfection of God."

Berkeley's view represents one extreme position on a theological issue of the utmost difficulty. According to him God is not only the creator or first cause, but the sole cause of everything which happens in the course of nature. There are no natural causes. Nature has no productive power. Everything is the work of God or the work of man—nothing the work of nature.

Within the limits of this issue, the other extreme consists in denying not the creativity of God, but the role of divine causality in the production of natural effects. It relegates them entirely to the efficacy of natural causes. Lucretius, of course, denies both the creation of the world and the intervention of the gods in the processes of nature. But others, like Descartes, seem to say that once God has created the physical world, once He has formed matter into bodies and given them their initial impetus, their motions henceforward need only the laws of nature which God laid down for them to follow. For everything that happens in the course of nature, natural causes, operating under these laws, suffice.

There is a third position which distinguishes between the work of God in the creation of nature, and the work of nature in the production of effects of all sorts, such as the natural motions of bodies or the propagation of animals. But though it ascribes efficacy to natural agents or second causes in the production of natural effects, it also regards natural causes as instrumental to the hand of God, the first or principal cause of everything which happens as well as of everything which is. Aquinas seems to hold that God acts alone only in the original creation of things; whereas in the preservation of created natures and in their causal interaction, God works through secondary, or natural, causes.

"Some have understood God to work in every agent," Aquinas writes, "in such a way that no created power has any effect in things, but that God alone is the immediate cause of everything wrought; for instance, that it is not fire that gives heat, but God in the fire, and so forth. But this is impossible. First, because the order of cause and effect would be taken away from created things, and this would imply a lack of power in the Creator . . . Secondly, because the operative powers which are seen to exist in things would be bestowed on things to no purpose, if things produced nothing through them ... We must therefore understand that God works in things in such a manner that things have also their proper operation."

In other words, according to Aquinas, "God is the cause of action in every agent." Furthermore, "God not only moves things to operate ... but He also gives created agents their forms and preserves them in being." With regard to the being of things, Aquinas holds that God "established an order among things, so that some depend on others, by which they are conserved in being, though He remains the principal cause of their conservation."

WITH REGARD TO NATURE itself this theological doctrine raises two sorts of problems. The first concerns the efficacy of natural causes, which are sufficient for the scientist to appeal to in explaining natural phenomena, yet are insufficient by themselves for the production of natural effects. The second concerns the distinction between the natural and the supernatural, now not in terms of the created and the uncreated, but in terms of what happens naturally (or even by chance) as opposed to what happens as a result of God's intervention in the course of nature.

Miracles, for example, are supernatural rather than natural events. They are not produced by natural causes; nor do they happen by accident. They are attributed by the theologian to divine causality, yet not in such a way that violence is done to nature. "The term *miracle*," Aquinas explains, "is derived from admiration, which arises when an effect is manifest, whereas its cause is hidden ... A miracle is so called as being full of wonder; in other words, as having a cause absolutely hidden from all. This cause is God. Therefore those things which God does outside the causes which we know are called miracles."

The miraculous is that which is beyond the power of nature to accomplish. "A thing is said to be above the ability of nature," Aquinas writes, "not only by reason of the substance of the thing done, but also because of the manner and the order in which it is done"; and "the more the power of nature is surpassed, the greater the miracle." Aquinas distinguishes three grades of miracles.

The first, he says, surpasses nature "in the substance of the deed; as, for example, if two bodies occupy the same place, or if the sun goes backwards, or if a human body is glorified. Such things nature is absolutely unable to do; and these hold the highest rank among miracles. Secondly, a thing surpasses the power of nature, not in the deed, but in that wherein it is done; as the raising of the dead, and giving sight to the blind, and the like. For nature can give life, but not to the dead, and it can give sight, but not to the blind. Such hold the second rank in miracles. Thirdly, a thing surpasses nature's power in the measure and order in which it is done; as when a man is cured of a fever suddenly by God, without treatment or the usual process of nature ... These hold the lowest place in miracles."

Though "each of these kinds has various degrees, according to the different ways in which the power of nature is surpassed," no miracle, according to Aquinas, transgresses the order of nature in the sense of accomplishing the impossible. Unlike the impossible, which would destroy nature, the improbable can be elicited by God's power within the general framework of nature.

Hume, on the other hand, thinks that "a miracle is a violation of the laws of nature." And since, in his view, a firm and unalterable experience has established these laws, the proof against a miracle, from the nature of the fact, is as entire as any argument from experience can be. "Why is it more than probable," he asks, "that all men must die; that lead cannot, of itself remain suspended in the air; that fire consumes wood, and is extinguished by water; unless it be, that these events are found agreeable to the laws of nature, and there is required a violation of these laws, or in other words, a miracle to prevent them?

"Nothing is esteemed a miracle," Hume continues, "if it ever happens in the common course of nature ... There must, therefore, be a uniform experience against every miraculous event, otherwise the event would not merit that appellation. And as a uniform experience amounts to proof, there is here a direct and full *proof,* from the nature of the fact, against the existence of any miracle; nor can such a proof be destroyed, or the miracle rendered credible, but by an opposite proof which is superior."

Hume does not think that miracles can be proved against our uniform experience of the order of nature. But he also thinks that they are "dangerous friends or disguised enemies to the *Christian religion*" who would try to defend its beliefs "by the principles of human reason . . . The *Christian religion* not only was at first attended with miracles," he declares, "but even at this day cannot be believed by any reasonable person without one. Mere reason is insufficient to convince us of its veracity: and whoever is moved by *Faith* to assent to it, is conscious of a continued miracle in his own person . . . which gives him a determination to believe what is most contrary to custom and experience."

ONE OTHER TRADITIONAL conception of nature, implicit in much of the foregoing, should be noted. The various senses of the term so far explicitly considered are alike in this: that they justify the use of the word "Nature" with a capital "N" and in the singular. This other sense of the term appears when we speak of each thing as having a nature of its own, and of the world as containing a vast plurality and radical diversity of natures.

In this sense we attribute a nature even to things which are contrasted with Nature and the natural. We speak of the nature of God and the nature of freedom, the nature of art, the nature of reason, the nature of ideas, the nature of the state, the nature of customs and habits. This could, of course, imply a theory that things which are not completely natural, nevertheless have a natural basis, as art, the state, or habit. Another meaning, however, seems to be involved.

The phrase "nature of" appears almost as frequently in the great books as the word "is," and frequently it is unaccompanied by any explicit theory of Nature or the natural. The discussion of the *nature of* anything seems, for the most part, to be a discussion of *what* it is. To state the nature of anything is to give its definition; or if for any reason definition in a strict sense cannot be given, then the attempt to state the nature of the thing consists in trying to say what characterizes this thing or kind of thing, in distinction from everything else or all other kinds.

Enumerating the senses of the term 'nature,' Aristotle gives this as the fifth meaning. The first four comprise senses which distinguish the natural from the artificial or the immutable, and which indicate that the natural or the physical has an immanent principle of movement in itself and involves matter or potency. The fifth sense is that in which 'nature' means "the *essence* of natural objects"; and, as he goes on to say, this implies the presence in them of form as well as matter. "By an extension of meaning from this sense of 'nature' every essence in general has come to be called a 'nature,' because the nature of a thing is one kind of essence." This is the sixth and most general sense, according to which the nature or essence of anything is the object of definition.

Does each individual thing have a nature peculiarly its own, even if it cannot be defined? Or is a nature or essence always something common to a number of individuals, according to which they can be classified into kinds, and the kinds ordered as species and genera? Do John and James, for example, have individual natures in addition to the common nature which they share through belonging to the human species; and does their human nature entail certain properties which are generic rather than specific, *i.e.,* which seem to be determined by their having the generic nature common to all animals as well as the specific nature common to all men?

Such questions about individual, specific, and generic natures raise problems of definition and classification which are discussed in the chapter on EVOLUTION. They also raise problems about the existence or reality of the *kinds* which men define and classify. Are they merely what Locke calls "nominal essences," or do our definitions signify real essences, *i.e.,* the natures of things as they really are? Is the real world one which, as William James says, "plays right into logic's hands"? Does Nature consist of a *hierarchy* of natures or distinct kinds; or is it a *continuum* of things all having the same nature and differing from each other only individually or accidentally, but not essentially? These problems are discussed elsewhere, in such chapters as Animal, Definition, Evolution, Life and Death, and Same and Other.

In the 20th century, Whitehead introduces what he calls an "organic theory of nature." This doctrine "cries aloud for a conception of organism as fundamental for nature," and he explains this by saying that "the whole point . . . is the evolution of the complex organisms from antecedent states of less complex organisms." For Whitehead, science is now "taking on a new aspect which is neither purely physical, nor purely biological. It is becoming the study of organisms. Biology is the study of the larger organisms; whereas physics is the study of the smaller organisms . . . The organisms of biology include as ingredients the smaller organisms of physics." In Whitehead's organismic view of nature, the old issue between mechanism and vitalism becomes irrelevant.

61

Necessity and Contingency

INTRODUCTION

THE basic meaning of the words *necessity* and *contingency* is made known to us by the fact that we can substitute for them the familiar words *must* and *may*. "Is there any being which *must* exist?" asks the same question as, "Does anything exist of *necessity?*" "Are all things of the sort which *may* or *may not* exist, or are they divided into those which *must* exist and those which *may* or *may not* exist?" means the same as, "Is everything *contingent* in being or do some things exist *necessarily* and some *contingently?*"

The great issues which involve the opposition between necessity and contingency are concerned with more than questions about being or existence. They also deal with cause and effect, judgment and reasoning, happenings or events, the actions and decisions of men, human history and social institutions. In each case, the problem is formulated by such questions as: Does everything which happens in nature or history happen necessarily? Is everything contingent? Or are some events necessary and others contingent? Is the relation between cause and effect a necessary connection, or do some causes produce their effects contingently?

Are there some propositions which the mind *must* affirm because their truth is necessary? Or are all propositions such that they *may* or *may not* be true, our affirmation or denial of them being contingent upon factors which lie outside the propositions themselves? In reasoning, does the conclusion always follow by necessity from the premises if it follows at all? And are all conclusions which follow necessarily from their premises necessarily true, or may some be necessary truths and some contingent?

Are men necessitated in all their acts, or are certain actions contingent upon the exercise of their will and in this sense free? Does human liberty consist merely in the freedom of a man's action from the external necessity of coercion or constraint; or does it consist in a man's being able to choose whatever he chooses, freely rather than necessarily? Is every act of the will necessarily determined, or are some acts of the will acts of free choice?

Are certain human institutions, such as the family and the state, necessary? Are men compelled to live socially or can they choose the solitary life? If domestic and political society are necessary, are the ways in which they are organized also necessary, or are such things as monogamy in the family and monarchy in the state contingent? Are such things as war, slavery, poverty, and crime necessary features of human society, or are they the result of circumstances which are contingent and which can therefore be remedied?

These questions indicate the range of subject matters in which issues are raised concerning the necessary and the contingent. They also indicate that the other ideas to which necessity and contingency have relevance are too manifold to permit an enumeration of all the other chapters in which some aspect of necessity and contingency is discussed. This chapter stands to the others as a kind of summary of the theme of necessity and contingency. It assembles in one place the various topics, problems, or subject matters which traditionally engage the human mind with that theme.

Two chapters alone demand specific mention as, in a sense, being concerned with ideas that seem to be inseparable from the notions of necessity and contingency. They are FATE and CHANCE. Though they stand opposed to one another as the necessary to the contingent, they do not cover every application of this opposition. They are largely concerned with necessity and contingency in the realm of change, in the causation of the events of nature or the happenings of history. They do not deal, at least not directly, with necessity and contingency in being or existence, in thought or knowledge, in human acts and social institutions.

THE NECESSARY AND the contingent do not seem to be opposed in exactly the same way in each of the four areas—namely, being, change, thought, and action—in which they raise basic issues.

In the sphere of human action, for example, writers like Hobbes, Locke, and Hume substitute the notion of liberty for contingency as the opposite of necessity. The meaning of necessity alters in consequence. Liberty, according to these authors, implies the absence not of all necessity, but only of external necessity in the form of compulsion. An internal necessity, they think, is quite compatible with complete freedom.

Hume therefore dismisses the supposed conflict between liberty and necessity as groundless. "By liberty," he writes, "we can only mean *a power of acting or not acting, according to the determinations of the will;* that is, if we choose to remain at rest, we may; if we choose to move, we also may. Now this hypothetical liberty is universally allowed to belong to everyone who is not a prisoner and in chains . . . Liberty, when opposed to necessity, not to constraint, is the same thing with chance; which is universally allowed to have no existence."

Similarly, Locke defines liberty as a man's power "to do or forbear doing any particular action, according as its doing or forbearance has the actual preference in the mind, which is the same thing as to say, according as he himself wills it." Liberty in this sense, he adds, belongs not to the will, the acts of which are necessitated by their causes, but to the man who is under no external necessity, in the form

of compulsion, to do what is contrary to his will or to refrain from doing what he wills.

Hobbes seems to go even further along the same line of thought. Holding that liberty is destroyed only by external impediments to action, he uses "necessity" in a sense which makes it consistent with liberty, or inseparable from it. "The actions which men voluntarily do," he says, "because they proceed from their will, proceed from *liberty;* and yet, because every act of man's will, and every desire, and inclination, proceeds from some cause, and that from another cause, in a continual chain (whose first link is in the hand of God, the first of all causes), they proceed from *necessity.*"

Yet if what Hobbes means by "external impediments" represents the same nullification of liberty which others call "compulsion" or "restraint," then there is at least one meaning of "necessity" which stands opposed to liberty. Enumerating the meanings of "necessary," Aristotle lists as one sense "the compulsory or compulsion, *i.e.,* that which impedes or tends to hinder, that which is contrary to impulse or purpose . . . or to the movement which accords with purpose and with reasoning." It is in a related sense that Plato opposes necessity to intelligence. Necessity represents for him those resistant factors in nature which the mind of man or God must overcome, or persuade to give way, if reason or purpose is to prevail in the coming to be of anything. In this sense, necessity like chance is opposed to purpose. Blind necessity and blind chance both exclude the operation of final causes; both exclude the possibility that the events of nature are directed toward an end.

WE SEEM TO HAVE found almost universal agreement on the point that there is one sense in which necessity conflicts with liberty. But this agreement does not affect the issue whether liberty is more than freedom from external coercion. There are those, like Aquinas, who think that man's will is free in its acts of choice with regard to "particular contingent means." Aquinas agrees that what is called "necessity of coercion" is "altogether repugnant to the will." The same act cannot be absolutely coerced and voluntary. But the question is whether the will's acts are necessarily determined by causes operating within the sphere of the will itself.

Aquinas names two modes of necessity which operate *within* the sphere of the will and restrict its freedom. One is the natural necessity that the will should desire an ultimate end, such as the complete good or happiness. If a man wills any object at all as the ultimate goal of his life, he cannot will anything other or less than that which can satisfy all his natural desires. The other necessity is that which concerns the use of those means which are absolutely indispensable conditions for reaching the end being sought. This may be an absolute or a conditional necessity. When the end is itself necessary (*e.g.,* happiness), whatever means are necessary thereto necessitate the will absolutely. When a certain end is not necessary, but has been freely adopted (*e.g.,* a certain destination), and when *only one* means is available (*e.g.,* one mode of transportation), then it becomes necessary to choose that means. But this necessity is conditional since it remains in force only on the condition that we continue to have a certain end in view—an end we can relinquish at any time as freely as we adopted it.

According to Aquinas, this leaves a great many acts of the will which are in no way necessitated: those in which there is no necessary connection between the means and a given end, and those in which a given means is necessary only on the condition that a certain end is sought. If the end need not be sought, then the will is free not to choose the means of achieving it; and if, when the end is necessarily sought, alternative means are available, then the will is free to choose one rather than another.

According to this theory, liberty consists in the absence of internal as well as external necessity. Furthermore, liberty seems to be related positively to contingency, insofar as freedom of choice depends on a contingent connection between means and ends, or upon the contingent, *i.e.,* the conditional, character of the end. On the other hand, those who hold that the will is never free from internal necessity insist that the act of choice, even

with respect to contingent means, is always caused. If being caused is equivalent to being determined—which seems to be the view of Hobbes, Locke, and Hume—then whether or not we know what causes a particular choice, our wills are so determined that we could not have chosen otherwise.

THE PROBLEM OF the freedom of the will in relation to the causes which determine its acts is considered in the chapter on WILL. The foregoing discussion suffices here for the purpose of throwing light on the meaning of necessity. If now we shift from human action to the realm of becoming, change, or motion, we face the question of the relation between necessity and causation in its most general form.

In the realm of nature the alternatives to necessity are referred to as "chance" and as "contingency." The significance of these alternatives depends on the theory of causation. According to one opinion, every effect is necessarily determined by its causes, and every cause necessarily produces certain effects. Given the causal chain of past events leading up to the present, every future event is necessarily determined. Nothing that ever happens could happen otherwise. Nothing happens contingently or by chance. This theory of causation is accordingly a doctrine of universal necessity or absolute determinism in the realm of change.

Calvin follows the teaching of Augustine on this point. Augustine, he says, "everywhere teaches, that if anything is left to fortune, the world moves at random . . . he also excludes the contingency which depends on human will, maintaining . . . that no cause must be sought for but the will of God."

"In nature," writes Spinoza, "there is nothing contingent, but all things are determined from the necessity of the divine nature to exist and act in a certain manner." Though nothing which exists or happens is contingent, "God alone exists from the necessity of His own nature and acts alone from the necessity of His own nature." The divine necessity is therefore different from the necessity of everything else which follows from the divine nature. One is the necessity of freedom or self-determination, the other the necessity of compulsion, or determination by another. "That thing is called free," says Spinoza, "which exists from the necessity of its own nature alone, and is determined to action by itself alone. That thing, on the other hand, is called necessary, or rather compelled, which by another is determined to existence and action in a fixed and prescribed manner."

Hume's statement that there is "no such thing as *Chance* in the world," would appear to agree with Spinoza's denial of contingency. But Hume also seems to deny the perception of any necessary connection between cause and effect. This is not to say that events happen without cause, but only that "our ignorance of the real cause of any event has the same influence on the understanding" as if nothing were necessarily determined by its causes.

"We are never able," Hume thinks, "to discover any power or necessary connexion, any quality, which binds the effect to the cause, and renders the one an infallible consequence of the other ... One event follows another; but we never can observe any tie between them. They seem *conjoined,* but never *connected* ... Our idea, therefore, of necessity and causation arises entirely from the uniformity observable in the operations of nature, where similar objects are constantly conjoined together, and the mind is determined by custom to infer the one from the appearance of the other. These two circumstances form the whole of that necessity, which we ascribe to matter. Beyond the constant *conjunction* of similar objects, and the consequent *inference* from one to the other, we have no notion of any necessity or connexion."

But the question remains whether in the order of nature itself particular events are necessarily determined or happen contingently. The fact that we may be ignorant of real necessities does not, as Hume seems to admit, imply their nonexistence. Our saying it is only probable that the sun will rise tomorrow may reflect our inadequate knowledge of causes rather than a real indeterminacy in the order of nature. On the other hand, to say as Hume does that chance has no place in nature, may mean only

that "nothing exists without a cause of its existence," rather than that whatever happens is necessarily determined by its causes.

As indicated in the chapter on CHANCE, two things must be distinguished here: the absolutely uncaused—the spontaneous or fortuitous—and the contingently caused, or that which depends upon the coincidence of a number of independent causes. A given condition may be necessary to produce a certain result, as, for example, oxygen may be necessary for combustion. But by itself it may not be sufficient for the production of that effect. If the maxim, "nothing exists without a cause of its existence," requires a cause or causes adequate to produce the effect, then the maxim is equivalent to the principle of sufficient reason. Whenever two or more causes, each of which may be necessary, are not sufficient in separation, the existence of the effect depends upon their combination; and the effect is contingent if the required combination of causes is itself not necessarily caused.

The issue concerning contingency in nature thus seems to be more sharply stated when there is no reference to our knowledge or ignorance of causes. On this issue, Aristotle and Spinoza appear to be more clearly opposed to one another than Hume is to either.

If things do not take place of necessity, "an event," according to Aristotle, "might just as easily not happen as happen; for the meaning of the word 'fortuitous' with regard to present or future events is that reality is so constituted that it may issue in either of two opposite directions." For example, "a sea-fight must either take place tomorrow or not, but it is not necessary that it should take place tomorrow, neither is it necessary that it should not take place, yet it is necessary that it either should or should not take place tomorrow." Though Aristotle holds that "one of the two propositions in such instances must be true and the other false," he also insists that "we cannot say determinately that this or that is false, but must leave the alternative undecided."

Aristotle's view with regard to propositions about future particular events is that our judgments cannot be either true or false, not because of insufficient knowledge on our part, but because future particulars are in themselves always contingent. Nothing in the nature of things or causes—existent in the past or present—necessarily determines them to happen. They will occur only if independent causes happen to coincide. Since these causes are independent—not determined to combination by their natures—the coincidence will be a matter of chance, not of necessity.

This theory of contingency in the realm of change—involving an affirmation of the real existence of contingent events—raises problems for the theologian concerning God's knowledge and will. Does the fact that nothing happens contrary to God's will imply that whatever happens happens necessarily? Aquinas answers that "God wills some things to be done necessarily, some contingently . . . Therefore, to some effects, He has attached necessary causes that cannot fail; but to others defectible and contingent causes, from which arise contingent effects . . . it being His will that they should happen contingently."

Similarly, the fact that God knows all things infallibly does not seem to Aquinas to be inconsistent with the real contingency of some things. He explains that "whoever knows a contingent effect in its causes only, has merely a conjectural knowledge of it." But "God knows all contingent things not only as they are in their causes, but also as each one of them is actually in itself . . . Hence it is manifest that contingent things are infallibly known by God, inasmuch as they are subject to the divine sight in their presentiality; yet they are future contingent things in relation to their own causes."

This has a bearing on the difference between human and divine apprehension of future contingent things. "Things reduced to actuality in time," Aquinas declares, "are known by us successively in time, but by God they are known in eternity, which is above time. Whence to us they cannot be certain, since we know future contingent things only as contingent futures; but they are certain to God alone, Whose understanding is in eternity above time. Just as he who goes along the road does not see those who come after him; whereas he who sees the whole road from a height sees at once all those travelling on it. Hence," Aquinas continues, "what is known by us must be necessary, even as it is in itself; for what is in itself a future contingent cannot be known by us. But what is known by God must be necessary according to the mode in which it is subject to the divine knowledge . . . but not absolutely as considered in its proper causes." It does not follow, therefore, that *everything known by God must necessarily be;* for that statement, according to Aquinas, "may refer to the thing or to the saying. If it refers to the thing, it is divided and false; for the sense is, *Everything which God knows is necessary.* If understood of the saying, it is composite and true, for the sense is, *This proposition, 'that which is known by God is,' is necessary.*"

With regard to human knowledge, Aquinas makes another distinction in answering the question whether man can have scientific or certain knowledge of contingent things. If, as Aristotle seems to hold, the objects of knowledge are necessary, not contingent things, then the realm of contingency belongs to opinion, conjecture, or probability. Insofar as the particular events of nature are contingent, they cannot be objects of scientific knowledge. But, according to Aquinas, "contingent things can be considered in two ways: either as contingent or as containing some element of necessity, since every contingent thing has in it something necessary; for example, that Socrates runs is in itself contingent; but the relation of running to motion is necessary, for it is necessary that Socrates moves if he runs."

The contingency that Socrates *may* or *may not* run does not alter the hypothetical necessity that *if* he runs, he *must* move. In its concern with contingent things, natural science is concerned only with such hypothetical necessities. Unlike physics, other sciences may deal with absolutely necessary things. That the objects of mathematics are of this sort seems to be an opinion shared by William James and Kant, Hume and Descartes, Plato and Aristotle. But they do not agree on whether the necessities of mathematics belong to reality or have only ideal existence, *i.e.,* whether they exist apart from or only in the human mind. This issue is connected with another major issue concerning necessity and contingency, namely, whether any reality has necessary existence.

AS WE HAVE SEEN, those who discuss necessity and contingency in the domain of human acts and natural events seem to construe these alternatives differently, according as they conceive liberty and chance in terms of different theories of causation. With regard to being or real existence, however, there seems to be a common understanding of the alternatives, even among those who do not agree that God alone is a necessary being because they think that this world is also determined to exist as a necessary consequence of God's existence.

In the preceding discussions, one meaning of contingency has repeatedly appeared. The contingent is that which can be otherwise. "That which cannot be otherwise is necessarily as it is," writes Aristotle, "and from this sense of 'necessary' all its other meanings are somehow derived." This insight is sometimes expressed by the statement that the opposite of the necessary is the impossible, whereas the contingent—which is neither necessary nor impossible—includes contrary possibilities.

In logical analysis what is called the "modality of necessity" is attributed to judgments the contradictories of which are self-contradictory; e.g., if the proposition 'the whole is *not* greater than any of its parts' represents an impossible judgment, then the contradictory proposition 'the whole *is* greater than any of its parts' represents a necessary judgment. In contrast, as Hume points out, *"that the sun will not rise tomorrow* is no less intelligible a proposition, and implies no more contradiction than the affirmation *that it will rise."* These two propositions represent contrary possibilities. No matter which turns out to be true, the event could have been otherwise.

In logical analysis some complication seems to arise from the fact that the necessary has two opposites: the impossible on the one hand, and the possible or contingent on the other. This is usually clarified by the recognition that the possible is the opposite of the impossible as well as of the necessary. In that sense of "possible" which excludes only the impossible, the necessary is, of course, possible, for what is necessary cannot be impossible. But in that sense of "possible" which implies contrary possibilities, the possible excludes the necessary as well as the impossible.

"From the proposition 'it may be' it follows," according to Aristotle, "that it is not impossible, and from that it follows that it is not necessary; it comes about therefore that the thing which must necessarily be need not be; which is absurd. But again, the proposition 'it is necessary that it should be' does not follow from the proposition 'it may be,' nor does the proposition 'it is necessary that it should not be.' For the proposition 'it may be' implies a twofold possibility, while, if either of the two former propositions is true, the twofold possibility vanishes. For if a thing may be, it may also not be, but if it is necessary that it should be or that it should not be, one of the two alternatives will be excluded. It remains, therefore, that the proposition 'it is not necessary that it should not be' follows from the proposition 'it may be.' For this is true also of that which must necessarily be."

Of the same thing we can say that it *may* be and that it *may not* be; but we cannot say of the same thing both that it *may* be and that it *must* be, or that it *may not* be and that it *cannot* be. As Aristotle traces the implications of these modes of 'to be,' we see that *may-be* implies *may-not-be,* which contradicts *must-be;* and similarly that *may-not-be* implies *may-be,* which contradicts *cannot-be.*

When we pass from the analysis of propositions or judgments to the consideration of being or existence, the situation is simpler. Since the impossible is that which cannot exist, whatever does exist must either be necessary or possible. Here the necessary and the possible are generally understood to exclude one another. The necessary is that which *cannot* not be, the possible that which *can* not be.

IN SPITE OF THIS common understanding of the alternatives, there are basic differences among the authors of the great books in regard to the analysis or demonstration of necessary being.

Aristotle, for example, tends to identify the possible with the perishable—with that which both comes into being and passes away. Those substances are necessary, in contrast, which are not subject to generation and corruption. Holding that the matter of the celestial bodies differs from that of terrestrial bodies with respect to the potentiality for substantial change, Aristotle seems to regard the heavenly bodies as necessary beings, eternal in the sense of always existing, even though changeable in regard to place, *i.e.,* subject to local motion. The changing things of this earth are all contingent in being, for the mutability to which their matter inclines them includes coming to be and passing away.

This analysis of necessity and contingency in terms of matter's potentialities leads to another conception of necessary being—that of a totally immutable being which has necessary existence because it lacks matter entirely and, since it consists of form alone, is purely actual. Whether or not there are for Aristotle substances other than the prime mover which are necessary because they are immaterial beings, he attributes pure actuality only to that one necessary being which is an *unmoved* mover.

Aquinas seems to adopt both of Aristotle's senses of "necessary being." He treats the celestial bodies and the angels as having necessity to the extent that they are immutable. But their immutability is limited in his opinion to the fact that they are by nature imperishable—the celestial bodies because of their matter; the angels because they are simple substances, not composed of matter and form. Since they are creatures they cannot be altogether immutable. "All creatures," Aquinas writes, "before they existed, were possible"— and in this sense contingent as regards their being, not necessary. "As it was in the Creator's power to produce them before they existed in themselves," he continues, "so likewise is it in the Creator's power when they exist in themselves to bring them to nothing." Furthermore, at every moment of their existence, their contingent being depends upon God's power. God preserves them in being, Aquinas says, "by ever giving them existence," for "if

He took away His action from them, all things would be reduced to nothing."

In the strict sense then of "necessary being," no creature, but only God, the uncreated being, is truly a necessary being—because in God alone existence is identical with essence. Only a being whose very essence it is to exist is incapable of not existing; only such a being is necessary in the sense of being purely actual. All created things must be contingent, for if in their case to exist belonged to their very natures, God could not have created them by causing their natures to exist, nor when they did exist would His power be necessary to sustain them in being.

Where Aquinas defines God's necessity in terms of the *identity* of essence and existence, Descartes and Spinoza tend to conceive God as necessary because his essence is such that his existence *follows from* it. The difference may affect the meaning with which it is said that God is uncaused or that God is self-caused. "If its existence is caused," Aquinas writes, "nothing can be the sufficient cause of its own existence." According to Descartes, to say that God is "cause of His own existence . . . merely means that the inexhaustible power of God is the cause or reason why he needs no cause."

Descartes's position seems to be that that which is self-caused in the sense of having its existence determined by its own nature or essence, is also uncaused in the sense that its existence is not caused by anything outside itself. "Existence," he writes, "is involved in the essence of an infinite being, no less than the equality of its angles to two right angles is involved in that of a triangle." But though this suggests the notion of God's existence following from His essence, Descartes also says that "in God existence is not distinguished from essence."

For Descartes as for Aquinas the basic point remains that that which does not depend for its being upon any external cause, exists necessarily. Descartes, furthermore, associates the necessary existence of an independent being with that being's infinity or perfection of nature. That which is conceived as infinite or perfect cannot be conceived as lacking existence. "The notion of possible or contingent existence," he says, "belongs only to the concept of a limited thing."

Like Descartes, Spinoza conceives God as the only infinite and immutable being which exists necessarily in the sense of being "that whose essence involves existence." But unlike him Spinoza also attributes necessity in another sense to every finite and mutable thing which God causes to exist; for in his view, God not only exists necessarily but, acting from the necessity of His own nature, God also necessitates whatever follows as a consequence of His action. No other world than this is possible. "Things could be produced by God," Spinoza writes, "in no other manner and in no other order than that in which they have been produced." Furthermore, since whatever is in God's power "necessarily follows from it, and consequently exists necessarily," it is impossible for this world not to have existed. The existence of this particular world is as inseparable from God's existence as God's own existence is inseparable from His essence or nature.

In the tradition of western thought, there is, perhaps, no deeper theological issue than that which opposes the freedom of God's will to the necessity of God's acting according to His nature; and which, in consequence, sets the possibility of other worlds (or even of no world at all) against the necessity that, if God exists, this particular world inevitably follows.

Taking the other side on both points, Aquinas, for example, argues that "since the goodness of God is perfect, and can exist without other things inasmuch as no perfection can accrue to Him from them, it follows that His willing things apart from Himself is not absolutely necessary." As for the particular features of this world, Aquinas says that "since God does not act from natural necessity" nor from a will that is "naturally or from necessity determined" to the things which exist, it follows that "in no way at all is the present course of events produced by God from any necessity, so that other things could not happen ... Wherefore, we must simply say that God can do other things than those He has done." Other, and even better, worlds than this are possible, for "God could make other things, or add something to the present creation; and then there would be another and a better universe."

Nor does the Christian theologian admit that the divine nature is subject to any necessity. "We do not put the life of God or the fore-knowledge of God under necessity," writes Augustine, "if we should say that it is necessary that God should live forever, and foreknow all things; as neither is His power diminished when we say that He cannot die or fall into error—for this is in such a way impossible to Him, that if it were possible for Him, He would be of less power. But assuredly He is rightly called omnipotent, though He can neither die nor fall into error. For He is called omnipotent on account of His doing what He wills, not on account of His suffering what He wills not; for if that should befall him, He would by no means be omnipotent. Wherefore, He cannot do some things for the very reason that He is omnipotent."

ONE OTHER TRADITIONAL issue is raised by the conception of God as a necessary being; or, more strictly, as the only necessary being in the sense of having a nature which involves existence. It is formed by opposite views of the validity of the so-called "ontological" or *a priori* argument for God's existence.

Both Descartes and Spinoza argue, like Anselm and others before them, that since God cannot be conceived as not existing, it is impossible in fact for God not to exist. Those who reject such reasoning do not deny that it is unintelligible or self-contradictory to think of God as merely possible rather than necessary, *i.e.*, as requiring a cause outside Himself in order to exist. Kant, for example, admits that existence must be included in the conception of God as *ens realissimum*—the most real and perfect being. But he denies that the real existence of the object so conceived is implied by the logical necessity of the conception itself.

This amounts to saying that it is possible for a being we cannot conceive except as existing, not to exist. Aquinas seems to make the same critical point when he says that even if everyone understood by the word "God" something than which nothing greater can be conceived, and therefore a being necessarily existing, still it would not follow that "he understands that what the word signifies actually exists, but only mentally."

Stated in its most general form, the problem is whether that which is inconceivable by the human mind is impossible in reality; or whether that which is logically necessary, or necessary in thought, is also necessary in fact or existence. However that issue is resolved, it must be noted that among the so-called *a posteriori* demonstrations of God's existence, or arguments from the existence of certain effects to the existence of their cause, one mode of reasoning turns upon the distinction between contingent and necessary being.

If contingent beings exist (as it is evident they do, from the mutability and perishabil-

ity of physical things), *and if* each contingent being is by definition incapable of causing its own existence, *and if* one contingent being cannot cause the existence of another, *and if* everything which exists must have a cause for its existence, either in itself or in another; *then* from all these premises it would seem to follow that a necessary being exists.

Here the conclusion may follow with logical necessity from the premises, but whether it is necessarily true depends upon the truth of the premises. That in turn seems to depend upon the understanding of what it means for anything to be contingent or necessary in being. It may also depend on whether or not the reasoning escapes Kant's criticism of all *a posteriori* arguments for the existence of a necessary being, namely, that such reasoning always implicitly contains the ontological argument, and is thereby invalidated.

62

Oligarchy

INTRODUCTION

IN the great books of political theory the word "oligarchy" is usually listed along with "monarchy" and "democracy" among the traditional names for the forms of government. According to the meaning of their Greek roots, "oligarchy" signifies the rule of the few as "monarchy" signifies the rule of one and "democracy" the rule of the people—or the many. These verbal meanings are somewhat altered, however, when we consider the actual conflict between oligarchy and democracy in Greek political life. It involved an opposition, not simply between the few and the many, but between the wealthy and the working classes. The contest between these factions for political power dominated more than a century of Greek history around the Periclean age; and that fact justifies Aristotle's remark that oligarchy and democracy are the two principal conflicting forms of government.

We would not so describe the political struggle of our time. We would not speak of oligarchy as one of the principal forms of government in the world today. Instead we tend to think in terms of the conflict between democracy and dictatorship or despotism. Even when we look to the background of present issues, it is the age-old struggle between absolute and constitutional government—or between monarchies and repubics—which seems to supply the obvious historical parallels for the contemporary conflict between the principles of arbitrary and legal government. The traditional terms of political theory, with the exception of oligarchy, thus appear to have a certain liveliness in the consideration of current problems. But though it does not have such frequency in our speech or familiarity in our thought, oligarchy may be much more relevant to the real issues of our day than appears on the surface.

Certainly within the framework of constitutional government oligarchic and democratic principles are the opposed sources of policy and legislation. In modern as in ancient republics the division of men into political parties tends to follow the lines of the division of men into economic factions. The ancient meanings of oligarchy and democracy, especially for those observers like Thucydides and Aristotle who see the rich and the poor as the major rivals for constitutional power, indicate the fusion of political and economic issues.

The difference between oligarchy and democracy, says Aristotle, is not well-defined by reference to the few and the many, unless it is understood that the few are also the rich and the many the poor. The issue is not whether the few are wiser than the many, or whether it is more efficient to have the government in the hands of the few rather than the many. Such issues have been debated in the history of political thought, but they are more appropriate to the alternatives of aristocracy and democracy than to the conflict between oligarchy and democracy.

The historic struggle between oligarchs and democrats—whether described as a struggle between rich and poor, nobility and bourgeoisie, landed gentry and agrarian peons, owners and workers, classes and masses—is a struggle over the political privileges of wealth, the rights of property, the protection of special interests. In the tradition of the great books, Marx and Engels may be the first to call this struggle "the class war," but they are only the most recent in a long line of political and economic writers to recognize that the economic antagonism of rich and poor generates the basic political conflict in any state. "Any city, however small," says Socrates, "is in fact divided into two, one the city of the poor, the other of the rich: these are at war with one another."

OLIGARCHY IS NOT always defined as the rule of the wealthy, nor is it always conceived as the opponent of democracy on constitutional questions. In the *Statesman,* for example, Plato first divides the forms of government into "monarchy, the rule of the few, and the rule of the many," and then divides "the rule of the few into aristocracy, which has an auspicious name, and oligarchy." Here aristocracy and oligarchy seem to be regarded as opposites, the one a government in which the few rule according to the laws, the other lawless government by the few. In both, the few are the wealthy; hence wealth is no more characteristic of oligarchy than of aristocracy.

Some political theorists make no reference to wealth at all in the discussion of oligarchy. Hobbes divides the forms of government according to whether the sovereign power is in the hands of one or more; and if in the hands of more than one, then whether it is held by some or all. He calls the several forms of government monarchy (one), aristocracy (some), and democracy (all). There are "other names of government in the histories and books of policy," he adds, such as "*tyranny* and *oligarchy.* But they are not the names of other forms of government, but of the same forms misliked. For they that are discontented under *monarchy* call it *tyranny,* and they that are displeased with aristocracy call it *oligarchy.*" Like Hobbes, both Locke and Rousseau use no criterion except numbers to distinguish the forms of government, Locke calling government by the few "oligarchy" and Rousseau calling it "aristocracy."

Barely outlined in this way, the alternatives of monarchy, aristocracy *or* oligarchy, and democracy seem to raise issues only of expediency or efficiency rather than of justice. Whether oligarchy is intrinsically a good or bad form of government tends to become a question only when other factors are con-

sidered; when, for example, the distinction between aristocracy and oligarchy is made to turn on whether the few are men of virtue or men of property, or when, in the comparison of oligarchy with democracy, the emphasis is not upon numbers but on the principles of wealth and liberty.

Nevertheless, the numerical criterion does not seem to be totally irrelevant to the comparison. "Oligarchy and democracy," Aristotle writes, "are not sufficiently distinguished merely by these two characteristics of wealth and freedom." Though the "real difference between democracy and oligarchy is poverty and wealth," and though "wherever men rule by reason of their wealth, whether they be few or many, that is an oligarchy," Aristotle does not seem to think we can neglect the political significance of what he calls the "accidental fact that the rich everywhere are few, and the poor numerous."

With regard to aristocracy and oligarchy, the chief question does not seem to be one of principle, but of fact. Plato in *The Republic* and Aristotle in the *Politics* define aristocracy as government by the few best men, or the most virtuous. They also place it next to what is for them the ideal government by the supremely wise man—the rule of the philosopher king, or what Aristotle calls "the divine sort of government." In this context, oligarchy represents a perversion of aristocracy, as tyranny represents a corruption of monarchy.

Plato describes oligarchy as arising when "riches and rich men are honored in the State" and when the law "fixes a sum of money as the qualification for citizenship" and allows "no one whose property falls below the amount fixed to have any share in the government." But according to Socrates, wealth does not qualify men to rule, as virtue and wisdom do. "Just think what would happen," he says, "if pilots were to be chosen according to their property, and a poor man were refused permission to steer, even though he were a better pilot." To which Adeimantus agrees that in government, as in navigation, the probable result would be shipwreck.

But though there may be no question of

the superiority of aristocracy over oligarchy in principle, the critics of aristocracy question whether any historic state in which the few hold political power is not in fact an oligarchy. It may not always be the case that the power of the few rests directly on wealth. The privileged class may be a military clique or a hereditary nobility. Yet these distinctions are seldom unaccompanied by the control of land or other forms of wealth, so that indirectly at least the oligarchic factor is thought to be operative.

THE CRITICISM OF aristocracies as masked oligarchies is discussed in the chapter on ARISTOCRACY. The critical point seems to be that nothing except superior virtue or talent justifies a political inequality between the few and the many. The meaning of oligarchy is generalized in consequence to include any government in which the special privileges or powers held by the few cannot be justified, whether it is wealth or some other title to preeminence that is substituted for superiority in virtue or talent. When it is so understood, the word "oligarchical" tends to become like "tyrannical," a term of reproach.

In describing different forms of democracy, Aristotle observes that their common principle is to give a share in the government to all who meet whatever minimum qualification is set by law. "The absolute exclusion of any class," he says, "would be a step towards oligarchy." To the same effect is J. S. Mill's comment on the steps away from oligarchy accomplished by English constitutional reforms in the 19th century.

"In times not long gone by," Mill writes, "the higher and richer classes were in complete possession of the government . . . A vote given in opposition to those influences . . . was almost sure to be a good vote, for it was a vote against the monster evil, the over-ruling influence of oligarchy." But now that the higher classes are no longer masters of the country, now that the franchise has been extended to the middle classes, a diminished form of oligarchy still remains. "The electors themselves are becoming the oligarchy"—in a population where many are still disfranchised. "The present electors," Mill continues, "and the bulk of

those whom any probable Reform Bill would add to the number, are the middle class; and have as much a class interest, distinct from the working classes, as landlords or great manufacturers. Were the suffrage extended to all skilled laborers, even those would, or might, still have a class interest distinct from the unskilled."

Oligarchy remains, according to Mill, so long as there is any unjustifiable discrimination among classes in the population. It is not in his view limited to discrimination based on the extremes of wealth and poverty, as he plainly indicates by his remarks on the special interests of different parts of the working class, or their relation as a whole to the lower middle classes. He makes this even plainer by what he has to say on political discrimination as between the sexes. Suppose the suffrage to be extended to all men, he writes, "suppose that what was formerly called by the misapplied name of universal suffrage, and now by the silly title of manhood suffrage, became the law; the voters would still have a class interest, as distinguished from women."

The oligarchic defect in representative government which Mill is here criticizing seems to have little or no basis in economic class divisions. The exclusion of any class in the population from a voice in government renders that government oligarchic with respect to them. The excluded class may even be a minority. So conceived, oligarchy no longer means the rule of either the rich or the few.

When the meaning of oligarchy is generalized in this way, the discussion of oligarchy seems to presuppose the typically modern conception of democracy. As indicated in the chapter on DEMOCRACY, the distinguishing feature of the modern democratic constitution is universal suffrage. By this criterion, the conflict between the democrats and the oligarchs of the ancient world appears to be a conflict between two forms of the oligarchic constitution—one in which the wealthier few and one in which the poorer many have political rights, but in neither of which membership in the political community includes all normal adult human beings in the population.

Where ancient political theory could conceive of a mixed constitution—somehow combining oligarchic and democratic principles—the modern conception of democracy seems to make any compromise with oligarchy impossible. Certain modern writers, notably Gaetano Mosca, Robert Michels, and Vilfredo Pareto, seem to insist, on the contrary, that oligarchy is present in all forms of government, and is especially prevalent in representative democracies where the actual conduct of government—the effective power—is in the hands of a bureaucracy or an elite, whether popularly chosen or self-appointed. But the contradiction may be more verbal than real if on one side the word "oligarchy" means some degree of restriction in the franchise or citizenship, and, on the other, it applies to any situation in which the whole people are not directly active in all the affairs of government and, consequently, a small number of men administers the state. Understood in the latter sense, the oligarchic principle does not seem to be incompatible with representative democracy. Those who use the word in this sense merely call attention to an inevitable characteristic of representative government. A representative democracy may also have an aristocratic aspect when it follows the principle that the men best qualified by virtue or talent for public office should be chosen by the suffrage of all their fellow citizens.

Tocqueville seems to express this point when he says, "Our contemporaries are ever a prey to two conflicting passions: they feel the need of guidance, and they long to stay free. Unable to wipe out these two contradictory instincts, they try to satisfy them both together. Their imagination conceives a government which is unitary, protective, and all-powerful, but elected by the people . . . Under this system the citizens quit their state of dependence just long enough to choose their masters and then fall back into it."

FULLER DISCUSSION of these aspects of oligarchy is found in the chapters on ARISTOCRACY and DEMOCRACY. Here we are primarily concerned with political issues which have their source in the opposition of economic classes in the state, primarily that extreme division of men into those who live by their labor and those who live on their property and the labor of others. It is in terms of this extreme division between men of leisure and workingmen that the conflict between oligarchy and democracy takes place in the ancient world.

At a time when citizenship meant a much more active and frequent participation in government than it does under the modern institutions of the ballot box and the representative assembly, the ancient defenders of oligarchy could argue that only men of wealth had the leisure requisite for citizenship. Oligarchy could be further defended on the ground that, in many of the Greek city-states, public officials were either not compensated at all or at least not substantially. Only men of sizable property could afford to hold public office.

Aristotle weighs the arguments for and against oligarchy. On the point of leisure, for example, he holds that "nothing is more absolutely necessary than to provide that the highest class, not only when in office, but when out of office, should have leisure." Yet "even if you must have regard to wealth in order to secure leisure," it is "surely a bad thing," he thinks, "that the greatest offices, such as those of kings and generals, should be bought. The law which allows this abuse makes wealth of more account than virtue."

Aristotle seems to regard democratic and oligarchic claims as complementary half-truths. "Both parties to the argument," he says, "are speaking of a limited and partial justice, but imagine themselves to be speaking of absolute justice." According to an adequate conception of political justice, it is as unjust to treat equals unequally as it is to treat unequals equally. The oligarch violates the first of these principles, the democrat the second. "Democracy arises out of the notion that those who are equal in any respect are equal in all respects; because men are equally free, they claim to be absolutely equal. Oligarchy is based on the notion that those who are unequal in one respect are in all respects unequal; being unequal, that is, in property, they suppose themselves to be unequal absolutely."

Both forms of government have "a kind of justice, but, tried by an absolute standard, they are faulty; and, therefore, both parties, whenever their share in the government does not accord with their preconceived ideas, stir up revolution . . . In oligarchies the masses make revolution under the idea that they are unjustly treated, because . . . they are equals and have not an equal share; and in democracies, the notables revolt, because they are not equal, and yet have only an equal share."

What can cure this situation in which perpetual revolution seems to be inevitable, as democracy succeeds oligarchy, or oligarchy democracy, in the government of the Greek cities? Aristotle describes many forms of oligarchy and democracy, but none seems to remove the cause of revolution. When, in an attempt to preserve their position, the wealthier families turn to the more extreme forms of oligarchic constitution, that tendency eventually leads to a kind of despotic government which Aristotle calls "dynasty," or the lawless rule of powerful families.

To establish a stable government which shall be less subject to revolution in favor of a contrary principle of government, and which shall resist the tendency toward lawless rule, by either the masses or the powerful few, Aristotle proposes the mixed constitution, which shall combine the elements of both democratic and oligarchic justice. But this will not work in actual practice, he thinks, unless the middle class "is large, and stronger if possible than both the other classes . . . Great then is the good fortune of a state in which the citizens have a moderate and sufficient property; for where some possess much, and the others nothing, there may arise an extreme democracy, or a pure oligarchy; or a tyranny may grow out of either extreme . . . These considerations will help us to understand why most governments are either democratical or oligarchical. The reason is that the middle class is seldom numerous in them, and whichever party, whether the rich or the common people, transgresses the mean and predominates, draws the constitution its own way, and thus arises either oligarchy or democracy."

From the point of view which sees no justice in granting any special privileges to property, Aristotle's position on oligarchy seems open to question. For one thing, in admitting a partial justice in the principle that those who are unequal in wealth should be treated unequally in the distribution of political power, Aristotle appears to affirm that the possessors of wealth *deserve* a special political status. For another thing, in his own formulation of an ideal polity, Aristotle advocates the exclusion of the working classes from citizenship. "The citizens must not lead the life of mechanics or tradesmen, for such a life is ignoble and inimical to virtue. Neither must they be husbandmen, since leisure is necessary both for the development of virtue and the performance of political duties." All these classes of men are necessary for the existence of the state, but they are to be no part of it in the sense of political membership. "The best form of state will not admit them to citizenship," though it will include as necessary "the slaves who minister to the wants of individuals, or mechanics and laborers who are the servants of the community."

Some of the great speeches in Thucydides' *The History of the Peloponnesian War,* which deal with domestic issues as well as the issues of war and peace, eloquently argue the opposite side of the case. Debating with Hermocrates before the Syracusan assembly, Athenagoras answers those who say that "democracy is neither wise nor equitable, but that the holders of property are the best fitted to rule. I say, on the contrary, first, that the word *demos,* or people, includes the whole state, oligarchy only a part; next, that if the best guardians of property are the rich, and the best counsellors the wise, none can hear and decide so well as the many, and that all these talents, severally and collectively, have their just place in a democracy. But an oligarchy gives the many their share of the danger, and not content with the largest part, takes and keeps the whole of the profit."

IN MODERN POLITICAL thought, the discussion of oligarchy seems to occur on two levels. There is a controversy on the level of constitutional principles with regard to suffrage and representation and the qualifications for public office. Here the issues concern the justice of the fundamental laws of republican or popular government. There is also a consideration of the way in which men of property or corporate concentrations of wealth are able to exert influence upon the actual course of government. Here the problem becomes, not so much the justice of the constitution or of the laws, but the weight which wealth seems able to throw onto the scales of justice.

The great modern defense of the oligarchic constitution does not seem to be as plainly or forcefully made in any of the great books as in the speeches of Edmund Burke, especially those in opposition to the suffrage reform measures proposed by Charles James Fox, wherein Burke argues for the principle of *virtual* representation. It is unnecessary, he claims, for the franchise to be extended to the working classes if their economic betters—who also happen to be their superiors in talent and education—deliberate on what is for the common good of all.

The Federalists seem to take an opposite view. Reflecting on the system of British representation in their day, they observe that, for the eight millions of people in the kingdoms of England and Scotland, "the representatives . . . in the House of Commons amount to five hundred and fifty-eight." But, they go on, "of this number one ninth are elected by three hundred and sixty-four persons and one half by five thousand seven hundred and twenty-three persons. It cannot be supposed," they argue, "that the half thus elected and who do not even reside among the people at large, can add anything either to the security of the people against the government, or to the knowledge of their circumstances and interests in the legislative councils. On the contrary, it is notorious that they are more frequently the representatives and instruments of the executive magistrate than the guardians and advocates of the popular rights." Nevertheless, they do not condemn such an oligarchic system of representation as entirely inimical to the virtues of parliamentary government. "It is very certain," they declare, "not only that a valuable portion of freedom has been preserved under all these circumstances, but that the defects in the British code are chargeable, in a very small

proportion, on the ignorance of the legislature concerning the circumstances of the people."

Some of the American constitutionalists may be influenced by Burke's defense of oligarchy in terms of the virtues of an aristocracy, but they state their own position in terms which are more plainly oligarchic. They argue for poll tax clauses and property qualifications for public office on the ground that the country should be run by the people who own it. Furthermore, those who are not economically independent are not in a position to exercise political liberty. "Power over a man's subsistence," Hamilton declares, "amounts to power over his will."

Facing the issue which had been raised on the floor of the constitutional convention, Madison remarks that "the most common and durable source of factions has been the various and unequal distribution of property. Those who hold and those who are without property have ever formed distinct interests in society." He proposes a representative—or what he calls a "republican"—system of government to avoid the excessive factionalism of the pure or direct democracies of Greek city-states.

"Theoretic politicians, who have patronized this species of government," Madison writes, "have erroneously supposed that by reducing mankind to perfect equality in their political rights, they would, at the same time, be perfectly equalized and assimilated in their possessions, their opinions, and their passions." By a weighted system of representation, the power of sheer numbers may be counterbalanced by the power given to other factors, thus preventing the "accomplishment of the secret wishes of an unjust and interested majority . . . A rage for paper money, for an abolition of debts, for an equal division of property, or for any other improper or wicked project, will be less apt to pervade the whole body of the Union than a particular member of it."

In another paper, the Federalists answer the charge that the constitution is oligarchic, because "the House of Representatives . . . will be taken from that class of citizens which will have least sympathy with the mass of the people and be most likely to aim at an ambitious sacrifice of the many to the aggrandizement of the few." This objection, they say, while "leveled against a pretended oligarchy," in principle "strikes at the very root of republican government."

The method of election provided for by the Constitution aims "to obtain for rulers men who possess most wisdom to discern, and most virtue to pursue, the common good of the society ... Who are to be the electors of the federal representatives? Not the rich, more than the poor; not the learned, more than the ignorant; not the haughty heirs of distinguished names, more than the humble sons of obscurity and unpropitious fortune ... Who are to be the objects of popular choice? Every citizen whose merit may recommend him to the esteem and confidence of the country. No qualification of wealth, of birth, of religious faith, or of civil profession, is permitted to fetter the judgment or disappoint the inclination of the people."

WHETHER THE AMERICAN Constitution in its original formulation is an oligarchic document has long been a matter of dispute. Whether the Federalists favor devices for protecting the rights of property or repudiate oligarchic restrictions in favor of the rights of man has also been the subject of controversy. That this is so may indicate at least a certain ambiguity in their position. But on the question of the oligarchic influences on government—the political pressures exerted by propertied classes to serve their special interests—the opinion of the modern authors of the great books seems much clearer.

The most extreme statement of this opinion is, of course, to be found in the *Manifesto of the Communist Party*. There government, in fact the state itself, is regarded as an instrument which the economic oppressors wield against the oppressed. The final step in the bourgeois revolution, according to Marx and Engels, occurred when the bourgeoisie "conquered for itself, in the modern representative State, exclusive political sway." In the bourgeois state, legislation is nothing but the will of this one class made into a law for all. One aim of the communist revolution, beyond the temporary dictatorship of the proletariat, is the withering away of that historic formation of the state in which "political power ... is merely the organized power of one class for oppressing another."

Though much less radical in intention than Marx, Adam Smith and J. S. Mill make statements which seem to be no less radical in their criticism of the oligarchic influences on modern parliamentary government. It has been said, Smith observes, that "we rarely hear ... of combinations of masters, though frequently of those of workmen. But whoever imagines, upon this account, that masters rarely combine, is as ignorant of the world as of the subject. Masters are always and everywhere in a sort of tacit, but constant and uniform combination, not to raise the wages of labor above their actual rate ... Masters too sometimes enter into particular combinations to sink the wages of labor even below this rate." Furthermore, the parties to the conflict do not have equal access to legislative protection. "Whenever the legislature attempts to regulate the differences between masters and their workmen, its counsellors are always the masters."

Almost a century later, Mill writes in a similar vein concerning "the persevering attempts so long made to keep down wages by law ... Does Parliament," he asks, "ever for an instant look at any question with the eyes of a working man? ... On the question of strikes, for instance, it is doubtful if there is so much as one among the leading members of either House who is not firmly convinced that the reason of the matter is unqualifiedly on the side of the masters, and that the men's view of it is simply absurd." The remedy for this inequity, according to Mill, is not communism, but constitutional reforms in the direction of universal suffrage which will no longer leave the working classes "excluded from all direct participation in the government."

63

One and Many

INTRODUCTION

IN *Pragmatism* and in his unfinished last work, *Some Problems in Philosophy,* William James uses the problem of the one and the many as one of the crucial tests of the philosophical mind. In his famous table of doctrines or "isms" he aligns monism with rationalism and idealism in the column headed "tender-minded," and in the other column, headed "tough-minded," he places their opposites—pluralism, empiricism, and materialism. But as his own theories show, "isms" like monism and pluralism tend to oversimplify the issues.

Whoever emphasizes the oneness of the world, for example, may also acknowledge its manyness and recognize that it is somehow a pluriverse as well as a universe. Some, like Francis H. Bradley, may qualify this view by regarding the unity as ultimate reality, the plurality as appearance or illusion. Whoever finds the multiplicity of things the primary fact may, nevertheless, find some unity in the order and connection of things. Some, like James himself, may insist that the connection is a loose concatenation of relatively independent parts of reality, rather than an interpenetration of each part with every other in the solid whole which James calls the "block universe."

There may be another oversimplification in James's consideration of the problem of the one and the many. He seems to be concerned largely, if not exclusively, with the alternatives of the block and the concatenated universe as conceptions of the structure of reality. But, as some of the great books of antiquity make evident, that is only one of the problems of the one and the many. Perhaps it should be said, not that there are many problems of the one and the many, but that there is one prob-

lem having many aspects or applications, for in every statement of the problem there is at least this singleness of theme; that the one and the many are opposed, that the one is *not* a many and the many *not* a one. Yet even that does not seem to be quite accurate for, as Socrates tells Protarchus in the *Philebus,* it may also be said that the one is a many and the many a one. These are "wonderful propositions," he says, wonderful because "whoever affirms either is very open to attack."

At this early moment in the recorded tradition of western thought, the dialogues of Plato, so thorough in their exploration of the problems of the one and many, make no claim to having discovered or invented them. They were ancient even then. They seem to hang in the very atmosphere of thought, usually befogging those who try to see the truth about anything else without first clearing away their obscurities.

Socrates refers to "the common and acknowledged paradoxes of the one and the many . . . that everybody has by this time agreed to dismiss as childish and obvious and detrimental to the true course of thought." These aside, some genuine perplexities remain. Protarchus asks Socrates to instruct him about "those other marvels connected with this subject which," as Socrates seems to have implied, "have not yet become common and acknowledged."

Socrates begins by calling his attention, not to the unity of *this* man or *this* ox, but to the sense in which it is said that "man is one, or ox is one, or beauty one, or the good one." It is necessary to ask, he says, first, whether such unities exist; then, such unities being always the same, and admitting neither generation nor destruction, how each is itself alone, is not only one but *this* one; finally, how these unities can be conceived as dispersed and multiplied in the world of things which come to be and pass away. This last question seems to be the most difficult because it asks about the *being* of the same and one as it *becomes* in the one and many.

Protarchus is impatient to begin clearing up these problems. Willing to undertake what he calls "this great and multifarious battle, in which such various points are at issue," Socrates is also anxious to let Protarchus and the other youths know the intellectual perils which lie ahead for novices who enter upon this inquiry. "The one and many," he tells them, "become identified by thought . . . They run about together, in and out of every word which is uttered . . . This union of them will never cease, and is not now beginning, but is . . . an everlasting quality of thought itself, which never grows old."

That is why, he explains, "any young man, when he first tastes these subtleties, is delighted, and fancies that he has found a treasure of wisdom; in the first enthusiasm of his joy, he leaves no stone, or rather no thought, unturned, now rolling up the many into the one, and kneading them together, now unfolding and dividing them; he puzzles himself first and above all, and then he proceeds to puzzle his neighbors, whether they are older or younger or of his own age—that makes no difference; neither father nor mother does he spare; no human being who has ears is safe from him, hardly even his dog; and a barbarian would have no chance of escaping him, if an interpreter could only be found."

WHETHER IT IS full of exasperating subtleties or is a treasure of true wisdom, the discussion of the one and the many—in itself and in relation to being and becoming, the intelligible and the sensible, the definite and the infinite, the same and other, universals and particulars, wholes and parts, the simple and the complex, the indivisible and the continuous—is a discussion which seems unavoidable to the ancients. In the dialogues of Plato and in Aristotle's treatises, especially his *Metaphysics,* the one and the many are connected with the basic terms of philosophical thought.

For Plato, the distinction between the one and the many enters into the analysis of almost any object—such as pleasure or virtue or knowledge. Anything, viewed under the aspect of its being or its becoming, its definite sameness or its indefinite otherness and variety, must be discussed both as a one and as a many. The motion of Plato's dialectic may be from the one to the many or from the many to the one; or it may be on the level of the many as an intermediate stage through which analysis must go in proceeding from the infinite to the one. Those who pass at once from unity to infinity, says Socrates, do not recognize "the difference between the mere art of disputation and true dialectic."

For Aristotle, first philosophy or metaphysics, concerned as it is with "being *qua* being and the attributes which belong to anything *qua* being," also investigates unity. Unity is the first property of being. The meanings of one or unity are as various as the meanings of 'to be.' If there is a difference between essential and accidental being, there is a parallel difference between essential and accidental unity. If natural and artificial things differ in substance or being, so too must they differ in unity. "Being and unity are the same," Aristotle says, "and are one thing in the sense that they are implied in one another as are principle and cause." Unity is nothing apart from being, and nothing can be without being one in some sense of unity which is determined by the way in which the thing exists. Aristotle's analysis of any subject matter, proceeding as it does by reference to contraries, always appeals to the one and the many. "All contraries," he says, "are reducible to being and non-being and to unity and plurality, as for instance, rest belongs to unity and movement to plurality . . . And everything else is evidently reducible to unity and plurality . . . For all things are either contraries or composed of contraries, and unity and plurality are the principles of all contrariety."

THE PROBLEMS IN whose analysis one and many seem to be involved recur in every period of western thought. The question, for example, whether there is an irreducible duality in the relation of knower and known, or whether, in the act of knowledge, knower and known are one, is discussed by Hobbes and James as well as Plotinus and Aristotle. The question whether the state—which is a multitude somehow united for a common life—has, or should have, the same degree of unity as the family, is discussed by Locke and Hegel as well as Plato and Aristotle.

The earlier controversy over the indivisibility of sovereignty becomes at a later stage the central issue of federal union, to which *e pluribus unum* is the solution offered by the Federalists. Questions concerning the simple and the complex, or wholes and parts, as objects of knowledge, or questions concerning the unity and divisibility of time, space, or matter, engage the attention of inquirers and analysts no less in modern than in ancient times.

But there are certain problems which are treated with unusual speculative vigor by the ancients alone. Unlike the problems just mentioned, which deal with applications of the contrast between unity and multiplicity, these are questions about the One itself—what it is, whether it exists, whether it is identical with Being, whether it is itself a substance or the substance of all things.

The sustained inquiry into such matters in antiquity seems to testify to the extraordinary power exerted upon ancient thought by Parmenides of Elea. The person called "the Eleatic Stranger" represents his theories in such dialogues of Plato as the *Sophist* and the *Statesman.* Parmenides, or his disciple Zeno, is probably the source of many of the paradoxes and riddles which Socrates, in the *Philebus,* dismisses as no longer worthy of serious attention. One whole dialogue, named *Parmenides* because of his part in the discussion, exhibits the Eleatic demonstration that 'all is one.' It abounds in the subtleties of the various arguments which try to defend the reality of the many or try to reduce that position to absurdity.

Questioned by Socrates concerning his paradoxes, Zeno says that his writings "were meant to protect the arguments of Parmenides against those who make fun of him and seek to show the many ridiculous and contradictory results which they suppose to follow from the affirmation of the one." When he addresses himself to the partisans of the many, Zeno says that he returns "their attack with interest by retorting upon them that their hypothesis of the being of many, if carried out, appears to be still more ridiculous than the hypothesis of the being of one."

Aristotle also deals with the Eleatic arguments. In the *Physics,* he says first that inquiring about whether being is one, cannot contribute to the study of nature. He then adds that such inquiry anyway would be "like arguing against any other position maintained for the sake of argument . . . or like refuting a merely contentious argument." This description, he says, "applies to the arguments both of Melissus and Parmenides: their premises are false and their conclusions do not follow . . . Accept one ridiculous proposition and the rest follows—a simple enough proceeding." Aristotle's treatment of Parmenides and Zeno in the *Metaphysics* seems to be no more sympathetic, though it tacitly admits the relevance of the Eleatic speculations to the study of being, if not to the study of change and the principles of nature. Nevertheless, many of the questions concerning the one and the many which both Plato and Aristotle deem worthy of discussion appear to have some connection with the perplexities propounded by Parmenides and his school.

THOSE WHO DO NOT deny either the unity of being or its multiplicity tend to make the primary fact about reality either its oneness or its manyness. This may seem at first to be of slight significance, but if the two views of the world which result from this difference are examined, it may be found that the disagreement on this single point changes the perspective on everything else. The philosophers who magnify either the one or the many behold universes more radically dissimilar than the same object looked at from opposite ends of a telescope. But that is not all. Almost every other fundamental conception—of God and man, of the mind and knowledge, of matter and motion, of cause and necessity—seems also to be altered.

Spinoza, for example, criticizes those who attribute to finite things, of which there are necessarily many, the properties which belong to the infinite being, of which there can be only one. This man, this stone, or any comparable individual thing, is not a substance, having the power to exist in and of itself; it consists merely "of certain modifications of the attributes of God," the one infinite substance in which everything else "both is and is conceived." According to Spinoza, those who suppose that the finite many are substances "have not observed a proper order of philosophic study."

They begin with the objects of sense which have the least reality and come last to the divine nature, the infinite one, which "ought to be studied first because it is first in the order of knowledge and in the order of things . . . Hence it has come to pass," Spinoza continues, "that there was nothing of which men thought less than the divine nature while they have been studying natural objects, and when they afterwards applied themselves to think about God, there was nothing of which they could think less than those prior fictions upon which they had built their knowledge of natural things, for these fictions could in no way help to the knowledge of the divine nature."

Starting with the definition of substance as that which exists in itself and is conceived through itself, and with the definition of God as absolutely infinite being, "that is to say, substance consisting of infinite attributes," Spinoza undertakes to prove that there cannot be two or more substances having the same nature or attributes, that substance is necessarily infinite, and hence that it is impossible for more than one substance to exist. Since he regards it as axiomatic that "everything which is, is either in itself or in another," it follows for Spinoza that if anything at all exists, God (or substance) must necessarily exist—as that which alone exists in itself and as that in which everything else has its finite being as a mode or affection of the attributes of God.

Certain other consequences seem to follow.

The one infinite substance is indivisible: it is not a whole made up of parts which can have independent existence, as the parts of a quantitative whole seem able to exist when the quantity is divided. Furthermore, God, according to Spinoza, "is the immanent, and not the transitive, cause of all things." God causes them not as one thing acting on another when both are independent in existence, but rather as the being *in which* all things are. God is not present in the world, as other theologians seem to think, in the manner in which a cause exists in an effect that depends upon it. Rather the whole world is in God as an effect which can in no way be separated from the existence of the cause, any more than an aspect can be separated from that of which it is an aspect.

For Spinoza, the unity and totality of being can be called "nature," as well as "infinite substance" or "God." His distinction between *natura naturans* and *natura naturata,* discussed in the chapter on NATURE, seems to permit him to distinguish between the infinite or eternal and the finite or temporal—the one and the many—without implying a real separation between God and the world. Since God is immanent in the world, and since God not only exists necessarily but also acts from the necessity of His own nature, it follows (as is indicated in the chapter on NECESSITY AND CONTINGENCY) that every finite and temporal aspect of nature is necessarily determined. Nothing is contingent. Nothing could be otherwise than it is.

THIS EXAMINATION of a doctrine in which the primacy of the one absorbs as well as subordinates the many, serves to exemplify the point that making the one primary is more than a matter of emphasis. It also shows that almost every fundamental question is affected. It presents a picture of what James appears to mean when he speaks of the block universe, though he himself usually seems to have in mind Hegel's Absolute rather than Spinoza's God.

Aristotle advances a contrary doctrine. Like Spinoza he uses the term 'substance.' Like Spinoza he defines substance as that which exists in itself, not as an accident (a quality, for example) which exists in another, *e.g.,* the redness in the rose. But for him substance is not necessarily infinite, nor is it indivisible. A rose or a man is a substance. Every physical thing which has a natural unity is a substance.

Each is a finite whole, or rather each is a whole in a number of different senses. Insofar as it has essential unity, it is a whole composed of matter and form which, according to Aristotle, are represented in the formulation of a definition by the genus and the differentia. Insofar as it is composed of matter, it also has the unity of a quantitative whole in virtue of which it moves as one thing or uniquely occupies a place. Since quantitative unity involves continuity, and continuity entails divisibility, a substance remains one only so long as it is not divided into its quantitative parts, just as it remains one essentially only so long as its matter and form are not separated.

A substance is individual not because it is absolutely indivisible—as for Lucretius the atom is because it is simple rather than composite. Its individuality rather consists, first, in its being divided from other substances in such a way that it can perish without necessarily destroying them, or they can perish without destroying it; and, second, in the fact that, though divisible into parts, it is one whole when these parts remain undivided. Yet as one substance it has more unity than a mere collection of things.

The difference between a man and a machine, according to Aristotle's differentiation between the unity of natural substances and of artificial things, is that a man is not composed of substances (though the parts of a living organism may come to exist as substances when it is decomposed or they are separated from it), whereas a machine, made up of separate pieces of metal, is nothing but a number of individual substances arranged in a certain way. The unity of man does not appear to be the same, therefore, when soul and body are conceived by Descartes as two substances and by Aristotle not as distinct substances but as form and matter which through their union constitute a single substance.

Unity, in short, belongs essentially to the individual natural substance. Because each individual substance is necessarily a one among a many, Aristotle, unlike Spinoza, cannot affirm the unity of substance without also affirming a plurality of substances. Not itself a substance, but only an aggregation of substances, the world is primarily a many rather than a one. The unity it possesses derives from the order and connection of the substances which are its component parts; and that in turn largely derives from the way in which distinct substances causally interact.

Since, according to Aristotle, causality includes contingency and chance, the causal interdependence of substances, with respect to their generation and their motions, does not lock them together into a solid block. To use James's imagery again, a vast plurality of individual substances, causally yet also contingently related, constitutes a loosely knit world, a concatenated universe.

THE RELATION OF the world as a whole to God does give it greater unity, if the supposition of a plurality of finite individual substances remains the fundamental feature of the world God creates. The Christian doctrine of creation may attribute to the world a greater unity than that possessed by any work of human art, in proportion as the infinitely greater wisdom of the divine plan orders the separate things of nature with an infinitely greater perfection than man can achieve in putting things together or in ordering them to his purpose. But if, according to the theologian, God in creating the world creates not one substance, but many substances, forming a single whole through the pattern of their connection with one another, then in a sense the world has less unity than each of its component substances.

For Aquinas, one kind of substance may have greater unity than another. The immaterial has more than the material; and God more than any finite substance, since each of these is composed of matter and form, or essence and accidents, or at least of essence and existence, whereas the infinite being of God is absolutely simple. The divine nature is without matter, without accidents; its attributes are identical with its essence, and its essence with its existence.

This cardinal point about the divine nature is crucial to the conception of God, and of the world's relation to God. In the formation of Christian theology, God's absolute simplicity seems to exclude all but one resolution of the issue concerning the Trinity. According to the position Augustine takes in criticizing the Arian heresy, the position which is expressed in the Nicene Creed and reaffirmed by Calvin, God is not a trinity of substances, but a trinity of persons—aspects of, or relations within, one substance. The plurality of things which constitutes the world puts the world entirely outside the divine substance. Immanent only as a cause, the simple being of God transcends the complex whole of the created world.

This transcendence seems, furthermore, to imply for theologians like Augustine and Aquinas a fundamental duality in the realm of existence. God and the world are two, not one. Infinite being is absolutely prior to and independent of finite beings. The one can exist without the many. Though the many are said to participate in being, when they do exist, they do not enter into the being of the one, or share it in any way. The being they have is not only separate from the being of God, but even their mode of being is only analogical to the divine being.

The doctrine that each thing has its own being, and that, as Aquinas says, "being is common to all things only in an analogical sense," seems to put diversity above unity in the structure of reality, and to leave the ultimate plurality of this world unaffected either by the fact that it was created as one or by the fact of its relation to a transcendent One.

IN THE TRADITION of the great books, the problem of the one and the many is often stated without using the notion of substance as the pivotal term.

It appears in Plato's consideration of being and becoming. It is sometimes present in his treatment of the relation between intelligible forms and sensible things—between the universal ideas and the particulars which resemble them through some manner of imitation or participation. It even runs through the discussion of the realm of ideas itself; for the idea of the one is one idea among many, and yet each of the many ideas is in some way one.

The problem of the one and the many appears in Hume's consideration of the absolute distinctness of each unit of experience from every other, accompanied as it is by his skepticism concerning our ability to discover any connections which might tie these units together into a real unity. It appears in Kant's theory of the transcendental unity of apperception, which reduces the sensory manifold to a unity of order; and in Hegel's theory of the one Absolute Idea which contains within itself all the variety that becomes manifest as the Idea unfolds in the processes of nature or history.

The substitution of one set of terms for another does not seem to alter the fundamental issue. Nor does it enable the mind to escape taking sides with those who give primacy to the one or to the many, except perhaps by trying to balance them as correlatives. Among the great books, however, *The Six Enneads* of Plotinus develops a theory of the One which, putting it above being and beyond knowing, seems to transfigure all the traditional terms of analysis.

The One of Parmenides is, after all, Being; and this identification of Being with One raises a question of the reality of the many. But, according to Plotinus, "there exists a Principle which transcends Being; this is The One, whose nature we have sought to establish so far as such matters lend themselves to proof. Upon The One follows immediately the Principle, which is at once Being and the Intellectual-Principle. Third comes the Principle, Soul." These are what Plotinus calls the three hypotases. He finds some analogy for his trinity in a doctrine he ascribes to Plato's *Parmenides,* in which he finds a threefold distinction "between the Primal One, a strictly pure Unity, and a secondary One which is a One-Many, and a third which is a One-and-Many."

The One, according to Plotinus, not only transcends being; it also transcends intelligence. Knowing or thinking requires an object. The relation of knower and known entails a duality which would fracture the utter simplicity of The One. Even the complete reflexivity of The One knowing only itself is excluded. The super-essential is for Plotinus also the supra-cogitative. "What stands above Being stands above intellection," he says; "it is no weakness in it not to know itself, since as pure unity it contains nothing which it needs to explore." Multiplicity begins with the effort of the Intellectual-Principle to know the Transcendent. "It knows the Transcendent in its very essence but, with all its efforts to grasp that prior as pure unity, it goes forth amassing successive impressions, so that, to it, the object becomes multiple . . . The Intellectual-Principle is established in multiplicity."

What is the All of which The One is not all, since the Intellectual-Principle and the Soul also belong to it? Plotinus answers that "The One is all things and no one of them. The source of all things is not all things . . . It is precisely because there is nothing within the One that all things are from it." Everything else in the totality of which the Transcendent is the source emanates from it.

"Seeking nothing, possessing nothing, lacking nothing," Plotinus declares, "The One is perfect and, in our metaphor, has overflowed, and its exuberance has produced the new: this product has turned again to its begetter and has filled and has become its contemplator and so an Intellectual-Principle . . . It is simultaneously Intellectual-Principle and Being; and, attaining resemblance in virtue of this vision, it repeats the act of the One in pouring forth a vast power. This second outflow is a Form or Idea representing the Divine Intellect as the Divine Intellect represented its own prior, The One. This active power sprung from essences (from the Intellectual-Principle considered as Being) is Soul. Soul arises as the idea and act of the motionless Intellectual-Principle . . . It takes fullness by looking toward its source; but it generates its image by adopting another, a downward, movement. This image of Soul is Sense and Nature, the vegetal principle."

Nothing, writes Plotinus, "is completely severed from its prior. Thus the human Soul appears to reach as far down as to the vege-

tal order." In these successive emanations "all that is not One is conserved by virtue of the One, and from the One derives its characteristic nature." Everything except the One is a one-many. "If it had not attained such unity as is consistent with being made up of multiplicity, we could not affirm its existence." The Transcendent alone is "a really existent One, wholly and truly One, while its sequent, poured down in some way from the One, is all, a total which has participation in unity and whose every member is similarly all and one."

If reason cannot fully grasp the Transcendent One, that may be because discursive reason is itself a thing of multiplicity. The unity of an all-embracing vision may be required to apprehend the ineffable unity of the Transcendent. But the mysteriousness of unity is not confined to the Transcendent One. It confronts the mathematician as well as the philosopher. It challenges Nicomachus and Euclid as well as Plotinus.

"Unity," writes Nicomachus, "occupying the place and character of a point, will be the beginning of intervals and numbers, but is not itself an interval or a number." What, then, is unity or a unit in itself? Euclid answers with this definition: "A unit is that by virtue of which each of the things that exist is called one." Unity is not only the measure of existence, but also of numbers; for, according to Euclid, "a number is a multitude composed of units." In mathematics no less than in metaphysics or in theology the relation of unity to number seems to be the heart of the problem of the one and the many.

"Number," according to Locke, "applies itself to men, angels, actions, thoughts; everything that either does exist, or can be imagined." Unity or *one* is, in his view, not only the simplest of all our ideas, but the most omnipresent. "Every object our senses are employed about; every idea in our understandings; every thought of our minds, brings this idea along with it. And therefore it is . . . in its agreement to all other things, *the most universal idea we have*."

64

Opinion

INTRODUCTION

THE noble Houyhnhnms are paragons of reason. They have no conceptions or ideas of what is evil in a rational nature. "Their grand maxim," according to Swift, their creator, "is to cultivate reason and to be wholly governed by it. Neither is reason among them a point problematical as with us, where men can argue with plausibility on both sides of the question; but strikes you with immediate conviction, as it needs must do where it is not mingled, obscured, or discolored by passion and interest."

What Captain Gulliver finds most striking in the contrast between men and this noble race of horses is that the perfect rationality of the Houyhnhnms lifts them entirely above the vagaries and vicissitudes of opinion. "I remember it was with extreme difficulty," he says, "that I could bring my master to understand the meaning of the word *opinion,* or how a point could be disputable; because reason taught us to affirm or deny only where we are certain, and beyond our knowledge we cannot do either. So that controversies, wranglings, disputes, and positiveness in false and dubious propositions, are evils unknown among the Houyhnhnms."

Among men it is not the meaning of "opinion" but of "knowledge" which causes trouble. If men had no conception of knowledge at all, as the Houyhnhnms seem to have no conception of opinion, they would find themselves disagreeing about many matters of opinion, but probably not about the nature of opinion itself. The great controversies concerning opinion in the tradition of western thought all relate to its distinction from knowledge, both with regard to the difference in their respective objects and with regard to the way in which the mind works when it knows and when it opines.

Only when something better than opinion is proposed as attainable do the characteristics of opinion come to be questioned. That something may stand in relation to opinion as certainty to probability, as fact to conjecture, as adequate to inadequate knowledge, as demonstration to persuasion. The chief source of disagreement about the nature of opinion seems to be the meaning of the other term in the comparison. Yet a few commonly recognized features of knowledge—if that is taken as the contrasting term—throw some light on the characteristics of opinion. Certain things which are never said about knowledge seem to be generally said of opinion.

AN OPINION, it is said, may be either true or false. But knowledge is never said to be false. For a great many writers, though not for all, doubt and belief are attitudes of mind which accompany the holding of opinions, but not the possession of knowledge. It is possible to opine and doubt at the same time, but not to know and doubt. Belief overcomes doubt with respect to opinion, but in those matters in which the mind is convinced of the truth of its judgments, an act of belief does not seem to be necessary.

In the sense in which belief implies a willingness to assent where assent might reasonably be withheld, belief seems to be appropriate to opinion but incompatible with knowledge. The opposite of an opinion may be reasonably maintained, whereas the opposite of that which is known must be error or falsehood, and therefore untenable. The traditional distinction between axioms and postulates (or assumptions) exemplifies this difference between knowledge and opinion. If a proposition is axiomatic, its contrary must be false. But if something is proposed as an assumption to be taken for granted, then its opposite can also be postulated, and probably will be postulated by those who are unwilling to grant what has been proposed. "What we firmly believe," Russell declares, "if it is neither knowledge nor error . . . may be called *probable opinion*. Thus the greater part of what would commonly pass as knowledge is more or less probable opinion."

This last point in the comparison of knowledge and opinion appears to have political significance. It is not merely that men are accustomed to expect more disagreement in the sphere of politics than in science; they take a different attitude toward scientific and political controversy, largely because one is supposed to occur in the domain of knowledge and the other in the realm of opinion. Men speak of having a right to their own opinions, which includes a right to persist in them despite the conflicting opinions of others. The notion of a right to a certain obstinacy in differing from one's fellowmen seems to follow from the nature of opinion and to accord with its distinction from knowledge. With regard to matters concerning which it is supposed that knowledge rather than opinion is possible, disagreement may of course occur, but never without the expectation that reasonable men should be able to reach agreement on the disputed point by reexamining the facts.

The differences between men which we appeal to a consensus to resolve are differences of opinion, not knowledge. Sometimes conflicts of opinion cannot be settled in any other manner, and for practical purposes it may be necessary to accept the opinion of the majority. The theory of majority rule raises many questions on which the great books take opposite views, but for the most part they restrict the application of the theory to matters of opinion. Disputed issues in mathematics or other theoretical sciences are seldom, if ever, settled by counting heads. The weight of numbers seems to be peculiarly relevant to measuring the worth of conflicting opinions. "In all matters not contrary to faith," Tocqueville tells us, "one must defer to the majority."

The traditional consideration of opinion naturally divides, therefore, into two major lines of discussion. The first deals with the theoretical problem of the difference between knowledge and opinion, and involves such related terms as doubt, belief, faith, certitude, and probability. The second assumes that distinction for the most part, and deals with the problems of decision and responsibility in the sphere of opinion—the problem of liberty of conscience, of freedom of thought and expression, of majorities and minorities, and of individual judgment in difficult cases of conscience.

THE DISTINCTION between knowledge and opinion is sometimes made in terms of a difference in their objects, and sometimes in terms of a difference in the way the mind works when it knows and when it opines. These two modes of differentiation may, of course, supplement one another—the object of opinion being such that the mind must operate in a certain way with respect to it. The same authors usually treat the matter both ways. But not all the great books in which these things are discussed use the words "knowledge" and "opinion" to signify the basic opposition.

Locke, for example, says that "the mind has two faculties conversant about truth and falsehood: first, knowledge, whereby it certainly *perceives* and is undoubtedly satisfied of the agreement or disagreement of any ideas; secondly, judgment, which is the putting ideas together, or separating them from one another in the mind, when their certain agreement or disagreement is not perceived, but *presumed* to be so." To the faculty of judgment belongs "belief, assent, or opinion, which is the admitting or receiving of any proposition for true, upon arguments or proofs that are found to persuade us to receive it as true, without certain knowledge that it is so."

As demonstration is to persuasion, as certainty is to probability, so for Locke knowing or perceiving stands to judging or presuming. Others, like Hume, tend to use the term 'belief' in the place of 'opinion' as the opposite of 'knowledge'; or, like Spinoza, to assign opinion along with imagination to the domain of inadequate as opposed to adequate knowledge. But such differences in vocabulary do not seem to obscure the fact that these authors are making distinctions which, if not identical, are at least analogous.

A certain parallelism or analogy exists between different statements of the objects of knowledge and opinion. The knowable seems to have the properties of necessity and immutability, of universality, clarity, and distinctness. That which is contingent and variable, or confused and obscure, is usually regarded as the object of opinion.

Plato, for example, says that that which is apprehended by intelligence and reason "always is, and has no becoming," whereas "that which is conceived by opinion with the help of sensation and without reason, is always in a process of becoming and perishing and never really is." As understanding and reason divide the realm of knowledge, whose object is the immutable being of the intelligible forms, so fancy and perception divide the realm of opinion, whose objects are the sensible things which come to be and perish.

According to Aristotle, the object of science is the essential and the necessary, the object of opinion the accidental and the contingent. To whatever extent sensible particulars involve contingent accidents of all sorts, they belong to opinion, while the intelligible essences of things, universal in the sense of being common to many individuals, belong to science. The parallel which so far seems to be present between Plato's and Aristotle's statements of the objects of knowledge and opinion does not continue when we consider the consequences of their analyses.

For Aristotle, it is possible to have scientific knowledge as well as probable opinion about the changing things of the physical world, to the extent that these things are both intelligible and sensible, and have aspects both of necessity and contingency. But for Plato the realm of becoming belongs exclusively to opinion, as the quite separate realm of being belongs exclusively to knowledge. In consequence, Aristotle's enumeration of the sciences includes physics along with mathematics and theology, whereas the study of the physical world does not yield a science, according to Plato, but only, as he says in the *Timaeus,* "a likely story"—a plausible composition of probable opinions.

At first glance, Hume seems to provide a closer parallel to Plato. "All the objects of human reason or enquiry may naturally be divided into two kinds," he writes, "*relations of ideas,* and *matters of fact.*" Objects of the first sort are capable of demonstratively certain knowledge, *e.g.,* the mathematical sciences. Matters of fact, which include questions concerning the real existence of anything or the causal connection of one thing with another, do not permit demonstration. They are objects of belief or opinion.

It would seem, therefore, that Hume, like Plato, regards the objects of knowledge and opinion, or science and belief, as belonging to altogether distinct realms. They even seem to agree that physics cannot be classified as a science, though the probabilities it establishes may be quite sufficient for action. But this agreement must be qualified by the fact that the realm of ideas is for Plato the reality which changing things image, while for Hume ideas have no reality at all. They exist only in the mind, which obtains them from the impressions of sense-experience.

A parallel between Hume and Aristotle might also be drawn, at least insofar as both connect opinion with the contingent—that which can be otherwise. If the opposite of a proposition is not impossible or does not lead to self-contradiction, then the proposition and its contrary are matters of opinion. This criterion, in Aristotle's terms, excludes all self-evident and demonstrable propositions. Such propositions, for both Hume and Aristotle, express knowledge, not opinion. Yet Aristotle, unlike Hume, does not seem to think that the real existence even of immaterial beings is indemonstrable, or that no necessary connections can be discovered between cause and effect.

THESE EXAMPLES might be extended to include similar observations concerning Locke,

Spinoza, Kant, William James—in fact, almost every writer who distinguishes between knowledge and opinion by reference to characteristically different objects. In the tradition of western thought the major controversies concerning the objects of knowledge and opinion occur with regard to the kind of being or reality assigned to each type of object; and, in consequence, with regard to applications of the distinction. One writer treats as knowledge what another, by apparently the same criterion, calls opinion. The term 'opinion' gets its skeptical impact from this circumstance. The skeptic never denies that men can form opinions about a given subject; he denies that the topic can be a matter of certain or unquestionable knowledge.

Skepticism approaches its limit when it is maintained that everything is a matter of opinion. At the furthest extreme, it is sometimes said that nothing is either true or false, though Aristotle and others argue that such skepticism is self-destructive since the proposition 'nothing is true or false' is inconsequential if it is false, and self-contradictory if it is true. But the proposition 'everything is a matter of opinion' can itself be an opinion, and its opposite an opinion also.

The position which Montaigne takes in the *Apology for Raymond Sebond* is not the provisional skepticism of universal doubt in order to discover the foundations of certain knowledge. It is rather a resolute skepticism which reduces all human judgments to the status of equally tenable opinions and gives man no hope that he will ever be able to do better than adopt opinions on insufficient grounds or else suspend judgment entirely. No axioms, according to Montaigne, have ever won the universal consent of mankind; no demonstrations have ever escaped the need to assume their initial premises. Unless men beg the question in this way, they cannot avoid an infinite regress in reasoning. There is no proposition about which men have not disagreed or changed their minds. Illusions and hallucinations suggest the pervasive unreliability of the senses, as errors of judgment and reasoning suggest the radical infirmity of the mind.

"How diversely we judge things!" writes Montaigne. "How many times we change our notions! What I hold today and what I believe," he continues, "I hold and believe it with all my belief . . . I could not embrace or preserve any truth with more strength than this one. I belong to it entirely, I belong to it truly. But has it not happened to me, not once, but a hundred times, a thousand times, and every day, to have embraced with these same instruments, in this same condition, something else that I have since judged false? . . . we must become wise at our own expense. If I have often found myself betrayed under just these colors, if my touchstone is found to be ordinarily false, and my scales uneven and incorrect, what assurance can I have in them this time more than at other times? . . . We should remember, whatever we receive into our understanding, that we often receive false things there, and by these same tools that are often contradictory and deceived."

Montaigne exempts religious faith from the uncertainty of all beliefs or opinions which man arrives at through the unaided efforts of his senses and his reason. Though we must "accompany our faith with all the reason that is in us," we must do so "always with this reservation, not to think that it is on us that faith depends, or that our efforts and arguments can attain a knowledge so supernatural and divine." Faith is distinguished from ordinary belief, according to Montaigne, only if it enters into us "by an extraordinary infusion."

What is an article of faith to one man may, however, be merely a matter of opinion to another. This seems to be generally recognized by all who differentiate religious faith from secular belief. The difference lies not in the object, but in the causes of belief.

Those who distinguish between knowledge and opinion also admit that a difference in the way the mind judges is able to produce either knowledge or opinion concerning the same object. It is impossible, according to Aristotle, for the same mind with regard to the same object to know and opine at the same time. A given individual, for example, cannot hold a proposition of geometry to be true *both* as a matter of knowledge and of opinion. But this does not prevent the individual who once held the proposition to be true merely on the authority of his teacher—and thus as a matter of opinion—from subsequently learning the reasons for its truth and thus coming to know what formerly he merely opined. Two individuals may likewise assert the same truth in different ways, the one as knowledge, the other as opinion.

The traditional account of the difference in the activity of the mind when it knows and when it opines appears to involve two related points. The point which both Plato and Aristotle emphasize is that the man who knows does not merely assert something to be true, but has adequate reasons for doing so. The truth of right opinion is no less true than the truth of knowledge. It differs, as the discussion in Plato's *Meno* and *Theaetetus* seems to show, in that the man of right opinion cannot explain why what he asserts is true. He cannot give the causes of its truth, or trace its connections with other truths which help to demonstrate it. The fact that an opinion is true does not prevent its being overturned or given up, since without adequate reasons it is insecure against attack. Unsupported by reasons, opinion is not only unstable as compared with knowledge, but it is also unteachable in the sense in which knowledge can be learned and taught. The man of right opinion, unable to explain satisfactorily why he thinks as he does, cannot help others understand the rightness of his opinions.

Russell writes of the dualism regarding knowledge of truths: "We may believe what is false as well as what is true. We know that on very many subjects different people hold different and incompatible opinions: hence some beliefs must be erroneous. Since erroneous beliefs are often held just as strongly as true beliefs, it becomes a difficult question how they are to be distinguished from true beliefs. How are we to know, in a given case, that our belief is not erroneous? This is a question of the very greatest difficulty, to which no completely satisfactory answer is possible."

The other characterization of the mind's activity in forming opinions seems to follow from the preceding observation. If reasons do not determine the mind to think *this* rather than *that,* what is the cause of its judgment? If the mind is not compelled by the object under consideration to think of it in a certain way, what does move the mind in its act of assent or dissent to that which is proposed? To such questions, the traditional answer seems to be wish or desire, whether an act of free choice on the part of the will or an inclination determined by the driving power of the emotions.

Pascal makes this point when he observes that there are two ways in which men come to think as they do. The more natural way "is that of the understanding, for one should only agree to demonstrated truths; but the more usual . . . is that of the will; for all men are nearly always led to believe, not by proof, but by inclination." Hobbes similarly differentiates knowledge, which rests upon definitions and demonstrations, from the opinions or beliefs which the mind adopts, not as the result of reasoning, but by an act of will.

The assent of reason is not, according to Aquinas, subject to command by the will in respect to all matters on which the reason can judge. If "that which the reason apprehends is such that it naturally assents thereto, *e.g.,* first principles, it is not in our power to assent to it or to dissent. For in such cases," he holds, "assent follows naturally, and consequently, properly speaking, is not subject to our command. But some things which are apprehended do not convince the intellect to such an extent as not to leave it free to assent or dissent, or at least suspend its assent or dissent for some cause or other; and in such things, assent or dissent is in our power, and is subject to our command." Knowledge, it would seem, consists in those judgments wherein the mind is moved to assent solely by the matter being considered, whereas all matters about which we are free to make up our minds one way or the other are matters of opinion.

Though they vary in the terms of their analyses, Descartes, Locke, and Hume seem also to agree that when the mind is moved to assent by the relations it perceives between ideas, especially when these are clear and distinct, it knows beyond doubt or the possibility of error. But when the mind, lacking such intuitive or rational grounds, nevertheless forms a judgment concerning what is not evident, then the result is opinion entertained as merely probable, accompanied by doubt, and subject to error.

For Descartes, the will, freely exercised, moves the mind to such fallible judgments. Except when it is so moved the mind, responding to its object alone, is naturally infallible. For Hume, the mind is free to imagine whatever it pleases, but its beliefs are determined by a sentiment or feeling of instinctive origin, "which depends not on the will, nor can be commanded at pleasure." The issue between those who connect opinion with free will and those who deny that beliefs are voluntarily formed is discussed in the chapter on WILL. It does not seem to affect the fairly general agreement on the point that opinion is an act of the mind caused by *something other than the object itself* which the mind is considering.

DOES THIS DISTINCTION between knowledge and opinion exhaustively divide all the acts of the mind? As we have seen, Montaigne appears to reject both alternatives and substitutes instead supernatural faith and ordinary belief. Aquinas, on the other hand, accepts knowledge and opinion as exhaustive on the plane of the mind's natural operations and makes religious faith a supernatural alternative to both.

He calls faith a mean or intermediate between science and opinion because he conceives it as having some of the characteristics of each. "To believe," he says, "is an act of the intellect assenting to the truth at the command of the will." In this faith resembles opinion. The act of faith is due to the will rather than to the rational evidence of the object. Faith is "the evidence of things unseen." But faith also resembles science because the affirmations of faith have the certitude or freedom from doubt which characterizes knowledge. According to Aquinas, faith has greater certitude than natural knowledge, since, as intellectual virtues, "science, wisdom, and understanding . . . are based upon the natural light of reason, which falls short of the certitude of God's word, on which faith is founded." Faith differs from knowledge in that the object of faith

exceeds the intellect's comprehension. That is why faith requires an act of the will to move the intellect to assent; but whereas ordinary opinions are adopted by a man's own volition, Aquinas attributes faith to God. "Faith," he writes, "as regards the assent which is the chief act of faith, is from God moving man inwardly by grace."

Just as skepticism with respect to science takes the form of reducing all human judgments to opinion, so skepticism with respect to religion takes the form of attributing all belief to purely natural causes. If Freud is correct that all beliefs are the product of wishful thinking, then it is difficult to separate religion from superstition or prejudice—or even, perhaps, to separate science from religion.

James finds the will to believe in science as well as religion. Like Freud, he explains belief in terms of emotion and desire. "Will and Belief, meaning a certain relation between objects and the Self," he writes, "are two names for one and the same *psychological* phenomenon." Except for those necessary truths which concern only ideal relationships, the mind in thinking about reality is free to choose between alternative theories, in the sphere of science as well as in religion. To believe is to attribute reality to a theory. Though the operation of the will to believe is not for James entirely independent of objective criteria, neither is it mainly determined thereby.

"That theory will be most generally believed," he says, "which, besides offering us objects able to account for our sensible experience, also offers those which are most interesting, those which appeal most urgently to our aesthetic, emotional, and active needs . . . So-called 'scientific' conceptions of the universe have so far gratified the purely intellectual interests more than the mere sentimental conceptions have. But . . . they leave the emotional and active interests cold. *The perfect object of belief would be a God or 'Soul of the World,' represented both optimistically and moralistically (if such a combination could be), and withal so definitely conceived as to show us why our phenomenal experiences should be sent to us by Him in just the very way in which they come.*"

OPINION RAISES moral and political as well as psychological issues of liberty. One of them is the problem of freedom of discussion. This problem has aspects which belong to other chapters—freedom in scientific inquiry to SCIENCE, freedom in artistic or poetic expression to ART and POETRY, freedom of conscience and worship to RELIGION, freedom in teaching to EDUCATION, and the general issue of freedom of thought and speech to the chapter on LIBERTY. Yet what is common to all these related questions seems to be determined by the nature of opinion, particularly in its distinction from knowledge.

None of the books which argue for freedom of expression—Milton's *Areopagitica,* Locke's letter *Concerning Toleration,* or J. S. Mill's essay *On Liberty*—defends the right to disseminate error or falsehood *knowingly.* All of them argue that the individual who claims the right to be heard is morally bound by the duty to speak the truth as it appears to him. Nor do those, like Plato and Hobbes, who recommend political censorship seek thereby to fortify the state by suppressing truth. In saying that the sovereign should "judge of what opinions and doctrines are averse, and what conducing to peace," Hobbes observes that "though in matters of doctrine, nothing ought to be regarded but the truth, yet this is not repugnant to regulating the same by peace. For doctrine repugnant to peace can no more be true, than peace and concord can be against the law of nature."

Since knowledge as distinct from opinion has the character of incontrovertible truth, the issue of freedom or censorship cannot be stated in terms of knowledge. But what some men hold to be knowledge others regard as opinion. The issue of free expression applies therefore to the entire range of human thought on the supposition that *no* proposition or doctrine is exempt from controversy, and no human judgment secure from contradiction. This supposition does not abolish the distinction between knowledge and opinion; nor does it flout the law of contradiction by treating opposite answers to the same question as in fact equally true.

"In formal logic," writes Whitehead, "a contradiction is the signal of a defeat: but in the evolution of real knowledge it marks the first step in progress towards a victory. This is one great reason for the utmost toleration of variety of opinion." Whitehead thus agrees with Mill, that for the pursuit of truth, such toleration is necessary.

"If all mankind minus one were of one opinion, and only one person were of the contrary opinion, mankind," according to Mill, "would be no more justified in silencing that one person, than he, if he had the power, would be justified in silencing mankind . . . The peculiar evil of silencing the expression of an opinion is, that it is robbing the human race; posterity as well as the existing generation; those who dissent from the opinion, still more than those who hold it. If the opinion is right, they are deprived of the opportunity of exchanging error for truth; if wrong, they lose, what is almost as great a benefit, the clearer perception and livelier impression of truth produced by its collision with error."

Mill advances four distinct reasons for recognizing "the necessity to the mental well-being of mankind (on which all their other well-being depends) of freedom of opinion, and freedom of the expression of opinion . . . First, if any opinion is compelled to silence, that opinion may, for aught we can certainly know, be true. To deny this is to assume our own infallibility. Secondly, though the silenced opinion be an error, it may, and very commonly does, contain a portion of truth; and . . . it is only by the collision of adverse opinions that the remainder of the truth has any chance of being supplied. Thirdly, even if the received opinion be not only true, but the whole truth; unless it is suffered to be, and actually is vigorously and earnestly contested, it will, by most of those who receive it, be held in the manner of a prejudice, with little comprehension or feeling of its rational grounds. And not only this, but, fourthly, the meaning of the doctrine itself will be in danger of being lost, or enfeebled."

The aim is not to perpetuate controversy; nor is it to keep all doctrines perpetually on the level of debatable opinion. "As mankind improve," Mill writes, "the number of doctrines which are no longer disputed or doubted will be constantly on the increase; and the well-being of mankind may almost be measured by the number and gravity of the truths which have reached the point of being uncontested. The cessation, on one question after another, of serious controversy, is one of the necessary incidents of the consolidation of opinion; a consolidation as salutary in the case of true opinions, as it is dangerous and noxious when the opinions are erroneous."

As Mill argues the case for freedom of thought and discussion, it appears to be based on the hypothesis that the public debate of all matters, carried on without any restriction except those minimum restraints needed to prevent violence, serves the end of separating true from false opinion and, by the clarification of opinion as well as the correction of error, discovering the reasons which turn opinion into knowledge. It is not to multiply opinions but to advance knowledge, not to encourage skepticism but to invigorate the search for truth, that Mill advocates the submission of all matters to open dispute so long as any disagreement remains.

His fundamental principle, like that of Locke, consists in divorcing political from logical criteria. Logically, the disputants may stand opposed to each other as one who knows and one who merely opines, or as one who holds a true and one a false opinion, or even as one who enjoys God's gift of supernatural faith and one who lacks such light; but considered politically, the opponents represent a conflict of opinion, with each party equally deserving the benefit of the doubt that it may have the truth on its side. If the state were to intervene, it would be deciding a disputed question, not by reason, but by force, in an area to which force is inapplicable.

"The business of laws," Locke writes, "is not to provide for the truth of opinions, but for the safety and security of the commonwealth, and for every particular man's goods and person. And so it ought to be. For the truth certainly would do well enough if she were once left to shift for herself . . . She is not taught by laws, nor has she any need of force to procure her entrance into the minds of men. Errors indeed prevail by the assistance of foreign and borrowed succours. But if Truth makes not her way into the understanding by her own light, she will be but the weaker for any borrowed force violence can add to her."

Those who argue that state censorship is justified, whether the matters whose debate is prohibited are speculative or practical, moral, political, or theological, appear to extend the safeguarding of the common good beyond security from immediate peril of violence; or to proceed upon the hypothesis of sufficient wisdom in the rulers to discriminate unerringly between truth and falsehood. Those who distinguish between church and state with regard to censorship tend to limit the application of ecclesiastical authority to questions of faith and morals, on which the church is supposed to have supernatural guidance in deciding what is true or sound.

THE PRINCIPLE OF majority rule in matters of opinion seems to be opposite to the principle that the voice of a minority should be heard. To settle a difference of opinion by taking a vote gives a decisive weight to numbers which, it may be thought, is as illegitimate as resolving a debate by force. But when it is necessary to legislate or to act, debate must be terminated and issues resolved.

On speculative questions, which may be answerable by knowledge rather than by opinion, and with respect to which agreement may be possible, the end of truth seems to be served by permitting discussion to go on as long as reason opposes reason. But if the discussion is for the sake of determining action and if, in addition, the subject under discussion is strictly a matter of opinion concerning which it is possible for reasonable men perpetually to disagree, then it may be necessary to appeal to some principle other than reason.

Traditional political theory appears to offer only two solutions. One principle of decision is to follow the opinion of a single man—an absolute monarch or an elected chief magistrate—whether or not that one man also has the wisdom commensurate with such responsibility. The other principle is to accept the opinion of the majority. According to Aristotle, this second principle is operative in every form of government except absolute monarchy. It is not only in democracy, he says, that "the greater number are sovereign, for in oligarchy, and indeed in every government, the majority rules." It is characteristic of every form of constitutional state that "whatever seems good to the majority of those who share in the government should have authority."

Considered in this way, the principle of majority rule leaves open the question whether the majority should be a preponderance of the many or the few. Should it be a democratic majority or, according to some aristocratic standard, the majority of the few who are wiser, more expert, or more virtuous than the many? With regard to some questions, Aristotle suggests, the multitude may be a better judge than any individual, even the most expert. "If the people are not utterly degraded, although individually they may be worse judges than those who have special knowledge, as a body they are as good or better."

The opposing claims of the greater number and the more competent, as well as the possibility of combining the merits of both, are discussed in the chapters on DEMOCRACY and ARISTOCRACY. The problem of majority rule also appears in those chapters as a factor in the theory of representation, especially the question considered by Mill—whether the representative shall exercise his own judgment or act on the opinion of the majority of his constituents.

Mill tries to separate those problems of government which should be submitted to representative assemblies and decision by majorities from those which should be solved by experts. But even on matters subject to deliberation by representatives of the people, Mill advocates such measures as plural voting and minority representation to offset the sheer weight of numbers and prevent its being the decisive force in settling political differences and determining action.

Such qualifications of the principle of majority rule do not seem necessary to those who, like Rousseau, think that "the general will is found by counting votes." What Rousseau says of any individual opinion applies to minority opinions as well, namely, that when a contrary opinion prevails, it proves that what the minority "thought to be the general will was not so." On the question of how large a majority should be decisive, he thinks that "the more grave and important the question discussed, the nearer should the opinion that is to prevail approach unanimity . . . The more the matter in hand calls for speed, the smaller the prescribed difference in the number of votes may be allowed to become."

There is, according to Rousseau, only one political decision which requires unanimity, and that is the decision to enter upon the social contract, to set up popular government under which individual liberty endures as long as "the qualities of the general will still reside in the majority." When the principle of majority rule is unanimously adopted, each individual agrees to substitute the general will for his own particular opinion.

65

Opposition

INTRODUCTION

Certain words in the vocabulary of common speech, used at almost every turn of discourse, indicate ideas so indispensable to human thought that they are often employed without analysis. The word "is" is one of these, signifying the idea of being or existence. The word "not" and the pair of words "either . . . or" have the same character. Taken together, "not" and "either . . . or" signify the idea of opposition. The quality of redness is *not* the same as the quality of hotness, yet this negative relation by itself does not make them opposite, for something can be red-hot. It is only when a thing can have *either* one quality *or* another, but *not* both, that the qualities are said to be opposed. Opposites are more than merely distinct; they exclude one another.

Opposition seems to be as pervasive as the familiar words which signify it. Even if it were not itself one of the great ideas, it would be manifest in all the other basic notions which come in antithetical pairs, *e.g.,* good and evil, life and death, war and peace, universal and particular, pleasure and pain, necessity and contingency, same and other, one and many, virtue and vice. Each of these notions seems to imply its opposite and to draw its meaning from the opposition. There are other terms in the list of great ideas which, though not paired in the same chapter, stand opposed to one another: art to nature, chance to fate, liberty to slavery, time to eternity, knowledge to opinion, matter to form, democracy to oligarchy and similarly other forms of government. Still other terms cannot be discussed without reference to their opposites, even though we have not explicitly listed them, such as being and nonbeing, truth and falsity, love and hate, justice and injustice, wealth and poverty.

The enumeration might extend to include every fundamental notion, except for the inconvenience in certain cases of not having readily familiar names to designate the opposites. In some instances, moreover, the opposition seems to involve more than a pair of terms, as, for example, is the case with poetry, history, and science; or physics, mathematics, and metaphysics.

In the tradition of the great books we not only find the opposition of one idea to another, but we also find opposite points of view, conflicting theories or doctrines, in the discussion of almost every basic topic under the heading of these ideas. We find the same word used with contrary meanings, the same proposition affirmed and denied. We find reasoning opposed to reasoning. The same conclusion is reached from apparently opposite principles, or opposite conclusions are drawn from premises apparently the same.

But though opposition seems to be inherent in the realm of ideas and in the life of thought, the idea of opposition is not itself explicitly thought about in many of the great books. This does not mean that in the consideration of other matters the significance and consequences of opposition go unnoted. On the contrary, all the chapters dealing with the nature and conduct of man, or with the institutions and history of society, give evidence of the general recognition—by poets and historians, by scientists and philosophers—that opposition in the form of active conflict characterizes the phenomena. The fact of warring opposites not only enters into descriptions of the way things are, but also poses problems for psychologists, moralists, economists, and statesmen to solve.

The study of nature, as well as of man and society, discovers opposition at the root of change. The physics of antiquity, for example, defines the elements or the bodily humors in terms of contrary qualities; according to Aristotle, contraries are among the ultimate principles of nature—the terms of change. The cosmology of Lucretius makes the conflict of opposites the principle of growth and decay in the universe. Destruction struggles against creativity, life against death:

The ways of death can not prevail forever,
Entombing healthiness, nor can birth and growth
Forever keep created things alive.
There is always this great elemental deadlock,
This warfare through all time.

Modern mechanics deals with action and reaction in the impact of bodies and the resolution of forces tending to produce opposite results. The theory of evolution pictures the world of living organisms as engaged in the struggle for survival, organism competing with organism or against an adverse environment for the means of subsistence or reproduction.

These indications of the prevalence of conflict in the realm of thought itself, or as a fundamental conception in man's thinking about nature and society, do not alter the point that only in logic or metaphysics is opposition abstracted from special subject matters, to become itself the object of thought. Even so, not all of the great speculative works develop an explicit theory of opposition—classifying its types, analyzing its structure, formulating it as a universal principle of being, mind, or spirit.

Four authors especially treat opposition as a primary theme, though not out of the context of such other notions as being, relation, one and many, same and other, or identity and difference. They are Plato, Aristotle, Kant, and Hegel. It should not be surprising that the same authors are the principal figures in the chapter on DIALECTIC. Their disagreement about the nature or meaning of dialectic has a parallel here in their conflicting theories of opposition.

SOCRATES ARGUES, in the *Protagoras,* for the unity of virtue by using the principle that "everything has one opposite and not more than one." If wisdom is the opposite of folly, and if it also appears that folly is opposed by temperance, then either wisdom and temperance are the same, or a thing may have more than one opposite. Protagoras reluctantly accepts the first alternative; he is apparently unwilling to reopen the question concerning the pairing of opposites. But the question is reopened by others. It is one of the great problems in the theory of opposition, relevant to the distinction of different kinds of opposites.

The problem can most readily be stated in terms of the logical processes of division and definition. On the hypothesis that opposites always come in pairs, every class can be divided into two subclasses which not only exclude each other, but also exhaust the membership of the divided class. Such division is called dichotomy. Many of the Platonic dialogues—notably the *Sophist* and the *Statesman*—exemplify the method of dichotomous division, used as a device for constructing definitions. The object to be defined, the character of the statesman or the sophist, is finally caught in the net of classification when, division after division having been made, two subclasses are reached which leave no other possibilities open. The thing is either one or the other.

In the *Sophist* a preliminary exercise is undertaken in the method of division as preparation for the use of this method to define the sophist. It will serve us here as an example of dichotomy. All the arts are first divided into two kinds, the productive and the acquisitive; then the acquisitive arts are divided into those making voluntary exchanges and those which obtain goods by coercion; the coercive divides into fighting and hunting according to the alternatives of open or secret attack; hunting into the hunting of the lifeless and the living; hunting of the living into hunting of swimming or walking animals; the hunting of swimming animals into the hunting of winged animals and the hunting of water animals; the hunting of water animals into opposite methods of catching fish, with further subdivisions made until the art of angling can be defined as an acquisitive art which, being coercive, is a form of hunting, distinguished from other forms of hunting by the character of its object—animals which swim in water rather than air—and by the method used to catch them—hooks or barbs rather than nets or baskets.

Aristotle objects to this process of division as a way of defining things. "Some writers," he says, "propose to reach the definitions of the ultimate forms of animal life by bipartite division. But this method is often difficult, and often impracticable." For one thing, it tends to associate or dissociate natural groups arbitrarily, *e.g.,* the classification of birds with water animals, or of some birds with fish and some birds with land animals. "If such natural groups are not to be broken up, the method of dichotomy cannot be employed, for it necessarily involves such breaking up and dislocation."

Aristotle also calls attention to the fact that the method of dichotomy often uses negative terms in order to make an exhaustive division into two and only two subclasses. But the class which is formed by negative characterization cannot be further subdivided. "There can be no specific forms of a negation, of feather-less for instance or of footless, as there are of feathered and of footed." It is impossible, Aristotle says, to "get at the ultimate specific forms of animal life by bifurcate division." He therefore proposes a method of defining by genus and difference, according to which it is possible in biological classification to sub-divide a genus into more than two species. To avoid subdivision into two and only two, that which differentiates each species from the others within the same genus must be some positive characteristic.

As ALTERNATIVE methods of definition, di-chotomous division and the differentiation of species within a genus are discussed in the chapter on DEFINITION. Here we are con-cerned with the problem of the number of opposites produced by the exhaustive division of a class or kind. For example, how many species of color are there? If the primary colors are more than two, it would appear that each primary color has more than one opposite, since the same object at the same time and in the same respect cannot be both red and yellow, red and green, green and yellow. But

Aristotle seems to restrict the notion of con-trariety to pairs of opposite qualities. "Red, yellow, and such colors, though qualities, have no contraries," he says. Whether or not he would have regarded them as contraries if he had been acquainted with the chromatic series of the spectrum, remains a conjecture.

To find a single opposite for red, it is neces-sary to employ the negative term 'not-red.' But then another difficulty arises which Aristotle recognizes when he calls the negative term "indefinite" and which Kant discusses when he treats the infinity of the negative. The not-red includes more than other colors which are not red, such as green and yellow. It includes everything in the universe, colored or color-less, which is *not* red, *e.g.,* happiness or atoms or poetry.

Perfect dichotomy can be achieved by using positive and negative terms as opposites, or what Aristotle sometimes calls "contradictory terms"—such as man and not-man or just and not-just. But the class which is thus divided is absolutely indeterminate. It is the universe, everything, the infinite. It is necessary, further-more, to distinguish between the opposition of 'just' and 'not-just' and the opposition of 'just' and 'unjust.' The term 'unjust' is the con-trary rather than the contradictory of 'just,' for these opposites apply only to men, or laws, or acts; only certain kinds of things are either just or unjust, and that is why it is said that contraries are always opposites within a genus or a definite kind. In contrast, 'not-just' is the contradictory rather than the contrary of 'just,' for these opposites apply to everything in the universe; everything is either the kind of thing to which just and unjust apply or it is the kind of thing to which neither of these terms apply, and so it is the not-just.

In addition to separating contraries (both of which are positive terms) from contradictory opposites (one of which is a positive, the other a negative term), Aristotle distinguishes two sorts of contraries. On the one hand, such contraries as odd and even exhaustively divide a limited class (*e.g.,* integral numbers): on the other hand, such contraries as white and black represent the extremes of a continuous series of shades, in which any degree of grayness can be considered as the opposite of either extreme or of a darker or a lighter gray.

There are still other kinds of opposite pairs, according to Aristotle, such as the terms 'double' and 'half,' which have the peculiarity of implying each other; or the terms 'blindness' and 'sight,' which are opposite conditions of the same subject. In this last case, one of the opposites naturally belongs to a certain kind of thing, and the other represents a loss of that natural property or trait. It is therefore called a "privation."

Considering these various modes of opposition, Aristotle proposes a fourfold classification of opposite terms: *correlative* opposites, like double and half; *contrary* opposites, like odd and even, white and black, just and unjust; the opposites of *possession* and *privation,* such as sight and blindness; the opposites of *affirmation* and *negation,* such as man and not-man, or just and not-just. He discusses the special characteristics of each type of opposition, but it is only contrariety which he thinks requires further subdivision.

Even though both are always positive terms, some contraries, like odd and even, exhaust a definite class, just as positive and negative opposites exhaust the infinite. They admit of no intermediate terms and hence they differ from contraries like white and black. White and black are extreme limits of a continuous series and thus permit an indefinite number of intermediates which fall between them. Things which differ only in degree are like the sort of contraries which find their place in a continuous series. Things which differ in kind are like the sort of contraries between which no intermediates are possible.

One of the great problems of classification, especially with respect to living organisms, is whether the diverse species which fall within a single genus differ in kind or only in degree. The answer would seem to depend on whether the several species are related by one or the other sort of contrariety. As the chapter on EVOLUTION indicates, the basic meaning of the word "species" changes when the possibility of "intermediate forms" is rejected or admitted. When a class is divided by contraries without intermediates, the genus can have only

two species, as for example, the division of animals into brutes and men. When a genus is divided into more than two subclasses (*e.g.,* the division of vertebrates into fish, amphibians, reptiles, birds, and mammals), it would seem to follow that the species are like points in a continuous series and admit the possibility of intermediate types.

According to Darwin's conception of species, their contrariety always tends to take the latter form. Aristotle, on the other hand, seems to use the word "species" in two distinct senses which correspond to the two kinds of contrariety—with and without intermediates. "A thing's difference from that from which it differs in species," he writes, "must be a contrariety." But though contrariety is always a "complete difference," the fact that "contraries are so-called in several senses" leads him to observe that "their modes of completeness will answer to the various modes of contrariety which attach to the contraries."

THE LOGICAL OPPOSITION of propositions or judgments depends in part on the opposition of terms or concepts. If contrary things are said about the same subject of discourse (*i.e.,* if the same number is called odd and even, or the same act is called cowardly and courageous, or the same animal is called a bird and a mammal), pairs of contrary statements are made, of which both cannot be true. But it does not seem to follow that one of the two statements must be true. Both can be false. In the examples given, the number may be a fraction and neither odd nor even; the act may be foolhardy and neither courageous nor cowardly; the animal may be a reptile and neither bird nor mammal.

This characteristic of contrary statements—the impossibility of their both being true combined with the possibility of their both being false—can also be found, according to Aristotle, in propositions which have the same subject and do not contain contrary terms as predicates. The propositions 'All men are white' and 'No men are white' cannot both be true, but they can both be false. The contrariety of these two statements, which can be taken as typifying the opposition of all universal affirmations and negations, does not depend on contrary predicates, but on the opposed meanings of 'all are' and 'none is.'

Keeping the terms constant and varying only the quality and quantity of the propositions, Aristotle formulates two other typical modes of opposition between pairs of statements. When both statements are particular or limited, but one is affirmative and the other negative, both cannot be false though both can be true, *e.g.,* 'Some men are white' and 'Some men are not white.' This pair of opposites Aristotle calls "sub-contraries." When one statement is universal and affirmative and the other is particular and negative—or when one is universal and negative, the other particular and affirmative—the two propositions are, according to Aristotle, contradictory. Contradiction is the most complete type of opposition, for contradictory statements are opposite in both quality and quantity. Of a pair of contradictories, both cannot be true and both cannot be false. One must be true and the other false, *e.g.,* it must be true either that all men are white or that some men are not white.

The formal scheme of opposite statements, traditionally known as "the square of opposition," appears to exhaust all possibilities. It indicates, moreover, that every statement may have two opposites, a contradictory and either a contrary or a subcontrary; for example, 'All men are white' is contradicted by 'Some men are not white' and opposed in a merely contrary fashion by 'No men are white.' The latter is a weaker form of opposition since it permits the dilemma to be avoided by the truth of a third statement, that some men are white and some are not. The dilemma set up by a contradiction cannot be avoided in this way.

The propositions 'God exists' and 'God does not exist,' or 'The world had a beginning' and 'The world did not have a beginning,' constitute contradictions from which there seems to be no escape. It would seem to make a difference, therefore, in facing the great controversies in the tradition of western thought, to know whether the opposite views which men have taken on fundamental issues are genuine contradictions, requiring everyone to take sides, or whether they are merely contrary positions. In the latter alternative, the inconsistency of the theories prevents us from agreeing with both parties to the dispute, but it does not require us to agree with either, for contrary doctrines never exhaust the possibilities. Between such extreme positions, for example, as that everthing is in flux and nothing changes, both of which cannot be true, the truth may lie in the doctrine that some elements of permanence are involved in all change; or it may be in the theory of a realm of becoming that lacks permanence and a realm of being that is free from change.

The principle that one should avoid contradicting oneself is often regarded as a rule of logical thinking or a law of thought. But, as Russell points out, "the law of contradiction is about things, and not merely about thoughts; and although belief in the law of contradiction is a thought, the law of contradiction itself is not a thought, but a fact concerning the things in the world."

ONE OF THE BASIC controversies in the tradition of the great books concerns opposition itself. Is the principle of contradiction the ultimate test of the truth of judgments and reasoning? Is the truth of indemonstrable propositions or axioms certified by the self-contradiction of their contradictories? For example, is the truth of the proposition 'The whole is greater than the part' made necessary by the impossibility of the contradictory statement 'The whole is *not* greater than the part,' on the theory that this latter statement is impossible because it is self-contradictory? And when a conclusion is demonstrated by propositions which seem to be necessarily true, must not the contradictory of this conclusion be false—or at least be incapable of demonstration by propositions which are also necessarily true?

On both these questions Kant and Aristotle seem to be opposed. According to Aristotle, no truths are necessary or axiomatic unless their contradictories are self-contradictory. But Kant makes a distinction between analytic and synthetic propositions (discussed in the chapter on JUDGMENT) and in terms of it he restricts the principle of contradiction to serving as a criterion of truth for analytic judgments alone. "In an analytical judgement," he writes, "whether negative or affirmative, its truth can always be tested by the principle of contradiction." But though we must admit, Kant continues, that "the principle of contradiction is the general and altogether sufficient principle of all analytical knowledge, beyond this its authority and utility, as a sufficient criterion of truth, must not be allowed to extend." In "the synthetical part of our knowledge, we must no doubt take great care never to offend against that inviolable principle, but we ought never to expect from it any help with regard to the truth of this kind of knowledge."

The reason, Kant explains, is that "in forming an analytical judgment I remain within a given concept, while predicating something of it. If what I predicate is affirmative, I only predicate of that concept what is already contained in it; if it is negative, I only exclude from it the opposite of it." For example, if the meaning of the concept 'whole' involves 'being greater than a part,' self-contradiction results from denying that the whole is greater than a part.

"In forming synthetical judgments, on the contrary, I have to go beyond a given concept, in order to bring something together with it, which is totally different from what is contained in it. Here," Kant declares, "we have neither the relation of identity nor of contradiction, and nothing in the judgment itself by which we can discover its truth or its falsehood"; for example, the judgment that everything which happens has a cause. The truth of such synthetic judgments, according to Kant, is as necessary and as *a priori* as the truth of analytic judgments, but the principle of contradiction does not provide their ground or validation.

For Aristotle, in contrast, those propositions which do not derive necessity from the principle of contradiction belong to the sphere of opinion rather than to the domain of knowledge. They can be asserted as probable only, not as true or false. In the domain of knowledge, it is impossible to construct valid arguments for contradictory conclusions, for if one must be true and the other false, one

can be validly demonstrated and the other cannot be demonstrated at all. But in the sphere of opinion, dialectical opposition is possible. Because the contradictory of a probable statement is itself also probable, probable arguments can be constructed on the opposite sides of every dialectical issue.

For Kant dialectical issues do not consist in a conflict of opposed probabilities. Far from setting probable reasoning against probable reasoning, dialectical opposition consists in what appear to be *demonstrations* of contradictory propositions. For example, in that part of *The Critique of Pure Reason* devoted to the Transcendental Dialectic, Kant presents opposed arguments which look like demonstrations of contradictory propositions—such as the thesis that "the world has a beginning in time" and its antithesis that "the world has no beginning"; or the thesis that "there exists an absolutely necessary being" and its antithesis that "there nowhere exists an absolutely necessary being." These are two of the four issues which Kant calls the "antinomies of a transcendental dialectic."

Such issues, Aristotle would agree with Kant, do not belong to the sphere of opinion or probability. But Kant would not agree with Aristotle that such issues belong to the domain of science or certain knowledge. The problem of the world's beginning or eternity, for example, is one which Aristotle treats in his *Physics* and appears to think is solved by the demonstration that motion can have neither beginning nor end. The problem of the existence of a necessary being is one which Aristotle treats in his *Metaphysics* and which he also appears to think is capable of a demonstrative solution. For him, therefore, both are problems to which scientific answers can be given. But for Kant the demonstration of the antitheses, or contradictory propositions, in both cases is as cogent as the demonstrations of the theses; and therefore, since we know that both of a pair of contradictory propositions cannot be validly demonstrated, we must conclude that the arguments advanced are only counterfeit demonstrations, or as Kant says, "illusory." He calls these demonstrations "dialectical," and the issues they attempt to resolve "antinomies," precisely because he thinks the reasoning goes beyond the limits of scientific thought and because he thinks the issues are problems reason cannot ever solve.

With respect to conclusions affirming or denying matters beyond experience, the antinomies can be interpreted either as showing that contradictory arguments are equally sound or as showing that they are equally faulty. On either interpretation, Kant and Aristotle seem to be opposed on the applicability of the principle of contradiction to conflicting arguments and conclusions (except, of course, those which are merely probable). This difference between them accords with the difference in their conceptions of science and dialectic, and in their theories of the scope and conditions of valid knowledge.

THE OPPOSITION between Kant and Aristotle may not present the only alternatives. Hegel's theory of the dialectical process seems to offer a third. Where Aristotle appears to think that all contradictions must be resolved in favor of one of the opposites, and where Kant appears to think that some contradictions cannot be resolved at all, Hegel proposes the resolution of all contradictions, not by a choice between them, but by a synthesis uniting the opposites and reconciling their differences.

According to Aristotle, opposites exclude one another in existence as well as in thought. A thing cannot both exist and not exist at the same time; nor in any particular respect can it simultaneously both be and not be of a certain sort. Only with the passage of time and in the course of change can opposites be realized, when a thing passes from being to nonbeing, or gives up one attribute in order to assume its contrary.

The difference for Aristotle between becoming and being (or between change and complete actuality) seems to be that the one includes and the other excludes opposites. Change cannot occur except as one opposite comes into existence *while* the other passes away. But opposites cannot coexist with complete actuality. So far as reality consists of co-existent actualities, it is limited by the principle of contradiction—as a principle of being—to

those which are not contradictory. All possibilities cannot, therefore, be simultaneously realized, for, as Leibniz states the principle, all possibilities are not "compossible."

According to Hegel, every finite phase of reality—everything except the Absolute Idea itself—has its contradictory, as real as itself, and coexistent with it. Contradictories imply one another and require each other, almost as correlative opposites do. Whatever is partial and incomplete presupposes something which is partial and incomplete in an opposite respect. The opposition between them can therefore be overcome by a synthesis which includes them both, and which complements each by uniting it with the other.

For example, the category of being is opposed by nonbeing. These opposites both exclude and imply one another. They are in a sense even identical with one another, insofar as the notion of being contains the notion of nonbeing, and, conversely, the notion of nonbeing, the notion of being. Except for the Absolute, everything which is also is not, and everything which is not also is. The apparent contradiction involved in this simultaneous application of opposite categories to the same thing is overcome by a third category, becoming, which is the synthesis of being and nonbeing. Being and nonbeing are united in becoming.

Not so, for Heidegger: nonbeing or "Nothing is the negation of the totality of what is . . . But at this point we bring Nothing into the higher category of the Negative and therefore of what is negated. But according to the overriding and unassailable teachings of 'logic' negation is a specific act of reason. How, then, in our enquiry into Nothing . . . can we dismiss reason?" If we must do so, it is only because the reality of Nothing is more original or fundamental than reason's act of negation.

Heidegger and Hegel thus take contrary views of being and nonbeing as irreconcilable or reconcilable opposites. The reconciling of opposites, by their union in a more inclusive whole embracing both, typifies the Hegelian dialectic of thesis, antithesis, and synthesis. The motion repeats itself as the synthesis of one contradiction faces its own opposite and requires a higher synthesis to overcome the contradiction it has generated. Thus every opposition in reality or thought is a phase in the progressive realization of the Absolute, wherein all contradictions are resolved.

In Hegel's *The Philosophy of History* and in his theory of the development of the state in *The Philosophy of Right,* the dialectical process is exemplified at every stage of progress. The conflict of interdependent opposites—of opposite classes or forces in society, of opposite political institutions or principles—calls for a resolution which shall unite rather than exclude the opposites.

Considering the division of labor, for example, Hegel writes: "When men are dependent on one another and reciprocally related in their work and the satisfaction of their needs, subjective self-seeking turns into a contribution to the satisfaction of the needs of everyone else. That is to say, by a dialectical advance, subjective self-seeking turns into the mediation of the particular through the universal, with the result that each man in earning, producing, and enjoying on his own account is *eo ipso* producing and earning for the enjoyment of everyone else." The opposition between the particular good of each individual and the universal good of all is thus overcome by that advance in social organization which is the division of labor.

Each of the stages of world history is, according to Hegel, "the presence of a necessary moment in the Idea of the world mind." But the world mind itself is a synthesis, a resolution of the conflicting opposites—of the various national minds "which are wholly restricted on account of their particularity. Their deeds and destinies in their reciprocal relations to one another are the dialectic of the finitude of these minds, and out of it arises the universal mind, the mind of the world, free from all restrictions, producing itself as that which exercises its right—and its right is the highest right of all—over these finite minds in the 'history of the world which is the world's court of judgment.' "

66

Philosophy

INTRODUCTION

THE difficulties which attend the consideration of any great idea—by philosophers or others—appear with peculiar force in the traditional discussion of philosophy itself. The word "philosophy" not only varies in its descriptive significance, now designating one part of learning, now another, and sometimes even an attitude of mind or a way of life; but it also varies as a term of evaluation. It is seldom used without expressing either praise or dispraise of the methods and accomplishments of philosophy, or of the calling and character of the philosopher.

On the descriptive side the meaning of the word ranges from a conception of philosophy which covers *all* branches of scientific knowledge and which contrasts philosophy with poetry, history, and religion, to a conception of philosophy in which the primary point is its contrast to science and its association with poetry and religion as works of vision, speculation, or belief rather than of knowledge.

On its evaluative side, the word "philosophy" sometimes eulogizes the love and search for truth, the pursuit and even the attainment of wisdom. At the other extreme, it derogates vain learning, idle disputation, and the dogmatism of unsupported opinion. At one time, the good name of the philosopher stands in contrast to the questionable reputation of the sophist. At another, "philosopher" carries almost the same invidious connotation as "sophist." The dismissal of philosophy as useless, or at best ornamental, in the practical affairs of society is sharply opposed to the vision of an ideal state which can come to pass only if philosophers are kings, or kings philosophers.

THESE SHIFTS IN the meaning of the words "philosophy" and "philosopher" record crises in the history of western thought. They reflect the characteristic formations of our culture in its major epochs.

The great books of antiquity, for example, seem to give no intimation of a division between science and philosophy. Particular bodies of knowledge, such as physics or mathematics, are indifferently regarded as sciences or branches of philosophy. The crown of knowledge is wisdom, approached as one rises in the hierarchy of knowledge to the highest science or the first philosophy. Aristotle and Plato may disagree in naming or defining the type of knowledge which deserves to be called wisdom, yet for both it is the ultimate attainment of philosophical inquiry or scientific work.

The differences between Plato and Aristotle discussed in the chapters on DIALECTIC and METAPHYSICS—the one using "dialectic" as the name for the supreme form of knowledge, the other using "theology" to name the summit of the sciences—do not affect their agreement that the philosopher is a man of knowledge, not opinion, and that his ultimate goal is wisdom.

If there is any distinction in antiquity between science and philosophy, it seems to find expression in the sense in which Socrates speaks of philosophy as the love of wisdom, implying thereby its pursuit rather than its attainment. A man would not be called a scientist in a particular field—mathematics, let us say—unless he actually had some mathematical knowledge; but a man who is not actually wise can be called a philosopher by virtue of his effort to become wise. Apart from this point of distinction, the Greeks tend to identify philosophy with the fundamental sciences, which somehow yield speculative or practical wisdom.

Considering the whole of human learning, all its arts and disciplines, we see that the things the ancients distinguish from philosophy are poetry, history, and the particular productive arts or crafts. Here again Plato and Aristotle do not make the distinction in the same terms. Plato compares the poet unfavorably with the philosopher in *The Republic*. The poet is an imitator of imitations and moves on the level of images and beliefs, whereas the philosopher rises above the imagination to the level of ideas which are the only true objects of knowledge. Aristotle, on the other hand, seems to pay poetry a compliment when in *On Poetics* he says that it is more philosophical than history because it deals with the universal rather than the particular. These attitudes toward poetry in relation to philosophy are somewhat reversed by the fact that for Plato myth and poetry provide materials from which philosophical insights can sometimes be distilled, whereas for Aristotle sense-experience is the source from which, by induction, the principles or axioms of philosophical knowledge are obtained. Despite these differences their accord on the supremacy of the philosopher remains unaffected.

More than poetry and history—and all the knowledge that can be applied productively—philosophy represents the highest use of man's faculties. On this Aristotle and Plato seem to be agreed, even though Aristotle distinguishes the philosophical from the political life and assigns the most perfect happiness to the contemplative activity of the philosopher, whereas Plato—in *The Republic* at least—brings the philosopher back to the shadows of the cave after he has seen the light of truth itself, so that he can put his wisdom to practice in the government of his less fortunate fellowman.

THE PRACTICE OF philosophy seems to become, for the Roman writers, more important than the content of philosophy as a body of doctrine. "What is that which is able to conduct a man?" asks Marcus Aurelius. "One thing and only one, philosophy." It keeps the inner man "free from violence and unharmed, superior to pains and pleasures, doing nothing without a purpose." It enables him to "accept all that happens and all that is allotted . . . and finally to wait for death with a cheerful mind, as being nothing else than a dissolution of the elements of which every living being is compounded." To Aurelius his imperial court is like a stepmother to whom one must be dutiful, philosophy like a mother from whom one gains solace and help. "Return to philosophy frequently and repose in her," he tells himself, so that "what thou meetest with in the court appears to thee tolerable, and thou tolerable in the court."

The Stoic conception of philosophy as a moral discipline and as a consolation creates that sense of the word in which the familiar injunction to a person in distress—"Be philosophical"—carries the same meaning as "Be stoical." Philosophy provides only peace of mind, not worldly riches or external power. "Philosophy does not promise to secure to man anything outside himself," says Epictetus. Nor does it fulfill its promise of inner strength without stern resolution to withdraw desire from the goods of fortune.

"Do you suppose that you can be a philosopher if you do as you do now?" Epictetus asks. "Do you suppose that you can eat and drink as you do now, and indulge your anger and displeasure just as before? No, you must sit up late, you must work hard, conquer some of your desires . . . When you have carefully considered these drawbacks, then come to us . . . if you are willing to pay this price for peace of mind, freedom, tranquility." Do not try to be "first a philosopher, then a tax-collector, then an orator, then one of Caesar's procurators. These callings do not agree . . . You must be busy either with your inner man, or with things outside, that is, you must choose between the position of a philosopher and that of an ordinary man."

There seems to be no difference between the Stoic and Epicurean conception of philosophy. Lucretius praises Epicurus, who was "first to raise / The shining light out of tremendous dark / Illumining the blessing of our life . . . Once your reason, your divining sense, / Begins its proclamation, telling us / The way things are, all terrors of the mind / Vanish."

But for Lucretius philosophy achieves this boon not merely by curbing the passions and quieting desires, but also, and primarily, by the truth of its teachings about the constitution of the world and the causes of things. Nor is it merely that the philosophical mind is able to dwell in "those calm heights, well built, well fortified / By wise men's teaching, to look down from here / At others wandering below, men lost, / Confused, in hectic search for the right road." Philosophy provides a more specific remedy for the deepest of human ills by freeing "men's spirit from the ties . . . which religion binds around them."

Men fear the thunderbolts of the gods, their intervention in the course of nature and human affairs, and the punishments of the afterlife. Before Epicurus taught them the mortality of the soul and the atomic determination of all things, "human life . . . lay foully grovelling on earth, weighed down / By grim Religion." His teaching concerning "what can be / And what cannot," rids the mind of the terrors fostered by religion. This "darkness of mind / Must be dispelled . . . by insight into nature, and a scheme / Of systematic contemplation."

EXCEPT FOR Lucretius, the triumph of philosophy over religion does not seem to be central to ancient conceptions of philosophy's contribution to the mind and life of man. In the pagan world, religious belief is either combined with philosophy to constitute the worship of the gods, which seems to be Plato's view in the *Laws;* or it represents the superstitions of the ignorant as opposed to the sophistication of the educated. Gibbon describes the rift between religion and philosophy not as a matter of intellectual controversy, but as a division of society into classes lacking or having the benefits of education—or, what is the same in the ancient world, instruction in philosophy.

But in the medieval world, the distinction between philosophy and religion seems to be essential to the consideration of the nature and value of philosophy. The importance of the distinction appears alike in the great books

of the Christian tradition and in the great writings of the Islamic and Jewish cultures—in Augustine and Aquinas, Avicenna, Averroës, and Maimonides—though the problem of philosophy's relation to religion and theology may be quite differently solved by each. In all three religious communities secular learning and sacred doctrine are set apart by their origin—the one from the efforts of human reason, the other from the word of God as revealed to the faithful. Even when it is held in highest esteem as the best achievement of secular learning, philosophy is for the most part regarded as inferior to the teachings of religion.

There are those—the simply religious, the devout, the mystical—who abominate the pretensions of reason and the vanity of philosophers who claim either merit or need for any knowledge beyond the truths which God himself has revealed. This position is expressed by such Christian writers as Tertullian, Peter Damian, Bernard de Clairvaux; or, in the Arabic tradition, by al-Ghazālī's *The Destruction of Philosophy.* Al-Ghazālī is answered by Averroës in his *Destruction of the "Destruction"* which asserts the supremacy of philosophy. Averroës reserves philosophy for men of requisite intellectual strength and relegates theology and religion to those who must substitute opinion and imagination for reason.

Neither Augustine nor Aquinas goes to these extremes. They do not dismiss philosophy as useless learning or as dangerous folly, subversive of the wisdom of faith; but neither do they admit the sufficiency of philosophy for knowledge of God—the mysteries of the divine nature, God's providence and His gracious gift of salvation to man.

Quoting Saint Paul's warning to "beware lest any man spoil you through philosophy and vain deceit according to the tradition of men and the rudiments of the world, and not according to Christ," Augustine defends his praise of the Platonic philosophy which in his judgment comes nearest to the Christian faith, on the ground that the Apostle also said to the gentiles that "that which is known of God is manifest among them, for God has manifested it to them." Yet he adds that "the Christian man who is ignorant of their writings . . . is not, therefore, ignorant that it is from the one true and supremely good God that we have that nature in which we are made in the image of God, and that doctrine by which we know Him and ourselves, and that grace with which, by cleaving to Him, we are blessed."

Philosophy, according to Augustine, can thus be dispensed with in all the major concerns of knowledge, love, or action. But Augustine does not argue that it should therefore be discarded. "If those who are called philosophers," he says, "and especially the Platonists, have said aught that is true and in harmony with our faith, we are not only not to shrink from it, but to claim it for our own use from those who have unlawful possession of it," even as the spoils of the Egyptians belong to the Jews.

Though Augustine and Aquinas conceive the relation of faith and reason differently, they seem to share a conception of philosophy as the handmaiden of theology when faith seeks understanding. For Aquinas this does not appear to imply lack of dignity or even the loss of a certain autonomy on the part of philosophy. On the contrary, so highly does he regard the demonstrations of Aristotle, whom he calls "the philosopher," that he opens the *Summa Theologica* with the question "Whether, besides the philosophical sciences, any further doctrine is required."

He answers that "it was necessary for the salvation of man that certain truths which exceed human reason should be made known to him by divine revelation. Even as regards those truths about God which human reason can investigate, it was necessary that man be taught by a divine revelation. For the truth about God, such as reason can know it, would only be known by a few, and that after a long time, and with the admixture of many errors; whereas man's whole salvation, which is in God, depends upon the knowledge of this truth ... It was, therefore, necessary that besides the philosophical sciences investigated by reason, there should be a sacred science by way of revelation." That sacred science is theology—not the theology which is a part of philosophy, but the theology whose principles come from faith rather than from reason.

"There is no reason," Aquinas writes, "why those things which are treated by the philosophical sciences, so far as they can be known by the light of natural reason, may not also be treated by another science so far as they are known by the light of the divine revelation." On this view, sacred theology may treat of certain things, such as the mystery of the Trinity, which do not belong properly to the philosopher because they exceed the power of reason to demonstrate; but other matters concerning nature, man, and God may belong both to the philosopher and to the theologian, who consider them according to their different lights. Since a truth cannot conflict with a truth, though reason sponsors one and faith the other, there can be no conflict between philosophy and theology.

Some modern philosophers, like Francis Bacon and John Locke, seem to agree with medieval theologians about the subordination of philosophy to theology. But for the most part the modern tendency, increasingly evident in the writings of Descartes, Spinoza, Kant, and Hegel, is to insist upon the complete autonomy of philosophy.

Hegel, for example, challenges "the imputation against Philososphy of being shy of noticing religious truths, or of having occasion to be so," and the insinuated "suspicion that it has anything but a clear conscience in the presence of these truths. So far from this being the case," Hegel remarks, "the fact is that in recent times Philosophy has been obliged to defend the domain of religion against the attacks of several theological systems."

The diverse aspects of the problem of the relation of philosophy to theology, and of theology to faith, are discussed in the chapters on Metaphysics, Theology, and Religion. The problem which is more characteristic of the modern consideration of philosophy concerns its relation to science.

To state the problem some distinction between the two is necessary, and making this distinction represents a novel departure, both in thought and language. As we have seen, philosophy and science are almost identified throughout the ancient and medieval tradition.

Insofar as the word "science" means knowledge rather than opinion, the result of philosophical inquiry is science, and philosophy as a whole is divided into a number of sciences. There may be, as ancient writings seem to suggest, sciences which aim at useful productions rather than at speculative or practical wisdom, and fall below the level of philosophy; or there may be, as some Christian theologians hold, a sacred science superior in its wisdom to all philosophical sciences. But these exceptions to the identity of philosophy and science merely confirm the point that in the ancient or medieval view philosophy is scientific and consists of sciences, even though there may be sciences which are not philosophical.

This use of the words "science" and "philosophy" persists well into modern times. Hobbes, for example, presents his classification of the types of knowledge under the heading "science, that is, Knowledge of Consequences, which is also called Philosophy." Bacon proposes to "divide sciences into theology and philosophy." Descartes uses the words "science" and "philosophy" interchangeably. "Among the different branches of Philosophy," he says, "I had in my younger days to a certain extent studied Logic; and in those of Mathematics, Geometrical Analysis and Algebra—three arts or sciences which seemed as though they ought to contribute to the design I had in view." In the Prefatory Letter to his *Principles of Philosophy,* he likens "philosophy as a whole" to "a tree whose roots are metaphysics, whose trunk is physics, and whose branches, which issue from this trunk, are all the other sciences. These reduce themselves to three principal ones, *viz.,* medicine, mechanics, and morals."

Even as near the end of the 18th century as Hume, the word "philosophy" continues to be the general name for the particular sciences. It covers the experimental study of natural phenomena as well as what are for Hume the nonexperimental sciences of mathematics and psychology. But it excludes divinity or theology, insofar as "its best and most solid foundation is *faith* and divine revelation"; metaphysics, which is "nothing but sophistry and illusion"; and all inquiries into particular as opposed to general facts, such as "history, chronology, geography, and astronomy."

Nor is this use of terms confined to what readers today would call books of philosophy. The authors of the books which are today regarded as among the foundations of modern science—Galileo, Newton, Huygens, Lavoisier, and Faraday—refer to themselves as philosophers and to the science in which they are engaged, *e.g.,* mathematics, mechanics, physics, chemistry, as parts or aspects of natural philosophy. They do, however, indicate an awareness of how they differ from ancient and medieval scientists (who also called themselves philosophers) by calling their own work "experimental philosophy."

In this phrase lies the root of the distinction between philosophy and science as that distinction is generally understood by writers since the 18th century. The word "experimental" applied to philosophy signifies a radical difference in the method of inquiry and even in the objects to be investigated, for certain objects can be known only by experimental or empirical research. Kant appears to be the first (in the great books at least) to make a sharp separation between the investigation of either nature or mind by what he calls "empirical" as opposed to "rational" methods. He still uses the name "science" for both sorts of investigation, but he appears to restrict "philosophy" to the latter—the pure, the *a priori,* the rational sciences.

Two other innovations must be noted. Though Kant regards it as a rational discipline, he excludes mathematics entirely from philosophy and criticizes its misleading influence upon those philosophers who have tried to imitate mathematical thought. And though he sometimes uses "metaphysic" narrowly to designate the critical examination of pure reason itself, he also says that "this name of metaphysic may be given to the whole of pure philosophy . . . excluding all that belongs to the empirical and the mathematical employment of reason." Considering that it has only two objects, nature and freedom—that which *is* and that which *ought to be*—Kant divides philosophy into the speculative and the practical use of pure reason, which gives rise to a *meta-*

physic of nature and a *metaphysic of morals.*
"Metaphysic, therefore, that of nature as well
as that of morals, and particularly the criticism
of our adventurous reason which forms the
introduction to and preparation for it, constitute together," Kant writes, "what may be
termed philosophy in the true sense of the
word. Its only goal is wisdom, and the path to
it, science."

Kant's innovations in vocabulary plainly announce the separation of philosophy from
mathematics and experimental science, which
is only intimated by earlier modern writers.
But Kant still uses the word "science" for
both the philosophical and the empirical sciences. The final step is taken in the 19th
century when the word "science" is restricted
to mathematics and to such knowledge of
nature, man, and society as can be obtained
by the methods of experimental or empirical
research. William James, for example, stresses
the fact that he is trying to expound psychology as one of the natural sciences, and to that
end he tries to separate the problems which
are capable of empirical investigation from
those which belong to philosophical speculation. For Freud that separation is an accomplished fact, and one which leaves to philosophy no problem that can be solved by science.

According to Freud, "it is inadmissible to
declare that science is one field of human
intellectual activity, and that religion and philosophy are others, at least as valuable, and
that science has no business to interfere with
the other two." On the contrary, Freud thinks
it is right for scientific research to look "on
the whole field of human activity as its own,"
and to criticize the unscientific formulations
of philosophy. The trouble with philosophy
is that "it behaves itself as if it were a science . . . but it parts company with science, in
that it clings to the illusion that it can produce a complete and coherent picture of the
universe." It is this illusion which science continually punctures, since, in Freud's opinion,
"that picture must needs fall to pieces with
every new advance in our knowledge."

WHEN SCIENCE AND philosophy are set apart
at last, it is possible to make sense of the

typically modern questions concerning philosophy. How does it stand in relation to science? Does it consist of verifiable knowledge
comparable to that which can be obtained in
the natural and social sciences? If not, what
is the standard of truth in philosophy? Does
it consist of definitions and postulates leading
to rigorously demonstrated conclusions in a
manner comparable to mathematics, especially
in its modern construction? If not, must it not
be regarded as opinion or speculation rather
than as knowledge in any strict sense? Or if
philosophical thought can be compared with
mathematics, does not the diversity of definitions and postulates employed by different
philosophers reduce philosophy to a collection
of competing "systems" rather than a single
discipline in which philosophers work cooper-
atively as do scientists and mathematicians?

However the foregoing questions are answered, there are still others. Does philosophy have distinct branches, divided according
to their objects of study like the natural sciences, or is philosophy to be identified with
metaphysics? If, in addition to metaphysics,
there is a philosophy of nature, how are its
principles and conclusions related to the findings of the natural sciences which appear to
study the same object? Similarly, if psychology is a branch of philosophy, how is it related
to experimental or clinical psychology? What
is the relation of moral and political philosophy to the empirical social sciences concerned
with describing, not judging or regulating, human conduct and social institutions? Is economics a science or is it a branch of moral
philosophy; or, if it is both, how are the two
related?

What is the use of philosophy, especially in
its theoretical branches, if, unlike science, it
cannot be applied to the mastery of physical
nature and the production of utilities, whether
bridges or bombs? What, finally, at the end of
its long history, does philosophy come to if,
in such marked contrast to the continuously
accelerated progress of the sciences, it cannot
claim any signal advance on which all philosophers are agreed, but instead must admit that
most of its problems seem to be perennially
debated, now as in every preceding century?

SOME OF THESE questions, as well as certain answers to them, are considered in other chapters: the comparison of empirical research and philosophical thought as constituting different types of science, in the chapter on SCIENCE; the distinction and relation between natural philosophy and natural science, in the chapter on PHYSICS; the difference between philosophical and scientific psychology, in the chapter on MAN; the function of definitions, hypotheses, postulates, or axioms in the foundation and method of philosophy and science, in the chapter on PRINCIPLE; the difference between the practical use of philosophy in the sphere of morals and the use of science in the sphere of the productive arts, in the chapter on KNOWLEDGE; the accumulation of truth as measuring advances in science and philosophy, in the chapter on PROGRESS.

Here we must observe that such answers to these questions as tend to subordinate philosophy to science originate exclusively with modern views of the nature of knowledge, of the criteria of truth, and of the capacities of the human mind, especially the power of reason. Even those modern authors who write at a time when the words "science" and "philosophy" are, for the most part, interchangeable tend in this direction. The points they make about the nature, aim, and method of what they call either science or philosophy have the effect of giving the status of *knowledge* only to mathematics and the empirical sciences, and of reducing philosophical speculation to the status of *opinion*.

Bacon's insistence, for example, that genuine knowledge gives us power over nature and generates productions, seems to have this effect, certainly upon any part of traditional philosophy which cannot meet this test. Hume's insistence upon experimental reasoning with respect to all matters of fact seems to eliminate not only metaphysics, but any science or philosophy of nature which is not experimental. The methodological reforms in philosophy which these philosophers and others, like Hobbes, Descartes, and Spinoza, propose seem to be reforms which eliminate whatever in philosophy cannot become either experimental science or a quasi-mathematical system of thought.

Among the modern reformers of philosophy, Kant represents the exception. By his critical method he hopes to establish philosophy above and independent of all the empirical sciences; and to institute metaphysics as a science which neither imitates mathematics nor accepts it as an equal in the scale of reason's accomplishments. Yet even Kant seems to betray the typically modern attitude toward philosophy. The intellectual revolution which he projects as the philosophical parallel to the Copernican revolution in astronomy is motivated by his desire to secure for philosophy a stability and development comparable to that enjoyed by mathematics and the empirical sciences. Another German philosopher, Heidegger, goes further than Kant in identifying philosophy with metaphysics. It is in metaphysics, he says, that "philosophy comes to itself and sets about its explicit tasks."

"IN THE PROGRESS of society," writes Adam Smith, "philosophy or speculation becomes, like every other employment, the principal or sole trade and occupation of a particular class of citizens. Like every other employment too, it is subdivided into a great number of different branches, each of which affords occupation to a peculiar tribe or class of philosophers; and this subdivision of employment in philosophy, as well as in every other business, improves dexterity and saves time. Each individual becomes more expert in his own peculiar branch, more work is done upon the whole, and the quantity of science is considerable increased by it."

Despite his use of the word "philosophy," it seems likely that Smith is describing the division of labor in scientific research and the specialization of scientists. Though philosophy has divisions, and though the distinction and order of its parts are discussed by the great philosophers, their own work exhibits a spirit opposed to specialization. In fact, one measure of the greatness of a philosopher is the comprehensiveness of his thought, the range of subject matters and the scope of the problems with which he deals.

Those philosophers, like Aristotle, Bacon, Hobbes, or Kant, who show great interest in the divisions of philosophy seem to be largely concerned with distinguishing the different objects of philosophical thought and differentiating the concepts or principles peculiarly relevant to each. Other chapters deal with subject matters, sciences, or disciplines that have been regarded, by one philosopher or another, as major divisions of philosophy, *e.g.*, Logic, Metaphysics, Theology, Dialectic, Mathematics, Physics, and psychology (in the chapter on Man). But one group of sciences or disciplines is not discussed elsewhere and must be briefly noted here. Traditionally within the province of the philosopher, they are sometimes expanded to his whole domain. They come nearer to what the ordinary man means by "philosophy" when he speaks of having a philosophy of life—an overall yet personal view of the human situation, illuminated by a sense of the values which should direct conduct.

The disciplines in question are traditionally called ethics and politics, or moral philosophy. Socrates is credited with having accomplished the first great reform in philosophy when he turned to such subjects and away from the inquiries of his predecessors. "I do not mean to speak disparagingly of the students of natural philosophy," he says at his trial, "but the simple truth is, O Athenians, that I have nothing to do with physical speculations." Subsequently he tells his judges that he "will never cease from the practice and teaching of philosophy"—reproaching those whom he questions with "under-valuing the greater and over-valuing the less," enjoining them not to take thought of their persons or their properties, "but first and chiefly to care about the greatest improvement of the soul." He will not foreswear philosophy even to save his life. "I cannot hold my tongue," he says. "Daily discourse about virtue . . . is the greatest good of man," for "the unexamined life is not worth living."

The conception of ethics and politics and of their relation to other branches of philosophy seems to depend upon the acceptance or rejection of a fundamental principle in the division of philosophy. Aristotle and Kant, for example, divide the philosophical sciences into the theoretical or speculative and the practical or moral, according as they consider what *is* (the nature and causes of things) or what *ought to be* (the objects of choice, the ends and means, in the conduct of life and the institutions of society). According to this conception of the practical, the practical sciences are ethics and politics, and with them economics and jurisprudence; or in another statement of the same divisions, the parts of practical philosophy are moral philosophy, the philosophy of right, the philosophy of law. They are all conceived as normative, prescriptive, or regulative disciplines, determining what is good and evil or right and wrong, and directing action in the sphere of human freedom.

Hobbes proceeds on a different principle. He separates natural philosophy (including *philosophia prima*) from civil philosophy, or the theory of the body politic. But he includes ethics and poetics under natural philosophy as part of the theoretical study of human nature. The distinction between the theoretical and the practical seems to be here ignored, or even implicitly denied insofar as Hobbes would reject the basis of the distinction—the difference between natural necessity and human freedom. Necessity governs the motions of the human body and of the body politic as much as it does the bodies studied by the physicist, and so ethics, politics, and physics are alike sciences of determined consequences.

Still another view seems to be taken by Bacon who separates natural from human and civil philosophy and divides natural philosophy into two main speculative branches (physics and metaphysics) and two main practical branches (mechanics and magic). Psychology, logic, and ethics belong to human philosophy; politics and jurisprudence to civil philosophy. But with respect to all of these Bacon does not apply the distinction between the speculative and the practical which seems to him of the utmost importance in natural philosophy. The reason seems to be that Bacon uses the word "practical" to mean the production of effects resulting from the knowledge of causes, rather than actions to be performed by men as the result of choice. His practical sciences correspond, therefore, to what Aristotle conceives as arts, or productive sciences—the sphere of making or poetics in general—not to what Aristotle means by the practical, the sphere of doing rather than of making, of prudence rather than of art. These matters are discussed in the chapters on ART and POETRY.

The problem of the relation of science to art becomes, if restated in Bacon's terms, the problem of the relation of the theoretical to the practical (*i.e.*, productive) sciences. But in terms of Aristotle, Aquinas, or Kant, the problem of the relation between the speculative and practical branches of philosophy becomes the quite different problem of how knowledge of being or nature relates to knowledge of what should be sought or ought to be done. In Hobbes's terms the problem shifts in still another direction to the consideration of the bearing of physics upon psychology, ethics, and politics.

WHEN WE COME to the 20th century, we encounter views of philosophy that both elevate it above the claims of the positive sciences and also degrade it to the role of handmaiden to empirical science. On the one hand, James confers upon philosophy the honor of discovering by reflection and analysis the fundamental wisdom to be found in the basic categories of common sense. "*Our fundamental ways of thinking about things,*" he writes, "*are discoveries of exceedingly remote ancestors, which have been able to preserve themselves throughout the experience of all subsequent time.* They form a great stage of equilibrium in the human mind's development, the stage of *common sense.*"

On the other hand, Russell and Wittgenstein use their command of mathematical logic to cast contempt, if not ridicule, upon philosophy. "The results of philosophy," writes Wittgenstein, "are the uncovering of one or another piece of plain nonsense and of bumps that the understanding has got by running its head up against the limits of language." For him, "a philosophical problem has the form: 'I don't know my way about.'" In his view, "philosophy simply puts everything before us, and neither explains nor deduces anything."

Russell denies that there is any "special source of wisdom which is open to philosophy but not to science." Accordingly, for him, philosophy and science do not differ essentially. "The results obtained by philosophy are not radically different from those obtained from science." However, he also acknowledges that "the essential characteristic of philosophy, which makes it a study distinct from science, is *criticism*. It examines critically the principles employed in science and in daily life." Nevertheless, he counters that by saying, "the value of philosophy is, in fact, to be sought largely in its very uncertainty."

Whitehead has few kind remarks to make about modern philosophy. In his view, "modern philosophy has been ruined. It has oscillated in a complex manner between three extremes. There are the dualists, who accept matter and mind as on an equal basis, and the two varieties of monists, those who put mind inside matter, and those who put matter inside mind. But this juggling with abstractions can never overcome the inherent confusion introduced by the ascription of *misplaced concreteness* to the scientific scheme of the seventeenth century."

The three extremes mentioned above by Whitehead existed in ancient and medieval thought. Plato was a dualist, Democritus a materialist, Plotinus a spiritualist; Aristotle and Aquinas are eminent examples of philosophers who commit the fallacy of "misplaced concreteness," to use the term that was Whitehead's own essential innovation. Accordingly, one must conclude that, with few exceptions, the history of philosophy before Whitehead is a dismal story of intellectual failures.

Perhaps the worst drubbing that philosophy receives comes a little earlier than the 20th century in the writings of Nietzsche. In *Beyond Good and Evil,* in a chapter concerned with "the prejudices of philosophers," Nietzsche directs his characteristic nihilism against philosophy. "What makes one regard philosophers half mistrustfully and half mockingly is not that one again and again detects how innocent they are . . . but that they display altogether insufficient honesty, while making a mighty and virtuous noise as soon as the problem of truthfulness is even remotely touched on." Philosophers, in his opinion, are "for the most part no better than cunning pleaders for their prejudices, which they baptize 'truths.' " Considering Nietzsche's own nihilistic skepticism about the existence of truth, his contempt for the philosophical pursuit of truth should extend to scientific investigation as well.

How, on any of the foregoing views, do speculations concerning the nature of things affect the theory of human life and society, or the practical principles by which man tries to lead a good life and organize a good society? What relation do the truths of physics and metaphysics, or the major philosophical issues in these fields, bear to the truths and issues in psychology, ethics, and politics? Or, as James puts the question, must not any man who has a philosophy of life also have, implicitly at least, a metaphysics?

Upon the answers to such questions depends the varying esteem in which philosophy is held in the great periods of western culture. Unlike supernatural religion and empirical science, and especially when separated from them, philosophy does not promise eternal salvation or earthly prosperity. The uses of philosophy, as compared with religion and science, must somehow be assessed in the terms which, from the beginning of philosophy, are of its essence—the love of wisdom, and through it the search for a human wisdom which shall be at once speculative and practical.

67

Physics

INTRODUCTION

CONCERNING the subject matter of physics, one thing seems to be taken for granted. The object of the study is the sensible world of changing things, or matter in motion. Because that was the object of their concern and study, the pre-Socratic philosophers from Thales, Anaximander, Anaximenes down to Heraclitus and Democritus were all called physicists. It is in their tradition and with critical commentary on their views that Aristotle in the 4th century B.C. wrote the first great book bearing the title *Physics*.

Aristotle's teacher Plato was not a physicist in this sense. In his formulation of the liberal arts and sciences that was part of the early education of the guardians in *The Republic,* the four mathematical disciplines were enumerated as arithmetic, geometry, music, and astronomy. All four were strictly mathematical disciplines, not empirical sciences. However, in one dialogue, the *Timaeus,* Plato is concerned with what looks like a physical problem—the formation of the cosmos and its structure. Yet even here his process of thought relies heavily on mathematical concepts and configurations. He regards the elaborate theory that he develops as only a *likely* story, aimed at saving the appearances by explaining them in mathematical terms. Thus Plato is more nearly than Aristotle the precursor of mathematical physics—of Ptolemy, Copernicus, and Kepler, of Galileo, Newton, and Huygens.

In any case, whether it is admixed with mathematics or not, a science is not a physical science, in the modern sense of that term, unless it investigates, observes, and measures the sensible or instrumentally detectable phenomena. If it has no concern with the phenomena of change, then it does not have the character of a physical or natural science. The Latin word "*natura*" is equivalent in meaning to the Greek word "*phüsis*," and both, in their primary meanings, signify *change*.

The early Greek physicists, to whom both Plato and Aristotle refer, inaugurate the study of change with speculations about, not empirical research into, ultimate origins of the underlying principles of, and the causes of, natural phenomena. Since they did not engage in empirical research, they have in modern times been called philosophers rather than scientists, because the mark of science in modern times has become its engagement in empirical research, and the mark of philosophy is speculation. But there seems to be no difference of opinion about their title as physicists. Their undisputed claim to this title derives, not from the method they employ, but from the object they study—change. The realm of nature is the realm of change.

It is for this reason that Aristotle, considering the theories of his predecessors in the opening chapters of his *Physics,* sets Parmenides apart from all the rest. Parmenides' affirmation of the unity of being, which leads to his denial of the reality of change or motion, cannot be treated as a physical theory. On the contrary, it is, according to Aristotle, a complete negation of the subject matter of physics. No matter what other points physicists may dispute among themselves, they must all at least agree in taking a stand against Parmenides. Aristotle does not even seem to think that a book on physics is the proper place to argue against Parmenides. That argument belongs to another part of philosophy. The reality of change seems to him sufficiently evident to assure the physicist that he has a subject matter to investigate.

It is that which Heracleitus, a pre-Socratic opponent of Parmenides, regards as fundamental, and going further, insists that everything in reality, like fire, is constantly in flux. Heisenberg, a 20th-century physicist, declares that "modern physics is in some way extremely near to the doctrines of Heraclitus. If we replace the word 'fire' by the word 'energy' we can almost repeat his statements word for word from our modern point of view. Energy is in fact the substance from which all elementary particles, all atoms and therefore all things are made, and energy is that which moves."

THE QUESTION whether the early physicists were scientists or philosophers calls attention to different methods of investigating natural phenomena. Agreement on the subject matter of physics may prevail, therefore, only in very general terms. When, in a manner to accord with the method employed, the object of physical inquiry is more specifically defined, there seem to be two physics, not one—a philosophical and a scientific physics, a philosophy of nature and a natural science, or, to use Kant's phrasing, rational or pure physics and an empirical or experimental physics.

Though Newton may call his work a philosophy of nature, he also refers to it as an experimental philosophy, in order to distinguish it from the work of earlier natural philosophers who did not perform experiments. The difference between the physics of Newton and that of Aristotle seems, however, to involve more than a divergence in method. The problems which Newton and Aristotle try to solve indicate a difference in subject matter as well. Nevertheless, this difference falls within what, in the most general terms, must be conceived as the domain of physics. For all their differences, both are physicists, though both are not philosophers or scientists in the same sense.

There are other sources of variation in the definition of physics. The problem of the relation of physics to other disciplines—whether these are other branches of philosophy or other fields of empirical research—raises issues about the object and scope of physics.

Aristotle, Francis Bacon, Descartes, and Kant, for example, do not seem to have a common understanding of the relation of physics to mathematics and metaphysics. In consequence they conceive physics itself differently.

On the level of empirical research, physics is sometimes regarded as just one of the natural sciences and sometimes as the whole group of natural sciences. In the latter case it includes such fields as astronomy, mechanics, optics, acoustics, thermodynamics, magnetism, and electricity; and sometimes chemistry, biology, and even psychology are included under the head of physical or natural sciences, contrasted in the broadest terms to the social sciences. The conception of physics obviously changes when its scope is determined by a boundary line which separates it from chemistry, or from biology and psychology, or from the study of society.

The separation of these other sciences from physics does not necessarily imply a discontinuity in nature or the natural sciences. The biologist and the psychologist, for example, consider the physical bases of life and the physical conditions or correlates of mental phenomena. Hybrid sciences like biophysics and psychophysics have developed. Even the study of society draws upon physics to the extent that the laws of matter in motion and considerations of space and time must be appealed to for an understanding of the physical foundations of economic and political life.

OTHER CHAPTERS DEAL with specific physical sciences, e.g., ASTRONOMY AND COSMOLOGY and MECHANICS. The latter tries to cover the various branches of mechanics and related fields of study, such as dynamics, optics, the theory of heat, magnetism, and electricity; particularly so far as these are represented in the work of Galileo, Newton, Huygens, Gilbert, and Faraday. The basic concepts of mechanics and its branches or affiliates are also treated in that chapter. Still other chapters deal with fundamental terms representing concepts or problems in the larger domain of physics, philosophical or scientific, e.g., CAUSE, CHANGE, ELEMENT, INFINITY, MATTER, PRINCIPLE, QUANTITY, SPACE, and TIME—not to mention NATURE and WORLD, terms which represent in the most comprehensive way the reality studied by the physicist.

Our discussion here can therefore be restricted to the problems raised in the great books concerning the conception of physics, its subject matter and method, its relation to other sciences or other parts of philosophy. It will lead to such questions as whether physics is supreme among the sciences studying reality or the nature of things and, at the other extreme, whether physics is at all possible as a science, whether there can be scientific knowledge of bodies in motion or of the whole realm of change and becoming.

The problem of the distinction between philosophical and scientific physics would appear to be only a special case of the distinction between philosophy and science in general. But it is more than that. It is the case which tests the main distinction itself, since here both philosopher and scientist claim to be expounding the same subject matter or at least to be dealing with the same general field of phenomena.

Mathematics and metaphysics bear on the distinction between philosophy and science in a different way. If, for example, we take experimentation or empirical research to be characteristic of science in distinction from philosophy, then mathematics would seem to resemble philosophy rather than science. On no understanding of the nature of mathematical knowledge is mathematics ever divided into two kinds which are capable of being described as empirical and rational. The possibility of metaphysical knowledge may be challenged, but no one has ever proposed an experimental metaphysics to challenge the metaphysics of the philosophers.

But physics seems to permit both an experimental and a philosophical treatment. Whether they are to be regarded as in conflict with one another depends on whether they are attacking the same problems by different methods or whether they represent something like a division of labor. In the latter view, each would deal, according to its method, with different problems and tend to supplement rather than to exclude the other. Psychology is an-

other subject matter which seems to receive a dual treatment—philosophical and experimental—in the tradition of the great books. It raises issues similar to those just mentioned. They are considered in the chapter on MAN.

As the chapters on PHILOSOPHY and on SCIENCE indicate, the discussion of their difference from and relation to one another is complicated by the double use of both terms. The word "science," for example, is used for both the philosophical and the experimental sciences throughout the greater part of the tradition. Similarly, until the 19th century, the name of philosopher is taken by those who experiment as well as by those who do not. The term "scientist," used in the modern sense, was introduced in the 19th century.

It is impossible, therefore, to speak without confusion of a scientific and a philosophical physics unless the verbal ambiguities are resolved by some convention, such as the understanding that when the context indicates that the words "science" and "philosophy" are being used as opposites rather than as synonyms, then "science" shall signify the experimental and "philosophy" the nonexperimental mode of treatment. Physicists themselves make this distinction in terms of "experimenters" and "theorists." The discipline is now so complicated that no single individual is a master of both activities. The last person who worked with equal brilliance in both theory and experiment is said to have been Enrico Fermi.

Beyond this, it is necessary to proceed as if the chapters on PHILOSOPHY and SCIENCE formed a background for some of the matters to be discussed here. Otherwise the consideration of natural philosophy and natural science would tend to become a general discussion of philosophy and science.

THE GREAT BOOKS of experimental physics seem to have three characteristics in common. First, and most naturally, they insist upon experimentation as either the indispensable source or the ultimate test of scientific formulations. Second, they tend to rely upon mathematics as much as upon experiment, both for the formulation of nature's laws and for the demonstration of the consequences or corollaries of the primary laws. Third, though experiments and observations multiply as science develops, they seek to bring all the phenomena of nature under the smallest number of generalizations, which have the utmost simplicity in mathematical statement.

On the second and third points, Newton's declarations seem to be most explicit. "Nature," he says, "is pleased with simplicity and affects not the pomp of superfluous causes." Accordingly, Newton directs his efforts toward the simplest statement of the laws of motion, and these he seeks to give the universality requisite for covering every type of natural phenomenon. At the opening of the third book of the *Mathematical Principles of Natural Philosophy,* he explains that in the preceding books, he has "laid down the principles of philosophy, principles not philosophical but mathematical; such, namely, as we may build our reasonings upon in philosophical inquiries. These principles are the laws and conditions of certain motions, and powers or forces." From these same principles, he will now undertake to "demonstrate the frame of the System of the World."

In the Preface to the first edition of this work, Newton describes the third book as one in which he derives "from the celestial phenomena the forces of gravity with which bodies tend to the sun and the several planets. Then from these forces, by other propositions which are also mathematical," he goes on, "I deduce the motions of the planets, the comets, the moon, the sea." But he does not consider his work to have attained the goal of physics— the comprehension of all natural phenomena by a few simple mathematical formulas.

His confession of failure may also be read as a prognostication of what an experimental physics based on mathematical principles might some day be able to achieve. "I wish we could derive the rest of the phenomena of nature by the same kind of reasoning," he writes, "for I am induced by many reasons to suspect that they may all depend upon certain forces by which the particles of bodies, by some causes hitherto unknown, are either mutually impelled towards one another, and cohere in regular figures, or are repelled and

recede from one another." These words of Newton can be thought of as constituting a kind of "Holy Grail" for modern fundamental physics. Einstein tried unsuccessfully for nearly four decades to produce a unified field theory—one that would unite in a single set of equations electromagnetism and gravitation. His successors have come to believe that such a unification is impossible without the quantum theory. In addition, electromagnetism and gravitation are only two of the four forces in need of unification. One must also include nuclear forces and the weak forces responsible for the instability of many nuclear particles. Some physicists believe that such unified "theories of everything" may now be in view.

Midway between Newton and Einstein, Fourier also bears testimony to the ideal of physics as a science at once simple in its principles and universal in the scope of their application. The successors of Newton and Galileo, he writes, "have extended their theories and given them an admirable perfection; they have taught us that the most diverse phenomena are subject to a small number of universal laws which are reproduced in all the acts of nature. It is recognized that the same principles regulate all the movements of the stars, their form, the inequalities of their courses, the equilibrium and the oscillations of the seas, the harmonic vibrations of air and sonorous bodies, the transmission of light, capillary actions, the undulations of fluids, in fine the most complex effects of all natural forces. Thus has the thought of Newton been confirmed," he concludes, referring to Newton's praise of geometry, whose glory it is that the few mathematical principles it provided for use in physics should have been "able to produce so many things."

ON THE EXPERIMENTAL SIDE, the great works of physical science seem to contain diverse notions of the purposes served by experimentation, accompanied by a fairly uniform recognition of the dependence of natural science upon experiment. In the field of magnetism, for example, Gilbert sets aside as unscientific all those authors who "have written about amber and jet as attracting chaff . . . but with never a proof from experiments . . . These writers deal only in words . . . Such philosophy bears no fruit." The fruitfulness of experiments on the vacuum, the equilibrium of fluids, and the weight of air leads Pascal to conclude that the secrets of nature remain hidden until "the experiments which supply us with knowledge about it" can be performed and multiplied.

"We ought never to search for truth but by the natural road of experiment and observation," writes Lavoisier; and Faraday describes himself as "an experimentalist" who feels "bound to let experiment guide me into any train of thought which it may justify." The science of electricity, he finds, "is in that state in which every part of it requires experimental investigation, not merely for the discovery of new effects," but ultimately for "the more accurate determination of the first principles of action of the most extraordinary and universal power in nature."

Methods of experimentation necessarily differ in different fields of physical research. Newton's optical experiments with mirrors and prisms were adapted to the phenomena of light, as Galileo's experiment with the inclined plane, Pascal's experiment on the equilibrium of fluids, or Faraday's experiments with induction coils were adapted to the phenomena of dynamics, hydrostatics, and electricity. The materials employed, the apparatus or instruments devised, the factors controlled or isolated from irrelevant circumstances, and the units of measurement in which the results are recorded, naturally vary with the phenomena under observation. Yet one thing is common to the variety of experiments described in the great books of physical science. They all involve the construction of an artificial physical system which permits more accurate and refined observation than does nature uncontrolled or untampered with.

The student of nature must observe in any case, no matter whether he is a philosopher or a scientist. To say that philosophical physics is nonexperimental does not mean for Aristotle that knowledge of nature is possible without observation or induction from experience. But the experimentalists insist upon the distinction between the kind of observation which men normally make in the course of everyday experience and the kind which involve the special experience enjoyed only by those who observe and, in addition, measure the results of specially contrived experiments.

This point of distinction seems to be strikingly illustrated by a passage in Galileo's *Dialogues Concerning the Two New Sciences*. One of the persons in the dialogue, Simplicio, declares "everyday experience to show the propagation of light to be instantaneous." He explains that "when we see a piece of artillery fired at a great distance, the flash reaches our eyes without lapse of time; but the sound reaches the ear only after a noticeable interval." Sagredo replies that this familiar bit of experience permits him to infer only that "sound, in reaching our ear, travels more slowly than light." It does not inform us, he says, "whether the coming of light is instantaneous or whether, although extremely rapid, it still occupies time." The choice between these alternatives could not be determined by ordinary experience. An experiment had to be constructed in order to measure the velocity of light. Indeed, Galileo carried out such an experiment with lanterns stationed at some distance from each other. The speed of light (more than 186,000 miles per second) is much too great for him to have noticed any effect with such a crude system.

Recourse to experimentation to find by observation and measurement the answers which ordinary experience fails to yield does not exhaust the uses of experiment. The great experimental physicists indicate at least three distinct uses to which experiments can be put in addition to a merely exploratory use for "the discovery of new effects."

In natural philosophy as in mathematics, writes Newton, "the method of analysis ought ever to precede the method of composition" or synthesis. In physics, the method of analysis "consists in making experiments and observations, and in drawing conclusions from them by induction." In contrast, the synthetic method begins with the principles *assumed,* therefrom "explaining the phenomena . . . and proving the explanations."

Here experiments perform a probative

rather than an inductive function. As Huygens observes, proof in physics does not have the certitude of mathematical demonstration, but it can have an extremely high degree of probability—"very often scarcely less than complete proof"—as a result of the experimental confirmation of a conclusion deduced from the assumed principles. This occurs "when things which have been demonstrated by the principles that have been assumed, correspond perfectly to the phenomena which experiment has brought under observation, especially when there are a great number of them." A single crucial experiment, so perfect in construction that all relevant factors have been controlled, makes unnecessary the multiplication of experiments to establish the conclusion.

A third use of experiment is illustrated by Galileo when he measures the velocity of a ball rolling down an inclined plane, in order to decide whether a certain mathematical definition of uniformly accelerated motion describes the acceleration "which one meets in nature in the case of falling bodies." The persons in the dialogue seem to be satisfied with some mathematical reasoning which shows that the velocity increases with the units of time elapsed rather than with the intervals of space traversed. But when Simplicio asks for an experiment to show that the mathematical conclusion has physical reality, in the sense of describing observable phenomena, Salviati replies that this request "is a very reasonable one, for this is the custom—and properly so—in those sciences where mathematical demonstrations are applied to natural phenomena" and "where the principles once established by well-chosen experiments become the foundations of the entire superstructure." Here experiment does not confirm conclusions. It establishes principles, not by inductive generalization but by comparing actual measurements with mathematical expectations.

WITHOUT EXPERIMENT but not without inductions from experience, without measurements but not without recourse to observation, Aristotle's *Physics*—and with it such physical treatises as his works *On the Heavens* and *On Generation and Corruption*—represents a philosophy of nature. In Aristotle's meaning of the term 'science,' these treatises expound sciences, but they also constitute one part of philosophy, to be distinguished from mathematics and from what Aristotle regards as the first or highest part of philosophy, *i.e.,* the science of metaphysics.

Aristotle's tripartite division of the theoretical sciences or speculative philosophy into physics, mathematics, and metaphysics raises a question concerning his numerous biological works, and perhaps also his treatise *On the Soul.* Are these to be classified as physical sciences or parts of natural philosophy? The fact that Aristotle distinguishes between the forms and properties of living and nonliving matter does not seem to affect the answer. By his criteria of physical inquiry—namely, that it investigates what neither exists nor can be conceived apart from matter and motion, and that it is concerned with every type of change—all these works belong to the domain of physics. Accordingly, even such apparently psychological studies as those dealing with sensation, memory, and dreams, justify the title under which they have been traditionally grouped—*Parva Naturalia, i.e.,* short physical treatises.

For all these more specialized considerations of natural phenomena the *Physics* seems to serve as a general introduction, as well as being in its own right an exposition of the most fundamental science in the sphere of natural philosophy. It tries to define change and to state the principles underlying every type of change. It tries to classify the types of change, separating coming to be and passing away simply (or generation and corruption), from coming to be in a special respect (or change in quality, quantity, and place) which Aristotle usually calls "motion" in distinction from "becoming" or "generation." It undertakes to analyze the conditions or causes of change or motion, to distinguish what happens by chance from what happens of necessity, to discriminate between natural and unnatural or violent motions, to treat the relation of mover and moved, to deal with the continuity and divisibility of motions, to consider place and time as conditions or aspects of motion, and to ask about the infinity of body and of change, and about the eternity of motion or the whole order of becoming, the natural world of things in motion.

Aristotle's physics thus seems to stand in sharp contrast to the physics of the experimentalists, not merely in method, but in the questions it tries to answer and in the principles to which it appeals. The effort to define change in general and to state the principles and causes operative in every type of change might appear to correspond to the search for formulas of maximum generality to cover all natural phenomena. But where Newton and Fourier hope thereby to reduce nature's variety to the simplest terms—a few laws of motion comprehending the whole framework of nature—Aristotle tends on the contrary to insist upon an irreducible variety of types of motion, kinds of matter, and causes of change.

Furthermore, the principles to which Aristotle appeals are not mathematical. He criticizes the discussion of becoming which takes place in Plato's *Timaeus* on the ground that it tries to substitute mathematical for physical terms in the analysis of change. "Physical bodies contain surfaces and volumes, lines and points," he writes, "and these are the subject matter of mathematics"; but the mathematician is not concerned with these things as the attributes of physical bodies, but only as separated, in thought at least, from matter and motion. There are sciences which represent mixtures of mathematics and physics, such as optics and harmonics, but the existence of these mixed sciences—the equivalent of what is later called "mathematical physics"—seems to Aristotle to imply rather than deny the separation of purely physical science from pure mathematics.

Where Newton (who can be taken as the exemplary author of a physics which is at once mathematical and experimental) goes to mathematics for the principles of natural philosophy, Aristotle seems to think that physics has its own proper principles. If any deeper understanding of these principles is sought, it is not to be found in mathematics, but in metaphysics, or what Aristotle calls "the first philosophy."

For example, matter, form, and privation, are proposed by Aristotle as the basic physical principles. In such terms he is able to state his insight that all change involves a substratum (or *that which* changes) and contraries (or that *from which* and that *to which* the change occurs). But the analysis of matter and form in terms of potentiality and actuality as modes of being, and the consideration of form and privation in terms of being and nonbeing, belong to metaphysics rather than physics.

Furthermore, Aristotle as a physicist deals with bodies in motion and with the difference between the generation of bodies and their alteration, increase and decrease, or change of place. But he leaves to metaphysics—to the books which come after the books on physics—the discussion of physical bodies as substances composite of matter and form, and the distinction of substance and accident which bears on the difference between substantial and accidental change (*i.e.,* generation and corruption as opposed to the change in quality, quantity, or place).

Though for Aristotle physics is as separate from metaphysics as it is from mathematics in subject matter, physics depends upon metaphysics, as it does not upon mathematics, for the establishment as well as the elucidation of its principles. It is in this sense that metaphysics is logically prior to physics. But there may also be a sense in which philosophical physics is logically prior to experimental natural science. To the extent that the experimentalist employs physical as opposed to mathematical principles, he may have to derive these from a philosophy of nature. Galileo, for example, investigates the properties of natural and violent motions in the Third and Fourth Day of his *Two New Sciences* (*i.e.,* the motions of freely falling bodies and of projectiles). The problem of establishing the reality of this distinction and of defining the natural and the nonnatural types of motion seems to be a matter of philosophical analysis rather than of experimental investigation.

BACON AND KANT appear to agree with Aristotle about the separation of physics from mathematics. Rational (or pure, as opposed to empirical) physics is, according to Kant, "entirely separate from mathematics." It is not to be confused with "what is commonly called *physica generalis,* which is mathematics rather than a philosophy of nature." Criticizing the natural philosophy of the ancients because it is corrupted by logic in the school of Aristotle and by mathematics in the school of Plato, Bacon says that mathematics should "terminate natural philosophy rather than generate or create it. We may hope for better results," he adds, "from pure and unmixed natural philosophy."

Bacon elsewhere observes that "the investigation of nature is best conducted when mathematics are applied to physics." He does not deny "the great use of mathematics in physics," but rather insists that mathematics be regarded as "an appendage or auxiliary" of natural philosophy, not its master. He is writing against the mathematicians "who would have their science preside over physics."

But to whatever extent Aristotle, Bacon, and Kant are in agreement concerning the relation of physics and mathematics, their theories of the scope and subject matter of physics seem to be at variance. For Bacon, physics is only one of the theoretical parts of natural philosophy; the other is metaphysics. Both are sciences of nature or the physical world, though one investigates material and efficient causes, the other formal and final causes. Both studies, moreover, can be conducted experimentally and can yield practical fruits (in mechanics and what Bacon calls "magic") through the production of effects by the application of a knowledge of causes.

For Kant, the whole body of theoretical knowledge which is rational and *a priori*, not empirical and *a posteriori*, is the metaphysic of nature, of which one part is rational physics, and the other rational psychology. "The metaphysic of corporeal nature," he writes, "is called *physic,* or, because it must contain the principles of an a priori knowledge of nature only, *rational physic*." Here physics and metaphysics do not have distinct objects as they do for Aristotle; nor does Kant's conception of physics as purely *a priori* knowledge of nature seem to agree with Aristotle's conception of physics as inductive and empirical, if not experimental.

A 20th-century mathematician, such as G. H. Hardy, takes a radically different view of the spheres of mathematics and physics. He writes: "there is probably less difference between the positions of a mathematician and of a physicist than is generally supposed, and . . . the most important seems to me to be this, that the mathematician is in much more direct contact with reality. This may seem a paradox, since it is the physicist who deals with the subject-matter usually described as 'real'; but a very little reflection is enough to show that the physicist's reality, whatever it may be, has few or none of the attributes which common sense ascribes instinctively to reality. A chair may be a collection of whirling electrons, or an idea in the mind of God: each of these accounts of it may have its merits, but neither conforms at all closely to the suggestions of common sense . . . we cannot be said to know what the subject-matter of physics is; but this need not prevent us from understanding roughly what a physicist is trying to do. It is plain that he is trying to correlate the incoherent body of crude fact confronting him with some definite and orderly scheme of abstract relations, the kind of scheme which he can borrow only from mathematics."

These issues concerning the relation of physics to mathematics and metaphysics have significance for the experimental as well as the philosophical study of nature. If, for example, following the position taken by Hume, metaphysical inquiry is dismissed as incapable of yielding knowledge, and mathematical knowledge is restricted to the realm of ideal entities, then natural science, which for Hume consists in experimental reasoning about matters of fact, becomes the only knowledge of reality. Even though Hume looks upon the conclusions of experimental reasoning as at best probable, it remains the case that questions about nature which cannot be answered by physics cannot be answered scientifically.

The effect is the same as that achieved by Hobbes, who makes physics the primary science of reality on the ground that nothing exists except bodies in motion. The assertion of the primacy of physics, in short, may be due *either* to the denial that immaterial objects can be known by us, *or* to the denial that such objects have any real existence. Of quite opposite tenor is the view that only immaterial and eternal things can be scientifically known, and that the sensible world of things which come to be, pass away, and are forever undergoing change, belongs to the realm of probability and opinion, not knowledge.

For Plato, mathematics and dialectic can be, respectively, science and wisdom because they study the intelligible reality of being in its immutable forms. But the physicists who try to give an account of becoming in all its changing sensible appearances can do no better than "adduce probabilities as likely as any others." On such matters, Timaeus says, "we ought to accept a tale which is probable and inquire no further." After discoursing at length of physical matters, Timaeus apologizes for the merely conjectural character of his account of natural phenomena, saying that "a man may sometimes set aside meditations about eternal things, and for recreation turn to consider the truths of becoming which are probable only; he will thus gain a pleasure not to be repented of, and secure for himself a wise and moderate pastime."

This view goes further than Hume's in depreciating physics by contrasting its probability with the certitude of mathematics. It praises mathematics and dialectic, as Hume's theory does not, for something more than their certitude—for their being knowledge of reality rather than of appearances.

Furthermore, Hume, unlike Plato, does not think the probability of physics detracts from its utility, the sort of utility which Bacon magnifies more eloquently than Hume—the invention of machines and the technical applications of physics whereby man extends his dominion over nature. In the traditional discussion of the dignity and value of physics, Plato and Bacon seem to represent attitudes as far apart as are the theories of Aristotle and Newton in the discussion of the subject matter and method of physics.

The invention of the quantum theory in the 1920s by Werner Heisenberg, Erwin Schrödinger, P. A. M. Dirac, Niels Bohr, and others, introduced many physicists to the sort of metaphysical debates that they thought had been the domain of philosophers. It is sometimes said that Einstein rejected the quantum theory because of its reliance on probabilities: "God does not play dice with the world." His concerns were much deeper. He thought that the Copenhagen interpretation of quantum mechanics abandoned an objective external world. The sort of limitations to knowledge embodied in Heisenberg's uncertainty principle seemed to him to be a transitory state of affairs which would be swept away when a better theory was invented.

On these matters, Einstein and Bohr engaged in a debate that lasted three decades. Bohr found the limitations of knowledge in the quantum theory entirely acceptable and, indeed, consistent with limitations in other domains which also had what he called "complementary" aspects. He gave as an example " 'thoughts' and 'sentiments,' equally indispensable to illustrate the variety and scope of conscious life." The two men, who deeply respected each other, agreed to disagree. Meanwhile, quantum theory has shown itself to be the most effective scientific theory ever formulated.

68

Pleasure and Pain

INTRODUCTION

PLEASURE and pain, writes Locke, "like other simple ideas, cannot be described, nor their names defined; the way of knowing them is ... only by experience." That pleasure and pain are elementary experiences, attributed to animals as well as enjoyed or suffered by men, is attested by poets and physiologists alike, by economists and theologians, by historians and moralists. Yet in the tradition of western thought, few of the great writers are content to leave the nature or meaning of pleasure and pain to the intuitions of experience alone.

Conflicting definitions are proposed. Psychologists disagree about the conditions under which the feelings of pleasure and pain occur, their causes and consequences, their relation to sensation, to desire and emotion, to thought, volition, and action. Moralists dispute whether pleasure is the only good and pain the only evil, whether pleasure is only one good among others to be assessed according to its worth in the scale of goods, whether pleasure and pain are morally indifferent, whether some pleasures are good, others bad, or all are intrinsically evil.

Not only in the theory of good and evil, but also in the theories of beauty and truth, pleasure and pain are fundamental terms. They are affected by all the difficulties which belong to these great themes; and also with the difficulties attendant on the ideas of virtue, sin, and punishment, of duty and happiness, into the consideration of which pleasure and pain traditionally enter.

The traditional use of the words "pleasure" and "pain" is complicated by more than the variety of definitions which have been given. Other words are frequently substituted for them, sometimes as synonyms and sometimes to express only one part or aspect of their meaning. Locke, for example, uses "pleasure" or "delight," "pain" or "uneasiness," and he observes that "whether we call it satisfaction, delight, pleasure, happiness, etc., on the one side, or uneasiness, trouble, pain, torment, anguish, misery, etc., on the other, they are still but different degrees of the same thing." Other writers use "joy" and "sorrow" or "grief" as synonyms for "pleasure" and "pain."

The words "pleasure" and "pain" are closely associated in meaning with "pleasant" and "unpleasant," though Freud sometimes uses "unpleasure" (*Unlust*) to signify an opposite of pleasure which is not the same as ordinary pain (*Schmerz*). The pleasant is often called "agreeable," "enjoyable," or "satisfying." In the language of Shakespeare, the words "like" and "dislike" have currency as the equivalents of "please" and "displease." A person who is displeased by something says of it that "it likes me not."

THE PROBLEM OF what pleasure and pain are seems logically to precede the ethical consideration of their relation to good and evil, happiness and misery, virtue and duty. But in the tradition of the great books, the psychological questions about pleasure and pain are usually raised in moral or political treatises, and sometimes in connection with discussions of rhetoric. What pleasure is, how it is caused, and the effects it produces are seldom considered apart from whether pleasures should be sought or avoided, whether some pleasures should be preferred to others, and whether pleasure is the sole criterion of the good. Sometimes, as with Marcus Aurelius and Epictetus, the ethical point—that pleasure and pain are in one sense morally indifferent—is made without any psychological account of the nature and origin of these experiences. More frequently, as in Plato's *Philebus* and Aristotle's *Nichomachean Ethics,* or in the writings of Hobbes, Spinoza, Locke, and J. S. Mill, the psychological discussion is imbedded in an ethical or political context.

Even Lucretius and William James do not seem to be complete exceptions. James's theory that the feeling of pleasure accompanies activity which is unimpeded, whereas pain attends arrested activity, seems to be a purely psychological observation, and one which can be readily divorced from moral considerations on the ground that it makes no difference to the occurrence of pleasure and pain whether the activity in question is ethically good or bad. Yet James makes this observation the basis for arguing against those whom he calls "the pleasure-philosophers"—those who make pleasure the only motive or goal of conduct. They confuse, he thinks, the pursuit of pleasure itself with the pleasure which accompanies the successful achievement of other things which may be the goals of activity.

"A *pleasant act*," he writes, "and an act *pursuing a pleasure* are in themselves two perfectly distinct conceptions, though they coalesce in one concrete phenomenon whenever a pleasure is deliberately pursued . . . Because a pleasure of achievement *can* become a pursued pleasure upon occasion, it does not follow that everywhere and always that pleasure must be pursued." One might as well suppose that "because no steamer can go to sea without incidentally consuming coal, and because some steamers may occasionally go to sea to *try* their coal, that therefore no steamer *can* go to sea for any other motive than that of coal-consumption."

Psychological observations of this sort have an obvious relevance to Aristotle's theory of good and bad pleasures, as well as to Locke's and Mill's position that pleasure is the only good or the only object of desire. They reveal an ethical strain even in the psychologist's view of pleasure and pain. The same point can be made with regard to James's observation that "pleasures are generally associated with beneficial, pains with detrimental, experiences."

Lucretius appears to give a purely physiological account of pleasure and pain in terms of the effect upon the sense organs of various atomic configurations:

No sense-delighting object has been made
Without some elemental smoothness in it,
And, on the other hand, whatever seems
Noxious, disgusting, has, as its deep core,
The presence of rough matter. In between
Are things by no means absolutely smooth,
Yet not all barbs and hooks, but little spurs
Projecting just a bit, to tease our senses.

But Lucretius is concerned to point out not only the basis of pain in the atomic nature of things, but also the natural tendency of all sensible things to avoid pain as the one besetting evil. "Nature snarls, yaps, barks for nothing, really, / Except that pain be absent from the body / And mind enjoy delight, with fear dispelled."

Without giving any psychological explanation of the pleasures of the mind, Lucretius sets them above the pleasures of the body because the latter—as his diatribe against love makes clear—seem to be inevitably followed by bodily torments or even to be admixed with them. The first maxim of nature, then, is not to seek pleasure, but to avoid pain; and among pleasures to seek only the unmixed or pure, the pleasures of knowledge and truth. The distinction between different qualities of pleasure (pleasures of the body and of the mind, mixed and pure pleasures), which is made by Plato and Mill as well as by Lucretius, inevitably tends to have at once both moral and psychological significance.

If, in the great books, there is any purely psychological theory of pleasure and pain, divorced from moral considerations, it is probably to be found in Freud. The pleasure-principle, according to him, automatically regulates the operation of the mental apparatus. "Our entire psychical activity," he writes, "is bent upon *procuring pleasure* and *avoiding pain*." Though pleasure and pain are for him primary elements of mental life, Freud admits the difficulty they present for psychological analysis. "We should like to know," he writes, "what are the conditions giving rise to pleasure and pain, but that is just where we fall short. We may only venture to say that pleasure is *in some way* connected with lessening, lowering, or extinguishing the amount of stimulation in the mental apparatus; and that pain involves a heightening of the latter. Consideration of the most intense pleasure of which man is capable, the pleasure in the performance of the sexual act, leaves little doubt upon this point."

Yet for Freud the pleasure-principle is not the only regulator of mental life. In addition to the sexual instincts, which aim at gratification and pleasure, there are the ego-instincts which, "under the influence of necessity, their mistress, soon learn to replace the pleasure-principle by a modification of it. The task of avoiding pain becomes for them almost equal in importance to that of gaining pleasure; the ego learns that it must inevitably go without immediate satisfaction, postpone gratification, learn to endure a degree of pain, and altogether renounce certain sources of pleasure. Thus trained, the ego becomes 'reasonable,' is no longer controlled by the pleasure-principle, but follows the reality-principle, which at bottom also seeks pleasure—although a delayed and diminished pleasure, one which is assured by its realization of fact, its relation to reality."

This recognition of a conflict between pleasure and reality, with a consequent attenuation or redirection of the pleasure-principle, is not amplified by Freud into a moral doctrine. It does, however, bear a striking resemblance to the theories of moralists like Kant who oppose duty to pleasure; and also to the teachings of those who, like Aristotle and Aquinas, conceive virtue as the foregoing of certain pleasures and the endurance of certain pains, through a reasonable and habitual moderation of these passions.

IF PLEASURE AND pain were simply sensations, like sensations of color or sound, they would pose a problem for the physiological psychologist no different from the problems which arise in the fields of vision and audition. Modern physiological research claims to have discovered differentiated nerve endings for pain which, together with the specific sense organs for pressure, heat, and cold, make up the cutaneous senses. But whether there are special cells for the reception of pain stimuli or whether cutaneous pain results from the too intense stimulation of the pressure and thermal nerve endings, there seems to be no evidence of organs sensitized to pleasure as, for example, the nerve cells of the retina are sensitized to light. The feeling of pleasure, it would seem to follow, is not a sensation. This seems to be confirmed by the traditional observation that every type of sensation, including the sensation of pain, can be pleasant.

Even if pain, unlike pleasure, is found to be a specific mode of sensation with a special sense organ of its own, all other types of sensation—visual, auditory, olfactory, etc.—might still have painfulness or a feeling of unpleasantness as an attribute. That such is the case seems to be a matter of traditional observation. Locke, for example, says that "delight or uneasiness, one or the other of them, join themselves to almost all our ideas of sensation and reflection: there is scarce any affection of our senses from without . . . which is not able to produce in us pleasure or pain." So understood, pleasure and pain—or the pleasant and the unpleasant—are not opposite sensations, as are hot and cold, but contrary attributes with which every sort of sensation *can* be affected. All *need* not be. Some sensations may be neutral with respect to what psychologists call "affective tone" or "affective quality."

The kind of pleasure and pain which is called "bodily" or "sensuous" would thus be sensuous because it is an attribute of sensations, and bodily because sensations involve bodily organs. But in almost every great discussion of pleasure and pain, other types are recognized: intellectual delights, the pleasures and pains of learning, aesthetic pleasure in contemplating beauty with the mind as well as with the senses, and the pain of loss, the grief accompanying deprivation, which is so different from the torment of a painful affliction of the senses. The human suffering with which the great poems deal is much more often a torment of the spirit than of the flesh.

To cover these other types of pleasure and pain, we must go beyond sensation to two other terms traditionally connected with the psychological analysis of pleasure and pain. One is emotion, the other desire, the latter to be understood broadly as including both the sensitive and the rational appetites—both the passions and the will. Aquinas, for example, treats joy and sorrow as specific emotions which represent the appetite in a state of satisfaction or frustration. So, too, the will as an appetite can come to rest in the attainment of its object and, with fruition, be in a state of joy.

In the great books of fiction, pleasure and pain are interwoven with emotion and desire, particularly with love. The usual formula connects pain with unrequited or lost love, and pleasure with the uniting of the lovers in the end. This formula becomes more complex in the writings of Proust. Swann's love for Odette is only pleasurable as long as he possesses her, or more importantly, the idea of her in his mind. Proust would have us believe that it is only such ideas of the beloved that we do love, for Swann's love—with its alternating joys and torments—is strongest when Odette is not around.

As conditions of the appetite, pleasure and pain (or joy and sorrow) can be either passions and, like all other emotions, bodily states; or they can be acts of the will and, according to Aquinas at least, spiritual states. But either way pleasure and pain seem to represent the satisfaction or frustration of desire rather than objects desired or averted. To be pleased by the attainment of an object desired, such as food and drink or knowledge, is not the same as to desire pleasure itself, as, for example, the pleasant sensations which may be involved in eating or drinking.

Aquinas talks about the desire for pleasure and the aversion to pain, as well as the pleasure and pain of satisfied and unsatisfied desires. Since the same words are almost always used to express both meanings, the two senses of pleasure and displeasure may go unnoticed unless by context or by explicit mention the author refers to pleasure as an object of desire or identifies it with the satisfaction of any desire, whether for pleasure or for some other object. As a passage already quoted from James indi-

cates, and as we shall presently see more fully, the distinction between these two senses of pleasure has a critical bearing on the dispute between those who think that pleasure is the only good, and those who think that pleasure is one good among others.

The generally recognized difference between two kinds of pain—the pain of sense and the pain of loss or deprivation—parallels the distinction which most writers acknowledge between sensuous pleasure and the pleasure of possession or satisfaction. Plato's example of the pleasure involved in the relief of itching by scratching seems to catch both meanings, and, in addition, to show that bodily pleasures may be either sensual *objects* or sensual *satisfactions*. In contrast, the pleasures of the mind are satisfactions of intellectual desire, as in the contemplation of beauty or the knowledge of truth.

Aristotle deals with pleasure and pain as *objects* when he defines temperance as a moderate pursuit of bodily pleasures, and courage as controlling the fear of pain and its avoidance. But he also conceives pleasure as that which completes any activity, whether of the senses and the body or of thought and the mind. "Without activity," he writes, "pleasure does not arise, and every activity is completed by the attendant pleasure." This meaning of pleasure seems to be analogous to, if not identical with, pleasure as satisfaction, at least insofar as the satisfaction of a desire is that which completes the activity springing therefrom. There can be as many different kinds of pleasure as there are kinds of activity; the quality of the pleasure is determined by the character of the activity it accompanies.

Though Mill refers to pleasure and freedom from pain as "the only things desirable as ends," he admits many other objects of desire, in the attainment of which men find pleasure or satisfaction. It is wrong to suppose that human beings, he writes, are "capable of no pleasures except those of which swine are capable." Precisely because "human beings have faculties more elevated than the animal appetites," they have sources of pleasure or gratification not open to swine. Here as before two meanings of pleasure seem to be involved. In pointing out that "money, in many cases, is desired in and for itself," Mill is naming an object of desire which, like health, knowledge, power, or fame, is not pleasure, yet which, through being desired, is a source of pleasure (*i.e.,* satisfaction) when achieved. Like other objects of desire, sensual or bodily pleasures may also be sources of satisfaction.

THESE TWO MEANINGS of pleasure are most in need of clear distinction when the relation of pleasure to happiness is being discussed. If happiness, as Aristotle and Mill seem to say, consists in having all desires satisfied, then the content of the happy life can be described either in terms of the goods which the happy man possesses—the objects of desires fulfilled—or in terms of the pleasures which accompany the goods possessed, that is, the pleasures which are satisfactions of desire. If pleasure in the other meaning, especially sensual or bodily pleasure, is only one object of normal desire, then lack or deficiency of pleasure may, like loss of health or fortune, impair a man's happiness. But the pursuit of pleasure in this sense cannot be identified with the pursuit of happiness. A life including every sort of bodily pleasure and free from every sort of bodily pain, if it lacked other things men normally desire, would be marred by many dissatisfactions inconsistent with happiness.

Talking to Don Quixote of the island he would like to govern, Sancho Panza says: "When I'm king, I'll do as I please, and doing as I please, I'll be satisfied; and when you're satisfied, there's nothing more to be desired." Here, it would seem, Sancho conceives happiness as the sum of pleasures in the sense of satisfactions—all desires come to rest through the possession of their objects.

Dr. Johnson seems to make the opposite point about pleasure and happiness. Boswell asks him whether abstention from wine would be "a great deduction from life." "It is a diminution of pleasure to be sure," Johnson replies, "but I do not say a diminution of happiness." But, Boswell asks, "if we could have pleasure always, should we not be happy?" Johnson explains his negative answer by saying that "when we talk of pleasure, we mean sensual pleasure. When a man says, he had pleasure with a woman, he does not mean conversation, but something of a different nature. Philosophers tell you that pleasure is contrary to happiness."

This last observation does not seem to describe the position taken by those philosophers who make happiness the greatest good or ultimate end of human striving. Both Aristotle and Mill distinguish the life of pleasure, the bestial or swinish life, from one which employs the higher faculties peculiar to man. In this sense, perhaps, the life of pleasure can be regarded as contrary or opposed to what Johnson, along with Aristotle and Mill, calls "the rational life." But pleasure itself, far from being inimical to happiness, either represents the state of satisfaction which is identical with happiness, or one of the things a man desires and hence a constituent of the happy life.

Hobbes and Locke seem to go further in the direction of identifying pleasure with happiness or the good. "Pleasure," writes Hobbes, "is the appearance or sense of Good . . . and Displeasure, the appearance or sense of Evil." Similarly, Locke says that "things are good or evil only in reference to pleasure or pain. That we call *good* which is apt to cause or increase pleasure or to diminish pain in us . . . And, on the contrary, we name that *evil* which is apt to produce or increase any pain, or diminish any pleasure in us." As for happiness, it is, according to Locke, "the utmost pleasure we are capable of, and misery the utmost pain; and the lowest degree of what can be called happiness is so much ease from all pain, and so much present pleasure, as without which anyone cannot be content."

In which sense of the term is Locke identifying pleasure with happiness? Not sensual pleasure, nor even pleasure as an object of desire, it would seem, for he says: "Let one man place his satisfaction in sensual pleasure, another in the delight of knowledge; though each of them cannot but confess there is great pleasure in what the other pursues, yet neither of them making the other's delight a part of *his* happiness, their desires are not moved, but each is satisfied without what the other enjoys." Yet his understanding of happiness as consisting in the pleasures or satisfactions accompanying the possession of things desired leads him to criticize "the philosophers of old" who "did in vain inquire whether the *summum bonum* consisted in riches, or bodily delights, or virtue, or contemplation; they might have as reasonably disputed whether the best relish were to be found in apples, plums, or nuts, and have divided themselves into sects upon it. For as pleasant tastes depend not on the things themselves, but on their agreeableness to this or that particular palate, wherein there is great variety; so the greatest happiness consists in the having those things which produce the greatest pleasure . . . These, to different men, are very different things."

The difference between Locke's position and that of Mill seems, therefore, not to lie in a different conception of the relation of pleasure—as object or as satisfaction of desire—to happiness, but rather in Locke's conception of degrees of happiness as being determined only by larger and smaller quantities of pleasure, whereas Mill insists upon diverse qualities of pleasure, and upon the possibility of ordering pleasures as higher and lower. In consequence, Mill can say what Locke would seem unable to approve, namely, that "it is better to be a human being dissatisfied than a pig satisfied; better to be Socrates dissatisfied than a fool satisfied."

Locke's denial that happiness is the same for all men explicitly takes issue with Aristotle's contrary view. It also involves an issue about pleasure. For Locke, as apparently for Hobbes and Mill, the good and the pleasant are inseparable. Nothing which satisfies a desire can be evil. Whether, as in Locke's view, one satisfaction is as good as another, and the only thing which matters is the amount or number of satisfactions; or whether, as in Mill's view, one pleasure may be better than another, in no case is a pleasure bad so long as someone desires it, or desires the thing which produces satisfaction when possessed.

But, for Aristotle, desires themselves can be good or bad, and consequently there can be good and bad pleasures, as well as pleasures which vary in quality and in degree of goodness. "Since activities differ in respect of goodness and badness, and some are worthy to be chosen, others to be avoided, and others neutral, so, too," Aristotle writes, "are the pleasures; for to each activity there is a proper pleasure. The pleasure proper to a worthy activity is good, and that proper to an unworthy activity bad; just as the appetites for noble objects are laudable, those for base objects culpable."

Pleasure and pain, in Aristotle's judgment, are measured by virtue, not what is good and evil by pleasure and pain. Pleasure and pain are elements common to the good life and the bad, but only the pleasures which the good man enjoys, and the pains he willingly suffers, can be called good. That is why "in educating the young we steer them by the rudders of pleasure and pain . . . for to enjoy the things we ought and to hate the things we ought has the greatest bearing on virtue or character." Virtue is possessed only by those who habitually take pleasure in the right things.

Nietzsche dismisses pleasure and pain as having little or no ethical significance. "Whether it be hedonism or pessimism or utilitarianism or eudaemonism: all these modes of thought"—to be found in Aristotle, Hobbes, Locke, and Mill—"which assess the value of things according to *pleasure* and *pain*" should be regarded "with derision, though not without pity." To which Nietzsche adds that "there are higher problems than the problems of pleasure and pain and pity; and every philosophy that treats only of them is a piece of naïvety."

As indicated in the chapters on Happiness and Duty, the moralists who make duty rather than virtue the spring of right conduct, and who make the goodness of anything depend upon its rightness according to the moral law, see little difference among the various theories of pleasure and happiness as the ultimate good and the standard of conduct.

The most eloquent tribute which Kant can pay to the idea of duty is that it "embraces nothing charming or insinuating." Reason, he says, "will never let itself be brought around" to the view that "there is any intrinsic worth in the real existence of a man who merely lives for enjoyment . . . even when in so doing he serves others." Admitting that "the greatest aggregate of the pleasures of life, taking duration as well as number into account," would appear to merit "the name of a true, nay, even of the highest good," Kant adds that "reason sets its face against this, too." The line of duty is always set against the seductions of pleasure or any calculations of utility, whether in terms of the means to achieving happiness or the ways of augmenting life's satisfactions.

According to Stoics like Marcus Aurelius, "pleasure is neither good nor useful," nor is pain an evil, for when we are "pained by any external thing," we should remember that "it is not this thing which disturbs us, but our own judgment about it." Pleasure and pain are morally indifferent, for like death and life, honor and dishonor, pain and pleasure are things which "happen equally to good men and bad" and therefore "make us neither better nor worse . . . and are neither good nor evil."

From the same observation, that pleasure is enjoyed by good and bad men, Aristotle and Plato seem to draw the conclusion, not that it is morally indifferent, but, as we have seen, that there are good and bad pleasures. Plato uses pleasure and wisdom to typify fundamentally different kinds of good. Wisdom is always true and good, but like opinion, which can be either true or false, there are true and false pleasures, good and evil pleasures. Furthermore, wisdom or knowledge represents the kind of good which is definite or intrinsically measured, whereas pleasure, like wealth, is an indefinite good, requiring something external to itself, something like wisdom, to measure it and limit its quantity.

If wisdom be allowed to choose among pleasures, Socrates suggests in the *Philebus,* it will choose those associated with itself in the activities of the mind, not the bodily pleasures which are always mixed with pain. So far as pleasure belongs to the realm of change or becoming, it is, again like opinion, inferior to knowledge and wisdom, which draw their goodness from the realm of immutable being. Yet Plato does not seem to think that knowledge and wisdom are the only goods. The

argument against those who think so seems to be as conclusive as against those who think that pleasure is the only good.

Each of the simple lives—the life of pleasure or the life of wisdom—is deficient. Only the mixed life, the life which combines both pleasure and wisdom, is the complete life. Like the happy life in Aristotle's view, it includes every kind of good; and the difficult problem, for Plato as for Aristotle, seems to be finding the principle which determines the goodness of the mixture or the right order and proportion in which the variety of goods should be combined.

THE MORAL ISSUES which have been raised here with respect to pleasure and pain are more broadly considered in the chapters on GOOD AND EVIL and on VIRTUE AND VICE, TEMPERANCE, and SIN, as well as in the chapters on HAPPINESS and DUTY. Other issues are reserved entirely for discussion elsewhere, such as the role of pleasure in the perception of beauty and in judgments of taste (the chapter on BEAUTY), or the role of pain in relation to the government of men (the chapter on PUNISHMENT).

Two special problems which involve pleasure and pain remain to be briefly mentioned. The first concerns the contrast between asceticism and self-indulgence or even profligacy.

In the tradition of western thought and culture, and in the ancient as well as in the modern world, those who worship pleasure, though perhaps only as a minor deity to be celebrated in bacchic revels, stand opposed to those who turn away from pleasure, as from the world, the flesh, and the devil, even mortifying the flesh and sanctifying themselves with pain. In their less extreme forms these contrasting attitudes generate the traditional issue concerning the place of worldly recreations in man's life and in the state. Is the pleasure of play a necessary and proper relief from the pain of work, or is it always an indulgence which provides occasions for sin? Are the enjoyment of the theatre, of music and poetry, the gaiety of public festivals, and the diversions of games or sports things to be promoted or prohibited by the state?

Man's avidity for amusements and diversions of all sorts leads Pascal to say, "How hollow and full of ribaldry is the heart of man!" The fact that "men spend their time in following a ball or a hare" and that "it is the pleasure even of kings," indicates to him how deep is the misery from which men try to escape through play and pleasure. "If man were happy," Pascal suggests, "he would be the more so, the less he was diverted." But "so wretched is man that he would weary, even without any cause of weariness, from the peculiar state of his disposition; and so frivolous is he, that, though full of a thousand reasons for weariness, the least thing, such as playing billiards or hitting a ball, is sufficient to amuse him." Men need such diversions in order to "prevent them from thinking of themselves."

Men indulge in pastimes for another reason, according to Aristotle. They "need relaxation because they cannot work continuously" and "amusement is a sort of relaxation." But "happiness does not lie in amusement. It would, indeed, be strange," he says, "if the end were amusement, and one were to take trouble and suffer hardship all one's life in order to amuse one's self." It is true that "pleasant amusements" resemble happiness in having the nature of an end, because we engage in playful activity "not for the sake of other things," whereas we do serious work for some end beyond itself. But in Aristotle's opinion "a virtuous life requires exertion" and since "the happy life is thought to be virtuous," it follows that "serious things are better than laughable things and those connected with amusement."

These reflections on work and play, and the pains and pleasures they involve, lead us to the second of the two problems mentioned above. That concerns pleasure and pain in the life of learning. Here there seems to be no fundamental issue, for the tradition speaks with an almost unanimous voice of the pleasure all men find in knowing and the pain none can avoid in the process of seeking the truth. The problem is rather a practical and personal one which the great books put to their readers, to solve in their individual lives. Their invitation to learning should not be accepted, nor their promise of pleasure relied upon, by those unwilling to take the pains which, however great initially, gradually diminish as the mind, in the very process of learning, learns how to learn.

69

Poetry

INTRODUCTION

THE spirit in which the great poets have read their predecessors differs remarkably from the attitude toward the past which prevails in other fields. The philosophers and scientists frequently feel assured that they can improve upon their predecessors. The poets, for the most part, wish only to do as well. Virgil's admiration for Homer; Dante's accolade to Virgil; Milton's praise of Aeschylus, Sophocles, and Euripides as "the three tragic poets unequall'd yet by any"; the tributes which Cervantes pays to the poets of antiquity—these testify that there is no battle between the modern and the ancient books of poetry.

Contemporary novelists and dramatists—especially those who are proud of their innovations in the forms or materials of poetry—may constitute an exception. Yet even those writers whom we call most "modern"—in terms of experimenting with new styles—offer their innovations as steps in the evolution of the written word, or as dialogues with writers in the great conversation. In "Tradition and the Individual Talent," T. S. Eliot claims that a writer should write "not merely with his own generation in his bones, but with a feeling that the whole of the literature of Europe from Homer and within it the whole of the literature of his own country has a simultaneous existence and composes a simultaneous order."

The order that Eliot describes begins with Homer, but Aristotle's *On Poetics* enjoys the unique distinction of having founded the science of poetry. More than that, it seems to have gained from the poets a large measure of approval, and even adherence to its principles, during a period of more than 2,000 years.

Not that the *Poetics* is without sources. They exist in Plato's comments on the kinds of poetry; in Aristophanes' critical weighing of Aeschylus and Euripides; and, of course, in the original inventions of Homer and the great dramatic poets, both tragic and comic. Not that the acceptance of Aristotle's theory of poetry is unaccompanied by some dissent, but novelists and poets who quarrel with Aristotle's rules or "unities" more frequently adopt than reject Aristotle's basic insights. The claim that the originality of creative genius cannot be bound by the laws of art or held accountable to any established critical standards would certainly receive sympathetic consideration from the man who formulated the rules of poetry and its measures of excellence by the study of the productions of Greek genius.

One way in which later poets have expressed their disagreement with the *Poetics* confirms the primacy of creative ingenuity. Those who have violated Aristotle's rules and yet produced great poems have been men of exceptional genius. Where the genius has been lacking to create new forms, the violation of the rules has usually resulted in formlessness. But it is not only in the creative work of the poets that Aristotle's principles have been put to use and tested. His influence also appears in the comments which the poets make on the nature and purpose of poetry. The terms and distinctions of the *Poetics* are reflected in the writings of Dante, Chaucer, Shakespeare, Milton, Goethe, and Melville, as well as in many essays in criticism from Horace and Demetrius to Giovanni Boccaccio, Nicolas Boileau, John Dryden, and Alexander Pope.

Socrates once complained of the wisdom of the poets. Those whom he asked about their poetry were tongue-tied. They finally resorted to the mystery of inspiration or the inscrutability of genius. "There is hardly a person present," he tells his judges in the *Apology*, "who would not have talked better about their poetry than they did themselves." The poets of a later age were, through benefit of Aristotle, better able to discourse analytically of their art.

IF WE TURN FROM the poets themselves, or rather from their poems, to the analysis of poetry—by poets or others—we find a number of major issues. On what poetry is and on the end it serves, the tradition does not seem to be either unified or harmonious. Boswell hints at the scope of such questions when he asks Dr. Johnson what poetry is. "It is much easier to say what it is not," Johnson replies. "We all *know* what light is; but it is not easy to *tell* what it is." Disagreements concerning the definition and aim of poetry begin in antiquity, long before Johnson.

On the question, for example, whether the poets have the same obligation to speak the truth—and the same kind of truth—as do philosophers or scientists, Plato and Aristotle seem to be opposed. On the question whether the art of poetry lies in its use of language or is primarily the craft of fiction, Aristotle's *Poetics* and Horace's *Ars poetica* represent the opposite answers which have been points of departure for divergent discussions of poetry throughout the whole tradition of western thought.

With regard to the second of these two questions, it may be wondered whether we are in the presence of the sort of disagreement which requires us to take one side rather than the other. The fact that Aristotle, in his *Rhetoric,* writes about poetry in a vein contrary to the theory he advances in his *Poetics,* would suggest the possibility of different but not inconsistent points of view about poetry. Unless Aristotle unwittingly contradicts himself, the rhetorical consideration of poetry is simply a different way of conceiving what is poetic.

In the *Advancement of Learning,* Francis Bacon records this difference in the meaning of poetry, which had become traditional by his time. He treats it, moreover, as the sort of dif-

ference which does not require the rejection of either alternative as incorrect. Poetry, he writes, can be "taken in two senses: in respect of words or matter. In the first sense it is but a character of style, and belongeth to the arts of speech, and is not pertinent for the present. In the latter it is (as hath been said) one of the principal portions of learning, and is nothing else but feigned history, which may be styled as well in prose as in verse."

When Bacon says that the conception of poetry as a literary style—as an art of writing in verse rather than prose—"is not pertinent for the present," he does not reject that alternative entirely. He merely postpones it for the later section of his work in which he treats of grammar and rhetoric. The other alternative—poetry as "feigned history"—is germane to his present consideration of the kinds of learning. Just as Aristotle does not set his *Rhetoric* against his *Poetics* on the nature of poetry, so Bacon does not exclude one of these conceptions in favor of the other when he observes how different are the principles and considerations appropriate to each.

These two points of view about the nature of poetry are not always treated in this way. Sometimes one or the other is taken as the primary or even the only way of approaching the subject, and then a genuine issue ensues—either with those who take the excluded point of view or with those who find it possible to embrace both. The Alexandrian and Roman critics seem to create such an issue by considering poetry largely in terms of style. Modern criticism, especially since the beginning of the 19th century, goes even further in the direction of identifying poetry with verse.

When William Wordsworth discusses the art of poetry in his Preface to *Lyrical Ballads,* he is concerned largely with its language. His definition of poetry as "emotion recollected in tranquility" indicates his emphasis upon the lyrical aspect of even narrative poetry. When Edgar Allan Poe writes his *Poetic Principle* and Matthew Arnold his *Essays in Criticism,* each is concerned almost exclusively with lyric poetry, with that kind of poetry which is written in verse rather than prose. The poet tends to become more and more a composer of verses—so much so that the free-verse movement can appear to be a great revolution in poetry. In *The Brothers Karamazov,* Smerdyakov says, "Poetry is rubbish." At Maria's protest that she is very fond of poetry, he adds: "So far as it's poetry, it's essentially rubbish. Consider yourself, whoever talks in rhyme?"

Just as the word "art" has come in popular usage to mean only painting and sculpture, so its sister word "poetry" has also narrowed in significance. Contemporary readers who are accustomed to think of poems as lyrics and of poetry as verse may be surprised to learn that according to the significance of its Greek root, the word "poetry" can cover all the forms of art or human productivity; Percy Bysshe Shelley sees poetry in the institution of laws and civil society, even in the field of teaching, and Walt Whitman calls the United States "essentially the greatest poem."

The same readers are just as likely to be surprised by the reference to novels and plays, written in prose, as poems. Yet, in the tradition of the great books, novelists like Cervantes and Melville call themselves poets. The great books consider poetry primarily as narrative rather than lyrical, as story rather than song.

This does not mean that they exclude the other consideration of poetry. Speaking of "the sweet influence which melody and rhythm by nature have," Plato may observe "what a poor appearance the tales of the poets make when stripped of the colors which music puts upon them and recited in simple prose"; but for Plato as for Aristotle the poet is a teller of tales, either in prose or in verse. In *Candide,* Voltaire has a man of learning and taste remark that a great poet never lets "any character in the piece appear to be a poet"; he must know his "language perfectly, speak it with purity, with a continuous harmony, without ever making a rhyme at the expense of sense."

Aristotle does not ignore the devices of language. In the third book of the *Rhetoric,* where he considers problems of style in all sorts of compositions, he distinguishes "poetic" from "prosaic" writing; and in the *Poetics* also he devotes a few chapters to style. But when in the latter case he deals with the language of poetry, he is not concerned with the style of any sort of composition, but only of dramatic and epic narratives. Except for a brief mention of the form of verse known as the "dithyramb," Aristotle does not discuss the isolated lyric as a kind of poetry. He treats song and spectacle merely as embellishments of the drama. In the *Poetics* his emphasis is not upon the devices of language or the sentiments of the poet, but upon the construction of plot, the development of character, the diction and thought of the characters—in short, upon the subject matter of the poem rather than upon the feelings of the poet and the eloquence with which he expresses them.

Because he regards plot as the "soul of tragedy"—and, by extension, the primary principle of all narrative poetry—Aristotle insists that "the poet or 'maker' should be the maker of plots rather than of verses." He is therefore led to criticize the confusion—apparently prevalent in his day as in ours—which he thinks results from identifying the art of poetry with skill in writing verse. "Even when a treatise on medicine or natural science is brought out in verse," he writes, "the name of poet is given by custom to the author; and yet Homer and Empedocles have nothing in common except the metre, so that it would be better to call the one poet, the other physicist rather than poet." Just as Bacon later remarks that "a true narrative may be delivered in verse and a feigned one in prose," so Aristotle says that "the poet and the historian differ not by writing in verse or in prose. The work of Herodotus might be put into verse, and it would still be a species of history, with metre no less than without it."

That the difference between prose and verse may affect the style of writing but not the essence of storytelling is a point which has wide acceptance among writers who call themselves poets. In the Prologue to Melibee, Chaucer's host commands him to leave off rhyming and "tell a tale in prose—you might do worse—wherein there's mirth or doctrine good and plain." Thinking of his *History of Don Quixote* as a species of epic poetry, Cervantes declares that "the epic may be written in prose as well as in verse."

The use of the word "history" in the title of Cervantes' novel indicates the acceptance of the other point in the conception of poetry by reference to its subject matter rather than to its linguistic style. The great poets recognize that, as narratives, their works resemble histories, but they also know that the stories poets tell are, in the words of Bacon, "imaginary history." Throughout *Moby Dick,* Melville touches upon "the plain facts, historical and otherwise," of whale fishery, lest someone "scout at Moby Dick as a monstrous fable, or still worse and more detestable, a hideous and intolerable allegory." In his chapter on the Leviathan's tail, he says, "Other poets have warbled the praises of the soft eye of the antelope, and the lovely plumage of the bird that never alights; less celestial, I celebrate a tail."

THE CONCEPTION of poetry as feigned or imaginary history seems to have a direct bearing on the question of the poet's obligation to speak the truth. We shall return subsequently to other aspects of the comparison of poetry with history and philosophy. For the present we are concerned with the issue in the theory of poetry which arises from applying the standards of knowledge to the inventions of the poet.

Bacon, like Aristotle, denies that such standards are applicable. Though he treats poetry as "a part of learning," he holds that it is only restrained "in measure of words"; "in all other points," it is "extremely licensed, and doth truly refer to the imagination; which, being not tied to the laws of matter, may at pleasure join that which nature hath severed, and sever that which nature hath joined." Kant, on the other hand, like Plato, judges poetry in terms of its contribution to knowledge. A thing of the imagination, poetry, he maintains, serves the understanding, for it conducts "a free play of the imagination as if it were a serious business of the understanding."

Though "the *poet* promises merely an entertaining *play* with ideas," Kant continues, "yet for the understanding there enures as much as if the promotion of its business had been his one intention." He achieves a certain "combination and harmony of the two facul-

ties of cognition, sensibility and understanding, which, though doubtless indispensable to one another, do not readily permit of being united without compulsion and reciprocal abatement." In so doing, the poet, in Kant's opinion, "accomplishes something worthy of being made a serious business, namely, the using of play to provide food for the understanding, and the giving of life to its concepts by means of the imagination."

Yet Kant and Plato do not agree in their judgment of the poet. Regarding "the poet's promise" as "a modest one"—"a mere play with ideas is all he holds out to us"—Kant praises him for achieving more in actual performance than he promises. Plato, on the contrary, seems to think the poet promises more and achieves less. He seems to regard the poet not as assisting, but as competing with the philosopher. The reason why the poet must fail in this attempt is that he tries to do on the level of the imagination what the philosopher is better able to do on the level of reason.

Both are engaged in a process of imitation—for all knowledge is imitation, according to Plato—but whereas the notions of the philosopher imitate the reality of the Ideas, the images of the poet imitate sensible appearances, which are themselves imitations of the Ideas or eternal Forms. Even when it is accurate or truthful, poetry must, therefore, be an inferior form of knowledge. In Plato's terms, it is on the level of opinion, along with fancy and belief. In any case, it must submit to being judged by the same standards of accuracy as anything else which claims to be knowledge or right opinion. "Imitations," he writes, "are not to be judged of by pleasure and false opinion . . . They are to be judged of by the standard of truth, and by no other whatever." The competent judge of poetry must, therefore, "possess three things: he must know, in the first place, of what the imitation is; secondly, he must know that it is true; and thirdly, that it has been well executed in words and melodies and rhythms."

The issue concerning poetry and truth can be most sharply drawn between Plato and Aristotle, precisely because Aristotle thinks that poetry is a form of imitation, but that knowledge does not have the character of imitation at all. Since poetry is not a kind of knowledge, the same standards do not apply to both. "There is not the same kind of correctness," he insists, "in poetry as in politics"—or "in medicine or any other special science." The poet's art is at fault if he "meant to describe the thing correctly but failed through lack of power of expression." But if a technical error in physiology enters into his description because he meant to describe the thing "in some incorrect way (*e.g.,* to make the horse in movement have both right legs thrown forward)," then, according to Aristotle, "his error in that case is not in the essentials of the poetic art." The poet's obligation is not to be truthful in such particulars but to make his whole story seem plausible. Aristotle summarizes his position in the statement of his famous rule concerning the probable and the possible. "For the purposes of poetry," he says, "a convincing impossibility is preferable to an unconvincing possibility."

Connected with this issue concerning the kind of truth to be expected from the poet is the controversy over the purpose of poetry—to instruct or to delight, or to do both. This in turn relates to the moral problem of the influence poetry can have on human character or virtue; and to the political problem of the regulation of poetry by the state or the right of poetry to be free from such censorship. It is not surprising that Plato, conceiving poetry as he does, should banish poets from the ideal state described in *The Republic;* or that he should lay down specific regulations for the content of poetry in the *Laws.*

At the opposite extreme are those who, like Milton and J. S. Mill, attack the principle of censorship itself—as applied to poetry as well as to other forms of communication. But the traditional defense of poetry, in essays bearing that title from the pen of Philip Sidney and Shelley or in the writings of Chaucer, Montaigne, and Cervantes, usually tries to answer Plato by praising poetry as an instrument of moral instruction as well as of delight. Waiving the question of its effect upon morals, some, like Adam Smith, answer the sort of criticism Augustine levels against pagan poetry and theatrical presentations by holding the theater to be a legitimate, a lawful, even a necessary means of recreation.

SOME OF THESE issues touch on considerations dealt with in other chapters. The problem of censorship is discussed in the chapters on ART and LIBERTY; and the theory of imitation as applied to the arts in general, useful as well as fine, is discussed in the chapter on ART. Here we are concerned with the bearing of that theory upon the nature of poetry. The difference we have observed between Plato and Aristotle concerning imitation itself does not seem to affect their use of this notion in treating works of fine art, and more particularly poetry. What Hamlet tells the players is the purpose of their play—"to hold, as 'twere, the mirror up to nature"—Aristotle says is the aim of such arts as poetry, sculpture, painting, music, and the dance, which give both instruction and delight through imitation.

Within the sphere of the fine arts, the distinction of poetry from the others is usually made in terms of the medium of imitation. Poetry, according to Aristotle, imitates through the medium of language; painting and sculpture through lines, planes, colors, and shapes; music through rhythm and harmony. Whether Aristotle's statement that "the objects of imitation are men in action" applies to poetry alone or to all the fine arts, is a question of interpretation to which opposite answers have been given. Some commentators seem to think that human action as the object of imitation specifically defines poetry, whereas music and sculpture have distinct objects as well as distinct mediums of imitation. Others hold that human action is the object of imitation common to all the arts.

However this issue is resolved, the differentiation of the kinds of poetry can be made neither in terms of the object nor the medium of imitation, but only in terms of the manner. "The medium being the same and the object the same," Aristotle writes, "the poet may imitate by narration—in which case he can either take another personality as Homer does, or speak in his own person, unchanged—or he may present all his characters as living and moving before us."

Plato makes the same distinction, pointing out that the Homeric type of poetry combines both the discourse of the poet and the discourse of his characters in dialogue. He calls stage plays pure imitations in the sense that the author never speaks directly, but tells his story entirely through the actions and speeches of the characters; whereas the type of poetry which he calls narrative as opposed to imitative may combine both methods of storytelling or may, in some extreme instances, never resort to dialogue at all.

Since all storytelling is narration, and since all poetry is imitation, it seems slightly confusing to call the two major types of poetry "narration" and "imitation," as Plato sometimes does, or "narrative" and "dramatic," as Aristotle sometimes does. Bacon also speaks of "narrative" and "dramatic" or "representative" poetry. He defines narrative poetry as "such an exact imitation of history as to deceive, did it not often carry things beyond probability," and dramatic poetry as "a kind of visible history, giving the images of things as if they were present, whilst history represents them as past."

The difficulties of language seem to be removed by other terms which both Plato and Aristotle use to express the main distinction. The manner of storytelling, exemplified by Homer, which either employs direct narration without dialogue or combines both, is *epic* poetry. That which uses dialogue alone is *dramatic.*

These words—"epic" and "dramatic"—may have their difficulties, too, especially for the contemporary reader, unless a number of things are remembered. First, epics and dramas may be written either in prose or verse. Second, the arts of theatrical representation are auxiliary to the art of the dramatic poet. The writing of a play is completely independent of its acting, "the production of spectacular effects depending," as Aristotle says, "more on the art of the stage machinist than on that of the poet." Third, epic poetry differs from dramatic poetry in other respects than the use of indirect discourse as well as dialogue.

On this last point, Aristotle observes that all the elements of epic poetry are found in drama, whereas the dramatic form may include the embellishments of song and spectacle in addition to plot, character, thought, and diction. Even more important is his distinction of the two in terms of the unities of time, place, and action. Because it need not be limited at all in time and place, epic narration may have a much more complicated plot structure or even, as Aristotle says, "a multiplicity of plots."

The word "epic" also implies a higher level of action and character within its more complicated plot structure. There are no fools or Falstaffs appearing as heroes in epics such as *The Iliad, The Odyssey,* or *The Aeneid.* The central character often represents all the good and virtuous qualities that a nation or race deems important: the strength of Achilles, the cunning of Ulysses, the duty of Aeneas. Herein lies the central irony of a mock-epic like *Don Quixote;* the title character, after going mad from reading old epics, attempts to reawaken chivalry in an age which precludes epic action. The high characters and high action expected in epic literature lead to interesting questions when we approach a work like *Paradise Lost,* in which, it has been argued, the epic hero is Satan.

With this understanding of the distinction between the two major types of storytelling, we can see why the great novels of Cervantes, Melville, Tolstoy, and Dostoevsky should be classified as epic poems, and were apparently so conceived by their authors, at least in the cases of Cervantes and Melville. As measured by the magnitude of its plot—its reach in time, and its scene the whole universe "from Heaven through the world and down to hell"—Goethe's *Faust,* even though dramatic in manner, seems to be no less epic in its structure and proportions than the poems of Homer, Virgil, Dante, and Milton. The story of a single white whale can be epic in its immensity if the storyteller, like Melville, makes it "include the whole circle of the sciences, and all the generations of whales, and men, and mastodons, past, present, and to come, with all the revolving panoramas of empire on earth, and throughout the whole universe, not excluding its suburbs."

ANOTHER TRADITIONAL division in the kinds of poetry is that between the tragic and the comic. This distinction is variously expressed. Some see the difference in terms of the misery or happiness to which the poet brings his principal characters in the end. Speaking of tragedy alone, Milton says that it has ever been held "the gravest, moralest, and most profitable of all other poems." In similar vein, Marcus Aurelius praises tragedy "for reminding men of the things which happen to them and that it is according to nature for things to happen so." He does not admit comedy to be of equal worth, though he does look with some favor upon the older forms of comedy which were "useful in reminding men to beware of insolence."

According to Aristotle, "comedy represents men as worse, tragedy as better than in actual life." He describes the action which tragic poetry imitates as serious, adding that tragedies "through pity and fear effect the proper purgation of these emotions." Whether comedies also arouse and purge certain emotions Aristotle does not say, for his promise to speak more fully of comic poetry is not fulfilled in the *Poetics.* Concerning the meaning of the tragic catharsis, there are questions enough.

Augustine asks: "Why is it that men enjoy feeling sad at the sight of tragedy and suffering on the stage, although they would be most unhappy if they had to endure the same fate themselves? . . . The more a man is subject to such suffering himself, the more easily he is moved by it in the theatre. Yet when he suffers himself, we call it misery: when he suffers out of sympathy with others, we call it pity. But what sort of pity can we really feel for an imaginary scene on the stage?"

Boswell begs Dr. Johnson to explain Aristotle's doctrine of the purging of the passions as the purpose of tragedy. "Why, Sir," Johnson replies, "you are to consider what is the meaning of purging in the original sense. It is to expel impurities from the body. The mind is subject to the same imperfections. The passions are the great movers of human actions; but they are mixed with such impurities, that it is necessary they should be purged or refined by means of terror and pity. For instance, am-

bition is a noble passion; but by seeing upon the stage, that a man who is so excessively ambitious as to raise himself by injustice is punished, we are terrified by the fatal consequences of such a passion. In the same manner a certain degree of resentment is necessary; but if we see that a man carries it too far, we pity the object of it, and are taught to moderate that passion." Johnson's interpretation seems to be more specific than Milton's notion that to purge the passions by tragedy is "to temper and reduce them to just measure with a kind of delight, stirr'd up by reading or seeing those passions well imitated."

It may be arguable whether the difference between tragedy and comedy is well defined by reference to the nobility or vulgarity of the leading characters; by the contrast between the pride of the tragic and the wit of the comic hero; by the seriousness or lightness of the tragic and comic themes and by the passions appropriate to each. In any case it seems clear that this division of poetry crosses the other division into epic and dramatic writing. The plays of Sophocles and *The Iliad* of Homer, Aristotle observes, are tragic poetry, yet dramatic and epic respectively in manner; but from another point of view, Sophocles is to be compared with Aristophanes, for though the one writes tragedies and the other comedies, both are dramatists. In the tradition of the great books, there are comic as well as tragic epics—Chaucer's *Troilus and Criseyde,* Rabelais's *Gargantua and Pantagruel,* and Cervantes' *Don Quixote*—just as there are tragic and comic plays. The examination of these suggests that talk rather than action is the essence of comedy.

The chief thing which Aristodemus remembers of Socrates' discourse the morning after the banquet, in Plato's *Symposium,* is Socrates' success in compelling Aristophanes and Agathon "to acknowledge that the genius of comedy was the same as that of tragedy, and that the true artist in tragedy was an artist in comedy also. To this they were constrained to assent, being drowsy, and not quite following the argument." Precisely what they assented to has never been entirely clear. What Pirandello says about comedy—"that the profession of the comedian is a noble one"—applies to tragedy as well.

On one interpretation of Socrates' remark, examples of his point are difficult to find in the great books—except, perhaps, for the plays of Shakespeare which, in the sphere of dramatic poetry, seem to represent an equal genius for tragic and comic writing. In the sphere of epic poetry, we have only Aristotle's reference to a lost poem of Homer's—the *Margites*—which he says "bears the same relation to comedy that the *Iliad* and *Odyssey* do to tragedy."

According to another interpretation the insight of Socrates is that the totality of the great tragic vision tends to approximate the totality of the great comic vision. The same poem may be both tragic and comic because the poet has been able to see far enough into the nature of things to reveal a world which is at once dreadful and ridiculous. In this sense *Moby Dick* may be both a tragedy and a comedy. "Though in many of its aspects," Melville writes, "this visible world seems formed in love, the invisible spheres were formed in fright"; but he also remarks that "there are certain queer times and occasions . . . when a man takes this whole universe for a vast practical joke."

IN THE SCIENCE of poetics, certain principles or rules seem to apply to all the major forms of poetry, where others relate specifically to epic or dramatic writing, or to tragedy or comedy. Aristotle implies that his most general formulations hold not only for long poems, but for dithyrambic poetry as well. If that is so, they should be capable of extension to other forms of lyric poetry, such as, for example, the sonnets of Shakespeare and Milton, and Milton's odes and elegies. Yet the two principal elements in Aristotle's analysis of poetry—plot and character—seem, superficially at least, to belong peculiarly to narrative poems, long or short. Whether they are present in any comparable manner in the structure of a lyric, or whether the form and content of lyric poetry require an analysis peculiar to itself, are among the most difficult questions in the theory of poetry.

In the tradition of the great books, there seems to be, as already observed, general agreement about the basic rules for writing narrative poetry. Since these rules aim to direct the artist toward the achievement of excellence, they are also the basic principles of criticism. The science of poetics is at once an organon of production and a canon of criticism.

The simple rules such as those of plot construction afford an example. A well-constructed plot must have a beginning, middle, and end. It must observe certain unities (at least of action, if not of time and place). Certain effects, it is held, can best be produced by the use of recognition scenes and reversals of fortune. Whether the events narrated are possible or impossible, the poet must at least invest them with plausibility or verisimilitude. Such rules, formulated by Aristotle and discussed by Cervantes, Racine, and others, provide standards for judging whether a poem is skillfully made, as well as give directions for the attainment of skill by the poet. In his Preface to *Phaedra,* Racine discusses Aristotle's rules of dramatic composition and maintains that Greek tragic poetry was "a school where virtue was not less well taught than in the schools of the philosophers."

When authors in the great books stretch the boundaries of Aristotle's rules, they are often quick to let the reader know that they are doing so, sometimes with an apology. In *The Winter's Tale,* Shakespeare introduces the character of Time, who explains the abrupt passage of years—a violation of Aristotle's unities:

. . . . Impute it not a crime
To me or my swift passage, that I slide
O'er sixteen years and leave the growth untried
Of that wide gap, since it is in my power
To o'erthrow law.

At the other extreme, Twain proclaims his transgression of all these rules at the opening of *Huckleberry Finn:* "Persons attempting to find a motive in this narrative will be prosecuted; persons attempting to find a moral in it will be banished; persons attempting to find a plot in it will be shot."

It may be held, of course, that the great poet works by inspiration, by a divine madness rather than by rule; that, as Theseus says in *A*

Midsummer-Night's Dream, "the lunatic, the lover, and the poet are of imagination all compact . . . The poet's eye, in a fine frenzy rolling, doth glance from heaven to earth, from earth to heaven; and as imagination bodies forth the forms of things unknown, the poet's pen turns them to shapes, and gives to airy nothing a local habitation and a name." But if there is an art of poetry, then like any other art it is a thing of rules, whether or not genius needs their guidance or can be regulated by them.

The pivotal question here is, Which takes precedence, the creative or the critical faculty? Does Aristotle's rule concerning the primacy of plot derive from the greatest poems of antiquity in which he found this principle observed? Does it set up an infallible measure of excellence in narration or, on the other hand, do certain modern novels have an impeccable greatness despite their violation of this rule by the emphasis they place on the development of character rather than on the action in which the characters are involved? The rule of probability and necessity may, on the other hand, be inviolable. Not even the most original genius may be able to tell a good story without giving it poetic truth, according to the necessities of the characters he has created and the probabilities of the situations in which he places them.

ON THE SIDE of language, poetic theory seems to draw much from the art of rhetoric. The relation of rhetoric to poetics, the nature of rhetorical devices such as metaphor and simile, the choice among existing words or the invention of new ones, are matters dealt with in the chapter on RHETORIC as well as here. Aristotle's treatment of these problems, both in his *Rhetoric* and his *Poetics,* lays the foundation for the traditional association of these two disciplines. In both, for example, he discusses the various modes of metaphor and their utility in achieving an expansion of meaning combined with a contraction of speech.

This, in turn, relates to his general maxim of style which directs the writer "to be clear without being ordinary. The clearest style," he says, "is that which uses only current or proper words," but in order to avoid being commonplace or ordinary, it must be admixed with lofty diction—"raised above the commonplace by the employment of unusual words . . . Nothing contributes more to produce a clearness of diction that is remote from commonness than the lengthening, contraction, and alteration of words . . . Phrases which are not part of current idiom give distinction to style . . . But the greatest thing by far is to have a command of metaphor. This alone cannot be imparted by another; it is the mark of genius for to make good metaphors implies an eye for resemblances."

One part of Aristotle's theory of style seems to be amplified by Pascal's observation that a certain perfection is achieved by the use of those words which, if altered, would spoil the discourse. In these terms, prosaic as opposed to poetic writing does not result from the lack of a fixed meter but rather from commonplaceness or lack of distinction in language. This standard of style does not apply to poetry alone; for just as history and philosophy may be written in prose or verse, so also may they be written poetically or prosaically.

Dr. Johnson's point that poetry cannot be translated, that "the beauties of poetry cannot be preserved in any language except that in which it was originally written," may be capable of the widest generalization. It may be extended to mean that writing which is poetic cannot be translated into any other form of words, even in the same language. A poetic sentence in English is untranslatable in this absolute sense when no alternative English phrasing is truly its equivalent. For example, it seems impossible to restate, without loss or ruin, Shakespeare's "Life is a tale told by an idiot, full of sound and fury, signifying nothing" or Hobbes's "Life in a state of nature is solitary, poor, nasty, brutish, and short." Because poetry is untranslatable, Johnson believes "it is the poets that preserve languages; for we would not be at the trouble to learn a language, if we could have all that is written in it just as well in a translation." In this respect, Johnson would agree with Shelley's claim that "Poets are the unacknowledged legislators of the world."

Lévi-Strauss repeats the point made by

Johnson when he writes that "poetry is a kind of speech which cannot be translated except at the cost of serious distortions; whereas the mythical value of the myth is preserved even through the worst translation."

The other part of Aristotle's theory of style, that concerning metaphors, seems to be converted by William James into a general distinction between poetic and philosophical thought, or what he calls "the splendid and the analytic" types of intellect. Poetic thought tends to develop the implications of an analogy without giving an explication of its grounds. This, in James's view, explains "the abrupt transitions in Shakespeare's thought," which "astonish the reader by their unexpectedness, no less than delight him by their fitness." Quoting a passage from Homer, unfathomably rich in metaphor, he says that "a man in whom all the accidents of an analogy rise up as vividly as this, may be excused for not attending to the ground of the analogy." The two types of intellect are rarely found in conjunction—Plato, according to James, being one of the few exceptions "whose strangeness proves the rule."

On the level of thought and knowledge, as opposed to that of language, poetry is traditionally contrasted to philosophy and history. As indicated in the chapter on History, historians like Herodotus, Thucydides, and Plutarch emphasize the difference rather than the similarity; the historian is a reporter of fact, the poet a creator of fables or fictions. The one gains credence by his display of evidence and reasons; the other, by the intrinsic plausibility of his tale. "In a good poem," writes Hobbes, "whether it be epic or dramatic . . . both judgment and fancy are required, but the fancy must be more eminent . . . In a good history, the judgment must be eminent, because the goodness consists in the method, in the truth . . . Fancy has no place but only in adorning the style."

Bacon associates poetry most intimately with history, both being concerned with "individuals, circumscribed by time and place," and differing only as one employs the imagination, the other the memory. Aristotle, on the other hand, finds poetry and philosophy more alike, at least to the extent that poetry, unlike history, "tends to express the universal," by which he means "how a person of a certain type will on occasion speak or act, according to the law of probability or necessity." Even if the poet "chances to take an historical subject, he is none the less a poet; for there is no reason why some events that have actually happened should not conform to the law of the probable and possible, and in virtue of that quality in them he is their poet or maker." In this sense the historian also may turn poet. Referring to the speeches in his history, Thucydides tells us that it was his habit "to make the speakers say what was in my opinion demanded of them by the various occasions, of course adhering as closely as possible to the general sense of what they really said."

Some of the great poems, notably *The Divine Comedy, Paradise Lost,* and *Faust,* are frequently called philosophical for what appear to be other reasons: either because the discourse of their characters is weighted with doctrine, or because the poet himself is expressing a doctrine, not in particular speeches, nor by argument, but in the symbolism of the poem as a whole. By these criteria, Lucretius' *The Way Things Are* is a philosophical work, but not a philosophical poem. It is argumentative throughout, not narrative at all; it aims to be a literal rather than an allegorical statement of the truth. Bacon's definition of allegorical poetry—as that "which represents intellectual things to the senses"—seems to characterize both the poetic aspect of philosophy and a distinctively philosophical type of poetry.

Yet Aristotle's point, that poetry and philosophy are alike, may remain valid. All poetry, certainly all the great narrative poems, the great epics and dramas, novels and plays, deal with the abiding problems of human action and the perennial themes of human thought. It is not this moral or metaphysical content, however, which makes poetry more philosophical than history. It is the poet's treatment of such matters. In the persons and events of his story he succeeds in giving the universal a concrete embodiment. Precisely because these are only imaginary, not real particulars, they permit the abstract universal to be readily disengaged. "The poet's function," writes Aristotle, "is to describe, not the thing that has happened, but a kind of thing that might happen, i.e. what is possible."

Poets like Chaucer and Cervantes, who insist that their function is to instruct as well as to delight, do not assume the role of pedagogues or preachers. They teach, not dogmatically, but as experience does, by affording the mind the materials or occasions for insight and inference. As an artistic imitation, poetry may be better than the experience it represents. It may improve upon experience as a teacher, because, born of the poet's mind, it is already impregnated with ideas.

70

Principle

INTRODUCTION

O F the three ways in which principles are considered in the tradition of the great books, the most familiar sense of the word is the one in which we speak of moral principles, principles of action, or political principles. The connotation of the word in this usage seems to be twofold. We think of principles as rules of conduct and we think of them as standards by which to measure and judge human acts or political events. Either conception attributes a certain generality to principles. Just as rules apply to an indefinite number of particular cases, so any principle we appeal to in order to decide a practical problem or to weigh the merits of an action undertaken, can be applied again and again in other circumstances. "In all our knowledge of general principles," Russell writes, "what actually happens is that first of all we realize some particular application of the principle, and then we realize that the particularity is irrelevant, and that there is a generality which may equally truly be affirmed."

In addition to this characteristic of generality, principles seem to have the quality of *underlying* or being the *source of* other things. In jurisprudence the search for principles consists in the attempt to discover those few most fundamental precepts from which the more detailed rules of law can be derived. The constitution of a state provides the principles which underlie its particular laws and sets the standards by which their legality is to be measured. Governments are judged by the principles they attempt to apply as well as by their success in putting these principles into practice. To say of a government that its acts are *unprincipled* is not to condemn the particular acts as wrong, but to accuse the government

of having no uniform policy to serve as a foundation for its acts.

This aspect of the meaning of principle—as the source from which a set of consequences follows—seems to be more characteristic of the idea of principle than the aspect of generality. According to its Latin derivation and the equivalent root in Greek, "principle" means a beginning or a foundation. Sometimes it means that which comes first absolutely, in the sense of being before everything else; sometimes it means that which comes first only relatively, taking precedence over some things, but having others prior to itself. Since priority may be either absolute or relative—first without qualification or first only in a certain respect—the traditional phrase "first principle" does not have the redundancy of "first first" or "beginning beginning."

If there are absolutely first beginnings, to which nothing else can be prior, they can legitimately be called "first principles" to distinguish them from principles which come first only in a certain respect. Only if there are first principles can regression to infinity be avoided in the search for origins. The propositions which lie at the foundation of a science may, for example, constitute its principles, but they may also be derived in turn from some prior science. Only the principles of a science which is prior to or independent of all others can be truly first principles.

THE FOREGOING example brings us to the other meaning of principle that is popularly recognized. It is the sense in which men speak of principles in relation to conclusions, or of principles as the foundations of a science.

The priority which belongs to principles in

the domain of thought need not be temporal. Principles may or may not be first in the order of learning. But if they are not first in the temporal order, they must be first logically, as premises are logically prior to a conclusion, or, as in Euclid's *Elements*, his principles—his definitions, postulates, and axioms—are logically prior to all the theorems he demonstrates by means of them.

It may be asked whether, among propositions related as premises and conclusions, the logical priority of one proposition to another is sufficient to make the prior proposition a principle. Can a proposition be a principle if, even though it is used as a premise in reasoning, it lacks generality? For example, is the particular proposition—that this bottle contains poison—a principle underlying the practical conclusion that its contents should not be swallowed?

Aristotle answers affirmatively. In the order of practical thinking, he holds, we deliberate neither about the end to be sought nor about the particular facts on which a choice of the means depends. "The end cannot be a subject of deliberation," he writes, "but only the means; nor indeed can the particular facts be a subject of it, as whether this is bread or has been baked as it should; for these are matters of perception." The perceived particulars thus function as principles along with the most general of all practical propositions, namely, what the end should be. Calling the faculty which apprehends first principles "intuitive reason," Aristotle says that "the intuitive reason involved in practical reasonings grasps the last and variable fact, *i.e.*, the minor premise. For these variable facts are the starting-points for the apprehension of the end, since the universals are reached from the particulars; of these therefore we must have perception, and this perception is intuitive reason."

Perception, at least in the form of *sense* perception, seems to be only one of the two ways in which we apprehend the particular facts which are principles in practical reasoning. Like Aristotle, Aquinas uses the judgment, that *this is bread or iron,* as an example of "facts received through the senses" which are "principles . . . accepted in the inquiry of

counsel." But the moral quality inherent in particular acts does not seem to be perceptible by the senses alone; and such particular moral judgments are also involved in moral reasoning. Aristotle suggests that habit (*i.e.,* the moral habits or virtues) are the immediate source of such judgments, which can be called "perceptions of the particular" even though they are not simply sense perceptions.

"Of first principles," Aristotle explains, "we see some by induction, some by perception, some by a certain habituation." By induction we see the general truths; by sense perception, the sensible particulars; and by habituation, the moral particulars. Hence Aristotle insists that "anyone who is to listen intelligently to lectures about what is noble and just and, generally, about the subjects of political science must have been brought up in good habits. For the fact is the starting-point, and if this is sufficiently plain to him, he will not at the start need the reason as well; for the man who has been well brought up has or can easily get the starting-points."

The word "principle" is used by Kant in a much more restricted sense. He reserves the status of principle to the general propositions which serve as the major premises in reasoning. In both the theoretical and the practical sciences, principles express reason's understanding of universal and necessary relationships.

Kant differs from Aristotle in other respects. He differentiates between ordinary general propositions which merely serve as major premises in reasoning and the propositions he classifies as "synthetic judgements *a priori*." He regards the former as principles only in a relative sense and treats the latter alone as principles absolutely. He also distinguishes between those principles of the *understanding* which he thinks are "constitutive of experience," and those principles of the *reason* which should be used in what he calls a "regulative," not a constitutive manner. They determine the direction and goals of thought beyond experience. But such differences concerning the nature and kinds of principles do not affect the commonly accepted meaning of principle as that from which, in the temporal order of learning, knowledge develops or that upon which, in the logical order, knowledge rests.

THE THIRD AND relatively unfamiliar sense in which principles are discussed in the great books does not refer to the sources of man's moral decisions, political acts, or scientific conclusions. The discussion in question refers to reality apart from man. Just as men try to discover the elements of matter, or the causes of motion, so they try to discover the principles of existence and of change. The issues which arise from this concern with the principles of reality are discussed in such chapters as BEING, CAUSE, CHANGE, FORM, MATTER, and NATURE.

If the word "principle" always connotes a beginning, every special sense of principle should involve some kind of priority. As we have already observed, principles may be either prior in time or prior logically. But the principles of the universe or the principles of change are not usually thought to be prior in either of these ways. From them Aristotle specifies another kind of priority—priority in nature—to explain the primacy of those principles which constitute the nature of a thing. In his view, for example, matter and form are the principles of a physical substance. Since a substance composite of matter and form cannot exist until its matter and its form coexist, matter and form are not prior to the substance they compose. Their priority to substance consists only in the fact that that which has the nature of a composite substance *results* from the union of matter and form as its natural components. Because the substance is the *natural resultant,* matter and form can properly be called its *natural principles.*

This way of considering principles at once suggests a close relationship among principles, elements, and causes; and also indicates the connection between the present chapter and the chapters on CAUSE and ELEMENT. The ultimate parts into which a whole can be divided may be its principles as well as its elements. The form or matter of a substance may be, in Aristotle's theory, not only one of its principles, but also a cause—a formal or a material cause. Among the great authors Aristotle

and Aquinas alone seem to dwell upon the relationship of these three terms. They give instances in which the same thing is principle, element, and cause, as well as instances in which a principle is neither a cause nor an element, *e.g.,* privation. In the sphere of human conduct, an end is both a principle and a final cause, but not an element. The last end is the highest final cause and the first principle—first in intention though last in attainment.

THE TRADITIONAL issues concerning this idea differ according to the general context in which the question of principles is raised. The main controversy, for example, with regard to principles in the order of reality is over their number and order.

Aristotle argues against an infinite number of principles as incompatible with the very notion of principle itself. In his analysis of change or motion, he tries to prove that no more than three principles are necessary, and no fewer will do. These are, as the chapter on CHANGE explains, matter, form, and privation. Considering the principles of the universe as a whole, Plotinus also enumerates three and tries to prove that none can be added or subtracted. But whereas Aristotle treats the three principles of change as coordinate, Plotinus places the cosmic principles in the absolute order of first, second, and third.

"We need not go seeking any other Principles," writes Plotinus. "This—the One and the Good—is our First, next to it follows the Intellectual Principle, the Primal Thinker, and upon this follows Soul. Such is the order in nature. The intellectual realm allows no more than these and no fewer. Those who hold to fewer Principles must hold the identity of either Intellectual Principle and Soul, or of Intellectual Principle and The First . . . To increase the Primals by making the Supreme Mind engender the Reason-Principle, and this again engender in the Soul a distinct power to act as mediator between Soul and the Supreme Mind, this is to deny intellection to the Soul, which would no longer derive its Reason from the Intellectual Principle, but from an intermediate . . . Therefore, we must affirm no more than these three Primals."

In the sense in which Plotinus conceives the three primals, they are not only principles in the order of reality, but are themselves the ultimate grades or modes of reality. Similarly for Plato soul is not only the principle of life and thought in the universe, but it also has its own existence in the realm of being. For Aristotle, in contrast, the principles of change do not have existence in and of themselves. Matter, form, and privation are not substances, but aspects of substance. They are present in every changing substance and in every change, but they are only the principles *of* mutable being; they are not mutable beings in themselves.

Lucretius states two principles as the basic laws of nature. The first is that nothing comes into being out of nothing; the second, that nothing is ever completely reduced to nothingness. The word "principle" is obviously not being used in the same sense here as when it designates The One for Plotinus, soul for Plato, matter for Aristotle, or the atoms which Lucretius calls the "first beginnings." Here it does not refer to an entity, or even to an aspect of some real being, but rather to a law—the statement of a universal and necessary condition which governs all that is or happens. It is in this sense that the proposition traditionally called "the law of contradiction"—that the same thing cannot both be and not be in the same respect at the same time—is said by Aristotle to be the first principle of being as well as of thought.

The conception of the law of contradiction and the related laws of identity and excluded middle as principles of thought raises problems about logical principles in general—whether they are axioms or postulates, whether they are merely rules of reasoning and demonstration or are themselves premises from which conclusions can be deduced. If, for example, the law of contradiction is *only* a rule of thought, which forbids the mind to affirm and deny the same proposition, then it is not a principle of knowledge in the sense in which the definitions and axioms of geometry function as premises in the demonstration of theorems. No conclusion can be drawn from it concerning the nature of things. But if, in addition to being a rule of thought, it is

a metaphysical axiom, which states the most fundamental fact about existence, then like the axioms in geometry it may be the source of conclusions in metaphysics.

On this second point Locke seems to differ sharply from Aristotle and Aquinas. He denies that the laws of identity and contradiction are fruitful principles of knowledge. "These magnified maxims," he writes, "are not the principles and foundations of all our other knowledge." Nor have they been, he adds, "the foundations whereon any science hath been built. There is, I know, a great deal of talk, propagated from scholastic men, of sciences and the maxims on which they are built; but it has been my ill luck, never to meet with any such sciences, much less any one built upon these two maxims, 'what is, is' and 'it is impossible for the same thing to be and not to be.' "

Bergson points out that the existence of principles in science does not imply the existence of metaphysical principles: "if all possible experience can be made to enter . . . into the rigid and already formed framework of our understanding, it is . . . because our understanding itself organizes nature, and finds itself again therein as in a mirror. Hence the possibility of science, which owes all its efficacy to its relativity, and the impossibility of metaphysics, since the latter finds nothing more to do than to parody with phantoms of things the work of conceptual arrangement which science practices seriously on relations."

WE SHALL PRESENTLY consider the issue concerning axioms or postulates—whether the principles of the sciences are self-evident truths or are only provisional assumptions. Those who are willing to admit the existence of axioms do not all agree, however, that such truths refer to reality. Hume, for example, limits the content of axioms to knowledge of the relations between our own ideas. They are not truths about real existence or matters of fact.

Locke also grants self-evidence only to perceptions of the agreement or disagreement between ideas. "Concerning the real existence of all other beings" except ourselves and God, we have, he writes, "not so much a demonstrative, much less a self-evident, knowledge; and therefore concerning these there are no maxims." But Locke does think that our demonstrative knowledge of God's existence depends upon an intuitive knowledge of our own existence; and in addition to knowing our own existence directly or without proof, he also thinks we have through our senses an equally direct knowledge of the existence of other things. Such intuitive and sensitive knowledge of particular existences is, like the truth of axioms, immediate—that is, something known directly or without proof, without any appeal to prior propositions. Hence Locke is not denying that we know some immediate truths about reality, but only that such truths consist exclusively of propositions about particular existences. Since axioms, or what Locke calls "maxims," are always general propositions, the self-evident truths which they express do not apply to reality.

William James uses the word "intuitive"—in a different sense from Locke—to characterize propositions that state "the necessary and eternal relations" which the mind "finds between certain of its ideal conceptions." Intuitive propositions are for him, therefore, what maxims are for Locke; and like Locke, James also denies that such axioms of reason hold for reality. "Only *hypothetically*," he says, "can we affirm intuitive truths of real things—by supposing, namely, that real things exist which correspond exactly with the ideal subject of the intuitive propositions ... The intuitive propositions of Locke leave us as regards outer reality none the better for their possession. We still have to 'go to our senses' to find what the reality is.

"The vindication of the intuitionist position," James continues, "is thus a barren victory. The eternal verities which the very structure of our mind lays hold of do not necessarily themselves lay hold on extramental being, nor have they, as Kant pretended later, a legislating character for all possible experience. They are primarily interesting only as subjective facts. They stand waiting in the mind, forming a beautiful ideal network; and the most we can say is that we *hope* to discover outer realities over which the network may be flung so that ideal and real may coincide."

The opposite view seems to be taken by Plato, Aristotle, Aquinas, Francis Bacon, Descartes, Spinoza, and Kant. Though they are far from being in complete agreement concerning the principles of knowledge, the propositions which they call axiomatic, self-evident, intuitive, or *a priori* synthetic judgments, are not restricted by them to the mind's perception of the relations between *its own* ideas. There are self-evident or immediate truths in physics and metaphysics, as well as in mathematics and logic. Whether these are inductions from experience or innate possessions of the mind, whether they are intuitive apprehensions of intelligible being or *a priori* judgments having a transcendental origin, these propositions are held to describe the world of experience, or the nature and existence of things outside the human mind.

THERE SEEM TO BE two degrees of skepticism with regard to principles in the order of knowledge. Complete skepticism would consist in denying principles in every sense. That would be the same as denying any beginning or basis for even the opinions which men hold. No one seems to go that far.

The issue with respect to the foundations of knowledge or opinion is therefore not between those who affirm and those who deny principles, but between different views of what the starting points are. It is sometimes said, for example, that sensations are the principles or beginnings of all human learning. This view is shared both by those who think that all our ideas or concepts are abstracted from the materials provided by the senses and by those who account for all the other contents of the mind—its memories and imaginations, its complex formations—in terms of the simple impressions originally received by the senses.

Concepts, as distinct from sense perceptions, are also sometimes regarded as principles of knowledge by those who think that concepts originate by abstraction from sensory materials, as well as by those who think that ideas are primary principles, *i.e.*, having no origin in any prior apprehensions. On either view, ideas or concepts function as principles insofar as they are the simples from which the more complex acts of the mind develop, such as the acts of judgment and reasoning. Just as on the level of language, words are the principles of all significant speech, out of which sentences and paragraphs are formed; just as, in the logical order, terms are said to be the principles of propositions and syllogisms; so concepts are the principles of judgments and reasonings. The definitions of Euclid, for example, state the notions of point, line, triangle, etc., which underlie his theorems and demonstrations.

One common characteristic of either sensations or concepts as principles of knowledge seems to be simplicity. Nothing more elementary, of which they can be formed, is prior to them. Another characteristic is that they are principles of knowledge or opinion without being themselves acts of knowledge or opinion. This point is made by all who hold that only propositions—whether statements of opinion or of knowledge—can be true or false.

The terms which express the simple apprehensions of the mind—its sensations or concepts—cannot be true or false, because, unlike propositions, which are composed of terms, they do not assert anything. If sensations and concepts cannot be true or false in the sense in which propositions or judgments are, then they lack the distinctive property of knowledge or opinion. In contrast, propositions or judgments—which are supposed to be principles, whether axioms or assumptions—can be treated as themselves expressions of knowledge or opinion, not merely as its starting points or sources.

THE TWO DEGREES of skepticism previously mentioned apply only to those principles of knowledge which are themselves capable of being regarded as knowledge or opinion and hence as either true or false.

We have already considered the skepticism of those who, admitting that the truth of some propositions can be immediately recognized by the mind, nevertheless deny that such self-evident truths describe reality. This may or may not be accompanied by a further depreciation of axioms on the ground that they are merely analytic propositions and hence trifling, uninstructive, or tautological.

The chapter on JUDGMENT considers the issue which revolves around the derogatory use of such words as "tautology" or "truism" to designate self-evident truths. Though the invidious connotation of the word "truism" does not make the truth to which this epithet is applied any less true, the dignity of a truth does seem to be affected by the refusal to regard it as a statement of reality. Furthermore, a certain degree of skepticism results from such refusal. Hume exemplifies this. He holds that self-evident truths are possible only in mathematics, which deals not with matters of fact, but with the relations between our own ideas. In consequence, he denies to the study of nature the certitude or demonstrative character which he finds in mathematical science. Since physics is concerned with real existences, no axioms or self-evident principles are available to it; and so, according to Hume, it cannot demonstrate its conclusions, but must advance them as probabilities.

A more thoroughgoing skepticism seems to consist in holding that there are absolutely no matters at all about which men have axiomatic knowledge. This appears to be the position of Montaigne. No truths are self-evident. None commands the universal assent of mankind; none belongs to the nature of the mind so that all men must agree to it. Montaigne almost holds it to be axiomatic that there are no axioms, for if there were, he says, "there would be one thing in the world . . . that would be believed by all men with universal consent. But this fact, that no proposition can be seen which is not debated and controverted among us, or which may not be, well shows that our natural judgment does not grasp very clearly what it grasps."

If it is objected that, in the absence of such principles, there is no starting point or foundation for science, Montaigne seems willing to accept the consequence. He does not flinch from an infinite regression of reasons. "No reason," he writes, "can be established without another reason; there we go retreating back to infinity." To those who say that there is no disputing with persons who deny principles, he replies that "there cannot be first principles for men, unless the Divinity has revealed them; all the rest—beginning, middle, and end—is nothing but dreams and smoke."

If, however, for practical purposes, a beginning must be made somewhere, Montaigne suggests that it can be done by taking things for granted and then getting others to grant our presuppositions. "It is very easy," he writes, "upon accepted foundations, to build what you please . . . By this path we find our reason well founded, and we argue with great ease. For our masters occupy and win beforehand as much room in our belief as they need in order to conclude afterward whatever they wish, in the manner of the geometricians with their axioms; the consent and approval that we lend them giving them the wherewithal to drag us left or right, and to spin us around at their will."

IF THE ONLY principles upon which reasoning can be based or from which conclusions can be drawn are assumptions, postulates, or hypotheses rather than axioms, then everything is a matter of opinion and probability; nothing can have the certitude of knowledge. As indicated in the chapters on KNOWLEDGE and OPINION, one theory of that distinction makes knowledge an act of the mind independent of our wishes or will and treats opinion as a judgment voluntarily accepted or rejected. Accordingly, assumptions or postulates are perfectly representative of opinion, and axioms express the very essence of knowledge. To assume or postulate anything is to take it for granted—voluntarily! A postulate neither compels assent, nor does it ever exclude the possibility of taking the opposite for granted. Where men make postulates, there dispute is possible. But to assert something as an axiom is to command assent on the ground that its opposite can be immediately recognized as impossible. No proposition can be regarded as an axiom if its acceptance or rejection is in any way a matter of choice.

For Aristotle the area in which men can dispute with some reason on both sides belongs to what he calls "dialectic," whereas what he calls "science" is the area from which dispute is excluded by demonstrations which rest on self-evident truths. One is the area of probability and opinion; the other, of certainty and knowledge. Contrary assumptions are the starting point of dialectical argument, whereas science begins with axioms. These may be the first principles which Aristotle and Bacon call "common notions" because they are common to diverse sciences; or they may be the axioms peculiar to a single subject matter.

The word "dialectic" is used by Plato in a quite different sense. It names the highest science. Whereas the mathematical sciences start from hypotheses which require further support, dialectic—in the conception of Plato—rises to the first principles of all knowledge. In the hierarchical ordering of the sciences, Plato's dialectic, Aristotle's metaphysics, and Bacon's *philosophia prima* seem to occupy respectively the same primary position and to perform the same function in virtue of being the discipline which contemplates or considers the absolutely first or most universal principles. For Bacon, as for Aquinas, the only higher science is sacred theology, whose principles are articles of supernatural faith, not axioms of reason.

These matters are more fully discussed in the chapters on DIALECTIC, METAPHYSICS, and THEOLOGY; questions concerning different kinds of principles or the principles of different sciences are considered in HYPOTHESIS and LOGIC. The chapter on INDUCTION, furthermore, discusses the inductive origin of axioms, as well as the disagreement between Bacon and Aristotle on the point of whether the highest axioms or first principles are immediately intuited from the particulars of experience, or are reached only through intermediate stages of generalization.

Since axioms are indemonstrable, they cannot be derived by reasoning as conclusions from any truths prior to themselves. Their indemonstrability is regarded by Aristotle and Pascal as a virtue rather than a defect, for if they were demonstrable, they could not be the principles or starting points of demonstration. If there were no axioms, then nothing could be demonstrated, because everything in turn would require proof in an endless regression.

To the ancient counterparts of the skeptical Montaigne, Aristotle replies that unless the law of contradiction is an indisputable axiom, any form of reasoning, even probable reasoning from assumptions, is impossible. The principle which underlies all disputation cannot itself be disputed. To those who, with skeptical intent, insist upon having everything demonstrated before they will accept it, Aristotle offers an indirect defense of the law of contradiction by asking the questioner to try denying that self-evident principle without reducing himself to absurdity.

Those who acknowledge the existence of axioms generally agree that they are indemonstrable truths, but some, like Descartes and Kant, do not agree that they are inductions from experience. The alternatives seem to be that axioms are innate possessions of the intellect or that they are transcendental *a priori* principles of pure reason, independent of experience. Yet Locke, who denies innate ideas and principles, or anything prior to experience, does not treat what he calls self-evident maxims as inductions from experience. They are rather direct perceptions of agreement or disagreement among the ideas we have acquired through experience.

Aquinas, who, no less than Locke, denies innate ideas and insists upon sense-experience as the source of all human knowledge, refers to the assent we give first principles as a *natural habit* of the mind—the intellectual virtue he calls "understanding," equivalent to what Aristotle calls "intuitive reason." As the chapter on HABIT indicates, axioms are called "natural" truths, not in the sense of being innate, instinctive, or congenital, but only in the sense that if the human reason functions naturally or normally it will come to recognize these truths. Again, like Locke, Aquinas seems to be saying that the truth of axioms is perceived by the human understanding as soon as their terms are known, but he does not concur with Locke in thinking that therefore such truths hold only for relations between our own ideas.

THE THEORY OF the possession of principles by natural habit has, for Aquinas, more than a verbal connection with the theory of natural law. Of the various meanings of the phrase "natural law" which are distinguished in the chapter on LAW, we are here concerned with what both Kant and Aquinas conceive as the moral law whose precepts are the fundamental principles of human conduct. Both also speak of the precepts of the natural law or the moral law as the first principles of man's practical reason.

For Aquinas, these principles are primary in the order of practical truth and the moral sciences, as metaphysical first principles are primary in the order of speculative truth and the theoretical sciences. "The precepts of the natural law," he writes, "are to the practical reason what the first principles of demonstration are to the speculative reason, because both are self-evident principles." As the proposition that "*the same thing cannot be affirmed and denied at the same time*" is the first principle of the speculative reason, so "the first precept of law, that *good is to be done, and evil is to be avoided,*" is the first principle of the practical reason.

For Kant, the principles of the pure practical reason, which legislate *a priori* for the realm of freedom, play an analogous role to the principles of the pure speculative reason, which legislate *a priori* for the realm of nature or experience. It is this parallelism between the two sets of principles which Kant seems to have in mind when he conceives a *metaphysic of nature* and a *metaphysic of morals* as twin disciplines founded on the speculative and the practical employment of the transcendental principles of pure reason.

The same fundamental issues which we have considered in connection with the axioms of theoretical knowledge occur here in connection with the first principles of moral knowledge. Aquinas and Kant disagree, for example, about the way in which we come into possession of these principles. For Kant, the principles of morality, like the principles of nature, belong to the transcendental structure of pure reason itself. For Aquinas, as already suggested, the precepts of the natural law are known in the same way as the axioms of the speculative reason. As the truth of the principle of contradiction is known when we understand the meaning of 'is' and 'not,' so the

truth of the first command of natural law—
'Seek the good'—is known when we understand the meaning of 'seek' and 'good.' We
hold such truths by the natural habit of our
minds, which in the case of the natural law is
given the special name of *synderesis*.

Just as we find a certain skepticism with
regard to the principle of contradiction and
other axioms, so we find doubts about the
existence of natural law, or about indisputable
and universally acceptable principles of morality. Referring to those who think that there
are some laws "firm, perpetual, and immutable,
which they call natural, which are imprinted
on the human race by the condition of their
very being," Montaigne declares that "the only
likely sign by which they can argue certain laws
to be natural is universality of approval"; and
he adds, "Let them show me just one law of
that sort."

The consequences of skepticism are here
the same as before. Without first principles,
moral science either fails entirely or is reduced
to systems of belief based upon one set of
assumptions or another. In either case, moral
judgments express, not knowledge, but opinion. As J. S. Mill observes, the utilitarians
must, despite all other differences, agree with
Kant that if there is to be a science of ethics,
"morality must be deduced from principles,"
and ultimately from one first principle, for "if
there be several, there should be a determinate
order of precedence among them."

What Mill says concerning the self-evidence
of the first principle of morality—which he
formulates as a statement of the ultimate end
of human conduct—closely resembles what
Aristotle says about the self-evidence of the
law of contradiction. "Questions of ultimate
ends are not amenable to direct proof," Mill
writes. "To be incapable of proof by reasoning
is common to all first principles: to the first
premises of our knowledge, as well as to those
of our conduct."

71

Progress

INTRODUCTION

Like the idea of evolution, with which it has some affinity, the idea of progress seems to be typically modern. Anticipations of it may be found in ancient and medieval thought, sometimes in the form of implicit denials of the idea. But in explicit formulation, in emphasis and importance, progress, like evolution, is almost a new idea in modern times. It is not merely more prominent in modern discussion; it affects the significance of many other ideas, and so gives a characteristic color or tendency to modern thought.

The idea of evolution affects our conceptions of nature and man. But the theory of evolution is itself affected by the idea of progress. Since it was a major theme at least two centuries before Darwin, progress does not depend for its significance upon the theory of biological evolution. The reverse relationship seems to obtain. The idea of evolution gets some of its moral, social, even cosmic significance from its implication that the general motion in the world of living things, perhaps in the universe, is a progress from lower to higher forms.

Darwin thinks "Von Baer has defined advancement or progress in the organic scale better than anyone else, as resting on the amount of differentiation and specialization of the several parts of a being"—to which Darwin adds the qualification that the organisms must be judged when they have arrived at maturity. "As organisms have become slowly adapted to diversified lines of life, their parts will have become more and more differentiated and specialized for various functions from the advantage gained by the division of physiological labour. The same part appears often to have been modified first for one pur-

pose, and then long afterwards for some other and quite distinct purpose; and thus all the parts are rendered more and more complex . . . In accordance with this view," Darwin writes, "it seems, if we turn to geological evidence, that organization on the whole has advanced throughout the world by slow and interrupted steps. In the kingdom of the Vertebrata it has culminated in man."

Whether strictly biological evolution has a single or uniform direction may be disputed in the light of evidences of regression and the multiplication of lower as well as higher forms. But Darwin seems to think that since "natural selection works solely by and for the good of each being, all corporeal and mental endowments will tend to progress toward perfection." Whatever the evidence may be, the popular notion of evolution, especially when applied by writers like Herbert Spencer to human society or civilization, connotes progress—the gradual yet steady march toward perfection.

According to Waddington, "there has been real evolutionary progress." He thinks that "the changes brought about by evolution will always be . . . an improvement," and it is such improvements that "we, quite justifiably, refer to as evolutionary progress." Other 20th-century scientists, notably Stephen Jay Gould, emphatically disagree. For them, the fact of evolution is wholly unrelated to any form of human progress.

APART FROM THIS APPLICATION of the idea of evolution to man's world, progress seems to be the central thesis in the modern philosophy of history. In the minds of some, the philosophy of history is so intimately connected with a theory of progress that the philosophy of history is itself regarded as a modern development. There seems to be some justification for this view in modern works on the tendency of history which have no ancient counterparts, such as the writings of Giambattista Vico, Marie-Jean Condorcet, Kant, Pierre-Joseph Proudhon, Auguste Comte, J. S. Mill, Hegel, and Marx.

These writers do not all define or explain progress in the same way. Nor do they all subscribe to an inviolable and irresistible law of progress which has the character of a divine ordinance, replacing or transforming less optimistic views of providence. But for the most part the moderns are optimists. They either believe in man's perfectibility and in his approach to perfection through his own efforts freely turned toward the realization of ideals; or they see in the forces of history—whether the manifestations of a world spirit or the pressure of material (*i.e.,* economic) conditions—an inevitable development from less to more advanced stages of civilization, according to a dialectical pattern of conflict and resolution, each resolution necessarily rising to a higher level.

As opposed to the optimism of expecting a continual improvement in all things or an irreversible ascent to new heights, the pessimistic view denies that progress is either the law or the hope of history. It believes rather that everything which goes up must come down. As indicated in the chapter on HISTORY, the theory of cycle after cycle of rise and decline—or even the notion that the golden age is past, that it is never to be regained, and that things are steadily getting worse—prevails more in the ancient than in the modern world.

The modern exceptions to optimism in the philosophy of history are notably Oswald Spengler and, to a much less extent, Arnold Toynbee. But modern pessimism never seems to reach the intensity of the Preacher's reiteration in Ecclesiastes that "there is no new thing under the sun" and that "all is vanity and vexation of spirit." Nor does the modern theory of cycles of civilization, even in Vico, seem to be as radical as that of the ancients. In his vi-

sion of cosmic cycles Lucretius sees the whole world crumbling into atomic dust to be reborn again. Herodotus does not relieve the gloom of his observation that, in the life of cities, prosperity "never continues long in one stay." The eternity of the world means for Aristotle that "probably each art and each science has often been developed as far as possible and has again perished."

LEAVING TO THE chapter on HISTORY the discussion of progress so far as it concerns an explicit philosophy of history, we shall here deal with considerations of progress as they occur in economics, in political theory, in the history of philosophy and the whole intellectual tradition of the arts and sciences.

In this last connection, the great books play a dual role. They provide the major evidence which, on different interpretations, points toward opposite answers to the question whether or not there has been progress in the tradition of western thought. Whatever their readers may think on this subject, the great authors, having read the works of their predecessors, offer their own interpretations of the intellectual tradition. In many cases, especially among the modern writers, their point of departure—even the conception they entertain of the originality and worth of their own contribution—stems from their concern with a deplorable lack of progress, for which they offer new methods as remedies.

Before we enter upon the discussion of economic, political, or intellectual progress, it seems useful to distinguish between the *fact* and the *idea* of progress. When men examine the fact of progress, they look to the past and find there evidence for or against the assertion that a change for the better has taken place in this or that respect. Two things are involved: a study of the changes which have occurred and the judgment—based on some standard of appraisal—that the changes have been for the better. But when men entertain the idea of progress, they turn from the past and present and look to the future. They regard the past merely as a basis for prophecy, and the present as an occasion for making plans to fulfill their prophecies or hopes. The fact of progress belongs to the record of achievement; the idea of progress sets a goal to be achieved.

This distinction seems to be exemplified by the difference between ancient and modern considerations of progress. The ancients observe the *fact* of progress in some particulars—almost never universally. Thucydides, for example, in the opening chapters of his *The History of the Peloponnesian War,* contrasts the power and wealth of the modern city-states of Greece with "the weakness of ancient times." "Without commerce, without freedom of communication either by land or sea, cultivating no more of their territory than the exigencies of life required, destitute of capital, never planting their land (for they could not tell when an invader might not come and take it all away, and when he did come they had no walls to stop him), thinking that the necessities of daily sustenance could be supplied at one place as well as another, they cared little for shifting their habitation, and consequently neither built large cities nor attained to any other form of greatness."

But Thucydides does not seem to draw from these observations any general idea of progress. He does not concretely imagine a future excelling the Periclean age in the magnitude of its wars and the magnificence of its wealth, as that period dwarfs antiquity. He does not infer that whatever factors worked to cause the advance from past to present may continue to operate with similar results. It might almost be said that he does not think about the future; certainly he does not think of it as rich in promise. "Knowledge of the past," he writes, is "an aid to the interpretation of the future, which in the course of human things must resemble if it does not reflect it."

Adam Smith's thinking about economic progress represents the contrasting modern emphasis upon the future. In one sense, both Thucydides and Smith measure economic progress in the same way, though one writes of the wealth of cities, the other of the wealth of nations. Both Smith and Thucydides judge economic improvement in terms of increasing opulence, the growth of capital reserves, the expansion of commerce, and the enlarged power in war or peace which greater wealth bestows. But Smith, in the spirit of Francis Bacon, seeks to analyze the causes of prosperity in order to make them work for further progress. He is the promoter of progress, not merely the historian who witnesses the beneficial effect on productivity of an increasingly refined division of labor and of the multiplication of machinery.

To know how these things have operated to bring about the opulence of modern nations as compared with the miserable poverty of primitive tribes or even the limited property of ancient cities is to know how to formulate policies which shall still further expand the wealth of nations. For Smith the study of the means and methods by which economic progress has been made serves to determine the policy which is most likely to ensure even greater increments of progress in the future.

MARX APPEARS TO measure economic progress by a different standard. The transition from the slave economies of antiquity through feudal serfdom to what he calls the "wage-slavery" of the industrial proletariat may be accompanied by greater productivity and vaster accumulations of capital stock. But the essential point for him about these successive systems of production is their effect upon the status and conditions of labor. The *Communist Manifesto* notes respects in which, under the capitalist system, the supposedly free workingman is worse off than were his servile ancestors. But if economic progress is conceived as the historically determined approach to the final liberation of labor from its oppressors, then capitalism represents both an advance over feudalism and a stage in the march to communism.

Each successive economic revolution brings mankind nearer to the goal of the ideal or classless economy. Capitalism creates the proletariat—the revolutionary class which is to be that system's own undoing. The overthrow of the landed aristocracy by the bourgeoisie thus prepares the way for the dictatorship of the proletariat, as that in turn liquidates the obstacles to the realization of the perfect communist democracy.

We are not here concerned with the details

of this history and prophecy but only with the theory of progress which it involves. In the first place, it seems to set an ultimate goal to progress, while at the same time it makes progress a necessary feature of what is for Marx, as it is for Hegel, the "dialectic of history." Those who think that the inevitability of progress ought to render progress as interminable as history itself, find some inconsistency in this tenet of dialectical materialism, as well as in Hegel's notion of the necessary dialectical stages by which the Absolute Idea reaches perfect realization in the German state. *Can progress be the inner law of history and yet reach its goal before the end of time?*

There may be some answer to this question in a second aspect of the theory of progress which goes with a dialectic of history. The progress which the successive stages of history represent resides in the quality of human institutions rather than in the nature of man. If more economic justice or greater political liberty is achieved, it is not because the later generations of men are born with a nature more disposed to goodness or virtue, but because better institutions have evolved from the conflict of historical forces. Furthermore, according to Marx, man's nature is only partly determined at birth. Part remains to be determined by the social and economic circumstances of his life—by the system of production under which he lives. Hence though institutional progress may arrive at its historical goal with the establishment of the ideal economy, it may be possible for further progress to be made throughout the rest of time by the improvement of men themselves, when at last their natures can develop under ideal circumstances.

WE HAVE NOTED TWO great issues in the characteristically modern discussion of progress. Is the goal of progress definitely attainable, or is its goal an ideal progressively approximated but never realized? Is progress accomplished by the betterment of human institutions or by improvements in the nature of man?

The second question has a critical bearing on the first, especially for those who conceive man as infinitely perfectible. It also relates to the problem of the evolutionist: whether a higher form of life on earth will evolve from man or whether the future belongs to the progressive development of human nature—biologically or culturally. Darwin is unwilling to admit that "man alone is capable of progressive improvement," but he does affirm that man "is capable of incomparably greater and more rapid improvement than is any other animal."

Rousseau, on the other hand, claims that "the faculty of self-improvement" is one distinction between man and brute "which will admit of no dispute." But he also thinks that this faculty is the cause of human decline as well as progress. "A brute, at the end of a few months," he writes, "is all he will ever be during his whole life, and his species, at the end of a thousand years, exactly what it was the first year of that thousand . . . While the brute, which has acquired nothing and has therefore nothing to lose, still retains the force of instinct, man, who loses, by age or accident, all that his *perfectibility* had enabled him to gain, falls by this means lower than the brutes themselves." According to Frazer, "The advance of knowledge is an infinite progression towards a goal that for ever recedes."

One other issue concerning progress remains to be stated. It raises the question of freedom or necessity in history. Is progress inevitable in the very nature of the case, or does it occur only when men plan wisely and choose well in their efforts to better themselves or the conditions of their lives?

In his *The Idea of a Universal History on a Cosmo-Political Plan* and his *The Principle of Progress,* Kant finds the possibility of progress in man's potentialities for improvement. He regards the realization of this possibility as a work of freedom rather than a manifestation of historical necessity. Political progress may have an ultimate goal—the world republic or federation of states. But this, according to Kant's conclusion in *The Science of Right,* is an impracticable idea, and serves only the regulative purpose of "promoting a continuous *approximation* to Perpetual Peace." Hegel's theory of the progressive realization of the idea of the state in history seems to represent the contrary position on both points. Progress is a historical necessity, and it reaches a historic consummation. For Tocqueville, the progress of democratic societies toward a universal equality of conditions is destined by Divine Providence.

THE CONTRAST BETWEEN ancients and moderns with respect to political progress seems to be the same as that which we observed between Thucydides and Smith with regard to wealth. The ancients assert the superiority of the present over the past, and even trace the stages by which advances have been made from primitive to civilized conditions. But they do not extend the motion they observe into the future. The moderns look to the future as to a fulfillment without which present political activity would be undirected.

According to Aristotle, for example, the state is the last stage in the development of social life which begins with the family. "When several families are united, and the association aims at something more than the supply of daily needs, the first society to be formed is the village." The village or tribal community, in turn, becomes the unit out of which a larger and more truly political community is formed. "When several villages are united in a single complete community, large enough to be nearly or quite self-sufficing, the state comes into existence."

Aristotle sees this development not merely as a progress from smaller and weaker societies to larger and more powerful ones, but also as an advance toward the realization of man's political nature. Absolute or despotic government by the eldest, natural to the family, still persists in the tribe. "This is the reason why the Hellenic states were originally governed by kings; because the Hellenes were under royal rule before they came together, as the barbarians still are." Not until the domestic or tribal form of government is replaced by political or constitutional government—not until kings and subjects are replaced by statesmen and citizens—is the state or political community fully realized.

But Aristotle does not conceive the development he describes as one continuing into the future. He does not imagine a larger po-

litical unity than the city-state, as Kant is able to envisage a world state as the ultimate formation toward which the progressive political unification of mankind should tend. Though Aristotle recognizes that new institutions have been invented and old ones perfected, his political theory, unlike Mill's, does not seem to measure the goodness of the best existing institutions by their devotion to further progress.

Considering the criterion of a good form of government, Mill criticizes those who separate the maintenance of order, or the preservation of existing institutions, from the cultivation of progress. "Progress includes Order," he writes, "but Order does not include Progress." Order "is not an additional end to be reconciled with Progress, but a part and means of Progress itself. If a gain in one respect is purchased by a more than equivalent loss in the same or in any other, there is not Progress. Conduciveness to Progress, thus understood, includes the whole excellence of government."

Progress fails to define good government, Mill adds, unless we understand by the term not merely "the idea of moving onward," but "quite as much the prevention of falling back. The very same social causes . . . are as much required to prevent society from retrograding, as to produce a further advance. Were there no improvement to be hoped for, life would not be the less an unceasing struggle against causes of deterioration; as it even now is. Politics, as conceived by the ancients, consisted wholly in this . . . Though we no longer hold this opinion; though most men in the present age profess a contrary creed, believing that the tendency of things, on the whole, is toward improvement; we ought not to forget that there is an incessant and everflowing current of human affairs toward the worse."

According to Mill, the ideally best polity is representative government on democratic principles. By a just distribution of political rights and by the fullest grant of liberties, it serves better than any other form of government "to promote the virtue and intelligence of the people themselves." This is the ultimate end of political progress. Inferior forms of government, such as despotic monarchy, may be justified for people as yet unfit for self-government, but only if they also work for progress, *i.e.,* "if they carry those communities through the intermediate stages which they must traverse before they can become fit for the best form of government."

The whole theory of good government is thus for Mill a theory of progress in which we must take "into account, not only the next step, but all the steps which society has yet to make; both those which can be foreseen and the far wider indefinite range which is at present out of sight." We must judge the merits of diverse forms of government by that ideal form "which, if the necessary conditions existed for giving effect to its beneficial tendencies, would, more than all others, favour and promote not some one improvement, but all forms and degrees of it."

IN THE FIELD OF THE ARTS and sciences or culture generally, the modern emphasis upon progress seems to be even more pronounced than in the spheres of economics and politics. Lack of progress in a science is taken to indicate that it has not yet been established on the right foundations or that the right method for discovering the truth has not yet been found. Lack of agreement in a particular field is the chief symptom of these defects. But whereas "scientific work is chained to the course of progress," Weber thinks that "in the realm of art there is no progress in the same sense." Lévi-Strauss goes even further, saying that "A primitive people is not a backward or retarded people; indeed it may possess, in one realm or another, a genius for invention or action that leaves the achievements of civilized peoples far behind."

The fact that philosophy "has been cultivated for many centuries by the best minds that have ever lived, and that nevertheless no single thing is to be found in it which is not a subject of dispute, and in consequence which is not dubious," leads Descartes to propose his new method. He hopes this may ensure progress in philosophy, of the same sort which the new method has, in his view, accomplished in mathematics. The *Novum Organum* of Bacon seems to be dedicated to the same end of progressively augmenting knowledge in all

those fields in which, according to the inventory made in the *Advancement of Learning* of the present state of the sciences, no or little progress has been made since antiquity. Similarly, Locke, Hume, and Kant insist that a study of the human mind should precede all other studies in order to save men from fruitless disputes concerning matters beyond their capacities for knowledge; they hope thereby to encourage research in areas where progress can be made.

The comparison of different disciplines or subject matters with respect to their progress leads to the condemnation of those which lag behind. The great scientific advances of the 17th century tend to intensify the complaint about philosophy, especially metaphysics. The progress which has been made from the beginning in mathematics and more recently in physics means to Kant that each of these disciplines has found the "safe way" or the "secure path" of a science. By comparison, metaphysics has not yet even made a beginning. A hundred years later, William James is still to say that, by comparison with the progress of knowledge in the natural sciences, metaphysics belongs to the future.

The notion that any field of learning has attained its full maturity seems to Bacon to be the presumption of those philosophers who, seeking "to acquire the reputation of perfection for their own art," try to instill the "belief that whatever has not yet been invented and understood can never be so hereafter." Whenever such belief prevails, learning languishes. "By far the greatest obstacle to the advancement of the sciences, and the undertaking of any new attempt or departure, is to be found in men's despair and the idea of impossibility."

THOUGH THE ANCIENTS do not evidence this presumption of perfection in their arts and sciences, neither do they fret about lack of progress. Nor does the disagreement of minds seem to them to signify an unhealthy condition which requires new and special methods to cure.

"The investigation of the truth is in one way hard, in another easy," writes Aristotle. "An indication of this is found in the fact that no one is able to attain the truth adequately, while, on the other hand, we do not collectively fail, but everyone says something true about the nature of things, and while individually we contribute little or nothing to the truth, by the union of all a considerable amount is amassed." Aristotle puts the intellectual tradition to use by adopting the policy of calling "into council the views of those of our predecessors who have declared any opinion" on whatever subject is being considered, "in order that we may profit by whatever is sound in their suggestions and avoid their errors."

But, in the opinion of the moderns, the intellectual tradition can also be the greatest impediment to the advancement of learning if it is received uncritically and with undue reverence for the authority of the ancients. "The respect in which antiquity is held today," Pascal says, "has reached such extremes in those matters in which it should have the least preponderance, that one can no longer present innovations without danger." This is the common complaint of Hobbes, Bacon, Descartes, and Harvey. "The reverence for antiquity and the authority of men who have been esteemed great in philosophy have," according to Bacon, "retarded men from advancing in science, and almost enchanted them."

Harvey agrees with Bacon that philosophers or scientists should not "swear such fealty to their mistress Antiquity, that they openly, and even in sight of all, deny and desert their friend Truth." Harvey has a much higher opinion than Bacon of the achievements of antiquity. "The ancient philosophers," he writes, "whose industry even we admire, went a different way to work, and by their unwearied labor and variety of experiments, searching into the nature of things, have left us no doubtful light to guide us in our studies. In this way it is that almost everything we yet possess of note or credit in philosophy, has been transmitted to us through the industry of ancient Greece."

His admiration for the ancients does not, however, lead Harvey to rest on their achievements. "When we acquiesce in the discoveries of the ancients, and believe (which we are apt to do through indolence) that nothing farther remains to be known," then, in his opinion, "we suffer the edge of our ingenuity to be taken off, and the lamp which they delivered us to be extinguished. No one of a surety," he continues, "will allow that all truth was engrossed by the ancients, unless he be utterly ignorant (to pass by other arts for the present) of the many remarkable discoveries that have lately been made in anatomy."

In his own anatomical researches, Harvey adopts an attitude toward the work of his predecessors, both ancient and recent, which remarkably resembles the attitude expressed by Aristotle toward his scientific forebears. "As we are about to discuss the motion, action, and use of the heart and arteries, it is imperative on us," Harvey declares, "first to state what has been thought of these things by others in their writings, and what has been held by the vulgar and by tradition, in order that what is true may be confirmed, and what is false set right by dissection, multiplied experience, and accurate observation." It is precisely this attitude which Bacon expressly condemns.

Bacon sees no genuine method of science, but merely a cultivation of opinion, in those who prepare themselves for discovery by first obtaining "a full account of all that has been said on the subject by others." Those who begin in this way, it is the judgment of Descartes, seldom go further. Particularly the followers of Aristotle, "would think themselves happy," he says, "if they had as much knowledge of nature as he had, even if this were on the condition that they should never attain to any more. They are like the ivy that never tries to mount above the trees which give it support, and which often even descends again after it has reached the summit; for it appears to me that such men also sink again—that is to say, somehow render themselves more ignorant than they would have been had they abstained from study altogether. For, not content with knowing all that is intelligibly explained in their author, they wish in addition to find in him the solution of many difficulties of which he says nothing, and in regard to which he possibly had no thought at all."

Pascal takes a more moderate view. We can profit, he thinks, from a limited respect for the ancients. "Just as they made use of those discoveries which have been handed down to them only as a means for making new ones and this happy audacity opened the road to great things, so," Pascal suggests, "must we accept those which they found for us and follow their example by making them the means and not the end of our study, and thus try to surpass them by imitating them. For what would be more wrong than to treat the ancients with more caution than they did those who preceded them, and to have for them this inviolable respect which they only deserve from us because they did not feel a similar respect for those who had the same advantage over them?"

MODERN WRITERS SEEM to conceive the law of intellectual progress by an analogy between the mind of the race and the individual mind. Where Aquinas says merely that "it seems natural to human reason to advance gradually from the imperfect to the perfect," adding, in the past tense, that hence the imperfect teaching of early philosophers "was afterwards perfected by those who succeeded them," Pascal generalizes the insight and gives it future significance. "Not only does each man progress from day to day in the sciences, but all men combined make constant progress as the universe ages, because the same thing happens in the succeeding generations of men as in the different ages of each particular man. So that the whole succession of men, in the course of so many centuries, should be regarded as the same man who exists always and learns continually."

At this point Pascal applies his metaphor to effect a reversal of the relation between the moderns and the ancients. "Since old age is the time of life most distant from childhood, who does not realize that old age in this universal man should not be sought in the times closest to his birth, but in those which are farthest

away from it? Those whom we call ancients were really novices in all things, and actually belonged to the childhood of man; and as we have added to their knowledge the experience of the centuries which followed them, it is in ourselves that may be found this antiquity which we revere in others."

As Frazer views it, "Intellectual progress, which reveals itself in the growth of art and science and the spread of more liberal views, cannot be dissociated from industrial or economic progress, and that in its turn receives an immense impulse from conquest and empire."

Whether by accident or borrowing, this characteristically modern view of the advantage progress confers upon modernity is expressed in similar language by Hobbes and Bacon. "Though I reverence those men of ancient times," writes Hobbes, "who either have written truth perspicuously or have set us in a better way to find it out for ourselves; yet to the antiquity itself I think nothing due; for if we will reverence age, the present is the oldest." "Antiquity, as we call it," writes Bacon, "is the young state of the world; for those times are ancient when the world is ancient; and not those we vulgarly account ancient by computing backwards; so that the present time is the real antiquity."

To secure a sound, not specious, progress in all things of the mind, Bacon recommends the avoidance of two extremes, the affectations of antiquity and novelty, for "antiquity envies new improvements, and novelty is not content to add without defacing." Since "antiquity deserves that men should stand awhile upon it, to view around which is the best way," the great books of the past can lay the foundations for progress, but only if they are properly read. "Let great authors, therefore, have their due," Bacon declares, "but so as not to defraud time, which is the author of authors, and the parent of truth."

72

Prophecy

INTRODUCTION

THE name of prophet signifies, throughout a great part of the western tradition, an eminence and dignity not shared by the scientist, the philosopher, the statesman, or even the sage. The soothsayer and the seer in pagan antiquity and the prophet of the Lord in Israel do not claim to speak from a merely human wisdom or to declare truths they have learned by inquiry or reflection. Nor are their utterances concerned with the nature of things. The prophet claims to know what men cannot know by any exercise of human powers. He enjoys special gifts. He is divinely inspired. He is instructed by God or has in some way been admitted to the secrets of the gods. His knowledge is not only of supernatural origin; it deals with supernatural matters.

Prophecy is more than a prediction of the future. It unveils what Fate holds in store for men; it foretells the course of providence. In most cases, the future predicted has deep moral significance, expressing the pleasure or displeasure of the gods with individuals or nations, or manifesting God's justice in the rewards promised those who keep His commandments, and the punishments awaiting those who break them. The prophet's foresight discerns more than the future; it discovers what men can hope for or must fear according to their merits, not in the eyes of men but in the sight of God.

This understanding of prophecy seems to be involved in the major issues which the great books raise about prophets. For example, the problem of distinguishing between true and false prophets goes beyond the mere truth or falsity of a prophet's utterances to the validity of his claim to special sources of knowledge or a supernaturally inspired understanding of

dreams and visions, omens and portents. The false prophet is not like the mistaken scientist or philosopher—just a person in error. He is either a deceiving impostor or a self-deceived victim of his own pathology.

Similarly, the Christian theologians who criticize the pagan cult of oracles and all forms of divination which seek to pry into divine mysteries, seem to imply that the seers and soothsayers of Greece and Rome, unlike the Hebrew prophets, did not have the gift of prophecy. The acceptance or rejection of prophets and of ways of foreseeing what has been planned in heaven cannot, it seems, be separated from a whole system of religious beliefs. In this respect, prophets are like miracles. Without faith, both are incredible. "There be two marks," writes Hobbes, "by which together, not asunder, a true Prophet is to be known. One is the doing of miracles; the other is the not teaching any other religion than that which is already established." In Hobbes's view, an already established religion among a people is the one indispensable condition for their reception of prophets or their experience of miracles.

Issues concerning prophecy may, therefore, occur within a single religious community, or be relative to differences between religious communities, as, for example, the opposition between the Jewish and Christian interpretation of the messianic prophecies in the Old Testament. Necessarily, then, there is an issue between the unbelievers and the religious of any faith. Those who deny the existence of God or the gods, or divine agency in the temporal affairs of men, and certainly those who deny the credentials of revelation, cannot but regard prophets as misled and misleading and those who accept prophecy as gullible or superstitious. In the pagan tradition, a philosopher like Aristotle may, however, be critical of divination, and a historian like Thucydides may cast doubt on oracles, without discrediting all other religious beliefs or being themselves atheists.

Some who reject religious prophecy do not concede that man's natural desire to peer into the future need be completely balked. But the secular substitutes for religious prophecy appear to alter the meaning of prophecy. Scientific predictions of the future of the world or of life on this planet (as, for example, those which occur in the writings of Lucretius or Darwin) may be accompanied by attributions of moral qualities to Nature, but usually they connote Nature's sublime indifference to man's welfare. They are seldom, if ever, read as promises or threats of what man deserves to have befall him.

Similarly, historians turned prophets, or philosophers of history who, like Oswald Spengler, prophesy decline and doom, do not exhort men to avert disaster, as do the prophets of the Old Testament. Nor do those who, like Hegel and Marx, foresee the ultimate goal toward which events inevitably march, urge men to prepare themselves for it as do the prophecies of the New Testament, which speak of the second coming of Christ. Secular prophecies which bespeak the inevitable operation of necessary causes are, in this respect, like pagan previsions of Fate. At most, they leave man only the illusion of free choice. Jewish and Christian prophecy, in contrast, addresses man as a responsible agent, who, even when he knows something of God's will, remains free to will good or evil for himself. If, according to the theologians, divine providence or predestination does not abolish human freedom, neither does prophetic knowledge of the divine plan.

These matters are discussed elsewhere—secular prophecy in the chapters on HISTORY and PROGRESS, and the problem of foreknowledge and freedom in the chapters on FATE and NECESSITY AND CONTINGENCY.

IN PAGAN ANTIQUITY, prophecy does not seem to be confined to men especially appointed by the gods. The gods themselves foretell the future to men. When people wish to know the future, they go or send emissaries to the temple at Delphi over which a goddess, the Pythoness, presides. The institution of the oracles, of which Delphi is perhaps the most illustrious example, leaves foresight in the hands of the gods; for, as most of the anecdotes in Herodotus and Thucydides show, only the Pythoness herself knows unequivocally the meaning of her oracular utterances.

To men is left the task of interpreting what the oracle means. The pagan unlike the Hebrew prophet seems to be a man of skill in penetrating the secrets of the gods—a skill which may itself be divinely bestowed—but he is not a man to whom the gods have spoken plainly, so that he may in turn unerringly advise others. "No man, when in his wits," according to Plato, "attains prophetic truth and inspiration." In Greek mythology, perhaps the only mortal who possesses an unerring vision of the future is the prophetess Cassandra, who appears in Euripides' *The Trojan Women,* Shakespeare's *Troilus and Cressida,* and, most prominently, in Aeschylus' *Agamemnon.* However, because she spurned the advances of Apollo, he assigned her a horrible fate: nobody would ever believe her.

There are passages in the Greek poets and historians which seem to suggest that the gods begrudge men too clear a vision of the future, and may even on occasion mislead them or at least permit them to be misled. In Aeschylus' *Prometheus Bound,* Prometheus declares that because "he stole and gave to men" gifts claimed by the gods, he is "bound . . . in chains unbreakable." He gave them radiant fire, the mechanical arts; he "caused mortals to cease foreseeing doom"; he gave them medicines and healing drugs. Last in his own enumeration and in a sense most significant, he endowed men with the divine gift of foresight.

"It was I who arranged all the ways of seercraft," Prometheus says, "and I first adjudged what things come verily true from dreams; and to men I gave meaning to the ominous cries, hard to interpret. It was I who set in order the omens of the highway and the flight of crooked-taloned birds, which of them were propitious or lucky by nature . . . It was I who made visible to men's eyes the flaming signs of the sky that were before dim." The chorus questions whether men, who are but "creatures of a day," shall by wisdom overpass the bounds set for their little lives by "the ordered law of Zeus." Does the wisdom of foreknowledge, gained through the arts of divination, give men strength to resist the will of the gods or to struggle against them?

Prometheus himself is the answer to the question. The power he wields over Zeus, which Zeus tries to wrest from him by bribes and threats and by the infliction of titanic pain, is the foreknowledge which Prometheus possesses of the doom to befall the son of Kronos. No threat of Zeus will get him to divulge it, Prometheus says, because "nought can surprise me who foreknow . . . Nought in his power shall bend me to reveal whom Fate prepares to work his overthrow."

A myth which Socrates relates in the *Gorgias* appears to contain a sequel to the legend as told by Aeschylus. It also seems to confirm the point that foresight is a divine privilege in which men should not share, lest they become too godlike. According to the myth, Zeus, in order to prevent men from evading the divine judgment, says: "In the first place, I will deprive men of the foreknowledge of death; this power which they have, Prometheus has already received my orders to take from them."

The oracles never make the future so plain that men can act with a foreknowledge equal to that possessed by the gods, but sometimes oracular utterances seem to be contrived not merely to veil the future, but to lead men astray. Herodotus tells the story of Miltiades who, on the advice of Timo, a priestess of the goddesses of the underworld, acted in a way which brought him to grief. When the Parians sent to Delphi to ask whether Timo should be punished for this, the Pythoness forbade them, saying, "Timo was not at fault; 'twas decreed that Miltiades should come to an unhappy end; and she was sent to lure him to his destruction."

There is also the story, told by Thucydides, of Cylon who, inquiring at Delphi, was told to seize the Acropolis of Athens on the grand festival of Zeus. This, too, turned into a disastrous misadventure, apparently because, as Thucydides observes, "whether the grand festival that was meant was in Attica or elsewhere was a question which he never thought of, and which the oracle did not offer to solve."

For the most part, however, the calamities which befall men who seek guidance from the oracle seem to be due to their own misinterpretation of the Delphic deliverance, itself always admittedly difficult to understand. Herodotus and Thucydides abound with such stories, and also with instances in which the same oracular statement is given conflicting interpretations, one of which must be wrong. Nevertheless, Herodotus declares himself unwilling "to say that there is no truth in prophecies," and he is certainly not willing to question "those which speak with clearness." Giving an example of a clear prediction, he adds, "When I look to this, and perceive how clearly Bacis spoke, I neither venture myself to say anything against prophecies, nor do I approve of others impugning them."

Thucydides appears to take a contrary view. He singles out one example as "an instance of faith in oracles being for once justified by the event." He puts into the speech of the Athenians at the Melian Conference the warning not to "be like the vulgar, who, abandoning such security as human means may still afford, when visible hopes fail them in extremity, turn to invisible, to prophecies and oracles, and other such inventions that delude men with hopes to their destruction."

THE PROBLEM OF THE reliability of prophecies, and of the faith or credulity of those who rely upon them, applies not only to oracles, but also to dreams or visions, and to omens and portents of all sorts. Two stories about Croesus, told by Herodotus, show that oracles and dreams can be equally ambiguous and are equally liable to misinterpretation. Croesus dreamed that his son Atys would die by the blow of an iron weapon. Subsequently when Atys wished to go boar hunting with Adrastus, he persuaded Croesus that the dream could not have been a warning against this undertaking because a boar does not have hands to strike with, nor does it wield iron weapons. But during the hunt Atys was killed by the spear which Adrastus intended for the boar.

On another occasion, Croesus inquired of Delphi how long his kingdom would last. The Pythoness answered, in effect, until "a mule is monarch in Media." This not only pleased him because "it seemed incredible to him that a mule should ever become king of the Medes," but also gave him confidence when he engaged in war with the Medes and Persians, led by Cyrus. The war ended in his defeat and capture but, according to Herodotus, he had no right to complain of the oracle because "he had misunderstood the answer which had been given him about the mule. Cyrus was that mule; for the parents of Cyrus were of different races and of different kinds"—his mother a Median princess, his father a Persian subject.

The attitude of the ancients toward these various instruments of prophecy or divination does not seem to be consistent or constant. Herodotus reports at one place how Xerxes, "despising the omens," carried out his plans against their forebodings; and at another how an eclipse of the moon, being interpreted as of good omen, rejoiced Xerxes who, "thus instructed, proceeded on his way with great gladness of heart." And again, when Xerxes reports to Artabanus the advice—concerning his war against the Greeks—which he received from a dream apparition, Artabanus scoffs, saying, "Such things, my son, have of truth nothing divine in them ... Whatever a man has been thinking of during the day, is wont to hover round him in the visions of his dreams at night." But when Artabanus himself experiences the same apparition which had occurred to Xerxes in his dream and, in addition to giving the same advice, the vision threatens him, Artabanus changes his mind about dreams and reverses his policy with regard to the expedition against Greece.

"As to the divination which takes place in sleep, and is said to be based on dreams," Aristotle writes, "we cannot lightly either dismiss it with contempt or give it implicit confidence." Nevertheless, he himself seems to conclude that most so-called prophetic dreams are "to be classed as mere coincidences"; and that "dreams are not sent by God, nor are they designed for this purpose," i.e., foretelling the future. One proof that they are not sent by God is, in his opinion, the fact that the persons having them "are not the best and wisest but merely commonplace persons." The fact that "the power of foreseeing the future and of having vivid dreams is found in persons of inferior type implies that God does not send them."

THE CHRISTIAN THEOLOGIANS, distinguishing between prophecy and divination, condemn the latter as a kind of presumption or impiety. Though their criticism seems to be directed especially against astrology, it applies to the interpretation of terrestrial as well as celestial signs. Augustine refers to the "insane and impious ritual" of the astrologers and "their illusory claims to predict the future," and Aquinas explains how the astrologers are able to foretell things in a general way without attributing to them any genuinely prophetic power.

In his consideration of the difference between true and false religion, Hobbes goes further than the theologians in condemning "the innumerable other superstitious ways of divination," such as "the ambiguous or senseless answers of the priests at Delphi, Delos, Ammon, and other famous oracles," or "the prediction of witches that pretended conference with the dead, which is called necromancy, conjuring, and witchcraft, and is but juggling and confederate knavery," or, in general, the recourse to omens, portents, and dreams for purposes of prognostication.

That the things Hobbes calls superstitious are not confined to pagan antiquity is manifest in Shakespeare's Macbeth. The witches and the omens there are like the soothsayers and the portents in Julius Caesar; and Macbeth's misunderstanding of " 'til Birnam Forest come to Dunsinane" is as fatal as Croesus' reliance on "until a mule is monarch in Media."

In one other respect, pagan and Christian cultures seem to exhibit a certain parallelism with regard to the belief in supernatural foreknowledge. The spirits of the departed, in The Odyssey and The Aeneid, are able to inform the visitor to the underworld of coming events on earth. They speak plainly and with perfect prescience. The veil which hides the future from mortal eyes has been lifted. So, too, the damned souls and the blessed foretell future things to Dante, no less accurately though less extensively than, in *Paradise Lost,* the archangel Michael unfolds to Adam the whole future history of mankind.

But so far as the foreknowledge of mortal men is concerned, the Hebrew prophets seem to be unique. Unlike pagan diviners or sooth-sayers, they do not probe the future in order to help men anticipate the turns of fortune or the lines of fate. They do not have to employ arts or devices for penetrating divine secrets. God speaks to them directly and, through them, to the Chosen People. For the most part their prophetic speeches, unlike those of the oracles, seem to be unambiguous. At least the intention seems to be to reveal, not to conceal, God's plan on such matters as He Himself wishes men to foresee the course of providence.

Where pagan prognosticators may claim to be divinely inspired in the sense of having special powers of interpretation, the Hebrew prophets speak from a different kind of su-pernatural inspiration. They are the vessels through which the Lord Himself speaks. They are interpreters only in that they make known to others what God has made known to them.

The content of the divine communication is seldom exclusively a foretelling of the fu-ture. It is often accompanied by instruction concerning the actions to be performed by the Jewish people—the direction of their conduct toward the Promised Land or the rebuilding of the Temple. Sometimes when the prophecy is one of doom rather than of hope, as in the case of the destruction of Jerusalem, the Bab-ylonian captivity, or the dispersion of Israel, the prediction of the future is accompanied by moral instruction of another sort—the lessons of the Law which the Jews have forsaken, meriting thereby the punishments the prophets foresee.

Mere prognostication does not seem to be the chief purpose of Hebrew prophecy. Just as the Covenant which God makes with Abra-ham, Isaac, and Jacob consecrates the Jewish people to a special mission; just as the Law which God hands down through Moses sets them apart from the Gentiles and prescribes for them the way of righteousness and sanc-tity; so the revelations of God's providence through the prophets tend to remind the Cho-sen People of the meaning of the Covenant and the Law as well as to disclose their destiny as a nation.

The prophets speak not only of the future, but of the present and the past. They are divinely appointed teachers, no less than the patriarchs and Moses. Yet they may rank be-low Moses (who is sometimes also regarded as a prophet) by reason of the manner in which they are addressed by God. As Hobbes points out, "God himself in express words declareth that to other prophets he spake in dreams and visions, but to his servant Moses, in such manner as a man speaketh to his friend"— face to face.

The content of Hebrew prophecy, in short, seems to be continuous with the rest of God's revelation of Himself to His Chosen People. The difference between the prophets as the instruments of God's teaching and the pagan philosophers as merely human teachers seems to Augustine plainly shown by the agreement of the prophets with one another and by their continuity with Moses and the patri-archs; whereas Augustine can find nothing but disagreement and dissension among even the best teachers of the pagans. Among them, false teachers or prophets seem to be accorded the same recognition and to attract the same fol-lowing as true.

"But that nation," Augustine writes, "that people, that city, that republic, these Israelites, to whom the oracles of God were entrusted, by no means confounded with similar license false prophets with the true prophets; but, agreeing together, and differing in nothing, acknowledged and upheld the authentic au-thors of their sacred books. These were their philosophers, these were their sages, divines, prophets, and teachers of probity and piety. Whoever was wise and lived according to them was wise and lived, not according to men, but according to God who hath spoken to them."

Hobbes also conceives the prophets of the Old Testament as more than foretellers of the future. "The name of prophet," he writes, "signifies in Scripture sometimes *prolocutor;* that is, he that speaketh from God to man, or from man to God; and sometimes predictor, or a foreteller of things to come." In addition to their being divinely appointed teachers, the prophets, according to Hobbes, seem to perform a political function. They check the power of the kings, or seek to awaken their consciences to the dictates of justice and mercy. "Through the whole history of the kings, as well of Judah as of Israel, there were prophets that always controlled the kings for transgressing the religion; and sometimes also for errors of state."

Centuries later, Weber, in his essay on "The Social Psychology of the World Religions," presents us with a secular view of religious prophecy. "Where prophecy has provided a religious basis," he writes, "this basis could be one of two fundamental types . . . : 'exemplary' prophecy, and 'emissary' prophecy." The former "points out the path to salvation by exemplary living"; the latter "addresses its *demands* to the world in the name of a god."

A secular view of the Hebrew prophets also seems to give prominence to their political role in the theocratic community of the Jews. Comparing the Jewish state with other sacerdotal societies, J. S. Mill observes that "neither their kings nor their priests ever obtained, as in those other countries, the exclusive moulding of their character. Their religion . . . gave existence to an inestimably precious unorganized institution—the Order (if it may be so termed) of the Prophets. Under the protection, generally though not always effectual, of their sacred character, the Prophets were a power in the nation, often more than a match for kings and priests, and kept up, in that little corner of the earth, the antagonism of influences which is the only real security for continued progress."

As THERE IS A BODY of prophetic doctrine in the Old Testament, so the religion of the Gospels contains a number of prophetic beliefs peculiar to Christian doctrine. Such, for example, is the prophecy of the second coming of Christ, the prophecy of the Last Judgment on that occasion, and the prophecy of a final conflagration to cleanse the world, which will precede the resurrection of the body as that in turn precedes the general judgment of souls.

Aquinas discusses the various signs which will foretell the imminence of these events. He also raises the question whether the time of the end of the world and of the resurrection can be known exactly. On this he agrees with Augustine that "that time is hidden from men." It cannot be calculated by natural reason, nor is it revealed. "Of that day and hour," it is written in Matthew, "no one knoweth, no, not the angels of heaven." When the apostles asked Christ about His second coming, He answered, according to Saint Paul, "It is not for you to know the times or moments which the Father hath put in His own power."

What Christ refused to tell the apostles, Aquinas adds, "He will not reveal to others. Wherefore all those who have been misled to reckon the aforesaid time have so far proved to be untruthful; for some, as Augustine says, stated from our Lord's ascension to His last coming 400 years would elapse, others 500, others 1,000. The falseness of these calculators is evident, as will likewise be the falseness of those who even now cease not to calculate."

The single greatest prophecy in the Judeo-Christian tradition is, perhaps, the messianic prophecy—the foretelling of a Messiah or of a messianic age. The prediction of a Messiah or Saviour, who shall be born of the house of David and shall be king of the Jews, runs throughout the prophetic books of the Old Testament, though with different degrees of explicitness and varying imagery in Daniel and Jeremiah, in Isaiah and Ezekiel.

"The Lord himself shall give you a sign," says Isaiah. "Behold a virgin shall conceive and bear a son, and shall call his name Immanuel . . . For unto us a child is born, unto us a son is given," Isaiah goes on, "and the government shall be upon his shoulder, and his name shall be called Wonderful Counsellor, The Mighty God, The Everlasting Father, The Prince of Peace. Of the increase of his government and peace, there shall be no end, upon the throne of David and upon his kingdom, to order it and to establish it with justice from henceforth even for ever." And Jeremiah tells his people, "Behold the days come, saith the Lord, that I will raise unto David a righteous Branch and a King shall reign and prosper and shall execute judgment and justice in the earth. In his days, Judah shall be saved, and Israel shall dwell safely."

Two of the great issues between the Jewish and Christian faiths concern these messianic prophecies in the Old Testament. One arises from opposite interpretations of the event predicted—a messianic age in which the kingdom of the Jews will be established on earth in perpetual righteousness and glory, or the coming to earth of God's only begotten son, incarnate in human form, for the salvation of all mankind. The other arises from opposite answers to the question whether the prediction—on either interpretation—has been fulfilled.

It is, of course, the Christian view that the prophets foretold the coming of Christ and that their prophecy has been fulfilled. But more than that, Christian apologists and theologians seem to make the fulfillment of Hebrew prophecies, interpreted as foreshadowing the truths of the Christian religion, a source of verification for these truths.

The difference between Jesus Christ and Mahomet, according to Pascal, is that "Mahomet was not foretold; Jesus Christ was foretold. I see many contradictory religions, and consequently all false save one," he writes.

"Each wants to be believed on its own authority, and threatens unbelievers. I do not therefore believe them. Everyone can say this; everyone can call himself a prophet. But I see the Christian religion wherein prophecies are fulfilled; and that is what everyone cannot do."

And in another place Pascal declares that "the prophecies are the strongest proof of Jesus Christ . . . If one man alone had made a book of predictions about Jesus Christ, as to the time and manner, and Jesus Christ had come in conformity to these prophecies, this fact would have infinite weight. But there is much more here. Here is a succession of men during four thousand years, who, consequently and without variation, come, one after another, to foretell this same event."

Centuries earlier Augustine writes in a similar vein. The Hebrew people as a whole are chosen to perform this prophetic function—to foretell, "sometimes through men who understood what they spake, and sometimes through men who understood not, all that has transpired since the advent of Christ until now, and all that will transpire." Not only the explicit "prophecies which are contained in words," but all the rituals and ceremonies, the offices and institutions, of the Jewish religion prefigure Christianity, signifying and fore-announcing "those things which we who believe in Jesus Christ unto eternal life believe to have been fulfilled, or behold in process of fulfillment, or confidently believe shall yet be fulfilled."

73

Prudence

INTRODUCTION

OF the qualities or virtues attributed to the intellect, prudence seems to be least concerned with knowledge and most concerned with action. When we call a man a scientist or an artist, or praise the clarity of his understanding, we imply only that he has a certain kind of knowledge. We admire his mind, but we do not necessarily admire him as a man. We may not even know what kind of man he is or what kind of life he leads. It is significant that our language does not contain a noun like "scientist" or "artist" to describe the man who possesses prudence. We must use the adjective and speak of a prudent man, which seems to suggest that prudence belongs to the whole man, rather than just to his mind.

Prudence seems to be almost as much a moral as an intellectual quality. We would hardly call a man prudent without knowing his manner of life. Whether he behaved temperately would probably be much more relevant to our judgment of his prudence than whether he had a cultivated mind. The extent of his education or the depth of his learning might not affect our judgment at all, but we probably would consider whether he was old enough to have learned anything from experience and whether he had actually profited from experience to become wise.

These observations not only express the ordinary sense of the word "prudence," but also give a summary indication of the idea for which that word stands in the great books. Like other fundamental traits of mind or character, prudence is considered by the poets and historians in terms of precept and example. For the definition of the term or for an analysis of its relation to other fundamental ideas, such as virtue and happiness, desire and duty,

one must go to the great works of moral and political theory or of theology.

Even there, however, the conception of prudence is used more frequently than it is expounded. Plato, Aristotle, Aquinas, Hobbes, and Kant seem to be the exceptions, and of these only Aristotle and Aquinas offer an extended analysis—Aristotle in his book on intellectual virtue in the *Nicomachean Ethics*, Aquinas in certain questions of his Treatise on Habits in the *Summa Theologica*, but more extensively in his Treatise on Prudence (see the questions from the *Summa Theologica* cited in the list of Additional Readings).

THAT PRUDENCE IS NOT knowledge in the ordinary sense of the term—that it is a product of experience and possession of reason which, unlike science or art, cannot be expressed in propositions—seems to be clearly implied by Hobbes. "When the thoughts of a man, that has a design in hand, running over a multitude of things, observes how they conduce to that design, or what design they may conduce to; if his observations are such as are not easy or usual; this wit of his is called Prudence, and depends on much experience and memory of the like things, and their consequences heretofore."

Whereas science can achieve some certainty, the judgments of prudence are, according to Hobbes, all uncertain, "because to observe by experience and remember all circumstances that may alter the success, is impossible." It is the opposition between experience and science which seems to lead Hobbes to distinguish prudence from wisdom. "As much experience is prudence, so is much science sapience. For though we usually have one name of wisdom for them both, yet the Latins did always distinguish between *prudentia* and *sapientia,* ascribing the former to experience, the latter to science."

The Greeks also had two words—*phronesis* and *sophia*—both of which are sometimes translated in English by "wisdom." But Aristotle, like Hobbes, insists upon the distinction between the wisdom which is the ultimate fruit of the speculative sciences or philosophy and the wisdom which belongs to the sphere of moral and political action. Wishing to preserve Aristotle's sense that *phronesis* and *sophia* have something in common which deserves the eulogistic connotation of "wisdom," his translators usually render these words in English by the phrases "practical wisdom" or "political wisdom" (for *phronesis*), and "speculative wisdom" or "philosophical wisdom" (for *sophia*). The English rendering of Aquinas, on the other hand, usually translates his *prudentia* by "prudence," and his *sapientia* by "wisdom."

Whether it is permissible to use "prudence" and "practical wisdom" as synonyms may be more than a question of verbal equivalence; for there is a fundamental issue in theory concerning the unity of wisdom, on which Plato differs from both Aristotle and Aquinas. The question about the relation of knowledge and virtue may be differently answered according to the view of wisdom which denies its division into speculative and practical, and according to the view which conceives the possibility that a man may be wise in one way without being wise in the other. In the language of Aquinas, a man may have acquired wisdom through science and understanding without having the moral character of a prudent man.

"That practical wisdom is not scientific knowledge is evident," Aristotle declares. This is confirmed, he adds, "by the fact that while young men become geometricians and mathematicians and wise in matters like these, it is thought that a young man of practical wisdom cannot be found. The reason is that such wisdom is concerned not only with universals but with particulars, which become familiar from experience, but a young man has no experience, for it is length of time that gives experience."

Hobbes and Aristotle seem to agree that experience is important for the development of prudence or practical wisdom precisely because "it is practical and practice is concerned with particulars." But though both also agree that this explains the distinction between prudence and scientific knowledge—which is concerned not with action but with the nature of things—Aristotle alone raises a further question about the distinction between practical wisdom and art.

In making something, the artist also deals with particulars. In this sense, art is also practical. But, according to Aristotle, the word "productive" should be used in the distinction from "practical" to signify the difference between making and doing—two kinds of human activity which, though alike as compared with scientific knowing, represent knowledge differently applied. The knowledge which the artist possesses can, furthermore, be formulated in a set of rules. An individual can acquire the skill of an art by practicing according to its rules. What a man knows when he is prudent seems to be much less capable of being communicated by precept or rule. What he knows is how to deliberate or calculate well about things to be done.

This, in Aristotle's view, marks prudence off from all other virtues. That prudence is a quality of mind seems to follow from the fact that it involves deliberation, a kind of thinking about variable and contingent particulars of the same sort which belong to the realm of opinion. That prudence is also a moral quality, an aspect of character, seems to follow no less from Aristotle's statement that prudence is not deliberation about the means to any sort of end, but only about those "which conduce to the good life in general."

PRUDENCE IS NOT ALWAYS described as skill of mind in deliberating about alternative courses of action, nor is it always regarded as entirely praiseworthy or admirable—inseparable from virtue and the good life.

It is, for example, sometimes identified with foresight or even conjecturing about the future. So conceived, prudence does not seem to require rational power so much as memory and imagination, in order to project past experience into the future. In this sense, Aristotle admits it may be said that "even some of the lower animals have practical wisdom, *viz.*, those which are found to have a power of foresight with regard to their own life."

Identifying prudence with foresight, Hobbes conceives perfect prudence as belonging only to God. When the event answers expectations, the prediction is attributed to prudence, yet human foresight being fallible, "it is but presumption. For the foresight of things to come, which is Providence, belongs only to him by whose will they are to come." Aquinas gives a quite different reason for saying that "prudence or providence may suitably be attributed to God." It is that the ordering of things toward their ultimate end is "the chief part of prudence, to which two other parts are directed—namely, remembrance of the past, and understanding of the present; inasmuch from the remembrance of what is past and the understanding of what is present, we gather how to provide for the future."

Prudence is sometimes described, not as a virtue of the mind, or even as the power of foresight, but as a temperamental trait, an emotional disposition. It is associated with timidity or caution in those who are fearful of risks or unwilling to take chances. It is in this sense that Francis Bacon seems to oppose hopefulness to prudence, "which is different upon principle and in all human matters augurs the worst." The cautiousness of the overdeliberate man may involve thought as well as fear. Hamlet thinks too much and on too many sides of every action. His action being "sicklied o'er by the pale cast of thought," he is irresolute. He laments his misuse of reason. "Whether it be bestial oblivion, or some craven scruple of thinking too precisely on the event—a thought, which quartered, hath but one part wisdom and ever three parts coward—I do not know why yet I live to say 'this thing's to do,' since I have cause, and will, and strength, and means to do it."

When prudence is conceived as excessive caution, its opposite is usually described as rashness, precipitateness, or impetuosity. Thucydides portrays these opposites in the persons of Nicias and Alcibiades. Their speeches to the Athenian assembly on the question of the Sicilian expedition do not merely present an opposition of reasons for and against the undertaking, but also represent an opposition of types of human character. Both come to grief: Nicias, the overcautious leader of the expedition, who earns a not inevitable defeat by his ever-delaying tactics, and Alcibiades, who does not stop at treachery or treason when the moment seems ripe for action which, if quickly taken, may succeed.

Aristotle and Aquinas would use such facts to argue against what, in their views, is the misconception of the prudent man as the opposite of the impetuous. The prudent man, in their opinion, does not stand at the other extreme of undue caution. In their theory of the virtues as means between extremes of excess and defect, prudence, like courage or temperance, represents a mean consisting in neither too much nor too little. As cowardice and foolhardiness are the opposite vices of too much and too little fear—and as both are opposed to the mean of courage which involves a moderation of fear—so excessive caution and impetuosity are the vices opposed to prudence as well as to each other.

Nor are prudence and imprudence simply matters of temperament. Men may differ in their temperamental dispositions; but, according to Aristotle and Aquinas, these are not to be confused with virtues and vices. One man may be by nature more fearful or fearless than another, but regardless of these differences in emotional endowment, either may become courageous, by forming the habit of controlling fear for the right reasons. So, too, one man may be naturally more impulsive or more circumspect than another, but either can acquire prudence through learning to take sufficient counsel and to deliberate enough before action, while also forming the habit of resolving thought into action by reaching decisions and commanding their execution. Failing to satisfy these conditions of prudence, either may develop the vices of imprudence, becoming, like Hamlet or Nicias, irresolute; or, like Alcibiades, impatient of counsel or ill advised, lacking care in deliberation and soundness in judgment.

THE CONCEPTION OF prudence as itself the extreme of caution, whether temperamental or habitual, is not the only challenge to the Aristotelian theory of prudence as a virtue. Other moralists, especially those who take a different view of virtue generally, do not seem to look upon prudence as wholly admirable. Even when they do not condemn prudence as an indisposition to act promptly or decisively enough, they seem to give prudent deliberation the invidious connotation of cold and selfish calculation.

A suggestion of this appears in J. S. Mill's contrast between duties to ourselves and duties to others, wherein he remarks that "the term duty to oneself, when it means anything more than prudence, means self-respect and self-development." It would seem to be implied that prudence means something less—something more selfish—than a proper and justifiable self-interest, the violation of which involves "a breach of duty to others, for whose sake the individual is bound to have care for himself."

Kant, more explicitly than Mill, associates prudence with expediency and self-seeking, and separates it from action in accordance with duty under the categorical imperative of the moral law. Prudence has meaning only in relation to a hypothetical imperative "which expresses the practical necessity of an action as a means to the advancement of happiness." Granted that a man seeks his individual happiness, then "skill in the choice of means to his own greatest well-being may be called *prudence*." Consequently, "the imperative which refers to the choice of means to one's happiness, *i.e.*, the precept of prudence, is still always hypothetical; the action is not commanded absolutely, but only as a means to another purpose," or, as Kant says elsewhere, "the maxim of self-love (prudence) only *advises;* the law of morality *commands*." Furthermore, he holds that "what *duty* is, is plain of itself to everyone; but what it is to bring true durable advantage, such as will extend to the whole of one's existence, is always veiled in impenetrable obscurity, and much prudence is required to adapt the practical rule founded on it to the ends of life, even tolerably, by making exceptions."

In terms of Kant's division of the imperatives of conduct into the pragmatic and the moral, according as they refer to welfare and happiness or duty and law, prudence is merely pragmatic. It does not belong to morality. The pragmatic imperative of prudence is more like the technical imperative of art, which is also conditional and concerned with determining means to an end—in this case, the thing to be produced by skill. "If it were only equally easy to give a definite conception of happiness, the imperatives of prudence would correspond exactly with those of skill."

As Kant sees it, "the sole business of reason in the moral philosophy of prudence is to bring about a union of all the ends, which are aimed at by our inclinations, into one ultimate end—that of *happiness,* and to show the agreement which should exist among the means of attaining that end. In this sphere, accordingly, reason cannot present to us any more than *pragmatical* laws of free action, for our guidance towards the aims set up by the senses, and is incompetent to give us the laws which are pure and determined completely *a priori*." Hence the precepts of prudence "are used by reason only as counsels, and by way of counterpoise against seductions to an opposite course."

The issue between Kant and Aristotle (or Aquinas) with respect to prudence thus appears to be part of the larger issue between them on the fundamental principles of morality, discussed in the chapters on DUTY and HAPPINESS. In Kant's view, Aristotle and Aquinas, no less than Mill, are pragmatists rather than moralists. They are all utilitarians in the sense that they regard happiness as the first principle of human conduct and concern themselves with the ordering of means to this end. Since the consideration of means necessarily involves the weighing of alternatives as more or less expedient, prudence becomes indispensable to the pursuit of happiness. The choice of the best means is second in importance only to the election of the right end.

Kant admits that those who live for happiness require a great deal of prudence, in order to adapt practical rules to variable circumstances and to make proper exceptions in applying them. None is required by those who live according to the moral law. "The moral law commands the most punctual obedience from everyone; it must, therefore, not be so difficult to judge what it requires to be done, that the commonest unpracticed understanding, even without worldly prudence, should fail to apply it rightly." That "the principle of *private* happiness" is "the direct opposite of the principle of morality" Kant seems to think is evident from the questionable worth of prudence; "for a man must have a different criterion when he is compelled to say to himself: I am a *worthless* fellow, though I have filled my purse; and when he approves himself, and says: I am a *prudent* man, for I have enriched my treasure."

Kant does not limit his criticism of prudence as pragmatic—or practical rather than moral—to the fact that it serves what he calls "private happiness." It may serve the public welfare. "A history is composed pragmatically," he writes, "when it teaches *prudence, i.e.,* instructs the world how it can provide for its interests better." But he also distinguishes between worldly and private prudence. "The former is a man's ability to influence others so as to use them for his own purposes. The latter is the sagacity to combine all these purposes for his own lasting benefit." Nevertheless, the prudence which aims at individual happiness is primary, for "when a man is prudent in the former sense, but not in the latter, we might better say of him that he is clever and cunning, but, on the whole, imprudent."

THOSE WHO TAKE THE view that happiness is the first principle of morality would still agree with Kant that the man who is skillful in exercising an influence over other men so as to *use* them for his own purposes, is clever or cunning rather than prudent. Hobbes, for example, says that if you permit to prudence "the use of unjust or dishonest means . . . you have that Crooked Wisdom, which is called Craft." Aristotle goes even further in his insistence that "it is impossible to be practically wise without being good," or, as the same point is made in the language of Aquinas, "one cannot have prudence unless one has the moral virtues; since prudence is right reason about things to be done, to which end man is rightly disposed by moral virtue."

"To be able to do things that tend towards the mark we have set before ourselves" is, according to Aristotle, to be clever. "If the mark be noble, the cleverness is laudable, but if the mark be bad, the cleverness is mere smartness." Hence the man of prudence has a certain cleverness, but the clever man who is merely smart cannot be called practically wise. By this criterion the clever thief who plans and executes a successful robbery, the shrewd businessman who, without regard to justice, calculates well how to maximize his profits, or Machiavelli's prince who exercises cunning to get or keep his power, exhibits, not prudence, but its counterfeits. In some cases, the cleverness or shrewdness may simulate prudence without involving the knavery of craft or cunning. Some men have what Aquinas conceives as artistic (or technical) rather than moral prudence. Those who are "good counsellors in matters of warfare or seamanship are said to be prudent officers or pilots, but not simply prudent. Only those are simply prudent who give good counsel about all the concerns of life."

Aristotle and Aquinas make the relation between prudence and moral virtue reciprocal. The moral virtues depend, for their formation and endurance, as much upon prudence as prudence depends upon them. "Virtue makes us aim at the right end," Aristotle writes, "and practical wisdom makes us take the right means." The rightness of the means requires not merely that they be adapted to an end, but that the end itself be right. The right end cannot be achieved unless the means to it be rightly chosen. Hence no skill of mind in deliberating about and choosing means is truly the intellectual virtue of prudence unless the man who habitually calculates well is also habitually inclined by the moral virtues to choose things for the right end, whether that be happiness or the common good of society.

Conversely, the moral virtues depend upon prudence because, in Aristotle's view, they are formed by the making of right choices. His definition of moral virtue names prudence as an indispensable cause. Since the mean between extremes, in which the virtues consist, is in most cases subjective or relative to the individual, it cannot be determined by objective measurements. Reason must determine it by a prudent consideration of the relevant circumstances.

The independence of prudence and the moral virtues seems to be the basis, for Aristotle, of the insight that it is impossible to have one moral virtue without having all. On this basis, Aristotle says, we can "refute the dialectical argument . . . that the virtues exist in separation from one another." As no moral virtue can exist apart from practical wisdom, so with it, all must be present.

Aquinas mentions another intellectual virtue as indispensable to the moral virtues, namely, the virtue of understanding which consists in knowing the first principles in practical as well as speculative matters. The first principles of the practical reason (*i.e.,* the precepts of the natural law) underlie prudence as well as the moral virtues. Just as sound reasoning in speculative matters "proceeds from naturally known principles . . . so also does prudence which is right reason about things to be done." Nevertheless, though prudence and the moral virtues depend upon it, Aquinas does not include understanding—as he does not include art, science, and wisdom—in his enumeration of the four cardinal virtues, cardinal in the sense of being the virtues indispensable to a good human life.

THESE MATTERS, especially the interconnection of the virtues and the theory of the cardinal virtues, are discussed in the chapter on VIRTUE AND VICE. The problem of the relative worth of the moral and the intellectual virtues is also considered there and in the chapter on WISDOM, where the contributions to happiness of prudence and wisdom—or of practical and speculative wisdom—are specifically compared.

Here there remains to be considered the Socratic conception of the relation between knowledge and virtue, for there seems to be an issue between his theory of this matter and the foregoing view of the relation between prudence and the moral virtues.

In the *Meno,* Socrates argues that whatever a man desires or chooses he either knows or deems to be good. The man who chooses something evil for himself does not do so knowingly, but only through the mistake of deeming that which is in fact evil to be advantageous or good. Except for such mistakes, "no man," says Socrates, "wills or chooses anything evil." Apart from error or ignorance, evil is never voluntarily chosen. Hence, if virtue consists "in willing or desiring things which are good, and in having the power to gain them," it would seem to follow that knowledge of the good is closely related to its practice.

Subsequently, Socrates suggests that "if there be any sort of good which is distinct from knowledge, virtue may be that good; but if knowledge embraces all good, then we shall be right in thinking that virtue is knowledge." To test these hypotheses, he proceeds to consider the various things which—whether or not they are the same as virtue—are like virtue in being advantageous to men. None of these things, such as courage or temperance, seems to profit men unless accompanied by what, in English translations, is sometimes called "wisdom" and sometimes "prudence."

Socrates points out that "everything the soul attempts, when under the guidance of wisdom"—or prudence—"ends in happiness; but in the opposite when under the guidance of folly"—or imprudence. "If then," he says, "virtue is a quality of the soul, and if it be of necessity always advantageous, then virtue must be wisdom or prudence, since none of the things of the soul are either advantageous or hurtful in themselves, but they are all made advantageous or hurtful by the addition to them of prudence or imprudence"—wisdom or folly. From this, says Socrates, we can conclude that "prudence is virtue, either the whole of virtue or some part of it at least"— or, as this is sometimes translated, "virtue is either wholly or partly wisdom."

In the light of his own view that all the moral virtues depend on practical wisdom, Aristotle criticizes the Socratic position. "Socrates in one respect was on the right track while in another he went astray. In thinking that all the virtues were forms of practical wisdom he was wrong, but in saying that they implied practical wisdom he was right ... Socrates thought the virtues were rules or rational principles ... while we think they involve a rational principle." Similarly, in considering the question whether there can be moral without intellectual virtue, Aquinas writes: "Although virtue be not right reason, as Socrates held, yet not only is it *according to right reason,* insofar as it inclines a man to do that which is in accord with right reason as the Platonists maintained; but it also needs to be *joined with right reason,* as Aristotle declares."

Aquinas furthermore interprets the opinion that "every virtue is a kind of prudence," which he attributes to Socrates, as meaning that when "a man is in possession of knowledge, he cannot sin, and that everyone who sins does so through ignorance." This, he says, "is based on a false supposition, because the appetitive faculty obeys the reason, not blindly, but with a certain power of opposition." Nevertheless, "there is some truth in the saying of Socrates that so long as a man is in possession of knowledge he does not sin; provided that this knowledge involves the use of reason in the individual act of choice."

Whether those who criticize the position of Socrates accurately perceive his intention and state the issue fairly are problems of interpretation as difficult as the question of where in this matter the truth lies. If Socrates is saying that a man will do good if he knows the good, what sort of knowledge is implied—knowledge of the good in general or knowledge of what is good in a particular case? Do both types of knowledge of the good lead as readily or surely to good or virtuous action?

Whether or not, in addition to knowledge, a good will or right desire is essential, it may be held that prudence is required to apply moral principles—aiming at the good in general—to particular cases. "There exists no moral system," writes Mill, "under which there do not arise unequivocal cases of conflicting obligation. These are the real difficulties, the knotty points, both in the theory of ethics and in the conscientious guidance of personal conduct. They are overcome practically, with great or less success, according to the intellect and virtue of the individual." Mill seems to imply that both prudence and virtue are essential to good action on the level of particulars, and that without them the kind of knowledge which is expressed in moral principles does not necessarily lead a man to act well.

Nietzsche writes about prudence in a contrary vein. "All these moralities which address themselves to the individual person, for the promotion of his 'happiness' as they say" are nothing but "prescriptions for behaviour in relation to the degree of *perilousness* in which the individual person lives with himself" and are merely "recipes to counter his passions." These include the "artifices and acts of prudence to which there clings the nook-and-cranny odour of ancient household remedies and old-woman wisdom ... all this is, from an intellectual point of view, of little value and far from constituting 'science,' not to speak of 'wisdom,' but rather, to say it again and to say it thrice, prudence, prudence, prudence, mingled with stupidity, stupidity, stupidity."

ONE OTHER PROBLEM OF interpretation must be mentioned. It occurs with respect to Aristotle's statement concerning diverse modes of prudence.

"Political wisdom and practical wisdom are the same state of mind," he writes, "but their essence is not the same. Of the wisdom concerned with the city, the practical wisdom which plays a controlling part is legislative wisdom, while that which is related to this as particulars to their universal is known by the general name of 'political wisdom' ... Practical wisdom also is identified especially with that form of it which is concerned with the individual man, and this is known by the general name 'practical wisdom.' Of the other kinds, one is called domestic, another legislative, a third political; and of this last, one part is called deliberative and the other judicial."

Does this mean that skill of mind in determining the best means to an end is different according to differences in the end—whether the happiness of an individual or the common good of a society? Does it mean, furthermore, that the prudence involved in managing a household is different from the prudence concerned with political affairs; and that, in the state, the prudence of the ruler (prince or statesman) is different from the prudence of the ruled (subject or citizen), because the one moves on the level of general laws, the other on the level of particular acts in compliance with law? Within the sphere of jurisprudence, or the prudence of laws, is the prudence of the legislator or lawmaker different from the prudence of the judge who applies the law?

In his Treatise on Prudence, Aquinas answers these questions affirmatively. He distinguishes between private, domestic, and political prudence, and within the political sphere places special emphasis upon what he calls "reignative prudence," the sort of prudence Dante calls "a kingly prudence," which sets the prince apart from ordinary men. Hobbes, on the other hand, asserts that "to govern well a family and a kingdom, are not different degrees of prudence, but different sorts of business; no more than to draw a picture in little, or as great, or greater than life, are different degrees of art."

This issue is intimately connected with the problem of the forms of government. If only a few men are fitted by nature to acquire the special mode of prudence which is reignative or legislative, would not government by the few or by the one seem to be naturally best? If, however, in a republic, those who are citizens rule and are ruled in turn, should not each citizen have the prudence requisite for both tasks, whether it be the same or different? Finally, if the democratic theory is that all men are capable of being citizens—though not all, perhaps, are equally eligible for the highest public offices—must not political prudence be conceived as attainable by all men?

The question remains open whether those who deserve the highest magistracies have a special mode of reignative prudence; or merely a higher degree of the same prudence by which they govern their private lives and their domestic establishments; or, as Hobbes suggests, have other abilities whereby they can apply the same prudence to a different kind of business.

74

Punishment

INTRODUCTION

THE problem of punishment divides into a number of questions. In what does punishment consist? What purpose should punishment serve, or what should be its principle or reason? Who has the authority to punish and under what conditions shall this authority be exercised? Who shall be punished and who shall be exempt from punishment? What are the forms or kinds of punishment? Are any of these reprehensible either in principle or for their consequences? Should there be a proportion between the severity of punishment and the gravity of the offense? Can a person punish himself? Do men desire to be punished?

These questions apply, though not with equal emphasis, to the three major types of wrongdoing in relation to which men discuss the nature and the need of punishment, its justice or its expediency. Punishment is traditionally considered in relation to vice, to crime, and to sin. According to the type of wrongdoing being considered, the punitive agent may be the wrongful individual himself or his family, his state, his church or God.

The lines which separate these areas of the problem of punishment cannot be sharply drawn in all cases, for as certain acts simultaneously violate the moral, the civil, and the divine law, they may also cause a person to be simultaneously subject to punishment from diverse sources. The wrong or injury which punishment is supposed to redress may in some cases fall under none of these headings, as, for example, acts of war or rebellion. It is sometimes questioned whether the theory of punishment remains the same when punitive steps are taken by one state against some or all the people of another; or again, when a government applies penalties for a rebellion engaged in by members of its own community.

In this chapter, we shall deal with the problem of punishment in its most general terms, for the most part considering the foregoing questions without regard to the distinction of sin, crime, and vice; or to the differences between divine and human punishment, or between punishment by the state and in the family (*i.e.*, punishment as involved in the enforcement of law and punishment as an instrument of education or training). These more specialized topics belong to other chapters: *e.g.*, punishment as affecting the formation of character to the chapters on EDUCATION and VIRTUE AND VICE; punishment as administered by parents to the chapter on FAMILY; divine rewards and punishments to the chapters on IMMORTALITY and SIN.

The basic ideas in terms of which any discussion of punishment proceeds are, of course, the subjects of the chapters on JUSTICE and LAW. One other chapter—PLEASURE AND PAIN—is of peculiar relevance to the question about the nature of punishment. Concerning the nature of punishment there seems to be no great difference of opinion in the tradition of western thought. Punishment is generally conceived as the infliction of pain, though some writers distinguish between corporeal and spiritual punishment according as the pain inflicted is the pain of sense or the pain of deprivation and loss. Imprisonment, for example, always entails the pain of loss—the loss of freedom—but it may also carry with it the suffering of physical·hardships or even tortures. The torment of the damned is, according to some theologians, both corporeal and spiritual—the agony of hellfire and the anguish of the soul deprived of God's love and presence.

IF THERE IS LITTLE DISPUTE about the nature of punishment, the opposite situation prevails concerning its purpose. Why men should be punished is one of the most controversial questions in the field of moral and political thought, and in psychology and theology as well.

The major opposition in the tradition of the great books is between those who think that punishment need only be inherently just, and those who think it cannot be justified without reference to its utility or expediency. While this debate goes on, for more than twenty centuries, punishments in actual practice—whether in accordance with the law or uncontrolled by it—tend generally to be severe and often fiendish or ferocious. Huizinga writes of the Middle Ages that "Man at that time is convinced that right is absolutely fixed and certain. Justice should prosecute the unjust everywhere and to the end. Reparation and retribution have to be extreme, and assume the character of revenge ... That the criminal deserved his punishment was not doubted for a moment. The popular sense of justice always sanctioned the most rigorous penalties ... Torture and executions are enjoyed by the spectators like an entertainment at a fair."

Not until Cesare Beccaria in the 18th, and Jeremy Bentham in the 19th century, does the discussion of punishment lead to major reforms in the spirit and provisions of the penal codes. But the opposite positions in the debate across the centuries are never without practical significance for penal institutions and punitive measures, even when theory is not immediately reflected in practice. The speculative significance of the issue is, however, always immediately apparent. Although justice and law are more fundamental and comprehensive ideas than punishment, this one problem of punishment—the question of its purpose—critically tests the meaning of anyone's theory of law and justice.

It may be that the issue cannot be fairly stated in terms of *purpose*. To use that word may beg the question, since one of the basic positions in the controversy appears to be that punishment has no purpose in the sense of *serving some end beyond itself,* or producing some desired consequence *in the future*. This is the theory—shared by Kant and Hegel—that punishment should be purely retributive.

According to this view the effect of the punishment upon the wrongdoer, or upon others whose conduct may be affected by punishments meted out or threatened, must not be taken into account at all. Nothing should be sought except the preservation of the balance sheet of justice, by seeing that every wrong is duly requited by a proportionate measure of punishment. Nor is the requital purely retributive if it considers any person except the wrongdoer himself. That punishment of the transgressor may assuage the feelings of those he has injured, or even satisfy a desire for revenge, should have no motivating force. The only pleasure the spectacle of punishment should yield, the only desire it should satisfy, is that of seeing the moral law upheld. We should punish only because we have, under the moral law, a duty to do so.

Kant castigates as utilitarian every theory of punishment which directs it to the service of anything besides strict justice—such as the reformation of the criminal, the deterrence of others, the welfare of society, or the slaking of the thirst for vengeance. "Juridical punishment," he says, "can never be administered merely as a means for promoting another good, either with regard to the Criminal himself, or to Civil Society, but must in all cases be imposed only because the individual on whom it is inflicted *has committed a Crime* ... The Penal Law is a Categorical Imperative; and woe to him who creeps through the serpent-windings of Utilitarianism to discover some advantage that may discharge him from the Justice of Punishment, or even from the due measure of it."

What shall determine the mode and measure of punishment? Kant answers: "It is just the Principle of Equality by which the pointer of the Scale of Justice is made to incline no more to one side than the other. It may be rendered by saying that the undeserved evil which anyone commits on another, is to be regarded as perpetrated on himself . . . This is the Right of Retaliation (*ius talionis*); and properly understood it is the only Principle which . . . can definitely assign both the quality and the quantity of a just penalty. All other standards are wavering and uncertain; and on account of other considerations involved in them, they contain no principle conformable to the sentence of pure and strict Justice."

RETRIBUTIVE PUNISHMENT or retaliation seems to express the principle of justice or fairness in exchange. The Mosaic injunction that "thou shalt give life for life, eye for eye, tooth for tooth, burning for burning, wound for wound, stripe for stripe," occurs in the context of other passages which declare the compensation in goods which an injured party shall receive for the loss of or damage to his chattel. But it is also accompanied by ordinances which impose the death penalty for wrongs other than the taking of a life.

"You have heard," Christ declares in the Sermon on the Mount, "that it hath been said, An eye for an eye, and a tooth for a tooth. But I say unto you, That ye shall resist not evil; but whosoever shall smite thee on thy right cheek, turn to him the other also. And if any man will sue thee at the law, and take away thy coat, let him have thy cloak also." This passage has sometimes been taken to mean that all punishment is simply vengeance; and that instead of returning injury for injury, the Christian should love his enemies and forgive them. "If you think someone has wronged you," Princess Mary says to Prince Andrew in *War and Peace*, "forget it and forgive! We have no right to punish."

But the Christian view of punishment may not be the same when the punishment of the evildoer is a question for the state rather than for the individual. "Avenge not yourselves," Saint Paul commands; "for it is written, Vengeance is mine, I will repay, saith the Lord." The individual need not avenge himself, for God punishes the wicked; not only God, but the ruler of the earthly state who, Saint Paul says, "is the minister of God to thee for good. But if thou do that which is evil, be afraid; for he beareth not the sword in vain;

for he is the minister of God, a revenger to execute wrath upon him that doeth evil."

A life for a life appears to be the symbolic statement of the *lex talionis* in the Greek as well as the biblical tradition. "The spirit of Right cries out aloud and extracts atonement," the Chorus explains in *The Libation Bearers* of Aeschylus. "Blood stroke for the stroke of blood shall be paid." This warning parallels the words of Saint Matthew: "Whoso'er shall take the sword, shall perish by the sword." But as Aristotle points out— and similarly Aquinas in his comment on the *lex talionis* of the Old Testament—simple reciprocity does not determine the mode of retribution. "People *want* even the justice of Rhadamanthus to mean this: Should a man suffer what he did, right justice would be done." Yet, Aristotle points out, "in many cases, reciprocity and rectificatory justice are not in accord, *e.g.*, if an official has inflicted a wound, he should not be wounded in return, and if someone has wounded an official, he ought not to be wounded only but punished in addition." Retaliation consists in reciprocity only if it is "in accordance with a proportion, and not on the basis of a precisely equal return."

Punishment as retaliation may seem to be inseparable from revenge. Yet, according to Lucretius, the surrender of primitive freedom for the restrictions of civilized life is motivated by the desire to substitute equitable retribution for unlimited vengeance. The ancient kings were, according to Lucretius,

Sick of their feuds and weary to exhaustion
Of violence piled on violence, where each man,
If he is judge, exacts in vengeance more
Than any decent law would ever inflict.
So men, being utterly tired of violence,
Are willing enough to suffer and submit
To legal codes.

Hegel tries to clarify what he regards as a popular confusion of retribution with revenge. "In that condition of society," he writes, "when there are neither magistrates nor laws, punishment always takes the form of revenge; revenge remains defective inasmuch as it is the act of a subjective will." It is understandable that retribution should be objected to on the ground that "it looks like something immoral, *i.e.*, like revenge, and that thus it may pass for something personal. Yet it is not something personal but the concept itself which carries out retribution. 'Vengeance is mine, saith the Lord,' as the Bible says . . . The Eumenides sleep, but crime awakens them, and hence it is the very act of crime itself which vindicates itself."

The apparent contradiction in the identity and difference of retribution and revenge can, in Hegel's opinion, be resolved. On the one hand, it can be said that "the annulment of crime is retribution insofar as retribution in *conception* is an 'injury of the injury.' " On the other hand, it can be said that "the annuling of crime in this sphere where right is immediate is principally revenge, which is just in its content insofar as it is retributive." The demand that this contradiction be resolved "is the demand for justice not as revenge but as punishment."

Hegel's resolution seems to be in terms of a distinction between the particular and the universal. "When the right against crime has the form of revenge, it is only right implicit, not right in the form of right, *i.e.*, no *act* of revenge is justified. Instead of the injured party, the injured *universal* now comes on the scene, and this has its proper actuality in the court of law. It takes over the pursuit and the avenging of crime, and this pursuit consequently ceases to be the subjective and contingent retribution of revenge, and is transformed into the genuine reconciliation of right with itself, *i.e.*, into punishment."

On this conception of punishment, Hegel like Kant decries every utilitarian purpose for punishment. Such misconceptions of punishment arise, he says, from the supposition that both crime and its annulment are "unqualified evils," which makes it seem "quite unreasonable to will an evil merely because 'another evil is there already.' To give punishment this superficial character of an evil is, amongst the various theories of punishment, the fundamental presupposition of those which regard it as a preventive, a deterrent, a threat, as reformative, etc., and what on these theories is supposed to result from punishment is characterized equally superficially as a good. But . . .

the precise point at issue is wrong and the righting of it. If you adopt that superficial attitude toward punishment, you brush aside the objective treatment of the righting of wrong."

The issue would seem to be a conflict between justice and expediency, with the utilitarians identifying retribution with revenge and demanding that punishment serve some good or mitigate some evil. But sometimes the question is whether justice and expediency are compatible.

In the debate on the treatment of the Mitylenians, which Thucydides reports, Cleon calls upon the Athenians to show no mercy to their rebellious subjects. "Their offence," he says, "was not involuntary, but of malice and deliberate," and they deserve to be punished. "If you follow my advice you will do what is just towards the Mitylenians, and at the same time expedient . . . For if they were right in rebelling, you must be wrong in ruling. However, if, right or wrong, you determine to rule, you must carry out your principle and punish the Mitylenians as your interest requires."

Diodotus objects to the policy of putting the Mitylenians to death on the ground that it is not a question of justice but of expediency. "We are not in a court of justice," he says, "but in a political assembly; and the question is not justice, but how to make the Mitylenians useful to Athens . . . I consider it far more useful for the preservation of our empire voluntarily to put up with injustice, than to put to death, however justly, those whom it is our interest to keep alive. As for Cleon's idea that in punishment the claims of justice and expediency can both be satisfied, facts do not confirm the possibility of such a combination."

In the chapter on justice in *Utilitarianism*, J. S. Mill seems to place justice above expediency, but he also seems to reduce retribution to revenge and call it just. "The sentiment of justice," which includes as "one of its elements . . . the desire to punish," Mill identifies with "the natural feeling of retaliation or vengeance." Retribution, or the giving of "evil for evil," he says, "becomes closely connected with the sentiment of justice and is universally included in the idea." The principle of "giving to each what they deserve," he adds, "that is, good for good as well as evil for evil, is not only included within the idea of Justice as we have defined it, but is a proper object of that intensity of sentiment, which places the Just, in human estimation, above the simply Expedient."

Other writers seem to think that the utility of punishment is not incompatible with its retributive justice. The great theologians, for example, considering the difference between the eternal punishment of the damned in hell, and the cleansing punishment of the repentant in purgatory, do not find it impossible for divine justice to include both absolute retribution and punishment which may be remedial as well as retributive. Purely retributive punishment seems justifiable to them, but they do not think that punishment can ever be justified simply by its utility—by the good it achieves— without any reference to the retaliation of evil for evil.

In the context of saying that the institution of slavery among men is a just punishment for Adam's sin, and that "God knows how to award fit punishments for every variety of offence," Augustine observes that "we must not only do harm to no man, but also restrain him from sin or punish his sin, so that either the man himself who is punished may profit by his experience or others be warned of his example." Here there seems to be no thought that retribution excludes a reformative or deterrent use of punishment. Aquinas even more explicitly combines the remedial and the deterrent utility of punishment with the function of punishment to preserve the order of justice by meting out an equitable retribution.

In willing justice, God wills punishment, according to Aquinas. "The order of justice belongs to the order of the universe; and this requires that penalty should be dealt out to sinners." But just retribution is not the only reason for punishment. Sometimes it is "for the good of those who are punished," sometimes "for the amendment of others." These reasons for punishment apply to human as well as to divine law. "When a thief is hanged, this is not for his own amendment, but for the sake of others, who at least may be deterred

from crime through fear of punishment." Punishment is a proper effect of human law, not merely because justice requires it, but because "the law makes use of the fear of punishment in order to ensure obedience."

In discussing the proportion between the severity of the penalty and the gravity of the fault in the punishment of sin under the Mosaic law, Aquinas explains that in addition to the reason of justice (that "a greater sin, other things being equal, deserves a greater punishment"), there is the purpose of reformation ("since men are not easily cured of habitual sin except by severe punishments") and the purpose of prevention ("for men are not easily deterred from such sins unless they be severely punished"). Here three reasons for punishment are stated side by side. But in the opinion of Aquinas retribution is more than the primary, it is the one indispensable reason; for punishment cannot be justified except as doing the work of justice.

THE VIEW OF KANT AND Hegel that retribution or retaliation is *the only basis* for punishment—not merely the primary or the indispensable reason—meets its exact opposite in what appears to be the completely utilitarian theory of punishment to be found in the writings of Plato, Hobbes, Locke, and Rousseau.

In the *Protagoras,* arguing for the proposition that virtue can be taught, Protagoras insists that "no one punishes the evil-doer for the reason that he has done wrong—only the unreasonable fury of a beast acts in that manner. But he who desires to inflict rational punishment does not retaliate for a past wrong which cannot be undone. He has regard to the future, and is desirous that the man who is punished, and he who sees him punished, may be deterred from doing wrong again. He punishes for the sake of prevention, thus clearly implying that virtue is capable of being taught."

Plato himself seems to adopt the opinion of Protagoras. In the *Laws*—wherein he sets forth the provisions of a penal code in a detail equaled, in the tradition of the great books, only by the proposals of Hobbes—Plato says no man is to be punished "because he did wrong, for that which is done can never be undone, but in order that, in the future times, he, and those who see him corrected, may utterly hate injustice, or at any rate abate much of their evil doing." Yet he also goes on to say that the law "should aim at the right measure of punishment, and in all cases at the deserved punishment." This qualification seems, in turn, to be balanced by his remarks on the death penalty which he thinks should be imposed only on the incurable who cannot profit from punishment and whose execution "would be an example to other men not to offend."

The notion of desert in Plato's theory of punishment appeals to justice without implying any separation between retribution and reform. In the *Gorgias,* Socrates says that "to suffer punishment is another name for being justly corrected when you do wrong." A wrongdoer who escapes punishment suffers a greater evil than one who is punished, for he "who is punished and suffers retribution, suffers justly." Thereby justice is restored to his soul. The judge who prescribes just punishments cures the soul, as the physician who prescribes the right remedies cures the body. The criminal who, having been unjust, goes unpunished "has no deliverance from injustice."

The fact that just punishments are deserved does not seem to be the reason why men should be punished. Considering the penalties imposed by gods and men, in the next world or in this, Socrates summarizes his argument by saying that "the proper office of punishment is twofold: he who is rightly punished ought either to become better and profit by it, or he ought to be made an example to his fellows, that they may see what he suffers, and fear and become better. Those who are improved when they are punished by gods and men, are those whose sins are curable; and they are improved, as in this world so also in another, by pain and suffering."

Like Plato, Hobbes places the reason for punishment in the future rather than in the past—in its utility to procure certain effects rather than in its effecting retaliation. He states it as a law of nature that "in revenges (that is, retribution of evil for evil), *men look not at the greatness of the evil past, but the greatness of the good to follow*. Whereby we are forbidden to inflict punishment with any other design than for the correction of the offender, or the direction of others." Anything else he calls "an act of hostility."

In *The Prince,* Machiavelli takes the idea of deterring wrongdoing one step further: "in seizing a state, the usurper ought to examine closely into all those injuries which it is necessary for him to inflict, and to do them all at one stroke so as not to have to repeat them daily . . . He who does otherwise, either from timidity or evil advice, is always compelled to keep the knife in his hand; neither can he rely on his subjects, not can they attach themselves to him."

The chief aim of punishment, in securing the reformation and the deterrence of criminals, Hobbes thinks, is to maintain public peace. "A punishment is an evil inflicted by public authority" on those who have transgressed the law, "to the end that the will of men may thereby the better be disposed to obedience." A law, without a penalty attached, is "not a law, but vain words." It fails to achieve the end of law, which is the same as the end of punishment. The worst offenses—those to be prevented by the most severe penalties—are crimes, not against individuals, but those that "are of most danger to the public."

Locke also derives from natural law the right to punish those who transgress that law, "for restraint and preventing the like offence," to which he adds that "each transgression may be punished to that degree, and with so much severity as to make it an ill bargain to the offender, give him cause to repent, and terrify others from doing the like." This theory of punishment applies not only to man living in a state of nature, but in civil society as well.

Though Rousseau describes the wise statesman as one who knows how, by punishing crimes, to prevent them, he lays greater emphasis on the other motive for punishment— the reformation of the criminal. "There is not a single ill-doer who could not be turned to some good. The State has no right to put to death, even for the sake of making an example, anyone whom it can leave alive without danger." Or, as Fetyukovitch says in his address to the jury in *The Brothers Karamazov:* "The Russian court does not exist for punishment only, but also for the salvation of the criminal. Let other nations think of retribution and the letter of the law, we will cling to the spirit and the meaning—the salvation and the reformation of the lost."

THIS GREAT ISSUE CONCERNING the reason for or purpose of punishment seems to affect most of the other questions which men raise about the penalties to be imposed for wrongdoing—whether the wrong is a sin, a crime, or a vicious act, and whether it is God or the state, nature or the individual himself, who inflicts the pain. The reverse also seems to be true. These other questions raise difficulties or issues which test the conflicting theories that punishment should be a just retaliation *exclusively,* or should be justified *only* by its consequences, or should somehow be a *combination* of awarding just deserts and securing good effects.

For example, the question of how the various modes and measures of punishment should be determined and assigned to diverse acts of wrongdoing does not seem to be answerable in the same way when the principle is simply retribution and when the purpose of punishment is reformation and deterrence. On the principle of retribution the gravity of the offense appears to be the only determinant of the severity of the punishment. The punishment should fit the crime, not the nature of the criminal as someone capable of being benefited by punishment.

Kant and Hegel do not think that the justification of the death penalty, for example, depends on the curability or incurability of the offender. Nor do they think that the taking of the criminal's life should be motivated, as Aquinas and Locke seem to suggest, by the desire to protect society from his future depredations. It is sufficient that he has taken a life, or committed some equally serious injury, which ought to be repaid by a proportionate requital.

"What is involved in the action of the criminal," Hegel writes, "is not only the concept of crime, the rational aspect in crime as such

whether the individual wills it or not, the aspect which the state has to vindicate, but also the abstract rationality of the individual's *volition*. Since that is so," Hegel argues, "punishment is regarded as containing the criminal's right and hence by being punished he is as honored as a rational being. He does not receive this due of honor unless the concept and measure of his punishment are derived from his own act. Still less does he receive it if he is treated either as a harmful animal who has to be made harmless, or with a view to deterring or reforming him."

On these grounds, Hegel criticizes Beccaria's unqualified opposition to the death penalty. In addition, he rejects Beccaria's theory that "it could not be presumed that the readiness of individuals to allow themselves to be executed was included in the social contract." Rousseau takes the diametrically opposite view. He argues for the death penalty on the ground that "we consent to die if we ourselves turn assassins" in order to protect ourselves from falling victims to assassins. In making this consent a part of the social contract, Rousseau holds that "we think only of securing [our own lives], and it is not to be assumed that any of the parties then expects to get hanged."

Hegel disagrees with both Beccaria and Rousseau. According to him, the state is not based upon a social contract; nor does he admit that "its fundamental essence [involves] the unconditional protection and guarantee of the life and property of members of the public as individuals. On the contrary," he holds, "it is that higher entity"—the state—"which even lays claim to this very life and property and demands its sacrifice."

The state, therefore, according to Hegel, cannot be denied the right of inflicting capital punishment. Hegel admits that "Beccaria's requirement that men should give their consent to being punished is right enough," but he adds that "the criminal gives his consent already by his very act. The nature of the crime, no less than the private will of the individual, requires that the injury initiated by the criminal should be anulled. However that may be," he continues, "Beccaria's endeavor to have capital punishment abolished has had beneficial effects." Because of the efforts made by Joseph II and Napoleon to abolish it, "we have begun to see," Hegel thinks, "which crimes deserve the death penalty and which do not. Capital punishment has in consequence become rare, as in fact should be the case with this most extreme punishment."

The attitude toward the death penalty as well as toward all other punishments is different when the *only* purpose of punishment is the welfare of society and the improvement of individuals, whether they are actual or potential offenders. The modes and degrees of punishment must then be determined by considering their effectiveness as means to the ends in view. Montesquieu discusses the penal codes in various systems of law entirely in terms of their success in preventing crime. Though he does not seem to think that punishment can improve the character of the individual, he believes that a certain proportion between the penalty and the offense may tend to reduce the extent and gravity of crimes. "In Russia," he says, "where the punishment of robbery and murder is the same, they always murder."

In general, Montesquieu is opposed to unduly severe punishments, and especially to cruel and unusual punishments, not so much on the grounds of injustice as for the protection of liberty and public morals. Hobbes, Locke, and Rousseau similarly discuss the severity of punishment with reference to its utility, and like Montesquieu, they face the problem that the same measure or degree of punishment may not be equally effective for the purposes of reformation and deterrence. Severe penalties, for example, may have a greater deterrent effect upon potential offenders than milder forms of punishment, but they may also tend to harden criminals instead of reforming them.

There have always been cruel and unusual punishments—in modern times as well as in antiquity and the Middle Ages. As the historian Huizinga points out, "The Middle Ages knew but the two extremes: the fulness of cruel punishment, and mercy." In his Preface to *Saint Joan,* Shaw calls our attention to the fact that "the penalty of hanging, drawing, and quartering, unmentionable in its details, was abolished so recently that there are men living who have been sentenced to it. We are still flogging criminals, and clamoring for more flogging. Not even the most sensationally frightful of these atrocities inflicted on its victim the misery, degradation, and conscious waste and loss of life suffered in our modern prisons, especially the model ones, without, as far as I can see, rousing any more compunction than the burning of heretics did in the Middle Ages. We have not even the excuse of getting some fun out of our prisons as the Middle Ages did out of their stakes and wheels and gibbets."

The conflict of principles in the determination of punishments seems to be even more marked in the case of those who try to combine retribution with utility. If, for example, the death penalty is the just desert for murder, should it be applied on the grounds of retribution, even though a particular murderer can be reformed by milder treatment? If heavy penalties were to prove highly effective as deterrents, should they be applied to minor offenses, which deserve less severe retaliations, in order to reduce the amount of crime?

THERE SEEMS TO BE AGREEMENT for the most part on who shall have the authority to punish and who shall be subject to punishment, in the relation of men to one another, to the state, and to God. Punishment seems to be annexed to law, as indispensable for its enforcement, so that whoever has the authority to set rules of conduct for another also has the authority to impose penalties for their violation. Yet the notion that punishment is a necessary sanction for law—which is apparently shared by those who take the retributive and those who take the utilitarian view of punishment—does not seem to fit both views equally well, at least not to the extent that the end of law and its enforcement is the common good or the public welfare.

Again, it seems to be generally agreed that moral responsibility on the part of offenders is an indispensable condition of just punishment for their misdeeds. Unless the sinful or the criminal act is voluntary, unless it is intentional rather than accidental—or if negligent, capable of being attributed to a willful error of judgment—the act is without fault and the agent without guilt. But although those who make punishment retributive and those who make it reformative or deterrent seem to agree upon responsibility as prerequisite, this principle does not seem to be equally consistent with both theories—at least not to the extent that the exemplary punishment may deter others quite apart from the responsibility of the person punished.

The question of responsibility raises other difficulties, *e.g.*, the metaphysical issue about personal identity, on which Locke takes the stand that unless the human individual is an enduring substance, he cannot deserve subsequent punishment for his prior acts; and the issue of free will and causality, on which Hume's position seems to be that unless human actions are subject to causal necessity, a man cannot be blamed for his acts or "become the object of punishment or vengeance."

Finally, there is the problem of a natural need for punishment and of the penalties which nature itself imposes for wrongdoing to fulfill this need. The familiar statement that virtue is its own reward and vice its own punishment, is sometimes interpreted to mean that virtue and vice are intrinsically good and evil, and sometimes to mean that through their natural consequences they heap benefit or injury on their possessor. This view appears to be Dickens' in *Little Dorrit*. The villain, Rigaud, escapes from prison, which has done nothing to reform his evil ways, while Little Dorrit's sense of duty allows her to live her entire childhood by the side of her father, who is jailed in debtor's prison (as was Dickens' own father).

Augustine, for example, says that by the sins which he committed God did justly punish him, for "every soul that sins brings its own punishment upon itself"; and Kant distinguishes juridical from natural punishment "in which Crime as Vice punishes itself, and does not as such come within the cognizance of the Legislator." The other interpretation seems to be represented by Hobbes's theory that "intemperance is naturally punished with diseases . . . injustice with the violence of enemies . . . cowardice with oppression." In the chain of consequences started by any action, he discerns the pains which are "the natural punishments of those actions that are the beginning of more harm than good."

But according to Freud it is the craving for punishment rather than the punishment which is natural, *i.e.*, psychologically determined. Individuals punish themselves or seek to be punished for what is either real or fancied guilt. "The unconscious need for punishment plays a part in every neurotic disease," Freud writes. "It behaves like a part of the conscience, like the prolongation of conscience into the unconscious; and it must have the same origin as conscience; that is to say, it will correspond to a piece of aggressiveness which has been internalized and taken over by the super-ego. If only the words were less incongruous, we should be justified . . . in calling it 'an unconscious sense of guilt.' "

Whatever its psychological validity, Freud's theory does not resolve the moral issue concerning the justice or utility of punishment. Nor does it eliminate the possibility of other motives for submitting to punishment voluntarily. Socrates in the *Crito* explains that he refuses to escape from the death penalty he thinks he does not deserve, in order to uphold the law which is itself just even though in his own case it has been unjustly applied by men. Henry David Thoreau, Mohandas K. Gandhi, and Martin Luther King, Jr. refuse to obey laws their consciences cannot approve, but do not resist the state's demand that they be punished for the law's infraction. In an unjust society, going to prison is for them the necessary fulfillment of the revolution begun by civil disobedience.

75

Quality

INTRODUCTION

IT is sometimes supposed that the fundamental categories in terms of which men think they are describing reality or their experience merely reflect the conventions of their language. Substance and attribute—and among attributes, quality and quantity—happen to be fundamental categories in western thought, it is held, only because the group of languages which the western cultures use all have a grammatical structure that involves a distinction between noun and adjective and between different kinds of adjectives. It is said, for example, that Aristotle's enumeration of the categories is merely a verbal classification based on Greek grammar. When he says that the basic terms of discourse represent substances, qualities, quantities, relations, and so forth, he is recognizing the grammatical difference between such words as "man" and "white," or between "white" and "six feet tall" and "double." The lineaments of reality, the varieties of being, or the modes of experience are not, it is held, thereby finally described.

In the tradition of the great books, another interpretation generally prevails. Even those who disagree in one way or another about the basic categories do not regard them as conventional or of linguistic origin. Kant, for example, disagrees with Aristotle's listing of the categories. He makes substance a mode of relation rather than coordinate with quality, quantity, and relation. He calls his categories "transcendental" to indicate that they are not drawn from experience and that, as *a priori* forms of thought, they determine the structure of all possible experience. Aristotle, on the other hand, draws his categories from experience. He thinks that they represent fundamental modes of being and that they are, therefore,

the basic concepts in terms of which thought apprehends reality. Despite all these differences, Kant and Aristotle agree that the categories signify real—not verbal—distinctions. Their agreement on this point seems to be shared even by those, like Hume, who question our ability to know whether substances exist; or those, like Berkeley, who question the validity of the distinction between quality and quantity.

In one sense, no one questions the existence of qualities, as they do the existence of substances—the enduring things, material or otherwise, in which qualities are supposed to inhere. Everyone somehow acknowledges the hot and the cold, the light and the dark, the moist and the dry, the hard and the soft. But such acknowledgment does not preclude a number of basic questions about quality on which much disagreement exists.

Are qualities attributes? Do they exist, that is, only as *qualifiers,* only as belonging to something else? Or do they exist independently, in and of themselves? If qualities are attributes, do they belong to things quite apart from our experience of them, or do they belong to things only as experienced and have no separate reality? Do things have in reality certain attributes that cause in us the experience of other traits which we then attribute to the things themselves?

Are all the attributes of things, whether in or apart from experience, to be conceived as qualities, and if so, are there different kinds of qualities? Or is quality only one kind of attribute, and if so, how is quality related to other kinds of attributes? Is quality, for example, distinct from quantity, dependent on quantity, reducible to quantity, affected by quantity?

These questions appear to be related in ways which make the issues they raise dependent on one another. If, in addition, their presuppositions and implications are observed, it will be seen that they cannot be fully discussed without entering into matters considered in other chapters, such as the notions of substance and accident in the chapter on BEING; the theory of experience and the various accounts of sense perception and the objects of sense in the chapters on EXPERIENCE and SENSE; and, of course, some of the principal topics considered in the closely related chapter on QUANTITY.

SPINOZA DISTINGUISHES between substance and mode as that which exists in itself and that which exists in another thing. He lays down as an axiom that "everything which is, is either in itself or in another." Whether or not qualities are modes of substance, it seems to be clear that Spinoza would not call them substances. The notion of qualities existing in themselves, and not as the qualities *of* anything, seems to be self-contradictory. As Descartes points out, to assert "the existence of real accidents," by which he means the existence of qualities or quantities apart from substances, is to deny the distinction between substance and accident. "Substance," he writes, "can never be conceived after the fashion of accidents, nor can it derive its reality from them"; whereas "no reality can be ascribed to [accidents], which is not taken from the idea of substance."

Anyone who acknowledges the distinction between substance and accident also conceives qualities as accidents or attributes, *i.e.,* as existing in the things they qualify. Spinoza, Descartes, Locke, and Aristotle do not conceive substance in the same way, nor do they all use the word "accident" to name the characteristics which inhere in substance. Locke, for example, uses the word "quality" with almost the same generality that Spinoza gives to the word "mode," or Descartes and Aristotle to "accident." And the word "substance" Locke uses in a sense that is nearer to Aristotle's meaning for the word "matter," when, in trying to conceive bare substance as the underlying "I know not what," Locke defines

this substratum as that which supports qualities. Apart from its qualities, substance has no positive characteristics.

Nevertheless, such differences in theory leave untouched the point of agreement that qualities do not float freely—without any support—in either reality or experience. Even Berkeley's denial of matter, or of bodies existing apart from their being perceived, does not turn qualities into substances, for qualities *as perceived* are the qualities of bodies *as perceived,* and both together have their existence *in* the perceiver.

The contrary view—that qualities exist in and of themselves—does not seem to receive clear or explicit expression in the tradition of the great books. It may be implied in the conception of experience which Hume develops more fully in *A Treatise of Human Nature* than in *An Enquiry Concerning Human Understanding.* There it seems to be supposed that each element of experience has the same reality as any other; that each stands by itself without any perceptible dependence upon any other; and that it has no existence beyond its momentary appearance. On this view no enduring substances exist. In addition, it is as appropriate to call the elements of experience "qualities" as it is to call them anything else. Experience can be described as nothing but qualities and relations—or as qualities related by succession and contiguity.

The notion that experience is a continual flux in which nothing has a continuing identity from moment to moment, seems to be basic to any theory which denies substances and affirms the independent reality of qualities. The theory of qualities which Plato attributes to Heracleitus or his followers illustrates this. "Their first principle," Socrates tells Theaetetus, "is that all is motion, and upon this all the affections of which we were just now speaking are supposed to depend; there is nothing but motion, which has two forms, one active and the other passive, both in endless number; and out of the union and friction of them is generated a progeny endless in number, having two forms, sense and the object of sense."

For example, "when the eye and the appropriate object meet together and give birth to whiteness and the sensation connatural with it . . . then, while the sight is flowing from the eye, whiteness proceeds from the object which combines in producing the color . . . This is true of all sensible objects, hard, warm, and the like, which are similarly to be regarded not as having any absolute existence, but as being all of them generated by motion in their intercourse with one another . . . for the agent has no existence until united with the patient, and the patient has no existence until united with the agent . . . And from all these considerations," Socrates says, "there arises a general reflection that there is no self-existent thing, but everything is becoming and in relation."

Socrates explains that, for those who assert a universal flux, qualities are not only the products of motion, but also are themselves in motion—"not even white continues to flow white, and whiteness itself is a flux or change which is passing into another color." There is no need to refute this doctrine, Socrates thinks, since it refutes itself by its unintelligibility or, worse, its inability to say anything definite in consequence of denying that words can have a constant meaning from moment to moment.

Aristotle concurs in this attitude toward "the most extreme view of the professed Heracliteans," but goes on to remark that "not even at different times does one sense disagree about the quality, but only about that to which the quality belongs. I mean, for instance, that the same wine might seem, if either it or one's body changed, at one time sweet and at another time not sweet; but at least the sweet, such as it is when it exists, has never yet changed." The sweet thing may become sour, either in itself or to us, but sweetness itself never becomes sourness.

THAT QUALITIES DO NOT change into one another, whereas substances undergoing alteration change from one quality to another, seems to Aristotle to distinguish quality from substance. "The most distinctive mark of substance," he writes, "appears to be that, while remaining numerically one and the same, it is capable of having contrary qualities . . . Thus, one and the same color cannot be white and

black . . . But the same individual person is at one time white, at another black, at one time warm, at another cold, at one time good, at another bad." The qualities do not change, but the substance in changing, passes from one quality to its contrary. (The difference between change of quality, or alteration, and the other types of change which substances can undergo, is discussed in the chapter on CHANGE.)

Aristotle suggests another mark of distinction between substance and quality. One substance, he says, never stands to another as its contrary, in the way in which qualities are contrary to one another, like hot and cold, white and black, good and bad. A quality may have a correlative as well as a contrary, e.g., if knowledge is a quality of mind, the object known is its correlative, whereas ignorance of the object is the contrary of knowledge. In some cases, the contrary qualities may be the extremes or limits of a continuous series of intermediates, e.g., white and black with all the intermediate grays. In some cases, as with knowledge and ignorance, the contrary qualities have no intermediates. (Contrariety and correlation, most frequently exemplified by qualities, are considered in the chapter on OPPOSITION.)

Still another mark of distinction between substance and quality, according to Aristotle, is that qualities *do* and substances *do not* admit of variation in degree. "One man cannot be more man than another," he writes, "as that which is white may be more or less white than some other white object . . . The same quality, moreover, is said to subsist in a thing in varying degrees at different times. A white body is said to be whiter at one time than it was before, or a warm body is said to be warmer or less warm than at some other time."

This observation raises a number of questions. Does variation in the degree of a quality from time to time imply that qualities themselves undergo change, just as substances undergo change in quality? Do they remain one and the same in kind while varying in degree? Is this change which qualities undergo as they increase or decrease in intensity, a change in quantity? Furthermore, does the fact that something white can become more or less white, mean that a quality can have a certain quantity even as a body can? Aquinas suggests an answer by distinguishing between what he calls the "dimensive quantity" of bodies and the "virtual quantity" of qualities. Virtual quantity is the degree or intensity which nonquantitative attributes may possess—such personal qualities as virtues and habits, or such corporeal qualities as colors and textures.

But this still seems to leave a very difficult question to be answered. How can qualities have the attribute of quantity without becoming substances? On the principle which both Aristotle and Aquinas accept—that accidents exist only in substances—how can one kind of accident (quantity) exist in another (quality)? The view which William James holds, namely, that variation in intensity creates differences in color as much as variation in hue, would solve the problem, or rather it would dismiss the problem as not genuine by denying Aristotle's thesis that a color can remain the same while varying in degree.

However handled, the problem is not peculiar to qualities. Actions and passions, Aristotle points out, also vary in degree. Nor are qualities distinguished from everything else in the world by having contraries. Correlatives can also have contraries, as can actions and passions. Furthermore, not all qualities have contraries. Not all admit of variation in degree. Shape, like triangular or square, which Aristotle regards as a kind of quality, cannot vary in this way. The square thing cannot become more or less square. In view of all this, Aristotle concludes that there is one characteristic alone which differentiates quality not only from substance, but also from everything else. Quality is the basis for saying that things are like or unlike, similar or dissimilar, as quantity is the basis for saying that things are equal or unequal.

Other contrasts between quality and quantity, especially those bearing on the reduction of quality to quantity, are discussed in the chapter on QUANTITY. Here it may be illuminating to apply the foregoing distinction between quality and quantity to shapes or figures. Shape or figure is a curious mixture of quality and quantity. It is a quantified quality or a qualified quantity or, as Aquinas says, "a quality about quantity, since the nature of shape consists in fixing the bounds of magnitude." This seems to be evident in the fact that shapes, like quantities, do not admit of variation in degree. But it may also be seen in the fact that Euclid deals quite separately with problems concerning the *equality* of triangles and problems concerning their *similarity*.

EXCEPT FOR THE QUESTION of whether qualities subsist by themselves or are the attributes of substances, most of the problems of quality seem to concern its distinction from or relation to quantity. As we have seen, the question of the degree or amount of a quality involves the notion of quantity. Even more explicitly a problem of how qualities and quantities are related, is the question of the order of these two attributes. Can it be said that quantities are the more fundamental attributes of things and that they somehow precede or underlie qualities? Is it the reverse? Or are qualities prior in certain respects and quantities in other respects?

Aristotle's theory of the elements seems to give absolute primacy to quality in the realm of material things. The four elements of matter are characterized by combinations of two pairs of contrary qualities, the hot and the cold, the dry and the moist. On the other hand, the atomic theory of Lucretius appears to make quantities, such as size and weight, the primary properties of matter. Newton's enumeration of what he calls "the universal qualities of all bodies whatsoever," including, of course, their "least particles," lists "extension, hardness, impenetrability, mobility, and inertia." As indicated in the chapter on QUANTITY, the very reason Newton gives for calling these qualities "universal" would seem to justify calling them "quantities" rather than qualities. In any case, Newton's view, like that of the ancient atomists, seems to be opposed to the theory of the *elementary* and *contrary* qualities.

But Aristotle himself also appears to hold a view which makes quantity prior to quality. Considering the way in which the quality *white* is in a body, he says that it is in the body in virtue of the body's extended surface. If surface or extension is interpreted as a physical quantity, then it would seem to follow that this quantity underlies a body's possession of visible and perhaps other qualities. Aquinas, for example, says that "quantity is the proximate subject of the qualities that cause alteration, as surface is of color," and, again, that "quantity is in substance before sensible qualities are."

This last statement can be interpreted to mean that quantity is universally prior to quality among the attributes of substance. Or it can be understood to mean that quantity is prior only to *sensible* qualities and then only among the physical attributes of bodies. Which interpretation is chosen depends in part on whether *all* qualities are sensible.

It would seem that all qualities are not sensible, according to Aristotle and Aquinas, and therefore quantity is not prior to every kind of quality among the accidents of substance. Natural qualities, Aquinas writes, "may be in the intellectual part or in the body and its powers." Certainly the qualities inherent in the intellectual part of man's nature are not sensible; nor are the first two of the four species of quality which both Aristotle and Aquinas enumerate.

In their enumeration, human qualities—the habits or dispositions of a man, such as knowledge and virtue, or beauty and health—are the first sort. The powers or inborn capacities whereby men and other animals act to develop their natures are a second type of quality; *e.g.,* the power of sensitivity in animals, the power of rationality in men, are qualities proper to these species and are, therefore, sometimes called "properties." This second type of quality does not seem to be restricted to living things. Inanimate bodies also have, among their properties, certain fundamental powers of action or reaction. The third and fourth types of quality differ from the first two in that both are sensible, *i.e.,* capable of affecting the senses directly and, therefore, sometimes called "affective qualities." Of these, the third type—shape or figure—has already been discussed. The fourth type—colors, sounds, textures, odors, tastes, and such thermal qualities as hot and cold—are, more than shape or figure, regarded as the principal affective or sensible qualities.

The fact that Aristotle regards certain qualities, such as hot and cold, or hard and soft, as being dispositions or powers as well as being affective qualities, need not invalidate his fourfold classification. His classification of the same attribute under two distinct species of quality seems to imply that it can be considered from two points of view. The elementary qualities, for example, are affective or sensible qualities but they are also the active qualities or powers—the properties—of the elements.

In view of this classification of qualities, it does not seem to be the case that quantities are prior to *all* the qualitative attributes of substance. On the conception of living things as composite of soul and body, the qualities which are vital powers are usually regarded as properties which the thing has in virtue of having a soul. They are certainly not founded upon the quantitative attributes of the organism's body. The moral and spiritual qualities of men seem to afford another example of qualities either prior to, or at least independent of, quantities. Even in the case of inanimate bodies, it may be that certain fundamental properties or powers are essentially qualitative rather than quantitative. The proposition that in substances, quantities are prior to qualities—or that qualities inhere in substances in virtue of their quantities—may apply only to sensible qualities, as, for example, colors in relation to surfaces.

ONE OF THE GREAT ISSUES in the tradition of western thought concerns our perception or knowledge of qualities. If certain characteristics which are not directly sensible are to be called "qualities," then the problem of how we know such qualities does not differ from the problem of how we know anything else that cannot be apprehended by our senses. We may, for example, be able to infer such qualities as habits or powers from the sensible evidences of a thing's behavior, even as in turn we infer the thing's nature or essence from its proper qualities or properties. With regard to sensible qualities, the problem does not seem to be *how* we know them—for the fact that they are sensible means that they are knowable by the senses. The question is rather one of the mode of existence—the objectivity or subjectivity—of the qualities sensed.

Descartes and Locke, as well as Galileo, make much of the distinction between primary and secondary qualities, a distinction that Whitehead questions in considering the relation of substances to their qualities. Locke's treatment of this matter is preceded by his distinction between the qualities of things and the ideas in our minds. "A snow-ball," he writes, has "the power to produce in us the idea of white, cold, and round. The powers to produce those ideas in us, as they are in the snow-ball, I call qualities; and as they are sensations or perceptions in our understandings, I call them ideas; which ideas, if I speak of them sometimes as in the things themselves, I would be understood to mean those qualities in the objects which produce them in us."

The primary qualities of bodies are those which are utterly inseparable from body—such as "sense constantly finds in every particle of matter which has bulk enough to be perceived, and the mind finds inseparable from every particle of matter, though less than to make itself singly perceived by our senses." Locke's enumeration of these "original or primary qualities of body, which we may observe to produce simple ideas in us, *viz.*, solidity, extension, figure, motion or rest, and number," closely resembles Newton's list of the universal qualities of perceptible bodies and of their "least particles" or atoms.

In contrast, the secondary qualities, such as colors, sounds, tastes, etc., are "nothing in the objects themselves, but powers to produce various sensations in us by their primary qualities, *i.e.*, by the bulk, figure, texture, and motion of their insensible parts . . . From whence," Locke declares, "I think it is easy to draw this observation, that the ideas of primary qualities of bodies, are resemblances of them, and their patterns do really exist in the bodies themselves, but the ideas produced in us by these secondary qualities, have no resemblance of them at all. There is nothing like our ideas existing in the bodies themselves. They are in the bodies we denominate from them, only a

power to produce those sensations in us: what is sweet, blue, or warm, in idea, is but the certain bulk, figure and motion of the insensible parts in the bodies which we call so."

Locke thinks the sensation of pain confirms this insight. As the piece of steel which by its corporeal properties has the power to produce pain in us, does not itself have the quality of pain, so it does not have anything corresponding to the ideas of blueness or coldness which it produces in us, except the power to produce these ideas through the action of its primary qualities on our senses. Yet Locke maintains that all our simple ideas of quality—not only of primary, but also of secondary qualities—"agree with the reality of things." By *agreement* he does not mean *resemblance* in the sense of copying; and therefore he thinks he can, without inconsistency, deny any *resemblance* between sensations of color or taste and the secondary qualities of bodies, while saying that "if sugar produces in us the ideas we call whiteness and sweetness, we are sure there is a power in sugar to produce those ideas in our minds, or else they could not have been produced by it."

Locke's point, however, is sometimes given exactly the opposite implication. Earlier thinkers who do not speak of primary and secondary qualities attribute to bodies only the characteristics which Locke calls primary, and give what he calls secondary qualities no reality at all, that is, no existence outside the mind. The secondary qualities are not qualities of things, but of sensations or images. Descartes, for example, says that nothing belongs "to the nature or essence of body except . . . length, breadth and depth, admitting of various shapes and various motions . . . On the other hand, colors, odors, savours, and the rest of such things are merely sensations existing in my thought, and differing no less from bodies than pain differs from the shape and motion of the instrument which inflicts it."

Hobbes similarly regards the various sensible qualities as feelings in us—the seemings or fancies of sense. All these "qualities called sensible are in the object that causes them, nothing but so many several motions of the matter . . . The object is one thing, the fancy is another." One type of "absurd assertion," in the opinion of Hobbes, consists in giving "the names of the accidents of bodies without us, to the accidents of our own bodies, as they do that say, *the color is in the body, the sound is in the air,* etc."

The attributes or accidents which Descartes and Hobbes assign to bodies seem to be quantities rather than qualities. Accordingly, whereas Locke attributes both primary and secondary *qualities* to bodies, Hobbes and Descartes seem to be saying that bodies differ from one another only quantitatively, and that qualities or qualitative differences occur only in the realm of sense or thought. Expounding the atomism of Democritus and Epicurus, Lucretius appears to make precisely this point when he says that the first-beginnings or atoms are characterized only by size, weight, shape, and motion. "Basic elements," he writes, "simply do not have color." They are bereft not only of color; they are also "devoid of warmth, of heat, of cold; / They are soundless, sapless; as they move along / They leave no trail of scent." These qualities, caused by the blows of the atoms upon the sense organs of animals, are the qualities of sensations, not of things.

THE CRITICISM OF THIS THEORY—whether in the formulation of Locke or in that of Descartes, Hobbes, and Lucretius—seems itself to take two forms. Aristotle, for example, criticizes Democritus and the atomists for treating perceptible qualities differently from perceptible quantities. According to his own theory of the objects of sense, some, like colors, sounds, odors, flavors—which Locke calls "secondary qualities" and the others simply "qualities"—are the proper objects of the special senses, such as sight, hearing, smell, taste. In contrast to these "proper sensibles," each exclusively perceived by one and only one sense, there are the "common sensibles," such as size and shape, number, movement and rest, which can be perceived commonly by several senses, *e.g.,* shape is visible and tangible, motion is visible and audible. Such sensible attributes of body, which Locke calls "primary qualities," Aristotle, no less than Hobbes or Lucretius, regards as quantities, not

qualities. Reporting his view, Aquinas writes that "the common sensibles are all reducible to quantity."

Aristotle's critical point seems to be that the atomists "reduce the proper to the common sensibles, as Democritus does with white and black; for he asserts that the latter is a mode of the rough and the former a mode of the smooth, while he reduces savours to the atomic figures." The atomists sometimes make the opposite error of representing "all objects of sense as objects of touch." But in either case they have no ground, in Aristotle's opinion, for giving to certain sensible attributes— whether these be tangible qualities or the commonly sensible quantities—an objective reality they deny to other sensible traits, like colors, sounds, and odors.

Aristotle's theory of sensation and the sensible is discussed more fully in the chapter on SENSE. According to it, the qualities, no less than the quantities, perceptible by sense have real or actual existence as the attributes of bodies. On this score Aristotle does not differentiate between qualities (the proper sensibles) and quantities (the common sensibles). Just as a body actually has the shape we perceive it to have, so it actually has the color we perceive it to have, on the supposition, of course, that our perception is accurate in both cases. If the senses are fallible at all, we are less prone to make errors, Aristotle thinks, in the field of the proper than of the common sensibles, *e.g.,* the stick in water which looks bent to the eye feels straight to the hand.

PRECISELY THE OPPOSITE direction seems to be taken by Berkeley and Hume. Where Aristotle criticizes the atomists for treating quantities (or common sensibles) as objective, and qualities (or proper sensibles) as subjective, Berkeley criticizes Locke for treating primary and secondary qualities differently. Where Aristotle's own theory assigns the same reality to all objects of sense, granting them an actuality apart from perception, Berkeley makes the actuality of the primary as well as the secondary qualities dependent upon their being perceived.

"Some there are," writes Berkeley, "who

make a distinction betwixt *primary* and *secondary* qualities. By the former they mean extension, figure, motion, rest, solidity or impenetrability and number; by the latter they denote all other sensible qualities, as colors, sounds, tastes and so forth. The ideas we have of these they acknowledge not to be the resemblances of anything existing without the mind or unperceived, but they will have our ideas of the primary qualities to be patterns or images of things which exist without the mind, in an unthinking substance which they call Matter."

Berkeley then argues that the so-called primary qualities are incapable of being separated, in reality or thought, from the secondary qualities, and that, therefore, the one like the other exists only in the mind. "In short, let anyone consider those arguments which are thought manifestly to prove that colors and tastes exist only in the mind, and he shall find they may with equal force be brought to prove the same thing of extension, figure, and motion." His own arguments, he thinks, "plainly show it to be impossible that any color or extension at all, or other sensible quality whatsoever, should exist in any unthinking subject without the mind, or in truth, that there should be any such thing as an outward object."

Hume professes to adopt Berkeley's reasoning. "It is universally allowed by modern enquirers," he writes, "that all the sensible qualities of objects, such as hard, soft, hot, cold, white, black, etc., are merely secondary, and exist not in the objects themselves, but are perceptions of the mind, without any external archetype or model which they represent. If this be allowed, with regard to secondary qualities, it must also follow with regard to the supposed primary qualities of extension and solidity . . . The idea of extension is entirely acquired from the senses of sight and feeling; and if all the qualities, perceived by the senses, be in the mind, not in the object, the same conclusion must reach the idea of extension . . . Nothing can save us from this conclusion, but the asserting that the ideas of those primary qualities are attained by *Abstraction,* an opinion, which, if we examine it accurately, we shall find to be unintelligible, and even absurd."

One fundamental point about sensible qualities may, however, remain unaffected by this long and many-sided controversy. No one denies that sensible qualities are the elements of human experience. That they are "the original, innate, or *a priori* properties of our subjective nature," James declares, must be allowed by "all schools (however they otherwise differ) . . . This is so on either of the two hypotheses we may make concerning the relation of the feelings to the realities at whose touch they become alive."

76

Quantity

INTRODUCTION

As indicated in the chapter on QUALITY, the traditional consideration of that fundamental notion involves questions concerning the relation of quality and quantity and the priority of one or the other in the nature of things. According to one theory of the elements, difference in quality rather than in quantity seems to be the defining characteristic. Certain kinds of qualities, it is thought, inhere in substances directly and without being based upon their quantitative aspects. But it is seldom if ever suggested that quality takes universal precedence over quantity.

In the tradition of western thought, the opposite view—that quantities are primary—seems to occur with some frequency, at least so far as the realm of material things is concerned. It is held that bodies have only quantitative attributes. Such sensible qualities as colors, odors, tastes, textures are thought to have no reality apart from experience; or, as it is sometimes put, red and blue, hot and cold, sweet and sour are the qualities of sensations, not of things.

Those who think that bodies can exist without being perceived, also tend to think that bodies can exist totally bereft of qualities, but never without the dimensions of quantity. The notions of matter and quantity seem to be inseparably associated. For matter to exist without existing in some quantity seems to be as inconceivable as for experience to exist without qualitative diversity. "As if there could be matter," says Hobbes, "that had not some determined quantity, when quantity is nothing else but determination of matter; that is to say, of body, by which we say that one body is greater or less than another by thus or thus much."

The use of the word "quality" where quantity appears to be meant only slightly obscures this point. Newton refers to "extension, hardness, impenetrability, mobility, and inertia" as "the qualities of bodies" which "are to be esteemed the universal qualities of all bodies whatsoever." Following him, Locke calls our simple ideas of "solidity, extension, figure, motion or rest, and number" ideas of "the original or primary qualities of bodies," and says that even if bodies are divided "till their parts become insensible, they must retain still each of them all those qualities. For division . . . can never take away either solidity, extension, figure, or mobility from any body, but only makes two or more distinct separate masses of matter, of that which was one before."

Though Locke uses the word "quality" for those attributes which belong to bodies even when they are not sensed or are not even sensible, he also appears to recognize that number, extension, and figure are, as the traditional objects of the mathematical sciences, traditionally regarded as quantities rather than qualities. "It has been generally taken for granted," he writes, "that mathematics alone are capable of demonstrative certainty; but to have such an agreement or disagreement as may intuitively be perceived, being, as I imagine, not the privilege of the ideas of number, extension, and figure alone, it may possibly be the want of due method and application in us . . . that demonstration has been thought to have so little to do in other parts of knowledge." Yet, he adds, "in other simple ideas, whose modes and differences are made and counted by degrees, and not quantity, we have not so nice and accurate a distinction of their differences

696

as to perceive, or find ways to measure, their just equality."

Newton also gives some indication that his "universal qualities" are quantities. He restricts them to attributes "which admit neither intensification nor remission of degrees." One difference between quantity and quality, according to an ancient opinion, is that qualities are subject to variation in degree, quantities not. One thing may be white or hot to a greater or lesser degree than another, Aristotle observes, but "one thing cannot be two cubits long in a greater degree than another. Similarly with regard to number: what is 'three' is not more truly three than what is 'five' is five . . . Nor is there any other kind of quantity, of all that have been mentioned, with regard to which variation in degree can be predicated."

GRANTED THAT WHAT Newton and Locke call "qualities" are not qualities, except in the sense in which the word "quality" means attribute, difficult questions remain concerning their enumeration of the *universal* or *primary* attributes of bodies. Do extension, hardness, impenetrability, motion and rest, figure and number constitute an exhaustive enumeration? Are these *all* the corporeal quantities, or only the basic ones from which others can be derived? Are they all of the same kind and, among them, are some more fundamental than others?

Descartes, for example, seems to make extension the one primary attribute of bodies. "I observed," he writes, "that nothing at all belonged to the nature or essence of bodies, except that it was a thing with length, breadth, and depth, admitting of various shapes and various motions. I found also that its shape and motions were only modes, which no power could make to exist apart from it . . . Finally, I saw that gravity, hardness, the power of heating, of attracting, and of purging, and all other qualities which we experience in bodies, consisted solely in motion or its absence, and in the configuration and situation of their parts."

With motion and figure modes of extension, and all the other properties of bodies the result of their motions or configurations, the three dimensions of extension (or spatial magnitude) become almost identical with body itself. Considering the statement *body possesses extension,* Descartes points out that, though "the meaning of *extension* is not identical with that of *body,* yet we do not construct two distinct ideas in our imagination, one of body, the other of extension, but merely a single image of extended body; and from the point of view of the thing it is exactly as if I had said: *body is extended,* or better, *the extended is extended.*"

But, Descartes adds, when we consider the expression *extension is not body,* "the meaning of the term *extension* becomes otherwise than as above. When we give it this meaning there is no special idea corresponding to it in the imagination." It becomes a purely abstract entity, which may properly be the object of the geometer's consideration; but then it should be treated as an abstraction and not as if it had independent reality.

Aquinas also distinguishes between physical and mathematical quantities, or the quantities which inhere in bodies and the quantities abstracted therefrom. "Quantities, such as number, dimension, and figure, which are the terminations of quantity, can be considered apart from sensible qualities, and this is to abstract them from sensible matter. But they cannot be considered without understanding the substance which is subject to quantity"— that is, corporeal or material substance. Like a body, a mathematical solid has three dimensions, but, as Aquinas points out, lacking matter, this three-dimensional object does not occupy space or fill a place. The three spatial dimensions are not for him, however, the only primary quantities of either the physical or the mathematical body. Number and figure are as fundamental.

Still another enumeration of corporeal quantities is given by Lucretius in his description of the properties of atoms. According to him, atoms vary in size, weight, and shape. Each of these attributes is a distinct quantity, not reducible to the others. In addition, atoms have the property which Newton calls "impenetrability" and Locke "solidity." But whereas atoms may be unequal in size and weight, and different in shape or configuration, they are all equal in their solidity, being absolutely indivisible through lack of void or pores.

THE DISTINCTION BETWEEN mathematical and physical quantity and the enumeration or ordering of diverse quantities seems to require the consideration of two prior questions. What is the nature of quantity? What are the kinds or modes of quantity?

Terms like quantity and quality do not appear to be susceptible of definition. Quantity is, perhaps, *the* fundamental notion in the mathematical sciences, yet neither it nor such terms as magnitude, figure, and number are defined in the great books of geometry or arithmetic. In Aristotle's theory of the categories as the highest genera, such terms as substance, quantity, quality, and relation are strictly indefinable, if to define a term is to give its genus and differentia.

With quite a different theory of the categories, Kant also treats them as indefinable. As indicated in the chapter on QUALITY, they are for him the transcendental concepts of the understanding. He uses such terms as quantity, quality, and relation, with modality as a coordinate fourth, to represent the four major groupings of the categories. In his table of the categories, Kant's treatment of quantity, under which he lists the concepts of unity, plurality, and totality, parallels the treatment of quantity in his table of judgments, according to which judgments are classified as universal, particular, and singular. All these considerations of quantity belong to what Kant calls his "transcendental logic." So far as Kant considers quantity in its mathematical or physical (rather than logical) significance, he discusses it in connection with the transcendental forms of space and time which provide, according to him, the *a priori* foundations of geometry and arithmetic—the sciences of magnitude and number. But in none of these connections are quantity and its principal modes, magnitude and number, defined.

Though indefinable, quantity can, according to Aristotle, be characterized by certain distinctive marks. As we have already observed, where qualities admit of variation in degree, quantities do not. With few exceptions, each quality has a contrary, whereas definite quantities such as an extent or a number are not opposed by contrary quantities. Aristotle considers the possibility that such apparently quantitative terms as 'large' and 'small' may also appear to be contrary to one another, as hot is to cold, or white is to black. But, he argues, these terms represent quantities only relatively, not absolutely. When things are compared with respect to size, one may be judged to be both larger and smaller than others, but the sizes of each of two things unequal in size are not contrary to one another.

These two characteristics (lack of contrariety and of variation in degree) do not, however, satisfy Aristotle's search for a distinctive mark of quantity. They apply to substances, such as tree or man, as well as to figures and numbers. This fact could have some bearing on the issue whether the objects of mathematics have a separate existence comparable to that of substances, but in Aristotle's view at least, quantities are not substances. Physical quantities are the attributes of bodies; the objects of mathematics consist of quantities abstracted from sensible matter.

Conceiving quantity as one of the attributes of substance, Aristotle says that "the most distinctive mark of quantity is equality and inequality." Only when things are compared quantitatively can they be said to be equal or unequal; and, conversely, in whatever respect things are said to be equal or unequal, in that respect they are determined in quantity.

"How far is it true," Plotinus asks, "that equality and inequality are characteristic of quantity?" It is significant, he thinks, that triangles and other figures are said to be similar as well as equal. "It may, of course, be the case that the term 'similarity' has a different sense here from that understood in reference to quality"; or another alternative, Plotinus adds, may be that "similarity is predicable of quantity only insofar as quantity possesses [qualitative] differences." In any case, comparison, whether in terms of equality or likeness, seems to generate the relationships fundamental to the mathematical treatment of quantities.

Euclid does not define magnitude in itself,

but only the relation of magnitudes to one another. The first four definitions in the fifth book of his *Elements* illustrate this. "1. A magnitude is a *part* of a magnitude, the less of the greater, when it measures the greater. 2. The greater is a *multiple* of the less when it is measured by the less. 3. A *ratio* is a sort of relation in respect of size between two magnitudes of the same kind. 4. Magnitudes are said to *have a ratio* to one another, which are capable, when multiplied, of exceeding one another."

Archimedes also states his understanding of the distinction between kinds of magnitudes—without defining these kinds—by reference to their comparability. Assuming that any given magnitude can, by being multiplied, exceed any other magnitude of the same kind, he is able to know that magnitudes are of the same kind if, by being multiplied, they can exceed one another. It follows that an indivisible point and a finite or divisible magnitude, such as a line, are not of the same kind, for they cannot have a ratio to one another. For the same reason, the length of a line, the area of a plane, and the volume of a solid are not magnitudes of the same kind. Since they bear no ratio to one another, they are quantitatively incomparable.

THE EMPHASIS UPON ratios has some significance for a controversial point in the definition of the subject matter of mathematics. In the tradition of the great books, mathematicians and philosophers seem to agree that arithmetic and geometry have as their objects the two principal species of quantity—number and magnitude. This is the opinion of Euclid, Nicomachus, Descartes, and Galileo; it is the opinion of Plato, Aristotle, Aquinas, Francis Bacon, Hume, and Kant. But writers like Russell and Whitehead, who reflect developments in mathematics since the 19th century, reject the traditional opinion as unduly narrowing the scope of mathematics.

To give adequate expression to the universality of mathematics, they sometimes propose that it should be conceived as the science not merely of quantity, but of relations and order. In view of the fact that the great books of mathematics deal with quantities largely in terms of their relationship or order to one another, the broader conception seems to fit the older tradition as well as more recent developments. Whether there is a genuine issue here concerning the definition of mathematical subject matter may depend, therefore, on whether the fundamental terms which generate the systems of relationship and order are or are not essentially quantitative. To this question the traditional answer seems to be that the mathematician studies not relations of any sort, but the relation of quantities.

The problem of the kinds of quantity seems to appeal for solution to the principle of commensurability. For example, Galileo's observation that finite and infinite quantities cannot be compared in any way, implies their utter diversity. But he goes further and says that "the attributes 'larger,' 'smaller,' and 'equal' have no place either in comparing infinite quantities with each other or in comparing infinite with finite quantities." If the notion of quantity entails the possibility of equality or inequality between two quantities *of the same kind,* then either infinite quantities are not quantities, or each infinite quantity belongs to a kind of its own.

The principle of incommensurability seems to be applied by mathematicians to distinguish quantities which are different species of the same generic kind. For example, the one-dimensional, two-dimensional, and three-dimensional quantities of a line, a plane, and a solid, are incommensurable *magnitudes*. The number of days in a year and the number of years in infinite or endless time are incommensurable *multitudes*.

The distinction between magnitude and multitude (or number) as two modes of quantity appears to be based upon another principle, that of continuity and discontinuity. Yet the question can be raised whether magnitudes are commensurable with numbers, at least to the extent of being measured by numbers. It may be necessary, however, to postpone answering it until we have examined the fundamental difference between magnitude and multitude as generic kinds of quantity.

What if magnitude and multitude, or continuous and discontinuous quantity, do not divide quantity into its ultimate kinds? Aquinas, for example, proposes that the two basic kinds are dimensive and virtual quantity. "There is quantity of *bulk* or dimensive quantity," he writes, "which is to be found only in corporeal things, and has, therefore, no place in God. There is also quantity of *virtue*, which is measured according to the perfection of some nature or form." It is in the latter sense, according to Aquinas, that Augustine writes: "In things which are great, but not in bulk, to be greater is to be better."

Just as dimensive quantities can be incommensurable with one another, so with respect to virtual quantities, God's infinite perfection makes him incommensurable with finite creatures. But a dimensive quantity cannot be either commensurable or incommensurable with a virtual quantity. The standard of measurement by which dimensive quantities are compared, and the standard by which virtual quantities are ordered, represent utterly diverse principles of commensurability. Euclid's statement that "those magnitudes are said to be commensurable which are measured by the same measure, and those incommensurable which cannot have a common measure," cannot be extended to cover dimensive and virtual quantities, for the very meaning of "measure" changes when we turn from the dimensions of a body to the perfections of a being.

The distinction which Aquinas makes between dimensive and virtual magnitudes has its parallel in the distinction he makes between two kinds of number, for both depend on the difference between *material* and *formal* quantity. "Division is twofold," he writes. "One is material, and is division of the continuous; from this results number, which is a species of quantity. Number in this sense is found only in material things which have quantity. The other kind of division is formal, and is effected by opposite or diverse forms; and this kind of division results in a multitude, which does not belong to a genus, but is transcendental in the sense in which being is divided by one and many. Only this kind of multitude is found in immaterial things." According to the example suggested in the context, such is the multitude which is the number of persons in the Trinity.

THE MATERIAL quantities of physics and mathematics seem to fall under the two main heads of magnitude and multitude. "Quantity is either discrete or continuous," writes Aristotle. "Instances of discrete quantities are number and speech; of continuous, lines, surfaces, solids, and, besides these, time and place." Nicomachus explains the two kinds of quantity by examples. "The unified and continuous," he says, is exemplified by "an animal, the universe, a tree, and the like, which are properly and peculiarly called 'magnitudes' "; to illustrate the discontinuous, he points to "heaps of things, which are called 'multitudes,' a flock, for instance, a people, a chorus, and the like."

The principle of this distinction appears to be the possession or lack of a common boundary. To take Aristotle's example of speech as a quantity, the letters of a written word or the syllables of vocal utterance comprise a multitude rather than a continuum or magnitude "because there is no common boundary at which the syllables join, each being separate and distinct from the rest." The continuity of magnitudes can be readily seen, according to Aristotle, in the possibility of finding a common boundary at which the parts of a line join or make contact. "In the case of a line," he says, "this common boundary is the point; in the case of a plane, it is the line ... Similarly, you can find a common boundary in the case of the parts of a solid, namely, either a line or a plane."

Accepting the principle of the distinction, Plotinus insists that "number and magnitude are to be regarded as the only true quantities." All others, like space and time, or motion, are quantities only in a relative sense, that is, insofar as they can be measured by number or involve magnitude. Galileo raises another sort of difficulty. The Aristotelian conception of magnitudes as continuous quantities implies their infinite divisibility. This means, in his terms, that "every magnitude is divisible into magnitudes" and that "it is impossible for anything continuous to be composed of indivisible parts." Galileo acknowledges the objections to "building up continuous quantities out of indivisible quantities" on the ground that "the addition of one indivisible to another cannot produce a divisible, for if this were so it would render the indivisible divisible." Suppose a line to comprise an odd number of indivisible points. Since such a line can, in principle, be cut into two equal parts, we are required to do the impossible, namely, "to cut the indivisible which lies exactly in the middle of the line."

To this and other objections which seem to him of the same type, Galileo replies that "a divisible magnitude cannot be constructed out of two or ten or a hundred or a thousand indivisibles, but requires an infinite number of them ... I am willing," he says, "to grant to the Peripatetics the truth of their opinion that a continuous quantity is divisible only into parts which are still further divisible, so that however far the division and subdivision be continued, no end will be reached; but I am not so certain that they will concede to me that none of these divisions of theirs can be a final one, as is surely the fact, because there always remains 'another'; the final and ultimate division is rather one which resolves a continuous quantity into an infinite number of indivisible quantities."

The question remains whether these indivisible units, an infinite number of which constitute the continuity of a finite magnitude, can properly be called quantities. At least they are not magnitudes, as is indicated by Euclid's definition of a point as "that which has no part," or by Nicomachus' statement that "the point is the beginning of dimension, but is not itself a dimension." If, in addition to having position, a point had size or extent, a finite line could not contain an infinite number of points.

WITHIN EACH OF THE two main divisions of quantity—magnitude and number—further subdivisions into kinds are made. Relations of equality and inequality, or proportions of these ratios, may occur between quantities different in kind—different plane figures, for example. But the great books of mathematics indicate other problems in the study of quantity than those concerned with the ratios and proportions of quantities. The classifications

of lines and figures results in the discovery of the properties which belong to each type. Possessing the same properties, all lines or figures of a certain type are similar in kind, not equal in quantity. In addition to developing the properties of such straight lines as perpendiculars and parallels, or such curved lines as circles and ellipses, parabolas and hyperbolas, the geometer defines the different types of relationship in which straight lines can stand to curves, e.g., tangents, secants, asymptotes.

As there are types of lines and figures, both plane and solid, so there are types of numbers. Euclid and Nicomachus divide the odd numbers into the prime and the composite—into those which are divisible only by themselves and unity, such as 5 and 7, and those which have other factors, such as 9 and 15. The composite are further differentiated into the variety which is simply secondary and composite and "the variety which, in itself, is secondary and composite, but relatively is prime and incomposite." To illustrate the latter, Nicomachus asks us to compare 9 with 25. "Each in itself," he writes, "is secondary and composite, but relatively to each other they have only unity as a common measure, and no factors in them have the same denominator, for the third part in the former does not exist in the latter nor is the fifth part in the latter found in the former."

The even numbers are divided by Nicomachus into the even-times-even (numbers like 64 which can be divided into equal halves, and their halves can again be divided into equal halves, and so on until division must stop); the even-times-odd (numbers like 6, 10, 14, 18 which can be divided into equal halves, but whose halves cannot be divided again into equal halves); and the odd-times-even (numbers like 24, 28, 40 which can be divided into equal parts, whose parts also can be so divided, and perhaps again these parts, but which cannot be divided in this way as far as unity). By another principle of classification, the even numbers fall into the superabundant, the deficient, and the perfect. The factors which produce superabundant or deficient numbers, when added together, amount to more or less than the number itself; but a number is perfect, Nicomachus writes, when, "comparing with itself the sum and combination of all the factors whose presence it will admit, it neither exceeds them in multitude nor is exceeded by them." It is "equal to its own parts"; as, for example, 6, "for 6 has the factors half, third, and sixth, 3, 2, and 1, respectively, and these added together make 6 and are equal to the original number." At the time of Nicomachus only four perfect numbers were known—6, 28, 496, 8128; since his day seven more have been discovered.

The further classification of numbers as linear, plane, and solid, and of plane numbers as triangular, square, pentagonal, etc., assigns properties to them according to their configurations. The analysis of figurate numbers by Nicomachus or Pascal represents one of the great bridges between arithmetic and geometry, of which the other, in the opposite direction, is the algebraic rendering of geometric loci in Descartes's analytic geometry.

In either direction of the translation between arithmetic and geometry, discontinuous and continuous quantities seem to have certain properties in common, at least by analogy. Euclid, for example, proposes numerical ratios as the test for the commensurability of magnitudes. "Commensurable magnitudes have to one another," he writes, "the ratio which a number has to a number." With the exception of infinite numbers, all numbers are commensurable and so provide the criterion for determining whether two magnitudes are or are not commensurable.

Introducing the notion of dimensionality into the discussion of figurate numbers, Nicomachus observes that "mathematical speculations are always to be interlocked and to be explained one by means of another." Though the dimensions by which linear, plane, and solid numbers are to be distinguished "are more closely related to magnitude . . . yet the germs of these ideas are taken over into arithmetic as the science which is the mother of geometry and more elementary than it." The translation does not seem to fail in any respect. The only nondimensional number, unity, finds its geometric analogue in the point, which has position without magnitude.

When diverse magnitudes are translated into numbers, the diversity of the magnitudes seems to be effaced by the fact that their numerical measures do not have a corresponding diversity. The numbers will appear to be commensurable though the magnitudes they measure are not, as magnitudes, comparable. As Descartes points out, it is necessary, therefore, to regard each order of magnitude as a distinct dimension.

"By dimension," Descartes writes, "I understand nothing but the mode and aspect according to which a subject is considered to be measurable. Thus it is not merely the case that length, breadth, and depth are dimensions; but weight also is a dimension in terms of which the heaviness of objects is estimated. So, too, speed is a dimension of motion, and there are an infinite number of similar instances. For that very division of the whole into a number of parts of identical nature, whether it exist in the real order of things or be merely the work of the understanding, gives us exactly that dimension in terms of which we apply number to objects."

The theory of dimensions can be illustrated by the choice of clocks, rulers, and balances as the fundamental instruments for the measurement of physical quantities. They represent the three dimensions in the fundamental equations of mechanics—time, distance, and mass. A thorough discussion of the measurement of quantities is to be found in Whitehead's *Introduction to Mathematics*.

Additional dimensions may be introduced in electricity or thermodynamics. In developing the theory of heat, Joseph Fourier, for example, enumerates five quantities which, in order to be numerically expressed, require five different kinds of units, "namely, the unit of length, the unit of time, that of temperature, that of weight, and finally the unit which serves to measure quantities of heat." To which he adds the remark that "every undetermined magnitude or constant has one *dimension* proper to itself, and that the terms of one and the same equation could not be compared, if they had not the same *exponent of dimension*."

A fuller discussion of the basic physical quantities, their definition, measurement, and their relation to one another, belongs to the chapter on MECHANICS. The consideration of time and space as quantities, or physical dimensions, occurs in the chapters devoted to those subjects.

77

Reasoning

INTRODUCTION

IN the tradition of western thought, certain verbal expressions have become shorthand for the fundamental ideas in the discussion of which they happen to be so often repeated. This may be due to the influence of the textbooks used in the schools, which copy one from another and hand down an easily recited jargon from generation to generation. In most cases the great books themselves are probably the original source, though they have usually suffered oversimplification or distortion when their insights are thus transmitted.

"Featherless biped" and "rational animal" are, for example, stock phrases to illustrate the idea that a definition consists of genus and differentia—the class to which man, in this instance, belongs and the attribute which differentiates him from other members of this class. Statements such as "the whole is greater than the part" or "two plus two equals four" similarly serve to represent axioms or at least statements which, whether or not they can be proved, are usually accepted as true without proof. In the field of reasoning, the familiar verbal landmark is "All men are mortal, Socrates is a man; therefore, Socrates is mortal." Even those who have never heard of syllogisms, or who are thoroughly innocent of the age-old controversies about the theory of the syllogism and the difference between deduction and induction, might offer this sequence of statements if, pressed to say what reasoning is, they tried to answer by giving an example.

The example, shopworn though it is and far from being the perfect paradigm, does convey certain insights into the nature of reasoning which are generally undisputed.

The word "therefore," which connects the third statement with the first two, signifies a relationship which is sometimes described in terms of cause and effect, as by Aristotle, and sometimes in terms of antecedent and consequent, as by Hobbes. The premises (*i.e.,* the statements which precede the "therefore") cause the conclusion, it is said. We know that Socrates is mortal *because* we know that Socrates is a man and that all men are mortal. The premises are the cause in the sense of the *reason why* the conclusion may be regarded as true.

The conclusion is also said to *follow from* the premises, or the premises are said to *imply* or *yield* the conclusion. *If* the premises are true, *then* the truth of the conclusion can be inferred or proved. The relationship between the premises and the conclusion seems to be the same whether the act of reasoning is called "proof" or "inference." The distinction in meaning between these two words seems to be one of direction. We speak of "proving" a conclusion when we look toward the premises as the foundation for its truth; we speak of "inferring" a conclusion when we look toward it as something which can be drawn from the premises.

The words "if" and "then" indicate that reasoning is a motion of the mind from one statement to another. Sometimes the inference is immediate, as when we argue that if all men are mortal, then some mortals are men. Here only two propositions are involved, one of which is simply the converse of the other. Those who deny that immediate inference is truly inference (because a proposition and its converse are merely two ways of stating the same fact), insist that, implicitly or explicitly, reasoning always involves *at least* three statements. In any case, a single statement like "Socrates is a man," or even a pair of statements connected by "and" rather than "if-then"—*e.g.*, "Socrates is a man and Socrates is mortal"—does not express what is commonly recognized as reasoning. The motion of reasoning does, however, appear in this sequence of statements, "If Socrates is a man, then Socrates is mortal," even though it omits a statement that may be necessary to the validity of the reasoning, namely, "All men are mortal."

Thus, the familiar grammatical distinctions of word (or phrase), sentence, and paragraph do not seem to provide a perfect parallel for the distinctions which the logicians make between terms, propositions, and syllogisms. But this much is clear. Just as a single word or phrase, like "man" or "rational animal," can never express a proposition, but only a term, so a simple sentence expresses only a proposition, and never a syllogism; and a compound sentence, one made up of a number of sentences, expresses a syllogism only if its verbal construction somehow indicates that they form a sequence in which one *follows* from the others, or if they are related in such a way that the truth of one is caused by the truth of the others.

THE CHAPTER ON IDEA (and perhaps also the chapter on DEFINITION) deals with that content or act of the mind—whether a percept or a concept, an image or an abstraction—which is verbally expressed in words or phrases and of which the *term* is the logical representative. The chapter on JUDGMENT (and perhaps also the chapter on PRINCIPLE) deals with the mental act or content that requires a sentence for its expression and is logically represented by the *proposition*. Here we are concerned with mental activity which involves not only two or more ideas, but also two or more judgments so connected that the mind passes from one to another.

Whether the logical structure that Aristotle calls a "syllogism" represents all forms of the mental activity called reasoning, is one of the great traditional issues. Hume suggests, for example, that animals reason without making use of syllogisms; and Descartes and Locke seem to hold that the highest forms of thinking, such as occur in mathematics or philosophy, cannot be reduced to syllogisms, except perhaps by a tour de force.

We face a different sort of problem when we compare reasoning with other acts of the mind—with conception (or the having of ideas) and with judgment (or the connecting of ideas with one another in the manner which medieval writers call "composition and division"). No one denies that reasoning is thinking, nor does anyone deny that there are forms of thinking which are not reasoning, since conceiving and judging are generally regarded as kinds of thinking or modes of thought. Reasoning is merely that mode of thought which is a *process*—the going step-by-step from one statement to another.

The problem which arises from the comparison of reasoning with other modes of thought turns on the question whether the mind can learn anything without having to think rationally. Can certain things be known by insight or instinct, by induction or intuition, rather than by reasoning? Are there truths which cannot be known by reasoning at all, but only by some other mode of thought? These questions in turn raise the problem of the priority or superiority of such modes of thought as do not consist in reasoning. The theory discussed in the chapter on INDUCTION—that induction is prior to reasoning because intuitive generalization from experience must provide the starting points for demonstration—indicates one solution of the problem. Our present concern, however, goes beyond the issue concerning induction and deduction to the most general contrast between the intuitive and the rational.

FOR PLOTINUS ANY FORM of thinking—not merely reasoning—signifies a deficiency or weakness. In the scale of intellectual beings man occupies the lowest rank because he reasons. But even the pure intelligences, which know intuitively, rank below the One, because even the simplest act of thought involves some duality of subject and object. The One, according to Plotinus, transcends thought even as it transcends being. "The super-essential," he says, "is the supra-cogitative." The One "has no need for intellection, being always self-sufficing."

Other writers do not go as far as this. Christian theologians do, however, contrast the human mind with the angelic intellect and the mind of God by saying that the latter are suprarational, *i.e.,* above the need to reason. They do not, like Plotinus, hold that the transcendent being transcends thought itself—certainly not insofar as they discuss the divine ideas. But the kind of thinking which is not an instantaneous act of vision or an immediate intuition involves the mind in a process thought, somehow akin to change or motion; and this, the theologians hold, cannot take place in any immutable being—the angels or God.

The human intellect, according to Aquinas, gradually comes to know the truth "by a kind of movement and discursive intellectual operation . . . by advancing from one thing known to another. But if from the knowledge of a known principle [men] were straightway to perceive as known all its consequent conclusions, then there would be no place for discursiveness in the human intellect. Such is the condition of the angels, because in the truths which they know naturally, they at once behold all things whatsoever that can be known in them."

That, says Aquinas, is why the angels "are called *intellectual* beings" and men "are called *rational.*" Recourse to reasoning on the part of men betrays "the feebleness of their intellectual light. For if they possessed the fullness of intellectual light, like the angels, then in the first grasping of principles they would at once comprehend all that they implied, by perceiving at once whatever could be reasoned out of them."

The type of intuitive apprehension which the angels enjoy is even more perfectly exemplified in God's knowledge. "In the divine knowledge," according to Aquinas, "there is no discursiveness"—no succession, neither the turning from one thought to another, nor the advance from the known to the unknown by reasoning from principles to conclusion. The divine knowledge, Aquinas explains, is a single all-embracing act of vision, in which "God sees all things in one thing alone, which is Himself," and therefore "sees all things together and not successively." Apart from participation in the vision of God through supernatural light, all human thinking on the natural plane is discursive. Even the conception and the judgment are discursive in the sense that the one involves an act of abstraction or definition and the other involves a composition or division of concepts. But though it is always discursive, human thinking is not, according to Aquinas, always involved in the *motion* of reasoning, that is, the transition from one thought to another. "Reasoning," he says, "is compared to understanding"—*i.e.,* the act of judgment by which we affirm or deny a single proposition—"as movement is to rest, or acquisition to possession."

DESCARTES USES THE word "intuition" to name the way in which we know certain truths immediately and with certitude. He distinguishes "intuition from deduction by the fact that into the conception of the latter there enters a certain movement or succession, into that of the former there does not . . . The first principles are given by intuition alone, while, on the contrary, the remote conclusions are furnished only by deduction." But while deduction, which Descartes says he understands to be "all necessary inference from other facts that are known with certainty," supplements intuition, it is never at any stage of the reasoning process independent of intuition.

Not only does intuition, according to Descartes, supply the first principles or ultimate premises of reasoning, but it also certifies each step in the process. He asks us to "consider this consequence: 2 and 2 amount to the same as 3 and 1. Now we need to see intuitively not only that 2 and 2 make 4, and that likewise 3 and 1 make 4, but further that the third of the above statements is a necessary conclusion from these two."

If in addition to knowing the premises by intuition, the drawing of a conclusion from them is, as Descartes says, itself "effected by intuition"—if the act of inference rests on the intuition that the conclusion follows logically from the premises—in what way does deduction or reasoning supplement intuition? To this question, Descartes replies that though the mind "has a clear vision of each step in the process," it cannot comprehend in one intuition all the connections involved in a long chain of reasoning. Only by taking the steps one after another can we "know that the last link in a long chain is connected with the first, even though we do not take in by means of one and the same act of vision all the intermediate links on which that connection depends, but only remember that we have taken them successively under review."

Like Descartes, Locke contrasts intuition and reasoning, or intuitive and demonstrative knowledge. "Sometimes the mind perceives the agreement or disagreement of two ideas immediately by themselves, without the intervention of any other: and this," says Locke, "we may call intuitive knowledge . . . When the mind cannot so bring its ideas together, as by their immediate comparison . . . to perceive their agreement or disagreement, it is fain by the intervention of other ideas . . . to discover the agreement or disagreement which it searches; and this is that which we call reasoning."

Again like Descartes, Locke asks, "What need is there of reason?" It is necessary, he thinks, "both for the enlargement of our knowledge and regulating our assent . . . Sense and intuition reach but very little of the way. The greatest part of our knowledge depends upon deductions and intermediate ideas; and in those cases where we are fain to substitute assent instead of knowledge, and take propositions for true without being certain they are so, we have need to find out, examine, and compare the grounds of their probability." But though reasoning enlarges our knowledge beyond what can be known intuitively, reasoning produces certain knowledge, according to Locke, only if "every step in reasoning . . . has intuitive certainty . . . To make anything a demonstration, it is necessary to perceive the immediate agreement of the intervening ideas, whereby the agreement or disagreement of the two ideas under examination (whereof the one is always the first, and the other the last, in the account) is found."

On this view of reasoning, nothing can be known demonstratively or by proof unless some things can be known intuitively, *i.e.*, without inference or proof. Locke and Descartes seem to agree with Aquinas and Aristotle that demonstration depends upon indemonstrable truths, whether these are called axioms, immediate propositions, first principles, or self-evident maxims. Locke and Descartes, on the one hand, stress the point that in reasoning the logical connection between premises and conclusion is also indemonstrable and must be intuitively perceived. Aquinas and Aristotle, on the other, repeatedly observe that the truth of the conclusion is implicitly contained in the truth of the premises, so that the advance which reasoning appears to make from the known to the unknown consists in coming to know actually what is already potentially known. Nevertheless they, unlike Descartes and Locke, maintain that reasoning extends knowledge, even though it may not be the method of initial discovery.

A somewhat contrary view seems to be taken by Hume. If the objects under consideration are matters of fact rather than the relations between our own ideas, the kind of reasoning which goes from premises to conclusion avails not at all. The beliefs we hold about such matters, according to Hume, result from mental operations which are "a species of natural instinct . . . which no reasoning or process of thought is able either to produce or to prevent." What he calls "experimental reasoning" or "reasoning concerning matters of fact" is founded, he says, "on a species of Analogy, which leads us to expect from any cause the same events which we have observed to result from similar causes."

Not only men, but also animals reason in this way. But Hume thinks "it is impossible that this inference of the animal can be founded on any process of argument or reasoning by which he concludes that like events must follow like objects . . . The experimental reasoning itself, which we possess in common with beasts, and on which the whole conduct of life depends, is nothing but a species of instinct or mechanical power, that acts in us unknown to ourselves; and in its chief operations is not directed by any such relations or comparisons of ideas, as are the proper objects of our intellectual faculties."

THE FOREGOING considerations indicate how diverse theories of the role of reasoning arise from diverse theories of the nature and kinds of knowledge in animals, men, angels, and God. According as various distinctions are made between human knowledge and opinion, or between the way in which different objects can be known, or between speculative and practical interests, so, too, different formulations are given of the nature of reasoning.

Aristotle's distinction, for example, between scientific and dialectical or rhetorical reasoning turns upon his understanding of the difference between the objects of certain knowledge and the objects of probable opinion. This difference, he says, makes it "equally foolish to accept probable reasoning from a mathematician and to demand from a rhetorician scientific proofs." Hume's distinction between *a priori* and *a posteriori* reasoning— *i.e.,* between reasoning from principles and reasoning from experience—depends upon his understanding of what matters must be submitted to experience and of the manner in which experience generates belief. The distinction which Aquinas makes between demonstrations *propter quid* and demonstrations *quia—i.e.,* between proving *what* something is from its causes and proving *that* it is from its effects—depends upon his understanding of the difference between essence and existence as objects of rational knowledge.

To take an example in the opposite vein, Locke's theory that the same type of demonstration is possible in both mathematics and the moral sciences, seems to rest upon his view that all knowledge consists in the comparison of ideas. In contrast to this, other theories, which hold that the mode of reasoning differs in different disciplines (especially in mathematics and morals, or in metaphysics and the natural sciences), seem to arise from the contrary view that, in these different fields of inquiry, the objects and conditions of knowledge are different.

Sometimes a distinction in the modes of reasoning is based upon the same considerations, but the distinction itself is expressed by different writers in different terms. The role of causes in reasoning appears to underlie Aquinas' distinction between *a priori* and *a posteriori* reasoning, or reasoning from cause to effect as opposed to reasoning from effect to cause. "Demonstration can be made in two ways," he writes; "one is through the cause and is called *a priori,* and this is to argue from what is prior absolutely. The other is through the effect, and is called a demonstration *a posteriori;* this is to argue from what is prior relatively only to us." Descartes appears to make a parallel distinction, though he makes it in different terms. "The method of proof is twofold," he says, "one being analytic, the other synthetic. Analysis shows the true way by which a thing was methodically discovered, as it were effect from cause . . . Synthesis employs an opposite procedure, one in which the search goes as it were from effect to cause." For both mathematical and metaphysical reasoning, Descartes prefers the analytic to the synthetic method.

According to Newton, the method of analysis, in natural science as well as mathematics, consists in going from effects to causes, while the method of synthesis goes from causes to effects. Newton relates the difference between analysis and synthesis to the difference between inductive and deductive reasoning. This way of distinguishing between inductive and deductive reasoning, in terms of going from effects to causes or from causes to effects, would also seem to be related to the distinction Aquinas makes between demonstration *quia* (*i.e.,* reasoning which proves only *that* something exists) and demonstration *propter quid* (*i.e.,* reasoning which proves *what* something is—its nature or properties). The proof that God exists is, according to Aquinas, a demonstration *quia;* it is also *a posteriori* reasoning or reasoning from effect to cause. But he would not call it "inductive." In one passage at least, he seems to regard induction as the method whereby we can come to some knowledge of what God is. "From natural things," he writes, "one does not come by a demonstration of reason to know non-natural things, but by the induction of reason one may know something above nature, since the natural bears a certain resemblance to the supernatural."

This sense of the word "induction," however, is like that in which Aristotle opposes induction to reasoning, not like that in which he distinguishes between inductive and deductive reasoning according to the order of terms in the inductive and deductive syllogism. In the ordinary deductive syllogism, the middle term establishes the connection between the two extreme terms (for example, 'being a man' establishes the connection between 'Socrates' and 'being mortal'). But "the syllogism which springs out of induction," according to Aristotle, establishes "a relation between one extreme and the middle by means of the other extreme, *e.g.,* if B is the middle term between A and C, it consists in proving through C that A belongs to B." Starting from C (particular cases of long-lived animals, such as man, horse, mule), we can argue inductively from the fact that these long-lived animals are bileless, to the general connection between B (being bileless) and A (being long-lived). Such reasoning is valid, Aristotle adds, only if we can treat C "as made up of all the particulars; for induction proceeds through an enumeration of all the cases."

DIFFERENT THEORIES of definition also affect the place which is assigned to definition in reasoning. Hobbes, for example, regards reasoning as a kind of calculation with names, which wholly depends upon the determination of their meanings. The operations of addition and subtraction when done with words rather than with numbers are, he thinks, equivalent to "conceiving of the consequence of the names of all the parts, to the name of the whole; or from the names of the whole and one part, to the name of the other part." It is "nothing but *reckoning* (that is, adding and subtracting) of the consequences of general names agreed upon." Aristotle, with the theory that definitions state the essential natures of things, not just the meanings of words, holds that a definition may be "the conclusion of a demonstration giving essential nature," as well as "an indemonstrable statement of essential nature." In the latter case, the definition functions as a principle in demonstration.

According to William James, reasoning, like definition, is "a selective activity of the mind" which serves an individual's interest or purpose. "My thinking," he says, "is first, last, and always for the sake of my doing . . . Reasoning is always for a subjective interest, to attain some particular conclusion, or to gratify some special curiosity." It makes no difference whether the interest is practical or the curiosity speculative. The process of reasoning will be the same, though the element which provides a solution to the problem in any emergency will be called a " 'reason' if the emergency be theoretical, a 'means' if it be practical."

Those writers who, like Aristotle and Aquinas, regard the speculative and the practical as distinct though related orders of thought and knowledge, seem to think that practical reasoning has its own syllogistic form. Practical deliberations for them are different from theoretical demonstrations. The conclusion of theoretical reasoning is an assertion that something is either true or false, whereas the conclusion of practical deliberation is a judgment that something is good or evil, and therefore should either be done or avoided. According to Aristotle, practical reasoning of the sort which ends in a decision that leads to action, takes the form of a syllogism which has one universal and one particular premise. The major premise is a general rule of conduct, the minor premise a particular perception of fact. In the example Aristotle gives of the practical syllogism, the major premise is the rule that *everything sweet ought to be tasted,* and the minor premise is the perception that *this particular thing is sweet.* These two premises lead to the practical conclusion that *this particular thing ought to be tasted.*

Not all practical reasoning, however, is concerned with reaching decisions or prompting action in particular cases. The rules of conduct which decisions and actions apply may themselves be the products of practical reasoning. The process by which general rules are derived from even more general principles—the precepts of law or morality—involves, according to Aquinas, a form of thinking distinctly different from the theoretical or speculative sort. He points out in his Treatise on Law that we are able to formulate certain practical rules only by making particular determinations of universal principles, not by drawing deductions from them. "Something may be derived from the natural law in two ways," he writes: "first, as a conclusion from premises; secondly, by way of determination of certain generalities. The first way is like that by which, in the speculative sciences, demonstrated conclusions are drawn from the principles; while the second mode is likened to that whereby, in the arts, general forms are particularized as to details." Of these two ways of thinking in the field of law, it would appear that it is only the second type which is peculiar to the practical as opposed to the speculative order.

THE DISCUSSION OF reasoning in relation to knowledge, opinion, and action, or in relation to different disciplines and sciences, usually presupposes a theory of the form which reasoning takes regardless of its subject matter or use. This fact is most explicitly attested by the order of three great books concerned with reasoning. Aristotle's *Posterior Analytics* deals with the theory of demonstration in the sciences. His *Topics* deals with the theory of probable argument or reasoning in the sphere of opinion. Both are preceded by his *Prior Analytics* which treats of the syllogism in terms of its purely formal structure and its various forms. In the later tradition, the distinction between the problems of the *Prior* and the *Posterior Analytics* comes to be represented by the separation between what are called "formal" and "material" logic.

The formal analysis of reasoning centers on the problem of its cogency. Quite apart from any consideration of the truth of its premises or conclusions, reasoning is true or false according as it is valid or invalid on purely logical grounds. From premises which are in fact false, a conclusion, which may be either true or false, can be truly inferred if the structure of the reasoning is formally valid—

that is, if the form of the premises stands in a certain logically prescribed relation to the form of the conclusion. The logical problem, then, is to prescribe the formal relationships among propositions which permit valid inference from certain propositions to others, without regard to the content of the propositions or their truth in fact.

Defining a syllogism as "discourse in which, certain things being stated, something other than what is stated follows of necessity from their being so," Aristotle says, "I call that a perfect syllogism which needs nothing other than what has been stated to make plain what necessarily follows; a syllogism is imperfect, if it needs either one or more propositions which are indeed the necessary consequences of the terms set down, but have not been expressly stated as premises." Using the letters S and P to symbolize the subject and predicate of the conclusion, and the letter M to symbolize the middle term, the term which appears in the premises but not in the conclusion, Aristotle states the form of a perfect syllogism in the following manner: "All M is P, all S is M; therefore all S is P."

The first of these propositions, the one which contains the predicate of the conclusion, is called the major premise; the second, the one which contains the subject of the conclusion, the minor premise; the subject of the conclusion is called the minor term, the predicate the major term. Aristotle classifies syllogisms into three figures, or formal types, according to the position of the middle term, either as subject of the major premise and predicate of the minor in the first figure, or as predicate in both or as subject in both in the second and third figures respectively. Then according to whether the premises are universal propositions or particular ('All M is P' or 'Some S is M'), and each is either affirmative or negative ('All M is P' or 'Some S is not M'), he further distinguishes within each figure a number of valid moods, or formally correct patterns of inference.

For example, in no figure can a valid mood be constructed with two particular or two negative premises. No conclusion can be drawn from the two particular statements that some poisons are liquids and that some liquids are indispensable to life; nor can any conclusion be drawn from the two negative statements that no triangles are parallelograms and no rhomboids are parallelograms. In the first figure, the minor premise can be particular and must be affirmative, the major can be negative and must be universal. In this figure the following combinations of premises—"some figures are not rectangular" with "all rectangular figures are parallelograms," or "all prime numbers are odd" with "some odd numbers are squares"—yield no conclusions. In the second figure, one premise must be negative. Here it is impossible to draw a valid conclusion from two affirmative premises. Nothing follows from the two affirmative statements that all fish swim and all whales swim. In the third figure, only a particular conclusion can be drawn from a pair of premises both of which are universal. From the proposition that no men are wise and the proposition that all men are mortal, we can conclude only that some mortals are not wise.

From these examples it will be seen that Aristotle's rules of the syllogism are rules concerning the quantity and quality of the premises required in each figure to permit a valid inference; and as in the third figure these rules permit only a particular conclusion to be drawn, so for all figures they determine the character of the conclusion which can be drawn from premises of a certain quantity and quality. If one premise is negative, the conclusion must be negative. If one premise is particular, the conclusion must be particular.

There seems to be one universal principle of the syllogism which underlies all these specific rules for the valid moods in different figures. "When one thing is predicated of another," Aristotle says, "all that which is predicable of the predicate will be predicable also of the subject." The negative aspect of this principle is immediately obvious. What cannot be predicated of a predicate, cannot be predicated of its subject. In the tradition of formal logic, this principle is sometimes stated in terms of the relation of classes rather than in terms of subjects and predicates: if one class is included in a second, and that second class is included

in a third, the first is included in the third; and if one class excludes another, the classes which it includes are also excluded from that other.

The principle of the syllogism is traditionally called the *dictum de omni et nullo*. The *dictum de omni,* which Kant in his *Introduction to Logic* calls "the supreme principle of affirmative syllogisms," is thus expressed by him: "Whatever is universally affirmed of a concept is also affirmed of everything contained under it." The *dictum de nullo,* according to Kant, states that "whatever is universally denied of a concept is also denied of everything that is contained under it." Kant appears to think that both these rules follow from even more general principles: that "an attribute of an attribute is an attribute of the thing itself" and that "whatever is inconsistent with the attribute of a thing is inconsistent with the thing itself."

James also attempts to make a more general formulation of the *dictum de omni et nullo.* This law of thought, he says, is "*only the result of the function of comparison* in the mind which has come by some lucky variation to apprehend a series of more than two terms at once." As James states what he calls the "principle of mediate comparison," it appears to be broader than the principle of the syllogism. It applies to any series of related terms—to the relation of equal and unequal quantities in mathematics, as well as to the relation of subjects and predicates in the logic of predication or classes.

James's principle of mediate comparison itself depends on what in mathematical logic and the logic of relations is called the "transitivity" of relations. The relation of *larger than,* for example, is transitive; for if one thing is larger than a second, and the second is larger than a third, it follows that the first is larger than the third. As stated in mathematical logic, the principle of the syllogism is merely a special case of transitivity as it appears in the relation of implication; for if P implies Q, and Q implies R, then P implies R.

James recognizes this when he writes that "*the principle of mediate predication or subsumption* is only the axiom of skipped intermediaries applied to a series of successive predications. It expresses the fact that any earlier term in the series stands to any later term, in the same relation in which it stands to any intermediate term; in other words, that *whatever has an attribute has all the attributes of that attribute;* or more briefly still, that *whatever is of a kind is of that kind's kind.*" Along with "the *axiom of mediate equality,* 'equals of equals are equal,' " the rule of mediate predication or subsumption is, according to James, a special case of the law that "skipping intermediary terms leaves relations the same. This AXIOM OF SKIPPED INTERMEDIARIES OR of TRANSFERRED RELATIONS ... seems to be on the whole the broadest and deepest law of man's thought."

JAMES'S ATTEMPT TO state a law of thought or principle of reasoning which relegates all the rules of the syllogism to the status of a special case represents one type of attack on the syllogism. Whether, for instance, the sample of reasoning which Descartes asks us to consider—that if 2 and 2 make 4, and 3 and 1 make 4, then 2 and 2 amount to the same as 3 and 1—can be reduced to the syllogistic form of subject and predicate, or must be formulated under a more general principle of "transferred relations," illustrates the basic issue here between subject-predicate logic and relational or mathematical logic. In arithmetic, Poincaré tells us, one "cannot conceive its general truths by direct intuition alone; to prove even the smallest theorem [one] must use reasoning by recurrence, for that is the only instrument which enables us to pass from the finite to the infinite."

Another type of criticism of the traditional theory of the syllogism accepts the syllogism as the form of *all* reasoning, but objects, as Kant does, to what he calls "the mistaken subtilty" of the classification of syllogisms according to figures and moods. But Kant does not deny all distinctions among syllogisms. On the contrary, he says that syllogisms are "three-fold, like all judgements, differing from each other in the manner in which they express the relation of knowledge in the understanding, namely, categorical, hypothetical, and disjunctive." Whether the hypothetical and disjunctive syllogisms are distinct types of reasoning, or only special cases which it would be a mistaken subtlety to treat as having principles of their own, is a problem considered in the chapter on HYPOTHESIS.

Of all criticisms, the most severe is that which either rejects the syllogism entirely as of no use in reasoning, or regards the deductive syllogism as useful only in argumentation or debate, not in the process of inquiry or discovery, where inductive reasoning alone is fruitful or instructive. From the conclusion of a syllogism, according to J. S. Mill, one learns nothing more than one already knew in the premises; whereas in inductive reasoning, Mill, like Francis Bacon, thinks that the mind goes beyond anything contained in the premises and genuinely discovers a new truth.

It seems to be Descartes's opinion that "the syllogistic forms are of no aid in perceiving the truth about objects." Locke makes the same point more extensively. Admitting that "all right reasoning may be reduced to [Aristotle's] forms of syllogism," he denies that they are "the best way of reasoning for the leading of those into truth who are willing to find it and desire to make the best use of their reason for the attainment of knowledge ... The rules of syllogism," he writes, "serve not to furnish the mind with those intermediate ideas that may show the connexion of remote ones. This way of reasoning discovers no new proofs, but is the art of marshalling and ranging the old ones we have already. The forty-seventh proposition of the first book of Euclid, is very true; but the discovery of it, I think, not owing to any rules of common logic. A man knows first, and then he is able to prove syllogistically; so that syllogism comes after knowledge, and then a man has little or no need of it ... Syllogism, at best, is but the art of fencing with the little knowledge we have, without making any addition to it."

It may be that the critics of the syllogism attribute to its exponents claims they do not make. Aristotle, for example, seems to present the syllogism as a method of expounding arguments rather than of discovering them, and of testing the validity of reasoning rather than of learning the truth about things. "All instruction given or received by way of argument," he writes, "proceeds from pre-existent knowledge. This becomes evident upon a survey of all the species of instruction. The mathematical sciences, and all other speculative disciplines, are acquired in this way, and so are the two forms of dialectical reasoning, syllogistic and inductive; for each of these latter makes use of old knowledge to impart new, the syllogism assuming an audience that accepts its premises, induction exhibiting the universal as implicit in the clearly known particular."

78

Relation

INTRODUCTION

Like quantity and quality, relation is generally recognized as a basic term or category. But its meaning, like theirs, cannot be defined. Relation is, perhaps, the prototype of an indefinable notion. As Russell points out, it seems to be impossible to make any statement of what relation is without using the notion of relation in doing so.

Any term which is essentially relative seems also to be incapable of definition. Its meaning cannot be stated without referring to its correlative; and since the meaning of the latter reciprocally involves the former as *its* correlative, each member of a pair of correlative terms draws upon the other for its meaning. A part is a part of a whole; a whole, a whole of parts. Similarly, the meaning of parent involves the notion of child, and the meaning of child the notion of parent.

Plato applies this maddening fact about correlative terms to all comparatives that presuppose the correlation of more and less. "Comparatives such as the hotter and the colder," he writes, "are to be ranked in the class of the infinite." They cannot be measured or defined. Terms like 'much' and 'little,' 'great' and 'small' look like quantities, but, according to Aristotle, they are "not quantities, but relatives, for things are not great or small absolutely; they are so called rather as the result of an act of comparison."

Concerning quantities and qualities, the ancients ask how they exist. The alternatives seem to be either that they exist in and of themselves, or that they exist as the attributes of substances such as stones and trees. But with regard to relations, the question seems to be whether they exist rather than how they exist.

The supposition that a relation cannot exist apart from the terms it relates may be thought to imply that the relation does exist when the terms it relates exist. The ancients, however, do not appear to regard the relation as something having a reality distinguishable from the reality of the correlative terms. It seems to be significant that both Plato and Aristotle discuss relative terms, rather than relations as such. For the most part, they signify relations by using a pair of words which name things standing in a certain relation to one another.

Thus in the *Categories*, Aristotle refers to 'double' and 'half,' 'master' and 'slave,' 'greater' and 'less,' or 'knowledge' and 'object known' as examples of correlative terms. "All relatives," he says, "have a correlative." Sometimes it is necessary to find the precise word, or even to invent the right word, for in order to indicate that a given term is relative, its correlative must be appropriately named. "Concubine," says Locke, "is, no doubt, a relative name, as well as wife; but in languages where this, and like words, have not a correlative term, there people are not so apt to take them to be so, as wanting that evident mark of relations which is between correlatives, which seem to explain one another, and not to be able to exist but together."

When "reciprocity of correlation does not appear to exist," Aristotle suggests that it may be the result of our failure to use words carefully. If we wish to use the term 'rudder' as relative, we cannot call its correlative a 'boat,' for "there are boats which have no rudders." Since there is no existing word, it would be "more accurate," Aristotle thinks, "if we coined some word like 'ruddered' to name the correlative of 'rudder.'" Similarly, in the case of 'slave' as a relative term, its correlative is not 'man' understood in any sense, but only man understood as 'master.'

The things which are designated by a pair of reciprocally relative terms must, according to Aristotle, coexist. One man cannot be called a master unless another man exists who can be called his slave; something cannot be called larger unless something coexistent with it can be called smaller. Aristotle considers possible exceptions to this principle of the simultaneity or coexistence of correlatives; as, for example, in the case of knowledge and the knowable. It seems possible, he thinks, for the knowable to exist before anyone has actual knowledge of it. But the exception may be due to an improper naming of the correlatives. If the correlative of knowledge is the known rather than the knowable, then knowledge and its object may be said to be necessarily coexistent, for nothing comes to be an object actually known, except simultaneously with someone's coming actually to know it.

THE COEXISTENCE OF things which are correlative to one another still leaves a question concerning the existence of the relation between them. When conceived as an attribute, a quality or a quantity can be said to exist in the thing it somehow modifies. In the language of Aristotle, such accidents *inhere in* substances, and accordingly have reality as long as the substances in which they inhere exist. But a relation does not seem to inhere in *a* substance. It cannot be the attribute of a single thing. It somehow lies between two things, inhering in neither, for if it belonged to either one alone it could have some reality if that one existed and the other did not. The question, therefore, is whether relations really exist at all, or are only in the mind of him who compares things or considers them relative to one another.

"A sign that the relative is least of all a substance and a real thing," writes Aristotle, "is the fact that it alone has no proper generation or destruction or movement; as in respect of quantity there is increase and diminution, in respect of quality alteration, in respect of place locomotion, in respect of substance simple generation and destruction. In respect to relation there is no proper change; for, without

changing, a thing will be now greater and now less or equal, if that with which it is compared has changed in quantity."

Plotinus also questions the reality of relations. "Has relation—for example, that of right and left, double and half—any actuality? . . . What can be the meaning of correlatives apart from our conception of their juxtaposition? 'Greater' may refer to very different magnitudes; 'different' to all sorts of objects. The comparison is ours; it does not lie in the things themselves." In the case of certain space and time relations he maintains that "right and left are in our conception, nothing of them in the things themselves. Before and after are merely two things; the relation is again of our making."

Yet Plotinus seems unwilling to say that "we do not mean anything by relation, but are victims of words," or that "none of the relations mentioned can exist." Recognizing what he calls "the elusive character of relation," he is willing to affirm the reality of relations "when the actuality of the relationships is derived from no other source than relation itself." He thinks that one quantity may be the double of another, "quite apart from our speech or thought." The fact that one quantity is the double of another is an additional fact about the two quantities over and above all their other properties. "In all the conditions in which we assert relation," Plotinus declares, "the mutual relation exists over and above the objects; we perceive it as already existent; our knowledge is directed upon a thing, there to be known—a clear testimony to the reality of relation."

The problem thus seems to become one of distinguishing between relations which have independent reality and those which exist only in the mind. "Some have said that relation is not a reality but only an idea. But this," Aquinas declares, "is plainly seen to be false from the very fact that things themselves have a mutual order and relation." Not all relations are real, however. "Relations which result in the things understood from the operation of the intellect alone are logical relations only, inasmuch as reason observes them as existing between two understood things." For example, "the relation of a thing to itself is not a real relation," for "reason, by apprehending one thing twice, regards it as two; and thus it apprehends a certain relation of a thing to itself . . . The same is true of those relations that follow upon an act of reason, as genus and species, and the like."

Aquinas offers, in contrast, "other relations which are realities with regard to both extremes; as when a relation exists between two things according to some reality that belongs to both. This is clear of all relations consequent upon quantity, great and small, double and half, and the like; for there is quantity in both extremes."

This distinction between real and logical relations seems to be qualified by the intermediate case of a relation which is partly logical and partly real; for, according to Aquinas, "sometimes a relation in one extreme may be a reality, while in the other extreme, it is only an idea. This happens whenever the two extremes are not of one order . . . Since God is outside the whole order of creation and all creatures are ordered to Him, and not conversely, it is manifest that creatures are really related to God Himself; whereas in God there is no real relation to creatures, but a relation only in idea, inasmuch as creatures are related to Him."

In the *Charmides,* Socrates raises some doubts about the admissibility of reflexive relations, or the relations of things to themselves. Others have questioned the partly real and partly logical relation, according to which one thing is related to another but the second is not related to the first. But the more important issues, in the tradition of western thought, seem to be whether there are both real and logical relations, *i.e.,* relations both in nature and in the mind, and whether, in either case, relations enter into the very nature of the things related or are merely external, so that the character of a thing is unaffected by the relations in which it stands.

As INDICATED IN THE chapters on JUDGMENT, REASONING, and LOGIC, relation tends to displace predication in certain typically modern theories of the proposition and of inference.

What is currently called "relational logic" is set against "subject-predicate logic." Relations themselves, without regard to the character of the terms related, become the primary object of logical analysis. It is said, for example, that the proposition 'John hit James' has the form 'aRb' or 'R(a,b),' and that the proposition 'John went to school with James' has the form 'R(a,b,c,).' The first is a dyadic relation, the second a triadic relation. As Russell points out, relations do not always involve only two terms, as is commonly supposed. "Some relations demand three terms, some four, and so on."

Relations are classified not only with respect to the number of the terms they relate, but also with respect to such formal properties as symmetry, transitivity, reflexivity. The relation of parent and child, for example, is asymmetrical. It cannot be said, if A is the parent of B, that B is also the parent of A; whereas the relation of brotherhood is symmetrical. Statements of symmetrical relationship are convertible. If we say that A is the brother of B, we can also say that B is the brother of A.

The type of relationship remains the same regardless of the character of the terms. Unequal quantities are asymmetrically related, equal quantities symmetrically; 'to-the-right-of' is an asymmetrical spatial relation, 'next-to' is symmetrical; in time, 'simultaneous-with' is symmetrical and 'prior-to' asymmetrical. The distinction between transitive and intransitive relations similarly holds for all kinds of terms. The relation of father to son or of 'standing-next-to' in space is intransitive, for if A is the father of B, and B the father of C, A is not the father of C; whereas the spatial relation of 'standing-to-the-right-of' is transitive, for if A is to the right of B, and B to the right of C, then A is to the right of C.

The modern analysis of propositions as relational structures which differ in type according to the character of the relations, not the character of the terms, has an antecedent in Locke's analysis of judgments as acts of comparison which look to the relation between ideas rather than to the ideas themselves. Both analyses lead to a theory of inference which is based on the *convertibility* of symmetrical relations and on the *transitivity* of certain relationships and the *intransitivity* of others. As indicated in the chapter on REASONING, the factor of transitivity appears in William James's discussion of the "principle of mediate comparison." He states this in the formula *"more than the more is more than the less."* Then he explains that "such a formula would cover all possible cases; as, earlier than early is earlier than late, worse than bad is worse than good, east of east is east of west; etc., etc., *ad libitum.* Symbolically, we might write it as $a < b < c < d$ ... and say that any number of intermediaries may be expunged without obliging us to alter anything in what remains written."

James thus formulates what he regards as the most fundamental law of thought. For series of "homogeneously related terms," the law is that *"skipping intermediary terms leaves the relations the same."* The factor of transitivity enters the picture when James distinguishes between relations which are and relations which are not *transferable.* "All skipping of intermediaries and transfer of relations occurs within homogeneous series," he writes. "But not all homogeneous series allow of intermediaries being skipped. It depends on which series they are, on what relations they contain. Let it not be said that it is a mere matter of verbal association, due to the fact that language sometimes permits us to transfer the *name* of a relation over skipped intermediaries, and sometimes does not; as where we call men 'progenitors' of their remote as well as of their immediate posterity, but refuse to call them 'fathers' thereof. There are relations which are *intrinsically* transferable, whilst others are not. The relation of *condition, e.g.,* is intrinsically transferable. What conditions a condition conditions what it conditions—'cause of cause is cause of effect.' The relations of negation and *frustration,* on the other hand, are not transferable: what frustrates a frustration does not frustrate what it frustrates. No changes in terminology would annul the intimate difference between these two cases."

THE FOREGOING PASSAGES from James reflect the general tenor of the theory of the cal-culus of relations. He himself does not systematically expound it. Its elaboration is to be found in the writings of George Boole, Louis Couturat, and Augustus De Morgan, of William Stanley Jevons, Charles Sanders Peirce, F. H. Bradley, Josiah Royce (whose works are cited in the Additional Readings), Russell, and Whitehead. Is this relational logic more general than the subject-predicate logic that is traditionally called "Aristotelian," or is the reverse the case?

The modern answer insists upon the greater generality of relational logic. Royce, for example, defining "subsumption" as a non-symmetrical, transitive relation which obtains between two classes when one includes the other, declares that "the entire traditional 'theory of the syllogism' can be expressed as a sort of comment upon, and relatively simple application of, the transitivity of the subsumption relation." According to Royce, James's axiom of skipped intermediaries represents a step in the right direction, but it fails to achieve complete generality.

Russell disposes of the traditional theory of the proposition in the same fashion that Royce disposes of the traditional theory of the syllogism. Traditional logic, he writes, "believed that there was only one form of simple proposition (*i.e.,* of proposition not stating a relation between two or more other propositions), namely, the form which ascribes a predicate to a subject." It is, therefore, "unable to admit the reality of relations; all relations, it maintains, must be reduced to properties of the apparently related terms." Russell insists, on the contrary, that "propositions stating that two things have a certain relation have a different form from subject-predicate propositions." This can be most easily seen, he thinks, in the case of asymmetrical relations. The proposition which states that A and B are related by the symmetrical relation of equality, can be interpreted to mean that A and B both possess a common property. "But when we come to asymmetrical relations, such as before and after, greater and less, etc., the attempt to reduce them to properties becomes," in Russell's opinion, "obviously impossible." The relational theory of the proposition, therefore, includes the subject-predicate theory as a special case.

A defense of the subject-predicate logic would not make the counterclaim that relational logic can be treated as a special case. Rather it would insist that the two logics are radically different in principle—that the one belongs to a philosophy of nature and a metaphysics, in which substance is the primary concept; whereas the other belongs to the empirical sciences and to modern mathematics, in which the concept of relation supplants substance. Whichever side of the controversy is taken, the undeniable difference between a relational and a subject-predicate logic represents one of the great differences between modern and ancient thought.

It is not only in logic that the modern emphasis seems to be upon relations rather than upon things related—on relations denuded of their terms rather than on terms treated as correlatives. The same tendency appears in modern mathematics, in algebra, in the calculus, and especially in the theory of equations and functions, of sets and series. It also appears in modern physics where, according to Ernst Cassirer, the great conceptual revolution consists in displacing substance by function, and the casual interaction of substances by functional relationships and systems of order. Such substitutions obviously parallel the shift in logic—from the consideration of terms related as subjects and predicates, to the consideration of relations without regard to differences in the terms related.

In the tradition of the great books, this conceptual revolution seems to be announced by the treatment which Hume and Kant accord to the notion of substance. Hume appears to conceive of experience as a series of events related, as he says, by "only three principles of connexion . . . namely, *Resemblance, Contiguity* in time or place, and *Cause or Effect*." These relations make up the fabric of experience. So long as it consisted in such connections, our experience would be the same whether or not there were enduring things or substances.

"Nature has established connexions among particular ideas," Hume writes, so that "no sooner does one idea occur to our thoughts than it introduces its correlative." All our knowledge of matters of fact depends upon the association of ideas, or the relations of resemblance, contiguity, and causation among the elements of experience. All other knowledge has for its object those relations between ideas which do not connect them causally or place them in a spatial or temporal order. In either case, relations of all sorts, rather than things and their properties (or substances and their attributes), seem to be the prime constituents of nature and of knowledge.

Kant presents a fourfold classification of judgments according to their quantity, quality, relation, and modality. Under the head of relation, he distinguishes the categorical, the hypothetical, and the disjunctive according to the following criteria: "*a*. Relation of the predicate to the subject. *b*. Relation of the cause to its effect. *c*. Relation of subdivided knowledge, and of the collected members of the subdivision to each other." These are, he writes, "all the relations of thought in judgements."

Pointing out that he borrows the term from Aristotle, Kant calls the pure concepts of the understanding "categories" and constructs a table of categories which runs parallel to his table of judgments; because, as he explains, "the same function which imparts unity to various representations in one judgement imparts unity likewise to the mere synthesis of various representations in one intuition, which in a general way may be called the pure concept of understanding." Kant's categories, in contrast to Aristotle's, afford a striking example of the shift from substance to relation.

Where for Aristotle substance is the primary category and all other categories signify the accidents of substance, among which relation seems to have least reality in the nature of things, Kant makes relation one of the four major groups of categories, and under relation places subsistence and inherence (or substance and accident) along with causality and dependence (or cause and effect) and community (or reciprocity between the active and the passive). It is not substance, but the relation of substance and accident, which is for Kant a transcendental category.

THE ISSUE CONCERNING substance and relation takes another form in the problem whether relations exist *in* the very nature of things, as belonging to their essence, or only exist as connections *between* things. In the latter alternative, there is still the question whether relations between things are externally affixed to them or are internally inherent in them and affect the natures of the things related.

According to the Christian doctrine of the Trinity, there are real relations *in* God, each really distinct from the others, yet each identical with the divine essence. These relations are the persons of the Trinity—the relations Aquinas calls "paternity, filiation, spiration and procession," the relation of the Father and the Son, and of the Holy Spirit to them both. "Relation in God," he writes, "is not as an accident in a subject, but is the divine essence itself; and so it is subsistent, for the divine essence is subsistent. Therefore, as the Godhead is God, so the divine paternity is God the Father, Who is a divine person. Therefore, a divine person signifies a relation as subsisting."

Since the three persons of the Trinity are of the same essence, the principle of their real distinction must be found elsewhere. Denying that "there can be discerned between them a real distinction in respect of the divine essence," Descartes does not reject the possibility of a distinction "in respect of their relation to one another." Aquinas considers "two principles of difference among the divine persons . . . *origin* and *relation*," but thinks it is "better to say that the persons or hypostases are distinguished by relations rather than by origin"; for, among other reasons, "when a relation is an accident, it presupposes the distinction of subjects; but when the relation is subsistent, it does not presuppose, but brings about, distinction."

It would seem to follow that, except in God, relations are not subsistent. In Aristotle's theory of corporeal substances, for example, the matter and the form which constitute a physical thing are united, not related. Though matter and form are conceived as really distinct principles in the composition of a composite substance—as essence and existence are also sometimes said to be really distinct principles in the being of all things except God—their real distinction does not imply that they are subsistent, as are the persons of the Trinity, nor that they are relations, or in relation to one another. If real as opposed to logical relations occur only between things which somehow really subsist, then those principles which must be united in order for a thing to subsist cannot be really related to one another.

WITH A SOMEWHAT different analysis, Locke seems to exclude relations from the constitution of what he calls "the complex idea of substance." All complex ideas, according to Locke, "are either modes, substances, or relations." The complex idea of substance is a "collection of those several simple ideas of sensible qualities, which we . . . find united in the thing called horse or stone; yet because we cannot conceive how they should subsist alone, nor one in another, we suppose them existing in, and supported by some common subject; which support we denote by the name substance, though it be certain we have no clear or distinct idea of that thing we suppose a support."

The various simple ideas of qualities which, together with the indistinct notion of a supporting substratum, constitute the complex idea of a particular substance, are, in Locke's theory, compounded, not related. Relation is itself a complex idea, consisting in "the consideration and comparing of one idea with another." The ideas related may be either simple or complex, but the relations are *between* ideas, not *in* them—certainly not in simple ideas, nor in complex ideas of modes and substances, which are combinations, not relations, of simple ideas.

The exception is, of course, a complex idea of relation, which involves several distinct ideas and, in addition, the idea of a relation between them which, Locke says, "it gets from their comparison one with another . . . Since any idea, whether simple or complex, may be the occasion why the mind thus brings two things together . . . any of our ideas may be the foundation of relation"; but, Locke adds, "there must always be in relation two ideas, or things, either in themselves really separate, or considered as distinct, and then ground or occasion for their comparison."

Locke's theory of relations not only seems to exclude them from the interior constitution of substances, but also seems to make them entirely extrinsic to the natures of the things related. "Ideas of relation," Locke says, "may be the same in men who have far different ideas of the things that are related or that are thus compared." The relation is unaffected by the things it relates, as they in turn are unaffected by it, for they are "not contained in the real existence of things, but [are] something extraneous and super-induced."

Berkeley and Hume also seem to agree that relations are entirely external. "Relations are distinct from the ideas or things related," writes Berkeley, "inasmuch as the latter may be perceived by us without our perceiving the former." To Hume, "all events seem entirely loose and separate. One event follows another; but we can never observe any tie between them. They seem *conjoined,* but never *connected.*" So far as our understanding goes, nothing in the nature of one event necessarily leads the mind to the consideration of another, as it would if the event could not be understood by us except as intrinsically related or connected with that other.

In the tradition of western thought, the issue concerning internality or externality of relations has profound implications for man's conception of the order of nature or the structure of the world. The difference, discussed in the chapter on CHANCE, between what James calls the "block" and the "concatenated" universe presupposes not only different views of causality, but also different positions with respect to the internality or externality of relations, as is indicated by James's criticism of Hegel and Bradley.

The relation of part and whole, and of one part to another in the structure of an organic whole, seems to be the prime example of internal relationship. Each part is thought to be constituted, both in its being and nature, by the being and nature of the whole to which it belongs and by the other parts which comprise that whole. This may be seen in Spinoza's theory of God or Nature as the one and only substance, in and through which everything else both is and is conceived. All things are locked together in a system of internal relationships—the finite parts with one another through the infinite whole which determines each to be what it is, in itself and in relation to all others.

RELATION SEEMS TO BE the principle of order. At least it can be said that the various conceptions of order which appear in the great books involve the idea of relation and of different kinds of relationship.

The order of the universe or of nature, for example, seems to be differently conceived according as things are causally related to one another, related as lower and higher species in a hierarchy of grades of being, or as the parts of one all-embracing whole. In each case, it makes a difference, as we have already observed, whether the relations involved are thought to be real or logical, and internal or external to the things related.

Relation similarly enters into conceptions of psychological, political, and moral order—the order of the parts of the soul, the order of classes or functions in the state, the order of goods, of means and ends, of duties, of loves. Just as the status of each thing in nature is affected by whether the universe is conceived as a whole of internally related parts or as a set of externally related wholes, so the status of the individual in society is affected by whether the state is conceived as an organic whole or merely as a political order formed by the free association of individuals.

The consideration of the various types of order occurs in other chapters, such as NATURE, WORLD, SOUL, STATE, GOOD AND EVIL, and BEAUTY. Particular types of relationship are also discussed in chapters concerned with the terms between which such relationships hold—the relation of cause and effect in the chapter on CAUSE; spatial and temporal relationships in the chapters on SPACE and TIME; the relation of species and genus in the chapters on EVOLUTION and IDEA; relations of equality and inequality in the chapter on QUANTITY; and relations of similarity and dissimilarity in the chapter on QUALITY.

This last type of relationship, more broadly

conceived as including not merely likeness in quality, but the sameness or similitude of things in every sort of respect, is the main consideration of the chapter on SAME AND OTHER. The theory of analogy is discussed there also, for though it is concerned with relation—a proportion being a ratio of ratios—the specific relationship by which relations are themselves related in analogies or proportions seems to be one of similitude (either identity or similarity).

Finally, the idea of relation seems to be involved in the contrast between the absolute and the relative. In Planck's view, "everything that is relative presupposes the existence of something that is absolute . . . The often-heard phrase, 'Everything is relative,' is both misleading and thoughtless. The Theory of Relativity, too, is based on something absolute, namely, the determination of the matrix of the space-time continuum; and it is an especially stimulating undertaking to discover the absolute which alone makes meaningful something given as relative."

Any value is absolute if it is immutable and does not vary with time, place, and circumstance; it is relative when it varies in relation to differences in time, place, and circumstances. Things are said to be considered absolutely when they are considered in themselves, and relatively when they are considered with reference to something else.

By extension of these meanings, relativism tends to assert that with regard to most things, if not all, what they are depends on the point of view, *i.e.*, their relation to man, to *this* group of men, or even to *this* man. Absolutism goes to the opposite extreme of saying that things are what they are independently of man's view of them. The opposition of these two tendencies creates familiar issues concerning the true, the good, and the beautiful, which are discussed in the chapters devoted to those subjects.

79

Religion

INTRODUCTION

ARGUMENT is unprofitable—worse than that, unintelligible—when opponents do not share some common ground. Between the complete skeptic who denies reason's competence and the philosopher or scientist who appeals to it, no common ground exists. Between the man who obeys the rule not to contradict himself and the man who finds nothing repugnant in answering Yes and No to the same question, there can be no argument. There is an issue between them, but the position each takes reduces the other to silence.

Lack of a common measure for judging opposed views tends to render them incommunicable to one another. For men to be in this plight is the exception in science and philosophy, but it seems to be the typical situation where the basic issues of religion are concerned. Of all subjects the most controversial, religious issues seem to be the least capable of being settled by controversy. No divisions among men—certainly not those which separate philosophers or scientists—are as unbridgeable as the chasm between the faithful and those they call infidels, between Jew and gentile, or Christian and pagan. Faith and lack of faith, or the diversity of faiths, seem to render certain questions as imponderable as they are weighty.

On the definition of religion itself, the deepest issue lies between those who conceive it as having a supernatural foundation in God's revelation and authority, and those who think of religion as having a purely natural origin in certain human tendencies, which makes it no different from philosophy and science as an element of culture.

This latter view is the basis for the field of anthropology, a science which came of age in the 20th century. "The anthropologist's task," writes Lévi-Strauss, "is to discover correlations between different types of religions and different types of social organization . . . The field of myth, ritual, and religion seems . . . to be one of the more fruitful for the study of social structure." Frazer, while admitting the difficulty of defining religion, claims that it universally includes "a belief in powers higher than man and an attempt to propitiate or please them." Both sides of this definition assume that "the course of nature is to some extent elastic or variable, and that we can persuade or induce the mighty beings who control it to deflect, for our benefit, the current of events from the channel in which they would otherwise flow." In this sense, both Frazer and Lévi-Strauss see religion closely linked to—and perhaps growing out of—magic. As scientists, they are concerned with the supernatural only insofar as it works its way into the structure of society.

Religion can be supernatural only for those whose faith declares it to be so. Those who deny that it is supernatural may offer many reasons for thinking so, and try in many ways to explain away faith. What they all come to is that it is an illusion to suppose faith is God's gift rather than man's own will to believe. To the man of faith this only means that his critic lacks the gift of faith or even the wish to have it.

Many consequences follow from this unarguable difference concerning the meaning of religion. Religion to the man of faith usually means much more than the acceptance of a creed. It means acts of piety and worship, recourse to prayer, the partaking of sacraments, the observance of certain rituals, the performance of sacrifices and purifications. It means rendering to God what is His due, obeying His commandments, beseeching and gaining the help of His grace, whereby to lead a life which shall seem worthy to Him. "Religion and thought concerning God," Barth declares, "have never meant the same thing." He also maintains that "the so-called 'religious experience' is a wholly derived, secondary, fragmentary form of the divine. Even in its highest and purest examples, it is form and not content."

When religion is conceived as nothing more than a set of beliefs which men have adopted, it is restricted to one part of life. It may or may not involve action as well as thought, but it is not the fabric of a whole life. It does not qualify every other part of it. It does not demand that inner devotion and external conduct constitute the practice of a man's belief if he is to avoid hypocrisy.

In this set of books we find quite the opposite views of religion in the writings of Augustine, Aquinas, Calvin, and Kierkegaard, on the one hand, and in the writings of Nietzsche, Weber, and Veblen, on the other hand. The first group of authors comprises persons of intense religious faith. The second group, lacking such faith, approaches religion as outsiders, as students of its social or cultural significance.

ACCORDING TO THIS difference in the conception of religion as supernatural or natural, men seem to hold incommunicably different views of religious belief, of revelation, miracles, and prophecies. But those who agree that religion is not man-made, that it requires, in some form, divine authority and inspiration, do not all have the same faith, worship in the same way, or conform to the same rites. The issue, therefore, between men of different faiths—men who live according to the rules of different religious communities—is almost as difficult as that between the religious and the irreligious.

In the western tradition, the plurality of religions necessarily raises a question of truth and falsity for any religionist whose faith excludes the possibility of several equally true religions. "Idolatrous" and "superstitious," "heretical"

and "schismatic," are epithets which draw their special significance from controversies about religion and religions. The word "pagan," as Gibbon points out, comes to mean idolatry or the worship of false gods. "The Latin Christians," he says, "bestowed it on their mortal enemies, the Mahometans." The Muhammadans, in turn, held the view, according to Gibbon, that "all except themselves deserved the reproach of idolatry and polytheism." The charges of idolatry and superstition occur also in the conflict between Jew and Christian, between Protestant and Catholic, countered often by charges of infidelity or heresy and schism.

Quite apart from the general problem of church and state, with its issues of political toleration and freedom of worship, the very meaning of religion raises the question of tolerance in its most acute form. It is not a question of political rights and liberties, but of being right or wrong in one's religious beliefs and acts. To the extent that the communicants of one religion regard themselves as believing what God has revealed to them, and to the extent that they hold their religious practices to be prescribed by divine law, they are not free in conscience, it seems, to entertain contrary beliefs and practices as conceivably true alternatives.

The conflict between men of diverse faiths, alike in their understanding of faith as divinely inspired, somehow appeals beyond any human decision to God himself for judgment. The controversy between men of any religious faith and those who treat such faith as a purely human prejudice seems to be even less susceptible of resolution by the ordinary processes of discourse.

IF THESE OBSERVATIONS are accurate and just, the materials of this chapter cannot be assembled dialectically—either as opposed views or as belonging together—simply by reference to the content of the various opinions which can be found in the great books. In this chapter, as in no other except, perhaps, those which treat of matters connected with religion—such as GOD, IMMORTALITY, SIN, and THEOLOGY—it seems necessary to pay some attention to the opinion's author as well as to the opinion, and even in some cases to the community or culture in which the opinion arises. It is not as necessary, for example, to know whether the man who writes about virtue is himself virtuous as it is to know whether the man who writes about religion is religious and to know furthermore in what sense he conceives himself as being religious and what religion he espouses.

The distinction between sacred and profane, and between religious and secular, applies to books as well as to other things. In the tradition of the great books, only one book is set apart as sacred. None of the writers included in this set regard the Koran as sacred scripture, though Gibbon as a historian reports the Islamic belief in the Koran. Muslims believe that the Koran is the word of God revealed to His one and only prophet, as Jews believe that the Old Testament is divinely inspired writing, and Christians believe in both Testaments as Holy Writ.

But though the Bible is *the* traditionally sacred book of the west, it is not read as such by all who write about it. The historian or the philosopher who is not himself a religious Jew or Christian may acknowledge the belief of others without sharing it. He reads the Bible as a collection of human writings which have exercised an unparalleled influence upon western culture. Whatever the merit of these writings as wisdom, history, preachment, or poetry, they do not command a special kind of reading unless they are distinguished from all others by being the word of God, not man. Controversies over interpretations of the Bible may thus begin with each side begging the main question in issue. Is the Bible sacred scripture, or is it no different in kind from the poetry of Homer and the sayings of the Greek wise men?

The two ways of reading the Bible are incommensurable. If the Bible is not sacred, a critical reading may be expected to disclose inconsistencies in it, and many of the things it says may be questioned in fact or in principle. But if, though humanly recorded, it is the repository of divine revelation, then it has an authority which puts it above questioning, though not beyond the need for interpretation.

There is one sort of proposition, says Locke, which challenges "the highest degree of our assent upon bare testimony, whether the thing proposed agree or disagree with common experience, and the ordinary course of things, or no. The reason whereof is, because the testimony is of such a one as cannot deceive, nor be deceived, and that is of God himself. This carries with it an assurance beyond doubt, evidence beyond exception. This is called by a peculiar name, revelation; and our assent to it, faith: which as absolutely determines our minds, and as perfectly excludes all wavering, as our knowledge itself; and we may as well doubt of our own being, as we can whether any revelation from God be true. So that faith is a settled and sure principle of assent and assurance, and leaves no manner of room for doubt or hesitation. Only we must be sure that it be a divine revelation, and that we understand it right."

Locke seems to be putting two qualifications upon his remark that "the bare testimony of revelation is the highest certainty." The first concerns our assurance that we are not mistaken in accepting something as revealed. The second concerns the correctness of our understanding of that which we take to be God's word.

On the first point, while Hobbes says that "faith is a gift of God, which man can neither give nor take away by promises of rewards or menaces of torture," he also says that faith depends "only upon certainty or probability of arguments drawn from reason or from something men believe already." Faith does not come "by supernatural inspiration or infusion" but, according to Hobbes, "by education, discipline, correction, and other natural ways, by which God worketh them in his elect, at such time as he thinketh fit." The object of faith is not God, but the men whom God has appointed to instruct us; belief, which Hobbes distinguishes from faith, goes beyond faith to the acceptance as true of what they say. "Consequently," Hobbes writes, "when we believe that the Scriptures are the word of God, having no immediate revelation from God himself, our belief, faith, and trust is in the Church, whose word we take, and acquiesce therein."

On this same point, Aquinas gives a different answer. He distinguishes between the material and the formal aspects of the object of faith. As in the object of science, so in the object of faith there is "that which is known . . . and is the material object, so to speak," and "that whereby it is known, which is the formal aspect of the object. Thus, in the science of geometry, the conclusions are what is known materially, while the formal aspect of the science consists in the means of demonstration, through which the conclusions are known. Accordingly, if in faith we consider the formal aspect of the object, it is nothing else than the First Truth. For the faith of which we are speaking does not assent to anything, except because it is revealed by God." The articles of religious faith may be drawn from the content of Holy Writ, but that Holy Writ is the revealed truth of God must first be accepted by an act of faith. Aquinas seems to be meeting Locke's point by saying that it is faith itself which makes us sure that the propositions to which we assent by faith are the matter of divine revelation.

According to Calvin, the creed "furnishes us with a full and every way complete summary of faith, containing nothing but what has been derived from the infallible word of God." Faith, thus understood, is, for Kierkegaard, "the highest passion in a man. There are perhaps many in every generation who do not even reach it, but no one gets further." In Shaw's *Saint Joan,* the Archbishop says that a miracle is "an event which creates faith . . . Frauds deceive. An event which weaves faith does not deceive: therefore it is not a fraud, but a miracle."

ON LOCKE'S OTHER point concerning the rightness of our interpretation of Scripture, Locke himself remarks that "though everything said in the text be infallibly true, yet the reader may be, nay, cannot choose but be, very fallible in the understanding of it. Nor is to be wondered that the will of God, when clothed in words, should be liable to that doubt and uncertainty, which unavoidably attends that sort of conveyance." From which he concludes that since "the precepts of natural religion are plain, and very intelligible to all mankind, and seldom come to be controverted; and other revealed truths, which are conveyed to us by books and languages are liable to the common and natural obscurities incident to words, methinks it would become us to be more careful and diligent in observing the former, and less magisterial, positive, and imperious, in imposing our own ideas and interpretations of the latter."

That Scripture is difficult to interpret and subject to various interpretations Augustine also acknowledges, but he differs somewhat from Locke concerning the task or duty which that fact imposes upon the religious man. "Let no one irritate me further," Augustine writes, "by saying, 'Moses did not mean what you say. He meant what I say.' If anyone were to ask me, 'How do you know that Moses meant his words to be taken in the way that you explain them?' it would be my duty to listen to the question with composure . . . But when a man says 'Moses did not mean what you say, but what I say,' and yet does not deny that both his interpretation and mine are consistent with the truth, then, O Life of the poor, O my God, in whose bosom there is no contradiction, I beg you to water my heart with the rain of forbearance, so that I may bear with such people in patience. They speak as they do, not because they are men of God or because they have seen in the heart of Moses, your servant, that their explanation is the right one, but simply because they are proud. They have no knowledge of the thoughts in his mind, but they are in love with their own opinions, not because they are true, but because they are their own."

Confronted by a variety of interpretations, Augustine remarks, "When so many meanings, all of them acceptable as true, can be extracted from the words that Moses wrote, do you not see how foolish it is to make a bold assertion that one in particular is the one he had in mind? . . . If I had been Moses and you had made it my task to write the book of Genesis, I should have wished you to give me such skill in writing and such power in framing words, that not even those who as yet cannot understand how God creates should reject my words as beyond their comprehension, and those who can should find expressed in the few words of your servant whatever true conclusions they had reached by their own reasoning." Those who thirst "not for vanity but for the truth" honor the human dispensers of God's revelation, Augustine thinks, by believing that, when under God's inspiration they wrote these words, they showed us "whichever meaning sheds the fullest light of truth and enables us to reap the greatest profit.

"For this reason, although I hear people say, 'Moses meant this' or 'Moses meant that,'" Augustine declares, "I think it more truly religious to say, 'Why should he not have had both meanings in mind, if both are true? And if others see in the same words a third, or a fourth, or any number of true meanings, why should we not believe that Moses saw them all? There is only one God, who caused Moses to write the Holy Scriptures in the way best suited to the minds of great numbers of men who would all see truths in them, though not the same truths in each case.'"

Augustine's position combines belief in the truth of Scripture, which is a consequence of the faith that it is God's word, with latitude of interpretation in determining what that truth is, appealing here to the ordinary standards of what seems to be true to the thinking mind. In the course of commenting on Augustine's own interpretation of certain passages in Genesis, Aquinas summarizes what he takes to be Augustine's two rules. "The first is, to hold the truth of Scripture without wavering. The second is that since Holy Scripture can be explained in a multiplicity of senses, one should adhere to a particular explanation only in such measure as to be ready to abandon it, if it be proved with certainty to be false; lest Holy Scripture be exposed to the ridicule of unbelievers, and obstacles be placed to their believing."

As THE QUESTION whether the Bible is sacred writing affects the way it is to be read, so the distinction between religious and secular writing seems relevant to what the great books have to say about religion.

In the pagan tradition, for example, Herodotus in his *The History* reports and discusses a great variety of religious doctrines and practices as characteristic of the peoples he visits or inquires about. There seems to be no indication that Herodotus is judging the truth or falsity of these various religions, either by reference to their reasonableness or from convictions born of his own adherence to one of these religions as against all the rest. For the most part, he is writing *about* religion rather than *religiously,* with the possible exception of those passages in which he expresses his own views, discussed in the chapter on PROPHECY, on the oracles, omens, and portents which reveal the will of the gods.

In contrast, the tragedies of Aeschylus, especially the Oresteian trilogy, are religious poetry, comparable to Dante's *The Divine Comedy* and Milton's *Paradise Lost*. These are not books *about* religion, as, in a sense, the great poem of Lucretius *The Way Things Are* is about religion—a passionate attack on religion by a man who is not religious; as passionate, but more savage, is the attack on Judaism and Christianity by Nietzsche in modern times. "Wherever the religious neurosis has hitherto appeared on earth," Nietzsche declares, "we find it tied to three dangerous dietary prescriptions: solitude, fasting and sexual abstinence." Lucretius dismisses the prevalent religions of his day only because they burden mankind with fear of the gods, of death, and of the afterlife.

It may be thought that the aim of Lucretius is to purify religion when he wishes to banish "thoughts unworthy of the gods" and "alien to their serenity," so that men can "go serenely to their altars." But even a person who thinks this will still find a marked contrast between Lucretius and poets like Aeschylus or Dante who are writing from religious convictions to which they adhere as members of a religious community.

Both kinds of writing may be found in the same author. Hobbes, for example, in examining the phenomena of religious belief, seems to make public acceptance the criterion of the distinction between religion and superstition. "Fear of a power invisible, feigned by the mind," he says, "or imagined from tales publicly allowed," is religion; when they are "not allowed, superstition." Still writing as an observer, he says that "this fear of things invisible is the natural seed of that which everyone in himself calls religion; and in them that worship or fear that power otherwise than they do, superstition." Originating from "natural seeds" which he enumerates, "religion," he says, "by reason of the different fancies, judgments, and passions of several men, has grown up into ceremonies so different, that those which are used by one man are for the most part ridiculous to another."

Yet Hobbes also writes religiously, when he treats all other religions from the standpoint of the special truth of his own. "These natural seeds of religion," he points out, "have received culture from two sorts of men. One sort have been they that have nourished and ordered them, according to their own invention. The other have done it by God's commandment and direction ... Of the former sort were all the founders of commonwealths and the law-givers of the Gentiles. Of the latter sort were Abraham, Moses, and our Blessed Saviour, by whom have been derived unto us the laws of the Kingdom of God."

It is as a Christian that Hobbes compares the state religion of the Romans with the divine religion of the Jews. The Romans, he writes, "made no scruple of tolerating any religion whatsoever in the city of Rome itself, unless it had something in it that could not consist with their civil government; nor do we read that any religion was there forbidden, but that of the Jews, who (being the peculiar Kingdom of God) thought it unlawful to acknowledge subjection to any mortal King or State whatsoever. And thus you see how the religion of the Gentiles was a part of their policy."

"But where God himself," Hobbes continues, "by supernatural revelation, planted religion; there he also made to himself a peculiar kingdom, and gave laws, not only of behavior toward himself, but also toward one another; and thereby in the Kingdom of God, the policy, and laws civil, are a part of religion; and therefore, the distinction of temporal and spiritual domination has there no place."

Again it is as a man of Christian faith that Hobbes ascribes belief in Christian teachings to that faith. "The causes why men believe any Christian doctrine are various," he writes. "For faith is the gift of God, and he worketh it in each man by such ways as it seemeth good to him. The most ordinary immediate cause of our belief, concerning any point of Christian faith, is that we believe the Bible to be the Word of God." But when Hobbes goes on to say that the "only article of faith, which the Scripture makes necessary to salvation, is this, that Jesus is The Christ," he becomes the theologian with whom other theologians within the Christian community may disagree, on this or other points of dogma.

The disagreements we find between Augustine or Aquinas and Hobbes or Locke, or the differences in dogma which appear in a comparison of *The Divine Comedy* and *Paradise Lost,* represent the division between Catholic and Protestant Christians. But such theological disagreements do not obliterate certain common tenets of religious belief among all who profess Christianity. Above all, they leave untouched the belief in religion itself as transcending all merely human teaching and as providing the precepts of life through which God himself directs and helps man to his salvation.

This belief—even if no other except the belief in one God Who created the universe and made man in His image—seems to be shared by Jews and Christians. It marks the difference between the religious writings of ancient polytheism and of those which draw their inspiration from the Pentateuch and the Gospels. It makes the issue, as Pascal suggests, between those who write about a religion which they themselves either have or seek, and those who, neither having nor seeking, oppose all religions equally or treat all with the same secular detachment.

WRITING AS A CHRISTIAN apologist, Pascal says that "it is the glory of religion to have for enemies men so unreasonable; and their opposition to it is so little dangerous that it serves on the contrary to establish its truths. For the Christian faith goes mainly to establish these two facts, the corruption of nature, and redemption by Christ. Now I contend that if these men do not serve to prove the truth of the redemption by the holiness of their behavior, they at least serve admirably to show the corruption of nature by sentiments so unnatural.

"Let them at least be honest men," he adds, "if they cannot be Christians . . . Let them recognize that there are two kinds of people one can call reasonable: those who serve God with all their heart because they know Him, and those who seek Him with all their heart because they do not know Him. But as for those who live without knowing Him and without seeking Him, they judge themselves so little worthy of their own care, that they are not worthy of the care of others; and it needs all the charity of the religion which they despise, not to despise them even to the point of leaving them to their folly."

The very existence of other religions, according to Pascal, helps to prove the truth of the Christian religion. "I should equally have rejected the religion of Mahomet and of China, of the ancient Romans and of the Egyptians, for the sole reason, that none having more marks of truth than another, nor anything which should necessarily persuade me, reason cannot incline to one rather than the other." As for Judaism, it seems to Pascal to be divinely intended as the historic foundation and the prophetic forerunner of Christianity.

Apart from these comparative judgments, Pascal attributes certain unique signs of truth to the Christian religion. "Every religion is false," he writes, "which as to its faith does not worship one God as the origin of everything, and which as to its morality does not love only God as the object of everything . . . The true religion must have as a characteristic the obligation to love God. This is very just, and yet no other religion has commanded this; ours has done so. It must also be aware of human lust and weakness; ours is so. It must have adduced remedies for this; one is prayer. No other religion has asked of God [the power] to love and follow him . . . That we must love one God only is a thing so evident, that it does not require miracles to prove it." Yet Pascal also interprets Christ's saying, "Though you believe not Me, believe at least the works," as meaning that miracles are the strongest proof of a religion. "Miracles," he writes, "furnish the test in matters of doubt, between Jews and heathens, Jews and Christians, Catholics and heretics, the slandered and slanderers, between the two crosses."

After criticizing the evidence for miracles on rational grounds, Hume appears to agree that "the *Christian religion* not only was at first attended with miracles, but even at this day cannot be believed by any reasonable person without one." But his meaning seems to be that belief in miracles is itself the miracle of faith. "Mere reason," he says, "is insufficient to convince us" of the veracity of the Christian religion; "and whoever is moved by *Faith* to assent to it, is conscious of a continued miracle in his own person, which subverts all the principles of his understanding, and gives him a determination to believe what is most contrary to custom and experience."

PHILOSOPHERS AND THEOLOGIANS disagree on another issue. Where Hume says that "our most holy religion is founded on *Faith,* not on reason"—with the further implication that to adhere to it with faith requires the abandonment of reason—Augustine and Aquinas think that there can be no conflict between faith and reason, though faith declares the truth of more than reason can prove; and that the support which reason can give to faith in no way lessens the merit of believing.

With this Hobbes seems to agree, at least to the extent of holding that it discredits supernatural religion to make it consist in believing impossibilities or contradictions. Revelation, he says, can consist "of nothing against natural reason." But for Hume the difference between supernatural and natural religion turns on what one must believe both without and against reason as contrasted to what one believes as the result of a reasonable interpretation of the evidence. Like philosophy, natural religion, "which is nothing but a species of philosophy, will never be able to carry us beyond the usual course of experience, or give us measures of conduct and behavior different from those which are furnished by reflections on common life."

Those who, like Marx and Freud, regard religion as a social imposture or the response to a neurotic need, not only impute falsity or worse to the traditional religions of the west; they also tend to reject natural religion. Science is enough—for truth's sake, for the conduct of life, for society's welfare. Yet in commenting on the following lines from Goethe,

He who has Science and has Art,
  Religion, too, has he;
Who has not Science, has no Art,
  Let him religious be!

Freud says that "on the one hand, these words contrast religion with the two highest achievements of man, and on the other, they declare that in respect of their value in life, they can represent or replace each other." In these terms Freud thinks the religion of the ordinary man is justified—"the only religion that ought to bear the name." If a man does not have science or art to live by, he must have religion, for "life as we find it is too hard for us" and "we cannot do without palliative remedies."

It is the religion of the philosophers and the theologians which Freud questions. He criticizes the philosophers for trying "to preserve the God of religion by substituting for him an impersonal, shadowy, abstract principle"; and he challenges the grounds on which he thinks the theologians hold it to be "an impertinence on the part of science to take religion as a subject for its investigations." They deny that science has any competence whatsoever "to sit in judgment on religion . . . If we are not deterred by this brusque dismissal," Freud declares, "but inquire on what grounds religion bases its claim to an exceptional position among human concerns, the answer we receive, if indeed we are honored with an answer at all, is that religion cannot be measured by human standards, since it is of divine origin, and has been revealed to us by a spirit which the human mind cannot grasp. It might surely be thought," he continues, "that nothing could be more easily refuted than this argument; it is an obvious *petitio principii*, a 'begging of the question.' The point which is being called in question is whether there is a divine spirit and a revelation; and it surely cannot be a conclusive reply to say that the question cannot be asked because the Deity cannot be called in question."

Marx takes a similar view of the theologians. According to him, the theologians beg the question in much the same way as do the classical economists for whom there are "only two kinds of institutions, those of art and those of nature. Feudal institutions are artificial institutions, those of the bourgeoisie are natural institutions. In this," Marx says, "they resemble the theologians who establish two kinds of religion. Every religion but their own is an invention of men, while their own religion is an emanation from God." In Marx's view, religion plays a large part in preventing revolution, which he sees as the only escape of the workers from oppression. "Religion," according to Marx, "is the opiate of the masses."

Plato excoriates those who think that "all religion is a cooking up of words and make-believe." It is almost as if he had Marx and Freud in mind when, in the *Laws,* the Athenian Stranger carries on the discussion of religion in terms of the distinction between nature and art, and refers to those who "would say that the Gods exist not by nature, but by art, and by the laws of states, which are different in different places, according to the agreement of those who make them." They are the very same people who hold that "the honorable is one thing by nature and another by law, and that the principles of justice have no existence at all by nature."

IN PLATO'S VIEW, the justice of the state and its laws must be founded not only on nature rather than art, but also upon religion and a right belief in the gods. The Athenian Stranger answers those who think it is "dreadful that [we] should legislate on the supposition that there are Gods," by saying why "it is a matter of no small consequence . . . to prove that there are Gods, and that they are good and regard justice more than men do." The reason he gives is that "no one who in obedience to the laws believed that there were Gods, ever intentionally did any unholy act, or uttered an unlawful word, but those who did must have supposed one of three things—either that [the Gods] did not exist, which is the first possibility, or secondly, that if they did, they took no care of man, or thirdly, that they were easily appeased and turned aside from their purpose by sacrifices and prayers." That is why the demonstration of the existence of the gods "would be the best and noblest prelude of all our laws."

Rousseau's legislator, like Plato's, is also concerned with the role which religion plays in the foundation and life of the state. But the question "Which religion?" arises at once for Rousseau, as it does not for Plato, who can treat the nature of the gods and the nature of the state as equally within the province of the political philosopher. But for Rousseau, living in a Christian civilization, the political philosopher cannot approach the subject of religion without being confronted by the theologian. He finds it necessary, therefore, to distinguish between a revealed religion like Christianity and the natural or civil religion of the citizen.

Christianity, says Rousseau, "not the Christianity of today, but that of the Gospel, which is entirely different," is the religion of man, not of the citizen. "So far from binding the hearts of the citizens to the State, it has the effect of taking them away from all earthly things. I know of nothing more contrary to the social spirit. We are told that a people of true Christians would form the most perfect society imaginable. I see in this supposition only one great difficulty: that a society of true Christians would not be a society of men . . . The country of the Christian is not of this world."

What the state needs, Rousseau goes on to say, is "a purely civil profession of faith, of which the Sovereign should fix the articles, not exactly as religious dogmas, but as social sentiments without which a man cannot be a good citizen or a faithful subject." He then enumerates what he calls "the dogmas of civil religion" which "ought to be few, simple, exactly worded, without explanation or commentary," such as "the existence of a mighty, intelligent, and beneficent Divinity, possessed of foresight and providence, the life to come, the happiness of the just, the punishment of the wicked, the sanctity of the social contract and the laws."

Montesquieu takes the diametrically opposite view. "With regard to the true religion," he writes, "I have never pretended to make its interests submit to those of a political nature, but rather to unite them . . . The Christian religion, which ordains that men should love each other, would, without doubt, have every nation blessed with the best civil, the best political laws; because these, next to this religion, are the greatest good that men can give and receive." Montesquieu meets the argument that "true Christians cannot form a government of any duration," by saying that the more men "believe themselves indebted to religion, the more they would think due to their country. The principles of Christianity, deeply engraved on the heart, would be infinitely more powerful than the false honor of monarchies, than the human virtues of republics, or the servile fear of despotic states."

ANY CONSIDERATION of the political significance of religion tends to lead into the controversy over the relation between church and state. Three main positions seem to be taken: one which calls for the integration of church and state, one which calls for a subordination of either state to church or church to state, and one which insists upon the autonomy of each as a basis for their relation to one another, or carries separation even further, to the point of complete divorce.

The theocratic state of the Old Testament represents the Jewish version of the first position, distinguished by the fact that the priesthood was in the service of the king. Hobbes defines a Christian commonwealth in almost parallel terms. It is indifferent whether it is called a "church" or a "state," because it is "a company of men professing Christian religion, united in the person of one sovereign." It follows, Hobbes argues, that "there is on earth, no such universal church as all Christians are bound to obey, because there is no power on earth, to which all other commonwealths are subject. There are Christians in the dominions of several princes and states; but every one of them is subject to that commonwealth, whereof he is himself a member; and consequently, cannot be subject to the commands of any other person. And therefore a church, such a one as is able to command, to judge, absolve, condemn, or do any another act, is the same thing with a civil commonwealth, consisting of Christian men; and is called a *civil state,* for that the subjects of it are *men;* and a *church* for that the subjects thereof are *Christians.*"

According to Hobbes, "*temporal* and *spiritual* government are but two words brought into the world, to make men see double, and mistake their lawful *Sovereign . . .* There is therefore no other government in this life, neither of state, nor religion, but temporal." Agreeing with Hobbes on the unity of government and the integration of church and state, writers like Augustine and Roger Bacon place kings in the service of the priesthood, and make the supreme pontiff, who governs both spiritually and temporally, the only earthly sovereign. Étienne Gilson summarizes their view by saying that for them "the definition of the Church includes the State," and that the church has a universality which embraces "the temporal and the spiritual domains alike."

The position of Aquinas is indicated in the Treatise on Law, in the passage in which he declares that no civil law can be valid or binding if what it commands is contrary to divine law. It is more explicitly developed in his little tract *On Kingship.* "It is not the ultimate end," he writes, "of an assembled multitude to live virtuously, but through virtuous living to attain to the possession of God. Furthermore, if it could attain this end by the power of human nature, then the duty of a king would have to include the direction of men to this end." But, Aquinas holds, men attain this end by divine, not human, power and therefore divine, not human, government is needed to direct men to their end. "Consequently," he maintains, "in order that spiritual things might be distinguished from earthly things, the ministry of this kingdom has been entrusted not to earthly kings, but to priests, and in the highest degree to the chief priest, the successor of St. Peter, the Vicar of Christ, the Roman Pontiff, to whom all the kings

of Christian peoples are to be subject as to our Lord Jesus Christ Himself. For those to whom pertains the care of intermediate ends should be subject to him to whom pertains the care of the ultimate end, and be directed by his rule."

This last statement indicates that Aquinas, unlike Augustine and Roger Bacon, assigns to the state a subsidiary dominion and to the king a subordinate jurisdiction. The opponent of Aquinas is usually thought to be Marsilius of Padua, whose *Defensor Pacis* separates church and state, but subordinates priest to king, in a manner which corresponds to the Averroistic subordination of theology to philosophy. Agreeing with both that church and state are distinct, Dante agrees with neither on the relation which should obtain between the temporal and the spiritual domains, or between civil and ecclesiastical government.

Whereas Aquinas holds that only man's spiritual end is ultimate and that all temporal ends are intermediate, Dante insists that man has two ultimate goals. "Man exists for a double purpose," he says in *De Monarchia.* "Since he alone among beings partakes of both corruptibility and incorruptibility, he alone among beings belongs in two final orders—one of which is his goal as a corruptible being, the other as incorruptible." Man has two beatitudes, or two forms of happiness—an earthly perfection which consists in the complete realization throughout time of the intellectual powers of mankind, and a heavenly perfection which consists in the vision of God. "These two states of bliss," Dante argues, "like two different goals, man must reach by different ways. For we come to the first as we follow the philosophical teachings, applying them to our moral and intellectual capacities; and we come to the second as we follow the spiritual teachings, which transcend human reason according to our theological capacities, faith, hope, and charity."

In terms of this theory of man's two ends, and of the distinct spheres of reason and faith, or philosophy and civil law on the one hand, and religion and divine law on the other, Dante formulates his doctrine of the autonomy of state and church. "The reins of man," he writes, "are held by a double driver according to man's two-fold end: one is the supreme pontiff, who guides mankind with revelations to life eternal, and the other is the emperor, who guides mankind with philosophical instructions to temporal happiness." Church and state may be related as sun and moon in the sense that the state receives some illumination from the church even about matters within its own jurisdiction; but, according to Dante, the state has its own source of light in reason. "Temporal power," he maintains, "receives from spiritual power neither its being, nor its power or authority, nor even its functioning, strictly speaking; but what it receives is the light of grace, which God in heaven and the pope's blessing on earth cause to shine on it in order that it may work more effectively."

All these medieval theories of what should be the relation between church and state—with the exception, perhaps, of the doctrine of Marsilius of Padua—conceive religion as having a supernatural source and the church as having a supernatural foundation, both being instituted for the sake of guiding man to his supernatural end. They differ from one another according to the view they take of man's earthly or temporal goods, the power of his reason, and the jurisdiction of his laws. Their difference, according to Gilson, verifies the principle that "the manner in which one conceives the relationship of the State to the Church, that in which one conceives the relationship of philosophy to theology, and in which one conceives the relationship of nature to grace, are necessarily correlated."

These medieval theories of church and state persist, with certain modifications, in modern times. But the characteristically modern view of the matter begins with a different view of religion itself. Its medieval prototype is to be found in the rationalism of Marsilius. Within the secular state, the church is a purely human institution, religion is defended by philosophy for the contribution it makes to the peace of the civil community—or, perhaps, condemned by the apostles of earthly progress as "the opiate of the masses." The principle of religious tolerance involves not merely tolerance of religion, but tolerance for a diversity of religions and often the complete rejection of all religion.

"I esteem it above all things necessary," writes Locke in *A Letter Concerning Toleration,* "to distinguish exactly the business of civil government from that of religion, and to settle the just bounds that lie between the one and the other . . . The commonwealth," Locke continues, "seems to me to be a society of men constituted only for the procuring, preserving and advancing their own civil interests." A church is "a voluntary society of men, joining themselves together of their own accord in order to the public worshipping of God in such manner as they judge acceptable to Him, and effectual to the salvation of their souls."

Locke's doctrine of the separation of church and state is reflected in the Constitution of the United States. In the form which Jefferson gives it, it appears in the declaration that "Congress shall make no law respecting an establishment of religion, or prohibiting the free exercise thereof." J. S. Mill carries out the same principles in his attack on "Sabbatarian legislation." Such laws, he thinks, exceed the power of civil government. They represent an "illegitimate interference with the rightful liberty of the individual . . . The notion that it is one's duty that another should be religious" is, in Mill's opinion, "the foundation of all the religious persecutions ever perpetrated." Hegel, on the other hand, holds that "the state should require all citizens to belong to a church," but he points out that "*a* church is all that can be said, because since the content of a man's faith depends on his private ideas, the state cannot interfere with it."

Examining America in its youth, Tocqueville praises the separation of church and state. "When a religion seeks to found its sway only on the longing for immortality equally tormenting every human heart, it can aspire to universality; but when it comes to uniting itself with a government, it must adopt maxims which apply only to certain nations." In Europe, the union of politics and religion prevents "the human spirit from following its inclination" and drives the human spirit "beyond those limits within which it should naturally remain." In America, religion "restricts itself to its own resources, of which no one can deprive it; it functions in one sphere only, but it pervades it and dominates there without effort."

The positions men take on the great issues of church and state thus seem to be determined in part by the diverse conceptions men have of religion. This is no less true of opposing views on religious liberty, on the treatment of heresy and schism, on religious education, the missionary calling, and the conversion of infidels. In the discussion of religion, perhaps more than anywhere else, the first Yea or Nay seems to determine all other affirmations or denials.

80

Revolution

INTRODUCTION

Most of the words commonly used as synonyms for "revolution," such as "insurrection," "uprising," "rebellion," or "civil war," carry the connotation of violence and the use of armed force. Most of the great revolutions in western history which come readily to mind—those in the city-states and empires of the ancient world, the Peasants' Revolt in Germany in the 15th century, the rebellion led by Cromwell in 17th-century England, the American and French Revolutions in the 18th century, the Russian and the Spanish Revolutions in the 20th century—have been affairs of bloodshed. Yet neither in political theory nor in historic fact does revolution always involve the use of force or the resort to violence.

Thucydides describes both violent and non-violent revolutions in the alternations of democracy and oligarchy in the constitution of the Greek city-states. In England, the Great Rebellion which, by civil war, succeeds in beheading one Stuart king, is followed by the Bloodless Revolution of 1688 which, without any war at all, unseats another. Some of the revolutions in the European states in the middle years of the 19th century are accompanied by barricades and fighting. Some, however, like the revolutions accomplished by the Reform Bills in England or by constitutional amendments in the United States, are fundamental changes in government effected by due process of law, by peaceful shifts in the distribution of political power.

A revolution may involve action in defiance of the law and yet be prosecuted without violence on the part of the revolutionists, as in the case of the rebellion which Gandhi led against British rule in India by the method of civil disobedience. The use of armed force may not, however, be the only technique of revolutionary violence. "Revolutions are effected in two ways," according to Aristotle, "by force and by fraud." Though fraud does no physical violence, it does violence to the will of those who are deceived. In some cases when fraud is used, "the citizens are deceived into acquiescing in a change of government, and afterwards," Aristotle observes, "they are held in subjection against their will." In other cases, they may subsequently be persuaded and their allegiance and goodwill won. But as Machiavelli's later consideration of these two techniques of seizing power indicates, the choice between force and fraud is one of expediency rather than of principle. He recommends guile as an alternative to force, with force held in reserve should cunning fail. Both methods, however, employ the strategy of warfare.

As opposed to both force and fraud, and even to the method of civil disobedience, which acts outside the law or in violation of it, the writers of *The Federalist* conceive the possibility of a revolutionary process which is at once peaceful and legal. It is precisely because they think that the Constitution of the United States affords the opportunity for achieving political change by constitutional amendment that they defend the clause which guarantees "to every State in this Union a republican form of government," and promises to protect each of them, upon application to the federal government, "against domestic violence." To the objection that such a guaranty may involve "an officious interference in the domestic concerns of the members," Hamilton replies: "It could be no impediment to reforms of the State constitutions by a majority of the people in a legal and peaceable mode. This right would remain undiminished. The guaranty could only operate against changes to be effected by violence. Towards the prevention of calamities of this kind, too many checks cannot be provided."

In another of the Federalist papers, Madison considers the possibility of "an insurrection pervading all the States, and comprising a superiority of the entire force, though not a constitutional right." He thinks such a case beyond "the compass of human remedies." It is enough if the Constitution "diminishes the risk of a calamity for which no possible constitution can provide a cure." Nor does "a conflagration through a whole nation, or through a very large proportion of it, proceeding either from weighty causes of discontent given by the government or from the contagion of some violent popular paroxysm" seem to Hamilton to "fall within any ordinary rules of calculation." In his estimation, "no form of government can always either avoid or control" such revolutions. But, he adds, "where the whole power of the government is in the hands of the people, there is the less pretence for the use of violent remedies in partial or occasional distempers of the State."

WHEN ARISTOTLE THINKS of revolution as taking place without violence, he does not have in mind the strictly modern device of constitutional amendment. Political change, he suggests, may be the result of accidents rather than of planned actions. "Political revolutions," he writes, sometimes "spring from a disproportionate increase in any part of the state . . . And this disproportion may sometimes happen by accident, as at Terentum, from a defeat in which many of the notables were slain in a battle with the Iapygians just after the Persian War, the constitutional government in consequence becoming a democracy." Or "when the rich grow numerous or properties increase, the form of government changes into an oligarchy or a government of families."

On the other hand, to writers like Hobbes and Locke, revolution means war and is inseparable from violence. Those who "deny the authority of the Commonwealth"—apart from which, according to Hobbes, men live in a state of war—by renouncing their subjection to the Sovereign, "relapse into the condition of war commonly called Rebellion . . . For *rebellion* is but war renewed." Unlike bees and ants, the peace of whose societies is never threatened by rebellion, there are "amongst men . . . very many that think themselves wiser, and abler to govern the public, better than the rest; and these strive to reform and innovate, one this way, another that way; and thereby bring it into distraction and civil war."

Locke's principle seems to be that "whoever uses force without right—as everyone does in society who does it without law—puts himself into a state of war with those against whom he so uses it." Having entered into society "and introduced laws for the preservation of property, peace and unity amongst themselves," men who "set up force again in opposition to the laws, do *rebellare*—that is, bring back again the state of war—and are properly rebels."

Aquinas also seems to align revolution (which he calls "sedition") with war and strife, though he thinks it differs from them in two respects: "First, because war and strife denote actual aggression on either side, whereas sedition may be said to denote either actual aggression or the preparation for such aggression . . . Secondly, they differ in that war is, properly speaking, carried on against external foes, being as it were between one people and another, whereas strife is between one individual and another, while sedition, in its proper sense, is between the mutually dissentient parts of one people, as when one part of the state rises in tumult against another part."

THOUGH THE WORD "revolution" may be used in both senses, it nevertheless seems to be the case that traditional discussions of the causes and prevention of revolution, theories of revolutionary strategy and tactics, and the great issue of the right of rebellion all seem to contemplate the resort to, or at least the threat of, force to gain an end. This also seems to be implied in the popular conception of the difference between revolution and evolution.

The contrast between revolution and evolution may explain why the note of violence, disorder, or disruption colors the idea of revolution. The word "evolution" usually signifies change which is gradual and which tends in one direction rather than another, that direction being for the most part toward a progressive development of changes already accomplished. Revolution is abrupt. Revolutions can occur in either direction, against the tide as well as with it. As action and reaction can be equal and opposite in physical motion, so in social change revolution and counter-revolution can aim in opposite directions. In either case, whether revolution reverses the direction of change or precipitates a radical transformation toward which things are moving too slowly, revolution seems to involve *overthrowing* the established order rather than *developing* its latent tendencies.

It is in this sense that the revolutionist is a radical. He may also be a reactionary in the sense that the radical change he is willing to use force to achieve, is a return to some earlier condition rather than one which, in the judgment of his opponents, is in the line of progress or evolution. But whether reactionary or progressive the revolutionist is never conservative. If the established order does not submit readily to the radical change which a revolutionary person or party seeks, or if it resists, it must be forced to yield. The revolutionist can be reluctant to use force, but he can never forswear it entirely.

This seems to be the sense in which Marx and Engels conceive the program of the *Communist Manifesto* as a revolutionary program. Their conception of a revolutionary class or party is not, however, limited to the proletariat in their struggle against the bourgeoisie. They apply it to the bourgeoisie, not in the contemporary world when the established order of capitalism makes the bourgeoisie conservative or reactionary, but in the 18th century when the bourgeoisie overthrew the landed aristocracy.

"The bourgeoisie," they write, "historically has played a most revolutionary part . . . The French Revolution, for example, abolished feudal property in favour of bourgeois property." And again: "When Christian ideas succumbed in the 18th century to rationalist ideas, feudal society fought its death-battle with the then revolutionary bourgeoisie." That the French Revolution represents the struggle not between the propertied and propertyless classes, but between two propertied classes— the bourgeoisie and the aristocrats—seems evident to Marx in the fact that "during the very first storms of the revolution, the French Bourgeoisie dared to take away from the workers the right of association just acquired."

No less than the *Communist Manifesto,* the American Declaration of Independence is a revolutionary document. Its signers are prepared to use force to overthrow the established order which, in their view, has worked grievous iniquities and injustices upon the colonies. But in the Marxist view the rebellion of the colonists, unlike the French Revolution, is political rather than economic, even if it has economic as well as political motivations. This distinction between economic and political revolution seems to be peculiarly modern.

It is not that the ancients—Thucydides, Plato, and Aristotle, for example—fail to recognize the "class war," which is paramount for Marx. They observe (as is indicated in the chapter on OLIGARCHY) the struggle between the rich and the poor for control of the state. They know that the opponents, in the frequent and violent revolutions which disturbed the Greek city-states, are the oligarchs and the democrats—the men of great property and the men of little or none.

The revolt of the helots in Sparta is the exceptional case of a rebellion of slaves against their master. For the most part, the struggle is between freemen belonging to different economic classes. The oligarchic and democratic revolutions which these classes in society foment are political in the sense of seeking to change the constitution rather than the economic system itself, even though the constitutional changes may have economic as well as political effects. "In the opinion of some," Aristotle reports, "the regulation of property is the chief point of all, that being the question upon which all revolutions turn."

Aristotle is willing to admit that "the equalization of property" may "prevent the citizens from quarrelling," but he does not think that economic injustice is the only cause of revolution, or economic justice its absolute cure. "The avarice of mankind," he writes, "is insatiable; at one time two obols was pay enough; but now, when this sum has become customary, men always want more and more without end; for it is of the nature of desire not to be satisfied, and most men live only for the gratification of it. The beginning of reform," in his opinion, "is not so much to equalize property as to train the nobler sorts of natures not to desire more, and to prevent the lower from getting more; that is to say, they must be kept down, but not ill-treated." Such a reform would hardly cure the evil of chattel slavery. That requires a revolution which effects the equalization of political status, not the equalization of property.

If a rebellion of slaves in the ancient world had succeeded in abolishing the institution of slavery, it would have been, in the modern view, an economic as well as a political revolution, for it would have radically altered the mode of production. It is in this sense that what Adam Smith describes as the change from an agrarian to a manufacturing economy, is strictly an economic revolution, though it is Marx, not Smith, who gives currency to the word "revolution" as used in this sense. It is exemplified in our common understanding of the phrase "the industrial revolution" which refers to the radical change in an economy based on manufactures, when mass production by machines in factories replaces the system of production by workers using their own tools in their own homes.

"In manufacture," writes Marx, "the revolution in the mode of production begins with labour-power; in modern industry it begins with the instruments of labour. Our first inquiry then is, how the instruments of labour are converted from tools into machines, or what is the difference between a machine and the implements of a handicraft?" But for Marx the meaning of economic revolution is not limited to radical changes in the physical conditions of production. Such changes necessarily involve equally radical changes in the social relationships of economic classes, and in their possession of political power. In the

Manifesto, "the modern bourgeoisie" is said to be "itself the product of a long course of development, of a series of revolutions in the modes of production and of exchange." The bourgeoisie, in turn, "cannot exist without constantly revolutionizing the instruments of production, and thereby the relations of production, and with them the whole relations of society."

According to Marx and Engels, "each step in the development of the bourgeoisie was accompanied by a corresponding political advance of that class. An oppressed class under the sway of the feudal nobility, . . . an armed and self-governing association in the mediaeval commune . . . afterwards, in the period of manufacture proper, serving either the semi-feudal or the absolute monarchy as a counterpoise against the nobility . . . the bourgeoisie has at last, since the establishment of modern industry and of the world market, conquered for itself, in the modern representative state, exclusive political sway."

ON THE QUESTION whether economic revolutions, in their social and political aspects, require violence, the writers of the *Manifesto* seem to be unambiguous—at least so far as the communist program is concerned. Since "the Communist revolution is the most radical rupture with traditional property relations," and "involves the most radical rupture with traditional ideas," it can hardly be expected to occur without open warfare, no less violent than the earlier struggle of the bourgeoisie against the aristocrats. Standing "face to face with the bourgeoisie today, the proletariat alone is a really revolutionary class," in whose development Marx and Engels see the transition from a "more or less veiled civil war raging within existing society, up to the point where that war breaks out into open revolution, and where the violent overthrow of the bourgeoisie lays the foundation for the sway of the proletariat."

It is precisely on the use of force that the *Manifesto* distinguishes between communism and socialism, especially the "utopian" variety of the latter. The Socialists "reject all political, and especially all revolutionary, action; they wish to attain their ends by peaceful means, and endeavour by small experiments, necessarily doomed to failure, and by the force of example, to pave the way for the new social gospel ... They, therefore, endeavour, and that consistently, to deaden the class struggle and to reconcile the class antagonisms." Communist strategy, on the contrary, everywhere supports "every revolutionary movement against the existing social and political order of things ... The Communists disdain to conceal their views and aims. They openly declare that their ends can be attained only by the forcible overthrow of all existing social conditions."

Though fundamentally economic, the communist revolution cannot help having political effects. "Political power," according to Marx and Engels, "is merely the organized power of one class for oppressing another." This applies to the proletariat's conquest of power. Yet they also seem to think that the dictatorship of the proletariat is only a temporary phase in the communist revolution. "If the proletariat during its contest with the bourgeoisie is compelled by the force of circumstances to organize itself as a class; if by means of a revolution it makes itself the ruling class and, as such, sweeps away by force the old conditions of production, then it will, along with these conditions, have swept away the conditions for the existence of class antagonisms and of classes generally, and will thereby have abolished its own supremacy as a class." In aiming at the economically classless society, with the consequent transformation of the state, the communist program seems to conceive its revolution as abolishing the possibility of or need for any further revolutions, peaceful or violent, economic or political.

Discussing why great revolutions will become rare with the advent of a politically as well as an economically classless society, Tocqueville asks, "Does equality of social conditions habitually and permanently drive men toward revolutions? Does it contain some disturbing principle which prevents society from settling down? ..." While Tocqueville tells us that he does not think so, he also fears that the democratic societies of the future "will end up by being too unalterably fixed with the same institutions, prejudices, and mores, so that mankind will stop progressing and will dig itself in."

IN ADDITION TO the issues raised by the economic theory and history which underlie revolutionary communism, there is the debatable question whether an economically classless society means the withering away of the state, or at least such changes in political institutions that revolution would cease to be possible or necessary. Even a hypothetical consideration of this question seems to call for attention to the various ways in which political revolutions take place. With the advent of the "classless society," no opportunity would remain, at least in theory, for the type of revolution in which one ruling class replaces another. But in such a society it is still conceivable that the equivalent of a palace revolution might substitute one ruling individual for another—by the old-fashioned methods of assassination or usurpation.

For Aristotle, however, all revolutions which produce a change from one form of government to another also involve the replacement of one ruling class by another. He distinguishes between such revolutions as affect the constitution, "when men seek to change from an existing form into some other, for example, from democracy into oligarchy, or from oligarchy into democracy," and those revolutions which do not affect the constitution, when men, "without disturbing the form of government, whether oligarchy or monarchy or any other, try to get the administration into their own hands." To these two types of revolution Aristotle adds a third, which "may be directed against only a portion of the constitution, e.g., the establishment or overthrow of a particular office; as at Sparta, it is said that Lysander attempted to overthrow the monarchy, and king Pausanias, the ephoralty."

Conceivably, any of these political changes might be accomplished without violence. In modern constitutional states, the basic principle of constitutions can be changed from oligarchy to democracy by amendments or legal reforms which extend the franchise. The structure of the government, as to its offices or their organization, can be changed by some form of peaceful plebiscite. As the Federalists point out, the polls provide a "natural cure for an ill-administration in a popular or representative constitution," namely, a change of men. But such changes of government in the ancient city-states, even when constitutional, appear to Aristotle to be revolutionary in the double sense of involving violence, or the threat of it, and of being radical transformations of the polity. What is true of constitutional changes in ancient republics is also true of monarchies and tyrannies, both ancient and modern.

When absolute power is concentrated in the hands of one man, his subjects are necessarily without juridical means for redressing their grievances by changing the occupant of the throne, much less for abolishing the monarchy entirely in favor of self-government. Machiavelli's advice to the prince on safeguarding his power against usurping rivals or rebellious subjects seems to be written against the background of force and fraud as the normal methods of changing rulers or modes of rule. They are the very same methods which the prince in power must employ to maintain his position.

"There are two ways of contesting," Machiavelli writes, "the one by law, the other by force; the first method is proper to men, the second to beasts; but because the first is frequently not sufficient, it is necessary to have recourse to the second. Therefore it is necessary for a prince to understand how to avail himself of the beast and the man . . . Being compelled knowingly to adopt the beast, [a prince] ought to choose the fox and the lion; because the lion cannot defend himself against snares and the fox cannot defend himself against wolves." It follows, according to Machiavelli, that the prince seldom can be, though he should always try to *appear* to be, "merciful, faithful, humane, religious, upright . . . A prince, especially a new one, cannot observe all those things for which men are esteemed, being often forced, in order to maintain the state, to act contrary to fidelity, friendship, humanity, and religion."

The stories of oriental despotism told by Herodotus, the account of the Caesars given by Tacitus and Gibbon, the chronicle of the English monarchy in the historical plays of Shakespeare, all seem to indicate that crowns seldom change heads without bloodshed. Machiavelli's rules for the prince do not greatly enlarge upon Aristotle's description of "the arts by which the tyrant preserves his power." Even when Aristotle proposes, as an alternative method, that the tyrant can try to be benevolent, he adds the Machiavellian suggestion that the tyrant should at least "appear to act" like a good king.

The tyrant, Aristotle writes, "should lop off those who are too high. He must put to death men of spirit . . . He must be on his guard against anything which is likely to inspire either courage or confidence among his subjects. He must prohibit literary assemblies or other meetings for discussion, and he must take every means to prevent people from knowing one another." After enumerating many similar practices which he calls "Persian and barbaric arts," Aristotle concludes that "there is no wickedness too great for the tyrant" if he is to maintain himself in power.

These matters are more fully discussed in the chapter on TYRANNY AND DESPOTISM. In our present consideration of the types of revolution, we must note one other political change which usually involves the widespread turbulence of civil war. That is the rebellion of subject peoples against their imperial masters. Unlike civil uprisings, which seek to overthrow governments or effect a change in the ruling classes or persons, these wars of rebellion seek to liberate one people from another or to establish the independence of colonies at the expense of empire.

Still another type of insurrection aims at the dissolution of the state itself. What Rousseau deals with in theory as the degeneration of the state into anarchy by the repudiation of the social contract, calls to mind no historic examples; but the few historic instances of "wars of secession" certainly illustrate the point. They aim to dissolve a federal state by severing ties of union which have something like a contractual character.

The distinction between these types of civil war may be clear in theory, yet difficult to apply to historic cases. Which sort of insurrection—a rebellion of colonies or a secession of states—does the Declaration of Independence announce? A theory current among American political writers in 1775 suggests that the thirteen colonies claimed the status of self-governing dominions in a confederacy united under the British crown. On this theory, does the principle stated in the Declaration—that it is sometimes "necessary for one people to dissolve the political bands which have connected them with another, and to assume among the powers of the earth the separate and equal station to which the laws of nature and of nature's God entitle them"—cover the secession of the Southern states from the American union, as well as the revolt of the American states from Great Britain, or the British Commonwealth of nations? Questions of fact are involved, of course, in any comparison of the Revolutionary War of 1776 and the war between the states in 1861; but the question of principle turns on the whole issue of whether revolution is a matter of might or right.

THE RIGHT OF REVOLUTION does not seem to be a central consideration in ancient political theory. The ancient discussion of revolutions appears to be more concerned with their causes, their methods, and their prevention. This does not mean that the ancients treat revolutions entirely as contests for power. On the contrary, Aristotle declares that "the universal and chief cause of the revolutionary impulse" is "the desire of equality, when men think that they are equal to others who have more than themselves; or, again, the desire of inequality and superiority, when conceiving themselves to be superior they think that they have not more but the same or less than their inferiors—pretentions which may or may not be just."

Nevertheless, Aristotle's elaborate treatise on revolution in the fifth book of his *Politics* deals alike with revolutions that spring from real and from fancied injustices. The object of his inquiry seems to be "what modes of destruction apply to particular states, and out of what and into what they mostly change; also what are the modes of preservation in states generally, or in a particular state, and by what means each state may be best preserved"— *not* how revolution can be justified or why rebellion is the crime of treason or the folly of anarchy. Such questions seem to come to the foreground in modern political theory, though they also have a certain prominence in medieval teaching.

Aquinas, for example, holds that sedition is "a special kind of sin" because it is "opposed to a special kind of good, namely, the unity and peace of a people." He qualifies this, however, in the case of an uprising against tyranny, even if it involves civil strife. Since in his view "a tyrannical government is not just, because it is directed, not to the common good but to the private good of the ruler . . . there is no sedition in disturbing a government of this kind, unless indeed the tyrant's rule be disturbed so inordinately that his subjects suffer greater harm from the consequent disturbance than from the tyrant's government. Indeed," Aquinas writes, "it is the tyrant rather who is guilty of sedition, since he encourages discord and sedition among his subjects, that he may lord over them more securely."

Holding that "the end of government is the good of mankind," Locke asks, in a similar vein, which is better: "that the people should be always exposed to the boundless will of tyranny, or that the rulers should be sometimes liable to be opposed when they grow exorbitant in the use of their power, and employ it for the destruction and not the preservation of the property of their people"? Since "force is to be opposed to nothing but unjust and unlawful force," Locke argues that a king may be resisted when he exceeds his authority or prerogative and uses his power unlawfully. Since such a king "has dethroned himself, and put himself in a state of war with his people, what shall hinder them from prosecuting him who is no king, as they would any other man who has put himself into a state of war with them?"

The right to resist a tyrant, or a king turned despot, may lead to regicide, but this seems no different to Locke from the punishment of any other criminal. "He who may resist must be allowed to strike"; and furthermore, Locke continues, "he has a right, when he prevails, to punish the offender, both for the breach of the peace, and all the evils that followed upon it." Rousseau is even less hesitant to condone tyrannicide. "The contract of government is so completely dissolved by despotism," writes Rousseau, "that the despot is master only so long as he remains the strongest; as soon as he can be expelled, he has no right to complain of violence. The popular insurrection that ends in the death or deposition of a Sultan is as lawful an act as those by which he disposed, the day before, of the life and fortunes of his subjects. As he was maintained by force alone, it is force alone that overthrows him."

In the 20th century, the century of the Russian Revolution, Orwell's *Animal Farm* is the bitter satiric attack on how revolutions undertaken with the highest aims can woefully miscarry. In *Animal Farm* the story begins with the old boar Major's dream of an animal rebellion against their human masters; and it ends with the betrayal of every hope that Major pictured in his dream. In the character of the pig Napoleon, we see Stalin perfectly portrayed.

Those who say that "it may occasion civil wars or intestine broils, to tell the people they are absolved from obedience when illegal attempts are made upon their liberties or properties . . . may as well say upon the same ground," in Locke's opinion, "that honest men may not oppose robbers and pirates because this may occasion disorder or bloodshed." Nor does Locke think that the right to resist injustice means that governments will be overthrown "upon every little mismanagement in public affairs. Great mistakes in the ruling part," he writes, "many wrong and inconvenient laws, and all the slips of human frailty will be borne by the people without mutiny or murmur. But if a long train of abuses, prevarications, and artifices, all tending the same way, make the design visible to the people . . . it is not to be wondered that they should then rouse themselves and endeavor to put the rule into such hands which may secure to them the ends for which government was at first erected."

Hence, to those who say that his revolutionary principle "lays a perpetual foundation for disorder," Locke replies that it will never operate until "the inconvenience is so great that the majority feel it, and are weary of it, and find it necessary to have it amended." Rebellions will occur only when the majority feel that "their laws, and with them their estates, liberties, and lives are in danger, and perhaps their religion too," and so will exercise their natural right to resist, with force if necessary, the illegal force used against them. But strictly, it is not the people who rebel; rather it is they who put down the sedition of the tyrant.

What Locke states as a right of resistance, the Declaration of Independence seems to put more positively as a right of rebellion, apparently deducing it from other natural rights— of life, liberty, and the pursuit of happiness. It is to secure these rights that "governments are instituted among men," so that "whenever any form of government becomes destructive of these ends, it is the right of the people to alter or to abolish it and to institute a new government." The Declaration admits that "governments long established should not be changed for light and transient causes"; but when a people suffer "a long train of abuses and usurpations . . . it is their right, it is their duty, to throw off such government, and to provide new guards for their security." Jefferson's view of the necessity of revolution is repeated in a famous letter to Madison: "I hold it that a little rebellion now and then is a good thing, and as necessary in the political world as storms in the physical."

AGAINST SUCH REVOLUTIONARY sentiments or principles Hobbes, Kant, and Hegel seem to take a stand, though in each case they place some qualification on their denial of a right of resistance or rebellion. Hobbes, for example, denies the right of men to change their form of government, or of subjects to resist their Sovereign, *except for the sake of self-preservation*. When men covenant to form a commonwealth, they are bound, Hobbes says, to uphold the actions and judgments of the Sovereign they have created; they "cannot lawfully make a new covenant amongst themselves, to be obedient to any other . . . without his permission . . . They that are subjects to a monarch, cannot without his leave cast off monarchy, and return to the confusion of a disunited multitude."

Furthermore, "because every subject is by this institution, author of all the actions and judgments of the Sovereign instituted, it follows," according to Hobbes, "that whatsoever he doeth, it can be no injury to any of his subjects; nor ought he to be by any of them accused of injustice." Yet "every subject has liberty in all those things, the right whereof cannot by covenant be transferred," such as the right of a man to defend his own body, "to resist those that assault him," or to have access to "food, air, medicine, or any other thing without which he cannot live."

Kant disallows rebellion as a matter of right, unless resistance is required to fulfill a moral duty outside the sphere of public right. " 'Obey the authority which has power over you' (in everything which is not opposed to morality) is a Categorical Imperative." Hence, though a juridical constitution "may be vitiated by great defects and coarse errors, it is nevertheless absolutely unallowable and punishable to resist it."

Since, in his view, public right is founded on the institution of "a *sovereign* will, uniting all particular wills by one law," Kant argues that "to allow a right of resistance to this sovereignty, and to limit its power, is a contradiction." It should be remembered also that for Kant the only legitimate form of government is a republic, resting on the founda-tion of popular sovereignty. Kant is not considering resistance to tyrannical or despotic power which lacks all juridical authority.

A similar qualification appears in Hegel's distinction between the rebellion of a conquered people and revolution in a well-organized state. Only the latter action is a crime, for only the latter situation corresponds to the Idea of the state—fully realized, for Hegel, only in a constitutional monarchy, never in a despotism or tyranny. "A rebellion in a province conquered by war," he says, "is a different thing from a rising in a well-organized state. It is not against their prince that the conquered are in rebellion, and they are committing no crime against the state, because their connexion with their master is not a connexion within the Idea, or one within the inner necessity of the constitution. In such a case, there is only a contract, no political tie."

With such qualifications on their position, those who disfavor revolution or deny its basis in right may not be completely opposed to those who apparently think rebellions can be justified. There may be qualifications on the other side too. Aquinas, for example, justifies sedition, not against any government or ruler, but only against tyranny. The signers of the Declaration of Independence speak of a right to alter or abolish "any form of government," but the writers of the Federalist papers do not seem equally willing to acknowledge a right to overthrow the Constitution of the United States.

81

Rhetoric

INTRODUCTION

RHETORIC is traditionally regarded as one of the liberal arts. When the liberal arts are counted as seven, and divided into the three and the four—the *trivium* and the *quadrivium*—rhetoric is grouped with grammar and logic, not with the mathematical arts of arithmetic and geometry, astronomy and music. The implication of this grouping seems to be that rhetoric, like grammar, has something to do with language or discourse; and that, like logic, it is concerned with thought, with reasoning or argument. But if grammar is the art of writing or speaking correctly, and if logic is the art of thinking correctly, it may be wondered what rhetoric can add to these other arts, either on the side of language or of thought.

Logic by itself does not suffice to ensure that words are properly used to express thought; nor does grammar guarantee that discourse which is flawless in syntax also complies with the demands of rationality. Hence neither grammar nor logic seems to challenge the function of the other, as together they challenge the function of rhetoric.

Upon the way this challenge is met depends not only the definition of rhetoric, but also the value put upon it. In the tradition of the great books, rhetoric is both praised as a useful discipline which liberally educated men should possess, and condemned as a dishonest craft to which decent men would not stoop. Like the words "sophistical" and "dialectical," the epithet "rhetorical" carries, traditionally as well as currently, a derogatory implication. The three words sometimes even tend to merge in meaning, expressing the same reproach against trickery. Yet of the three, "sophistical" alone implies an unqualified rebuke.

We do not speak of good and bad sophistry. But dialectic has its defenders as well as its detractors; and even those who, like Plato, charge rhetoric with being an art of enchantment or a form of flattery also distinguish between a true and a false rhetoric, the one associated with dialectic as a wholly admirable pursuit, the other classed with sophistry as a vocation divorced from virtue. According to Francis Bacon, the aim of rhetoric is to support reason, "not to oppress it." Rhetoric may be misused, but logic also has its abuses. "Rhetoric can be no more charged," in Bacon's opinion, "with the coloring of the worse part, than logic with sophistry, or morality with vice."

THE PURPOSE AND scope of rhetoric are capable of broad and narrow definitions. The broader view, which we shall consider subsequently, tends to merge rhetoric with poetics as together the art of eloquence in any sort of discourse. The narrower view tends to restrict rhetoric to the art of persuasion in the sphere of practical affairs. Rhetorical skill consists in getting others to embrace certain beliefs, to form the opinions or make the judgments which the speaker or writer wishes them to adopt. Usually action, not persuasion, is the ultimate goal. The rules of rhetoric are supposed to give one power not merely to move the minds of men to certain conclusions but, through persuasion of their minds, to move men to act or not act in a certain way.

The sphere of rhetoric, so conceived, is limited to moral and political problems. The things about which men deliberate before acting, the things on which they pass moral judgments or make political decisions, constitute the subject matter of oratory, or what Hobbes calls "exhortation and dehortation," that is, "counsel accompanied with signs in him that giveth it, of vehement desire to have it followed."

In the narrower conception, rhetoric seems to be confined to *oratory*. It is with oratory and orators that Socrates seems to be concerned when he discusses rhetoric with Phaedrus or with Gorgias. Gorgias, who was a teacher of rhetoric, praises the power of the orator to persuade "the judges in the courts, or the senators in the council, or the citizens in the assembly, or at any other public meeting." In view of this Socrates asks him whether he will accept the definition of rhetoric as "the artificer of persuasion." When Gorgias admits that "persuasion is the chief end of rhetoric," Socrates goes on to ask whether rhetoric is "the only art which brings persuasion, or do other arts have the same effect? Does he who teaches anything persuade men of that which he teaches or not?" If so, "then arithmetic as well as rhetoric is an artificer of persuasion."

Gorgias reminds Socrates of his initial point about the orator, that "rhetoric is the art of persuasion in courts of law and other assemblies . . . about the just and unjust." But Socrates is still not satisfied that rhetoric has been sharply defined. He introduces the distinction between knowledge and belief or opinion, and gets Gorgias to agree that, whereas there cannot be false knowledge as well as true, beliefs and opinions may be either true or false. Persuasion can, therefore, be of two sorts—"one which is the source of belief without knowledge, as the other is of knowledge."

Gorgias is willing to limit rhetoric to that form of persuasion "which only gives belief," to which Socrates adds the emphatic negative that "the rhetorician does not instruct the courts of law or other assemblies about things just and unjust, but creates beliefs about them." If an assembly wishes to learn about matters connected with medicine or shipbuilding, it consults the physician or shipwright, not the orator. But, says Gorgias, "when a decision has to be given in such matters, the rhetoricians are the advisers; they are

the men who win their point." He confirms this by reminding Socrates that the speeches of Themistocles and Pericles, not the suggestions of the builders, determined the Athenian assembly in the construction of the harbor, the docks and walls.

By way of further illustration, Gorgias tells of occasions when he has succeeded in getting patients to do what they would not do on the advice of their physicians. "I have persuaded the patient," he says, "to do for me what he would not do for the physician, just by the use of rhetoric." Similarly, in a contest for public office between a rhetorician and a man of any other profession, "the rhetorician more than any other would have the power of getting himself chosen, for he can speak more persuasively to the multitude than any of them, and on any subject. Such is the nature and power of the art of rhetoric!"

In comparing it with dialectic, Aristotle seems to have a different conception of the function of rhetoric. "Neither rhetoric nor dialectic," he says, "is the scientific study of any one separate subject; both are faculties for providing arguments." Both also are concerned with arguments which fall short of scientific demonstration, that is, with matters of opinion concerning which something probable can be said on either side of the issue.

Though for Aristotle rhetoric is the counterpart of dialectic, in that both deal with arguments on any subject, his differentiation between the two disciplines seems to indicate that rhetoric is limited to the consideration of oratory in the familiar sense of public speaking. The rhetorician is concerned with persuading an audience, not, as the dialectician is, with carrying on a dispute in which two individuals may be privately engaged. The persuasion, furthermore, is directed to obtaining a certain response from that audience—not merely agreement, but either action, or a decision to act, or approval which, charged with emotional force or enthusiasm, has practical significance.

The divisions of rhetoric, according to Aristotle, are determined by the kinds of oratory, as these, in turn, are determined by the types of audience to be addressed. "Of the three elements in speech-making—speaker, subject, and person addressed," Aristotle writes, "it is the last one, the hearer, that determines the speech's end and object. The hearer must be either a judge with a decision to make about things past or future, or an observer. A member of the assembly decides about future events, a juryman about past events; while those who merely decide on the orator's skill are observers.

"From this it follows that there are three divisions of oratory: (1) political, (2) forensic, and (3) the ceremonial oratory of display"—or, as these three are sometimes named, deliberative, legal, and epideictic. "Political speaking urges us either to do or not do something . . . Forensic speaking either attacks or defends somebody . . . The ceremonial oratory of display either praises or censures somebody. These three kinds of rhetoric refer to three different kinds of time. The political orator is concerned with the future; he tries to persuade men about things to be done or not done hereafter. The party in a case at law is concerned with the past; one man accuses the other, and the other defends himself, with reference to things already done. The ceremonial orator is, properly speaking, concerned with the present, since all men praise or blame in view of the state of things existing at the time, though they often find it useful also to recall the past and to make guesses about the future.

"Rhetoric has three distinct ends in view, one for each of its three kinds. The political orator aims at establishing the expediency or the harmfulness of a proposed course of action . . . Parties in a lawsuit aim at establishing the justice or injustice of some action . . . Those who praise or attack a man aim at proving him worthy of honor or the reverse."

THIS CONCEPTION OF rhetoric as concerned with oratory or public speaking gives one answer to the question of what rhetoric adds to grammar and logic as arts of discourse. In oratory more is involved than the communication of ideas, the marshaling of arguments, the making of proofs. Discourse, whether written or spoken, has an effect upon the emotions as well as upon the mind, and disposes a man to act as well as the mind to assent.

"The communicating of ideas by words," Berkeley observes, "is not the chief and only end of language, as is commonly supposed. There are other ends, as the raising of some passion, the exciting to or deterring from an action, the putting the mind in some particular disposition—to which the former is in many cases barely subservient, and sometimes entirely omitted . . . I entreat the reader to reflect with himself, and see if it doth not often happen, either in hearing or reading a discourse, that the passions of fear, love, hatred, admiration, disdain and the like, arise immediately in his mind upon the perception of certain words, without any ideas coming between."

Engaged in the oratorical task of persuading the people of New York to ratify the federal constitution, the writers of the Federalist papers are aware that "a torrent of angry and malignant passions will be let loose" in the debate of that issue. They realize that arguing for the adoption of certain political principles or conclusions is not like teaching geometry, the objects of which are "entirely abstracted from those pursuits which stir up and put in motion the unruly passions of the human heart."

Hamilton admits at once, in the opening paper, that "the plan offered to our deliberations affects too many particular interests, innovates upon too many local institutions, not to involve in its discussion, a variety of objects foreign to its merits, and of views, passions, and prejudices little favorable to the discovery of truth." Nevertheless, he tries to persuade his audience to judge the issue on the merits of the argument alone.

The opponents of the Constitution, he says, "may be actuated by upright intentions." The opposition may "spring from sources, blameless at least, if not respectable—the honest errors of minds led astray by preconceived jealousies and fears. So numerous indeed and so powerful are the causes which serve to give a false bias to the judgment, that we, upon many occasions, see wise and good men on the wrong as well as on the right side of questions of the first magnitude to society."

To recognize this, Hamilton tells his audience, is to be on guard "against all attempts, from whatever quarter, to influence your decision . . . by any impressions other than those which may result from the evidence of truth." He wishes them to consider him as relying upon nothing but the merits of his case. "I frankly acknowledge to you my convictions," he writes, "and I will freely lay before you the reasons on which they are founded . . . My motives must remain in the depository of my own breast. My arguments will be open to all, and may be judged by all. They shall at least be offered in a spirit which will not disgrace the cause of truth."

We can detect here another element in the art of rhetoric. The orator seems to be concerned, not only with the strength of his arguments and with the passions of the audience which he hopes to move by these arguments, but also with the impression he makes upon that audience as a person of good character and honest intentions, devoted to the truth and, above all, to the best interests of those whom he addresses.

The great speeches reported—or perhaps polished, if not invented—by Thucydides exemplify this effort on the part of the orator, as do also the orations written by Shakespeare for his characters, of which the speeches of Brutus and Antony in *Julius Caesar* are among the most notable as well as the most familiar. The point is also illustrated by the *Communist Manifesto,* which is denounced as "propaganda" by those who mistrust the writers, but to those who trust them is powerful and persuasive oratory. The great books abound with examples of great oratory, such as the hellfire sermon in Joyce's *A Portrait of the Artist as a Young Man* and the speech in Conrad's *Heart of Darkness* that the narrator reports as giving him "the notion of an exotic Immensity ruled by an august Benevolence. It made me tingle with enthusiasm. This was the unbounded power of eloquence—of words—of burning noble words."

Not all examples of oratory have the nobility of Conrad's narrator. In Orwell's *Animal Farm,* the pig Squealer is a master of diverting attention from the tyranny of Napoleon and the other pigs: "When he was arguing some difficult point he had a way of skipping from side to side and whisking his tail which was somehow very persuasive. The others said of Squealer that he could turn black into white." Squealer is not merely a totalitarian propagandist; he exemplifies Orwell's overall view, as written elsewhere, that "political language . . . is designed to make lies sound truthful and murder respectable, and to give an appearance of solidity to pure wind."

Separating the use of witnesses and documents by the forensic orator from what he calls the strictly artistic means of persuasion—*i.e.,* the means intrinsic to the art of rhetoric—Aristotle divides the latter into the three elements already noted. Persuasion, he says, depends "on the personal character of the speaker . . . on putting the audience into a certain frame of mind . . . [and] on the proof, or apparent proof, provided by the words of the speech itself. Persuasion is achieved by the speaker's personal character when the speech is so spoken as to make us think him credible . . . Secondly, persuasion may come through the hearers when the speech stirs their emotions . . . Thirdly, persuasion is effected through the speech itself when we have proved a truth or an apparent truth by means of the persuasive arguments suitable to the case in question."

These being the three technical means of effecting persuasion, Aristotle concludes that rhetorical skill must consist in the ability "(1) to reason logically, (2) to understand human character and goodness in their various forms, and (3) to understand the emotions . . . to know their causes and the way in which they are excited." The art of rhetoric, therefore, involves more than training in grammar and logic. It requires the study of ethics and psychology—particularly knowledge of the types of human character and knowledge of the passions.

The same consideration of the conditions of oratory seems to lead Socrates to tell Phaedrus that Thrasymachus or anyone else who teaches rhetoric ought "to give an exact description of the nature of the soul," to explain "the mode in which it acts or is acted upon." The rhetorician, he goes on, "having classified men and speeches, and their kinds and affections, and adapted them one to another," will be able to "tell the reasons of his arrangement, and show why one soul is persuaded by a particular form of argument, and another not."

THIS FACT ABOUT rhetoric—that it must adapt speech to persons as well as to subject matters—seems to occasion Socrates' definition of oratory as "the art of enchanting the soul." It is not, he tells Phaedrus, confined to courts and public assemblies. Whether this art is a good or evil thing depends on whether it requires the speaker to know—more than the nature of the person he is addressing—the truth about the matters spoken of. To engender probabilities in the minds of the many by the likeness of the truth, it is necessary, says Socrates, to know the truth. "He who knew the truth would always know best how to discover the resemblances of the truth." Such a man might be able, not only to please and so to persuade his audience, but also, perhaps, he might "be able to say what is acceptable to God."

The issue about rhetoric then—at least so far as that issue concerns its being an art consistent with virtue—seems to turn on the admixture of pleasure and truth. The question is whether, given a particular sort of audience to persuade, the orator does not have to choose between pleasing them and telling them the truth. Does the art of rhetoric extend to the persuasion of bad men as well as good? Is the skill of the orator to be measured by his success in persuading, without regard to the character of the audience he has persuaded and the means he has been forced to use? Does the goodness of the orator—and of his speech—depend upon his being morally virtuous as well as rhetorically skillful?

One view of rhetoric seems to identify persuasion with pleasure and to divorce it from truth. Pascal, for example, in his essay *On Geometrical Demonstration,* speaks of "two methods, the one of convincing, the other of pleasing." In order to persuade, he writes, "one must consider the person with whom one has to deal, whose spirit and heart one must know, the principles he accepts, the things he

loves." In view of such considerations, Pascal holds that "the art of persuasion consists more in pleasing than in convincing, to such an extent is it true that men are controlled more by whim than by reason." He does not doubt that "there are rules which are as reliable with respect to pleasing as there are for demonstrating"; nor does he seem to condemn rhetoric for being such an art, unless he writes with irony when he says that "pleasing is incomparably more difficult, more subtle, more useful, and more admirable."

Rhetoric so conceived appears to Locke to be a "powerful instrument of error and deceit"; and to Plato to be no art at all, but a form of flattery. As cookery tries to please the palate without caring what is good for the health of the body, so rhetoric, according to Plato, aims to delight without caring what is good for the soul or the state. Cookery and rhetoric are shams or simulations of the genuine arts of medicine and politics, which aim at the good, not at pleasure. "This is the sort of thing," Socrates tells Callicles, "which I term flattery, whether concerned with the body or the soul, or whenever employed with a view to pleasure and without any consideration of good and evil."

Socrates then asks Callicles whether he knows rhetoricians who "aim at what is best . . . and seek to improve the citizens by their speeches," or whether all "are bent upon giving them pleasure, forgetting the public good in the thought of their own interest, playing with the people as with children, and trying to amuse them, but never considering whether they are better or worse for this."

When Callicles replies that he thinks "there are some who have a real care for the public in what they say," Socrates says that he is "contented with the admission that rhetoric is of two sorts: one, which is mere flattery and disgraceful declamation; the other, which is noble and aims at the training and improvement of the souls of the citizens, and strives to say what is best, whether welcome or unwelcome, to the audience." But, he asks Callicles, "have you ever known such a rhetoric; or if you have, and can point out any rhetorician of this stamp, who is he?"

SOCRATES MAY NOT be asking a rhetorical question. He may be presenting the defenders of rhetoric with this critical dilemma: *either* the orator adheres to the truth and aims at the good, even if such high-mindedness defeats his efforts at persuasion with an audience whom he thus displeases; *or* the orator takes persuasion as his end and subordinates everything else to the rhetorical means for succeeding with any sort of audience.

Bacon rises to the defense by rejecting the dilemma as ungenuine. "The duty and office of rhetoric," he writes, "is to apply reason to the imagination for the better moving of the will." He admits that rhetoric is controlled by other considerations than the truth. Though "logic handleth reason exact and in truth," and though "the proofs and demonstrations of logic are toward all men indifferent and the same . . . the proofs and persuasions of rhetoric ought to differ according to the auditors."

Nevertheless, Bacon thinks "it was great injustice in Plato, though springing out of a just hatred for the rhetoricians of his time, to regard rhetoric as a voluptuary art, resembling it to cookery that did mar wholesome meats, and help unwholesome by a variety of sauces to please the taste. For we see that speech is much more conversant in adorning that which is good than in coloring that which is evil; for there is no man but speaketh more honestly than he can do or think; and it was excellently noted by Thucydides in Cleon, that because he used to hold on the bad side in causes of state, therefore he was ever inveighing against eloquence and good speech knowing that no man can speak fair of courses sordid and base."

Aristotle's defense of rhetoric seems to be implied in the remark that "its function is not simply to succeed in persuading, but rather to discover the means of coming as near such success as the circumstances of each case allow." Just as, for him, the sophist differs from the dialectician not in the skills of argument or dispute, but in moral purpose or respect for truth, so the name "rhetorician" may be applied to two sorts of men. Rhetoric may signify "either the speaker's knowledge of his art, or his moral purpose." For want of separate names, both the honest and the sophistical orator are called and can claim to be "rhetoricians," and it is this which confuses the issue.

IN THE TRADITION of the great books, Aristotle's *Rhetoric* occupies a place comparable to that which, as noted in the chapter on POETRY, his *On Poetics* unquestionably fills. It seems to be not merely the first but the standard treatise on oratory. It divides rhetoric into three parts—the first concerned with invention, the second with the disposition or order of a speech, the third with problems of expression. To the last of these belongs the analysis of the orator's use of language and his style in speaking; to the second, the analysis of the structure of an oration into such parts as proem, statement, argument, and epilogue; and to the first, under the head of invention, belongs the consideration of the means of persuasion.

As we have already noted, the artistic means of persuasion are, according to Aristotle, threefold—emotions, character, and argument. The orator must consider how to arouse and use the passions of his audience, as well as calculate how far to go in displaying his own emotions. He must consider the moral character of the audience to which he is appealing, and in this connection he must try to exhibit his own moral character in a favorable light. Finally, he must know the various types and sources of rhetorical argument—not only what sorts of argument are available for a particular purpose, but also how to employ each argument most persuasively. In this last respect, Aristotle distinguishes rhetorical proof from rhetorical induction—the use of what he calls the "enthymeme" as opposed to the use of examples—and he relates this distinction to the difference between dialectical proof and induction which he treats in the *Topics*.

Cicero and Quintilian may extend Aristotle's analysis in certain directions, but neither they nor modern writers like George Campbell and Richard Whately depart far from the framework Aristotle sets up for the discussion of oratory. Even those who reject Aristotle's authority in logic, natural philosophy, and metaphysics pay him the tribute of following (as does Hobbes) his treatment of oratory, or of approving (as does Bacon) his contribution to rhetoric. In the case of this science, as with few others, Bacon finds no serious deficiencies in the accepted tradition. He calls rhetoric "a science excellent and excellently well labored," and places "the emulation of Aristotle" first among the causes why later writers "in their works of rhetorics exceed themselves."

Yet by another standard Aristotle's *Rhetoric* may be judged deficient. Because he confines his attention almost exclusively to oratory, Aristotle's discussion leaves rhetoric in a larger sense almost untouched. This limitation of rhetoric to the subject matter of oratory does not go unexplained. "Every other art," Aristotle writes, "can instruct or persuade about its own particular subject matter; for instance, medicine about what is healthy and unhealthy, geometry about the properties of magnitudes, arithmetic about numbers, and the same is true of the other arts and sciences. But rhetoric," he says, "we look upon as the power of observing the means of persuasion on almost any subject presented to us."

This last statement would seem to give rhetoric complete generality. Aristotle qualifies it, however. "People fail to notice," he says, "that the more correctly they handle their particular subject the further they are getting away from pure rhetoric." So far as knowing good arguments and knowing how to use them are concerned, the physicist and the mathematician need no help from rhetoric. The art of rhetoric is necessary only in dealing with such topics as do not fall within the subject matters or systems of the established arts and sciences. Such topics are precisely those with which the orator must deal. "The duty of rhetoric," Aristotle writes in summary, "is to deal with such matters as we deliberate upon without arts or systems to guide us, in the hearing of persons who cannot take in at a glance a complicated argument, or follow a long chain of reasoning." This is his answer to those who have given rhetoric "a far wider subject matter than strictly belongs to it."

But Aristotle's explanation of his limitation of rhetoric is itself limited to only one of its major parts, namely, the construction of arguments. As contrasted with the mathematician, the physician, and the philosopher, whose mastery of the subject matter of their arts or sciences gives them a command of the relevant principles and methods of argument, only the orator needs the special art of rhetoric to provide him with the topics from which examples and enthymemes can be drawn and to give him skill in the use of such arguments. But it is not only the orator who must consider the character and emotions of his audience. It is not only the orator who must consider the best way in which to order the parts of an elaborate discourse. Above all, it is not only the orator who is faced with the problem of using language more or less effectively in the expression of thought, and especially in its communication to others. All these considerations and problems are common to the orator and the teacher. They are considerations and problems which must be faced not merely by the public speaker who tries to move an audience to action, but by anyone—poet, philosopher, or scientist—who tries to write whatever he has to say as effectively as possible.

Competence in a particular art or science may give a man competence with respect to arguments in the field of his particular subject matter, but it does not seem to give him competence with respect to these other considerations and problems, which he faces when he tries to communicate his knowledge or thought. Here, then, is the possibility of a broader conception of the art of rhetoric—an art concerned not merely with being persuasive in the sphere of action, but with eloquence or effectiveness in the expression of thought.

We find this view of rhetoric reflected in Chaucer's *The Canterbury Tales.* In his Prologue, the Franklin says, "I beseech / You to excuse me my untutored speech"; for, he explains,

They never taught me rhetoric, I fear,
So what I have to say is bare and clear.
I haven't slept on Mount Parnassus, no.
Nor studied Marcus Tullius Cithero. ·

The Squire also apologizes for the inadequacy of his English, when he tries to describe the beauty of Canace:

To tell her beauty is too much for me,
Lying beyond what tongue of mine can sing;
I dare not undertake so high a thing.
My English too is insufficient for it,
It asks a rhetorician to explore it,
A poet in the colours of that art,
To give a fair account of every part.

Though Aristotle's *Rhetoric* for the most part neglects this broader conception of rhetoric in order to expound the rules of oratory, the third book of his treatise, which deals with the use of language, indicates that problems of style are common to oratory and poetry and to other types of discourse as well.

Kant seems to hold this broader conception of rhetoric when he says that "the arts of speech are *rhetoric* and *poetry*." In the tradition of western thought, the two arts tend to become identified when each is separated from any particular subject matter. As appears in the chapter on POETRY, poetry like rhetoric has a broader and a narrower meaning. In the narrower meaning, it is the art of the narrative, just as in its narrower meaning, rhetoric is the art of oratory. The other sense in which poetics as an art can be understood is, according to Bacon, with respect to words, not matter. "In this sense," he writes, "it is but a character of style, and belongeth to arts of speech."

In this sense the poetic art is hardly distinguishable from the rhetorical art. The problems involved in composing a good speech are not the same as those involved in writing a good poem (or what Bacon calls a "feigned history"). But when poetics and rhetoric are each separated from such problems to become the arts of writing or speaking well about anything, then, in becoming as general as discourse itself, they tend to become one and the same art—an art of style or expression, an art of preaching or teaching the truth about any matter on which one mind seeks to communicate with another.

Nietzsche expatiates on the mastery of style in antiquity. "In those days," he writes, "the rules of written style were the same as those of spoken style; and these rules depended in part on the astonishing development, the refined requirements of ear and larynx, in part on the strength, endurance, and power of ancient lungs . . . Periods such as appear with Demosthenes or Cicero, rising twice and sinking twice and all within a *single* breath: these are delights for men of *antiquity,* who knew from their own schooling how to value the virtue in them, the rarity and difficulty of the delivery of such a period—*we* have really no right to the *grand* period, we moderns, we who are short of breath in every sense!" In Nietzsche's view, the ancients "were one and all themselves dilettantes in rhetoric, consequently connoisseurs, consequently critics—and so they drove their orators to extremes."

IN THE TRADITION of the great books, no book does for the art of rhetoric in general what Aristotle's *Rhetoric* does for that art in the limited sphere of oratory. But Augustine's treatise *On Christian Doctrine* engages in a general rhetorical analysis that is in a way comparable to Aristotle's analysis of oratory. In this work Augustine brings his own professional training as an orator to bear on the problems of reading, interpreting, and expounding Sacred Scripture. The fact that he is dealing with Sacred Scripture and hence, in his view, with the teaching of the most fundamental truths, lifts him above the limited concerns of the orator; but the fact that he limits himself to Sacred Scripture also prevents him from formulating his rules of interpretation and exposition with the complete generality they would have to possess in order to be the rules of a general art of rhetoric.

At the opening of the fourth book of *On Christian Doctrine,* Augustine declares that, having considered in the preceding books "the mode of ascertaining the proper meaning" of Scripture, he will now treat "the mode of making known the meaning when it is ascertained." He disclaims any intention "to lay down rules of rhetoric"; he wishes merely "to engage it on the side of truth." To this end he tries to show how Scripture itself, and such holy men as Saint Cyprian and Saint Ambrose in commenting on Scripture, have employed the art of rhetoric.

"It is the duty," Augustine writes, "of the interpreter and teacher of Holy Scripture . . . both to teach what is right and refute what is wrong; and in the performance of this task to conciliate the hostile, to rouse the careless, and to tell the ignorant both what is occurring at present and what is probable in the future. But once his hearers are friendly, attentive, and ready to learn, whether he has found them so, or has himself made them so, the remaining objects are to be carried out in whatever way the case requires." The first rule of a general rhetoric would thus seem to be one of creating a receptive frame of mind in the persons being addressed. This accomplished, the teacher must proceed with various alternatives in mind.

"If the hearers need teaching," Augustine writes, "the matter treated of must be made fully known by means of narrative. On the other hand, to clear up points that are doubtful requires reasoning and the exhibition of proofs. If, however, the hearers require to be roused rather than instructed, in order that they may be diligent to do what they already know, greater vigor of speech is needed. Here entreaties and reproaches, exhortations and upbraidings, and all the other means of rousing the emotions, are necessary."

In Scripture and its great commentators, Augustine finds "wisdom not aiming at eloquence, yet eloquence not shrinking from wisdom." He also finds examples of the three kinds of style which Cicero had distinguished—the eloquence of those "who can say little things in a subdued style, moderate things in a temperate style, and great things in a majestic style." These three styles Augustine connects with the three ends which Cicero had assigned to eloquence—teaching, giving pleasure, and moving. The subdued style, he says, should be used "in order to give instruction," the temperate style "in order to give pleasure," and the majestic style "in order to sway the mind."

"In elegance and beauty, nay, splendour," Calvin writes, "the style of some of the prophets is not surpassed by the eloquence of heathen writers." In his view, their writings "rise far higher than human reach. Those who feel their works insipid must be absolutely devoid of taste."

The great books of history, science, and philosophy provide additional materials for general rhetorical analysis. They offer us the light of examples at least, even if they do not, like Augustine's commentary on Scripture, give us the guidance of rules. Such historians as Herodotus, Thucydides, Tacitus, and Gibbon exhibit a diversity of styles in the writing of history. The diversity is not only on the grammatical level of the use of language, but also on the logical level of order and argument. Rhetorical principles control the way in which the language and the organization of the parts are suited to each other and to the historian's purpose—to the effect he wishes to produce upon his reader.

The way in which Euclid writes the *Elements* is a style of exposition, having rhetorical as well as logical features. In its rhetorical (if not its strictly logical) form it is applicable to other subject matters. This may be seen in Spinoza's adoption of it in his *Ethics* and in Newton's adaptation of it in his *Mathematical Principles of Natural Philosophy*. The dialogue form which Plato seems to have invented for writing philosophy appears to recommend itself rhetorically not only to other philosophers, but also to a scientist like Galileo in the composition of his *Concerning Two New Sciences*. If the doctrines of the *Summa Theologica* or of *The Critique of Pure Reason* were separated from the very special styles of these two works, they would probably not have the same effect upon the reader; and as they are written, they affect different readers differently, as differently as do the styles of Dante, Milton, Melville, Dostoevsky, Adam Smith, and Marx.

Some methods of exposition may be more appropriate than others to certain subject matters. "There is a great difference in the delivery of mathematics," says Bacon, "and of politics." But in every subject matter or field of learning, there is the common problem of how to make language serve most effectively to enlighten or convince in the communication of thought. The problem arises in the writing of a single sentence as well as in the organization of a whole discourse.

THE CHOICE OF WORDS and the formation of new words, the invention and employment of figures of speech, by which abbreviation or amplification of discourse may be achieved and the imagination freshened—these are some of the considerations of style which Aristotle discusses (both in his *Rhetoric* and in his *On Poetics*) and which Augustine illustrates in his analysis of Scripture. They suggest the rules of a general rhetoric, founded on principles as universal as Pascal's insight that "words differently arranged have a different meaning, and meanings differently arranged have a different effect."

This observation indicates a further answer to the question raised much earlier, namely, why the art of rhetoric is needed over and above the skills of grammar and logic. For oratory the question has been answered by reference to those rules of rhetoric which deal with the passions and with moral character. But for a more general rhetoric, concerned with all discourse, the answer must be in terms of rules of style of the sort Pascal's observation suggests.

If there were never more than one grammatically and logically correct way of saying anything, then grammatical and logical standards would suffice for the regulation of sound discourse. But if there are always several ways of stating something and if each of them satisfies the rules of grammar and logic, but differs in the impression it makes on the mind, then criteria other than those of grammar and logic will be needed to determine our choice of which to use.

Such criteria may take the passions and the imagination into account, but they may also look primarily to the manner in which the mind itself naturally works. The fact that there are several ways of presenting the same truth to the mind—and usually several ways in which the mind can interpret the same statement—defines the scope of a general rhetoric and the relation of its rules to those of grammar and logic.

Nevertheless, some of the great authors seem to doubt the worth of rhetoric in science or philosophy. Locke, for example, admits that "in discourses where we seek pleasure and delight rather than information and improvement, such ornaments"—as "figurative speeches and allusion in language"— "can scarce pass for faults. But," he adds, "if we would speak of things as they are, we must allow that all the art of rhetoric, besides order and clearness, all the artificial and figurative application of words eloquence hath invented, are for nothing else but to insinuate wrong ideas, move the passions, and so, indeed, are perfect cheats . . . and where truth and knowledge are concerned, cannot but be thought a great fault, either of the language or person that makes use of them."

Descartes also declares that "those who have the strongest power of reasoning, and who most skilfully arrange their thoughts in order to render them clear and intelligible, have the best power of persuasion even if they can but speak the language of Lower Britanny and have never learned rhetoric." Yet he qualifies this severity somewhat by identifying dialectic with rhetoric and granting its "possible use . . . to serve to explain at times more easily to others the truths we have already ascertained."

Plato for the most part tends in the opposite direction, keeping dialectic and rhetoric poles apart. But if there were a true as opposed to a false rhetoric, a rhetoric concerned with knowledge and truth, not merely opinion and pleasure, he would be willing, it seems, to admit it to the company of dialectic, and regard it as an aid in the teaching, if not the discovery, of the truth. The pedagogical utility of rhetoric as well as dialectic appears in the summary which Socrates gives to Phaedrus, after they have finished examining the speeches about love.

"Until a man knows the truth of the several particulars of which he is writing or speaking," Socrates says, "and is able to define them as they are, and having defined them again to divide them until they can no longer be divided, and until in like manner he is able to discern the nature of the soul, and discover the different modes of discourse which are adapted to different natures, and to arrange and dispose them in such a way that the simple form of speech may be addressed to the simpler nature, and the complex and the composite to the more complex nature—until he has accomplished all this, he will be unable to handle arguments according to rules of art . . . either for the purpose of teaching or persuading."

82

Same and Other

INTRODUCTION

THE problems of identity and diversity—of sameness and otherness, similarity and difference—occur at that level of philosophical thought which deals with being and with unity. Plotinus, for example, says that in addition to Being, Motion, and Rest, "we are obliged to posit the further two, Identity and Difference, so that we have in all five genera."

In Aristotle's conception, terms like 'being,' 'one,' and 'same' have a greater universality than the terms he calls the highest genera, *e.g.*, 'substance,' 'quantity,' 'quality,' 'relation,' and so forth. These latter represent categories or classes under which certain things fall and others do not. Not everything is a substance or a quantity, but in Aristotle's opinion there is nothing of which it cannot be said that it is a being in some sense, that it has some kind of unity, that it is identical with itself, and that, compared with anything else in the whole universe, it is in certain respects the same, in others different.

The fundamental relation of quantities with one another, namely, equality, consists in their being the same. The fundamental relation of qualities consists in their being alike, or the same in spite of some difference in degree or intensity, *e.g.*, a brighter and a darker red of the same hue. The notion of relation itself seems to be as fundamental as that of sameness, since in comparisons one thing is said to be the same or different only in relation to something else; yet it also seems to be true that relations can be the same or similar, for the essence of proportion or analogy lies in one thing's being related to a second as a third is to a fourth. The sameness of two relationships is the object of the comparison.

Such considerations are sometimes called "metaphysical" with an invidious tone. But no one, not even those who would eliminate metaphysical discussion as indulging in "vicious abstractions" or as verging on the meaningless, can easily avoid such notions as identity and diversity. It is not merely that ordinary speech, as well as scientific discourse, must use such words as "same" and "other" almost as frequently as the words "is" and "not" or "one" and "many." Those who are critical of theorizing and who want to save discourse itself from becoming "too metaphysical" are still obliged to give some account of what it means for things to be the same or different and of how we know when they are.

Semantics currently has vogue as a critical instrument for safeguarding discourse from ambiguity and nonsense and perhaps also for spotting metaphysical legerdemain. But semantics itself cannot go far in its own analysis of words and meanings without having to explain how the *same* word can have *different* meanings or how the *same* meaning can be expressed by *different* words. It does not seem likely that an adequate explanation could be developed without some theory of sameness and otherness.

THE "SENSE OF SAMENESS," says William James, "is the very keel and backbone of our thinking." He is here speaking "of the sense of sameness from the point of view of the mind's structure alone, and not from the point of view of the universe . . . Whether there be any *real* sameness in *things* or not, or whether the mind be true or false in its assumptions of it," he goes on, the point remains that "the mind makes continual use of the *notion* of sameness, and if deprived of it, would have a different structure from what it has . . . Without the psychological sense of identity, sameness might rain down upon us from the outer world forever and we be none the wiser. With the psychological sense, on the other hand, the outer world might be an unbroken flux, and yet we should perceive a repeated experience."

James distinguishes three principles of identity. In addition to the *psychological* law according to which we feel a later experience to be the same as an earlier one, he refers to the *ontological* principle which "asserts that every real thing is what it is, that *a* is *a*, and *b, b*"; and the *logical* principle which declares that "what is once true of the subject of a judgment is always true of that subject." James seems to think that "the ontological law is a tautological truism," whereas the logical and the psychological principles have further implications not immediately obvious. Locke appears to take a contrary view. He finds the identity of all *ideas* self-evident, while to him the real identity of *things* is much more difficult to grasp.

The principle of identity and its companion principle of contradiction are, according to Locke, expressed in the propositions 'Whatsoever is, is' and 'It is impossible for the same thing to be and not to be'—"these two general propositions amounting to no more, in short, but this, that the same is the same, and the same is not different." But, Locke adds, "the mind, without the help of any proof or reflection on either of these general propositions, perceives so clearly, and knows so certainly, that 'the idea of white is the idea of white, and not the idea of blue,' and that 'the idea of white, when it is in the mind, is there and is not absent,' that the consideration of these axioms can add nothing to the evidence or certainty of its knowledge . . . I appeal to everyone's own mind, whether this proposition 'A circle is a circle' be not as self-evident a proposition as that consisting of more general terms 'Whatsoever is, is.' "

But unlike the comparing of an idea with itself, real identity, according to Locke, requires us to consider a thing "as existing at any determined time and place" and to "compare it with itself existing at another time . . . When, therefore, we demand whether anything be the same or no? it refers always to something that existed at such a time in such a place, which, it was certain, at that instant, was the same with itself and no other; from whence it follows that one thing cannot have two beginnings of existence, nor two things one beginning, it being impossible for two things of the same kind to be or exist in the same instant in the very same place, or one and the same thing, in different places. That, therefore, that had one beginning is the same thing; and that which had a different beginning in time and place from that, is not the same, but diverse." In short, across a lapse of time a thing remains identical, in Locke's view, or maintains its identity, if existence having made it "one particular thing under any denomination, the same existence continued preserves it the same individual under the same denomination."

THIS UNDERSTANDING OF real identity Locke applies without difficulty to an atom of matter which, being at a given instant "what it is and nothing else . . . is the same and so must continue as long as its existence is continued; for so long it will be the same, and no other. In like manner, if two or more atoms be joined together into the same mass, every one of those atoms will be the same by the foregoing rule; and whilst they exist united together, the mass consisting of the same atoms, must be the same mass or the same body, let the parts be ever so differently jumbled. But," Locke continues, "if one of these atoms be taken away, or one new one added, it is no longer the same mass or the same body."

The problem of identity in living organisms Locke does not find so easy to solve. "In the state of living creatures," he says, "their identity depends not on a mass of the same particles, but on something else. For in them the variation of great parcels of matter alters not the identity; an oak growing from a plant to a great tree, and then lopped, is still the same oak; and a colt grown up to a horse, sometimes fat, sometimes lean, is all the while the same horse, though in both these cases there may be a manifest change of the parts, so that truly they are not, either of them, the same masses of matter."

The problem of the real identity or continuity of living things through time and change is, as we shall see presently, only a special case of the larger problem of whether anything at all remains identical for more than an instant in the universal flux of things. But supposing that problem solved in favor of enduring substances, or things which somehow remain continuously the same while changing in this or that respect, the point of Locke's observation about living things still holds, for their identity does not seem to lie in the continuity or permanence of the matter—the particles—of which they are composed.

The familiar riddle about the pipe—whether it is in any respect the same after it has its broken bowl replaced by a new one, and then has a new stem added to the new bowl—may be propounded for living organisms. But in their case, Locke argues, a principle of identity can be found. A plant, he says, "continues to be the same plant as long as it partakes of the same life, though that life be communicated to new particles of matter vitally united to the living plant, in a like continued organization conformable to that sort of plant."

The principle, he thinks, applies to animals and men. "The case is not so much different in brutes but that anyone may hence see what makes an animal and continues it the same. Something we have like this in machines, and may serve to illustrate it. For example, what is a watch? It is plain it is nothing but a fit organization or construction of parts to a certain end, which, when a sufficient force is added to it, it is capable to attain. If we would suppose this machine one continued body, all whose organized parts were repaired, increased, or diminished by a constant addition or separation of insensible parts, with one common life, we should have something very much like the body of an animal . . . This also shows wherein the identity of the same man consists; *viz.*, in nothing but a participation of the same continued life by constantly fleeing particles of matter, in succession, vitally united to the same organized body."

IN THE CASE OF MAN, however, Locke thinks we must face the additional problem of personal identity. What makes a man the same person from moment to moment, sleeping and waking, remembering or not remembering his past? In what does the continuity of the self consist, on the identity of which, Locke insists, "is founded all the right and justice of reward and punishment"? His answer seems to be that, as a living organism is identical throughout one and the same life, it is the continuity of the same consciousness which "makes a man be himself to himself" and establishes his personal identity.

"Whatever has the consciousness of present and past actions," Locke writes, "is the same person to whom they both belong . . . That with which the consciousness of this present thinking thing *can* join itself, makes the same person, and is one self with it, and with nothing else . . . If the same Socrates, waking and sleeping, do not partake of the same consciousness, Socrates, waking and sleeping, is not the same person. And to punish Socrates waking for what sleeping Socrates thought, and waking Socrates was never conscious of, would be no more right than to punish one twin for what his brother twin did, whereof he knew nothing, because their outsides were so like that they could not be distinguished."

James also attributes the sense of personal identity to continuity of consciousness, but for him there still remains a problem of explaining that continuity. In the flow of consciousness from moment to moment, "continuity," he thinks, "makes us unite what dissimilarity might otherwise separate; similarity makes us unite what discontinuity might hold apart . . . The sense of our personal identity, then, is exactly like any one of our other perceptions of sameness among phenomena. It is a conclusion grounded either on the resemblance in a fundamental respect, or on the continuity before the mind, of the phenomena compared."

In his opinion, "*resemblance among the parts of a continuum* of feelings (especially bodily feelings) experienced along with things widely different in all other regards, *thus constitutes the real and verifiable 'personal identity' which we feel*. There is no other identity than this in the 'stream' of subjective consciousness . . . Its parts differ, but under all their differences they are knit in these two ways; and if either way of knitting disappears, the sense of unity departs. If a man wakes up some fine day unable to recall any of his past experiences, so that he has to learn his biography afresh . . . he *feels* and he *says* that he is a changed person. He disowns his former me, gives himself a new name, identifies his present life with nothing from out of the older time. Such cases are not rare in mental pathology."

In the tradition of the great books, other solutions are offered to the problem of personal identity. Kant thinks, for example, that a "transcendental unity of apperception" is necessary to constitute "in all possible phenomena which may come together in our experience, a connection of all these representations according to laws. Unity of consciousness," he writes, "would be impossible if the mind, in the knowledge of the manifold, could not become conscious of the identity of function by which it unites the manifold synthetically in one knowledge. Therefore, the original and necessary consciousness of the identity of one's self is at the same time a consciousness of the equally necessary unity of the synthesis of all phenomena according to concepts."

Where Kant posits a transcendental ego to account for the experienced identity of the self, other philosophers who hold one or another theory of the soul as an imperishable substance or an unchanging principle seem to find no special subtleties in the problem of the identity of living organisms or persons. So far as such theories bear upon that problem, the consideration of them belongs to the chapter on Soul. Here we are concerned with the notions of same and other as they apply to everything in the universe. Hence we must face all the problems of how two things can be the same, not merely the problem of self-sameness or the identity of a thing with itself.

The word "identical" is sometimes used as a synonym for "same," as when we say that two things are identical in a certain respect. But without the qualification expressed by "in a certain respect," it is seldom if ever said that

two things are identical, for if they can be discriminated from one another in any respect at all, they are two, not one, and therefore not identical. This seems to be the sense of Leibniz's principle of the identity of indiscernibles, concurred in by all who understand identity as the self-sameness of that which is one in number and existence. A plurality of things involves a numerical diversity—each of the many being an *other*. To this extent at least, the traditional discussion of same and other tends to merge with matters discussed in the chapter on One and Many.

For both Plato and Aristotle, the relation between these two pairs—*one and many* and *same and other*—seems to be much closer. In the comparison of two things, Aristotle appears to treat sameness as a kind of oneness, referring to the various ways in which two things can be "one and the same." Of sameness, he says that "it is a unity of the being, either of more than one thing or of one thing when it is treated as more than one"; and of the one he says that to it "belong . . . the same and the like and the equal, and to plurality belong the other and the unlike and the unequal."

The enumeration he gives of kinds of unity seems to be paralleled by his enumeration of kinds of similitude. As a thing may be one essentially or one by accident, so two things may be the same essentially or by accident. Aristotle's statement that "some things are one in number, others in species, others in genus, others by analogy," finds its counterpart in his statement that " 'different' is applied to those which, though other, are the same in some respect, only not in number, but either in species or in genus or by analogy."

As indicated in the chapter on Relation, a distinction is traditionally made between relationships which really exist among things apart from the mind, and logical relationships which occur in thought alone. This distinction seems to separate self-sameness or identity from all relations of similitude which obtain between two things. "The relation signified by the term *the same*," Aquinas says, "is a logical relation only if it is taken in regard to absolutely the same thing, because such a relation can exist only in a certain order observed by reason as regards the order of anything to itself. The case is otherwise, however, when things are called the same, not numerically, but generically or specifically."

Nevertheless, identity seems to underlie all other relations of sameness, for among things or ideas lacking identity no comparisons can be made. Those who deny identity on the ground that everything is in flux, nullify all further discussion of sameness. The theory of a universal flux, which Plato attributes to Heracleitus, permits nothing ever to remain stationary or the same for an instant; and "the professed Heraclitean," Cratylus, went even further, according to Aristotle: he "criticized Heraclitus for saying that it is impossible to step twice into the same river; for *he* thought one could not do it even once."

In saying of men that "they are *nothing but a bundle or collection of different perceptions,* which succeed each other with an inconceivable rapidity, and are in a perpetual flux and movement," Hume does more than deny personal identity. He affirms an utter diversity— "as if there were no manner of relation" at all—between distinct perceptions, each of which is for him a distinct existence. The opposite point of view affirms things which have an enduring existence and which can, as Aristotle says of substances, undergo change in many respects "while remaining numerically one and the same."

According to Wittgenstein, "We seem to have an infallible paradigm of identity in the identity of a thing with itself." But he goes on to say of the phrase, "a thing is identical with itself," that "there is no finer example of a useless proposition, which yet is connected with a certain play of the imagination. It is as if in imagination we put a thing into its own shape and saw that it fitted."

TIME AND CHANGE raise the question of how any one thing can be the same from moment to moment. The question of how two things can be one and the same in any respect arises from the simple fact that, at the instant of comparison, they are two. If they were the same only for the comparing mind, then their sameness would be a logical and not a real relationship. For two things to be the same in reality seems to imply that, although two in number, they are one in some respect. To use Hegel's language, there is identity in diversity; or, in the language of Aquinas, a real community exists, according to which some one thing is common to two.

The problem of the sameness of two things can be stated in terms of the significance of what Hobbes, Berkeley, and Hume call common or general names. Denying that such words as "man" or "tree" or "stone" express abstract or general ideas, they seem to say that common names like these signify what is common to two or more individuals—whether things, perceptions, or ideas. Those who, like Aristotle, Aquinas, and Locke, take general or common names to signify abstract ideas, seem to say such ideas themselves signify that in reality two or more things have something in common. Still another view is that, apart from all individual things, real universals exist as the objects of the mind's conceptions.

If the latter alternative is chosen, then two individuals—two men, for example—may be thought alike only because both somehow resemble, as Plotinus suggests, the separate archetype Man. What is common to the two men lies in a third and separate reality, of which Plotinus says that it is "present in multiplicity," as if "in multi-impression . . . from one seal." But as Parmenides observes, in Plato's dialogue of that name, if a separate idea of Man is required to explain how two individuals are alike in being men, then still another idea is needed to account for the likeness between each individual man and the idea Man.

On the other hand, the view that the real sameness of two individuals, or the reality of the one kind to which both belong, resides in them—in their common possession of the same nature, quality, or other attribute— seems to lead to the difficulty already intimated, namely, the difficulty of understanding how distinct existences can have anything in common—how they can be two in number and yet also one in nature. If John and James are alike as men because they share a common humanity, then can it be said that each has *his own* human nature? If their natures and properties are as individual as their existences, how can two things be *really the same* in any respect? Must not kinds or universals—or whatever is supposed to be common to many and the source of their sameness—exist only in the general meaning of words, or in the mind's abstract concepts, or as separate archetypes? But, then, what truth is there in the familiar statement that two individual things are in some respect *really* alike or the same?

THESE QUESTIONS indicate that the traditional discussion of the same and the other tends to involve not merely the theory of the one and the many, but also, in certain issues at least, the problem of the individual and the universal. As the chapter on UNIVERSAL AND PARTICULAR shows, the several positions traditionally taken with regard to universals afford different answers to the problem of how any sameness between two or more things exists. The factor of similitude in knowledge (the nature of the likeness between image or idea and its object) and the function of similitude in love (the attraction, or repulsion, of like by like) also extend the consideration of sameness in diversity into the field of problems dealt with in other chapters. Here attention must be given to the meaning of sameness itself, as that is affected by the distinction between the same and the similar, by the enumeration of various kinds or degrees of likeness, and by the range of opposite meanings in the notions of diversity and difference.

Discussing discrimination and comparison, James, for example, draws a sharp line between the simple and complex components of our experience. Simple impressions, he seems to think, are either absolutely alike or absolutely unlike. Here there can be no degrees of resemblance or similarity. "Two resembling things," he writes, "owe their resemblance to their absolute identity in respect to some attribute or attributes, combined with the absolute nonidentity of the rest of their being. This, which may be true of compound things, breaks down when we come to simple impressions." The latter, apart from their numerical nonidentity or otherness, are either the same in quality or diverse. But compound things may be more or less alike, varying in degree of similarity or difference according to the number of simple respects in which they are or are not the same.

"Similarity, in compounds," says James, "is partial identity," and he gives the following illustrations. "The moon is similar to a gas-jet, it is also similar to a foot-ball; but a gas-jet and a foot-ball are not similar to each other . . . Moon and gas-jet are similar in respect of luminosity and nothing else; moon and foot-ball in respect of rotundity, and nothing else. Football and gas-jet are in no respect similar—that is, they possess no common point, no identical attribute."

Other writers seem to agree on this distinction between the same and the similar, the diverse and the different. The latter in both cases combine elements of sameness and diversity to give degrees of likeness. Aquinas, for example, says that "we seek for difference where we also find resemblance. For this reason, things which differ must in some way be composite, since they differ in some respect and in some respect they resemble each other. In this sense, although all things that differ are diverse, yet all things that are diverse do not differ . . . For simple things are diverse through themselves, and do not differ from one another by differences as their components. For instance, a man and an ass differ by the difference of rational and irrational, but we cannot say that these again differ by some further difference."

The specific difference between man and ass with respect to rationality, accompanied by their generic sameness with respect to animality, makes them similar. If they were utterly diverse, *i.e.*, the same in no respect, they would not be said to differ; just as if they were identical in all respects except number, they would not be called similar. "The other and the same," writes Aristotle, "are thus opposed. But difference is not the same as otherness. For the other and that which it is other than need not be other in some definite respect . . . but that which is different is different from some particular thing in some particular respect, so that there must be something identical by which they differ."

But within the area of this agreement on fundamental terms, there seems to be some disagreement about whether two things can be utterly diverse. Since they are two, they cannot be the same in *all* respects—certainly not in number—but can they be totally incomparable? James appears to say Yes in his remark about the football and the gas jet having "no common point, no identical attribute." Yet he also seems to hold that no two things are ever absolutely incomparable. They may not differ or be similar as the diverse species of the same genus, *e.g.*, man and ass; but regarding them as " 'thinkables' or 'existents,' " he writes, "even the smoke of a cigarette and the worth of a dollar bill are comparable—still more so as 'perishables' or as 'enjoyables.' " The gas jet and the football would appear to be comparable also as 'existents' or 'usables'—or even, perhaps, as 'bodies.'

The question thus arises whether—all things being somehow comparable—they are all the same in genus, as, for example, all three-dimensional material things may be said to belong to the genus 'body' no matter how much else they differ as species or subordinate kinds within this genus. Kant answers this question by affirming a principle of ultimate homogeneousness. According to this principle, "there are no different original and first *genera,* as it were isolated and separated from each other, but all diverse *genera* are divisions only of one supreme and general *genus.*" Kant states a correlative principle of variety or specification, according to which "every *genus* requires *species,* and these again *sub-species,* and as none even of these *sub-species* is without a sphere . . . reason in its utmost extension requires that no species or sub-species should in itself be considered as the lowest."

Aristotle's theory of species and genera appears to be exactly opposite to Kant's on both points. For Aristotle, there is no single all-embracing genus, but rather a number of diverse yet supreme genera, such as substance, quantity, quality, etc. There is a finite, not an infinite variety of species. The lowest species is further divisible only into kinds which differ, as individuals of the same species do, in accidental, not essential respects, *e.g.,* white

man and red man differ in the same way as John and James do within the species 'man,' not as the species 'man' and 'ass' differ within the genus 'animal.' Furthermore, where Kant insists upon a third principle of continuity, according to which between any two species "there always remain possible intermediate species, differing from the first and the second by smaller degrees than those by which these differ from each other," Aristotle seems to find no intermediates possible between the contrary species of a single genus. The order of species is for him a discontinuous series like the order of the whole numbers, between proximate members of which no fractions are admitted.

Does Aristotle's position with respect to the *heterogeneity* of an animal and the color blue—the one in the genus 'substance,' the other in the genus 'quality'—mean that such things, *absolutely diverse in genus,* are absolutely incomparable? His answer seems to be twofold. In one place he says that things which are diverse in genus may still be the same by analogy: "things that are one by analogy are not all one in genus." In another, he gives us an example of analogical resemblance (between the soul and the hand): "As the hand is a tool of tools, so the mind is the form of forms and sense the form of sensible things."

If the example seems inappropriate on the ground that the soul and the hand are of the same genus, *i.e.,* both substances or parts of the same substance *man,* it may be necessary to introduce the distinction between natural and logical genera. According to this distinction, a material and a spiritual substance can both be called "substances" as a matter of logical classification, but they are not in the same genus by their own natures. In this sense, Aquinas assigns a geometric solid and a physical body to the same logical genus 'body' but regards them as of heterogeneous natures; and Descartes, calling an extended and a thinking substance both "substances," insists upon the utter diversity of their natures.

An easier example, however, may not be too difficult to find. A man and a number belong to different genera, according to Aristotle—one a substance, the other a quantity. But the man can be related to his sons as the number *one* is related to any other whole number. The relation which is the same in both cases is that of priority, according to which the man and unity are the principles or generators respectively of his sons and other numbers. Here, then, we see two heterogeneous things—a substance and a quantity—which are, nevertheless, the same by analogy, *each standing to another in the same relationship;* both, therefore, can be called "principle" or "generator" analogically.

Aristotle's other indication that a special mode of similitude obtains between heterogeneous things, occurs in all those passages in which he says that terms like 'being' can be predicated of things in every category or genus. Just as James seems to think that any two things may be comparable as 'thinkables' or 'existents,' so Aristotle seems to hold that all things, though otherwise heterogeneous, are at least alike in *being, i.e.,* in having some mode of existence. Yet the term 'being' cannot be equated with Kant's single supreme genus. Though Aristotle agrees with Kant that every genus must be capable of division into species, he does not think that 'being' can be so divided by specific differences.

Two POINTS MUST be observed concerning Aristotle's theory of the predication of a term like 'being' of everything in the universe.

First, he repeatedly asserts that 'being' is not said *in the same sense* of substances, quantities, qualities, and so forth. Hence when such heterogeneous things are all called 'beings,' the implication cannot be that, as beings, they are all the *same.* The point seems to be that they are somehow *at once both the same and diverse.* As, to use an example from Aristotle's *Physics,* a tone and a taste can both be sharp, though the sharpness of a tone is as diverse from the sharpness of a taste as tone and taste are qualitatively diverse from each other; so a man and a number can both have being, though their modes of being are as diverse as substance is from quantity. If the word "similarity" were to be used to signify not the combination of separable elements of sameness and diversity, but rather the inseparable

fusion of the two to constitute a *diversified sameness,* then heterogeneous things should be called *similar,* not the same, in being.

Second, Aristotle does not identify such similarity of heterogeneous things with the sameness by analogy which heterogeneous things can have. 'Being' is not a relative term and therefore it cannot be predicated analogically, as 'principle' or 'generator' can be. Terms which are predicated analogically, as 'principle' can be predicated of a father and the number one, may signify *similarity* (in the sense of *diversified sameness*) rather than simple sameness in a single respect. The relation of generation which creates the analogical similitude between the father and the number one seems to be the same relation in the two cases (between a father and his sons, and between one and other numbers); it is not, however, simply the same, for that relation is diversified according as the things related—substances in the one case, quantities in the other—are absolutely diverse in genus. But in Aristotle's analysis it does not follow that because some analogical predicates signify *diversified* rather than *simple* sameness, all do; or that because some instances of *diversified sameness* happen to be analogical (*i.e.,* sameness in a relation), all are.

The interest in Aristotle's separation of these two points lies in the fact that Aquinas combines them in a theory which states that, when being and other terms (which are not genera and yet are above all genera) are predicated of heterogeneous things, they must be predicated analogically of them. The existence which is found in all things, he says, "is common to all only according to some sort of analogy," not "according to the same specific or generic formality." This is most easily seen in the "likeness of creatures to God," which is "solely according to analogy, inasmuch as God is essential being, whereas other things are beings by participation."

Aristotle's statement that "things which are one by analogy are not all one in genus," seems to be converted by Aquinas into the proposition that *things which are not one in genus, and yet are alike in some way, are all one by analogy.* For Aristotle, sameness by analogy may be either simple sameness or diversified sameness (*i.e.,* similarity); and diversified sameness may or may not be analogical, that is, it may be the kind of similarity which two heterogeneous things have in respect to being or in respect to some relation in which they stand to other things. For Aquinas, on the other hand, whenever heterogeneous things are the same in any single respect, their diversified sameness is *always analogical;* and whenever the similitude between two things is truly analogical, then it is *always similarity,* that is, a diversified, not a simple sameness. Likeness in being, according to Aquinas, affords us the prime example of a similitude which is at once an analogical and a diversified sameness.

Aquinas applies his theory of the analogy of being to the great traditional issue, which puts all theories of similitude to the test—the question of the resemblance between God and creatures, or between infinite and finite being. Against the answer first given by Maimonides, and later expressed by Spinoza when, of all comparisons between God and man, he says that "His essence . . . could resemble ours in nothing except in name"; and against those,

on the other hand, who think that whatever names apply to both God and creatures (such as "being" or "good" or "one"), apply simply in the *same* sense, Aquinas seems to take the middle ground. The names which are properly applicable to both God and creatures, according to him, are said of them, not equivocally and not univocally, but analogically.

This threefold distinction of univocal, equivocal, and analogical names, especially as it concerns the names of God, is discussed in the chapter on SIGN AND SYMBOL. The theological problem of the similitude between God and creatures confronts us with three basic alternatives in man's speculation about the sameness and diversity which exists among all things. We can say, (1) that infinite and finite being are utterly diverse, and have no similarity *even* in being. We can say, (2) that they are homogeneous—that, with respect to being, for example, they have the kind of sameness which things have when they belong to the same genus. Or we can say, (3) that they are only similar in the sense of a diversified sameness, whether such similarity is or is not always analogical in character.

83

Science

INTRODUCTION

IN our time, science, philosophy, and religion have come to represent three quite distinct intellectual enterprises. Each appeals for allegiance not merely on the ground that it can answer fundamental questions, but also because of its contribution to human life and culture. In other periods, philosophy and religion competed for supremacy, though, as appears in the chapter on PHILOSOPHY, some philosophers and theologians tried to remove this conflict by arguing for the complete compatibility of reason and faith. Nevertheless, before the 19th century, the issue, if one existed, was between philosophy and religion. Science had not yet become sufficiently distinct from philosophy to complicate the picture.

When science and philosophy are not themselves sharply distinguished, men are not confronted with three separate claims upon their intellectual allegiance. Modern science as something quite distinct in method and subject matter from traditional philosophy may actually make its appearance as early as the 17th century. But not until Kant are two kinds of science plainly set apart. Not until then are they so defined that one becomes identified with what men have always called "philosophy" and the other gradually appropriates the name of "science" and regards itself as a quite separate enterprise.

Kant differentiates between the empirical and the rational sciences. This differentiation tends to correspond with the distinction by others before him of experimental and abstract philosophy. It also corresponds with a later division into the experimental or inductive and the philosophical or deductive sciences. But Kant does not seem to contemplate the possibility of conflict between science and philosophy—between the experimental study of nature and metaphysics or, what is for him the same, between empirical and rational physics.

Hume is willing to admit only mathematics to the status of a rational science, capable of demonstrating its conclusions with certainty. He insists upon experimental reasoning in the study of nature, wherein only probable conclusions can be attained. But he does not make these critical points in terms of science versus philosophy. If the traditional metaphysics is to be rejected, it is not because it is philosophy rather than science, but because it represents a failure in philosophy *or* science, resulting from the wrong method of dealing with matters of fact.

In the 19th century, however, Auguste Comte formulated a doctrine which, under the title of *Positive Philosophy,* explicitly declares that only the positive sciences—the study of natural, mental, and social phenomena by empirical methods—deserve to be called "sciences" in the eulogistic sense of that term. In contrast, philosophy is mere speculation, and religion is superstition. The word "speculation" is for the positivist only slightly less invidious than "superstition." Whereas superstition implies irrational belief, speculation represents a futile attempt by reason to go behind the phenomena in order to discover ultimate causes or substances. This cannot result in anything but guesswork or conjecture—never in knowledge or science, which are the same for the positivist. For all its show of logic and system, philosophy cannot produce conclusions which have the validity or objectivity of science, because it tries to do more than explore and describe the phenomena and because it tries to do whatever it does without investigation or experiment.

From many sources in addition to Comte similar views converge to form an attitude generally prevalent in the world today under the name of positivism. All its current varieties seem to have this much in common: the identification of science with knowledge of fact, and further, the restriction of such knowledge to conclusions obtained and verified empirically. Whatever does not accord with this conception of science is either, like mathematics or logic, a purely formal discipline or, like philosophy and religion, it is conjecture, opinion, or belief—personal, subjective, even wishful.

FREUD IS THE AUTHOR in this set of great books who provides us with a declaration of positivism and sets science against philosophy and religion. It is also fitting that he should be a scientist in the field of psychology, since psychology is a latecomer among the disciplines that, once branches of philosophy, now claim to be positive sciences. Not only late, but last, according to Freud, for "sociology, which deals with the behavior of man in society, can be nothing other than applied psychology. Strictly speaking, indeed, there are only two sciences—psychology, pure and applied, and natural science."

In his *New Introductory Lectures on Psycho-Analysis,* Freud concludes with a statement of what he calls the "scientific *Weltanschauung.*" In essence, he thinks, "it asserts that there is no other source of knowledge of the universe, but the intellectual manipulation of carefully verified observations, in fact, what is called *research,* and that no knowledge can be obtained from revelation, intuition, or inspiration." Freud makes the drastic implications of this statement quite explicit. "It is inadmissible to declare," he writes, "that science is one field of human intellectual activity, and that religion and philosophy are others, at least as valuable, and that science has no business to interfere with the other two, that they all have an equal claim to truth, and that everyone is free to choose whence he shall draw his convictions and in which he shall place his belief.

"Such an attitude," he goes on, "is considered particularly respectable, tolerant, broadminded, and free from narrow prejudices. Unfortunately, it is not tenable; it shares all the pernicious qualities of an entirely unscientific *Weltanschauung* and in practice comes to much the same thing. The bare fact is that truth cannot be tolerant and cannot admit compromise or limitations, that scientific research looks on the whole field of human activity as its own, and must adopt an uncompromisingly critical attitude towards any other power that seeks to usurp any part of its province."

As a threat to the dominion of science over man and society, "religion alone is a really serious enemy." Philosophy, Freud thinks, "has no immediate influence on the great majority of mankind"; whereas "religion is a tremendous force, which exerts its power over the strongest emotions of human beings." Religion and science might be compatible if religion, offering men something "incomparably more beautiful, more comforting, and more ennobling than anything they could ever get from science," would only say: 'It is a fact that I cannot give you what men commonly call truth; to obtain that, you must go to science.' "

But religion cannot say that, Freud thinks, without losing "all influence over the mass of mankind," and science cannot, on its side, yield at all in its claim to being the *only* avenue to truth. Employing a method which "carefully examines the trustworthiness of the sense perceptions on which it bases its conclusions," which "provides itself with new perceptions ... not obtainable by everyday means," and which "isolates the determinants of these new experiences by purposely varied experimentation," science alone can "arrive at correspondence with reality." It is "this correspondence with the real external world we call truth"; and thus when "religion claims that it can take the place of science and that, because it is beneficent and ennobling, it must therefore be true, that claim is, in fact, an encroachment, which, in the interests of everyone, should be resisted." In a little book entitled *Cosmic Religion,* Einstein appeared to have a more benign attitude toward the relation between science and religion. Elsewhere he wrote, "Science without religion is lame, religion without science is blind."

Philosophy does not seem to Freud to offer men a genuine alternative to scientific truth. Unlike religion, it is not in his view necessarily opposed to science; at times it even behaves "as if it were a science," and to some extent makes "use of the same methods." But insofar as it parts company with science by clinging "to the illusion that it can produce a complete and coherent picture of the universe," philosophy must be regarded as an impostor in the halls of knowledge.

The picture philosophy tries to construct, Freud says, "must needs fall to pieces with every new advance in our knowledge." Not itself knowledge, but mere opinion or speculation, philosophy does not, any more than religion, offer a substitute for science. Both together fall under Freud's interdict. Both together would be outcasts from human culture if what he calls "our best hope for the future," that is, "the intellect—the scientific spirit, reason— should in time establish a dictatorship over the human mind."

WILLIAM JAMES, ALMOST contemporary with Freud, also draws a sharp line between science and philosophy. Writing his *The Principles of Psychology* at a time when the experimental methods of the natural sciences, especially physiology, had just been introduced into the study of mental phenomena, he is at pains to define the scope of psychology as a natural science, and to separate the questions which can be properly considered by a scientist from those which belong to the philosopher. But, unlike Freud, James does not seem to regard the philosopher as engaged in a futile effort to solve problems which are either insoluble or better left until science finds means for solving them.

For James the distinction between science and philosophy does not seem to lie only in the methods they employ, though the empirical or experimental approach does have a bearing on the kind of problems scientists can undertake to solve and the conclusions they can reach. The problems and the conclusions are themselves characteristically different from those of the philosopher.

The scientist *describes* the phenomena, according to James, as precisely as possible and as comprehensively, but without any implication of finality or totality. He recognizes that his descriptive formulations are tentative and incomplete, always subject to the discovery of new data or a more refined presentation of the evidence. Above all, he admits that he is only describing, not *explaining*—not laying bare the ultimate reality which gives the phenomena their deepest intelligibility, or ascertaining the causes which show why, not merely how, things happen as they do.

In the Preface to his *Principles,* James says that he has "kept close to the point of view of natural science throughout the book . . . This book, assuming that thoughts and feelings exist and are vehicles of knowledge, thereupon contends that psychology, when she has ascertained the empirical correlation of the various sorts of thought or feeling with definite conditions of the brain, can go no farther—can go no farther, that is, as a natural science. If she goes farther, she becomes metaphysical. All attempts to *explain* our phenomenally given thoughts as products of deeper-lying entities . . . are metaphysical."

This scientific point of view, James admits, "is anything but ultimate . . . The data assumed by psychology, just like those assumed by physics, must sometime be overhauled. The effort to overhaul them clearly and thoroughly is metaphysics." James does not imply that metaphysics cannot "perform her task well," but he does think that "she . . . spoils two good things when she injects herself into a natural science."

Science and metaphysics should be kept quite separate, he states, even though the sciences, in accumulating "a mass of descriptive details," run "into queries which only a metaphysics alive to the weight of her task can hope successfully to deal with. That will perhaps be centuries hence; and meanwhile the best mark of health that a science can show is this unfinished-seeming front."

The variance of James's conception of metaphysics and its future from other traditional views on that subject is discussed in the chapter on METAPHYSICS. Here it is relevant to observe that James has a conception of science broad enough to include both the empirical natural sciences and what he calls the "pure or *a priori* sciences of Classification, Logic, and Mathematics." Yet in his view metaphysics does not represent philosophy as opposed to science, because it aims at ultimate reality or underlying causes. For example, he rejects the theory of a soul, not because he knows it to be false, but because he thinks it has no place in "a psychology which contents itself with verifiable laws" and which is to "remain positivistic and non-metaphysical."

James in *Pragmatism* does not embrace the positivist view, prevalent in the 19th century and our own day. He limits science to, as well as excludes philosophy from, the domain of empirical knowledge. In discussing the possibility of free will, he says that "Psychology will be Psychology and Science, Science, as much as ever (as much and no more) in this world, whether free-will be true in it or not. Science, however, must be constantly reminded that her purposes are not the only purposes, and that the order of uniform causation which she has use for, and is therefore right in postulating, may be enveloped in a wider order, in which she has no claims at all."

The 20th-century authors included in this set deal in a variety of ways with the problem of distinguishing the spheres of science, philosophy, and religion, and also of relating them to one another: notably Whitehead in *Science and the Modern World,* Planck in his *Scientific Autobiography,* Russell in *The Problems of Philosophy,* Weber in his essay on "Science as a Vocation," and Heisenberg in *Physics and Philosophy.*

EARLIER MODERN SCIENTISTS and philosophers who do not make a sharp distinction between science and philosophy and who antedate any explicit formulation of the positivist doctrine, nevertheless do for the most part conceive natural science as experimental in its method and as having for its goal the formulation of general laws describing and correlating the phenomena. They do not all exclude causes

from the consideration of the natural scientist; nor do they all, as stringently as James, rule out explanation in favor of description or correlation. Furthermore, the almost universal emphasis by modern writers upon the experimental character of the natural sciences does not mean a universal identification of science with the experimental disciplines.

Mathematics, for example, is usually regarded as a science in spite of its being non-experimental. For Locke and Hume, as well as for Descartes, it exhibits certain characteristics—the self-evidence of principles, the certainty of demonstrations—which make it more genuinely worthy of the high name of science than are the tentative hypotheses and probable conclusions of experimental physics. Other disciplines are called "sciences" by comparison with mathematics rather than physics. Descartes, for instance, seems to think that metaphysics can as surely be made a science as mathematics can be. Locke argues that demonstration from axioms is not limited to the science of quantity. As much clarity and certainty is attainable in reasoning about moral matters. Thus, ethics is no less a science than mathematics.

Hobbes appears to take a similar view of politics, though it must be noted in his case that he differs from Descartes and Locke, from Francis Bacon, Hume, and others, in not distinguishing mathematics from physics with respect to the latter's need for experimental evidence. All the sciences are for him alike in being "the demonstrations of consequences of one affirmation to another," regardless of "the diversity of the matter." The "certain and infallible" sign that a man is a scientist in any field of subject matter is that he can "demonstrate the truth thereof perspicuously to another."

Hobbes, furthermore, seems to think that what is true of geometry is true of every science, namely, that it must begin with definitions. "In geometry," he says, "men begin at settling the signification of their words; which settling of significations, they call *definitions.*" Without definitions, science is impossible. "In the right definition of names," Hobbes maintains, "lies the first use of speech, which is the acquisition of science; and in the wrong, or no definitions, lies the first abuse, from which proceed all false or senseless tenets."

Freud expresses the opposite view, which is generally more characteristic of the attitude of the modern scientist, especially the experimentalist or empiricist in method. "The view is often defended," he writes, "that sciences should be built on clear and sharply defined basal concepts." But "in actual fact, no science, not even the most exact, begins with such definitions. The true beginning of scientific activity," Freud holds, "consists rather in describing phenomena and then proceeding to group, classify and correlate them. Even at the stage of description, it is not possible to avoid applying certain abstract ideas to the material in hand, ideas derived from various sources and certainly not the fruit of new experience only ... They must at first necessarily possess some measure of uncertainty; there can be no question of any clear limitation of their content. So long as they remain in this condition, we come to an understanding about their meaning by repeated references to the material of observation, from which we seem to have deduced our abstract ideas, but which is in point of fact subject to them."

The basic concepts or definitions of a science are, according to Freud, "in the nature of conventions; although," he adds, "everything depends on their being chosen in no arbitrary manner, but determined by the important relations they have to the empirical material ... It is only after more searching investigation of the field in question that we are able to formulate with increased clarity the scientific concepts underlying it ... Then indeed, it may be time to immure them in definitions. The progress of science, however, demands a certain elasticity even in these definitions." This may not be true of mathematical concepts or definitions, but, Freud points out, the science of physics illustrates "the way in which even those 'basal concepts' that are firmly established in the form of definitions are constantly being altered in their content."

WITH THE EXCEPTION of Hobbes, the notion that scientific conclusions can be drawn from definitions or can be established without recourse to experiment, is not usually extended by modern writers from mathematics and metaphysics to physics. As the chapter on PHYSICS shows, the basic division of the study of nature into philosophical and scientific physics becomes equivalent, in modern times, to a separation of the philosophy of nature from the experimental natural sciences. We shall return presently to that sense of "science" in which physics is associated with mathematics and metaphysics as a branch of theoretical philosophy or as one of the speculative sciences. All three disciplines are thought of as proceeding in the same way: by the demonstration of conclusions from principles obtained by induction from experience—ordinary sense-experience, that is, not the special experiences artificially contrived in a laboratory under experimental conditions. But it should be observed that, in the modern period, even those authors who use "science" in the foregoing sense when they discuss mathematics and metaphysics, treat physics differently. They hold that physics must be experimental if it is to be scientific.

In proportion as modern physics becomes more and more the model of science, the meaning of the word "science" tends to become reserved for experimental study, or at least for empirical investigation, so that nonexperimental disciplines, like metaphysics or ethics, are questioned when they call themselves "sciences." Other disciplines try to establish themselves as sciences by imitating physics. Marx, for example, in presenting his own work as economic *science,* seeks to explain how it can be scientific even if it is not experimental.

"The physicist," he writes, "either observes physical phenomena where they occur in their most typical form and most free from disturbing influence, or, wherever possible, he makes experiments under conditions that assure the occurrence of the phenomenon in its normality." If experiment, in the strict sense, is impossible in economics, at least the student of economics can be scientific in his effort to observe the phenomena "in their most typical form." England, Marx thinks, offers the most typical example of "the capitalist mode of production, and the conditions of production and exchange corresponding to that mode." Hence, for scientific purposes, he has used England "as the chief illustration in the development of [his] theoretical ideas."

THE EXPERIMENTAL CHARACTER of modern physics, whether it is called natural science or natural philosophy, is discussed in the chapter on PHYSICS. The distinction between the construction or use of experiments and the appeal to experience—apart from experiment—either as a source or as a test of scientific formulations, is discussed in the chapter on EXPERIENCE, as well as in the chapters on HYPOTHESIS and INDUCTION. Here it seems pertinent to note that neither the distinction between induction and deduction, nor the distinction between hypotheses and axioms, unequivocally marks the line which separates science from philosophy.

Aristotle and Bacon, for example, regard induction as the source of axioms in metaphysics or *philosophia prima* as well as in physics or the philosophy of nature. They may have different theories of induction, but only insofar as one conceives induction as an intuitive generalization from *ordinary sense-experience,* and the other makes induction an inference from *experiments,* does the difference between them seem to have a bearing on the distinction between philosophy and science.

Similarly, the difference between the scientist's and the philosopher's consideration of hypotheses seems to lie not in the role they play in reasoning or argument, but rather in their having or not having a special relation to experimentation, either to guide it or to submit to its test.

Experiment, then, seems to be the distinguishing mark of science on the side of method; and, by an extension of meaning, even in those subject matters where experiments in the strict sense—in laboratories, with apparatus, under controlled conditions—are impossible, the scientist differs from the philosopher in an analogous point of method. The scientist investigates, does research, makes observations which go beyond experi-

ences which ordinary men have in the course of daily life.

It seems to be in this spirit that Newton opens the *Optics* with the statement that "my design in this book is not to explain the properties of light by hypotheses, but to propose and prove them by reason and experiments." In the same spirit Faraday says of himself: "As an experimentalist, I feel bound to let experiment guide me into any train of thought which it may justify; being satisfied that experiment, like analysis, must lead to strict truth if rightly interpreted; and believing also that it is in its nature far more suggestive of new trains of thought and new conditions of natural power."

Lavoisier imposes upon himself the rule "never to form any conclusion which is not an immediate consequence necessarily flowing from observation and experiment." Gilbert criticizes those who write about magnetism without recourse to experiments—philosophers who are not themselves investigators and have no firsthand acquaintance with things. Referring to "what has been held by the vulgar and by tradition" concerning the motion of the heart and arteries, Harvey proposes to separate true from false opinions "by dissection, multiplied experience and accurate observation."

Even a scientist like Joseph Fourier, who conceives physical theory as a kind of applied mathematics, says that "no considerable progress can hereafter be made which is not founded on experiments . . . for mathematical analysis can deduce from general and simple phenomena the expression of the laws of nature; but the special application of these laws to very complex effects demands a long series of exact observations." Like Fourier, Galileo also combines mathematics and experiment in the study of nature. But though he is willing to introduce experiments where they are necessary in order to test rival hypotheses or alternative mathematical formulations of the laws of motion, he seems to express a preference for the rigor of purely mathematical physics.

In the Fourth Day of Galileo's *Concerning Two New Sciences,* discussing the parabolic path of projectiles, one person in the dialogue, Sagredo, says that "the force of rigid demonstrations such as occur only in mathematics fills me with wonder and delight." The understanding thus derived, he adds, "far outweighs the mere information obtained by the testimony of others or even by repeated experiment." Agreeing with this, Salviati, another person in the dialogue, claims that "the knowledge of a single fact acquired through a discovery of its causes prepares the mind to understand and ascertain other facts without need of recourse to experiment, precisely as in the present case, where by argumentation alone the Author proves with certainty that the maximum range occurs when the elevation is 45°. He thus demonstrates what has perhaps never been observed in experience, namely, that of other shots those which exceed or fall short of 45° by equal amounts have equal ranges."

THE CONCEPTION OF SCIENCE as consisting in a rigorous demonstration of conclusions from axioms—whether in mathematics or other subject matters—seems to be modern as well as ancient. It is found in Descartes and Spinoza, in Hobbes and Locke, as well as in Plato and Aristotle. Holding that "science in its entirety is true and evident cognition," Descartes may add that "it has been mathematicians alone who have been able to succeed in making any demonstrations, that is to say, producing reasons which are evident and certain"; yet he also hopes to make metaphysics a science after the model of mathematics.

This conception of science is somewhat qualified by Descartes when he discusses the study of nature. Here he tends toward experimentalism. Here he says that "experiments . . . become so much the more necessary the more one is advanced in knowledge." Referring to particular effects which "might be deduced from the principles in many different ways," he thinks that the only way to overcome the difficulty of discovering the principles on which the effects do depend is "to try to find experiments of such a nature that their result is not the same if it has to be explained by one of the methods, as it would be if explained by the other."

On the other hand, the conception of science as knowledge founded upon experiment, or at least upon extended observation, seems to be ancient as well as modern. Aristotle criticizes those of his predecessors in physics whose "explanation of the observations is not consistent with the observations." The test of principles "in the knowledge of nature," he says, "is the unimpeachable evidence of the senses as to each fact." It is for this reason that he praises the method of Democritus as scientific.

"Lack of experience," Aristotle writes, "diminishes our power of taking a comprehensive view of the admitted facts. Hence those who dwell in intimate association with nature and its phenomena grow more and more able to formulate, as the foundations of their theories, principles such as to admit of a wide and coherent development; while those whom devotion to abstract discussions has rendered unobservant of the facts are too ready to dogmatize on the basis of a few observations. The rival treatments of the subject now before us will serve to illustrate how great is the difference between a 'scientific' and a 'dialectical' method of inquiry. For whereas the Platonists argue that there must be atomic magnitudes 'because otherwise "The Triangle" will be more than one,' Democritus would appear to have been convinced by arguments appropriate to the subject, i.e., drawn from the science of nature."

There are many passages in which Aristotle rejects an astronomical hypothesis because it does not account for the observations, or favors one theory against all others because it alone seems to fit the sensible phenomena. So, too, in his biological works, he makes experience the test of theories. Speaking of the generation of bees, for example, he says that if we ever learn the truth about this matter, "credit must be given to observation rather than to theories, and to theories only if what they affirm agrees with the observed facts." And in his treatise *On the Motion of Animals,* he calls for "reference to particulars in the world of sense, for with these in view we seek general theories, and with these we believe that general theories ought to harmonize."

But Aristotle also defines science as the certain demonstration of universal and necessary conclusions from self-evident principles. "Scientific knowledge," he writes, "is judgment about things that are universal and necessary; and the conclusions of demonstration . . . follow from first principles (for scientific knowledge involves apprehension of a rational ground)." The emphasis here is on knowledge of causes, and on the certainty and necessity of conclusions which can be demonstrated from axiomatic truths.

By these criteria, metaphysics and mathematics are, in Aristotle's conception of the three philosophical sciences, perfect examples of scientific knowledge. Physics as a general philosophy of nature is also scientific knowledge in this sense; but the particular natural sciences, such as astronomy or zoology, are more empirical than philosophical in character. At least they involve admixtures of demonstration from principles with the verification of hypotheses by observation. To the extent that they are empirical, they are qualified by an uncertainty and a tentativeness in formulation which do not seem to be present in Aristotle's conception of the purely philosophical sciences.

It might even be said that the knowledge of nature which depends on empirical research is not strictly scientific at all. Locke appears to say just that. "How far soever human industry may advance useful and experimental philosophy in physical things," he writes, "scientifical will still be out of our reach." Holding that "our knowledge of bodies is to be improved only by experience," Locke adds: "I deny not but a man accustomed to rational and regular experiments, shall be able to see farther into the nature of bodies, and guess righter at their yet unknown properties, than one that is a stranger to them; but yet, as I have said, this is but judgment and opinion, not knowledge and certainty. This way of getting and improving our knowledge in substances only by experience and history . . . makes me suspect that natural philosophy is not capable of being made a science."

WHETHER THE EXPERIMENTAL study of nature is the type of all scientific knowledge (in its object, its method, and the character of its conclusions) or whether, according to another conception, the philosophical disciplines are the more perfect, perhaps even the only examples of science, there seems to be no question that different values attach to these two meanings of science—or, as it is currently expressed, to science and philosophy.

The philosophical sciences may be either theoretical or practical according as they aim at wisdom or at action, but they are seldom praised as being useful productively. The practical sciences which are also traditionally regarded as branches of moral philosophy—such as ethics, politics, and economics—may be knowledge put to use in the guidance of individual conduct or the affairs of society, but apart from poetics, which may direct production in the sphere of the fine arts, there does not seem to be any philosophical science, or branch of philosophy, that provides a mastery of matter or some control over nature. None has applications in the sphere of the useful arts.

As indicated in the chapters on ART, KNOWLEDGE, and PHILOSOPHY, Bacon appears to take a contrary view. Using the word "practical" to mean productive rather than moral or civil, he divides the philosophy of nature into speculative and practical branches. He regards mechanics as the application of physics to useful purposes, and finds a productive counterpart to metaphysics in what he calls "magic."

Nor is Bacon's point merely that "the real and legitimate goal of the sciences is the endowment of human life with new inventions and riches," in opposition to those whom he criticizes for thinking that "the contemplation of truth is more dignified and exalted than any utility or extent of effects." In addition, he thinks that the truth of science can be tested by its productive utility. "That which is most useful in practice," he writes, "is most correct in theory."

Bacon's position with regard to the productive utility of science would not be contrary to the traditional view if by "the philosophy of nature" he meant science in the experimental rather than the philosophical sense. His emphasis upon experimentation in all parts of the study of nature suggests that that is the case. The fact that he places equal emphasis upon machinery and inventions and power over nature also suggests that technology is the other face of any science which is experimental in method.

Bacon and Descartes seem to be the first to perceive that knowledge which is experimental in origin must be by its very nature capable of technological applications. The instruments and apparatus which Bacon regards as necessary implements of science, no less than the machinery and inventions which science can be expected to produce, represent the very same techniques of operating upon nature. Experimental science is thus seen to be at once the creature and creator of technology. As Plato's *The Republic* projects a society which cannot be realized unless it is ruled by the science of the philosopher, so Bacon's *New Atlantis* prophesies a civilization which the dominance of experimentalism and technology have brought to present reality.

IT IS A STRIKING fact about the 20th-century view of science that it introduces aesthetic considerations. In contemporary physics, Einstein, as much as anyone, is responsible for emphasizing the role of aesthetic criteria— simplicity, beauty, elegance—in the formulation of theories. When, in his early work, Einstein found his theories challenged by apparent experimental results which, if true, would have required unaesthetic theoretical explanations, he rejected the experiments. It usually turned out that the experiments were wrong and the theory correct. These criteria are subjective, in the first instance, but, in due course, scientists came to agree on which theories are truly beautiful.

It appears to be a deep fact about nature, at least as we perceive it, that beautiful theories are also true; *i.e.,* fit the facts. This requirement of fitting the facts distinguishes the scientific aesthetic from that of the artist. A beautiful work of art is not, in any obvious sense, the solution to a problem. It just is. Nonetheless, the same sensibilities illuminate science, at its highest level, and the arts.

As Heisenberg writes, "the two processes, that of science and that of art, are not very different. Both science and art form in the course of the centuries a human language by which we can speak about the more remote parts of reality, and the coherent sets of concepts as well as the different styles of art are different words or groups of words in this language."

84

Sense

INTRODUCTION

THE nature of sensation seems at first to be as obvious as its existence. In the tradition of the great books there may be controversy concerning the existence of sense in plants as well as in animals, and there may be controversy over the existence in man of faculties higher than sense. But no one disputes that men and other animals are endowed with a power of sense.

The extent of this power may be questioned, but not the fact that animals and men, when awake, experience sensations or perceive through their senses. Sleep, according to Aristotle, can occur only in those living things which have the power of sense perception. "If there be an animal not endowed with sense-perception, it is impossible that this should either sleep or wake, since both these are affections of the activity of the primary faculty of sense-perception."

The existence of the sensible—of an external something which causes sensation and can be sensed—also seems to escape denial or dispute. The existence of a purely intelligible reality—of a world of immaterial things incapable of being sensed—is subject to debate in all periods of western thought. The sensible world is sometimes regarded as the only reality; sometimes it is regarded as mere seeming, or appearance, in comparison with the reality of purely intelligible being. Men may also differ on the question whether things possess sensible qualities when they are not being sensed. But with few exceptions, notably Berkeley and Hume, the existence of a sensible world of material things is not denied or seriously doubted.

The controversies and issues indicated above are, for the most part, discussed elsewhere. The chapter on ANIMAL considers the sensitivity of plants. There also, as well as in the chapters on MAN, IDEA, and MIND, is considered the distinction between the senses and the higher faculties of reason or intellect. The chapter on MEMORY AND IMAGINATION deals with these two functions in their relation to sense and sense perception; and the contrast between sensible and intelligible reality is discussed in the chapters on BEING, FORM, IDEA, and MATTER. Some of these topics necessarily recur here, especially as they bear on what for this chapter are the primary problems—the nature of sensation, the analysis of the power of sense, and the character of the knowledge which is afforded by the senses.

AS WE HAVE ALREADY observed, no difficulty seems to arise at first concerning the nature of sensation. It is supposed by many inquirers, early and late in the tradition, that matter is sensitive as well as sensible. Animals have sense organs which react to physical stimulation. Bodies either act directly upon the sense organs, as in the case of touch and taste; or, as in the case of vision, hearing, and smell, they exert their influence through an intervening medium, yet in a manner which seems to be no less the action and reaction of bodies.

Those who distinguish between living organisms and inanimate bodies tend to regard sensitivity as a property of living matter, but it does not follow for all who make this distinction that other than material factors are needed to explain sensation. On the contrary, some writers seem to think that the motions of matter account for sensation as readily as the laws of mechanics account for all the sensible changes we are able to perceive.

Lucretius, for example, holds that living things consist of body and soul, and that the soul (or mind) differs from the body only in the size, the fineness of texture, and the mobility of the material particles which compose it. Sensation occurs when the particles of body and soul together are set in motion by the impact of external bodies upon the organs of sense. "Our eyes receive / One kind of impulse when they look at white / And quite another from black." Similarly, "Noise is audible / Because its body penetrates the ears, / Impinging on the sense; voices and sounds / Are bodily in nature, since they strike / With impact on the senses."

Either the external body itself, as in touch, strikes the sense and sets up those bodily motions in the animal which are sensation; or, according to Lucretius, minute replicas or images—composed of atoms, as all things are—fly off from the surface of distant bodies and enter through the pores of our sense organs to awaken in us vision, hearing, or smell. In either case, sensation is a bodily reaction; and, for Lucretius, imagination and memory, even thought, are consequent motions in the atoms of the mind—further bodily reverberations, as it were, of sensation.

"The cause of sense," writes Hobbes, "is the external body, or object, which presseth the organ proper to each sense, either immediately, as in the taste and touch; or mediately, as in seeing, hearing, and smelling: which pressure, by the mediation of nerves and other strings and membranes of the body, continued inwards to the brain and heart, causeth there a resistance, or counter-pressure, or endeavour of the heart to deliver itself: which endeavour, because outward, seemeth to be some matter without. And this seeming, or fancy, is that which men call *sense*."

The object seems to be colored or hot or sweet when it causes certain sensations in us which are projected outward upon it, in response or counteraction to the inward motions it sets up. But, says Hobbes, these sensible qualities are, in the object, nothing but "so many several motions of the matter, by which it presseth our organs diversely. Neither in us that are pressed are they anything else but diverse motions (for motion produceth nothing but motion)."

THE FOREGOING THEORY, reducing sensation to bodily motion, seems to draw its cogency from the fact that only bodies are sensible, that sense organs are bodily parts, and that sense organs must be activated by some sort of physical contact for sensations to occur. Some writers, like Descartes, accept the theory for animals, but reject it for men; or they distinguish, in the case of men, between thought and sensation. They regard sensation, with its subsidiary functions of memory and imagination, as reducible to corporeal motions, but refuse to grant that external sense impressions or interior fancy can produce knowledge without the activity of an immaterial soul.

To animals, Descartes declares, "we can ascribe . . . no knowledge at all, but only fancy of a purely corporeal kind." In contrast, "that power by which we are said to know things is purely spiritual, and not less distinct from every part of the body than blood from bone, or hand from eye." In men as well as animals, the external senses, "in so far as they are part of the body . . . perceive in virtue of passivity alone, just in the way that wax receives an impression from a seal." Fancy or imagination is also "a genuine part of the body"; and "memory, at least that which is corporeal and similar to that of the brutes, is in no respect distinct from imagination."

These corporeal faculties are, according to Descartes, of use to the understanding or the mind only when it "proposes to examine something that can be referred to the body"; but if it "deal with matters in which there is nothing corporeal or similar to the corporeal, it cannot be helped by those faculties." Hence, for Descartes, the "mind can act independently of the brain; for certainly the brain can be of no use in pure thought; its only use is for imagining and perceiving."

For others, like William James, the distinction between sensation and thought, so far as their relation to matter is concerned, seems quite untenable. He objects to those who look upon sensational consciousness as "something *quasi*-material, hardly cognitive, which one need not much wonder about," while they regard rational consciousness as "quite the reverse, and the mystery of it [as] unspeakable." We can correlate consciousness with the brain's workings only in an empirical fashion, James thinks, and we ought to confess that "no glimmer of explanation of it is yet in sight. That brains should give rise to a knowing consciousness at all, this is the one mystery which returns, no matter what sort the consciousness or of what sort the knowledge may be. Sensations, aware of mere qualities, involve the mystery as much as thoughts, aware of complex systems, involve it."

Still others, like Plotinus and Aristotle, think that the mystery of conscious matter is not essentially different from the mystery of living matter, for if there is anything mysterious about nutrition and growth, or sensation and imagination, it consists in the same thing—the union of material and immaterial principles, of body and soul.

"If the soul were a corporeal entity," Plotinus writes, "there could be no sense-perception, no mental act, no knowledge . . . If the sentient be a material entity (as we are invited to believe), sensation could only be of the order of seal-impressions struck by a ring on wax." Perception is not a passively received impression. It is, according to Plotinus, an act of awareness "determined by the nature and character of the living being in which it occurs . . . In any perception we attain by sight, the object is grasped there where it lies in the direct line of vision . . . The mind looks outward; this is ample proof that it has taken and takes no inner imprint, and does not see in virtue of some mark made upon it, like that of the ring on the wax; it need not look outward at all if, even as it looked, it already held the image of the object, seeing by virtue of an impression made upon itself."

According to Aristotle, "two characteristic marks have above all others been recognized as distinguishing that which has soul in it from that which has not—self-movement and sensation." By self-movement he appears to mean such things as the nutrition and growth which is found in plants, as well as the additional animal faculty of local motion. Both self-movement and sensation require soul as well as body. "Nothing grows or decays naturally," he writes, "except what feeds itself, and nothing feeds itself except what has a share of soul in it." So, too, "nothing except what has soul in it is capable of sensation." But "the exercise of sense-perception does not belong to soul or body exclusively." Sensation "is not an affection of the soul" by itself, nor has a soulless body "the potentiality of perception."

But, Aristotle asks, are all affections of the soul "affections of the complex body and soul, or is there any one among them peculiar to the soul by itself? . . . If we consider the majority of them, there seems to be no case in which the soul can act or be acted upon without involving the body; e.g., anger, courage, appetite, and sensation generally. Thinking seems to be the most probable exception; but if this too proves to be a form of imagination, or to be impossible without imagination, it too requires a body as a condition of its existence."

Aquinas tries to answer the question Aristotle asks, with a threefold distinction which places sensation and imagination midway between the vegetative functions and rational thought. The power of thought, or "the intellectual power," Aquinas says, "does not belong to a corporeal organ, as the power of seeing is the act of the eye; for understanding is an act which cannot be performed by a corporeal organ, like the act of seeing."

At the other extreme from this "operation of the soul which so far exceeds the corporeal nature that it is not even performed by any corporeal organ," are those "operations of the soul . . . performed by a corporeal organ and by virtue of a corporeal quality." Because it is a kind of self-movement, digestion requires soul as well as body, but it is a corporeal action in the way in which, according to Aquinas, it involves "the action of heat." Between these extremes, Aquinas places sensation and imagination, operations "performed through a corporeal organ, but not through a corporeal quality."

He explains this further by means of a distinction between natural and spiritual immutation—physical and psychic change. "Natural immutation takes place by the form of the thing which causes the immutation being received, according to its natural existence, into the thing in which the immutation is effected, as heat is received into the heated thing." Vegetative activities, while remaining psychic in the sense of occurring only in living or besouled matter, involve only natural immutations in the vital organs involved.

In contrast, "spiritual immutation takes place by the form of the thing causing the immutation being received, according to a spiritual mode of existence, into the thing in which the immutation is effected, as the form of color is received into the eye, which does not thereby become colored." Though some sensations may require a natural immutation of the sense organ, as hot and cold do, all sensations necessarily involve a spiritual immutation, which enables the sense organ to perform its proper act of knowing, as the eye knows color without becoming colored. "Otherwise," Aquinas says, "if a natural immutation alone sufficed for the sense's action, all natural bodies would feel when they undergo alteration."

THESE DIVERSE VIEWS of the nature of sensation seem to be paralleled by diverse views of the sensitive faculty. That the function of the senses is somehow to apprehend or know does not seem to be disputed. But whether the senses—including memory and imagination— are the only faculty of knowing is an issue to which the great books seem to give a variety of answers.

The opposite answers appear to be correlated, not only with conflicting positions in respect to body and soul, but also with opposing theories of the distinction between men and other animals. Those who hold that the motions of matter are adequate to explain the phenomena of knowing and thinking, tend to make sense perception the primary function of the mind and to treat not only memory and imagination, but also reasoning or thought as subsequent activities of the same general faculty which receives impressions from external sources in the first instance. Since other animals possess senses and give evidence that per-

ception in them has consequences for memory and imagination, those who hold this view also tend to attribute thought to animals and to regard man as differing from them only in degree.

Those who take the contrary view that knowing involves an immaterial principle or cause—a soul as well as a body—tend to distinguish the various functions of sense from the activities of thought—such as conception, judgment, and reasoning. They also take the position that man, while sharing sense perception, memory, and imagination with other animals, alone possesses the higher faculty. The difference between men and brutes is thus conceived as one of kind, not of degree, when the difference between the senses and the reason in man is also conceived as a difference in kind. A functional relationship between sensation and thought is not thereby denied, but a distinct faculty is affirmed to be necessary for going beyond the apprehension of particulars to knowledge of the universal, or for rising above the imagination to abstract thought.

The distinction between sense and reason as faculties of knowing is sometimes stated in terms of a difference in their objects—the particular versus the universal, becoming versus being, the material versus the immaterial. Sometimes it is stated in terms of the difference between a corporeal power requiring a bodily organ and a spiritual power which belongs exclusively to the soul. Sometimes it is stated in terms of the contrast between sense as intuitive and reason as discursive, the one beholding its objects immediately, the other forming concepts, judgments, or conclusions about objects which are either beheld by the senses or cannot be intuitively apprehended at all.

The exceptions to the foregoing summary are almost as numerous as the exemplifications of the points mentioned. Nothing less than this intricate pattern of agreements and differences will serve, however, to represent the complexity of the discussion and the way in which diverse theories of sense imply different views of nature and man, of mind and knowledge. The situation can be illustrated by taking certain doctrines which seem to be opposite on most points, and then considering other theories which seem to agree, on this point or that, with both extremes.

WE HAVE ALREADY observed the opposition between Hobbes and Aquinas with regard to matter and spirit in relation to the activity of the senses. Hobbes, like Lucretius, not only treats all mental phenomena as manifestations of bodily motion, but also reduces thought to the train or sequence of images. Images are in turn reducible to the sensation from which they derive.

"As we have no imagination," Hobbes writes, "whereof we have not formerly had sense, in whole or in parts; so we have no transition from one imagination to another, whereof we never had the like before in our senses." Using the word "thoughts" to stand for the images derived from sense, Hobbes goes on to say that "besides sense, and thoughts, and the train of thoughts, the mind of man has no other motion; though by the help of speech, and method, the same faculties may be improved to such a height as to distinguish men from all other living creatures."

Only man's use of words makes the difference in the exercise of the imagination "that we generally call understanding," and which, according to Hobbes, "is common to man and beast." Similarly, it is only the fact that common names have general significance which gives human discourse the appearance of abstract thought, for Hobbes denies abstract ideas. Thoughts or images are no less particular than sensations, "there being nothing in the world universal but names."

Berkeley and Hume seem to agree with Hobbes that a man has no abstract ideas or universal concepts; that all the operations of thought are merely elaborations of the original impressions of sense; and that no special power, but only the use of language, distinguishes men from other animals.

Berkeley uses the word "idea" to stand for sense impressions—"ideas actually imprinted on the senses"—and for whatever is "perceived by attending to the passions and operations of the mind." To these two he adds a third: "ideas formed by the help of memory and imagination, either compounding or dividing, or barely representing those originally perceived in the aforesaid ways." The only difference between the first and the third is that "the ideas of sense are more strong, lively, and distinct than those of the imagination." But our ideas of sense and imagination do not cover all the objects of which we can think. He admits, therefore, the possibility of our having *notions,* whereby we understand the meaning of a word like "spirit" or "soul" which refers to a substance of which we can form no idea.

Hume divides "all the perceptions of the mind into two classes or species, which are distinguished by their different degrees of force and vivacity. The less forcible and lively are commonly denominated *thoughts* or *ideas.*" The other he calls "impressions," meaning thereby "all our more lively perceptions." Impressions are the source of all other ideas, the creative power of the mind consisting in "no more than the faculty of compounding, transposing, augmenting, or diminishing the materials afforded us by the senses" and every simple idea being "copied from similar impression."

Yet, though Berkeley and Hume seem to agree with Hobbes in reducing all thought to primary sense perceptions and derived memories or imaginations, Hume does not attempt to explain thought by the motions of matter. Berkeley differs even more radically. He denies that matter or bodies exist, and so he regards sense perception, like all the rest of thought, as purely spiritual. The soul passively receives its original impressions directly from God and actively forms the ideas it is able to derive from these impressions.

NOR DO ALL THOSE who somehow conceive man as composed of both body and soul agree upon the function of sense in relation to the rest of thought. Locke, for example, uses "understanding" to cover all sorts of mental activity. Mental activity begins with the passive reception of the simple ideas of sense— the impressions produced in us when "the bodies that surround us do diversely affect our organs"—and the simple ideas of reflection which arise from an awareness of our own mental operations. But mental activity also includes the formation of complex ideas by the compounding of simple ones, and even the act whereby we form abstract ideas, in doing which man, in Locke's opinion, is distinguished from brutes.

All these activities require soul as well as body. All are somehow nothing more than a reworking of the original sensations passively received. In this last respect, Locke's view accords with that of Hobbes, Berkeley, and Hume, though he differs from them with respect to abstract ideas and in his theory of body and soul. On the very point which he holds in common with Hobbes, Berkeley, and Hume, Locke seems to disagree with Descartes.

Thinking, for Descartes, is the activity of a purely spiritual substance—the rational soul—peculiar to the dual nature of man; whereas sensation and imagination, common to men and brutes, are purely corporeal functions. In man, the soul or thinking substance may form certain of its ideas, those relative to bodies, under the influence of sense or fancy; but with regard to other ideas, such as those we have of geometric figures, Descartes says he cannot admit that they "have at any time entered our minds through the senses." He objects to the use of the word "idea" for images, or what he calls "pictures in the corporeal imagination, *i.e.,* in some part of the brain." He criticizes those who "never raise their minds above the things of sense," so accustomed are they "to consider nothing except by imagining it," with the result that whatever "is not capable of being imagined appears to them not to be intelligible at all."

Against the maxim which Locke, no less than Hobbes or Berkeley, would approve—that "there is nothing in the understanding which has not first of all been in the senses"—Descartes offers the ideas of God and of the soul as plainly contrary examples, ideas clearly in the mind which have no origin in sensation or fancy. "Those who desire to make use of their imagination to understand these ideas," he adds, "act in the same way as if, to hear sounds or smell odours, they should wish to make use of their eyes."

In making a sharp distinction between the faculties of sense and understanding or reason, Descartes seems to share the position of Plato, Aristotle, Aquinas, Spinoza, and Kant. Yet for Descartes as for Plato, the intellect in its own sphere of objects is like the senses in theirs, since each is able to behold its proper objects intuitively; whereas for Kant as for Aristotle, sense alone is a faculty of intuition. The ideas by which we apprehend intelligible objects, according to Plato, Descartes, and Spinoza, are not derived from sensations or images. According to Aristotle and Aquinas, on the other hand, the intellect abstracts all its ideas, or universal concepts, from the particulars of sense.

In this respect Aristotle and Aquinas seem to be in agreement with Locke, even though that agreement must be qualified by the observation that Locke sees no need for a special faculty to obtain abstract ideas. On the other hand, Plato, Aristotle, Aquinas, and Descartes all seem to agree in holding that understanding is as immaterial as its objects. Unlike sense, which requires bodily organs, rational thought is, according to them, an activity peculiar either to the soul itself or to a power of the soul which is not embodied in an organ, as the power of vision is embodied in the eye or the powers of memory and imagination are embodied in the brain.

James denies this. He holds the view that all forms of consciousness are somehow functions of the brain. Yet he also insists that percept and concept are radically distinct forms of consciousness. To this extent, James makes as sharp a separation as the authors above mentioned between the sensory and the rational phases of thought. He places sensation, perception, memory and imagination on one side, and conception, judgment, and reasoning on the other. But this is for him not a distinction of faculties of powers, but only of different functions which one and the same mind is able to perform.

CERTAIN POINTS OR problems in the traditional discussion of sense are unaffected by the basic issues just considered. For example, most writers tend to make some distinction between the special exterior senses, such as vision and hearing, touch and taste, and the several interior senses, which Aquinas enumerates as the common sense, memory, imagination, and the estimative or cogitative powers. Yet not all who consider memory and imagination as activities consequent upon sense perception call them "interior senses." Not all recognize a distinct estimative or cogitative power even when they recognize a kind of thinking about particulars done by animals and men with sensory materials. Nor do all who discuss discrimination or comparison, and the collation or combining of the impressions received from the special senses, attribute these functions to the special faculty which Aristotle first calls "the common sense."

Frequently the same analytic point is made in different ways. As indicated in the chapter on QUALITY, the distinction which Aristotle and Aquinas make between proper and common sensibles, according as the quality, such as color and odor, belongs to a single sense, or, like shape and motion, can be perceived by two or more senses, seems to parallel the distinction between what Locke calls "secondary" and "primary" qualities. But where Locke and others treat the so-called "secondary qualities" as entirely subjective, occurring only in the experience of the sentient organism and having no reality in the sensible thing, Aristotle takes a contrary view.

When it is not actually seen or smelled, the sensible thing, according to Aristotle, is potentially colorful or odoriferous; just as when it is not actually seeing or smelling, the sense of vision or smell is also in a state of potentiality with respect to these qualities. But when the sensible thing is actually sensed, then, Aristotle says, "the actuality of the sensible object and of the sensitive faculty is *one* actuality." The thing is actually colored when it is actually seen, though it is only potentially colored when it is merely able to be so seen. "Earlier students of nature," he writes, "were mistaken in their view that without sight there was no white or black, without taste no savor. This statement of theirs is partly true, partly false: 'sense' and 'the sensible object' are ambiguous terms, *i.e.,* they may denote either potentialities or actualities. The statement is true of the latter, false of the former."

Another example of the same analytic point (which is made differently by different writers) concerns the distinction between sensation and perception. According to Russell, as well as many other writers in the 20th century, a sharp distinction must be made between sense data and physical objects, the latter being objects of sense perception, but not of any one or another of the special senses. "If the physical sun had ceased to exist within the last eight minutes, that would make no difference to the sense-data which we call 'seeing the sun' "; and this, Russell adds, illustrates "the necessity of distinguishing between sense-data and physical objects." Ten people sitting around a dinner table all perceive one and the same table and all the physical objects on it, but "the sense-data are private to each separate person."

According to James, "perception involves sensation as a portion of itself, and sensation in turn never takes place in adult life without perception also being there." The difference between them is that the function of sensation is "that of mere acquaintance with a fact," whereas "perception's function . . . is knowledge *about* a fact, and this knowledge admits of numberless degrees of complication." Hearing a sound is having a sensation, but perception occurs when, as James points out, we "hear a sound, and say 'a horse-car.' "

But James does not agree that, when perception is so described, it is, as other psychologists have suggested, a species of reasoning. "If, every time a present sign suggests an absent reality to our mind, we make an inference, and if every time we make an inference we reason; then," James admits, "perception is indubitably reasoning. Only one sees no room in it for any unconscious part." No inference is consciously made in perception; and James thinks that "to call perception unconscious reasoning is either a useless metaphor, or a positively misleading confusion between two different things." In his opinion, "perception differs from sensation [simply] by the consciousness of further facts associated with the objects of sensation." For him, "perception and reasoning are coordinate varieties of that deeper sort of process known psychologically as the association of ideas."

What James treats as the object of sensation, Aristotle refers to as a quality sensed by one or more of the special senses, either a proper or a common sensible. What James treats as the object of perception, Aristotle calls an "accidental object of sense," because it is strictly not sensible at all by any of the exterior senses, singly or in combination. When we call "the white object we see" the son of Diares or a man, we have an example of an accidental sensible or an object incidentally perceived, because " 'being the son of Diares' is incidental to the directly visible white patch" we see with our eyes.

This distinction between sensation and perception seems to have a bearing on the problem of the fallibility of the senses. Again the same point seems to be differently made. Aristotle, for example, holds that whereas each of the senses is normally infallible in the apprehension of its proper object or appropriate quality, error is possible in the perception of the complex thing, which is not strictly an object of special senses. "While the perception that there is white before us cannot be false," he writes, "the perception that what is white is this or that may be false." Planck points out that "when a person happens to be deceived by a mirage, the fault lies not with his ... visual image, which is actually present, but in his inferences which draw false conclusions from the given sensory data. The sensory impression is always a given fact, and therefore incontestable. What conclusions the individual attaches to it, is another story."

Lucretius likewise insists that the senses themselves are never deceived, but that all the errors attributed to the senses are the result of a false inference or judgment which reason makes on the basis of the evidence presented by the senses. That also seems to be the opinion of Descartes, who thinks that "no direct experience can ever deceive the understanding if it restricts its attention accurately to the object presented to it ... Thus if a man suffering from jaundice persuades himself that the things he sees are yellow, this thought of his will be composite, consisting partly of what his imagination presents to him, and partly of what he assumes on his own account, namely,

that the color looks yellow, not owing to the defect in his eye, but because the things he sees really are yellow ... We can go wrong only when the things we believe are in some way compounded by ourselves." Descartes holds that "no falsity can reside" in sensations themselves, but only in those judgments which, on the basis of sensations, we are "accustomed to pass about things external to us."

THE MOST FUNDAMENTAL judgment which men make on the basis of sensation is that an external world exists—a reality not of our own making. Descartes argues from the evidence of the senses to the independent existence of a world of bodies. Though Berkeley argues, on the contrary, that bodies do not exist except as objects of perception, he attributes the sense impressions, over which we seem to have no control, to the action of an external cause—to God, who uses them as signs for instructing us.

Locke defines sensitive knowledge as that which informs us of "the existence of things actually present to our senses." We may know our own existence intuitively, and God's existence demonstratively, but "the knowledge of the existence of any other thing we can have only by sensation." And though he adds, "the notice we have by our senses of the existing of things without us ... be not altogether so certain as our intuitive knowledge or the deductions of our reason ... yet it is an assurance that deserves the name of knowledge."

Whitehead agrees with Locke. "There is not one world of things for my sensations and another for yours, but one world in which we both exist." For Russell, common sense "unhesitatingly" asserts the existence of a world that is independent of our individual sense impressions. Whenever any of us say that we are perceiving this or that physical object, we are at the same time asserting that that physical object really exists in a world that is independent of our sense. "We want," Russell writes, "the *same* object for different people ... But the sense-data are private to each separate person; what is immediately present to the sight of one is not immediately present to the sight of another."

Against such views, the most fundamental skepticism goes further than doubting the veracity of the senses because of the illusions and hallucinations they cause us to suffer. "By what arguments," Hume asks, "can it be proved that the perceptions of the mind must be caused by the external objects . . . and could not arise either from the energy of the mind itself or from the suggestion of some visible or unknown spirit?"

"It is a question of fact," he adds, "whether the perception of the senses be produced by external objects, resembling them. How shall this question be determined? By experience surely; as all other questions of a like nature. But here experience is, and must be, entirely silent. The mind has never anything present to it but the perceptions, and cannot possibly reach any experience of their connexion with objects. The supposition of such a connexion is, therefore, without any foundation in reasoning." If Hume's skepticism is unfounded, it arises from his failure to distinguish between sensation and perception.

85

Sign and Symbol

INTRODUCTION

A SIGN points to something. A symbol stands for or takes the place of another thing. Sign and symbol are sometimes differentiated according to whether emphasis is placed on that which is signified or pointed out, or on that which functions as a surrogate or substitute.

Yet "sign" and "symbol" are often used interchangeably. We call the notations of music or mathematics either "signs" or "symbols"; though mathematicians, such as Whitehead, prefer the latter usage when they discourse about "the symbolism of mathematics." Words, too, are traditionally spoken of as signs or symbols. Words and other conventional notations for expressing meaning both point to and stand for something else. It is only in certain cases that one of these two functions seems to predominate, as the road marker points out the direction to take, and paper money takes the place of the precious metal whose value it represents.

On what is common to signs and symbols of all sorts there seems to be no disagreement throughout the tradition of western thought. From Augustine's statement that "a sign is a thing which, over and above the impression it makes on the senses, causes something else to come into mind as a consequence of itself," to Freud's analysis of the symbolism of dreams, of symptoms, and symptomatic acts, the great books consider sign or symbol as one term in a relation, the relation being one of meaning or, as Freud says, of "significance, intention, tendency." The fundamental problems traditionally discussed concern the nature of meaning itself, and the modes of signification which vary with the kinds of things that function as signs and the kinds of things they signify.

WITH RESPECT TO THINGS which function symbolically, the primary distinction seems to be that between natural and conventional signs. Augustine at first suggests a threefold division. Some things are simply things, and not signs at all. Some (for example, "the ram which Abraham offered up instead of his son") are not only things, but "also signs of other things." And some things, such as words, "are never employed except as signs." Augustine adds that words are not merely signs. "Every sign," he writes, "is also a thing, for what is not a thing is nothing at all."

The distinction between natural and conventional signs falls within this threefold division. "Natural signs," Augustine says, "are those which, apart from any intention or desire of using them as signs, do yet lead to the knowledge of something else, as, for example, smoke when it indicates fire. For it is not from any intention of making it a sign that it is so, but through attention to experience we come to know that fire is beneath, even when nothing but smoke can be seen. And the footprint of an animal passing by belongs to this class of signs."

Augustine seems to find natural signs in things that are related as cause and effect. Berkeley, on the other hand, tends to substitute the relation of sign and thing signified for the relation of cause and effect. "The fire which I see," he writes, "is not the cause of the pain I suffer upon my approaching, but the mark that forewarns me. In like manner the noise that I hear is not the effect of this or that motion or collision of the ambient bodies, but the sign thereof."

Every natural thing or event thus tends to become the sign of something else, so that the whole of nature constitutes a vast symbolism or language by which God informs us of his plan. Aristotle tends, in the opposite direction, to limit natural signs to those things which, according to our knowledge and experience, permit a necessary or probable inference to something else. The fact that a woman is giving milk he regards as an infallible sign that she has lately borne a child; the fact that a man is breathing fast is merely a probable and refutable sign that he has a fever.

In any case, signs are generally acknowledged to be natural if they satisfy Augustine's criterion that they were not intentionally devised by men for the purpose of signifying. "Conventional signs, on the other hand," he writes, "are those which living beings mutually exchange for the purpose of showing, as well as they can, the feelings of their minds, or their perceptions, or their thoughts." Of conventional signs, Augustine goes on to say, words hold the chief place, because everything which can be expressed by gestures, or by such nonverbal symbols as flags or bugle calls, can also be expressed in words, whereas many thoughts which words readily express do not lend themselves easily to other modes of expression.

Except for the hypothesis (discussed in the chapter on LANGUAGE) of a natural form of speech common to all men and consisting of words perfectly adapted to the objects they name, it is never proposed that words are anything but conventional signs. As Aristotle says, "nothing is by nature a noun or a name—it is only so when it becomes a symbol." The audible sound or the visible mark becomes a symbol only by human institution or convention.

Yet not all the audible sounds which men and other animals make to express their feelings or desires are, in Aristotle's opinion, to be regarded as words. "Inarticulate sounds, such as those which brutes produce, are significant, yet none of these constitutes a noun." Nor are such cries, whereby one animal calls another or communicates fear or anger, strictly conventional signs; for, as Augustine points out, they are instinctive modes of expression, and so are natural rather than conventional. They are not voluntarily instituted.

IN TERMS OF THE ancient distinction between the conventional and the natural—that which changes from time to time and place to place and that which is everywhere and always the same—no one would question the conventionality of words and all other nonverbal symbols which are peculiar to one people, one culture, or one epoch. That words are conventional signs raises the central problem concerning their meaning or significance. Utterly dissimilar words in different languages can have the same meaning, and identical sounds or marks in different languages can mean quite different things. Since the sounds or marks which constitute spoken and written words do not possess meaning naturally, from what source do such conventional signs get the meanings they have?

The usual answer, given by Aristotle, Locke, and others, is that words get their meanings from the ideas, thoughts, or feelings which men use them to express. "Spoken words," writes Aristotle, "are the symbols of mental experience and written words are the symbols of spoken words. Just as all men do not have the same writing, so all men do not have the same speech sounds, but the mental experiences, which these directly symbolize, are the same for all, as also are those things of which our experiences are the images."

In addition to being able to make articulate sounds, it was necessary for man, Locke says, to "be able to use these sounds as signs of internal conceptions, and to make them stand as marks for the ideas within his own mind, whereby they might be made known to others." Thus words came to be used by men "as the signs of their ideas; not by any natural connexion that there is between particular articulate sounds and certain ideas, for then there would be but one language amongst all men; but by a voluntary imposition, whereby such a word is made arbitrarily the mark of such an idea. The use then of words is to be sensible marks of ideas, and the ideas they stand for are their proper and immediate signification."

Locke goes further. Not only does the immediate signification of words lie in the ideas they stand for, but in his view words "can be signs of nothing else." Yet he also considers the fact that men, because they "would not be thought to talk barely of their own imaginations, but of things as they really are . . . often suppose their words to stand also for the reality of things." Locke thinks, nevertheless, that "obscurity and confusion" enter into the signification of words "whenever we make them stand for anything but those ideas we have in our own minds."

But though the meaning of a word may come from the idea it signifies, the word which is thus made meaningful seems, in the common usage of mankind, to serve as the name or designation of some real thing. It refers to something other than ideas or concepts in the human mind. Locke himself talks of "the application of names to things," and in his consideration of the distinction between proper and common names is concerned to point out that, though they differ in meaning (*i.e.,* differ in the type of idea they signify), both refer to the same sort of reality—individual existences. Aristotle and other writers who distinguish between things in the order of nature and the concepts we form of them, tend to take both views of the significance of words. Words signify the real things which they name as well as the ideas whose meanings they express. If we waive for the moment the possibility that some words may signify *only* ideas, whereas others signify both ideas and things, two questions may be asked. Are there any words which signify things alone? What is the relation between the idea and the thing a word signifies, when a word signifies them both; that is, when a word has both sorts of significance, how are they related to one another?

Aquinas answers the second question by saying that since "words are the signs of ideas, and ideas the similitudes of things, it is evident that words function in the signification of things through the conceptions of the intellect." Ideas may be the immediate or proximate object which words signify, but through them words ultimately signify the real things which are themselves the objects of ideas. According to this theory, an idea may be both the *object signified* by a word and the *medium through which* that word also signifies the thing of which we have the idea. Aquinas

seems to think that ideas are always required as the medium whereby words signify things. "We can give a name to anything," he says, "only insofar as we can understand it." Accordingly, it is impossible for words to signify things directly, *i.e.,* without the mediation of ideas.

In the 20th century an opposite theory of how words get their meanings is attributed to Wittgenstein. He is again and again cited as holding that to determine the meaning of a word one must look to "its use in the language." This raises the question whether the use of a word is not itself determined by the idea that confers meaning on that word, which is the traditional view of how words get their meanings.

THE TRADITIONAL VIEW has a number of consequences for the theory of signs and raises a number of issues. Augustine's statement that "every sign is also a thing" has a different meaning when it is said of the sensible things which also happen to be signs and of the things of the mind—concepts or ideas—which cannot *be* without *being signs*. The understanding of this difference helps to explain the relation between verbal signs and the mental signs through which they signify or from which they get their meanings.

Whereas words are in the first instance meaningless marks and sounds which get meaning when men use them to express their thoughts or feelings, ideas and images are at once meaningful, however they arise in the mind. They are natural signs in the sense that it seems to be their very nature to signify. They do not get meaning. They do not even have meaning, in the way in which smoke as a natural sign of fire has a meaning which is distinct from, though a consequence of, its nature as smoke. An idea *is* a meaning, an intention of the mind, as it is sometimes called, a reference to an object thought about. The idea of fire is the meaning the word "fire" has when it designates the natural phenomenon which that word is conventionally used to name; and as Aristotle suggests, the conventional signs of different languages [*e.g.,* "fire" and "*Feuer*"]— have the same meaning because the idea of fire is the same, and the natural phenomenon experienced and thought about is the same, for men of diverse tongues.

That ideas or mental images are themselves meanings or intentions—the symbols of things thought about—seems to be recognized in different ways by many writers in the tradition of the great books. In the *Cratylus,* Socrates suggests that signs should be like the things they signify. Some conventional signs, he thinks, are better than others in this respect. He implies that all words are inferior to mental images, which, by their very nature, imitate or resemble their objects.

The act of memory, according to Aristotle, requires a memory image which is "something like an impression or picture" of the thing remembered. If the memory image, through its resemblance to something once experienced, did not function as the sign of that absent thing, memory would not be memory, for, Aristotle argues, it would consist in beholding the memory image itself, which is present, rather than the absent thing it stands for.

Aquinas, perhaps, is the writer most explicit in his treatment of images and ideas as in their very nature meanings or intentions of the mind. His calling them "mental words" seems to indicate that in his view they, like physical and sensible words, are signs; but the added qualification of "mental" also implies their difference. "The vocal sound which has no signification," he writes, "cannot be called a word; wherefore the exterior vocal sound is called a word from the fact that it signifies the interior concept of the mind. It follows that, first and chiefly, the interior concept of the mind is called a word." The mental word or concept suffices "when the mind turns to the actual consideration of what it knows habitually," for then, he adds, "a person speaks to himself." But unlike angels, who can make their concepts known to one another immediately, men require the medium of external speech. They must use sensible physical signs to communicate their thoughts.

Without referring to ideas as mental words, Locke does appear to identify ideas with meanings and to regard them as signs. The definition of a word, he says, is an attempt to make known "the meaning or idea it stands for." Denying that the general and the universal belong to the real existence of things, he holds that they "concern only signs, whether words or ideas. Words are general . . . when used for signs of general ideas . . . and ideas are general when they set up as the representatives of many particular things; but universality belongs not to things themselves, which are all of them particular in their existence, even those words and ideas which, in their signification, are general."

The basic issue to which Locke is addressing himself is discussed in the chapter on UNIVERSAL AND PARTICULAR. Locke's solution seems to involve the affirmation of abstract ideas, which are general or universal in their significance and through which common names come to have a different sort of meaning from the meaning of proper names. "Ideas become general by separating them from the circumstances of time and place, and any other ideas that may determine them to this or that particular existence." Common nouns like "man" or "cat" become general in their significance, according to Locke, "by being made the signs of general ideas." For Russell, the distinction between the significance of proper and common names is best expressed in terms of definite and indefinite descriptions, such as *the* first President of the United States (George Washington) and *a* domesticated species in the feline family (cat).

To the question of what kind of signification it is that general words have, Locke replies: "As it is evident, that they do not signify barely one particular thing; for then they would not be general terms, but proper names; so, on the other side, it is as evident, they do not signify a plurality; for man and men would then signify the same . . . That, then, which general words signify," Locke declares, "is a sort of things, and each of them does that by being a sign of an abstract idea in the mind."

It seems to follow, therefore, that those who, like Hobbes and Berkeley, deny the existence of abstract ideas or universal concepts, must offer a different explanation of the meaning of common nouns or general names. "There being nothing in the world universal but names," Hobbes writes, a name is universal when it "is imposed on many things for their similitude in some quality, or other accident: and whereas a proper name bringeth to mind one thing only, universals recall any one of those many."

On similar grounds, Berkeley criticizes Locke's theory of how words acquire general significance. His own theory is that words become general "by being made the sign, not of an abstract general idea, but of several particular ideas, any one of which it indifferently suggests to the mind." And, in another place, he says that "an idea which, considered in itself, is particular becomes general by being made to represent or stand for all other particular ideas of the same sort." He does not himself explain how we come by the notion of "the same sort," or how one particular idea can represent the sort to which other particular ideas belong. But he rejects Locke's explanation because it involves ideas which are not only general, but also abstract.

The attempt to account for the meaning of general names is, in Berkeley's view, the cause of Locke's acceptance of abstract ideas. "If there had been no such thing as speech or universal signs," he writes, "there never [would have] been any thought of abstraction." Not only do men mistakenly suppose that "every name has, or ought to have, one only precise and settled signification, which inclines [them] to think there are certain abstract, determinate ideas that constitute the true and only immediate signification of each general name"; but they also suppose that "it is by the mediation of these abstract ideas that a general name comes to signify any particular thing. Whereas, in truth," Berkeley concludes, "there is no such thing as one precise and definite signification annexed to any general name." Where Locke would say that a common name gets its general meaning by signifying one idea which itself has general significance, Berkeley reiterates that a general name gets its meaning from "a great number of particular ideas," all of which it signifies indifferently.

THE RELATION OF WORDS to ideas raises still other problems in the theory of signs, problems which have peculiar interest in the tradition of the liberal arts. One of these problems has already been mentioned. It is the question whether some words signify ideas alone, in contrast to words which signify ideas and, through them, things. This suggests the parallel problem of words which signify words, in contrast to words which are the names of things.

In his little tract *Concerning the Teacher,* Augustine points out that some words, such as "noun" and "adjective," signify kinds of words, just as other words, such as "man" and "stone," signify kinds of things. Furthermore, in the sentence "man is a noun," the word "man" signifies itself as the object referred to; whereas in the sentence "man is an animal," the word "man" signifies a living organism of a certain sort. The same word, therefore, may signify both itself and some thing other than itself.

These differences which Augustine observes in the signification of words come to be formulated in the traditional distinction between the first and second imposition of words. A word is used in the first imposition when it is used to signify things which are not words, as, for example, the word "man" when it refers to a human being. A word is used in the second imposition when it is applied to words rather than things, as, for example, the word "noun" said of "man," or the word "man" when it is used to refer to itself in the sentence "man is a noun."

A parallel distinction is that between words used in the first and the second intention. When the word "man" is used to signify a living organism of a certain sort, it is used in the first intention because it signifies a reality, not an idea. A word is said to be used in the second intention when it signifies an idea rather than a thing. For example, in the sentence, "man is a species," the word "species" signifies a logical classification and so is in the second intention; and the word "man" is also in the second intention because it refers to the idea which is denominated a species.

In some cases, an idea may not signify things at all, but only other ideas, such as the logical notions of *genus* and *species.* Words like "genus" and "species," unlike the words "man" and "stone," can therefore be used only in the second intention. The idea *man* is called a "first intention of the mind" because its primary function is to signify the living thing. Only secondarily does it signify itself as an object able to be considered. The idea *species,* on the other hand, is called a "second intention" because its sole function is to signify ideas which stand to other ideas in a certain relation.

Hobbes concisely summarizes most of these points when he points out that some words "are the names of the things conceived," whereas "others are the names of the imaginations themselves, that is to say, of those ideas or mental images we have of all the things we see and remember. And others again are names of names . . . as 'universal,' 'plural,' 'singular,' are the names of names." The names which we apply to particular species and genera, such as "man" and "animal," Aquinas says, "signify the common natures themselves, but not the intentions of these common natures, which are signified by the terms *genus* or *species.*"

ANOTHER TRADITIONAL distinction in the modes of signification is that between intrinsic and extrinsic denomination. A name is said to be an intrinsic denomination when it is applied to a thing in order to signify its nature or its inherent properties and attributes, as, for example, when we call a thing "animal" or "rational," "white" or "square." A name is said to be an extrinsic denomination when it is applied to a thing only in order to signify some relation in which that thing stands to something else, as, for example, when we call sunshine "healthy" because it helps to produce healthy organisms or when we apply the names of animals, such as "pig" or "fox," to men because we think the men bear certain resemblances to these animals. The same word can be used in different connections both as an intrinsic and as an extrinsic denomination. "Healthy" means an inherent quality when it is applied to living organisms, and a causal relation to organic health when it is applied to sunshine; "pig" means a certain kind of animal when it is applied to the four-footed mammal, and only a resemblance to this animal in certain characteristics when it is applied to men.

This double use of the same word exemplifies what is traditionally called "equivocal speech" or the equivocal use of a name. Some writers tend to identify equivocation with ambiguity, on the ground that both involve a multiplicity of meanings for the same word. Others seem to think that a word is used ambiguously only if its user is indefinite as to which of its several meanings he intends to express; but they hold that a word can be used equivocally without ambiguity if its user makes plain that he is employing it now in this sense, now in that.

Aristotle says that two things are named equivocally "when though they have the same name, the definition corresponding with the name differs for each"; and "on the other hand, things are said to be named univocally which have both the name and the definition answering to the name in common." When we call a man and a pig an "animal," we are using that word univocally because we are using it with the same definition or meaning in both cases; but when we call a pig and a man a "pig," we are using that word equivocally because we are using it with different meanings, signifying *having the nature of a pig* in one instance and *being like a pig in certain respects* in the other.

Aristotle distinguishes several types of equivocation, of which we have already noted two. The use of the word "healthy" to describe an animal and sunshine is that type of equivocation in which the same word is used to name an inherent attribute and also a cause of that attribute; in other instances of the same type, it might be used to name the nature or attribute and the effect rather than the cause. Speaking of a man and a pig as a "pig" represents the metaphoric type of equivocation, in which the same word is used to name the nature of a thing and something else of a different nature which has only a likeness to that nature.

Metaphors, in turn, can be divided into types. Some are based on a direct similitude between two things in some accidental respect, *e.g.,* the man who is like a pig in manner of eating. Some, Aristotle says, are based on analogies or proportions, as, for example, when we call a king the "father of his people." Here the metaphor is based on the similarity of the relationship of a king to his subjects and of a father to his children. The name "father" is used metaphorically when it is transferred from one term in this proportion to the term which stands in an analogous position.

A third kind of metaphor, according to Aristotle, consists in the use of the same word now in a more generic, now in a more specific sense, or with broader and narrower meanings. Of this he gives an example in the *Nicomachean Ethics* when he discusses general and special justice, using the word "justice" narrowly to signify one of the special virtues and broadly to mean all the virtues considered in their social aspect. There is a sense of the word "justice," he writes, in which it signifies "not part of virtue but virtue entire"; "this form of justice is complete virtue, though not absolutely, but only in relation to our neighbor." The word "injustice" is also used in a correspondingly wide sense. But there is "another kind of injustice which is a part of injustice in the wide sense." This "particular injustice," Aristotle says, "shares the name and nature of the first, because its definition falls within the same genus." As Aristotle treats this type of equivocation in the *Rhetoric* and the *On Poetics,* it includes three possibilities: the transfer of the name of a genus to one of its species, the transfer of the name of a species to its genus, and the transfer of the name of one species to another in the same genus.

It may be questioned whether this type of equivocation is properly classified as metaphoric, on Aristotle's own definition of metaphor as "giving a thing a name that belongs to something else." In the type of equivocation exemplified by the use of the word "justice," now with a generic and now a specific meaning, the name does not seem to belong to the genus any more than it does to the species, or conversely. In contrast, when the name "father" is given to a king in relation to his people, the usage is metaphoric, because the name "father" belongs to something else, *i.e.,* the man who is a progenitor.

The same point can be made in terms of intrinsic and extrinsic denomination. When "justice" is used as the name for the whole of virtue (regarded socially) and also for one particular virtue, the word is an intrinsic denomination in both instances. In all other types of equivocation, the equivocal word is used once as an intrinsic and once as an extrinsic denomination; for example, as applied to the animal, the word "pig" is an intrinsic denomination, but it is an extrinsic denomination when it is applied to a man in order to signify a certain resemblance to the animal to which the name belongs. The same is true in the case of the word "healthy" as said of an animal and of sunshine.

In all these cases of equivocation, the two meanings of the same word are not totally distinct. On the contrary, the two senses have something in common. One of the meanings seems to be derived from the other; one appears to be secondary (usually the one involved in the extrinsic denomination) and the other primary. What is traditionally called "equivocation by chance," in contrast to equivocation by intention, is the extreme case in which the same word is used in two utterly distinct senses, having no common element of meaning at all; *e.g.,* the word "pen" used for a writing instrument and an enclosure for animals. Equivocation by intention, in which the different meanings of a word have something in common, thus appears to be intermediate between equivocation by chance (in which the meanings share no common element) and univocal usage (in which the meaning is exactly the same each time the word is used).

In the *Physics,* Aristotle seems to discover still another type of equivocation. "A pen, a wine, and the highest note in a scale are not commensurable," he writes. "We cannot say whether any one of them is sharper than any other . . . because it is only equivocally that the same term 'sharp' is applied to them." This does not seem to be equivocation by chance, for the word "sharp" seems to have some common meaning as applied to the three objects which affect the diverse senses of touch, taste, and hearing; nor is it like all other cases of equivocation by intention, in that no one of these three meanings of "sharp" seems to be primary and the others derived from it. Furthermore, in all three meanings, the word "sharp" is used as an intrinsic denomination.

In the *Metaphysics,* Aristotle also considers the special pattern of meaning which words like "being" or "one" have when they are applied to such heterogeneous things as substances, quantities, etc. He refers to these words as ambiguous or equivocal, comparing them with the word "healthy" as said of an animal, and of other things which either cause health or are effects of health. It may be questioned, however, whether "being" is equivocal in the same way that "healthy" is, since it always carries the significance of an intrinsic, never of an extrinsic denomination. "Being" as said of heterogeneous things seems to be more like "sharp" said of diverse sensible qualities—having a meaning which remains somehow the same while it is diversified in each case according to the diversity of the objects to which it applies.

THESE CONSIDERATIONS of the univocal and the equivocal sign, along with the treatment of ambiguity and intrinsic and extrinsic denomination, indicate the extent and manner in which the great books anticipate the kind of analysis which in our time has come to be called "semantics." The chapter on LANGUAGE gives further evidence of the fact that many of the points and distinctions made in contemporary semantics have a long history in the tradition of the liberal arts. Furthermore, as the chapter on LANGUAGE indicates, contemporary semantics cannot even claim novelty for its great interest in freeing men from the tyranny of words or in serving as a critical instrument to cut through the "vicious abstractions" of metaphysics. Hobbes and Locke frequently dismiss theories not on the ground that they are false, but rather because they think that the statement of them consists in so many meaningless words.

In the tradition of the great books, the analysis of words and their modes of signification seems to be motivated by other interests as well as these. The distinction between the univocal and the equivocal sign, for example, is considered in its bearing on the logical problems of definition and demonstration as well as for the sake of proposing remedies to safeguard discourse against ambiguity. It is also brought to bear upon the theological problem of the meaning of the names men apply to God and on the way in which they interpret the words of Sacred Scripture.

The problem of the names of God is discussed in the chapter on SAME AND OTHER in terms of the kind of likeness which can obtain between an infinite being and finite creatures. As there appears, Aquinas takes the position that God and creatures are neither the same in any respect, nor are they in all respects so diverse as to be utterly incomparable. Though an infinite and a finite being are in his view incommensurable, yet they can also have some sort of similitude—not an unqualified sameness, but the kind of similarity which can be described as an intrinsically diversified sameness.

Aquinas holds, therefore, that no names can be applied to God and creatures univocally, for "no name belongs to God in the same sense that it belongs to creatures." Nor, he goes on, "are names applied to God and creatures in a purely equivocal sense," for it would follow then that "from creatures nothing at all could be known or demonstrated about God," which supposition Aquinas denies. Between these two extremes of the simply univocal and the purely equivocal, he finds a middle ground in a type of signification which he calls "analogical." The meaning of an analogical name, he says, "is not, as it is in univocals, one and the same; yet it is not totally diverse as in equivocals."

What he means by "pure equivocation" seems to be what earlier writers call "equivocation by chance," and what he means by the "analogical" seems to correspond to what they call "equivocation by intention." "Univocal names have absolutely the same meaning," he writes, "while equivocal names have absolutely diverse meanings; whereas in analogicals, a name taken in one signification must be placed in the definition of the same name taken in other significations; as, for instance, "being" which is applied to *substance* is placed in the definition of "being" as applied to *accident;* and "healthy" applied to *animal* is placed in the definition of "healthy" as applied to *urine* and *medicine.*"

But, as we have seen, there are many types of equivocation by intention—the attributive, based on cause and effect, as exemplified by the word "healthy"; that involving broader and narrower meanings, exemplified by the word "justice"; metaphors, of the sort exemplified by calling a man "pig," and of the sort based on analogies, when we speak of a king as the "father" of his people; and, finally, the very special type of equivocation found in "sharp" applied to a tone, a taste, and a touch.

If Aquinas places the kind of signification he calls "analogical" in the general area of equivocation by intention, it may be asked whether the various names of God are all analogical *in the same way.* The answer seems to be negative, for he distinguishes those names which have only a metaphoric sense when said of God, such as "angry" or "jealous"; and he denies the opinion of those who say that God is called "good" only in an attributive sense, *i.e.,* signifying him to be the cause of the goodness found in creatures. On the contrary, he thinks that words like "good" and "wise," and especially the name "being," are to be interpreted as intrinsic denominations when applied to both God and creatures.

For Aquinas, as for Aristotle, that would appear to make the pattern of meaning exhibited by the word "sharp" the model for the significance of "being" rather than that found in the merely attributive equivocation of the word "healthy"—whether "being" is said of substance and accidents, or of God and creatures. The point seems to be unaffected by the fact that Aquinas calls this type of signification "analogical," whereas Aristotle always refers to "being" as equivocal. Aristotle never treats any type of equivocation as analogical except the metaphor which results from transferring the name of one term in a proportion to another term standing in the same or a similar relationship.

THE DISTINCTION BETWEEN literal and figurative or metaphoric speech seems to be of prime importance in the theologian's rules for interpreting the word of God. As indicated in the chapter on RELIGION, Augustine insists that the language of Holy Writ must be read in many senses. Aquinas distinguishes a basic literal sense from three modes of spiritual meaning. That signification "whereby words signify things belongs to the first sense, the historical or literal. That signification whereby things signified by words have themselves also a signification is called the spiritual sense, which is based on the literal and presupposes it." The spiritual sense Aquinas divides into the allegorical, the moral, and the analogical.

To grasp the various spiritual meanings, the reader must understand that in Holy Scripture "divine things are metaphorically described by means of sensible things." As in the symbolism of the sacraments, physical things serve as the outward and visible signs of an inward and spiritual grace, so also "in Holy Scripture spiritual truths are fittingly taught under the likeness of material things."

A theologian like Aquinas thus justifies metaphors not only in Scripture, but also in sacred doctrine or theology, as "both necessary and useful," whereas in his view the poet's employment of them is solely for the sake of pleasure. Philosophers and scientists, on the other hand, often take the opposite view—that metaphors have a place only in poetry and should be avoided in the exposition of knowledge.

In the writing of poetry, "the command of metaphor," says Aristotle, "is the mark of genius," but all his rules for the construction of scientific definitions and demonstrations require the avoidance of metaphors, as of all other forms of equivocation. So, too, Hobbes inveighs against metaphors and figures of speech, giving as one of the main causes of absurdity in science "the use of metaphors, tropes, and other rhetorical figures, instead of words proper. For though it be lawful to say, for example, in common speech, *the way goeth, or leadeth hither, or thither; the proverb says this or that* (whereas ways cannot go, nor proverbs speak); yet in reckoning, and seeking of truth, such speeches are not to be admitted."

Darwin looks forward to the day when "the terms used by naturalists, of affinity, relationship, community of type, paternity, morphology, adaptive characters, rudimentary and aborted organs, and so forth, will cease to be metaphorical and will have a plain significance." Freud, on the other hand, aware of how pervasive symbolism is in all works of man, normal and neurotic, dreaming and awake, seems to be reconciled to the inevitability of metaphors in scientific discourse. The difficulty we meet with in picturing certain psycho-logical processes, he writes, "comes from our being obliged to operate with scientific terms, *i.e.,* with the metaphorical expressions peculiar to psychology . . . Otherwise we should not be able to describe the corresponding processes at all, nor in fact even to have remarked them. The shortcomings of our description would disappear if for the psychological terms we could substitute physiological or chemical ones. These, too, only constitute a metaphorical language, but one familiar to us for a much longer time and perhaps also simpler."

86

Sin

INTRODUCTION

THE sin of Satan and the sin of Adam are among the great mysteries of the Christian religion. Satan is highest among the angels, the first of God's spiritual creatures. He is only less than God in the perfection of his nature. Adam is created with supernatural graces and gifts, his immortal body is completely responsive to his spirit, his appetite in all things is submissive to his reason, and his reason is turned toward God, according to the original justice which harmonized his faculties and the elements of his nature.

The only evil latent in either Satan or Adam would seem to reside in the privation of infinite being, power, and knowledge. But this is not a moral evil in them; it is neither a sin nor a predisposition to sin. Hence the only cause of their sinning, if God himself does not predestine them to sin, must be a free choice on their part between good and evil. If God positively predestines them to sin, then they would seem to be without responsibility, and so without sin. If they are not predetermined to evil—if, except for the weakness of being finite, they are without positive blemish—how does the conflict arise in them which opens the choice between good and evil and impels them, almost against the inclination of their natures, away from good and toward evil?

In Milton's *Paradise Lost,* God says of Adam: "I made him just and right, sufficient to have stood, though free to fall." Of Satan and fallen angels, as well as of Adam, God observes:

They therefore as to right belongd,
So were created, nor can justly accuse
Thir maker, or thir making, or thir Fate:
As if Predestination over-rul'd
Their will, dispos'd by absolute Decree

Of high foreknowledge; they themselves decreed
Thir own revolt, not I: if I foreknew,
Foreknowledge had no influence on their fault,
Which had no less prov'd certain unforeknown.

Yet there is a difference between Adam and Satan. The fallen angels "by their own suggestion fell, self-tempted, deprav'd." Satan, having sinned, becomes man's tempter. "Man falls deceiv'd by the other first: Man therefore shall find grace, the other none."

As Satan approaches the Garden of Eden to work his will on man, he contemplates his plight. He does not deny his sin, he does not repent it, he does not seem fully to understand it. Thus Milton has him speak:

O thou that with surpassing Glory crowned,
Look'st from the sole Dominion like the God
Of this new World; at whose sight all the Starrs
Hide thir diminisht heads; to thee I call,
But with no friendly voice, and add thy name
O Sun, to tell thee how I hate thy beams
That bring to my remembrance from what state
I fell, how glorious once above thy Spheare;
Till Pride and worse Ambition threw me down
Warring in Heav'n against Heav'ns matchless King;
Ah wherefore! he deserved no such return
From me, whom he created what I was
In that bright eminence, and with his good
Upbraided none; nor was his service hard.
What could be less than to afford him praise,
The easiest recompense, and pay him thanks,
How due! yet all his good prov'd ill in me,
And wrought but malice; lifted up so high
I sdeind subjection, and thought one step higher
Would set me highest, and in a moment quit
The debt immense of endless gratitude,
So burthensome, still paying, still to owe . . .
O had his powerful Destiny ordained
Me some inferior Angel, I had stood
Then happie; no unbounded hope had rais'd
Ambition. Yet why not? some other Power
As great might have aspir'd, and me through mean
Drawn to his part; but other Powers as great
Fell not, but stand unshak'n, from within

Or from without, to all temptations arm'd.
Hads't thou the same free Will and Power to stand?
Thou hads't: whom has thou then or what to
    accuse,
But Heav'ns free Love, dealt equally to all?
Be then his Love accurst, since love or hate
To me alike, it deals eternal woe.
Nay cursed be thou; since against his, thy will
Chose freely what it now so justly rues.
Me miserable! which way shall I flie
Infinite wrauth, and infinite despaire?
Which way I flie is Hell; my self am Hell;
And in the lowest deep a lower deep
Still threatning to devour me opens wide,
To which the Hell I suffer seems a Heav'n.
O then at last relent: is there no place
Left for Repentance, nor for Pardon left?
None left but by submission; and that word
Disdain forbids me, and my dread of shame
Among the spirits beneath, whom I seduc'd
With other promises and other vaunts
Then to submit, boasting I could subdue
Th' Omnipotent.

Before Satan approaches Eve, Adam reminds
her of their debt of obedience, saying that God
requires

From us no other service than to keep
This one, this easie charge, of all the Trees
In Paradise that beare delicious fruit
So various, not to taste that onely Tree
Of Knowledge, planted by the Tree of Life.
So neer grows Death to Life, what ere Death is,
Some dreadful thing no doubt; for well thou
    knowst
God hath pronounc'd it death to taste that Tree,
The only sign of our obedience left
Among so many signes of power and rule
Conferrd upon us, and Dominion giv'n
Over all other Creatures that possesse
Earth, Aire, and Sea. Then let us not think hard
One easie prohibition, who enjoy
Free leave so large to all things else, and choice
Unlimited of manifold delights.

The temptation to disobey first moves Eve
in a dream in which the apparition of an angel
speaks of the forbidden fruit

. . . . as onely fit
For Gods, yet able to make Gods of Men;
And why not Gods of Men, since good, the more
Communicated, more abundant growes,
The Author not impair'd, but honourd more?

"Here, happie Creature," the vision says
to her,

Happier thou mayst be, worthier canst not be:
Taste this, and be henceforth among the Gods
Thy self a Goddess, not to Earth confind,
But sometimes in the Air, as wee, sometimes

Ascend to Heav'n, by merit thine, and see
What life the Gods live there, and such live thou.

Later when Satan in the guise of the Serpent
actually addresses Eve, he argues in the same
vein, that as he, by tasting of this fruit, speaks
as a man, so Eve and Adam, if they too partake, "shall be as Gods, knowing both Good
and Evil as they know." Eve succumbs and,
as Milton tells the story, Adam, knowing fully
the evil of his act, joins Eve in disobedience,
not from envy of the gods, but out of love
for her, willing to die because unwilling to live
without her.

Willing "to incurr divine displeasure for her
sake, or Death . . .

. . . . he scrupl'd not to eat
Against his better knowledge, not deceav'd,
But fondly overcome with Femal charm.
Earth trembled from her entrails, as again
In pangs, and Nature gave a second groan,
Skie lowr'd, and muttering Thunder, som sad drops
Wept at compleating of the mortal Sin
Original.

IN THE POET's expansion of the third chapter
of Genesis, the basic elements in the Judeo-
Christian conception of sin seem to be plainly
accented: the pride and envy which move Satan and Eve, the disobedience which results
from the disorder of Adam's loving Eve more
than he loves God. In *The Divine Comedy*,
another great poem of sin and salvation, Adam
speaks to Dante in Paradise and tells him
that "the tasting of the tree was not in itself
the cause of so long an exile, but solely the
overpassing of the bound." Earlier Beatrice explains why, in order to redeem man from sin,
the Word of God assumed human nature—
"the nature which had estranged itself from
its Maker." She tells Dante that "this nature,
which was thus united to its Maker, was, when
it was created, pure and good; but by its own
self it had been banished from Paradise, because it turned aside from the way of the truth
and its proper life." Man can fall from his
nobility by "sin alone . . . which disfranchises
it and makes it unlike the Supreme Good, so
that it is little illumined by Its light; and to its
dignity it never returns unless, where fault has
emptied, it fill up with just penalties against
evil delight."

The preacher in Joyce's *A Portrait of the Artist as a Young Man* notes that "Sin ... is a twofold enormity. It is a base consent to the promptings of our corrupt nature to the lower instincts, to that which is gross and beastlike; and it is also a turning away from the counsel of our higher nature, from all that is pure and holy, from the Holy God Himself. For this reason mortal sin is punished in hell by two different forms of punishment, physical and spiritual."

In both the pagan and the Christian conceptions of sin, man's pride and his disobedience of divine commandment are usually connected with the very notion of sin. The heroes of the Greek tragedies, exhibiting the tragic fault of pride, seem to forget that, though they strive with gods, they are only men, subject to laws they cannot disobey without catastrophe. In *The Iliad,* Phoinix cautions Achilles to rid himself of pride and "beat down your great anger. It is not yours to have a pitiless heart. The very immortals can be moved; their virtue and honour and strength are greater than ours are, and yet with sacrifices and offerings for endearment, with libations and with savour men turn back even the immortals in supplication, when any man does wrong and transgresses."

In pride and disobedience we find the deep disorder of love which lies at the heart of sin. Pride is self-love in excess of what the self deserves. Disobedience, as in the case of Milton's Adam, may be prompted by a love which, too, exceeds the worth of the object loved. The measure of that worth, or the bounds put upon the love of self or other, is set by the Supreme Good which, ordering all other goods, should also order our loves in proportion to their goodness.

This seems to be the central insight of *The Divine Comedy.* It is given a summary statement in "Purgatorio," where Virgil explains how love is the root both of virtue and of sin. "Neither Creator nor creature," he says to Dante, "was ever without love, either natural or of the mind, and this you know. The natural is always without error; but the other may err either through an evil object, or through too much or too little vigor. While it is directed on the Primal Good, and on secondary goods observes right measure, it cannot be the cause of sinful pleasure. But when it is turned awry to evil, or speeds to good with more zeal, or with less, than it ought, against the Creator works His creature. Hence you can comprehend that love must needs be the seed in you of every virtue and of every action deserving punishment."

Dostoevsky offers us further thoughts concerning the relation of love and sin. In *The Brothers Karamazov,* Father Zossima makes lack of love the punishment as well as the substance of sin. To those who ask, "What is Hell?" Father Zossima replies: "I maintain that it is the suffering of being unable to love ... They talk of hell fire in the material sense. I don't go into that mystery and I shun it. But I think if there were fire in the material sense, they would be glad of it, for, I imagine, that in material agony, their still greater spiritual agony would be forgotten for a moment ... Oh, there are some who remain proud and fierce even in hell, is spite of their certain knowledge and contemplation of the absolute truth; there are some fearful ones who have given themselves over to Satan and his proud spirit entirely. For such, hell is voluntary and ever consuming; they are tortured by their own choice. For they have cursed themselves, cursing God and life."

To avoid sin, the only positive commandment, according to Father Zossima, is to love in accordance with God's love. "Love a man even in his sin," he counsels, "for that is the semblance of Divine Love and is the highest love on earth ... And let not the sin of men confound you in your doings. Fear not that it will wear away your work and hinder its being accomplished. There is only one means of salvation; then take unto yourself, and make yourself responsible for, all men's sins; that is the truth, you know, friends, for as soon as you sincerely make yourself responsible for everything and for all men, you will see at once that it is really so, and you are to blame for everyone and for all things. But throwing your own indolence and impotence on others, you will end by sharing the pride of Satan and murmuring against God. Of the pride of Satan, what I think is this: it is hard for us on earth to comprehend it, and therefore it is so easy to fall into error and to share it, even imagining that we are doing something grand and fine."

In the disorder of love which leads to sin, sin is itself enjoyed for its own sake, and the disobedient act is pleasant because it is forbidden. In that also there is the pride of supposing one's self to be a law unto one's self. In his *The Confessions,* concerned most immediately with his own sinfulness, Augustine reflects upon the pears he stole in his youth, not, as he says, from any desire "to enjoy the things I coveted by stealing, but only to enjoy the theft itself and the sin . . . If the crime of theft which I committed that night as a boy of sixteen were a living thing, I could speak to it and ask what it was that, to my shame, I loved in it." He had no need of the pears. "No sooner had I picked them," he says, "than I threw them away, and tasted nothing in them but my own sin, which I relished and enjoyed. If any part of one of those pears passed my lips, it was the sin that gave it flavour."

He keeps on asking himself what it was that attracted him in that theft, what it was that he enjoyed in that childish act of stealing. Since he could not break God's law, he wonders, "Was it that I enjoyed at least the pretence of doing so, like a prisoner who creates for himself the illusion of liberty by doing something wrong, when he has no fear of punishment, under a feeble hallucination of power? Here was the slave who ran away from his master and chased a shadow instead! What an abomination! What a parody of life! What abysmal death! Could I enjoy doing wrong for no other reason than that it was wrong?"

IN THE PAGAN AND Judeo-Christian conceptions of sin, the fundamental meaning seems to depend upon the relation of man to the gods or to God, whether that itself be considered in terms of law or love. The vicious act may be conceived as one which is contrary to nature or reason. The criminal act may be conceived as a violation of the law of man, injurious to the welfare of the state or to its members. Both may involve the notions of responsibility and fault. Both may involve evil and wrongdoing. But unless the act transgresses the law

of God, it is not sinful. The divine law which is transgressed may be the natural law that God instills in human reason, but the act is sinful if the person who commits the act turns away from God to the worship or love of other things.

To disbelieve in God, in divine law and divine punishment, is also to disbelieve in sin— at least in the sense in which religious men have distinguished between saints and sinners, between the righteous and the wicked in the eyes of God. "There are only two kinds of men," writes Pascal: "the righteous who believe themselves sinners; the rest, sinners, who believe themselves righteous."

Those who reject the religious meaning of sin do not deny the wide prevalence of a sense of sin, nor do they deny that many men suffer remorse for transgressions which they suppose to be evil in God's eyes; but, with Freud, they interpret these feelings of guilt in terms of natural causes. They hold that the person who is tormented by conscience suffers from an illusion concerning the true nature of his guilt. When the sense of sin is intensely active and is, in addition, apparently unexplained by the character and conduct of the person, the guilt feelings, according to the Freudian view, take on the attributes of pathological distortion and become part of the symptomology of the neuroses. There is no question about the sincerity of the person who is thus agonized, but only about the true causes of the agony.

"When one asks how a sense of guilt arises in anyone," Freud says, "one is told something one cannot dispute: people feel guilty (pious people call it 'sinful') when they have done something they know to be 'bad.' But then one sees how little this answer tells one." What accounts for the judgment a man makes of himself as good or bad? Freud's answer is that "what is bad is, to begin with, whatever causes one to be threatened with a loss of love; because of the dread of this loss, one must desist from it. That is why it makes little difference whether one has already committed the bad deed or only intends to do so."

The external authority of the father and, through him, of society becomes, according to Freud, "internalized by the development of a super-ego. The manifestations of conscience are then raised to a new level; to be strict one should not call them conscience and sense of guilt before this . . . At this second stage of development, conscience exhibits a peculiarity which was absent in the first . . . That is, the more righteous a man is, the stricter and more suspicious will his conscience be, so that ultimately it is precisely those people who have carried holiness farthest who reproach themselves with the deepest sinfulness . . . A relatively strict and vigilant conscience is the very sign of a virtuous man, and though saints may proclaim themselves sinners, they are not so wrong, in view of the temptations of instinctual gratifications to which they are peculiarly liable—since, as we know, temptations do but increase under constant privation, whereas they subside, at any rate, temporarily, if they are sometimes gratified."

Freud applies his theory of the origin of feelings of guilt (in "the dread of authority" first and later in "the dread of the super-ego") to the religious sense of sin. "The people of Israel," he writes, "believed themselves to be God's favorite child, and when the great Father hurled visitation after visitation upon them, it still never shook them in this belief or caused them to doubt His power and His justice; they proceeded instead to bring their prophets into the world to declare their sinfulness to them, and out of their sense of guilt they constructed the stringent commandments of their priestly religion."

In general, Freud thinks, the great religions "have never overlooked the part played by the sense of guilt in civilization. What is more, they come forward with a claim . . . to save mankind from this sense of guilt which they call sin. We have drawn our conclusion from the way in which in Christianity this salvation is won—the sacrificial death of one who therewith takes the whole of the common guilt of all upon himself, about the occasion on which this primal sense of guilt was first acquired." The conclusion referred to is developed in two of Freud's works which are devoted to the consideration of religion and sin—*The Future of an Illusion* and *Totem and Taboo*. In the latter of these books, Freud tells us, he had first

"expressed a suspicion that perhaps the sense of guilt in mankind as a whole, which is the ultimate source of religion and morality, was acquired in the beginning of history through the Oedipus complex."

OTHER WRITERS, who approach the problem of sin in legalistic rather than psychological terms, either make no distinction between crime and sin or make the distinction without referring to God. Spinoza, for example, prefaces his explanation of the meanings of "praise and blame, merit and crime," with a discussion of the difference between "the natural and civil state of man." In a state of nature, he says, no one is "bound by any law to obey any one but himself. Hence in a natural state sin cannot be conceived, but only in a civil state, where it is decided by universal consent what is good and what is evil, and where everyone is bound to obey the State. Sin, therefore, is nothing but disobedience, which is punished by the law of the State alone."

Though Hobbes does not identify crime and sin, his distinction between them does not seem to be based on the contrast between the civil law and the divine law, unless the latter is equated with the law of nature. "A crime is a sin," he writes, "consisting in the committing (by deed or word) of that which the law forbiddeth, or the omission of that which it hath commanded. So that every crime is a sin, but not every sin a crime. To intend to steal or kill is a sin, though it never appear in word or fact, for God that seeth the thoughts of man, can lay it to his charge; but till it appear by something done, or said, by which the intention may be argued by a human judge, it hath not the name of crime.

"From this relation of sin to the law," Hobbes continues, "and of crime to the civil law, may be inferred, first, that where law ceaseth, sin ceaseth. But because the law of nature is eternal, violation of covenants, ingratitude, arrogance, and all facts contrary to any moral virtue, can never cease to be sin. Secondly, that the civil law ceasing, crimes cease; for there being no other law remaining, but that of nature, there is no place for accusation; every man being his own judge, and accused only by his own conscience, and cleared by the uprightness of his own intention. When therefore his intention is right, his fact is no sin; if otherwise, his fact is sin, but not crime."

The more strictly religious conception of sin seems to be exemplified by Pascal's remark that "all that God does not permit is forbidden" and that "sins are forbidden by the general declaration that God has made, that He did not allow them." Whatever God does not permit, "we ought to regard as sin," for "the absence of God's will, which is all goodness and all justice, renders it unjust and wrong."

With the precision of a theologian in these matters, Aquinas defines the peculiar type of evil which is sin. "Evil," he writes, "is more comprehensive than sin, as also is good than right ... Now in those things that are done by the will, the proximate rule is the human reason, while the supreme rule is the eternal law. When, therefore, a human act tends to the end according to the order of reason and of the eternal law, then that act is right; but when it turns aside from that rectitude, then it is said to be a sin." Elsewhere he says that "every created will has rectitude of act only so far as it is regulated according to the divine will ... Thus only in the divine will can there be no sin, whereas in the will of every creature, considered according to its nature, there can be sin."

THE THEOLOGICAL DISCUSSION of sin involves a tremendous range of topics, and problems as significant as they are subtle. The dogma of original sin, for example, raises questions not only about the cause and character of Adam's transgression, but also about the punishment which is visited upon the children of Adam in perpetuity, and about the conditions under which man can be reclaimed from his bondage to sin, both original and actual or personal.

There seems to be some resemblance between the Christian doctrine that Adam's sin merits a penalty to be paid by all subsequent generations, and the Jewish doctrine of the collective responsibility of the people of Israel for the sins of their ancestors, even unto the third and fourth generation. But the points

of difference appear to be more fundamental than the similarity.

In the first place, the sins of the fathers from which later generations suffer are the individual sins of men whose natures are predisposed to sin, as Adam's, before the fall, was not. In the second place, the punishment is visited not upon the whole human race, but only upon the Chosen People, and in the form of temporal scourges rather than in a corruption of human nature itself.

Furthermore, the Hebrew prophet Ezekiel questions the justice of collective responsibility. "What mean ye," he asks,

that ye use this proverb concerning the land of Israel, saying, The fathers have eaten sour grapes, and the children's teeth are set on edge?

As I live, saith the Lord God, ye shall not have occasion any more to use this proverb in Israel ...

The soul that sinneth, it shall die. The son shall not bear the iniquity of the father, neither shall the father bear the iniquity of the son: the righteousness of the righteous shall be upon him, and the wickedness of the wicked shall be upon him.

But if the wicked will turn from all his sins that he hath committed, and keep all my statutes, and do that which is lawful and right, he shall surely live, he shall not die.

All his transgressions that he hath committed, they shall not be mentioned unto him: in his righteousness that he hath done he shall live.

Have I any pleasure at all that the wicked should die? saith the Lord God: and not that he should return from his ways, and live?

But when the righteous turneth away from his righteousness, and committeth iniquity, and doeth according to all the abominations that the wicked man doeth, shall he live? All his righteousness that he hath done shall not be mentioned: in his trespass that he hath trespassed, and in his sin that he hath sinned, in them shall he die.

According to Christian teaching, the justice of individual punishment for the sins which individuals commit in their own lifetime does not apply to the penalty which all men must pay for the sin of Adam. "Wherefore, as by one man sin entered into the world," Saint Paul writes to the Romans,

and death by sin; and so death passed upon all men, for that all have sinned:

(For until the law sin was in the world: but sin is not imputed when there is no law.

Nevertheless, death reigned from Adam to Moses, even over them that had not sinned after the similitude of Adam's transgression, who is the figure of him that was to come.

But not as the offence, so also is the free gift. For if through the offence of one many be dead, much more the grace of God, and the gift by grace, which is by one man, Jesus Christ, hath abounded unto many.

And not as it was by one that sinned, so is the gift: for the judgment was by one to condemnation, but the free gift is of many offences unto justification.

For if by one man's offence death reigned by one; much more they which receive abundance of grace and of the gift of righteousness shall reign in life by one, Jesus Christ.)

Therefore as by the offence of one judgment came upon all men to condemnation; even so by the righteousness of one the free gift came upon all men unto justification of life.

For as by one man's disobedience many were made sinners, so by the obedience of one shall many be made righteous.

The Christian doctrine of original sin thus appears to be closely connected with the Christian doctrine of the need for a divine savior—God Himself become man to redeem man from the taint of sin, and through the sacraments He instituted to provide the instruments of healing grace and the means of repentance for, and absolution from, both original sin and the individual's own personal sins.

The understanding of the sacraments; the theory of grace in relation to the original and fallen nature of man; the issue concerning grace and good works, or God's justification and man's merit, in the achievement of sanctity and salvation; the distinction between the everlasting perdition of hell and the expiatory punishments of purgatory—all these fundamental theological problems are involved in the consideration of sin and its consequences, both temporal and eternal.

Some of these problems are discussed in the chapters on MAN, ANGEL, IMMORTALITY, and PUNISHMENT. Other matters, such as the classification of sins according to the distinction between spiritual and carnal, mortal and venial, and the enumeration of the various species of both mortal and venial sin in the order of their gravity, are problems of moral theology. Though they belong primarily to this chapter, they are also related to the classification of virtues and vices, especially to the theory of the theological virtues; and among the theological virtues, especially to charity, which is the principle of sanctity, even as pride is the principle of sin.

Of all points in the consideration of sin, the distinction between original and acquired sin is perhaps the most important, not only because inherited sinfulness is conceived as the predisposing cause of all other sins, but also because the human nature corrupted by sin is conceived as fallen below the perfection of a purely natural man as well as below the state of grace in which Adam was created. As Adam had gifts which made him superior to the natural man—immortality, infused knowledge and freedom from error, immunity from concupiscence, exemption from labor and servility—so the children of Adam, cast out of Eden, have ingrained weaknesses which make them unable to achieve the goods or attain the ends proportionate to their human nature.

Among all Christian theologians, Calvin takes the most extreme view of the consequences of original sin which has flawed the fallen nature of the children of Adam. Before he disobeyed God by an exercise of his free will, Adam was free to choose between good and evil and had the power to work freely for his salvation. But after Adam's fall, the human race, cast out of Eden, lost its freedom of choice. "When the will is enchained as the slave of sin, it cannot make a movement towards goodness, far less steadily pursue it." It is only by faith, the gift of God's grace, not by good works voluntarily done, that souls can be saved. Calvin comments on the "great darkness of the philosophers" who think free choice is inherent in human nature without recognizing that man's fallen nature is flawed primarily by the loss of that gift. Thus, Calvin is more anti-Pelagian than Augustine.

According to some theologians, the purely

natural man, without either the gifts of grace or the wounds of sin, has never existed. It is this mystery of man, having natural aspirations which exceed the weakened powers of his fallen nature, that Pascal seems to contemplate in all his observations on "the greatness and wretchedness of man"—the "astonishing contradictions" which he thinks only the Christian religion explains. In the state in which men now are, he writes, "there remains to them some feeble instinct of the happiness of their former state; and they are plunged in the evils of their blindness and their lust, which have become their second nature."

"As the result of original justice," Aquinas writes, "the reason had perfect hold over the lower parts of the soul, while reason itself was perfected by God in being subject to Him. Now this same original justice was forfeited by the sin of our first parent . . . so that all the powers of the soul are left, as it were, destitute of their proper order, whereby they are naturally directed to virtue. This destitution is called a wounding of nature . . . In so far as the reason is deprived of its order to the true, there is the wound of ignorance; in so far as the will is deprived of its order to the good, there is the wound of malice; in so far as the irascible is deprived of its order to the arduous, there is the wound of weakness; and in so far as the concupiscible is deprived of its order to the delectable as moderated by reason, there is the wound of concupiscence. Accordingly, these are the four wounds inflicted on the whole of human nature as a result of our first parent's sin."

Aquinas rejects the supposition that "the entire good of human nature can be destroyed by sin," arguing that what sin diminishes is "the natural inclination to virtue, which is befitting to man from the very fact that he is a rational being." But "sin cannot entirely take away from man the fact that he is a rational being, for then he would no longer be capable of sin."

Other theologians take a more extreme view than Aquinas and Augustine. They attribute depravity rather than weakness to human nature as a consequence of original sin. "On the Calvinistic theory," J. S. Mill writes, "the one great offense of man is self-will." Under the maxim that "whatever is not a duty, is a sin," men are left with no choice. "Human nature being radically corrupt," Mill continues, "there is no redemption for any one until human nature is killed within him." But, according to Augustine and Aquinas, original sin does not deprive the individual man entirely of the power to establish his worth, though it puts him in need of God's help to be worthy of salvation. Between the one extreme which holds that men can be saved by God's grace alone, and the other extreme which supposes that men can win salvation by the merit of their own good works, Augustine and Aquinas try to take the middle position, according to which neither grace without good works nor good works without grace will avail.

87

Slavery

INTRODUCTION

MORALISTS and political philosophers who appear to be in substantial agreement on the principles of justice differ remarkably from one another on whether slavery is just. The sharpness of this disagreement is made all the more remarkable by the almost unanimous condemnation of slavery—in two senses of that term.

As appears in the chapter on TYRANNY AND DESPOTISM, the condition of those who live under tyrannical rule is generally conceived as a kind of slavery, involving not only the loss of political freedom but also the suffering of other abuses or injuries. With the possible exception of Hobbes, who says that tyranny is merely monarchy "misliked," none of the great authors from Plato and Aristotle to Rousseau, Hegel, and J. S. Mill, writes of tyranny except as a perversion of government—unjust, lawless, or illegitimate. The evil of tyranny for them lies in the enslavement of men who deserve to be free, who should govern themselves or at least should be governed for their own good, not exploited by a ruler who uses them for his own private interests.

Some writers, like Montesquieu, who tend to identify despotism and tyranny see little difference between subjection and slavery, regarding both alike as degradations. Yet Montesquieu—and with him Aristotle—also thinks that for certain races of mankind subjection or slavery may be justified. Mill later makes the comparable point that for a people at a certain stage of political development, subjection may be necessary for a time in preparation for citizenship. The two basic distinctions in political status which are here implied—between slavery and subjection and between subjection and citizenship—are developed more fully in the chapter on CITIZEN. The first of these distinctions relates to the difference in the condition of men under tyranny and under benevolent despotism; the second, to the difference in the condition of men under absolute and under constitutional government.

The other sense in which the word "slavery" seems always to be used with the connotation of evil is the sense in which Augustine speaks of man's slavery to lust as a consequence of original sin; or in which Spinoza writes of human bondage—the condition of men enslaved by the tyranny of their passions—as compared with human freedom under the rule of reason. This meaning of slavery is discussed in other chapters, such as EMOTION and LIBERTY.

The slavery which results from the tyranny of the passions is a disorder from which any man may suffer; it stems from a weakness in the human nature which is common to all. Similarly, the slavery of a whole people under tyrannical rule is a perversion of government for all the members of the community, not just for some. But whenever slavery is defended, it is justified only for *some men* within a community, not for all; or if for a whole people, not for all mankind, but only for *certain peoples* under certain conditions. With regard to slavery, the basic issue of justice is, therefore, whether *some* men should be slaves or *all* should be free, not whether *all* should be slaves or *all* free.

THE DISTINCTION BETWEEN the slavery of some men within a community and the enslavement of a whole people appears to be related to the distinction between economic and political enslavement. In the ancient meaning of the word "economic," the economic slave is the slave of the household or family. "A complete household," writes Aristotle, "consists of slaves and freemen." The elements of a family are "master and slave, husband and wife, father and children."

That the distinction between the chattel slave and the freeman signifies economic rather than political status for Aristotle, and for the ancients generally, seems to be indicated by the fact that, under certain types of oligarchic constitution, freemen are excluded from citizenship without thereby becoming slaves. But in all ancient republics, democratic as well as oligarchic, chattel slaves are ineligible for citizenship.

Though the relation of master and slave is essentially economic rather than political, such slavery has a political aspect in the sense that some men have no function in the state except to serve other men. Aristotle speaks of them as necessary to the state, but not, as are citizens, parts of it. "The necessary people," he says, "are either slaves who minister to the wants of individuals, or mechanics and laborers who are the servants of the community."

The mark of economic slavery seems to be the kind of work human beings do and the conditions under which they labor, whereas political slavery seems to depend upon the kind of life human beings lead and the conditions under which they live in society. The economic slave serves a master by his work. The political slave lives under a tyrant. In Aristotle's view it is only the man who is economically free who has anything to lose from being enslaved by a tyrant. "No free man, if he can escape from it, will endure such government," he writes; but the barbarians, who "are by nature slaves," do not rebel against tyranny. Where some men are by nature free, there is also a natural distinction between women and slaves, "but among barbarians," according to Aristotle, "no distinction is made between women and slaves, because there is no natural ruler among them: they are a community of slaves, male and female." Veblen, in *The Theory of the Leisure Class,* opts for a purely economic interpretation of slavery: "There is reason to believe that the institution of ownership has begun with the ownership of

persons, primarily women. The incentives to acquiring such property have apparently been: (1) a propensity for dominance and coercion; (2) the utility of these persons as evidence of the prowess of their owner; (3) the utility of their services."

The difference between economic bondage—which can include what Marx calls the wage slavery of the proletariat, as well as chattel slavery and other forms of serfdom—and the political condition of those enslaved by a tyrant does not seem to affect the issue of justice. Those, like Hobbes and Locke, who think that the vanquished in war must pay for being allowed to live by submitting to slavery, do not seem concerned whether the servitude takes the form of private possession by an individual master or the subjugation of a whole people by the conquering state. Nor do those, like Aristotle and Montesquieu, who regard some men or some races as naturally servile, seem to offer reasons for political slavery different from those which they think justify economic servitude.

What does seem to affect the issue concerning the justice of slavery is the difference between the natural slave and the slave by force or law. This is the difference between the man who is born a slave (not merely born of slaves and into slavery) and the man who, born with a nature fit for freedom, is made a slave, either because his parents before him were slaves, because he is sold into slavery, or because, for one reason or another, he forfeits his birthright to freedom.

If no men are by nature slaves, then the only questions of justice concern the conditions which justify making slaves of freemen. These may remain the only questions even if there are natural slaves, since it cannot be unjust to treat as slaves those who are by nature slaves, any more than it is unjust to treat animals as brutes.

In both cases some consideration may be given to how slaves or animals should be treated. "The right treatment of slaves," Plato declares in the *Laws,* "is to behave properly to them, and to do to them, if possible, even more justice than to those who are our equals." Justice also requires, according to

Plato, that if a slave or an animal do any harm, the master shall pay for the injury.

WE HAVE ALREADY observed that, with regard to natural slavery, the main issue is one of fact. The fact in question concerns human equality and inequality. Within that equality of all men which rests upon their common possession of human nature, are some men by nature inferior to others in their use of reason or their capacity for leading the life of reason? Does such inferiority prevent them from directing their own lives or even their own work to the ends which are the natural fulfillment of man's powers? And if so, do not such men profit from being directed by their superiors, as well as from serving them and, through serving them, participating in the greater good their betters are able to achieve?

These are the questions of fact which Aristotle seems to answer affirmatively as he develops his theory of natural slavery. If the facts are granted, then no issue of justice arises, for Aristotle can say that "the slave by nature and the master by nature have in reality the same interests." It is by the justice inherent in the relation of master and slave *when both are naturally so related* that Aristotle can criticize the injustice of all *conventional* forms of slavery. But the question of fact must be faced, as Aristotle himself is aware.

"Is there any one intended by nature to be a slave," he asks, "and for whom such a condition is expedient and right, or is all slavery a violation of nature?" Aristotle recognizes that "others affirm the rule of a master over slaves to be contrary to nature and that the distinction between slave and free man exists by law only, and not by nature, and being an interference with nature is therefore unjust." He himself questions the justice of making slaves of captives taken in war, for that may violate the natures of men of high rank who have had the misfortune to be captured or sold. But he thinks that the same kind of difference which exists between male and female—the male being by nature superior, the female inferior; the one ruling, the other submitting to rule—can be extended to all mankind.

"Where there is such a difference," Aristot-

le explains, "as that between soul and body, or between men and animals . . . the lower sort are by nature slaves, and it is better for them as for all inferiors that they should be under the rule of a master. For he who can be, and therefore is, another's and he who participates in a rational principle enough to apprehend, but not to have, such a principle, is a slave by nature; whereas the lower animals cannot even apprehend a principle; they obey their instincts. And indeed the use made of slaves and of tame animals is not very different; for both with their bodies minister to the needs of life . . . If men differed from one another in the mere forms of their bodies as much as the statues of the gods do from men, all would acknowledge that the inferior class should be slaves of the superior. And if this is true of the body, how much more just that a similar distinction should exist in the soul . . . It is clear, then, that some are by nature free, and others slaves, and that for these latter slavery is both expedient and right."

According to the theory of natural slavery, it is as good for the slave to have a master as for the master to have a slave. This reciprocity of interest does not occur in legal or conventional slavery. In both types of slavery, the slave is a piece of property, a possession. Whether by nature or by institution, a slave does not own himself; he is another's man. "He may be called another's man," Aristotle says, "who, being a human being, is also a possession." Does this mean that the slave belongs wholly to the master, in all that he is and has? He would seem to belong to his master insofar as he is a *possession;* but not wholly—in all that he is and has—insofar as he is a *human being.* Aristotle does not introduce such a qualification where he says that "the slave is a part of the master, a living but separated part of his bodily frame"; yet he adds: "where the relation of master and slave is natural they are friends and have a common interest, but where it rests merely on law and force, the reverse is true."

Aristotle considers the difference between the natural slave and other forms of personal property, whether domestic animals, beasts of burden, or the inanimate instruments used in the household for productive purposes. Do slaves, he asks, have any excellence "beyond and higher than merely instrumental and ministerial qualities" of the sort to be found in tools and animals? Do they have virtues, and if so, then "in what way will they differ from freemen?"

Aristotle answers by saying that "since they are men and share in the rational principle, it seems absurd to say that they have no virtue." But since the rational principle in them is weak and consists only in the ability to execute decisions—not to make them or to know the end for which they are made—the slave will have a capacity for only so much virtue as he requires; enough virtue, for example, to "prevent him from failing in his duty through cowardice or lack of self-control."

It is precisely because of his limited competence and virtue that the slave needs, and profits by having, a master. Aristotle thinks that he is better off than the artisan out of bondage. "The slave shares in his master's life; the artisan is less closely connected with him, and only attains excellence in proportion as he becomes a slave. The meaner sort of mechanic has a special and separate slavery, and whereas the slave exists by nature, not so the shoemaker or other artisan."

The "separate slavery" of the artisan makes him more like an animal or an inanimate tool in the way he is used; for, according to Aristotle, he is an instrument of production, while the natural slave participates in his master's life by being an instrument not of production, but of action. The work the slave does enables the master to live well—to achieve the happiness of the political or contemplative life—and since "life is action, not production . . . the slave is a minister of action." If the slave had in his own nature the capacity for human happiness, he would not be by nature a slave, nor be limited to the good of serving another man's happiness.

"Slaves and brute animals cannot form a state," Aristotle says, because "the state exists for the sake, not of life, but the good life" and slaves "have no share in happiness or in a life of free choice . . . No one assigns to a slave a share in happiness," he says in another place,

"unless he assigns to him also a share in human life." At best, that share could come only from being a part of the master and contributing to the master's happiness. But though to this extent "the slave by nature and the master by nature have in reality the same interests," the rule under which the slave lives "is nevertheless exercised primarily with a view to the interest of the master."

ARISTOTLE'S DOCTRINE OF natural slavery is rejected by those who affirm the fundamental equality of all men in their common humanity and who, in addition, insist that their inequality as individuals in talent or capacity, should not affect their status or determine their treatment. On these grounds, Roman Stoics and Christian theologians seem to agree—and with them such modern thinkers as Rousseau, Kant, Hegel, and Mill—that all men are by nature born to be free. Freedom, writes Kant, belongs "to every man in virtue of his Humanity. There is, indeed, an innate Equality belonging to every man which consists in his right to be independent of being bound to others . . . in virtue of which he ought to be *his own master by Right*." That "all persons are deemed to have a *right* to equality of treatment" seems to follow for Mill from the principle that "one person's happiness, supposed equal in degree (with the proper allowance made for kind), is counted for exactly as much as another's." The "equal claim of everybody to happiness" involves "an equal claim to all the means of happiness," among them freedom.

But though theologians like Augustine and Aquinas deny that slavery is instituted by nature, they do not seem to regard it as contrary to natural law or to the will of God. Something can be according to natural law in two ways, Aquinas says: "First, because nature inclines thereto . . . Secondly, because nature does not require the contrary." Just as we can say, in the second sense, that nakedness is natural for man, "because nature did not give him clothes, but art invented them," so we can say that all men are by nature free because slavery was not instituted by nature, "but devised by human reason for the benefit of human life."

The institution of slavery, whereby one man

belongs to another for his use, seems due to the fallen nature of man, as one of the penal consequences of original sin. If man had remained in a state of innocence, one man would have ruled another for the latter's good, but no man would have been the master of slaves to be used for the master's good. Since "it is a grievous matter to anyone to yield to another what ought to be one's own," it follows, says Aquinas, that "such dominion necessarily implies a pain inflicted on the subject." This painfulness of slavery in turn seems to imply a contradiction to Aristotle's view that slavery fits certain natures and is for their benefit.

"By nature, as God first created us," writes Augustine, "no one is the slave either of man or of sin." Both sorts of slavery are "introduced by sin and not by nature." Both are punishments for sin, though one seems to Augustine more grievous than the other. "It is a happier thing," he says, "to be the slave of a man than of a lust; for even this very lust of ruling ... lays waste men's hearts with the most ruthless dominion. Moreover, when men are subjected to one another in a peaceful order, the lowly position does as much good to the servant as the proud position does harm to the master."

Not sin, but climate, according to Montesquieu, is the cause of slavery and to some extent its excuse. Though he thinks that "the state of slavery is in its own nature bad ... neither useful to the master nor to the slave," Montesquieu, like Hippocrates before him, regards the Asiatics as reduced to servility by the physical conditions of their life. "There reigns in Asia," he writes, "a servile spirit which they have never been able to shake off." Under Asiatic despotism, where whole peoples live in political servitude, domestic slavery is more tolerable than elsewhere. In those countries "where the excess of heat enervates the body, and renders men so slothful and dispirited that nothing but the fear of chastisement can oblige them to perform any laborious duty: slavery is ... more reconcilable to reason."

Montesquieu seems to accept Aristotle's doctrine with some qualifications. "Aristotle endeavours to prove that there are natural slaves; but what he says is far from proving it. If there be any such, I believe they are those of whom I have been speaking." Slavery is both natural and unnatural. "As all men are born equal," Montesquieu declares, "slavery must be accounted unnatural, though in some countries it be founded on natural reason ... Natural slavery, then, is to be limited to some particular parts of the world." But in arguing the right of Europeans "to make slaves of the negroes," he concludes with the equivocal remark that "it is impossible for us to suppose these creatures to be men, because, allowing them to be men, a suspicion would follow that we ourselves are not Christians."

Writing about conditions in the United States toward the middle of the 19th century, Tocqueville compares the status of the indigenous Indians with that of the imported African blacks. "The Indians die as they have lived, in isolation; but the fate of the Negroes is in a sense linked with that of the Europeans. The two races are bound one to the other without mingling; it is equally difficult for them to separate completely or to unite." He then goes on to say that "the most formidable evil threatening the future of the United States is the presence of the blacks on their soil." Whether 20th-century efforts at integration will be able finally to overcome the evils of segregation still remains to be seen.

Hegel's comment on the enslavement of African negroes by Europeans runs somewhat differently. "Bad as this may be," he writes, "their lot in their own land is even worse, since there a slavery quite as absolute exists." But though Hegel thinks that the negroes are naturally given to slavery, he regards "the 'natural condition' itself as one of absolute and thorough injustice." To remove this injustice, however, is not easy. "Man must be matured" for freedom, Hegel writes. "The gradual abolition of slavery is therefore wiser and more equitable than its sudden removal."

Tocqueville distinguishes between ancient and modern slavery by the fact that "in antiquity the slave was of the same race as his master and was often his superior in education and enlightenment ... The modern slave differs from his master not only in lacking freedom but also in his origin. You can make the Negro free, but you cannot prevent him facing the European as a stranger."

Mill, like Hegel, also looks upon slavery as a stage in the rise of certain peoples from savagery to political life, and maintains that the transition to freedom must be gradually effected. "A slave properly so called," he says, "is a being who has not learnt to help himself. He is, no doubt, one step in advance of a savage. He has not the first lesson of political life still to acquire. He has learnt to obey. But what he obeys is only a direct command. It is the characteristic of *born* slaves to be incapable of conforming their conduct to a rule, or a law . . . They have to be taught self-government, and this, in its initial stage, means the capacity to act on general instructions." Extenuations of the injustice of ruling men as slaves, such as those proposed by Hegel and Mill, are rejected by Rousseau.

The notion that some men are by nature slaves, whether in Asia or in Europe, seems to Rousseau to be an illusion due to the fact that those who are made slaves by force have had their natures debased to slavishness. Aristotle, he says, "took the effect for the cause. Nothing can be more certain than that every man born in slavery is born for slavery. Slaves lose everything in their chains, even the desire of escaping from them . . . If then there are slaves by nature, it is because there have been slaves against nature. Force made the first slaves, and their cowardice perpetuated the condition."

It is sophistry, he thinks, for philosophers to "attribute to man a natural propensity to servitude, because the slaves within their observation are seen to bear the yoke with patience; they fail to reflect that it is with liberty as with innocence and virtue; the value is known only to those who possess them, and the taste for them is forfeited when they are forfeited themselves."

THE ISSUE CONCERNING slavery as a social or legal institution does not seem to be resolved by the views men take of natural slavery. Aristotle, who holds that *only* natural slavery is justified, criticizes those who "affirm to be unjust and inexpedient in their own case what they are not ashamed of practising towards others; they demand just rule for themselves," he writes, "but where other men are concerned they care nothing about it. Such behavior is irrational, unless the one party is, and other is not, born to serve." This cannot be determined by conquest. Aristotle questions, therefore, the convention "by which whatever is taken in war is supposed to belong to the victors," or the principle that "because one man has the power of doing violence and is superior in brute strength, another shall be his slave and subject." Those who "assume that slavery in accordance with the custom of war is justified by law," are confronted by Aristotle with the question: "What if the cause of the war be unjust?"

Hobbes and Locke appear to take an opposite view. Men in a state of nature are free, though they can actually enjoy only as much freedom as they have power to secure. Yet the natural inequality in their powers does not establish a natural right on the part of the stronger to enslave the weaker. Hobbes makes the right of mastership or what he calls "despotical dominion" depend not merely upon victory in war, but upon a covenant into which the vanquished enter voluntarily, "when the vanquished, to avoid the present stroke of death, covenanteth . . . that so long as his life, and the liberty of his body, is allowed him, the victor shall have the use thereof at his pleasure." Only "after such covenant is made, the vanquished is a servant, and not before . . . It is not, therefore, the victory, that giveth the right of dominion over the vanquished, but his own covenant." That Hobbes means chattel slave when he says "servant," seems to be indicated by his remark that "the master of the servant is master also of all he hath, and may exact the use thereof; that is to say, of his goods, of his labour, of his servants, and of his children, as often as he shall think fit."

Locke disagrees with Hobbes that one man can give another the right to enslave him by contracting to become a slave in order to avoid death. "A man not having the power of his own life," he writes, "cannot by compact, or his own consent, enslave himself to anyone . . . Nobody can give more power than he has himself; and he that cannot take away his own life, cannot give another power over it." As among the ancient Jews, men can sell themselves into temporary service to requite a debt. But this was a kind of drudgery, not slavery; "the person sold was not under an absolute, arbitrary, despotical power, for the master could not have the power to kill him at any time, whom at a certain time he was obliged to let go free out of his service." No Jew, Aquinas concurs, "could own a Jew as a slave absolutely, but only in a restricted sense, as a hireling for a time. And in this way the Law permitted that through stress of poverty a man might sell his son or daughter."

Absolute slavery, for Locke, "is nothing else but the state of war continued between a lawful conqueror and a captive." It is lawful, he thinks, to kill a violent aggressor, "for to that hazard does he justly expose himself whoever introduces a state of war, and is aggressor in it." But he who has forfeited his life necessarily forfeits his freedom. Slaves, then, are those "who, being captives taken in a just war, are by right of nature subjected to the absolute dominion and arbitrary power of their masters." In contrast to the limited servitude which a man can contract for wages, absolute slavery "is the effect only of forfeiture which the aggressor makes of his own life when he puts himself into the state of war with another."

Against Locke and Hobbes, as well as Aristotle, Rousseau denies that there is any justice in slavery—by nature, by covenant or compact, or by right of war. To think as Hobbes appears to, that "the child of a slave comes into the world as a slave," is, in Rousseau's opinion, to say that "a man shall come into the world not a man." Holding that slavery is "contrary to nature," Rousseau also holds that it "cannot be authorized by any right or law." A man cannot alienate his freedom by selling himself into slavery, for "to renounce liberty is to renounce being a man."

In Kant's language, "a contract by which the one party renounces his *whole* freedom for the advantage of the other, ceasing thereby to be a person and consequently having no duty even to observe a contract, is self-contradictory, and is therefore of itself null and void." Agreeing that such a contract is a nullity,

Hegel holds that the "slave has an absolute right to free himself," but he adds that "if a man is a slave, his own will is responsible for his slavery . . . Hence the wrong of slavery lies at the door not simply of enslavers or conquerors, but of the slaves and the conquered themselves."

As for Hugo Grotius and the others who "find in war another origin for the so-called right of slavery"—on the ground that "the victor having . . . the right of killing the vanquished, the latter can buy back his life at the price of his liberty"—Rousseau thinks their argument begs the question. "The right of conquest," he says, "has no foundation other than the right of the strongest. If war does not give the conqueror the right to massacre the conquered peoples, the right to enslave them cannot be based upon a right which does not exist."

Since Rousseau denies that victory gives the victors a right to kill those who have laid down their arms, he regards it unfair to make the captive "buy at the price of his liberty his life, over which the victor holds no right . . . From whatever aspect we regard the question," he concludes, "the right of slavery is null and void, not only as being illegitimate, but also because it is absurd and meaningless. The words *slave* and *right* contradict each other and are mutually exclusive."

IN MODERN AS WELL AS ancient times, in the European colonies in the New World if not in Europe itself, slave labor characterizes a certain type of economy and determines the mode of production, especially in agriculture and mining. The slave as chattel is bought and sold like other property. He may be a source of profit to his owner in exchange as well as in production. The traffic in slaves depends upon an original acquisition, either through the spoils of war or by the activity of slave traders who hunt men as if they were animals, to transport them in chains and sell them into slavery.

In the ancient world, individual slave owners emancipated their slaves, even as, under modern feudalism, a great landowner like Prince Andrew in *War and Peace* freed his serfs. Aristotle speaks of those in his own time who opposed the institution of slavery; and the Roman Stoics did a great deal to ameliorate the condition of the slave and to protect him legally against abuse. But there seems to have been no political party or active political movement among the ancients corresponding to the abolitionists and their struggle in the 18th and 19th centuries. Even then, however, the abolitionists were looked upon as a radical minority who had no respect for the rights of property in their overzealous sentimentality about the rights of men. Those who were willing to outlaw the African slave trade as outrageous were less outraged by the treatment of men as chattel, once they were possessed.

Madison, for example, referring to the prohibition affecting the importation of slaves into the United States, which the Constitution postponed until 1808, thinks it "a great point gained in favor of humanity, that a period of twenty years may terminate forever, within these States, a traffic which has so long and so loudly upbraided the barbarism of modern policy." But in another paper the writers of *The Federalist* present their version of the Southern argument defending the Constitution's apportionment of representation, "determined by adding to the whole number of free persons, including those bound to service for a term of years, and excluding Indians not taxed, three-fifths of all other persons." They do not object to the view of the negro slave as two-fifths property and three-fifths a person, confessing themselves reconciled to reasoning which, though "it may appear a little strained in some points," appeals to a principle they themselves approve, namely, that "government is instituted no less for the protection of property than of persons."

There are even those, in the 18th century, who defend the slave trade. Boswell reports an argument set forth by Dr. Johnson in favor of granting liberty to a negro, who claimed his freedom before a Scottish Court of Session. The sum of Dr. Johnson's argument, according to Boswell, came to this: "No man is by nature the property of another; the defendant is, therefore, by nature free. The rights of nature must be in some way forfeited before they can be justly taken away . . . and if no proof of such forfeiture can be given, we doubt not but the justice of the court will declare him free." Admitting that Johnson may have been right in the particular case at hand, Boswell protests his general attitude toward slavery and the slave trade.

"To abolish a status," Boswell writes, "which in all ages God has sanctioned, and man has continued, would not only be robbery to an innumerable class of our fellow-subjects; but it would be extreme cruelty to the African savages, a portion of whom it saves from massacre, or intolerable bondage in their own country, and introduces into a much happier state of life, especially now when their passage to the West Indies and their treatment there is humanely regulated."

Issues of justice aside, economists like Adam Smith and Marx question the productivity of slave labor. Improvements in machinery "are least of all to be expected," writes Smith, when the proprietors "employ slaves for their workmen. The experience of all ages and nations, I believe, demonstrates that the work done by slaves, though it appears to cost only their maintenance, is in the end the dearest of any. A person who can acquire no property, can have no interest but to eat as much, and to labor as little as possible." He explains the lack of mechanical progress in Greece and Rome by the fact that "slaves . . . are very seldom inventive; and all the most important improvements in machinery, or in the arrangement and distribution of work, which facilitate and abridge labor, have been the discoveries of free men."

Marx also judges "production by slave labor" to be "a costly process . . . The principle, universally applied in this method of production," is "to employ the rudest and heaviest implements and such as are difficult to damage owing to their sheer clumsiness. In the slave-states, bordering on the Gulf of Mexico, down to the date of the civil war, ploughs constructed on old Chinese models, which turned up the soil like a hog or a mole, instead of making furrows, were alone to be found."

But Marx does not limit his judgment of slavery to criteria of efficiency, nor does he limit his consideration of servitude to its more obvious forms of chattel slavery and feudal serfdom. For him, all use of labor by those who own the instruments of production involves exploitation; it differs only in the degree to which the owner derives a surplus value from the labor power he possesses, through property rights or wage payments.

According to Marx, "the essential difference between the various economic forms of society, between, for instance, a society based on slave labor and one based on wage labor, lies only in the mode in which this surplus-labor is in each case extracted from the actual producer, the laborer." As all the value produced by a slave, in excess of the cost of keeping him alive, profits his owner, so during "the period of surplus-labor, the usufruct of the labor-power creates a value for the capitalist that costs him no equivalent . . . In this sense it is that surplus-labor can be called unpaid labor"—whether it is the labor of chattel or wage slaves.

Because a laborer is forced to sell his labor power in the open market in order to subsist, Marx regards his so-called "freedom" as a pious fiction. "The contract by which he sold to the capitalist his labor-power proved in black and white," Marx writes, "that he disposed of himself freely. The bargain concluded, it is discovered that he was no 'free-agent,' that the time for which he is free to sell his labor-power is the time for which he is forced to sell it."

Others take the view that there is a fundamental moral difference between chattel slaves and men who work for wages. Hobbes, for example, thinks that between slaves who "are bought and sold as beasts" and servants "to whose service the masters have no further right than is contained in the covenants made betwixt them," there is only this much in common—"that their labor is appointed them by another." In slightly varying terms, Aquinas, Locke, and Kant make a similar distinction between the free servant, or paid worker, and the slave. The point is summarized by Hegel as a difference between alienating to someone else "products of my particular physical and mental skill," and alienating "the whole of my time, as crystallized in my work." In the latter case, "I would be making into another's property the substance of my being."

Debating with Douglas, Lincoln insisted that political freedom was the difference between the white slaves of the North and the black slaves of the South. The legal right, won by the proletariat, to organize and strike, seems to be a difference which Marx himself recognizes between the wage earner and the bonded slave. Until his chains are struck, the slave is not in the position of the free workingman to fight for political rights and privileges. Citizenship is not always extended to the laboring classes, but it is never conferred upon slaves.

88

Soul

INTRODUCTION

In the language of the poets as well as in the discourse of the philosophers, body and soul are correlative terms. Each affects the meaning of the other. The words are used together in daily speech. Men who are unaware of, or deny, the metaphysical and theological significance of having a soul, nevertheless use the word "soul" with a sense of contrast to body, even if only to refer to vague manifestations of spirit—feelings and sympathies which seem to be alien to the world of matter.

With few exceptions, traditional theories of the soul involve its distinction from and relation to the body. Berkeley represents one of the major exceptions. Denying the reality of matter, he conceives the soul as existing in and by itself; souls or spirits differ from God as finite from infinite spiritual beings. The something "which knows and perceives" and which "exercises divers operations, as willing, imagining, remembering," Berkeley says, "is what I call *mind, spirit, soul,* or *myself.*" Berkeley, therefore, would not speak of himself or other men as having souls, but rather as *being* souls.

The other major exception is exemplified by Lucretius. It is not that Lucretius denies soul as Berkeley denies body. Nor does he deny that soul adds something to body which differentiates living organisms from inorganic things. On the contrary, he declares the mind to be "a part / Of a man's make-up, every bit as much / As are his hands and feet and seeing eyes." Distinct from mind, soul is also part of a living being. "Mind and spirit are held close together, / Compose one unity," but whereas the mind is, as it were, the lord or head of the whole body, "The rest of spirit is dispersed all through / The entire frame, and it obeys the mind, / Moves, gains momentum, at its nod and beck."

But when Lucretius refers to mind and soul as parts of the body, he means no more than is implied in speaking of the hand and eye as parts of the body. "The nature of both mind and spirit / Must be corporeal," he writes. Just as flesh and bones are composed of atomic particles, so the mind is formed "of particles which are small and smooth and round," and the soul consists of "very tiny seeds, / All sown minutely in sinew, flesh, and veins."

Apart from these exceptions, the traditional discussion of soul considers it as somehow conjoined with body to constitute a whole of which it is the immaterial principle or part. Even those who, like Descartes, define the soul as an immaterial substance, capable of existing by itself, do not actually ascribe to the human soul complete independence of the human body. Nor do the theologians who think of God as a purely spiritual being and of angels as immaterial substances attribute soul to them.

The primitive tribes described by Frazer in *The Golden Bough* believe that "the soul may temporarily absent itself from the body without causing death." This notion of an "external soul" has its advantages and disadvantages. Wizards of certain tribes are believed to hide their souls outside their bodies—sometimes in trees or animals—because they are afraid of someone capturing their magical powers. However, as Frazer tells us, "Such temporary absences of the soul are often believed to involve considerable risk," because the soul, although absent from the body, is still united to the body by a type of sympathetic magic. "So long as this object which he calls his life or soul remains unharmed, the man is well; if it is injured, he suffers; if it is destroyed, he dies."

Precisely because God and the angels do not have bodies, neither do they have souls. Whether everything which has a body also has a soul is another question. It is variously answered; but certainly those who, like Plato and Plotinus, speak of a world-soul or a soul of the universe, confirm the point that soul is the co-principle or complement of body. The same point appears in theories of the celestial bodies which conceive them as being alive and as therefore having souls.

Unfolding to Socrates the story of the creation, Timaeus says: "Using the language of probability, we may say that the world became a living creature endowed with soul and intelligence by the providence of God." To the world, Timaeus explains, God "gave a body, smooth and even, having a surface in every direction equidistant from the center, a body entire and perfect, and formed out of perfect bodies. And in the center, he put the soul which he diffused throughout the body, making it also to be the exterior environment of it."

Comparing the magnetic force of the loadstone with the animation of a soul, Gilbert says that "this one eminent property is the same which the ancients held to be a soul in the heavens, in the globes, and in the stars, in sun and moon . . . The ancient philosophers . . . all seek in the world a certain universal soul, and declare the whole world to be endowed with a soul. Aristotle held that not the universe is animate, but the heavens only . . . As for us," Gilbert writes, "we deem the whole world animate, and all globes, stars, and this glorious earth, too, we hold to be from the beginning by their own destinate souls governed . . . Pitiable is the state of the stars, abject the lot of earth, if this high dignity of soul is denied them, while it is granted to the worm, the ant, the roach, to plants and morels; for in that case, worms, roaches, moths, were more beauteous objects in nature and more perfect, inasmuch as nothing is excellent, nor precious, nor eminent, that hath not a soul."

On the question whether the earth, each heavenly body, or the whole world is endowed with life, intelligence, and soul, Kepler differs from Gilbert, Augustine from Plato and Plotinus, Aquinas from Aristotle. Nevertheless, the many-sided controversy indicates the traditional connection of soul with life and mind on the one hand, and with animate or organic bodies on the other—bodies which manifest certain properties and tendencies to motion.

THE MAJOR ISSUES CONCERNING soul seem to follow from these traditional associations. Does the soul which is somehow conjoined with a body exist as an immaterial substance or principle, in such a way that the being composed of body and soul consists of two distinct substances or entities, united as related parts of a whole? Or is the soul the substantial form of an organic body, with the consequence that the form and matter together constitute a single composite substance, which is the living thing? In the latter alternative the unity of soul and body, according to Aristotle, is like that of "the wax and the shape given to it by the die."

On either conception of soul and its relation to body or matter, further questions arise concerning the soul's existence apart from the body. Does it exist before being united to the body? Does it exist after the union is dissolved? How does it exist when it exists separately or apart from matter? For those, like Lucretius, who conceive the soul as itself composed of material particles within the framework of the body, such questions can have little meaning. For those, like Plato and Descartes, who conceive the soul as an immaterial entity having being in its own right, these questions can be immediately answered in favor of the soul's capacity for separate existence. Only when the soul is conceived as a form which, together with matter, constitutes the substance of a living body, does there seem to be both meaning and difficulty to the question whether the soul continues to endure separately when a plant, an animal, or a man dies, i.e., when such composite substances decompose.

If the individual soul ceases to be when the body with which it is somehow united perishes, it is as mortal as the body. The traditional theories of personal immortality—such as the Platonic myths concerning the transmigration or reincarnation of souls, and the Christian doctrine of man's immortal soul, specially created for union with the body, but destined to survive its separation from the body—are theories which involve conceptions of the soul as capable of self-subsistence. The controversy over these doctrines is dealt with in the chapter on IMMORTALITY. Here are we concerned to see how different implications for immortality necessarily follow from various theories of the soul.

Still other issues concerning soul arise in connection with other chapters. For example, the question whether soul is to be found only in living things, or only in animals but not in plants, or in man alone, is discussed in the chapters on LIFE AND DEATH and on MIND. If soul, on any conception, is the principle or cause of life, then the distinction between animate and inanimate bodies is identical with the distinction between things which have and things which do not have a soul. If, furthermore, the kind of life possessed by a vegetable or plant is radically different from animal life, and that in turn from human life, then souls, too, may have to be differentiated in kind according to the mode of life or the range of vital powers of which each type is the principle.

Some writers, however, tend to equate "soul" with "mind" or "understanding." When, as by Descartes, soul is identified with rational soul or thinking substance, it is usually attributed to man alone. Soul is then not thought necessary to explain the phenomena of life in plants and animals, at least in no sense of soul which implies either an incorporeal or a formal principle; that is, anything beyond the complex interaction of organic parts. Other authors, like Locke, who conceive soul or understanding not merely in terms of rational thought, but also in terms of sensation, imagination, and memory, may exclude plants, but not animals, from the possession of soul or mind.

Descartes takes notice of these ambiguities in the traditional use of the word "soul." Probably because "men in the earliest times," he writes, "did not distinguish in us that principle in virtue of which we are nourished, grow, and perform all those operations which are common to us with the brutes . . . from that by which we think, they called both by the single name *soul;* then, perceiving the distinction between nutrition and thinking, they called that which thinks *mind,* believing also that this was the chief part of the soul. But I, perceiving that the principle by which we are nourished is wholly distinct from that by means of which we think have declared that the name *soul* when used for both is equivocal; and I say that, when soul is taken to mean the *primary actuality* or *chief essence of man,* it must be understood to apply only to the principle by which we think, and I have called it by the name *mind* as often as possible to avoid ambiguity; for I consider the mind not as part of the soul, but as the whole of that soul which thinks."

In another place, he uses the word "soul" to stand for "that subtle fluid styled the animal spirits" which, pervading the organs of brute animals, accounts for their peculiar type of animation. "We can recognize no principle of motion in them beyond the disposition of their organs and the continual discharge of the animal spirits that are produced by the beat of the heart as it rarefies the blood." Soul in this sense is not to be confused with "the incorporeal and spiritual nature of man's soul." It is "something corporeal, of a fine structure and subtle, spread throughout the external body, and the principle of all sensation, imagination, and thought. Thus there are three grades of being, Body, the Corporeal or soul, and Mind or spirit."

IN THE OPENING PAGES of his treatise *On the Soul,* Aristotle says that "to attain any assured knowledge about the soul is one of the most difficult things in the world." The difficulty seems to apply both to *what the soul is* and to *whether it exists.* The questions are connected. Even Lucretius, who regards the soul as material in nature, does not claim to know its existence by direct observation. It is not, like the body itself or like other parts of the body, a sensible object. It must be inferred to exist. Just as the existence of unobservable atoms is inferred in order to explain the constitution and change of all natural objects, so the existence of soul is inferred in order to explain the constitution and motion of living things. Those who conceive the soul as immaterial—whether as substance, principle, or form—would seem to face an even greater difficulty in establishing its existence and in describing its nature. Admittedly, the soul as some sort of immaterial being cannot be discovered by observation and experiment. The alternatives, which represent traditional solutions of the problem, seem to include the soul's reflexive knowledge of its own existence, inferential knowledge about the soul based on observed facts, various religious beliefs concerning the nature and destiny of the soul, and the postulation of the soul's existence on practical, not theoretical, grounds.

Not all writers agree with Aristotle that the soul is an object difficult to know, or with Kant that it is absolutely impossible for us to reach any sound theoretical conclusions about the soul's existence. Descartes, for example, says that if there are "any persons who are not sufficiently persuaded of the existence of God and of the soul by the reasons which I have brought forward, I wish them to know that all other things of which they perhaps think themselves more assured (such as possessing a body, and that there are stars and an earth and so on) are less certain."

The argument for the soul's existence which precedes this remark is the famous *Cogito, ergo sum*—"I think; therefore, I am." From the fact that, in the very act of doubting the existence of everything else, he could not doubt that he was doubting, and hence thinking, Descartes assures himself of his own existence, or, more precisely, of the existence of himself as a thinking being. "I knew," he writes, "that I was a substance the whole essence or nature of which is to think, and that for its existence there is no need of any place, nor does it depend on any material thing; so that this 'me,' that is to say, the soul by which I am what I am, is entirely distinct from body, and is even more easy to know than is the latter; and even if the body were not, the soul would not cease to be what it is."

Locke appears to agree that "if I doubt of all other things, that very doubt makes me perceive my own existence, and will not suffer me to doubt of that . . . I have as certain perception of the existence of the thing doubting," he goes on, "as of that thought which I call doubt. Experience then convinces us that we have an intuitive knowledge of our own existence, and an internal infallible perception that we are."

But Locke does not turn the proposition that a thinking being exists into the assertion that a spiritual being, the soul as an immaterial substance, exists. "We have the idea of matter and thinking," he writes, "but possibly shall never be able to know whether any mere material being thinks or no; it being impossible for us, by the contemplation of our own ideas, without revelation, to discover whether Omnipotency has not given to some systems of matter fitly disposed, a power to perceive and think, or else joined and fixed to matter so disposed, a thinking immaterial substance: it being, in respect of our notions, not much more remote from our comprehension to conceive that God can, if he pleases, superadd to matter a faculty of thinking, than that he should superadd to it another substance with a faculty of thinking."

For Locke, however, our idea of soul is as clear as our idea of body. "Our idea of body," he says, "is an extended, solid substance capable of communicating motion by impulse; and our idea of soul, as an immaterial spirit, is of a substance that thinks, and has a power of exciting motion in body, by willing or thought . . . I know that people whose thoughts are immersed in matter, and have so subjected their minds to their senses, that they seldom reflect on anything beyond them, are apt to say, that they cannot comprehend a thinking thing; which, perhaps, is true: but I affirm, when they consider it well, they can no more comprehend an extended thing." And in another place, he adds: "If this notion of immaterial spirit may have, perhaps, some difficulties in it, not easy to be explained, we have, therefore, no more reason to deny or doubt the existence of such spirits, than we have to deny or doubt the existence of body, because the notion of body is cumbered with some difficulties, very hard, and, perhaps, impossible to be explained or understood by us."

Berkeley differs from Locke not only in maintaining that we have no idea of matter at all, but also in holding that, if we use the word "idea" for sense impressions or the images derived from them, we can have no idea of soul or spiritual substance. But we can, he thinks, form what he calls a "notion" of the soul, which grasps the meaning of the word "spirit" as signifying "that which thinks, wills, or perceives." He differs from Locke further in proportion as he tends to agree with Descartes, asserting that the existence of a spiritual substance, a thinking being, necessarily follows from the undeniable existence of thinking itself.

For both Descartes and Berkeley, the immortality of the soul can be directly concluded from our knowledge of the soul's existence and nature. "The soul," writes Berkeley, "is indivisible, incorporeal, unextended, and it is consequently incorruptible. Nothing can be plainer than that the motions, changes, decays and dissolutions which we hourly see befall natural bodies . . . cannot possibly affect an active, simple, uncompounded substance; such a being therefore is indissoluble by the force of nature; that is to say, 'the soul of man is naturally immortal.' "

The arguments in Plato's *Phaedo* for the proper existence of the soul before it joins a particular body, and for its existence after it leaves the body to dwell apart before entering another body—arguments, in short, for the soul's immortality—seem to stem from a slightly different principle. It is not merely that the soul is simple or uncompounded and hence indissoluble, or that the knowledge we have of the absolute ideas requires us to posit a principle of knowledge other than the bodily senses which can apprehend only changing things. In addition, Socrates argues that the knower must be like the known. If it is the soul which knows the unchangeable and eternal essences, it must be as unchangeable and eternal as they are. When the soul uses "the body as instrument of perception," Socrates says, it is "then dragged by the body into the region of the changeable . . . But when return-ing into herself she reflects, then she passes into the other world, the region of purity, and eternity, and immortality, and unchangeableness, which are her kindred."

AGAINST ANY FORM of argument for the existence and immortality of the human soul which proceeds from the nature of our thought or knowledge, Kant takes the position that the premises do not warrant the conclusion. He claims to expose the fallacies in what he calls the "paralogism of a rational psychology." The "I" of the *Cogito, ergo sum* may be the necessary logical subject of all our judgments, but this does not give us intuitive knowledge of a really existing substance which has the attributes of simplicity, spirituality, and permanence or immortality.

"In all our thinking," Kant writes, "the I is the subject in which our thoughts are inherent; nor can that I ever be used as a determination of any other thing. Thus everybody is constrained to look upon himself as the substance, and on thinking as the accident of his being." But, he goes on, "though the I exists in all thoughts, not the slightest intuition is connected with that representation by which it might be distinguished from other objects of intuition . . . Hence it follows that in the first syllogism of transcendental psychology reason imposes upon us an apparent knowledge only, by representing the constant logical subject as the knowledge of the real subject in which that knowledge inheres. Of that subject, however, we have not and cannot have the slightest knowledge . . . In spite of this, the proposition that the soul is a substance may well be allowed to stand, if only we see that this concept cannot help us on in the least or teach us any of the ordinary conclusions of rational psychology, as, for instance, the everlasting continuance of the soul amid all changes and even in death; and that it therefore signifies a substance in idea only, and not in reality."

Similarly with respect to the simplicity of the soul, Kant contends that the absolute, but merely logical, unity of apperception or thought is illegitimately converted into the absolute unity of a real substance. The proposition, *I am a simple substance,* he declares, "teaches us nothing at all with reference to myself as an object of experience." Its only value is to enable us "to distinguish the soul from all matter, and thus to exempt it from that decay to which matter is at all times subject."

To this extent, rational psychology may "guard our thinking self against the danger of materialism." The concept of the soul as an immaterial and simple substance may thus function regulatively, but we deceive ourselves with the illusion of knowledge when we treat that concept as if it had intuitive content— when, as he says, we change "thoughts into things." Kant does not deny that the "I" is substantial in concept or simple in concept. Though these propositions are "incontestably true," he says, "nevertheless, what we really wish to know of the soul, becomes by no means known to us in that way, because all these predicates are with regard to intuition non-valid, entailing no consequences with regard to objects of experience, and therefore entirely empty."

The existence and immortality of the soul is, for Kant, a postulate or demand of the practical reason. "Of the psychic substance, regarded as an immortal soul, it is absolutely impossible to obtain any proof from a theoretical point of view," but if such an object must be thought *a priori* in order for "pure practical reason to be used as duty commands," it becomes what Kant calls "matter of faith." Immortality seems to him rationally required as the practically necessary condition for the fulfillment of the moral law and the endless progress of the soul toward holiness of will.

William James questions even such practical arguments for the soul. The imperishability of a simple substance does not, he thinks, guarantee "immortality of a sort *we care for.*" Nor, following Locke, does it seem to him that a substantial soul is required for personal identity and moral responsibility. Writing as an empirical or scientific psychologist, who feels "entirely free to discard the word Soul" because he finds the concept useless "so far as accounting for the actually verified facts of conscious experience goes," James tells those

who may find "any comfort in the idea" that they are "perfectly free to continue to believe in it; for our reasonings have not established the non-existence of the Soul; they have only proved its superfluity for scientific purposes."

JAMES'S CONCLUSION THAT "the substantial Soul . . . explains nothing and guarantees nothing," along with the arguments of Kant and Locke, may not apply to the soul conceived as the principle of life rather than as the agent of thought, or to the soul conceived as the form of an organic body rather than as a spiritual being associated with or somehow imprisoned in the body. Precisely because this other conception affirms reality of soul as something other than a complete substance, precisely because it applies to plants and animals as well as men, this other conception of soul would seem to require a different sort of criticism.

The Greek and Latin words—*psyche* and *anima*—which we translate by "soul" seem to have life as their primary connotation. In the *Cratylus,* Socrates suggests that "those who first used the name *psyche* meant to express that the soul when in the body is the source of life, and gives the power of breath and revival." Other dialogues express the Greek conception of the living thing as that which has the power of self-motion, and ascribe this power to the soul as source. In the *Phaedo,* for example, Socrates asks, "What is that the inherence of which will render the body alive?" to which Cebes answers, "Soul," and agrees with Socrates' further statement that "whatever the soul takes possession of, to that she comes bearing life." In the *Laws,* Cleinias having identified the power of self-motion with life, the Athenian Stranger gains his assent to the proposition that whatever has life or self-motion also has soul.

To this much Aristotle also agrees. "What has soul in it," he says, "differs from what has not, in that the former displays life"; to which he adds that "living may mean thinking or perception or local movement, or movement in the sense of nutrition and growth," so that we must "think of plants also as living," and as having souls. But Aristotle goes further. In defining soul as the cause of life, and in differentiating three kinds of souls—vegetative, sensitive, and rational—according to the vital powers manifested by the activities of plants, animals, and men, he uses his general theory of corporeal substances to state precisely what the soul is and how it is related to the body.

Corporeal substances are, according to him, all composite of two principles, form and matter. "What is called matter is potentiality, what is called form, actuality." As exemplified in works of art, wood is the matter which has the potentiality for a certain shape and a certain function that is the actuality or form of a chair. In the case of natural things, that which determines "the essential whatness" of a body is its form or, as Aristotle sometimes says, "its formulable essence."

If living things are essentially distinct from inert bodies, as Aristotle supposes them to be, then the forms which determine their essences must be different from the forms of inanimate substances. It is this difference in forms which Aristotle appropriates the word "soul" to signify. In each kind of living thing, the soul is the substantial form or "the first grade of actuality of a natural body having life potentially in it."

He speaks of the first grade of actuality here to distinguish merely being alive or besouled from the various acts which, as operations of the vital powers, constitute living. If an ax or an eye had a soul, it would consist of its power to cut or to see, not in its actually cutting or seeing. While nourishing or thinking "is actuality corresponding to the cutting and the seeing, the soul is actuality in the sense corresponding to the power of sight and the power in the tool . . . As the pupil *plus* the power of sight constitutes the eye, so the soul *plus* the body constitutes the animal."

From this conception of soul as the form or actuality of a living substance, "it indubitably follows," Aristotle says, "that the soul is inseparable from its body, or at any rate certain parts of it are—for the actuality of some of them is nothing but the actualities of their bodily parts." Where Plato holds that the soul is prior in existence to the body, Aristotle holds that soul and body come into existence together when the organism is generated. Where Plato attributes an independent

mode of being to the soul, distinct in character from that of bodies, Aristotle says that "the soul cannot be without a body. Yet it cannot *be* a body; it is not a body, but something relative to a body. That is why it is *in* a body and a body of a definite kind," being nothing more than "the actuality or formulable essence of something that possesses the potentiality of being besouled."

Aquinas is an Aristotelian with regard to soul, but Calvin is a Platonist: "man consists of a body and a soul; meaning by soul, an immortal though created essence, which is his nobler part. Sometimes he is called a spirit . . . When spirit is used by itself it is equivalent to soul."

FURTHER CONSEQUENCES follow from these conflicting conceptions of soul. In the *Timaeus,* Plato advances the view that only the lowest grade of soul—the plant soul—is mortal, in contrast to the souls of animals and men. Aristotle would seem to attribute mortality to every grade of soul. If any exception is to be made, it is only for the human soul because it involves the power of rational thought. Mind or the power to think, he writes, "seems to be a widely different kind of soul, differing as what is eternal from what is perishable."

The critical point is whether thinking, unlike all other psychic powers, is an activity of the soul alone. For the most part, "there seems to be no case in which the soul can act or be acted upon without involving the body . . . Thinking seems the most probable exception; but," Aristotle adds, "if this too proves to be a form of imagination or to be impossible without imagination, it too requires a body as the condition of its existence. If there is any way of acting or being acted upon proper to soul, soul will be capable of separate existence; if there is none, its separate existence is impossible."

Is there any way of acting or being acted upon proper to soul? Aristotle seems to answer this question affirmatively when he says that "insofar as the realities it knows are capable of being separated from their matter, so is it also with the powers of mind." On one interpretation this means that the mind or intellect is as immaterial in its mode of operation as some of its objects are in their mode of being; with the further consequence that what is capable of acting apart from body is also able to exist apart from body. But whether Aristotle's further statement that "mind set free from its present conditions . . . is immortal and eternal" applies to the intellect alone or to the rational soul as a whole, has been disputed by various interpreters. Adopting Aristotle's conception of soul as the form which is the actuality of life in an organic body, Aquinas for one seems to think that the immortality of a rational soul can be demonstrated from the special character of its intellectual powers.

A theory of the soul which regarded it as a simple and incorporeal substance, or as having a being independent of the body, would seem to harmonize more readily with the Christian belief in the human soul's special creation and its individual survival after death. But Aquinas rejects such a theory on the ground that then man would be two substances or two beings, not one; or else if the human person is identified with the soul, man would be a soul using a body rather than a single substance of composite nature. The doctrine of body and soul which holds them to be related as matter and form, preserves the unity of man and, in the opinion of Aquinas, fits the way in which man learns through his senses, experiences passions, and, in thinking, depends upon imagination.

But though he admits that men cannot think without images, Aquinas also insists, contrary to Locke, that thinking, insofar as it involves abstract concepts, cannot be performed by matter. To make matter think is beyond even the power of God. Unlike nourishing or sensing, *understanding* is not and cannot be "the act of a body, nor of any corporeal power."

This theory—that the acts of understanding by which the intellect abstracts and receives universal concepts cannot be accounted for by the motions of the brain—is further discussed in the chapter on UNIVERSAL AND PARTICULAR. Here we are concerned simply to note that, for Aquinas, the fact that the concepts with which men think are universal, means that they are abstracted from matter; and the fact that they are abstracted from matter means that the various acts of understanding must also be imma-

terial—that is, not acts of bodily organs like the brain. To these premises Aquinas adds one further principle, namely, that a thing's mode of being is indicated by its mode of operation. In these terms he concludes that, since the intellect has "an operation *per se* apart from the body," the human soul, which is called rational because of its power of understanding, can have a being *per se* apart from the body. Hence it is "something incorporeal and subsistent."

Nevertheless, according to Aquinas, though the human soul can subsist separately, it belongs to its nature to be embodied, that is, to be the form of a material substance. "The soul, as part of human nature," he writes, "has its natural perfection only as united to the body. Therefore it would have been unfitting for the soul to be created without the body." Furthermore, if the entire nature of man were to be a soul—the soul making "use of the body as an instrument, or as a sailor uses a ship"—there would be no need for the resurrection of the body after the Last Judgment. The Christian dogma of the resurrected body more properly accords, in Aquinas' view, with a conception of soul "united to the body as form to matter"; for, as he says in another place, "if it is natural to the soul to be united to the body, it is unnatural for it to be without a body, and as long as it is without a body it is deprived of its natural perfection."

In the consideration of the relation of body and soul, an opposite estimation of the body's role goes with an opposite theory of the soul's nature. Socrates, in the *Phaedo,* describes the body as the soul's prison house, or worse, the source of the soul's contamination by the impurities of sense and passion. "In this life," he says, "we make the nearest approach to knowledge when we have the least possible intercourse or communion with the body, and are not surfeited with the bodily nature." But complete purification requires "the separation of the soul from the body . . . the release of the soul from the chains of the body." That is why, Socrates tells his friends gathered in the cell where he is to drink the hemlock, "true philosophers are ever seeking to release the soul" and "are always occupied in the practice of dying."

It is also the opinion of Plotinus that it is evil

for the soul to be in the body. But Christian theologians, for the most part, take a contrary view. Aquinas, for example, criticizes Origen for holding that "souls were embodied in punishment of sin." To him there is nothing "of a penal and afflicting nature" in the soul's union with the body. Though Scripture says that "the corruptible body weigheth down the soul, and the earthly tabernacle presseth down the mind," Augustine interprets this to mean, not that the flesh is evil in itself, but that man is beset by sin when "the flesh lusteth against the spirit."

"There is no need, therefore," according to Augustine, "that in our sins and vices we accuse the nature of the flesh to the injury of the Creator, for in its own kind and degree the flesh is good." Man is both body and soul, human nature is a thing of both flesh and spirit, and "he who extols the nature of the soul as the chief good," Augustine continues, "and condemns the nature of the flesh as if it were evil, assuredly is fleshly both in his love of the soul and his hatred of the flesh."

89

Space

INTRODUCTION

On the level of our everyday observations, space and time seem to be the obvious, the common, and the connected properties of physical things. We distinguish things from one another by their position in space, as we mark happenings by the date of their occurrence. The where and when of a thing is often used to identify it, for it is generally agreed that two bodies cannot occupy the same place at the same time, and that at the same time two distinct places cannot be occupied by the same body. According to a theologian like Aquinas, these limitations of space and time apply even to bodiless things, *i.e.,* to angels.

"An angel and a body are said to be in a place," he writes, "in quite a different sense." Whereas a body is in the place which contains it, "an angel is said to be in a corporeal place by application of the angelic power . . . not as being contained, but as somehow containing it." It follows, nevertheless, that at a given time an angel "is not everywhere, nor in several places, but in only one place." Nor does the incorporeality of angels permit more than one angel to be at the same time in the same place. According to the manner in which an angel is at a place—by the action of his power—"there can be only one angel in one place," Aquinas declares, even as there can be only one body in one place at a time.

Location or position in space, and spatial relationships such as higher and lower, nearer and farther, are so familiar and intelligible that they provide terms of reference whereby men speak metaphorically of the moral hierarchy and spiritual distances. The whole of Dante's *The Divine Comedy,* for example, involves a spatial metaphor which sets forth the gradation of sin and the degrees of blessedness in

terms of places beneath the earth and in the heavens above.

As he mounts from sphere to sphere in Paradise, Dante meets Piccarda Donati in the Heaven of the Moon. She explains to him that this place "which appears so lowly," is assigned to those who have violated their vows in some particular. Dante wonders why she and the others do not "desire a more exalted place, to see more." Piccarda replies: "Brother, the power of love quiets our will and makes us wish only for that which we have and gives us no other thirst . . . so that our being thus from threshold to threshold throughout this realm is a joy to all the realm as to the King, who draws our wills to what He wills; and in His will is our peace."

This speech of Piccarda's makes it clear to Dante "how everywhere in Heaven is Paradise, even if the grace of the Supreme Good does not there rain down in one same measure." These different measures of beatitude in the diffusion of God's love and light are represented by the celestial spheres from the earth-adjacent moon to the Crystalline Heaven, the outermost bound of the physical universe, of which Dante says that it "has no other *Where* than the Divine Mind."

When the whole expanse of physical space or the boundary of the universe is considered, Newton no less than Dante conceives the omnipresence and eternity of God as that which somehow encompasses all space and time. God "is not duration or space," Newton writes at the end of the *Mathematical Principles of Natural Philosophy,* "but He endures and is present . . . and by existing always and everywhere, He constitutes duration and space." In the concluding queries of the *Optics,* Newton appears to think of infinite space as the Divine Sensorium in which all things are at once present to God, who "being in all places is more able by His will to move the bodies within His boundless uniform sensorium, and thereby to form and reform the parts of the Universe, than we are by our will to move the parts of our own bodies."

The physicist does not have to turn theologian, however, to be confronted with the mysteries of space. Even without the modern complication of the relation of its three dimensions to time as a fourth dimension, the physical concept of space raises difficulties for analysis.

In the tradition of western thought, conflicting definitions of space seem to result from a fundamental difference in the object being defined—whether it is an inseparable property of bodies, perhaps even identical with unformed matter, or a reality apart from the bodies which move and have their being in it. Sometimes this difference is signified by a difference between the meaning of the word "place" or "extension" and the meaning of "space." It appears also to be involved in the contrast between filled space and empty space (*i.e.,* the void or vacuum); and it bears some relation to Aristotle's distinction between space and place, and to Newton's distinction between absolute and relative space.

The controversial character of space in physical theory may be appreciated in terms of these oppositions in meaning, and the issues which they raise. In addition, physical theory is confronted with the problem of action-at-a-distance (*i.e.,* action through a void or through an ethereal medium), the problem of the infinity of space (or the question of a bounded or unbounded universe), and the distinction between one physical space and the variety of geometric spaces.

Space, which at first seems easily apprehended by sense and susceptible to measurement, becomes upon examination so subtle as to be almost a vanishing object. Reason finds it difficult to say precisely *what* space is in itself, and how it is related to matter and motion. Even the familiar space of ordinary

sense perception seems to have its puzzles. A psychologist like William James is concerned with how the different fields of touch, vision, and hearing coalesce to form the single space of our experience; and in dealing with the process by which we learn to perceive the spatial manifold of positions and directions, he cannot avoid the issue of innate as opposed to acquired space perception. But what for James is the single space of our experience is not, according to Poincaré, the mathematical space of geometry.

PLATO'S THEORY OF SPACE is set forth in the *Timaeus* as part of "the likely story" which Timaeus tells about the production and constitution of the universe. The sensible things which come into being and pass away are, according to him, patterned after the eternal forms. To the eternal patterns and their copies in the world of change, Timaeus finds it necessary to add a third factor in order to account for the physical elements and their generation. This factor, he says, is "difficult to explain and dimly seen ... It is the receptacle, and in a manner the nurse, of all generation." In contrast to the elements which are perpetually changing into and out of one another, the receptacle "never departs from her own nature, and never in any way assumes a form like that of any of the things which enter into her ... The forms which enter into and go out of her are the likenesses of real existences modelled after their patterns in a wonderful and inexplicable manner."

Timaeus distinguishes the three principles as (1) that which comes to be and passes away in the process of generation, (2) that in which the generation takes place, and (3) that which the generated thing resembles and which is its source. He likens the receptacle or "receiving principle to a mother, the source to a father, and the intermediate nature to a child," and adds that "if the model is to take every variety of form, then the matter in which the model is fashioned will not be duly prepared, unless it is formless and free from the impress of any of those shapes which it is hereafter to receive from without ... Wherefore, that which is to receive all forms should have no form ... The mother and receptacle of all created, visible, and in any way sensible things, is not to be termed earth, or air, or fire, or water, or any of their compounds, or any of the elements from which these are derived, but is an invisible and formless being which receives all things, and in some mysterious way partakes of the intelligible, and is most incomprehensible."

This third factor which Timaeus sometimes calls "matter" as well as "receptacle," he also sometimes calls "space." When matter and space are identified with each other under the conception of a receptacle for the forms, they have the characteristics of being absolutely formless and imperceptible to the senses. Nor are they, as are the forms, genuinely intelligible to reason. "The third nature, which is space, and is eternal," Timaeus says, "admits not of destruction and provides a home for all created things, and is apprehended without the help of sense, by a kind of spurious reason, and is hardly real; which we beholding as in a dream, say of all existence that it must of necessity be in some place and occupy a space, but that which is neither in heaven nor on earth has no existence."

The precise meaning of this conception of space is difficult to determine. Does it, for example, find an echo in Plotinus' statement that "space is a container, a container of body; it is the home of such things as consist of isolated parts"? But he also says that space "in a strict sense is unembodied and is not, itself, body," and that "body is not a void," but rather that "the void must be that in which body is placed," seeming thereby to imply that space is essentially the void. The statement in the *Timaeus* that "there can be no such thing as a vacuum," may apply only to the filled space of the created heaven and earth. May it not also be said that space is a void when it is identified with the formless matter of the receptacle prior to creation?

This raises further questions. Is the receptacle space or matter? And is the conception of space in the *Timaeus* rightly interpreted by Aquinas, in commenting on Augustine's reading of "the earth was void and empty" in Genesis 1:2? Augustine holds that by the word "earth" in this passage formless matter is

to be understood. Because of its formlessness, Aquinas writes, "the earth is said to be *void and empty,* or *invisible and shapeless,*" and, he adds, "that is why Plato says matter is place."

HOWEVER THESE QUESTIONS are answered, one thing seems to be clear. Space, functioning as receptacle, can be identified only with matter devoid of form, not with the matter of three-dimensional bodies. The relation of space to matter seems to be differently conceived by Descartes. Space is for him not an antecedent principle involved in the original production of sensible things, but rather—as the extension of bodies—it is inseparable in existence from them. This attitude of Descartes finds its echo in Einstein, whose general theory of relativity is built around the idea that gravitating matter determines the nature of space. Of space itself, Einstein once remarked that "space is not a thing." It is a property which signifies the essence of material substances, as thinking signifies the essence of mind or soul. "By extension," Descartes writes, "we understand whatever has length, breadth, and depth, not inquiring whether it be a real body or merely space." Nevertheless, he goes on to say that "by extension we do not here mean anything distinct and separate from the extended object itself."

Descartes considers the significance of three statements: "*extension occupies place, body possesses extension,* and *extension is not body.*" The first statement, he thinks, means no more than "*that which is extended occupies place.*" The second statement seems to imply that "the meaning of *extension* is not identical with that of *body; yet,*" Descartes insists, "we do not construct two distinct ideas in our imagination, one of body, the other of extension, but merely a single image of extended body; and from the point of the view of the thing it is exactly as if I had said: *body is extended,* or better, *the extended is extended.*" Finally, in the statement that *extension is not body,* the word "extension," according to Descartes, expresses a purely abstract conception—nothing which in itself has any sensible reality. So far as its existence is concerned, the thing conceived as extension cannot be separated from body. Those who think otherwise, Descartes asserts, are involved in "the contradiction of saying that *the same thing is at the same time body and not body.*"

The point is summarized in his *Principles of Philosophy* by the statement that "the nature of matter or of body in its universal aspect, does not consist in being hard, or heavy, or colored . . . but solely in the fact that it is a substance extended in length, breadth, and depth." But, it may be asked, are the dimensions of a body the same as space? Descartes replies that "the same extension which constitutes the nature of a body constitutes the nature of space . . . not only that which is full of body, but also of that which is called a vacuum."

If there were a vacuum, or empty space, extension might be separated from body. This Descartes flatly denies. "As regards a vacuum in the philosophic sense of the word, *i.e.,* a space in which there is no substance, it is evident that such cannot exist, because the extension of space or internal place is not different from that of body." And even "when we take this word vacuum in its ordinary sense," Descartes goes on, "we do not mean a place or space in which there is absolutely nothing, but only a place in which there are none of those things which we expected to find there."

These points made in the *Principles* confirm the identification of three-dimensional space or extension with body which appears in the *Rules for the Direction of the Mind.* They seem to be further confirmed in the *Discourse on the Method* by the reference to "a continuous body, or a space indefinitely extended in length, height or depth" which is "the object of the geometricians." Descartes does not, however, neglect the distinction between space as the extension of body, and place as the position one body occupies in relation to another. According to common usage, he says, the word "place" signifies that "in virtue of which a body is said to be here or there." He objects to those who, like Aristotle, mean by "place" the surrounding surface of a body. Local motion or change of place is not, he argues, a change in the body's surrounding surface, but a change in its relative position.

The most revolutionary change with regard to the idea of space occurred in the 20th century with Einstein's adoption of Hermann Minkowski's four-dimensional space. "The non-mathematician," Einstein writes, "is seized by a mysterious shuddering when he hears of 'four-dimensional' things, by a feeling not unlike that awakened by thoughts of the occult. And yet there is no more commonplace statement than that the world in which we live is a four-dimensional space-time continuum . . . The world of physical phenomena which was briefly called 'world' by Minkowski is naturally four-dimensional in the space-time sense. For it is composed of individual events, each of which is described by four numbers, namely, three space co-ordinates x, y, z and a time co-ordinate, the time-value t." To which Einstein adds: "The four-dimensional mode of consideration of the 'world' is natural on the theory of relativity, since according to this theory time is robbed of its independence."

IT IS PLACE RATHER THAN space which Aristotle seeks to define, and place in the sense of the circumference of a body rather than its position in space. He rejects the notion that place is the extension of a magnitude, for that would, he thinks, identify it with matter. Place belongs to body, not as matter or a property of matter, but as its boundary. It is, Aristotle writes, "the innermost motionless boundary . . . a kind of surface and, as it were, a vessel, *i.e.,* a container of the thing." This boundary is itself made at the surface of a body by a surrounding body or bodies. "If a body has another body outside it and containing it," Aristotle writes, "it is in place, and if not, not."

The consequences of this conception of place are, first, a denial of space in the sense of void or empty place, since place is always "coincident with the thing" contained or bounded; second, a denial of any infinite place, since that would presuppose an actually infinite body—to Aristotle, an impossibility; and third, the conclusion that the whole universe itself does not have a place, for outside the outermost heaven which bounds the world, there can be no containing body by which the universe is bounded.

Aristotle explains that by "heaven" he means "the extreme circumference of the whole"—a whole "composed of all natural perceptible body." In describing space, Einstein discussed the possibility of a "finite" and yet "unbounded" universe. This has a verbal similarity to Aristotle's conception of a world finite in body or matter, yet unbounded, *i.e.,* without anything outside itself to determine or define its boundary. However, Einstein had in mind a possible cosmology in which a light ray, when emitted in the universe, would eventually return to its point of origin. Experiments have not yet been able to decide whether Einstein's cosmology applies to our universe or whether our universe is actually infinite.

Aristotle's view of the world seems to be directly opposed to that of the ancient atomists. For them, the whole of matter is discontinuous, existing in indivisible units or atoms, each of which is a plenum—that is, a unit of matter absolutely continuous without void in it—but between which there is void or empty space. For Aristotle, the material world as a whole is a plenum, *i.e.,* continuous body without void. Hence if by "space" is meant not place but void—a bodyless interval between or within bodies—there is no space. Aristotle considers the arguments of Democritus that without void local motion would be impossible, but he thinks "there is no necessity for there being a void if there is movement."

Following Democritus, Lucretius gives another reason for positing void or empty space. As the indivisibility of the simple bodies or atoms consists in their absolute solidity—their lack of void—so the divisibility of composite bodies derives from their being constituted by both atoms and void. "Where space exists, or what we call the void," Lucretius writes, "Matter cannot be found; what substance holds / Void cannot occupy. So atoms are / Solid and therefore voidless . . . Were there nothing which we label *void,* / All would be solid substance; and again, / Were there no substance to fill up the spaces, / All would be void and emptiness."

For Aristotle, in contrast, the divisibility of matter seems to depend upon its being continuous. On his view, the composite body,

constituted by atoms separated from one another by void, is not divisible, but is already actually divided; whereas the very thing which Lucretius regards as indivisible because it is continuous—the voidless atom—is for Aristotle divisible. To call an atom divisible is, of course, to deny that it is atomic or, in the language of Lucretius, an uncuttable bit of "solid singleness."

Thus diametrically opposite theories of space and place seem to be connected with opposite theories of matter or body. Space as the empty interval or void *between* solid bodies goes along with atomism, whereas place as "the boundary of the containing body at which it is in contact with the contained body" goes along with the theory of the world as a material plenum.

The atomic theory and the plenum theory are opposed in one other fundamental respect concerning space. According to Aristotle, the impossibility of an actually infinite body makes the largest place finite. According to Lucretius, the infinite number of atoms requires an infinite space. Asking whether void or space must have "finite limits or . . . reach / Unmeasurable in deep wide boundlessness," Lucretius answers that "the universe is limitless, unbounded / In any of its areas." His argument seems to be like Aristotle's for an "unbounded universe." Since there can be "nothing beyond the sum of things," writes Lucretius, "therefore that sum is infinite, limitless." But where Aristotle's meaning seems to be that the universe has no place, since all places are inside it, Lucretius appears to mean that empty space extends infinitely in all directions.

MODERN ATOMISTS like Newton and Locke hold a theory of space which accords with the view of matter existing in discontinuous units, separated by intervals of emptiness. Newton's distinction, for example, between absolute and relative space acknowledges a space that is relative to bodies, but also affirms an absolutely independent space, which has being in separation from matter or bodies. "Absolute space, in its own nature, without relation to anything external," he writes, "remains always similar and immovable. Relative space is some movable dimension or measure of the absolute spaces, which our senses determine by its position to bodies and which is commonly taken for immovable space." As for place in distinction from space, Newton holds that it is "a part of space which a body takes up, and is according to the space, either absolute or relative." In opposing Aristotle's view, he adds that place is "not the situation, nor the external surface of the body. For the places of equal solids are always equal; but their surfaces, by reason of their dissimilar figures, are often unequal."

Locke also distinguishes between space and place, the one consisting in "the relation of distance between any two bodies or points," the other in "the relation of distance betwixt any thing and any two or more points which are considered as keeping the same distance one with another and, so considered, as at rest." With this conception of place, he holds in apparent agreement with Aristotle that "we can have no idea of the place of the universe, though we can of all the parts of it." Yet he goes on to say that what lies beyond the universe is "one uniform space or expansion, wherein the mind finds no variety or marks."

This seems to indicate that Locke's idea of space, like that of Lucretius, conceives an infinite void. "Those who assert the impossibility of space existing without matter must," he writes, "make body infinite." Furthermore, "those who dispute for or against a vacuum, do thereby confess that they have distinct ideas of vacuum and plenum, *i.e.*, that they have an idea of extension void of solidity, though they deny its existence, or else they dispute about nothing at all. For they who so much alter the signification of words, as to call extension, body, and consequently make the whole essence of body to be nothing but pure extension, must talk absurdly whenever they speak of vacuum, since it is impossible for extension to be without extension: for vacuum, whether we affirm or deny it, signifies space without body, whose very existence no one can deny to be possible who will not make matter infinite, and take from God a power to annihilate any particle of it."

Precisely because he thinks no one can affirm an infinite body, and because he conceives space to be a void, distinct from bodies, Locke finds it necessary to affirm the infinity of space. "I would ask," he says, "whether if God placed a man at the extremity of corporeal beings, he could not stretch his hand beyond his body. If he could, then he would put his arm where there was before space without body." Furthermore, if "it be impossible for any particle of matter to move but into empty space, the same possibility of a body's moving into a void space, beyond the utmost bounds of body, as well as into a void space interspersed amongst bodies, will always remain clear and evident . . . So that, wherever the mind places itself by any thought, either amongst or remote from all bodies, it can, in this uniform idea of space, no where find any bounds, any end; and so must necessarily conclude it . . . to be actually infinite."

IT MAY SEEM PARADOXICAL that pure space—space existing without matter—is denied by one who also denies the existence of matter. "When I speak of pure or empty space," Berkeley writes, "it is not to be supposed that the word 'space' stands for an idea distinct from or conceivable without body or motion." What is meant, he suggests, is merely that the resistance one body gives to another in motion is absent when space is relatively empty. But this is always relative. "In proportion as the resistance is lesser or greater," Berkeley says, "the space is more or less *pure*." There would be absolutely pure space only if all bodies other than his own were annihilated. "If that, too, were annihilated," Berkeley concludes, "then there could be no motion, and consequently no Space."

All these contradictions concerning space enter into Kant's statement of the first cosmological antinomy, in which the thesis that the world is limited with regard to space and the antithesis that the world is infinite in space seem to be equally susceptible to proof—and so to disproof! Both alternatives violate our empirical concepts.

If space "is *infinite* and unlimited," Kant writes, "it is *too large* for every possible empirical concept. If it is *finite* and limited, you have a perfect right to ask what determines that limit. Empty space is not an independent correlate of things, and cannot be a final condition, still less an empirical condition forming part of possible experience—for how can there be experience of what is absolutely void? But in order to produce an absolute totality in an empirical synthesis, it is always requisite that the unconditioned should be an empirical concept. Thus it follows that a *limited world* would be *too small* for your concept."

Space itself, however, is for Kant "not an empirical concept which has been derived from external experience." Rather it "is a necessary representation *a priori* forming the very foundation of all external intuitions" and, as Kant explains in his *Prolegomena,* it establishes geometry as an *a priori* science. "Space is nothing but the form of all phenomena of the external senses; it is the subjective condition of our sensibility, without which no external intuition is possible for us . . . Nothing which is seen in space is a thing by itself," nor is "space a form of things supposed to belong to them by themselves." (This is exactly Einstein's view.) The external objects which we perceive in space "are nothing but representations of our senses, the form of which is space."

So far as the experience of space is concerned, James seems to take an opposite view. Time and space relations, he says, "are impressed from without" and "*stamp copies of themselves within.*" To the Kantian theory that space is "a *quality produced* out of the inward resources of the mind, to envelope sensations which, as given originally, are not spatial," James replies that he can find "no introspective experience of mentally producing or creating space."

He proposes two other alternatives: "either (1) there is no spatial *quality* of sensation at all, and space is a mere symbol of succession; or (2) there is an *extensive quality given immediately* in certain particular sensations." The second seems to James best suited to explain the development of our perceptions of space, and he does not think it inconsistent with the *a priori* or nonempirical character of geometry,

whose necessary truths refer to ideal objects, not to experienced things in physical space.

THE CHAPTER ON MATHEMATICS considers the relation of the postulates of diverse geometries to the diversity of Euclidean and non-Euclidean spaces, such as that of the flat plane, the surface of a sphere, and the surface of a pseudosphere. Just as different parallel postulates select different spaces for geometric construction, so a postulate like Euclid's concerning the equality of all right angles seems to assume a uniformity of space which permits geometric figures to be transposed without alteration. "If translation through space warped or magnified forms," James remarks, "then the relations of equality, etc., would always have to be expressed with a position-qualification added."

Confronted with a variety of purely mathematical spaces, the physicist is concerned with the problem of which geometry is, as Einstein says, in "correspondence with a 'real' object," or true of the real world. "According to the general theory of relativity, the geometrical properties of space are not independent," Einstein writes, "but are determined by matter." It follows that our assumptions about the distribution of matter determine the character of the world's space, or, more precisely, space and time, or space-time. In the general theory of relativity, space and time become inseparable in strong gravitational fields.

On the assumption of a world "not inhabited by matter everywhere," in whose infinite space "the average density of matter would necessarily be *nil,*" Einstein says we can imagine "a quasi-Euclidean universe" analogous to "a surface which is irregularly curved in its individual parts, but which nowhere departs appreciably from a plane: something like the rippled surface of a lake." But if the "average density of matter . . . differs from zero, however small may be that difference, then the universe cannot be quasi-Euclidean." It would be spherical (or elliptical) if the matter were uniformly distributed; but "since in reality the detailed distribution of matter is not uniform," Einstein concludes that "the real universe will deviate in individual parts from the spherical, *i.e.,* the universe will be quasi-spherical. But it will be necessarily finite."

The nature of the actual space-time of the universe is determined by the density of matter in it. At the present time, this is not known precisely. However, theoretical prejudice favors a universe which is both essentially Euclidean in character and closed. Experiments are not inconsistent with this possibility.

Defining a vacuum as "a space empty of all bodies known to the senses," Pascal insists that "there is as much difference between nothingness and space, as there is between empty space and a material body," so that "empty space occupies the mean between matter and nothingness." Evangelista Torricelli's experiments with a vacuum seem to him complete proof against the disciples of Aristotle, for they upset the belief that "nature abhors a vacuum."

Gilbert's observations on magnetic influences, Newton's observations on the transmission of light and heat as well as gravitational pull, and Faraday's on electrical phenomena, all seem to admit the possibility of action-at-a-distance, or through a vacuum. But the question remains whether the so-called physical vacuum is an absolute void or merely empty of "all bodies known to the senses." Contemporary quantum theory confirms Pascal's view that there is no such thing as a vacuum in nature, if by vacuum is meant a volume of space devoid of matter.

"Is not the heat of the warm room conveyed through the *vacuum*," Newton asks, "by the vibrations of a much subtiler medium than air which after the air was drawn out remained in the *vacuum?* And is not this medium the same with that medium by which light is refracted and reflected, and by whose vibrations light communicates heat to bodies? . . . And is not this medium exceedingly more rare and subtile than the air, and exceedingly more elastic and active? And does it not readily pervade all bodies? And is it not (by its elastic force) expanded through all the heavens?"

Huygens also refers to an ethereal matter as the medium for the propagation of light. "One will see," he writes, "that it is not the same that serves for the propagation of sound . . . It is not the same air, but another kind of matter in which light spreads; since if the air is removed from the vessel, the light does not cease to traverse it as before." But this ethereal medium, without which bodies would act at a distance upon one another—gravitationally, magnetically, electrically—through an absolute void, seems to have contrary properties. It is not only "subtiler" than air, but, as Newton suggests, it may be "denser than quick-silver or gold," since "planets and comets, and all gross bodies perform their motions more freely, and with less resistance in this aethereal medium than in any fluid, which fills all space adequately without leaving any pores." And, in still another place, he asks: "What is there in places almost empty of matter, and whence is it that the Sun and Planets gravitate towards one another, without dense matter between them?"

Whatever may be thought of the ether as a physical hypothesis (it is dispensed with entirely in Einstein's theory of relativity), the problem still remains whether action can take place at a distance through a void or must employ what Faraday calls "*physical* lines of force" through filled space. Faraday thinks the evidences support the latter alternative for both electricity and magnetism. He quotes a letter from Newton to Richard Bentley to show that Newton was "an unhesitating believer in physical lines of gravitating force."

In that letter, posthumously discovered, Newton says: "That gravity should be innate, inherent and essential to matter, so that one body may act upon another at a distance through a *vacuum,* without the mediation of anything else, by and through which their action and force may be conveyed from one to another, is to me so great an absurdity, that I believe no man who has in philosophical matters a competent faculty of thinking, can ever fall into it."

Along with dispensing with the ether, Einstein also dispensed with Newton's notion of absolute space and time. Implicit in Newton's scheme was the postulate that simultaneity was absolute. Two events, Newton claimed, that appeared simultaneous to any pair of observers would so appear to all observers, moving or not.

Einstein also argued that this ignored both the finite speed of light and the actual way in which simultaneous measurements were made. If these are correctly accounted for, observers moving relative to each other no longer can agree on the simultaneity of events. This leads to the relativity of both space and time. Moving clocks go more slowly and moving rulers contract. These effects have now been routinely observed in laboratory experiments.

90

State

INTRODUCTION

Is man gregarious in the same sense as other animals are? Is he, unlike other social animals, the only political animal? Does man pattern the state after his own nature, or does he, in imitation of the angels, try to live up to a "city in the skies"—a model of rationality or a utopian illusion? According to the way such questions are answered, different theories of the state develop in the tradition of western thought.

But it is not only the view man takes of his social nature which affects his view of society or the state. His conception of the state is also colored by his understanding of man's place in nature and by his understanding of man's relation to God. On one view the state is ordered to the service of man; on another, man is thought to be a creature of the state, and the state is made God; on still another, man—like Antigone in Sophocles' play—seems to be torn between serving the state and serving God.

If man admits anything to be his superior, he acknowledges his inferiority only to God or to the state. That the idea of God and the idea of the state compete for maximum attention in the tradition of western thought is a significant and readily intelligible fact. That the word "sovereign," which connotes *absolute supremacy,* has both political and religious significance throws further light on this rivalry. It immediately suggests all the issues of church and state, of the spiritual and the temporal power, of the city of God and the city of man.

Even without the aura of divinity, the state, in the conception of many writers, assumes by comparison with the individual man the proportions of the greatest living thing on earth. For Plato it is the counterpart of the human soul, many times magnified. For Aristotle it is like an organic whole to which the individual belongs, just as his own arm or leg belongs to him as an organic part. For Hobbes it is the body politic—that Leviathan which dwarfs its members. For Rousseau it is the corporate person, having a general will more perfect than the individual will—infallible, or almost infallible. When to these images of the state is added the highest transfiguration—that by which the state becomes, according to Hegel, the image of God on earth or the embodiment of Absolute Spirit—the greatness of the state cannot be magnified further.

Huizinga refers to this when he notes that "medieval political speculation is imbued to the marrow with the idea of a structure of society based upon distinct orders" and that each of these orders "represents a divine institution, an element of the organism of Creation emanating from the will of God, constituting an actual entity, and being, at bottom, as venerable as the angelic hierarchy."

THE PASSAGES IN WHICH these conceptions first appear are among the most famous in the literature of the theory of the state. In *The Republic,* Socrates proposes that "we inquire into the nature of justice and injustice, first as they appear in the State and secondly in the individual, proceeding from the greater to the lesser and comparing them." After the structure of the state has been examined in terms of its constituent classes and their functions or relations to one another, Socrates returns to the individual. We may assume, he says, that "he has the same three principles in his own soul which are found in the state"; and in another place he adds that "there appear to be as many forms of the soul as there are distinct forms of the State."

Whereas Plato analogizes the social classes in the state with the parts of the soul, Aristotle compares the state in relation to the individual with the body in relation to its members. "The state is by nature clearly prior to the family and to the individual," Aristotle writes, "since the whole is of necessity prior to the part; for example, if the whole body be destroyed, there will be no foot or hand, except in an equivocal sense . . . The proof that the state is a creation of nature and prior to the individual is that the individual, when isolated, is not self-sufficing; and therefore he is like a part in relation to the whole."

The analogical conception of the state takes a different turn with Hobbes. The state is a work of art, not a creation of nature. "Nature (the art whereby God hath made and governs the world)," says Hobbes, "is by the art of man, as in many other things, so in this also imitated, that it can make an artificial animal." The machines men make—"engines that move themselves by springs and wheels as doth a watch"—seem to Hobbes to "have an artificial life." But "art goes yet further, imitating that rational and most excellent work of Nature, *man*. For by art is created that great Leviathan called a Commonwealth, or State (in Latin, *Civitas*), which is but an artificial man, though of greater stature and strength than the natural, for whose protection and defence it was intended; and in which the sovereignty is an artificial soul, as giving life and motion to the whole body."

Hobbes also speaks of the multitude being "united in one person" as the "generation of that great Leviathan, or rather, to speak more reverently, of that mortal god to which we owe, under the immortal God, our peace and defence." It is both divine and human, for "that which is compounded of the powers of most men, united by consent in one person, natural or civil" is, according to Hobbes, "the greatest of human powers."

Rousseau has a number of different names for the "moral and collective body" formed by the association of individuals. "This public person," he says, "formerly took the name

city, and now takes that of *Republic* or *body politic;* it is called by its members *State* when passive, *Sovereign* when active, and *Power* when compared with others like itself." But Rousseau's primary emphasis seems to be upon the personality of the State; it is a corporate person, with moral qualities and intellectual faculties. He refers repeatedly to the State "as a *persona ficta*" and as "a moral person whose life is in the union of its members."

Many of these comparisons or analogies recur in Hegel's theory of the state. But for Hegel they are no longer metaphors, they are the elements of a literal definition. "The state is an organism," says Hegel. It is the organic whole no part of which can have a separate life. As "occurs with life in the physical organism," he writes, "life is present in every cell" and "separated from that life, every cell dies. This is the same as the ideality of every single class, power, and Corporation as soon as they have the impulse to subsist and be independent. It is with them as with the belly in the organism. It, too, asserts its independence, but at the same time its independence is set aside and it is sacrificed and absorbed into the whole."

But the state is not merely a living organism. "To the mature state," says Hegel, "thought and consciousness essentially belong . . . As high as mind stands above nature, so high does the state stand above physical life. Man must therefore venerate the state as the divine on earth, and observe that if it is difficult to comprehend nature, it is infinitely harder to understand the state." In saying this Hegel seems to go beyond analogy to the assertion of a definition. "The march of God in the world, that is what the state is," he declares. "The basis of the state is the power of the reason actualizing itself as will. In considering the Idea of the state, we must not have our eyes on particular states or on particular institutions. Instead we must consider the Idea, this actual God, by itself."

To those who object that the state is finite, Hegel replies that "to hold that mind on earth, *i.e.,* the state, is only a finite mind, is a one-sided view, since there is nothing irrational about actuality. Of course, a bad state is worldly and finite and nothing else. But the rational state is inherently infinite." As simply stated by Hegel in the Introduction to his *The Philosophy of History*, "the State is the Divine idea as it exists on Earth."

THE DIVERSE CONCEPTIONS of the state raise major issues in political theory concerning the origin of the state and the ends it serves, in both of which is involved the problem of the individual's relation to the state. That problem is touched on in the chapter on CITIZEN, and wherever the problem of the common good or the general welfare is discussed. Here the question whether the state is made for man or man for the state, whether the state subordinates the individual in every phase of his life or only in those matters wherein the public welfare takes precedence over private interests, serves critically to test the practical significance of different theories of the state. Here also questions concerning the relation of the family to the state—discussed from the point of view of the domestic community in the chapter on FAMILY—throw light on the nature and origin of the political community.

The word "community" and its synonym "society" seem to be more inclusive in meaning than "state." The family and the state are both communities—associations of individuals for a common purpose and sharing in a common life. The word "state" is customarily used only for the developed political society—whether a city-state, a feudal state, or a nation-state; the word "society" usually covers the tribal community, the village, or any community which is politically primitive and has some of the characteristics of a large family. In addition there are within the state, at least in its modern formation, many organized groups which deserve the name "society"—economic corporations and other associations, religious, educational, professional, recreational; and more comprehensive than any particular political community are the cities of God and man which, in Augustine's conception of them, are not to be identified with either the Church or the State.

With the rise of the science of sociology in our time, the idea of society has come to be re-garded as more general than that of state. But in the tradition of the great books, particularly those of political theory, the state seems to be considered the epitome of human society. All other forms of association are, for the most part, discussed only in their relation to the state, either as the antecedents from which the state develops, or as the subordinate organizations which it includes, or sometimes, as in the case of the church, a distinct but coordinate community.

The nature of society in general and the problem of different types of social organization and development are not treated in the great books except in their bearing on the family, the church, or the state—the three communities which seem to be taken as representative or basic. Hence there is no chapter on society or community as such. What for modern sociology is a unified subject matter here divides into a number of related yet distinct ideas—the domestic community being treated in the chapter on FAMILY, the religious community in the chapter on RELIGION, the various forms of economic organization in the chapters on LABOR and WEALTH. In this chapter, therefore, we shall confine our attention to the specifically political community, both in itself and in relation to these other communities or social groups.

CONCEIVED IN POLITICAL terms, the problems of the state would seem to be inseparable from the problems of government. Yet the ideas of state and government may be separated to the extent that one signifies the political community as a whole and the other the organization of its members according to relationships of ruler and ruled. Furthermore, the state may in one sense remain the same while in another it changes with changes in its form of government.

Some writers, like Aristotle and Hegel, tend to identify state and government. Aristotle, for example, says that "the sameness of the state consists chiefly in the sameness of its constitution." Others, like Locke and Rousseau, seem to regard government as part of the state, the chief institution of a civil society or political community, but definitely a means for securing the ends for which the state is formed. For Locke government is primarily the legislative power, for Rousseau it is "the supreme administration, the legitimate exercise of the executive power," but for both it is a representative body—an organ of the whole body politic.

Insofar as the great political theorists distinguish problems of the external relation of states with one another from those which concern the internal organization of the state, and the relation of the state to its own members, they also tend to distinguish state from government. Hegel's distinction between external and internal sovereignty, for example, conceives the whole community as a sovereign state in relation to other communities and the state as a sovereign government in relation to its own members.

Such questions of sovereignty, or more generally of the relation of states to one another, belong to this chapter as well as to the chapter on WAR AND PEACE; but the theory of government is for the most part treated elsewhere—in the chapters on GOVERNMENT and CONSTITUTION, and in all the chapters dealing with the special forms of government. Still other problems of government, which have a bearing on the nature of the state, its powers, and its limits, are dealt with in the chapters on JUSTICE and LAW.

THAT IT IS SOMEHOW natural for men to associate politically is generally affirmed, even by those who also think the state is artificial or conventional. No one takes either of the possible extreme positions: that the state as a purely voluntary association is without any basis at all in man's nature and needs; or that the state, like the beehive and the ant mound, is purely a production of instinct.

Saying that "man is by nature a political animal," Aristotle goes on to remark that "man is more of a political animal than bees or other gregarious animals." But the difference Aristotle points out between man and other social animals may make man the *only* political animal. It consists in the fact that man, being "the only animal . . . endowed with the gift of speech," can communicate with his fellows concerning "the expedient and inexpedient, and therefore likewise the just and the unjust." What characterizes human associations, according to Aristotle, is that they are built upon a shared sense of the expedient and the just. "Justice," he writes, "is the bond of men in states."

Hobbes also distinguishes between human and animal societies, but seems to interpret the distinction differently "Bees and ants live sociably one with another," he says, "and yet have no other direction than their particular judgements and appetites; nor speech, whereby one of them can signify to another what he thinks expedient for the common benefit." Inquiring "why mankind cannot do the same"—that is, live sociably without government and law—Hobbes offers a number of explanations, of which the last is that "the agreement of these creatures is natural; that of men is by covenant only, which is artificial: and therefore it is no wonder if there be somewhat else required, besides covenant, to make their agreement constant and lasting; which is common power to keep them in awe and to direct their actions to the common benefit."

But though Hobbes calls the state artificial because he holds it to be the product of a contract, he does not deny the natural necessity which drives men to the creation of a commonwealth. Man quits the state of nature, which is a "war of every man against every man," to achieve self-preservation, or at least to enjoy the security of civil peace and the freedom from fear of violence.

As natural as it may be for men to be "in that condition which is called war" when "they live without a common power to keep them all in awe," it is equally natural, according to Hobbes, for men to seek peace. "The passions that incline men to peace are: fear of death; desire of such things as are necessary to commodious living; and a hope by their industry to obtain them. And reason suggesteth convenient articles of peace upon which men may be drawn to agreement." The commonwealth is therefore natural, to the extent that man's needs and passions require it and man's reason recognizes certain natural laws for constructing it.

The state is naturally necessary, not as the

effect of instinctive determinations, but as the rationally determined means to an end. If the end the state serves were not naturally sought, or if there were any other means which reason could devise for accomplishing that end, the state would be purely conventional—and dispensable. "The final cause, end, or design of men in the introduction of that restraint upon themselves (in which we see them live in commonwealths) is," according to Hobbes, "the sight of their own preservation and of a more contented life thereby."

In this main particular Aristotle's account of the origin of the state seems to be the same. Though he does not attribute its formation to a contract, and does not make fear the predominant motive, he does regard the state as natural *only because* of its indispensability as a means for achieving the ends men naturally seek. The family is natural, Aristotle suggests, because it is necessary for the perpetuation of the race and "for the supply of men's everyday wants." When men aim "at something more than the supply of daily needs, the first society to be formed is the village"—normally, an association of families. And "when several villages are united in a single complete community, large enough to be nearly or quite self-sufficing, the state comes into existence, originating in the bare needs of life, and continuing in existence for the sake of a good life. Therefore, if the earlier forms of society are natural, so is the state."

The implication seems to be that if men were not naturally impelled to seek a better life than the family or the tribal community can provide—in other words, if the family or village satisfied all of man's natural needs for society—the larger community, the state, would be neither natural nor necessary. That man is by nature a political animal does not, therefore, mean that men have always and everywhere lived in states.

Aristotle refers to the man who lives apart from society, describing the natural outcast— "the 'tribeless, lawless, heartless one' whom Homer denounces"—as "a lover of war." He conceives the state as coming into being subsequent to more primitive forms of social life, each type of community being successively

"established with a view to some good, for mankind always act in order to obtain that which they think good." Since he thinks that the state "aims at good in a greater degree than any other, and at the highest good," he praises the man "who first founded the state" as "the greatest of benefactors."

FOR ARISTOTLE, THEN, there seems to be no inconsistency in saying that the state is as natural as the family and also that it is the result of a convention, *i.e.*, a voluntary association of men. Nor does there seem to be any inconsistency between Hobbes's view that the state is produced by a "covenant of every man with every man" and his understanding of the naturalness of the state in terms of the impulses which lead men to enter into this contract. The same double note appears in the account of the state's origin which Locke, Rousseau, and Kant give. The issue raised by the contract theory thus seems to turn on the interpretation of the original convention—whether or not it has legal significance and what obligations or limitations it imposes.

Where Hobbes, for example, interprets the contract as creating, along with the commonwealth, a sovereign person having absolute power, Locke seems to make majority rule the legal consequence of the original compact. God "designed man for a sociable creature," according to Locke, "with an inclination and under a necessity to have fellowship with those of his own kind." Yet even what he calls "the first society . . . between man and wife," Locke says, "is made by a voluntary compact." It makes no difference to Locke's theory whether political societies develop by expansion from the family (which he takes to be the normal course of events) or result from a voluntary association of independent men.

In either case, political as distinguished from domestic society does not begin until "every man, by consenting with others to make one body politic under one government, puts himself under an obligation to every one of that society, to submit to the determination of the majority . . . This is done by barely agreeing to unite into one political society, which is all the compact that is, or needs be, between the individuals that enter into or make up a commonwealth. And thus that which begins and actually constitutes any political society is nothing but the consent of any number of free men capable of a majority to unite and incorporate into such a society."

If it is "that, and that only, which did or could give beginning to any lawful government in the world," it seems to be equally evident to Locke that "absolute monarchy, which by some men is counted the only government in the world, is indeed inconsistent with civil society, and so can be no form of civil government at all."

Though Rousseau says that the most ancient of all societies, the family, is "the only one that is natural," he qualifies this by adding that it remains natural only so long as the children need the family for their preservation. If the members of the family remain united thereafter, "they continue so no longer naturally, but voluntarily; and the family itself is then maintained only by convention." By the same criterion, civil society would seem to be natural, at least on Rousseau's own supposition that "the obstacles in the way of their preservation in the state of nature" are greater than the power of isolated individuals or families to maintain themselves, and so "the human race would perish unless it changed its manner of existence."

Rousseau, furthermore, explicitly denies that the transition from a state of nature to a state of civil society can be treated as a historical fact. It is a hypothesis "calculated to explain the nature of things, [rather] than to ascertain their actual origin." The social contract, which Rousseau sometimes calls the "first convention," is, therefore, the legal, not the historical, origin of the state. As he formulates the compact, "each of us puts his person and all his power in common under the supreme direction of the general will, and, in our corporate capacity, we receive each member as an indivisible part of the whole."

Though "all the qualities of the general will" may "reside in the majority," so that the general will can be discovered by a majority vote, unanimity is required to create the sovereign body politic, with the right as well as the power to compel "whoever refuses to obey the general will." Rousseau points out that "the law of majority voting is itself something established by convention, and presupposes unanimity, on one occasion at least." To this extent Rousseau agrees with Locke about the juridical significance of the original convention or the universal consent which establishes a civil society; and just as Locke calls absolute monarchy inconsistent with the very nature of the state, so Rousseau uses the words "republic" and "body politic" interchangeably. "To be legitimate," he writes, "the government must be, not one with the sovereign, but its minister."

But Rousseau identifies government with the executive, rather than primarily with the legislative as Locke does. He therefore denies that the original convention institutes government as well as the body politic itself—"the Sovereign having no force other than the legislative power." In consequence, Rousseau and Locke differ somewhat in their discussion of the dissolution of government as distinguished from the dissolution of society, or the death of the body politic. Rousseau regards no law as irrevocable, "not excluding the social compact itself; for if all the citizens assembled of one accord to break the compact, it is impossible to doubt that it would be very legitimately broken."

According to Kant, "a state is the union of a number of men under juridical laws"—the opposite of the state of nature, "in which there is no distributive justice." It is incumbent on men, says Kant, "to accept the principle that it is necessary to leave the state of nature, in which every one follows his own inclinations, and to form a union of all those who cannot avoid coming into reciprocal communication, and thus subject themselves in common to the external restraint of public compulsory laws."

Kant refers to this principle as the "postulate of public right" which obliges "all men to enter into the relations of a civil state of society." The state thus seems to be both necessary and voluntary; for though he says that "the act by which a people is represented as constituting itself into a state is termed *the original contract*," yet he also adds that "this is properly only an outward mode of representing the idea by which the rightfulness of the process of organizing the constitution may be made conceivable."

AGAINST ALL THESE notions of the original contract, Hegel, criticizing Kant's treatment of marriage under the concept of contract, says that "it is equally far from the truth to ground the nature of the state on the contractual relation, whether the state is supposed to be a contract of all with all, or of all with the monarch and the government." Contract, according to Hegel, belongs to the sphere of "relationships concerning private property generally." Hence "the intrusion of this contractual relation . . . into the relation between the individual and the state has been productive of the greatest confusion in both constitutional law and public life."

A contract, Hegel explains, "springs from a person's arbitrary will, an origin which marriage too has in common with contract. But the case is quite different with the state; it does not lie with an individual's arbitrary will to separate himself from the state, because we are already citizens of the state by birth. The rational end of man is life in the state, and if there is no state there, reason at once demands that one be founded. Permission to enter a state or leave it must be given by the state; this then is not a matter which depends on an individual's arbitrary will and therefore the state does not rest on contract, for contract presupposes arbitrariness. It is false to maintain that the foundation of the state is something at the option of all its members. It is nearer the truth to say that it is absolutely necessary for every individual to be a citizen."

Hegel dismisses all questions concerning historical origins in general or particular as "no concern of the Idea of the state." In the Idea itself, its antecedents are to be found. The family and civil society are the earlier—logical—moments in the development of the Idea of the State. "Civil society," Hegel writes, "is the [state of] difference which intervenes between the family and the state, even if its formation follows later in time than that of the state." The social contract theory applies only to what he calls "civil society," by which he means the modern conception of the state "as a unity which is only a partnership . . . Many modern constitutional lawyers," Hegel goes on, "have been able to bring within their purview no theory of the state but this. In civil society each member is his own end" and, "except by contract with others, he cannot attain the whole compass of his ends, and therefore these others are means to the end of the particular members."

In another place, Hegel describes civil society as a system of complete interdependence for the attainment of selfish ends, "wherein the livelihood, happiness, and legal status of one man is interwoven with the livelihood, happiness, and rights of all." In still another, he observes that only when the state is confused with civil society, only when "its specific end is laid down as the security and protection of property and personal freedom," does "the interest of the individuals as such become the ultimate end of their association." Whence "it follows that membership in the state is something optional. But the state's relation to the individual is quite different from this. Since the state is mind objectified, it is only as one of its members that the individual himself has objectivity, genuine individuality, and an ethical life."

The unity of the state, unlike that of civil society, is, according to Hegel, "an absolute unmoved end in itself, in which freedom comes into its supreme right . . . This final end has supreme right against the individual, whose supreme duty is to be a member of the state."

IT DOES NOT SEEM to be an inevitable corollary of the social contract theory that the state be conceived as serving the private interests of individuals. "The welfare of the state," Kant declares, "is its own highest good." It is not to be understood merely as "the individual *well-being* and *happiness* of the citizens of the state; for—as Rousseau asserts—this end may perhaps be more agreeably and more desirably attained in the state of nature." Kant and Locke both affirm a social contract, but where Kant makes the safety of the republic itself the highest law (*salus reipublicae suprema lex*),

Locke makes it the security of the people (*salus populi*).

"The reason why men enter into society is the preservation of their property," writes Locke. The property of the individual is insecure in a state of nature; to avoid this insecurity "men unite into societies that they may have the united strength of the whole society to secure and defend their properties." When Locke says that the chief end of civil society is "the preservation of property," he does not refer solely to economic goods, but to all the goods to which he thinks man has a natural right—"his life, liberty, and estate." Men would not quit the state of nature, he writes, "were it not to preserve their lives, liberties and fortunes, and by stated rules of right and property to secure their peace and quiet."

In the light of Locke's conception of "property," his position resembles Hobbes's statement of the end which men seek in forming a commonwealth: "to live peaceably amongst themselves and be protected against other men" and to get "themselves out from that miserable condition of war" in which life is "solitary, poor, nasty, brutish, and short."

It seems to be in a different sense of property that Rousseau holds that "the foundation of the social compact is property; and its first condition, that everyone should be maintained in the peaceful possession of what belongs to him." Restricting "property" to economic possessions, Rousseau asks, "Are not all the advantages of society for the rich and powerful?" Society, he observes, "provides a powerful protection for the immense possessions of the rich, and hardly leaves the poor man in quiet possession of the cottage he builds with his own hands." Tawney agrees, pointing out, with reference to the 18th century, that "No one has forgotten the opposition offered in the name of the rights of property to factory legislation, to housing reform, to interference with the adulteration of goods, even to the compulsory sanitation of private houses."

This and Adam Smith's statement that "civil government, so far as it is instituted for the security of property, is in reality instituted for the defence of the rich against the poor, or of those who have some property against those who have none at all," seem to anticipate the Marxist view of the state as the bulwark of property rights and an instrument of class oppression. If the protection of property and the maintenance of economic inequalities is the sole purpose of the state, then the ultimate resolution of the class war in favor of a classless society will, in the opinion of Marx and Engels, be accompanied by what they call "the withering away of the state"—an atrophy from loss of function.

But even in a classless society, the state would not cease to function if its end were to secure not merely the individual's wealth, but his whole well-being. Then, however, we must face another question—whether the happiness of the individual is the end of the state. Plato, for example, seems to answer this question in opposite ways.

In the *Protagoras*, it is said that "the desire for self-preservation gathered men into cities." This is part of the Promethean legend of the origin of civilization. As told by Aeschylus— and in a similar account of early history by Lucretius—the story intimates that men contract to live together for protection against violence and to enjoy a better life—the fruits of civil society or civilization.

But in *The Republic,* Socrates says that, in constructing the ideal state, the aim is "not the disproportionate happiness of any one class, but the greatest happiness of the whole." To the objection of Adeimantus that the citizens may be miserable in such a state, Socrates replies that we must consider whether "we would look to their greatest happiness individually, or whether this principle of happiness does not rather reside in the State as a whole." Later Socrates reminds Glaucon, who wonders whether the members of the guardian (or ruling) class will not be unhappy, that we are "fashioning the State with a view to the greatest happiness, not of any particular class, but of the whole."

Aristotle criticizes Socrates for depriving even the guardians of happiness and for saying that "the legislator ought to make the whole state happy." In his own view, "the whole cannot be happy unless most, or all, or some of its parts enjoy happiness. In this respect, happiness is not like the even principle in numbers, which may exist only in the whole, but in neither of the parts." When Aristotle asserts that "the state exists for the sake of a good life," he seems to have the happiness of individuals in mind, for he excludes slaves and brute animals from membership in the state on the ground that they can have "no share in happiness or in a life of free choice."

But Aristotle also seems to give the state preeminence over the individual. "Even if the end is the same for a single man and for a state," he writes, "that of the state seems at all events something greater and more complete, whether to attain or to preserve." This does not seem to him inconsistent with thinking that that "form of government is best in which every man, whoever he is, can act best and live happily."

Nor is Hegel reluctant to embrace both horns of the dilemma. Civil society rather than the state in its perfect realization seems to be devoted to the "attainment of selfish ends," such as individual happiness. But Hegel also says it is "perfectly true" that "the end of the state is the happiness of the citizens . . . If all is not well with them, if their subjective aims are not satisfied, if they do not find that the state as such is the means to their satisfaction, then the footing of the state is itself insecure."

THE FOREGOING CONSIDERATIONS of the nature, origin, and end of political society enter into the various conceptions of the ideal state which appear in the tradition of western thought. They also have a bearing on the division of social classes in the state, on the duties of the statesman or prince, and the principles of statecraft—the art or science of the ruler. Finally, they have implications for the relation of states to one another and for the different historic formations of the state.

All the modern writers who make some distinction between the state of nature and the state of civil society seem to agree that independent or sovereign states in their relation to one another are in a state of nature. Identifying the state of nature with the state of war, Hobbes remarks that "though there had never been any time wherein particular men were in

a condition of war one against another, yet in all times kings and persons of sovereign authority" are "in the state and posture of gladiators . . . which is a posture of war."

Similarly, to the question, "Where are or ever were there any men in a state of nature?" Locke replies, "all princes and rulers of independent governments all through the world are in a state of nature." Because "bodies politic" remain "in a state of nature among themselves," they experience, according to Rousseau, "all the inconveniences which had obliged individuals to forsake it." With the same intent, Montesquieu observes that "princes who live not among themselves under civil law are not free; they are governed by force; they may continually force or be forced."

In Kant's opinion, "states, viewed as nations in their external relations to one another— like lawless savages—are naturally in a nonjuridical condition," and he adds that "this natural condition is a state of war." Similarly, Hegel writes that "since the sovereignty of a state is the principle of its relations to others, states are to that extent in a state of nature in relation to each other."

On any of the theories concerning the origin of the state, it may be asked why political society cannot be enlarged to include all mankind. If, for example, in Aristotle's view, the state is a union of villages, as the village is a union of families, why may not a further expansion of political society be brought about by a union of states?

The question is not simply one of geographic limits or extent of population. The modern national state, though normally larger than the ancient city-state, remains an individual state and in the same external relationship to other states. Even the expansion of a city-state like Rome, at the greatest extent of its imperial domain, does not exemplify the principle of the world state unless it is proposed that the political unification of mankind be brought about by conquest and maintained by despotism.

Though Aristotle describes the state as formed by a combination of villages, he does not propose a combination of states to form a larger community. His reason may be that the essence of the state lies in its self-sufficiency. Consequently, "the best limit of the population of a state is the largest number which suffices for the purposes of life, and can be taken in at a single view"; and the territory need be no larger than one which enables the population to be "most entirely self-sufficing."

The moderns, in contrast, propose the expansion of the political community by the amalgamation of separate political units. Montesquieu, for example, suggests that by entering into a "confederate republic," a number of small states can obtain the security which none of them has by itself. "If a republic be small," he writes, "it is destroyed by a foreign force; if it be large, it is ruined by an internal imperfection." A confederate republic, he thinks, "has all the internal advantages of a republican, together with the external force of a monarchical, government . . . This form of government," Montesquieu continues, "is a convention by which several petty states agree to become members of a larger one, which they intend to establish. It is a kind of assemblage of societies, that constitute a new one, capable of increasing by means of further associations, till they arrive at such a degree of power as to be able to provide for the security of the whole body."

It is not security against external aggression, but internal peace, which leads Rousseau to propose an association more extensive than anything Montesquieu seems to have in mind—a confederation of *all* the states of Europe. But he does not see beyond Europe to all the states of the world. He regards "the great city of the world" as something less than a political society with civil laws, for he speaks of it as "the body politic whose general will is always the law of nature."

Nor are the American Federalists, Hamilton, Madison, and Jay, able, at the end of the 18th century, to envisage the unlimited extension of the principle of federal union. They content themselves with arguing for the possibility of so extensive a union as the projected United States of America, against those who quoted "the observations of Montesquieu on the necessity of a contracted territory for a Republican Government."

Before our own day Kant alone seems to contemplate the possibility of a world state *through federal union.* The "cosmopolitical ideal," he says, is "a universal union of states analogous to that by which a nation becomes a state." The postulate of reason which obliges men to quit the state of nature and form a civil union applies to states as well. "The natural state of nations, as well as of individual men," Kant writes, "is a state which it is a duty to pass out of, in order to enter into a legal state." But the ideal is impracticable in Kant's opinion—again because of the supposed limits of government with respect to extended territories and populations.

"With the too great extension of such a union of states over vast regions, any government of it, and consequently the protection of its individual members, must at last become impossible." Kant therefore proposes as an alternative a "permanent congress of nations," but one which, being "a voluntary combination of states . . . would be dissolvable at any time"—a mere league or confederacy, and not such a federal union "as is embodied in the United States of America, founded upon a political constitution, and therefore indissoluble."

The further implications of Kant's proposal, the alternative it replaces, and Hegel's objections to either, are discussed in the chapter on WAR AND PEACE. Here it seems appropriate to conclude with that vision of the world state which appears early in the tradition of the great books. It is conceived not as a worldwide federal union, but as a universal or unlimited community in which all men are citizens together even as they belong to one human brotherhood.

"If our intellectual part is common," argues the philosophical Roman emperor, Marcus Aurelius, "the reason also, in respect of which we are rational beings, is common; if this is so, common also is the reason which commands us what to do, and what not to do; if this is so, there is a common law also; if this is so, we are fellow-citizens; if this is so, we are members of some political community; if this is so, the world is in a manner a state."

Centuries later Dante, in the first book of

his *De Monarchia,* recaptures this ancient vision of the world state. Because "a plurality of authorities is disorder," authority must be single; and therefore, Dante argues, "world government is necessary . . . for the well-being of the world." It must be conceived as governing "mankind on the basis of what all have in common." By that "common law, it leads all toward peace."

THE PHILOSOPHICAL DOCTRINE of anarchy holds up the vision of human beings living together in peace and harmony without government and coercive force. They can get along in peace without states that impose order by the use of coercive force as well as by the laws to which coercive force must be attached to make the laws effective. Weber quotes with approval Leon Trotsky's statement that "every state is founded on force." Without the use of force, Weber declares, states would not exist, and "a condition would emerge that could be designated as 'anarchy,' in the specific sense of this word." This leads Weber to define the state as "a human community that (success-

fully) claims the *monopoly of the legitimate use of physical force* within a given territory." All other use of force, being illegitimate and unauthorized, is therefore violence.

Weber adds the note "that 'territory' is one of the characteristics of the state." Its significance in the definition of state is that, in a given tract of territory, the state is the most inclusive organized community. In that territory, families, corporations, and other organizations and associations are members of the state, but the state is not a member of any other organized community, unless it be something like the United Nations, which is not a state because it does not have a monopoly of authorized force.

If a federal world government ever comes into existence, it will be a world state because it will have a monopoly of legitimate force; and thus, in the global territory which it thereby governs, the several national states will become members of it, having internal but not external sovereignty, as is the case with the several states that constitute the federal union of the United States of America.

91

Temperance

INTRODUCTION

MOST outstanding figures in history, most heroes of legend or fiction, are men of strong passions, of ambition, and of pride. They are driven by desires which tend to be limitless. Few exemplify moderation. Few stop short of excess in anger or love, or in their striving for power and pleasure. They may curb their appetites in one direction, only to indulge them without rein in another. They do not follow in all things the counsels of temperance, expressed by the ancient maxim "Nothing overmuch."

Achilles is not temperate in his wrath, nor does Odysseus, for all his craft and cunning, exhibit self-control when his vanity or curiosity is at stake. The tragedies of Euripides, more perhaps than those of Sophocles and Aeschylus, embody the hubris, or pride, which is common to all tragic figures in some particular form of intemperance, such as the boundless hate of Medea or the abstemiousness of Hippolytus. One play especially, *The Bacchae,* takes intemperance for its central theme and sets the disciples of the Dionysiac spirit in mortal conflict with the puritans and their prohibitions. Comedy as well as tragedy flows from intemperance, as when we smile at the exaggerated sentimentality, or frown at the excessive sensuality, of the lovers described by Cervantes and Molière, Chaucer and Shakespeare, Voltaire and Balzac, George Eliot and Jane Austen, James Joyce and Marcel Proust; or find merriment in the indulgences of Sir John Falstaff, or Pantagruel and Panurge.

The great books of history add their evidence. They make fiction seem pale by comparison with the excesses of cruelty and sensuality which, if they were not presented as fact, might be dismissed as unimaginable. Page after page of Tacitus, Gibbon, and Huizinga often describe, in an unrelieved sequence, human debauchery, brutalities, and revelries ingeniously designed to reach some new extreme in order to procure, through novelty, satisfaction for appetites already overindulged and weary of familiar pleasures.

Nor is the historian's panorama of intemperance limited to the uncontrolled indulgences of the few—the oriental despots described by Herodotus, or the Caesars and their retinues in the imperial court of Rome. Armies in the field and the mob-formations of civilian life are depicted in wanton and riotous behavior. Whole peoples are described as being given to luxurious living or as wanting in standards of public decency. The few exceptions in antiquity, such as Spartan rigor or the chastity, if not the sobriety, of the primitive Germans, only accentuate by contrast the immoderate tenor of life in most ancient societies.

DARWIN SEEMS TO think that a much greater degree of self-control characterizes modern life, both public and private, though his opinion on this score may give undue weight to the conventions so much insisted upon in England under Queen Victoria. Temperance, according to him, is a virtue peculiar to civilized life. "The greatest intemperance," he writes, "is no reproach with savages."

Darwin places temperance along with prudence among the "so-called self-regarding virtues, which do not obviously, though they may really, affect the welfare of the tribe" and which "have never been esteemed by savages, though now highly appreciated by civilized nations." That Darwin has modern society in mind when he speaks of "civilized nations," may be inferred from his remarks about the sensuality of the Greeks and Romans. This seems to be confirmed by his statement that "the hatred of indecency . . . which is so valuable an aid to chastity, is a modern virtue, appertaining exclusively . . . to civilized life."

What may be noted here and questioned—in addition to the validity of Darwin's comparison of modern and ancient culture—is the tendency to identify temperance with chastity, or at least with restraint, if not abstinence, in the sphere of the sexual impulses. In our day, the general notion of virtue is often restricted to the virtue of chastity, as when we use the words "virtuous woman" to signify one who is chaste, or "woman of easy virtue" to signify one who is not. But spectacles of gluttony and drunkenness, of avarice or greed, are ever present to remind us that man can be intemperate in more ways than one. Darwin's implication of progress from licentious to moderate living may have less justification when we consider all the forms which intemperance can take.

Darwin, furthermore, seems to distinguish between courage and temperance in relation to the level or degree of civilization. Unlike temperance, courage, he thinks, is demanded by primitive as well as civilized life because it concerns the welfare of society as much as the well-being of the individual. Since "no man can be useful or faithful to his tribe without courage, this quality," he says, "has universally been placed in the highest rank." On the point of this comparison between the two virtues, Freud appears to disagree. Though he too considers temperance or self-control largely in the sphere of the sexual instincts, he seems to think that any form of organized social life, whether regarded as primitive or civilized, exacts certain restraints from the individual for the sake of the common good. Temperance no less than courage serves the tribe or the state.

"Civilization has been built up," Freud writes, "under the pressure of the struggle for existence, by sacrifices in gratification of the primitive impulses, and that is to a great extent forever being re-created as each individual, successively joining the community, repeats the sacrifice of his instinctive pleasures for the common good. The sexual are amongst the most important of the instinctive forces thus utilized; they are in this way sublimated, that is to say, their energy is turned aside from its sexual goal and diverted towards other ends, no longer sexual, and socially more valuable."

Society may depend on the temperance of its members without being able to exact temperance from them. Writers like J. S. Mill, for example, question the right of society to enforce temperance upon its members by the enactment of sumptuary laws, especially with regard to food and drink. The supposition seems to be that the intemperate man injures only himself—to do which is the prerogative of his personal liberty—whereas the unjust man injures others. We shall return to the consideration of this issue later, after we have examined the nature of temperance and its relation to other virtues, such as justice, courage, and wisdom or prudence.

IF THE POETS AND the historians describe the prevalence and the range of man's intemperance, the moralists tend to be unanimous in recommending self-control or moderation. There is hardly any variety of moral theory—whether developed in terms of law and duty or in terms of happiness and virtue, whether appealing to *a priori* principles or to criteria of utility empirically applied—which does not recommend the discipline of desire by reason and which does not condemn sensuality, self-indulgence, unchecked appetites, or passions run wild.

The word "temperance" itself is not always used, nor is the technical notion of virtue always implied, by those who advocate what Milton calls "the rule of not too much, by temperance taught." For some writers, on the other hand, temperance and virtue are almost identical. They think the essence of temperance is moderation and the virtuous life is the reasonable one. It is one in which reason moderates the passions and limits the pursuit of pleasure.

For example, Freud's theory of the reality principle seems to reflect traditional notions of temperance. A person dominated by the pleasure principle is infantile in character. "The transition from the pleasure-principle to the reality-principle," he points out, "is one of the most important advances in the development of the ego." When "the ego learns that it must inevitably go without immediate satisfaction, postpone gratification, learn to endure a degree of pain, and altogether renounce certain sources of pleasure," it "becomes 'reasonable,' is no longer controlled by the pleasure-principle, but follows the reality-principle," which seeks "a delayed and diminished pleasure, one which is assured by its realization of fact, its relation to reality."

So, too, Spinoza's doctrine that human bondage consists in being subject to the tyranny of the passions, whereas human freedom stems from the rule of reason, can be read as an apostrophe to temperance. Descartes's maxim, "to try always to conquer myself rather than fortune, and to alter my desires rather than change the order of the world," is still another expression of the insight that peace of mind comes from self-control. Though Kant does not think temperance deserves "to be called good without qualification," he does affirm that "moderation in the affections and passions, self-control and calm deliberation, are not only good in many respects, but even seem to constitute part of the intrinsic worth of the person."

Nietzsche stands alone as being completely against any form of temperance. *On the Genealogy of Morals* is an extensive critique of the ascetic spirit in western culture. In *Beyond Good and Evil*, he mocks various types of temperance, "whether it be that indifference and statuesque coldness towards the passionate folly of the emotions which the Stoics advised and applied; or that no-more-laughing and no-more-weeping of Spinoza, that destruction of the emotions through analysis and vivisection which he advocated so naively; or that depression of the emotions to a harmless mean at which they may be satisfied, the Aristotelianism of morals." Nietzsche calls all such doctrines "Morality as Timidity."

IT IS MONTAIGNE WHO magnifies temperance beyond virtue, and makes it the measure of the sound pursuit of every sort of good, even virtue itself. Without temperance, he writes in his essay "Of moderation," we can "corrupt things that of themselves are beautiful and good. We can grasp virtue in such a way that it will become vicious, if we embrace it with too sharp and violent a desire." Montaigne opposes "those who say that there is never any excess in virtue." On the contrary, he thinks that "a man may both love virtue too much, and perform excessively in a just action . . . I like temperate and moderate natures. Immoderation, even in the direction of the good, if it does not offend me, astonishes me and gives me trouble to name it."

As with virtue, so with wisdom or philosophy. He quotes Plato to the effect that we should be soberly wise, not try to be wiser than befits our natures. Regarding philosophy, we should not "plunge into it beyond the limits of profit . . . Taken with moderation, it is pleasant and advantageous." There is, in short, no pleasure "so just that excess and intemperance in it are not a matter of reproach."

Montaigne sees temperance as augmenting the pleasure of life rather than diminishing it. He subscribes to Plato's statement in the *Laws* that "the temperate life is in all things gentle, having gentle pains and gentle pleasures; whereas the intemperate life . . . has violent pains and pleasures, and vehement and stinging desires, and loves utterly insane; and in the temperate life the pleasures exceed the pains, but in the intemperate life the pains exceed the pleasures in greatness and number and frequency." To overlook this, Montaigne elsewhere suggests, is to suppose that "the regimen that stops the drinker short of drunkenness, the eater short of indigestion, the lecher short of baldness, is an enemy of our pleasures." Yet, in his love of "temperate and moderate natures," Montaigne repeatedly counsels us to avoid being overzealous even about temperance itself. The maxim "Nothing overmuch" applies to virtue as well as to the pleasure-seeking that virtue tries to control.

CONSIDERED IN TERMS of Aristotle's theory that all the moral virtues consist in a mean between excess and defect, Montaigne seems to be identifying moderation with the observance of the mean, so that moderation becomes an aspect of every virtue, including temperance itself as one virtue among others. Thus the courageous man is one who fears neither too much nor too little, but is moderate with respect to peril and pain. Accordingly, a man cannot be too courageous, but only too fearless, and so rash or foolhardy.

But it may be supposed that if moderation enters into all the virtues, such virtues as temperance and courage are not distinct. Holding them to be distinct in regard to the objects with which they deal, Aquinas admits that each of the major virtues can be "taken to denote certain general conditions of virtue," so that in a sense "they overflow into one another." He defines temperance as "a disposition of the soul, moderating any passions or acts, so as to keep them within bounds," and fortitude as "a disposition whereby the soul is strengthened for that which is in accord with reason, against any assaults of the passions or the toil involved in any work to be done." So conceived, Aquinas thinks it is possible to see how temperance and fortitude are in some sense one.

The man who can curb his desires for the pleasures of touch is more able to check his daring in the face of danger, "and in this sense fortitude is said to be temperate." The man who is able to stand firm against the dangers of death is more able to remain firm against the onslaught of pleasures, and so "temperance can be said to be brave." Thus temperance enters into other virtues, insofar as it leads men to "observe the mean in all things," just as fortitude enters into temperance because it strengthens men against "the enticements of pleasure" as well as against the fear of pain.

The general theory of virtue, in terms of which the several virtues are distinguished and their connections traced, is discussed in the chapter of VIRTUE AND VICE; and the special virtues to which temperance is related are considered in the chapters on COURAGE, JUSTICE, and PRUDENCE. Here we must be concerned to observe how the general conception of virtue is exemplified in the definitions of temperance given by those who, like Plato, Aristotle, and Aquinas, consider it to be, not the whole of virtue, but one of the major virtues and distinct from the others.

THOUGH PLATO AND Aristotle do not conceive virtue in the same way, and though they diverge in analyzing particular virtues, such as justice or wisdom, and in describing how particular virtues are related to one another, they nevertheless seem to concur on a number of points in their treatment of temperance.

In the *Gorgias*, Callicles asserts that only those who are unable to satisfy their desire for pleasures praise temperance, and call intemperance base. But, he asks, "what could be more truly base or evil than temperance to a man . . . who might freely be enjoying every good and has no one stand in his way?" And he concludes by saying that "luxury and intemperance and license, if they be provided with means, are virtue and happiness."

In reply, Socrates tries to persuade Callicles that "instead of the intemperate and insatiate life," one should "choose that which is orderly and sufficient and has a due provision for daily needs." He compares the intemperate man "to a vessel full of holes, because it can never be satisfied." By analogy with the sound and the leaky vessel, Socrates describes the temperate man as able to satisfy his limited desires, whereas the intemperate man, of boundless desire, can never pause in his search for pleasure. "If he pauses for a moment, he is in an agony of pain. Such are their respective lives," he adds, "and now would you say that the life of the intemperate is happier than that of the temperate?"

Callicles claims to be unconvinced, but later Socrates gets him to admit that in all things—in a house or a ship, in the body or the soul—order is good, and disorder evil. He then proceeds to point out that order is the principle of health in the body and of temperance in the soul. It is in these terms that Socrates defines temperance in *The Republic* as "the ordering or controlling of certain pleasures and desires." In the human soul, he explains, "there is a better and also a worse principle; and when the better has the worse under control, then a man is said to be master of himself."

The words "temperance" and "self-mastery" are almost interchangeable; both signify "the rule of the better part over the worse." Just as the courageous man is one "whose spirit retains in pleasure and in pain the commands of reason about what he ought or ought not to fear," so the temperate man is one in whom the "ruling principle of reason and the two subject ones of spirit and desire are equally agreed that reason ought to rule."

In somewhat similar terms, Aristotle defines temperance and courage by reference to pleasure and pain. "The man who abstains from bodily pleasures and delights in this very fact is temperate, while the man who is annoyed at it is self-indulgent; and he who stands his ground against things that are terrible and delights in this or at least is not pained is brave, while the man who is pained is a coward." Like Plato, Aristotle makes the rational principle the source of these virtues. It is reason, or more precisely one of reason's virtues, prudence, which determines the mean between excess and defect with regard to pleasure and pain, or fear, anger, and the other passions.

Like Freud, Aristotle regards self-indulgence as infantile or childish. Children "live at the beck and call of appetite, and it is in them that the desire for what is pleasant is strongest." When such desire is not regulated by reason, "it will go to great lengths; for in an irrational being the desire for pleasure is insatiable even if it tries every source of gratification." Where Freud speaks of the pleasure principle submitting to the reality principle, Aristotle says, "as the child should live according to the direction of his tutor, so the appetitive element should live according to the rational principle. The appetitive element in a temperate man should harmonize with the rational principle."

According to Aristotle, temperance is concerned not with all pleasures, but "with the kind of pleasures that other animals share in, which therefore appear slavish and brutish; these are touch and taste." Self-indulgence is a matter of reproach "because it attaches to us not as men but as animals. To delight in such things and to love them above all others is brutish."

The endurance of pain, which is central to the nature of courage, enters into temperance incidentally. The self-indulgent man "is pained more than he ought at not getting pleasant things," whereas the temperate man "is not pained at the absence of what is pleasant or at his abstinence from it." But total abstinence is not temperance, any more than over indulgence is. "The temperate man occupies a middle position" between those who have an insatiable craving for pleasure and those "who fall short with regard to pleasures and delight in them less than they should." Such insensibility, Aristotle declares, is not human either.

When reason curbs the desire for bodily pleasures, "it is not to lessen sensual pleasure," in the opinion of Aquinas, "but to prevent the force of concupiscence from cleaving to it immoderately. By *immoderately*," he explains, "I mean going beyond the bounds of reason, as a sober person does not take less pleasure in food eaten in moderation than the glutton, but his conscupiscence lingers less in such pleasures." Though Aquinas agrees with Aristotle in defining temperance strictly as moderation with respect to the pleasures of taste and touch, "such as the pleasures of the table or of sex," he associates with temperance those virtues which involve moderation with respect to other pleasures.

For example, there is liberality with respect to money as an object of love or pleasure. Neither the spendthrift nor the miser is temperate. Friendliness or affability and gentleness represent temperance in the relation of a man to the pleasures of fellowship; and the virtue which Aristotle calls *eutrapelia* is similarly classified by Aquinas, as being a moderate indulgence in the pleasures of recreation, of sport and games, the opposites of which, in excess and defect, can be called "buffoonery" and "boorishness." Even the pleasures of learning can be pursued intemperately, so that an undue craving for knowledge—beyond the proper limits and for the wrong reasons—is, according to Aquinas, the vice of curiosity.

THE NOTIONS OF ABSTINENCE and continence seem to be closely related to the idea of temperance. The words are often used interchangeably. But as we have seen, according to the theory of virtue as a mean between extremes of excess and defect, temperance calls for a moderate indulgence in pleasures, not abstinence from them entirely. This raises the question whether the asceticism of the religious life violates the rule of reason by a kind of immoderate withdrawal from ordinary pleasures. What to the psychoanalyst may look like pathological self-denial, or to the philosopher like a violation of nature, takes, in the eyes of the Christian theologian, the form of heroic temperance, a supernatural perfection of the virtue.

When in the religious life a man does "his utmost to strive onward to divine things," then, according to Aquinas, in those who are "tending towards the divine similitude," temperance is a *perfecting* virtue. "So far as nature allows," it "neglects the needs of the body." In those "who have already attained to the divine likeness, the *perfect* virtue of temperance" is one which "knows no earthly desires."

Since "use of sexual union hinders the mind from giving itself wholly to the service of God," and since "the use of venery withdraws the mind from that perfect intentness on tending to God," the perpetual continence of the celibate life, as well as the voluntary poverty of the monastic life, seem to Aquinas "requisite for religious perfection."

Augustine, in *The Confessions,* tells of the time when "I thought it would be too much for me to bear if I were to be deprived of woman's love. In your mercy you have given us a remedy to cure this weakness, but I gave it no thought because I had never tried it for myself. I believed that continence was to be achieved by man's own power, which I knew that I did not possess. Fool that I was, I did not know that no man *can be master of himself, except of God's bounty,* as your Bible tells us."

Though he separated from his mistress in order to prepare for marriage, he discovered that he was "more a slave of lust than a true lover of marriage." He recounts the struggles which finally enabled him turn in the other direction and to "see the chaste beauty of Continence in all her serene, unsullied joy"; and with her, he adds, "were countless boys and girls, great numbers of the young and people of all ages, staid widows and women

still virgins in old age. And in their midst was Continence herself, not barren but a fruitful mother of children, of joys born on you, O Lord, her Spouse."

But there is another meaning of continence according to which it is condemned by the philosopher who conceives temperance as a natural virtue. The reason for Aristotle's condemnation of continence differs from the reason he gives for his disapproval of abstinence. Abstinence—at least on the natural plane— is an immoderate denial of pleasure. Continence is opposed to temperance because it merely represents reason's inhibition of the act prompted by a licentious desire for pleasure. It is not a habitual moderation of desire itself. Aristotle's emphasis on habit, therefore, leads him to insist upon the distinction between temperance and continence.

"We group together the incontinent and the self-indulgent, the continent and the temperate man," Aristotle writes, "because they are concerned somehow with the same pleasures and pain; but though they are concerned with the same objects, they are not similarly related to them." The difference lies in the fact that a man acts continently in a particular situation when his reason is able to overcome an immoderate desire for pleasure, and incontinently when the force of his desire brushes reason aside; whereas a man not only acts temperately, but is temperate in character, when his desires are themselves habitually moderated to be in accord with reason.

The temperate man, therefore, has no need for continence. Nor is the incontinent man to be confused with the intemperate, for the latter is not convinced that his desires are inordinate. The continent man is one who, when acting against reason, knows that he is doing so. Though both the continent and the temperate man do nothing contrary to the rule of reason for the sake of bodily pleasures, the one, according to Aristotle, has bad appetites, the other is free from them. Calvin approves what seems to him to be Aristotle's "very shrewd distinction between incontinence and intemperance. Where incontinence . . . reigns," Calvin explains, the individual's desires tend to suppress relevant knowledge "so that the individual sees not in his own misdeed the evil which he sees generally in similar cases."

THE CONTINENT MAN is not the only one who gives the appearance of temperance without being really temperate in character. Some men, says Aristotle, are moderate by nature—"from the very moment of birth fitted for self-control." What appears to be temperance in them, therefore, is not, in his opinion, a virtuous habit acquired by good acts, but simply a natural capacity to control their desires or a temperamental constitution which happens not to be ridden by very strong desires. They do not deserve to be praised for their apparent self-control; neither do those who manage to be moderate about certain pleasures but give themselves free rein with respect to other desires. The miser who limits his bodily comforts in order to amass a pile of gold is hardly temperate.

Gibbon writes of the Emperor Julian that he "seldom recollected the fundamental maxim of Aristotle, that true virtue is placed at an equal distance between the opposite vices." Julian's lack of temperance appears, however, not merely in the opposite extreme to which he went to express his contempt for luxury, sleeping on the ground and renouncing the decencies of dress and cleanliness. Though genuinely moderate in some things, such as his diet, he went to excess in others, overdoing his preoccupation with affairs of state and working incessantly for long hours day after day. He "considered every moment as lost that was not devoted to the advantage of the public or the improvement of his own mind. By this avarice of time," Gibbon observes, "he seemed to protract the short duration of his reign."

Temperance in a particular respect is sometimes praised as a virtue relative to a specific and limited goal. Considering the wealth of nations, Adam Smith looks upon prodigality as a major vice, and regards parsimony as an indispensable virtue. "Capitals are increased by parsimony," he writes, "and diminished by prodigality and misconduct ... Parsimony, and not industry, is the immediate cause of the increase of capital ... By what a frugal man annually saves, he not only affords maintenance to an additional number of productive hands, for that or the ensuing year, but, like the founder of a public workhouse, he establishes as it were a perpetual fund for the maintenance of an equal number in all times to come."

Capital funds are perverted by the prodigal. "By not confining his expenses within his income," Smith declares, "he encroaches upon his capital ... By diminishing the funds designed for the employment of productive labor, he necessarily diminishes ... the quantity of that labor which adds a value to the subject upon which it is bestowed, and, consequently, the value of the annual produce of the land and labour of the whole country ... If the prodigality of some was not compensated by the frugality of others, the conduct of every prodigal, by feeding the idle with the bread of the industrious, tends not only to beggar himself, but to impoverish his country."

From the point of view of augmenting wealth, Smith may be right in calling every prodigal "a public enemy and every frugal man a public benefactor." Marx, however, raises the question whether thrift or parsimony represents moral virtue in the capitalist himself. He mocks the classical, or what he calls the "vulgar," economic theory which tends to identify capital with abstinence, and, taking Smith's statement that "industry furnishes the material which saving accumulates," he interprets *saving* to mean the *reconversion of the greatest possible portion of surplus-value or surplus-product into capital.*

For Marx the question is, in addition to being economic, a moral and psychological one. He describes the capitalist as suffering from "a Faustian conflict between the passion for accumulation and the desire for enjoyment." His parsimony, or abstinence from certain pleasures, hardly signifies genuine temperance; for, according to Marx, the capitalist is like the hoarder who "makes a sacrifice of the lusts of the flesh to his gold fetish." Elsewhere he says that the "boundless greed after riches ... is common to the capitalist and the miser; but while the miser is merely a capitalist gone mad, the capitalist is a rational miser."

In Marx's opinion the capitalist cannot even boast of personal thrift to any great extent. "The capitalist gets rich, not like the miser, in proportion to his personal labor and restricted consumption, but at the same rate as he squeezes out the labor-power of others, and enforces on the laborer abstinence from all life's enjoyments." The kind of intemperance exhibited by the nonworking capitalist—consumption beyond need and even pleasure in superficial goods—Veblen calls conspicuous waste.

THESE CONSIDERATIONS OF political economy lead us naturally back to the issue raised earlier, concerning the significance of temperance for society, or the effect of private intemperance on the public welfare.

What is the relation between temperance and justice? Aristotle answers this question in terms of his conception of general justice as including the social aspect of all the other moral virtues. To the extent that his courage or temperance can affect others or the common good, a man is required by justice to be temperate and brave. It is proper for the law, he says, to bid us do "both the acts of a brave man (*e.g.,* not to desert our post nor take flight nor throw away our arms) and those of a temperate man (*e.g.,* not to commit adultery nor to gratify one's lust)."

Though he accepts Aristotle's notion of general justice, Aquinas puts a limitation on the extent to which the positive law of the state can regulate or enforce the acts of virtue like temperance. Because it is "framed for a multitude of human beings, the majority of whom are not perfect in virtue . . . human laws do not forbid all vices, from which the virtuous abstain, but only the more grievous vices, from which it is possible for the majority to abstain; and chiefly those that are injurious to others, without the prohibition of which human society could not be maintained." The point is not that some acts of temperance cannot be prescribed by law, but rather that the human law does not command every act of temperance, but only those "which are ordainable to the common good."

The principle being clear, the problem remains extremely difficult when the question is one of regulating certain types of behavior, such as insobriety, extravagance, or adultery.

Montesquieu discusses the difficulties of administering, under the Julian law, the "punishments decreed by the Roman emperors against the incontinence of women." He considers the advantages and disadvantages, relative to different forms of government, of sumptuary laws directed at maintaining frugality and avoiding luxury; as, for example, in Venice, where the rich were "compelled by laws to moderation" and were thus so "habituated to parsimony that none but courtesans could make them part with their money." As for sobriety, he seems to think that the problem varies with the climate, the Muhammedan law against the drinking of wine being "improper for cold countries where the climate seems to force them to a kind of national intemperance, very different from personal inebriety . . . A German drinks through custom, and a Spaniard by choice."

The reasons which have been offered against the legal prohibition of intoxicants are many and various. To those who hold that temperance consists in moderation, not abstinence, "temperance laws" are misguided as well as misnamed. To others, like William James, "drunkenness . . . as teetotalers use the word, is one of the deepest functions of human nature. Half of both the poetry and tragedy of human life would vanish if alcohol were taken away." To still others, like Mill, such sumptuary laws are wrong in principle because consumption, which they try to regulate, is a private matter.

If an individual's intemperance injures only himself, he may be morally reprobated, but, Mill holds, he ought not to be prosecuted by law. A man who, "through intemperance or extravagance, becomes unable to pay his debts," or becomes incapable of supporting his family, "might be justly punished; but it is for the breach of duty to his family or creditors, not for the extravagance." Again Mill writes: "No person ought to be punished simply for being drunk; but a soldier or a policeman should be punished for being drunk on duty. Whenever, in short, there is a definite damage, or a definite risk of damage, either to another individual or to the public, the case is taken out of the province of liberty, and placed in that of morality or law."

92

Theology

INTRODUCTION

IT has seldom been disputed that the questions with which theology deals are of critical significance for all the rest of human knowledge. Even those who deny that theology is or can be a science might be willing to concede that, if it were, it would deserve its traditional title, "queen of the sciences."

It has been said that the great questions of theology are unanswerable. It has been said that theological dispute or controversy is futile because the issues are not resolvable by argument. But it has rarely been asserted, or even implied, that our outlook would be unaltered and our actions unaffected if we could know, in any degree, the answers to questions concerning the existence of the supernatural and its relation to the visible world of nature. To Plato it is of such importance that he asks: "Who can be calm when he is called upon to prove the existence of the gods?"

The main controversy, not in, but about, theology turns on the use of such words as "knowledge" and "science" for a discipline which, both in method and conclusion, seems compelled to go beyond experience and to push reason to (or even beyond) the limit of its powers. In the minds of many, especially in our day, theology is associated with religion and is opposed to science or, if not opposed, at least it is set apart from science as entirely different. Those who conceive science as limited by its empirical methods to the investigation of observable phenomena might not quarrel with the allocation of theology to philosophy, but whether or not they did would in turn depend on their conception of philosophy.

As the chapters on SCIENCE and PHILOSOPHY indicate, these two terms are identified through a large part of the western tradition. The various sciences are regarded as branches of philosophy. But we also find a distinction being made in the 18th century between the empirical and rational or philosophical sciences; and in our day those who regard philosophy as mere speculation or opinion contrast it to the experimental disciplines which are thought to be the *only* established bodies of knowledge, that is, sciences.

The question whether theology is a science may, therefore, embrace a number of alternatives. That it is an empirical or experimental science has seldom been proposed. It may be treated as a science, however, by those who consider it as a part of philosophy; or it may be denied that honor precisely because it belongs to philosophy. A third alternative remains—that theology is separate from philosophy, that it is a science as distinct in character from the philosophical sciences as they are from the experimental disciplines. In this third alternative, the association of theology with religion or religious faith seems to determine the character of theology.

It is this third alternative which Hume seems to have in mind at the conclusion of his *An Enquiry Concerning Human Understanding*. "Divinity or Theology, as it proves the existence of a Deity and the immortality of souls . . . has," he writes, "a foundation in *reason,* so far as it is supported by experience. But its best and most solid foundation is *faith* or divine revelation." To the extent that its principles come from religious faith, theology does not seem to fit perfectly into Hume's twofold division of the sciences into those which involve "abstract reasoning concerning quantity or number" and those which

846

involve "experimental reasoning concerning matter of fact and existence."

When he says that he would commit to the flames "any volume of divinity or school metaphysics which does not contain either of these two kinds of reasoning"—for then "it can contain nothing but sophistry and illusion"—he can hardly be condemning the theology he has himself described as resting primarily on faith or divine revelation, though it may also have some foundation in reasoning from experience.

THE DISCUSSION OF THE nature and scope of theology, its principles and methods, may refer either to the theology which is a part of philosophy or to the theology which is sometimes called "dogmatic" because it expounds and explains the dogmas of a religious faith. Furthermore, those who make the distinction between the two kinds of theology raise questions concerning their relation to one another. In so doing they enter into the larger problem of the relation of faith and reason, and the limited part which reason can play in the development of a theology which rests on faith.

The distinction itself is made by many writers and in diverse ways. The theology which is entirely philosophical and independent of any religious faith is usually called "natural theology." The name "sacred theology" is given to a body of doctrine which finds its fundamental principles in the articles of a religious faith. The ultimate source of these articles of faith in Jewish, Christian, and Islamic theology is the truth revealed in a sacred scripture—the Old and New Testament or the Koran—from which, by interpretation, the articles of faith are drawn.

Francis Bacon, for example, defines "divine philosophy or natural theology" as "that knowledge or rudiment of knowledge concerning God, which may be obtained by the contemplation of his creatures; which knowledge may be truly termed divine in respect of the object, and natural in respect of the light. The bounds of this knowledge are that it suffices to convince atheism, but not to inform religion." In contrast, "inspired theology" or "sacred theology (which in our idiom we call divinity) is grounded only upon the word and oracle of God, and not upon the light of nature."

Kant makes a similar distinction when he says that theology is based either "on reason alone (*theologia rationalis*) or upon revelation (*theologia revelata*)." But for Kant "natural theology" designates only one kind of rational theology. Another kind is "transcendental theology," which differs from the first in the method which reason employs. He also differentiates between speculative and moral theology. Though both fall within the sphere of reason, one is the work of the pure theoretical reason, the other of the pure practical reason.

In the opening question of the *Summa Theologica*, Aquinas tries to explain why, in addition to the "philosophical science built up by reason, there should be a sacred science learned through revelation." To an objection which claims that "there is no need of any further knowledge," because philosophical science can attain to knowledge even of God Himself, he replies that "there is no reason why those things which may be learnt from philosophical science, so far as they can be known by natural reason, may not also be taught us by another science so far as they fall within revelation." Though they may deal with the same object, "sciences are differentiated according to the various means through which knowledge is obtained . . . Hence the theology included in sacred doctrine differs in kind from that theology which is part of philosophy."

In another place, Aquinas refers to the theological conclusions which the philosopher thinks he can demonstrate—"the existence of God and other like truths about God which can be known by natural reason." Of these he says that they "are not articles of faith, but are preambles to the articles . . . Nevertheless," he adds, "there is nothing to prevent a man, who cannot grasp a proof, accepting as a matter of faith, something which in itself is capable of being scientifically known and demonstrated." But such propositions, which belong to both reason and faith, are only part of sacred doctrine. In addition, there are the propositions which belong to faith alone.

"It is impossible," Aquinas writes, "to attain to the knowledge of the Trinity by natural reason." The triune nature of the Godhead cannot be demonstrated philosophically; nor can the dogma be fully comprehended by human understanding. In Purgatory, Dante learns that "Foolish is he who hopes that our reason may compass the infinite course taken by One Substance in Three Persons."

Though it is not a theological mystery in the same sense, another example of a dogma not demonstrable by reason is the proposition that the world began to be. "That the world did not always exist," Aquinas declares, "we hold by faith alone; it cannot be proved demonstratively; which is what was said above of the mystery of the Trinity." We find in Sacred Scripture the words *In the beginning God created heaven and earth,* "in which words the newness of the world is stated" and so "the newness of the world is known only by revelation."

With respect to such matters as belong to faith alone, a theologian like Aquinas cautions against the misuse of reason. "When anyone in the endeavor to prove what belongs to faith, brings forward arguments which are not cogent, he falls under the ridicule of the unbelievers; since they suppose that we base ourselves upon such arguments, and that we believe on their account. Therefore, we must not attempt to establish what is of faith, except by authority alone" and only "to those who accept the authority." For those who do not accept the authority of Scripture, the most that reason can do concerning propositions peculiar to faith is "to prove that what faith teaches is not impossible." Elsewhere Aquinas points out that "although the argument from authority based on human reason is the weakest, yet the argument from authority based on divine revelation is the strongest."

THE FOREGOING THROWS some light on Montaigne's defense of a book by Raymond Sebond, bearing the title *La theologie naturelle.* Though he calls his work "natural theology," Sebond, according to Montaigne, "undertakes by human and natural reasons to establish and prove against the atheists all the articles of the Christian religion." What his opponents reprehend in his work is that "Christians do themselves harm in trying to support their belief by human reasons, since it is conceived only by faith and by a particular inspiration of divine grace."

Montaigne agrees that it is "faith alone that embraces vividly and surely the high mysteries of our religion." But he also thinks that it is "a very fine and very laudable enterprise to accommodate also to the service of our faith the natural and human tools that God has given us. There can be no doubt," he says, "that this is the most honorable use that we could put them to, and that there is no occupation or design more worthy of a Christian man than to aim, by all his studies and thoughts, to embellish, extend, and amplify the truth of his belief."

The conception of natural theology which Montaigne appears to entertain in his "Apology for Raymond Sebond" does not seem to differentiate it from sacred theology, insofar as all its principles are articles of faith. Quite apart from Sebond, Montaigne himself does not think that the existence of God or the immortality of the soul can be demonstrated by reason. Montaigne observes that "those most obstinate in this most just and clear persuasion of the immortality of our spirit . . . have fallen short and found themselves powerless to prove it by their human powers . . . Let us confess frankly that God alone has told us so, and faith; for a lesson of nature and of our reason it is not."

Though the denial of God's existence is, according to Montaigne, "a proposition as it were unnatural and monstrous, difficult too and not easy to establish in the human mind," he thinks the affirmation to be no less beyond reason's power to establish with certitude, for "we should remember, whatever we receive into our understanding, that we often receive false things there, and by these same tools that are often contradictory and deceived."

In this, Montaigne differs not only from a theologian like Aquinas, who assigns certain truths to natural theology as capable of being demonstrated by reason without the aid of faith, but also from such philosophers as

Descartes, Spinoza, and Locke, who hold that we can know God by reason with more certainty, and even (according to Spinoza) more adequately, than we can know most other things. "I have always considered," Descartes writes, "that the two questions respecting God and the Soul were the chief of those that ought to be demonstrated by philosophical rather than theological argument. For although it is quite enough for us faithful ones to accept by means of faith the fact that the human soul does not perish with the body, and that God exists, it certainly does not seem possible ever to persuade infidels of any religion . . . unless, to begin with, we prove these two facts by means of the natural reason."

Descartes, it appears, reserves the use of the word "theology" for sacred doctrine. What others, like Bacon, call "natural theology," he treats simply as philosophy, or that branch of it which he calls "metaphysics." Dedicating his *Meditations on First Philosophy* to "the dean and doctors of the sacred faculty of theology in Paris," he says: "I have noticed that you, along with all the theologians, did not only affirm that the existence of God may be proved by the natural reason, but also that it may be inferred from the Holy Scriptures, that knowledge of Him is much clearer than that which we have of many created things, and, as a matter of fact, is so easy to acquire that those who have it not are culpable in their ignorance."

But Descartes wishes to confess the limitations of the mere philosopher's knowledge of God. When he came to inquire "how God may be more easily and certainly known than the things of this world," no matter how much "certainty and evidence I find in my reasons," he could not persuade himself, he says, that "all the world is capable of understanding them . . . There are not so many in the world who are fitted for metaphysical speculations as there are for those of geometry."

Answering a critic who quotes Aquinas against him, he later writes: "I admit along with all theologians that God cannot be comprehended by the human mind, and also that He cannot be distinctly known by those who try mentally to grasp Him at once in His entirety . . . Wherever I have said that God can

be clearly and distinctly known, I have understood this to apply only to this finite cognition of ours, which is proportionate to the diminutive capacity of our minds."

So FAR WE HAVE considered the distinction between natural and sacred theology—or between philosophy and theology—as it is made in the Christian tradition by writers conscious of the difference between faith and reason, or revelation and demonstration. In pagan antiquity, there seems to be no equivalent of sacred theology. "The various modes of worship, which prevailed in the Roman world," Gibbon tells us, "were all considered by the people as equally true; by the philosopher as equally false; and by the magistrate as equally useful . . . The superstition of the people was not embittered by theological rancour; nor was it confined by the chains of any speculative system." It was "the elegant mythology of Homer," he says, not reasoning, which "gave a beautiful, and almost a regular form to the polytheism of the ancient world."

Of the Greek philosophers, Gibbon remarks that "they meditated on the Divine Nature as a very curious and important speculation," but only the Stoics and the Platonists "endeavored to reconcile the jarring interests of reason and piety." Plato's criticism of the poets in *The Republic* for their impiety, and his rational defense of piety in the *Laws*, accompanied by a demonstration of the existence of the gods, may be taken as examples of ancient theological discourse within a religious context. Another example, and from quite another point of view, is Cicero's *De Natura Deorum*, which Gibbon praises as the best guide to the opinions of the philosophers concerning the tenets of polytheism.

But neither Cicero nor Plato treats theology as a science. The ancient philosopher who does and who, moreover, regards theology as the highest of the speculative sciences, seems to proceed without reference to or benefit of prevailing religious beliefs. Aristotle dismisses "the school of Hesiod and all the theologians [who] thought only of what was plausible to themselves." He refers to the legends of the gods which "our forefathers in the most remote ages have handed down to their posterity ... in the form of a myth ... with a view to the persuasion of the multitude and to its legal and utilitarian expediency." But the highest science, which Aristotle sometimes calls "first philosophy," he also calls "theology." It deals with the immaterial and the insensible, the immovable and eternal. We may call it "theology," he writes, "since it is obvious that if the divine is present anywhere, it is present in things of this sort." In another place he says, "there are three kinds of theoretical sciences—physics, mathematics, theology ... and of these the last named is best, for it deals with the highest of existing things."

At the beginning of the *Metaphysics,* Aristotle gives another reason for thinking that theology is a divine science: not that it is divinely inspired, but that, having the divine for its object, it is the science "most meet for God to have ... Such a science either God alone can have, or God above all others." The title given the book in which Aristotle attempts to develop this science comes in the later tradition to be the name given to speculation concerning immaterial and insensible substances. What Aristotle calls "theology," Descartes, as we have seen, calls "metaphysics" in order to distinguish it from the theology based on revelation.

Whether the theology of a pagan philosopher is commensurable with the theology of Jewish or Christian thinkers, even when the latter attempt to be purely philosophical or natural theologians, is a question which deeply probes the relation of reason to faith. For even when reason tries to proceed independently of faith, the religious faith of a community may tinge the concepts the philosopher uses and define the problems he undertakes to solve. It may be one thing to prove the existence of a Prime Mover, and another to know by reason the nature and existence of the God who in the beginning created heaven and earth—the God of Abraham, Isaac, and Jacob, the God of the Christians, whom Pascal distinguishes from the God of the philosophers.

Augustine explains his attitude as a theologian toward the theories of the philosophers touching divine matters. "I have not under-

taken," he says, "to refute all the vain theological opinions of all the philosophers, but only of such of them as, agreeing in the belief that there is a divine nature, and that this divine nature is concerned about human affairs, do nevertheless deny that the worship of the one unchangeable God is sufficient for the obtaining of a blessed life after death, as well as at the present time." Since "Plato defined the wise man as one who imitates, knows, and loves this God, and who is rendered blessed through fellowship with Him in His own blessedness, why discuss with the other philosophers? It is evident that none come nearer to us than the Platonists."

Plato, according to Augustine, "is justly preferred to all the other philosophers of the Gentiles"; those among his followers who show "the greatest acuteness in understanding him ... entertain such an idea of God as to admit that in Him are to be found the cause of existence, the ultimate reason for the understanding, and the end in reference to which the whole life is to be regulated." So amazing, to his mind, are the parallels between certain insights expressed by Plato and the wisdom of Sacred Scripture, that Augustine is almost inclined to believe that "Plato was not ignorant of those writings." But he does not think it necessary to determine whether Plato had acquaintance with the writings of Moses and the prophets, because certain basic truths, which were revealed to the Hebrews, were made known to the gentiles through the light of nature and reason. "That which is known of God," the apostle had said, "has been manifested among them, for God hath manifested it to them."

Therefore Augustine feels justified in taking any truth from Plato which is consistent with Christian faith. Aquinas, borrowing much from Aristotle, explains that "sacred doctrine makes use of the authority of philosophers in those questions in which they were able to know the truth by natural reason." Sacred theology uses the doctrines of the philosophers, he adds, "not as though it stood in need of them, but only in order to make its teaching clearer." It is in this sense that Aquinas calls philosophy the handmaiden of theology.

Others seem to take a different view of this relationship. Montaigne wonders whether it would not be better if "the divine doctrine keeps her rank better apart, as queen and mistress," and he quotes Saint John Chrysostom to the effect that philosophy "has long been banished from the holy schools as a useless handmaid." Hobbes goes further. He describes the traditional theology as a mingling of Aristotle's metaphysics with Scripture, and claims that the "bringing of the philosophy and doctrine of Aristotle into religion by the Schoolmen" caused the "many contradictions and absurdities" which "brought the clergy into a reputation both of ignorance and of fraudulent intention, and inclined people to revolt from them."

Hegel, however, dismisses the criticism that is often made concerning the dependence of Christian theology, at least in its formative period, on pagan philosophy. "The Fathers of the Church and the Councils," he writes, "constituted the dogma; but a chief element in this constitution was supplied by the previous development of *philosophy*." That certain dogmas were introduced into the Christian religion through "the instrumentality of philosophy . . . is not sufficient ground for asserting that they were foreign to Christianity and had nothing to do with it. It is a matter of perfect indifference where a thing originated; the only question," Hegel insists, "is, 'Is it true in and for itself?' Many think that by pronouncing the doctrine to be Neo-Platonic, they have *ipso facto* banished it from Christianity. Whether a Christian doctrine stands exactly thus and thus in the Bible . . . is not the only question. The Letter kills, the Spirit makes alive."

COMPARED WITH SACRED theology, the subject matter of natural theology and the scope of its problems seem to be extremely narrow. At most, it is only a part of philosophy, and some writers treat it as no more than one part of metaphysics.

Kant, for example, divides metaphysics into three parts—theology, cosmology, and psychology—according to his conception of metaphysics as having "for the proper object of its inquiries only three grand ideas: God, Freedom, and Immortality." As a branch of transcendental speculation, theology is concerned primarily with the problem of God's existence. Similarly, Aristotle's metaphysical inquiries include more than his theology. His theology begins only after he has discussed the nature and being of sensible substances. It is stated mainly in Book XII of the *Metaphysics* where he considers the existence and character of immaterial substances, and of the one purely actual being which is God.

Descartes's conception seems to be broader, for he regards the immortality of the soul as well as the existence and nature of God as being characteristically theological problems even when they are treated in metaphysics and by the methods of the philosopher. Because these two problems concern spiritual beings, Adam Smith also groups them together under the name "pneumatics" or "pneumatology," which he identifies with metaphysics—that part of philosophy most emphasized "in the universities of Europe where philosophy was taught only as subservient to theology." Bacon alone seems to separate natural theology entirely from metaphysics, which, along with physics, is for him a part of natural rather than divine philosophy. But though he would limit natural theology to that knowledge of God which can be drawn from nature, and excludes attempts to induce from nature "any verity or persuasion concerning the points of faith," he grants that natural as well as divine theology may treat of "the nature of angels and spirits," as "neither inscrutable nor interdicted."

The subject matter of sacred theology, or what he calls "divinity," is, according to Bacon's account, much more extensive. He first divides it into "matter of belief" and "matter of service and adoration"; and from these two derives the "four main branches of divinity: faith, manners, liturgy, and government." The matter of faith contains "the doctrine of the nature of God, of the attributes of God, and of the works of God." Under manners, Bacon lists the consideration of divine law and the breach of it by sin; liturgy concerns the sacraments and rituals of religion; government, the organization, offices, and jurisdictions of the church.

As its title indicates, the *Summa Theologica* of Aquinas endeavors to set forth the sum of theological knowledge. In addition to the topics and problems peculiar to sacred doctrine, the subject matters treated in the *Summa* seem to represent the whole range of human inquiry—almost coextensive with the scope of the natural sciences and philosophy, both speculative and moral.

Aquinas explains the encyclopedic character of the *Summa* by pointing out that to have God as the subject matter of theology means that sacred doctrine treats "all things under the aspect of God, either because they are God Himself, or because they refer to God as their beginning and end." The unity of theology in covering so wide a diversity of matters consists in the single formality under which they are considered—the formality of being divinely revealed. That is why "objects which are the subject matter of different philosophical sciences can yet be treated by this one single sacred science under one aspect, namely, insofar as they can be included in revelation."

Thus, for example, in the preamble to his *Treatise on Man*, Aquinas writes: "The theologian considers the nature of man in relation to the soul; but not in relation to the body, except insofar as the body has relation to the soul." This emphasis is dictated by the articles of Christian faith which concern man, in both body and soul. Similarly, with respect to moral matters, Aquinas explains that the theologian "considers human acts inasmuch as man is thereby directed to happiness," and he takes account of the circumstances of human acts because they may excuse from sin, "the consideration of which belongs to the theologian." It belongs to the theologian only when sin is conceived "as an offense against God," but to the moral philosophers when it is conceived "as something contrary to reason."

IT APPEARS FROM THE foregoing that sacred theology is both speculative and practical (or moral). It deals with the nature of divine things and with human acts, but with the latter only so far as they have God for their rule or end.

"Although among the philosophical sciences," Aquinas writes, "some are speculative and others practical, sacred doctrine includes both."

Even though it is made on the level of the philosophical sciences, Kant's distinction between speculative and moral theology seems to be based on a different principle. For Aquinas the speculative and the practical parts of theology deal with different problems, such as God, the Trinity, creation, and the angels on the one hand, and beatitude, the virtues, divine law, sin, grace, and sacraments on the other. But for Kant both speculative and moral theology deal with the problem of God's existence. They differ only according to the manner in which the theoretical and the practical reason undertake to solve this problem.

"All attempts of reason to establish a theology by the aid of speculation alone are fruitless," writes Kant. Consequently, "a rational theology can have no existence unless it is founded upon the laws of morality." The postulates of pure practical reason—of immortality, free will, and the existence of God—"all proceed from the principle of morality, which is not a postulate but a law by which reason determines the will directly." The moral law involves, as a necessary condition, "the existence of the *summum bonum*," and that in turn involves "the supposition of the supreme independent good, that is, the existence of God."

According to Kant, a Supreme Being is "for the speculative reason, a mere ideal, though a faultless one—a conception which perfects and crowns the system of human cognition, but the objective reality of which can neither be proved nor disproved by pure reason." It is this defect which moral theology remedies. "We must assume," he says, "a moral world-cause, that is, an Author of the world, if we are to set before ourselves a final end in conformity to the moral law." But, he adds, "this moral argument is not intended to supply an objectively valid proof of the existence of God. It is not meant to demonstrate to the skeptic that there is a God, but that he *must adopt* the assumption of this proposition as a maxim of his practical reason, if he wishes to think in a manner consistent with morality."

THE PROBLEM OF THE proof of God's existence, though central in theology, is more fully discussed in the chapter on GOD. Here we are concerned with the nature of theology itself as a branch of learning or inquiry. Since the chapter on METAPHYSICS necessarily touches on theology as a philosophical discipline, it seems advisable to devote attention here to some of the things which are peculiarly the concern of sacred theology.

Heresy is one of these. A scientist or philosopher may be criticized for his errors, but only a theologian, only the man who tries to explain some article of faith, can be called a heretic in the strict sense of that word. According to his view of the relation between church and state, Hobbes defines heresy in political terms. "Heresy," he writes, "is nothing else but a private opinion, obstinately maintained, contrary to the opinion which the Public Person"—*i.e.,* the Sovereign—"has commanded to be taught." But, according to Pascal, "none but God was able to instruct the Church in the faith," and so "it is heresy to resist the decisions of the faith, because this amounts to an opposing of our own spirit to the spirit of God." But, he adds, "it is no heresy, though it may be an act of presumption, to disbelieve certain particular facts, because this is no more than opposing reason—it may be enlightened reason—to an authority which is great indeed, but in this matter is not infallible."

The aspect of choice, of obstinately preferring one's own opinion against a superior authority, is emphasized by Aquinas, but he adds the specification that heresy is a corruption of Christian faith, a species of unbelief in which the heretic defies the authority of the Church, choosing "not what Christ really taught, but the suggestion of his own mind." He quotes a statement by Augustine that we should not accuse of heresy "those who, however false and perverse their opinion may be, defend it without obstinate fervor" and are "ready to mend their opinion when they have found the truth because they do not make a choice in contradiction to the doctrine of the Church." It is not the falsity of the opinion which makes it heresy, for until the point of faith has been defined by the authority of the

Church, theologians may differ, and even be in error, without being heretical.

The inference may be drawn that progress is made in the refinement and precision of theological doctrine as the dogmas of a religion are more fully stated and the line between orthodoxy and heresy becomes more clearly defined. Augustine, who is one of the great formative theologians for the Protestant as well as the Catholic tradition, devotes a large part of his writing to the criticism of heresies—the great Arian heresy concerning the Trinity, the Nestorian or Monophysite heresy concerning the Incarnation, the Manichaean heresy concerning the existence of evil, and the Pelagian heresy concerning grace and good works.

"While the hot restlessness of heretics," Augustine writes, "stirs questions about many articles of the catholic faith, the necessity of defending them forces us . . . to investigate them more accurately, to understand them more clearly, and to proclaim them more earnestly"; and the question mooted by an adversary becomes the occasion of instruction. According to Aquinas, "the profit that ensues from heresy is beside the intention of heretics, for it consists in the constancy of the faithful being put to the test and makes us shake off our sluggishness and search the Scriptures more carefully."

To Augustine and Aquinas, theological argument and controversy seem to be serviceable in the propagation and defense of the faith. Aquinas, for example, distinguishes the various types of dispute in which a Christian theologian can engage—with heretics, with Jews, with infidels. "We can argue with heretics from texts in Holy Scripture," he writes, "and against those who deny one article of faith we can argue from another. If our opponent believes nothing of divine revelation, there is no longer any means of proving the articles of faith by argument, but only of answering his objections—if he has any—against faith."

But it is necessary to add the qualification that the reasons employed "to prove things that are of faith are not demonstrations; they are either persuasive arguments showing that what is proposed by faith is not impossible; or else they are proofs drawn from the principles of faith, *i.e.*, from the authority of Holy Writ . . . Whatever is based on these principles is as well-proved in the eyes of the faithful, as a conclusion drawn from self-evident principles is in the eyes of all."

Furthermore, Aquinas points out, "since faith rests upon infallible truth, and since the contrary of a truth can never be demonstrated, it is clear that the proofs brought against faith are not demonstrations, but arguments that can be answered." Descartes seems to hold a similar view. Defending his opinions in a letter to Father Dinet, he declares: "As to theology, as one truth can never be contrary to another, it would be a kind of impiety to fear that the truths discovered in philosophy were contrary to those of the true Faith."

A SOMEWHAT CONTRARY view of the relation of faith and reason seems to be taken by Locke. "Whatever God hath revealed," he says, "is certainly true; no doubt can be made of it. This is the proper object of faith; but whether it be a divine revelation, or no, reason must judge." Reason, not faith, is the ultimate test of truth, in theology as in philosophy. "Reason must be our last judge and guide in everything." If reason finds something "to be revealed from God, reason then declares for it, as much as for any other truth, and makes it one of her dictates."

In many of the great books we find a less favorable view of the merit or profit in theological controversy. Its excesses and mumbo jumbo are travestied and caricatured by Rabelais; its futility and folly are the subject of bitter complaint by Hobbes and Bacon; its intolerance is condemned by Locke and J. S. Mill. Gibbon, who reports the disputes which raged through ten centuries of Christendom, seldom speaks kindly of the disputants. He refers to "the exquisite rancor of theological hatred"; and in describing the fury of the conflict between the Arians and the defenders of the Nicene creed, he says that, "in the midsts of their fierce contentions, they easily forgot the doubt which is recommended by philosophy, and the submission which is enjoined by religion."

In the Middle Ages, mystical theologians, like Peter Damian or Bernard de Clairvaux, attack as impious or irreligious the kind of theology which borrows from the philosophers and makes use of the liberal arts, especially the techniques of the dialectician. In similar vein Protestant reformers, like Martin Luther, later attack theology itself as detrimental to the purity of Christian faith and the spirit of religion. It is in this vein also that Bacon deplores the "unprofitable subtility or curiosity" and the "fruitless speculation or controversy" in divinity, and speaks of the "extreme prejudice which both religion and philosophy have received and may receive by being commixed together." Here, too, we must place Erasmus, who, in his satirical essay *Praise of Folly* pokes fun at the subtleties of the scholastic theologians of the Middle Ages. "I fancy the apostles themselves would need the help of another holy spirit if they were obliged to join issue on these topics with our new breed of theologian."

When the Student in *Faust* says that "theology has claims more strong" than other disciplines, Mephistopheles replies:

Sir, I should grieve to see you going wrong.
The aspirants who choose that learned field
May fail to see the pitfalls, oversure;
And zealotry has virus so concealed,
It's hard to tell the poison from the cure!

That, however, is the voice of the devil; and from the point of view of those who see no conflict between faith and reason or between piety and inquiry, the attempt to separate religion from theology often looks diabolic.

TWO 20TH-CENTURY comments on theology remain to be added. Weber points out that theologies "regularly proceed from the further presupposition that certain 'revelations' are facts relevant for salvation and as such make possible a meaningful conduct of life. Hence, these revelations must be believed in. Moreover, theologies presuppose that certain subjective states and acts possess the quality of holiness, that is, they constitute a way of life, or at least elements of one, that is religiously meaningful. Then the question of theology is: How can these presuppositions, which must simply be accepted be meaningfully interpreted in a view of the universe? For theology, these presuppositions as such lie beyond the limits of 'science.' They do not represent 'knowledge,' in the usual sense, but rather a 'possession.' Whoever does not 'possess' faith, or the other holy states, cannot have theology as a substitute for them, least of all any other science. On the contrary, in every 'positive' theology, the devout reaches the point where the Augustinian sentence holds: *credo non quod, sed quia absurdum est.*"

Discussing the development of religion and science in the modern era, Whitehead observes the similarity between scientific growth and change in theology. "This fact is a commonplace to theologians, but is often obscured in the stress of controversy." Calling attention to Cardinal Newman's epoch-making treatise on the development of Christian doctrine, in which quite radical theological changes are noted and explained, Whitehead goes on to say that "science is even more changeable than theology. No man of science could subscribe without qualification to Galileo's beliefs, or to Newton's beliefs, or to all his own scientific beliefs of ten years ago." But "when Darwin or Einstein proclaim theories which modify our ideas, it is a triumph for science." In contrast, changes in theology and religious thought are regarded as a retreat, not as progress, and in Whitehead's view this "has at last almost entirely destroyed the intellectual authority of religious thinkers."

Barth is completely negative in his view of the kind of rational discourse that is to be found in traditional theology. "There is no way from us to God—not even a *via negativa*—not even a *via dialectica* nor *paradoxa.* The god who stood at the end of some human way—even of this way—would not be God." And in another place, he writes, "Faith and revelation expressly deny that there is any way from man to God and to God's grace, love, and life. Both words indicate that the only way between God and man is that which leads *from* God *to* man." God's revelation of Himself remains while man's theological approach to God disappears.

93

Time

INTRODUCTION

DEVOURING Time," "wasteful Time," "this bloody tyrant, Time"—Time is the predatory villain with whom not only the lover, but all men must contend. The sonnets of Shakespeare make war upon Time's tyranny—to stay "Time's scythe," to preserve whatever of value can be kept from "the wastes of time," and to prove that "Love's not Time's fool" entirely.

Yet, viewing the almost universal depredations of Time, the poet fears that love may not escape Time's ruin.

When I have seen by Time's fell hand defaced
The rich-proud cost of outworn buried age;
When sometime lofty towers I see down-razed,
And brass eternal slave to mortal rage;
When I have seen the hungry ocean gain
Advantage on the kingdom of the shore,
And the firm soil win of the watery main,
Increasing store with loss and loss with store;
When I have seen such interchange of state,
Or state itself confounded to decay;
Ruin hath taught me thus to ruminate,
That Time will come and take my love away.
　　This thought is as a death, which cannot choose
　　But weep to have that which it fears to lose.

The lover knows that he cannot save his love from change and her beauty from decay. Time is too much for him. But when the lover is also a poet he may hope to defeat Time, not by making his love last forever, but by making the memory of it immortal. "Do thy worst, old Time," he can say, "despite thy wrong, My love shall in my verse ever live young." Or again:

Since brass, nor stone, nor earth, nor boundless sea,
But sad mortality o'er-sways their power,
How with this rage shall beauty hold a plea,
Whose action is no stronger than a flower?
O, how shall summer's honey breath hold out
Against the wreckful siege of battering days,
When rocks impregnable are not so stout,
Nor gates of steel so strong, but Time decays?

O fearful meditation! where, alack,
Shall Time's best jewel from Time's chest lie hid?
Or what strong hand can hold his swift foot back?
Or who his spoil of beauty can forbid?
　　O, none, unless this miracle have might,
　　That in black ink my love may still shine bright.

But the poet may have the cast of a theologian rather than a lover. He may, as Milton does, stand not in awe or fear but in contempt of Time, willing to wait while Time runs out its race. Milton bids Time

. . . glut thyself with what thy womb devours,
Which is no more than what is false and vain,
And merely mortal dross;
So little is our loss,
So little is thy gain.
For when as each thing bad thou hast entomb'd,
And last of all thy greedy self consum'd,
Then long Eternity shall greet our bliss
With an individual kiss . . .
Then all this Earthly grossness quit,
Attir'd with Stars, we shall forever sit,
　　Triumphing over Death, and Chance, and thee
　　　O Time.

A philosopher like Marcus Aurelius neither defies nor despises time. He enjoins himself to accept the mutability of all things as fitting and "suitable to universal nature . . . Dost thou not see," he asks himself, "that for thyself also to change is just the same, and equally necessary for the universal nature?" To him it seems "no evil for things to undergo change"; nor is he oppressed by the image of Time as "a river made up of the events which happen, and a violent stream; for as soon as a thing has been seen, it is carried away, and another comes in its place, and this will be carried away too."

For man to resign himself to time's passage, Pascal thinks, requires no special effort. "Our nature consists in motion," he says; "complete rest is death." Time fits our nature, not only because it "heals griefs and quarrels," but because time's perpetual flow washes away the desperate ennui men suffer when they feel themselves imprisoned in the present.

Just as we seek and multiply diversions as means to escape from ourselves, so, according to Pascal, when we are dissatisfied with the present, "we anticipate the future as too slow in coming . . . or we recall the past, to stop its too rapid flight . . . For the present is generally painful to us . . . Let each one examine his thoughts, and he will find them all occupied with the past and the future . . . The past and present are our means; the future alone is our end. So we never live, but we hope to live; and, as we are always preparing to be happy, it is inevitable we should never be so."

THESE ARE ONLY SOME of the conflicting attitudes toward time and mutability which express man's desire for permanence, for the eternity of a now that stands still, or his restless weariness, his avidity for the novelties time holds in store. Wherever in the great books of poetry, philosophy, or history men reflect upon their loves and aspirations, their knowledge and their institutions, they face man's temporality. It is not that man alone of earthly things has a time-ridden existence, but that his memory and imagination enable him to encompass time, and so save him from being merely rooted in it. Man not only reaches out to the past and future, but he also sometimes lifts himself above the whole of time by conceiving the eternal and the immutable. Or, in the case of a 20th-century writer like Proust, man feels conquered by time. The past cannot be recollected to any satisfactory degree; it is lost—as the title of Proust's work suggests—and we can only regain it through artificial means, as his narrator manages to do by eating the "petites madeleines," the smell and taste of which set off the entire narrative.

Man's apprehension of the past and future is discussed in the chapter on MEMORY AND IMAGINATION. The bent of his mind or his striving toward the unchanging, the everlasting, the eternal, is considered in the chapter on CHANGE. Here we are concerned with his examination of time itself.

Though the idea of time is traditionally linked with that of space, it seems to be much more difficult to grasp. In addition to provoking opposite emotions from the poets, it seems to engage the philosophers in a dispute about its intelligibility. This goes deeper than conflicting definitions or analyses, such as occur in the discussion of both space and time. Whereas time seems no less clear than space to some thinkers, to others it is irremediably obscure. Struggling to say what it is and how it exists, they are exasperated by its evanescence as an object of thought.

Aristotle indicates some initial difficulties in the consideration of time. It is not itself a movement, yet "neither does time exist without change . . . Time is neither movement nor independent of movement." Furthermore, according to Aristotle, time is a continuous quantity. "Time, past, present, and future, forms a continuous whole." T. S. Eliot repeats this notion in *Four Quartets:* "Time present and time past are both perhaps present in time future, and time future contained in time past." But the very nature of a continuous quantity is to be divisible. The present moment, however—the 'now' which is "the link of time" and the dividing line between past and future—seems to be an indivisible instant.

If the present had an extended duration, Aristotle points out, it would have to include parts, some of which would be past and some future. Hence though the present seems to be a part of time, it is, unlike the rest of time, indivisible; and though it separates past and future, yet it must also somehow belong to both, for otherwise time would not be continuous. "The 'now' is an end and a beginning of time, not of the same time however, but the end of that which is past and the beginning of that which is to come."

According to Augustine, we try to define the present as "an instant . . . that cannot be divided even into the most minute fractions," and yet "a point of time as small as this passes so rapidly from the future to the past that its duration is without length." Only past time and future time can be called long or short. Only they have duration. "But how can anything which does not exist be either long or short?" Augustine asks. "The past is no more and the future is not yet."

The past and future, it seems, have duration, or at least extent, but no existence. The present exists but does not endure. "What, then, is time? I know well enough what it is," Augustine says, "provided that nobody asks me; but if I am asked what it is and try to explain, I am baffled." All the words with which we speak of time could not be "plainer or more commonly used. Yet their true meaning is concealed from us. We have still to find it out."

Augustine returns again and again to the point that we can measure time "only while it is passing." But, he says, "If I am asked how I know this, my answer is that I know it because we do measure time. We could not measure a thing which did not exist, and time does not exist when it is past or future. How, then, do we measure present time, when present time has no duration?" While we measure time, Augustine asks, "where is it coming from, what is it passing through, and where is it going? It can only be coming from the future, passing through the present, and going into the past. In other words, it is coming out of what does not yet exist, passing through what has no duration, and moving into what no longer exists."

The more he reflects on time and its measurement, the more Augustine is perplexed, the more he is forced to say, "I still do not know what time is." He realizes that he has been "talking about time for a long time, and that this long time would not be a long time if it were not for the fact that time had been passing all the while. How can I know this, when I do not know what time is?" It seems to him true that we measure time, and yet he must say, "I do not know what I measure." It seems to him that "time is merely an extension, though," he must add, "of what it is an extension I do not know."

Berkeley suggests that the difficulties in understanding time may be of our own making. "Bid your servant meet you at such a *time* in such a place, and he shall never stay to deliberate on the meaning of those words . . . But if *time* be taken exclusive of all those particular actions and ideas that diversify the day, merely for the continuation of existence or duration

in the abstract, then it will perhaps gravel even a philosopher to comprehend it.

"For my own part," Berkeley goes on to say, "whenever I attempt to frame a simple idea of *time*, abstracted from the succession of ideas in my own mind, which flows uniformly and is participated by all beings, I am lost and embrangled in inextricable difficulties. I have no notion of it at all."

To those who conceive time as a mathematical magnitude or as a physical dimension, there seems to be no difficulty about its definition or a precise statement of its properties. So considered, time appears to be no less intelligible than space, for when it is so considered it is being treated exactly like space—not as a property of things, not as relative to bodies or their motions, but as an extensive manifold capable of being occupied by things, and in which they exist and move.

As in what Einstein calls "the four-dimensional space-time continuum" (which comprises three space coordinates and one time coordinate) time is merely one dimension among others, so in Newton's theory time and space are also given parallel treatment. "Times and spaces," Newton writes, "are as it were, the places as well of themselves as of all other things. All things are placed in time as to order of succession; and in space as to order of situation." Einstein criticizes Newtonian mechanics for its "habit of treating time as an independent continuum," yet Newton no less than Einstein appears to conceive time and space alike as dimensions, even if he conceives them in separation from one another.

But if time and space are something to be occupied or filled, they can also be thought of as unoccupied or empty. The opposition, discussed in the chapter on SPACE, between those who think of space in itself as empty, and those who deny a void or vacuum, seems to be paralleled here by the issue concerning empty time—time apart from all change or motion, time in itself. Waiving for the moment the question whether such time exists or is only a mathematical abstraction, we can see that this time may be more susceptible to analysis than the time of ordinary experience, the time which, according to Lucretius, "exists apart from things at rest or moving."

Newton explains that he does not define time, space, place, and motion, because they are "well known to all." But he observes that men commonly "conceive these quantities under no other notions but from the relation they bear to sensible objects." He finds it necessary, therefore, to distinguish each of them "into absolute and relative, true and apparent, mathematical and common."

By "absolute, true, and mathematical time," Newton means that which "of itself, and from its own nature, flows equably without relation to anything external, and by another name is called duration." In contrast, "relative, apparent, and common time, is some sensible and external (whether accurate or unequable) measure of duration by the means of motion, which is commonly used instead of true time, such as an hour, a day, a month, a year." In astronomy, Newton points out, absolute time "is distinguished from relative, by the equation or correction of the apparent time. For the natural days are truly unequal, though they are commonly considered as equal, and used for measures of time; astronomers correct this inequality that they may measure the celestial motions by a more accurate time."

Newton seems to be saying that time measures motion and also that it is measured by it. If his distinction between absolute and relative time is ignored, his theory of time does not appear to be very different from that of Aristotle, who says, "not only do we measure the movement by the time, but also the time by the movement." Insofar as movement or change involves a sequence in which one part comes after another, time measures it by numbering the *befores* and *afters*. But we also judge the length of the time according to the duration of the movement, and in this sense the movement measures time.

As both Aristotle and Augustine point out, time measures rest as well as motion, for, in Aristotle's words, "all rest is in time . . . Time is not motion, but the 'number of motion' and what is at rest can be in the number of motion. Not everything that is not in motion can be said to be 'at rest'—but only that

which can be moved, though it actually is not moved."

But where Aristotle, in defining time as the measure of motion or rest, makes time an attribute of movement, Newton regards absolute time as the perfect measure of motion precisely because its nature is independent of all physical change. Only relative time depends on motion, and that is the time which is measured by motion, not the measure of it. Those "who confound real quantities with their relations and sensible measures," Newton declares, "defile the purity of mathematical and philosophical truths."

Distinguishing between duration and time, Locke expresses in another way the difference between Newton and Aristotle. Time for Locke is that portion of duration which consists of definite periods and is measured by the motion of bodies. "We must, therefore, carefully distinguish betwixt duration itself, and the measures we make use of to judge its length. Duration in itself is to be considered as going on in one constant, equal uniform course; but none of the measures which we make use of, can be known to do so." It seems wrong to Locke to define time as the measure of motion when, on the contrary, it is motion—"the motion of the great and visible bodies of the world"—which measures time.

What Locke calls "duration" seems to be the same as Newton's absolute time. It is in no way relative to the existence of bodies or motion. Just as space or, as he calls it, "expansion," is not limited by matter, so duration is not limited by motion. As place is that portion of infinite space "which is possessed by and comprehended within the material world, and is thereby distinguished from the rest of expansion," so time is "so much of infinite duration, as is measured by, and coexistent with, the existence and motions of the great bodies of the universe."

MANY ISSUES ARE RAISED by absolute time or infinite duration conceived as independent of all bodily motions. Einstein, for example, challenges the classical notion of simultaneity, according to which two events taking place a great distance from one another are said to occur *at the same time,* that is, at the same moment in the absolute flow of time.

According to this notion, events that appear simultaneous to a pair of observers would appear simultaneous to all observers. Einstein illustrates this with the example of two bolts of lightning striking "simultaneously" at the front and back ends of a moving train. He notes that a careful analysis shows that these "simultaneous" events cannot appear simultaneous for an observer at rest in the train and an observer at rest on the ground. The Newtonian physicist, on the other hand, who ignores the fact that light propagates with a finite speed, would argue that simultaneity was absolute. Einstein argues that any actual time measurement—such as the time of arrival of a train in a railway station at a given hour—is, in fact, a measurement of two simultaneous events: the arrival of the train at some place and the arrival of the hands of a clock at some configuration. Since, in his theory, simultaneity is relative to the state of motion of the observers, so then is the time duration of events relative to the state of motion of observers.

"Before the advent of the theory of relativity," Einstein writes, "it had always been tacitly assumed in physics that the statement of time had an absolute significance, *i.e.,* that it is independent of the state of motion of the body of reference." But if the world of physical events is a four-dimensional manifold in which the time coordinate is always associated with the space coordinates for any reference-body under observation, then "every reference-body (coordinate system) has its own particular time"; and, Einstein adds, "unless we are told the reference-body to which the statement of time refers, there is no meaning in a statement of the time of an event."

There is also the issue of the emptiness of that part of absolute time or infinite duration which comes before or after the existence of the world, comparable to the issue concerning the void or empty space beyond the borders of the material universe. Those who regard time as relative to and inseparable from motion deny the possibility of such empty time.

For Plato, as for Christian theologians like Augustine and Aquinas, time itself is created

with the creation of the heavenly bodies and their motions. As the story of the world's becoming is told in the *Timaeus,* the maker "resolved to have a moving image of eternity, and when he set in order the heaven, he made this image eternal but moving according to number, while eternity itself rests in unity; and this image we call time . . . Time, then, and the heaven came into being at the same instant."

Augustine undertakes to answer "those who agree that God is the Creator of the world, but have difficulties about the time of its creation." He asserts that "there is no time before the world . . . For if eternity and time are rightly distinguished by this, that time does not exist without some movement and transition, while in eternity there is no change, who does not see that there could have been no time had not some creature been made, which by some motion could give birth to change . . . I do not see," Augustine continues, "how God can be said to have created the world after spaces of time had elapsed, unless it be said that prior to the world there was some creature by whose movement time could pass." But the existence of a creature prior to creation is impossible. Hence Augustine concludes that "if in the world's creation change and motion were created," then "the world and time were simultaneously created."

Though the existence of a creature prior to creation is impossible, it is not impossible, according to Aquinas, for the created world to be coeval with its Creator. While he rejects the opinion of those who assert that the world now exists without any dependence on God, and who deny that it was ever made by God, he entertains, as possible, the view that "the world has a beginning, not of time, but of creation." Those who hold this view, he explains, mean that "it was always made . . . For just as, if a foot were always in the dust from eternity, there would always be a footprint which without doubt was caused by him who trod on it, so also the world always was, because its Maker always existed."

It does not necessarily follow, Aquinas admits, that "if God is the active cause of the world, He must be prior to the world in duration, because creation, by which He produced the world, is not a successive change." But Aquinas does not think that the question whether the world and time began with creation or has always coexisted with its Creator, can be resolved by reason. "The newness of the world," he says, "is known only by revelation . . . That the world did not always exist we hold by faith alone; it cannot be proved demonstratively." In saying this, he is not unmindful of the fact that Aristotle advances arguments to show that there can be no beginning to either time or motion. "Since time cannot exist and is unthinkable apart from the moment, and the moment is a kind of middle point, uniting as it does in itself both . . . a beginning of future time and an end of past time, it follows that there must always be time . . . But if this is true of time, it is evident that it must also be true of motion, time being an attribute of motion."

Newton himself believed that the universe had an initiating origin in time, that time began at the instant of creation, as stated in Genesis 1: "In the beginning God created heaven and earth." For Aquinas that belief is an article of faith, based on divinely inspired Scripture; it is not a truth that reason can affirm by argument from empirical evidence. As for Kant much later, so for Aquinas, neither one or the other of the two conflicting assertions— that time has a beginning or that time ever began—can be established by rational argument or by empirical evidence.

From the point of view of Aquinas as a theologian, the understanding of God as the indispensable cause of the existence of this cosmos in which we live remains exactly the same whether it had a beginning or has always existed with no beginning in time.

Contemporary philosophical theologians agree with Aquinas on this point against the position taken by many 20th-century scientific cosmologists who suppose that the big bang origin of the development of this cosmos can be interpreted as the creative instant in which it came into being out of absolute nothing. For them, the big bang is not *ex nihilo;* for them, it is not the beginning of time, though they would concede that our physical measurements of time cannot go back further

than 15,000,000,000 years ago when the big bang occurred. Accordingly, Stephen Hawking's book should have been entitled *A Brief History of Measurable Time.*

With one exception, all his predecessors, according to Aristotle, are in agreement that time is uncreated. "In fact," he says, "it is just this that enables Democritus to show that all things cannot have had a becoming . . . Plato alone asserts the creation of time, saying that it had a becoming together with the universe." But Aristotle's own arguments for the eternity of time and motion do not seem to Aquinas to be "absolutely demonstrative, but only relatively so—*viz.,* as against the arguments of some of the ancients who asserted that the world began to be in some actually impossible ways." As for the present moment, or the *now* of time, always requiring something which comes *before* as well as *after,* Aquinas admits that "time cannot be made except according to some *now,"* yet "not because there is time in the first *now,* but because from it time begins."

The position of Aquinas, that arguments for the initiation or the endlessness of time are only dialectical, seems to be confirmed by Kant. In the Transcendental Dialectic of *The Critique of Pure Reason,* Kant sets forth as one of the cosmological antinomies the opposed arguments for the beginning of the world and for a world without beginning. The reasoning on either side being equal in its *appearance* of cogency, neither conclusion, according to Kant, is genuinely demonstrated.

But those who, like Newton and Locke, separate absolute time or infinite duration from the existence of a world in motion, seem to be unaffected by arguments which concern only the time of the material world, the time that is relative to motion. For them, absolute or infinite time is eternity. It may be empty of motion, but it is filled with God's everlasting being. "Though we make duration boundless, as certainly it is," Locke writes, "we cannot yet extend it beyond all being. God, every one easily allows, fills eternity." God is not eternity, says Newton, but He is eternal. "His duration reaches from eternity to eternity . . . He endures forever, and is everywhere present;

and, by existing always and everywhere, He constitutes duration and space."

The issue is again brought into focus by the denial that God's eternity can be identified with infinite or absolute time. "Even supposing that the world always was," Aquinas writes, it would not be eternal in the sense in which God is, "for the divine being is all being simultaneously without succession." He distinguishes "the *now* that stands still" as the eternal present from the continually shifting *now* in the flow of time's passing moments. For him God's everlasting being does not endure through endless time, but rather exists unchanging in the eternal present. "As eternity is the proper measure of being, so time is the proper measure of movement; and hence," Aquinas writes, "according as any being recedes from permanence in being, and is subject to change, it recedes from eternity and is subject to time."

THE TWO MEANINGS of eternity—infinite time and utter timelessness—are discussed in the chapter on ETERNITY. The distinction between time and eternity, which is considered both there and here, seems to be understood differently by those who contrast timelessness with temporality and by those who equate eternity with endless time. For the latter, the point of difference between eternity and time seems to be only one of infinite as opposed to limited duration. Yet, as we have just observed, writers like Newton and Locke also distinguish absolute or infinite time (which they tend to identify with eternity) from definite periods or limited spans of time, by making the one independent of, the other relative to and measured by, motion.

The question remains whether absolute time is real time or only a mathematical abstraction, whether it exists apart from perceived time—the experienced duration of observable motions or the elapsed time of events in succession.

Considering this question, Kant says that "those who maintain the absolute reality of time and space, whether as essentially subsisting, or only inhering, as modifications in things, must find themselves at utter variance with the principles of experience itself. For, if they decide for the first view, and make space and time into substances, this being the side taken by mathematical natural philosophers, they must admit two self-subsisting nonentities, infinite and eternal, which exist (yet without their being anything real) for the purpose of containing in themselves everything that is real. If they adopt the second view of inherence, which is preferred by some metaphysical natural philosophers, and regard space and time as relations ... abstracted from experience ... they find themselves in that case necessitated to deny the validity of mathematical doctrine *a priori* in reference to real things."

On Kant's own view, the synthetic judgments of mathematics can have the absolute certainty of *a priori* propositions only if space and time are themselves *a priori* forms of intuition. As the *a priori* form of space makes possible the pure science of geometry, according to Kant, so the *a priori* form of time makes possible the pure science of numbers, *i.e.*, arithmetic. But whereas "space, as the pure form of external intuition is limited ... to external phenomena alone," time, as "the form of the internal sense," is for Kant "the formal condition *a priori* of all phenomena whatsoever."

Without sharing Kant's theory of *a priori* forms of intuition, or of the foundations of pure mathematics, other writers appear to agree to some extent with his denial of independent reality to time. Aristotle raises the question "whether if soul did not exist, time would exist or not." He thinks the question may be fairly asked because "if there cannot be someone to count, there cannot be anything that can be counted, so that evidently there cannot be number"—for number is the counted or the countable. "But if nothing but soul, or in soul reason, is qualified to count, there would not be time unless there were soul." Yet Aristotle qualifies this somewhat by adding that "if *movement* can exist without soul, and the before and after are attributes of movement," time may exist as "these *qua* numerable."

Augustine takes a less qualified position. Asking what it is that time is the "extension of," he wonders whether it is "the mind itself." Insisting that neither future nor past time can be measured because neither exists, Augustine concludes that it is only passing time we can measure, and that we can measure it only in the mind. "It is in my own mind," he says, "that I measure time . . . Everything which happens leaves an impression on it, and this impression remains after the thing itself has ceased to be. It is the impression that I measure, since it is still present, not the thing itself, which makes the impression as it passes and then moves into the past. When I measure time it is this impression that I measure."

Yet William James, while giving a similar analysis of our experience of time, insists that time is objective as well as subjective. Time and space relations, he writes, "*are* impressed from without." The time and space in which the objects of our thought exist, exist as independently of the mind as do those objects themselves. "*The time- and space-relations between things do stamp copies within*"; as, for example, when "things sequent in time impress their sequence on our memory."

JAMES THEN PROPOSES a solution of the mystery of how time exists—at least how it exists in experience. So far as our experience goes, past and future can exist only in the present. But how can these extended parts of time exist in the present if the present is but a fleeting moment, without any extent of duration, "gone," as James says, "in the instant of becoming"? His answer is in terms of something he calls "the specious present."

Commenting on the present moment in the light of the theory of relativity, Heisenberg tells us that "in classical theory we assume that future and past are separated by an infinitely short time interval which we may call the present moment. In the theory of relativity we have learned that the situation is different: future and past are separated by a finite time interval the length of which depends on the distance from the observer. Any action can only be propagated by a velocity smaller than or equal to the velocity of light."

Unlike the real present, what James calls the specious present is "no knife-edge but a saddle-back, with a certain breadth of its own on which we sit perched, and from which we look in two directions into time. The unit of composition of our perception of time is a *duration,* with a bow and a stern, as it were— a rearward- and a forward-looking end. It is only as parts of this *duration-block* that the relation of *succession* of one end to the other is perceived."

On the basis of some experimental evidence, James estimates that the specious present may vary in length "from a few seconds to probably not more than a minute." It has "a vaguely vanishing backward and forward fringe; but its nucleus is probably the dozen seconds or less that have just elapsed."

The irreversible flow of time—the succession of moments which constitute the motion of the future through the present into the past—occurs in the specious present, though not, according to James, without the accompaniment of observed or experienced change. "Awareness of *change* is . . . the condition on which our perception of time's flow depends." But that awareness must take place in the specious present "with its content perceived as having one part earlier and the other part later." In consequence, James considers the specious present to be, not only "the original intuition of time," but also *the original paragon prototype of all conceived times.*"

In the 19th century, with the work of people like James Clerk Maxwell, Ludwig Eduard Boltzmann, and others, a new puzzle about the nature of time arose. Viewed on a microscopic level, all the collisions of a gas appear to be "time reversible." This means that if a film of such collisions were made and then run backward, the collisions viewed from this perspective would be indistinguishable in kind from the collisions viewed in the forward-running film. Nonetheless, the system, studied microscopically, "ages." The resolution of this paradox, which has exercised several generations of scientists, appears to be in the initial conditions in which these systems are prepared. If a system is prepared in an improbable initial condition, it will tend to evolve toward more and more probable states even though each collision is time reversible. In the language of entropy, the system tends to evolve toward states of greater and greater entropy. In this sense, the system ages.

THE PROBLEMS OF TIME, its own process and being as well as its relation to all other existence and change, its character as an aspect of experience and as an object of thought, seem to belong to many subject matters—to psychology and to experimental or mathematical physics, to the philosophy of nature, metaphysics, and theology.

For some thinkers—in the 20th century notably Bergson, Whitehead, and Dewey—the concept of time, of the burgeoning future, of the continuum of events, seems to determine a whole philosophical outlook. Bergson, for example, writes that "reality is mobility. Not *things* made, but things in the making, not self-maintaining *states,* but only changing states, exist. Rest is never more than apparent, or, rather, relative."

If the concept of time is not equally decisive throughout the tradition of the great books, it is at least of critical significance in speculations about the origin and end of the world, in the contrast between physical and spiritual modes of being, in the consideration of the processes of life, thought, and feeling, and in the analysis of more inclusive concepts, such as that of order.

The temporal relationships of succession and simultaneity, for example, may be the source from which we derive the notions of prior, posterior, and simultaneous, but they are traditionally viewed as exemplifying rather than exhausting these types of order. When Augustine deals with the perplexing theological question of the priority of eternity to time, he finds it necessary to distinguish "priority in eternity, in time, in choice, and in origin."

When Aristotle deals with metaphysical questions concerning the order of cause and effect, of potentiality and actuality, of essence and accident, he differentiates between temporal and logical priority, and between priority in thought and priority in nature. When Harvey tries to solve the familiar biological riddle (which came first, the chicken or the egg?), he also finds his solution in a distinction. "The fowl is prior by nature," he writes, "but the egg is prior in time."

Space and spatial relationships, no less than time and the temporal, figure in the general analysis of order or relatedness and have a bearing on other problems in physics and philosophy. But in addition to time's having more significance than space for the theologian, time also has peculiar importance for one subject matter in which space is of much less concern, namely, history and the philosophy of history.

Besides the general view which the historian takes of time as the locus of history, or the medium in which the pattern of history unfolds, the writer of history usually employs certain conventional time divisions to mark the major phases or epochs of the story he has to tell. Clocks and calendars record or represent the passage of time in conventional units, but these conventions have some natural basis in astronomical time, solar or sidereal. In contrast, the distinction between historic and prehistoric time, or the division of history into such periods as ancient, medieval, and modern, seems to be purely a matter of social or cultural convention.

With Hegel, however, the division of the whole of history into three epochs, and of each epoch again into three periods, follows from the dialectical triad of thesis, antithesis, and synthesis which is the indwelling form of history's development. The division of each of the three phases of world history—the Oriental, the Greco-Roman, and the German worlds—into a first, second, and third period produces in each case the same pattern of origin, conflict, and resolution. For the most part, Hegel does not identify these three periods with ancient, medieval, and modern times; yet in one case, that of the German world, he does refer to the second period as "the middle ages" and the third as "the modern time."

Such words as "ancient" and "modern" have conventional significance for most historians. Furthermore, the meanings of modernity and antiquity are themselves subject to historical relativity. In the tradition of the great books, this appears most plainly in the references made to ancients and moderns by writers whom we today classify as ancient and medieval.

Thucydides, for example, begins his history with a description of what is for him the antiquity of Greece. Nicomachus opens his *Introduction to Arithmetic* with a remark about "the ancients, who under the leadership of Pythagoras first made science systematic, defined philosophy as the love of wisdom." Mathematics, Aristotle says, "has come to be identical with philosophy for modern thinkers."

In another place, Aristotle contrasts "the thinkers of the present day" with "the thinkers of old"; and in still another he speaks of "ancient and truly traditional theories." Like Aristotle in the sphere of thought, so Tacitus in the sphere of politics frequently compares ancient and modern institutions or practices.

In the Middle Ages, Aquinas speaks of the "teachings of the early philosophers" and, as frequently as Aristotle, he refers to ancient and modern doctrines. In the Renaissance, Kepler treats as ancient a scientist who, in point of time, comes much later than those whom Aristotle and Aquinas call modern. Classifying three schools of astronomical thought, he distinguishes an ancient one, which had "Ptolemy as its coryphaeus," from two modern ones, respectively headed by Copernicus and Tycho Brahe.

Such references, which have occurred in all three periods of the western tradition, suggest the probability that at some future date the whole tradition with which we are now acquainted will be referred to as the thought and culture of ancient times.

94

Truth

INTRODUCTION

Not everyone knows Josiah Royce's definition of a liar as a man who willfully misplaces his ontological predicates, but everyone who has ever told a lie will recognize its accuracy. To restate the definition less elegantly, lying consists in saying the contrary of what one thinks or believes. To speak truthfully we must make our speech conform to our thought, we must say that something is the case if we think it is, or that it is not, if we think it is not. If we deliberately say "is" when we think *is not,* or say "is not" when we think *is,* we lie.

Of course, the man who speaks truthfully may in fact say what is false, just as the man whose intent is to falsify may inadvertently speak the truth. The intention to speak one's mind does not guarantee that one's mind is free from error or in possession of the truth. Herein lies the traditional distinction between truth as a social and as an intellectual matter. What Dr. Johnson calls *moral* truth consists in the obligation to say what we mean. In contrast what he calls *physical* truth depends not on the veracity of what we say but on the validity of what we mean.

The theory of truth in the tradition of the great books deals largely with the latter kind of truth. The great issues concern whether we can know the truth and how we can ever tell whether something is true or false. Though the philosophers and scientists, from Plato to Freud, seem to stand together against the extreme sophistry or skepticism which denies the distinction between true and false or puts truth utterly beyond the reach of man, they do not all agree on the extent to which truth is attainable by men, on its immutability or variability, on the signs by which men tell whether they have the truth or not, or on the causes of error and the means for avoiding falsity.

Much that Plato thinks is true Freud rejects as false. Freud searches for truth in other quarters and by other methods. But the ancient controversy in which Socrates engages with the sophists of his day, who were willing to regard as true whatever anyone wished to think, seems to differ not at all from Freud's quarrel with those whom he calls "intellectual nihilists." They are the persons who say there is no such thing as truth or that it is only the product of our own needs and desires. They make it "absolutely immaterial," Freud writes, "what views we accept. All of them are equally true and false. And no one has a right to accuse anyone else of error."

Across the centuries the arguments against the skeptic seem to be the same. If the skeptic does not mind contradicting himself when he tries to defend the truth of the proposition that all propositions are equally true or false, he can perhaps be challenged by the fact that he does not act according to his view. If all opinions are equally true or false, then why, Aristotle asks, does not the denier of truth walk "into a well or over a precipice" instead of avoiding such things. "If it were really a matter of indifference what we believed," Freud similarly argues, "then we might just as well build our bridges of cardboard as of stone, or inject a tenth of a gramme of morphia into a patient instead of a hundredth, or take tear-gas as a narcotic instead of ether. But," he adds, "the intellectual anarchists themselves would strongly repudiate such practical applications of their theory."

Whether the skeptic can be refuted or merely silenced may depend on a further step in the argument, in which the skeptic substitutes probability for truth, both as a basis for action and as the quality of all our opinions about the real world. The argument takes different forms according to the different ways in which probability is distinguished from truth or according to the distinction between a complete and limited skepticism. Montaigne, for example, seems to think that the complete skeptic cannot even acknowledge degrees of probability to be objectively ascertainable without admitting the criterion of truth, whereas Hume, defending a mitigated skepticism, offers criteria for measuring the probability of judgments about matters of fact.

The self-refuting character of total or nihilistic skepticism with regard to truth pervades all of Nietzsche's works. What claim can they make upon the judgment of readers? In what way are they persuasive if, denying the traditional values of truth and falsity, they cannot assume the guise of truth?

THE POSITION OF THE skeptic, in its bearing on truth and probability, is discussed in the chapters on KNOWLEDGE and OPINION. Here we shall proceed to other controversial questions concerning truth. But we must first observe that there is one major question which does not seem to cause much dispute. Not only do the great authors (with the possible exception of Montaigne and Hume) seem to be unanimous in their conviction that men can attain and share the truth—at least some truths—but they also appear to give the same answer to the question, What is truth?

The apparently unanimous agreement on the nature of truth may seem remarkable in the context of the manifold disagreements in the great books concerning what is true. As already indicated, some of these disagreements occur in the theory of truth itself— in divergent analyses of the sources of error, or in conflicting formulations of the signs of truth. But even these differences do not affect the agreement on the nature of truth. Just as everyone knows what a liar is, but not as readily whether someone is telling a lie, so the great philosophers seem able to agree on

what truth is, but not as readily on what is true. That the definitions—of lying and of truth—are intimately connected will be seen from Plato's conception of the nature of truth as a correspondence between thought and reality. If truthfulness, viewed socially, requires a man's words to be a faithful representation of his mind, truth in the mind itself (or in the statements which express thought) depends on their conformity to reality.

A false proposition, according to Plato, is "one which asserts the non-existence of things which are, and the existence of things which are not." Since "false opinion is that form of opinion which thinks the opposite of the truth," it necessarily follows, as Aristotle points out, that "to say of what is that it is, and of what is not that it is not, is true," just as it is false "to say of what is that it is not, or of what is not that it is."

In one sense, the relation between a true statement and the fact it states is reciprocal. "If a man is," Aristotle declares, then "the proposition in which we allege that he is, is true; and conversely, if the proposition wherein we allege that he is, is true, then he is." But the true proposition "is in no way the cause of the being of the man," whereas "the fact of the man's being does seem somehow to be the cause of the truth of the proposition, for the truth or falsity of the proposition depends on the fact of the man's being or not being."

THIS SIMPLE STATEMENT about the nature of truth is repeated again and again in the subsequent tradition of western thought. What variation there is from writer to writer seems to be in phrasing alone, though the common insight concerning truth as an agreement or correspondence between the mind and reality may occur in the context of widely varying conceptions concerning the nature of the mind and of reality or being.

Plotinus may be an exception, insofar as his theory of knowledge involves a relation of identity rather than of mere correspondence. "The object known," he writes, "must be identical with the knowing act . . . If this identity does not exist, neither does truth . . .

Truth cannot apply to something conflicting with itself; what it affirms it must also be."

But others, like Augustine, Aquinas, Descartes, and Spinoza, adopt the conception of truth as an agreement between the mind and reality. "Falsehood," says Augustine, "is nothing but the supposed existence of something which has no being." According to Aquinas, "any intellect which understands a thing to be otherwise than it is, is false." Truth in the human intellect consists "in the conformity of the intellect with the thing." The same point is implied, at least, in Descartes's remark that if we do not relate our ideas "to anything beyond themselves, they cannot properly speaking be false." Error or, for that matter, truth can only arise in "my judging that the ideas which are in me are similar or conformable to the things which are outside me." Spinoza states it as an axiom rather than a definition that "a true idea must agree with that of which it is the idea."

Making a distinction between verbal and real truth, Locke writes: "Though our words signify nothing but our ideas, yet being designed by them to signify things, the truth they contain, when put into propositions, will be only verbal, when they stand for ideas in the mind that have not an agreement with the reality of things." Precisely because he considers truth to consist "in the accordance of a cognition with its object," Kant holds that, so far as the content (as opposed to the form) of a cognition is concerned, it is impossible to discover a universal criterion of truth.

We shall return to Kant's point in a subsequent discussion of the signs of truth, as also we shall have occasion to return to Locke's distinction between real and verbal truth. Neither affects the insight that truth consists in the agreement of our propositions or judgments with the facts they attempt to state, unless it is the qualification that truth so defined is real, not verbal.

In *Pragmatism,* William James puts the matter into a nutshell by saying that " '*the true*'. . . *is only the expedient in the way of our thinking, just as 'the right' is only the expedient in the way of our behaving.*" Theories that "*work satisfactorily*" are true. In his Preface to *The Meaning of Truth,* James comments on the excitement caused by his earlier lectures on pragmatism, in which, offering the pragmatist's conception of truth, he had spoken of an idea's "working successfully" as the sign of its truth. He warns his critics that this is not a new definition of the nature of truth, but only a new interpretation of what it means to say that the truth of our ideas consists in "their agreement, as falsity means their disagreement, with reality. Pragmatists and intellectualists," he adds, "both accept this definition as a matter of course.

"To agree in the widest sense with reality," James then explains, "can only mean to be guided either straight up to it or into its surroundings, or to be put into such working touch with it as to handle either it or something connected with it better than if we disagreed. Better either intellectually or practically . . . Any idea that helps us to deal, whether practically or intellectually, with either the reality or its belongings . . . that *fits,* in fact, and adapts our life to the reality's whole setting, will agree sufficiently to meet the requirement. It will be true of that reality." James sums this up with the statement that "*true ideas are those that we can assimilate, validate, corroborate and verify. False ideas are those that we cannot.*"

Without enlarging on its meaning as James does, Freud affirms that the ordinary man's conception of truth is that of the scientist also. Science, he says, aims "to arrive at correspondence with reality, that is to say with what exists outside of us and independently of us . . . This correspondence with the real external world we call truth. It is the aim of scientific work, even when the practical value of that work does not interest us."

THE DEFINITION OF TRUTH as the agreement of the mind with reality leaves many problems to be solved and further explanations to be given by those who accept it. As James indicates, the theory of truth begins rather than ends with its definition. How do we know when our ideas—our statements or judgments—correspond with reality? By what signs or criteria shall we discover their truth or falsity? To this question the great books give various answers which we shall presently consider. There are other problems about the nature of truth which deserve attention first.

For example, one consequence of the definition seems to be that truth is a property of ideas rather than of things. Aristotle says that "it is not as if the good were true and the bad were in itself false"; hence "falsity and truth are not in things . . . but in thought." Yet he also applies the word "false" to nonexistent things or to things whose appearance somehow belies their nature. Aquinas goes further. He distinguishes between the sense in which truth and falsity are primarily in the intellect and secondarily in things.

The equation between intellect and thing, he points out, can be looked at in two ways, depending on whether the intellect is the cause of the thing's nature, or the nature of the thing is the cause of knowledge in the intellect. When "things are the measure and rule of the intellect, truth consists in the equation of the intellect to the thing . . . But when the intellect is the rule or measure of things, truth consists in the equation of things to the intellect"—as the product of human art may be said to be true when it accords with the artist's plan or intention. Thus "a house is said to be true that fulfills the likeness of the form in the architect's mind."

But, according to Aquinas, not only artificial things, but natural things as well, can have truth when they are viewed in relation to the intellect on which they depend. The divine intellect which is the creative cause of natural things measures their truth, as the human intellect measures the truth of artificial things. "Natural things are said to be true," Aquinas writes, "in so far as they express the likeness of the ideas that are in the divine mind; for a stone is called true, which possesses the nature proper to a stone, according to the preconception in the divine intellect."

Aquinas' conclusion—that "truth resides primarily in the intellect and secondarily in things according as they are related to the intellect as their source"—at once suggests the profound difference between truth in the divine and in the human intellect. The difference

is more than that between infinite and finite truth. The distinction between uncreated and created truth affects the definition of truth itself.

The definition of truth as an equation of thought to thing, or thing to thought, does not seem to hold for the divine intellect. The notion of "conformity with its source," Aquinas acknowledges, "cannot be said, properly speaking, of divine truth." Divine truth has no source. It is not truth by correspondence with anything else. Rather it is, in the language of the theologian, the "primal truth." "God Himself, Who is the primal truth . . . is the rule of all truth," and "the principle and source of all truth."

IN THE HUMAN SPHERE, the definition of truth seems to be differently interpreted according as truth is made a property of words or of ideas. "To form a clear notion of truth," Locke writes, "it is very necessary to consider truth of thought and truth of words distinctly from one another." The truth of signs, or what is sometimes called "truth of signification," is "nothing but the joining or separating of words in propositions as the ideas they stand for agree or disagree in men's minds." In contrast to such verbal truth, what Locke calls mental truth consists in the joining or separating of our ideas themselves in a manner to accord with the realities they represent.

For Locke, verbal truth is "chimerical" or "barely nominal" because it can exist without any regard to "whether our ideas are such as really have, or are capable of having, an existence in nature." The signs we use may truly represent our thought even though what we think or state in words is false in fact. Hobbes takes a somewhat contrary view. "True and false," he writes, "are attributes of speech, not of things. And where speech is not, there is neither truth nor falsehood."

What is the cause of truth in speech? Hobbes replies that, since it consists "in the right ordering of names in our affirmations," a man needs only "to remember what every name he uses stands for." If men begin with definitions or "the settling of significations," and then abide by their definitions in subsequent discourse, their discourse will have truth. From want of definitions or from wrong definitions arise "all false and senseless tenets."

Agreement with reality would seem to be the measure of truth for Hobbes only to the extent that definitions can be right or wrong by reference to the objects defined. If definitions themselves are merely nominal and have rightness so far as they may be free from contradiction, then truth tends to become, more than a property of speech, almost purely logistic—a matter of playing the game of words according to the rules. Reasoning is reckoning with words. It begins with definitions and if it proceeds rightly, it produces "general, eternal and immutable truth . . . For he that reasoneth aright in words he understandeth, can never conclude in error."

Hobbes's position seems to have a bearing not only on the issue concerning verbal and real truth, but also on the question whether the logical validity of reasoning makes the conclusion it reaches true as a matter of fact. Some writers, like Kant, distinguish between the truth which a proposition has when it conforms to the rules of thought and the truth it has when it represents nature. Valid reasoning alone cannot guarantee that a conclusion is true in fact. That depends on the truth of the premises—upon their being true of the nature of things. Aristotle criticizes those who, accepting certain principles as true, "are ready to accept any consequence of their application. As though some principles," he continues, "did not require to be judged from their results, and particularly from their final issue. And that issue . . . in the knowledge of nature is the unimpeachable evidence of the senses as to each fact."

BUT NOT ALL TRUTH may require or admit of such certification. The truths of mathematics may be different from those of physics or metaphysics, and those of philosophy or religion from those of the empirical natural sciences. It is sometimes supposed, for example, that the truths of mathematics are purely formal or without reference to real existence. That seems to be the position of Hobbes and

Hume, both of whom take geometry as the model of truth. For them statements of fact about real existence are at best probable opinions. For others, like James, there can be truth in the natural sciences, but such empirical truth is distinct in type from what he calls the "necessary" or "*a priori*" truths of mathematics and logic.

Does the definition of truth as agreement with reality apply to all kinds of truth, or only to truths about the realm of nature? The question has in mind more than the distinction between mathematics and physics. It is concerned with the difference between the study of nature and the moral sciences, or between the theoretical and the practical disciplines. "As regards nature," writes Kant, "experience presents us with rules and is the source of truth," but not so in ethical matters or morality. A theoretical proposition asserts that something exists or has a certain property, and so its truth depends on the existence of the thing or its real possession of an attribute; but a practical or moral judgment states, not what is, but what should occur or ought to be. Such a judgment cannot be true by correspondence with the way things are. Its truth, according to Aristotle, must consist rather "in agreement with right desire."

On this theory, all that remains common to speculative and practical truth is the conformity of the intellect to something outside itself—to an existing thing or to desire, will, or appetite. Stressing the difference, Aquinas declares that "truth is not the same for the practical as for the speculative intellect." The "conformity with right appetite" upon which practical truth depends, he goes on to say, "has no place in necessary matters, which are not effected by the human will, but only in contingent matters which can be effected by us, whether they be matters of interior action or the products of external work." In consequence, "in matters of action, truth or practical rectitude is not the same for all as to what is particular, but only as to the common principles"; whereas in speculative matters, concerned chiefly with necessary things, "truth is the same for all men, both as to principles and as to conclusions."

THE PROBLEM OF THE criteria or signs of truth does not seem to be of equal concern to all who discuss the nature of truth. For the ancients, at one extreme, it seems to be hardly a problem at all. For James, at the other extreme, it seems to be the central problem. In the controversy over the pragmatic theory of truth, in which James engages with F. H. Bradley and Bertrand Russell, some confusion tends to result from the fact that James seldom discusses what truth is except in terms of how we know what is true, while his opponents often ignore the signs of truth in discussing its nature. The important point for James is not that truth consists in agreement with reality, but that "true ideas are those we can assimilate, validate, corroborate, and verify." Whether we can assimilate or validate or verify an idea in turn depends upon its consequences, either for thought or action, or what James calls "truth's cash-value in experiential terms."

In his *The Principles of Psychology,* James suggests another aspect of his theory of the expediency of a true idea, which he later developed in *Pragmatism.* Not only must our conceptions or theories be "able to account satisfactorily for our sensible experience," but they are also to be weighed for their appeal "to our aesthetic, emotional, and active needs." Apart from this added criterion, which became the subject of much dispute, the pragmatic theory of truth represents one of the traditional solutions of the problem of how to tell whether something is true or false. It looks mainly to extrinsic signs—not to some feature of the idea or thought itself, but to its consequences.

"The test of real and vigorous thinking," writes J. S. Mill, "the thinking which ascertains truths instead of dreaming, is successful application to practice." In similar vein, Francis Bacon says that "of all the signs there is none more certain or worthy than that of the fruits produced, for the fruits and effects are the sureties and vouchers, as it were, for the truth of philosophy." The man who supposes that the end of learning lies in contemplation of the truth will "propose to himself as the test of truth, the satisfaction of his mind and understanding, as to the causes of things long

since known." Only those who recognize that "the real and legitimate goal of the sciences is the endowment of human life with new inventions and riches," will submit truth to the test of its leading "to some new earnest of effects." To take effects as "pledges of truth" is, for Bacon, equivalent to declaring that truth and utility are "perfectly identical."

Verification by appeal to observation or sensible evidences may be regarded as one way of testing the truth of thought in terms of its consequences, but it also involves the principle of contradiction as a criterion of truth. When Aristotle recommends, for example, that we should accept theories as true "only if what they affirm agrees with the observed facts," he is saying that when the truth of a particular perception is indisputable, because the observed fact is evident, the general or theoretical statement which it contradicts must be false.

But the principle of contradiction as a criterion of truth goes further than testing theories by their consistency with observation. One of two contradictory statements must be false and the other must be true "if that which it is true to affirm is nothing other than that which it is false to deny." Heisenberg points to indeterminacy in quantum mechanics as an exception to this axiom. "In quantum theory," he writes, the law " 'Tertium non datur,' "—which states that there cannot be a middle term between two contradictory terms—"is to be modified."

Even a single statement may show itself false by being self-contradictory, and in consequence its opposite can be seen to be true. What Aristotle calls axioms, or self-evident and indisputable truths, are those propositions immediately known to be true, and necessarily true, because their contradictories, being self-contradictory, are impossible statements, or necessarily false. The truth of any proposition which is neither a self-evident axiom nor the statement of an evident, perceived fact, is tested, according to the principle of contradiction, by its consistency with axioms or perceptions.

As opposed to consequences or effects, contradiction or consistency as a sign of truth seems to be an intrinsic criterion. But this

criterion is not universally accepted. "Contradiction," writes Pascal, "is not a sign of falsity,
nor the want of contradiction a sign of truth."
Nor, even when accepted, is it always judged
adequate to solve the problem. It is, for Kant,
a "merely logical criterion of truth . . . the *con-
ditio sine qua non,* or negative condition of all
truth. Farther than this logic cannot go, and
the error which depends not on the form, but
on the content of the cognition, it has no test
to discover."

Some thinkers seem to rely upon an intrinsic
mark by which each idea reveals its own truth
or falsity. Augustine, for example, considers
by what criterion he would know whether
what Moses said was true. "If I knew this," he
writes, "it could not be from him that I got
such knowledge. But deep inside me, in my
most intimate thought, Truth, which is neither
Hebrew nor Greek nor Latin nor any foreign
speech, would speak to me, though not in
syllables formed by lips and tongue. It would
whisper, 'He speaks the truth.' "

For Augustine, God is the warranty of the
inner voice which plainly signifies the truth.
For Spinoza, the truth of an idea depends
upon its relation to God. Because "a true
idea in us is that which in God is adequate,
in so far as He is manifested by the nature of the human mind," it follows, according to Spinoza, that "he who has a true idea
knows at the same time that he has a true idea,
nor can he doubt the truth of the thing"; for
"he who knows a thing truly must at the same
time have an adequate idea or a true knowledge of his knowledge, that is to say (as is self-
evident) he must be certain."

It is impossible, Spinoza maintains, to have
a true idea without at the same time knowing
that it is true. To the question, "How can a
man know that he has an idea which agrees
with that of which it is the idea?" he replies
that "he knows it simply because he has an
idea which agrees with that of which it is the
idea, that is to say, because truth is its own
standard." For what can be clearer, Spinoza
asks, "or more certain than a true idea as the
standard of truth? Just as light reveals both
itself and the darkness, so truth is the standard
of itself and of the false."

Spinoza defines an adequate idea as one
which, "in so far as it is considered in itself,
without reference to the object, has all the
properties or internal signs of a true idea."
He explains, moreover, that by "internal" he
means to exclude even "the agreement of the
idea with its object." This, he thinks, meets
the objection that "if a true idea is distinguished from a false idea only in so far as it
is said to agree with that of which it is the
idea, the true idea [would have] no reality or
perfection above the false idea (since they are
distinguished by an external sign alone), and
consequently the man who has true ideas will
have no greater reality or perfection than he
who has false ideas only."

Although Descartes and Locke also employ
an intrinsic criterion of truth—not the adequacy, but the clarity and distinctness, of
ideas—they do not seem to mean, as Spinoza
does, that a single idea, in and of itself, can
be true or false. Like Aristotle before them or
Kant later, they regard a simple idea or concept as, strictly speaking, incapable of being
either true or false.

"Truth and falsity," writes Locke, "belong
. . . only to propositions"—to affirmations or
denials which involve at least two ideas; or,
as Kant says, "truth and error . . . are only to
be found in a judgement," which explains why
"the senses do not err, not because they always judge correctly, but because *they do not
judge at all.*"

Nevertheless, for Locke the clarity and distinctness of the ideas which enter into the
formation of propositions enable the mind to
judge intuitively and certainly of their truth.
When ideas are clear and distinct, "the mind
perceives the agreement or disagreement of
two ideas immediately by themselves . . . Such
kind of truths the mind perceives at the first
sight of the ideas together by bare intuition . . .
and this kind of knowledge is the clearest and
most certain that human frailty is capable of."

THE PROBLEM OF the criterion of truth is sometimes closely connected with the problem of
the causes of error. Descartes seems to pass
by natural steps from one to the other. Having decided that "the things which we con-

ceive very clearly and distinctly are all true," he reminds himself that there may be "some difficulty in ascertaining which are those that we distinctly conceive." The mystery of error looms large for Descartes because it seems to him that the human intellect, being created by God, must have a kind of natural infallibility, the infallibility of an instrument designed by God for knowing the truth, not for ignorance or error.

"If we did not know," Descartes reflects, "that all that is in us of reality and truth proceeds from a perfect and infinite being, however clear and distinct were our ideas, we should not have any reason to assure ourselves that they had the perfection of being true." But once we have "recognized that there is a God . . . and also recognized that all things depend upon Him, and that He is not a deceiver," we can infer that whatever we "perceive clearly and distinctly cannot fail to be true."

What, then, is the source of our errors? "I answer," writes Descartes, "that they depend on a combination of two causes, to wit, on the faculty of knowledge that rests in me, and on the power of choice or free will." Each perfect in its own sphere, neither the will nor the understanding by itself causes us to fall into error. "Since I understand nothing but by the power which God has given me for understanding, there is no doubt," Descartes declares, "that all that I understand, I understand as I ought, and it is not possible that I err in this."

The trouble lies in the relation of the will to the intellect. "Since the will is much wider in its range and compass than the understanding, I do not restrain it within the same bounds, but extend it also to things which I do not understand." It is not God's fault, says Descartes, if, in the exercise of my freedom, I do not "withhold my assent from certain things as to which He has not placed a clear and distinct knowledge in my understanding." But as long as "I so restrain my will within the limits of knowledge that it forms no judgment except on matters which are clearly and distinctly represented to it by the understanding, I can never be deceived."

There are other accounts of error, less elaborate than Descartes's, which are similar to the extent that they place the cause in some combination of human faculties rather than in their simple and separate operation. Socrates explains to Theaetetus that false opinions arise when the senses and the mind do not cooperate properly. Aristotle suggests that it is the imagination which frequently misleads the mind. Looking at the problem from the point of view of the theologian, Aquinas holds that Adam, in his state of innocence before the fall, could not be deceived. "While the soul remained subject to God," he writes, "the lower powers in man were subject to the higher, and were no impediment to their action." But man born in sin can be deceived, not because the intellect itself ever fails, but as a result of the wayward influence "of some lower power, such as the imagination or the like."

Lucretius, for whom sense, not mind, is infallible, attributes error to the fault of reason, which misinterprets the veridical impressions of the senses. "What can there be more certain than our senses," he asks, "to mark true things and false?" He explains that the mind, not the senses, is responsible for illusions and hallucinations. "Don't blame flaws of judgment on your eyes."

Other writers, like Descartes, take the opposite view, that the senses are much less trustworthy than the intellect. Still others, like Montaigne, seem to find that error and fallacy, rather than any sort of infallibility, are quite natural to all human faculties, and beset sense and reason alike. "Man," says Pascal, is "full of error, natural and ineffaceable, without grace. Nothing shows him the truth. Everything deceives him. Those two sources of truth, reason and the senses, besides being both wanting in sincerity, deceive each other in turn."

Considering the extremes to which men have gone in their appraisal of human prowess or frailty, Locke's moderate statement of the matter is worth pondering. "Notwithstanding the great noise made in the world about errors and opinions," he writes, "I must do mankind that right, as to say, there are not so many men in errors and wrong opinions as is commonly supposed. Not that I think they embrace the truth; but, indeed, because concerning these doctrines they keep such a stir about, they have no thought, no opinion at all ... And though one cannot say that there are fewer improbable or erroneous opinions in the world than there are, yet this is certain, there are fewer that actually assent to them, and mistake them for truths, than is imagined." As Planck sees it, "A new scientific truth does not triumph by convincing its opponents and making them see the light, but rather because its opponents eventually die, and a new generation grows up that is familiar with it."

95

Tyranny and Despotism

INTRODUCTION

I F any point in political theory is indisputable, it would seem to be that tyranny
is the worst corruption of government—a vicious misuse of power and a violent abuse of
the human beings who are subject to it. Aristotle's remark that "no freeman, if he can escape
from it, will endure such government," would
seem to express the sentiments of all who,
loving liberty and abhoring slavery, look upon
tyranny as destroying the one and establishing
the other.

Certainly the word "tyranny" is seldom if
ever used eulogistically. Such phrases as "a
just tyranny" or "a good tyrant" are at once
seen to be as self-contradictory as "a round
square." The great books of history give
the impression that tyrants and despots, who
vastly outnumber good rulers, are always objects of hate and fear, never of love and admiration. If there are exceptions, if there are
peoples who willingly submit to or even deserve the yoke of despotism and tyranny, they
are, in the judgment of ancients and moderns
alike, politically primitive.

The traditional association of the word
"despotism" with "tyranny" requires us to
consider whether our understanding of these
terms is as uniformly clear as the denunciation
of what they denote seems to be universal.
Are despotism and tyranny the same? It may
be thought that the tyrant must always have
despotic power at his disposal, power unlimited by law, so that the lawless ruler is at once
both despot and tyrant. But need the despot,
the absolute ruler, always rule tyrannically?

The familiar phrase, "benevolent despotism," at once suggests the negative answer,
and also some line of distinction between
despotism and tyranny. Tyranny can never be

benevolent. But despotism may be no worse
than paternalism. While its injustice may consist in treating adults, able to govern themselves, as if they were children, it may also
derive an air of justice from the fact that the
despot, like the father, rules his subjects for
their own good. If he treats them like slaves
rather than children, exploiting them to serve
his own interests, then he is not a benevolent but a tyrannical despot.

This understanding of the meaning of
"despotism" and "tyranny" seems to be only
partly supported by their etymology. The
Greek word from which "despot" comes signifies the head of a household, the *paterfamilias*
(as he is called by the Romans) who exercises
the absolute authority of a master over chattel
slaves, and of a parent over his children. In
contrast, the Greek word *týrannos* refers to
the ruler of a state rather than a family and
is sometimes used as if it were equivalent in
meaning to "king." Yet both words carry the
connotation of absolute power, and when, in
addition, the subjects of a tyrant are considered to be no better off than slaves, the difference in the meaning of the two words almost
disappears.

The difficulty of grasping what is essential
to the nature of tyranny and despotism seems
to be complicated by certain criteria, originally
proposed by the Greeks, for distinguishing between king and tyrant, or between royal and
despotic rule. Both Plato and Aristotle speak
of the king as a good monarch and the tyrant
as a bad one. Both say that monarchy, or rule
by a single man, is royal when it is for the welfare of the ruled and tyrannical when it serves
only the interests of the ruler. Both make lawlessness—either a violation of existing laws or

government by personal fiat without settled laws—a mark of tyranny.

Yet, for Aristotle at least, some of these criteria also apply to despotism, and even to royal government, insofar as these are distinguished from political or constitutional government—government by law rather than by men. Furthermore, the association of either tyranny or despotism with monarchy—rule by *one* man, whether just or unjust—seems to be counterbalanced by Aristotle's discussion of the tyranny of the *few* and of the *many*. In a monarchy, the king can turn tyrant; but so can the wealthy become despotic in an oligarchy, or the poor in a lawless democracy.

The nature of tyranny thus seems to be more difficult to define precisely than would at first appear from the almost universal condemnation of it as the worst perversion of government.

To some extent, the difficulties may be verbal. The word "tyranny" is used with many meanings, not only by the Greeks, but throughout the tradition of the great books. Some writers identify tyranny and despotism; some distinguish the two sharply. Some writers consider tyranny and despotism only in connection with monarchy; some extend the consideration to other forms of government. The words are sometimes used descriptively, without the connotation of good or evil; and sometimes they are more derogatory than descriptive.

Even when the necessary verbal classifications are achieved, genuine issues still remain. Conflicting accounts are given of the causes of tyranny or the circumstances from which it develops. Concerning despotism, some writers take the position that it may be justified by conquest, or by the need of a people for absolute government, or, in the form of a temporary dictatorship, by emergency conditions. Not even the condemnation of tyranny seems to be unanimous, if the views of Hobbes are to be reckoned with; nor, among those who condemn tyranny, is the fairly general approval of tyrannicide free from the strong dissenting voice of Kant.

THE FOREGOING INDICATES how the notions of tyranny and despotism are involved in other chapters dealing with the various forms of government and, in addition, such chapters as JUSTICE, LIBERTY, and SLAVERY. The distinction, for example, between domestic and political slavery bears on one of the ways in which despotism and tyranny are distinguished; and the discussion in the chapters on MONARCHY and CONSTITUTION concerning absolute and limited government raises a question which must also be considered here, namely, whether absolute monarchy can be distinguished from despotism and whether it has an inveterate tendency to become tyrannical.

That question deserves immediate attention, because its answers are connected with opposed views of the justice or defensibility of tyranny and despotism. Plato and Aristotle, for example, treat tyranny as the prototype of political injustice, and the tyrant as the extreme case of the vicious man; yet there are passages which appear to have a contrary tenor. In the *Laws,* the Athenian Stranger proposes a good tyrant as the best means for establishing the laws. To the question, "What are the conditions which you require in a state before you can organize it?" he thinks the legislator's answer should be: "Give me a state which is governed by a tyrant, and let the tyrant be young and have a good memory; let him be quick at learning and of a courageous and noble nature"—in short, let him have temperance and every other virtue.

More readily than monarchy, democracy, or oligarchy, tyranny is the stepping-stone to the best state, according to the Athenian Stranger, because it involves the greater power concentrated in a single man. The combination of virtue and power may rarely be found, but, he says, "when the supreme power in man coincides with the greatest wisdom and temperance, then the best laws and the best constitution come into being, and in no other way."

Aristotle's classification of the types of kingship, or the forms of royal government, seems to include tyranny among them. He refers to the kind of monarchy which prevails among the barbarians who, "being more servile in character than Hellenes . . . do not rebel against a despotic government. Such royalties," he goes on, "have the nature of tyrannies because the people are by nature slaves, but there is no danger of their being overthrown, for they are hereditary and legal." Even among the Hellenes in ancient times, Aristotle points out, there was a form of monarchy or "dictatorship" that may be defined "as an elective tyranny, which like the barbarian monarchy, is legal, but differs from it in not being hereditary."

These two forms of tyranny, Aristotle says elsewhere, "are both according to law, and therefore easily pass into royalty." The line between king and tyrant is not, however, as shadowy as might first appear. "Kings rule according to law over voluntary subjects, but tyrants over involuntary; and the one are guarded by their fellow citizens, the others are guarded against them." The forms of monarchy which Aristotle also calls "tyrannies" seem to him to have a mixed character. "They are royal," he says, "in so far as the monarch rules according to law over willing subjects; but they are tyrannical in so far as he is despotic and rules according to his own fancy." But there is also a kind of tyranny which, being unmixed, is "the counterpart of perfect monarchy. This tyranny is just that arbitrary power of an individual which is responsible to no one, and governs all alike, whether equals or better, with a view to its own advantage, not to that of its subjects, and therefore against their will."

Aristotle explains his association of tyranny with monarchy on the ground that "both are forms of one-man rule, but," he adds, "there is the greatest difference between them; the tyrant looks to his own advantage, the king to that of his subjects." Tyrannical government is "monarchy exercising the rule of a master over political society," and therefore deserves to be called "despotic" as well as tyrannical. When it has no admixture of royalty, tyranny is not only self-serving but lawless rule. It is "the very reverse of a constitution," or rule by law. Except for the hypothetical case in which the truly superior, the almost godlike man is king, Aristotle seems to identify absolute or unconstitutional monarchy with tyranny and despotism, and he condemns both for violating the very nature of the state conceived as "a community of free men."

THE LINE BETWEEN KING and tyrant is similarly drawn by Plato. Monarchy for him "divides into royalty and tyranny" according as one man rules by law or lawlessly, over voluntary or involuntary subjects. If the one man were like a god in relation to other men, it would be fitting for him to rule the state by his wisdom or science and without recourse to laws. "If there could be such a despot," the Eleatic Stranger says in the *Statesman,* "he alone would be the happy ruler of a true and perfect state," but men "can never be made to believe that any one can be worthy of such authority." (History suggests the contrary in such cases as Caesar, Napoleon, and Hitler.)

Giving the name of "king" to the monarch who abides by and maintains established laws, the Stranger gets Socrates to agree that the ruler should be called a "tyrant" when he "governs neither by law nor by custom, but, imitating the true man of science, pretends that he can only act for the best by violating the laws, while in reality appetite and ignorance are the motives of the imitation."

In *The Republic,* Socrates refers to Euripides' praise of "tyranny as god-like," and gives, as another reason for excluding the poets from the state, the fact that "they are the eulogists of tyranny." Far from being godlike, the tyrannical man is described by Socrates as "drunken, lustful, passionate." Tyrants "are always either the masters or servants and never the friends of anybody; the tyrant never tastes of true freedom or friendship." Oriental despotism, Hegel later writes, appears to give freedom to one man, but "the freedom of that one is only caprice, ferocity—brutal recklessness of passion . . . That *one* is therefore only a despot; not a *free man.*"

According to Plato, tyranny is not only the greatest evil a state can suffer, but the tyrant is also the unhappiest of men. "Will not he who has been shown to be the wickedest," Socrates asks, "be also the most miserable?" Polus, in the *Gorgias,* tries to prove that, like the successful criminal who goes unpunished, the tyrant who does injustice to everybody, but suffers none, achieves more happiness than other men. But Socrates, taking the position that it is better to suffer than to do injustice, argues to the contrary that the tyrant is more miserable than those whom he oppresses.

If this is true, the confirmed tyrant is probably the man least able to perceive or acknowledge it. Plutarch reports the story of Plato's first meeting with Dionysius, the tyrant of Syracuse. When Plato tried to prove to him that "tyrants, of all men, had the least pretence to virtue," and that, since they lacked justice, they suffered "the miserable condition of the unjust," Dionysius would not hear the argument out. "He asked the philosopher in a rage," Plutarch relates, "what business he had in Sicily. To which Plato answered, 'I come to seek a virtuous man.' 'It seems, then,' replied Dionysius, 'you have lost your labor.' " According to Plutarch, Dionysius tried to have Plato killed on his return voyage to Greece; or failing that, to have him sold into slavery. He would not be harmed by that, Dionysius reasoned, because, "being the same just man as before, he would enjoy his happiness, though he lost his liberty."

ON THE WHOLE, THEN, Aristotle's and Plato's disapproval of tyrants and tyranny seems to be unequivocal. The passages which might cause this to be questioned can perhaps be accounted for by the ancient tendency to use the word "tyrant" descriptively to denote the possessor of absolute power. Yet even in the *Laws,* where such usage occurs, Plato observes that kings, unable "to sustain the temptation of arbitrary power," tend to overthrow the laws and so become tyrannical in the invidious sense of the word.

With the exception of Hobbes, medieval and modern writers are no less disapproving than the ancients. "Tyrannical government," according to Aquinas, "is altogether corrupt" and completely lawless. It is the tyrant himself, rather than those who may rebel against a government so lacking in justice, who is "guilty of sedition, since he encourages discord and sedition among his subjects, that he may lord over them more securely." When a king, by becoming a tyrant, "has dethroned himself and put himself in a state of war with his people, what shall hinder them," asks Locke, "from prosecuting him who is no king, as they would any other man who has put himself in a state of war with them?"

In Locke's view, it is a mistake to think that the fault of tyranny "is proper only to monarchies. For wherever the power that is put in any hands for the government of the people and the preservation of their properties is applied to other ends, and made use of to impoverish, harass, or subdue them to the arbitrary irregular commands of those that have it, there it presently becomes tyranny, whether those that thus use it are one or many . . . Wherever law ends, tyranny begins, if the law be transgressed to another's harm."

Tyranny is thus defined by Locke as "the exercise of power beyond right, which nobody can have a right to." Such "absolute arbitrary power, or governing without settled standing laws, can neither of them consist with the ends of society and government." Tyranny so defined may not be limited to monarchies; but, according to Locke, absolute monarchy is always tyrannical. For that very reason it is, he writes, "inconsistent with civil society, and so can be no form of civil government at all."

What Locke calls "tyranny" or, without change of meaning, "absolute monarchy," Kant calls "autocracy." But Kant distinguishes the monarch "who has the *highest* power" from the autocrat "who has *all* power." Hegel calls "despotism" that "state of affairs where law has disappeared and where the particular will as such, whether of a monarch or a mob, counts as law or rather takes the place of law." The writers of *The Federalist* use the words "tyranny" and "despotism" interchangeably, but do not vary from the definition which Montesquieu gives of despotic government as "that in which a single person directs everything by his own will and caprice." In all other governments, even in monarchy when it is constitutional, the separation of power puts some limitation on the power entrusted to the offices of state.

Following Montesquieu's doctrine, Madison declares: "The accumulation of all powers, legislative, executive, and judiciary, in the same hands, whether of one, a few, or many, and whether hereditary, self-appointed, or elective, may justly be pronounced the very definition of tyranny." He reinforces his point by quoting Jefferson's dictum that concentrating "all the powers of government . . . in the same hands, is precisely the definition of despotic government."

HOBBES SEEMS TO BE the one exception in the great books to this variously expressed opinion of the evil of absolute power. Locke may have him in mind when he says that absolute monarchy is "by some men . . . counted the only government in the world." Certainly Hobbes would not repudiate the charge that he thinks none but absolute government feasible; nor is he dismayed by the tendency of other writers to call absolute government "tyrannical" or "despotic." On the contrary, he dismisses this as so much empty name-calling.

In every form of government, according to Hobbes, the sovereign power must be absolute to be effective. "Though of so unlimited a power, men may fancy many evil consequences, yet the consequences of the want of it, which is perpetual war of every man against his neighbor, are much worse." Describing the absolute dominion of the father over his children, and the equally absolute dominion of the master over his slaves, Hobbes says that "the rights and consequences of both paternal and despotical dominion are the very same with those of a sovereign by institution," for unless the sovereign is also absolute, "there is no sovereignty at all."

To the cry "Tyranny," Hobbes replies that just as men who "find themselves grieved under a democracy call it *anarchy,*" or those who "are displeased with aristocracy, call it *oligarchy,*" so "they that are discontented under monarchy, call it *tyranny.*" He holds Aristotle's *Politics* responsible for spreading the fallacy of regarding anything except popular government as tyrannical; and in general he blames the Greek and Roman writers for fomenting sedition against kings by treating tyrannicide as lawful.

Hobbes offers a historical explanation of the origin of these confusions. "A *tyrant,*" he writes, "originally signified no more, simply, but a *monarch.* But when afterwards in most parts of Greece that kind of government was abolished, the name began to signify, not only the thing it did before, but with it the hatred which the popular states bore towards it: as also the name of *king* became odious after the deposing of the kings in Rome."

A word like "tyranny" carries only emotional force. Used descriptively, Hobbes declares, it "signifieth nothing more nor less than the name of sovereignty . . . saving that they that use the former word are understood to be angry with them they call *tyrants.*" He is willing to make himself the object of that anger by identifying "a professed hatred of tyranny" with "hatred to Commonwealth in general," and by regarding the toleration of both hatreds alike as evil seeds of sedition.

IN ONE NEGATIVE RESPECT, Rousseau seems to agree with Hobbes. Not that the man who holds that only republican institutions are legitimate, in any way accepts the identification of either prince or popular government with sovereign power. But he, like Hobbes, rejects Aristotle's distinction between the king and the tyrant as good and bad monarchs, the one governing for the good of his subjects, the other in his own interest. Rousseau contends not only that most Greek authors used "the word *tyrant* in a different sense . . . but also," he adds, "it would follow from Aristotle's distinction that, from the very beginning of the world, there has not yet been a single king."

It is only according to a vulgar usage that a tyrant is conceived as "a king who governs violently and without regard for justice or law." The more precise conception, Rousseau insists, defines the tyrant as "an individual who arrogates to himself the royal authority without having a right to it. This is how the Greeks understood the word 'tyrant'; they applied it indifferently to good and bad princes whose authority was not legitimate. *Tyrant* and *usurper* are thus perfectly synonymous terms."

The usurpation of power is, according to Rousseau, the root of both tyranny and despotism, but they are not for that reason to be confused. "I call him who usurps the royal authority a tyrant," Rousseau writes, "and him who usurps the sovereign power a *despot*. The tyrant is he who thrusts himself in contrary to the laws to govern in accordance with the laws; the despot is he who sets himself above the laws themselves. Thus the tyrant cannot be a despot, but the despot is always a tyrant."

Other writers distinguish between tyranny and despotism on different principles. They accept, where Rousseau rejects, the notion that tyranny is not merely a usurpation of power, but always a self-serving or unjust use of that power. They reject Rousseau's conception of despotism as inseparable from usurpation. Absolute power can be gained and held in other ways.

Locke, for example, conceives despotic dominion as the rule of a master over slaves, or the government of a vanquished people by their conquerors in a just war. "Despotical power," in his opinion, "is an absolute arbitrary power one man has over another to take away his life whenever he pleases." Unlike tyranny, it is not "power beyond right," for "the conqueror, if he have a just cause, has a despotical right over the persons of all that actually aided and concurred in the war against him." Since, in Locke's view, "a usurper can never have right on his side," despotic dominion, when justified, is not achieved by usurpation.

For Montesquieu, despotisms constitute one of the three major forms of government, the other two being republics (aristocratic or democratic) and monarchies. Though he regards despotism as an intrinsically corrupt form of government, in which the rulers wield personal power without the restraint of law, he also judges it to be appropriate to the servile natures or temperaments of certain peoples. Like Aristotle and Hippocrates before him, he attributes to the climate and disposition of the Asiatic peoples their submissiveness to the worst excesses of despotism.

Montesquieu does not so much condemn despotism as he deplores the conditions which seem to render it necessary or natural for a large part of mankind. He does not suggest, as J. S. Mill does, that despotic government can and should serve to civilize those who are as yet unprepared for self-government. Despo-

tism is benevolent, according to Mill, only if it prepares a people for freedom; if it tries to perpetuate itself, it is tyrannical or enslaving.

Though Mill holds the view that, relative to a free society, there cannot be a "good despot" no matter how benevolent his intentions, he also thinks that, in dealing with barbarians, "despotism is a legitimate mode of government . . . provided the end be their improvement, and the means justified by actually effecting that end. Liberty, as a principle, has no application to any state of things anterior to the time when mankind has become capable of being improved by free and equal discussion. Until then, there is nothing for them but implicit obedience to an Akbar or a Charlemagne, if they are so fortunate as to find one."

Under certain "conditions of society . . . a vigorous despotism," according to Mill, "is in itself the best mode of government for training the people in what is specifically wanting to render them capable of a higher civilization." In his opinion, still other conditions justify despotism. "I am far from condemning," he writes, "in cases of extreme exigency, the assumption of absolute power in the form of a temporary dictatorship." In another place, he says that "the establishment of the despotism of the Caesars was a great benefit to the entire generation in which it took place" because "it put a stop to civil war, and abated a vast amount of malversation and tyranny by praetors and proconsuls."

But in all these cases the essential point is that the despotic rule should be temporary. Mill applies the same criterion to the despotism which occurs in the government of colonial dependencies. It should aim to benefit a subject people by training them in the arts of government, and it should not seek to outlast the conferring of this benefit. "The ruling country," he thinks, "ought to be able to do for its subjects all that could be done by a succession of absolute monarchs, guaranteed by irresistible force against the precariousness of tenure of barbarian despotisms . . . Such is the ideal rule of a free people over a barbarous or semi-barbarous one."

This may be the ideal, but critics of imperialism, like Swift or Marx, think that colonial policies are in fact otherwise motivated—by land-grabbing, by the desire for national aggrandizement, and by the profits to be made from the economic exploitation of colonies or subject peoples. Throughout the pages of Thucydides and Tacitus, the spokesmen for empire dwell upon the blessings which Athenian or Roman rule bestows, only to be answered by the protests of the colonists or the conquered, who seem to prefer the insecurities and uncertainties of liberty to the mixed motives of even the best despot.

As ALREADY INDICATED, the political significance of tyranny and despotism is broader than the conception of the tyrant as an unjust king or of the despot as an absolute monarch. The reign of the Thirty Tyrants at Athens and of the Decemviri at Rome are classical examples of oligarchic tyranny. Advocates of republican or democratic institutions, like the writers of *The Federalist* or Mill, are as much concerned to safeguard constitutional or representative government from the tyranny of special interests—whether of a dominant majority or of concentrated wealth—as they are to protect the rule of law from the encroachments of despotism which begin with usurpations of power by elected officials.

Moderns and ancients alike fear the susceptibility of the mob to the wiles of the demagogue, who encourages their lawlessness in order to take the law into his own hands. Both Hegel and Plato see in the alliance between a scheming demagogue and an unruly populace the step by which a corrupt democracy turns into a tyranny. Though Aristotle disagrees with what he takes to be the theory of Socrates in *The Republic,* that tyranny normally arises from democracy in the progressive degeneration of the state, his own opinion seems to be that "tyranny is a compound of oligarchy and democracy in their most extreme forms" and that "almost all tyrants have been demagogues who gained the favor of the people by their accusation of the notables."

In Tocqueville's *Democracy in America,* there is a striking passage on a form of oppression to which democratic societies are prone that he thinks worse than the tyrannies and despotisms known to earlier centuries. According to him, "The type of oppression which threatens democracies is different from anything there has ever been in the world before . . . Such old words as 'despotism' and 'tyranny' do not fit." The word that Tocqueville could not come up with, we, in the 20th century, call "totalitarianism." The oppression that he describes, 20th-century authors often call "totalitarian democracy."

These aspects of tyranny are discussed in the chapters on DEMOCRACY and OLIGARCHY. The traditional emphasis, however, is on the individual tyrant, whether he is a hereditary prince who misuses his autocratic power, the usurper of an established throne, or the demagogue who makes himself dictator. However tyranny arises, monarchy is the form it usually takes in the pages of history or poetry—the domination of the state by one man. But while the great political philosophers offer conflicting theories of the origin of tyranny, there seems to be remarkable agreement concerning the methods the tyrant uses to maintain himself in power.

Other political practices may vary greatly from one historical epoch to another, but the devices of tyranny seem to have a certain timelessness. When they are describing the actions of the tyrant, Herodotus, Plutarch, Tacitus, and Gibbon tell stories of iniquity, of cruelty, of cowardly and unscrupulous stratagems, so alike in detail that the reader loses all sense of time and place. Nor need he exert any effort of imagination to place the figure of the tyrant thus delineated in the setting of contemporary events.

The past also speaks with contemporary relevance in Plato's enumeration of the tyrant's desperate measures, his stirring up of foreign wars to smother domestic discord, his assassination of enemies, his purging of friends or followers, and his confiscation of property as well as his generally indiscriminate bloodletting. The resort to unwarranted searches and seizures, the creation of *ex post facto* crimes, the arrest and punishment of men without trial "have been," writes Hamilton, "in all ages the favorite and most formidable instruments of tyranny." So, too, in all ages, the tyrant, fearing reprisal and revenge, lives in a state of war, turns his palace into an armed camp, and goes nowhere without a numerous bodyguard which, as both Aristotle and Machiavelli suggest, functions most efficiently when composed of hirelings or mercenaries.

The great books contain not only the record of tyrannical perfidy and violence, but also recommendations to the would-be tyrant of the best means to use for his nefarious purposes. Though Rousseau refers to Machiavelli's *The Prince* as "the book of Republicans," and thinks that "the choice of his detestable hero, Caesar Borgia, clearly enough shows his hidden aim," the rules which Machiavelli formulates for the prince seem, on the surface at least, to be essentially similar to the advice Aristotle gives the tyrant.

The end in both cases is the same—success in the effort to gain and keep power. The means, in general, are force and fraud or, as Machiavelli phrases it, the methods of the lion and the fox. Machiavelli counsels the prince "to inspire fear in such a way that, if he does not win love, he avoids hatred." He tells him that he should appear to keep faith without hesitating to break his promises, that he should avoid flatterers and sycophants, and that he should acquire a reputation for liberality without cost to himself. Not very different

is Aristotle's advice to the tyrant—to lop off the heads of those who are too high and to humble all the rest, to sow discord among his subjects, to impoverish the people by multiplying taxes, to employ informers, and to encourage the betrayal of one faction by another.

But in his suggestion of another course for the tyrant to take—the policy of not merely pretending, but of actually trying, to conduct himself like a just king—Aristotle seems to deviate from the spirit of Machiavelli's maxim that the appearance of virtue is profitable so long as it does not interfere with doing whatever is expedient, however vicious. Yet even here Aristotle says that "the tyrant must be careful . . . to keep power enough to rule over his subjects, whether they like him or not, for if he once gives this up he gives up his tyranny."

The best commentary on these recommendations seems to be indirectly expressed by their authors. Both Aristotle and Machiavelli draw one striking conclusion from the history of those—call them princes or tyrants—who have tried to put such rules into practice. Whether its collapse is due to the inherent weakness of might without right, as Aristotle suggests, or, in Machiavelli's terms, to the unforeseeable mishaps of fortune, tyranny, of all forms of government, seems to be the shortest-lived.

96

Universal and Particular

INTRODUCTION

On such speculative problems as the existence of God, the immortality of the soul, the infinity of time and space, or the limits of human knowledge, the conversation of philosophers seems to make contact with the discourse of scientists, the language of poets, and the speech of ordinary men. The philosophers usually begin at least by propounding questions which correspond to those asked by men who do not profess to be philosophers. But throughout the tradition of western thought, the problem of the universal, unlike these others, seems to have the character of a professional secret.

The various solutions of the problem of the universal are so many esoteric doctrines, each with its own sectarian name. The initiated can distinguish themselves from the novices by their proficiency in this area; and the outsider who overhears the discussion of professionals may be completely left behind, wondering as much about how the question arose as about the meaning of the conflicting answers.

No genuine philosophical problem, it seems reasonable to suppose, can be so remote from questions intelligible to common sense. If it is not just a specious riddle to amuse the experts, the problem of the universal, despite its technical appearance, should raise issues from which, in some form or other, no one can escape. Whether or not this is so can be tested by considering the various ways in which the problem occurs in other chapters under different guises and in different contexts.

In the chapter on SAME AND OTHER, we find the question how two individuals can be the same in some particular respect—how in spite of their separate existence they can share in the possession of a common nature or attribute. Anyone who classifies things or tries to make definitions may be led to wonder whether classifications are entirely verbal and definitions fictions of the mind, or whether things themselves belong together in some real community based upon an inherent sameness or similarity.

In the chapter on ONE AND MANY, the question takes the form of asking how two or more things can be one in any way. Again, both science and common sense seem able to deal with an infinite number of individuals by applying a single name to them or apprehending them all under a single concept or notion. But it may be asked what justifies the denomination of many things by one name. What unity in the things verifies the tendency of thought to unify them conceptually? Does a real unity exist in things, by virtue of their being somehow one as well as many, or as a result of the many somehow participating in a one which exists separately from them?

In the chapters on DEFINITION and SIGN AND SYMBOL the same questions are at least implicit. In connection with the object of definition, one issue is whether what Aristotle calls "the formulable essence" exists as the common nature of many individuals, or whether, as Locke suggests, definitions formulate only the nominal, not the real, essences of things. As that and related issues are faced, anyone who acknowledges the familiar distinction between proper and common names may become involved in questioning what common or general names signify and how they get the meanings with which they are used in everyday discourse.

The problem of the sameness of things distinct from one another, the problem of the one *in* the many or the one *and* the many, the problem of essences and common names, are other statements of the problem of the universal and the particular. Attention to the words themselves confirms this. The word "*universal*" connotes a unity—the one as opposed to the many, the common as opposed to the unique or special. The word "*particular*" connotes participation—the part as opposed to the whole, the member as opposed to the class. As the reference already made to essence and individual indicates, these are not the only pairs of terms which somehow correspond in significance to universal and particular, but others, like model and imitation, form and matter, abstract and concrete, are more obscure in meaning. The discussion of universal and particular throws light on them rather than gains clarity from them.

THE READER OF THE great books can witness the origin of the problem of the universal and particular as it occurs in a conversation, not between technical philosophers, but between Socrates and his friends. In the *Meno*, Socrates and Meno get into a discussion of how virtue is acquired. Socrates thinks it is necessary to inquire first what virtue is. Meno responds by enumerating different virtues, but Socrates is not satisfied. He wants a definition which will cover all the virtues. Even if Meno could say what justice or temperance is, that would not do, for each of these is, as Socrates says, *a* virtue, not *virtue*—a particular virtue or a part of virtue, not the whole of it.

"In searching after one virtue," Socrates tells Meno, "we have found many . . . but we have been unable to find the common virtue which runs through them all." To help Meno, who claims he is not able to follow Socrates in his "attempt to get at one common notion of virtue," Socrates shifts the discussion to colors and figures. He warns Meno that color cannot be defined by naming colors, and that, even if he could define a square, a circle, and all other figures, he would not be saying what *figure* is. To proceed in this way is to be "landed in particulars."

"Tell me then," Socrates says, "since you call them by a common name, and say that

they are all figures, even when opposed to one another, what is that common nature which you designate as figure?"

If Meno were to reply, "I do not know what you want," not much further explanation could be given. To someone who remained perplexed at this point, we could only say, Socrates suggests, "Do you not understand that we are looking for the same in the many?" Or, put in another form, we might ask, he says, "What is that [one in many] which you call figure, and which includes not only the round and straight figures, but all?"

Thus stated, the problem of the universal seems inescapable—a problem for everyone, not just for philosophers. But the philosophers complicate the problem almost as soon as it is stated. Giving his version of the history of philosophy, Aristotle offers an explanation of how the problem shifted to another level. Socrates, he writes, "was busying himself about ethical matters" and, "seeking the universal in these ethical matters, [he] fixed thought for the first time on definitions. Plato accepted his teaching, but held that the problem applied not to sensible things, but to entities of another kind—for this reason, that the common definition could not be a definition of any sensible thing, as they were always changing. Things of this other sort he called Ideas, and sensible things, he said, were all named after these, and in virtue of a relation to these; for the many existed by participation in the Ideas that have the same name as they."

It is at this point, according to Aristotle, that the great philosophical controversy begins. Whereas "the thinkers of old ranked particular things as substances, *e.g.*, fire and earth, not what is common to both, body," the Platonists or idealists—"the thinkers of the present day"—"tend to rank universal as substances, for genera are universal." Aristotle repeatedly tries to distinguish between the Socratic inquiry and what he regards as the Platonic doctrine—the theory of Ideas. "The first to raise the problem of universal definition . . . Socrates," he writes, "did not make the universals or the definitions exist apart; they, however,"—the Platonists—"gave them separate existence, and this was the kind of thing they called Ideas."

As between Socrates and his disciple, Aristotle does not hesitate to take sides. "Socrates gave the impulse to this theory of ideas . . . but he did not *separate* universals from individuals; and in not separating them," Aristotle adds, "he thought rightly." The issue between Aristotle and his own teacher, Plato, cannot, however, be stated by so simple an affirmation and denial.

On Aristotle's side, it involves the fundamental principles of his metaphysics, especially his doctrine of substance, as well as his theory of what and how the intellect knows, as contrasted with the perceptions of the senses. On Plato's side, it involves many questions, concerning the intelligible and the sensible, being and becoming, the one and the many—questions the Aristotelian answers to which would not satisfy Plato.

Wherever the truth lies, Aristotle recognizes that on this issue, perhaps more than on any other, he is most sharply opposed to Plato. It is the one matter wherein he feels a conflict between devotion to his teacher and to the truth as he sees it. The consideration of the universal good, he declares in the *Nicomachean Ethics,* is made difficult "by the fact that the Forms have been introduced by friends of our own," but "while both are dear, piety requires us to honor truth above our friends."

THE HISTORIANS OF PHILOSOPHY, beginning with Aristotle, attribute one solution of the problem of universals to Plato. That solution comes to be called "realism" because it affirms the independent reality of universals as separately existing Ideas or Forms. But all the commentators do not, like Aristotle, dissent from Plato's solution. In our own time, for example, Russell, treating of "the world of universals" in *The Problems of Philosophy,* says, "the problem with which we are now concerned is a very old one, since it was brought into philosophy by Plato. Plato's 'theory of ideas' is an attempt to solve this very problem, and in my opinion it is one of the most successful attempts hitherto made. The theory to be advocated in what follows is largely Plato's, with merely such modifications as time has shown to be necessary."

For one thing, Russell thinks "the word 'idea' has acquired in the course of time many associations which are quite misleading when applied to Plato's 'ideas.' We shall, therefore," he writes, "use the word 'universal' instead of the word 'idea' to describe what Plato meant . . . We speak of whatever is given in sensation . . . as a *particular;* by opposition to this, a *universal* will be anything which may be shared by many particulars . . . Broadly speaking, proper names stand for particulars, while other substantives, adjectives, prepositions, and verbs stand for universals."

Russell here calls attention to another point which he thinks has too seldom been observed, namely, that universals are not exclusively signified by common nouns and adjectives, but that, in addition, there are relational universals signified by prepositions and verbs. This sort of universal, according to him, most readily shows that universals have being apart from particulars. It can also be shown, he argues, "that their being is not merely mental . . . that whatever being belongs to them is independent of their being thought of or in any way apprehended by minds."

If the word "existence" implies definite location in time and space, then, Russell concludes, in the sense in which "thoughts and feelings, minds and physical objects *exist* . . . universals do not exist." We must say instead that "they *subsist* or *have being,* where 'being' is opposed to 'existence' as being timeless. The world of universals, therefore, may also be described as the world of being. The world of being is unchangeable . . . The world of existence is fleeting . . . According to our temperaments, we shall prefer the contemplation of the one or the other. The one we do not prefer will probably seem to us a pale shadow of the one we prefer, and hardly worthy to be regarded as in any sense real. But the truth is that both have the same claim on our impartial attention, both are real, and both are important to the metaphysician. Indeed no sooner have we distinguished the two worlds than it becomes necessary to consider their relations."

What Russell calls timeless subsistence,

Whitehead calls eternal objects. "These transcendent entities," Whitehead writes, "have been termed 'universals.' I prefer to use the term 'eternal objects,' in order to disengage myself from presuppositions which cling to the former term owing to its prolonged philosophical history."

IT IS THIS CONSIDERATION which seems to be for Plato *the* problem of the universal—the central difficulty in the theory of Ideas or separate Forms. As indicated in the chapters on FORM and IDEA, the separation of the two worlds—the sensible world of becoming and the intelligible world of being—always calls for some explanation of their resemblance.

Socrates sometimes refers to the doctrine of Ideas as if its truth could be assumed, and sometimes argues the necessity of a realm of immutable and intelligible being as the object of thought, comparable to sensible, changing things as the object of perception. In the *Phaedo,* for example, he gets Cebes to admit that the ideas, "which in the dialectical process we define as essences or true existences," are not subject to change, but that they are "always what they are, having the same simple self-existent and unchanging forms." In contrast to absolute beauty or goodness, the many beautiful or good things "are always in a state of change." These, Socrates says, "you can touch and see and perceive with the senses, but the unchanging things you can only perceive with the mind. Let us suppose then," he adds, "that there are two sorts of existences—one seen, the other unseen."

Later in the same dialogue, Socrates repeats the assumption that "there is an absolute beauty and goodness and greatness and the like." No other assumption seems to him to provide as satisfactory an explanation of how particular things can be beautiful or good or have any other characteristics. "Nothing makes a thing beautiful," he declares, "but the presence and participation of beauty in whatever way or manner obtained; for as to the manner I am uncertain, but I stoutly contend that by beauty all beautiful things become beautiful."

In later Platonic dialogues, the question of the manner comes to the fore. Though the Eleatic Stranger in the *Sophist* refers to the "endless conflict raging" between the materialists and the idealists concerning the existence of the unseen world of ideas, he himself seems to be doubtful only on the point of how the changing things of sense participate in the immutable forms. One answer is suggested in the *Timaeus.* According to the story of creation which Timaeus tells, the artificer of the world made its sensible particulars copy an eternal pattern. When many things seem to be of one nature or to share the same quality, they are so by virtue of imitating the eternal forms, which are not only absolute essences in themselves, but are also the models for created or generated things.

But in the *Parmenides* Socrates seems unable to defend the view that "the ideas are, as it were, patterns fixed in nature, and other things are like them, and resemblances of them—for what is meant by the participation of other things in the ideas, is really assimilation to them." Nor can he meet other objections which Parmenides raises, such as the difficulty of two or more individuals participating in one idea; for if the idea is wholly in one individual, it cannot be in another, and if each of the many partake of the idea only in part, then the idea cannot be one and indivisible. "In what way, Socrates," Parmenides asks, "will all things participate in ideas, if they are unable to participate in them as parts or wholes?"

In the course of the discussion Parmenides rebukes Socrates for being squeamish about positing absolute essences for "such things as hair, mind, dirt, or anything else which is vile and paltry," as well as for things which are beautiful and good. But his main intention seems to be to leave Socrates with an unresolved dilemma. On the one hand, the difficulties with the theory of Ideas make the denial of their separate existence reasonable; on the other, the denial of their existence seems to make thought and reasoning impossible, because it deprives the mind of its proper objects.

SOME OF ARISTOTLE'S arguments against the separate existence of universals repeat the objections raised by Parmenides, to which no answer is given in the dialogues of Plato. If it were not for the fact that Aristotle attributes to Plato himself the theory he criticizes, the dialogues would leave us in some doubt as to whether it is Plato or his followers, the Platonists, who hold that theory. But whether or not Aristotle's criticisms apply to Plato—and even if they involve some misunderstanding of his doctrine—the objections Aristotle raises help define his own position.

To say that the Forms "are patterns and that other things share in them," Aristotle writes, "is to use empty words and poetical metaphors." In his view, "the most paradoxical thing of all is the statement that there are certain things besides those in the material universe, and that these are the same as sensible things except that they are eternal while the latter are perishable." To posit the separate being of the forms of things seems to him a useless multiplication of existences. To say that "there must be Ideas of all things that are spoken of universally" is to make substances of ideas.

Those who say the Forms exist would be right, Aristotle concedes, "*if* they are substances." He does not think it is impossible to establish the existence of imperishable and insensible substances, but such substances, if they exist, would not stand in relation to sensible substances as universal to particular, or as one to many. His objection to the theory of Ideas is that, in speaking of absolute beauty or beauty-itself, of the idea Man or man-itself, the Platonists do no more than add words like "absolute" or "itself" to the names of sensible things, and posit the existence of these absolutes or universals over and above the existence of the sensible particulars having the same name.

Aristotle's own position seems to be that only individual substances exist, whether they are sensible or intelligible, perishable or eternal, and that "no universal can be a substance" or exist separately in and of itself. He does not thereby deny the reality of the universal. On the contrary, he holds that "without the universal it is not possible to get knowledge," *i.e.,* scientific knowledge in distinction from

mere sense perception. "All knowledge is of the universal and of the 'such,' " he writes; yet in adding that "substance is not a universal, but is rather a 'this,' " Aristotle indicates what is for him the central problem of the universal.

Aristotle's theory that the mind abstracts universal concepts from the particulars of sense-experience, and that such concepts are the terms of the universal propositions constituting scientific knowledge, leaves a question concerning the object of science. If science is knowledge of real existence, not of our own concepts, and if only individual things really exist, then how can the object of science be the universal, not the individual? What is the object apprehended by the universal concept 'man' or 'horse'?

Aristotle's answer seems to be that if the universal term 'man' can be truly predicated of an indefinite number of individuals, it must signify something common to them all. The common nature or properties shared by a number of individuals cannot be actually universal, however, since, in Aristotle's opinion, whatever exists in the individual—the form as well as the matter of the concrete substance— is itself individual. He finds it necessary to say, therefore, that the universal exists potentially, not actually, whenever a number of individuals have something in common.

The form which constitutes human nature, for example, is an individual form in Socrates and Callias; but it has the potentiality of being universal insofar as it is capable of being separated from the individual matter of these two men by the abstractive power of the mind. When the abstraction takes place and results in the universal concept 'man,' the form thus received in the mind becomes actually universal and enables the mind to apprehend the nature common to all individual men.

ARISTOTLE'S DOCTRINE THAT the universal exists potentially in individual things and actually in the abstract concepts of the mind, later comes to be called "moderate realism," in contrast to the extreme realism of the position which asserts the actual subsistence of universals, outside of minds as well as apart from individual things. It affirms that the universal has what Russell calls "extra-mental reality," even though it severely qualifies the real being of the universal by saying it is neither actual nor subsistent.

As Aristotle denies unqualified reality to universals, later philosophers deny that they have any reality at all. Those who are sometimes called "conceptualists" admit the existence of universals only as abstract ideas in the mind. The "nominalist" position, taken by Hobbes and Berkeley, goes further and even denies abstract ideas or universal notions in the mind. It holds that universality is a property of words alone, which manifests itself in the meaning of general or common names.

In the progressive complication of the controversy, each of the theories which has acquired a traditional title undergoes modification as it is reformulated in different contexts. This is especially true of the two middle positions which tend to lean toward one or the other of the extremes.

Locke, for example, may be called a conceptualist because he thinks that general names derive their universal significance from the abstract ideas they signify. But though he denies that by means of our universal notions or abstract ideas we can know the real essences of things, he does not deny real essence. To this extent, he may lean toward moderate realism more than a philosopher like William of Ockham, or a psychologist like William James who says, *We must decide in favor of the conceptualists,* and affirm that the power to think things, qualities, relations . . . isolated and abstracted from the total experience in which they appear, is the most indisputable function of our thought." Similarly, the development which Aquinas gives to Aristotle's views, especially in the point he adds concerning ideas in the mind of God—the "eternal exemplars"— may be a form of moderate realism which, more than Aristotle's, has some affinity with the theory of self-subsistent ideas as the eternal archetypes for sensible particulars.

Aquinas presents his own theory in the context of stating his understanding of the issue between Plato and Aristotle. "Plato supposed," he declares, "that the forms of natural things subsisted apart from matter, and conse-

quently that they are intelligible, for a thing is actually intelligible from the very fact that it is immaterial. And he called such forms *species* or *ideas*. From a participation in these, he said that even corporeal matter was formed, in order that individuals might be naturally established in their proper genera and species . . . But since Aristotle did not allow that the forms of natural things exist apart from matter, and since forms existing in matter are not actually intelligible, it follows that the natures or forms of the sensible things which we understand are not actually intelligible."

Aquinas speaks of the forms (which exist only in union with matter in individual things) as "universal forms," even though they are not actually intelligible. "We abstract universal forms from their particular conditions," he says, and by doing so we "make them actually intelligible." The Platonic error, in his opinion, consists in thinking that "the form of the thing known must be in the knower in the same manner as in the thing known." From the fact that "the form of the thing understood is in the intellect under conditions of universality, immateriality, and immobility," Plato concluded, erroneously, according to Aquinas, "that the things which we understand must subsist in themselves under the same conditions of immateriality and immobility."

As Aquinas states what he takes to be Aristotle's correction of this error, it consists in distinguishing two ways in which the universal can be considered. "First, the universal nature may be considered together with the intention of universality. And since the intention of universality—*viz.,* the relation of one and the same to many—is due to intellectual abstraction, the universal thus considered is subsequent, in our knowledge . . . Secondly, the universal can be considered according to the nature itself (for instance, *animality* or *humanity*) as existing in the individual." In the order of generation and time, the potential universal precedes the actual universal; that is, the universal form or common nature exists in individual things under conditions of particularity before it exists in the human mind under conditions of abstraction.

Even as forms exist in things (though they

are not actually universal prior to their existence as universal concepts of the mind), so they have a mode of being prior to their existence in things. Here Aquinas attributes to Augustine the correction of a pagan error and the substitution for it of a Christian truth. "Whenever Augustine, who was imbued with the doctrines of the Platonists," he writes, "found in their teaching anything consistent with the faith, he adopted it; and those things which he found contrary to faith, he amended."

Plato, positing "the forms of things subsisting of themselves apart from matter," had supposed that, "just as corporeal matter, by participating in the Idea of stone, becomes a stone, so our intellect, by participating in the same Idea, has knowledge of the stone." But, according to Aquinas, "it seems contrary to faith that the forms of things should subsist of themselves without matter outside the things themselves . . . Therefore, in place of the Ideas defended by Plato, Augustine said that the exemplars of all creatures existed in the divine mind. It is according to these that all things are formed, as well as that the human soul knows all things."

THE SOLUTION TO THE problem of universals which Aquinas proposes seems to involve a threefold distinction with respect to the being of forms: they are (1) in the human mind by abstraction from our experience of sensible particulars; (2) in individual things; and (3), prior to their existence in things, in the divine mind.

But Aquinas himself says that in God there is no distinction between universal and particular; nor does knowledge "exist in God after the mode of created knowledge, so as to be universal or particular." The divine ideas, whether considered as the exemplars by which God creates things or as the types and likeness by which God knows them, are not abstractions and so do not have the universality characteristic of human concepts. Whereas our abstract universals do not give us knowledge of individual things in their singularity, the divine ideas, according to Aquinas, are the principles whereby God at once knows the singular and the universal.

If the universal *as such* is not in the divine mind, neither, in Ockham's opinion, is it really in things—not even potentially. Everything that exists in an individual—its form and matter, all its parts and properties—is the unique and singular possession of that individual. If there were something common to two things, it would have to be one and two at the same time. As common to both, it would have to be somehow one and the same in both, yet as existing in each, it would have to be as singular in each as each individual thing in which it existed. But since Ockham regards this as impossible, he concludes that "no universal really exists outside the soul in an individual substance; nor is it of the substance or the being of things, but is only in the soul."

The old riddle thus returns in another form. If abstract concepts are in the mind—or if, as Ockham suggests, the logical "terms 'animal' and 'man' are universals because predicable of many, not through themselves, but for the things they signify"—then what in reality is the object signified by the universal term or concept? It cannot be the many unless the numerically distinct individuals are also alike as men or animals; and how can they be really alike, as opposed to being merely conceived as such, unless they have a common nature or attribute and to that extent are one and the same?

Locke puts the question another way. "Since all things are only particulars," he asks, "how come we by general terms, or where find we those general natures they are supposed to stand for?" He answers that "words become general, by being made the signs of general ideas; and ideas become general by separating from them the circumstances of time and place, and other ideas that may determine them to this or that particular existence. By this way of abstraction, they are made capable of representing more individuals than one; each of which having in it a conformity to that abstract idea is (as we call it) of that sort."

But if, as Locke goes on to say, general natures (or genera and species) are "nothing else but abstract ideas, more or less comprehensive, with names annexed to them," then in what way do the many individuals represented by one abstract idea have in them "a conformity to that abstract idea"? Locke's position seems to avoid this problem. "Abstract ideas," he writes, give us "no knowledge of existence at all." Only particular propositions are about real existences. "Universal propositions, of whose truth or falsehood we can have certain knowledge, concern not existence." Such propositions express nothing but "the agreement or disagreement of our abstract ideas."

In addition to denying their reference to reality, Locke regards abstract ideas as "fictions or contrivances of the mind," which are imperfect precisely to the extent that they succeed in being universal. The general idea of triangle, he observes, must be neither equilateral, isosceles, nor scalene, "but all and none of these at once. In effect, it is something imperfect, that cannot exist." Where Locke seems to mean only that there can be no counterpart in reality to our general ideas, Berkeley, observing the same "imperfection" in what are supposed to be abstract ideas, denies that they can exist even in the mind. "I deny," he writes, "that I can abstract from one another, or conceive separately, those qualities which it is impossible should exist so separated, or that I can frame a general notion by abstracting from particulars."

Berkeley admits that "a man may consider a figure merely as triangular, without attending to the particular qualities of the angles or relations of the sides. So far he may abstract; but this will never prove that he can frame an abstract, general, inconsistent idea of a triangle." He recognizes also that all our common names have general significance, but he rejects Locke's explanation of their general meaning. "A word becomes general," he says, "by being made the sign, not of an abstract general idea, but of several particular ideas, any one of which it indifferently suggests to the mind."

Does a nominalist like Berkeley escape the persistent riddle? Does it not reappear in the question which must be asked: what is there in this set of particular ideas, as opposed to some other set, which makes it possible for a general name to signify any one of them indifferently? If each particular idea were absolutely unique and had nothing in common with any other,

would the universal have any truth even on the level of names?

James thinks the nominalists are somehow forced to "admit a *quasi*-universal, something which we think *as if it were* universal, though it is not; and in all that they say about this something which they explain to be 'an indefinite number of particular ideas,' the same vacillation between the subjective and objective points of view appears. The reader never can tell," James continues, "whether an 'idea' spoken of is supposed to be a knower or a known. The authors themselves do not distinguish. They want to get something in the mind which shall *resemble* what is out of the mind, however vaguely, and they think that when that fact is accomplished, no farther questions will be asked."

SOME PHILOSOPHERS DEAL with the universal and particular in a manner which leads away from rather than into the traditional problem.

To Spinoza, for example, the universal terms, such as *man, horse, dog,* represent confused images drawn from sense-experience. They provide us with an inadequate knowledge of things. To know things adequately we must proceed "from an adequate idea of the formal essence of certain attributes of God to the adequate knowledge of the essence of things." Quite opposite to the abstract universal (or indeterminate image from experience), the adequate idea is universal in the totally different sense of comprehending an infinite whole.

Hegel also distinguishes between abstract universality and "true infinity or concrete universality." The former is "something determinate; *i.e.,* being abstraction from all determinacy, it is itself not without determinacy; to be something abstract and one-sided constitutes its determinacy, its defectiveness, its finitude." The antithesis of the abstract universal is the particular, the determinate content implicitly contained in an abstract universal. The synthesis is the individual; not the particular individual, but the infinite individual which is the concrete universal.

The concrete universal is neither "the universal as a common characteristic, nor the abstract universality which stands outside and over against the individual, the abstract identity of the Understanding." It is "the universality which has the particular as its opposite, but the particular which by its reflection into itself has been equalized with the universal. This unity is individuality, not individuality in its immediacy as a unit . . . but individuality in accordance with its concept." For Hegel, the concrete universal is the immanent Idea itself. It is the manifestation of the Absolute Spirit or God.

HOWEVER IT IS formulated and whether or not it is or can be solved, the problem of the universal seems to have a critical bearing on the discussion of many other great ideas. In addition to the chapters enumerated at the beginning, we can now see that the universal, the particular, and the individual are implicated in the consideration of BEING and INFINITY, FORM and IDEA, MATTER and MIND, EXPERIENCE, INDUCTION, JUDGMENT, and SCIENCE. These chapters, in turn, do more than throw light on the various solutions proposed to the problem of the universal. They help us understand the importance of the problem—certainly to the philosophers of the western tradition. If in the broader context of connected issues, it is discovered that the proof of man's distinctive rationality, or even the possibility of an immortal soul, may depend on the affirmation or denial of universals, at least as concepts in the mind, then, perhaps, some tolerance and patience may be won for the burdensome technicalities of the problem.

Virtue and Vice

INTRODUCTION

I N their currently popular connotations, the words "virtue" and "vice" have extremely limited significance. Virtue tends to be identified with chastity or at least with conformity to the prevailing standards of sexual behavior. The popular notion of vice retains a little more of the traditional meaning, insofar as it implies injury to a person's character or health as the result of strong *habitual* addictions. But, as in the case of virtue, the things which are popularly called "vices" are largely concerned with pleasures or sensual indulgences.

In the tradition of the great books, however, the scope of these terms and the range of the problems in which they are involved seem to be coextensive with morality; or, in other words, with the broadest consideration of good and evil in human life, with what is right and wrong for man not only to do, but also to wish or desire, and even to think. For some of the great moral philosophers, other terms—such as duty for Marcus Aurelius and Kant, or pleasure and utility for J. S. Mill—seem to be more central. But for Plato, Aristotle, and Aquinas virtue is a basic moral principle. By reference to it they define the good man, the good life, and the good society. Yet even for them it is not the first principle of ethics. They define virtue itself by reference to a more ultimate good—happiness. For them the virtues promote and serve happiness as means to an end.

T HE ANCIENT ENUMERATION of particular virtues may show the range of things comprehended under the notion of virtue generally. It may also further sharpen the contrast with the contemporary tendency to use the words "virtue" and "vice" as if they applied only to

matters which fall within the sphere of one of the virtues. That one is the virtue which both Plato and Aristotle call "temperance," and which they conceive as concerned chiefly with the bodily appetites and pleasures. Plato and Aristotle give somewhat different enumerations, but courage and justice are as fundamental for them as temperance; and when certain virtues come later to be classified as the cardinal or principal virtues, these three are always named together. In that classification, there is a fourth—prudence or, as it is sometimes called, "practical wisdom."

Plato's enumeration of the virtues in *The Republic* also adds wisdom to temperance, courage, and justice. This indicates at once that the ancient conception of virtue as the quality which makes a man good, extends to his mind as well as to his character—to the sphere of thinking and knowing as well as to desire, emotion, and action. Aristotle makes this explicit by dividing all the virtues into moral and intellectual, or excellences of character and of mind. He names five intellectual virtues: in addition to wisdom and prudence (which he distinguishes as speculative and practical wisdom), he lists art, science, and what he calls "intuitive reason," which Aquinas later calls "understanding."

The division of the virtues into moral and intellectual leads, in Aristotle's analysis, to the further distinction between those intellectual virtues—understanding, science, wisdom—which represent the possession of speculative insight or theoretical knowledge, and those—art and prudence—which represent skill in practical thinking or in the application of knowledge to production and action respectively. Because it is concerned with action, or moral conduct, the virtue of prudence is most closely associated with the moral virtues of justice, courage, and temperance. The grouping together by Aquinas of these four as the cardinal virtues carries the implication that the remaining four (*i.e.*, art and the three virtues of the speculative reason) play a secondary role. The implication is simply that a man may be made good as a scientist or good as an artist by the acquisition of these secondary virtues, but he is not made good as a man by these virtues, nor do they enable him to lead a good life and achieve happiness, as do the moral virtues accompanied by prudence.

In line with the principle by which he regards certain virtues as cardinal or indispensable for human rectitude and welfare, the Christian moralist goes further than the moral philosopher in developing the theory of virtue. Considering man's limitations and his fallen nature, he holds that more than all the natural virtues (*i.e.*, the virtues which men can attain by their own effort) is required for salvation—for the supernatural end of eternal happiness. Faith, hope, and charity, according to Saint Paul, are indispensable to lift man's life to a plane, and direct it to a goal, which exceed his nature. These gifts of God's grace are subsequently treated by Augustine, Aquinas, and Calvin as virtues—supernatural, not natural virtues. Aquinas specifically calls them "theological virtues" to distinguish them from other supernatural endowments, such as the infused moral virtues and the gifts of the Holy Ghost.

THE READER MAY OBSERVE that of all the virtues so far named, only the three theological virtues are not the subject of separate chapters in this collection of great ideas. The chapters on COURAGE, JUSTICE, TEMPERANCE, PRUDENCE, WISDOM may include discussions of these qualities which do not specifically treat them as virtues. Certainly that is true of the chapters on ART and SCIENCE, and the chapter on PRINCIPLE, wherein the virtue of intuitive reason or the understanding of first principles is considered. Nevertheless, that all but one of these chapters bear the name of the traditionally recognized virtues indicates how

widely and variously they make their appearance throughout the great books—by example and comment in poetry and history as well as by definition and analysis in the ethical and political treatises. In contrast, the theological virtues appear only in Christian, not pagan literature, and then mainly in religious rather than secular writing.

It is also of interest to note the relation which this chapter bears to those dealing with other fundamental concepts of moral philosophy or theology. Some of the terms mentioned in the foregoing paragraphs—duty, pleasure, happiness, good—name chapters which are co-implicated with this one in the problem of how men should live and what they should seek. The Outline of Topics will reveal still others—knowledge, desire, emotion, reason, will, wealth, honor, friendship, teaching, family, state, citizen, law, sin, and grace—each of which is (or indicates) the title of a chapter that treats of matters related to virtue as cause or consequence, as psychological factor or external condition.

One chapter not yet mentioned has maximum relevance for most of the authors who offer some analysis of virtue. The chapter on HABIT treats an idea that is crucial to the definition of virtue. Aquinas, for example, allocates the discussion of virtue and vice to his "Treatise on Habits" in the *Summa Theologica*. He divides this treatise into questions concerning habits in general and questions concerning good and evil habits—or virtues and vices—in particular. But the notion that virtue combines the elements of habit and goodness is not peculiarly his. With varying degrees of emphasis and explicitness, it appears in Plato and Aristotle, in Augustine, Francis Bacon, Hegel, and William James. Kant alone expressly dissents, declaring that virtue "is not to be defined and esteemed merely as *habit*, and . . . as a long *custom* acquired by the practice of morally good actions."

THE DISCUSSION OF VIRTUE originates in the dialogues of Plato and the *Nicomachean Ethics* of Aristotle with a number of related questions. Meno's opening question—"Can you tell me, Socrates, whether virtue is acquired by teaching or by practice; or if neither by teaching nor practice, then whether it comes to man by nature, or in what other way?"—requires, in the opinion of Socrates, other questions to be faced: what virtue is, how virtue is related to knowledge, whether virtue is one or many, and if many, how the several particular virtues are related to one another.

In the course of the dialogue, each of the alternatives is considered. If virtue were identical with knowledge, it could be taught and learned just as geometry is. If virtue were simply a habit, it could be acquired by practice, that is, by the repetition of similar acts. But neither practice nor teaching seems by itself to explain how men come by virtue, and even less why virtuous fathers should so often fail to produce virtue in their sons. Yet Socrates does not completely dismiss these possibilities or the possibility considered at the end, that "virtue comes to the virtuous by the gift of God." What truth there is in each of them, he concludes, cannot be determined until we know precisely what virtue is.

Another dialogue, the *Protagoras*, pursues a similar inquiry and seems to reach a similarly indeterminate conclusion. The relation of virtue to knowledge here leads to the question whether "wisdom and temperance and courage and justice and holiness" are "five names of the same thing." To the extent that each depends on knowledge of what is good and evil, they would seem to be, if not identical, at least inseparable aspects of the same thing. Protagoras objects on the score that a man may be courageous and at the same time "utterly unrighteous, unholy, intemperate, ignorant." But Socrates finally gets him to admit reluctantly that courage consists in knowledge, and cowardice in ignorance, of what is and is not dangerous.

It was Protagoras, however, who originally contended against Socrates that virtue can be taught. The reduction of all the virtues to some form of knowledge would therefore seem to confirm his opinion. Socrates, in winning the argument about virtue and knowledge, seems to overthrow his own view that virtue cannot be taught. "The result of our discussion," Socrates says at the end, "appears to me to be singular. For if the argument had a human voice, the voice would be heard laughing at us and saying: 'Protagoras and Socrates, you are strange beings; there are you, Socrates, who were saying that virtue cannot be taught, contradicting youself now by your attempt to prove that all things are knowledge, including justice and temperance and courage—which tends to show that virtue can certainly be taught . . . Protagoras, on the other hand, who started by saying that it might be taught, is now eager to prove it to be anything rather than knowledge.' "

The only way "this terrible confusion of our ideas" might be cleared up, Socrates suggests, is for the conversation to go on "until we ascertain what virtue is." But that particular conversation does not go on; nor do the definitions of virtue which are proposed in other Platonic dialogues seem to be decisive on the point whether virtue is knowledge or whether it can be taught. In the *Laws,* for example, the Athenian Stranger, saying that "harmony of the soul, taken as a whole, is virtue," proposes that education should consist in training "the first instincts of virtue in children" by producing suitable habits in them. But his training does not seem to be, like ordinary teaching, the inculcation of knowledge. It is "training in respect of pleasure and pain," whereby we are led to hate what we ought to hate and love what we ought to love.

In *The Republic,* Socrates compares the harmony produced by virtue in the soul with the harmony of the parts in a healthy body. "Virtue is the health and beauty and well-being of the soul," he declares, "and vice the disease and weakness and deformity of the same." Though wisdom consists in the rule of the other parts of the soul by reason in the light of "knowledge of what is for the interest of each of the parts and of the whole," it does not seem to be the whole of virtue, nor does Socrates suggest that men become virtuous simply by becoming wise. On the contrary, he intimates that "good practices lead to virtue, and evil practices to vice," and that, like certain bodily qualities, the "virtues of the soul . . . can be implanted by habit and exercise."

IT IS SOMETIMES SUPPOSED that Aristotle differs from Plato on fundamental points in the theory of virtue. The fact that Aristotle criticizes Socrates for "thinking that all the virtues are forms of practical wisdom," seems to imply a basic disagreement on the relation of virtue to knowledge. But Aristotle also remarks that Socrates was right "in saying they implied practical wisdom." His own view that the moral virtues of courage, temperance, and justice are inseparable from the intellectual virtue of prudence does not seem to differ substantially from the statements of Socrates that "virtue must be a sort of wisdom or prudence" and that "virtue is either wholly or partly wisdom." Such difference as there is appears to be not so much in what is being affirmed or denied as in the manner of statement or analysis, and beyond that, perhaps, in a method of exposition which permits Aristotle to give definite answers to questions Plato's dialogues often leave unanswered.

Aristotle's analysis, of course, sometimes changes the questions themselves to make them answerable, but this is not always so. His summary of existing opinions concerning the acquisition of virtue—that "some think we are made good by nature, others by habituation, others by teaching"—is nearly equivalent, as an enumeration of possibilities, to Meno's opening question. But where Socrates in answering Meno contents himself with suggesting that there may be some truth in each possibility as against the others, Aristotle definitely affirms that the whole truth about the matter combines all three factors. "There are three things," he writes, "which make men good and virtuous: these are nature, habit, rational principle." Even Socrates' final point, that virtue may be a gift of God, seems to be affirmed by Aristotle's comment that, in effecting virtue, "nature's part evidently does not depend on us, but as a result of some divine causes is present in those who are truly fortunate."

But in the case of two Platonic questions— the one about the relation of virtue to knowledge and the other about the unity of virtue— Aristotle's analysis transforms the problem. His basic distinction between moral and intel-lectual virtue turns the question about virtue and knowledge into one concerning the role which one very special kind of knowledge, represented by the virtue of prudence, plays in the formation and operation of good moral habits—habits in the sphere of action and passion or of the will and the emotions. By substituting a number of distinct intellectual virtues for the single term 'knowledge,' Aristotle can definitely answer both Yes and No to the question. Not all the intellectual virtues, not art and science, or even speculative wisdom, are needed for courage, temperance, and justice; but if by "knowledge" is meant nothing more than prudence, then Aristotle affirms these moral virtues to involve knowledge of a sort.

The distinction between moral and intellectual virtue also enables Aristotle to reformulate the problem of the unity of virtue. Instead of asking whether there is only one virtue, having many aspects, or many distinct virtues, he considers which virtues are interdependent and which can exist separately from one another. Virtue has unity in the inseparability of the moral virtues from one another and from prudence. The sailor who appears to be courageous without being temperate, or the thief who appears to be prudent without being just, has only the appearance of these virtues. But though Aristotle uses the phrase "perfect virtue" to signify both the integration of these virtues and the perfection of each when it is integrated with the others, he does not include all the particular virtues in the unity of virtue. Some, like art and science, can exist apart from prudence or the moral virtues, and they from it.

By showing how all of the moral virtues depend upon prudence or practical wisdom, Aristotle thinks he is able to "refute the argument . . . that the virtues exist in separation from each other." But he does not find any greater unity of the virtues than is involved in their inseparability as a result of their common dependence on prudence. Following Aristotle, Aquinas criticizes those who assert a more profound unity by claiming that prudence, temperance, fortitude, and justice signify "only certain general conditions . . . to be found in all the virtues." This, according to Aquinas, is tantamount to denying that they are distinct habits.

Insisting that they are really distinct as habits, Aquinas nevertheless suggests that "these four virtues qualify one another by a kind of overflow. For," he explains, "the qualities of prudence overflow into the other virtues in so far as they are directed by prudence. And each of the others overflows into the rest, for the reason that whoever can do what is more difficult, can do what is less difficult." The man who "can curb his desires for the pleasures of touch, which is a very hard thing to do ... is more able to check his daring in dangers of death ... which is much easier"; the man who can withstand the "dangers of death, which is a matter of great difficulty, is more able to remain firm against the onslaught of pleasures."

As for justice, Aquinas holds that legal justice, "by commanding the other virtues ... draws them all into the service of the commonweal." Aristotle also sees a certain unification of the virtues, at least all the moral virtues, in terms of justice—the kind of justice he calls "general" to distinguish it from the special virtue of justice. He conceives general justice as comprising all the moral virtues, including special justice, insofar as all these virtues are directed toward the welfare of society and the good of other men. "Justice in this sense," he writes, "is not a part of virtue, but virtue entire." Holding that it "is complete virtue, not absolutely, but in relation to our neighbor," he adds that "it is complete because he who possesses it can exercise his virtue not only in himself, but towards his neighbor as well."

Some writers tend in the opposite direction toward a greater separation of the virtues. Justice, according to Marcus Aurelius, is prior to the other virtues, for "in justice the other virtues have their foundation." In suggesting that a man can secure "a favorable and commodious interpretation of his vices" by coloring them in the light of his virtues, Bacon seems to accept the conjunction of virtue with vice which is expressed in the familiar phrase, "the defects of one's virtues." That a gentleman may with honor be permitted certain failings is similarly implied by Dr. Johnson's reference to "the genteel vices."

This comfortable doctrine that a man can be truly virtuous in some aspects of character while vicious in others seems, however, to be rejected by Montaigne and Kant, as well as by Plato and Aristotle. The standard of Christian virtue is even more stringent. What may appear to be virtues are, according to Augustine, "rather vices than virtues so long as there is no reference to God in the matter. For although some suppose that virtues which have a reference only to themselves, and are desired only on their own account, are yet true and genuine virtues, the fact is that even they are inflated with pride, and are therefore to be reckoned vices."

The theological virtue of charity—the love of God—is held by the theologians to be indispensable to the perfection of all the other virtues in a Christian life. Not only, according to Aquinas, do faith and hope lack "the perfect character of virtue without charity," but all the other virtues are imperfect in its absence.

"It is possible by means of human works," he writes, "to acquire the moral virtues in so far as they produce good works that are directed to an end not surpassing the natural ability of man. And when they are acquired thus, they can be without charity, even as they were in many of the pagans. But in so far as they produce good works in relation to a supernatural last end, thus they have the character of virtue truly and perfectly, and cannot be acquired by human acts, but are infused by God. Such moral virtues cannot be without charity ... Only the infused virtues are perfect, and deserve to be called virtues absolutely ... The other virtues, those, namely, that are acquired, are virtues in a restricted sense."

THAT VIRTUE IS GOOD and vice evil seems to go undisputed in the tradition of the great books, even by Machiavelli who bemoans the "necessity" of vice in a successful prince. But unanimity on this point does not preclude a variety of answers to the question, What is the good of virtue?

Is it an end in itself, or a means, and if a means, what end does it serve? Moreover, what is the principle of goodness in the virtues? Does it lie in the rule of reason, in conformity to nature, in obedience to the moral law and the imperative of duty, in submission to God's will? Or are the virtues good only to the extent that they are useful and profitable? To the individual alone or to society as well? As these questions are differently answered, different conceptions of virtue appear.

Marcus Aurelius gives the simplest and most familiar answer. Virtue is its own reward. "What more dost thou want," the Stoic asks, "when thou hast done a man a service? Art thou not content that thou hast done something conformable to thy nature, and dost thou seek to be paid for it?" The virtues are not only self-rewarding but they are the only things in which a good man can take delight. "When thou wishest to delight thyself," Aurelius says, "think of the virtues of those who live with thee ... For nothing delights so much as the examples of the virtues."

Locke seems to make profit or utility the source of goodness in the virtues. "God, having by an inseparable connexion, joined virtue and public happiness together," Locke writes, "and made the practice thereof necessary to the preservation of society, and visibly beneficial to all with whom the virtuous man has to do, it is no wonder that everyone should not only allow, but recommend and magnify those rules to others, from whose observance of them he is sure to reap advantage to himself."

The virtues seem to become conventional in Locke's view. They are whatever the members of a particular society deem advantageous. "Virtue and vice are names pretended, and supposed, everywhere to stand for actions in their nature, right and wrong; and as far as they are really so applied, they are so far coincident with the divine law ... But yet, whatever is pretended," Locke adds, "this is visible, that these names, virtue and vice, in the particular instances of their application, through the several nations and societies of men in the world, are constantly attributed only to such actions as, in each country and society, are in reputation or discredit ... Thus, the measure

of what is everywhere called and esteemed virtue and vice, is the approbation or dislike, praise or blame," which establishes itself in a society "according to the judgment, maxims, or fashion of that place ... That this is the common measure of virtue and vice, will appear," Locke thinks, "to anyone who considers, that though that passes for vice in one country, which is counted a virtue, or at least not a vice, in another; yet everywhere, virtue and praise, vice and blame, go together."

Hobbes also regards the names of the virtues as "inconstant names" varying according to "the nature, disposition and interest of the speaker ... for one man calleth *wisdom*, what another calleth *fear*; and one *cruelty*, what another *justice*; one *prodigality*, what another *magnanimity*." Yet this does not prevent Hobbes from proposing a list of virtues which derive their goodness from the natural law. "All men agree on this," he writes, "that peace is good, and therefore also the ways or means of peace, which ... are *justice, gratitude, modesty, equity, mercy,* and the rest of the laws of nature, are good; that is to say, moral virtues; and their contrary vices, evil."

Moral philosophy, according to Hobbes, is "the science of virtue and vice" and "therefore the true doctrine of the laws of nature is the true moral philosophy." Though other writers of moral philosophy "acknowledge the same virtues and vices," Hobbes thinks they do not see "wherein consisted their goodness, nor that they come to be praised as the means of peaceable, sociable, and comfortable living."

Like Kant, he criticizes Aristotle's doctrine of the mean; or, as Hobbes refers to it, the notion that virtue consists in "a mediocrity of the passions: as if not the cause, but the degree of daring, made fortitude; or not the cause, but the quantity of a gift, made liberality." The cause of virtue, according to Hobbes, is the natural law, commanding men to do whatever is required for peace and self-preservation. In terms of a quite different conception of law and duty, Kant also says that "the difference between virtue and vice cannot be sought in the degree in which certain maxims are followed, but only in the specific *quality* of the maxims. In other words, the vaunted principle of Aristotle, that virtue is the *mean* between two vices, is false."

It is not Kant but Spinoza who seems to bear an affinity to Hobbes in the theory of virtue. Both make self-preservation the end which determines the direction of virtuous conduct. Both consider civil peace or the good of others in relation to self. Both draw up lists of moral virtues from their enumeration of the passions, Hobbes by reference to natural law, Spinoza in terms of adequate ideas of God's nature. Spinoza identifies virtue with power and holds that "the more each person strives and is able to seek his own profit, that is to say, to preserve his own being, the more virtue does he possess." But though he makes "the endeavor after self-preservation . . . the primary and only foundation of virtue," he conceives self-preservation itself to have its foundation in knowledge of God.

"To act in conformity with virtue," Spinoza maintains, "is to act according to the guidance of reason, and every effort which we make through reason is an effort to understand, and therefore the highest good of those who follow after virtue is to know God, that is to say, it is a good which is common to all men, and can be equally possessed by all in so far as they are of the same nature." In direct consequence, he declares that "the good which everyone who follows after virtue seeks for himself, he will desire for other men; and his desire on their behalf will be greater in proportion as he has greater knowledge of God."

ALL THOSE WHO RELATE virtue to happiness do not do so in the same way. "The multiplication of happiness," writes Mill, "is, according to the utilitarian ethics, the object of virtue." He attributes to "a very imperfect state of the world's arrangements" the fact that "anyone can best serve the happiness of others by the absolute sacrifice of his own; yet so long as the world is in that imperfect state," he goes on to say, "the readiness to make such a sacrifice is the highest virtue which can be found in man."

But Mill repeatedly insists that only an increase of happiness justifies sacrifice, and only its contribution to happiness makes virtue good. He criticizes the Stoics for striving "to raise themselves above the concern about anything but virtue" and for supposing that "he who has that has everything . . . No claim of this description is made for the virtuous man by the utilitarian doctrine."

While admitting that virtue may come to be desired disinterestedly, as an ingredient of happiness rather than as a means to it, Mill does not regard virtue as a natural and necessary condition of happiness. "Virtue, according to the utilitarian doctrine, is not naturally and originally part of the end, but it is capable of becoming so." If there are some who do not desire virtue, either because it gives them no pleasure or because the lack of it causes them no pain, they can be happy without it.

The view taken by Plato and Aristotle seems to be directly contrary. All things which have ends appointed by their nature, Socrates argues at the beginning of *The Republic,* must also be capable of virtues or excellences whereby to achieve their ends. If happiness is the end of the soul or of human life, then we must look to such excellences as the virtue of justice and temperance to provide the means. When Glaucon and Adeimantus ask Socrates to prove that only the virtuous man can be happy, he undertakes the long analysis of the parts of the soul and the parts of the state to discover the virtues appropriate to each and to the whole. When the virtues are defined, Glaucon admits that the question he originally asked "has now become ridiculous."

The answer to the question is evident as soon as virtue and happiness are seen to be reciprocal notions, like cause and effect. Yet Aristotle's definition of moral virtue as a habit of choice, consisting in a mean—a mean relative to ourselves, determined by reason or as the prudent man would determine it—does not immediately explain why happiness is defined as "the realization and perfect exercise of virtue." The connection between virtue as means and happiness as end becomes apparent only in terms of the conception that happiness is the ultimate end *because* it includes all good things and leaves nothing to be desired.

As an object of desire, as something worth having in itself, virtue is only one type of good. It does not constitute happiness. Happiness, according to Aristotle, includes as well such bodily and external goods as health and pleasure, friendship and wealth. But unlike these other goods, the virtues alone are capable of producing happiness because, in Aristotle's view, they are the causes of our thinking and acting well with respect to all other goods.

"We do not acquire or preserve virtue by the help of external goods," Aristotle says, "but external goods by the help of virtue." This applies to health and pleasures, no less than to wealth and friends. Because the moral virtues, together with prudence, direct our desires, determine our choices, and govern our actions in accordance with reason's discrimination between real and apparent goods, the exercise of these habits results in happiness or living well. But since external goods are goods of fortune and not entirely within our control, Aristotle finds it necessary to qualify the definition of happiness. To the statement that the happy man is one "who is active in accordance with complete virtue," he adds that he is one "who is sufficiently equipped with external goods, not for some chance period, but throughout a complete life."

According to Kant, "the connexion of virtue and happiness may be understood in two ways: either the endeavor to be virtuous and the rational pursuit of happiness are not two distinct actions, but absolutely identical . . . or the connexion consists in this, that virtue produces happiness as something distinct from the consciousness of virtue, as a cause produces an effect." Kant thinks that both the Stoic and Epicurean doctrines choose the first of these alternatives. They differ from each other, in his opinion, only in the way they conceive the identity of virtue and happiness. "The Epicurean notion of virtue," he writes, "was already involved in the maxim: to promote one's own happiness. According to the Stoics, on the other hand, the feeling of happiness was already contained in the consciousness of virtue."

Kant's own resolution of what he calls "the antinomy of practical reason" seems to depend on his conception of the *summum bonum*. For him it is not happiness; it consists rather in being worthy of happiness through doing one's duty. "Morality," he says, "is not properly the doctrine how we should *make* ourselves happy, but how we should become *worthy* of happiness." Under the moral law, to be happy is not a duty, but to be worthy of happiness is. In Kant's view, therefore, virtue is related to happiness through the medium of duty. Virtue, he declares, is "a coincidence of the rational will with every duty firmly settled in the character." It is "the moral strength of a man's will in his obedience to duty."

But in addition to being the will's strength in overcoming obstacles—"the natural inclination which may come into conflict with the moral purpose"—virtue, or rather "the imperative, which commands the duty of virtue," includes "besides the notion of constraint, that of an end." Not an end that we have, Kant explains, but one that "we ought to have," an end "which, therefore, pure practical reason has in itself, whose highest, unconditional end (which, however, continues to be a duty) consists in this: that virtue is its own end, and by deserving well of men is also its own reward."

The issue between Kant and Aristotle concerning the good of virtue, as a means or an end, involves the whole of their moral philosophy. It goes to the central conflict between their fundamental principles, which is discussed in the chapters on Duty and Happiness. Fundamental differences in political philosophy also arise from different views of virtue in relation to the forms of government and the ends of the state.

The ancients, for example, define aristocracy in terms of virtue. The point is not only that aristocracy is a form of government in which the few who are most virtuous rule; it is also that form of government the principle of which is virtue, as liberty is the principle of democracy, and wealth of oligarchy. Nietzsche believes, "Every elevation of the type 'man' has hitherto been the work of an aristocratic society."

Montesquieu makes virtue the principle in republican government, in contrast to honor as the principle in monarchies and fear in despotism. "What I distinguish by the name of virtue, in a republic," he explains, "is the love

of one's country—that is, the love of equality. It is not a moral, nor a Christian, but a
political virtue; and it is the spring which sets
republican government in motion, as honor is
the spring which gives motion to monarchy."
Since for Montesquieu both democracy and
aristocracy are forms of republican government, the former rests on virtue as much as
the latter.

Agreeing that the conditions Montesquieu
sets for republican government "could not
exist without virtue," Rousseau criticizes him
for failing to see that, "the sovereign authority
being everywhere the same, the same principle should be found in every well-constituted
state, in a greater or less degree, it is true,
according to the form of government." So
for Mill, virtue defines the aim of good government itself, without respect to particular
forms. "The most important point of excellence which any form of government can possess," he writes, "is to promote the virtue and
intelligence of the people themselves."

The virtues which a government promotes,
however, may be those of the good citizen
rather than the good man. This distinction
between civic and moral virtue occupies the
ancients, related as it is to the problem of the
virtuous man living in a bad society—a problem which Socrates actually faces, as well as
discusses, in the *Apology* and the *Crito*.

"The virtue of the citizen," Aristotle writes,
"must be relative to the constitution of the
state of which he is a member . . . Hence it is
evident that the good citizen need not of necessity possess the virtue which makes a good

man." Yet "in some states, the good man and
the good citizen are the same."

In this vein Aquinas, considering whether
the laws should try to make men good, says of
a tyrannical or unjust law that "in so far as it
has something of the nature of law, its aim is
that the citizens be good." At least "it aims at
being obeyed by them; and this," he adds, "is
to make them good, not absolutely, but with
respect to that particular government."

It is this type of moral relativism with respect
to one's form of government that Tocqueville
finds repugnant. "There are some universal and
permanent needs of mankind on which moral
laws are based," and nations have always rede-
fined virtue for their own purposes. Quoting
Plutarch, Tocqueville cites the example that
courage in ancient Rome became so valued that
"in Latin 'virtue' came to mean 'courage.'"
Other societies have equated virtue with skill
in war or loyalty to a monarch. In America, as
Tocqueville foresees it, "all those quiet virtues
which tend to regularity in the body social and
which favor trade are sure to be held in special honor," while "all those turbulent virtues
which sometimes bring glory but more often
trouble to society will rank lower in the public
opinion."

Although Aquinas believes virtue is relative
to particular governments, he also contemplates the need for disobeying a civil ordinance
if it demands too great a sacrifice of virtue
by requiring the citizen to violate the natural
or the divine law. As Rousseau later says, "a
man's duty" takes precedence over "that of
a citizen."

98

War and Peace

INTRODUCTION

THE 20th century may go down in history as the century of war and peace—the first in which world wars were fought, the first in which men established world peace, and so, perhaps, the last in which peace among nations was merely an armed truce, a breathing spell between wars. Even if world peace is not actually begun in our time, we may prove to be the first generation of men on earth who, under the impact of world wars, have made a firm attempt to draw a decisive conclusion from all the accumulated wisdom concerning war and peace.

It may be thought that antiquity anticipates, and that at all times the tradition contains, the fundamental notions which have recently gained so wide a currency. Socrates and Epictetus, for example, speak of world citizenship. Marcus Aurelius and Zeno of Citium even more explicitly envision a world community. Alexander tries to conquer the world to make it one; Virgil proclaims a peace which will be as universal as the Roman Empire; and Dante, recasting Virgil's vision, advocates the reenactment of that empire and with it monarchy—by which he means *one* government—to give all Christendom political as well as spiritual unity.

To neglect these anticipations would be to overlook wisdom's perennial aspirations for unity. But if, because of their significance for peace, they should not be neglected here, neither should their importance be exaggerated. For one thing, man has always acted at variance with his wisdom, nullifying the hope of peace by preparing always for the next war. For another thing, it is doubtful that peace by conquest or by empire—the only ways in which the past could conceive the world's

coming to the unity of peace—would be a peace perpetual as well as universal. The latter without the former is but a fraction of the ideal.

Even when in modern times the ideal is at last stated in terms of peaceful methods for achieving peace—by law, not by force; by consent, not by imposition—something less than the whole world in its global reality is the object of consideration. William Penn and Rousseau, for example, state the indispensable legal conditions for turning Europe from a continent perpetually wracked by wars into a society able to perpetuate peace, but their historical location causes them to limit their proposals to Europe.

Kant alone first makes the generalization which lies dormant in their reasoning, and which almost begs to be inductively drawn from the conceptions of war and peace so plainly stated by Hobbes and Locke. He conceives the possibility of a peace not only perpetual but truly worldwide. Yet for all the rightness he perceives in what he calls "the cosmopolitical ideal," it seems to remain for him an ideal—not attainable except by approximation. Yet because it is right, he holds that it must be pursued even though it is impossible. We are the first generation to argue for world peace as a conclusion on the level of reality and to conclude that it is possible because it is necessary.

The argument is not yet won, nor the conclusion enacted, but henceforth the problem of war and peace can hardly be discussed without stating the issue as a choice of world government and peace, or of world anarchy and war. If it does no more than seriously face that choice for the first time, the 20th century makes a signal advance in understanding one of the great ideas—an advance which can change the course of history and the life of man more than the discovery of atomic fission, which is only an instrument of war or a tool of peace. But just as the release of heat and energy from nuclear combustion has its prototype in ordinary fire, which the ancients associate with the beginning of civilization, so the insight which may exert a new civilizing force has its origin in the fundamental thinking man does about war and peace as soon as he begins to think about society.

IN THE TRADITION OF the great books, war and peace are usually discussed in political terms, or at least in terms of the relation of men to one another, individually or in groups. But the psychologist, the moralist, and the theologian sometimes use the word "peace" in another sense to signify the absence of conflict within the individual or to signify an inner harmony—peace of mind on earth or the heavenly rest of the blessed in the presence of God.

In their spiritual meanings, war and peace are considered in other chapters; *e.g.*, interior conflict is a topic in the chapter on OPPO-SITION and interior peace is discussed in the chapter on HAPPINESS. We shall not treat these matters here except in their bearing on the social and political discussion; nor shall we consider civil war except for the light it throws on war and peace in general. The special problem of discord and strife within a single community belongs to the chapter on REVOLUTION.

Certain attitudes toward war between states seem to recur in every century. In the face of the ever-present fact of war, men deplore its folly or find some benefit to compensate for its devastation. But throughout most of the tradition, those who see only suffering, no less than those who celebrate the martial spirit, seem to accept the necessity of war. Good or bad, or a mixture of the glorious and the horrible, war seems, to most of those who write about it, an inevitable thing—as ineradicable as disease and death for the living body, as inescapable as tragedy. Only in recent times has the inevitability of war been questioned, and the possibility of lasting peace proposed.

The two books which look most steadily and searchingly on the face of war—Homer's *The Iliad* and Tolstoy's *War and Peace*—seem to behold it as a mixed thing. Battle with sword and javelin on the plains of Troy or with musket and howitzer on the Russian steppes lets loose a fury which sweeps human nature to extremes of nobility and baseness, to actions of heroic strength and cringing weakness. To both Homer and Tolstoy, war is the realm of force and chance, and though both see in it occasions for courage and magnanimity and even for a kind of charity or at least compassion, the whole spectacle is one of agony, pervaded by darkness and dismay, torn bodies and ruined minds. "Grievous war" is Homer's repeated epithet. "Pale fear" and "black death" are the colors of battle. They are everywhere that Ares reigns, "Ares, manslaughtering, blood-stained," "insatiate of fighting."

To the poet of any century, Homer or Tolstoy, Virgil or Shakespeare, war's human features appear to be unchanged even if its mechanical dress and physical lineaments are altered—its weapons and armor, its organization of men and materials, its scope of operations in space and time. The historian who measures the contestants and keeps the score of victories and defeats takes a different view. He dwells on all the differences which mark progress in the art of war, or which enable wealthier and more advanced societies to wage wars of greater magnitude. To Herodotus, no military undertaking ever assumed the proportions of Xerxes' army on the march, raising a cloud of dust from horizon to horizon. Yet Thucydides says that before the Peloponnesian War "there was nothing on a great scale either in war or in other matters."

The historian is attentive not only to weights and numbers, to the changing accoutrement of war and its mechanical elaboration, but also to inventions in the sphere of strategy and tactics. The Alexandrian phalanx, the patience of Fabius, the forced marches of Caesar, Hannibal's outflanking and enveloping movements at the battle of Cannae, the deployment in depth of the Roman legions on the Rhine—these are but a few of the inventions of military genius which, as Plutarch, Tacitus, and Gibbon recognize, have an effect far beyond the advantage that novelty initially gives them. They become the classical models of war's art and the principles of its science.

Tolstoy may scoff at the historians who stand in awe of military genius. He may be right that Kutuzov's lack of plans rather than Napoleon's air of outwitting all contingencies is the essence of great generalship. Nevertheless Tolstoy magnifies the campaign of 1812 as beyond comparison the greatest mass movement of humanity, from west to east and then from east to west, just as Herodotus apotheosizes the movement of the Persian horde from east to west and Thucydides the rise of Athenian naval power.

Writing from the center of a whole continent in arms a century later, Freud in 1915 gives his impression of what was yet to become the first world war. A war of such proportions and ferocity was almost incredible before it happened. "Then the war in which we had refused to believe broke out," and, Freud writes, "not only is it more sanguinary and more destructive than any war of other days, because of the enormously increased perfection of weapons of attack and defense; but it is at least as cruel, as embittered, as implacable as any that preceded it . . . It tramples in blind fury on all that comes in its way, as though there were to be no future and no goodwill among men after it has passed. It rends all bonds of fellowship between the contending peoples, and threatens to leave such a legacy of embitterment as will make any renewal of such bonds impossible for a long time to come."

THE ENEMIES OF WAR use a variety of weapons in their attack. *The Trojan Women* of Euripides cries out with the bitterness of Andromache and Hecuba against the misery of war's innocent victims—the women and children who are left to mourn the vanquished or to become the victors' spoils. Aristophanes turns laughter rather than pity and fear against the waste of war. Such comedies as *Peace, The Acharnians, Lysistrata* make light of the issues over which men fight and give war the aspect of a wearisome business, preposterous

in its motives and hollow in its victories. In the 20th century, Brecht's *Mother Courage and Her Children* is a biting satire on the folly and cruelty of war.

The genial satire of Rabelais exposes the impostures of war, but beneath the horseplay which deflates by its exaggerations, there is the earnest, serious note of Grangousier's resolution not to "undertake war until I have first tried all the ways and means of peace." Swift's satire is not so amiable. In the eyes of the truly rational Houyhnhnms, war appears to be as senseless and despicable as the Yahoos who wage it. Gulliver tries to tell the Houyhnhnm who is his master about the wars of Europe, their causes and their cost. "I was going on to more particulars," he relates, "when my master commanded me silence. He said whoever understood the nature of the Yahoos might easily believe it possible for so vile an animal to be capable of every action I had named, if their strength and cunning equalled their malice . . . When a creature pretending to reason could be capable of such enormities, he dreaded lest the corruption of that faculty might be worse than brutality itself. He seemed therefore confident that, instead of reason, we were only possessed of some quality fitted to increase our natural vices." And Voltaire, in *Candide,* after referring to the opposing armies as "so handsome, so smart, so brilliant, so well trained," calls their ensuing clash "heroic butchery."

According to Augustine, it is not man's nature but his sinfulness which degrades him below the beasts "devoid of rational will," who "live more securely and peaceably with their own kind than men . . . For not even lions or dragons have ever waged with their kind such wars as men have waged with one another." Calling it "the greatest and most pompous of human actions," Montaigne asks whether war is not "testimony of our imbecility and imperfection; as indeed the science of undoing and killing one another, of ruining and destroying our own species, seems to have little to make it alluring to the beasts who do not have it."

But in his essay "Of evil means employed to a good end," Montaigne also quotes Juvenal's remark that "we bear the evils of long peace;

fiercer than war, luxury weighs us down."
He seems to approve the Roman policy of
maintaining wars "not only to keep their men
in condition, for fear that idleness, mother
of corruption, might bring them some worse
mischief . . . but also to serve as a bloodletting
for their republic and to cool off a bit the
too vehement heat of their young men." War
as a purgative is a familiar theme. Hobbes,
like Malthus later, suggests that "when all the
world is overcharged with inhabitants, then
the last remedy of all is war; which provideth
for every man, by victory or death."

Many writers seem to be ambivalent about
war. Plato, for example, seems to see both
sides of the question though he does not give
them equal weight. In *The Republic,* Socrates
proclaims the discovery that war is "derived
from causes which are also the causes of almost all the evils in states, private as well as
public." In the *Laws,* the Athenian Stranger
admits to Cleinias the Cretan that the laws of
his city, devised primarily with a view to war,
can be justified insofar as they aim at courage;
but he reminds him later that insofar as such
laws "regarded a part only, and not the whole
of virtue, I disapproved of them."

That he regards permanent peace as the
ideal toward which the moral law commands
us to strive, does not prevent Kant from saying
that "a prolonged peace favours the predominance of a mere commercial spirit, and with it
a debasing self-interest, cowardice, and effem-
inacy, and tends to degrade the character of
the nation." Nor is war to be absolutely condemned. "Provided it is conducted with order
and a sacred respect for the rights of civilians,"
war itself, says Kant, "has something sublime
about it, and gives nations that carry it on
in such a manner a stamp of mind only the
more sublime the more numerous the dangers
to which they are exposed, and which they are
able to meet with fortitude." Yet even while
thinking that war can be a "spur for developing to the highest pitch all talents that minister
to culture," Kant reflects that the underlying
purpose of war may be "to prepare the way
for a rule of law governing the freedom of
states, and thus bring about their unity in a
system established on a moral basis."

Hegel alone is not ambivalent. Not only
is war not "to be regarded as an absolute
evil," but it is, according to Hegel, a necessary corrective for the corrosive influence of
peace. "War is a state of affairs," he writes,
"which deals in earnest with the vanity of temporal goods and concerns—a vanity at other
times the common theme of edifying sermon-
izing . . . War has the higher significance that
by its agency, as I have remarked elsewhere,
'the ethical health of peoples is preserved in
their indifference to the stabilization of finite
institutions; just as the blowing of the winds
preserves the sea from foulness which would
be the result of a prolonged calm, so also the
corruption in nations would be the product of
prolonged, let alone "perpetual," peace.'"

Far from agreeing with those who advocate
"perpetual peace . . . as an ideal towards which
humanity should strive," Hegel points out
that "in peace civil life continually expands;
all its departments wall themselves in, and in
the long run men stagnate . . . As a result of
war, nations are strengthened, and people involved in civil strife also acquire peace at home
through making wars abroad."

To Prince Andrew in *War and Peace* who
says that "the aim of war is murder; the methods of war are spying, treachery, and their
encouragement"; or to Freud who says that
"the warring state permits itself every such
misdeed, every such act of violence, as would
disgrace the individual man," Hegel has an
answer. "States are not private persons," he
says, "but completely autonomous totalities in
themselves, and so the relation between them
differs from a moral relation and a relation
involving private rights . . . The relation between states is a relation between autonomous
entities which make mutual stipulations, but
which at the same time are superior to these
stipulations."

Self-interest, or "a will for its own welfare pure and simple," is, according to Hegel,
"the highest law governing the relation of one
state to another." Therefore, "when politics is
alleged to clash with morals . . . the doctrine
propounded rests on superficial ideas about
morality, the nature of the state, and the state's
relation to the moral point of view."

In Hegel's view, "wars occur when the necessity of the case requires." He is not alone in thinking war inevitable, but others who think the same do not do so in the same mood, or with the same opinion of the reason for its inevitability. "Drain the blood from men's veins," declares Prince Andrew's father, "and put in water instead, then there will be no more war!" It is an illusion, Freud thinks, to suppose that civilization so transforms human nature as to lift it above the impulses of war. In war, he says, "our fellow-citizens have not sunk so low as we feared, because they have never risen so high as we believed." The sad fact, he concludes, is that "war is not to be abolished; so long as the conditions of existence among the nations are so varied, and the repulsions between peoples so intense, there will be, there must be, wars."

William James finds the human race as bellicose as its individual members are instinctively pugnacious; and Hamilton says that if we "judge from the history of mankind, we shall be compelled to conclude that the fiery and destructive passions of war reign in the human breast with much more powerful sway than the mild and beneficent sentiments of peace; and that to model our political systems upon speculations of lasting tranquility, is to calculate on the weaker springs of human character."

To the extent that even those who deplore war despair of lasting peace, Machiavelli may not be too cynical a realist when he advises the prince that he "ought to have no other aim or thought, nor select anything else for his study, than war and its rules and discipline . . . When princes have thought more of ease than of arms, they have lost their states." The prince "ought never, therefore, to have out of his thoughts this subject of war, and in peace he should addict himself more to its exercise than in war." The prince who delays in order to save himself from war makes a serious mistake. War, Machiavelli tells him, "is not to be avoided, but is only deferred to your disadvantage."

Like Machiavelli, Cleinias the Cretan in Plato's *Laws* justifies his city's constant preoccupation with war or preparation for war.

The world is foolish, he thinks, "in not understanding that all men are always at war with one another . . . For what men in general term peace [is] only a name; in reality every city is in a natural state of war with every other, not indeed proclaimed by heralds, but everlasting."

Both Plato and Aristotle seem to agree that war is somehow rooted in the nature of things—in the nature of men and the nature of cities. Yet both also look upon war as transitory, even if recurrent. "No one can be a true statesman," the Athenian Stranger tells Cleinias, "who looks only, or first of all, to external warfare; nor will he ever be a sound legislator who orders peace for the sake of war, and not war for the sake of peace." The whole of life, according to Aristotle, is "divided into two parts, business and leisure, war and peace . . . There must be war for the sake of peace, business for the sake of leisure, things useful and necessary for the sake of things honorable . . . Men must be able to engage in business and go to war, but leisure and peace are better; they must do what is necessary and indeed what is useful, but what is honorable is better."

But how does war produce peace? One answer may be Virgil's. In the opening book of *The Aeneid*, Jove predicts the coming of a Caesar "whose empire / Shall reach to the ocean's limits, whose fame shall end in the stars." When at last Rome has conquered the world, the golden age of peace—or as least the *pax Romana*—will supplant war's age of iron.

Then shall the age of violence be mellowing into
     peace:
Venerable Faith, and the Home, with Romulus and
     Remus,
Shall make the laws; the grim, steel-welded gates
     of War
Be locked; and within, on a heap of armaments, a
     hundred
Bronzen knots tying his hands behind him, shall sit
Growling and bloody-mouthed the godless spirit of
     Discord.

In accordance with this heaven-laid destiny, Anchises bids his son Aeneas to make war for the sake of peace. "Be this your art:—to practise men in the habit of peace, / Generosity to the conquered, and firmness against aggressors." But some of the proud who are subjugated by Rome's legions take a different view of the peace that is imposed by force of arms. Tacitus reports the speech of the British chieftain Galgacus, in which he refers to those "terrible Romans, from whose oppression escape is vainly sought by obedience and submission ... To robbery, slaughter, plunder, they give the lying name of empire; they create a wilderness and call it peace."

Augustine more soberly reflects on the inevitable frustration of the Roman kind of peace. "The imperial city," he writes, "has endeavored to impose on subject nations not only her yoke, but her language, as a bond of peace ... How many great wars, how much slaughter and bloodshed, have provided this unity. And though these are past, the end of these miseries has not yet come. For though there have never been wanting, nor are yet wanting, hostile nations beyond the empire, against whom wars have been and are waged, yet supposing there were no such nations, the very extent of the empire itself has produced wars of a more obnoxious description—social and civil wars—and with these the whole race has been agitated, either by the actual conflict or the fear of a renewed outbreak."

Considering war and peace in relation to democratic societies, Tocqueville comes to "the strange conclusion that of all armies those which long for war most ardently are the democratic ones, but that of all peoples those most deeply attached to peace are the democratic nations."

DESPITE HIS PERCEPTION of war's failures, despite his enjoining the wise men, not merely to wage, but "to lament the necessity of just wars," Augustine holds that it is "with the desire for peace that wars are waged ... Every man seeks peace by waging war, but no man seeks war by making peace. For even they who intentionally interrupt the peace in which they are living have no hatred of peace, but only wish it changed into a peace that suits them better ... Even those whom they make war against they wish to make their own, and impose on them the laws of their own peace."

Peace, according to Augustine, consists in harmony and concord. "Peace between man and man is well-ordered concord. Domestic peace is the well-ordered concord between those of the family who rule and those who obey. Civil peace is a similar concord among the citizens ... The peace of all things is the tranquility of order." Without disagreeing essentially, Aquinas explains that peace involves more than concord. "Wherever peace is," he says, "there is concord, but there is not peace wherever there is concord, if we give peace its proper meaning." The peace between men may consist in concord, "not indeed any kind of concord, but that which is well-ordered, through one man agreeing with another in respect of something befitting to them both. For if one man agree with another, not of his own accord, but through being forced ... such concord is not really peace."

For men to be at peace with one another, Aquinas believes, each must be at peace with himself, but "man's heart is not at peace, so long as he has not what he wants, or if, having what he wants, there still remains something for him to want." This, according to Aquinas, explains why Augustine defined peace not simply as concord, but as *the tranquility of order,* for by "tranquility" is meant all the desires of each individual man "being set at rest together." It also explains why "those who seek war and dissension, desire nothing but peace, which they deem themselves not to have. For," Aquinas reminds us, "there is no peace when a man enters into concord with another counter to what he would prefer. Consequently men seek by means of war to break this concord, because it is a defective peace, in order that they may obtain peace, where nothing is contrary to their will. Hence all wars are waged that men may find a more perfect peace than that which they had heretofore."

The fundamental insight here seems to be that, though charity or love produces the unity of peace, peace is also "the work of justice"—indirectly, as Aquinas says, "insofar as justice removes the obstacles to peace." Thucydides gives us a historian's confirmation of the theologian's point. He tells us why he considers the long truce or armistice—a period of no actual fighting—to be a part of the war. "Only a mistaken judgment," he writes, "can object to including the interval of treaty in the war. Looked at by the light of facts it cannot, it will be found, be rationally considered a state of peace, where neither party either gave or got back all that they had agreed upon."

To the same effect is the speech of Hermocrates the Syracusan, which Thucydides reports. "That war is an evil is a proposition so familiar to everyone that it would be tedious to develop it. No one," he declares, "is forced to engage in it by ignorance, or kept out of it by fear, if he fancies there is anything to be gained by it ... I suppose that no one will dispute that we went to war at first, in order to serve our several interests; that we are now, in view of the same interests, debating how we can make peace; and that if we separate without having as we think our rights, we shall go to war again."

THUCYDIDES' OBSERVATION that periods of armistice or truce are part of war, and the remark of Cleinias in Plato's *Laws* that "every city is in a natural state of war with every other," may anticipate Hobbes, but full clarity on the point is not reached until Hobbes explicitly distinguishes between war as battle and the state of war which always prevails between men or nations when they do not live together under a common government.

"War consisteth not in battle only," Hobbes explains, "or in the act of fighting, but in a tract of time, wherein the will to contend by battle is sufficiently known: and therefore the notion of *time* is to be considered in the nature of war, as it is in the nature of weather. For as the nature of foul weather lieth not in a shower or two of rain, but in an inclination thereto of many days together: so the nature of war consisteth not in actual fighting, but in the known disposition thereto during all the time there is no assurance to the contrary. All other time is *peace*."

Hobbes does not exclude from the condition of peace differences between men or even discord, but only fighting or the need to resort to fighting as a way of settling differences or resolving conflicts. He is cognizant of the distinction which Machiavelli paraphrases from Cicero. "There are two ways of contesting," Machiavelli writes, "the one by law, the other by force; the first method is proper to men, the second to beasts." Here Machiavelli adds the comment that "because the first is frequently not sufficient, it is necessary to have recourse to the second." But Hobbes does not think it is always necessary. At least there is a cure for "the war of every man against every man." That cure is the formation of a commonwealth and the institution of government with sufficient coercive force to maintain law and secure peace. "Anarchy and the condition of war," according to Hobbes, are one and the same, a condition in which each man, being a law unto himself and judge in his own case, must of necessity resort to force if he would impose his will upon, or resist the will of, another.

Since men are everywhere found in societies, living under law and government, it might seem that the universal state of war to which Hobbes refers is now abolished. Not so, according to Hobbes, for "though there had never been any time wherein particular men were in a condition of war one against another, yet," in his opinion, "in all times kings and persons of sovereign authority, because of their independency, are in continual jealousies, and in the state and posture of gladiators, having their weapons pointing, and their eyes fixed on one another; that is, their forts, garrisons, and guns upon the frontiers of their kingdoms, and continual spies upon their neighbours, which is a posture of war."

This notion that sovereigns are always in a state of war with one another—because being sovereigns they are autonomous, *i.e.*, not subject to any superior government—seems to be accepted by most of the great political writers who come after Hobbes. The point is sometimes differently formulated, but the basic insight remains essentially the same.

Locke, for example, makes a threefold distinction between the state of nature, which is anarchy or complete independence; the state of war, in which force without authority is resorted to by men to settle their differences; and the state of civil society, which provides law and government for the arbitration of disputes. "Civil society," he writes, is "a state of peace amongst those who are of it, from whom the state of war is excluded by the umpirage which they have provided in their legislative for the ending all differences that may rise amongst any of them."

Since Locke holds that "want of a common judge with authority puts all men in a state of nature," it follows for him that, though the state of nature and the state of war may not be identical, the state of nature, unlike that of civil society, inevitably lapses into the state of war. If in a state of nature men fail to settle their differences by reason, they enter into the state of war which is the realm of force "or a declared design of force . . . where there is no common superior on earth to appeal to for relief."

With these qualifications, Locke not only agrees with Hobbes that "all princes and rulers of independent governments all through the world are in a state of nature," but also draws from this the same implication for war and peace. Since "the whole community is one body in the state of nature in respect of all other states or persons out of its community," Locke argues that the government of each state must have "the power of war and peace, leagues and alliances," in relation to everything external to itself.

Montesquieu and Rousseau slightly alter Hobbes's point by attributing the origin of war itself to the existence of separate societies. War, writes Rousseau, "is a relation, not between man and man, but between State and State." Because they are "in a state of nature among themselves," bodies politic experience, in his opinion, "the inconveniences which had obliged individuals to forsake it . . . Hence arose national wars, battles, murders and reprisals, which shock nature and outrage reason."

Hegel's ultimate reason for thinking that war is ineradicable seems to be not merely that sovereign states are "in a state of nature in relation to each other," but that they must always remain so. "There is no Praetor to judge between states," he writes; "at best there may be an arbitrator or a mediator, and even he exercises his functions contingently only, i.e., in dependence on the particular wills of the disputants."

That is why Hegel dismisses Kant's idea "for securing 'perpetual peace' by a League of Nations to adjust every dispute . . . This idea," Hegel writes, "presupposes an accord between states; this would rest on moral and religious or other grounds and considerations, but in any case would always depend ultimately on a particular sovereign will and for that reason would remain infected with contingency." Hence, he concludes, "if states disagree and their particular wills cannot be harmonized, the matter can only be settled by war."

KANT AGREES THAT, in the absence of what he calls a "cosmo-political constitution" or world state, "war is inevitable." In their external relations to one another, states, "like lawless savages, are naturally in a non-juridical condition," and this, according to Kant, "is a state of war, in which the right of the stronger prevails; and although it may not in fact be always found as a state of actual war and incessant hostility . . . yet the condition is wrong in itself in the highest degree, and the nations which form States contiguous to each other are bound mutually to pass out of it."

How shall this be accomplished? Is Kant's idea the one Hegel attributes to him? Is the "alliance of nations," of which he speaks, to be a "league of nations" or does he have something more than that in mind when he says that "this mutual connection by alliance" must "take the form of a Federation"?

On the one hand, he calls for "a universal Union of States analogous to that by which a Nation becomes a State," and argues that "it is only thus that a real state of Peace could be established." But on the other, he explains that he means "only a voluntary combination of different States that would be dissoluble at any time, and not such a union as is embodied in the United States of America, founded upon a political constitution and therefore indissoluble."

The arguments for the federal constitution of the United States help to make this issue clear. The authors of the Constitution regard it as providing "a more perfect union" than the Articles of Confederation under which the thirteen separate colonies are banded together by little more than treaties or alliances. To the writers of *The Federalist,* who advocate the adoption of a federal union to replace the loose confederacy or league of states, there is no middle ground between the establishment of peace through federal union and the continuation of the state of war between separate states.

"A man must be far gone in Utopian speculations," Hamilton declares, "who can seriously doubt that, if these States should either be wholly disunited, or only united in partial confederacies, the subdivisions into which they might be thrown would have frequent and violent contests with each other . . . To look for a continuation of harmony between a number of independent, unconnected sovereignties in the same neighborhood, would be to disregard the uniform course of events, and to set at defiance the accumulated experience of ages." In another paper, Hamilton admits that "there is nothing absurd or impracticable in the idea of a league or alliance between independent nations for certain defined purposes precisely stated in a treaty," but he thinks that Europe has taught "an instructive but afflicting lesson to mankind, how little dependence is to be placed on treaties which have no other sanction than the obligations of good faith."

He returns therefore to attack the "visionary or designing men, who stand ready to advocate the paradox of perpetual peace between the States, though dismembered and alienated from each other." What reason have we to expect, he asks, "peace and cordiality between the members of the present confederation, in a state of separation"? It seems to him "an established truth that the several states, in the case of disunion . . . would be subject to those vicissitudes of peace and war, of friendship and enmity with each other, which have fallen to the lot of all neighboring nations not united under one government."

The Federalists do not seriously recommend their prescription for peace as a plan for the whole world. Yet they see the generalization that is implicit in all their reasoning. "Happy would it be," Madison says, "if such a remedy for its infirmities could be enjoyed by all free governments; if a project equally effectual could be established for the universal peace of mankind!"

J. S. Mill, writing somewhat later and in the light of the experience of American federation as a peace plan, seems to be even less ready to propose world federal government as the indispensable condition of world peace. He has no doubt that federal union "puts an end to war and diplomatic quarrels." But he does not think that abrogating the distinction between fellow countrymen and foreigners by making them all fellow citizens of an encompassing state—an object which is "one of the worthiest to which human endeavor can be directed"—can, "in the present state of civilization, be promoted by keeping different nationalities of anything like equivalent strength under the same government."

Not only does Kant definitely dismiss the notion of a world union formed along American lines, but even the less perfect union of states which would have the form of a *"Permanent Congress of Nations,"* seems to him an impracticable idea in the world as it is at the end of the 18th century. "With the too great extension of such a Union of States over vast regions," he writes, "any government of it, and consequently the protection of its individual members, must at last become impossible; and thus a multitude of such corporations would again bring round a state of war."

Nevertheless, Kant refuses to yield completely to this conclusion. "The morally practical reason," he affirms, "utters within us its irrevocable *Veto: 'There shall be no War'* . . . Hence the question no longer is as to whether Perpetual Peace is a real thing or not a real thing, or as to whether we may not be deceiving ourselves when we adopt the former alternative, but we must *act* on the supposition of its being real. We must work for what may perhaps not be realized . . . and thus we may put an end to the evil of wars, which have been the chief interest of the internal arrangements of all States without exception."

And in his *The Idea of a Universal History on a Cosmo-Political Plan,* Kant does more than urge upon us our moral duty to work for perpetual peace as prerequisite to "the highest political good." He engages in prophecy. He pictures the nations of the world "after many devastations, overthrows, and even complete internal exhaustion of their powers" as "driven forward to the goal which Reason might well have impressed upon them, even without so much sad experience. This is none other than the advance out of the lawless state of savages and the entering into a Federation of Nations . . . However visionary this idea may appear to be . . . it is nevertheless the inevitable issue of the necessity in which men involve one another."

THE ARGUMENT FOR world government as the means to world peace is nowhere made in the great books as explicitly as in Dante's *De Monarchia.* "Wherever there can be contention," Dante writes, "there judgment should exist; otherwise things should exist imperfectly, without their own means of adjustment or correction . . . Between any two governments, neither of which is in any way subordinate to the other, contention can arise either through their own fault or that of their subjects. This is evident. Therefore there should be judication between them. And since neither can know the affairs of the other, not being subordinate (for among equals there is no authority), there must be a third and wider power which rules both within its own jurisdiction.

"This third power," Dante continues, "is either the world-government, or it is not. If it is, we have reached our conclusion; if it is not, it must in turn have its equal outside its jurisdiction, and then it will need a third party as a judge, and so *ad infinitum,* which is impossible. So we must arrive at a first and supreme judge for whom all contentions are judicable either directly or indirectly . . . Therefore, world-government is necessary for the world." Aristotle, according to Dante, "saw this argument when he said, Things hate to be in disorder, but a plurality of authorities is disorder; therefore authority is single." But Aristotle certainly did not draw the conclusion that a single government embracing all mankind should be instituted so that "by com-

mon law it might lead all toward peace." Nor, with the exception of Kant, does any other great author argue to this conclusion. But, as we have seen, Kant, unlike Dante, reaches this conclusion only to qualify his acceptance of it and his advocacy of world government.

Nevertheless, several of the great books do contain the nerve of the argument. It is contained in one fundamental proposition that is variously enunciated by Hobbes and Locke, Rousseau and the Federalists. That proposition is: *As anarchy leads to war, government establishes peace, and just laws preserve it.* By inductive generalization, it seems to follow that, if local peace depends on local government, world peace depends on world government.

But if, except for Dante and Kant, no one until the present made this inference, the tradition of western thought does include, not only the essential premise for making the inference, but also the controlling vision of a politically united humanity—all men as fellow citizens in a single political society embracing the earth.

Kant speaks of "the right of man as a citizen of the world to *attempt* to enter into communion with all others." Epictetus says, "there is but one course open to men, to do as Socrates did: never to reply to one who asks his country, 'I am an Athenian,' or 'I am a Corinthian,' but 'I am a citizen of the universe.' "

Reflecting on the fact that man's "nature is rational and social," Marcus Aurelius declares: "My city and my country, so far as I am Antoninus, is Rome, but so far as I am a man, it is the world." If we look at "what value everything has with reference to the whole," we will perceive that man "is a citizen of the highest city, of which all other cities are like families." The reason which is common to all men dictates a common law of human life. "If this is so," Aurelius argues, "we are fellow citizens; if this is so, we are members of one political community; if this is so, the world is in a manner a state."

Aristotle describes how the family is formed by the union of man and wife, parents and children; and from this first of all social units, the tribe or village is formed by a union of families, and the city or state by a union of villages. He does not carry this series on to its natural terminus, but Augustine does. "After the state or city," Augustine says, "comes the world, the third circle of human society—the first being the family, the second the city."

Yet Augustine, who orders earthly peace to the peace of heaven, does not prophesy a single political community of all men living together under one government. The heavenly city, he says, "while it sojourns on earth, calls citizens out of all nations, and gathers together a society of pilgrims of all languages, not scrupling about diversities in the manners, laws, and institutions whereby earthly peace is secured and maintained, but recognizing that, however various these are, they all tend to one and the same end of earthly peace."

One and the same end of earthly peace may require one city of man as well as one city of God. That, according to Dostoevsky, seems to be implied in the fact that "the craving for universal unity is the third and last anguish of men. Mankind as a whole," he writes, "has always striven to organize a universal state. There have been many great nations with great histories, but the more highly developed the more unhappy they were, for they felt more acutely than other people the craving for world-wide union."

99

Wealth

INTRODUCTION

IF the only questions about wealth concerned the means of getting and keeping it, the causes of its increase and decrease, the idea of wealth would be confined to economics. "The end of the medical art is health," writes Aristotle in the *Nicomachean Ethics,* and "that of economics, wealth." But as the *Ethics* indicates, the moralist and the statesman are also concerned with health and wealth—not simply as things to get and keep, but in relation to all other goods and as constituents of the good life and the good society. What is regarded as the end in economics may be only a means in ethics and politics; in which case, Aristotle suggests, the latter sciences subordinate economics, even as politics subordinates military strategy, and military strategy the making and use of armaments.

The discussion of riches in the tradition of the great books exhibits these two ways of considering wealth. The Bible, the poets, historians, and philosophers deal with wealth as a factor in the life of men and societies. They scrutinize the desire for wealth or the love of money in relation to sin and virtue. They raise questions of justice concerning the distribution of wealth, the rights of property, and fairness in exchange—in buying and selling, borrowing and lending, and in compensating the laborer. They describe the effect of poverty and prosperity or opulence upon states, and prescribe the attitude which individual men as well as societies should take toward wealth and poverty.

Throughout it seems to be assumed that wealth is merely a means, however important or indispensable. Though wealth may also be viewed as an end when the problem is one of how to acquire, produce, or increase it, the fact that, when possessed, it should be treated as a means, leads the moralist to condemn not only the miser, the hoarder, or the man who devotes his whole life to making money, but also those who elevate wealth into the sort of end which justifies any means that can advance its pursuit.

The other approach is that of the economist. Five of the great books—Adam Smith's *The Wealth of Nations,* Marx's *Capital,* Veblen's *The Theory of the Leisure Class,* Tawney's *The Acquisitive Society,* and Keynes's *General Theory of Employment, Interest and Money*—deal not with wealth as a means, but with the means to wealth. Another, though by title *On Political Economy,* is concerned with the principles of government, and with wealth only insofar as, in Rousseau's conception, government includes "the administration of property" as well as the protection of persons. "Provision for the public wants," he writes, is "the third essential duty of government."

Rousseau explains the title of his treatise by reference to the etymology of the word "economy," which "meant originally only the wise and legitimate government of the household for the common good of the whole family." It is in this sense that Aristotle employs the word and that a work sometimes attributed to him bears it as the title. "The meaning of the term," Rousseau goes on, "was then extended to the government of that great family, the State. To distinguish these two senses of the word, the latter is called *general* or *political* economy, the former domestic or particular economy."

Smith uses the term more narrowly. Not only does he limit his inquiry to the nature and causes of wealth, but by specifying "the wealth of nations," he restricts himself to political economy which, he says, has "two distinct objects: first, to provide a plentiful revenue or subsistence for the people, or more properly to enable them to provide such a revenue or subsistence for themselves; and secondly, to supply the state or commonwealth with a revenue sufficient for the public services." In saying that the political economist aims "to enrich both the people and the sovereign," and that "the great object of the political economy of every country is to increase the riches and power of that country," Smith takes wealth as an end (though it may also be a means, "so far as power depends upon riches") and tries to formulate the natural laws of wealth-making.

Nowhere does he define the quantity of wealth which should satisfy a nation. The natural resources of a country, the size and industry of its population, and various unfavorable contingencies, may set certain bounds to the maximization of wealth. Within these bounds the country which adopts and follows a sound system of political economy—one which accords with the right conception of wealth and its causes—can (and deserves to) become as wealthy as possible.

Yet Smith, in treating wealth as an end and its increase without limit as a good, does not make economics absolutely autonomous. He regards political economy as a part of politics—"a branch of the science of a statesman or legislator"—and to that extent implies that other considerations than wealth may control the policies of a nation in its regulation of agriculture, industry, domestic commerce, and foreign trade.

Furthermore, the larger moral questions which accompany Smith's economic speculations in his *Lectures on Jurisprudence* and his earlier treatise *The Theory of Moral Sentiments* are not entirely absent from *The Wealth of Nations*. But to the extent that he writes purely as an economist concerned with securing "cheapness or plenty" or, what for him is the same, "wealth and abundance," he adheres to considerations of expediency and only infrequently permits himself *obiter dicta* on justice or questions of right and wrong.

Marx also writes as an economist. He details the factors which govern the production and distribution of wealth as these manifest themselves in the great historic systems of production—the slave economy, the feudal economy, and the bourgeois or capitalist economy. So far he is a scientist and, even more than Smith, a historian who describes how wealth is acquired and how it multiplies by reproducing itself. But Marx is much less content than Smith to stop there. Smith tries to describe the economic process scientifically in order to prescribe the means a nation should use to become increasingly prosperous, but Marx undertakes to describe it in order to criticize the way in which some men get richer than they need be while others become poorer than they should be.

His critical purpose makes inevitable the expression of moral judgments concerning such inequities; and by implication they are everywhere present. For example, a descriptive phrase like "surplus value" connotes "unearned increment"; an apparently neutral economic term like "profit" is given the invidious moral significance traditionally attached to "usury." Nor does Marx rest with criticism. He has an economic program to propose, a program he reveals more clearly with Engels in the *Communist Manifesto* than in *Capital*. The aim is not primarily to increase the production of wealth, but to remedy its inequitable distribution under all past economic systems. This program looks forward to the final revolution which will bring the necessary historic motion of progress to its culmination when socialism replaces capitalism.

SMITH AND MARX, IT appears, are not economists in the same sense. But it may be supposed that, in spite of their different purposes, they would as scientists agree in their description of economic phenomena. To some extent they do, yet the difference in their point of view and aim leads to a quarrel about facts, or at least about their interpretation.

Classical economists in the tradition of Smith dispute the consequences which Marx draws from the labor theory of value, especially with regard to the origin of profit from the surplus product of unpaid labor time.

Profit seems to them as much a part of the natural price of commodities as the wages paid to labor and the rent paid to the landlord.

"In exchanging the complete manufacture either for money, for labor, or for other goods, over and above what may be sufficient to pay the price of the materials, and the wages of the workmen, something," writes Smith, "must be given for the profits of the undertaker of the work who hazards his stock in this adventure. The value which the workmen add to the materials, therefore, resolves itself in this case into two parts, of which the one pays their wages, the other the profits of their employer upon the whole stock of materials and wages which he advanced. He could have no interest to employ them, unless he expected from the sale of their work something more than what was sufficient to replace his stock to him; and he could have no interest to employ a great stock rather than a small one, unless his profits were to bear some proportion to the extent of his stock."

It is precisely on this point of profit as a return for risking one's capital stock that Marx charges Smith, and after him, David Ricardo and J. S. Mill, with being apologists for the capitalistic system. He quotes Mill's statement that "the cause of profit is that labor produces more than is required for its support." The fact that Mill does not question the validity of this surplus value, which accrues as profit to the *entrepreneur;* the fact that Ricardo treats surplus value, according to Marx, "as a thing inherent in the capitalist mode of production, which mode, in his eyes, is the natural form of social production," is explicable, in Marx's view, only if we recognize that their economic theories mix special pleading with science. "These bourgeois economists instinctively saw, and rightly so," he says, "that it is very dangerous to stir too deeply the burning question of the origin of surplus value."

Though he distinguishes between its classical and vulgar forms, political economy for Marx is a bourgeois science, which "first sprang into being during the period of manufacture." Political economy "has generally been content to take, just as they were, the terms of commercial and industrial life," Engels remarks in a prefatory note to *Capital,* and so it "never went beyond the received notions of profit and rent, never examined this unpaid part of the product (called by Marx surplus-product) in its integrity as a whole, and therefore never arrived at a clear comprehension, either of its origin and nature, or of the laws that regulate the subsequent distribution of its value."

Marx's work is, in his own conception of it, at one and the same time a criticism of the capitalist economy and of the science of economics which accepts and defends that economic system. In his own preface to *Capital,* Marx tells the reader that the "volume which I now submit to the public forms the continuation" of an earlier work—*A Contribution to the Critique of Political Economy.* Within the sphere of political economy as defined by the problem of augmenting a nation's wealth, the author of *The Wealth of Nations* similarly finds a critique of prevalent economic fallacies—those of the physiocrats and the mercantilists—inseparable from the constructive statement of his own theory.

THE ANCIENTS CONCEIVE wealth as consisting in the variety of external goods which sustain life—food, clothing, and shelter. But wealth may include more than the bare necessities. When Socrates in *The Republic* outlines a simple economy which aims to satisfy only basic needs, Glaucon tells him that he is "providing for a city of pigs." More is required, he says, for "the ordinary conveniences of life. People who are to be comfortable are accustomed to lie on sofas, and dine off tables, and they should have sauces and sweets in the modern style." Socrates replies by projecting "a luxurious State"—"a State at fever heat"—which goes beyond the necessaries, "such as houses and clothes and shoes. The arts of the painter and the embroiderer," he says, "will have to be set in motion, and gold and ivory and all sorts of materials procured"; and the city will "have to fill and swell with a multitude of callings which are not required by any natural want."

This distinction between necessaries and luxuries, which has many implications for ethics and economics as well as for politics, does not draw the line between natural and artificial wealth. Nor is natural wealth identified exclusively with natural resources in their pure state, unconverted by labor for use or consumption. Wealth is generally thought to comprise all consumable goods, whether necessaries or luxuries, whether products of hunting, agriculture, or manufacture, and all the means of producing them. Only money is excluded. Only money is declared to be either not wealth at all or artificial wealth.

Yet the identification of money with wealth seems to be prevalent at all times, as repeated attempts to correct the fallacy indicate. The use of money originates, according to Aristotle, with retail trade, which is "not a natural part of the art of getting wealth"; for, he goes on, "had it been so, men would have ceased to exchange when they had enough." What Aristotle calls retail trade replaces "the barter of necessary articles." Made possible by the use of coin, retail trade, he says, comes to be thought of as "the art which produces riches and wealth.

"Indeed," Aristotle continues, "riches is assumed by many to be only a quantity of coin." But he agrees with those who maintain, to the contrary, that "coined money is a mere sham, a thing not natural, but conventional only . . . because it is not useful as a means to any of the necessities of life, and he who is rich in coin may often be in want of necessary food. But how can that be wealth of which a man may have a great abundance and yet perish with hunger, like Midas in the fable, whose insatiable prayer turned everything that was set before him into gold?"

To say that money in itself cannot satisfy any natural need does not imply that it serves no economic purpose. Plato and Aristotle, Hobbes, Locke, and Kant, as well as Smith and Marx, understand the utility of money as a medium of exchange, indispensable for "the circulation of commodities"—to use Marx's phrase—beyond the stage of barter. Money is not only a medium of exchange, according to Plato; it "reduces the inequalities and incommensurabilities of goods to equality and common measure"; and Aristotle seems to anticipate Marx's conception of money as the universal form in which all economic values can be expressed when he defines "wealth" to mean "all things whose value is measured by money."

The economic utility of money in exchange and as a measure of value, or even the fact that gold and silver coin may have some intrinsic value because of the labor involved in mining and minting the metals, does not alter the distinction between natural and artificial wealth. "Natural wealth," Aquinas explains, "is that which serves man as a remedy for his natural wants, such as food, drink, clothing, conveyances, dwellings, and things of this kind, while artificial wealth is that which is not a direct help to nature, as money, but is invented by the art of man for the convenience of exchange and as a measure of things saleable."

The same point is restated by Locke in the 17th century, but it is still necessary for Smith a century later to argue against the mercantilist theory of national prosperity, on the ground that it confuses wealth with money. "It would be too ridiculous to go about seriously to prove," Smith writes, "that wealth does not consist in money, or in gold or silver; but what money purchases, and is valuable only for purchasing . . . Goods can serve many other purposes besides purchasing money, but money can serve no other purpose besides purchasing goods. Money, therefore, necessarily runs after goods, but goods do not always or necessarily run after money. The man who buys, does not always mean to sell again, but frequently to use or consume; whereas he who sells, always means to buy again."

Nevertheless, that "wealth consists in money, or in gold and silver, is a popular notion which naturally arises from the double function of money, as the instrument of commerce, and as the measure of value." The notion is so familiar that, Smith observes, "even they, who are convinced of its absurdity, are very apt to forget their own principles, and in the course of their reasonings to take it for granted as a certain and undeniable truth. Some of the best English writers on commerce set out with observing that the wealth of a country consists, not in its gold and silver only, but in its lands, houses, and consumable goods of all different kinds. In the course of their reasonings, however, the land, houses, and consumable goods seem to slip out of their memory, and the strain of their argument frequently supposes that all wealth consists in gold and silver, and to multiply these metals is the great object of national industry and commerce."

The two principles of the mercantilist policy are, according to Smith, that "wealth consisted in gold and silver, and that those metals could be brought into a country which had no mines only by the balance of trade, or by exporting to a greater value than it imported." A favorable balance of trade thus necessarily became the sole object of the mercantilists; and, Smith adds, "its two great engines for enriching the country, therefore, were restraints upon importation, and encouragements to exportation."

Since in his opinion the wealth of a nation consists in "the whole annual produce of its land and labor," Smith opposes all such restraints, and with them the protection of monopolies. He advocates free trade and the free competition of producers, within a country as well as between domestic and foreign producers, on the ground that "consumption is the sole end and purpose of all production; and the interest of the producer ought to be attended to, only so far as it may be necessary for promoting that of the consumer. But in the mercantile system," Smith claims, "the interest of the consumer is almost constantly sacrificed to that of the producer." A laissez-faire economy, he thinks, not only reverses this situation, but also, by preferring more consumable commodities to more gold and silver, tends to increase the real, not the artificial wealth of a nation.

Marx also criticizes the mercantilist error, but in terms of his theory that "since the production of surplus-value is the chief end and aim of capitalist production . . . the greatness of a man's or a nation's wealth should be measured, not by the absolute quantity produced, but by the relative magnitude of the surplus-value."

Surplus value cannot be produced by exchange. Against the mercantilists who "derived the excess of the price over the cost of production of the product, from the act of exchange, from the product being sold above its value," Marx quotes Mill's statement that "profit arises, not from the incident of exchange, but from the productive power of labor; and the general profit of the country is always what the productive power of labor makes it, whether any exchange takes place or not."

But this is not the whole picture, according to Marx. Although it is impossible for capital or surplus value "to be produced by circulation," or the exchange of commodities, he also thinks it is "impossible that outside the sphere of circulation, a producer of commodities can, without coming into contact with other commodity owners, expand value, and consequently convert money or commodities into capital." The two sides of the picture are brought together, in Marx's view, by the treatment of labor itself as a commodity, and the buying and selling of labor power in the open market.

THE DISTINCTION BETWEEN real wealth and money and the distinction between necessities and luxuries have more than economic significance. They are basic to the moralist's strictures concerning the desire for wealth, its place in the order of goods, and the way it can be put to good use.

It is not only Saint Paul who says that "the love of money is the root of all evil." It is not only Christian theologians like Augustine and Aquinas who explain how "lust of the eyes" or covetousness is a capital sin and as such the principle of many other transgressions. As Marx points out, the Greeks also "denounced money as subversive of the economical and moral order of things." In the passage in Sophocles' *Antigone* which he quotes, Creon declares: "Nothing so evil as money ever grew to be current among men. This lays cities low, this drives men from their homes, this trains and warps honest souls till they set themselves to works of shame; this still teaches folk to practice villainies, and to know every godless deed." Dickens strikes a similar note in *Little Dorrit;* in a chapter entitled "The Progress of an Epidemic," he compares the London citizens' lust for wealth—occasioned by the success of a fraudulent entrepreneur—to a plague without a cure.

Plato condemns the oligarchic state by comparing it to the miser and money-maker among men. "Such a State," he says, "aims to become as rich as possible, a desire which is insatiable." In the *Laws,* the Athenian Stranger explains why the reasonable statesman should not aim to make "the state for the true interests of which he is advising . . . as great and as rich as possible," if he also "desires to have the city the best and happiest possible"; for though each may be possible alone, they are not possible together. It is impossible, he holds, to be "good in a high degree and rich in a high degree at the same time."

What Plato says of the oligarch, Marx says of the capitalist: "He shares with the miser the passion for wealth as wealth." But, Marx adds, "that which in the miser is a mere idiosyncrasy is, in the capitalist, the effect of the social mechanism, of which he is but one of the wheels." Involved as he is by the system in "the restless never-ending process of profit-making," the individual capitalist, like the miser, exhibits "this boundless greed after riches, this passionate chase after exchange-value."

The root of the evil in the love of money—of "gold, yellow, glittering, precious gold," which Shakespeare calls the "common whore of mankind"—is the boundlessness of the lust. The hoarding of anything springs from an insatiable desire, but because money can be converted into every sort of commodity, it is, according to Marx, the ideal object of hoarding. "The antagonism between the quantitative limits of money and its qualitative boundlessness," he writes, "continually acts as a spur to the hoarder in his Sisyphus-like labor of accumulating."

In the light of such observations, Marx cites with approval Aristotle's distinction between "economic" and "chrematistic" or what Aristotle differentiates as the two arts of wealth-getting. Considering economics as the management of a household, Aristotle says that the art of acquisition which is a natural part of it "must either find ready to hand, or itself provide, such things necessary to life, and useful for the community of the family or state, as can be stored. They are the elements of true riches; for the amount of property which is needed for a good life is not unlimited." But "there is another variety of the art of acquisition which is commonly and rightly called an art of wealth-getting, and has in fact suggested that riches and property have no limit."

The two arts tend to become confused in men's minds. "Some persons are led to believe," Aristotle observes, "that getting wealth is the object of household management, and the whole idea of their lives is that they ought either to increase their money without limit, or at any rate not to lose it. The origin of this disposition in men is that they are intent upon living only, and not upon living well; and as their desires are unlimited, they also desire that the means of gratifying them should be without limit." Even "those who do aim at a good life seek the means of obtaining bodily pleasures; and, since the enjoyment of these appears to depend upon property, they are absorbed in getting wealth; and thus there arises the second kind of wealth-getting."

Plato, like Aristotle, while admitting the service of retail trade in effecting the exchange of commodities, condemns the tendency of its practitioners to make "gains without limit." In the *Laws,* furthermore, he prohibits interest on loans; and in *The Republic,* he describes this form of money-making as a process in which "men of business . . . insert their sting—that is, their money—into someone else who is not on his guard against them, and recover the parent sum many times over multiplied into a family of children." This biological metaphor for making money out of money appears also in Aristotle. The term "interest," he says, "means the birth of money from money." Of all forms of money-making, this "breeding of money" is, in his opinion, the most unnatural. "Usury, which makes a gain out of money itself," Aristotle writes, violates the natural object of money—"intended to be used in exchange, but not to increase at interest."

INTEREST AND USURY are not distinguished in the Old Testament. "Take thou no usury of him, or increase," is the command in Leviticus. But this rule does not apply to the stranger. "Unto a stranger thou mayst lend upon usury," Deuteronomy says, "but unto thy brother thou shalt not lend upon usury."

A theologian like Aquinas, following both Scripture and Aristotle, condemns, for Christians, all interest as usury; and Martin Luther also appeals to pagan precept as well as to Scriptural warrant. "The heathen were able, by the light of reason, to conclude that a usurer is a double-dyed thief and murderer," Luther says in a passage which Marx quotes under the comment that the usurer is "that old-fashioned but ever renewed specimen of the capitalist." Castigating his fellow Christians for holding usurers "in such honor that we fairly worship them for the sake of their money," Luther declares that "whoever eats up, robs, and steals the nourishment of another, that man commits as great a murder (so far as in him lies) as he who starves a man or utterly undoes him. Such does a usurer."

It seems to be a later consequence of the Protestant reformation, as Weber and Tawney point out, that the exaction of interest for the loan of money or goods is defended, and only exorbitant rates of interest are denounced as usurious. The signs of the change may be seen in Pascal's diatribe against the specious casuistry which tries to exempt some forms of interest-taking from the charge of usury; and also in the fact that Montesquieu attributes to the schoolmen, "who adopted from Aristotle, a great many notions on lending upon interest," the mistake of condemning it "absolutely and in all cases." In his own opinion, "to lend money without interest is certainly an action laudable and extremely good; but it is obvious that it is only a counsel of religion, and not a civil law."

Montesquieu thinks a price for the use of money is necessary for the carrying on of trade. If a fair rate of interest is not allowed, nobody will lend money; or rather, Montesquieu says, because "the affairs of society will ever make it necessary," moneylending will inevitably take the form of usury. "Usury increases in Mohammedan countries," he points out, "in proportion to the severity of the prohibition. The lender indemnifies himself for the danger he undergoes of suffering the penalty."

Smith agrees that prohibition, "instead of preventing, has been found from experience to increase the evil of usury." A fair rate of interest is justified, he thinks, because "as something can everywhere be made by the use of money, something ought everywhere to be paid for the use of it ... In countries where interest is permitted, the law, in order to prevent the extortion of usury, generally fixes the highest rate which can be taken without incurring a penalty. This rate ought always to be somewhat above the lowest market price, or the price which is commonly paid for the use of money by those who can give the most undoubted security." Smith offers the British practice as a good example. "Where money is lent to government at three per cent, and to private people upon good security at four, and four and a half, the present legal rate, five per cent, is perhaps as proper as any."

Interest and profit, while not the same in Smith's view, are closely connected. As the revenue from land is rent, from labor wages, and "that derived from stock, by the person who manages or employs it, is called profit," interest is "the compensation which the borrower pays to the lender, for the profit which he has an opportunity of making by the use of the money. Part of that profit naturally belongs to the borrower, who runs the risk and takes the trouble of employing it; and part to the lender, who affords him an opportunity of making this profit." Conceiving interest as a derivative revenue, Smith holds it to be a maxim that "wherever a great deal can be made by the use of money, a great deal will be commonly given for the use of it," so that we may expect to find "the usual market rate of interest" to vary with "the ordinary profits of stock."

THE THEORY WHICH PLACES wealth lowest in the order of goods determines its contribution to human happiness accordingly, and leads to a disapproval of luxuries, on the part of both the individual and society.

"Riches are for the sake of the body, as the body is for the sake of the soul. The latter are good," writes Plato, "and wealth is intended by nature to be for the sake of them, and is therefore inferior to them both, and third in the order of excellence." Aristotle similarly orders wealth, or external goods, to health and other goods of the body, as these in turn are subordinate to the virtues, or goods of the soul; and Hobbes, in somewhat different terms, holds that, of all goods, "those that are dearest to a man are his own life and limbs; and in the next degree (in most men), those that concern conjugal affection; and after them riches and means of living."

While Aristotle admits that happiness requires some external prosperity, he always adds that only a moderate amount of external goods is needed. "Happiness, whether consisting in pleasure or virtue, or both," he writes, "is more often found with those who are most highly cultivated in their mind and in their character, and have only a moderate share of external goods, than among those who possess external goods to a useless extent, but are deficient in higher qualities." Aristotle praises Solon for telling Croesus, one of the world's wealthiest men, that happiness requires more than riches. The conversation is narrated by Herodotus.

"What, stranger of Athens," Herodotus reports Croesus as saying, "is my happiness, then, valued so little by you, that you do not even put me on a level with private men?" To which, Solon replies: "Croesus, I see that you are wonderfully rich, and the lord of many nations," but "he who possesses a great store of riches is no nearer happiness than he who has what suffices for his daily needs, unless luck attends him, and so he continue in the enjoyment of all his good things to the end of his life." Aristotle adds the further observation that "one can with but moderate possessions do what one ought" and that "a good life requires a supply of external goods in a less degree when men are in a good state and in a greater degree when they are in a lower state."

Aquinas agrees with Aristotle so far as the happiness of the active life is concerned, but he holds that wealth "does not conduce to the happiness of the contemplative life; rather is it an obstacle thereto." With regard to achieving

"the happiness of heaven" in the life hereafter, Aquinas not only thinks wealth an obstacle, but he also explains why the religious orders take the vow of voluntary poverty. "Man is directed to future happiness by charity," he writes; and "in the attainment of the perfection of charity the first foundation is voluntary poverty, whereby a man lives without property of his own."

The opinion that wealth is an obstacle or that it should be sought in moderation does not seem to be universally shared. As Herodotus, Plato, and Aristotle report the prevalence in the ancient world of the notion that "external goods are the cause of happiness," so Melville reflects that in modern society "the urbane activity with which a man receives money is really marvellous, considering that we so earnestly believe money to be the root of all earthly ills, and that on no account can a monied man enter heaven. Ah! how cheerfully we consign ourselves to perdition!" Marx quotes a still more extravagant claim. In a letter from Jamaica in 1503, Christopher Columbus exclaims: "Gold is a wonderful thing! Whoever possesses it is lord of all he wants. By means of gold one can even get souls into Paradise."

Against Rousseau's attack upon opulence as the cause of civilization with all its miseries, Dr. Johnson rises in the defense of luxuries and the advantages of wealth. "Rousseau's treatise on the inequality of mankind," Boswell writes, "was at this time a fashionable topick. It gave rise to an observation by Mr. Dempster that the advantages of fortune and rank were nothing to a wise man." To this, Dr. Johnson replies: "If a man were a savage, living in the woods by himself, this might be true," but "in civilized society, external advantages make us more respected . . . Sir, you may make the experiment. Go into the street, and give one man a lecture on morality, and another a shilling, and see which will respect you the most . . .

"And, Sir," he continues, "if six hundred pounds a year procure a man more consequence, and, of course, more happiness than six pounds, the same proportion will hold as to six thousand, and so on as far as opulence can be carried. Perhaps he who has a large fortune may not be so happy as he who has a small one; but that must proceed from other causes than from his having the large fortune; for, *ceteris paribus,* he who is rich in a civilized society, must be happier than he who is poor."

On one occasion, Dr. Johnson seems to share Solon's view. When Boswell suggests that the proprietor of a great estate "must be happy," he exclaims: "Nay, Sir, all this excludes but one evil—poverty." But for the most part, his opinion is that "it is in refinement and elegance that the civilized man differs from the savage," and that it is right for every society to be as luxurious as it can be.

"Many things which are false are transmitted from book to book," he says to General Oglethorpe, "and gain credit in the world. One of these is the cry against the evil of luxury. Now the truth is that luxury produces much good. You will hear it said, very gravely, Why was not the half-guinea, thus spent in luxury, given to the poor? To how many might it have afforded a good meal. Alas! has it not gone to the *industrious* poor, whom it is better to support than the *idle* poor? You are much surer that you are doing good when you *pay* money to those who work as the recompense of their labor, than when you *give* money in charity . . . And as to the rout that is made about people who are ruined by extravagance, it is no matter to the nation that some individuals suffer. When so much general productive exertion is the consequence of luxury, the nation does not care though there are debtors in gaol."

Dr. Johnson's pronouncements may silence Mr. Dempster and General Oglethorpe, but not Smith or Marx. To Smith, spendthrift extravagance squanders wealth which might have been capitalized for productive purposes; to Marx, the multiplication of luxury products diverts labor power that is socially necessary for producing the means of subsistence into what Veblen later calls "conspicuous consumption" and "conspicuous waste." Not only, in Marx's view, can the capitalistic system be charged with indifference as to whether its profits are made out of the production of luxuries or necessities; but the

workers on starvation wages engaged in the luxury trades constitute a signal indictment of the inequitable distribution of wealth.

As the needs of the individual are thought to set a natural limit to his acquisition of wealth, or at least to provide him with a rational standard for stopping short of wanton luxuries when he seeks the decencies or amenities of life, so the needs of society as a whole are thought to establish a criterion of justice in the distribution of wealth.

"God gave the world to men in common," says Locke, and "the measure of property nature has well set by the extent of man's labor and the convenience of life . . . No man's labor could subdue or appropriate all; nor could his enjoyment consume more than a small part; so that it was impossible for any man, this way, to intrench upon the right of another, who would still have room for as good and as large a possession (after the other had taken out his) as before it was appropriated. Which measure did confine every man's possession to a very moderate proportion, and such as he might appropriate to himself without injury to anybody, in the first age of the world."

This rule of property—"that every man should have as much as he could make use of" without prejudice or injury to others—worked well in the beginning when, as Locke puts it, "all the world was America." It "would still hold in the world without straitening anybody," Locke thinks, "since there is land enough in the world to suffice double the inhabitants, had not the invention of money . . . introduced (by consent) larger possessions and a right to them"; for gold and silver being relatively imperishable, men can hoard excesses of them without appearing to waste them, as they would if they amassed perishable commodities which they could not consume or use.

It is not money but property itself which Rousseau claims to be the origin of inequality among men and of the inequitable distribution of wealth. "The first man who, having enclosed a piece of ground, bethought himself of saying *This is mine,* and found people simple enough to believe him, was the real founder of civil society." Once established as a right, property tends to expand. The larger proprietors avoid the question, "Do you not know that numbers of your fellow-creatures are starving, for want of what you have too much of?" Instead, according to Rousseau, they conceive "the profoundest plan that ever entered the mind of man" to protect their possessions against invasion or plunder. They institute civil government, ostensibly for the security of all, but really to secure for themselves their property and power.

"Such was, or may well have been," Rousseau writes, "the origin of society and law, which bound new fetters on the poor, and gave new powers to the rich; which irretrievably destroyed natural liberty, eternally fixed the law of property and inequality, converted clever usurpation into unalterable right, and, for the advantage of a few ambitious individuals, subjected all mankind to perpetual labor, slavery, and wretchedness." Smith seems to agree. "Where there is no property," he says, "or at least none that exceeds the value of two or three days labor, civil government is not so necessary . . . Civil government, so far as it is instituted for the security of property, is in reality for the defense of the rich against the poor, or of those who have some property against those who have none at all."

But, unlike Smith, Rousseau has an alternative to propose. "Since it is plainly contrary to the law of nature . . . that the privileged few should gorge themselves with superfluities while the starving multitude are in want of the bare necessities of life," he thinks it is "one of the most important functions of government to prevent extreme inequalities of fortunes; not by taking away wealth from its possessors, but by depriving all men of means to accumulate it; not by building asylums for the poor, but by securing the citizens from becoming poor."

THIS STATES AN END, but not the means for achieving it. The problem of poverty is not so easily solved, if it can be solved at all, once the right of property is admitted. Rousseau, for example, no less than Locke and others before him, affirms this right which, for Kant and Hegel later, is almost the whole substance of private or abstract right. "The right of property," says Rousseau, "is the most sacred of all the rights of citizenship, and even more important in some respects than liberty itself." Yet it is difficult, he admits, "to secure the property of individuals on one side, without attacking it on another; and it is impossible that all the regulations which govern the order of succession, wills, contracts, etc., should not lay individuals under some constraint as to the disposition of their goods, and should not consequently restrict the right of property."

To Hegel, poverty seems to be an inevitable consequence of property, as war is an inevitable consequence of sovereignty, and in neither case can the cause be abolished. "When the masses begin to decline into poverty," as they must, they can be supported from public funds and private charities, thus receiving "subsistence directly, not by means of their work," or as an alternative, "they might be given subsistence indirectly through being given work." But, Hegel adds, "in this event the volume of production would be increased, but the evil consists precisely in an excess of production and in the lack of a proportionate number of consumers who are themselves also producers, and thus it is simply intensified by both of the methods by which it is sought to alleviate it." Hence, Hegel concludes, it "becomes apparent that despite an excess of wealth civil society is not rich enough . . . to check excessive poverty and the creation of a penurious rabble. This inner dialectic of civil society thus drives it— or at any rate a specific civil society—to push beyond its own limits and seek markets, and . . . its necessary means of subsistence, in other lands which are either deficient in the goods it has over-produced, or else generally backward in industry."

Imperialism, according to Marx, will not long work as a cure for what Tawney later calls "the sickness of an acquisitive society"—the inner frustration which Marx sees manifested in recurring economic crises and depressions of greater and greater magnitude. Nor does he propose the abolition of all private property as the remedy for poverty, when he calls for "the expropriation of the expropriators." On the contrary, only the possession by each individual of an adequate supply of consumer's goods can abolish poverty. Differentiating between individual and capitalist property, according as its owners are or are not laborers, and according as it consists in consumable goods or the means of production, Marx would transfer the latter from private property to public ownership.

The socialist economy he outlines with Engels also includes "abolition of property in land, and application of all rents of land to public purposes; a heavy progressive or graduated income tax; abolition of all right of inheritance." It includes "centralization of credit in the hands of the state, by means of a national bank with State capital and an exclusive monopoly," and also "centralization of the means of communication and transport." Last but not least, it includes "equal liability of all to labor."

More radical than Marx's socialism is the communism Plato proposes in *The Republic*. Plato's aim is not to solve the problem of poverty or economic injustice. By abolishing for his guardian class *all* private property, he hopes that his guardians through sharing common possessions (including wives and children) will have no cause for rivalry, dissension, or personal ambition. Common possessions should mold them into a fraternity and free them from private interests to work for the common good. In this matter of property, the condition of Plato's imagined guardians was not so different from that of Jesus' disciples as recounted in the Book of Acts, or of the monastic orders whose vows include that of voluntary poverty.

Aristotle's criticisms of the arrangements for the guardian class in *The Republic* are largely directed against the community of women and children and the elimination of private property. "Property," he says, "should be in a certain sense common, but as a general rule private; for, when everyone has a distinct interest, men will not complain of one another, and they will make more progress, because everyone will be attending to his own business." He thinks "it is clearly better that property should be private, but the use of it common," in the sense that its use have the common welfare in mind.

Not only does Aristotle defend private property on many counts, but he objects to schemes for equalizing it, such as Plato sets forth in the *Laws*. For one thing, "the legislator ought not only to aim at the equalization of properties, but at moderation in their amount." Yet if the legislator "prescribe this moderate amount equally to all, he will be no nearer the mark; for it is not the possessions but the desires of mankind which need to be equalized, and this is impossible unless a sufficient education is provided by the laws."

Whether or not communism is desirable, there are those who think it is impossible, not so much on the level of the economic, as on the level of the moral, revolution for which Aristotle looks to education. The skeptic thinks human nature cannot be so transformed. It may be only in the 20th century that the world is divided into two camps on this subject, but the issue is as old as the western tradition. At its beginning Aristophanes expresses the skeptical position in a form that is still current. *The Assemblywomen* simply laughs at the idea that inequalities of property can ever be done away with—by law or by education.

WHEN ONE COMES to more recent writing on wealth, the book most centrally concerned is Tawney's *The Acquisitive Society*. Tawney sees wealth as the result of the release of all men to pursue without social conscience or inhibition their personal self-interests. Thus are all relieved by the system "of the necessity of discriminating between different types of economic activity and different sources of wealth, between enterprise and avarice, energy and unscrupulous greed, property which is legitimate and property which is theft, the just enjoyment of the fruits of labor and the idle parasitism of birth and fortune."

These being the diverse sources of wealth, it is evident that Tawney does not have a highly favorable view either of riches or of those who possess them. Under the impulse to possession, "men do not become religious or wise or artistic; for religion and wisdom and art imply the acceptance of limitations. But they become powerful and rich. They inherit the earth and change the face of nature, if they do not possess their own souls ... The temper which dedicates itself to the cultivation of opportunities, and leaves obligations to take care of themselves, is set upon an object which is at once simple and practicable. The eighteenth century defined it. The twentieth century has very largely attained it." Not many writers, at least in the social sciences, have so fully stated their position in so few words.

Tawney then prescribes, on the whole, a more difficult matter. He does not condemn indiscriminately the pursuit of wealth; it can be a means to better ends and not an end in itself. (All men, he notes, are very likely to confuse means and ends.) He seeks a social order in which industrial activity is professionalized. In the manner of the good physician or scholar, money should be earned with a larger commitment to good or anyhow acceptable behavior. Acceptable behavior, in turn, includes a willingness to see and concede to the conflicting goals of others. Tawney would encourage such professionalism in a practical way by the organization of workers and other economic groups to exercise power countervailing the power of those motivated by greed and other acquisitive impulses. Tawney also presses hard against the tendency to divorce religion and its obligations and restraints from economic motives. The latter, he strongly feels, should be kept subordinate to religious ethic. When there is uninhibited pursuit of wealth as an end in itself, nothing can prevent collision with others so motivated or those, workers in particular, who stand in the way.

Veblen's *The Theory of the Leisure Class,* published in 1899, appeared amid the most intense discussion of wealth and its social justifications and effects that the United States, perhaps any country, has ever experienced. The robber barons—Vanderbilt, Rockefeller, Jay Gould, the exceptionally visible James Fisk—were or had recently been large on the economic landscape. Congress had enacted the Sherman Antitrust Act in the hope that competition would curb their greed or, as was more often seen, their compulsive piracy, and the

Interstate Commerce Act was specifically directed at rate abuse by the railroads. Theodore Roosevelt would soon condemn the "malefactors of great wealth," and a generation of muckraking writers—Theodore Dreiser, Upton Sinclair, Ida Tarbell—who criticized the rich and their presumed greed was about to enter on the literary scene. None of these, all notable in the American experience, would quite match in practical effect that of Veblen.

Veblen's instrument is a wonderfully solemn, seemingly scientific ridicule. The relevant discipline for viewing wealth in general and the American rich in particular is not economics but anthropology. The rich are anthropological specimens to be examined sequentially with members of the most primitive Pacific tribal communities. Their behavior, Veblen, on occasion, accommodates to his needs. "The institution of a leisure class," he writes, "is found in its best development at the higher stages of the barbarian culture." In Newport as in Papua, both seek competitive display: "Costly entertainments, such as the potlatch or the ball, are peculiarly adapted to serve this end." The tribal leader in both cases sets great store by the adornment of his women—painful tattooing and mutilation in the one case, more or less equally painful constriction by corsets in the other. However, the modern man of wealth has moved on to make the wife, "who was at the outset the drudge and chattel of the man," now "the ceremonial consumer of goods which he produces." From the characterization of such display come Veblen's enduring contributions to the language—"conspicuous consumption" and "conspicuous waste."

Related to these is the role of conspicuous leisure. "In order to gain and to hold the esteem of men," he writes, "it is not sufficient merely to possess wealth or power. The wealth or power must be put in evidence ... a life of leisure is the readiest and most conclusive evidence of pecuniary strength."

Veblen and *The Theory of the Leisure Class* brought into being a distinctive American reaction to wealth. In Europe wealth was regarded with envy, resentment, and social disapproval, and from its possessors came indignant affirmation of the righteousness of its possession and enjoyment. These attitudes and behavior patterns were not lacking in the United States, but to them Veblen added a new dimension. The rich might have their wealth and the associated entertainments. However, no truly sensitive and sensible person would be so captured; no one so endowed would want to be guilty of "invidious" display; who would casually risk the charge of conspicuous consumption? Veblen accomplished the nearly impossible: he made wealth and its display a subject of amusement, maybe even scorn.

In the United States, at least until recent times, it is possible, in consequence, that the legacy of Veblen was more influential in restraining the pleasures and extravagances of the rich than any other force, except perhaps the progressive income tax. Such was the social effect of *The Theory of the Leisure Class*.

KEYNES, IN NEITHER his *General Theory of Employment, Interest and Money* nor in his other writings, was very interested in the moral, social, or even economic aspects of wealth. He largely accepted what existed; he devoted a substantial amount of his personal time to amassing (and once or twice losing) a modest fortune. He is remembered for investment operations verging on speculation on behalf of King's, his Cambridge college, where he long served as bursar. Yet, in an unintended way, his work had a profound influence on attitudes toward wealth and the accumulation of wealth.

Keynes's concern, as discussed also in the chapter on LABOR, was to have an economy that functioned with the full or near full employment of its labor force. This, not the need for the goods produced, was his central interest. But in order to employ labor and industrial plants it was essential that production increase

from year to year as more workers became available and as the productivity of the individual worker increased. From this, in turn, came the standard and all but universally accepted test of economic performance, the one now enunciated daily and without thought: the rate of economic growth of the country, the growth being that in the aggregate production of goods and services—of wealth in the particular national community. If a country has a high rate of such growth, it is doing well, is successful. A low rate of growth is a matter for anxiety and serious attention. No one dreams of examining the needs behind this incremental wealth; the justification lies not in what is produced but in the employment and income provided by the production or merely in the growth itself.

In the socialist world the supply of goods—wealth *per se*—remains a major issue. So also, needless to say, in the poor lands of, as it is now called, the Third World. In the rich countries a steady increase in wealth is what ensures the employment and well-being of those who produce it. Here economic growth—the annual increase in wealth—is the culmination of the long history of changing attitudes on this subject. The question is not the power that increasing wealth affords the individual. There is almost no mention of the pleasure or prestige that it provides. Rather, as noted, the increase in wealth is in some measure a social end in itself, to the extent that it does have functional justification, which comes not from the goods produced but from the employment provided.

Such is the legacy of Keynes. Although, to repeat, he was not himself concerned with the economic and moral justification of wealth, it was the unintended consequence of his *General Theory* that he profoundly reshaped both social thought and political action on the subject.

100

Will

INTRODUCTION

THE great controversy over the freedom of the will tends to overshadow the theory of the will itself. For some thinkers the two notions are inseparable. As the word "choice" popularly connotes freedom in choosing between alternatives, so for them liberty belongs to the very nature of the will. But others who affirm that men can act freely or voluntarily also deny that the will itself is ever free.

Still others who distinguish between voluntary and reflex actions—on the part of brute animals as well as men—also distinguish between the voluntary and the free. They reserve freedom to men alone on the ground that men alone have wills. Far from identifying will with free will, they differentiate between those acts of the will which are necessitated and those which are free.

It would appear from this sampling of conflicting opinions that the issue concerning free will presupposes, and often conceals, diverse theories of the will—different conceptions of its nature, its various acts, and its relation to other faculties. Those who affirm and those who deny the will's freedom of action hardly meet on that issue if they proceed from different conceptions of what the will is and how it operates.

The matter is further complicated by different conceptions of freedom. Even those who define will in somewhat similar terms conceive its liberty differently. As the chapter on LIBERTY indicates, freedom has many meanings—theological, metaphysical, psychological, moral, natural, and civil. What is called free in one of these senses may not be so regarded in another. But one thing is clear. If, as Hobbes thinks, the only sense in which freedom can be affirmed is that of natural or political liberty—the sense in which a man can *do* what he *wills* without restraint or compulsion—then the will is not free, for its freedom depends on how its own acts are caused, or how it causes other acts, not on how the acts it causes are affected by outward circumstances beyond its control.

The problem of the freedom of the will seems, therefore, to be primarily psychological and metaphysical. It requires us to consider freedom in terms of *cause* and *necessity*. It appeals to such distinctions as that between the caused, the uncaused, and the self-caused, or to the difference between the predetermined, the contingent, and the spontaneous event. To this extent the problem is metaphysical. But it is psychological insofar as the kind of event with which we are concerned is an interior act of a living thing and, even more specifically, of an intelligent being, a being which has *mind* in some sense of that term. We do not ask whether stones and vegetables have free will because we do not usually suppose that they have will. Even those who, like Aristotle, attribute *desire* to all things or who, like William James, find a striving toward goals in at least all living things, do not refer to volition or the voluntary in the absence of imagination or thought.

The italicized words in the foregoing paragraph indicate ideas which have the most fundamental bearing on the discussion of will, and hence the relation of this to other chapters. The chapters on CAUSE and NECESSITY (and those on FATE and CHANCE) deal with doctrines which both affect and are affected by various theories of the will's freedom. But if we are to postpone the question of free will until the nature of will itself is considered, we must begin with definitions which employ terms discussed in the chapters on MIND and DESIRE.

THE DISTINCTION BETWEEN thought and action sets the stage for the discovery of a factor or faculty which serves to connect them. Acting may follow upon thinking, but not without the intervention of a determination or a desire to translate thought into deed. Plato, in *The Republic,* divides the soul into three parts, of which one, reason, is the faculty of thought and knowledge, and the other two, spirit and appetite, are principles of action. Both spirit and appetite need to be guided and ruled by reason but, according to Plato, reason depends also upon spirit, for without its support even wisdom must fail to influence conduct. Though he does not use the word, the role he assigns to spirit as the auxiliary of reason corresponds to the function performed by what later writers call "will."

The word "will" appears in the English translation of Aristotle. It is used less frequently than other words—such as "wish," "choice," "purpose," "impulse," "appetite," "desire"—to designate a motivating force, but along with them it signifies the factor which turns thought into action. Unlike Plato, who separates spirit and appetite, Aristotle makes appetite the generic notion, and treats will and desire as modes of appetite. But sometimes "desire" is used as a synonym for "appetite," and sometimes "wish" or "choice" is substituted for "will."

In his treatise *On the Motion of Animals,* we find Aristotle saying that "the living creature is moved by intellect, purpose, wish, and appetite. All these are reducible to mind and desire. For both imagination and sensation have this much in common with mind, that all three are faculties of judgment. However, will, impulse, and appetite are all three forms of desire, while purpose belongs both to intellect and to desire." But in the treatise *On the Soul,* we find him insisting that appetite be considered as the single "faculty of originating local movement," though if the soul were to be divided into a rational and an irrational part, he would assign wish to the calculative or

deliberative reason, desire and passion to the irrational part. "Wish," he writes, "is a form of appetite, and when movement is produced according to calculation, it is also according to wish, but appetite can originate movement contrary to calculation, for desire is also a form of appetite."

What is said of purpose and wish is also said of choice. All three somehow combine reason and desire. Giving choice as the cause of specifically human action, and desire combined with deliberation as the origin of choice, Aristotle speaks of choice as "either desiderative reason or ratiocinative desire." Lacking reason, animals do not have choice, according to Aristotle, or for that matter wish or purpose either; but insofar as their appetites are stirred by sensation or imagination, and the desires aroused lead to action, animals behave voluntarily.

When the words "desire" and "appetite" are so used, not to name the generic faculty of originating movement, but to signify a motivation different in kind from wish, purpose, or choice, they correspond to what Aquinas later calls "animal appetite" or "sensitive desire." This is for him the sphere of the emotions or passions. He treats the impulses of fear and anger, for example, as acts of the sensitive appetite.

The kind of desire which, for Aristotle, depends upon practical reason, Aquinas calls "intellectual appetite" or "rational desire." Since "will" is for him just another name for the desire or appetite which is determined by reason rather than sense, he necessarily holds that irrational animals do not have will.

Aristotle says that "the apparent good is the object of appetite, and the real good is the primary object of rational wish." Aquinas distinguishes somewhat differently between the object of the passions and the object of the will. For each sort of appetite or desire, the object takes its special character from the faculty by which it is apprehended. The sensible good, perceived or imagined, stands to the sensitive appetite as the intelligible good, judged by reason, stands to the intellectual appetite or will.

In one place Aristotle differentiates between wish and choice by saying that we can wish for the impossible, whereas choice is always of things within our power. But his more usual distinction is in terms of means and ends. "The end is what we wish for," he writes, "the means what we deliberate about and choose." Aquinas also divides the acts of the will according as they concern means or ends, but where Aristotle mentions only choice and wish, Aquinas enumerates three acts of the will with respect to ends (volition, intention, and enjoyment) and three with respect to means (consent, choice, and use).

According to Aquinas, each of these acts of the will responds to a distinct act of the practical reason and, except for the will's last acts, each may in turn be followed by further practical thought. This progressive determination of the will by reason goes on until the *use* of means leads to action, and action leads to the enjoyment of the end accomplished. As in practical reasoning ends come before means, so for the will the end comes first in the order of intention; but in the order of execution action begins with the means.

LIKE ARISTOTLE AND Aquinas, Kant and Hegel conceive will as a faculty of desire or activity founded upon reason, and so they attribute will, as they attribute reason, to man alone. But both Kant and Hegel go further and almost identify will in its pure state with reason.

"The faculty of desire," writes Kant, "in so far as its inner principle of determination as the ground of its liking or predilection lies in the reason of the subject, constitutes the will"; and he goes on to say that the will, "in so far as it may determine the voluntary act of choice . . . is the practical reason itself." Only man can claim "possession of a will which takes no account of desires and inclinations, and on the contrary conceives action as possible to him, nay, even necessary, which can only be done by disregarding all desires and sensible inclinations."

In this last statement, Kant seems to use the word "desire" in a sense which is opposed to will. The context indicates that he has in mind something like the distinction made by Aquinas between sensitive and rational desire. This indication is confirmed by his own

distinction between brute and human choice. "That act which is determinable only by inclination as a sensuous impulse or stimulus would be irrational brute choice (*arbitrium brutum*). The human act of choice, however, as human, though in fact *affected* by such impulses or stimuli, is not *determined* by them; and it is, therefore, not pure in itself when taken apart from the acquired habit of determination by reason." But, according to Kant, the human act of choice can be determined solely by reason. Only then is it "determined to action by the pure will."

One point must be observed, to which we shall subsequently return. The pure will is for Kant a free will. "The act of choice that is determined by pure reason," he writes, "is the act of free will . . . The freedom of the act of volitional choice is its independence of being determined by sensuous impulses or stimuli. This forms the negative conception of the free will. The positive conception of freedom is given by the fact that the will is the capability of pure reason to be practical of itself." Insofar as pure reason is able to become practical, that is, to determine choices and direct action, independently of all sensuous impulses or inclinations, that reason is in itself the pure will, and that will is in its very essence free.

For Hegel also, freedom is of the essence of will. "Freedom," he writes, "is just as fundamental a character of the will as weight is of bodies. Heaviness constitutes the body and is the body. The same is the case with freedom and will, since the free entity is the will. Will without freedom is an empty word, while freedom is actual only as will, as subject."

Though the passions enter into the sphere of the subjective will, according to Hegel, will transforms them. "Subjective volition—Passion—is that which sets men in activity, that which effects 'practical' realization." When it is occupied with the passions, the subjective will, Hegel writes, "is dependent and can gratify its desires only within the limits of this dependence." The passions, however, are common to both men and animals. "An animal too has impulses, desires, inclinations," Hegel says, "but it has no will and must obey its impulses if nothing external deters it." Only man, "the wholly undetermined, stands above his impulses and may make them his own, put them into himself as his own. An impulse is something natural, but to put it into my ego depends on my will."

Hegel explains this aspect of the will by reference to that "element of pure indeterminacy or that pure reflection of the ego into itself which involves the dissipation of every restriction and every content either immediately presented by nature, by needs, desires, and impulses, or given and determined by any means whatever." But indeterminacy is only one moment of the will, its negative aspect. The second moment occurs in "the transition from undifferentiated indeterminacy to the differentiation, determination, and positing of a determinacy as a content and object." Both of these moments are partial, each the negation of the other. "The indeterminate will," in Hegel's opinion, is "just as one-sided as the will rooted in sheer determinacy. What is properly called the will includes in itself both the preceding moments."

As the unity of both these moments, the will "is particularity reflected into itself and so brought back to universality, *i.e.,* it is individuality. It is," Hegel continues, "the *self-*determination of the ego, which means that at one and the same time the ego posits itself as its own negative, *i.e.,* as restricted and determinate, and yet remains by itself, *i.e.,* in its self-identity and universality." While the two previous moments of the will are "through and through abstract and one-sided," the third moment gives us the individual will and freedom in the concrete. "Freedom lies neither in indeterminacy nor in determinacy; it is both of these at once . . . Freedom is to will something determinate, yet in this determinacy to be by oneself and to revert once more to the universal."

IN THE TRADITION OF the great books, other writers place the essence of the will not in its freedom, but in its being the cause of the voluntary acts performed by animals and men. The students of physiology from Aristotle to William James distinguish the movements of the various bodily organs—the heart, the lungs, the organs of digestion, excretion, and reproduction—from those movements of the whole animal or of its members which are somehow based upon desire and imagination or thought.

Aristotle sometimes calls these physiological changes "non-voluntary" and sometimes "involuntary," though he has another meaning for "involuntary" when he describes the conduct of a man, compelled by fear, to do something contrary to his wishes, *e.g.,* the captain who throws his cargo overboard to save his ship. The completely nonvoluntary motion is one which occurs quite apart from any *knowledge* of the end, or without conscious desire, whereas the involuntary involves some conflict of desires. When the involuntary in this special sense is not considered, only a twofold division is made, as in James's distinction between reflex and voluntary movements, Harvey's distinction between natural and animal motions, or Hobbes's distinction between vital and animal motions.

"There be in animals," Hobbes writes, "two sorts of motions peculiar to them: one called vital . . . such as are the course of the blood, the pulse, the breathing, the concoction, nutrition, excretion, etc.; to which motions there needs no help of imagination. The other is *animal motion,* otherwise called *voluntary motion,* as to go, to speak, to move any of our limbs, in such manner as is first fancied in our minds . . . Because going, speaking, and the like voluntary motions, depend always upon a precedent thought of *whither, which way,* and *what,* it is evident that the imagination is the first internal beginning of all voluntary motion."

But the imagination, according to Hobbes, gives rise to voluntary motions through arousing desire or appetite. When desires and aversions, hopes and fears, alternately succeed one another, what Hobbes means by "deliberation" takes place; and, he declares, "in deliberation, the last appetite, or aversion, immediately adhering to the action, or to the omission thereof, is that we call the will; the act, not the faculty, of *willing.* And beasts that have deliberation must necessarily also have will. The definition of the will, given commonly by the Schools, that it is a *rational appetite,* is not good. For if it were, then could there be no voluntary act against reason. For a voluntary act is that which proceedeth from the will, and no other."

Locke disagrees with Hobbes's view that willing is an act of desire. "That the will is perfectly distinguished from desire," he thinks, may be seen in the fact that desire "may have a quite contrary tendency from that which our wills set us upon." Desire, according to Locke, "is an uneasiness of the mind for want of some absent good"; whereas will is the "power to begin or forbear, continue or end, the several actions of our minds, and motions of our bodies, barely by a thought or preference of the mind ordering or, as it were, commanding the doing or not doing, such or such a particular action ... The actual exercise of that power, by directing any particular action or its forbearance, is that which we call volition or willing."

Though volition is not an act of desire, Locke holds that it is the uneasiness of desire which "determines the will to the successive voluntary actions." And though Locke speaks of willing as if it were an act of thought, he distinguishes between the mind's power of understanding and of willing. The one is a passive, the other is an active power. Understanding or perceptivity is "a power to receive ideas or thoughts"; will or motivity is the "power to direct the operative faculties to motion or rest."

In this conception of the will as the power the mind has to control the faculties, or the motions of the body, which can be voluntarily exercised, Locke, like Hobbes before him and James after, explains the will's action in terms of thinking of the motion to be performed or the deed to be done. Discussing the theory of what he calls "ideo-motor action," James says that "a supply of ideas of the various movements that are possible, left in the memory by experiences of their involuntary performance, is thus the first prerequisite of the voluntary life." Reflexive or other innately determined movements do not depend upon consciousness of the movement to be performed. That is why "voluntary movement must be secondary, not primary functions of our organism"; or as he says in another place, the action which is performed voluntarily "must before that, at least once, have been impulsive or reflex."

The kind of idea which initiates a voluntary movement James calls a "kinaesthetic image"—an image of the sensations which will be experienced when the movement takes place. "In perfectly simple voluntary acts," he writes, "there is nothing else in the mind but the kinaesthetic image, thus defined, of what the act is to be." In certain cases, however, there must be "an additional mental antecedent, in the shape of a fiat, decision, consent, volitional mandate ... before the movement can follow." This becomes necessary when contrary kinesthetic images vie with one another to initiate antagonistic movements. "The express fiat, or act of mental consent to the movement, comes in when the neutralization of the antagonistic and inhibitory idea is required.

"With the prevalence, once there as a fact, of the motive idea," James goes on, "the *psychology* of volition properly stops. The movements which ensue are exclusively physiological phenomena, following according to physiological laws upon neural events to which the idea corresponds. The *willing* terminates with the prevalence of the idea ... We thus find that we reach the heart of our inquiry into volition when we ask by what process it is that the thought of any given object comes to prevail stably in the mind." The answer James gives is that it is "the essential achievement of the will ... to attend to a difficult object and hold it fast before the mind. The so-doing *is* the *fiat* ... Effort of attention is thus the essential phenomenon of the will."

Though Freud does not use the word "will," or analyze voluntary movements in ideomotor terms, he does attribute to what he calls "the ego" the function which Locke and James ascribe to will. "In popular language," he writes, "we may say that the ego stands for reason and circumspection, while the id stands for the untamed passions." To the ego is given "the task of representing the external world for the id," and so of protecting it from destructive conflicts with reality.

In discharging this function, "on behalf of

the id, the ego controls the path of access to motility, but," Freud continues, "it interpolates between desire and action the procrastinating factor of thought, during which it makes use of the residues of experience stored up in memory. In this way it dethrones the pleasure-principle, which exerts undisputed sway over the processes in the id, and substitutes for it the reality-principle, which promises greater security and greater success."

Treating the will metaphysically, not psychologically, Heidegger regards "will" as "the basic feature of the 'is-ness' of what-is," and, so conceived, it is "the equation of what-is with the Real, in such a way that the reality of the Real becomes invested with the sovereign power to effect a general objectivisation."

As the problem of the will's freedom involves the question of whether or how its acts are caused, so the will's action raises a problem concerning how it causes the voluntary effects it produces. In Locke's view, we are equally at a loss to explain how one body moves another and how our own bodies are moved by our will. "The passing of motion out of one body into another," he thinks, "is as obscure and inconceivable as how our minds move or stop our bodies by thought; which we every moment find that they do."

If we could "explain this and make it intelligible," Locke says in another place, "then the next step would be to understand creation." Hume agrees that "it must forever escape our most diligent inquiry" how "the motion of our body follows upon the command of our will." That it does, he says, "is a matter of common experience, like other natural events. But the power and energy by which this is effected, like that in other natural events, is unknown and inconceivable."

No less mysterious to Hume is the coming into "existence of an idea, consequent to the command of the will," which seems to imply a "creative power, by which it raises from nothing a new idea, and with a kind of *Fiat*, imitates the omnipotence of its Maker." How "this operation is performed, the power by which it is produced," seems to him "entirely beyond our comprehension."

Spinoza and Descartes take a different view of the relation between the will and the intellect or understanding. Neither admits that the human will forms new ideas, or, as Spinoza says, that there are "mere fancies constructed by the free power of the will." Both conceive the will's activity as consisting in assent or dissent to ideas, their affirmation or negation. But beyond this point they part company.

For one thing, Descartes distinguishes between the will as a faculty of choice and the understanding as a faculty of knowledge, where Spinoza holds that "the will and the intellect are one and the same." Since Spinoza denies that will and intellect are anything except "the individual volitions and ideas themselves," it is more precise, he suggests, to say that the individual volition (*i.e.*, the affirmation or negation of *this* idea) and the individual idea affirmed or denied are one and the same.

In consequence, they differ with respect to the power of volition. Spinoza criticizes the supposition he finds in Descartes, that "the will extends itself more widely than the intellect, and is therefore different from it." Whereas Descartes thinks that "the faculty of comprehension which I possess . . . is of very small extent and extremely limited," Spinoza says, "I am conscious of a will so extended as to be subject to no limits." We can affirm or deny much more than we can know with certitude.

This difference between Spinoza and Descartes reveals itself most strikingly in their conception of God's will. According to Descartes, the omnipotence of God lies in the supremacy of his will—in its absolute independence even with respect to the divine intellect. "It is self-contradictory that the will of God should not have been from eternity indifferent to all that has come to pass or ever will occur . . . Thus, to illustrate, God did not will . . . the three angles of a triangle to be equal to two right angles because he knew that they could not be otherwise. On the contrary . . . it is because he willed the three angles of a triangle to be necessarily equal to two right angles that this is true and cannot be otherwise." Against Descartes's voluntarism, Spinoza declares it absurd to say that "God could bring it about that it should not follow from the nature of a triangle that its three angles should be equal to two right angles."

Such different conceptions of the will or of its power necessarily lead to opposite conclusions concerning free will—in man or God. The human mind, according to Spinoza, "cannot be the free cause of its own actions." In each of its volitions, as in each of its ideas, it is determined by a cause. The supposition of an infinite will in God does not exempt that will from the need to be determined in its acts; nor can God "on this account be said to act from freedom of will." Yet Spinoza also affirms that "God alone is a free cause, for God alone exists and acts from the necessity of his own nature." Freedom does not reside in the will, nor in the absence of necessity or causal determination, but rather in self-determination. It does not consist in choice, but in the absence of compulsion by causes which lie outside one's own nature. Hence only an infinite being—a *causa sui* in Spinoza's sense—can be free.

Calvin also denies the freedom of the will, not because man is a finite being, but because his nature is corrupted by sin. "In the perverted and degenerate nature of man there are still some sparks which show that he is a rational animal, and differs from the brutes, inasmuch as he is endued with intelligence, and yet, that this light is so smothered by clouds of darkness, that it cannot shine forth to any good effect. In like manner, the will, because inseparable from the nature of man, did not perish, but was so enslaved by depraved lusts as to be incapable of one righteous desire."

Descartes, on the other hand, places freedom in the will and identifies it with the power of choice. "The faculty of will," he writes, "consists alone in our having the power of choosing to do a thing or choosing not to do it . . . or rather it consists alone in the fact that in order to affirm or deny, pursue or shun, those things placed before us by the understanding, we act so that we are unconscious that any outside force constrains us in so doing." Descartes seems to conceive the will as cause of itself in its acts of choice. But he does not attribute to the human will the autonomy

Spinoza ascribes to God. "The knowledge of the understanding," he writes, "should always precede the determination of the will"; and in another place he says that "our will impels us neither to follow after nor to flee from anything, except as our understanding represents it as good or evil."

In order to be free, Descartes explains, "it is not necessary that I should be indifferent as to the choice of one or the other of two contraries; but contrariwise the more I lean to the one—whether I recognize clearly that the reasons of the good and the true are to be found in it, or whether God so disposes my inward thought—the more freely do I choose and embrace it." The will always retains "the power of directing itself towards one side or the other apart from any determination by the understanding." The human will is, in this sense, always undetermined from without, though it is not always indifferent to the alternatives confronting it. It is indifferent, Descartes holds, only when a man "does not know what is the more true or the better, or at least when he does not see clearly enough to prevent him from doubting about it. Thus the indifference which attaches to human liberty is very different from that which belongs to the divine."

THE DENIAL OF FREE WILL in the tradition of western thought seems to follow from the principle that every happening must have a cause. In the sphere of human conduct, voluntary acts are no less determined effects of prior causes than involuntary acts. Though both are equally necessitated, the difference between the voluntary and the involuntary, according to Hobbes, Locke, and Hume, consists in the fact that when a man acts voluntarily, he does what he himself has decided to do.

The fact that his decision to act in a certain way is itself caused, does not, in the opinion of these writers, abolish the freedom of his action, but only the freedom of his will. If freedom is attributed not to a man's will, but to the man who can do what he wills, then, these writers think, there is no conflict between freedom and necessity—or between freedom and the universal reign of causality.

For them freedom is abridged only by external forces which coerce a man to act contrary to his wishes or constrain him from acting as he wills. Freedom in this sense is incompatible only with exterior compulsion, not with the inner causal determination of every act of the will.

To those who deny free will, it does not seem to be an entirely satisfactory answer to say, as Descartes does, that we are immediately conscious of our freedom of choice. In the Third Set of Objections, urged by Thomas Hobbes against Descartes, Objection XII (which is directed against Meditation IV wherein Descartes discusses free will) contains this statement: "We must note here also that the freedom of the will has been assumed without proof, and in opposition to the opinion of the Calvinists." In replying, Descartes merely repeats his original statement of the evidence for free will.

"I made no assumption concerning freedom," he writes, "which is not a matter of universal experience. Though there are many who, looking to the divine foreordination, cannot conceive how that is compatible with liberty on our part, nevertheless no one, when he considers himself alone, fails to experience that to will and to be free are the same thing (or rather that there is no difference between what is voluntary and what is free)." To Pierre Gassendi who, in another set of objections, also denies "the indeterminateness of the will," Descartes replies: "These matters are such that anyone ought to experience them in himself rather than be convinced of them by ratiocination . . . Refuse then to be free, if freedom does not please you; I at least shall rejoice in my liberty, since I experience it in myself, and you have assailed it not with proof but with bare negations merely."

The experience of free will is no proof either, the opponents reply, for the experience is open to the suspicion that it is illusory rather than real. It may be, Hume suggests, only "a false sensation or seeming experience which we have . . . of liberty or indifference in many of our actions." We suffer this illusion, even foist it upon ourselves, he further suggests, because we are motivated by "the fantastical desire of shewing liberty." In the same vein, Freud later discounts objections to the determinism of psychoanalysis on the part of those who refuse to recognize the hidden causes which control their actions. "You have an illusion of a psychic freedom within you which you do not want to give up," he says. But this "deeply rooted belief in psychic freedom and choice" must be given up because it "is quite unscientific . . . It must give way before the claims of a determinism which governs even mental life."

Nietzsche dismisses the whole issue of determinism versus free will by saying, "What is called 'freedom of will' is essentially the emotion of superiority over him who must obey." Elsewhere Nietzsche lists the notion of the will's freedom as one of "the four great errors." In another place, Nietzsche writes: "It is certainly not the least charm of a theory that it is refutable: it is with precisely this charm that it entices subtler minds. It seems that the hundred times refuted theory of 'free will' owes its continued existence to this charm alone—: again and again there comes along someone who feels he is strong enough to refute it."

THE DILEMMA OF FREE WILL or determinism does not seem to other writers to be so easily resolvable. "All theory is against the freedom of the will," says Dr. Johnson; "all experience for it." Tolstoy states the dilemma in similar terms. "Regarding man as a subject of observation" by the rational methods of the sciences, Tolstoy writes, "we find a general law of necessity to which he (like all that exists) is subject. But regarding him from within ourselves as what we are conscious of, we feel ourselves to be free. This consciousness is a source of self-cognition quite apart from and independent of reason. Through his reason man observes himself, but only through consciousness does he know himself . . . You say: I am not free. But I have lifted my hand and let it fall. Everyone understands that this illogical reply is an irrefutable demonstration of freedom. That reply is the expression of a consciousness that is not subject to reason."

The problem cannot be solved, Tolstoy thinks, by ignoring one side of the question.

To do that is to put the problem "on a level on which the question itself cannot exist. In our time," Tolstoy continues, "the majority of so-called advanced people—that is, the crowd of ignoramuses—have taken the work of the naturalists who deal with one side of the question for a solution of the whole problem." But to admit that "from the point of view of reason man is subject to the law of necessity . . . does not advance by a hair's breadth the solution of the question, which has another, opposite, side, based on the consciousness of freedom." Not only does this "unshakable, irrefutable consciousness of freedom, uncontrolled by experiment or argument" constitute for Tolstoy "the other side of the question," but it is also for him that "without which no conception of man is possible."

James takes a somewhat different view of the dilemma of free will or determinism. Conceiving the act of free will in terms of the exertion of an effort on our part which is not determined by its object, James is willing to admit that our consciousness of freedom may be a delusion. "Even in effortless volition we have the consciousness of the alternative being also possible. This is surely a delusion here," he writes; "why is it not a delusion everywhere?" Hence it seems to him that "the question of free will is insoluble on strictly psychological grounds."

But if the existence of free will cannot be proved from experience, neither, in his opinion, can determinism be scientifically demonstrated. "The most that any argument can do for determinism," he says, "is to make it a clear and seductive conception, which a man is foolish not to espouse, so long as he stands by the great scientific postulate that the world must be one unbroken fact, and that prediction of all things without exception must be ideally, if not actually, possible." For those who accept this postulate, "a little fact like effort can form no real exception to the overwhelming reign of deterministic law."

Yet it remains a postulate, and postulation is not proof. Furthermore, there is "a *moral* postulate about the Universe . . . which would lead one to espouse the contrary view . . . the postulate that *what ought to be can be, and that*

bad acts cannot be fated, but that good ones must be possible in their place." As scientific law and prediction seem to call for the postulate of determinism, so moral responsibility and the genuineness of moral options seem to demand free will.

In *Pragmatism,* James has this to say about free will and determinism:

Both free-will and determinism have been inveighed against and called absurd, because each, in the eyes of its enemies, has seemed to prevent the "imputability" of good or bad deeds to their authors. Queer antinomy this! Free-will means novelty, the grafting on to the past of something not involved therein. If our acts were predetermined, if we merely transmitted the push of the whole past, the free-willists say, how could we be praised or blamed for anything? We should be "agents" only, not "principals," and where then would be our precious imputability and responsibility?

But where would it be if we *had* free-will? rejoin the determinists. If a "free" act be a sheer novelty, that comes not *from* me, the previous me, but *ex nihilo,* and simply tacks itself on to me, how can I, the previous I, be responsible? How can I have any permanent *character* that will stand still long enough for praise or blame to be awarded?

Hume recognizes that "it may be said . . . that, if voluntary actions be subjected to the same laws of necessity with the operations of matter, there is a continued chain of necessary causes, pre-ordained, and pre-determined, reaching from the original cause of all to every single volition of every human creature." But he does not think that the assertion of "no contingency anywhere in the universe; no indifference; no liberty," requires us to give up our notions of moral responsibility, and to abstain from making judgments of praise or blame concerning human actions. "The mind of man is so formed by nature," he writes, "that, upon the appearance of certain characters, dispositions, and actions, it immediately feels the sentiment of approbation or blame. The characters which engage our approbation are chiefly such as contribute to the peace and security of human society; as the characters which excite blame are chiefly such as tend to public detriment and disturbance."

In Hume's opinion, "remote and uncertain speculations" concerning the causation of human character or conduct, or concerning the general structure of the universe, do not affect "the sentiments which arise from the natural and immediate view of the objects . . . Why should not the acknowledgement of a real distinction between vice and virtue," he asks, "be reconcileable to all speculative systems of philosophy, as well as that of a real distinction between personal beauty and deformity?" James takes the exactly opposite view. A doctrine of necessity or determinism is for him incompatible with moral responsibility, or with the distinction between virtue and vice. Holding that free will is indispensable to the moral life, James chooses "the alternative of freedom." In doing so he confesses that "the grounds of his opinion are ethical rather than psychological."

He does go one step further into what he calls "the logic of the question." Since postulation is not proof—since a postulate is not an undeniable axiom but an expression of what James elsewhere calls "the will to believe"—the kind of dilemma which is formed by conflicting postulates can be resolved only by the exercise of free choice. The alternatives of free will and determinism constitute that kind of dilemma for James, and so it seems to him quite proper that the first act of free will should be to believe in free will.

"When scientific and moral postulates war thus with each other," he writes, "and objective proof is not to be had, the only course is voluntary choice, for skepticism itself, if systematic, is also voluntary choice." Hence belief in free will "should be voluntarily chosen from amongst other possible beliefs. Freedom's first deed should be to affirm itself. We ought never to hope for any other method of getting at the truth if indeterminism be a fact. Doubt of this particular truth will therefore probably be open to us to the end of time, and the utmost that a believer in free will can *ever* do will be to show that the deterministic arguments are not coercive. That they are seductive," James concludes, "I am the last to deny; nor do I deny that effort may be needed to keep the faith in freedom, when they press upon it, upright in the mind."

IN THE TRADITION OF THE great books, not all who affirm free will think that to do so

requires them to deny the universal reign of causality in nature; nor do they base their affirmation on our immediate consciousness of free choice or make it an act of faith—a pragmatic postulate. Kant, for example, explicitly disclaims that freedom is a matter of faith. "It is the only one of all the ideas of pure reason," he says, "whose object is a matter of fact." This means for him that its objective reality can be proved. In contrast, "the existence of God and the immortality of the soul are matters of faith," by which Kant means that they must be postulated by the practical reason as conditions necessary for the conceivability of the *summum bonum* which the moral law commands us to seek.

In order to understand Kant's proof of freedom, it is necessary to remember that he conceives the freedom of the will in terms of its autonomy, and its autonomy in terms of the fact that the practical reason, with which the pure will is identical, legislates for itself in proclaiming, and obeys only itself in upholding, the moral law. "Autonomy of the will," he writes, "is that property of it by which it is a law unto itself . . . Now the idea of freedom is inseparably connected with the conception of *autonomy,* and this again with the universal principle of morality." The moral law, Kant goes on, "expresses nothing else than the *autonomy* of the pure practical reason," and "this *self-legislation* of the pure and, therefore, practical reason is freedom in the positive sense."

In saying that "a free will and a will subject to moral laws are one and the same," Kant thinks that he may be suspected of circular reasoning, in that he appears to make freedom a condition of morality and at the same time to infer freedom from the existence of the moral law. There is no question that for him freedom "must be the foundation of all moral laws and the consequent responsibility." But, he explains, no inconsistency results from calling "freedom the condition of the moral law" and also maintaining that "the moral law is the condition under which we can first *become conscious* of freedom," if it be understood that "freedom is the *ratio essendi* [ground of being] of the moral law, while the moral law is the *ratio cognoscendi* [ground of knowing] of freedom."

We know that our will is free from knowing the existence of the moral law. We know that the moral law exists, for otherwise reason could never judge, as it does, that we ought to have done what we did not do. It is not freedom but the moral law "of which we become directly conscious (as soon as we trace for ourselves maxims of the will)." This, Kant says, "first presents itself to us, and leads directly to the concept of freedom." Whenever a man judges that "he can do a certain thing because he is conscious that he ought," then, according to Kant, "he recognizes that he is free, a fact which but for the moral law he would never have known."

The freedom which Kant thinks can be directly deduced from the moral law is a very special kind of causality. In the sensible world of nature, each cause is in turn the effect of some prior cause. None is the first or unconditioned cause, an uncaused cause. But for Kant freedom is "a faculty of absolute spontaneity" and consists in "the unconditioned causality of the cause . . . a causality capable of producing effects independently of and even in opposition to the power of natural causes, and capable, consequently, of *spontaneously* originating a series of events."

How are these two modes of causality—which Kant calls "the causality of *nature* and of *freedom*"—compatible with one another? To affirm both would appear to get us into the antinomy in which the thesis that "causality according to the laws of nature is not the only causality . . . a causality of freedom is also necessary," is contradicted by the antithesis that "there is no such thing as freedom, but everything in the world happens solely according to the laws of nature." Yet Kant thinks he can show that "this antinomy is based upon a mere illusion, and that nature and freedom are at least *not opposed*."

It would be impossible, he admits, "to escape this contradiction if the thinking subject, which seems to itself free, conceived itself in *the same sense* or in *the very same relation* when it calls itself free as when in respect to the same action it assumes itself to be subject

to the laws of nature." But the contradiction is only apparent or illusory if man belongs to two worlds—the sensible world of natural phenomena and the supersensible world of intelligible beings or noumena. "The notion of a being that has free will," writes Kant, "is the notion of a *causa noumenon*"—of a cause which does not operate under the temporal conditions of natural causality. "The notion of causality as *physical necessity* . . . concerns only the existence of things so far as it is determinable *in time* and, consequently, as phenomena, in opposition to their causality as things in themselves."

To remove "the apparent contradiction between freedom and the mechanism of nature in one and the same action, we must remember . . . that the necessity of nature, which cannot co-exist with the freedom of the subject, appertains only to the attributes of the thing that is subject to time-conditions, consequently only to those of the acting subject as a phenomenon . . . But the very same subject," Kant continues, "being on the other side conscious of himself as a thing in himself, considers his existence also *in so far as it is not subject to time-conditions*, and regards himself as only determinable by laws which he gives himself through reason."

In the latter mode of supersensible existence, man exercises the causality of a free will. He is not in any way subject to the natural necessity which governs all physical things. Yet the two worlds—the moral world of freedom and the physical world of necessity—meet in the same act. "The rational being," Kant explains, "can justly say of every unlawful action that he performs, that he could very well have left it undone; although as appearance it is sufficiently determined in the past, and in this respect is absolutely necessary."

THE APPARENT CONFLICT between freedom and nature arises for Kant because he conceives the act of free will to be absolutely spontaneous. It is as uncaused as the swerve of the atoms (discussed in the chapter on CHANCE) on which Lucretius bases the existence of free will. There is another conception of freedom that does not attribute to free will any special character which brings it into conflict with or-dinary causality. It does not belong to liberty, Aquinas thinks, that "what is free should be the first cause of itself." Not only is God the ultimate cause of what a man freely chooses to do, as He is the first cause of every natural event, but the will as a natural faculty of man never moves itself to operation. It is always moved by the reason, even in its acts of choice, and so these acts, wherein the will is free, are also caused.

Where Kant identifies will with free will (which implies that the will is free in all its acts), Aquinas distinguishes between those acts of the will which are necessitated and those which are free. He quotes Augustine to the effect that "natural necessity does not take away the liberty of the will," for that liberty exists only in the will's choice of means, not in its volition of the end. "Just as the intellect naturally and of necessity adheres to first principles," Aquinas explains, "so the will adheres to the last end." And just as the in-tellect assents of necessity to those "proposi-tions which have a necessary connection with first principles, namely, demonstrable conclu-sions," so the will adheres of necessity only to those things "which have a necessary connec-tion with happiness." With regard to all else—the whole realm of particular goods which are merely contingent means—the will is not necessitated, and so its choice among them is free.

Although Aquinas says that unless man has free choice, "counsels, exhortations, com-mands, prohibitions, rewards and punishments would be in vain," he does not postulate free will as an indispensable condition of moral conduct. Rather he shows how reason in caus-ing the will's choices at the same time leaves them free. "The root of liberty," he writes, "is the will as the subject thereof, but it is the reason as its cause. For the will can tend freely towards various objects precisely because the reason can have various perceptions of good." When, for example, "the deliberating reason is indifferently disposed to opposite things, the will can be inclined to either." The freedom of the will's choice with respect to particular means thus lies in the fact that, with respect

to all contingent matters, "the judgment of reason may follow opposite courses, and is not determinate to one."

"In all particular goods," Aquinas writes, "the reason can consider an aspect of some good and the lack of some good, which has the aspect of evil; and in this respect it can apprehend any single one of such goods as something to be chosen or to be avoided. The perfect good alone, which is happiness, cannot be apprehended by reason as an evil, or lacking in any way. Consequently man wills happiness of necessity, nor can he will not to be happy, or to be unhappy. Now since choice is not of the end, but of the means, it is not of the perfect good, which is happiness, but of par-ticular goods. Therefore, man chooses not of necessity, but freely."

Like Aquinas, Locke holds that "to be de-termined by our own judgment is no restraint to liberty." But where Locke thinks the "con-stant determination to a pursuit of happiness, no abridgment of liberty," Aquinas holds that because "man wills happiness of necessity," his will is not free in the volition of its nat-ural end. Yet Locke does mention the case "wherein a man is at liberty in respect of will-ing"—the case in which "a man may suspend the act of his choice from being determined for or against the thing proposed, till he has examined whether it be really of a nature in itself and consequences to make him happy or not."

In this type of case Aquinas locates what is peculiar to the causality of freedom. Some-times the judgment of reason is determined by its object, as when it contemplates the final end of actions. But when it deliberates about alternative means (which are both particular and contingent), reason can judge either way. What determines it to judge this way rather than that? Aquinas' answer is that such judg-ments of the reason are voluntary, in contrast to reason's involuntary assent to self-evident truths, wherein it is determined entirely by the object being considered. But if a voluntary judgment is one in which the will determines the reason's assent, and if reason's judgments concerning means are voluntary in this sense, then the act of the reason which causes the will's act of choice is itself an act caused by the will. The will's choice is, therefore, not uncaused; but, as Aquinas conceives it, the way in which it is caused makes it self-determining, and to this extent free.

THE GENERAL THEORY OF the will figures most prominently in the theology of Aquinas and in the philosophy of Kant and Hegel. They not only present the most elaborate analyses of its nature and its relation to reason but, in the tradition of the great books, they are the most stalwart defenders of its freedom. Their differences in principle and in reasoning may, however, obsure the common ground they share.

This may be seen in their conception of freedom. Aquinas does not attribute autonomy or spontaneity to the will. Yet in his view of free choice as a self-determining act of the will, there is something analogous to Kant's autonomy; and where Kant makes the pure will essentially free and spontaneous, Aquinas holds that the will, with respect to willing or not willing, is always free and inviolable. It is absolutely within "the power of the will," he writes, "not to act and not to will." He does not try to explain such freedom of exercise in the same way as freedom of choice.

It is only with regard to the latter that Aquinas appeals to the causal reciprocity between reason and will to show how the will's act of choice can be both free and caused. The kind of causation which Aquinas thinks takes place in free choice—the will determining the reason to make the practical judgment by which it is itself determined—seems to involve a circularity, or perhaps simultaneity, in action and reaction. If this is possible only because reason and will are *spiritual* powers, then here too there is some likeness to Kant's theory of the will's action as belonging to the supersensible world rather than to the domain of physical movement.

On one other point, they tend to agree even more plainly. "Free choice," writes Aquinas, "is part of man's dignity." Man's dignity for Kant—his membership in what Kant calls "the kingdom of ends"—is "rendered possible by the freedom of the will." But though they share this opinion of the source of human dignity in rationality and freedom, they do not draw the same moral consequences from their affirmation of free will as pivotal in human life.

Aquinas, like Aristotle, does not find moral goodness only in the will. On the contrary, the rectitude of the will depends on the goodness of the end it adheres to and the means it chooses. But like the Stoics, Kant makes the will the sole repository of moral goodness.

As Epictetus says that all good and evil lie in man's will, and that the morally neutral sphere is "in the region outside the will's control," so Kant begins his moral philosophy with the statement, "Nothing can possibly be conceived in the world, or even out of it, which can be called good without qualification, except a Good Will." In his view, "a good will is good not because of what it performs or effects, not by its aptness for the attainment of some proposed end, but simply by virtue of the volition; that is, it is good in itself." In another place, he adds that "though not indeed the sole and complete good," the will, *good in itself,* "must be the supreme good and the condition of every other, even of the desire of happiness."

These fundamental issues concerning the will in moral philosophy are more fully treated in the chapter on DUTY. The problems of the will in political theory are considered in the chapters on LAW and STATE—especially those problems which involve the concept of the sovereign will and the distinction of the particular will and the general will, the majority will and the will of all. The strictly theological problems concerning God's freedom and man's freedom in relation to God's will are also reserved for treatment elsewhere.

101

Wisdom

INTRODUCTION

THE special character of wisdom among the attainments of the mind shows itself in the things which everyone will agree can be said about wisdom—things which cannot be said about art and science, or knowledge and learning generally. We believe that, with the centuries, knowledge can be steadily increased and learning advanced, but we do not suppose that the same progress can be achieved in wisdom. The individual may grow in wisdom. The race does not seem to.

In the tradition of the great books, the moderns usually assert their superiority over the ancients in all the arts and sciences. They seldom claim superiority in wisdom. The phrase "modern science" needs no elucidation, but if anyone were to speak of modern wisdom, he would have to explain his meaning. As "modern" seems to have an immediately acceptable significance when it qualifies "science," so "ancient" seems to go with "wisdom," and to suggest that, with the centuries, far from increasing, wisdom may be lost.

Wisdom is more frequently and extensively the subject of discussion in the ancient and medieval than in the modern books. The ancients seem to have not only a greater yearning for wisdom, but also a greater interest in understanding what wisdom is and how it can be gained. The traditional discussion of wisdom, furthermore, has its foundations in the literature of the Old and the New Testament, as well as in the books of pagan antiquity.

This is not true of other forms of knowledge. The teachings of revealed religion open a path to the "heart of wisdom." They do not propose methods of scientific research. Again and again the Scriptures proclaim that "fear of the Lord is the beginning of wisdom"—a wisdom which develops with piety and worship, as science develops with experiment and proof.

Still another distinctive mark of wisdom is that it cannot be misused. We recognize that bad men as well as good may possess other kinds of knowledge. We have seen artistic skill and scientific truth put to evil use. But we do not ordinarily think a man wise unless he acts wisely. To act wisely is to act well, even as to have wisdom is to use it. The satirist's praise of folly condemns a useless wisdom. The theologian's condemnation of "worldly wisdom" dismisses it as the worst of folly—a counterfeit of wisdom.

Other forms of learning may separate knowledge from action; wisdom tends to unite them. Other forms of inquiry may be content with knowing and understanding the facts; the pursuit of wisdom aspires to a knowledge of good and evil. Plato, for example, makes the vision of the good the goal of a dialectic which ascends to wisdom, yet which does not rest there, but returns enlightened to the realm of action. This conception of wisdom is hinted at whenever we refrain from calling a man wise simply because he is learned—a scholar, scientist, or philosopher.

Again it is Plato who respects wisdom so highly that he will not call the philosopher wise, but only a lover of wisdom. "No god is a philosopher or seeker after wisdom, for he is wise already," Socrates says in the *Symposium;* "nor does any man who is wise seek after wisdom. Neither do the ignorant seek after wisdom." The lovers of wisdom are neither the wise nor the ignorant and foolish. As Socrates points out, they are "in a mean between the wise and the ignorant."

Aristotle would seem to disagree, not from a lower regard for wisdom, but because he identifies wisdom with philosophical knowledge, and especially with that highest branch of speculative science which is called "theology," "first philosophy," or "metaphysics." His use of the phrase "philosophical wisdom" to distinguish speculative from practical or political wisdom suggests that the philosopher may attain the wisdom he pursues. Yet Aristotle, like Plato, speaks of "philosophers or lovers of wisdom"; and Plato, like Aristotle, treats wisdom as one of the basic human virtues.

WE SHALL RETURN TO THE distinction which both Aristotle and Aquinas make between practical and speculative wisdom; they often call the latter simply "wisdom," in contrast to "prudence," which is their name for practical wisdom. Other writers, who treat wisdom as one, sometimes emphasize its speculative, and sometimes its practical, aspect. But for all of them, this double aspect remains part of wisdom's special character.

Lucretius, for example, believes,

Nothing is more sweet than full possession
Of those calm heights, well built, well fortified
By wise men's teaching, to look down from here
At others wandering below, men lost,
Confused, in hectic search for the right road.

The way of life, free from pain, the distress of fear, and futile struggle, is known only to the wise. Calm and repose are here suggested as attributes of the wise man. That also seems to be the implication of Dr. Johnson's "approbation of one who had attained to the state of the philosophical wise man, that is, to have no want of anything." When Boswell observes that then "the savage is a wise man," Johnson retorts: "Sir, I do not mean simply being without—but not having a want."

For Plotinus, wisdom seems to be purely speculative, and its repose a condition of the reasoning mind at rest. "Wisdom," he writes, "is a condition in a being that possesses repose. Think what happens when one has accomplished the reasoning process; as soon as we have discovered the right course, we cease to reason. We rest because we have come to wisdom." Still wisdom has a moral or, for Plotinus, an aesthetic aspect. "One Soul," he says, is "wise and lovely, another foolish and ugly. Soul-beauty is constituted by wisdom."

The practical or moral aspect of wisdom predominates in Milton, Rabelais, and Tolstoy. In *Paradise Lost,* Adam communicates his reflections on human knowledge to Raphael.

But apte the Mind or Fancie is to roave
Uncheckt, and of her roaving is no end;
Till warn'd, or by experience taught, she learn
That not to know at large of things remote
From use, obscure and suttle, but to know
That which before us lies in daily life,
Is the prime Wisdom; what is more, is fume,
Or emptiness, or fond impertinence,
And renders us in things that most concerne
Unpractis'd, unprepar'd, and still to seek.

Gargantua, writing a letter to his son Pantagruel while the latter is a student in Paris, admonishes him in the words of Solomon that "Wisdom entereth not into a malicious mind, and that knowledge without conscience is but the ruin of the soul." In *War and Peace,* Pierre, after reiterating that "All we can know is that we know nothing. And that's the height of human wisdom," learns from the Mason that "the highest wisdom is not founded on reason alone, nor on those worldly sciences of physics, chemistry, and the like, into which intellectual knowledge is divided." The highest wisdom, the Mason continues, is "but one science—the science of the whole—the science explaining the whole creation and man's place in it. To receive that science it is necessary to purify and renew one's inner self . . . And to attain this end, we have the light called conscience that God has implanted in our souls."

Though Plato defines wisdom as the virtue of reason—that part of the soul which is for him the faculty of knowledge—he gives it the function of directing conduct as well as contemplating truth. "Him we call wise," Socrates declares in *The Republic,* "who has in him that little part which rules" and which has "a knowledge of what is for the interest of each of the three parts and of the whole." In the state as in the soul, "how can there be the least shadow of wisdom," the Athenian Stranger asks in the *Laws,* "where there is no harmony?"

There is no harmony or wisdom "when fair reasonings have their habitation in the soul, and yet do no good, but rather the reverse of good" because reason fails to rule or be obeyed. "When the soul is opposed to knowledge, or opinion, or reason, which are her natural lords," the Athenian Stranger goes on, "that I call folly, just as it is in the state, when the multitude refuses to obey their rulers or the laws."

The four virtues which Plato enumerates in both *The Republic* and the *Laws* are wisdom, temperance, courage, justice. Justice is given a certain preeminence in *The Republic* as somehow embracing the other three, but in the *Laws,* the ruling virtue is wisdom. Calling the virtues "divine goods" to distinguish them from such things as health, beauty, strength, and wealth, the Athenian Stranger makes wisdom "chief and leader of the divine class of goods . . . Next," he says, "follows temperance; and from the union of these two with courage springs justice, and fourth in the scale of virtue is courage." As the principle of these other virtues, wisdom like them engages in the life of action. It does not move solely in the realm of thought.

When he refers to wisdom as one of the five intellectual virtues, Aristotle uses the word "wisdom" as if it named a single virtue. In the passage in the *Politics* in which he says that "the courage, justice, and wisdom of a state have the same form and nature as the qualities which give the individual who possesses them the name of just, wise or temperate," he does not divide wisdom into the speculative and the practical. But he seldom overlooks that separation. The passage just cited, for instance, begins with the statement that "each one has just so much happiness as he has of virtue and wisdom, and of virtuous and wise action."

Here the reference to virtue *and* wisdom places wisdom outside the virtues, when the latter are conceived exclusively as *moral* virtues. Wisdom for Aristotle is a virtue only in the order of intellectual excellence, not of moral excellence or character. As an intellectual virtue, wisdom is not even involved in the growth or exercise of the moral virtues. It is

as possible, Aquinas says, following Aristotle, to have the cardinal moral virtues without wisdom, as it is to have them without art or science. But for both Aquinas and Aristotle this is neither true nor intelligible unless we bear in mind the distinction between philosophical and practical wisdom, or between wisdom and prudence.

Though prudence is, no less than wisdom, an intellectual virtue—a quality of mind rather than of character—it belongs with the moral virtues. As the chapter on Virtue and Vice indicates, the cardinal virtues according to Aquinas include prudence, not wisdom. Similarly, as may be seen in the chapter on Prudence, Aristotle's theory holds it impossible to be good "without practical wisdom," just as it is impossible to be "practically wise without moral virtue."

Practical wisdom, Aristotle writes, "is concerned with things human and things about which it is possible to deliberate." Philosophical wisdom, on the other hand, "will contemplate none of the things that make a man happy." To explain the difference, Aristotle uses the example of the early Greek sages. "We say Anaxagoras, Thales, and men like them have philosophic but not practical wisdom, when we see them ignorant of what is to their own advantage . . . They know things that are remarkable, admirable, difficult, and divine, but useless; *viz.,* because it is not human goods they seek."

If "wisdom" connotes the highest form of knowledge, then the name, according to Aristotle, is more properly applied to speculative than to practical wisdom. The highest form of knowledge, in his view, is concerned with the highest objects. Hence, he says, "it would be strange to think that . . . practical wisdom is the best knowledge, since man is not the best thing in the world . . . But if the argument be that man is the best of the animals, this makes no difference; for there are other things much more divine in their nature than man," and wisdom is knowledge "of the things that are highest by nature."

When Hobbes distinguishes between prudence and sapience, he does not assign a special object to wisdom. "As much experience is *prudence*," he writes, "so is much science *sapience*." It is the amount of science a man possesses, not his possession of a particular kind of knowledge, which makes him wise. Descartes seems to take a similar view when he says that "the sciences taken all together are identical with human wisdom." But for Aristotle and Aquinas, philosophical wisdom can be differentiated from the other spec, lative virtues, such as the understanding of first principles or the scientific knowledge of the conclusions which can be demonstrated from them. It involves them, but it is distinct from them insofar as it uses principles to demonstrate conclusions concerning the highest causes. Wisdom can be called a science if it is understood that by reason of its object it stands at the apex of the sciences, crowning and perfecting them.

In the opening pages of his *Metaphysics*, Aristotle identifies wisdom with the supreme philosophical science—the science which investigates first principles and causes. He calls it a "divine science" or "theology," for, as he says, "God is thought to be among the causes of all things and to be a first principle." It is not the most useful science, but the most "desirable on its own account and for the sake of knowing . . . It alone exists for its own sake . . . All the sciences, indeed, are more necessary than this, but none is better."

While adopting Aristotle's conception of wisdom, Aquinas finds it most eminently represented among the sciences, not by metaphysics or the theology of the philosophers, but by sacred doctrine or the theology based on revelation. "Since it is the part of a wise man to order and to judge," he writes, "and since lesser matters can be judged in the light of some higher cause . . . therefore, he who considers absolutely the highest cause of the whole universe, namely God, is most of all called wise . . . But sacred doctrine essentially treats of God viewed as the highest cause, for it treats of Him not only so far as He can be known through creatures just as the philosophers know Him . . . but also so far as He is known to Himself alone and revealed to others. Hence," Aquinas concludes, "sacred doctrine is especially called wisdom."

THE CONTRAST BETWEEN THE wisdom of the philosopher and the wisdom of the theologian is more fully discussed in the chapters on METAPHYSICS and THEOLOGY. But we are concerned here with the further implications of the difference between natural and supernatural wisdom, or the wisdom of man and of God.

The Greeks insistently raise the question whether man can have wisdom. In the *Apology*, Socrates tells his accusers that his "cross-examination of the pretenders to wisdom" was a duty imposed upon him by the oracle which declared that there was no man wiser than himself. To understand the oracle's meaning, he tried to seek out wisdom in other men but, he says at his trial, "I found that the men most in repute were all but the most foolish." This gave him an insight into the kind of wisdom which he himself possessed.

"My hearers always imagine," Socrates declares, "that I myself possess the wisdom which I find wanting in others; but the truth is, O men of Athens, that God only is wise; and by his answer he intends to show that the wisdom of men is worth little or nothing; he is not speaking of Socrates, he is only using my name by way of illustration, as if he said, He, O men, is the wisest, who, like Socrates, knows that his wisdom is in truth worth nothing." Again in the *Phaedrus*, Socrates refuses to call any man wise, "for that is a great name which belongs to God alone." For men, "lovers of wisdom or philosophers is the modest and befitting title."

Aristotle also says of the science which most deserves the name of wisdom, because it is a science of divine things, that "such a science either God alone can have, or God above all others." He does not think that the divine power can be jealous, but if there were any truth in what the poets say about the jealousy of the gods, "it would probably occur in this case above all, and all who excelled in this knowledge would be unfortunate." To whatever extent the possession of wisdom "might be justly regarded as beyond human power," it would be unfitting, in Aristotle's opinion, "for man not to be content to seek the knowledge that is suited to him."

This is even more typically a Christian than a

pagan sentiment. "Christians have a particular knowledge," writes Montaigne, "of the extent to which curiosity is a natural and original evil in man. The urge to increase in wisdom and knowledge was the first downfall of the human race; it was the way by which man hurled himself into eternal damnation." In *Paradise Lost,* as he is about to leave the Garden of Eden, Adam says to the angel Michael:

Greatly instructed I shall hence depart.
Greatly in peace of thought, and have my fill
Of knowledge, what this vessel can containe;
Beyond which was my folly to aspire.

To which the angel replies:

This having learnt, thou hast attained the summe
Of wisdom . . .

But Sacred Scripture does more than enjoin man to humble himself before the chasm between human wisdom at its best and the infinite wisdom of God. It does more than say in the words of Jeremiah: "Let not the wise man glory in his wisdom," for it also says that "fools despise wisdom." In the Epistle of James we find true wisdom set apart from false. If the knowledge of the wise man is not accompanied by the "meekness of wisdom," if instead there is "bitter envying and strife in your hearts," then "this wisdom descendeth not from above, but is earthly, sensual, devilish . . . But the wisdom that is from above is first pure, then peaceable, gentle, and easy to be intreated, full of mercy and good fruits, without partiality, and without hypocrisy."

Saint Paul asks: "Hath not God made foolish the wisdom of this world? When

. . . the world by wisdom knew not God, it pleased God by the foolishness of preaching to save them that believe.
For the Jews require a sign, and the Greeks seek after wisdom:
But we preach Christ crucified, unto the Jews a stumbling block, and unto the Greeks foolishness;
But unto them which are called both Jews and Greeks, Christ the power of God, and the wisdom of God.
Because the foolishness of God is wiser than men; and the weakness of God is stronger than men.

"My speech and my preaching," Saint Paul continues to the Corinthians,

. . . was not with enticing words of man's wisdom, but in demonstration of the Spirit and of power:

That your faith should not stand in the wisdom of men, but in the power of God.
Howbeit we speak wisdom among them that are perfect; yet not the wisdom of this world, nor of the princes of this world, that come to nought:
But we speak the wisdom of God in a mystery, even the hidden mystery, which God ordained before the world unto our glory.

Wonder is the beginning of the kind of natural wisdom which a philosopher like Aristotle regards as the ultimate goal of human inquiry. But the supernatural wisdom of which Scripture speaks begins with the fear of God and comes to man not through his efforts at learning, but only as a divine gift. "If any of you lack wisdom," Saint James declares, "let him ask God, that giveth to all men liberally and upbraideth not; and it shall be given him." It is wrong for a man to take pride in his own learning but, according to Pascal, "the proper place for pride is in wisdom, for it cannot be granted to a man that he has made himself wise . . . God alone gives wisdom, and that is why *Qui gloriatur, in Domino glorietur.*"

The theologians dwell at length on the text of the Psalmist that "the fear of the Lord is the beginning of wisdom." Enumerating seven steps to wisdom, Augustine writes: "First of all, it is necessary that we should be led by the *fear of God* to seek the knowledge of His will, what He commands us to desire and what to avoid. Now this fear will of necessity excite in us the thought of our mortality and of the death that is before us, and crucify all the motions of pride as if our flesh were nailed to the tree." Then in succession come the steps of piety, knowledge, resolution, counsel, purification of heart; and, finally, the "holy man will be so single and so pure in heart that he will not step aside from the truth, either for the sake of pleasing men or with a view to avoid any of the annoyances which beset this life. Such a man ascends to *wisdom,* which is the seventh and the last step, and which he enjoys in peace and tranquility."

Only the wisdom which begins with faith, according to Aquinas, also begins with fear. "A thing may be called the beginning of wisdom in two ways," he explains; "in one way, because it is the beginning of wisdom itself as to its essence; in another way, as to its effect.

Thus the beginning of an art as to its essence consists in the principles from which that art proceeds, while the beginning of an art as to its effect is that wherefrom it begins to operate." Aquinas then points out that wisdom is considered by theologians "in one way, and in another way by philosophers." As the wisdom of the philosophers does not begin with articles of faith but with axioms of reason, so it does not begin with fear but with wonder.

The wisdom of the philosophers and the wisdom of the religious both consist in knowledge of divine things, but "wisdom, as we look at it," Aquinas writes, "is considered not only as being cognizant of God, as it is with the philosophers, but also as directing human conduct, since this is directed not only by the human law, but by the divine law . . . Accordingly the beginning of wisdom as to its essence consists in the first principles of wisdom, *i.e.,* the articles of faith, and in this sense faith is said to be the beginning of wisdom. But as regards the effect, the beginning of wisdom is the point where wisdom begins to work, and in this way fear is the beginning of wisdom, yet servile fear in one way and filial fear in another."

"For servile fear," Aquinas explains, "is like a principle disposing a man to wisdom from without, in so far as he refrains from sin through fear of punishment, and is thus fashioned for the effect of wisdom . . . On the other hand, chaste or filial fear is the beginning of wisdom, as being the first effect of wisdom. For since the regulation of human conduct by the divine law belongs to wisdom, in order to make a beginning, man must first of all fear God and submit himself to Him."

The special character of wisdom which we noted earlier—that it is at once speculative and practical knowledge, that it is concerned both with the ultimate nature of things and the ultimate good for man—seems to be strikingly exemplified in what the theologian calls "the gift of wisdom." Wisdom as Plato conceives it may have this double character, but for Aristotle, as we have seen, wisdom, as opposed to prudence, is purely speculative. It remains speculative even when it deals with the end which is the good of each thing "and

in general with the supreme good in the whole of nature." It considers the end or the good, as Aristotle indicates, only under the aspect of investigating "the first principles and causes; for the good, *i.e.,* the end, is one of the causes." It does not thereby direct man to his own end, or lay down the rules of a good life.

The supernatural gift of wisdom, Aquinas tells us, "is not merely speculative but also practical . . . It belongs to wisdom as a gift, not only to contemplate divine things, but also to regulate human acts." Such infused wisdom not only extends "to the hidden mysteries of divine things," which are beyond the greatest wisdom man can acquire by his natural efforts, but this wisdom also directs man's actions to "the sovereign good which is the last end, by knowing which man is said to be truly wise."

CHRISTIAN THEOLOGIANS LIKE Augustine and Aquinas do not hold the wisdom of the philosophers in contempt because they fail to penetrate the divine mysteries, or to guide man to his salvation. Augustine finds in Plato's teaching a marvelous foreshadowing of Christian wisdom. "It is evident that none come nearer to us than the Platonists," he says, when he attributes to Plato the conception of "the wise man as one who imitates, knows, loves this God, and who is rendered blessed through fellowship with Him in His own blessedness." Though Aquinas holds that "wisdom as a gift is more excellent than wisdom as an intellectual virtue, since it attains to God more intimately by a kind of union of the soul with Him," he certainly regards Aristotle as the epitome of natural wisdom when he refers to him as *the* philosopher."

The admonition of Saint Paul, "to beware lest any man spoil you through philosophy and vain deceit, after the tradition of men, after the rudiments of the world," does not seem to be interpreted by Augustine and Aquinas to mean, as Montaigne later suggests, that "the plague of man is the opinion of knowledge. That is why ignorance is so recommended by our religion." But the theologians do condemn the counterfeits of wisdom to which men are susceptible. These are false wisdoms; the wisdom of the philosophers is not false, but imperfect.

We find three types of false worldly wisdom listed by Aquinas. If a man "fixes his end in external earthly things," he writes, "his wisdom is called *earthly;* if in the goods of the body, it is called *sensual* wisdom; if in some excellence, it is called *devilish* wisdom, because it imitates the devil's pride." These worldly wisdoms constitute for him the sin of folly. "It is the wisdom of the world," Aquinas says, "which deceives and makes us foolish in God's sight . . . Though no man wishes to be a fool," he adds, "yet he wishes those things of which folly is a consequence, *viz.* to withdraw his sense from spiritual things and to plunge it into earthly things." The essence of such folly, according to the Psalmist, lies in denial: "The fool hath said in his heart, There is no God."

But there is another meaning of folly, in which it is neither a sin nor the opposite of wisdom. "If any man among you seem to be wise in this world," Saint Paul declares, "let him become a fool, that he may be wise." Commenting on this text, Aquinas explains that "just as there is an evil wisdom called *worldly wisdom* . . . so too there is a good folly opposed to this evil wisdom, whereby man despises worldly things." If there is wisdom in such folly, so also, according to Aquinas, there can be wisdom in those whom the world regards as natural fools or innocents. If they have grace, he writes, "baptized idiots, like little children, have the habit of wisdom, which is a gift of the Holy Ghost, but they have not the act, on account of the bodily impediment which hinders the use of reason in them."

Throughout the tradition of the great books those who praise folly do not take exception to the Psalmist's remark that only "fools despise wisdom." Rather they find wisdom in the appearances of folly, and use the wisdom of fools to expose the folly of those who pretend to be wise. "The wise have more to learn from the fools than the fools from the wise," writes Montaigne, quoting Cato the Elder; and in a similar vein, Touchstone, the clown in *As You Like It,* complains: "The more pity that fools may not speak wisely what wise men do foolishly." To which Celia replies: "By my troth,

thou sayest true; for, since the little wit that fools have was silenced, the little foolery that wise men have makes a great show." And later, after a conversation with Touchstone about the passing of time, Jaques observes: "When I did hear the motley fool thus moral on the time, my lungs began to crow like chanticleer that fools should be so deep contemplative."

Erasmus, quoting scripture, Cicero, the Stoics, and others, declares that only God is wise and that all men are fools. He even goes so far as to say that Christ, "though he is the wisdom of the Father, was made something of a fool himself in order to help the folly of mankind, when he assumed the nature of man."

Nevertheless, the jesters and clowns in Shakespeare's comedies have a kind of wisdom. In *Twelfth Night,* the clown who banters with Viola denies that he is the Lady Olivia's fool, but says he is simply "her corrupter of words." The trouble, he explains, is not that he lacks reason, but that "words are grown so false that I am loath to prove reason with them"; and he ends by telling Viola: "Foolery, sir, does walk about the orb like the sun; it shines everywhere. I would be sorry, sir, but the fool should be as oft with your master as with my mistress. I think I saw your wisdom there."

Pantagruel persuades Panurge to take counsel of a fool. "The wise may be instructed by a fool," he says. "You know how by the advice and counsel and prediction of fools, many kings, princes, states, and commonwealths have been preserved, battles gained, and diverse doubts of a most perplexed intricacy resolved." As he who "is called a worldly wise man," Pantagruel goes on to remark, may "in the second judgment of the intelligences which are above . . . be esteemed a fool," so he may be thought a sage who lays "quite aside those cares which are conducible to his body or his fortunes . . . All which neglects of sublunary things are vulgarly imputed folly."

To the same general effect are Pierre's reflections in *War and Peace* on the period of his blissful insanity after the burning of Moscow. When he recalls the views he formed of men and circumstances at the time of his madness, he always finds them correct. "I may have appeared strange and queer then," he says to himself, "but I was not so mad as I seemed. On the contrary, I was wiser and had more insight than at any other time, and understood all that is worth understanding in life, because . . . because I was happy."

FOLLY IS NOT ALWAYS PRAISED in paradox, nor is it seriously condemned only by the Christian theologian who equates it with denying or turning away from God. "Delusion is the elder daughter of Zeus," says Agamemnon in *The Iliad*, "the accursed who deludes all; her feet are delicate and they step not on the firm earth, but she walks the air above men's heads and leads them astray . . . Yes, for once Zeus even was deluded." Agamemnon concludes the story of Zeus's befuddlement by relating how in his rage Zeus "caught by the shining hair of her head the goddess Delusion in the anger of his heart, and swore a strong oath, that never after this might Delusion, who deludes all, come back to Olympos and the starry sky. So speaking, he whirled her about in his hand and slung her out of the starry heaven, and presently she came to men's establishments."

On the earthly plane, folly takes many forms, of which, in Montaigne's judgment, the most exasperating are dullness of wit, the boldness of stupidity, and contentiousness in argument. "Obstinacy of opinion and heat in argument are the surest proofs of folly," he observes. "Is there anything so assured, resolute, disdainful, contemplative, serious, and grave as the ass?"

Whatever the forms or aspects of folly, and however the wisdom it implies or opposes be conceived, one thing is clear throughout the tradition of western thought. No one who can separate true wisdom from folly in disguise places anything but the highest value on it in the order of human goods.

The final utterance of the Chorus in *Antigone*, that "our happiness depends on wisdom"; the Aristotelian doctrine that "the ac-

tivity of philosophic wisdom is admittedly the pleasantest of virtuous activities" and "all the other attributes ascribed to the supremely happy man are evidently those connected with this activity"; the statement by Plato in his *The Seventh Letter*, in which he demands that his myth of the philosopher-king be taken seriously, for "the human race will not see better days until either the stock of those who rightly and genuinely follow philosophy acquire political authority, or else the class who have political control be led by some dispensation of providence to become real philosophers"— all these express the tribute which pagan antiquity pays to wisdom in human life and society.

To the Christian—theologian, mystic, or poet—it is in heaven with the saints who dwell in God's presence that wisdom, like love, reigns supreme. Nor are these two unconnected. As charity is the perfection of the will, so wisdom is the perfection of the intellect. In *The Divine Comedy*, Aquinas explains to Dante when they meet in Paradise how lack of wisdom's order in the mind goes hand in hand with love's disorder. "He is right low down among the fools," the spirit says, "who affirms or denies without distinguishing; because it happens that oftentimes hasty opinion inclines to the wrong side, and then fondness for it binds the intellect."

With the accent on earth rather than on heaven, with reliance upon reason rather than upon faith, Spinoza voices a comparable insight that to have wisdom is to love wisely, for to know wisely is to love God. "It is therefore most profitable to us in this life," he writes, "to make perfect the intellect or reason as far as possible, and in this one thing consists the highest happiness or blessedness of man; for blessedness is nothing but the peace of mind which springs from the intuitive knowledge of God." Not only does "the highest possible peace of mind" arise from this kind of knowledge but, he adds, from it also "necessarily springs the intellectual love of God."

102

World

INTRODUCTION

"HE who does not know what the world is," writes Marcus Aurelius, "does not know where he is. And he who does not know for what purpose the world exists, does not know who he is, nor what the world is." According to the Stoic emperor, for whom "there is one universe made up of all things, and one God who pervades all things," man has only to exercise the divine spark of reason in himself in order to be at home in a world which reason rules.

He does not hesitate long before the dilemma that "it is either a well-arranged universe or a chaos huddled together." In the belief that it is through and through an orderly world—a cosmos rather than a chaos, governed by providence rather than by chance—Aurelius is willing to assume whatever place destiny allots him in the universal scheme. "Everything harmonizes with me," he says, "which is harmonious to thee, O Universe."

With a Christian's faith in God's plan and providence, Montaigne is also willing to conceive the universe as the stage on which man acts his destined part. But suppose, Montaigne adds, that we consider "man alone, without outside assistance, armed solely with his own weapons, and deprived of divine grace and knowledge, which is his whole honor, his strength, and the foundation of his being." How then does the world appear? Is it, in all its vastness, the human habitat—the home of man, its lord and master?

Man deceives himself, Montaigne thinks, if he pictures the world thus, in terms of his own reason and knowledge. What could lead him to believe, he asks, that the "admirable motion of the celestial vault, the eternal light of those torches rolling so proudly above his head, the fearful movements of that infinite sea, were established and have lasted so many centuries for his convenience and his service? Is it possible to imagine anything so ridiculous as that this miserable and puny creature, who is not even master of himself . . . should call himself master and emperor of the universe, the least part of which it is not in his power to know, much less to command?"

If, as Montaigne thinks he should, man "feels and sees himself lodged here, amid the mire and dung of the world, nailed and riveted to the worst, the deadest, and the most stagnant part of the universe, on the lowest story of the house and the farthest from the vault of heaven," how absurd for him to imagine himself "above the circle of the moon, and bringing the sky down beneath his feet." Except "by the vanity of this same imagination" by which "he equals himself to God," how can he regard himself as occupying an exalted position in the universe?

Deprived of the religious faith that he is made in God's image and that all the rest of the visible universe is made for him, only presumption or conceit can save man from being dwarfed by the world. But science robs man of such conceit, according to Freud. The cosmology that "is associated in our minds with the name of Copernicus" displaces man and shrinks him. Humanity cannot hold on to "its naive self-love," Freud writes, when it realizes that the earth is "not the center of the universe, but only a tiny speck in a world-system of a magnitude hardly conceivable."

NOT ONLY IN THE reflections of Marcus Aurelius, Montaigne, and Freud, but throughout the tradition of the great books, the conception of the world or universe is inseparable from the ideas of God and man. These three ideas always interpenetrate each other, though the resulting pattern of thought varies according to the direction in which thought moves from any one of the three to the other two.

Sometimes the whole universe lies on one side of the infinite distance between the Creator and His creation, and man has a special place of honor in the hierarchy of beings which constitutes the order of the created world. Though man is greater than the earth he treads or the skies he watches, the whole world is less than God, Who has made it out of nothing and Who, in the freedom of His act of creation, is unaffected by the world's coming to be or passing away. On this view, taken by Christian theologians, God is not part of the world, the world is not part of God, nor is there any whole which embraces both; and if "world" means the physical totality, then man belongs both to this world and to another—the realm of spiritual creatures which is also part of the created universe.

Sometimes "world" means the all-embracing universe, uncreated and coeternal with the divinity which dwells in it, a thing of soul as well as body, including mind as well as matter. Whether God is the prime mover of the universe; the transcendent One from which emanates in all degrees of being the multiplicity of intelligible and sensible things; the infinite substance which exceeds the sum of all the finite things that exist only as its modifications; or the Absolute Spirit which manifests itself historically in both physical and psychical nature—on any of these views cosmology merges with theology, as in the theories of Aristotle, Plotinus, Spinoza, and Hegel. For Spinoza and Hegel, as for the Stoics, to know the world is to know God. Its order or structure is more than divinely instituted. It is the indwelling divinity itself.

Such views of the world tend, for the most part, to look upon the individual man as a microcosm mirroring the macrocosm. The world's body and soul, its matter and mind, are there to be seen in miniature. Considering the philosophers who assert that "mind is the king of heaven and earth," Socrates suggests in the *Philebus* that "in reality they are magnifying themselves." Nevertheless, the doctrine of a world soul animating the body of the universe is repeatedly proposed in the dialogues of Plato as a way of understanding man; and that mad or at least cryptic Platonist, Captain Ahab, gazing on the gold doubloon he has nailed to the mast as a reward for sighting Moby Dick, observes in soliloquy that "this round gold is but the image of the rounder globe, which, like a magician's glass, to each and every man in turn but mirrors back his own mysterious self."

A third alternative remains. Sometimes, as with Lucretius and later philosophers of a materialist cast, the world is all there is, and all there is of it can be reduced to atoms and the void. It is thrown together by blind chance rather than designed by a presiding intelligence. The universe obeys no laws except the laws of its own matter in motion. "Nature has no tyrants over her," writes Lucretius, "But always acts of her own will; she has / No part of any godhead whatsoever." For their own happiness, Lucretius exiles his papier-mâché gods to the interspaces where they "lead lives supremely free of care." But man is not so fortunate.

In a world that is not made for him, and in which, godless, he must be entirely self-reliant, man is burdened with heavy cares. Since he is one of nature's progeny, he may not be wholly alien in this world of material forces; but neither is he, like a beloved son, assured of nature's hospitality. The dominant note here is that of man *against* the world; and in this unequal struggle science alone gives him the sense—or perhaps the illusion—that at least in his little corner of the world his mind may dominate. Yet from time to time defeat reminds him that the world remains unruly. Bridle its matter and harness its energies as he will, he holds no checkrein to prevent his being overthrown.

AS THE CHAPTER ON NATURE indicates, the word "nature" in one of its meanings seems to be synonymous with "world." This fact, as well as the various ways in which "world" has been used in the foregoing discussion, requires us to note a certain ambiguity. When we speak of the world, our meaning may range from the earth or globe which man inhabits to the solar system in which our planet revolves and beyond that to the whole physical universe, however far-flung. We also use "world" to signify an entire realm of things which is distinctively set apart from another order of existence, as when we speak of material and spiritual worlds, or when we refer to the world of thought or the world of sense. Such phrases as "world government" and "world peace" use "world" in a political sense which evokes the image of the whole order of human society upon this globe.

We shall restrict ourselves in this chapter to that sense of "world" in which it signifies the object of cosmological speculations and controversies. We are concerned with the idea of the universe or cosmos. As we have already observed, the universe may be quite differently conceived according to the way in which it is related to God, but it is almost always conceived as that totality in which man and his earth and solar system exist, and outside of which nothing can exist except God. According to the theologians, the angelic hierarchies are no exception, for they fall within the created universe. But philosophers like Plato and Plotinus, who identify the world with the physical universe, set apart from it the eternal ideas or the order of the pure intelligences.

The traditional issues concerning the world or universe, so understood, can be summarized by three basic questions: Are there many worlds or is there only one? What is the structure of the world? Does the world have a beginning and does it have an end?

The first of these questions seems to violate the meaning of "world" as *the* universe—the complete totality of things. How can there be more than one *all*? But that difficulty, as we shall see, may be avoided by the hypothesis of a plurality of worlds succeeding one another in infinite time. It may even be met by the supposition that the infinity of space permits the possibility of two or more coexistent but unrelated worlds. Considerations of the time and space of the world, amplified in the chapters on SPACE and TIME, have a bearing on this issue of one or many worlds.

The second question presupposes agreement that the world has a structure, for if it does not, no problem arises concerning what that structure is. Such agreement is present in the tradition, and is unaffected by the dispute over the role of chance or design in the world's production, and by the controversy concerning the world's creation. As Harvey points out, the Greek word "cosmos" connotes order and beauty. Its opposite is chaos.

Writers may disagree about an original chaos prior to the formation of the cosmos. Plato, for example, refers to a time when the elements "were all without reason and measure"—"before they were arranged so as to form a universe." Milton also writes of a time when "yet this world was not, and *Chaos* wilde reign'd where these Heav'ns now rowl." In the "dark illimitable Ocean with out bound"—before "Heav'ns and Earth rose out of *Chaos*"— "eldest Night and *Chaos,* Ancestors of Nature, held eternal *Anarchie*." In contrast, Aristotle maintains that "chaos or Night did not exist for an infinite time" prior to the world, and he argues against "the theologians who generate the world from Night."

But these differences of opinion leave the main point unaffected. The world is a cosmos, not a chaos. The universe has some order. Even those who doubt the perfection of its order, or who point out how it is marred by evil and irrationality, affirm an order or structure, according to which the universe hangs together and is in some degree intelligible to man. The disputed question of the world's structure, therefore, centers on what the structure is. What precisely is the principle or pattern of cosmic coherence? By what image or analogy shall man try to hold the world before his mind as if it were a single intelligible object?

This problem, as well as the issue concerning one or many worlds, cannot be completely discussed apart from the last of the three questions—the question of the world's beginning and end. For example, if world follows world in succession, each must have a beginning and an end. So, too, the world's structure takes on a different aspect for those who affirm and those who deny its creation by a divine intelligence; and according to at least one view of the order in the universe, men are persuaded that it must be made or ruled by reason, and argue against its being the result of chance.

But the question of the world's beginning must not be confused with the issue of creation, or the problem of the world's relation to God. Aquinas may agree with Berkeley's criticism of "the ancient philosophers who maintained the being of a God," while holding "Matter to be uncreated and co-eternal with Him"; but he does not wholly agree with Hobbes that "to say the world was not created, but eternal, seeing that which is eternal has no cause, is to deny there is a God." For Aquinas, to deny creation is to deny God, but whether the created world ever began to be is a question for faith, not reason. Nor does the denial of creation necessarily imply the eternity of the world—at least not in the sense in which Lucretius imagines the world to have both a beginning and an end.

Two great exponents of atomism in the tradition of the great books—Lucretius and Newton—show us that agreement on some of the basic questions of cosmology does not preclude disagreement on others. Both conceive the world as built of indestructible atomic particles. They conceive its structure to be determined by the motions of its parts, both large and small, through the forces exerted by body upon body. Both, furthermore, favor the hypothesis of a plurality of worlds, but only Lucretius holds that this world had a chance beginning and will come to a similar end.

When Lucretius refers to the infinite universe, which, "unmeasurable in deep wide boundlessness . . . is limitless," he does not mean this world in which man now lives. He means the void in which our world as well as other worlds are formed out of the infinite number of atoms which, combining and separating, cause the birth and death of worlds. "The universe," he writes,

Is infinitely wide; its vastness holds
Innumerable seeds, beyond all count,
Beyond all possibility of number,

Flying along their everlasting ways.
So it must be unthinkable that our sky
And our round world are precious and unique
While all those other motes of matter flit
In idleness, achieve, accomplish nothing.

The existence of worlds other than this seems probable to him, not only because of the infinity of the universe in respect to its space and matter, but also because the atoms form each world "quite by chance, / Quite casually and quite intentionless." As chance produced this world, so it can produce others. Hence, Lucretius argues, "There are, elsewhere, other assemblages / Of matter, making other worlds . . .

Let's admit—
We really have to—there are other worlds,
More than one race of men, and many kinds
Of animal generations.

Furthermore,
Adding up all the sum, you'll never find
One single thing completely different
From all the rest, alone, apart, unique.

On this principle, he thinks "you must admit that earth, sun, moon, / Ocean, and all the rest, are not unique, / But beyond reckoning or estimate."

By calling the atoms eternal bodies and first-beginnings, Lucretius indicates that it is each particular world, not the universe of matter and the void, which has a beginning and an end. The atoms or first-beginnings were not arranged, he explains, by "a conscious pact, a treaty with each other . . .

More likely, being so many, in many ways
Harassed and driven through the universe
From an infinity of time, by trying
All kinds of motion, every combination,
They came at last into such disposition
As now establishes the sum of things.

Thus a world is born, and so even does it grow by the addition of bodies from without. But as a world is born and grows, it also decays and dies. "There is always diminution, ebb, retreat," Lucretius writes, "But for a while our gain exceeds our loss / Until we reach that highest point of ripeness. / From there we go, a little at a time, / Downhill; age breaks our oak, dissolves our strength," until finally, "In just this way the ramparts of the world . . . will some day face assault, / Be stormed, collapse in ruin and in dust."

According to Newton, the atoms are indestructible but not eternal bodies. Upon their indestructibility or permanence depends the uniform and enduring texture of nature in all ages. "That Nature may be lasting," Newton says, "the changes of corporeal things are to be placed only in the various separations and new associations and motions of these permanent particles." But for Newton the indivisibility of the ultimate particles of matter does not preclude their being created. "It seems probable to me," he writes, "that God in the beginning formed matter in solid, massy, hard, impenetrable movable particles, of such size and figures, and with such other properties . . . as most conduced to the end for which he formed them."

Not through the chance colligation of atoms, but through their being "variously associated in the first creation by the counsel of an intelligent agent," is the world formed. "For it became him who created them to set them in order. And if he did so," Newton adds, "it's unphilosophical to seek for any other origin of the world, or to pretend that it might arise out of a chaos by the mere laws of nature; though being once formed, it may continue by those laws through many ages."

Newton differs from Lucretius in these particulars, but shares his view of the probability of many worlds. "Since space is divisible *in infinitum,* and matter is not necessarily in all places, it may also be allowed," Newton declares, "that God is able to create particles of matter of several sizes and figures, and in several proportions to space . . . and thereby to vary the laws of nature, and make worlds of several sorts in several parts of the universe. At least," he continues, "I see nothing of contradiction in all this."

OTHER WRITERS SEEM TO FIND a plurality of worlds repugnant to reason, if not flatly contradictory. Plato, for example, appears to think that the possibility of other worlds is inconsistent with the perfection of this one—certainly if this world is made in the image of the eternal ideas. Because "the original of the universe contains in itself all intelligible beings," Plato's Timaeus argues that there cannot be many worlds, but "one only, if the created copy is to accord with the original." It belongs to the world's perfection to be solitary, and for this reason, Timaeus explains, "the creator made not two worlds or an infinite number of them; but there is and ever will be one only-begotten and created heaven."

Aristotle reasons differently to the conclusion that "there cannot be more worlds than one." The conclusion follows in his view from the impossibility of an infinity of body or matter, and with it an infinity of space. "The universe is certainly a particular and a material thing," he writes. "If it is composed not of a part but of the whole of matter, then though the being of 'universe' and of 'this universe' are still distinct, yet there is no other universe, and no possibility of others being made, because all the matter is already included in this." He thinks it a tenable hypothesis that "the world as a whole includes *all* its appropriate matter"; hence, he concludes, "neither are there now, nor have there ever been, nor can there ever be formed, more heavens than one, but this heaven of ours is one and unique and complete."

On theological grounds, Augustine challenges those who suppose "either that this is not the only world, but that there are numberless worlds, or that indeed it is the only one, but that it dies, and is born again at fixed intervals, and this times without number." On theological grounds also, though with a different conception of God and the universe, Spinoza maintains that "besides God no substance can be or be conceived"; that "God is one, which is to say, in nature there is but one substance, and it is absolutely infinite"; that all finite things have their existence in the one infinite substance of God; and that God is "not only the cause of the commencement of their existence, but also of their continuance in existence." Because God's liberty consists, in Spinoza's conception, in acting according to the necessity of His own nature, not in freedom of will, he insists that "things could be produced by God in no other way and in no other order than that in which they have been produced." This is not merely the only actual but the only possible world.

Aquinas agrees that there is only one actual world. "The very order of things created by God," he writes, "shows the unity of the world." Since "whatever things come from God have relations of order to each other and to God himself . . . it is necessary that all things should belong to one world. Therefore," Aquinas continues, "only those were able to assert the existence of many worlds who do not acknowledge any ordaining wisdom, but rather believed in chance; as did Democritus, who said that this world, besides an infinite number of other worlds, was made by a coming together of atoms."

Aquinas places God's liberty in freedom of choice, and so he contemplates the possibility of other worlds than this. This is the only world God actually created, but since, in creating, "God does not act from natural necessity," and since, in the act of creation, the divine will "is not naturally and from any necessity determined to these creatures," Aquinas concludes that "in no way is the present scheme of things produced by God with such necessity that other things could not come to be."

As the chapter on WILL indicates, Spinoza holds that God does not have the power of free choice. He therefore argues that the actual world, being the only possible one, cannot be bettered. All things, he writes, have been "produced by God in the highest degree of perfection, since they have necessarily followed from the existence of a most perfect nature." Aquinas, on the other hand, denies that this is the best of all possible worlds. "Given the things which actually exist," he says, "the universe cannot be better, for the order which God has established in things, and in which the good of the universe consists, most befits things . . . Yet God could make other things, or add something to the present creation; and then there would be another and a better universe."

OTHER SPECULATIONS CONCERNING the cosmos seem to divide into three sorts, according as they consider the matter and space, the size and shape, of the universe; or they try to discover the principle by which all things are ordered together in one world; or they examine whatever order is found, and judge its perfection, its goodness, and its beauty.

The first of these three types of cosmological theory belongs primarily to the physicist and the astronomer. From Aristotle to Einstein, observation, mathematical calculation, and imaginative hypotheses have propounded the alternatives of a finite or infinite universe or, as Einstein prefers to put it, of a "finite yet unbounded universe," as opposed to one which is either simply finite or both infinite and unbounded. Einstein also points out that spherical surface beings, such as the inhabitants of this planet, "have no means of determining whether they are living in a finite or in an infinite universe, because the 'piece of universe' to which they have access is in both cases practically plane, or Euclidean."

Archimedes in *The Sand-Reckoner* undertakes to show that the number of the grains of sand in a universe whose outer space extends to the distance of the fixed stars, is, however large, a finite rather than an infinite number. Lucretius and Newton, as we have seen, embrace the opposite hypothesis, while Aristotle defends the proposition that the universe is finite, bounded, and spherical in shape. Among the great astronomers, Copernicus and Kepler, no less than Ptolemy, conceive the world as bounded by an outer sphere. Copernicus opens his treatise by remarking that "the world is like a globe; whether because this form is the most perfect of all . . . or because it is the figure having the greatest volume . . . or because the separate parts of the world, *i.e.,* the sun, moon, and stars, are seen under such a form; or because all things seek to be delimited by such a form, as is apparent in the case of drops of water and other liquid bodies, when they become delimited through themselves."

A spherical or (if matter is not distributed uniformly) an elliptical or quasi-spherical universe, "will be necessarily finite," according to Einstein, but it will also "have no bounds." Among the conceivable "closed spaces without limits," Einstein points out that "the spherical space (and the elliptical) excels in its simplicity, since all points on it are equivalent." But "whether the universe in which we live is infinite, or whether it is finite in the manner of the spherical universe," he thinks is a question that "our experience is far from being sufficient to enable us to answer." Recent astronomical observations of the velocity of the receding nebulas have suggested the hypothesis of an infinitely expanding universe.

These cosmological theories are more fully discussed in the chapter on SPACE. Another point of physical speculation concerning the uniformity of the world's matter—not the uniformity of its distribution, but the sameness or difference in kind of terrestrial matter and the matter of the heavenly bodies—is considered in the chapters on ASTRONOMY AND COSMOLOGY and MATTER. We turn, therefore, to the question of the world's structure, apart from its size, its shape, and the disposition of its matter.

THREE METAPHORS SEEM to express the great traditional images of the world's structure. The world is a living organism. *It is like an animal* with a soul, even a soul endowed with reason. The world is a multitude of diverse and unequal individual things, forming a hierarchy and associated, according to their natures and functions, for the common good of the whole. This view was first proposed by Plato. *It is like a society,* a society under divine law and government. The conception of the world as a divinely instituted and governed society seems to be a product of Jewish and Christian faith. Though that expression of it, which includes a hierarchical ordering of all things from the elemental bodies to the angels, belongs to Christian theologians and poets, there may be a pre-Christian version in the Stoic theory of the world as governed by a divine intelligence. *It is like a machine,* a system of interdependent moving parts, linked together from the least to the greatest in an unbroken chain of causation. This may be the earliest of the three theories, if the atomistic cosmology of Democritus, which Lucretius later expounds, can be interpreted as adopting the mechanical analogy. Full-fledged mechanism may, however, be thought to await 17th-century developments in the science of

mechanics, when, for Descartes, Newton, and others, the laws of mechanics become the only laws of nature.

According to Plato, in the *Timaeus,* "God desired all things to be good and nothing bad," and he "found that no unintelligent creature taken as a whole was fairer than the intelligent taken as a whole; and that intelligence could not be present in anything which was devoid of soul. For which reason," Timaeus explains, "when he was framing the universe, he put intelligence in soul, and soul in body . . . Wherefore, using the language of probability, we may say that the world became a living creature truly endowed with soul and intelligence by the providence of God." Since his intention was that "the animal should be as far as possible a perfect whole and of perfect parts," he gave it self-sufficiency, a spherical body—which figure "comprehends within itself all other figures"—and circular movement. The universe did not require, therefore, sense organs or hands or feet.

"Such was the whole plan of the eternal God about the god that was to be, to whom for this reason he gave a body, smooth and even, having a surface in every direction equidistant from the center . . . And in the center," according to Timaeus, "he put the soul, which he diffused throughout the body, making it also to be the exterior environment of it; and he made the universe a circle moving in a circle . . . Having these purposes in view he created the world a blessed god."

The theory of a world soul and of an animated, organic universe appears not only in the *Timaeus,* but also in other Platonic dialogues. In the *Phaedrus,* for example, Socrates says that "the soul in her totality has the care of inanimate being everywhere"; and in the *Laws,* the Athenian Stranger, asking whether "it is the soul which controls heaven and earth, and the whole world," replies that "the best soul takes care of the world and guides it along the good path."

In somewhat different form, the theory of a world soul appears in Plotinus, according to whom the cosmic soul belongs only to the material universe and is, therefore, third and lowest in the scale of the "authentic existents." It appears in Gilbert and Kepler, though in the latter largely as the expansion of a metaphor. It is considered by William James, whose comment on the "materialistic, or so-called 'scientific,' conceptions of the universe" is that "they leave the emotional and active interests cold," whereas he thinks "the perfect object of belief would be a God or 'Soul of the World,' represented both optimistically and moralistically . . . All science and all history would thus be accounted for in the deepest and simplest fashion."

Precisely because exponents of the doctrine attribute divinity to the world soul, Augustine and Aquinas object to it. "Impious and irreligious consequences follow," in Augustine's opinion, from the notion that "God is the soul of the world, and the world is as a body to Him." To those who compare the microcosm with the macrocosm by saying that "the soul is in the body as God is in the world," Aquinas replies that "the comparison holds in a certain respect, namely, because as God moves the world, so the soul moves the body. But it does not hold in every respect, for the soul did not create the body out of nothing as God created the world."

Furthermore, according to Aquinas, "God is not a part of it, but far above the whole universe, possessing within Himself the entire perfection of the universe in a more eminent way." God in relation to the world should not be conceived by analogy with soul and body, but by comparison to a king who "is said to be in the whole kingdom by his power, although he is not everywhere present." This analogy fits better with the conception of the universe as a society under divine government.

Although Aurelius reminds himself to "regard the universe as one living being, having one substance and one soul," he also takes the view that the world is a community of things ordered to one another. "The intelligence of the universe is social," he writes. "Accordingly it has made the inferior things for the sake of the superior, and it has fitted the superior to one another . . . It has subordinated, co-ordinated, and assigned to everything its proper portion." This view of the universe as a community is the one most fully developed in Christian thought. Augustine and Aquinas go much further than Aurelius in depicting the hierarchy of things and their ordination to one another under the eternal law. Both take as a basic text from Scripture the statement that God has "ordered all things in measure, and number, and weight." According to its dignity or worth, each thing occupies a place and plays its part in the general scheme of things.

"The parts of the universe are ordered to each other," Aquinas writes, "according as one acts on another, and according as one is the end and exemplar of the other." The government of the universe by the divine reason produces a perfection of order in the whole, which is the intrinsic common good of the universe, and directs each thing to the attainment of its end, in which consists its own perfection. "It belongs to the divine goodness," Aquinas says, "as it brought things into being, to lead them to their end. And this is to govern." But neither the perfection of each thing, nor the order of the universe itself, is the ultimate end of divine government. "Some good outside the whole universe," he says, "is the end of the government of the universe"— for the end of all things, as their beginning, lies in the goodness of God.

THE CONCEPTION OF THE WORLD as divinely governed, and cared for by divine providence, excludes chance as a factor in the formation of the world or in its structure. With Democritus and Epicurus in mind, Aquinas points out that "certain ancient philosophers denied the government of the world, saying that all things happened by chance." But the rejection of chance does not seem to be peculiar to Christian faith or theology.

Plato and Plotinus also deny that the order in the universe can be the result of chance. For Plato it is not merely that the world is animated by a rational soul, but also, as the Athenian Stranger suggests in the *Laws,* that it is a work of art rather than of nature or chance.

" 'Atoms' or 'elements'—it is in either case an absurdity, an impossibility," writes Plotinus, "to hand over the universe and its contents to material entities, and out of the disorderly swirl thus occasioned to call order

. . . into being." According to him, "there is nothing undesigned, nothing of chance, in all the process." Aristotle, too, speaks against the atomists who "ascribe this heavenly sphere and all the worlds to spontaneity" or chance. "When one man," he writes, referring to Anaxagoras, "said that reason was present—as in animals, so throughout nature—as the cause of order and of all arrangement, he seemed like a sober man in contrast with the random talk of his predecessors."

It might be supposed that those who view the world through the eyes of Newton or Descartes would be inclined to favor chance rather than reason or design. But this does not seem to be the case, at least not for Newton or Descartes. "This most beautiful system of the sun, planets, and comets," Newton declares, "could only proceed from the counsel and dominion of an intelligent and powerful Being."

Descartes asks us to consider what would happen if God were now to create a new world "somewhere in an imaginary space." Suppose that He agitated its matter in various ways "so that there resulted a chaos as confused as the poets ever feigned, and concluded His work by merely lending His concurrence to Nature in the usual way, leaving her to act in accordance with the laws which He had established." Something like this orderly universe would be the result. The laws of matter in motion, Descartes thinks, are "of such a nature that even if God had created other worlds, He could not have created any in which these laws would fail to be observed."

In the tradition of the great books, only the ancient atomists seem to take the position that the universe is a thing of chance. But this does not mean that, except for the atomists, agreement prevails concerning the manifestation of purpose or design in the world's structure. "Is the Kosmos an expression of intelligence, rational in its inward nature, or," James asks, "a brute external fact pure and simple?" James finds two answers to this question which he calls "the deepest of all philosophic problems"—one which regards the world "as a realm of final purposes, that . . . exists for the sake of something," and one which sees "the present only as so much mere mechanical sprouting from the past, occurring with no reference to the future."

As the chapter on MECHANICS indicates, Newton and Descartes are, in a sense, mechanists; yet they also affirm final causes—ends or purposes—in the plan of the universe. Newton speaks of God's "most wise and excellent contrivance of things, and final causes." It is true that Descartes, while referring to the universe as a work of divine art, says that God's purpose may not be visible to us in all its arrangements. Therefore "the species of cause termed final finds no useful employment in physical (or natural) things; for it does not appear to me," he explains, "that I can without temerity seek to investigate the (inscrutable) ends of God." But this states a rule of method in natural science, not the denial of a cosmic plan.

That denial is to be found, however, most plainly in Spinoza. "It is commonly supposed," he writes, "that all things in nature, like men, work to some end; and indeed it is thought to be certain that God Himself directs all things to some sure end, for it is said that God has made all things for man, and man that he may worship God." Against this view, which he regards as the most besetting of all human prejudices, Spinoza holds that "nature does nothing for the sake of an end, for that eternal and infinite Being whom we call God or Nature acts by the same necessity by which He exists." Since "He exists for no end, He acts for no end; and since He has no principle or end of existence, He has no principle or end of action. A final cause, as it is called," Spinoza continues, "is nothing, therefore, but human desire, in so far as this is considered as the principle or primary cause of anything."

Because man discovers things in nature which serve as means to his own ends, man is led to infer, Spinoza declares, that "some ruler or rulers of nature exist, endowed with human liberty, who have taken care of all things for him, and have made all things for his use . . . and hence he affirmed that the gods direct everything for his advantage, in order that he may be bound to them and hold them in the highest honor . . . Thus has this prejudice been turned into a superstition, and has driven deep roots into the mind—a prejudice which was the reason why everyone has so eagerly tried to discover and explain the final causes of things." The attempt, however, to show that nature does nothing in vain (that is to say, nothing which is not profitable to man) seems, in Spinoza's opinion, "to end in showing that nature, the gods, and man are alike mad."

WHERE SPINOZA DENIES purpose or plan in the universe because everything exists or happens from the necessity of efficient, not final, causes (and ultimately from the necessity of nature or God himself), Lucretius argues against design or providence from the imperfection of the world. To those who "think that gods / Have organized all things for the sake of men," Lucretius says:

I might not know a thing about the atoms,
But this much I can say, from what I see
Of heaven's ways and many other features:
The nature of the world just could not be
A product of the gods' devising; no,
There are too many things the matter with it.

Spinoza would dismiss this argument. He thinks he can easily answer those who ask, "How is it that so many imperfections have arisen in nature—corruption, for instance, of things till they stink; deformity, exciting disgust; confusion, evil, crime, etc.?" He holds that "the perfection of things is to be judged by their nature and power alone; nor are they more or less perfect because they delight or offend the human senses, or because they are beneficial or prejudicial to human nature."

Others deal differently with the apparent imperfections in the world. Descartes, for example, makes the point that "the same thing which might possibly seem very imperfect . . . if regarded by itself, is found to be very perfect if regarded as part of the whole universe." Marcus Aurelius goes further. "Nothing is injurious to the part," he writes, "if it is for the advantage of the whole . . . By remembering, then, that I am part of such a whole, I shall be content with everything that happens."

In terms of another principle, Berkeley asks us to "consider that the very blemishes and defects of nature are not without their use, in that they make an agreeable sort of variety, and augment the beauty of the rest of cre-

ation, as shades in a picture serve to set off the brighter and more enlighted parts . . . As for the mixture of pain or uneasiness which is in the world, pursuant to the general laws of nature," he thinks that "this, in the state we are in at present, is indispensably necessary to our well-being."

In the opinion of those "philosophers who, after an exact scrutiny of all the phenomena of nature, conclude that the *whole,* considered as one system is, in every period of its existence, ordered with perfect benevolence," Hume sees only a specious, if also sublime, consolation for all human ills. But he does not think such convictions ever really work in practice. "These enlarged views may, for a moment," he says, "please the imagination of a speculative man, who is placed in ease and security; but neither can they dwell with constancy on his mind, even though undisturbed by the emotions of pain or passion; much less can they maintain their ground when attacked by such powerful antagonists."

But according to theologians like Augustine and Aquinas, evil does not and cannot exist in the world except as a privation or corruption of some good. "Evil neither belongs to the perfection of the universe, nor comes under the order of the universe," writes Aquinas, "except accidentally, that is, by reason of some good joined to it." But how does evil enter into a world created by a supremely good deity? What "God chiefly intends in created things," Aquinas answers, "is the good of the order of the universe. Now the order of the universe requires . . . that there should be some things that can, and sometimes do, fail. And thus God, by causing in things the good order of the universe, consequently and, as it were by accident, causes the corruptions of things." Furthermore, "the order of justice belongs to the order of the universe; and this requires that penalty should be dealt out to sinners. And so God is the author of the evil which is penalty, but not of the evil which is fault."

ON THIS POINT OF THE perfection of the universe, the great conversation passes from the order of the world to the problem of evil and to related issues.

In Voltaire's *Candide,* there is much talk about Doctor Pangloss' philosophy that this is the best of all possible worlds. Candide is not persuaded by Pangloss. He tells Cunégonde that "we are going to another universe," and adds, "in that one all is well. For it must be admitted that one might deplore a little what goes on in ours in the physical and moral realms"—earthquakes and tidal waves, rapture and torture.

When Freud, in commenting on what he calls "the religious Weltanschauung," says that "earthquakes, floods and fires do not differentiate between the good and devout man, and the sinner and unbeliever," he raises questions which are considered in the chapters on Justice, Punishment, and Good and Evil. The perfection of the universe also leads to a discussion of the beauty of its order. The praises which are differently voiced by the astronomers, the theologians, and the poets extol not the visible beauties of nature, but the intelligible beauty of the cosmic structure—perceptible to a Kepler in his mathematical and musical formulation of the harmonies of the world.

In addition to questions of its goodness and beauty, the problem of the world's order is sometimes stated in terms of its rationality. For some writers, such as Hegel, rationality is affirmed as the very foundation of existence. *What is rational is actual and what is actual is rational,*" he writes. "On this conviction the plain man like the philosopher takes his stand, and from it philosophy starts in its study of the universe of mind as well as the universe of nature." According to Russell, "we cannot prove that the universe as a whole forms a single harmonious system such as Hegel believes that it forms." To others, like James, "the whole war of the philosophies is over that point of faith. Some say that they can see their way already to the rationality; others that it is hopeless in any other but the mechanical way. To some the very fact that there is a world at all seems irrational."

Against the Hegelian notion of the world as a perfectly ordered whole (to which James applies the epithet "block universe"), James proposes the conception of a "concatenated universe." "The real world as it is given at this moment," James declares, "is the sum total of all its beings and events now. But can we think of such a sum? Can we realize for an instant what a cross-section of all existence at a definite point in time would be? While I talk and the flies buzz, a sea-gull catches a fish at the mouth of the Amazon, a tree falls in the Adirondack wilderness, a man sneezes in Germany, a horse dies in Tartary, and twins are born in France.

"What does that mean?" James asks. "Does the contemporaneity of these events with each other, and with a million more as disjointed as they, form a rational bond between them, and unite them into anything that means for us a world?" It would certainly not mean a universe or cosmos for those who, like Hegel, insist upon the pervasive unity of the universe as a whole which completely and rationally relates all its parts. But for James, who conceives the universe in a pluralistic rather than in a monistic fashion, the "collateral contemporaneity" of all things, "and nothing else, is the *real* order of the world."

All of these issues carry the discussion back to what is perhaps the decisive question—the question of the world's origin. According as men believe it to be the purposeful work of a beneficent intelligence or the product of blind chance or of equally blind necessity, their other judgments about the world tend in the general directions of optimism or pessimism. Yet this is only true for the most part.

The problem of the world's origin involves some technical issues which do not seem to have such consequences for man's appraisal of the universe. One is the question whether a created world has a beginning in time or is co-eternal with its creator. As is indicated in the chapters on Eternity and Time, whichever way the disputed question concerning the eternity of the world is answered, its creation may be affirmed or denied. Those who think the world is created declare that the power needed to maintain the world in being is identical with the creative power needed to initiate it. "The divine conversation," as Berkeley points out, is conceived as "a continual creation."

The most difficult point in issue concerns the meaning of creation itself. According to Christian doctrine, the essence of creation consists in making something out of nothing. On this principle Aquinas, for example, contrasts creation with generation or procreation and with artistic production. In biological generation, the offspring is produced out of the substance of its progenitors. In artistic production, some preexistent material is transformed by the craftsman. But according to the theologian, creation is not change, "for change means that the same thing should be different now from what it was previously."

In becoming or alteration, some being is presupposed. "Creation is more perfect and more excellent than generation and alteration," Aquinas says, "because the term *whereto* is the whole substance of the thing; whereas what is understood as the term *wherefrom* is absolutely non-being," which, as he remarks, is the same as *nothing*. Since the distance between total nonbeing and being is infinite, only an infinite power can create, or make something out of nothing.

Lucretius flatly denies this possibility when he asserts as a first principle that "*Nothing comes from nothing*." Not even the gods can violate this principle. "*Nothing at all*," he declares, "*is ever born from nothing / By the god's will*." To Locke, on the other hand, the inconceivability of creation constitutes no argument against it. Writers like Lucretius "must give up their great maxim, *Ex nihilo nihil fit* . . . It is not reasonable to deny the power of an infinite Being because we cannot comprehend its operations. We do not deny other effects upon this ground," Locke continues, "because we cannot possibly conceive the manner of their production . . . It is an overvaluing of ourselves, to reduce all to the narrow measure of our capacities, and to conclude all things impossible to be done, whose manner of doing exceeds our comprehension."

But may not the world be related to a supreme cause or principle in some way which does not involve *exnihilation*? The great books present various alternatives. Aristotle's prime mover is the unmoved and eternal cause of the world's eternal motion, not of its coming

into being or its conservation in being. Plato's demiurge is a divinity which, according to the myth of the world's origin in the *Timaeus,* fashions the universe after the model of the eternal ideas, artistically producing their sensible replicas in the matter or space which is called "the receptacle."

The emanation of the sensible as well as the intelligible world from the transcendent All-One in the cosmogony of Plotinus, or the production of finite things from the infinite substance of God in Spinoza's theory, seem to be more like generation or procreation than like creation in the meaning of the opening chapter of Genesis.

Such theories, according to theologians like Augustine and Aquinas, or philosophers like Berkeley and Locke, deny what is meant by creation in the Judeo-Christian tradition. To Berkeley they are all equally forms of atheism. Yet it should be remarked that to Spinoza a theory like that of Plato's is also impious; for it places "something outside of God which is independent of Him, to which He looks while He is at work as to a model, or at which He aims as if at a certain mark. This is indeed nothing else than to subject God to fate, the most absurd thing which can be affirmed of Him whom we have shown to be the first and only free cause of the essence of all things as well as of their existence."

THE VARIOUS THEORIES of the world's origin usually extend also to the problem of the world's end. Aristotle, for example, who denies a beginning to the motions of the heavens and all other cycles of natural change, affirms them to go on in everlasting perpetuity. But it is not merely those who think the world has no beginning or source who attribute endless endurance to it. If the world did not have endless duration, it would not be for Plato the moving image of eternity. And though they conceive the world as somehow a divine emanation or production, Plotinus and Spinoza, no less than Aristotle, hold it to be everlasting if not eternal. "We hold that the ordered universe, in its material mass," Plotinus writes, "has existed for ever and will for ever endure."

The proposition that nothing is ever reduced to nothing is, for Lucretius, as true as the principle that nothing ever comes from nothing. He applies these principles, however, only to the eternal atoms, uncreated and indestructible, not to the world after world which arises and perishes as the atoms come together and disperse. Just as any compound body which atoms form can be dissolved into its simple bodies, so whole worlds are subject to similar dissolution, and will suffer it in the course of long ages. Yet though world succeeds world in the ceaseless activity of the eternal atoms, Lucretius contemplates a universe without beginning or end.

Since annihilation (or reduction to nothingness) is the opposite of exnihilation (or creation out of nothing), it might be expected that the doctrine which rests on the faith that "in the beginning God created heaven and earth," would also foresee an end to all things—a return of the whole created universe to the nothingness from which it came. Sacred Scripture does contain the prophecy of a final cataclysm. "The earth shall reel to and fro like a drunkard, and shall be removed like a cottage," says Isaiah. Reciting the parable of the tares in the field, Matthew explains that as "the tares are gathered and burned in the fire, so shall it be in the end of this world." In the Gospel according to Luke, Christ foretells His second coming:

And there shall be signs in the sun, and in the moon, and in the stars; and upon the earth distress of nations, with perplexity; the sea and the waves roaring;

Men's hearts failing them for fear, and for looking after those things which are coming on the earth: for the powers of heaven shall be shaken;

And then shall they see the Son of man coming in a cloud with great power and great glory . . .

Heaven and earth shall pass away; but my word shall not pass away.

But there is one other text which exercises a controlling influence on the theologian's interpretation of Scripture. In the second Epistle of Peter, we find:

. . . the day of the Lord will come as a thief in the night; in the which the heavens shall pass away with a great noise, and the elements shall melt with fervent heat, the earth also and the works that are therein shall be burned up . . .

Nevertheless we, according to his promise, look for new heavens and a new earth, wherein dwelleth righteousness.

The final conflagration will be the end of the world as we know it, but it will bring about the re-formation, not the annihilation, of the material universe. As God has the power to create, so, according to Aquinas, He has the power to annihilate, but "since the power and goodness of God are rather manifested by the conservation of things in being . . . we must conclude by denying absolutely that anything at all will be annihilated." In the concluding treatises of the *Summa Theologica*—dealing with the end of the world, the Last Judgment, and the resurrection of the body—the final cataclysm is described as the cleansing of the world by fire to bring into being a new earth and a new heaven.

In our time, men talk of the end of the world as an event which might by chance occur if a chain reaction set up by atomic fission got out of control and exploded the whole material universe. The physicist's theory of entropy also forecasts the eventual dissipation of energy to the point at which the universe will be a frozen mass of inert matter. These are secular alternatives to the religious prophecy of the world's end. But what Jesus said of the Last Judgment—that its time is a secret hidden from men—may be applicable to any termination of the world, certainly if it lies in the hands of God, and not merely at the disposal of man or nature.